PRENTICE HALL
LITERATURE

Timeless Voices, Timeless Themes

COPPER

BRONZE

SILVER

GOLD

PLATINUM

THE AMERICAN EXPERIENCE

THE BRITISH TRADITION

CONTRIBUTING AUTHORS

The contributing authors guided the direction and philosophy of *Prentice Hall Literature: Timeless Voices, Timeless Themes*. Working with the development team, they helped to build the pedagogical integrity of the program and to ensure its relevance for today's teachers and students.

Kate Kinsella

Kate Kinsella, Ed.D., is a faculty member in the Department of Secondary Education at San Francisco State University. A specialist in second-language acquisition and adolescent reading and writing, she teaches coursework addressing language and literacy development across the secondary curricula. She has taught high-school ESL and directed SFSU's *Intensive English Program* for first-generation bilingual college students. She maintains secondary classroom involvement by teaching an academic literacy class for second-language learners through the University's *Step to College* partnership program. A former Fulbright lecturer and perennial institute leader for TESOL, the California Reading Association, and the California League of Middle Schools, Dr. Kinsella provides professional development nationally on topics ranging from learning-style enhancement to second-language reading. Her scholarship has been published in journals such as the *TESOL Journal,* the *CATESOL Journal,* and the *Social Studies Review.* Dr. Kinsella earned her M.A. in TESOL from San Francisco State University and her Ed.D. in Second Language Acquisition from the University of San Francisco.

Kevin Feldman

Kevin Feldman, Ed.D., is the Director of Reading and Early Intervention with the Sonoma County Office of Education (SCOE). His career in education spans thirty-one years. As the Director of Reading and Early Intervention for SCOE, he develops, organizes, and monitors programs related to K–12 literacy and prevention of reading difficulties. He also serves as a Leadership Team Consultant to the California Reading and Literature Project and assists in the development and implementation of K–12 programs throughout California. Dr. Feldman earned his undergraduate degree in Psychology from Washington State University and has a Master's degree in Special Education, Learning Disabilities, and Instructional Design from U.C. Riverside. He earned his Ed.D. in Curriculum and Instruction from the University of San Francisco.

Colleen Shea Stump

Colleen Shea Stump, Ph.D., is a Special Education supervisor in the area of Resource and Inclusion for Seattle Public Schools. She served as a professor and chairperson for the Department of Special Education at San Francisco State University. She continues as a lead consultant in the area of collaboration for the California State Improvement Grant and travels the state of California providing professional development training in the areas of collaboration, content literacy instruction, and inclusive instruction. Dr. Stump earned her doctorate at the University of Washington, her M.A. in Special Education from the University of New Mexico, and her B.S. in Elementary Education from the University of Wisconsin–Eau Claire.

Joyce Armstrong Carroll

In her forty-year career, Joyce Armstrong Carroll, Ed. D., has taught on every grade level from primary to graduate school. In the past twenty years, she has trained teachers in the teaching of writing. A nationally known consultant, she has served as president of TCTE and on NCTE's Commission on Composition. More than fifty of her articles have appeared in journals such as *Curriculum Review, English Journal, Media & Methods, Southwest Philosophical Studies, English in Texas,* and the *Florida English Journal.* With Edward E. Wilson, Dr. Carroll co-authored *Acts of Teaching: How to Teach Writing* and co-edited *Poetry After Lunch: Poetry to Read Aloud.* She co-directs the New Jersey Writing Project in Texas.

Edward E. Wilson

A former editor of *English in Texas,* Edward E. Wilson has served as a high-school English teacher and a writing consultant in school districts nationwide. Wilson has served on both the Texas Teacher Professional Practices Commission and NCTE's Commission on Composition. Wilson's poetry appears in Paul Janeczko's anthology *The Music of What Happens.* With Dr. Carroll, he co-wrote *Acts of Teaching: How to Teach Writing* and co-edited *Poetry After Lunch: Poetry to Read Aloud.* Wilson co-directs the New Jersey Writing Project in Texas.

PROGRAM ADVISORS

The program advisors provided ongoing input throughout the development of *Prentice Hall Literature: Timeless Voices, Timeless Themes*. Their valuable insights ensure that the perspectives of the teachers throughout the country are represented within this literature series.

Diane Cappillo
English Department Chair
Barbara Goleman Senior High School
Miami, Florida

Anita Clay
Language Arts Instructor
Gateway Institute of Technology
St. Louis, Missouri

Ellen Eberly
Language Arts Instructor
Catholic Memorial High School
West Roxbury, Massachusetts

Nancy Fahner
L.A.M.P. Lansing Area Manufacturing
   Partnership
Ingham Intermediate School District
Mason, Michigan

Terri Fields
Instructor of Language Arts,
   Communication Arts, and Author
Sunnyslope High School
Phoenix, Arizona

Susan Goldberg
Language Arts Instructor
Westlake Middle School
Thornwood, New York

Margo L. Graf
English Department Chair, Speech,
   Yearbook, Journalism
Lane Middle School
Fort Wayne, Indiana

Christopher E. Guarraia
Language Arts Instructor
Lakewood High School
Saint Petersburg, Florida

V. Pauline Hodges
Teacher, Educational Consultant
Forgan High School
Forgan, Oklahoma

Karen Hurley
Language Arts Instructor
Perry Meridian Middle School
Indianapolis, Indiana

Lenore D. Hynes
Language Arts Coordinator
Sunman-Dearborn Community
   Schools
Sunman, Indiana

Linda Kramer
Language Arts Instructor
Norman High School North
Norman, Oklahoma

Thomas S. Lindsay
Assistant Superintendent of Schools
Mannheim District 83
Franklin Park, Illinois

Agathaniki (Niki) Locklear
English Department Chair
Simon Kenton High School
Independence, Kentucky

Ashley MacDonald
Language Arts Instructor
South Forsyth High School
Cumming, Georgia

Mary Ellen Mastej
Language Arts Instructor
Scott Middle School
Hammond, Indiana

Nancy L. Monroe
English, Speed Reading Teacher
Bolton High School
Alexandria, Louisiana

Jim Moody
Language Arts Instructor
Northside High School
Fort Smith, Arkansas

David Morris
Teacher of English, Writing,
   Publications, Yearbook
Washington High School
South Bend, Indiana

Rosemary A. Naab
English Department Chair
Ryan High School
Archdiocese of Philadelphia
Philadelphia, Pennsylvania

Ann Okamura
English Teacher
Laguna Creek High School
Elk Grove, California

Tucky Roger
Coordinator of Languages
Tulsa Public Schools
Tulsa, Oklahoma

Jonathan L. Schatz
English Teacher/Team Leader
Tappan Zee High School
Orangeburg, New York

John Scott
Assistant Principal
Middlesex High School
Saluda, Virginia

Ken Spurlock
Assistant Principal, Retired
Boone County High School
Florence, Kentucky

Dr. Jennifer Watson
Secondary Language Arts
   Coordinator
Putnam City Schools
Oklahoma City, Oklahoma

Joan West
Assistant Principal
Oliver Middle School
Broken Arrow, Oklahoma

CONTENTS IN BRIEF

UNIT 1

THEME: *Coming of Age*

SKILLS WORKSHOPS

THEME: *Meeting Challenges*

SKILLS WORKSHOPS

UNIT 3

THEME: *Quest for Justice*

SKILLS WORKSHOPS

UNIT 4

THEME: *From Sea to Shining Sea*

SKILLS WORKSHOPS

UNIT 5

THEME: *Extraordinary Occurrences*

UNIT 6

GENRE: *Short Stories*

SKILLS WORKSHOPS

UNIT 7

GENRE: *Nonfiction*

SKILLS WORKSHOPS

UNIT 8

Genre: *Drama*

SKILLS WORKSHOPS

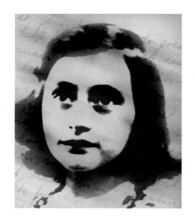

UNIT 9

GENRE: *Poetry* (continued)

SKILLS WORKSHOPS

UNIT 10 · GENRE: *The American Folk Tradition*

COMPLETE CONTENTS BY GENRE

COMPLETE CONTENTS BY GENRE

POETRY

COMPARING LITERARY WORKS

READING INFORMATIONAL MATERIALS

CONNECTIONS

HOW TO READ LITERATURE

WRITING WORKSHOPS

LISTENING AND SPEAKING WORKSHOPS

ASSESSMENT WORKSHOPS

Learn About Literature

Forms of Literature

*Novel and Novella • Short Story • Nonfiction •
Poetry • Drama • The American Folk Tradition*

Just as various types of government and society have developed over the course of history, so have different forms of literature. Each of these forms, called a genre (zhän´ rə), has its own characteristics. In this introduction, you can find explanations and examples of each genre.

Novel and Novella

Novels and **novellas** are long works of prose fiction that tell a story about imaginary people or animals called characters who live in a made-up world, or setting. A novella is briefer than a novel. However, each has a plot, a series of events linked by cause and effect that reveals a conflict, or struggle, and usually shows its resolution. These works of longer fiction may also have subplots, smaller plots related to the main one. The plot and subplots explore a theme, or central idea or question about life.

● **What do you learn about the main character and setting of this novel from this passage?**

Buck did not read the newspapers, or he would have known that trouble was brewing, not alone for himself, but for every tide-water dog, strong of muscle and with warm, long hair, from Puget Sound to San Diego. . . .

FROM *CALL OF THE WILD,* JACK LONDON
PRENTICE HALL LITERATURE LIBRARY

Short Story

A **short story** is a brief work of prose fiction. It tells a story about imaginary people or animals called characters. The plot of a short story is simple and focused, and the story explores an insight into life.

● **Which details show that the story is set during the Civil War?**

He saw a general on a black horse gazing over the lines of blue infantry at the green woods which veiled his problems.

FROM "AN EPISODE OF WAR," STEPHEN CRANE, PAGE 16

Nonfiction

Nonfiction tells the story of a person's life, narrates a series of true events, describes a real scene, or presents information.

● **Who is the subject of this nonfiction piece?**

Of all the great artists of Japan, the one Westerners probably like and understand best is Katsushika Hokusai. . . .

FROM "HOKUSAI: THE OLD MAN MAD ABOUT DRAWING," STEPHEN LONGSTREET, PAGE 636

Poetry

Poetry is literature that appears in verse form. Many poems have a regular rhythm and possibly a rhyme scheme. Most poems use highly concise, musical, and powerful language to tell a story or to convey a single image or idea.

⬤ **What qualities of the passage at right reveal that it is poetry?**

Slowly, silently, now the moon
Walks the night in her
    silver shoon;
This way, and that, she peers,
    and sees
Silver fruit upon silver trees . . .

FROM "SILVER," WALTER DE LA MARE, PAGE **868**

Drama

Drama, which can be written in prose or poetry, tells a story through the words and actions of actors who impersonate the characters. The text of a drama contains the characters' spoken words, or dialogue, and bracketed information, called stage directions, telling actors how to move and speak. Most dramas are meant to be performed, and you should imagine actors speaking the dialogue as you read it.

⬤ **Which part of this dramatic text is dialogue and which is stage directions?**

MIEP. Are you all right, Mr. Frank?
MR. FRANK. [*Quickly controlling himself*] Yes, Miep, yes.

FROM *THE DIARY OF ANNE FRANK*, FRANCES GOODRICH AND ALBERT HACKETT, PAGE **700**

The American Folk Tradition

The myths, tales, ballads, and tall tales that make up the **American folk tradition** are a kind of rugged, outdoor literature. They were shaped by singers and storytellers around campfires for generations before being brought to the "indoors" of a printed page.

The literature of the American folk tradition expresses the insights, explanations, values, hopes, and fears of the groups and individuals that created them. It often explains natural phenomena like thunder and hurricanes. It may also celebrate the heroes of the American frontier. To get the full flavor of these works, imagine them as being told or sung to you rather than lying quietly on a page.

⬤ **What natural fact does this folk tale "explain" in the African American dialect, or regional speech, of the South?**

De wind is a woman, and de water is a woman too. . . .When you see a storm on de water, it's de wind and de water fightin' over dem chillun.

FROM "WHY THE WAVES HAVE WHITECAPS," ZORA NEALE HURSTON, PAGE **923**

Short Stories

Plot and Conflict • Characters •
Point of View • Setting • Theme

   **Short stories can transport you to cities you have never
seen or to historical events that occurred long ago. Generally,
the ideas for short stories are inspired and developed in an
author's imagination. These pages introduce the key elements
of short stories.**

Plot and Conflict

   The **plot** of a story is a sequence of
actions. A typical plot, diagrammed
below, involves a **conflict** or problem.
As the plot develops, the story builds
to the point of greatest tension, the
climax. The characters may or may
not address and resolve the conflict
as the story moves to its conclusion.

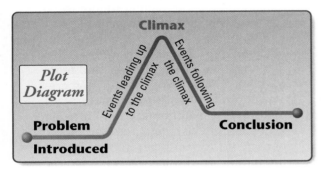

Plot Diagram

Climax

Events leading up to the climax

Events following the climax

Problem Introduced

Conclusion

● **What plot details does this passage
from a short story reveal?**

   One of his eyes resembled that of a
vulture—a pale blue eye, with a
film over it. Whenever it fell upon me,
my blood ran cold; and so by degrees—
very gradually—I made up my mind to
take the life of the old man, and thus
rid myself of the eye forever.
   FROM "THE TELL-TALE HEART," EDGAR
ALLAN POE, PAGE 522

Characters

   The **characters** in a story are the imaginary
people, animals, or other beings that take
part in the action. To bring them to life,
authors use characterization, telling you
directly what they are like or revealing their
traits indirectly through their thoughts,
words, actions, and reactions to situations.
   If an author does not tell you a character's
motivations, or reasons for acting, you must
use evidence from the story to determine
them for yourself. As you read a variety of
stories, compare and contrast the motivations and reactions of characters from different historical eras as they encounter similar
situations or conflicts.

● **In this passage, does the narrator tell you
directly what a character is like or reveal the
character through her words and actions?
Explain.**

   Susan didn't really feel interested in Saleh
Hamadi until she was a freshman in high
school carrying a thousand questions around. . . .
   FROM "HAMADI," NAOMI SHIHAB NYE, PAGE 539

> *[S]tories are truthful dreams, actually. But they are dreamt."*
>
> —Grace Paley

Point of View

A story's **point of view** is the vantage point from which a story is told.

- In **first person,** the narrator, involved in the action, refers to himself or herself as "I."
- In **third person,** the narrator, outside the action, refers to characters as "he" or "she."
- In **omniscient** (äm nish′ ənt) **third person,** the narrator knows all characters' thoughts.

● **What clues to the point of view can you find in the opening of this story?**

> The day my son Laurie started kindergarten he renounced corduroy overalls . . .
>
> FROM "CHARLES," SHIRLEY JACKSON, PAGE 22

Setting

When you think of the world that a short story evokes, you are thinking of its **setting.** This world includes not only the time and place of the story's action, but also the customs and beliefs of that time and place. The setting can provide clues to the story's meaning, influence the story's conflict, or play a central role in that conflict.

● **What details in this passage help you identify the setting of the story?**

> Hana Omiya stood at the railing of the small ship that shuddered toward America in a turbulent November sea. She shivered as she pulled the folds of her silk kimono close to her throat. . . .
>
> FROM "TEARS OF AUTUMN," YOSHIKO UCHIDA, PAGE 564

Theme

The **theme** of a story is an insight into life that it offers directly or indirectly. Certain recurring themes appear in many stories because they have meaning for numbers of readers. One such theme involves the battle between good and evil.

Authors communicate themes in different ways, sometimes stating them directly. More often, however, they imply or suggest the theme. To determine an implied theme, consider clues like the meaning of a story's title, how a character solves a problem, and a passage that conveys powerful emotions. In some cases, an author does not even imply a theme that you can summarize, but instead explores an important question without answering it.

● **What clues in the title and opening paragraph of this story suggest that its theme may relate to people's attitude toward their heritage? Explain.**

> My kid sister Cheryl and I always bragged about our Sioux grandpa, Joe Iron Shell. Our friends, who had always lived in the city and only knew about Indians from movies and TV, were impressed by our stories. . . .
>
> FROM "THE MEDICINE BAG," VIRGINIA DRIVING HAWK SNEVE, PAGE 582

Nonfiction

Autobiography • Biography • Exposition • Essay • Informational Text

Nonfiction is the mind's workshop. In this workshop, an author is hammering, carving, and shaping ideas about the real world. Readers explore this genre to learn about the lives of others, find valuable information, reflect on new ideas, and weigh arguments about important issues. These pages will help you discover the characteristics and varied purposes of nonfiction.

Autobiography

An **autobiography** is the story of part or all of a person's life, written by that person. As a story, a prose narrative of events, it shares certain characteristics with fiction, such as point of view, setting, and theme.

Unlike fiction, however, autobiography presents a version of what actually happened to the author rather than a made-up world. The author's purposes for telling this life-story may be to explain his or her values, to teach lessons in life, to tell how he or she developed, to entertain, or any combination of these.

● **What does this passage from Eudora Welty's autobiography reveal about her purpose or purposes for writing?**

Learning stamps you with its moments. Childhood's learning is made up of moments. It isn't steady. It's a pulse. . . .

FROM *ONE WRITER'S BEGINNINGS*, EUDORA WELTY, PAGE **628**

Biography

In a **biography**, an author tells the story of someone else's life. Usually, the subject of a biography is a person, famous or not, whose life has special meaning or value. Like an autobiography, this literary form is a factual prose narrative with elements such as plot, setting, and theme. It can also share many of the purposes of autobiography, such as teaching and entertaining. With biography, however, there is often a special emphasis on explaining the causes and effects of a subject's actions.

● **According to this biographer of the artist Hokusai, which of Hokusai's traits explain many of his actions?**

He was a restless, unpredictable man who lived in as many as a hundred different houses and changed his name at least thirty times. For a very great artist, he acted at times like P.T. Barnum or a Hollywood producer with his curiosity and drive for novelty.

FROM "HOKUSAI: THE OLD MAN MAD ABOUT DRAWING," STEPHEN LONGSTREET, PAGE **636**

"The essayist . . . can . . . be any sort of person, according to his mood or his subject matter—philosopher, scold, jester . . ." —E.B. White

Exposition

The purpose of **exposition** is to present and explain information. This type of writing plays a valuable role when the exchange of accurate information is important.

● **Why is the definition of *de facto* useful in this passage from an expository essay?**

[Until] the early 1950s, many public schools in both the North and South were segregated. . . . In the North most of the schools were segregated *de facto;* that is, the law allowed blacks and whites to go to school together, but they did not actually always attend the same schools.

FROM "BROWN VS. BOARD OF EDUCATION," WALTER DEAN MYERS, PAGE 230

Essay

Essays are brief prose works about a particular subject.

- **Reflective essays** explore an author's thoughts about ideas or experiences.
- **Narrative essays** tell the story of actual events.
- **Descriptive essays** present people, situations, or places.
- **Persuasive essays** try to convince readers to think or act in a certain way.

● **Basing your answer on the first sentence of this essay, how would you classify it? Why?**

I first saw her one autumn day when I was called to see one of Mrs. Ainsworth's dogs, and I looked in some surprise at the furry black creature sitting before the fire.

FROM "DEBBIE," JAMES HERRIOT, PAGE 652

Informational Text

Imagine a friendly guide who could help you buy the right clothes, discover what is happening in the world, learn a subject, figure out how to work gadgets and machines, or master a sport. **Informational texts** are such a guide. Ranging from directions and warranties to maps and contracts, they are the real-world texts that you encounter as you manage your daily life. Informational texts help you perform necessary tasks or enjoy your recreation.

● **A warranty is a guarantee offered by a seller or manufacturer to the consumer purchasing a product. According to the passage shown here from a warranty, what does a company guarantee about its fire extinguisher?**

BRK Brands, Inc. warrants its enclosed Fire Extinguisher to be free from defects in materials and workmanship under normal use and service for a period of five years from date of purchase. . . .

FROM "WARRANTY FOR A FIRE EXTINGUISHER," PAGE 662

Drama

Staging • Historical Context • Plot and Subplot • Dialogue

Drama is a form of literature that asks you, the reader, to play many roles. You are the director, guiding the actors; the set designer, creating the right environment; the lighting designer, making sure scenes are properly lit; the actors, portraying the characters; and the audience, appreciating it all. Such active reading allows you to transform a page into a stage alive with action. This introduction will prepare you for your "performance" by explaining the characteristics of drama.

Staging

The term **staging** refers to all the elements that turn words on a page into a full-scale dramatic production: scenery, lighting, sound effects, and costumes, as well as instructions to the actors about how to speak their lines and move. The playwright summarizes this information in the italicized and bracketed stage directions. Directors use this information as a blueprint for "constructing" the drama. You can also use the directions to picture the drama in your mind as you read it.

● **What information about the set do these stage directions provide?**

[. . . The three rooms of the top floor and a small attic space above are exposed to our view. The largest of the rooms is in the center, with two small rooms, slightly raised, on either side. On the right is a bathroom, out of sight. A narrow steep flight of stairs at the back leads up to the attic. . . .]

FROM *THE DIARY OF ANNE FRANK*, FRANCES GOODRICH AND ALBERT HACKETT, PAGE 700

Historical Context

Often a drama captures the atmosphere and conflicts of a past era. When this is the case, you must be alert to the drama's **historical context**, the political forces, beliefs, and events that influenced the characters in the play. For example, the context for *The Diary of Anne Frank* is the Holocaust, the systematic destruction of over six million European Jews by the Nazis before and during World War II. In 1942, the Frank family and other Jews living in Nazi-controlled Holland went into hiding to escape being imprisoned by the Nazis.

● **How does the historical context explain the mood of the scene below?**

MRS. VAN DAAN. [*Rising, nervous, excited*] Something's happened to them! I know it!

MR. VAN DAAN. Now, Kerli!

MRS. VAN DAAN. Mr. Frank said they'd be here at seven o'clock. He said . . .

FROM *THE DIARY OF ANNE FRANK*, FRANCES GOODRICH AND ALBERT HACKETT, PAGE 700

> "A play, I think, ought to make sense to commonsense people."
>
> —Arthur Miller

Plot and Subplot

As in a work of fiction, the **plot** in a drama is a linked sequence of events involving a conflict, a struggle between opposing forces. The problem or conflict is introduced, tension builds to its greatest point, the climax, and then the problem is solved.

Like longer works of fiction, dramas also have **subplots**, smaller sequences of events related to the main plot and the themes, or insights, it explores. In *The Diary of Anne Frank*, for example, the plot concerns the attempt of the Franks, the Van Daans, and others to hide from the Nazis. However, a subplot concerns a blossoming relationship between Anne Frank and Peter Van Daan, both teenagers.

● **What does this first exchange between Anne and Peter suggest will happen in the subplot involving them?**

ANNE. What's your cat's name?

PETER. Mouschi.

ANNE. Mouschi! Mouschi! Mouschi! [*She picks up the cat, walking away with it. To* PETER] I love cats. . . .

PETER. He's a tom. He doesn't like strangers. [*He takes the cat from her, putting it back in its carrier.*]

FROM *THE DIARY OF ANNE FRANK*, FRANCES GOODRICH AND ALBERT HACKETT, PAGE **700**

Dialogue

Playwrights can use narrators, or characters who serve as narrators, only in a limited way. Much more than fiction writers, playwrights tell a story through **dialogue**, the words of the characters. Dialogue can express dramatic irony, when characters' words have a meaning known to the audience but not understood by the characters. Dialogue also serves to reveal the traits of the characters. As you read dialogue, use the stage directions to see and hear the characters delivering their lines. Then, analyze this "performance" to determine the characters' personalities.

● **What does this passage of dialogue reveal about Mr. Frank and his role among the people who are in hiding?**

MR. FRANK. . . . This is the way we must live until it is over, if we are to survive.
[*There is silence for a second.*]

MRS. FRANK. Until it is over.

MR. FRANK. [*Reassuringly*] After six we can move about . . .

FROM *THE DIARY OF ANNE FRANK*, FRANCES GOODRICH AND ALBERT HACKETT, PAGE **700**

Poetry

Purpose and Form • Narratives and Ballads •
Lyric Poetry • Symbols • Imagery •
Figurative Language

Arranged in lines and groups of lines called stanzas, rather than in sentences and paragraphs, poetry makes greater use of the sounds of words than prose does. Whether telling a story or expressing feelings, poetry presents surprising but accurate comparisons. This introduction will help you understand the special characteristics, purposes, and forms of poetry.

Purpose and Form

Different **forms** of poetry often have different **purposes**, as follows:

- An **elegy** is a relatively long formal poem about death or another serious topic.
- An **epic** is a long narrative poem written in an elevated style. The epic conveys the adventures of heroic characters and the story is connected to the history of a nation, race, or religion.
- An **ode** is a dignified uplifting lyric written to celebrate a person, place, thing or event.
- A **sonnet** is a 14-line lyric poem with one of several rhyme schemes.

● **Which qualities in this passage suggest that it is the beginning of an ode?**

Under the trees light
has dropped from the top of the sky
light
like a green latticework of branches,
shining
on every leaf . . .
FROM "ODE TO ENCHANTED LIGHT," PABLO
NERUDA, PAGE 848

Narratives and Ballads

Narrative poems are poems that tell a story. A special type of narrative poem is the **ballad**, a form of verse meant to be sung or recited. Ballads use simple language to tell stories with dramatic action.

● **What evidence suggests that this stanza is the beginning of a ballad?**

It was the schooner Hesperus,
    That sailed the wintry sea;
And the skipper had taken his little daughter,
    To bear him company. . . .
FROM "THE WRECK OF THE HESPERUS," HENRY
WADSWORTH LONGFELLOW, PAGE 818

Lyric Poetry

A **lyric poem** expresses thoughts and feelings. Once, lyric poems were actually sung to the accompaniment of a stringed instrument called a lyre. Today, they rely on their own rhythm and sound.

● **What emotion do these lines express?**

Blow, blow, thou winter wind.
    Thou art not so unkind
        As man's ingratitude. . . .
FROM "BLOW, BLOW, THOU WINTER WIND,"
WILLIAM SHAKESPEARE, PAGE 836

Symbols

A **symbol** is an object, person, or place that stands for something beyond itself. Some symbols in a culture come ready-made—for example, an eagle stands for the United States. Often, however, poets and other writers create symbols in their work by writing about an object, person, or place in such a way that it suggests meanings beyond itself.

⦿ **In these couplets, or pairs of rhyming lines, what feelings might the father's hands symbolize?**

. . . The man had struck a match to see
If his son slept peacefully.

He held his palms each side the spark
His love had kindled in the dark.

His two hands were curved apart
In the semblance of a heart. . . .

FROM "THE SECRET HEART," ROBERT P. TRISTRAM COFFIN, PAGE **810**

Imagery

Imagery is the descriptive language that appeals to one or more senses. The images in a poem supply details of sight, sound, taste, touch, smell, or movement and help readers sense the experience the poet describes.

⦿ **To what senses do the images in these lines appeal?**

At dusk / the gray / foxes / stiffen / in cold; / blackbirds / are fixed / in the / branches. . . .

FROM "NEW WORLD," N. SCOTT MOMADAY, PAGE **878**

Figurative Language

Poets use **figurative language**, words not meant in their exact dictionary sense, to surprise you. These types of figurative language are based on a comparison of apparently unlike items:

- **Similes** use *like* or *as* to compare items as in "sunset hovers like a sound/Of golden horns."
- **Metaphors** describe one item as if it were another as in "turning/his feet to swift half-moons."
- **Personifications** give human qualities to something nonhuman as in "Sir I encountered Death Just now among our roses."

⦿ **Which type of figurative language is this poet using?**

Stars are great drops
Of golden dew.

FROM "HARLEM NIGHT SONG," LANGSTON HUGHES, PAGE **834**

The American Folk Tradition

Folk Tale • Myth • Tall Tale

Imagine that instead of reading literature, you heard it told to you around a flickering campfire. That way of telling, rather than writing down, stories is what shaped American folk literature. The word *folk* indicates that these stories were made up by the folk, or people, for the people. That is why folk tales are a welcoming kind of literature. Because they were eventually written down, you can pick up a book and join in the campfire circle of a particular culture or group to appreciate tales of talking animals and wondrous events. These pages will introduce you to different types of folk literature and their characteristics.

Folk Tale

A **folk tale** is a story passed on by word of mouth for the purpose of teaching the ideas and values of a culture. Folk tales originated among groups of people who could not read or write. Instead, the people told the stories aloud, passing them from generation to generation. In the modern era, folk tales were collected and written down by scholars so folk wisdom could be shared with a wider audience.

As you read folk tales, notice the following elements of the culture that produced them:

- A specific **setting** such as a desert or riverside landscape
- The unique **rituals** and **customs** of a group
- The **values** or beliefs the people hold
- Specific **dialect,** or the patterns of speech that are characteristic of a cultural group or region

● **What values does the first paragraph of this African American folk tale teach?**

> Back in the days when the animals could talk, there lived ol' Brer Possum. He was a fine feller. Why, he never liked to see no critters in trouble. He was always helpin' out, a-doin' somethin' for others.
>
> FROM "BRER POSSUM'S DILEMMA," RETOLD BY JACKIE TORRENCE, PAGE 917

"... the folk tale or the fairy tale ... come out of the most distant deeps of human experience ..."

—John Buchan

Myth

How? Why? When? If you have ever spent time with a younger child, you have heard those questions a thousand times. To answer these questions, and satisfy a small child's curiosity, you have probably had to tell many true or made-up stories. That is exactly what some people did when humanity itself was younger. To answer questions like *why are there seasons like winter and spring?*, storytellers created **myths**—tales of gods, heroes, and animals that explain natural occurrences or customs and beliefs.

As a member of a scientifically-minded society, you may read these folk "explanations" with disbelief. However, a story that is not scientifically true can still contain other kinds of truth. For example, its explanation may truthfully reflect human or animal nature and be true to our wish for a memorable and satisfying story.

● **Which natural facts do you think this Native American myth will "explain"?**

At this time the world was still dark; the sun and moon had not yet been put in the sky. "Friend," Coyote said to Eagle, "no wonder I can't catch anything; I can't see. Do you know where we can get some light?"

"You're right, friend, there should be some light," Eagle said. "I think there's a little toward the west. Let's try and find it."

FROM "COYOTE STEALS THE SUN AND MOON," ZUÑI MYTH RETOLD BY RICHARD ERDOES AND ALFONSO ORTIZ, PAGE 920

Tall Tale

A **tall tale** is a humorous story that recounts exaggerated events in a matter-of-fact way, using the everyday speech of the common people. Tall tales associated with the American frontier show how the imaginations of storytellers and listeners expanded in response to the vast geography of the United States. The Mississippi River, the Great Plains, and the Rocky Mountains seemed to call for heroes, heroines, and deeds that could match their geographical majesty.

● **Which exaggerations indicate that this passage comes from a tall tale?**

In one respect Bill even welcomed the cyclone, for it blew so hard it blew the earth away from his wells. The first time this happened, he thought the wells would be a total loss. There they were, sticking up several hundred feet out of the ground. As wells they were useless. But he found he could cut them up into lengths and sell them for postholes to farmers in Iowa and Nebraska. It was very profitable, especially after he invented a special posthole saw to cut them with. He didn't use that type of posthole himself. He got the prairie dogs to dig his for him. He simply caught a few gross of prairie dogs and set them down at proper intervals. . . .

FROM "PECOS BILL: THE CYCLONE," RETOLD BY HAROLD W. FELTON, PAGE 938

Coming of Age

The Cat, Robert Vickrey, licensed by VAGA, New York

Exploring the Theme

Laughter, tears, failure, and triumph are part of growing up and of growing older. By reading about the experiences of fictional characters and real-life people in this unit, you may gain insights that apply to your own coming of age.

As you read, you can think about characters' situations and writers' thoughts and discuss them with your classmates.

◀ **Critical Viewing** What elements of this picture seem to be about the process of coming of age, or growing up? [**Analyze**]

Why **Read Literature?**

Whenever you read, you have a purpose, or reason. Your purpose will vary, depending on the genre, content, and style of the work you plan to read. Preview the three purposes you might set before reading the works in this unit.

1 Read for the love of literature.

Leo Tolstoy is considered one of the great masters of Russian fiction. See what a powerful story he can tell in five paragraphs when you read the folk tale **"The Old Grandfather and His Little Grandson,"** page 72.

Maya Angelou read one of her poems at the inauguration of a president, but there was a time when she would not even read out loud in class. Share a moment in the early life of this shy child who grew up to be a best-selling author in the excerpt from *I Know Why the Caged Bird Sings,* page 32.

2 Read to appreciate an author's style.

Poems about love are not always sweet and sentimental. Laugh at the sarcastic sting of Dorothy Parker's love poem **"The Choice,"** page 48.

The poems of Robert Frost are known for their use of simple, everyday language. Discover what else makes his style memorable when you read **"The Road Not Taken,"** page 44.

3 Read for information.

Can a computer giant like Bill Gates be reached through e-mail? Find out when you read the excerpt from John Seabrook's article, **"E-Mail from Bill Gates,"** page 54.

Like other forms of communication, e-mail has its own rules of politeness. Learn what they are when you read Virginia Shea's article, **"How to Be Polite Online,"** page 62.

 Take It to the Net

Visit the Web site for online instruction and activities related to each selection in this unit.

www.phschool.com

How to Read Literature

Use Literal Comprehension Strategies

The first step in understanding any communication is to achieve literal comprehension—the actual meaning of words and sentences. In this unit, you will learn and practice the following literal comprehension strategies.

1. Use context to determine meaning.

The context, or situation in which an unfamiliar word is used, can provide clues to a word's meaning. In the following example, the writer uses two words that are related in meaning.

> . . . forty thousand men . . . lay *crazily askew* in their uniforms.
> —from "The Drummer Boy of Shiloh"

The word *askew* may be unfamiliar, but the word *crazily* suggests something "out of order." Men lying *askew* must therefore be lying in some crazy, disordered way.

2. Identify word origins.

By learning the origins of words and different influences on the English language, you will understand how groups of words are related. In this unit, you will learn to identify words with

- Latin Roots
- Latin Prefixes
- Latin Suffixes

In later units, you will learn about other influences on the English Language.

3. Distinguish between literal and figurative meaning.

In this unit, you will learn to distinguish between words and sentences that are meant literally and words and sentences that are not. Recognizing the difference will help you avoid confusion.

4. Paraphrase.

Pause occasionally in your reading to restate a sentence or passage in your own words. This para-phrasing will help you make sense of figurative language and difficult passages. The example shows one reader's paraphrase of the first lines of "The Road Not Taken" by Robert Frost.

Poet's Words

Two roads diverged in a yellow wood,
And sorry I could not travel both
And be one traveler, long I stood
And looked down one as far as I could
To where it bent in the undergrowth.

Paraphrase

There were two roads in the forest. I wished I could travel on both, but one person can't be in two places. So I tried to see as far as I could down one road, but eventually it turned. The bushes got in the way of seeing any further.

Prepare to Read

The Drummer Boy of Shiloh

 Take It to the Net

Visit www.phschool.com for interactive activities and instruction related to "The Drummer Boy of Shiloh," including
- background
- graphic organizers
- literary elements
- reading strategies

Preview

Connecting to the Literature

In "The Drummer Boy of Shiloh," a frightened boy finds courage in the inspiring words of a general on the night before a battle. Connect with the drummer boy by thinking about a time when the words of someone you admire helped you through a difficult time.

Background

Ray Bradbury's story "The Drummer Boy of Shiloh" is about a Civil War drummer boy. Although drummer boys accompanied troops into battle, they carried no weapons. There was no age requirement, so some drummer boys were as young as ten. Because few parents were willing to send their young sons to battle, many drummer boys were runaways or orphans.

Literary Analysis

Historical Setting

A **historical setting** is a real time and place from history. The italicized words in the following example contain several historically accurate details.

> It was indeed a solemn time and a solemn *night* for a boy just turned fourteen *in the peach field near the Owl Creek not far from the church at Shiloh.*

Shiloh is the location of a bloody Civil War battle. It is near Owl Creek. Look for the answers to the following focus questions.

1. What details indicate where the story takes place?
2. What details tell when the story takes place?

Connecting Literary Elements

Often, the setting contributes to the **mood**—the feeling or atmosphere of the work. The details shown here in italics establish the mood.

> In the *April night,* . . . blossoms fell from the *orchard trees* and lit with *rustling taps* on the drumskin. *At midnight* a peach stone . . . *fell swift and unseen,* struck once, like panic, . . .

These details of unexpected noises in an otherwise quiet night create a nervous, anxious mood.

Reading Strategy

Finding Word Meaning in Context

The **context** of a word is the situation in which it is used, as indicated by the surrounding words and phrases. When you come across an unfamiliar word, look for clues in the context to help you find the meaning. Here, the words *crazily* and *helter-skelter* give you clues to the meanings of *askew* and *strewn.*

> . . . forty thousand men . . . lay *crazily askew* in their uniforms.
> A mile yet farther on, another army was *strewn helter-skelter.* . .

The clues suggest that *askew* and *strewn* mean "crooked" and "scattered." As you read, jot down any unfamiliar words and the page number on a chart like the one shown. Then, go back and use context to find the meaning of each word you wrote.

Word	Page	Context
ramrod	8	gunpowder, ramrod, Minié ball
lag	11	The heart would beat slow in the men. They would lag by the wayside.

Vocabulary Development

benediction (ben´ ə dik´ shən) *n.* blessing (p. 8)

riveted (riv´ it əd) *adj.* fastened or made firm (p. 8)

compounded (käm pound´ əd) *adj.* mixed or combined (p. 8)

resolute (rez´ ə lळ्ōt´) *adj.* showing a firm purpose; determined (p. 11)

THE Drummer Boy OF Shiloh

RAY BRADBURY

In the April night, more than once, blossoms fell from the orchard trees and lit with rustling taps on the drumskin. At midnight a peach stone left miraculously on a branch through winter, flicked by a bird, fell swift and unseen, struck once, like panic, which jerked the boy upright. In silence he listened to his own heart ruffle away, away—at last gone from his ears and back in his chest again.

After that, he turned the drum on its side, where its great lunar face peered at him whenever he opened his eyes.

His face, alert or at rest, was solemn. It was indeed a solemn time and a solemn night for a boy just turned fourteen in the peach field near the Owl Creek not far from the church at Shiloh.[1]

". . . thirty-one, thirty-two, thirty-three . . ."

Unable to see, he stopped counting.

Beyond the thirty-three familiar shadows, forty thousand men, exhausted by nervous expectation, unable to sleep for romantic dreams of battles yet unfought, lay crazily askew in their uniforms. A mile yet farther on, another army was strewn helter-skelter, turning slow, basting themselves[2] with the thought of what they

---

1. Shiloh (shī´ lō) site of a Civil War battle in 1862; now a national military park in southwest Tennessee.
2. basting themselves here, letting their thoughts pour over them as they turn in their sleep.

would do when the time came: a leap, a yell, a blind plunge their strategy, raw youth their protection and <u>benediction</u>.

Now and again the boy heard a vast wind come up, that gently stirred the air. But he knew what it was—the army here, the army there, whispering to itself in the dark. Some men talking to others, others murmuring to themselves, and all so quiet it was like a natural element arisen from South or North with the motion of the earth toward dawn.

What the men whispered the boy could only guess, and he guessed that it was: "Me, I'm the one, I'm the one of all the rest who won't die. I'll live through it. I'll go home. The band will play. And I'll be there to hear it."

Yes, thought the boy, that's all very well for them, they can give as good as they get!

For with the careless bones of the young men harvested by night and bindled[3] around campfires were the similarly strewn steel bones of their rifles, with bayonets fixed like eternal lightning lost in the orchard grass.

Me, thought the boy, I got only a drum, two sticks to beat it, and no shield.

There wasn't a man-boy on this ground tonight who did not have a shield he cast, <u>riveted</u> or carved himself on his way to his first attack, <u>compounded</u> of remote but nonetheless firm and fiery family devotion, flag-blown patriotism and cocksure immortality strengthened by the touchstone of very real gunpowder, ramrod, Minié ball[4] and flint. But without these last, the boy felt his family move yet farther off away in the dark, as if one of those great prairie-burning trains had chanted them away never to return—leaving him with this drum which was worse than a toy in the game to be played tomorrow or some day much too soon.

The boy turned on his side. A moth brushed his face, but it was a peach blossom. A peach blossom flicked him, but it was a moth. Nothing stayed put. Nothing had a name. Nothing was as it once was.

If he lay very still, when the dawn came up and the soldiers put on their bravery with their caps, perhaps they might go away, the war with them, and not notice him lying small here, no more than a toy himself.

"Well, now," said a voice.

The boy shut up his eyes, to hide inside himself, but it was too late. Someone, walking by in the night, stood over him.

"Well," said the voice quietly, "here's a soldier crying *before* the fight. Good. Get it over. Won't be time once it all starts."

---

3. bindled (bin′ dəld) *adj.* bedded.
4. Minié (min′ ē) **ball** cone-shaped rifle bullet that expands when fired.

Reading Strategy
Finding Word Meaning in Context What do you think *murmuring* means based on the context clues "whispering" and "quiet"?

riveted (riv′ it əd) *adj.* fastened or made firm

compounded (käm pound′ əd) *adj.* mixed or combined

◀ **Critical Viewing**
Does the drummer boy in this photograph seem to want to "hide inside himself"? Explain.
[Assess]

And the voice was about to move on when the boy, startled, touched the drum at his elbow. The man above, hearing this, stopped. The boy could feel his eyes, sense him slowly bending near. A hand must have come down out of the night, for there was a little *rat-tat* as the fingernails brushed and the man's breath fanned his face.

"Why, it's the drummer boy, isn't it?"

The boy nodded, not knowing if his nod was seen. "Sir, is that *you*?" he said.

"I assume it is." The man's knees cracked as he bent still closer.

He smelled as all fathers should smell, of salt sweat, ginger tobacco, horse and boot leather, and the earth he walked upon. He had many eyes. No, not eyes—brass buttons that watched the boy.

He could only be, and was, the general.

"What's your name, boy?" he asked.

"Joby," whispered the boy, starting to sit up.

"All right, Joby, don't stir." A hand pressed his chest gently, and the boy relaxed. "How long you been with us, Joby?"

"Three weeks, sir."

✓ **Reading Check**

What is the boy thinking about as he lies in the orchard?

The Drummer Boy of Shiloh ◆ 9

"Run off from home or joined legitimately, boy?"

Silence.

"Fool question," said the general. "Do you shave yet, boy? Even more of a fool. There's your cheek, fell right off the tree overhead. And the others here not much older. Raw, raw, the lot of you. You ready for tomorrow or the next day, Joby?"

"I think so, sir."

"You want to cry some more, go on ahead. I did the same last night."

"*You*, sir?"

"It's the truth. Thinking of everything ahead. Both sides figuring the other side will just give up, and soon, and the war done in weeks, and us all home. Well, that's not how it's going to be. And maybe that's why I cried."

"Yes, sir," said Joby.

The general must have taken out a cigar now, for the dark was suddenly filled with the smell of tobacco unlit as yet, but chewed as the man thought what next to say.

"It's going to be a crazy time," said the general. "Counting both sides, there's a hundred thousand men, give or take a few thousand out there tonight, not one as can spit a sparrow off a tree, or knows a horse clod from a Minié ball. Stand up, bare the breast, ask to be a target, thank them and sit down, that's us, that's them. We should turn tail and train four months, they should do the same. But here we are, taken with spring fever and thinking it blood lust, taking our sulfur with cannons instead of with molasses, as it should be, going to be a hero, going to live forever. And I can see all of them over there nodding agreement, save the other way around. It's wrong, boy, it's wrong as a head put on hindside front and a man marching backward through life. More innocents will get shot out of pure enthusiasm than ever got shot before. Owl Creek was full of boys splashing around in the noonday sun just a few hours ago. I fear it will be full of boys again, just floating, at sundown tomorrow, not caring where the tide takes them."

The general stopped and made a little pile of winter leaves and twigs in the darkness, as if he might at any moment strike fire to them to see his way through the coming days when the sun might not show its face because of what was happening here and just beyond.

Literature in Context Social Studies Connection

Battle of Shiloh

The Battle of Shiloh took place when a southern Confederate army unexpectedly struck Union forces commanded by General Ulysses S. Grant on April 6, 1862, near Shiloh Church in Tennessee. The North won the battle on April 7. Of the nearly 100,000 men involved, about 13,000 Union soldiers and 10,000 Confederate soldiers were killed, wounded, or captured. It was the bloodiest single battle that had taken place in the United States up to that time.

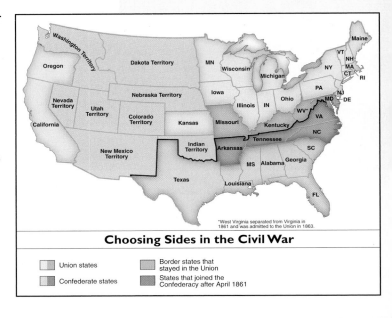

*West Virginia separated from Virginia in 1861 and was admitted to the Union in 1863.

Choosing Sides in the Civil War

Union states

Confederate states

Border states that stayed in the Union

States that joined the Confederacy after April 1861

The boy watched the hand stirring the leaves and opened his lips to say something, but did not say it. The general heard the boy's breath and spoke himself.

"Why am I telling you this? That's what you wanted to ask, eh? Well, when you got a bunch of wild horses on a loose rein somewhere, somehow you got to bring order, rein them in. These lads, fresh out of the milkshed, don't know what I know, and I can't tell them: men actually die, in war. So each is his own army. I got to make *one* army of them. And for that, boy, I need you."

"Me!" The boy's lips barely twitched.

"Now, boy," said the general quietly, "you are the heart of the army. Think of that. You're the heart of the army. Listen, now."

And, lying there, Joby listened. And the general spoke on.

If he, Joby, beat slow tomorrow, the heart would beat slow in the men. They would lag by the wayside. They would drowse in the fields on their muskets. They would sleep forever, after that, in those same fields—their hearts slowed by a drummer boy and stopped by enemy lead.

But if he beat a sure, steady, ever faster rhythm, then, then their knees would come up in a long line down over that hill, one knee after the other, like a wave on the ocean shore! Had he seen the ocean ever? Seen the waves rolling in like a well-ordered cavalry charge to the sand? Well, that was it, that's what he wanted, that's what was needed! Joby was his right hand and his left. He gave the orders, but Joby set the pace!

So bring the right knee up and the right foot out and the left knee up and the left foot out. One following the other in good time, in brisk time. Move the blood up the body and make the head proud and the spine stiff and the jaw <u>resolute</u>. Focus the eye and set the teeth, flare the nostrils and tighten the hands, put steel armor all over the men, for blood moving fast in them does indeed make men feel as if they'd put on steel. He must keep at it, at it! Long and steady, steady and long! Then, even though shot or torn, those wounds got in hot blood—in blood he'd helped stir—would feel less pain. If their blood was cold, it would be more than slaughter, it would be murderous nightmare and pain best not told and no one to guess.

The general spoke and stopped, letting his breath slack off. Then, after a moment, he said, "So there you are, that's it. Will you do that, boy? Do you know now you're general of the army when the general's left behind?"

The boy nodded mutely.

"You'll run them through for me then, boy?"

"Yes, sir."

"Good. And, maybe, many nights from tonight, many years from now, when you're as old or far much older than me, when they ask you what you did in this awful time, you will tell them—one part

Literary Analysis
Historical Setting and Mood Find two historical details that help create a positive mood.

resolute (rez´ ə loot´) *adj.* showing a firm purpose; determined

Reading Check

What does the drummer boy promise to do?

humble and one part proud—'I was the drummer boy at the battle of Owl Creek,' or the Tennessee River, or maybe they'll just name it after the church there. 'I was the drummer boy at Shiloh.' Good grief, that has a beat and sound to it fitting for Mr. Longfellow. 'I was the drummer boy at Shiloh.' Who will ever hear those words and not know you, boy, or what you thought this night, or what you'll think tomorrow or the next day when we must get up on our legs and *move!*"

The general stood up. "Well, then. Bless you, boy. Good night."

"Good night, sir." And tobacco, brass, boot polish, salt sweat and leather, the man moved away through the grass.

Joby lay for a moment, staring but unable to see where the man had gone. He swallowed. He wiped his eyes. He cleared his throat. He settled himself. Then, at last, very slowly and firmly, he turned the drum so that it faced up toward the sky.

He lay next to it, his arm around it, feeling the tremor, the touch, the muted thunder as, all the rest of the April night in the year 1862, near the Tennessee River, not far from the Owl Creek, very close to the church named Shiloh, the peach blossoms fell on the drum.

Review and Assess

Thinking About the Selection

1. **Respond:** Do you think Joby should have enlisted as a drummer boy? Why or why not?

2. **(a) Recall:** What frightens Joby about the upcoming battle? **(b) Compare and Contrast:** How are his fears like and unlike those of the other soldiers? **(c) Compare and Contrast:** In what other ways are Joby and the soldiers alike and not alike?

3. **(a) Recall:** What is Joby doing when the general stops to talk to him? **(b) Infer:** Why do you think the general stops to talk to Joby?

4. **(a) Recall:** Why does the general say he needs Joby? **(b) Evaluate:** Is the drummer boy's role as crucial as the general says? Explain.

5. **(a) Recall:** What does Joby agree to do for the general at the end of the story? **(b) Draw Conclusions:** How do you think Joby feels after his talk with the general? Explain.

6. **(a) Speculate:** Do you think the general has motivated Joby to keep his promise? Why or why not? **(b) Make a Judgment:** Is the general's request fair or unfair to Joby? Explain.

Ray Bradbury

(b. 1920)
Ray Bradbury grew up in Waukegan, Illinois, and later moved with his family to California. As a teenager, he read science fiction stories and soon began writing his own. The young writer eventually became an award-winning science fiction author, known for such works as *The Martian Chronicles.*

Bradbury wrote this story after reading the death notice of an actor whose grandfather had been "the drummer boy of Shiloh." This phrase inspired him to write his tale. To paint an accurate description of the setting, he went to the Los Angeles library before writing and did research on the weather conditions during the Battle of Shiloh.

Review and Assess

Literary Analysis

Historical Setting

1. Describe the **historical setting** of "The Drummer Boy of Shiloh."
2. **(a)** What are three details from the story that tell where the story is set? **(b)** What are three details that tell when the story takes place? Record these details on a chart like the one below.

Details that show time	Details that show place

3. In what way does the setting reveal what happens after the story ends?

Connecting Literary Elements

4. Describe the **mood** of the story.
5. What details of the setting help create the mood?

Reading Strategy

Finding Word Meaning in Context

6. Write the following sentences. Circle the word or words in each sentence that give clues to the meaning of the italicized word.

   a. . . . You will tell them—one part *humble* and one part proud—"I was the drummer boy. . ."

   b. Make the head proud and the spine stiff and the jaw *resolute*.

7. Explain how making a contrast between the italicized parts of the sentence helps you find the meaning of *legitimately*.

   Run off from home or *joined legitimately*, boy?

Extend Understanding

8. **Social Studies Connection:** What are two additional details of clothing, transportation, or forms of communication that Bradbury might have used to reinforce the Civil War setting?

Quick Review

A **historical setting** is an actual time and place from history in which the events of a narrative occur. To review historical setting, see page 5.

Mood is the overall feeling or atmosphere of a literary work. To review mood, see page 5.

The **context** of a word is the situation in which it is used, including the surrounding words, sentences, and paragraphs. To review context, see page 5.

 Take It to the Net
www.phschool.com
Take the interactive self-test online to check your understanding of the selection.

Integrate Language Skills

Vocabulary Development Lesson

Word Analysis: Latin Root -bene-

The Latin word root -bene- means "well" or "good." It appears in each of these English words that name or describe something good:

benediction   beneficial
benevolence   benefit

Write one word from the list to complete each sentence. Use a dictionary to check your answers.

1. The general's visit to Joby was ____?____ because it raised Joby's spirits.
2. The young, inexperienced soldier appreciated the general's kindness and ____?____.
3. Before he left, the general gave a ____?____, or blessing, to Joby.
4. The general believes Joby's drumbeat can ____?____ the army.

Concept Development: Synonyms

On your paper, write the word closest in meaning to the first word.

1. riveted (a) fastened (b) drilled (c) split
2. compounded (a) flattened (b) guarded (c) mixed
3. resolute (a) determined (b) absolute (c) calm
4. benediction (a) curse (b) wealth (c) blessing

Spelling Strategy

When you add -ed to a two-syllable word, do not double the final consonant if the stress is on the first syllable:

riv´et + -ed = riveted

On your paper, add -ed to the following verbs:

1. travel   2. hinder   3. savor

Grammar Lesson

Nouns

A **noun** names a person, animal, place, thing, or idea. All sentences contain at least one noun.

Person	boy, general, Joby
Thing	book, snow, branch, Liberty Bell
Animal	bird, macaw, Tweety
Idea	freedom, age, silence
Place	field, Shiloh, Owl Creek

A noun can be singular (one individual thing), plural (more than one individual thing), or collective (a group of things acting as a single unit).

Singular	soldier, person
Plural	soldiers, people
Collective	army, assembly

▶ For more practice, see page R28, Exercise A.

Practice Copy the sentences. Underline each noun.

1. Fear kept the young drummer boy awake.
2. A moth gently brushed against his face.
3. The anxious soldiers dreamed of battles.
4. Raw youth was their protection.
5. The fears kept Joby awake.

Writing Application Write four sentences using nouns that

- give the specific name of a place.
- name more than one animal.
- name an idea.
- name a group of people acting as a unit.

W̸G Prentice Hall Writing and Grammar Connection: Chapter 14, Section 1

Writing Lesson

Letter Home from a Soldier

Write a letter as Joby about the night before the battle. Include details about Joby's feelings as well as other facts you know about the Civil War.

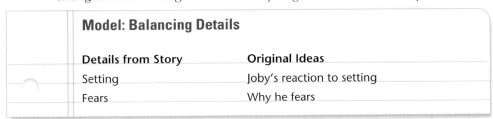

Prewriting Gather details about Joby's feelings and observations by completing a character wheel like the one shown here. Fill each section with details from the story that match the section label.

Drafting Write your letter as Joby, using the first-person pronoun *I* to refer to yourself as Joby. Balance your original ideas about Joby's thoughts and feelings with details you gather from the story.

Model: Balancing Details	
Details from Story	**Original Ideas**
Setting	Joby's reaction to setting
Fears	Why he fears

Revising Reread your draft, eliminating repeated nouns by using synonyms—words that have almost the same meaning.

W/G Prentice Hall Writing and Grammar Connection: Chapter 4, Section 3

Extension Activities

Research and Technology Prepare a **Civil War "photo album"** of scenes Joby could have witnessed.

- Use a search engine to do an Internet key word search using *Shiloh* or another battle site.
- Search the Library of Congress site using key words as well.

Download any available photos of people, battles, or documents. Choose the ones that will bring Joby's experiences to life. Label each picture with captions that reflect what Joby might have thought or written about the picture.

Listening and Speaking With a partner, **debate** this proposition: An age requirement should be established for joining the army as a drummer boy.

- Prepare notes in favor of or against it.
- Take notes on supporting facts and statistics.
- As you listen to your opponent, make additional notes about which points you want to stress in your answer. **[Group Activity]**

Take It to the Net www.phschool.com

Go online for an additional research activity using the Internet.

CONNECTIONS
Literature and Social Studies

The Civil War in Literature

Fiction writers Ray Bradbury and Stephen Crane each use an individual character to communicate the feelings and experiences shared by hundreds and thousands who fought in the Civil War.

Bradbury includes realistic details in "The Drummer Boy of Shiloh," but his main focus is on creating sympathetic characters. Stephen Crane, who was born five years after the Civil War ended, is famous for the realism of his Civil War stories. He focuses on the war's effect on a character, more than on the character's thoughts and feelings.

An Episode of War Stephen Crane

The lieutenant's rubber blanket lay on the ground, and upon it he had poured the company's supply of coffee. Corporals and other representatives of the grimy and hot-throated men who lined the breast-work[1] had come for each squad's portion.

The lieutenant was frowning and serious at this task of division. His lips pursed as he drew with his sword various crevices in the heap, until brown squares of coffee, astoundingly equal in size, appeared on the blanket. He was on the verge of a great triumph in mathematics, and the corporals were thronging forward, each to reap a little square, when suddenly the lieutenant cried out and looked quickly at a man near him as if he suspected it was a case of personal assault. The others cried out also when they saw blood upon the lieutenant's sleeve.

He had winced like a man stung, swayed dangerously, and then straightened. The sound of his hoarse breathing was plainly audible. He looked sadly, mystically, over the breast-work at the green face of a wood, where now were many little puffs of white smoke. During this moment the men about him gazed statuelike and silent, astonished and awed by this catastrophe which happened when catastrophes were not expected—when they had leisure to observe it.

---

1. breast-work low wall put up quickly as a defense in battle.

▶ **Critical Viewing** What does this picture indicate about medical care on the battlefield? **[Analyze]**

As the lieutenant stared at the wood, they too swung their heads, so that for another instant all hands, still silent, contemplated the distant forest as if their minds were fixed upon the mystery of a bullet's journey.

The officer had, of course, been compelled to take his sword into his left hand. He did not hold it by the hilt. He gripped it at the middle of the blade, awkwardly. Turning his eyes from the hostile wood, he looked at the sword as he held it there, and seemed puzzled as to what to do with it, where to put it. In short, this weapon had of a sudden become a strange thing to him. He looked at it in a kind of stupefaction, as if he had been endowed with a trident, a sceptre, or a spade.[2]

Finally he tried to sheathe it. To sheathe a sword held by the left hand, at the middle of the blade, in a scabbard hung at the left hip, is a feat worthy of a sawdust ring.[3] This wounded officer engaged in a desperate struggle with the sword and the wobbling scabbard, and during the time of it breathed like a wrestler.

Thematic Connection
How and why does the lieutenant's attitude toward his weapon change?

But at this instant the men, the spectators, awoke from their stone-like poses and crowded forward sympathetically. The orderly-sergeant took the sword and tenderly placed it in the scabbard. At the time, he leaned nervously backward, and did not allow even his finger to brush the body of the lieutenant. A wound gives strange dignity to him who bears it. Well men shy from his new and terrible majesty. It is as if the wounded man's hand is upon the curtain which hangs before the revelations of all existence—the meaning of ants, potentates,[4] wars, cities, sunshine, snow, a feather dropped from a bird's wing; and the power of it sheds radiance upon a bloody form, and makes the other men understand sometimes that they are little. His comrades look at him with large eyes thoughtfully. Moreover, they fear vaguely that the weight of a finger upon him might send him headlong, precipitate the tragedy, hurl him at once into the dim, grey unknown. And so the orderly-sergeant, while sheathing the sword, leaned nervously backward.

precipitate (prē sip′ ə tāt′) v. cause to happen before expected or desired

There were others who proffered assistance. One timidly presented his shoulder and asked the lieutenant if he cared to lean upon it, but the latter waved him away mournfully. He wore the look of one who knows he is the victim of a terrible disease and understands his helplessness. He again stared over the breast-work at the forest, and then, turning, went slowly rearward. He held his right wrist tenderly in his left hand as if the wounded arm was made of very brittle glass.

And the men in silence stared at the wood, then at the departing lieutenant; then at the wood, then at the lieutenant.

As the wounded officer passed from the line of battle, he was

✔**Reading Check**

What has happened to the lieutenant?

---

2. **a trident, a sceptre, or a spade** (trīd′ ənt; sep′ tər) symbols of royal authority.
3. **sawdust ring** ring in which circus acts are performed.
4. **potentates** (pōt′ ən tāts) n. rulers; powerful people.

enabled to see many things which as a participant in the fight were unknown to him. He saw a general on a black horse gazing over the lines of blue infantry at the green woods which veiled his problems. An aide galloped furiously, dragged his horse suddenly to a halt, saluted, and presented a paper. It was, for a wonder, precisely like a historical painting.

To the rear of the general and his staff a group, composed of a bugler, two or three orderlies, and the bearer of the corps standard,[5] all upon maniacal horses, were working like slaves to hold their ground, preserve their respectful interval, while the shells boomed in the air about them, and caused their chargers to make furious quivering leaps.

A battery, a tumultuous and shining mass, was swirling toward the right. The wild thud of hoofs, the cries of the riders shouting blame and praise, menace and encouragement, and, last, the roar of the wheels, the slant of the glistening guns, brought the lieutenant to an intent pause. The battery swept in curves that stirred the heart; it made halts as dramatic as the crash of a wave on the rocks, and when it fled onward this <u>aggregation</u> of wheels, levers, motors had a beautiful unity, as if it were a missile. The sound of it was a war-chorus that reached into the depths of man's emotion.

The lieutenant, still holding his arm as if it were of glass, stood watching this battery until all detail of it was lost, save the figures of the riders, which rose and fell and waved lashes over the black mass.

Later, he turned his eyes toward the battle, where the shooting sometimes crackled like bush-fires, sometimes sputtered with exasperating irregularity, and sometimes reverberated like the thunder. He saw the smoke rolling upward and saw crowds of men who ran and cheered, or stood and blazed away at the <u>inscrutable</u> distance.

He came upon some stragglers, and they told him how to find the field hospital. They described its exact location. In fact, these men, no longer having part in the battle, knew more of it than others. They told the performance of every corps, every division, the opinion of every general. The lieutenant, carrying his wounded arm rearward, looked upon them with wonder.

At the roadside a brigade was making coffee and buzzing with talk like a girls' boarding-school. Several officers came out to him and inquired concerning things of which he knew nothing. One, seeing his arm, began to scold. "Why, man, that's no way to do. You want to fix that thing." He appropriated the lieutenant and the lieutenant's wound. He cut the sleeve and laid bare the arm, every nerve of which softly fluttered under his touch. He bound his handkerchief over the wound, scolding away in the meantime. His tone allowed one to think that he was in the habit of being wounded every day. The lieutenant

---

5. **corps standard** (kôr) flag or banner representing a military unit.

Thematic Connection
Why wouldn't the lieutenant normally notice these details?

aggregation
(ag′ grə gā′ shən) *n.* group or mass of distinct objects or individuals

inscrutable (in skrōōt′ ə bəl) *adj.* impossible to see or understand

Thematic Connection
What does this incident suggest about the kind of medical care Civil War soldiers received?

hung his head, feeling, in this presence, that he did not know how to be correctly wounded.

The low white tents of the hospital were grouped around an old schoolhouse. There was here a singular commotion. In the foreground two ambulances interlocked wheels in the deep mud. The drivers were tossing the blame of it back and forth, gesticulating and berating, while from the ambulances, both crammed with wounded, there came an occasional groan. An interminable crowd of bandaged men were coming and going. Great numbers sat under the trees nursing heads or arms or legs. There was a dispute of some kind raging on the steps of the schoolhouse. Sitting with his back against a tree a man with a face as grey as a new army blanket was serenely smoking a corncob pipe. The lieutenant wished to rush forward and inform him that he was dying.

A busy surgeon was passing near the lieutenant. "Good-morning," he said, with a friendly smile. Then he caught sight of the lieutenant's arm, and his face at once changed. "Well, let's have a look at it." He seemed possessed suddenly of a great contempt for the lieutenant. This wound evidently placed the latter on a very low social plane. The doctor cried out impatiently, "What mutton-head had tied it up that way anyhow?" The lieutenant answered, "Oh, a man."

When the wound was disclosed the doctor fingered it disdainfully. "Humph," he said. "You come along with me and I'll 'tend to you." His voice contained the same scorn as if he were saying: "You will have to go to jail."

The lieutenant had been very meek, but now his face flushed, and he looked into the doctor's eyes. "I guess I won't have it amputated," he said.

"Nonsense, man! Nonsense! Nonsense!" cried the doctor. "Come along, now. I won't amputate it. Come along. Don't be a baby."

"Let go of me," said the lieutenant, holding back wrathfully, his glance fixed upon the door of the old schoolhouse, as sinister to him as the portals of death.

And this is the story of how the lieutenant lost his arm. When he reached home, his sisters, his mother, his wife, sobbed for a long time at the sight of the flat sleeve. "Oh, well," he said, standing shamefaced amid these tears, "I don't suppose it matters so much as all that."

Stephen Crane

(1871–1900)
The son of a minister, Crane grew up in New Jersey and attended Syracuse University. After playing baseball in college, Crane seriously considered becoming a shortstop in the newly formed National League. He decided instead that he wanted to be a writer. He became internationally famous as a writer of stories so realistic that they seemed to be true. His novel *The Red Badge of Courage* is considered one of the best war novels ever written by an American.

Connecting Literature and Social Studies

1. In what ways is this story similar to and different from "The Drummer Boy of Shiloh"?
2. How do the two stories together give you a more complete picture of the Civil War experience than either story can give alone?

Prepare to Read

Charles

 Take It to the Net

Visit www.phschool.com for interactive activities and instruction related to "Charles," including

- background
- graphic organizers
- literary elements
- reading strategies

Preview

Connecting to the Literature

Recall how you and your classmates felt and behaved when you first started school. In "Charles," you will read about a young boy who brings home some startling stories from his first weeks at school.

Background

Beginning school is often a time of difficult adjustment for children. In kindergarten, children learn social skills as well as academic lessons. For the characters in this story, the adjustment to a school situation is made interesting and exciting by a boy named Charles.

Literary Analysis

Point of View

The perspective from which a story is told is its **point of view.** A story can be told from one of two overall points of view.

- **First person:** The narrator participates in the action of the story and can tell only what he or she sees, knows, thinks, or feels.
- **Third person:** The narrator is not a character in the story but tells events from the "outside."

"Charles" is told from the first-person point of view. Think about the following focus questions as you read "Charles."

1. In what way does the first-person point of view increase your curiosity about the boy Charles?
2. In what ways would the story be different if Laurie were the first-person narrator?

Connecting Literary Elements

Dialogue is conversation between characters. In stories, novels, and poems, a speaker's exact words in dialogue are set off by quotation marks.

> "Why did Charles hit the teacher?" I asked quickly.

As you read, notice what you learn about Charles from dialogue. On a graphic organizer like the one shown here, write words that each character uses and what you think the words mean.

Character's Words	Meaning
"Throw him out of school, I guess."	Laurie thinks students who misbehave are kicked out of school.
"This Charles boy sounds like a bad influence."	

Reading Strategy

Identifying Word Origins

In the sixth century, Latin-speaking missionaries arrived in England. Their Latin words soon mixed with the Anglo-Saxon language of England. As a result, many current English words or word parts have Latin **word origins.**

- simulate: *sim-* means "together with"
- regain: *re-* means "back" or "again"
- incredible: *cred-* means "believe"

Knowing the origins of words can help you recognize that words with the same origins or parts often have related meanings. Look for the words in the story that have the parts explained above.

Vocabulary Development

renounced (ri nounst´) *v.* gave up (p. 22)

insolently (in´ sə lənt lē) *adv.* boldly disrespectful in speech or behavior (p. 22)

simultaneously (sī məl tā´ nē əs lē) *adv.* at the same time (p. 24)

incredulously (in krej´ o͞o ləs lē) *adv.* with doubt or disbelief (p. 25)

Charles

Shirley Jackson

The day my son Laurie started kindergarten he <u>renounced</u> corduroy overalls with bibs and began wearing blue jeans with a belt; I watched him go off the first morning with the older girl next door, seeing clearly that an era of my life was ended, my sweet-voiced nursery-school tot replaced by a long-trousered, swaggering[1] character who forgot to stop at the corner and wave good-bye to me.

He came home the same way, the front door slamming open, his cap on the floor, and the voice suddenly become raucous[2] shouting, "Isn't anybody *here*?"

At lunch he spoke <u>insolently</u> to his father, spilled his baby sister's milk, and remarked that his teacher said we were not to take the name of the Lord in vain.

"How *was* school today?" I asked, elaborately casual.

"All right," he said.

"Did you learn anything?" his father asked.

Laurie regarded his father coldly. "I didn't learn nothing," he said.

"Anything," I said. "Didn't learn anything."

"The teacher spanked a boy, though," Laurie said, addressing his bread and butter. "For being fresh," he added, with his mouth full.

"What did he do?" I asked. "Who was it?"

Laurie thought. "It was Charles," he said. "He was fresh. The teacher spanked him and made him stand in a corner. He was awfully fresh."

"What did he do?" I asked again, but Laurie slid off his chair,

renounced (ri nounst´) *v.* gave up

insolently (in´ sə lənt lē) *adv.* boldly disrespectful in speech or behavior

---

1. **swaggering** (swag´ ər iŋ) *v.* strutting; walking with a bold step.
2. **raucous** (rô´ kəs) *adj.* harsh, rough-sounding.

took a cookie, and left, while his father was still saying, "See here, young man."

The next day Laurie remarked at lunch, as soon as he sat down, "Well, Charles was bad again today." He grinned enormously and said, "Today Charles hit the teacher."

"Good heavens," I said, mindful of the Lord's name, "I suppose he got spanked again?"

"He sure did," Laurie said. "Look up," he said to his father.

"What?" his father said, looking up.

"Look down," Laurie said. "Look at my thumb. Gee, you're dumb." He began to laugh insanely.

"Why did Charles hit the teacher?" I asked quickly.

"Because she tried to make him color with red crayons," Laurie said. "Charles wanted to color with green crayons so he hit the teacher and she spanked him and said nobody play with Charles but everybody did."

The third day—it was Wednesday of the first week—Charles bounced a see-saw on to the head of a little girl and made her bleed, and the teacher made him stay inside all during recess. Thursday Charles had to stand in a corner during story-time because he kept pounding his feet on the floor. Friday Charles was deprived of blackboard privileges because he threw chalk.

On Saturday I remarked to my husband, "Do you think kindergarten is too unsettling for Laurie? All this toughness, and bad grammar, and this Charles boy sounds like such a bad influence."

"It'll be all right," my husband said reassuringly. "Bound to be people like Charles in the world. Might as well meet them now as later."

On Monday Laurie came home late, full of news. "Charles," he shouted as he came up the hill; I was waiting anxiously on the front steps. "Charles," Laurie yelled all the way up the hill, "Charles was bad again."

"Come right in," I said, as soon as he came close enough. "Lunch is waiting."

"You know what Charles did?" he demanded, following me through the door. "Charles yelled so in school they sent a boy in from first grade to tell the teacher she had to make Charles keep quiet, and so Charles had to stay after school. And so all the children stayed to watch him."

"What did he do?" I asked.

"He just sat there," Laurie said, climbing into his chair at the table. "Hi, Pop, y'old dust mop."

"Charles had to stay after school today," I told my husband. "Everyone stayed with him."

"What does this Charles look like?" my husband asked Laurie. "What's his other name?"

"He's bigger than me," Laurie said. "And he doesn't have any

Reading Strategy
Identify Word Origins
What Latin word part is used at the beginning of *reassuringly*?

Reading Check
What does Laurie tell his parents about Charles?

rubbers and he doesn't ever wear a jacket."

Monday night was the first Parent-Teachers meeting, and only the fact that the baby had a cold kept me from going; I wanted passionately to meet Charles's mother. On Tuesday Laurie remarked suddenly, "Our teacher had a friend come to see her in school today."

"Charles's mother?" my husband and I asked <u>simultaneously</u>.

"Naaah," Laurie said scornfully. "It was a man who came and made us do exercises, we had to touch our toes. Look." He climbed down from his chair and squatted down and touched his toes. "Like this," he said. He got solemnly back into his chair and said, picking up his fork, "Charles didn't even do exercises."

"That's fine," I said heartily. "Didn't Charles want to do exercises?"

"Naaah," Laurie said. "Charles was so fresh to the teacher's friend he wasn't let do exercises."

"Fresh again?" I said.

"He kicked the teacher's friend," Laurie said. "The teacher's friend told Charles to touch his toes like I just did and Charles kicked him."

"What are they going to do about Charles, do you suppose?" Laurie's father asked him.

Laurie shrugged elaborately. "Throw him out of school, I guess," he said.

Wednesday and Thursday were routine; Charles yelled during story hour and hit a boy in the stomach and made him cry. On Friday Charles stayed after school again and so did all the other children.

With the third week of kindergarten Charles was an institution in our family; the baby was being a Charles when she cried all afternoon; Laurie did a Charles when he filled his wagon full of mud and pulled it through the kitchen; even my husband, when he caught his elbow in the telephone cord and pulled the telephone, ashtray, and a bowl of flowers off the table, said, after the first minute, "Looks like Charles."

simultaneously
(sī′ məl tā′ nē əs lē) *adv.*
at the same time

▶ **Critical Viewing**
Examine the expression on these children's faces. Which of them might have a personality like that of Charles?
[Connect]

During the third and fourth weeks it looked like a reformation in Charles; Laurie reported grimly at lunch on Thursday of the third week, "Charles was so good today the teacher gave him an apple."

"What?" I said, and my husband added warily, "You mean Charles?"

"Charles," Laurie said. "He gave the crayons around and he picked up the books afterward and the teacher said he was her helper."

"What happened?" I asked <u>incredulously</u>.

"He was her helper, that's all," Laurie said, and shrugged.

"Can this be true, about Charles?" I asked my husband that night. "Can something like this happen?"

"Wait and see," my husband said cynically.[3] "When you've got a Charles to deal with, this may mean he's only plotting." He seemed to be wrong. For over a week Charles was the teacher's helper; each day he handed things out and he picked things up; no one had to stay after school.

"The PTA meeting's next week again," I told my husband one evening. "I'm going to find Charles's mother there."

"Ask her what happened to Charles," my husband said. "I'd like to know."

"I'd like to know myself," I said.

On Friday of that week things were back to normal. "You know what Charles did today?" Laurie demanded at the lunch table, in a voice slightly awed. "He told a little girl to say a word and she said it and the teacher washed her mouth out with soap and Charles laughed."

"What word?" his father asked unwisely, and Laurie said, "I'll have to whisper it to you, it's so bad." He got down off his chair and went around to his father. His father bent his head down and Laurie whispered joyfully. His father's eyes widened.

"Did Charles tell the little girl to say *that*?" he asked respectfully.

"She said it *twice*," Laurie said. "Charles told her to say it *twice*."

"What happened to Charles?" my husband asked.

"Nothing," Laurie said. "He was passing out the crayons."

Monday morning Charles abandoned the little girl and said the evil word himself three or four times, getting his mouth washed out with soap each time. He also threw chalk.

My husband came to the door with me that evening as I set out for the PTA meeting. "Invite her over for a cup of tea after the meeting," he said. "I want to get a look at her."

"If only she's there," I said prayerfully.

"She'll be there," my husband said. "I don't see how they could hold a PTA meeting without Charles's mother."

At the meeting I sat restlessly, scanning each comfortable matronly face, trying to determine which one hid the secret of

---

3. **cynically** (sin´ i klē) *adv.* with disbelief as to the sincerity of people's intentions or actions.

Reading Strategy
Identify Word Origins
If the word root -*form*- means "shape" or "form," what do you think the word *reformation* means?

incredulously
(in krej´ ōō ləs lē) *adv.* with doubt or disbelief

Reading Check

How does Laurie's family respond to his stories about Charles?

Charles ◆ 25

Charles. None of them looked to me haggard enough. No one stood up in the meeting and apologized for the way her son had been acting. No one mentioned Charles.

After the meeting I identified and sought out Laurie's kindergarten teacher. She had a plate with a cup of tea and a piece of chocolate cake; I had a plate with a cup of tea and a piece of marshmallow cake. We maneuvered[4] up to one another cautiously, and smiled.

"I've been so anxious to meet you," I said. "I'm Laurie's mother."

"We're all so interested in Laurie," she said.

"Well, he certainly likes kindergarten," I said. "He talks about it all the time."

"We had a little trouble adjusting, the first week or so," she said primly, "but now he's a fine little helper. With occasional lapses, of course."

"Laurie usually adjusts very quickly," I said. "I suppose this time it's Charles's influence."

"Charles?"

"Yes," I said, laughing, "you must have your hands full in that kindergarten, with Charles."

"Charles?" she said. "We don't have any Charles in the kindergarten."

---

4. **maneuvered** (mə nōō′ vərd) v. moved in a planned way.

Review and Assess

Think About the Selection

1. **Respond:** Were you surprised to learn that Charles and Laurie were the same person? Why or why not?

2. **(a) Recall:** Describe the change in Laurie's clothing on the day he starts school. **(b) Infer:** Why does he make this change?

3. **(a) Recall:** Give three examples of Charles's behavior at school. **(b) Recall:** Give three examples of Laurie's behavior at home. **(c) Compare and Contrast:** How is Charles's behavior at school similar to and different from Laurie's behavior at home?

4. **(a) Recall:** Who is Charles? **(b) Infer:** Why do you think Laurie invented Charles? **(c) Speculate:** How do you think Laurie will react after his parents learn his secret?

5. **(a) Recall:** What does Laurie suggest will happen to Charles? **(b) Infer:** Why does Laurie misbehave in school? **(c) Draw Conclusions:** Why does Laurie begin to cooperate at school?

6. **Evaluate:** What should Laurie's mother say to him after she meets his teacher and learns the truth?

Shirley Jackson

(1919–1965)

As the mother of four energetic children, Shirley Jackson once said that she wrote because "It's the only chance I get to sit down." As a writer, she produced mainly two types of stories—spine-tingling tales of supernatural events and hilarious stories about daily life.

Like many other writers, Jackson borrowed real characters and events from her own life and enlarged them in her fictional stories. The main character in "Charles," for example, is modeled on Jackson's son Laurie. Among her family-inspired books are the fictionalized memoirs *Life Among the Savages* (1953) and *Raising Demons* (1957).

Review and Assess

Literary Analysis

Point of View

1. In what way does the first-person **point of view** increase your curiosity about the boy Charles? Explore the question by filling out a graphic organizer like the one below.

What narrator knows	What she wants to know	What do you want to know?
Charles misbehaves in school. Charles is in Laurie's class.		

2. In what ways would the story be different if Laurie were the first-person narrator?
3. How does the first-person point of view help make the ending a surprise?

Connecting Literary Elements

4. Whose words reveal that Charles is Laurie?
5. Identify two examples of **dialogue** in which Laurie gives a hint that he is Charles.

Reading Strategy

Identify Word Origins

6. Complete a chart like the one shown here to identify the origins of words found in the story.

Word From Story	Other Words with Same Origin	Shared Word Part	Origin and Meaning of Shared Word Part
renounce	announce, pronounce, denounce	nounce	Latin *nuntius,* "messenger"
simultaneously	simulate, similar		
influence	fluctuate, fluent		

Extend Understanding

7. **Career Connection:** What techniques can a teacher use to get children like Laurie to behave in class?

Quick Review

Point of view is the perspective from which a story is told.

A narrative in the **first-person point of view** is told by a character who participates in the action.

To review point of view, see page 21.

Dialogue is the conversation between characters. To review dialogue, see page 21.

Identify **word origins** to recognize relationships between words. To review word origins, see page 21.

 Take It to the Net
www.phschool.com
Take the interactive self-test online to check your understanding of the selection.

Integrate Language Skills

Vocabulary Development Lesson

Word Analysis: Latin Root -cred-

In *incredulous*, the Latin word root *-cred-* means "believe." Write a definition of each word below, using the meaning of the Latin root *-cred-*. Use a dictionary to check your definitions.

1. incredible   2. credible   3. credence

Spelling Strategy

When you add the word ending *-ed* or *-ing* to a word that ends with *-e*, drop the *e* before adding the ending.
Example: renounce + *ed* = renounced
           renounce + *ing* = renouncing

Correct any misspellings in the following passage.

> Laurie's mother considered invitieng Laurie's teacher home for a cup of tea. Laurie elaborated on Charles's behavior. She thought that he might be influenceing Laurie's behavior.

Grammar Lesson

Common and Proper Nouns

Common nouns name any person, place, thing, or idea. **Proper nouns** name a particular person, place, thing, or idea. Always capitalize proper nouns. Capitalize common nouns only when they begin a sentence.

Common Nouns	Proper Nouns
boy	Charles
day	Thursday
school	Primrose School

Fluency: Words in Context

On your paper, complete the following passage so that it makes sense, using the vocabulary words from "Charles."

Zita's teacher, Mr. Acevedo, stared at her paper ____?____.

"I have ____?____ language in favor of Art," Zita declared.

Mr. Acevedo laughed but would not accept the paper. Zita stamped her foot ____?____.
____?____, she started to pout.

For each numbered item, use both words correctly in a single sentence.

1. renounced/enjoyed
2. insolently/politely
3. simultaneously/separately
4. incredulously/trustingly

▶ *For more practice, see page R28, Exercise A.*
Practice Write each of these sentences, underlining the nouns. Then, write C or P above each noun to tell whether it is common or proper.

1. Laurie regarded his father coldly.
2. "What does this Charles look like?" my husband asked Laurie.
3. On Friday things were back to normal.
4. Our teacher had a friend, Mr. Simmons.
5. Jackson is a good writer.

Writing Application Rewrite the following items, replacing bracketed proper nouns with common nouns and common nouns with proper nouns.

1. We have music class on [a day].
2. We are taught by [Mr. Rando].
3. [A girl] is very musical.

𝒲𝒢 *Prentice Hall Writing and Grammar Connection: Chapter 14, Section 1*

Writing Lesson

Humorous Anecdote

Write a humorous anecdote—a funny, brief story—about another of Laurie's school experiences. In your anecdote, include details that form a single, main impression of Laurie.

Prewriting   Choose one word that gives the overall impression. On a graphic organizer like the one shown here, write actions that demonstrate how Laurie shows that quality. In the outer sections jot down ideas for events that result from Laurie's actions.

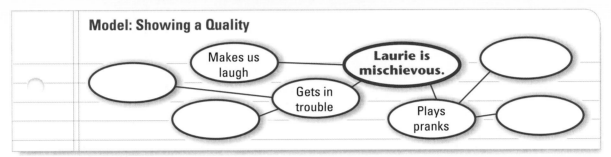

Model: Showing a Quality

Makes us laugh

Gets in trouble

Laurie is mischievous.

Plays pranks

Drafting   Incorporate the events and actions from your graphic organizer. Use specific words to name actions and strengthen your overall impression.

Revising   Eliminate any details that do not directly contribute to the main impression. Strengthen your main impression by replacing vague action words with more specific ones.

W͞G Prentice Hall Writing and Grammar Connection: Chapter 6, Section 2

Extension Activities

Listening and Speaking Imagine that you are Laurie in the eighth grade. Perform a **retelling** of the story of "Charles" as you now see it. Use your voice and expression to add to the humor of your retelling.

1. Use a childish voice when you are speaking as the kindergarten Laurie.

2. Show an exaggerated innocent expression when kindergarten Laurie tells about Charles's actions.

Practice your story, and deliver it to a small group of classmates. Ask them to comment on how effectively you used your voice and expression.

Research and Technology With a small group of classmates, conduct an **interview** with a kindergarten teacher to discuss the challenges of teaching children Laurie's age. Prepare a list of questions that your group would like to ask the teacher. During the interview, ask follow-up questions—questions for clarifying an answer. Present the results to the rest of your class in a written or an oral report.

Take It to the Net   www.phschool.com

Go online for an additional research activity using the Internet.

Prepare to Read

from I Know Why the Caged Bird Sings

Parkville, Main Street (Missouri), 1933, Gale Stockwell, National Museum of American Art, Washington, DC

Take It to the Net

Visit www.phschool.com
for interactive activities
and instruction related to *I
Know Why the Caged Bird
Sings,* including

- background
- graphic organizers
- literary elements
- reading strategies

Preview

Connecting to the Literature

In this true-life story from *I Know Why the Caged Bird Sings*, a distinguished adult helps a young girl overcome shyness and begin to have pride in herself. Connect to her experience by remembering a time when someone helped you feel proud of yourself.

Background

When Maya Angelou, the author of *I Know Why the Caged Bird Sings*, was growing up in the 1930s and 1940s, African Americans and whites attended separate schools. African Americans were excluded from many public facilities. As an African American woman, Angelou experienced both racial and gender discrimination. With the help of a family friend, she learned to rise above it.

Literary Analysis

Memoir

A **memoir** is autobiographical writing—true writing from a person's own life—in which a writer shares a memory of a significant person or event. Angelou writes about her memories of working in the family store and learning "lessons in living" from a remarkable woman.

As you read the excerpt from *I Know Why the Caged Bird Sings*, use these focus questions to explore the significance of the events.

1. Why is the store Angelou's favorite place?
2. What change occurs in Angelou after her visit with Mrs. Flowers?

Connecting Literary Elements

In a memoir, writers use **descriptive details**—details that appeal to the senses—to bring their memories to life. In the following example, the italicized words provide details of the sights, feelings, and scents that Angelou associates with her memories of pineapples.

> Although the *syrupy golden rings* sat in their exotic cans on our shelves year round, we only tasted them during Christmas. . . . Bailey and I received one slice each, and I carried mine around for hours, *shredding off the fruit* until nothing was left except the *perfume on my fingers*.

Reading Strategy

Analyze Figurative Language

In the excerpt from *I Know Why the Caged Bird Sings*, Angelou uses several types of **figurative language**—words, phrases, and expressions not meant to be interpreted literally. The chart shows different types of figurative language. When you encounter examples in the text, think about what the author really means, not just what the words say.

Idiom
Expression that has a meaning particular to a language or region

Analogy
Comparison of the particular resemblances of things that are otherwise not like each other

Metaphor
Figure of speech in which one thing is referred to as if it were another

Simile
Figure of speech in which two unlike things are compared using the word *like* or *as*

Vocabulary Development

fiscal (fis′ kəl) *adj.* having to do with finances (p. 33)

taut (tôt) *adj.* tightly stretched (p. 34)

benign (bi nīn′) *adj.* kindly (p. 34)

infuse (in fyo͞oz′) *v.* put into (p. 36)

intolerant (in täl′ ər ənt) *adj.* unable or unwilling to accept (p. 37)

couched (koucht) *v.* put into words; expressed (p. 37)

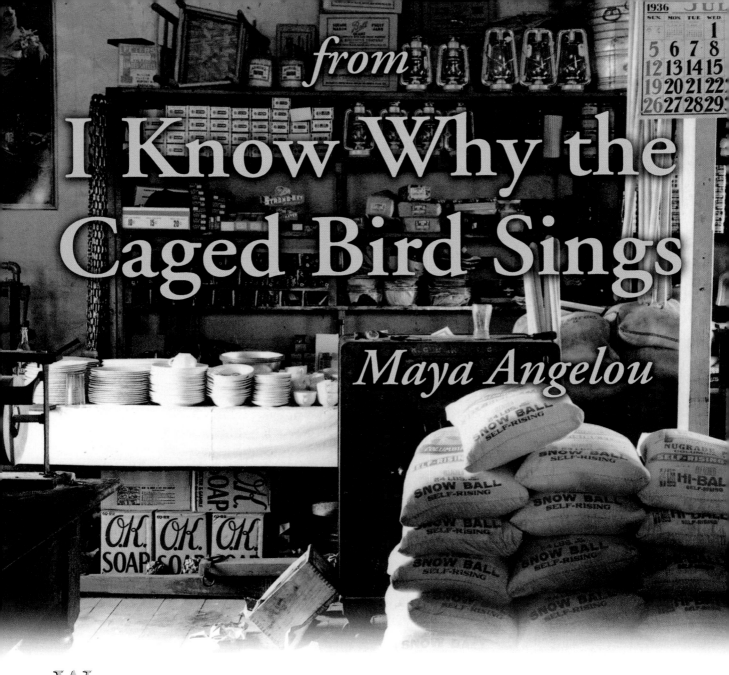

from

I Know Why the Caged Bird Sings

Maya Angelou

1936 JUL
SUN MON TUE WED
1
5 6 7 8
12 13 14 15
19 20 21 22
26 27 28 29

W e lived with our grandmother and uncle in the rear of the Store (it was always spoken of with a capital *s*), which she had owned some twenty-five years.

Early in the century, Momma (we soon stopped calling her Grandmother) sold lunches to the sawmen in the lumberyard (east Stamps) and the seedmen at the cotton gin (west Stamps). Her crisp meat pies and cool lemonade, when joined to her miraculous ability to be in two places at the same time, assured her business success. From being a mobile lunch counter, she set up a stand

▲ **Critical Viewing**
Why might the narrator enjoy spending time in a place like this? **[Connect]**

between the two points of <u>fiscal</u> interest and supplied the workers' needs for a few years. Then she had the Store built in the heart of the Negro area. Over the years it became the lay center of activities in town. On Saturdays, barbers sat their customers in the shade on the porch of the Store, and troubadours[1] on their ceaseless crawlings through the South leaned across its benches and sang their sad songs of The Brazos[2] while they played juice harps[3] and cigar-box guitars.

The formal name of the Store was the Wm. Johnson General Merchandise Store. Customers could find food staples, a good variety of colored thread, mash for hogs, corn for chickens, coal oil for lamps, light bulbs for the wealthy, shoestrings, hair dressing, balloons, and flower seeds. Anything not visible had only to be ordered.

Until we became familiar enough to belong to the Store and it to us, we were locked up in a Fun House of Things where the attendant had gone home for life. . . .

Weighing the half-pounds of flour, excluding the scoop, and depositing them dust-free into the thin paper sacks held a simple kind of adventure for me. I developed an eye for measuring how full a silver-looking ladle of flour, mash, meal, sugar or corn had to be to push the scale indicator over to eight ounces or one pound. When I was absolutely accurate our appreciative customers used to admire: "Sister Henderson sure got some smart grandchildrens." If I was off in the Store's favor, the eagle-eyed women would say, "Put some more in that sack, child. Don't you try to make your profit offa me."

Then I would quietly but persistently punish myself. For every bad judgment, the fine was no silver-wrapped kisses, the sweet chocolate drops that I loved more than anything in the world, except Bailey. And maybe canned pineapples. My obsession with pineapples nearly drove me mad. I dreamt of the days when I would be grown and able to buy a whole carton for myself alone.

Although the syrupy golden rings sat in their exotic cans on our shelves year round, we only tasted them during Christmas. Momma used the juice to make almost-black fruit cakes. Then she lined heavy soot-encrusted iron skillets with the pineapple rings for rich upside-down cakes. Bailey and I received one slice each, and I carried mine around for hours, shredding off the fruit until nothing was left except the perfume on my fingers. I'd like to think that my desire for pineapples was so sacred that I wouldn't allow myself to steal a can (which was possible) and eat it alone out in the garden, but I'm certain that I must have weighed the possibility of the scent exposing me and didn't have the nerve to attempt it.

fiscal (fis′ kəl) *adj.* having to do with finances

Literary Analysis
Memoir What does this paragraph tell about Marguerite?

 **Reading Check**

What does the narrator do in the store?

---

1. **troubadours** (tr$\overline{oo}$′ bə dôrz′) *n.* traveling singers.
2. **The Brazos** (bräz′ əs) area in central Texas near the Brazos River.
3. **juice** (j$\overline{oo}$s) **harps** small musical instruments held between the teeth and played by plucking.

Until I was thirteen and left Arkansas for good, the Store was my favorite place to be. Alone and empty in the mornings, it looked like an unopened present from a stranger. Opening the front doors was pulling the ribbon off the unexpected gift. The light would come in softly (we faced north), easing itself over the shelves of mackerel, salmon, tobacco, thread. It fell flat on the big vat of lard and by noontime during the summer the grease had softened to a thick soup. Whenever I walked into the Store in the afternoon, I sensed that it was tired. I alone could hear the slow pulse of its job half done. But just before bedtime, after numerous people had walked in and out, had argued over their bills, or joked about their neighbors, or just dropped in "to give Sister Henderson a 'Hi y'all,'" the promise of magic mornings returned to the Store and spread itself over the family in washed life waves. . . .

When Maya was about ten years old, she returned to Stamps from a visit to St. Louis with her mother. She had become depressed and withdrawn.

For nearly a year, I sopped around the house, the Store, the school and the church, like an old biscuit, dirty and inedible. Then I met, or rather got to know, the lady who threw me my first lifeline.

Mrs. Bertha Flowers was the aristocrat[4] of Black Stamps. She had the grace of control to appear warm in the coldest weather, and on the Arkansas summer days it seemed she had a private breeze which swirled around, cooling her. She was thin without the <u>taut</u> look of wiry people, and her printed voile[5] dresses and flowered hats were as right for her as denim overalls for a farmer. She was our side's answer to the richest white woman in town.

Her skin was a rich black that would have peeled like a plum if snagged, but then no one would have thought of getting close enough to Mrs. Flowers to ruffle her dress, let alone snag her skin. She didn't encourage familiarity. She wore gloves too.

I don't think I ever saw Mrs. Flowers laugh, but she smiled often. A slow widening of her thin black lips to show even, small white teeth, then the slow effortless closing. When she chose to smile on me, I always wanted to thank her. The action was so graceful and inclusively <u>benign</u>.

She was one of the few gentlewomen I have ever known, and has remained throughout my life the measure of what a human being can be. . . .

One summer afternoon, sweet-milk fresh in my memory, she stopped at the Store to buy provisions. Another Negro woman of

Reading Strategy
Analyze Figurative Language Marguerite says that Mrs. Bertha Flowers threw her a "lifeline." What does she mean to communicate with this expression?

taut (tôt) *adj.* tightly stretched

benign (bi nīn′) *adj.* kindly

---

4. **aristocrat** (ə ris′ tə krat) *n.* person belonging to the upper class.
5. **voile** (voil) *n.* light cotton fabric.

Woman in Calico, 1944, William Johnson, National Museum of American Art, Washington, DC

▲ **Critical Viewing** Read the description of Mrs. Flowers on page 34. Does this portrait resemble her? Explain. **[Assess]**

her health and age would have been expected to carry the paper sacks home in one hand, but Momma said, "Sister Flowers, I'll send Bailey up to your house with these things."

She smiled that slow dragging smile, "Thank you, Mrs. Henderson. I'd prefer Marguerite, though." My name was beautiful when she said it. "I've been meaning to talk to her, anyway." They gave each other age-group looks.

Momma said, "Well, that's all right then. Sister, go and change your dress. You going to Sister Flowers's. . . ."

There was a little path beside the rocky road, and Mrs. Flowers walked in front swinging her arms and picking her way over the stones.

She said, without turning her head, to me, "I hear you're doing very good school work, Marguerite, but that it's all written. The teachers report that they have trouble getting you to talk in class." We passed the triangular farm on our left and the path widened to

✔ Reading Check

What details about Mrs. Flowers are still vivid in Angelou's memory?

from *I Know Why the Caged Bird Sings* ◆ 35

allow us to walk together. I hung back in the separate unasked and unanswerable questions.

"Come and walk along with me, Marguerite." I couldn't have refused even if I wanted to. She pronounced my name so nicely. Or more correctly, she spoke each word with such clarity that I was certain a foreigner who didn't understand English could have understood her.

"Now no one is going to make you talk—possibly no one can. But bear in mind, language is man's way of communicating with his fellow man and it is language alone which separates him from the lower animals." That was a totally new idea to me, and I would need time to think about it.

Literary Analysis
Memoir What does this paragraph reveal about Marguerite's personality?

"Your grandmother says you read a lot. Every chance you get. That's good, but not good enough. Words mean more than what is set down on paper. It takes the human voice to <u>infuse</u> them with the shades of deeper meaning."

infuse (in fyooz′) v. put into

I memorized the part about the human voice infusing words. It seemed so valid and poetic.

She said she was going to give me some books and that I not only must read them, I must read them aloud. She suggested that I try to make a sentence sound in as many different ways as possible.

"I'll accept no excuse if you return a book to me that has been badly handled." My imagination boggled at the punishment I would deserve if in fact I did abuse a book of Mrs. Flowers'. Death would be too kind and brief.

The odors in the house surprised me. Somehow I had never connected Mrs. Flowers with food or eating or any other common experience of common people. There must have been an outhouse, too, but my mind never recorded it.

The sweet scent of vanilla had met us as she opened the door.

"I made tea cookies this morning. You see, I had planned to invite you for cookies and lemonade so we could have this little chat. The lemonade is in the icebox."

It followed that Mrs. Flowers would have ice on an ordinary day, when most families in our town bought ice late on Saturdays only a few times during the summer to be used in the wooden ice cream freezers.

She took the bags from me and disappeared through the kitchen door. I looked around the room that I had never in my wildest fantasies imagined I would see. Browned photographs leered or threatened from the walls and the white, freshly done curtains pushed against themselves and against the wind. I wanted to gobble up the room entire and take it to Bailey, who would help me analyze and enjoy it.

"Have a seat, Marguerite. Over there by the table." She carried a platter covered with a tea towel. Although she warned that she hadn't tried her hand at baking sweets for some time, I was certain that like everything else about her the cookies would be perfect.

They were flat round wafers, slightly browned on the edges and butter-yellow in the center. With the cold lemonade they were sufficient for childhood's lifelong diet. Remembering my manners, I took nice little ladylike bites off the edges. She said she had made them expressly for me and that she had a few in the kitchen that I could take home to my brother. So I jammed one whole cake in my mouth and the rough crumbs scratched the insides of my jaws, and if I hadn't had to swallow, it would have been a dream come true.

As I ate she began the first of what we later called "my lessons in living." She said that I must always be <u>intolerant</u> of ignorance but understanding of illiteracy. That some people, unable to go to school, were more educated and even more intelligent than college professors. She encouraged me to listen carefully to what country people called mother wit. That in those homely sayings was <u>couched</u> the collective wisdom of generations.

When I finished the cookies she brushed off the table and brought a thick, small book from the bookcase. I had read *A Tale of Two Cities* and found it up to my standards as a romantic novel. She opened the first page and I heard poetry for the first time in my life.

"It was the best of times and the worst of times . . ." Her voice slid in and curved down through and over the words. She was nearly singing. I wanted to look at the pages. Were they the same that I had read? Or were there notes, music, lined on the pages, as in a hymn book? Her sounds began cascading gently. I knew from listening to a thousand preachers that she was nearing the end of her reading, and I hadn't really heard, heard to understand, a single word.

"How do you like that?"

It occurred to me that she expected a response. The sweet vanilla flavor was still on my tongue and her reading was a wonder in my ears. I had to speak.

I said, "Yes, ma'am." It was the least I could do, but it was the most also.

"There's one more thing. Take this book of poems and memorize one for me. Next time you pay me a visit, I want you to recite."

I have tried often to search behind the sophistication of years for the enchantment I so easily found in those gifts. The essence escapes but its aura[6] remains. To be allowed, no, invited, into the private lives of strangers, and to share their joys and fears, was a chance to exchange the Southern bitter wormwood[7] for a cup of mead with Beowulf[8] or a hot cup of tea and milk with Oliver Twist.

Literary Analysis
Memoir and Descriptive Details Which descriptive details in this paragraph help bring to life Angelou's memory of her visit with Mrs. Flowers?

intolerant (in täl´ ər ənt) *adj.* not able or willing to accept

couched (koucht) *v.* expressed in softer or more flowery terms

Reading Check

What does Marguerite learn from Mrs. Flowers?

6. **aura** (ôr´ ə) *n.* atmosphere or quality.
7. **wormwood** (wurm´ wood´) *n.* plant that produces a bitter oil.
8. **Beowulf** (bā´ ə woolf´) hero of an old Anglo-Saxon epic. People in this poem drink mead, (mēd), a drink made with honey and water.

When I said aloud, "It is a far far better thing that I do, than I have ever done . . ."[9] tears of love filled my eyes at my selflessness.

On that first day, I ran down the hill and into the road (few cars ever came along it) and had the good sense to stop running before I reached the Store.

I was liked, and what a difference it made. I was respected not as Mrs. Henderson's grandchild or Bailey's sister but for just being Marguerite Johnson.

Childhood's logic never asks to be proved (all conclusions are absolute). I didn't question why Mrs. Flowers had singled me out for attention, nor did it occur to me that Momma might have asked her to give me a little talking to. All I cared about was that she had made tea cookies for *me* and read to *me* from her favorite book. It was enough to prove that she liked me.

---

9. **"It is . . . than I have ever done"** speech from *A Tale of Two Cities* by Charles Dickens.

Review and Assess

Thinking About the Selection

1. **Respond:** Does Mrs. Flowers remind you of anyone you know? Explain.

2. **(a) Recall:** What does Marguerite do in the store?
   (b) Infer: What can you tell about Marguerite's character from her actions at the Store?

3. **(a) Recall:** According to Mrs. Flowers, for what two reasons is language important? **(b) Interpret:** Why does Mrs. Flowers tell Marguerite to read aloud and in as many different ways as possible?

4. **(a) Recall:** What does Mrs. Flowers tell Marguerite in the first of her "lessons in living"? **(b) Compare and Contrast:** Describe the change in Marguerite after her first meeting with Mrs. Flowers. **(c) Draw Conclusions:** In what ways do you think Marguerite will change as a result of her meetings with Mrs. Flowers?

5. **(a) Recall:** What does Mrs. Flowers do when Marguerite visits? **(b) Infer:** What do Mrs. Flowers' actions prove to Marguerite? **(c) Interpret:** Why has Mrs. Flowers remained for Angelou "the measure of what a human being can be"?

6. **Apply:** Mrs. Flowers helped build a sense of self-worth for young Maya Angelou. What social conditions of the time may have contributed to her low self-esteem before her meetings with Mrs. Flowers?

Maya Angelou

(b. 1928)
Born Marguerite Johnson in St. Louis, Missouri, Maya Angelou received her unusual first name from her brother, Bailey, who referred to her as "mya sister." Maya and Bailey were raised by their grandmother, who owned a country store in rural Arkansas.

Growing up in the segregated South did not prevent Angelou from breaking through the barriers of racism and poverty. She has been a streetcar conductor in San Francisco, a journalist, an actress, a civil rights worker, a teacher, and a poet. In January 1993, she read "On the Pulse of Morning" at President-elect Bill Clinton's inauguration, a poem that she had been asked to write for the occasion.

Review and Assess

Literary Analysis

Memoir

1. In a chart like the one below, list two details that we learn about Marguerite from her **memoir**. In the second column, explain how we know about each detail.

What we know about Marguerite	How we know it

2. Why is the store Angelou's favorite place?
3. What change occurs in Angelou after her visit with Mrs. Flowers?

Connecting Literary Elements

4. Complete a sensory details chart like the one shown here.

	Sights	Sounds	Touch	Tastes	Smells
The Store					
Mrs. Flowers's house					

5. Explain why sensory details are important in the memoir.

Reading Strategy

Analyze Figurative Language

6. Explain the difference between the literal and **figurative** meanings of the idiom "I developed an eye for measuring."
7. Explain what Angelou means by the following analogy: "Opening the front doors was pulling the ribbon off the unexpected gift."
8. What simile does Marguerite use to communicate her low self-esteem before she goes to Mrs. Flowers's house?

Extend Understanding

9. **Social Studies Connection:** Angelou's memoir takes place during a time when segregation laws governed most of the South. How do Mrs. Flowers's life lessons prepare Marguerite to challenge unjust laws?

Quick Review

A **memoir** is a form of autobiography that focuses on a writer's memory of a significant person or event. To review memoir, see page 31.

Descriptive details are words that appeal to the five senses—sight, smell, taste, touch, and hearing.

Figurative language is speech or writing that is not meant to be taken literally. To review figurative language, see page 31.

 Take It to the Net
www.phschool.com
Take the interactive self-test online to check your understanding of the selection.

Integrate Language Skills

Vocabulary Development Lesson

Word Analysis: Forms of *tolerate*

The verb *tolerate* means "to accept." Other forms of *tolerate* include the following:

tolerance   tolerable   intolerant   tolerant

Knowing the meaning of *tolerate*, you can determine the meanings of its related forms. On your paper, complete the following sentences with the correct related word from the list above.

1. Mrs. Flowers suggested that Marguerite show ___?___ toward people who are illiterate but to always be ___?___ of ignorance.
2. Marguerite's working at Momma's store was ___?___.
3. Mrs. Bertha Flowers was ___?___ of Marguerite's shyness but wanted her to overcome it.

Fluency: Sentence Completions

On your paper, write the vocabulary word that best completes each sentence.

1. The rope was pulled ___?___ for security.
2. Although stern, Mrs. Flowers's actions were ___?___.
3. She used lemons to ___?___ her tea.
4. Her advice was ___?___ in stories and sayings.
5. For ___?___ reasons, the Store was open late.
6. Marguerite learned not to be ___?___ of others.

Spelling Strategy

In some words, like *benign*, the *īn* sound is spelled *ign*—with a silent *g*. Complete the following with an *ign* word.

1. A pattern or arrangement of parts: ___?___
2. A publicly displayed billboard: ___?___
3. To leave a job: ___?___

Grammar Lesson

Plural and Possessive Nouns

Plural and possessive nouns are sometimes confused. A **plural noun** indicates more than one person, place, thing, or idea. Most plural nouns end with the letter *-s*.

Plural Nouns: "On *Saturdays*, *barbers* sat their *customers* in the shade on the porch. . . ."

A **possessive noun** shows ownership, belonging, or some other close relationship. A possessive noun can be **singular,** ending in *-'s*, or **plural,** usually ending in *-s'*.

Singular Possessive: "If I was off in the *Store's* favor, the eagle-eyed women would . . ."

Plural Possessive: "[S]he . . . supplied the *workers'* needs for a few years."

▶ *For more practice, see page R28, Exercise B.*
Practice On your paper, copy the following sentences. Correct errors of plural and possessive nouns as needed.

1. Mrs. Flowers's home smelled like vanilla.
2. There are many picture's in the book. All the picture's colors are fading.
3. The book's Mrs. Flowers' allowed Marguerite to borrow were her favorite's.
4. Take this book of poems.
5. Read each poems words carefully.

Writing Application Write a paragraph that includes the following nouns: *store, owner,* and *customer.* Use two of the nouns as plurals and one as a possessive.

WG Prentice Hall Writing and Grammar Connection: Chapter 26, Section 5

Writing Lesson

Memoir About a Turning Point

Marguerite's visit with Mrs. Flowers was a turning point that changed her outlook. Think of a time when you experienced a turning point. Write a memoir about the event.

Prewriting   List specific details that describe your turning point. Include explanations of how events and people made you feel and why. Then, organize the details into a sequence.

Drafting   Use your organized list as the basis for drafting your memoir. Add descriptive details that will make the event or experience vivid in your readers' minds.

Model: Add Descriptive Details

I clutched the trophy proudly.

+ **silver**

+ **heavy**

_____

I clutched the heavy, silver trophy proudly.

> Descriptive details like *heavy* and *silver* appeal to sight, sound, taste, smell, or touch and help paint a more memorable picture of what happened.

Revising   Reread your memoir and underline the descriptive details you have used. Add details to appeal to senses you have not included.

*W*G   *Prentice Hall Writing and Grammar Connection: Chapter 6, Section 2*

Extension Activities

Listening and Speaking Angelou describes the effect of Mrs. Flowers's reading aloud as "a wonder in my ears." Prepare a **reading** of a portion of Angelou's memoir.

With a group, discuss **delivery techniques** that can enhance a listener's appreciation for what is being read. Techniques include

- volume (the loudness or softness of your voice).
- tone of voice (the feelings expressed through your voice).
- enunciation (the clear, precise pronunciation of words).

Research and Technology Photographers Walker Evans and Dorothea Lange recorded the lives of Americans during the Great Depression. Use museums, museum Web sites, or the Library of Congress Web page to locate historical photographs. Print copies of the photos. Identify the photographer and where and when the photo was taken. Display your **photo collection** in the classroom.

 **Take It to the Net**   www.phschool.com

Go online for an additional research activity using the Internet.

Prepare to Read

The Road Not Taken ◆ All But Blind ◆ The Choice

 Take It to the Net

Visit www.phschool.com for interactive activities and instruction related to these selections, including

- background
- graphic organizers
- literary elements
- reading strategies

Preview

Connecting to the Literature

Connect to the decision makers who speak in these poems by thinking about decisions you have made in your own life and where those decisions have led or may lead.

Background

The speaker of Walter de la Mare's poem, "All But Blind," compares himself to three creatures with poor vision. Moles are small, nearly blind rodents that live underground. Bats rely more on their sense of hearing than on their sight. Because owls have keen night vision and often appear disoriented during the day, they are thought to be "blinded" by sunlight. In fact, an owl is clumsy in daylight because daytime is supposed to be its sleeping time!

Literary Analysis

Identify the Speaker in a Poem

The **speaker** in a poem is the character or voice assumed by the writer. In some poems, the speaker may be the poet, but do not be fooled by the pronoun "I." The speaker may be a character who is not even human—perhaps a tree or an old rocking chair. As you read each poem, notice clues that reveal the personality of the speaker.

Comparing Literary Works

Each of these works gives a view of decisions and choices in life. As you read, think about the **tone** of each work—the writer's attitude toward the subject and the reader. Compare and contrast the tones of the works by focusing on the following questions:

1. What examples and images does each writer use to show how choices are made?
2. What is the attitude expressed in the last line of each poem?

Reading Strategy

Paraphrasing

Poetry often expresses ideas in language that does not sound like everyday speech. **Paraphrasing,** or restating the lines in your own words, can help you make sense of the ideas. Some words may be arranged in an unusual order.

- **Original lines:** All but blind / In his chambered hole / Gropes for worms / The four-clawed Mole.
- **Paraphrase:** Almost blind in his underground tunnel, the mole digs for worms.

Idioms and analogies may use familiar words in new ways.

- **Idioms:** expressions that are unique to a region or language.
- **Analogies:** comparisons of similarities between unlike things.

For each poem, prepare a chart like the one shown. Record your paraphrase of passages from the poems.

Original Phrase	Paraphrase
And sorry I could not travel both / And be one traveler	and wishing that even though I'm only one person I could try both roads
as just as fair	because it looked just as good

Vocabulary Development

diverged (dī vʉrjd´) v. branched off (p. 44)

blunders (blun´ dərz) v. moves clumsily or carelessly (p. 47)

smoldering (smōl´ dər iŋ) adj. burning or smoking without flame (p. 48)

lilting (lilt´ iŋ) adj. singing or speaking with a light, graceful rhythm (p. 48)

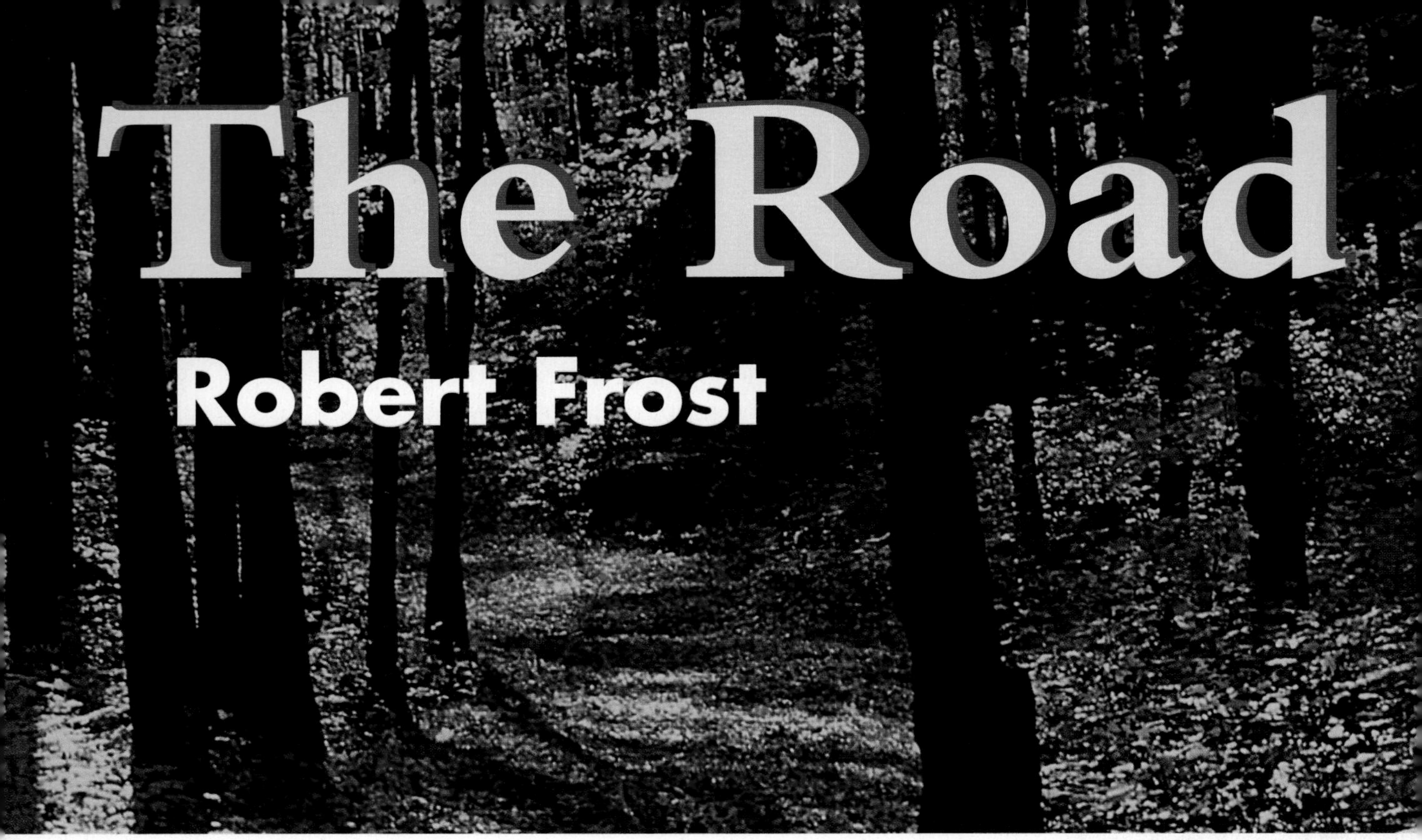

The Road
Robert Frost

Two roads <u>diverged</u> in a yellow wood,
And sorry I could not travel both
And be one traveler, long I stood
And looked down one as far as I could
5 To where it bent in the undergrowth;

Then took the other, as just as fair,
And having perhaps the better claim,
Because it was grassy and wanted wear;
Though as for that, the passing there
10 Had worn them really about the same,

And both that morning equally lay
In leaves no step had trodden black.
Oh, I kept the first for another day!
Yet knowing how way leads on to way,
15 I doubted if I should ever come back.

I shall be telling this with a sigh
Somewhere ages and ages hence:
Two roads diverged in a wood, and I—
I took the one less traveled by,
20 And that has made all the difference.

diverged (dī vʉrjd′) v.
branched off

Reading Strategy
Paraphrasing Restate the
first two lines of the
second stanza, or group of
lines, in your own words.

Not Taken

Robert Frost

(1874–1963)

Review and Assess

Thinking About the Selection

1. **Respond:** Do you think the speaker in "The Road Not Taken" made a wise choice? Explain.

2. **(a) Recall:** In the first five lines of the poem, where does the speaker remember being? **(b) Infer:** What can you tell about the speaker's character and attitude toward life from these lines?

3. **(a) Compare and Contrast:** How are the two roads alike and different? **(b) Interpret:** What kind of choice might these two roads represent?

4. **(a) Recall:** Which road does the speaker finally choose? **(b) Deduce:** Why does the speaker choose one road over the other? **(c) Analyze:** Find two statements suggesting that the speaker believes he has made a significant choice.

5. **(a) Speculate:** Why does the speaker predict that he will remember this decision? **(b) Generalize:** What message does the poem communicate about decisions in general?

One memorable moment for poetry in the twentieth century was Robert Frost's reading of his poem "The Gift Outright" at the 1961 inauguration of President John F. Kennedy. One of the best-known and best-loved American poets, Frost was a four-time winner of the Pulitzer Prize. Although he was born in San Francisco, his family moved to New England when he was eleven, and he later settled on a farm in New Hampshire. Many of Frost's poems are set in or are about some aspect of life in rural New England.

All But Blind

Walter de la Mare

All but blind
    In his chambered hole
Gropes for worms
    The four-clawed Mole.

5 All but blind
    In the evening sky
The hooded Bat
    Twirls softly by.

All but blind
10   In the burning day
The Barn-Owl <u>blunders</u>
    On her way.

And blind as are
    These three to me,
15 So, blind to Some-One
    I must be.

Reading Strategy
Paraphrasing In your own words, explain the analogy the speaker makes between animals being unaware of him and his own unawareness of "Some-One."

blunders (blun´ dərz) v. moves clumsily or carelessly

Review and Assess

Thinking About the Selection

1. **Respond:** Does the life of one of these three animals seem more appealing to you than the lives of the others? Explain your answer.

2. **(a) Recall:** What three words does the speaker use to describe the ways the three animals move? **(b) Analyze:** How do these words reinforce the idea that the animals do not see well? **(c) Support:** Which of these words describes negative aspects of the animals' lives?

3. **(a) Recall:** What do all three creatures in this poem have in common? **(b) Interpret:** In what way does the speaker assume that he is like them? **(c) Infer:** Why is the comparison between the animals and the speaker a surprise?

4. **(a) Deduce:** Who might be the "Some-One" the speaker mentions? **(b) Interpret:** What does the reference reveal about the speaker's world view?

Walter de la Mare

(1873–1956)
British poet and novelist Walter de la Mare has been called the "last poet of the Romantic tradition." De la Mare believed that the world beyond human experience could best be understood through the imagination. His poetry often deals with childhood, nature, dreams, and the uncanny.

The Choice

Dorothy Parker

He'd have given me rolling lands,
    Houses of marble, and billowing farms,
Pearls, to trickle between my hands,
    <u>Smoldering</u> rubies, to circle my arms.
5   You—you'd only a <u>lilting</u> song.
    Only a melody, happy and high,
You were sudden and swift and strong,—
    Never a thought for another had I.

He'd have given me laces rare,
10   Dresses that glimmered with frosty sheen,
Shining ribbons to wrap my hair,
    Horses to draw me, as fine as a queen.
You—you'd only to whistle low,
    Gaily I followed wherever you led.
15   I took you, and I let him go,—
    Somebody ought to examine my head!

smoldering (smōl′ dər iŋ)
adj. burning or smoking
without flame

lilting (lilt′ iŋ) *adj.* singing
or speaking with a light,
graceful rhythm

Review and Assess

Thinking About the Selection

1. **Respond:** Would you enjoy the company of the speaker in "The Choice"? Explain.

2. **(a) Recall:** What choice does the speaker make? **(b) Analyze:** Why does she choose as she does?

3. **(a) Recall:** What would the rejected suitor have given the speaker? **(b) Infer:** Does the speaker regret the decision she made? **(c) Support:** What in the poem makes you think so?

4. **(a) Analyze:** In what way is the last line of "The Choice" different from what the poem leads you to predict?
(b) Make a Judgment: Do you think the speaker's attitude is appropriate? Explain.

5. **Take a Stand:** Would you advise the speaker to make a practical choice or a romantic one? Why?

Dorothy Parker

(1893–1967)

Dorothy Parker is known for her poetry, short stories, and biting comments on the subject of love. In New York literary circles of the 1920s, Parker was a member of the Algonquin Round Table. This group of writers lunched regularly at the Algonquin Hotel, trading brilliant insults and witty observations.

Review and Assess

Literary Analysis

Identify the Speaker in a Poem

1. What is the main concern of the **speaker** in "The Road Not Taken"?
2. How does the speaker in "All But Blind" view his or her place in the world?
3. What do the details in "The Choice" reveal about the speaker's personality?

Comparing Literary Works

4. Complete a comparison and contrast diagram like the one shown here to examine the similarities and differences among the **tones** of the three poems. Where the circles overlap, use words and phrases to describe attitudes the poems' speakers share.

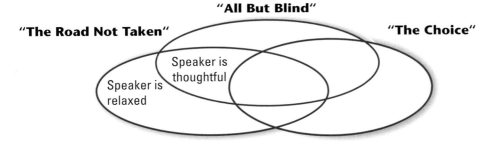

"All But Blind"

"The Road Not Taken"   "The Choice"

Speaker is thoughtful

Speaker is relaxed

5. What examples and images does each writer use to show how choices are made?
6. What is the attitude expressed in the last line of each poem?

Reading Strategy

Paraphrasing

7. Paraphrase lines 14–15 of "The Road Not Taken."
8. Explain the similarity between the three animals and the speaker in "All But Blind." What is the point of this analogy?
9. Explain the meaning of the idiom "Somebody ought to examine my head" in line 16 of "The Choice."

Extend Understanding

10. **Evaluate:** Which of these poems do you think offers the most useful message or lesson? Explain your choice.

Quick Review

The **speaker** in a poem is the character or voice that the writer of the poem assumes. To review the speaker in a poem, see page 43.

Tone is the writer's attitude toward the subject and toward the audience. To review tone, see page 43.

Paraphrasing is the restatement of phrases or lines in your own words.

 Take It to the Net
www.phschool.com
Take the interactive self-test online to check your understanding of these selections.

Integrate Language Skills

Vocabulary Development Lesson

Word Analysis: Latin Root -verg-

The Latin root -verg- means "to bend or turn." In the word *diverged*, which Robert Frost uses in "The Road Not Taken," the prefix *di-*, meaning "apart," is added to -verg-. Combining the root and prefix, you can figure out that *diverge* means "to go or move in different directions." The prefix *con-* means "together." What does *converge* mean? Complete the following sentences using a form of either *diverge* or *converge*.

1. Because of that large boulder, the stream ____?____.
2. All the groups will ____?____ at noon for a combined lunch meeting.
3. Since he and I have different points of view, our opinions ____?____ on that issue.
4. The Missouri River ____?____ with the Mississippi River in St. Louis.

Grammar Lesson

General and Specific Nouns

Nouns name people, places, things, or ideas. **General nouns,** like *tree* and *flower*, convey broad information. **Specific nouns,** like *maple* and *rose*, give more precise information. Although it is not necessary to use only specific nouns in your writing, you should recognize that they give writing clarity.

For example, the writer of "The Choice" could have written that one suitor offered her many *jewels*. Instead, she created this vivid image:

> He'd have given me . . .
> **Pearls,** to trickle between my hands,
> Smoldering **rubies** . . .

Fluency: Word Choice

Rewrite by replacing each italicized phrase with a word from the vocabulary list.

1. Late at night, the campfire was still *burning without a flame*.
2. The path to the farm *went in a different direction* from the main road.
3. During the audition, the soprano showed off her *gracefully rhythmic* voice.
4. The puppy *stumbles clumsily* into everything.

Spelling Strategy

When adding *-ing* to a verb that has more than one syllable, ends in a consonant, and is not accented on the last syllable, do not change the spelling of the original word. Just add *-ing*. On your paper, add *-ing* to the following verbs.

1. travel   2. blunder   3. billow

▶ *For more practice, see page R28, Exercise A.*
Practice Copy these sentences, and underline each general noun.

1. The traveler in "The Road Not Taken" once walked on a path through trees.
2. The speaker in "All But Blind" compares himself to several small animals.
3. In "The Choice," one suitor offered the speaker many items.
4. Robert Frost and Dorothy Parker are people known to have written many memorable lines.

Writing Application Make sentences 1–4 clearer by substituting a specific noun for each general noun you have underlined.

WG *Prentice Hall Writing and Grammar Connection: Chapter 4, Section 4*

Writing Lesson

Memo

Decisions are based on information. One of the most common methods of communicating information is in a memo—a brief business message. Write a memo recommending that one of these poems be read at graduation. Briefly explain your proposal, include a reference to expert advice that supports your position, and request that action be taken or a response be given.

Prewriting   Choose the poem you think would be most appropriate for a graduation. Interview an expert—such as an English teacher—to get expert support for your suggestion.

Drafting   Use a standard memo format. In the body of your memo, include the expert's opinion and give the expert's credentials.

Revising   Edit your paragraphs to make them short and clear. Check the accuracy of your facts and the spellings of names.

Model: Support from an Authority

TO: Student Government Officers Sue Sullivan and Dave Bell

FROM: Joe Anderson

DATE: February 10, 2002

RE: Graduation Poem

Mrs. Allen, who has taught American literature for ten years, says that Frost is one of the most important American poets of the twentieth century.

 Prentice Hall Writing and Grammar Connection: Chapter 2, Section 4

Extension Activities

Research and Technology Work with a small group to research and compare the animals that the poet describes in "All But Blind."

Present your group's findings in an **oral report**. Point out any features of the animals that reinforce the analogy in the poem. **[Group Activity]**

Listening and Speaking "The Road Not Taken" is a poem that many people love and know by heart. Memorize Frost's poem and give an **oral recitation** to a group. Adjust your voice and your body language to indicate your hesitation and determination in the appropriate places.

 Take It to the Net   www.phschool.com

Go online for an additional research activity using the Internet.

Prepare to Read

from E-Mail from Bill Gates

 Take It to the Net

Visit www.phschool.com for interactive activities and instruction related to "E-Mail from Bill Gates," including

- background
- graphic organizers
- literary elements
- reading strategies

Preview

Connecting to the Literature

This excerpt from "E-Mail from Bill Gates" tells of one writer's unexpected e-mail correspondence. Do you use e-mail? Think about the forms of communication you use, and whether or not a famous person would be likely to respond in any of those forms.

Background

While preparing an article on Bill Gates, John Seabrook sent an e-mail to the famous computer whiz. To Seabrook's surprise, Gates responded, and the interview was conducted almost entirely through e-mail.

Literary Analysis

Magazine Article

A **magazine article** is a short nonfiction text written in prose. It may present or explore ideas, insights, explanations, or facts.

John Seabrook's magazine article explains a technical subject of current interest. It also gives insight into one of the key figures involved in the topic. As you read, notice how Seabrook alternates explanations and insights. Use the following focus questions to guide your reading:

1. What information and insights does this article give about Bill Gates?
2. What was the author's purpose for writing this article?

Connecting Literary Elements

A magazine article is a form of **journalism**—the gathering, writing, and editing of current information to be presented in the **media**. Media include:

- magazines and newspapers
- radio and television
- Web sites and other internet resources

Media text is quickly outdated. When gathering information from media sources, check the date and consider whether it is recent.

Reading Strategy

Using Context Clues

Use **context clues**—the words in the surrounding text—to make an informed guess about the meaning of unfamiliar words and terms.

> At the moment, the best way to communicate with another person on the information highway is to exchange <u>electronic mail</u>: *to write a message on a computer and send it through the telephone lines into someone else's computer.*

Here, the context (in italics) gives a definition of "electronic mail." As you read, look for the types of context clues shown on the chart. Record unfamiliar words and technical terms on a similar chart.

Vocabulary Development

interaction (in´ tər ak´ shən) *n.* actions that affect each other (p. 55)

misinterpret (mis´ in tʉr´ prit) *v.* to understand or explain incorrectly (p. 55)

intimate (in´ tə mət) *adj.* private or personal (p. 56)

etiquette (et´ i kit) *n.* rules for behavior (p. 56)

spontaneously (spän tā´ nē əs lē) *adv.* naturally, without planning (p. 56)

Example
composition book standards like "It may have come to <u>your attention.</u>"

Comparison
there was a *pause* after each response to think; <u>it was like</u> football players huddling up after each play.

Contrast
I give out my home phone number to <u>almost no one but</u> my e-mail address is known *very broadly.*

Restatement
How about *immortality*—<u>being remembered for a thousand years after you're dead</u> . . .

from

E-MAIL FROM
BILL GATES

John Seabrook

At the moment, the best way to communicate with another
person on the information highway[1] is to exchange electronic mail:
to write a message on a computer and send it through the telephone lines into someone else's computer. In the future, people
will send each other sound and pictures as well as text, and do it
in real time,[2] and improved technology will make it possible to
have rich, human electronic exchanges, but at present E-mail is
the closest thing we have to that. Even now, E-mail allows you to
meet and communicate with people in a way that would be impossible on the phone, through the regular mail, or face to face, as I
discovered while I was working on this story. Sitting at my computer
one day, I realized that I could try to communicate with Bill Gates,
the chairman and co-founder of the software giant Microsoft, on the
information highway. At least, I could send E-mail to his electronic
address, which is widely available, not tell anyone at Microsoft I was
doing it, and see what happened. I wrote:

Dear Bill,

   I am the guy who is writing the article about you for The
New Yorker. It occurs to me that we ought to be able to do
some of the work through e-mail. Which raises this fascinating question—What kind of understanding of another person
can e-mail give you? . . .

   You could begin by telling me what you think is unique
about e-mail as a form of communication.

John

I hit "return," and the computer said, "mail sent." I walked out
to the kitchen to get a drink of water and played with the cat for
a while, then came back and sat at my computer. Thinking that
I was probably wasting money, I nevertheless logged on again and
entered my password. "You have mail," the computer said.

   I typed "get mail," and the computer got the following:

Reading Strategy
Using Context Clues
What clues could help
someone unfamiliar with
computers figure out the
meaning of "logged on"?

---

1. information highway network of computers and file servers that allows for the
rapid exchange of electronic information.
2. in real time in actual time (with little delay between the moment of sending and
the moment of receiving the sound, picture, and text).

From: Bill Gates <billg@microsoft.com>
Ok, let me know if you get this email.

According to my computer, eighteen minutes had passed between the time I E-mailed Bill and he E-mailed me back. His message said:

E-mail is a unique communication vehicle for a lot of reasons. However email is not a substitute for direct <u>interaction</u>. . . .

There are people who I have corresponded with on email for months before actually meeting them—people at work and otherwise. If someone isn't saying something of interest its easier to not respond to their mail than it is not to answer the phone. In fact I give out my home phone number to almost no one but my email address is known very broadly. I am the only person who reads my email so no one has to worry about embarrassing themselves or going around people when they send a message. Our email is completely secure. . . .

Email helps out with other types of communication. It allows you to exchange a lot of information in advance of a meeting and make the meeting far far more valuable. . . .

Email is not a good way to get mad at someone since you can't interact. You can send friendly messages very easily since those are harder to <u>misinterpret</u>.

We began to E-mail each other three or four times a week. I would have a question about something and say to myself, "I'm going to

E-mail Bill about that," and I'd write him a message and get a one- or two-page message back within twenty-four hours, sometimes much sooner. At the beginning of our electronic relationship, I would wake up in the middle of the night and lie in bed wondering if I had E-mail from Bill. Generally, he seemed to write messages at night, sleep (maybe), then send them the next morning. We were <u>intimate</u> in a curious way, in the sense of being wired into each other's minds, but our contact was elaborately stylized, like ballroom dancing.

In some ways, my E-mail relationship with Bill was like an ongoing, monthlong conversation, except that there was a pause after each response to think; it was like football players huddling up after each play. There was no beginning or end to Gates' messages—no time wasted on stuff like "Dear" and "Yours"—and I quickly corrected this <u>etiquette</u> breach in my own messages. Nor were there any fifth-grade-composition-book standards like "It may have come to your attention that" and "Looking forward to hearing from you." Social niceties are not what Bill Gates is about. Good spelling is not what Bill Gates is about, either. He never signed his messages to me, but sometimes he put an "&" at the end, which, I learned, means "Write back" in E-mail language. After a while, he stopped putting the "&," but I wrote back anyway. He never addressed me by name. Instead of a letterhead, there was this:

```
Sender: billg@microsoft.com
Received: from netmail.microsoft.com by dub-img-
2.compuserve.com (5.67/5.930129sam) id AA03768;
Wed, 6 Oct 93 14:00:51-0400
Received: by netmail.microsoft.com (5.65/25—eef)
id AA27745; Fri, 8 Oct 93 10:56:01-0700
Message-Id:
<9310081756.AA27745@netmail.microsoft.com>
X-Msmail-Message-Id: 15305A55
X-Msmail-Conversation-Id: 15305A55
From: Bill Gates <billg@microsoft.com>
To: 73124.1524@CompuServe.COM
```

I sometimes felt that this correspondence was a game I was playing with Gates through the computer, or maybe a game I was playing against a computer. What is the right move? What question will get me past the dragon and into the wizard's star chamber, where the rich information is stored? I had no idea where Gates was when he wrote to me, except that once he told me he was on a "think week" at his family's summer place on Hood Canal. I could not tell whether he was impatient or bored with my questions and was merely answering them because it served his interest. Because we couldn't talk at the same time, there was little chance for the conversation to move <u>spontaneously</u>. On the other hand, his answers meant more, in a certain way, being written, than answers I would have received on the phone. I worried that he might think I was

intimate (in´ tə mət) *adj.* private or personal

etiquette (et´ i kit) *n.* rules for behavior

Reading Strategy
Using Context Clues
What context clues help you guess the meaning of the term *letterhead*?

spontaneously (spän tā´ nē əs lē) *adv.* naturally, without planning

being "random" (a big putdown at Microsoft) because I jumped from topic to topic. I sometimes wondered if I was actually communicating with Bill Gates. How hard would it be for an assistant to write these messages? Or for an intelligent agent to do it?

I wrote a message titled "What motivates you?":

> You love to compete, right? Is that where your energy comes from—love of the game? I wonder how it feels to win on your level. How much do you fear losing? How about immortality—being remembered for a thousand years after you're dead—does that excite you? How strong is your desire to improve people's lives (by providing them with better tools for thinking and communicating)? Some driven people are trying to heal a wound or to recover a loss. Is that the case with you?

Reading Strategy
Using Context Clues
What words restate the meaning of *immortality*?

Gates wrote back:

> Its easy to understand why I think I have the best job around because of day to day enjoyment rather than some grand long term deep psychological explanation. It's a lot of fun to work with very smart people in a competitive environment. . . . We get to hire the best people coming out of school and give them challenging jobs. We get to try and figure out how to sell software in every part of the world. Sometimes our ideas work very well and sometimes they work very poorly. As long as we stay in the feedback loop and keep trying it's a lot of fun.
>
> It is pretty cool that the products we work on empower individuals and make their jobs more interesting. It helps a lot in inventing new software ideas that I will be one of the users of the software so I can model what's important. . . .
>
> Just thinking of things as winning is a terrible approach. Success comes from focusing in on what you really like and are good at—not challenging every random thing. My original vision of a personal computer on every desk and every home will take more than 15 years to achieve so there will have been more than 30 years since I first got excited about that goal. My work is not like sports where you actually win a game and its over after a short period of time.
>
> Besides a lot of luck, a high energy level and perhaps some IQ I think having an ability to deal with things at a very detailed level and a very broad level and synthesize[3] between them is probably the thing that helps me the most. This allows someone to take deep technical understanding and figure out a business strategy that fits together with it.
>
> It's ridiculous to consider how things will be remembered after you are dead. The pioneers of personal computers including Jobs, Kapor, Lampson, Roberts, Kaye,[4] are all great people but

☑ **Reading Check**

Why does Bill Gates think he has "the best job around"?

---

3. **synthesize** to form by bringing together separate parts.
4. **Jobs, . . . Kaye** important developers of the computer and software industries.

I don't think any of us will merit an entry in a history book.

I don't remember being wounded or losing something big so I don't think that is driving me. I have wonderful parents and great siblings. I live in the same neighborhood I grew up in (although I will be moving across the lake when my new house is done). I can't remember any major disappointments. I did figure out at one point that if I pursued pure mathematics it would be hard to make a major contribution and there were a few girls who turned me down when I asked them out.

At the end of one message, I wrote:

This reporting via e-mail is really fascinating and I think you are going to come across in an attractive way, in case you weren't sure of that.

Gates wrote:

I comb my hair everytime before I send email hoping to appear attractive. I try and use punctuation in a friendly way also. I send :) and never :(.

Review and Assess

Think about the Selection

1. **Respond:** Would you like to meet Bill Gates? Why or why not?
2. **(a) Recall:** Why does Seabrook first send e-mail to Bill Gates? **(b) Analyze:** What does Seabrook accomplish by letting Gates speak for himself?
3. **(a) Recall:** What does Seabrook learn about the etiquette of sending and receiving e-mail? **(b) Compare and Contrast:** How is Seabrook's first e-mail to Gates similar to and different from later e-mails? **(c) Infer:** What does Gates's e-mail style reveal about him?
4. **(a) Speculate:** Do you think Seabrook would use this method of communication to conduct other interviews? **(b) Support:** Why or why not?
5. **(a) Apply:** Why is Bill Gates of current interest? **(b) Evaluate:** Based on the topic of the article, how important is the date of the article? Explain. **(c) Extend:** What media sources could you use to find information about Bill Gates's most recent activities and accomplishments?
6. **Take a Stand:** Do you think that "basic computer skills" should be a required class? Why or why not?

John Seabrook

(b. 1959)

John Seabrook grew up in a tomato-farming community in New Jersey. Years later, when writing about biotechnology and a new kind of tomato, he mentioned this boyhood experience. Readers' reactions made him realize that science writers need to add a personal touch.

Bill Gates

(b. 1955)

As co-founder of Microsoft, Bill Gates helped launch the computer revolution. His phenomenal success and astounding wealth have made him a legend in the business world. In 2000 Gates stepped down as chief executive officer of Microsoft to become chairman and chief software architect of the company.

Review and Assess

Literary Analysis
Magazine Article

1. List facts about e-mail and details about Bill Gates that you learned from this **magazine article**. Record them on a chart like this.

Facts About E-Mail	Details About Bill Gates
1.	1.
2.	2.

2. What do you think was Seabrook's purpose for writing this article?

Connecting Literary Elements

3. Identify two topics related to this article that a journalist might investigate.
4. Complete a chart like the one below to compare the strengths and weaknesses of different **media**.

	Television	Newspaper	Internet
Speed			
Problems			
Use of visuals			
How easy to deliver to many people at once			

Reading Strategy
Using Context Clues

For each of the following sentences, give the meaning of the italicized words. Explain the context clues that help you determine the meaning.

5. "Our contact was elaborately *stylized*, like ballroom dancing."
6. "I have wonderful parents and great *siblings*."

Extend Understanding

7. **Career Connection:** (a) What personal qualities do you think are useful for people who work in the computer field? (b) What academic subjects should a person study to prepare for a career in computers?

Quick Review

A **magazine article** is a short, informational work of nonfiction published in a periodical. To review a magazine article, see page 53.

Journalism is informational writing about real people, places, events, and ideas of current interest.

Media forms include magazines, newspapers, television, radio, and the Internet.
To review journalism and media, see page 53.

Context clues are words and phrases from the surrounding text that help you figure out the meaning of unfamiliar words and phrases. To review context clues, see page 53.

 Take It to the Net
www.phschool.com
Take the interactive self-test online to check your understanding of the selection.

Integrate Language Skills

Vocabulary Development Lesson

Word Analysis: Latin Prefix *inter-*

The Latin prefix *inter-* in *interaction* means "between" or "among." On your paper, write the correct word in each blank by adding *inter-* to one of these words:

national   state   active

1. An ___?___ highway system runs from California to Maine.
2. Many people play ___?___ video games.
3. E-mail speeds up ___?___ communications.

Spelling Strategy

Before adding the suffix *-tion*, you will probably have to drop the final letter or letters of the base word:

interact + *-tion* = interaction.

On your paper, add *-tion* to the following verbs.

1. connect   2. relate   3. reflect

Grammar Lesson

Pronouns and Antecedents

Pronouns are words that take the place of a noun or nouns. Some common pronouns include *we, he, they, I, each other, it,* and *us.*

The noun to which a pronoun refers is the pronoun's **antecedent.** Many pronouns must have an antecedent in order for their meaning to be clear. In the following example, the pronoun *those* refers to the antecedent *messages.*

Example: You can send friendly *messages* easily since *those* are harder to misinterpret.

Concept Development: Antonyms

Antonyms are words with opposite meanings, such as *happy* and *sad* or *light* and *dark.* Copy each sentence. Underline the antonym of the italicized word.

1. Use symbols and words that are easy to understand so that the receiver does not *misinterpret* your message.
2. It is strange to have such *intimate* correspondence with such a public figure.
3. I had hoped we could communicate *spontaneously,* but I had to settle for planned exchanges.
4. His messages followed e-mail *etiquette,* but mine contained examples of bad form.

▶ *For more practice, see page R28, Exercise B.*
Practice Copy each of the following sentences. Circle the pronoun. Underline the antecedent.

1. Seabrook e-mailed Gates to ask him questions.
2. Seabrook and Gates corresponded because they were working on an interview.
3. The ability to recognize problems and find solutions for them is important.

Writing Application Revise the following passage so that it is clear to which noun *he* refers. Replace some uses of *he* with a name.

Seabrook wrote to Gates and he wrote back to him. He told him that he was writing his article about him. He wrote back to him.

Prentice Hall Writing and Grammar Connection: Chapter 14, Section 2

Writing Lesson

Comparison of Forms of Communication

Choose two forms of communication, such as e-mail and conventional letter-writing, and write a short essay comparing and contrasting them.

Prewriting   Choose the two forms of communication you will compare. List ways in which these forms are alike and different.

Drafting   Organize your comparison point by point. Describe a feature of e-mail, then describe the same or related feature of your other form of communication. When you compare or contrast ideas or features of equal weight, use parallel structure—similar or repeated grammatical forms and structures.

Revising   Look for passages where the similarities or differences would be shown more sharply if you used parallel structure. Revise to produce parallel structure.

Model: Parallel Structure

Not Parallel: E-mail transmits in moments; someone receiving conventional mail might wait days.

Parallel: E-mail takes moments; conventional mail takes days.

> Each part of the revised sentence has the same structure. This makes the difference between the two types of mail stand out.

W͟G Prentice Hall Writing and Grammar Connection: Chapter 8, Section 3

Extension Activities

Listening and Speaking Do an **oral presentation** on the history of forms of communication, such as the telephone, facsimile machine, or e-mail. First, tell about early versions. Then, describe the development. Conclude by explaining how the system functions today and what experts predict for the future. Follow these tips:

1. Use strong action verbs such as *transmit, communicate,* and *deliver.*
2. Use active voice rather than passive voice. Passive: The file is stored on the drive. Active: The drive stores the file.

Research and Technology Work with a group to produce a **manual** explaining how to use e-mail. Each group member can research and explain one function, such as how to develop an e-mail address book or how to save a message. Organize the topics of your manual in a logical sequence and prepare a table of contents.

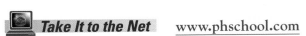 **Take It to the Net**   www.phschool.com

Go online for an additional research activity using the Internet.

READING INFORMATIONAL MATERIALS

Magazine Articles

About Magazine Articles

Magazines are a form of print media. Although most are published monthly or weekly, some appear quarterly, or four times a year. Magazines either appeal to certain special interest groups (such as gardeners, skiers, or opera lovers), or they offer feature stories on current topics to a general audience with more detail than newspapers can give. Magazines often contain opinions as well as facts.

Reading Strategy

Headings

Informational text in magazines, newspapers, and textbooks is often divided into sections. **Headings,** or **heads**, usually stand out from the regular text in one of the following ways:

- color
- boldface
- larger print
- placement on page

Heads organize the material in an easy-to-follow pattern, which helps readers find information quickly. They also visually break up the type on a page so that the article is easy to read. Look, for instance, at the heads in "How to Be Polite Online." The first three paragraphs of the article introduce the article. Then, the first head, "Tone of voice online," tells the reader what information will be covered in the first section. Use headings to help you organize notes and summaries as outlined on the chart below.

Section	Summary
Title	
Introductory Text	
Tone of Voice Online	
Table 1	
Table 2	
Flame On/Flame Off	
Looking Good Online	

How to Be Polite Online
from Netiquette VIRGINIA SHEA

The truth is that computer networking is still in its infancy. Probably nothing illustrates this more clearly than the "ASCII[1] jail": 90% of network communications are still limited to plain old ASCII text—that is, the characters of the alphabet, the numerals 0 through 9, and the most basic punctuation marks. It's bad enough that multimedia communications have not been implemented in most of cyberspace.[2] Most of the time you can't even put a word in bold or italics!

Because people cannot see or hear you in cyberspace, you need to pay close attention to the style of your electronic communications if you hope to make a good impression there. The *style* of electronic communications encompasses everything about your correspondence except its content, from your use of network conventions like "smileys" and "sigs" to the number of characters per line in your email messages.

Style considerations are influenced by several of the rules of Netiquette, especially *Rule 4,* Respect other people's time, and *Rule 5,* Make yourself look good online. It doesn't matter how brilliant your messages are if they're formatted in such a way that no one can read them.

Tone of voice online The fact that most network interactions are limited to written words can be the source of misunderstandings. Fortunately, clever network users have had years to deal with this. They've created a shorthand to help communicate the tone that you'd otherwise get from the other person's voice, facial expressions, and gestures. These shorthand expressions are known as smileys or emoticons. They're easy to figure out once you get the hang of it. Just remember that they're all sideways faces.

See Table 1 for a list of the most commonly used emoticons. There are whole books about smileys for those who are interested, including the enjoyable *Smiley Dictionary* by Seth Godin.

Table 1: Emoticons	
:-)	Smile; laugh; "I'm joking"
:-(	Frown; sadness; "Bummer"
:)	Variant of :-) or "Have a nice day"
;-)	Wink; denotes a pun or sly joke
:-O	Yelling or screaming; or completely shocked
:-()	Can't (or won't) stop talking
:-D	Big, delighted grin
:-P	Sticking out your tongue
:-] or :-)	Sarcastic smile
%-)	Confused but happy
%-(	Confused and unhappy
:-|	Can't decide how to feel; no feelings either way
*	Kiss
{ } or [ ]	Hug
{{{***}}}	Hugs and kisses

1. **ASCII** acronym for American Standard Code for Information Interchange, a standard computer code used to assist the interchange of information among various types of data-processing equipment.
2. **cyberspace** popular term for the borderless world of computers and telecommunication on the Internet.

Table 2: Abbreviations	
BTW	By the way
IMHO	In my humble opinion
IMNSHO	In my not so humble opinion
IOW	In other words
IRL	In real life
ITRW	In the real world
LOL	Laughing out loud
OTF	On the floor (laughing)
ROTFL	Rolling on the floor laughing
WRT	With regard to
YMMV	Your mileage may vary
<g> or <G>	Grin
<bg>	Big grin

People also use abbreviations to express emotional states or to qualify what they're saying. See Table 2 for a list of common abbreviations.

The "FLAME ON/FLAME OFF" notifier
When you really want to run off at the keyboard—but you want your readers to know that you know that you're not expressing yourself in your usual measured, reasoned manner—you need to let them know that you know that you're flaming.[3] So before you begin your rant, simply enter the words FLAME ON. Then rant away. When you're done, write FLAME OFF and resume normal discourse.

Looking good online One of the neat things about computers is that they let us use all kinds of special effects in our documents that we didn't even dream of back in the days of typewriters (if you're old enough to remember those days). But when you're communicating online, in most cases it's back to the typewriter as far as effects go. Even if your mail system lets you use boldface, italics, and tabs, there's no guarantee that your correspondent's system will understand them. At worst, your communication will turn into unreadable gibberish.

What to do?

- Forget about boldface, italics, tabs, and font changes. Never use any effect you couldn't get on an old-fashioned typewriter. In fact, you can't even use all of those. Underlining won't work, for example. Nor can you use the old "required backspace" trick to put a diacritical mark[4] (a tilde or an accent mark, for example) over another character.
- Most systems won't read the diacritical marks anyway, so just leave them out. If you feel an accent mark is absolutely necessary, type an apostrophe after the letter the accent would have gone over.
- Use only ASCII characters. This includes all 26 letters of the alphabet (upper and lower case), the numerals 0 through 9, and most commonly used punctuation marks. For any publishing mavens out there, however, it excludes em dashes (" — "), en dashes ("–"), and bullets.
- Limit your line length to 80 characters, or better yet, 60 characters.

Otherwise, your lines may break in weird places and your readers
will have to wade through notes that look like this.
Believe me,
it gets annoying after a very short while.

- NEVER TYPE YOUR NOTES IN ALL CAPS, LIKE THIS. It's rude—like shouting constantly. And, like constant shouting, it makes people stop listening. All caps may be used, IN MODERATION, for emphasis.
- To indicate italics, you may *surround the material to be italicized with asterisks.*

---

3. flaming slang for "ranting."
4. diacritical (dī′ ə krit′ ik əl) **mark** mark added to a letter or symbol to show its pronunciation.

Text is organized into chunks using bullets and tables.

Check Your Comprehension

1. What elements contribute to the style of electronic communication?
2. What are some possible online substitutes for voice, facial expressions, and gestures?
3. Why is it suggested that you not type in all capitals or write lines longer than sixty characters?

Applying the Reading Strategy

Headings

4. What are three main ideas identified by the headings in this article?
5. What information do you learn from Table 1?
6. What is the abbreviation for "In other words"? How do you know?

Activity

Use Online Etiquette

Many products now carry e-mail addresses so that customers can give feedback online. Find the e-mail addresses for two companies that produce products you use. Send an e-mail to each company, expressing your satisfaction or dissatisfaction with the product. Follow the etiquette outlined in "How to Be Polite Online." Tell the class when and if you receive a reply.

Comparing Informational Materials

Compare Articles

This article, and the article from "E-Mail from Bill Gates," both discuss the way people communicate through e-mail. Each writer, however, has a unique purpose that affects the scope, or range, of ideas that are covered and the way those ideas are organized. In "E-Mail from Bill Gates," the author's purpose is to give you a glimpse through e-mail at a famous computer whiz. The author of "How to Be Polite Online" wants to inform readers about the do's and don'ts of e-mailing. Fill out a chart like the one shown here to find similarities and differences between the two texts.

	E-mail from Bill Gates	How to Be Polite Online
Main subject of article		
Three main ideas		
Types of details included		

Prepare to Read

Grandma Ling ◆ Old Man ◆ The Old Grandfather and His Little Grandson

Second Circle Dance, Phoebe Beasley

Take It to the Net

Visit www.phschool.com for interactive activities and instruction related to these selections, including
- background
- graphic organizers
- literary elements
- reading strategies

Preview

Connecting to the Literature

"Grandma Ling," "Old Man," and "The Old Grandfather and His Little Grandson" are about the relationships between grandchildren and grandparents. Think about an older person who holds a special place in your life.

Background

In the poem "Grandma Ling," Chinese American poet Amy Ling tells about meeting her grandmother in Taiwan. Taiwan, a group of islands near China, has been occupied by Portugal, China, Holland, and Japan. Today, it is an independent nation. Many people living in Taiwan moved there from China when communist forces won control of the Chinese government.

Literary Analysis

Sensory Language

Writers use **sensory language** to describe sights, sounds, smells, tastes, and sensations of touch. The italicized words in this excerpt from "Grandma Ling" give details that appeal to the sense of hearing.

> Before she came to view, I heard
> her *slippered feet softly measure*
> the tatami floor with *even step;*

As you read each selection, look for the sensory language.

Comparing Literary Works

Through sensory language, writers create **images**—specific pictures in the reader's mind. In addition to visual details, these "pictures" may include details of sound, smell, taste, or touch. Compare and contrast the imagery in "Grandma Ling," "Old Man," and "The Old Grandfather and His Little Grandson." Use these focus questions to guide your comparison:

1. To what senses does the imagery in each work appeal?
2. What is the strongest, most memorable image in each work?

Prepare a graphic organizer like the one shown here to record the sensory details of the images in each work.

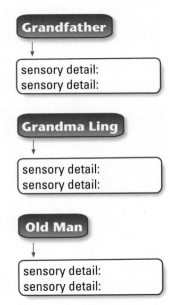

Reading Strategy

Using Words in Context

Many English words have more than one meaning or can be used as different parts of speech in different situations. When you read, make sure you understand the meaning of a word in **context**—the situation in which it is used. For instance, in the following example, the word *blood* means *heritage* or *ancestry*, not the liquid that pumps through your heart.

> ". . . before the coming of coronado,
> other of our blood
>   came with los españoles,"

Vocabulary Development

sturdy (stŭr´ dē) *adj.* firm; strong (p. 69)

rivulets (riv´ yoo lits) *n.* little streams (p. 70)

furrows (fŭr´ ōz) *n.* deep wrinkles (p. 70)

supple (sup´ əl) *adj.* flexible and pliant (p. 71)

stoic (stō´ ik) *adj.* calm and unbothered in spite of suffering (p. 71)

scolded (skōld´ əd) *v.* criticized harshly (p. 72)

Amy Ling

Grandma Ling

Woman with White Kerchief (Uygur), Lunda Hoyle Gill

▲ **Critical Viewing** Compare and contrast the woman in this painting with Grandma Ling, as she is described in the poem. **[Compare and Contrast]**

If you dig that hole deep enough
you'll reach China, they used to tell me,
a child in a backyard in Pennsylvania.
Not strong enough to dig that hole,
5   I waited twenty years,
then sailed back, half way around the world.

In Taiwan I first met Grandma.
Before she came to view, I heard
her slippered feet softly measure
10   the tatami[1] floor with even step;
the aqua paper-covered door slid open
and there I faced
my five foot height, <u>sturdy</u> legs and feet,
square forehead, high cheeks, and wide-set eyes;
15   my image stood before me,
acted on by fifty years.

She smiled, stretched her arms
to take to heart the eldest daughter
of her youngest son a quarter century away.
20   She spoke a tongue I knew no word of,
and I was sad I could not understand,
but I could hug her.

Literary Analysis
Sensory Language What words in lines 9–11 appeal to one or more of the five senses?

sturdy (stʉr´ dē) *adj.* firm; strong

---

1. tatami (tə tä´ mē) *adj.* woven of rice straw.

Review and Assess

Thinking About the Selection

1. **Respond:** What is the most surprising or unusual feature of the speaker's meeting with her grandmother?

2. **(a) Recall:** What was the speaker told as a child about China? **(b) Analyze:** How might what she was told affect her ideas and feelings about China?

3. **(a) Recall:** Where did the speaker first meet her grandmother? **(b) Infer:** Why didn't she wait for the grandmother to visit her? **(c) Interpret:** What does the expression "my image stood before me, / acted on by fifty years" mean?

4. **(a) Recall:** What prevents the grandmother and granddaughter from communicating in their first meeting? **(b) Speculate:** What might they want to tell or ask each other? **(c) Analyze:** How do they finally communicate, and what are they saying?

Amy Ling

(1939–1999)
Amy Ling was born in China and lived there with her family for six years before moving to the United States.

In the 1960s, Ling visited her grandmother in Taiwan. The writer described this first meeting in her poem "Grandma Ling."

OLD MAN

Ricardo Sánchez

remembrance
(smiles/hurts sweetly)
October 8, 1972

old man
with brown skin
talking of past
    when being shepherd
5   in utah, nevada, colorado and
         new mexico
was life lived freely;

old man,
    grandfather,
 wise with time
10 running <u>rivulets</u> on face,
deep, rich <u>furrows</u>,
    each one a legacy,
deep, rich memories of life . . .
15   "you are indio,[1]
        among other things,"
he would tell me
      during nights spent
so long ago
20   amidst familial gatherings
in albuquerque . . .

old man, loved and respected,
he would speak sometimes
of pueblos,[2]
25   san juan, santa clara,
    and even santo domingo,
and his family, he would say,
    came from there:
    some of our blood was here,

El Pan Nuestro (Our Daily Bread), c. 1905, Ramon Frade, Instituto de Cultura Puertorriquena, San Juan

▲ **Critical Viewing** Does this painting convey an old man "wise with time"? Explain. **[Make a Judgment]**

rivulets (riv´ yoo lits) *n.* little streams

furrows (fur´ ōz) *n.* deep wrinkles

---

1. indio (ēn´ dyō) *n.* Indian; Native American.
2. pueblos (pweb´ lōz) *n.* here, Native American towns in central and northern New Mexico.

30   he would say,
          before the coming of coronado,[3]
     other of our blood
          came with los españoles,[4]
     and the mixture
35   was rich,
          though often painful . . .
     old man,
     who knew earth
          by its awesome aromas
40   and who felt
     the heated sweetness
          of chile verde[5]
     by his supple touch,
     gone into dust is your body
45   with its stoic look and resolution,
     but your reality, old man, lives on
     in a mindsoul touched by you . . .

     Old Man . . .

---

3. **coronado** (kô rô nä´ dô) Coronado explored what is today the American Southwest.
4. **los españoles** (lōs es pä nyōl´ es) *n.* the Spaniards.
5. **chile verde** (chē´ le vehr´ de) *n.* green pepper.

Review and Assess

Think About the Selection

1. **Respond:** How does Sánchez make you feel about his grandfather?

2. **(a) Recall:** What groups of ancestors did the grandfather teach the poet about? **(b) Analyze:** What feelings about their heritage did the grandfather pass on to the poet?

3. **(a) Recall:** How do you know that the grandfather is no longer living? **(b) Interpret:** Explain the meaning of the lines "but your reality, old man, lives on / in a mindsoul touched by you . . ."
(c) Generalize: Explain how those lines could apply to older people of any culture or family.

Literary Analysis
Sensory Language and Imagery How does the image in lines 9–12 appeal to one of the five senses?

supple (sup´ əl) *adj.* flexible and pliant

stoic (stō´ ik) *adj.* calm and unbothered in spite of suffering

Ricardo Sánchez

(1941–1995)
    The poet Ricardo Sánchez was born in El Paso, Texas. His family had roots in Spanish, Mexican, North American, and Native American cultures. Most of Sánchez's work is an exploration and celebration of his rich cultural heritage. His writing often includes both Spanish and English words. In the poem "Old Man," Sánchez offers a portrait of a grandfather who is remembered with love.

The Old Grandfather and His Little Grandson
Leo Tolstoy

The grandfather had become very old. His legs would not carry him, his eyes could not see, his ears could not hear, and he was toothless. When he ate, bits of food sometimes dropped out of his mouth. His son and his son's wife no longer allowed him to eat with them at the table. He had to eat his meals in the corner near the stove.

One day they gave him his food in a bowl. He tried to move the bowl closer; it fell to the floor and broke. His daughter-in-law <u>scolded</u> him. She told him that he spoiled everything in the house and broke their dishes, and she said that from now on he would get his food in a wooden dish. The old man sighed and said nothing.

A few days later, the old man's son and his wife were sitting in their hut, resting and watching their little boy playing on the floor. They saw him putting together something out of small pieces of wood. His father asked him, "What are you making, Misha?"

The little grandson said, "I'm making a wooden bucket. When you and Mamma get old, I'll feed you out of this wooden dish."

The young peasant and his wife looked at each other, and tears filled their eyes. They were ashamed because they had treated the old grandfather so meanly, and from that day they again let the old man eat with them at the table and took better care of him.

scolded (skōld′ əd) *v.* criticized harshly

Review and Assess

Thinking About the Selection

1. **Respond:** What would you like to say to the old grandfather's son and his wife?

2. **(a) Recall:** What are the grandfather's physical problems? **(b) Evaluate:** Is this tale a positive view of aging? Explain.

3. **(a) Recall:** How do the son and his wife react to the grandfather's problems? **(b) Infer:** Why do they react as they do? **(c) Contrast:** How is the boy's reaction different from his parents' reaction?

4. **(a) Recall:** What happens at the end of the story? **(b) Analyze:** Why do the son and his wife change their behavior?

5. **(a) Recall:** What did the grandson do that helped make his parents change their treatment of the grandfather? **(b) Evaluate:** How valuable is the lesson the parents learn? Explain.

Leo Tolstoy

(1828–1910)

Many experts have called Russian author Leo Tolstoy one of the best novelists who ever lived. Tolstoy's mother and father both died when he was young. As a boy, Tolstoy discovered the joy of reading books. He read Russian folk tales, stories from the Bible, and poems.

In his short story "The Old Grandfather and His Little Grandson," Tolstoy shows the importance of caring for the elderly.

Review and Assess

Literary Analysis

Sensory Language

1. Prepare a **sensory language** chart like the one below. Fill in as many sensory details as you can find in each work.

	sound	touch	sight	smell	taste
"Grandma Ling"					
"Old Man"					
"Grandfather"					

2. In "Grandma Ling," the speaker hears the grandmother before she sees her. What is the effect of highlighting these sounds?

3. What scents are included in "Old Man" to reflect the closeness the speaker feels to the land?

Comparing Literary Works

4. To what senses does the **imagery** in each work appeal?

5. What is the strongest, most memorable image in each work? Use note cards like the one below to jot them down.

"Grandma Ling"

Strongest and most memorable image:

Explanation:

Reading Strategy

Using Words in Context

6. Copy the sentence that uses *tongue* in the same context as it is used in "Grandma Ling."
   a. A cat's tongue is rough.
   b. In the midst of familiar voices, I heard a foreign tongue.

7. How does context affect your understanding of the word "old" when you read "Old Man" and "The Old Grandfather . . . "?

Extend Understanding

8. **Social Studies Connection:** What do these works suggest about the bond between a grandparent and a grandchild?

Quick Review

Sensory language describes sights, sounds, smells, tastes, and sensations of touch. To review sensory language, see page 67.

Imagery is the combination of sensory details that create specific images, or pictures, in the reader's mind. To review imagery, see page 67.

The **context** of a word is the situation in which it is used—the surrounding words, phrases, and sentences. To review context, see page 67.

 Take It to the Net
www.phschool.com
Take the interactive self-test online to check your understanding of these selections.

Integrate Language Skills

Vocabulary Development Lesson

Word Analysis: Forms of *supple*

The word *supple*, which means "flexible," comes from the Latin word *supplicare*, meaning "humble," "not resisting," or "easily bent."

Use *supplication*, *supple*, and *supplicate* to complete these sentences.

1. The athlete's legs were long and ___?___.
2. The little boy's ___?___ for more food was heart-rending.
3. The hungry dog seems to ___?___ for food.

Spelling Strategy

When spelling most two-syllable words with a consonant sound in the middle that follows a short vowel sound, double the middle consonant. On your paper, correct any misspelled words.

1. britle   2. battle   3. ridle

Grammar Lesson

Personal Pronouns

Personal pronouns refer to the person speaking, the person spoken to, or the person spoken about. Personal pronouns are singular or plural.

	Singular	**Plural**
First Person	I, me, my, mine	we, us, our, ours
Second Person	you, your, yours	you, your, yours
Third Person	he, him, his, she, hers, it, its	their, theirs

A personal pronoun must refer clearly to its **antecedent**—the noun that the pronoun replaces. First- and second-person pronouns often have understood antecedents. It is understood that the pronouns refer to the person speaking or the person being spoken to.

Fluency: Sentence Completions

Choose the word or words in parentheses that would best replace the italicized word.

1. The girl kept a *stoic* look on her face, showing no emotion. (calm, still)
2. The wooden bench was *sturdy* enough for two people to sit on it. (firm, strong)
3. The sprinkler had made a *rivulet* in the garden. (river, small stream)
4. The *furrows* in his face made him look older. (deep wrinkles, rows)
5. The woman *scolded* the slow clerk. (punished, spoke sharply to)

▶ *For more practice, see page R28, Exercise B.*
Practice Write the pronoun(s) in each sentence. After each pronoun, write the antecedent. If it is understood, write *understood*.

1. I heard Grandma before she came into view.
2. Old man, you look tired.
3. The man and his wife knew they were wrong.

Writing Application Revise the passage. Change or rearrange words to avoid repeating nouns and to make each pronoun's antecedent clear.

Two poets write about the poets' grandparents. Amy Ling writes about Ling's grandmother. Ricardo Sánchez writes about Sánchez's grandfather. He told many stories.

W̶G Prentice Hall Writing and Grammar Connection: Chapter 14, Section 2

Writing Lesson

Description of an Older Person

Each of the three selections in this group paints a portrait of an older person. Follow their lead by writing your own description of a senior citizen.

Prewriting   Choose an older person you know well. Make a two-column list. In one column, list personal qualities. In the other, list actions that illustrate those qualities.

Drafting   Use sensory language to create powerful images that show the person's qualities, rather than just telling about them. If the person is adventurous, describe him or her in an adventurous situation.

Revising   Identify several descriptive words you have used. Evaluate whether they appeal to one or more of the senses. Change words as needed to convey a powerful image.

Model: Revise Word Choice

Draft: She has a nice smile and her laugh is fun to hear.

Revision: Her smile lights up her whole face, and the music of her laugh bubbles around you until you're laughing, too.

WG Prentice Hall Writing and Grammar Connection: Chapter 6, Section 2

Extension Activities

Listening and Speaking With a small group, prepare a **Public Service Announcement** on the benefits of hiring senior citizens.

1. Interview managers or owners of several local businesses.
2. Organize your information to call attention to the qualities of senior citizens that will interest potential employers. Repeat your most important information near the end of the announcement. **[Group Activity]**

Research and Technology Search for information on changes in life expectancy in the United States from 1900 to the present. Use the key words "life expectancies" with quotation marks to avoid Web sites containing only one of the words. Prepare a **presentation with visual aids** such as diagrams or flowcharts to show the process you followed to locate the information.

 **Take It to the Net**   www.phschool.com

Go online for an additional research activity using the Internet.

Prepare to Read

Ring Out, Wild Bells ◆ Winter Moon ◆ Poets to Come

 Take It to the Net

Visit www.phschool.com for interactive activities and instruction related to these selections, including
- background
- graphic organizers
- literary elements
- reading strategies

Preview

Connecting to the Literature

The speakers in these poems reflect on new beginnings. They mark the coming of the new year, the new moon, and a new generation. Think about times when you have felt the anticipation of a fresh start—such as the beginning of the school year or the first day of summer vacation.

Background

In "Ring Out, Wild Bells," Alfred, Lord Tennyson, calls on bells to "ring out" the negatives of the past and "ring in" hope for the future. The ringing of bells, clanking of pans, shouting, and generally "wild" noise-making at midnight are traditional New Year's customs in many countries.

Literary Analysis

Repetition in Poetry

Repetition in poetry is the use, more than once, of certain sounds, words, and phrases within a poem. Repetition is used

- to emphasize an important idea.
- to produce unity by tying the lines to the repeated word or phrase.
- to create a musical sound.

As you read these poems, pay attention to repeated words and phrases. Notice their sounds and rhythms as well as their meanings. Think about the purpose the poet may have had for using repetition.

Comparing Literary Works

These poems are very different from one another in structure and style, yet each poet is dealing with a similar moment: a moment of change, of beginning. Compare and contrast the way the poems show change and the speakers' thoughts and feelings about change. Use the following focus questions to guide your comparison.

1. What is the specific topic of each poem?
2. How does the speaker of each poem feel about the change being observed or described?

Reading Strategy

Reading Poetry According to Punctuation

Every poem comes equipped with a set of instructions on how to read it. Those instructions are its **punctuation** marks. Commas, periods, exclamation points, semicolons, and colons tell you when to pause or stop. They also indicate relationships between groups of words; when you recognize these relationships you will read with greater understanding and expression.

As you read, make sure you are clear about the poet's reading instructions. Use a chart like the one shown to remember when to pause and when to stop.

Punctuation mark	Instructions
Comma ,	Brief pause
Period .	Pause at the end of a thought
Exclamation Point !	Speak with force and pause
Semicolon ;	Pause between related but distinct thoughts
Colon :	Pause before giving explanations or examples

Vocabulary Development

strife (strīf) *n.* conflict (p. 78)

orators (ôr´ ət ərz) *n.* public speakers (p. 80)

indicative (in dik´ ə tiv) *adj.* giving a suggestion; showing (p. 80)

sauntering (sân´ tər iŋ) *v.* walking slowly and confidently (p. 80)

RING OUT, WILD BELLS

Alfred, Lord Tennyson

Ring out, wild bells, to the wild sky,
    The flying cloud, the frosty light:
    The year is dying in the night;
Ring out, wild bells, and let him die.

5 Ring out the old, ring in the new,
    Ring, happy bells, across the snow:
    The year is going, let him go;
Ring out the false, ring in the true.

Ring out the grief that saps[1] the mind,
10   For those that here we see no more;
    Ring out the feud of rich and poor,
Ring in redress[2] to all mankind.

Ring out a slowly dying cause,
    And ancient forms of party <u>strife</u>;
15   Ring in the nobler modes[3] of life,
With sweeter manners, purer laws.

Ring out the want, the care, the sin,
    The faithless coldness of the times;
    Ring out, ring out thy mournful rhymes,
20 But ring the fuller minstrel[4] in.

Ring out false pride in place and blood,
    The civic[5] slander and the spite;
    Ring in the love of truth and right,
Ring in the common love of good.

25   Ring out old shapes of foul disease;
Ring out the narrowing lust of gold;
    Ring out the thousand wars of old,
    Ring in the thousand years of peace.

---

1. **saps** (saps) *v.* drains; exhausts.
2. **redress** (ri dres´) *n.* the righting of wrongs.
3. **modes** (mōdz) *n.* ways; forms.
4. **fuller minstrel** (min´ strəl) *n.* singer of the highest rank.
5. **civic** (siv´ ik) *adj.* of a city.

strife (strīf) *n.* conflict

Alfred, Lord Tennyson

(1809–1892)

Born in rural England, Tennyson left home as a teenager to attend Cambridge University. While at Cambridge, Tennyson won a university prize for poetry, his first step on the way to becoming a famous poet. In 1850, Queen Victoria appointed him Poet Laureate of England.

"Ring Out, Wild Bells" is part of the long poem "In Memoriam A.H.H." This poem's title means "In Memory," and Tennyson wrote it in memory of his close friend, Arthur Henry Hallam, who died in 1833. The section "Ring Out, Wild Bells" marks a New Year's holiday after his friend's death.

Winter Moon

Langston Hughes

How thin and sharp is the moon tonight!
How thin and sharp and ghostly white
Is the slim curved crook of the moon tonight!

Review and Assess

Thinking About the Selections

1. **Respond:** What is a New Year's hope that you have expressed?

2. **(a) Recall:** List three phrases that describe what Tennyson wants to "ring out." **(b) Infer:** How does the poet seem to feel about the past? **(c) Draw Conclusions:** In what way is this poem about more than the passing of the old year?

3. **(a) Recall:** List three phrases that describe what Tennyson wants to "ring in." **(b) Infer:** Explain what the poet hopes the future will bring.

4. **(a) Recall:** Which phrases are repeated in "Winter Moon"? **(b) Interpret:** What qualities of the moon appeal to Hughes?

5. **(a) Apply:** How does Hughes's poem make you feel about the moon? **(b) Interpret:** In your own words, describe the moon the speaker sees.

6. **Make a Judgment:** What, if anything, is the value of making New Year's resolutions?

Langston Hughes

(1902–1967)
Langston Hughes incorporated the rhythms of blues, jazz, and African American speech in his poetry. He came of age during the Harlem Renaissance of the 1920s. This renaissance, or rebirth, was a flowering of African American writers, musicians, and painters in New York City's neighborhood of Harlem.

Poets to Come
Walt Whitman

Poets to come! <u>orators</u>, singers, musicians to come!
Not to-day is to justify me and answer what I am for,
But you, a new brood, native, athletic, continental,
    greater than before known,
Arouse! for you must justify me.

5 I myself but write one or two <u>indicative</u> words for
    the future,
I but advance a moment only to wheel and hurry
    back in the darkness.

I am a man who, <u>sauntering</u> along without fully
    stopping, turns a casual look upon you and then
    averts his face,
Leaving it to you to prove and define it,
Expecting the main things from you.

Review and Assess

Thinking About the Selection

1. **Respond:** Do you feel that Whitman is speaking directly to you in "Poets to Come"? Why or why not?
2. **(a) Recall:** Whom does Whitman call on to justify himself? **(b) Infer:** On what topic is Whitman asking to be justified?
3. **(a) Recall:** In the second stanza, how does Whitman describe what he is writing? **(b) Connect:** How does this description relate to the future poets?
4. **(a) Recall:** What does Whitman say he does after "advanc[ing] a moment"? **(b) Interpret:** How does Whitman present himself and his influence on the world of poetry? **(c) Evaluate:** How accurate or inaccurate is his summary of his influence?

Walt Whitman

(1819–1892)

The course of American poetry was influenced by Walt Whitman's *Leaves of Grass*, first published in 1855. Whitman, a New Yorker who worked at a variety of jobs, created bold new poems to suit a new country. He discarded the regular rhythms and rhymes of traditional poetry in favor of his own invented rhythms and unrhymed lines.

Review and Assess

Literary Analysis

Repetition in Poetry

1. In "Poets to Come," how does the repetition of the pronouns *I* and *you* emphasize the poem's meaning?
2. What words are repeated in "Winter Moon"? Based on the description, to what could you compare the moon?
3. Complete a chart like the one below to examine the use of repetition of "ring out" and "ring in" in Tennyson's poem. Explain the change in emphasis you discover.

Line number	1	2	3	4	5	6	7	8	9	10	11	12	13	14	15	16	17	18	19	20	21	22	23	24	25	26	27	28
Ring out	X		X	X																								
Ring in												X																

Comparing Literary Works

4. What is the specific topic of each poem?
5. How does the speaker of each poem feel about the change being observed or described?
6. Make a chart like the one below to note similarities among the three poems. Place checkmarks in the appropriate boxes.

	"Ring Out, Wild Bells"	"Winter Moon"	"Poets to Come"
use of repetition	√		
use of rhyme			
moment of change			

Reading Strategy

Reading Poetry According to Punctuation

7. Explain where you would pause and where you would stop in lines 21–24 of "Ring Out, Wild Bells."
8. Which of these poems calls for no pauses and just two stops? Explain.

Extend Understanding

9. **Social Studies Connection:** Explain how the words of "Ring Out, Wild Bells" could be applied to specific events and social conditions in the United States in the first half of the nineteenth century.

Quick Review

Repetition in poetry is the use, more than once, of certain sounds, words, and phrases in a poem. To review repetition in poetry, see page 77.

Punctuation marks are instructions for reading a poem. They tell you when to pause and when to stop. To review punctuation marks, see page 77.

 Take It to the Net
www.phschool.com
Take the interactive self-test online to check your understanding of these selections.

Integrate Language Skills

Vocabulary Development Lesson

Word Analysis: Latin Suffix -or

The Latin suffix -or signals that a word means "a person or thing that does something." In "Poets to Come," Whitman addresses future *orators*, "people who give public speeches." The word *orator* combines *orate*, "to give a speech," and -or.

Use your knowledge of the Latin suffix -or to explain the meaning of the italicized words in the following paragraph. Write the definitions on your paper.

A new movie featured a fight among the *Terminator*, the *Eliminator*, and the *Hesitator*. While the *Hesitator* was waiting, the first two guys destroyed each other. Then, the movie *projector* caught on fire. I had to stop applauding to dial the emergency *operator*.

Fluency: True or False?

On your paper, answer these true-or-false questions. Then, explain your answers.

1. The best *orators* usually win debates.
2. A jogger is accustomed to *sauntering*.
3. The color red may be *indicative* of danger.
4. *Strife* is what ends when a war begins.

Spelling Strategy

When adding a suffix beginning with a vowel to words ending in e, drop the e.

    indicate + -ive = indicative
    advise + -or = advisor

On your paper, spell the word that results from combining these words and suffixes.

1. create + -or
2. face + -ial
3. senate + -or
4. machine + -ist

Grammar Lesson

Intensive Pronouns

Intensive pronouns are formed by combining a personal pronoun and the suffix -self or -selves.

> *myself; ourselves; yourself, yourselves; herself, himself, itself; themselves*

Intensive pronouns emphasize the person's role or indicate that a person performs an action alone. In a sentence, an intensive pronoun stresses the importance of the noun or other pronoun that comes before it.

Emphasizes Person: "I *myself* but write one or two indicative words for / the future, . . ."

Indicates Person Acts Alone: I'll do it *myself*, thanks.

▶ For more practice, see page R28, Exercise A.
Practice On your paper, identify the intensive pronoun in each sentence. Tell whether it emphasizes the person or indicates that the person acts alone.

1. I myself read "Poets to Come" aloud.
2. Did you yourself see the winter moon?
3. Whitman himself addresses future poets, without a backup chorus of voices.
4. We ourselves can ring the bells.

Writing Application On your paper, fill in each blank with a suitable intensive pronoun.

1. I ___?___ was born on January fifth.
2. Have you ___?___ seen a crescent moon?
3. They made the poetry book ___?___.

*W*G *Prentice Hall Writing and Grammar Connection: Chapter 14*

Writing Lesson

Literary Response

Choose one of the poets, read an article or essay about him or his work, and then write a composition in which you agree or disagree with the writer of the article.

Prewriting As you read your article, take notes on words used to describe the poet's work and the examples used to illustrate the descriptions.

Drafting Give an overview of what you have read and state whether or not you agree with the writer. Include details from your reading and quotations from the poem. When you include someone else's ideas, either word for word or paraphrased, you must credit the source.

Model: Citing Sources

Although Whitman seemed larger-than-life in his poetry, people who met him were surprised at how "conventional" he seemed. (Townsend 12) The following lines from "Poets to Come" create the impression of a forceful man: "But you, a new brood, native, athletic, continental, greater than before known./Arouse! for you must justify me" (3–5).

> Townsend's reaction is paraphrased but must be credited as his original thought. Whitman's lines are quoted exactly and are also cited.

Revising Check the accuracy of your citations and the spellings of all names.

Prentice Hall Writing and Grammar Connection: Chapter 11, Section 5

Extension Activities

Speaking and Listening Choose one of the poems to deliver as a **recitation**—a performance of a memorized poem. Before reading, prepare a rehearsal copy of the poem.

1. Use a red pen to emphasize punctuation that indicates where to pause or stop.
2. Use a yellow highlighter to mark words and phrases that you want to emphasize by speaking more slowly or loudly than you do in the rest of the poem.

Memorize the poem from your rehearsal copy. After your recitation, ask listeners to suggest improvements.

Research and Technology Work with a group to prepare a **presentation** on the phases of the moon. Make a chart showing all the phases and how long each one lasts. Research in online encyclopedias, astronomy Web sites, and the NASA Web site for facts and photographs. Identify the phase Hughes is probably describing in his poem. Discuss words he might have used in a poem about the other phases.

 **Take It to the Net**   www.phschool.com

Go online for an additional research activity using the Internet.

READING INFORMATIONAL MATERIALS

Eyewitness Accounts

About Eyewitness Accounts

In your everyday life, each time you observe and report on something you have seen, you are making an **eyewitness account.** Eyewitness accounts are used for a number of different reasons: police investigations, lawsuits, news stories, and historical reference, to name just a few. The following selection, from *A Tour on the Prairies*, is an eyewitness account written by Washington Irving after his journey to the western frontier of the United States in the mid 1800s. At the time this account was written, its purpose was to give people information about a region that was still largely unknown to them. Today, this account serves a different purpose; it is now a historical account of the West as it was before it was settled.

When reading eyewitness accounts, it is important to remember that they may not always be reliable. For example, a number of people may witness the same event, but their accounts will always be different because they each have a different perspective. Nonetheless, as historical **primary sources**—documents written during the time period being studied—eyewitness accounts can offer readers an unromantic view of the past.

Reading Strategy

Evaluating a Text

When reading informational texts critically, it is important to evaluate the texts for internal consistency and logic. Internal consistency includes coherent ideas that build upon one another as well as a solid logical development. A text that develops logically has

- ideas that build toward an overall theme or purpose.
- sentences and paragraphs that flow in a logical sequence.
- reliable facts, statistics, or quotations that support main points.

When writing is not consistent or logical, it often loses its credibility with readers. Use a chart like the one below to help you evaluate the text of the beginning of *A Tour on the Prairies*.

Logical Technique	Examples
Sentences and paragraphs flow logically	• Irving tells how people wanted to know about his journey west, thereby explaining his reason for writing his book.
	•
Ideas fit together toward a main goal	•
	•

A Tour on the Prairies
Washington Irving, 1835

Having, since my return to the United States, made a wide and varied tour, for the gratification of my curiosity, it has been supposed that I did it for the purpose of writing a book; and it has more than once been intimated in the papers, that such a work was actually in the press, containing scenes and sketches of the Far West.

These announcements, gratuitously made for me, before I had put pen to paper, or even contemplated anything of the kind, have embarrassed me exceedingly. I have been like a poor actor, who finds himself announced for a part he had no thought of playing, and his appearance expected on the stage before he has committed a line to memory.

I have always had a repugnance, amounting almost to disability, to write in the face of expectation; and, in the present instance, I was expected to write about a region fruitful of wonders and adventures, and which had already been made the theme of spirit-stirring narratives from able pens; yet about which I had nothing wonderful or adventurous to offer.

Irving reveals that he has read other writers' descriptions of his topic.

Since such, however, seems to be the desire of the public, and that they take sufficient interest in my wanderings to deem them worthy of recital, I have hastened, as promptly as possible, to meet, in some degree, the expectation which others have excited. For this purpose, I have, as it were, plucked a few leaves out of my memorandum book, containing a month's foray beyond the outposts of human habitation, into the wilderness of the Far West. It forms, indeed, but a small portion of an extensive tour; but it is an episode, complete as far as it goes. As such, I offer it to the public, with great diffidence. It is a simple narrative of every-day occurrences; such as happen to every one who travels the prairies. I have no wonders to describe, nor any moving accidents by flood or field to narrate; and as to those who look for a marvellous or adventurous story at my hands, I can only reply, in the words of the weary knife-grinder: "Story! God bless you, I have none to tell, sir."

Irving identifies his purpose.

Here Irving gives an indication of what readers will find in his account.

In the often vaunted regions of the Far West, several hundred miles beyond the Mississippi, extends a vast tract of uninhabited country, where there is neither to be seen the log-house of the white man, nor the wigwam of the Indian. It consists of great grassy plains, interspersed with forests and groves, and clumps of trees, and watered by the Arkansas, the grand Canadian, the Red River, and their tributary streams. Over these fertile and verdant wastes still roam the elk, the buffalo, and the wild horse, in all their native freedom. These, in fact, are the hunting grounds of the various tribes of the Far West. Hither repair the Osage, the Creek, the Delaware and other tribes that have linked themselves with civilization, and live within the vicinity of the white settlements. Here resort also, the Pawnees, the Comanches, and other fierce, and as yet independent tribes, the nomads of the prairies, or the inhabitants of the skirts of the Rocky Mountains. The regions I have mentioned form a debatable ground of these warring and vindictive tribes; none of them presume to erect a permanent habitation within its borders.

This section gives readers a picture of the region as it once was.

Check Your Comprehension

1. Why did Irving make a journey west?
2. What did people believe was Irving's reason for traveling west?
3. Give three details Irving uses to describe the prairie.

Applying the Reading Strategy

Evaluating the Text

4. Does this text build toward a main idea or an overall purpose?
5. What was Irving's original writing purpose?
6. How has that purpose affected the organization of the writing?
7. What words or phrases does Irving use to connect sentences and paragraphs?

Activity

Comparing Works by Washington Irving

Washington Irving was a well-known American writer during the 1800s. He wrote numerous works of both fiction and nonfiction. Find and read a fictional work by Irving. Then, compare it with *A Tour on the Prairies*. How are the writing styles different? In a brief essay, explain which work you prefer and why.

Contrasting Informational Materials

Eyewitness Accounts and Biographies

A **biography** is an account of a person's life written by another individual. The biographer gathers information from **primary sources,** such as letters, diaries, and interviews with the subject or people who knew the subject, and then weaves together and interprets the information.

Autobiographical writing, which includes eyewitness accounts, is less objective. The writer is the subject of the writing and presents events and observations from a personal viewpoint. Look at the Venn diagram for an overview of the differences between biography and autobiography.

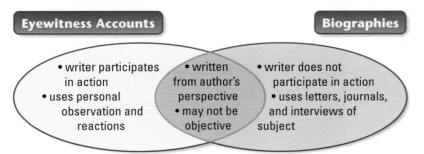

Eyewitness Accounts
- writer participates in action
- uses personal observation and reactions

- written from author's perspective
- may not be objective

Biographies
- writer does not participate in action
- uses letters, journals, and interviews of subject

Writing WORKSHOP

Narration: Autobiographical Writing

Narrative writing is writing that tells a story. An **autobiographical narrative** tells the story of a memorable event, person, period, or situation in the writer's life. In this workshop, you will write about an interesting incident that happened to you.

Assignment Criteria. Your autobiographical narrative should have the following characteristics:

- a consistent first-person point of view
- a clear sequence of true events from your life, presented in a logical order
- a central conflict, problem, or shift in perspective
- your thoughts and feelings about the experience
- vivid details that describe people, setting, and actions
- dialogue that helps reveal your characters' personalities

See the Rubric on page 91 for the criteria on which your autobiographical narrative may be assessed.

Prewriting

Choose a topic. Draw and label a **blueprint** of a familiar place—a friend's house, your school, or a park. List the people, things, and incidents you associate with each spot on the blueprint. Pick one as your topic. The blueprint at right shows the events and experiences one writer associates with the town baseball field.

Consider your audience and purpose. Knowing who your readers will be and why you want to tell them your story can help you decide how and what to tell. If your purpose is to entertain your audience, focus on the funny, moving, or exciting parts of your story. If your purpose is to share a lesson you learned, focus on the events that illustrate the lesson and the conclusions you draw from them.

Model: Blueprint

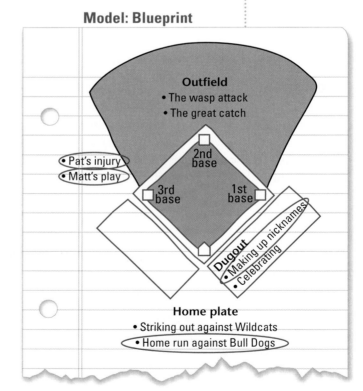

Student Model

Before you begin drafting your autobiographical narrative, read this student model and review the characteristics of a successful autobiographical narrative.

Chris Kleinhen
Palos Verdes, California

Baseball, a Sport I Love

I remember the day my dad placed a glove in one of my hands and a bat in the other and told me the combination was an eight-letter word called baseball. Ever since then, most of my memories have been related to the sport. When I was eleven, I played in a game I'll remember forever.

> The writer begins by identifying when the action of the narrative begins.

We were facing the West Torrance Bull Dogs. We had a great team that year. Our pitcher, Frank (The Smasher) was tough to hit. The nick-names of other players— "Hot Glove," "Fireball," and "Maguire, Jr." were earned with outstanding play during the season. We had a team of stars. The only one who had not earned a "star" nickname was Matt.

The nine starters took the field at five o'clock on a warm afternoon. The small crowd of parents and friends made enough noise for a major league game. For most of the game the two teams were evenly matched. Then, in the last inning, Pat "The Runstopper" at third base was injured as one of the Bull Dogs accidentally rammed his ankle while sliding into third base. We had two choices: forfeit the game or play Matt.

> Details about the warmth and the noise help bring the scene to life.

> The injury increases the tension of the conflict between the two teams.

"You can do it, Matt!" the coach said as he sent Matt out to take Pat's place on third base.

"All right, Matt!" we encouraged from our places in the field as he trotted out nervously.

The score was tied with two outs. Unfortunately, the next ball took a sharp bounce toward third—and toward Matt. Matt ran forward and made an awkward catch, followed by an even more awkward lob toward first. Amazingly it made it there in time!

As we jogged back in the players called out "Way to go, Matt!" "You came through in the clutch!"

> Dialogue helps readers feel as if they are witnessing this important conversation.

That's when I realized the truth of something the coach is always telling us. When you play as a team, everyone is a star. And that's exactly what I told Matt, whose new nickname is "Clutch."

> Here, the writer reveals how his experience has helped him look at his favorite sport in a new way.

Drafting

Order events. Identify the **conflict,** or problem, that makes your narrative worth reading. Organize events that are related to the conflict in **chronological** (time) **order.** As you introduce people, places, and things into your narrative, add details that bring these elements of your narrative to life. In your first draft, you can use sticky notes to jot down details that you would like to add when you revise.

West Torrance Bull Dogs

Model

We were facing (our rivals) in a game that put the pride of both teams at stake. Neither team wanted to lose, and neither team planned to lose. We had a great team that year. We had a (team of stars) —except maybe the benchwarmer, Matt.

Add examples— great pitching, nicknames earned

Use a consistent point of view. Stick to first-person point of view, using the pronoun *I* to refer to yourself. Avoid telling what *other* people in your narrative are thinking or feeling. As a first-person narrator, you can only know and tell your own thoughts and feelings.

Revising

Revise sentence patterns. Look over your sentences to see how sentence variety can make your story more interesting. Color-code the first word of each sentence in your draft. For example, use green to highlight or circle articles; orange for pronouns; blue for adjectives; red for adverbs; and yellow for prepositions. When writing in the first person, you may find that many of the sentences begin with *I.* Revise to make some of them begin with another kind of word.

Model

Draft: I remember the first time I held a baseball. I knew then I would love the game. I remember one game especially.

Revision: I remember the first time I held a baseball. Even then, I knew I would love the game. One game, especially, stands out in my memory.

Revise for word choice. Look for vague nouns that might leave readers asking *What kind?* Replace them with **precise nouns**.

> **Example:** Weeds filled the *place*.
> Weeds filled the *playground*.

Identify vague verbs, and replace them with vivid, **precise verbs**.

> **Example:** Weeds *filled* the playground.
> Weeds *overran* the playground.

Compare the model and the nonmodel. Why is the model more effective than the nonmodel?

Nonmodel	Model
People cheered as we headed out. Usually, I feel comfortable as I go out to my spot. On this day, though, I was so nervous, I barely felt my shoes hitting the ground.	Fans cheered as we headed out. Usually, I feel comfortable as I jog out to third base. On this day, though, I was so nervous, I barely felt my cleats hitting the ground.

Publishing and Presenting

Choose one of the following ways to share your writing with classmates or a wider audience.

Present an autobiographical storytelling or a speech. Use your autobiographical narrative as the basis for a narrative presentation.

Make a comic strip. Create a comic strip based on your narrative. Draw pictures to show important scenes. Exaggerate actions or facial expressions for effect, and use speech bubbles to show what people say. Post your comic strip in the classroom.

 Prentice Hall Writing and Grammar Connection: Chapter 4.

Speaking Connection

To learn more about presenting an autobiographical narrative, see the **Listening and Speaking Workshop: Organizing and Presenting a Narrative Presentation,** page 92.

Rubric for Self-Assessment

Evaluate your autobiographical narrative using the following criteria and rating scale:

Criteria	Rating Scale Not very				Very
How consistently does the writer use first-person point of view?	1	2	3	4	5
Is the central conflict, problem, or shift in perspective clearly explained?	1	2	3	4	5
How often does the writer include thoughts, feelings, and reactions?	1	2	3	4	5
How vivid are the details of people, setting, and action?	1	2	3	4	5
How well does the writer use dialogue to reveal characters' personalities?	1	2	3	4	5

Organizing and Presenting a Narrative Presentation

Narratives tell a story. Narratives can be written stories or stories told aloud by a narrator. In this workshop, you will present a true narrative account—a story from your life or the life of someone else. (To review the characteristics of autobiographical narratives, see the writing workshop, pp. 88–91.) The following strategies will help you to deliver an effective account.

Organize and Rehearse

Like a written narrative, an oral narrative should spin out a story, telling the events in chronological order and focusing on the central conflict, or struggle, in the story. Follow these guidelines to plan your presentation.

Plot the story. Write each event in your narrative on one note card. Label the card that contains the first event with a *B* for beginning; the card that describes the high point of the story with a *C* for climax; and the card that describes the last event with an *E* for ending. Check to see that each event is related to the story's central conflict. Then, put the cards in the correct sequence and discard any that are not related.

Model: Plot Card
B
I went outside one late night with my little sister when she discovered that her cat Samantha was missing.

Add details. On each note card, add details that you will tell about the people and setting of your story. Jot down lines of dialogue to bring the incident to life. Include on your cards notes about how you or the subject of the narrative felt about the events as they occurred.

Rehearse. Practice in front of a mirror. Use note cards to jog your memory, but put them aside when you no longer need them. Think about word choice and grammar.

- For your dialogue, choose words that the people would actually use.
- Think about your audience and setting. While you might use casual language to deliver your narrative at a campfire, you will want to choose your words carefully for a classroom presentation.

Deliver Your Account. Remember these points as you present your narrative.

- Stand confidently, balancing your weight on both feet.
- Pronounce each word carefully so your audience will hear it.
- Do not rush. Take breaths as you need them.
- Slow down to build suspense. Speed up for exciting action.
- Look at different people. Do not stare at the floor or the ceiling.

Activity:
Presentation and Feedback With a partner, take turns rehearsing your narratives. Provide feedback for each other on the flow of the story, enunciation, pacing, and word choice. Mention the strengths of each presentation, and brainstorm ideas for improvement.

Assessment WORKSHOP

Context Clues

The reading sections of some tests ask you to read a passage and answer questions about word meanings. Some questions require you to determine the meanings of words by using context clues—words or phrases near an unfamiliar word that can help you figure out the word's meaning. The following strategies will help you answer such test questions:

- A context clue may be a synonym (word with the same meaning) or an antonym (word with the opposite meaning) of the unfamiliar word.

- Sometimes the passage contains a definition or an explanation of the unfamiliar word or a description with details or examples that can help you figure out the word's meaning.

Sample Test Item

Directions: Read the passage, and then answer the item that follows.

The town's first Amateur Scientists Night was a huge success. The most popular participant was a local **ornithologist,** who showed slides of birds he had studied all over the world.

1. The word **ornithologist** in this passage means—
   - **A** worldwide traveler
   - **B** person who studies birds
   - **C** photographer
   - **D** endangered species

Answer and Explanation

The context tells you that the correct answer has to be an amateur scientist, so A and C are incorrect. D does not make sense since humans are not an endangered species. *B* is correct.

Practice

Directions: Read the passage, and then answer the items that follow.

On her way home from work, Janice saw the sign in the storefront: Cooking Classes Start Tonight at 8 P.M. She imagined herself surprising her family with one **culinary** treat after another. Promptly at eight, she returned to the store, only to discover that **preregistration** was required.

1. In this passage, the word **culinary** means—
   - **A** related to school
   - **B** related to money
   - **C** related to cooking
   - **D** related to dessert

2. The word **preregistration** in this passage means—
   - **A** wearing specialized clothing
   - **B** bringing supplies
   - **C** paying cash
   - **D** signing up ahead of time

UNIT 2 *Meeting Challenges*

The Idleness of Sisyphus, 1981, Sandro Chia, Museum of Modern Art

Exploring the Theme

From taking your first steps, to learning to ride a two-wheeled bicycle, to graduating with honors, to making a scientific breakthrough or winning a writing prize—challenges occur throughout life. Some challenges make headlines; others are personal.

◄ **Critical Viewing** What message about meeting challenges might this painting express? **[Interpret]**

Why Read Literature?

The literature in this unit explores the theme of meeting challenges—the exciting, dangerous, or unfamiliar opportunities that people face. Depending on the content, genre, and style of the works you plan to read, you will set various purposes for reading. Preview three of the purposes you might set before reading the works in this unit.

1 Read for the love of literature.

A person who weighs 120 pounds on Earth would weigh only 20 pounds on the moon! The reason for this is that gravity on the moon is only one-sixth as strong as it is on Earth. Imagine living on such a world when you read **"The Secret,"** page 118.

The state name *Texas* comes from the way Spanish adventurers pronounced the Native American word *Tejas,* meaning "friends" or "allies." Explore the early days of the American West by reading the poems **"Western Wagons"** and **"The Other Pioneers,"** page 146.

3 Read for information.

During the 1800s, rewards offered for the capture of Harriet Tubman, the African American woman who led many enslaved Africans to freedom, were as high as $40,000. That amount is eight times as much as the $5,000 reward offered by the Governor of Missouri for the capture of outlaw Jesse James. Find out why slave owners were willing to pay such a high sum to stop this daring rescuer. Read **"Harriet Tubman: Guide to Freedom"** on page 130.

Learn the ins and outs of reading and understanding contracts by reading the **Employment Contract** on page 113.

2 Read to be entertained.

The average winter temperature in the Yukon is twenty degrees below zero. Frostbite can damage unprotected skin in moments. Experience the danger and suspense of a Yukon adventure when you read about a character who battles the Yukon winter in **"Up the Slide,"** page 156.

 Take It to the Net

Visit the Web site for online instruction and activities related to each selection in this unit.

www.phschool.com

How to Read Literature

Use Literal Comprehension Strategies

Reading is like any challenging process: When you know the basics, it becomes easier. In reading, knowing the basics means understanding the literal meaning of the text. Once you know that you understand the meanings of the words and phrases, you can begin interpreting and analyzing. Preview the literal comprehension strategies that you will use in this unit to understand what you are reading.

1. Interpret idioms.

An **idiom** is a word or phrase whose literal meaning is different from its intended meaning. The idiom in the following example is italicized.

> Now came this shriek: "Here! You going to set there all day?"
>
> I *lit in the middle of the floor*, shot there by the electric suddenness of surprise.

You can figure out from the surrounding text that Twain does not mean he did something to brighten the floor. After reading the whole passage, you interpret "lit" to mean that he "moved in a hurry" or that he fell back on the floor. Recognizing when writers are using figures of speech will help you understand what writers mean.

2. Paraphrase.

Restating unfamiliar phrases and sentences in your own words can help you understand them. To paraphrase, ask yourself these questions:

- What is the main point?
- What additional details are provided?
- Which words would I use to express the main point and details?

Organize details of a passage in your mind by paraphrasing.

3. Recognize word roots.

A word root is the most basic part of a word. For example, the word *microbe,* meaning "small form of life," contains the Greek word roots *micro,* meaning "small," and *bio (be),* meaning "life."

> micro + be = microbe
>
> small + life = small form of life

In this unit, you will learn to use word roots and origins to determine the meanings of unfamiliar words.

Original: "But the descent was precipitate and dangerous in the uncertain moonlight, and he elected to go down the mountain by its gentler northern flank."

You might paraphrase this sentence in this way:

Paraphrase: The way down was steep and dangerous with only the light of the moon, and he chose to go down the side of the mountain with the more gradual slope.

As you read the selections in this unit, review the reading strategies and look at the notes in the side column. Use the suggestions to apply the strategies and comprehend the text.

Prepare to Read

Cub Pilot on the Mississippi

The Great Mississippi Steamboat Race, 1870, Currier & Ives

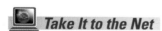 **Take It to the Net**

Visit www.phschool.com
for interactive activities
and instruction related
to "Cub Pilot on the
Mississippi," including
- background
- graphic organizers
- literary elements
- reading strategies

Preview

Connecting to the Literature

In "Cub Pilot on the Mississippi," Mark Twain describes his experience working for an ill-tempered boss. Connect to the story by thinking of how you have dealt with bullies or other difficult people.

Background

In the 1800s, steamboats carried goods and people on the nation's waterways. On the wide, long Mississippi River, people could travel quickly and sometimes luxuriously on steamboats. However, there were also dangers. Fires broke out, boilers burst, hidden rocks and sandbars could damage ships, and steamboat crews had to negotiate ever-changing currents.

Literary Analysis

Conflict Between Characters

"Cub Pilot on the Mississippi" tells of a **conflict between characters**—a struggle between two characters with opposite needs or wants. In this story, the conflict is between young Twain and the steamboat pilot for whom he works.

As you read, look for details that contribute to this conflict. Use the following focus questions to guide you.

1. What are the two sides of the conflict between Twain and Pilot Brown?
2. How is the conflict between them finally worked out?

Connecting Literary Elements

Often, the way characters or people react to a conflict is guided by the **historical context**—the customs, laws, and expectations of the time period. In the historical context of "Cub Pilot on the Mississippi," a young man like Twain would not challenge authority. Decide how a character today would respond to a similar conflict. Use a graphic organizer like the one shown to help you make your comparison.

Today

Laws protect employees

Conflict with bullying authority

Apprentices (young employees) have no rights

Twain's Time

Reading Strategy

Identifying Idioms

An **idiom** is an expression that has a certain understood meaning in a particular language or region. The italicized idioms in the example are understood by most English speakers. These expressions would not have the same meaning if they were translated word for word into another language.

> I *lit in* the middle of the floor, *shot* there by the electric suddenness of the surprise.

As you read the story, notice how idioms give a feeling of reality to each speaker's words.

Vocabulary Development

furtive (fur´ tiv) *adj.* sly or done in secret (p. 101)

pretext (prē´ tekst) *n.* false reason or motive used to hide a real intention (p. 103)

intimation (in´ tə mā´ shən) *n.* hint or suggestion (p. 105)

judicious (jōō dish´ əs) *adj.* wise and careful (p. 105)

indulgent (in dul´ jənt) *adj.* very mild and tolerant; not strict or critical (p. 107)

emancipated (i man´ sə pā´ təd) *v.* freed from the control or power of another (p. 108)

Cub Pilot
on the Mississippi

Mark Twain

During the two or two and a half years of my apprenticeship[1] I served under many pilots, and had experience of many kinds of steamboatmen and many varieties of steamboats. I am to this day profiting somewhat by that experience; for in that brief, sharp schooling, I got personally and familiarly acquainted with about all the different types of human nature that are to be found in fiction, biography, or history.

---

1. **apprenticeship** (ə pren′ tis ship) *n.* time a person spends working for a master craftsperson in a craft or trade in return for instruction.

▼ **Critical Viewing**
Imagine the activity that might be happening in this scene. Why were riverboats important to the life of Mississippi towns like this? **[Analyze]**

The fact is daily borne in upon me that the average shore-employment requires as much as forty years to equip a man with this sort of an education. When I say I am still profiting by this thing, I do not mean that it has constituted me a judge of men—no, it has not done that, for judges of men are born, not made. My profit is various in kind and degree, but the feature of it which I value most is the zest which that early experience has given to my later reading. When I find a well-drawn character in fiction or biography I generally take a warm personal interest in him, for the reason that I have known him before—met him on the river.

The figure that comes before me oftenest, out of the shadows of that vanished time, is that of Brown, of the steamer *Pennsylvania*. He was a middle-aged, long, slim, bony, smooth-shaven, horse-faced, ignorant, stingy, malicious, snarling, fault-hunting, mote[2] magnifying tyrant. I early got the habit of coming on watch with dread at my heart. No matter how good a time I might have been having with the off-watch below, and no matter how high my spirits might be when I started aloft, my soul became lead in my body the moment I approached the pilothouse.

I still remember the first time I ever entered the presence of that man. The boat had backed out from St. Louis and was "straightening down." I ascended to the pilothouse in high feather, and very proud to be semiofficially a member of the executive family of so fast and famous a boat. Brown was at the wheel. I paused in the middle of the room, all fixed to make my bow, but Brown did not look around. I thought he took a furtive glance at me out of the corner of his eye, but as not even this notice was repeated, I judged I had been mistaken. By this time he was picking his way among some dangerous "breaks" abreast the woodyards; therefore it would not be proper to interrupt him; so I stepped softly to the high bench and took a seat.

There was silence for ten minutes; then my new boss turned and inspected me deliberately and painstakingly from head to heel for about—as it seemed to me—a quarter of an hour. After which he removed his countenance[3] and I saw it no more for some seconds; then it came around once more, and this question greeted me: "Are you Horace Bigsby's cub?"[4]

"Yes, sir."

After this there was a pause and another inspection. Then: "What's your name?"

---

2. **mote** (mōt) *n.* speck of dust.
3. **countenance** (koun′ tə nəns) *n.* face.
4. **cub** (kub) *n.* beginner.

Literary Analysis
Conflict Between Characters What clues here indicate that the conflict is between Twain and Brown?

furtive (fur′ tiv) *adj.* sly or done in secret

✔**Reading Check**

Why does Twain not like going to the pilothouse?

I told him. He repeated it after me. It was probably the only thing he ever forgot; for although I was with him many months he never addressed himself to me in any other way than "Here!" and then his command followed.

"Where was you born?"

"In Florida, Missouri."

A pause. Then: "Dern sight better stayed there!"

By means of a dozen or so of pretty direct questions, he pumped my family history out of me.

The leads[5] were going now in the first crossing. This interrupted the inquest.[6] When the leads had been laid in he resumed:

"How long you been on the river?"

I told him. After a pause:

"Where'd you get them shoes?"

I gave him the information.

"Hold up your foot!"

I did so. He stepped back, examined the shoe minutely and contemptuously, scratching his head thoughtfully, tilting his high sugar-loaf hat well forward to facilitate the operation, then ejaculated, "Well, I'll be dod derned!" and returned to his wheel.

What occasion there was to be dod derned about it is a thing which is still as much of a mystery to me now as it was then. It must have been all of fifteen minutes—fifteen minutes of dull, homesick silence—before that long horse-face swung round upon me again—and then what a change! It was as red as fire, and every muscle in it was working. Now came this shriek: "Here! You going to set there all day?"

I lit in the middle of the floor, shot there by the electric suddenness of the surprise. As soon as I could get my voice I said apologetically: "I have had no orders, sir."

"You've had no *orders*! My, what a fine bird we are! We must have *orders*! Our father was a *gentleman* —and *we've* been to *school*. Yes, *we* are a gentleman, *too*, and got to have *orders*! Orders, is it? Orders is what you want! Dod dern my skin, *I'll* learn you to swell yourself up and blow around *here* about your dod-derned *orders*! G'way from the wheel!" (I had approached it without knowing it.)

I moved back a step or two and stood as in a dream, all my senses stupefied by this frantic assault.

"What you standing there for? Take that ice-pitcher down to the texas-tender![7] Come, move along, and don't you be all day about it!"

The moment I got back to the pilothouse Brown said: "Here! What was you doing down there all this time?"

---

5. **leads** (ledz) *n.* weights that were lowered to test the depth of the river.

6. **inquest** (in′ kwest) *n.* investigation.

7. **texas-tender** the waiter in the officers' quarters (On Mississippi steamboats, rooms were named after the states. The officers' area, which was the largest, was named after what was then the largest state, Texas.)

"I couldn't find the texas-tender; I had to go all the way to the pantry."

"Derned likely story! Fill up the stove."

I proceeded to do so. He watched me like a cat. Presently he shouted: "Put down that shovel! Derndest numskull I ever saw—ain't even got sense enough to load up a stove."

All through the watch this sort of thing went on. Yes, and the subsequent watches were much like it during a stretch of months. As I have said, I soon got the habit of coming on duty with dread. The moment I was in the presence, even in the darkest night, I could feel those yellow eyes upon me, and knew their owner was watching for a pretext to spit out some venom on me. Preliminarily he would say: "Here! Take the wheel."

Two minutes later: "*Where* in the nation you going to? Pull her down! pull her down!"

After another moment: "Say! You going to hold her all day? Let her go—meet her! meet her!"

Then he would jump from the bench, snatch the wheel from me, and meet her himself, pouring out wrath upon me all the time.

George Ritchie was the other pilot's cub. He was having good times now; for his boss, George Ealer, was as kind-hearted as Brown wasn't. Ritchie had steered for Brown the season before; consequently, he knew exactly how to entertain himself and plague me, all by the one operation. Whenever I took the wheel for a moment on Ealer's watch, Ritchie would sit back on the bench and play Brown, with continual ejaculations of "Snatch her! Snatch her! Derndest mudcat I ever saw!" "Here! Where are you going *now*? Going to run over that snag?" ♦ "Pull her *down*! Don't you hear me? Pull her *down*!" "There she goes! *Just* as I expected! I *told* you not to cramp that reef. G'way from the wheel!"

So I always had a rough time of it, no matter whose watch it was; and sometimes it seemed to me that Ritchie's good-natured badgering was pretty nearly as aggravating as Brown's dead-earnest nagging.

I often wanted to kill Brown, but this would not answer. A cub had to take everything his boss gave, in the way of vigorous comment and criticism; and we all believed that there was a United States law making it a penitentiary offense to strike or threaten a pilot who was on duty.

However, I could *imagine* myself killing Brown; there was no law against that; and that was the thing I used always to do the

Literature in context — Science Connection

♦ *River Navigation*

Snags are submerged trees that may not be visible from the surface. In the 1820s, riverboat builder Henry Shreve invented a boat to pull up and remove snags. This boat rammed a heavy iron wedge into a snag. Then lifting machinery hoisted the large, sodden trunks. By 1830, the snag boats, called "Uncle Sam's Tooth Pullers," had cleared most of the snags. Sometimes, a pilot would still have to steer around one that the snag boats had missed.

This snag puller clears a tree from the river.

pretext (prē′ tekst) *n.* false reason or motive used to hide a real intention

Literary Analysis
Conflict and Historical Context In what ways does the historical context prevent the conflict from being settled?

✔**Reading Check**

How does Twain feel about Brown? Explain.

moment I was abed. Instead of going over my river in my mind, as was my duty, I threw business aside for pleasure, and killed Brown. I killed Brown every night for months; not in old, stale, commonplace ways, but in new and picturesque ones—ways that were sometimes surprising for freshness of design and ghastliness of situation and environment.

Brown was *always* watching for a pretext to find fault; and if he could find no plausible pretext, he would invent one. He would scold you for shaving a shore, and for not shaving it; for hugging a bar, and for not hugging it; for "pulling down" when not invited, and for *not* pulling down when not invited; for firing up without orders, and *for* waiting for orders. In a word, it was his invariable rule to find fault with *everything* you did and another invariable rule of his was to throw all his remarks (to you) into the form of an insult.

One day we were approaching New Madrid, bound down and heavily laden. Brown was at one side of the wheel, steering; I was at the other, standing by to "pull down" or "shove up." He cast a furtive glance at me every now and then. I had long ago learned what that meant; viz., he was trying to invent a trap for me. I wondered what shape it was going to take. By and by he stepped back from the wheel and said in his usual snarly way:

"Here! See if you've got gumption enough to round her to."

This was simply *bound* to be a success; nothing could prevent it; for he had never allowed me to round the boat to before; consequently, no matter how I might do the thing, he could find free fault with it. He stood back there with his greedy eye on me, and the result was what might have been foreseen: I lost my head in a quarter of a minute, and didn't know what I was about; I started too early to bring the boat around, but detected a green gleam of joy in Brown's eye, and corrected my mistake. I started around once more while too high up, but corrected myself again in time. I made other false moves, and still managed to save myself; but at last I grew so confused and anxious that I tumbled into the very worst blunder of all—I got too far *down* before beginning to fetch the boat around. Brown's chance was come.

His face turned red with passion; he made one bound, hurled me across the house with a sweep of his arm, spun the wheel down, and began to pour out a stream of vituperation[8] upon me which lasted till he was out of breath. In the course of this speech he called me all the different kinds of hard names he could think of, and once or twice I thought he was even going to swear—but he had never done that, and he didn't this time. "Dod dern" was the nearest he ventured to the luxury of swearing.

Two trips later I got into serious trouble. Brown was steering; I was "pulling down." My younger brother Henry appeared on the hur-

Reading Strategy
Identifying Idioms What is the figurative meaning of "I lost my head"?

---

8. vituperation (vī too̅′ pə rā′ shən) *n.* abusive language.

The Champions of the Mississippi, Currier & Ives

ricane deck, and shouted to Brown to stop at some landing or other, a mile or so below. Brown gave no <u>intimation</u> that he had heard anything. But that was his way: he never condescended to take notice of an underclerk. The wind was blowing; Brown was deaf (although he always pretended he wasn't), and I very much doubted if he had heard the order. If I had had two heads, I would have spoken; but as I had only one, it seemed <u>judicious</u> to take care of it; so I kept still.

Presently, sure enough, we went sailing by that plantation. Captain Klinefelter appeared on the deck, and said: "Let her come around, sir, let her come around. Didn't Henry tell you to land here?"

"*No*, sir!"

"I sent him up to do it."

"He *did* come up; and that's all the good it done, the dod-derned fool. He never said anything."

"Didn't *you* hear him?" asked the captain of me.

Of course I didn't want to be mixed up in this business, but there was no way to avoid it; so I said: "Yes, sir."

I knew what Brown's next remark would be, before he uttered it. It was: "Shut your mouth! You never heard anything of the kind."

I closed my mouth, according to instructions. An hour later Henry entered the pilothouse, unaware of what had been going on. He was a thoroughly inoffensive boy, and I was sorry to see him come, for I

intimation (in´ tə mā´ shən) *n.* hint or suggestion

judicious (joō dish´ əs) *adj.* showing sound judgment; wise and careful

Reading Check

Describe Brown's treatment of Twain and Henry.

Cub Pilot on the Mississippi ◆ 105

knew Brown would have no pity on him. Brown began, straightway: "Here! Why didn't you tell me we'd got to land at that plantation?"

"I did tell you, Mr. Brown."

"It's a lie!"

I said: "You lie, yourself. He did tell you."

Brown glared at me in unaffected surprise; and for as much as a moment he was entirely speechless; then he shouted to me: "I'll attend to your case in a half a minute!" then to Henry, "And you leave the pilothouse; out with you!"

It was pilot law, and must be obeyed. The boy started out, and even had his foot on the upper step outside the door, when Brown, with a sudden access of fury, picked up a ten-pound lump of coal and sprang after him; but I was between, with a heavy stool, and I hit Brown a good honest blow which stretched him out.

I had committed the crime of crimes—I had lifted my hand against a pilot on duty! I supposed I was booked for the penitentiary sure, and couldn't be booked any surer if I went on and squared my long account with this person while I had the chance; consequently I stuck to him and pounded him with my fists a considerable time. I do not know how long, the pleasure of it probably made it seem longer than it really was; but in the end he struggled free and jumped up and sprang to the wheel: a very natural solicitude, for, all this time, here was this steamboat tearing down the river at the rate of fifteen miles an hour and nobody at the helm! However, Eagle Bend was two miles wide at this bank-full stage, and correspondingly long and deep: and the boat was steering herself straight down the middle and taking no chances. Still, that was only luck—a body *might* have found her charging into the woods.

Perceiving at a glance that the *Pennsylvania* was in no danger, Brown gathered up the big spyglass, war-club fashion, and ordered me out of the pilothouse with more than ordinary bluster. But I was not afraid of him now; so, instead of going, I tarried, and criticized his grammar. I reformed his ferocious speeches for him, and put them into good English, calling his attention to the advantage of pure English over the dialect of the collieries[9] whence he was extracted. He could have done his part to admiration in a crossfire of mere vituperation, of course; but he was not equipped for this species of controversy; so he presently laid aside his glass and took the wheel, muttering and shaking his head; and I

9. **collieries** (kal´ yər ēz) *n.* coal mines.

▼ Critical Viewing
Put yourself in the place of this pilot. What challenges does the river pose? [Assess]

retired to the bench. The racket had brought everybody to the hurricane deck, and I trembled when I saw the old captain looking up from amid the crowd. I said to myself, "Now I *am* done for!" for although, as a rule, he was so fatherly and <u>indulgent</u> toward the boat's family, and so patient of minor shortcomings, he could be stern enough when the fault was worth it.

I tried to imagine what he *would* do to a cub pilot who had been guilty of such a crime as mine, committed on a boat guard-deep[10] with costly freight and alive with passengers. Our watch was nearly ended. I thought I would go and hide somewhere till I got a chance to slide ashore. So I slipped out of the pilothouse, and down the steps, and around to the texas-door, and was in the act of gliding within, when the captain confronted me! I dropped my head, and he stood over me in silence a moment or two, then said impressively: "Follow me."

I dropped into his wake; he led the way to his parlor in the forward end of the texas. We were alone now. He closed the afterdoor, then moved slowly to the forward one and closed that. He sat down; I stood before him. He looked at me some little time, then said: "So you have been fighting Mr. Brown?"

I answered meekly: "Yes, sir."

"Do you know that that is a very serious matter?"

"Yes, sir."

"Are you aware that this boat was plowing down the river fully five minutes with no one at the wheel?"

"Yes, sir."

"Did you strike him first?"

"Yes, sir."

"What with?"

"A stool, sir."

"Hard?"

"Middling, sir."

"Did it knock him down?"

"He—he fell, sir."

"Did you follow it up? Did you do anything further?"

"Yes, sir."

"What did you do?"

"Pounded him, sir."

"Pounded him?"

"Yes, sir."

"Did you pound him much? that is, severely?"

"One might call it that, sir, maybe."

"I'm deuced glad of it! Hark ye, never mention that I said that. You have been guilty of a great crime; and don't you ever be guilty of it again, on this boat. *But*—lay for him ashore! Give him a good sound

---

10. **guard-deep** here, a wooden frame protecting the paddle wheel.

indulgent (in dul′ jənt) *adj.* very mild and tolerant; not strict or critical

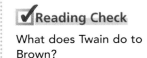

Reading Check

What does Twain do to Brown?

thrashing, do you hear? I'll pay the expenses. Now go—and mind you, not a word of this to anybody. Clear out with you! You've been guilty of a great crime, you whelp!"[11]

I slid out, happy with the sense of a close shave and a mighty deliverance; and I heard him laughing to himself and slapping his fat thighs after I had closed his door.

When Brown came off watch he went straight to the captain, who was talking with some passengers on the boiler deck, and demanded that I be put ashore in New Orleans—and added: "I'll never turn a wheel on this boat again while that cub stays."

The captain said: "But he needn't come round when you are on watch, Mr. Brown."

"I won't even stay on the same boat with him. One of us has got to go ashore." "Very well," said the captain, "let it be yourself," and resumed his talk with the passengers.

During the brief remainder of the trip I knew how an <u>emancipated</u> slave feels, for I was an emancipated slave myself. While we lay at landings I listened to George Ealer's flute, or to his readings from his two Bibles, that is to say, Goldsmith and Shakespeare, or I played chess with him—and would have beaten him sometimes, only he always took back his last move and ran the game out differently.

---

11. whelp (hwelp) *n.* here, a disrespectful young man.

emancipated
(iē man´ sə pā´ təd) *v.*
freed from the control
or power of another

Mark Twain

(1835–1910)

Growing up in Hannibal, Missouri, Mark Twain was enchanted by the nearby Mississippi River. Born Samuel Langhorne Clemens, Twain took his pen name from a riverman's call, "By the mark—twain," which means "the river is two fathoms (twelve feet) deep."

Although Twain traveled all over the United States and worked as a printer, a prospector, a reporter, and an editor, his boyhood experiences on the Mississippi were the strongest influences on his most memorable writing. *The Adventures of Tom Sawyer* is a coming-of-age story about a boy in a small Missouri town. In *The Adventures of Huckleberry Finn,* Twain tells about a boy and a runaway slave who travel on the river together.

Review and Assess

Thinking About the Selection

1. **Respond:** Would you want to be an apprentice pilot? Why or why not?

2. **(a) Recall:** For about how long did Twain serve as a pilot's apprentice? **(b) Infer:** Why are cub pilots assigned to work with experienced pilots? **(c) Interpret:** Why is Brown's treatment of Twain unfair?

3. **(a) Recall:** How does George Ritchie tease Twain? **(b) Deduce:** How do you know that Brown treated other cub pilots the same way he treated Twain? **(c) Analyze Cause-and-Effect:** Is Brown's treatment of Twain the result of a personal dislike or an overall attitude? Explain.

4. **(a) Recall:** How does the captain react to Twain's beating of Brown? **(b) Draw Conclusions:** What are the captain's feelings about Brown? How do you know?

5. **(a) Take a stand:** Do you think Twain should have hit Brown? Explain. **(b) Apply:** Under what circumstances, if any, should physical force be used to solve a problem?

Review and Assess

Literary Analysis
Conflict Between Characters
1. List three occasions in the narrative in which Twain and Brown are involved in a conflict.
2. What are the two sides of the conflict between Twain and Pilot Brown? Fill out a graphic organizer like this one to show details that contribute to the conflict.

Twain is inexperienced. ....▶

................................▶

................................▶

Twain vs. Brown

◀........ Brown is demanding.

◀................................

◀................................

3. How is the conflict between Twain and Mr. Brown finally worked out?

Connecting Literary Elements
4. Explain how Twain's reactions are influenced by the laws, customs, and expectations of his time.
5. What unexpected action does Twain do, given the historical context?

Reading Strategy
Identifying Idioms
6. Complete a chart like the one below to show the difference between the literal and figurative meanings of idioms.

Idiom	Literal Meaning	Figurative Meaning
He would scold you for *shaving a shore* . . .	cutting hair close to the face with a razor	steering very close to a shore
I ascended to the pilot-house *in fine feather* . . .		
I *lost my head* in a quarter of a minute . . .		

Extend Understanding
7. **Social Studies Connection:** What other forms of transportation would people have used when Twain was a cub pilot? (Use Twain's birth year to figure out the year Twain's story takes place.)
8. **Extend:** Do you think "apprenticeship" is an effective way to learn a job? Why or why not?

Quick Review

Conflict between characters is the struggle between two or more characters with opposing needs or wants. To review conflict between characters, see page 99.

The **historical context** is the customs, laws, and expectations of the time period. To review historical context, see page 99.

An **idiom** is an expression that has a certain meaning understood in a particular language or region. To review idioms, see page 99.

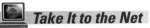 **Take It to the Net**
www.phschool.com
Take the interactive self-test online to check your understanding of the selection.

Integrate Language Skills

Vocabulary Development Lesson

Word Analysis: Forms of *judge*

The verb *judge* means "to decide [in a court of law]." On your paper, complete each sentence using *judicious* or *judgment*.

1. I do not make a ___?___ about his behavior.
2. My gym teacher is a ___?___ referee.

Spelling Strategy

• When a word ends with *e* and the suffix begins with a consonant, do not drop the *e* spelling: *severe + ly = severely.*
• When a word ends with *e* and the suffix begins with a vowel, drop the *e: close + ing =closing.*
Add the suffixes to these words.

1. offensive + ly
2. emancipate + ed
3. time + ly
4. false + hood

Fluency: Matching Words and Definitions

On your paper, match each vocabulary word with the word or phrase closest in meaning.

1. furtive
2. indulgent
3. pretext
4. judicious
5. intimation
6. emancipated

a. wise and careful
b. false motive used to hide a real intention
c. freed from the control of another
d. done in secret, hidden from view
e. mild and tolerant
f. hint or suggestion

Grammar Lesson

Verbs and Verb Phrases

A **verb** is a word that expresses an action or the fact that something exists.

I *closed* my mouth, according to instructions.
My profit *is* various in kind and degree.

A **verb phrase** consists of a main verb and its helping verbs. In the following sentence, *closed* is the main verb; *had* is the helping verb.

I *had closed* my mouth.

Common Helping Verbs:
be, been, am, are, is, was, were; do, does, did; have, has, had; can, could, will, would, may, might, shall, should, must

▶ *For more practice, see page R28, Exercise B.*
Practice Copy the following passages from the story. Underline the verb phrase once and the main verb twice. Then, circle each helping verb.

1. Then he would jump from the bench . . .
2. The racket had brought everybody to the hurricane deck . . .
3. He would scold you for shaving a shore . . .
4. I had long ago learned what that meant . . .
5. I could feel those yellow eyes upon me . . .

Writing Application Write a paragraph about what it might have been like to be a riverboat pilot. Use the verbs *concentrate* and *steer* along with the helping verbs *would* and *have.*

 Prentice Hall Writing and Grammar Connection: Chapter 15, Section 3

Writing Lesson

Autobiographical Anecdote

"Cub Pilot on the Mississippi" is an example of autobiographical writing. Choose a memorable experience you have had, and write an **autobiographical anecdote**—a brief, true narrative of something that has happened to you.

Prewriting Choose an experience that has a conflict that changed the way you look at things or taught you a lesson. Conflicts can be related to decisions, misunderstandings, or personality differences.

Drafting Begin your story by setting up the conflict. Identify the situation. Then, tell the events that lead up to the conflict being settled. Include your observations and comments on events. Tell why the experience is important to you.

Model: Show the Significance

Topic: My First Dive

Conflict: Fear of diving vs. wanting to be a big kid

Events: *Got laughed at, asked brother for help, finally did it*

What I learned: It's better to try something new than to always be afraid.

> The words in italics show the events leading up to the resolution of the conflict.

Revising Revise your draft by adding details and comments that make clear the importance of characters and events. Proofread for spelling and punctuation.

 Prentice Hall Writing and Grammar Connection: Chapter 4, Section 3

Extension Activities

Listening and Speaking With a group, produce an **interview show** with Twain and Pilot Brown as the guests. Have several classmates watch the show.

1. Assign roles for Twain, Brown, the interviewer, Henry, and the captain.
2. Have the interviewer ask each "guest" about the fighting incident.
3. Each guest should tell the story from his or her point of view.
4. After the show, evaluate the credibility of each guest. Discuss reasons why each guest's account may or may not be accurate.

Research and Technology Create a **transportation brochure** on Mississippi River steamboat travel in the 1800s. Use keywords such as *steamboat, Mississippi,* and *river travel* to find information on the Internet. Provide details of the accommodations on board and information about the towns and cities along the route. Post your brochure on a class bulletin board.

 **Take It to the Net**   www.phschool.com

Go online for an additional research activity using the Internet.

Contracts

About Contracts

A **contract** is an agreement between two or more people, organizations, or companies. Most contracts are written documents that are legally binding: Once the contract is signed, the signers are required by law to stick to the agreement.

Contracts are used in a variety of business situations. The details of a contract are very specific so that no possibility is left in question. For some complicated contracts, such as contracts for the sale of property or the joining of two businesses, lawyers are hired to give advice to the signers. Other contracts, such as a contract for a specific home repair or an employment contract, are straightforward enough for the average person to understand. It is important to read all contracts carefully and question any detail with which you do not agree or that you do not understand. Signing a contract is like saying "I understand everything that is written here and will do exactly what it says."

Reading Strategies

Use Information to Make a Decision

Before a contract is signed, it is not a binding agreement. You can choose to sign or not sign. Read contracts carefully and use the information in the contract to make a decision.

- **Check dates:** Do you agree to the dates and times that are stated in the contract?

- **Check amounts:** Are the amounts of money stated in the contract what you are willing to pay or accept as payment? Are any sizes, weights, and numbers what you are willing to give or take?

- **Check the fine print:** Are there any special events, conditions, or situations in the contract? Are you willing to do what the contract says if one of those events or situations occurs?

In order to understand the information in a contract, you need to know some legal terms that are commonly used in contracts. Preview the list at right.

Words in Contracts	
execute	make complete, final, and legal
hereinafter	after this moment
party/parties	person or people referred to in the contract
terminate	put an end to
appendix	additional material, usually attached to the end
limited	restricted, going no further than, confined

Omicron Corporation, Inc.
Employment Contract

1   THIS CONTRACT executed as of this 5th day of May,
2   2003 by the Omicron Corporation, Inc. (hereinafter called
3   Omicron), a New Jersey corporation, with its principal place
4   of business in Newark, New Jersey, and Leslie Johnson
5   (hereinafter called the Candidate), a citizen of the United States
6   of America.
7   The parties hereto mutually agree as follows:
8   1. Omicron has need for the Candidate's services and the
9   Candidate wishes to work for Omicron.
10   2. The Candidate shall report to 100 Front Steet, Newark, New
11 Jersey, not later than July 7, 2003 at 8:30 am for processing, which
12 shall consist of photographing, fingerprinting, and signing Omicron
13 standard secrecy and patent agreements.
14   3. The Candidate shall prepare and sign all documents necessary
15 to apply for clearance of the Candidate to have access to classified
16 material in accordance with the Department of Defense regulations.
17 In the event such clearance is denied, this agreement of employ-
18 ment shall be immediately terminated.
19   4. The Candidate's base monthly salary is to be Dollars ($4,833)
20 based upon a normal work week schedule of five days per week,
21 eight hours per day.
22   5. Upon execution of this contract by both parties, Omicron
23 shall pay to the Candidate the reasonable costs of transporting the
24 Candidate (and dependent(s), if applicable), from origin to
25 destination, paying per diem to Candidate and dependents while in
26 travel status, and paying per diem for a period not to exceed seven
27 days from date of Candidate's arrival at destination, or until settled,
28 whichever is less. Omicron shall arrange for shipment and pay for
29 actual cost of moving the Candidate's household goods and personal
30 property, storing them for a period not to exceed sixty (60) days and
31 then moving them to his permanent quarters. Payments will be
32 made based upon the conditions and limitations noted above and as
33 set forth in Appendix A attached hereto and by this reference made
34 a part hereof. This sum or sums will be reported to the appropriate
35 federal, state, and local taxing authorities, and taxes will be withheld
36 on that portion which Omicron is required to withhold.

Lines are numbered so signers can easily refer to specific details.

The conditions under which the company can end the agreement are specified in lines 17-18 and 41-51.

This section tells what Omicron will pay for.

37   6. In consideration of the sums to be paid to the Candidate
38 pursuant to paragraph 5 hereof, the Candidate shall work for
39 Omicron for a period of not less than twelve (12) months from the date
40 upon which he reports for work.
41   7. (a) In the event Omicron should terminate this contract prior to
42 the Candidate's completion of twelve (12) months employment
43 with Omicron, on account of either (1) the Candidate's failure to
44 report by the date specified in paragraph 2 hereof or (2) the
45 discharge of the Candidate for cause, then in either such event, the
46 Candidate shall forthwith refund to Omicron the full amount of
47 the sums paid to paragraph 5 hereof, provided, however, that if the
48 Candidate is discharged for cause said refund shall be applicable
49 only if the cause is one of the following: sabotage, espionage,
50 subversive activity, commission of a crime or violation of the
51 secrecy agreement referred to in paragraph 2 hereof.
52 (b) In the event Omicron should terminate this contract for any
53 other reason including, without limitation, (1) denial of clearance
54 specified in paragraph 3 hereof or (2) lack of work suitable for the
55 Candidate, then in either such event, the Candidate shall retain all
56 sums paid to him pursuant to paragraph 5 hereof.
57 (c) In the event the Candidate voluntarily terminates his employment
58 with Omicron prior to the expiration of twelve (12) months employ-
59 ment, the Candidate shall forthwith refund to Omicron the full amount
60 of the sums advanced to him pursuant to paragraph 5 hereof.
61 In the event the contract is not signed by the Candidate and
62 returned to Omicron within thirty (30) days from the date first
63 above written, this contract shall be null and void. IN WITNESS
64 WHEREOF, the parties hereto have executed this contract as of the day
65 and year first above written.
66
67 OMICRON CORPORATION, INC.
68
69 By_____   By_____
70   OC   the Candidate
71
72 _____   _____
73   Date   Date

> These lines outline the various situations in which the contract might be terminated.

> This tells how long the candidate has to decide whether or not to sign the contract.

Check Your Comprehension

1. Who is "the Candidate"?
2. If you sign this contract, on what day do you have to report for work?
3. How many hours will you work each week?
4. What is one reason the company can legally end your employment?

Applying the Reading Strategy

Use Information to Make a Decision

Use the information in the contract to make a decision about each situation. Explain the reasons for your answer using details from the contract.

5. Tyrell is twenty-two years old and has just graduated from college. His family lives in Michigan. Should he take this job? Explain.
6. Mary has always lived in California and has two children in middle school. Her husband is a freelance writer. Their combined incomes equal $55,000 per year. Should Mary take this job? Explain.
7. Cleo is single and lives in Maryland. Most of her family live in New Jersey. She works approximately fifty hours each week at a job she loves that pays $60,000 per year. Should she take this job? Explain.

Activity

Be a Cautious Consumer

Prepare a chart like the one shown here. Identify one question you would expect the contract to answer before you would sign it. Questions for the other two contracts will differ. If possible, get samples of the type of contracts shown on the chart. Look for the answers to your questions.

	Contract between you and a plumber who will fix your kitchen sink	Contract between you and a CD of the month club	Contract between you and a cell phone service provider
Dates	On what day will the repair be done?		
Amounts	How much will it cost?		
Other	Does the cost include parts?		

Comparing Informational Materials

Contracts and Warranties

A warranty is similar to a contract because it outlines an agreement between two parties (people, businesses, or groups). In a brief essay, compare and contrast the amount of detail and types of information found in this contract and the warranty on page 860.

Prepare to Read

The Secret

Preview

Connecting to the Literature

In "The Secret," a reporter struggles over whether or not to publish a fascinating, but upsetting, discovery. Connect to the story by thinking about what you would do in a similar situation.

Background

"The Secret," by Arthur C. Clarke, takes place in a colony on the moon. For years, astronauts have conducted experiments to learn about what it would be like to live in space. For example, they evaluate how the human body adapts to extreme changes in atmosphere and gravity. Information collected in space is then analyzed on Earth. The results help scientists develop new strategies for survival in space.

Literary Analysis

Science Fiction

Science fiction combines elements of fiction and fantasy with scientific fact. Science fiction writers balance realistic details with fantasy details. In the following example, fantasy details are italicized.

> So here he was, doing the *lunar circuit* . . . and *beaming* back two thousand words of copy a day.

In the example, the reporter's "two thousand words a day" is a detail that gives a sense of realism in a world where a reporter does a "lunar circuit" and "beams" assignments in to the office.

Connecting Literary Elements

The **setting** of a story is the time and place of the action. In science fiction, the setting is often the future and a place other than Earth such as another planet or an imaginary universe. This story takes place on the moon, a good indication that it happens in the future. Use these focus questions to guide you as you read.

1. How does the setting affect the meaning of the story?
2. What details of the setting are only possible at a time in the future?

Reading Strategy

Using Word Origins

You will encounter many words related to science in a science fiction story. Many science words come from Latin and Greek. Use the origins of words to help you see the relationships between words and remember their meanings. Look at the chart on this page for examples of the origins of some groups of words. Copy the chart. As you read, notice the word or words in the story that fit into each of these groups. Add any appropriate words to the first column.

Science words	Origin
microscope, microchip, microbiology	*micro-* from Greek *mikro* meaning "small"
transparent, translucent, transform	from Latin *trans* meaning "over, across, beyond, or through"
technical, technician, technique	*tech-*, from Greek *tekton* meaning "to build"

Vocabulary Development

receding (ri sēd´ iŋ) *n.* moving back; fading (p. 119)

competent (käm´ pə tənt) *adj.* well qualified and capable (p. 120)

microbes (mī´ krōbes´) *n.* extremely small organisms (p. 121)

hemisphere (hem´ i sfir´) *n.* half of a sphere; dome (p. 121)

radial (rā´ dē əl) *adj.* branching out in all directions from a common center (p. 121)

heedless (hēd´ lis) *adj.* unmindfully careless (p. 123)

implications (im´ pli kā´ shəns) *n.* possible conclusions (p. 123)

looming (lo͞om´ iŋ) *adj.* ominous and awe-inspiring (p. 124)

The Secret

Arthur C. Clarke

Henry Cooper had been on the Moon for almost two weeks before he discovered that something was wrong. At first it was only an ill-defined suspicion, the sort of hunch that a hard-headed science reporter would not take too seriously. He had come here, after all, at the United Nations Space Administration's own request. UNSA had always been hot on public relations—especially just before budget time, when an overcrowded world was screaming for more roads and schools and sea farms, and complaining about the billions being poured into space.

So here he was, doing the lunar circuit for the second time, and beaming back two thousand words of copy a day. Although the novelty had worn off, there still remained the wonder and mystery of a world as

Literary Analysis
Science Fiction What elements in this paragraph seem scientifically possible? Which ones seem impossible?

big as Africa, thoroughly mapped, yet almost completely unexplored. A stone's throw away from the pressure domes, the labs, the spaceports, was a yawning emptiness that would challenge humankind for centuries to come.

Some parts of the Moon were almost too familiar, of course. Who had not seen that dusty scar on the Mare Imbrium, with its gleaming metal pylon and the plaque that announced in the three official languages of Earth:

> ON THIS SPOT
> AT 2001 UT
> 13 SEPTEMBER 1959
> THE FIRST MAN-MADE OBJECT
> REACHED ANOTHER WORLD

Cooper had visited the grave of Lunik II—and the more famous tomb of the men who had come after it. But these things belonged to the past; already, like Columbus and the Wright brothers,[1] they were <u>receding</u> into history. What concerned him now was the future.

receding (ri sēd′ iŋ) v. moving back, fading

When he had landed at Archimedes Spaceport, the Chief Administrator had been obviously glad to see him, and had shown a personal interest in his tour. Transportation, accommodation, and official guide were all arranged. He could go anywhere he liked, ask any questions he pleased. UNSA trusted him, for his stories had always been accurate, his attitudes friendly. Yet the tour had gone sour; he did not know why, but he was going to find out.

He reached for the phone and said: "Operator? . . . Please get me the Police Department. I want to speak to the Inspector General."

Presumably Chandra Coomaraswamy possessed a uniform, but Cooper had never seen him wearing it. They met, as arranged, at the entrance to the little park that was Plato City's chief pride and joy. At this time in the morning of the artificial twenty-four-hour "day" it was almost deserted, and they could talk without interruption.

As they walked along the narrow gravel paths, they chatted about old times, the friends they had known at college together, the latest developments in interplanetary politics. They had reached the middle of the park, under the exact center of the great blue-painted dome, when Cooper came to the point.

Literary Analysis
Science Fiction and Setting In this paragraph, which details of the setting indicate that the story is science fiction? Which do not?

"You know everything that's happening on the Moon, Chandra," he said. "And you know that I'm here to do a series for UNSA—hope to make a book out of it when I get back to Earth. So why should people be trying to hide things from me?"

It was impossible to hurry Chandra. He always took his time to

Reading Check

Who is Henry Cooper?

---

1. **Columbus . . . Wright brothers** Christopher Columbus (15th-century Italian navigator) and Orville and Wilbur Wright (20th-century American inventors of the airplane) were great explorers.

answer questions, and his few words escaped with difficulty around the stem of his hand-carved Bavarian[2] pipe.

"What people?" he asked at length.

"You've really no idea?"

The Inspector General shook his head.

"Not the faintest," he answered; and Cooper knew that he was telling the truth. Chandra might be silent, but he would not lie.

"I was afraid you'd say that. Well, if you don't know any more than I do, here's the only clue I have—and it frightens me. Medical Research is trying to keep me at arm's length."

"Hmmm," replied Chandra, taking his pipe from his mouth and looking at it thoughtfully.

"Is that all you have to say?"

"You haven't given me much to work on. Remember, I'm only a cop; I lack your vivid journalistic imagination."

"All I can tell you is that the higher I get in Medical Research, the colder the atmosphere becomes. Last time I was here, everyone was very friendly, and gave me some fine stories. But now, I can't even meet the Director. He's always too busy, or on the other side of the Moon. Anyway, what sort of man is he?"

"Dr. Hastings? Prickly little character. Very <u>competent</u>, but not easy to work with."

"What could he be trying to hide?"

"Knowing you, I'm sure you have some interesting theories."

"Oh, I thought of narcotics, and fraud, and political conspiracies—but they don't make sense, in these days. So what's left scares the heck out of me."

Chandra's eyebrows signaled a silent question mark.

"Interplanetary plague," said Cooper bluntly.

---

2. **Bavarian** (bə ver′ ē ən) *adj.* of or related to Bavaria, a region in Germany.

Reading Strategy
Using Word Origins Find the root of *journalistic*. Explain how the affixes change the meaning of the word.

competent (käm′ pə tənt) *adj.* well qualified and capable

"I thought that was impossible."

"Yes—I've written articles myself proving that the life forms of other planets have such alien chemistries that they can't react with us, and that all our <u>microbes</u> and bugs took millions of years to adapt to our bodies. But I've always wondered if it was true. Suppose a ship has come back from Mars, say, with something *really* vicious—and the doctors can't cope with it?"

There was a long silence. Then Chandra said: "I'll start investigating. *I* don't like it, either, for here's an item you probably don't know. There were three nervous breakdowns in the Medical Division last month—and that's very, very unusual."

He glanced at his watch, then at the false sky, which seemed so distant, yet was only two hundred feet above their heads.

"We'd better get moving," he said. "The morning shower's due in five minutes."

The call came two weeks later in the middle of the night—the real lunar night. By Plato City time, it was Sunday morning.

"Henry? . . . Chandra here. Can you meet me in half an hour at air lock five? . . . Good. I'll see you."

This was it, Cooper knew. Air lock five meant they were going outside the dome. Chandra had found something.

The presence of the police driver restricted conversation as the tractor moved away from the city along the road roughly bulldozed across the ash and pumice. Low in the south, Earth was almost full, casting a brilliant blue-green light over the infernal landscape. However hard one tried, Cooper told himself, it was difficult to make the Moon appear glamorous. But nature guards her greatest secrets well; to such places men must come to find them.

The multiple domes of the city dropped below the sharply curved horizon. Presently, the tractor turned aside from the main road to follow a scarcely visible trail. Ten minutes later, Cooper saw a single glittering <u>hemisphere</u> ahead of them, standing on an isolated ridge of rock. Another vehicle, bearing a red cross, was parked beside the entrance. It seemed that they were not the only visitors.

Nor were they unexpected. As they drew up to the dome, the flexible tube of the air-lock coupling groped out toward them and snapped into place against their tractor's outer hull. There was a brief hissing as pressures equalized. Then Cooper followed Chandra into the building.

The air-lock operator led them along curving corridors and <u>radial</u> passageways toward the center of the dome. Sometimes they caught glimpses of laboratories, scientific instruments, computers—all perfectly ordinary, and all deserted on this Sunday morning. They must have reached the heart of the building, Cooper told himself, when their guide ushered them into a large circular chamber and shut the door softly behind them.

It was a small zoo. All around them were cages, tanks, jars

microbes (mī′ krōbes′) *n.* extremely small organisms

Literary Analysis
Science Fiction and Setting What details of the setting combine the possible and the less possible?

hemisphere (hem′ i sfir′) n. half of a sphere; dome

radial (rā′ dē əl) *adj.* branching out in all directions from a common center

✔ **Reading Check**

What does Cooper ask Chandra to investigate?

▲ Critical Viewing
How does this picture
illustrate Hastings's
explanation? [Connect]

containing a wide selection of the fauna and flora of Earth. Waiting
at its center was a short, gray-haired man, looking very worried,
and very unhappy.

"Dr. Hastings," said Coomaraswamy, "meet Mr. Cooper." The
Inspector General turned to his companion and added, "I've convinced the Doctor that there's only one way to keep you quiet—
and that's to tell you everything."

"Frankly," said Hastings, "I'm not sure if I care anymore." His
voice was unsteady, barely under control, and Cooper thought,
Hello! There's another breakdown on the way.

The scientist wasted no time on such formalities as shaking
hands. He walked to one of the cages, took out a small bundle of
fur, and held it toward Cooper.

"Do you know what this is?" he asked abruptly.

"Of course. A hamster—the commonest lab animal."

"Yes," said Hastings. "A perfectly ordinary golden hamster. Except
that this one is five years old—like all the others in this cage."

"Well? What's odd about that?"

"Oh, nothing, nothing at all . . . except for the fact that hamsters

live for only two years. And we have some here that are getting on for ten."

For a moment no one spoke; but the room was not silent. It was full of rustlings and slitherings and scratchings, of faint whimpers and tiny animal cries. Then Cooper whispered, "My God—you've found a way of prolonging life!"

"No," retorted Hastings. "We've not found it. The Moon has given it to us . . . as we might have expected, if we'd looked in front of our noses." He seemed to have gained control over his emotions—as if he was once more the pure scientist, fascinated by a discovery for its own sake and <u>heedless</u> of its <u>implications</u>.

"On Earth," he said, "we spend our whole lives fighting gravity. It wears down our muscles, pulls our stomachs out of shape. In seventy years, how many tons of blood does the heart lift through how many miles? And all that work, all that strain is reduced to a sixth here on the Moon, where a one-hundred-and-eighty-pound human weighs only thirty pounds?"

"I see," said Cooper slowly. "Ten years for a hamster—and how long for a man?"

heedless (hēd′ lis) *adj.* unmindfully careless

implications (im′ pli kā′ shəns) *n.* possible conclusions

Reading Check

What have the doctors in the Medical Division discovered?

The Secret ◆ 123

"It's not a simple law," answered Hastings. "It varies with the sex and the species. Even a month ago, we weren't certain. But now we're quite sure of this: on the Moon, the span of human life will be at least two hundred years."

"And you've been trying to keep this a secret!"

"You fool! Don't you understand?"

"Take it easy, Doctor—take it easy," said Chandra softly.

With an obvious effort of will, Hastings got control of himself again. He began to speak with such icy calm that his words sank like freezing raindrops into Cooper's mind.

"Think of them up there," he said, pointing to the roof, to the invisible Earth, whose <u>looming</u> presence no one on the Moon could forget. "Six billion of them, packing all the continents to the edges— and now crowding over into the sea beds. And here—" he pointed to the ground—"only a hundred thousand of *us*, on an almost empty world. But a world where we need miracles of technology and engineering merely to exist, where a man with an IQ of only a hundred and fifty can't even get a job.

"And now we find that we can live for two hundred years. Imagine how they're going to react to that news! This is your problem now, Mister Journalist; you've asked for it, and you've got it. Tell me this, please—I'd really be interested to know—*just how are you going to break it to them?*"

He waited, and waited. Cooper opened his mouth, then closed it again, unable to think of anything to say.

In the far corner of the room, a baby monkey started to cry.

looming (lo͞om′ iŋ) *adj.* ominous and awe-inspiring

Arthur C. Clarke

(b. 1917)

As a youth, Arthur C. Clarke built his own telescope and used it to create a map of the moon. This English writer has always been ahead of his time. In 1945, when he was a radar technician for the Royal Air Force, Clarke outlined ideas for a world-wide satellite system. Today, we rely on satellites to transmit radio, television, and telephone communica-tions. One common satel-lite orbit is named in Clarke's honor.

The author of more than eighty books, Clarke has presented many versions of what our future might hold. One of his works inspired the movie *2001: A Space Odyssey*.

Review and Assess

Thinking About the Selection

1. **Respond:** Do you think Cooper should write about the secret or hide this information from people on Earth? Why or why not?

2. **(a) Recall:** What is Cooper's profession? **(b) Connect:** How is this information important to the action of the story?

3. **(a) Recall:** What is the secret? **(b) Analyze Causes and Effects:** What is the scientific reason for this phenomenon? **(c) Predict:** What would be the effect of sharing the information with the people on Earth?

4. **(a) Recall:** What is Cooper's first reaction upon learning the secret? **(b) Interpret:** How does Dr. Hastings' interpretation cause Cooper to change his mind?

5. **(a) Generalize:** Do you think this story supports or discourages the idea of human colonies in space? **(b) Support:** Give examples from the story to support your answer.

Review and Assess

Literary Analysis

Science Fiction

1. On a chart like the one shown, list three elements in "The Secret" that are based on scientific fact and three that are not.

Elements based on scientific fact	Elements not based on scientific fact

2. How does Clarke contrast life on the moon with life on Earth?

Connecting Literary Elements

3. How does the **setting** affect the meaning of the story?
4. What details of the setting are only possible at a time in the future?
5. Identify details from the story that describe the setting. Record them on a chart like the one shown here.

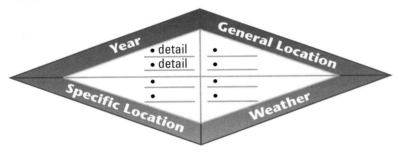

Reading Strategy

Using Word Origins

6. What is the common part of the words *atmosphere* and *hemisphere*? In a dictionary, find the origin of the shared word part.
7. Find the origin of the word *gravity*. From what language does it come? What is the meaning of the word from which it comes?

Extend Understanding

8. **Science Connection:** Why do you think many words used in science and math come from Latin and Greek?
9. **Take a Position:** Are there circumstances in which the media should not report the truth? Explain.

Quick Review

Science fiction combines elements of fiction and fantasy with scientific fact. To review science fiction, see page 117.

The **setting** of a story is the time and place of the action. To review setting, see page 117.

Word origins are the languages and parts from which words come.

 Take It to the Net

www.phschool.com
Take the interactive self-test online to check your understanding of the selection.

Integrate Language Skills

Vocabulary Development Lesson

Word Analysis: Greek Word Part *micro*

The Greek word part *micro* means "small." The word *microbe* means "small form of life" or "tiny organism." It combines *micro* and the word part *bio*, meaning "life."

Determine the meanings of the following words by analyzing the word parts.

1. microscopic **2.** microwave **3.** microfilm

Spelling Strategy

When adding *-ing* to words that end with *-cede*, drop the *e* and then add the ending.

recede + *-ing* = receding

On your paper, add *-ing* to the following words.

1. precede   **2.** accede   **3.** concede

Concept Development: Synonyms

Write the word or phrase that is a **synonym**—a word with a similar meaning—for the vocabulary word.

1. competent: **(a)** simple, **(b)** good, **(c)** able
2. receding: **(a)** vanishing, **(b)** surging, **(c)** preceding
3. heedless: **(a)** unmindful, **(b)** cautious, **(c)** sly
4. implications: **(a)** possible effects, **(b)** facts, **(c)** styles
5. hemisphere: **(a)** pyramid, **(b)** cube, **(c)** dome
6. radial: **(a)** from outside, **(b)** from outer space, **(c)** from a central point
7. microbes: **(a)** scientists, **(b)** tiny forms of life, **(c)** substances
8. looming: **(a)** inspiring, **(b)** failing, **(c)** appearing

Grammar Lesson

Action Verbs and Linking Verbs

An **action verb** expresses action.

> **Example:** Cooper *followed* Chandra.

A **linking verb** expresses a state of being. It connects the subject to a noun, pronoun, or adjective that identifies or describes it later in the sentence. Linking verbs include forms of the verb *to be* as well as *seem, appear, look, feel, become, sound, stay, remain,* and *grow.*

> **Example:** That *sounds* impossible.
> That *is* impossible.

To determine whether a verb is an action or a linking verb, replace it with a form of *to be.* If the sentence still makes sense, it is a linking verb.

▶ *For more practice, see page R28, Exercise B.*
Practice On your paper, copy the following sentences. Underline each verb. Above each verb, write *AV* if it is an action verb and *LV* if it is a linking verb.

1. The space colony orbits Mars.
2. Last year was the settlement's first anniversary.
3. Radiation shields protect the inhabitants.
4. Life became routine for the colonists.
5. They remain optimistic about their future.

Writing Application Write a paragraph describing Cooper's search for the truth. Use action verbs and linking verbs to express the characters' actions and state of being.

𝒲𝒢 *Prentice Hall Writing and Grammar Connection: Chapter 15, Section 2*

Writing Lesson

Story Continuation

What might happen after "the secret" is revealed? What if the secret is never revealed? Write a continuation of the story based on one of these two possibilities.

Prewriting Use a timeline to help you plan the sequence of events.

Drafting Use your timeline to describe what happens as the story continues. Refer to "The Secret" to help you with characters and details. To make the sequence of events clear, use transitions.

Model: Support Ideas

Presently, the tractor turned aside from the main road to follow a scarcely visible trail. *Ten minutes later,* Cooper saw a single glittering hemisphere ahead of them. . . .

> The words in italics are transitional words or phrases that help put the sequence of events in order.

Revising Underline transitional words and phrases you have used. Add transitions where meaning is unclear. Place a check mark where science fiction details will make the setting more vivid.

𝒲𝒢 *Prentice Hall Writing and Grammar Connection: Chapter 4, Section 3*

Extension Activities

Listening and Speaking Give a two-minute speech on whether or not "The Secret" would make a good television movie.

1. Begin by stating your position.
2. Use action verbs as you give reasons for your opinion. Action verbs will make your speaking more powerful and convincing.
   Strong: The secret shocks the reporter.
   Weak: The secret is shocking to the reporter.
3. Adapt your speaking voice and facial expression to the meaning of the action verbs you use.

Research and Technology Work with a partner to research other science fiction works that are set in space in the future. Do a subject search through a library online catalog. Use *science fiction* as your keyword. Review the results of your search and make a **list of ten recommendations** based on the information provided in the catalog. Display your lists with illustrations.

 **Take It to the Net** www.phschool.com

Go online for an additional research activity using the Internet.

Prepare to Read

Harriet Tubman: Guide to Freedom

Harriet Tubman Series, #16, Jacob Lawrence, Hampton University Museum

 Take It to the Net

Visit www.phschool.com for interactive activities and instruction related to "Harriet Tubman: Guide to Freedom," including
- background
- graphic organizers
- literary elements
- reading strategies

Preview

Connecting to the Literature

"Harriet Tubman: Guide to Freedom" tells the true story of a woman who risked her life for a cause she believed in. Connect to the story by thinking of issues about which you feel strongly and what you would be willing to risk for these causes.

Background

Harriet Tubman was born into slavery but escaped to freedom. She became one of the leading forces behind the Underground Railroad, a network of people who helped African American slaves escape from the South in the mid-1800s. Tubman made nineteen trips on this "railroad," bringing 300 people north to freedom.

Literary Analysis

Third-Person Narrative

All narratives (stories) have narrators who describe the action. In a **third-person narrative,** the narrator tells the story from outside the action. As you read, focus on these questions:

1. How do you know that the narrator does not take part in the events being narrated?
2. How would the story be different if it were told by one of the escaping African Americans in Harriet's group?

Connecting Literary Elements

The perspective of the narrator affects the amount, type, and treatment of information readers learn.

- A **third-person limited narrator** tells readers only what one character knows, thinks, and feels.
- A **third-person omniscient narrator** tells readers what several or all characters know as well as some information that the characters themselves do not know.

"Harriet Tubman: Guide to Freedom" is told by a third-person omniscient narrator. The narrator knows and tells more than any single character in the narrative knows.

Reading Strategy

Setting a Purpose for Reading

Just as you have reasons for seeing a movie—for example, to be entertained or to be scared—you should have a reason, or **purpose,** for reading. Your purpose in reading this narrative might be to learn about Harriet Tubman. Ask yourself *who, what, when, where, why,* and *how* questions like those in the chart. On your own chart, answer the questions as you read.

Questions	Harriet Tubman
Who was . . .?	
What did she do?	
When did she live?	
Where did she work and live?	
Why is she important?	
How did she help slaves escape?	

Vocabulary Development

fugitives (fyoo´ ji tivs´) *n.* people fleeing (p. 131)

incentive (in sent´ iv) *n.* something that stimulates one to action; encouragement (p. 132)

disheveled (di shev´ əld) *adj.* untidy; messy (p. 132)

guttural (gut´ ər əl) *adj.* made in back of the throat (p. 134)

mutinous (myoot´ ən əs) *adj.* rebellious (p. 134)

cajoling (kə jōl´ iŋ) *v.* coaxing or persuading gently (p. 136)

indomitable (in däm´ it ə bəl) *adj.* not easily discouraged (p. 136)

fastidious (fas tid´ ē əs) *adj.* refined in an oversensitive way, so as to be easily disgusted or displeased (p. 137)

Harriet Tubman

Guide to Freedom

ANN PETRY

Along the Eastern Shore of Maryland, in Dorchester County, in Caroline County, the masters kept hearing whispers about the man named Moses, who was running off slaves. At first they did not believe in his existence. The stories about him were fantastic, unbelievable. Yet they watched for him. They offered rewards for his capture.

They never saw him. Now and then they heard whispered rumors to the effect that he was in the neighborhood. The woods were searched. The roads were watched. There was never anything to indicate his whereabouts. But a few days afterward, a goodly number of slaves would be gone from the plantation. Neither the master nor the overseer had heard or seen anything unusual in the quarter. Sometimes one or the other would vaguely remember having heard a whippoorwill call somewhere in the woods, close by, late at night. Though it was the wrong season for whippoorwills.

Sometimes the masters thought they had heard the cry of a hoot owl, repeated, and would remember having thought that the intervals between the low moaning cry were wrong, that it had been repeated four times in succession instead of three. There was never anything more than that to suggest that all was not well in the quarter. Yet when morning came, they invariably discovered that a group of the finest slaves had taken to their heels.

▲ **Critical Viewing**
What is the artist's opinion of Harriet Tubman? How can you tell?

Literary Analysis
Third-Person Narrative
What details indicate that this story is a third-person narrative?

Unfortunately, the discovery was almost always made on a Sunday. Thus a whole day was lost before the machinery of pursuit could be set in motion. The posters offering rewards for the <u>fugitives</u> could not be printed until Monday. The men who made a living hunting for runaway slaves were out of reach, off in the woods with their dogs and their guns, in pursuit of four-footed game, or they were in camp meetings[1] saying their prayers with their wives and families beside them.

Harriet Tubman could have told them that there was far more involved in this matter of running off slaves than signaling the would-be runaways by imitating the call of a whippoorwill, or a hoot owl, far more involved than a matter of waiting for a clear night when the North Star was visible.

In December 1851, when she started out with the band of fugitives that she planned to take to Canada, she had been in the vicinity of the plantation for days, planning the trip, carefully selecting the slaves that she would take with her.

She had announced her arrival in the quarter by singing the forbidden spiritual[2] —"Go down, Moses, 'way down to Egypt Land"—singing it softly outside the door of a slave cabin, late at night. The husky voice was beautiful even when it was barely more than a murmur borne on the wind.

Once she had made her presence known, word of her coming spread from cabin to cabin. The slaves whispered to each other, ear to mouth, mouth to ear, "Moses is here." "Moses has come." "Get ready. Moses is back again." The ones who had agreed to go North with her put ashcake and salt herring in an old bandanna, hastily tied it into a bundle, and then waited patiently for the signal that meant it was time to start.

There were eleven in this party, including one of her brothers and his wife. It was the largest group that she had ever conducted, but she was determined that more and more slaves should know what freedom was like.

She had to take them all the way to Canada. The Fugitive Slave Law[3] was no longer a great many incomprehensible words written

Harriet Tubman Quilt made by the Negro History Club of Marin City and Sausalito (detail). Designed by Ben Irvin, Atlanta University Center, Robert W. Woodruff Library

fugitives (fyōō′ ji tivs′) *n.* people fleeing

Reading Strategy
Setting a Purpose for Reading What purpose for reading does this paragraph suggest?

✔**Reading Check**

Who is Harriet Tubman?

---

1. **camp meetings** religious meetings held outdoors or in a tent.
2. **forbidden spiritual** In 1831, a slave named Nat Turner encouraged an unsuccessful slave uprising in Virginia by talking about the biblical story of the Israelites' escape from Egypt. Afterwards, the singing of certain spirituals was forbidden for fear of encouraging more uprisings.
3. **Fugitive Slave Law** This part of the Compromise of 1850 held that escaped slaves, even if found in free states, could be returned to their masters. As a result, fugitives were not safe until they reached Canada.

down on the country's lawbooks. The new law had become a reality. It was Thomas Sims, a boy, picked up on the streets of Boston at night and shipped back to Georgia. It was Jerry and Shadrach, arrested and jailed with no warning.

She had never been in Canada. The route beyond Philadelphia was strange to her. But she could not let the runaways who accompanied her know this. As they walked along she told them stories of her own first flight, she kept painting vivid word pictures of what it would be like to be free.

But there were so many of them this time. She knew moments of doubt when she was half-afraid, and kept looking back over her shoulder, imagining that she heard the sound of pursuit. They would certainly be pursued. Eleven of them. Eleven thousand dollars' worth of flesh and bone and muscle that belonged to Maryland planters. If they were caught, the eleven runaways would be whipped and sold South, but she—she would probably be hanged.

They tried to sleep during the day but they never could wholly relax into sleep. She could tell by the positions they assumed, by their restless movements. And they walked at night. Their progress was slow. It took them three nights of walking to reach the first stop. She had told them about the place where they would stay, promising warmth and good food, holding these things out to them as an <u>incentive</u> to keep going.

When she knocked on the door of a farmhouse, a place where she and her parties of runaways had always been welcome, always been given shelter and plenty to eat, there was no answer. She knocked again, softly. A voice from within said, "Who is it?" There was fear in the voice.

She knew instantly from the sound of the voice that there was something wrong. She said, "A friend with friends," the password on the Underground Railroad.

The door opened, slowly. The man who stood in the doorway looked at her coldly, looked with unconcealed astonishment and fear at the eleven <u>disheveled</u> runaways who were standing near her. Then he shouted, "Too many, too many. It's not safe. My place was searched last week. It's not safe!" and slammed the door in her face.

She turned away from the house, frowning. She had promised her passengers food and rest and warmth, and instead of that, there would be hunger and cold and more walking over the frozen ground. Somehow she would have to instill courage into these eleven people, most of them strangers, would have to feed them on hope and bright dreams of freedom instead of the fried pork and corn bread and milk she had promised them.

They stumbled along behind her, half-dead for sleep, and she urged them on, though she was as tired and as discouraged as they were. She had never been in Canada but she kept painting

incentive (in sent´ iv) *n.* something that stimulates one to action; encouragement

disheveled (di shev´ əld) *adj.* untidy; messy

wondrous word pictures of what it would be like. She managed to dispel their fear of pursuit, so that they would not become hysterical, panic-stricken. Then she had to bring some of the fear back, so that they would stay awake and keep walking though they drooped with sleep.

Yet during the day, when they lay down deep in a thicket, they never really slept, because if a twig snapped or the wind sighed in the branches of a pine tree, they jumped to their feet, afraid of their own shadows, shivering and shaking. It was very cold, but they dared not make fires because someone would see the smoke and wonder about it.

She kept thinking, eleven of them. Eleven thousand dollars' worth of slaves. And she had to take them all the way to Canada. Sometimes she told them about Thomas Garrett, in Wilmington. She said he was their friend even though he did not know them. He was the friend of all fugitives. He called them God's poor. He was a Quaker and his speech was a little different from that of other people. His clothing was different, too. He wore the wide-brimmed hat that the Quakers wear.

She said that he had thick white hair, soft, almost like a baby's, and the kindest eyes she had ever seen. He was a big man and strong, but he had never used his strength to harm anyone, always to help people. He would give all of them a new pair of shoes. Everybody. He always did. Once they reached his house in Wilmington, they would be safe. He would see to it that they were.

She described the house where he lived, told them about the store where he sold shoes. She said he kept a pail of milk and a loaf of bread in the drawer of his desk so that he would have food ready at hand for any of God's poor who should suddenly appear before him, fainting with hunger. There was a hidden room in the store. A whole wall swung open, and behind it was a room where he could hide fugitives. On the wall there were shelves filled with small boxes—boxes of shoes—so that you would never guess that the wall actually opened.

While she talked, she kept watching them. They did not believe her. She could tell by their expressions. They were thinking. New shoes, Thomas Garrett, Quaker, Wilmington—what foolishness was this? Who knew if she told the truth? Where was she taking them anyway?

That night they reached the next stop—a farm that belonged to a German. She made the runaways take shelter behind trees at the edge of the fields before she knocked at the door. She hesitated before she approached the door, thinking, suppose that he, too, should refuse shelter, suppose—Then she thought, Lord, I'm going to hold steady on to You and You've got to see me through—and knocked softly.

 **Reading Check**

What is the overall mood among the runaways?

She heard the familiar <u>guttural</u> voice say, "Who's there?"

She answered quickly, "A friend with friends."

He opened the door and greeted her warmly. "How many this time?" he asked.

"Eleven," she said and waited, doubting, wondering.

He said, "Good. Bring them in."

He and his wife fed them in the lamplit kitchen, their faces glowing, as they offered food and more food, urging them to eat, saying there was plenty for everybody, have more milk, have more bread, have more meat.

They spent the night in the warm kitchen. They really slept, all that night and until dusk the next day. When they left, it was with reluctance. They had all been warm and safe and well-fed. It was hard to exchange the security offered by that clean, warm kitchen for the darkness and the cold of a December night.

Harriet had found it hard to leave the warmth and friendliness, too. But she urged them on. For a while, as they walked, they seemed to carry in them a measure of contentment; some of the serenity and the cleanliness of that big warm kitchen lingered on inside them. But as they walked farther and farther away from the warmth and the light, the cold and the darkness entered into them. They fell silent, sullen, suspicious. She waited for the moment when some one of them would turn <u>mutinous</u>. It did not happen that night.

Two nights later she was aware that the feet behind her were moving slower and slower. She heard the irritability in their voices, knew that soon someone would refuse to go on.

She started talking about William Still and the Philadelphia Vigilance Committee.[4] No one commented. No one asked any questions. She told them the story of William and Ellen Craft and how they escaped from Georgia. Ellen was so fair that she looked as though she were white, and so she dressed up in a man's clothing and she looked like a wealthy young planter. Her husband, William, who was dark, played the role of her slave. Thus they traveled from Macon, Georgia, to Philadelphia, riding on the trains, staying at the finest hotels. Ellen pretended to be very ill— her right arm was in a sling, and her right hand was bandaged,

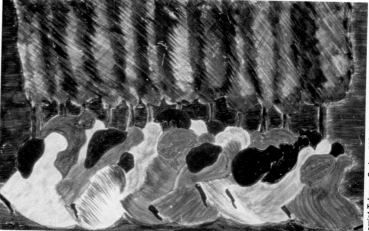

Harriet Tubman Series, #16, Jacob Lawrence, Hampton University Museum

▲ **Critical Viewing**
This painting depicts fugitive slaves fleeing north. Why might the artist have chosen not to include details showing faces and clothing? **[Draw Conclusions]**

guttural (gut´ ər əl) *adj.* made in back of the throat

mutinous (myo͞ot´ ən əs) *adj.* rebellious

Literary Analysis
Third-Person Narrative
How can you tell that the narrator does not take part in these events?

---

4. **Philadelphia Vigilance Committee** group of citizens who helped escaped slaves. Its secretary was a free black man named William Still.

because she was supposed to have rheumatism. Thus she avoided having to sign the register at the hotels for she could not read or write. They finally arrived safely in Philadelphia, and then went on to Boston.

No one said anything. Not one of them seemed to have heard her.

She told them about Frederick Douglass, the most famous of the escaped slaves, of his eloquence, of his magnificent appearance. Then she told them of her own first vain effort at running away, evoking the memory of that miserable life she had led as a child, reliving it for a moment in the telling.

But they had been tired too long, hungry too long, afraid too long, footsore too long. One of them suddenly cried out in despair, "Let me go back. It is better to be a slave than to suffer like this in order to be free."

She carried a gun with her on these trips. She had never used it—except as a threat. Now as she aimed it, she experienced a feeling of guilt, remembering that time, years ago, when she had prayed for the death of Edward Brodas, the Master, and then not too long afterward had heard that great wailing cry that came from the throats of the field hands, and knew from the sound that the Master was dead.

One of the runaways said, again, "Let me go back. Let me go back," and stood still, and then turned around and said, over his shoulder, "I am going back."

She lifted the gun, aimed it at the despairing slave. She said, "Go on with us or die." The husky low-pitched voice was grim.

He hesitated for a moment and then he joined the others. They started walking again. She tried to explain to them why none of them could go back to the plantation. If a runaway returned, he would turn traitor, the master and the overseer would force him to turn traitor. The returned slave would disclose the stopping places, the hiding places, the cornstacks they had used with the full knowledge of the owner of the farm, the name of the German farmer who had fed them and sheltered them. These people who had risked their own security to help runaways would be ruined, fined, imprisoned. She said, "We got to go free or die. And freedom's not bought with dust."

This time she told them about the long agony of the Middle Passage on the old slave ships, about the black horror of the holds, about the chains and the whips. They too knew these stories. But she wanted to remind them of the long hard way

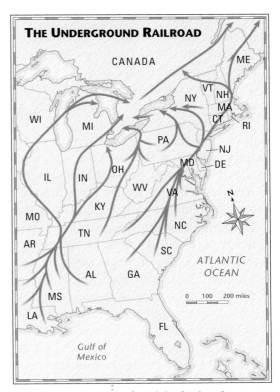

THE UNDERGROUND RAILROAD

▲ **Critical Viewing**
What conclusions about the underground railroad and its routes can you draw from this map? **[Draw Conclusions]**

 **Reading Check**

Why do some of the runaways want to return?

Harriet Tubman: Guide to Freedom ◆ 135

they had come, about the long hard way they had yet to go. She told them about Thomas Sims, the boy picked up on the streets of Boston and sent back to Georgia. She said when they got him back to Savannah, got him in prison there, they whipped him until a doctor who was standing by watching said, "You will kill him if you strike him again!" His master said, "Let him die!"

Thus she forced them to go on. Sometimes she thought she had become nothing but a voice speaking in the darkness, cajoling, urging, threatening. Sometimes she told them things to make them laugh, sometimes she sang to them, and heard the eleven voices behind her blending softly with hers, and then she knew that for the moment all was well with them.

She gave the impression of being a short, muscular, indomitable woman who could never be defeated. Yet at any moment she was liable to be seized by one of those curious fits of sleep, which might last for a few minutes or for hours.[5]

Even on this trip, she suddenly fell asleep in the woods. The runaways, ragged, dirty, hungry, cold, did not steal the gun as they might have, and set off by themselves, or turn back. They sat on the ground near her and waited patiently until she awakened. They had come to trust her implicitly, totally. They, too, had come to believe her repeated statement, "We got to go free or die." She was leading them into freedom, and so they waited until she was ready to go on.

Finally, they reached Thomas Garrett's house in Wilmington, Delaware. Just as Harriet had promised, Garrett gave them all new shoes, and provided carriages to take them on to the next stop.

By slow stages they reached Philadelphia, where William Still hastily recorded their names, and the plantations whence they had come, and something of the life they had led in slavery. Then he carefully hid what he had written, for fear it might be discovered. In 1872 he published this record in book form and called it *The Underground Railroad.* In the foreword to his book he said: "While I knew the danger of keeping strict records, and while I did not then dream that in my day slavery would be blotted out, or that the time would come when I could publish these records, it used to afford me great satisfaction to take them down, fresh from the lips of fugitives on the way to freedom, and to preserve them as they had given them."

William Still, who was familiar with all the station stops on the Underground Railroad, supplied Harriet with money and sent her and her eleven fugitives on to Burlington, New Jersey.

---

5. **sleep . . . hours** when she was about 13, Harriet accidentally received a severe blow on the head. Afterwards, she often lost consciousness and could not be awakened until the episode was over.

cajoling (kə jōl′ iŋ) *v.* coaxing or persuading gently

indomitable (in däm′ it ə bəl) *adj.* not easily discouraged

Literary Analysis
Third-person Narrative
What do you learn about William Still in this paragraph that you would not have known if this were not a third-person narrative?

Harriet felt safer now, though there were danger spots ahead. But the biggest part of her job was over. As they went farther and farther north, it grew colder; she was aware of the wind on the Jersey ferry and aware of the cold damp in New York. From New York they went on to Syracuse, where the temperature was even lower.

In Syracuse she met the Reverend J.W. Loguen, known as "Jarm" Loguen. This was the beginning of a lifelong friendship. Both Harriet and Jarm Loguen were to become friends and supporters of Old John Brown.[6]

From Syracuse they went north again, into a colder, snowier city—Rochester. Here they almost certainly stayed with Frederick Douglass, for he wrote in his autobiography:

"On one occasion I had eleven fugitives at the same time under my roof, and it was necessary for them to remain with me until I could collect sufficient money to get them to Canada. It was the largest number I ever had at any one time, and I had some difficulty in providing so many with food and shelter, but, as may well be imagined, they were not very <u>fastidious</u> in either direction, and were well content with very plain food, and a strip of carpet on the floor for a bed, or a place on the straw in the barnloft."

Late in December 1851, Harriet arrived in St. Catharines, Canada West (now Ontario), with the eleven fugitives. It had taken almost a month to complete this journey; most of the time had been spent getting out of Maryland.

That first winter in St. Catharines was a terrible one. Canada was a strange frozen land, snow everywhere, ice everywhere, and a bone-biting cold the like of which none of them had ever experienced before. Harriet rented a small frame house in the town and set to work to make a home. The fugitives boarded with her. They worked in the forests, felling trees, and so did she. Sometimes she took other jobs, cooking or cleaning house for people in the town. She cheered on these newly arrived fugitives, working herself, finding work for them, finding food for them, praying for them, sometimes begging for them.

Often she found herself thinking of the beauty of Maryland, the mellowness of the soil, the richness of the plant life there. The climate itself made for an ease of living that could never be duplicated in this bleak, barren countryside.

In spite of the severe cold, the hard work, she came to love St. Catharines, and the other towns and cities in Canada where black men lived. She discovered that freedom meant more than

---

fastidious (fas tid′ ē əs) *adj.* refined in an over-sensitive way, so as to be easily disgusted or displeased

Reading Check

What jobs do the fugitives take?

---

6. John Brown white abolitionist (1800–1859) who was hanged for leading a raid on the arsenal at Harpers Ferry, Virginia, as part of a slave uprising.

black men lived. She discovered that freedom meant more than the right to change jobs at will, more than the right to keep the money that one earned. It was the right to vote and to sit on juries. It was the right to be elected to office. In Canada there were black men who were county officials and members of school boards. St. Catharines had a large colony of ex-slaves, and they owned their own homes, kept them neat and clean and in good repair. They lived in whatever part of town they chose and sent their children to the schools.

When spring came she decided that she would make this small Canadian city her home—as much as any place could be said to be home to a woman who traveled from Canada to the Eastern Shore of Maryland as often as she did.

In the spring of 1852, she went back to Cape May, New Jersey. She spent the summer there, cooking in a hotel. That fall she returned, as usual, to Dorchester County, and brought out nine more slaves, conducting them all the way to St. Catharines, in Canada West, to the bone-biting cold, the snow-covered forests—and freedom.

She continued to live in this fashion, spending the winter in Canada, and the spring and summer working in Cape May, New Jersey, or in Philadelphia. She made two trips a year into slave territory, one in the fall and another in the spring. She now had a definite crystallized purpose, and in carrying it out, her life fell into a pattern which remained unchanged for the next six years.

Review and Assess

Thinking About the Selection

1. **Respond:** Would you have trusted Harriet Tubman to take you on a long, difficult journey? Why or why not?

2. **(a) Recall:** What kinds of stories does Tubman tell the fugitives? **(b) Analyze:** Why does she tell them these stories? **(c) Evaluate:** How effective are the stories?

3. **(a) Recall:** What does Tubman do when one of the fugitives insists he is going back? **(b) Analyze Causes and Effects:** Explain why Tubman feels she cannot let anyone go back.

4. **(a) Interpret:** Explain one of the several possible meanings of Tubman's statement "We live free or die." **(b) Make a Judgment:** Do you think the results of Tubman's trips are worth the danger she puts herself in?

5. **(a) Synthesize:** Describe Harriet Tubman's character. **(b) Connect:** What modern leaders have qualities similar to Harriet Tubman's?

Ann Petry

(1908–1997)
Growing up in Old Saybrook, Connecticut, in a predominantly white community, Ann Petry sometimes encountered racism. However, she was inspired by her mother's tales about the strength and courage of her ancestors.

Although Petry began writing in high school, she earned her degree as a pharmacist. She later returned to writing, becoming a fiction writer and a newspaper reporter in New York City.

Petry greatly admired Harriet Tubman. She pays tribute to her in her biography, *Harriet Tubman, Conductor of the Underground Railroad*, from which this selection is taken.

Review and Assess

Literary Analysis

Third-Person Narrative

1. How do you know that the **narrator** does not take part in the events being narrated?
2. How would the story be different if it were told by one of the escaping African Americans in Harriet's group?
3. Fill out a graphic organizer like the one shown to analyze details that only a contemporary third-person narrator could know.

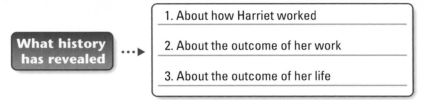

What history has revealed ...▶

1. About how Harriet worked
2. About the outcome of her work
3. About the outcome of her life

Connecting Literary Elements

4. Explain how two details from the story would be presented differently for each type of narrator on the chart. An example is done for you.

Third-person omniscient	Third-person limited
They had come to trust her implicitly, totally.	The narrator would only tell how one of the characters in the story felt.

Reading Strategy

Setting a Purpose for Reading

5. What was your purpose for reading "Harriet Tubman"?
6. How did having a purpose help you focus your reading of this story?
7. What are three details that helped you achieve your purpose?

Extend Understanding

8. **Social Studies Connection:** What historical event caused Tubman to stop making the journeys she made in the 1850s? Explain why.

Quick Review

A **third-person narrative** is a story told by a narrator who is outside the story. To review third-person narrative, see page 129.

Setting a purpose for reading is defining your reason for reading a work of literature.

 Take It to the Net
www.phschool.com
Take the interactive self-test online to check your understanding of the selection.

Integrate Language Skills

Vocabulary Development Lesson

Word Analysis: Latin Root -fug-

The word *fugitives*, meaning "persons running from the law," is built on the Latin root *-fug-*, meaning "to flee." Using the dictionary, define the words listed below. Then, write a sentence explaining how the root *-fug-* contributes to the meaning of each word. Use a dictionary to help you.

1. subterfuge   **2.** refuge   **3.** centrifugal

Spelling Strategy

In the word *incentive*, the *s* sound is spelled with a *c*. When *c* is followed by *e*, *i*, or *y*, it usually has an *s* sound. Identify the words below that have an *s* sound spelled with a *c*.

1. existence   **2.** cajoling   **3.** magnificent

Concept Development: Synonyms

Synonyms are words with similar meanings, such as *courageous* and *brave*. On your paper, match each vocabulary word with a synonym.

1. guttural	**a.** escapees
2. disheveled	**b.** harsh
3. incentive	**c.** unconquerable
4. fugitives	**d.** picky
5. mutinous	**e.** encouragement
6. cajoling	**f.** rebellious
7. indomitable	**g.** messy
8. fastidious	**h.** coaxing

Grammar Lesson

Transitive and Intransitive Verbs

A verb is **transitive** when it expresses an action directed toward a person or thing. The action passes from the doer to the receiver of the action. The person or thing receiving the action is the object of the verb.

> **Transitive:** They never *saw* him.
>   V. OBJ.
> Harriet *believed* her friends.
>   V.   OBJ.

A verb is **intransitive** when it expresses action (or tells something about the subject) without passing the action to the receiver.

> **Intransitive:** They *did* not *believe* in his existence.
>   V.   V.
> She *hoped* for a quick escape.
>   V.

Some verbs can be transitive or intransitive, depending on the way they are used in a sentence.

▶ *For more practice, see page R28, Exercise B.*
Practice On your paper, identify each verb as transitive or intransitive. If the verb is transitive, write its object.

1. At night she guided the fugitives.
2. She knocked on the farmhouse door.
3. One fugitive pleaded to go back.
4. They arrived safely in Philadelphia.
5. The abolitionist gave them food and money.

Writing Application Write a summary of Tubman's journey. When you revise, look for places where using an object and a transitive verb would be more effective than using an intransitive verb. In at least one sentence, use *hide* as a transitive verb. In another, use *run* as an intransitive verb.

𝒲𝒢 *Prentice Hall Writing and Grammar Connection: Chapter 15, Section 1*

Writing Lesson

Introduction

Heroes like Harriet Tubman deserve to be honored. Imagine you are to give a speech at the opening of a museum display on Tubman. In your speech, tell why she is an inspiration to you.

Prewriting   Gather biographical details about Tubman. Organize the details into groups.

Drafting   Begin with an attention-grabbing statement or an anecdote about Tubman. Then, from the details you have gathered, give specific examples to support statements you make about her.

Model: Give Specific Examples

General: She was an extraordinary person.

Specific: Harriet Tubman's extraordinary efforts *to help enslaved people find freedom and a new life in Canada* deserve admiration.

> The words in italics are specific examples of Tubman's efforts.

Revising   Underline each claim you make about Harriet Tubman. For each claim, circle one example. If you cannot find an example, revise to add an example or remove the claim from your introduction.

W̶G̶ Prentice Hall Writing and Grammar Connection: Chapter 5, Section 2

Extension Activities

Listening and Speaking Using an outline you prepare in advance, give a **brief speech** in which you persuade people to contribute money to a memorial for Harriet Tubman.

1. In the introduction of your outline, state your purpose and preview the reasons you will give.
2. In the body of your outline, list details and facts that will help you develop and support your reasons.
3. In the conclusion of your outline, jot down a quotation or question with which you can end your speech.

Research and Technology Work with a group to create a **map** of the Underground Railroad. Include the following:

- routes
- approximate location of safe houses
- final destinations

Research by using encyclopedias, library books, and Web sites. Display your map in the classroom.

 **Take It to the Net**   www.phschool.com

Go online for an additional research activity using the Internet.

Prepare to Read

Columbus ◆ Western Wagons ◆ The Other Pioneers

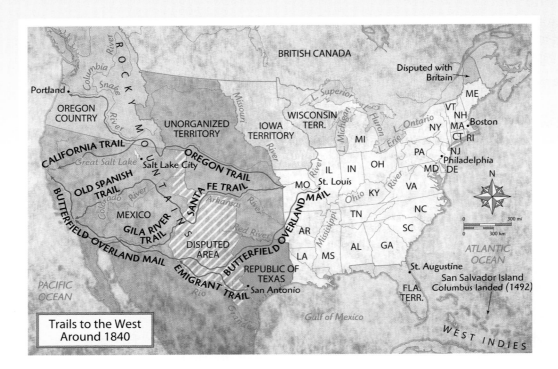

Trails to the West
Around 1840

Preview

Connecting to the Literature

The three poems in this section celebrate people who took risks as explorers and pioneers. Make a connection with the adventurous spirit in the poems by thinking about a time you have "explored the unknown"—either by traveling to a new place or trying a new experience.

Background

These three poems celebrate the pioneer spirit of people who left their homes to explore the unknown. The map above shows trails to the West that were used by pioneers described in Stephen Vincent Benét's "Western Wagons." Also shown is the Republic of Texas, where the "other pioneers" that are the subject of Roberto Félix Salazar's poem settled after crossing the Rio Grande from Mexico.

Literary Analysis

Author's Perspective

An **author's perspective** is the unique viewpoint from which he or she writes. This perspective is a combination of the following factors:

- the author's heritage and traditions
- the author's attitudes and beliefs
- the culture of the time during which the author lived.

Stephen Vincent Benét and Roberto Félix Salazar both write about pioneers. Their perspectives, however, are very different. As you read the three poems, notice details that reflect each author's perspective.

Comparing Literary Works

Compare and contrast the authors' perspectives in these works. To focus your comparison, look for answers to the following focus questions:

1. What topic or subject do the works share?
2. What is the poet's attitude toward the topic?
3. What details from the poet's background may have helped shape the poet's attitude?

Reading Strategy

Relating to What You Know

One way to understand a poem is by **relating** it **to what you know**. For example, you know that Columbus landed on American shores in the late 1400s and that sea voyages were dangerous at that time. This information helps you appreciate the depth of Columbus's determination and the extent of the crew's fear in Joaquin Miller's poem "Columbus."

As you read and respond to these poems, think about how the details fit in with what you already know. Use a KWL chart to take notes. Before reading, write what you know in the "K" column. Write what you want to know under "W." After reading, write what you have learned under "L." Add any additional questions you want to investigate under "W."

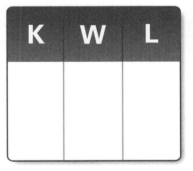

Vocabulary Development

mutinous (myo͞ot′ ən əs) *adj.* rebellious (p. 144)

wan (wän) *adj.* pale (p. 144)

swarthy (swôr′ thē) *adj.* having a dark complexion (p. 144)

unfurled (un furld′) *adj.* unfolded (p. 145)

stalwart (stôl′ wərt) *adj.* resolute; firm; unyielding (p. 150)

Columbus

Joaquin Miller

The Landing of Columbus, 1876, Currier & Ives, Museum of the City of New York

◄ **Critical Viewing**
What qualities of Columbus depicted in the poem are revealed or suggested by the figure of Columbus standing at the front of the boat in this painting? **[Compare and Contrast]**

Behind him lay the gray Azores,[1]
Behind the Gates of Hercules;[2]
Before him not the ghost of shores;
Before him only shoreless seas.
5   The good mate said: "Now must we pray,
For lo! the very stars are gone.
Brave Adm'r'l, speak; what shall I say?"
"Why, say: 'Sail on! sail on! and on!'"

"My men grow <u>mutinous</u> day by day;
10   My men grow ghastly <u>wan</u> and weak."
The stout mate thought of home; a spray
Of salt wave washed his <u>swarthy</u> cheek.
"What shall I say, brave Adm'r'l, say,
If we sight naught[3] but seas at dawn?"
15   "Why, you shall say at break of day:
'Sail on! sail on! sail on! and on!'"

mutinous (myo͞ot′ ən əs) *adj.* rebellious

wan (wän) *adj.* pale

swarthy (swôr′ thē) *adj.* having a dark complexion

---

1. Azores (ā′ zôrz) group of Portuguese islands in the North Atlantic west of Portugal.
2. Gates of Hercules (gāts uv hʉr′ kyə lēz′) entrance to the Strait of Gibraltar between Spain and Africa.
3. naught (nôt) *n.* nothing.

They sailed and sailed, as winds might blow,
Until at last the blanched mate said:
"Why, now not even God would know
20 Should I and all my men fall dead.
These very winds forget their way,
For God from these dread seas is gone.
Now speak, brave Adm'r'l; speak and say—"
He said: "Sail on! sail on! and on!"

25 They sailed. They sailed. Then spake[4] the mate:
"This mad sea shows his teeth to-night.
He curls his lip, he lies in wait,
With lifted teeth, as if to bite!
Brave Adm'r'l, say but one good word:
30 What shall we do when hope is gone?"
The words leapt like a leaping sword:
"Sail on! sail on! sail on! and on!"

Then, pale and worn, he kept his deck,
And peered through darkness. Ah, that night
35 Of all dark nights! And then a speck—
A light! A light! A light! A light!
It grew, a starlit flag unfurled!
It grew to be Time's burst of dawn.
He gained a world; he gave that world
40 Its grandest lesson: "On! sail on!"

---

4. **spake** (spāk) v. old-fashioned word for "spoke."

unfurled (un fʉrld´) *adj.*
unfolded

Joaquin Miller

(1837–1913)

Joaquin Miller was born near Liberty, Indiana, though he once claimed that his cradle was "a covered wagon pointed West." Miller later settled in Oregon, where he owned a newspaper, worked as a county judge, and helped establish a pony express route. As a tribute to the Mexican bandit Joaquin Murieta, Miller changed his given name, Cincinnatus Hiner Miller, to Joaquin Miller.

Miller wrote several books of poetry, often depicting the beauty and excitement of the frontier. In 1870 he visited England, where his book *Songs of the Sierras* was well received. "Columbus" is his best-known poem.

Review and Assess

Thinking About the Selection

1. **Respond:** Would you like to have been on Columbus's voyage? Why or why not?

2. **(a) Recall:** Who are the two characters speaking in the poem? **(b) Compare and Contrast:** Compare and contrast these two speakers' reactions to the voyage.

3. **(a) Recall:** To what does the mate compare the sea in lines 26–28? **(b) Interpret:** What do you think he means by this comparison?

4. **(a) Recall:** In the last stanza, what does Columbus see during the night? **(b) Draw Conclusions:** What is its importance?

5. **(a) Recall:** What words does Columbus repeat throughout the poem? **(b) Evaluate:** How do these words provide the "grandest lesson" to the world?

Western Wagons

Stephen Vincent Benét

A New Beginning, Duane Bryers, Courtesy of the artist

▲ **Critical Viewing** What do the expressions on the faces of the couple in the painting reveal about their emotions? **[Infer]**

They went with axe and rifle, when the trail was still to blaze,
They went with wife and children, in the prairie-schooner days,
With banjo and with frying pan—Susanna, don't you cry!
For I'm off to California to get rich out there or die!

5   We've broken land and cleared it, but we're tired of where we are.
They say that wild Nebraska is a better place by far.
There's gold in far Wyoming, there's black earth in Ioway,
So pack up the kids and blankets, for we're moving out today!

    The cowards never started and the weak died on the road,
10 And all across the continent the endless campfires glowed.
    We'd taken land and settled—but a traveler passed by—
    And we're going West tomorrow—Lordy, never ask us why!

    We're going West tomorrow, where the promises can't fail.
    O'er the hills in legions, boys, and crowd the dusty trail!
15 We shall starve and freeze and suffer. We shall die,
        and tame the lands.
    But we're going West tomorrow, with our fortune in our hands.

Reading Strategy
Relating to What You Know Why does the poet insert "Susanna, don't you cry!" in this stanza?

Review and Assess

Thinking About the Selection

1. **Respond:** Does the life of a westward pioneer appeal to you? Explain.

2. **(a) Recall:** With what items do the pioneers travel? **(b) Analyze:** Why are these items important to the pioneers? **(c) Interpret:** How do these details help you understand the meaning of the phrase "the trail was still to blaze"?

3. **(a) Recall:** To what places do the people in "Western Wagons" want to go? **(b) Infer:** Why do they want to go to these places? **(c) Apply:** What qualities characterized the age of westward expansion?

4. **(a) Recall:** In line five, what do you learn about the life of the pioneers? **(b) Interpret:** What do you think drives the pioneers to keep moving?

5. **(a) Make a Judgment:** What do you think is the most compelling reason most of the pioneers had for moving on? **(b) Evaluate:** Do you think the rewards of their move are worth the risks they face? Explain.

Stephen Vincent Benét

(1898–1943)

A poet, short-story writer, and dramatist, Stephen Vincent Benét had his first collection of poetry published when he was only seventeen years old. Benét grew up in a literary family. His father read poetry to the children, and Benét's brother, William Rose, and sister, Laura, also were writers.

Benét often wrote on historical themes. *A Book of Americans,* which he wrote with his wife Rosemary Carr, consists of poems on historical characters. His epic poem on the Civil War, *John Brown's Body,* won the Pulitzer Prize in 1929.

The Other Pioneers

Roberto Félix Salazar

Now I must write
Of those of mine who rode these plains
Long years before the Saxon[1] and the Irish came.
Of those who plowed the land and built the towns
5   And gave the towns soft-woven Spanish names.
Of those who moved across the Rio Grande
Toward the hiss of Texas snake and Indian yell.
Of men who from the earth made thick-walled homes
And from the earth raised churches to their God.
10 And of the wives who bore them sons
And smiled with knowing joy.

Literary Analysis
Author's Perspective
What historical event does this poem describe?

---

1. Saxon (sak´ sən) *n.* English.

They saw the Texas sun rise golden-red with promised wealth
And saw the Texas sun sink golden yet, with wealth unspent.
"Here," they said. "Here to live and here to love."
15 "Here is the land for our sons and the sons of our sons."
And they sang the songs of ancient Spain
And they made new songs to fit new needs.
They cleared the brush and planted the corn
And saw green stalks turn black from lack of rain.
20 They roamed the plains behind the herds
And stood the Indian's cruel attacks.
There was dust and there was sweat.
And there were tears and the women prayed.

✓**Reading Check**

Where are the people in this poem going?

East Side Main Plaza, San Antonio, Texas,
1844, William G.M. Samuel. Courtesy of Bexar County
and the Witte Museum, San Antonio, Texas

◀ **Critical Viewing** This painting depicts San Antonio, Texas, in the mid-1800s. What does the painting reveal about the landscape of the area? **[Infer]**

And the **years** moved on.
25   Those **who** were first placed in graves
Beside **the** broad mesquite[2] and the tall nopal.[3]
Gentle **mothers** left their graces and their arts
And <u>stalwart</u> fathers pride and manly strength.
Salinas, **de** la Garza, Sánchez, García,
30   Uribe, González, Martinez, de León:[4]
Such **were** the names of the fathers.
Salinas, **de** la Garza, Sánchez, García,
Uribe, González, Martinez, de León:
Such **are** the names of the sons.

stalwart (stôl′ wərt) *adj.* resolute; firm; unyielding

---

2. mesquite (mes kēt′) *n.* thorny tree or shrub common in the southwestern United States and Mexico
3. nopal (nō′ pəl) *n.* cactus with red flowers
4. Salinas (sä lē′ näs), **de la Garza** (dā lä gär′sä), **Sánchez** (sän′ chās), **García** (Gär sē′ ä), **Uribe** (ōō rē′ bā) **Gonzáles** (gōn sä′ lās), **Martinez** (mär tē′ nās), **de León** (dā lā ōn′)

Review and Assess

Thinking About the Selection

1. **Respond:** Would you have liked to have been a part of the life described in this poem? Why or why not?

2. **(a) Recall:** Who are the "other pioneers" referred to in the title?
   (b) Infer: Why does Salazar refer to them as "other"?
   (c) Contrast: Identify the diffferences between these two groups.

3. **(a) Recall:** What did these pioneers do in their new land?
   (b) Apply: Identify evidence of their actions in modern times.

4. **(a) Synthesize:** Describe the life of these pioneers. **(b) Evaluate:** Were the rewards of their efforts worth the risks they faced?

5. **(a) Connect:** Who are today's pioneers? **(b) Analyze:** What do they risk? **(c) Assess:** Is it worth the risk?

Roberto Félix Salazar

(b. 1913)

In his writing, Roberto Félix Salazar aims to dramatize his Mexican American heritage as well as challenge his readers' assumptions about the beginnings of the United States. According to Philip Ortego, a professor of Chicano Studies, "The Other Pioneers" was written to remind Hispanic Americans and others that the first pioneers to settle the Southwest had Spanish names—and that their descendants still do, although they are American citizens.

Review and Assess

Literary Analysis

Author's Perspective

1. Complete a chart like the one shown to indicate details that contribute to each author's perspective.

Author	Heritage	An experience that shaped attitudes or beliefs
Joaquin Miller		Helped establish pony express routes
Stephen Vincent Benét		
Roberto Félix Salazar		

2. What are two different details of early American culture that are included in Benét's "Western Wagons"?
3. How does Salazar honor his heritage in "The Other Pioneers"?

Comparing Literary Works

4. What topic or subject do the works share?
5. What is each poet's attitude toward the topic?
6. What details from each poem are shaped by the poet's background?

Reading Strategy

Relating to What You Know

7. Complete an organizer like this one for "Western Wagons" and "The Other Pioneers" to illustrate prior knowledge you brought to each poem.

Poem	Subject of poem	Details in poem	What I already know	How it fits together
"Columbus"	Columbus's voyage	The men are mutinous.	Sea voyages were unpredictable and dangerous then.	They are frightened and want to turn back.

8. Based on what you know about pioneer life, explain why the pioneers in "Western Wagons" travel with axes and rifles.

Extend Understanding

9. **Social Studies Connection:** What legacy do the characters in the poems leave to people living today?

Quick Review

An **author's perspective** is the unique viewpoint from which he or she writes based on heritage, traditions, beliefs, attitudes, and the culture of the times in which the author lives. To review author's perspective, see page 143.

To fully appreciate a work of literature, **relate to what you know.** That is, see how details in the work fit together with your prior knowledge of the subject.

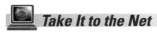 **Take It to the Net**

www.phschool.com
Take the interactive self-test online to check your understanding of these selections.

Integrate Language Skills

Vocabulary Development Lesson

Concept Development: Antonyms
wan and *swarthy*

Antonyms are words with opposite meanings, such as *light* and *dark*. Joaquin Miller uses the antonyms *wan* and *swarthy* in "Columbus." If you know that *wan* means "pale," you can guess that *swarthy* means "having a dark complexion."

A. Copy the following sentences on your paper. Fill in each blank with *wan* or *swarthy*.

   1. The sick child looked ___?___ and tired.

   2. The rancher, who had worked outside for years, had a ___?___ complexion.

   3. Hours after the accident, the driver still looked ___?___ and startled.

B. Write a sentence describing the mate in "Columbus." Tell when he is *swarthy* and when he looks *wan*.

Grammar Lesson

Active and Passive Voice

A verb is in the **active voice** when the subject of the sentence performs the action. It is in the **passive voice** when the subject receives the action. The passive voice uses a form of the helping verb *be*.

> **Active Voice:** The settlers crossed the prairie.
>
> **Passive Voice:** The prairie was crossed by settlers.

Although you should aim to use the active voice in your writing, sometimes you need to use the passive voice. Use the passive voice when you do not know who or what performed the action or when you want to place emphasis on the result of the action rather than on the performer of the action.

Spelling Strategy

When adding the suffix *-ous* to a word that ends in y, drop the y if the sound it represents disappears: mutiny + *-ous* = mutinous.

Keep the y or change it to *e* or *i* if the sound it represents remains: harmony + *-ous* = harmonious.

On your paper, add *-ous* to these words.

   1. larceny   **2.** glory   **3.** beauty

Fluency: Matching Words and Definitions

Match the vocabulary words with their definitions.

   1. unfurled   **a.** rebellious

   2. wan   **b.** having a dark complexion

   3. stalwart   **c.** unfolded

   4. mutinous   **d.** pale

   5. swarthy   **e.** resolute or unyielding

Practice On your paper, write whether each verb is in active or passive voice.

   1. Pioneers crossed the empty land.

   2. The trail was marked by wagon tracks.

   3. The plains echoed with coyote howls.

   4. Benét was impressed by the pioneers.

Writing Application Rewrite this passage, changing any use of the passive voice to the active voice.

The voyage was made by Columbus. The ships sailed for days without direction. After a time, threats were muttered by the crew. The crew was relieved, however, when land was sighted by Columbus.

Prentice Hall Writing and Grammar Connection: Chapter 22, Section 2

Writing Lesson

Written Proposal

These poems honor courageous trailblazers. Write a persuasive speech in which you propose naming a public area or building after a historical figure you admire.

Prewriting   Choose a historical figure you would like to honor. Write down what you already know about the person. Then, make a list of questions you have about the person. Do research to answer the questions.

Drafting   Use your research notes to identify qualities or achievements you admire in your subject. Use these to support your proposal.

Model: Supporting Ideas With Reasons

We should name the new science lab Carver Memorial Science Facility. George Washington Carver performed research that benefits many people today. His determination and curiosity are an example to all science students.

> The writer gives two specific reasons why the science lab should be named after George Washington Carver.

Revising   Read your speech, underlining each reason you use to support your main idea. Revise any underlined reasons that are not specific.

Prentice Hall Writing and Grammar Connection: Chapter 7, Section 1

Extension Activities

Listening and Speaking In an **oral presentation,** compare and contrast the pictures of the American West shown in "Western Wagons" and "The Other Pioneers."

1. Use the active voice rather than the passive voice.
   Passive: Settlers are described in both poems.
   Active: Both poems describe settlers.
2. Use action verbs to show the emphasis of each poem. For example, *explored* and *roamed* are two verbs that identify important action in "Western Wagons." *Settled* and *built* identify important actions in "The Other Pioneers."

Research and Technology With a group, develop **historical marker**s for an area mentioned in one of the poems.

1. Use place names and names of people as keywords in an Internet search.
2. Use search conventions to get only the hits that apply to your specific search. For example, "Texas + settlers" will give hits related to the combination of Texas and settlers rather than many hits about Texas or many hits about settlers.

 **Take It to the Net**   www.phschool.com

Go online for an additional research activity using the Internet.

Prepare to Read

Up the Slide

 Take It to the Net

Visit www.phschool.com for interactive activities and instruction related to "Up the Slide," including

- background
- graphic organizers
- literary elements
- reading strategies

Preview

Connecting to the Literature

In "Up the Slide," a young man sets out to do something simple that turns into a hair-raising, life-threatening adventure. Connect to the character's experience by thinking of a time when you have gotten yourself into a situation that was more difficult to get out of than you thought it would be.

Background

The young man in Jack London's story "Up the Slide" was one of many prospectors who traveled to the Yukon Territory in search of gold in the 1890s. The Yukon Territory is located in the northwestern corner of Canada. It is part of the subarctic zone where temperatures have been known to plunge to −80°F!

Literary Analysis

Conflict

A **conflict** is a struggle between opposing forces. In literature, the conflict may be between characters, within a character's mind, or between a character and nature. In "Up the Slide," the conflict is between Clay Dilham and the cold and snowy rock face of a mountain.

> He clawed desperately with his hands, but there was little to cling to, and he sped downward faster and faster.

As you read, notice how natural elements are in conflict with Clay's plans.

Connecting Literary Elements

The way characters in a story deal with a conflict often depends on the **historical context**—the laws, beliefs, and expectations of the time period. In the late 1800s, people in the Yukon expected to live without the comforts of civilization, so Clay is not surprised that he must struggle to survive. A character from a modern city might have a very different reaction.

As you read, think about the following focus questions:

1. In what ways is Clay different from modern teenagers?
2. In what ways does the time period of the story affect the way Clay deals with the conflict?

Reading Strategy

Predicting

When you read an adventure story, you can sometimes **predict**, or make educated guesses about, story events. Predictions are usually based on one or both of the following factors:

- clues in the story that suggest a certain outcome
- your own experience in a similar situation

Use a chart like the one shown to record and check the accuracy of your predictions about events in the story.

Vocabulary Development

exhausted (eg zôst′ əd) *v.* used up; expended completely (p. 157)

thoroughly (thʉr′ ō lē) *adv.* accurately and with regard to detail (p. 157)

manifestly (man′ ə fest′ lē) *adv.* clearly (p. 158)

exertion (eg zʉr′ shən) *n.* energetic activity; effort (p. 160)

maneuver (mə nōō′ vər) *n.* series of planned steps (p. 161)

ascent (ə sent′) *n.* the act of climbing or rising (p. 162)

descent (dē sent′) *n.* the act of climbing down (p. 162)

Clue or Event

Clay is expected to be back in half an hour.

Prediction

Something will happen to delay him.

Actual Outcome

Up the SLIDE

JACK LONDON

When Clay Dilham left the tent to get a sled-load of firewood, he expected to be back in half an hour. So he told Swanson, who was cooking the dinner. Swanson and he belonged to different outfits, located about twenty miles apart on the Stewart River, but they had become traveling partners on a trip down the Yukon to Dawson[1] to get the mail.

Swanson had laughed when Clay said he would be back in half an hour. It stood to reason, Swanson said, that good, dry firewood could not be found so close to Dawson; that whatever firewood there was originally had long since been gathered in; that firewood would not be selling at forty dollars a cord if any man could go out and get a sled-load and be back in the time Clay expected to make it.

---

1. **Yukon** (yōo´ kän) **. . . Dawson** (dô´ sən) The Yukon River is in the Yukon Territory of northwestern Canada, and Dawson is a town nearby.

Then it was Clay's turn to laugh, as he sprang on the sled and *mushed* the dogs on the river-trail. For, coming up from the Siwash village the previous day, he had noticed a small dead pine in an out-of-the-way place, which had defied discovery by eyes less sharp than his. And his eyes were both young and sharp, for his seventeenth birthday was just cleared.

A swift ten minutes over the ice brought him to the place, and figuring ten minutes to get the tree and ten minutes to return made him certain that Swanson's dinner would not wait.

Just below Dawson, and rising out of the Yukon itself, towered the great Moosehede Mountain, so named by Lieutenant Schwatka long ere[2] the Yukon became famous. On the river side the mountain was scarred and gullied and gored; and it was up one of these gores or gullies that Clay had seen the tree.

Halting his dogs beneath, on the river ice, he looked up, and after some searching, rediscovered it. Being dead, its weatherbeaten gray so blended with the gray wall of rock that a thousand men could pass by and never notice it. Taking root in a cranny, it had grown up, <u>exhausted</u> its bit of soil, and perished. Beneath it the wall fell sheer for a hundred feet to the river. All one had to do was to sink an ax into the dry trunk a dozen times and it would fall to the ice, and most probably smash conveniently to pieces. This Clay had figured on when confidently limiting the trip to half an hour.

He studied the cliff <u>thoroughly</u> before attempting it. So far as he was concerned, the longest way round was the shortest way to the tree. Twenty feet of nearly perpendicular climbing would bring him to where a slide sloped more gently in. By making a long zigzag across the face of this slide and back again, he would arrive at the pine.

Fastening his ax across his shoulders so that it would not interfere with his movements, he clawed up the broken rock, hand and foot, like a cat, till the twenty feet were cleared and he could draw breath on the edge of the slide.

The slide was steep and its snow-covered surface slippery. Further, the heelless, walrus-hide shoes of his *muclucs* were polished by much ice travel, and by his second step he realized how little he could depend upon them for clinging purposes. A slip at that point meant a plunge over the edge and a twenty-foot fall to the ice. A hundred feet farther along, and a slip would mean a fifty-foot fall.

He thrust his mittened hand through the snow to the earth to steady himself, and went on. But he was forced to exercise such care that the first zigzag consumed five minutes. Then, returning across the face of the slide toward the pine, he met with a new difficulty. The slope steepened considerably, so that little snow collected, while bent flat beneath this thin covering were long, dry last-year's grasses. The surface they presented was as glassy as that of his muclucs,

---

2. **ere** (er) *prep.* archaic for before.

◀ **Critical Viewing** What does this picture of the Yukon tell you about the difficulties of making contact with the outside world? **[Connect]**

exhausted (eg zôst´ əd) *v.* used up; expended completely

thoroughly (thur´ ō lē) *adv.* accurately and with regard to detail

Literary Analysis
Conflict and Historical Context Do you think a character from modern times would take on the challenge of climbing "The Slide"?

✔**Reading Check**

What is the slide?

and when both surfaces came together his feet shot out, and he fell on his face, sliding downward and convulsively clutching for something to stay himself.

This he succeeded in doing, although he lay quiet for a couple of minutes to get back his nerve. He would have taken off his muclucs and gone at it in his socks, only the cold was thirty below zero, and at such temperature his feet would quickly freeze. So he went on, and after ten minutes of risky work made the safe and solid rock where stood the pine.

A few strokes of the ax felled it into the chasm, and peeping over the edge, he indulged a laugh at the startled dogs. They were on the verge of bolting when he called aloud to them, soothingly, and they were reassured.

Then he turned about for the trip back. Going down, he knew, was even more dangerous than coming up, but how dangerous he did not realize till he had slipped half a dozen times, and each time saved himself by what appeared to him a miracle. Time and again he ventured upon the slide, and time and again he was balked when he came to the grasses.

He sat down and looked at the treacherous snow-covered slope. It was <u>manifestly</u> impossible for him to make it with a whole body, and he did not wish to arrive at the bottom shattered like the pine tree.

He must be doing something to keep his blood circulating. If he could not get down by going down, there only remained to him to get down by going up. It was a herculean task, but it was the only way out of the predicament.

From where he was he could not see the top of the cliff, but he reasoned that the gully in which lay the slide must give inward more and more as it approached the top. From what little he could see, the gully displayed this tendency; and he noticed, also, that the slide extended for many hundreds of feet upward, and that where it ended the rock was well broken up and favorable for climbing. . . .

So instead of taking the zigzag which led downward, he made a new one leading upward and crossing the slide at an angle of thirty degrees. The grasses gave him much trouble, and made him long for soft-tanned moosehide moccasins, which could make his feet cling like a second pair of hands.

He soon found that thrusting his mittened hands through the snow and clutching the grass roots was uncertain and unsafe. His mittens were too thick for him to be sure of his grip, so he took them off. But this brought with it new trouble. When he held on to a bunch of roots the snow, coming in contact with his bare warm hand, was melted, so that his hands and the wristbands of his woolen shirt were dripping with water. This the frost was quick to attack, and his fingers were numbed and made worthless.

Literary Analysis
Conflict How is the slide an opposing force to Clay?

manifestly (man´ ə fest´ lē) *adv.* clearly

Reading Strategy
Predicting Clay encounters problem after problem. What do you predict will happen?

Then he was forced to seek good footing, where he could stand erect unsupported, to put on his mittens, and to thrash his hands against his sides until the heat came back into them.

This constant numbing of his fingers made his progress very slow; but the zigzag came to an end finally, where the side of the slide was buttressed by a perpendicular rock, and he turned back and upward again. As he climbed higher and higher, he found that the slide was wedge-shaped, its rocky buttresses pinching it away as it reared its upper end. Each step increased the depth which seemed to yawn for him.

While beating his hands against his sides he turned and looked down the long slippery slope, and figured, in case he slipped, that he would be flying with the speed of an express train ere he took the final plunge into the icy bed of the Yukon.

He passed the first outcropping rock, and the second, and at the end of an hour found himself above the third, and fully five hundred feet above the river. And here, with the end nearly two hundred feet above him, the pitch of the slide was increasing.

☑ **Reading Check**

What is the challenge Clay faces?

Each step became more difficult and perilous, and he was faint from exertion and from lack of Swanson's dinner. Three or four times he slipped slightly and recovered himself; but, growing careless from exhaustion and the long tension on his nerves, he tried to continue with too great haste, and was rewarded by a double slip of each foot, which tore him loose and started him down the slope.

On account of the steepness there was little snow; but what little there was was displaced by his body, so that he became the nucleus of a young avalanche. He

exertion (eg zʉr´ shən) *n.* energetic activity; effort

▼ Critical Viewing
What does this photograph reveal about the hardships endured by gold prospectors in the Yukon? **[Connect]**

clawed desperately with his hands, but there was little to cling to, and he sped downward faster and faster.

The first and second outcroppings were below him, but he knew that the first was almost out of line, and pinned his hope on the second. Yet the first was just enough in line to catch one of his feet and to whirl him over and head downward on his back.

The shock of this was severe in itself, and the fine snow enveloped him in a blinding, maddening cloud; but he was thinking quickly and clearly of what would happen if he brought up head first against the outcropping. He twisted himself over on his stomach, thrust both hands out to one side, and pressed them heavily against the flying surface.

This had the effect of a brake, drawing his head and shoulders to the side. In this position he rolled over and over a couple of times, and then, with a quick jerk at the right moment, he got his body the rest of the way round.

And none too soon, for the next moment his feet drove into the outcropping, his legs doubled up, and the wind was driven from his stomach with the abruptness of the stop.

There was much snow down his neck and up his sleeves. At once and with unconcern he shook this out, only to discover, when he looked up to where he must climb again, that he had lost his nerve. He was shaking as if with a palsy, and sick and faint from a frightful nausea.

Fully ten minutes passed ere he could master these sensations and summon sufficient strength for the weary climb. His legs hurt him and he was limping, and he was conscious of a sore place in his back, where he had fallen on the ax.

In an hour he had regained the point of his tumble, and was contemplating the slide, which so suddenly steepened. It was plain to him that he could not go up with his hands and feet alone, and he was beginning to lose his nerve again when he remembered the ax.

Reaching upward the distance of a step, he brushed away the snow, and in the frozen gravel and crumbled rock of the slide chopped a shallow resting place for his foot. Then he came up a step, reached forward, and repeated the <u>maneuver</u>. And so, step by step, foothole by foothole, a tiny speck of toiling life poised like a fly on the face of Moosehide Mountain, he fought his upward way.

Twilight was beginning to fall when he gained the head of the slide and drew himself into the rocky bottom of the gully. At this point the shoulder of the mountain began to bend back toward the crest, and in addition to its being less steep, the rocks afforded better handhold and foothold. The worst was over, and the best yet to come!

The gully opened out into a miniature basin, in which a floor of soil had been deposited, out of which, in turn, a tiny grove of pines had sprung. The trees were all dead, dry and seasoned, having long since exhausted the thin skin of earth.

Literary Analysis
Conflict Which force appears to be winning the conflict?

maneuver (mə nōō′ vər) *n.* series of planned steps

 **Reading Check**

How does Clay "brake" himself?

Clay ran his experienced eye over the timber, and estimated that it would chop up into fifty cords at least. Beyond, the gully closed in and became barren rock again. On every hand was barren rock, so the wonder was small that the trees had escaped the eyes of men. They were only to be discovered as he had discovered them—by climbing after them.

He continued the <u>ascent</u>, and the white moon greeted him when he came out upon the crest of Moosehide Mountain. At his feet, a thousand feet below, sparkled the lights of Dawson.

But the <u>descent</u> was precipitate and dangerous in the uncertain moonlight, and he elected to go down the mountain by its gentler northern flank. In a couple of hours he reached the Yukon at the Siwash village, and took the river-trail back to where he had left the dogs. There he found Swanson, with a fire going, waiting for him to come down.

And although Swanson had a hearty laugh at his expense, nevertheless, a week or so later, in Dawson, there were fifty cords of wood sold at forty dollars a cord, and it was he and Swanson who sold them.

ascent (ə sent′) *n.* the act of climbing or rising

descent (dē sent′) *n.* the act of climbing down

Review and Assess

Thinking About the Selection

1. **Respond:** Do you think the risks that Clay takes are reasonable or foolish? Why?

2. **(a) Recall:** How long does Clay say he will be gone collecting firewood? **(b) Recall:** What is Swanson's reaction to Clay's estimate? **(c) Apply:** Why do you think London begins his story with the description of the two men's disagreement?

3. **(a) Recall:** How old is Clay? **(b) Deduce:** How is Clay's age reflected in his actions?

4. **(a) Infer:** Identify three specific skills Clay possesses that aid his survival. **(b) Deduce:** How do these skills save his life? **(c) Contrast:** Which of his actions endanger his life? Explain.

5. **(a) Recall:** What does Clay find after reaching the top of the slide? **(b) Draw Conclusions:** How does this discovery reward him for his dangerous climb? **(c) Make Judgments:** Is the discovery worth the risks Clay takes?

6. **(a)Infer:** What lesson does Clay learn from his experiences? **(b) Generalize:** What lesson does the story hold for readers who will never visit the Yukon?

7. **Connect:** What risks today are not worth taking in spite of potential millions?

Jack London

(1876–1916)

Jack London was the most popular novelist and short-story writer of his day. His exciting tales of adventure and courage were inspired by his own experiences.

At age seventeen, London sailed with a seal-hunting ship to Japan and Siberia. After two years, London returned to high school, vowing to become a writer.

In 1897, London journeyed to the Yukon Territory in search of gold. Although he did not find it, he did find inspiration for his writing.

London's best-known works depict strong characters facing the powerful elements of nature—from Buck, the dog in *The Call of the Wild*, to the ruthless Wolf Larson in *The Sea-Wolf*.

Review and Assess

Literary Analysis

Conflict

1. In a diagram like the one shown, show three instances of nature in conflict with Clay.

2. Explain how elements of nature oppose Clay's efforts to find firewood.
3. How is the conflict between Clay and forces of nature resolved?

Connecting Literary Elements

4. In what ways is Clay different from modern teenagers?
5. In what ways does the time period of the story affect the way Clay deals with the conflict?
6. Complete an organizer like the one shown to compare and contrast the way Clay deals with the conflict to the way a contemporary character might deal with it.

Clay		Contemporary Teenager
	Usual daily activities	
	How food is obtained	
	Kinds of transportation used	
	Other	

Reading Strategy

Predicting

7. What clues at the beginning of the story could lead you to predict that Clay's task may take him longer than he expects?
8. What clues might lead you to predict that Clay will survive?

Extend Understanding

9. **Career Connection:** Based on his actions in the story, for what kinds of jobs do you think Clay is suited? Why?

Quick Review

Conflict in a story means a struggle between the main character and either another character or some force of nature. To review conflict, see page 155.

The **historical context** of a story includes the laws, beliefs, and expectations of the time period. To review historical context, see page 155.

Predicting means making educated guesses about story events based on clues that suggest a certain outcome.

 Take It to the Net
www.phschool.com
Take the interactive self-test online to check your understanding of the selection.

Up the Slide ◆ 163

Integrate Language Skills

Vocabulary Development Lesson

Concept Development: Forms of *exhaust*

Exhausted is a form of the verb *exhaust*, meaning "to use up" or "expend completely." Other forms of exhaust include *exhaustion*, *exhaustive*, *exhausting*, and *exhaust*.

Copy these sentences and fill in the blanks with the correct form of the word *exhaust*. Use the suffixes *-ion*, *-ing*, and *-ive* where necessary.

1. It was ___?___ to climb the mountain.
2. The hiker collapsed from ___?___ when he reached the top.
3. They had made an ___?___ study of the trail map.
4. She fell asleep from sheer ___?___.
5. The ___?___ from the car choked us.

Fluency: Definitions

Match the vocabulary words in the left column with their definitions in the right column.

1.	manifestly	a.	energetic activity
2.	descent	b.	expended completely
3.	maneuver	c.	with regard to detail
4.	exhausted	d.	act of climbing up
5.	exertion	e.	act of climbing down
6.	thoroughly	f.	clearly
7.	ascent	g.	series of planned steps

Spelling Strategy

The long *o* sound is occasionally spelled *ough*, as in *thoroughly* and *although*. Correctly complete these senteces with *thoroughly* or *although*.

1. We were ___?___ exhausted by the journey.
2. ___?___ it was still light, we went to bed.

Grammar Lesson

Principal Parts of Regular Verbs

Every verb has four principal parts. A regular verb forms its past and past participle by adding *-d* or *-ed* to the base form. The following chart explains the principal parts of regular verbs.

Principal Part	Description	Examples
Base Form:	basic form	listen, care
Past:	adds *-ed* or *-d*	listened, cared
Present Participle:	adds *-ing*	listening, caring
Past Participle:	adds *-ed* or *-d*	listened, cared

▶ *For more practice, see page R32, Exercise A.*
Practice On your paper, write the principal parts of each verb.

1. look   3. invite   5. subtract
2. trap   4. compel

Writing Application On your paper, write sentences about the story, using each verb in the principal part indicated. Add helping verbs where necessary.

stare (past)
listen (base)
long (present participle)
end (past participle)

 Prentice Hall Writing and Grammar Connection: Chapter 22, Section 1

Writing Lesson

Yukon Description

Write a description of the Yukon Territory based on the details you learned in the story.

Prewriting   Decide on the main impression you want to convey. Think about the kind of words and phrases that could contribute to that impression. Then, write a statement conveying this main impression. The model shows two different main impressions of the Yukon.

Model: Creating a Main Impression

mean and heartless: The brutal force of the Yukon can break a person's neck in a sudden, thundering avalanche.

beautiful but cruel: The crystal mountains of ice and snow can sweep away the life of anyone standing in the way.

Drafting   Begin by stating a main impression in your introduction. Supply specific examples and details that contribute to your main impression. Organize related details about weather, landscape, or size.

Revising   Use a thesaurus to consider alternatives to words you have used more than once. Replace overused words such as *good* and *great*.

*W*G *Prentice Hall Writing and Grammar Connection: Chapter 6, Sections 2, 3, and 4*

Extension Activities

Listening and Speaking With a group, **analyze the effects of language choice and delivery** on listeners.

1. Choose a passage from the story.
2. Take turns reading it aloud. Each reader should try something different with the speed, loudness, or tone of voice.
3. After each reader, discuss how the delivery affected listeners. Discuss also London's word choices and how they influenced the effect of the reading.

Research and Technology Write a **résumé** for Jack London that shows why he is qualified to write an adventure column for a magazine.

1. Use details from his author biography and other sources as details of his experience.
2. Find sample résumés and résumé guidelines online. Use a word-processing program to develop a standard résumé format.
3. Include details about London's life experiences as well as his writing experiences.

 **Take It to the Net**   www.phschool.com

Go online for an additional research activity using the Internet.

Look at the literature of almost any time period, and you will find writers who specialize in adventure stories in which a character struggles to survive in a harsh natural setting. Classic writers like Jack London and contemporary authors like Gary Paulsen and Jean Craighead George are known for their novels and stories that take place outside of civilization, far from cities and towns. These authors show nature in a realistic way: They love nature's beauty, but they also respect nature's power.

How a character reacts to a conflict with nature depends on the character's personality and background and the historical period in which the conflict takes place. The character of Clay in Jack London's "Up the Slide" lives in the late 1800s—before television, air travel, computers, and microwaves. To Clay, going out to collect firewood, hiking from one place to another, and cooking food over a fire are just part of everyday life. In Gary Paulsen's contemporary novel *Hatchet*, Brian, a young man about Clay's age, lives in the late twentieth century. He is used to telephones, automobiles, and air conditioning. Yet, through an accident, Brian finds himself alone in a natural setting, needing to collect firewood, hike from one place to another, and cook his food over a fire. As you read the excerpt from *Hatchet*, compare and contrast the way Brian and Clay confront their conflicts with nature. Think about how the circumstances of their individual time periods affect the way they react.

from Hatchet
Gary Paulsen

What had he read or seen that told him about food in the wilderness? Hadn't there been something? A show, yes, a show on television about air force pilots and some kind of course they took. A survival course. All right, he had the show coming into his thoughts now. The pilots had to live in the desert. They put them in the desert down in Arizona or someplace and they had to live for a week. They had to find food and water for a week.

For water they had made a sheet of plastic into a dew-gathering device and for food they ate lizards.

That was it. Of course Brian had lots of water and there weren't too many lizards in the Canadian woods, that he knew. One of the pilots had used a watch crystal as a magnifying glass to focus the sun and start a fire so they didn't have to eat the lizards raw. But Brian had a digital watch, without a crystal, broken at that. So the show didn't help him much.

Wait, there was one thing. One of the pilots, a woman, had found some kind of beans on a bush and she had used them with her lizard meat to make a little stew in a tin can she had found. Bean lizard stew. There weren't any beans here, but there must be berries. There had to be berry bushes around. Sure, the woods were full of berry bushes. That's what everybody always said. Well, he'd actually never heard anybody *say* it. But he felt that it should be true.

There must be berry bushes.

He stood and moved out into the sand and looked up at the sun. It was still high. He didn't know what time it must be. At home it would be one or two if the sun were that high. At home at one or two his mother would be putting away the lunch dishes and getting ready for her exercise class.

He shook his head. Had to stop that kind of thinking. The sun was still high and that meant that he had some time before darkness to find berries. He didn't want to be away from his—he almost thought of it as home—shelter when it came to be dark.

He didn't want to be anywhere in the woods when it came to be dark. And he didn't want to get lost—which was a real problem. All he knew in the world was the lake in front of him and the hill at his back and the ridge—if he lost sight of them there was a really good chance that he would get turned around and not find his way back.

▼ **Critical Viewing**
What is the danger in eating unidentified berries such as these?
[Speculate]

So he had to look for berry bushes, but keep the lake or the rock ridge in sight at all times.

He looked up the lake shore, to the north. For a good distance, perhaps two hundred yards, it was fairly clear. There were tall pines, the kind with no limbs until very close to the top, with a gentle breeze sighing in them, but not too much low brush. Two hundred yards up there seemed to be a belt of thick, lower brush starting—about ten or twelve feet high—and that formed a wall he could not see through. It seemed to go on around the lake, thick and lushly green, but he could not be sure.

If there were berries they would be in that brush, he felt, and as long as he stayed close to the lake, so he could keep the water on his right and know it was there, he wouldn't get lost. When he was done or found berries, he thought, he would just turn around so the water was on his left and walk back until he came to the ridge and his shelter.

▼ **Critical Viewing**
What difficulties might Brian face in a natural setting such as this one? **[Connect]**

Simple. Keep it simple. I am Brian Robeson. I have been in a plane crash. I am going to find some food. I am going to find berries.

He walked slowly—still a bit pained in his joints and weak from hunger—up along the side of the lake. The trees were full of birds singing ahead of him in the sun. Some he knew, some he didn't. He saw a robin, and some kind of sparrows, and a flock of reddish orange birds with thick beaks. Twenty or thirty of them were sitting in one of the pines. They made much noise and flew away ahead of him when he walked under the tree. He watched them fly, their color a bright slash in solid green, and in this way he found the berries. The birds landed in some taller willow type of undergrowth with wide leaves and started jumping and making noise. At first he was too far away to see what they were doing, but their color drew him and he moved toward them, keeping the lake in sight on his right, and when he got closer he saw they were eating berries.

He could not believe it was that easy. It was as if the birds had taken him right to the berries. The slender branches went up about twenty feet and were heavy, drooping with clusters of bright red berries. They were half as big as grapes but hung in bunches much like grapes and when Brian saw them, glistening red in the sunlight, he almost yelled.

His pace quickened and he was in them in moments, scattering the birds, grabbing branches, stripping them to fill his mouth with berries.

Gary Paulsen

(b. 1939)

Painfully shy as a child, Gary Paulsen ran away and joined a traveling carnival at the age of fourteen. He has since worked as a teacher, an electronics field engineer, an army sergeant, an actor, a farmer, a truck driver, a singer, and a sailor. However, as he says, writing remains his passion: "I write because it's all I can do. Every time I've tried to do something else, I cannot." Paulsen's love of reading began one cold day when he went into the library to get warm. To his surprise, the librarian handed him a library card. "When she handed me the card, she handed me the world," Paulsen says.

Paulsen has written more than 175 books and has won three Newbery Honor Awards—for his books *Hatchet, Dogsong,* and *The Winter Room.*

Connecting Literature Past and Present

1. Where does Brian get his knowledge of the wilderness?
2. Brian and Clay each study the place they are going to travel through before beginning their journeys. What does each character notice? What do the details that each one notices tell him?
3. What is each character thinking about as he makes his journey?
4. How confident is each character that he will survive his conflict with nature?
5. What is each character's greatest concern, worry, or fear during his conflict with nature?
6. How does the time period in which each character lives affect the way he deals with his conflict with nature?

Prepare to Read

Thank You, M'am

Empire State, Tom Christopher, Vicki Morgan Associates

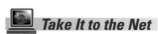 **Take It to the Net**

Visit www.phschool.com for interactive activities and instruction related to "Thank You, M'am," including
- background
- graphic organizers
- literary elements
- reading strategies

Preview

Connecting to the Literature

In "Thank You, M'am," a boy learns an important lesson about kindness and trust from a surprising source. Before reading, think about an unexpected act of kindness you have done for someone or someone has done for you.

Background

"Thank You, M'am," by Langston Hughes, is set in Harlem, a community in New York. Like many urban areas, Harlem experienced rapid population growth early in the twentieth century. Many single-family buildings were converted into small apartments. The character Mrs. Jones lives in one of these "kitchenette" apartments—a bathroom and one large room with a mini-kitchen in the corner of the room.

Literary Analysis

Implied Theme

The **theme** of a literary work is the major idea or underlying message that it communicates.

- A **stated theme** is directly expressed by the narrator or a character.
- An **implied theme** is suggested by story events as well as the characters' actions and reactions.

"Thank You, M'am" has an implied theme about the effects of kindness and trust. Themes of kindness and trust appear in literature of all time periods. As you read "Thank You, M'am," identify what message this contemporary short story communicates.

Connecting Literary Elements

The theme or message that is suggested by characters' actions often depends on a **character's motives**—the reasons for his or her actions. In this story, a boy snatches a purse because he wants money to buy shoes. By the end of the story, he discovers he wants something much more valuable. When his motives change, so do his actions. Use these focus questions to help you recognize characters' motives in "Thank You, M'am":

1. How do Roger's actions change during the story?
2. Why do they change?

Reading Strategy

Responding to Characters' Actions

Reading a story is more enjoyable if you become involved with the people in it. One way to do this is to **respond to the characters' actions.** Ask yourself,

- "Would I do that?"
- "Do I think the character should do that?"
- "How would I feel if that happened to me?"

As you read the story, record your responses to the characters' actions in a chart like the one shown.

Story Event
Purse snatching

My Response	
1	I wouldn't do that.
2	He shouldn't do that
3	If I were Mrs. Jones, I would be furious.

Vocabulary Development

presentable (prē zent′ ə bəl) *adj.* in proper order for being seen, met, etc., by others (p. 174)

mistrusted (mis′ trust′ əd) *v.* doubted (p. 175)

latching (lach′ iŋ) *v.* grasping or attaching oneself to (p. 176)

barren (bar′ ən) *adj.* sterile; empty (p. 176)

Empire State, Tom Christopher, Vicki Morgan Associates

Thank You, M'am

Langston Hughes

She was a large woman with a large purse that had everything in it but hammer and nails. It had a long strap and she carried it slung across her shoulder. It was about eleven o'clock at night, and she was walking alone, when a boy ran up behind her and tried to snatch her purse. The strap broke with the single tug the boy gave it from behind. But the boy's weight, and the weight of the purse combined caused him to lose his balance. Instead of taking off full blast as he had hoped, the boy fell on his back on the sidewalk, and his legs flew up. The large woman simply turned around and kicked him right square in his blue-jeaned sitter. Then she reached down, picked the boy up by his shirt front, and shook him until his teeth rattled.

After that the woman said, "Pick up my pocketbook, boy, and give it here."

She still held him. But she bent down enough to permit him to stoop and pick up her purse. Then she said, "Now ain't you ashamed of yourself?"

Firmly gripped by his shirt front, the boy said, "Yes'm."

The woman said, "What did you want to do it for?"

The boy said, "I didn't aim to."

She said, "You a lie!"

By that time two or three people passed, stopped, turned to look, and some stood watching.

"If I turn you loose, will you run?" asked the woman.

"Yes'm," said the boy.

"Then I won't turn you loose," said the woman. She did not release him.

"Lady, I'm sorry," whispered the boy.

"Um-hum! Your face is dirty. I got a great mind to wash your face for you. Ain't you got nobody home to tell you to wash your face?"

"No'm," said the boy.

"Then it will get washed this evening," said the large woman starting up the street, dragging the frightened boy behind her.

He looked as if he were fourteen or fifteen, frail and willow-wild, in tennis shoes and blue jeans.

The woman said, "You ought to be my son. I would teach you right from wrong. Least I can do right now is to wash your face. Are you hungry?"

"No'm," said the being-dragged boy. "I just want you to turn me loose."

"Was I bothering you when I turned that corner?" asked the woman.

"No'm."

"But you put yourself in contact with me," said the woman. "If you think that that contact is not going to last awhile, you got another thought coming. When I get through with you, sir, you are going to remember Mrs. Luella Bates Washington Jones."

Sweat popped out on the boy's face and he began to struggle. Mrs. Jones stopped, jerked him around in front of her, put a half nelson[1] about his neck, and continued to drag him up the street. When she got to her door, she dragged the boy inside, down a hall, and into a large kitchenette-furnished room at the rear of the house. She switched on the light and left the door open. The boy could hear other roomers laughing and talking in the large house. Some of their

---

1. **half nelson** wrestling hold using one arm.

◀ **Critical Viewing**
In what ways does the picture at left show that it would be easy to "disappear" in the scene? **[Analyze]**

Literary Analysis
Theme How does this dialogue point to the author's message?

Reading Check

How do Roger and Mrs. Jones meet?

doors were open, too, so he knew he and the woman were not alone. The woman still had him by the neck in the middle of her room.

She said, "What is your name?"

"Roger," answered the boy.

"Then, Roger, you go to that sink and wash your face," said the woman, whereupon she turned him loose—at last. Roger looked at the door—looked at the woman—looked at the door—and went to the sink.

"Let the water run until it gets warm," she said. "Here's a clean towel."

"You gonna take me to jail?" asked the boy, bending over the sink.

"Not with that face, I would not take you nowhere," said the woman. "Here I am trying to get home to cook me a bite to eat and you snatch my pocketbook! Maybe you ain't been to your supper either, late as it be. Have you?"

"There's nobody home at my house," said the boy.

"Then we'll eat," said the woman. "I believe you're hungry—or been hungry—to try to snatch my pocketbook."

"I wanted a pair of blue suede shoes," said the boy.

"Well, you didn't have to snatch my pocketbook to get some suede shoes," said Mrs. Luella Bates Washington Jones. "You could of asked me."

"M'am?"

The water dripping from his face, the boy looked at her. There was a long pause. A very long pause. After he had dried his face and not knowing what else to do dried it again, the boy turned around, wondering what next. The door was open. He could make a dash for it down the hall. He could run, run, run, run, run!

The woman was sitting on the day bed. After awhile she said, "I were young once and I wanted things I could not get."

There was another long pause. The boy's mouth opened. Then he frowned, but not knowing he frowned.

The woman said, "Um-hum! You thought I was going to say *but,* didn't you? You thought I was going to say, *but I didn't snatch people's pocketbooks.* Well, I wasn't going to say that." Pause. Silence. "I have done things, too, which I would not tell you, son—neither tell God, if He didn't already know. So you set down while I fix us something to eat. You might run that comb through your hair so you will look <u>presentable</u>."

In another corner of the room behind a screen was a gas plate and an icebox. Mrs. Jones got up and went behind the screen. The woman did not watch the boy to see if he was going to run now, nor did she watch her purse which she left behind her on the day bed. But the boy took care to sit on the far side of the room where he thought she could easily see him out of the corner of her eye, if she wanted to. He did not trust the woman not to

Literary Analysis
Theme and Characters' Motives What does this speech tell you about Mrs. Jones's reasons for helping Roger?

presentable (prē zent′ ə bəl) *adj.* in proper order for being seen, met, etc., by others

Minnie, 1930, William Johnson, National Museum of American Art, Washington, DC

▲ **Critical Viewing** Does the woman in the painting resemble Mrs. Jones as described in the story? Explain. **[Make a Judgment]**

trust him. And he did not want to be <u>mistrusted</u> now.

"Do you need somebody to go to the store," asked the boy, "maybe to get some milk or something?"

"Don't believe I do," said the woman, "unless you just want sweet milk yourself. I was going to make cocoa out of this canned milk I got here."

"That will be fine," said the boy.

mistrusted (mis′ trust′ əd)
v. doubted

☑**Reading Check**

What does the woman do with Roger?

Thank You, M'am ◆ 175

She heated some lima beans and ham she had in the icebox, made the cocoa, and set the table. The woman did not ask the boy anything about where he lived, or his folks, or anything else that would embarrass him. Instead, as they ate, she told him about her job in a hotel beauty shop that stayed open late, what the work was like, and how all kinds of women came in and out, blondes, redheads, and brunettes. Then she cut him a half of her ten-cent cake.

"Eat some more, son," she said.

When they were finished eating she got up and said, "Now, here, take this ten dollars and buy yourself some blue suede shoes. And next time, do not make the mistake of <u>latching</u> onto *my* pocketbook *nor nobody else's*—because shoes come by devilish like that will burn your feet. I got to get my rest now. But from here on in, son, I hope you will behave yourself."

She led him down the hall to the front door and opened it. "Goodnight! Behave yourself, boy!" she said, looking out into the street.

The boy wanted to say something other than, "Thank you, m'am," to Mrs. Luella Bates Washington Jones, but although his lips moved, he couldn't even say that as he turned at the foot of the <u>barren</u> stoop and looked up at the large woman in the door. Then she shut the door.

latching (lach´ iŋ) *v.* grasping or attaching oneself to

barren (bar´ ən) *adj.* sterile; empty

Langston Hughes

(1902–1967)

Born in Joplin, Missouri, Langston Hughes moved often as a young boy. He turned to writing as a way of dealing with his ever-changing home address and with the difficulties of being a young African American in the early 1900s. People first noticed Hughes in 1921 when his poem "The Negro Speaks of Rivers" was published shortly after he graduated from high school. He soon won other prizes and opportunities, including a college scholarship. His first book of poetry, *The Weary Blues*, was published in 1926. Hughes wrote fiction, plays, and essays; translated other poets; and collected African American folklore.

Review and Assess

Thinking about the Selection

1. **Respond:** Do you think Mrs. Jones is wise or foolish to trust Roger? Why?

2. **(a) Recall:** What does Mrs. Jones do when Roger tries to steal her purse? **(b) Interpret:** What can you tell about her character from this action? **(c) Connect:** How are her actions connected to her past experiences?

3. **(a) Recall:** What does Roger do when Mrs. Jones leaves him alone with her purse? **(b) Infer:** Why does he do this? **(c) Compare and Contrast:** How have Roger's behavior and attitude changed?

4. **(a) Recall:** What do Mrs. Jones and Roger talk about during their meal? **(b) Draw Conclusions:** Why doesn't Mrs. Jones ask Roger any personal questions?

5. **(a) Recall:** What does Roger say when he leaves the apartment? **(b) Infer:** What more does he wants to say? **(c) Interpret:** Why can't he say more?

6. **(a) Predict:** What effect will Mrs. Jones's actions have on Roger's future? **(b) Make a Judgment:** Does Mrs. Jones make good choices about how to treat Roger?

Review and Assess

Literary Analysis

Implied Theme

1. What **theme** about kindness and trust is communicated in the story?
2. Why do you think the theme is implied rather than stated?
3. In a chart like the one shown, give three examples of clues that reveal the story's theme.

Type of Clue	Example from Story
Words	
Character's actions	
Ideas	

4. How does the title "Thank you, M'am" relate to the theme?

Connecting Literary Elements

5. What is Roger's motivation for stealing the purse? On your paper, fill in a diagram to show this cause-and-effect relationship.

Motive ··············▶ Action

_____ ··············▶ _____

6. How do Roger's motives and actions change during the story?

Reading Strategy

Responding to Characters' Actions

7. How did you respond when Mrs. Jones physically dragged Roger to the apartment?
8. Were you surprised by any of Mrs. Jones's actions? Why or why not?
9. Describe your responses to both characters at the end of the story.

Extend Understanding

10. **Social Studies Connection:** Compare Mrs. Jones's treatment of Roger to the punishment for stealing in the American West in the 1800s.
11. **Take a Position:** What do you think is the most effective treatment for criminals? Explain.

Quick Review

The **implied theme** of a literary work is the message suggested by the work. A **stated theme** is directly expressed by the narrator or a character. To review theme, see page 171.

The **motives** of characters are their reasons for taking certain actions. To review characters' motivations, see page 171.

Responding to the characters' actions helps you understand the characters and get involved in the story.

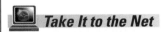 **Take It to the Net**
www.phschool.com
Take the interactive self-test online to check your understanding of the selection.

Integrate Language Skills

Vocabulary Development Lesson

Word Analysis: Latin Suffix -able

You can add the Latin suffix -able to some verbs to form adjectives that show an ability or quality. For example: wash + -able = washable.

Add -able to the verbs *disagree* and *present*. Use one of the new words in each sentence.

1. "You might run that comb through your hair so you will look ____?____."
2. The first encounter between Roger and Mrs. Jones was ____?____.

Spelling Strategy

When you add the prefix *mis-* to a word, do not change the original spelling: *mis-* + *spell* = *misspell*.

Add *mis-* to the following words.

1. take   2. trust   3. step

Concept Development: Synonyms

Synonyms are words with the same or similar meanings, such as *big* and *large*. Sometimes a synonym is a phrase, not a single word. On your paper, rewrite these sentences substituting a vocabulary word as a synonym for the word or phrase in italics.

1. There was little furniture in the cold, *empty* apartment.
2. Roger *was suspicious of* kindness from adults.
3. After putting on a clean sweater, she felt *neat* enough to meet her new neighbors.
4. My little sister was always *clinging* onto us when we wanted to go to the mall.

Grammar Lesson

Principal Parts of Verbs

Every verb has four **principal parts**: the base form (present tense), past tense, present participle, and past participle. Regular verbs form the past and past participle by adding -ed or -d to the base, but **irregular verbs** follow different patterns. You need to memorize them.

Here are some common irregular verbs and their irregular principal parts:

Base (Present)	Past	Participle
eat	ate	eaten
have	had	had
sing	sang	sung
drink	drank	drunk
grow	grew	grown

▶ For more practice, see page R32, Exercise A.
Practice On your paper, replace each verb in parentheses with the form of that verb that is correct in the sentence. Use the past participle after a helping verb such as *had* or *have*.

1. When Roger grabbed her purse, the strap (break).
2. He had (steal) the purse to get money.
3. With the money, Roger (buy) a pair of blue suede shoes.
4. Mrs. Jones (speak) to him calmly.

Writing Application Go through some of your previous writing. Circle any incorrect use of the past tense and past participles of irregular verbs and then write the verb correctly.

W͟G͟ Prentice Hall Writing and Grammar Connection: Chapter 22, Section 1

Writing Lesson

Letter of Guidance

Imagine that you are Roger twenty years later. Write a short letter to a young relative who needs guidance. Explain how meeting Mrs. Jones changed your life.

Prewriting   Picture what Roger is like and what he has done with his life in the past twenty years. Then, brainstorm as many points of advice as you can think of. Circle three or four that seem the most important, and build your letter around them.

Drafting   To support your ideas, use quotations from the story, opinions from experts, or an **analogy**—a specific likeness between things that are quite different.

Model: Support Ideas

The feeling that Mrs. Jones was giving me a chance to be trustworthy was both exciting and scary—*like getting ready to jump off a diving board.* I was jumping into a new kind of life.

> The words in italics show an analogy, one way of supporting ideas.

Revising   Reread your letter, underlining any analogies, opinions, and quotations you have used. Add them if they are missing.

Prentice Hall Writing and Grammar Connection: Chapter 7, Sections 3 and 4

Extension Activities

Listening and Speaking Prepare a **speech outline** for a talk in which you persuade your audience that Mrs. Jones did—or did not—do the right thing in dealing with Roger. In your outline, include the following:

- an introduction in which you state your position
- several reasons for your position
- a conclusion in which you leave your listeners with a memorable idea or quotation

Then, deliver a **speech** following the outline. Ask for feedback from your audience to determine whether you have convinced them of your position.

Research and Technology Write the copy for a **book jacket** for a new collection of poems and stories by Langston Hughes. Research the Harlem Renaissance and Hughes's role in it, as well as his influence on later writers. Use this information to write three paragraphs that point out the importance of Hughes's career and make readers want to buy the book. Include quotations.

 **Take It to the Net**   www.phschool.com

Go online for an additional research activity using the Internet.

Prepare to Read

Flowers for Algernon

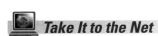 **Take It to the Net**

Visit www.phschool.com for interactive activities and instruction related to "Flowers for Algernon," including

- background
- graphic organizers
- literary elements
- reading strategies

Preview

Connecting to the Literature

Charlie Gordon, the main character in "Flowers for Algernon," takes a huge risk because he wants to "be like everyone else." Make a connection between his decision and situations you have observed in which people misjudged or made fun of someone whom they saw as "different."

Background

The scientists in "Flowers for Algernon" focus on the main character's "IQ," which is short for *intelligence quotient*. Although one's IQ has traditionally been the most common measure of "intelligence," contemporary researchers have come to recognize that one test cannot accurately measure the wide range of abilities and learning potential that people have.

Literary Analysis

First-Person Point of View

Point of view is the perspective from which a story is told. In a story told from the **first-person point of view,** the narrator participates in the action and events are seen from the narrator's perspective. "Flowers for Algernon" is told in the first person. As you read, notice that the details of the story are seen through Charlie's eyes.

Connecting Literary Elements

As the story develops, Charlie changes in the way he writes, thinks, and reacts to other people. He is a **dynamic character,** a character that grows and changes. Characters that do not change are **static characters.**

Use these focus questions to help you identify why Charlie is a dynamic character:

1. How do Charlie's relationships with other people change before and after the operation?
2. How does Charlie's view of himself change?

Reading Strategy

Using Context to Verify Meaning

When you encounter an unfamiliar word, use the **context** (the surrounding words and sentences) to help you verify or determine the word's meaning. You may find clues such as restatements, comparisons, contrasts, definitions, and examples. The graphic organizer shows how context can be used to determine the meaning of the word *ignorance* in the example below.

> Before they laughed at me and despised me for my ignorance and dullness; now they hate me for my knowledge and understanding.

Use context clues as you read "Flowers for Algernon."

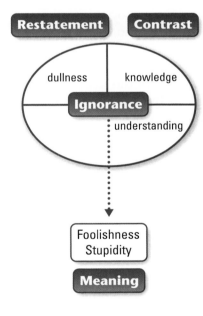

Vocabulary Development

psychology (sī käl′ ə jē) *n.* science dealing with the mind and with mental and emotional processes (p. 194)

tangible (tan′ jə bəl) *adj.* that which can be understood; definite; objective (p. 199)

specter (spek′ tər) *n.* a ghost; frightening image (p. 199)

refute (ri fyo͞ot′) *v.* give evidence to prove (an argument or statement) false (p. 200)

illiteracy (il lit′ ər ə sē) *n.* inability to read or write (p. 202)

obscure (əb skyoor′) *v.* conceal or hide (p. 204)

syndromes (sin′ drōmz′) *n.* a number of symptoms occurring together and characterizing a specific disease or condition (p. 204)

introspective (in′ trō spekt′ iv) *adj.* inward looking; thoughtful (p. 205)

Flowers for
ALGERNON

Daniel Keyes

progris riport 1—march 5 1965

Dr. Strauss says I shud rite down what I think and evrey thing that happins to me from now on. I dont know why but he says its importint so they will see if they will use me. I hope they use me. Miss Kinnian says maybe they can make me smart. I want to be smart. My name is Charlie Gordon. I am 37 years old and 2 weeks ago was my brithday. I have nuthing more to rite now so I will close for today.

progris riport 2—march 6

I had a test today. I think I faled it. and I think that maybe now they wont use me. What happind is a nice young man was in the room and he had some white cards with ink spillled all over them. He sed Charlie what do you see on this card. I was very skared even tho I had my rabits foot in my pockit because when I was a kid I always faled tests in school and I spillled ink to.

I told him I saw a inkblot. He said yes and it made me feel good. I thot that was all but when I got up to go he stopped me. He said now sit down Charlie we are not thru yet. Then I dont remember so good but he wantid me to say what was in the ink. I dint see nuthing in the ink but he said there was picturs there other pepul saw some picturs. I coudnt see any picturs. I reely tryed to see. I held the card close up and then far away. Then I said if I had my

glases I coud see better I usally only ware my glases in the movies or TV but I said they are in the closit in the hall. I got them. Then I said let me see that card agen I bet Ill find it now.

I tryed hard but I still coudnt find the picturs I only saw the ink. I told him maybe I need new glases. He rote somthing down on a paper and I got skared of faling the test. I told him it was a very nice inkblot with littel points all around the eges. He looked very sad so that wasnt it. I said please let me try agen. Ill get it in a few minits becaus Im not so fast somtimes. Im a slow reeder too in Miss Kinnians class for slow adults but I'm trying very hard.

He gave me a chance with another card that had 2 kinds of ink spilled on it red and blue.

He was very nice and talked slow like Miss Kinnian does and he explained it to me that it was a *raw shok*.[1] He said pepul see things in the ink. I said show me where. He said think. I told him I think a inkblot but that wasnt rite eather. He said what does it remind you—pretend somthing. I closd my eyes for a long time to pretend. I told him I pretned a fowntan pen with ink leeking all over a table cloth. Then he got up and went out.

I dont think I passd the *raw shok* test.

progris report 3— martch 7

Dr Strauss and Dr Nemur say it dont matter about the inkblots. I told them I dint spill the ink on the cards and I coudnt see anything in the ink. They said that maybe they will still use me. I said Miss Kinnian never gave me tests like that one only spelling and reading. They said Miss Kinnian told that I was her bestist pupil in the adult nite scool becaus I tryed the hardist and I reely wantid to lern. They said how come you went to the adult nite scool all by yourself Charlie. How did you find it. I said I askd pepul and sumbody told me where I shud go to lern to read and spell good. They said why

Literary Analysis
First-Person Point of View
What elements in this paragraph indicate that this story is told from the first-person point of view?

☑ **Reading Check**
Who is Charlie?

---

1. **raw shok** misspelling of Rorschach (rôr´ shäk) test, a psychological test involving inkblots that the subject describes.

did you want to. I told them becaus all my life I wantid to be smart and not dumb. But its very hard to be smart. They said you know it will probly be tempirery. I said yes. Miss Kinnian told me. I dont care if it herts.

Later I had more crazy tests today. The nice lady who gave it me told me the name and I asked her how do you spellit so I can rite it in my progris riport. THEMATIC APPERCEPTION TEST.[2] I dont know the frist 2 words but I know what *test* means. You got to pass it or you get bad marks. This test lookd easy becaus I coud see the picturs. Only this time she dint want me to tell her the picturs. That mixd me up. I said the man yesterday said I shoud tell him what I saw in the ink she said that dont make no difrence. She said make up storys about the pepul in the picturs.

I told her how can you tell storys about pepul you never met. I said why shud I make up lies. I never tell lies any more becaus I always get caut.

She told me this test and the other one the raw-shok♦ was for getting personalty. I laffed so hard. I said how can you get that thing from inkblots and fotos. She got sore and put her picturs away. I dont care. It was sily. I gess I faled that test too.

Later some men in white coats took me to a difernt part of the hospitil and gave me a game to play. It was like a race with a white mouse. They called the mouse Algernon. Algernon was in a box with a lot of twists and turns like all kinds of walls and they gave me a pencil and a paper with lines and lots of boxes. On one side it said START and on the other end it said FINISH. They said it was *amazed*[3] and that Algernon and me had the same *amazed* to do. I dint see how we could have the same *amazed* if Algernon had a box and I had a paper but I dint say nothing. Anyway there wasnt time because the race started.

One of the men had a watch he was trying to hide so I woudnt see it so I tryed not to look and that made me nervus.

Anyway that test made me feel worser than all the others because they did it over 10 times with difernt *amazeds* and Algernon won every time. I dint know that mice were so smart. Maybe thats because Algernon is a white mouse. Maybe white mice are smarter than other mice.

2. THEMATIC (thē mat´ ik) **APPERCEPTION** (ap´ ər sep´ shən) **TEST** personality test in which the subject makes up stories about a series of pictures.
3. amazed Charlie means a maze, or confusing series of paths. Often, the intelligence of animals is assessed by how fast they go through a maze.

Literature in context Science Connection

♦ *Intelligence and Psychological Testing*

At the time this story was written, the usual measure of intelligence was the IQ, or "intelligence quotient." A Stanford University psychologist, Lewis Terman, established the standard IQ test in about 1916, based on earlier work by psychologists in France. While IQ tests are still given, people have recognized that there are many kinds of intelligence and that one test cannot accurately measure all of them.

A Rorschach test does not measure intelligence. The subject identifies what an inkblot looks like. Psychologists make interpretations about personality and mental condition. Charlie is unable to understand that there is no right or wrong answer to the question about what he sees in the inkblot.

A Rorschach inkblot

progris riport 4—Mar 8

Their going to use me! Im so exited I can hardly write. Dr Nemur and Dr Strauss had a argument about it first. Dr Nemur was in the office when Dr Strauss brot me in. Dr Nemur was worryed about using me but Dr Strauss told him Miss Kinnian rekemmended me the best from all the pepul who she was teaching. I like Miss Kinnian becaus shes a very smart teacher. And she said Charlie your going to have a second chance. If you volenteer for this experament you mite get smart. They dont know if it will be perminint but theirs a chance. Thats why I said ok even when I was scared because she said it was an operashun. She said dont be scared Charlie you done so much with so little I think you deserv it most of all.

So I got scaird when Dr Nemur and Dr Strauss argud about it. Dr Strauss said I had something that was very good. He said I had a good *motor-vation.*[4] I never even knew I had that. I felt proud when he said that not every body with an *eye-q*[5] of 68 had that thing. I dont know what it is or where I got it but he said Algernon had it too. Algernons *motor-vation* is the cheese they put in his box. But it cant be that because I didnt eat any cheese this week.

Then he told Dr Nemur something I dint understand so while they were talking I wrote down some of the words.

He said Dr Nemur I know Charlie is not what you had in mind as the first of your new brede of intelek** (coudnt get the word) superman. But most people of his low ment** are host** and uncoop** they are usualy dull apath** and hard to reach. He has a good natcher hes intristed and eager to please.

Dr Nemur said remember he will be the first human beeng ever to have his intelijence trippled by surgicle meens.

Dr Strauss said exakly. Look at how well hes lerned to read and write for his low mentel age its as grate an acheve** as you and I lerning einstines therey of **vity without help. That shows the intenss motorvation. Its comparat** a tremen** achev** I say we use Charlie.

I dint get all the words and they were talking to fast but it sounded like Dr Strauss was on my side and like the other one wasnt.

Then Dr Nemur nodded he said all right maybe your right. We will use Charlie. When he said that I got so exited I jumped up and shook his hand for being so good to me. I told him thank you doc you wont be sorry for giving me a second chance. And I mean it like I told him. After the operashun Im gonna try to be smart. Im gonna try awful hard.

---

4. **motor-vation** motivation, or desire to work hard and achieve a goal.
5. **eye-q** IQ, or intelligence quotient. A way of measuring human intelligence.

Literary Analysis
First-Person Point of View How does Charlie's reaction to being chosen for the operation show his motivation?

Reading Strategy
Using Context
What context clues help you know what the partial words *intelek, ment-, host-, uncoop-,* and *apath-* mean?

**Reading Check**

What will happen to Charlie's intellect after the operation?

progris ript 5—Mar 10

Im skared. Lots of people who work here and the nurses and the people who gave me the tests came to bring me candy and wish me luck. I hope I have luck. I got my rabits foot and my lucky penny and my horse shoe. Only a black cat crossed me when I was comming to the hospitil. Dr Strauss says dont be supersitis Charlie this is sience. Anyway Im keeping my rabits foot with me.

I asked Dr Strauss if Ill beat Algernon in the race after the operashun and he said maybe. If the operashun works Ill show that mouse I can be as smart as he is. Maybe smarter. Then Ill be abel to read better and spell the words good and know lots of things and be like other people. I want to be smart like other people. If it works per-minint they will make everybody smart all over the wurld.

They dint give me anything to eat this morning. I dont know what that eating has to do with getting smart. Im very hungry and Dr Nemur took away my box of candy. That Dr Nemur is a grouch. Dr Strauss says I can have it back after the operashun. You cant eat befor a operashun . . .

Progress Report 6—Mar 15

The operashun dint hurt. He did it while I was sleeping. They took off the bandijis from my eyes and my head today so I can make a PROGRESS REPORT. Dr Nemur who looked at some of my other ones says I spell PROGRESS wrong and he told me how to spell it and REPORT too. I got to try and remember that.

I have a very bad memary for spelling. Dr Strauss says its ok to tell about all the things that happin to me but he says I shoud tell more about what I feel and what I think. When I told him I dont know how to think he said try. All the time when the bandijis were on my eyes I tryed to think. Nothing happened. I dont know what to think about. Maybe if I ask him he will tell me how I can think now that Im suppose to get smart. What do smart people think about. Fancy things I suppose. I wish I knew some fancy things alredy.

Progress Report 7—Mar 19

Nothing is happining. I had lots of tests and different kinds of races with Algernon. I hate that mouse. He always beats me. Dr Strauss said I got to play those games. And he said some time I got to take those tests over again. Thse inkblots are stupid. And those pictures are stupid too. I like to draw a picture of a man and a woman but I wont make up lies about people.

I got a headache from trying to think so much. I thot Dr Strauss was my frend but he dont help me. He dont tell me what to think or when Ill get smart. Miss Kinnian dint come to see me. I think writing these progress reports are stupid too.

Reading Strategy
Using Context
What context clues help you know what Charlie means by the word *bandijis?*

▲ **Critical Viewing** In what ways are Charlie and Algernon alike?
[Compare and Contrast]

Progress Report 8—Mar 23

Im going back to work at the factery. They said it was better I shud
go back to work but I cant tell anyone what the operashun was for
and I have to come to the hospitil for an hour evry night after work.
They are gonna pay me mony every month for lerning to be smart.

Im glad Im going back to work because I miss my job and all my
frends and all the fun we have there.

Dr Strauss says I shud keep writing things down but I dont
have to do it every day just when I think of something or something speshul happins. He says dont get discoridged because
it takes time and it happins slow. He says it took a long time
with Algernon before he got 3 times smarter then he was before.
Thats why Algernon beats me all the time because he had that

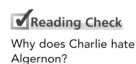

Reading Check

Why does Charlie hate
Algernon?

Flowers for Algernon ◆ 187

operashun too. That makes me feel better. I coud probly do that *amazed* faster than a reglar mouse. Maybe some day Ill beat Algernon. Boy that would be something. So far Algernon looks like he mite be smart perminent.

Mar 25   (I dont have to write PROGRESS REPORT on top any more just when I hand it in once a week for Dr Nemur to read. I just have to put the date on. That saves time)

We had a lot of fun at the factery today. Joe Carp said hey look where Charlie had his operashun what did they do Charlie put some brains in. I was going to tell him but I remembered Dr Strauss said no. Then Frank Reilly said what did you do Charlie forget your key and open your door the hard way. That made me laff. Their really my friends and they like me.

Sometimes somebody will say hey look at Joe or Frank or George he really pulled a Charlie Gordon. I dont know why they say that but they always laff. This morning Amos Borg who is the 4 man at Donnegans used my name when he shouted at Ernie the office boy. Ernie lost a packige. He said Ernie what are you trying to be a Charlie Gordon. I dont understand why he said that. I never lost any packiges.

Reading Strategy
Using Context
What is the *amazed* Charlie talks about? How do you know?

▼ **Critical Viewing**
Compare and contrast your vision of Charlie as described in the story with this photograph showing the actor's portrayal of the character. **[Compare and Contrast]**

Mar 28   Dr Straus came to my room tonight to see why I dint come in like I was suppose to. I told him I dont like to race with Algernon any more. He said I dont have to for a while but I shud come in. He had a present for me only it wasnt a present but just for lend. I thot it was a little television but it wasnt. He said I got to turn it on when I go to sleep. I said your kidding why shud I turn it on when Im going to sleep. Who ever herd of a thing like that. But he said if I want to get smart I got to do what he says. I told him I dint think I was going to get smart and he put his hand on my sholder and said Charlie you dont know it yet but your getting smarter all the time. You wont notice for a while. I think he was just being nice to make me feel good because I dont look any smarter.

Oh yes I almost forgot. I asked him when I can go back to the class at Miss Kinnians school. He said I wont go their. He said that soon Miss Kinnian will come to the hospitil to start and teach me speshul. I was mad at her for not comming to see me when I got the operashun but I like her so maybe we will be frends again.

Mar 29   That crazy TV kept me up all night. How can I sleep with something yelling crazy things all night in my ears. And the nutty pictures. Wow. I dont know what it says when Im up so how am I going to know when Im sleeping.

Dr Strauss says its ok. He says my brains are lerning when I sleep and that will help me when Miss Kinnian starts my lessons in the hospitl only I found out it isnt a hospitil its a labatory. I think its all crazy. If you can get smart when your sleeping why do people go to school. That thing I dont think will work. I use to watch the late show and the late late show on TV all the time and it never made me smart. Maybe you have to sleep while you watch it.

PROGRESS REPORT 9—April 3

Dr Strauss showed me how to keep the TV turned low so now I can sleep. I don't hear a thing. And I still dont understand what it says. A few times I play it over in the morning to find out what I lerned when I was sleeping and I dont think so. Miss Kinnian says Maybe its another langwidge or something. But most times it sounds american. It talks so fast faster then even Miss Gold who was my teacher in 6 grade and I remember she talked so fast I coudnt understand her.

I told Dr Strauss what good is it to get smart in my sleep. I want to be smart when Im awake. He says its the same thing and I have two minds. Theres the *subconscious* and the *conscious* (thats how you spell it). And one dont tell the other one what its doing. They dont even talk to each other. Thats why I dream. And boy have I

Literary Analysis
Point of View and Dynamic Character What changes can you see in Charlie so far?

Reading Strategy
Using Context
Based on what Charlie says, what do the words *subconscious* and *conscious* mean?

✔**Reading Check**

What do Charlie's friends mean when they say someone "pulled a Charlie Gordon"?

been having crazy dreams. Wow. Ever since that night TV. The late late late late late show.

I forgot to ask him if it was only me or if everybody had those two minds.

(I just looked up the word in the dictionary Dr Strauss gave me. The word is *subconscious*. adj. *Of the nature of mental operations yet not present in consciousness; as, subconscious conflict of desires*.) There's more but I still dont know what it means. This isnt a very good dictionary for dumb people like me.

Anyway the headache is from the party. My frends from the factery Joe Carp and Frank Reilly invited me to go with them to Muggsys Saloon for some drinks. I dont like to drink but they said we will have lots of fun. I had a good time.

Joe Carp said I shoud show the girls how I mop out the toilet in the factory and he got me a mop. I showed them and everyone laffed when I told that Mr Donnegan said I was the best janiter he ever had because I like my job and do it good and never come late or miss a day except for my operashun.

I said Miss Kinnian always said Charlie be proud of your job because you do it good.

Everybody laffed and we had a good time and they gave me lots of drinks and Joe said Charlie is a card when hes potted. I dont know what that means but everybody likes me and we have fun. I cant wait to be smart like my best frends Joe Carp and Frank Reilly.

I dont remember how the party was over but I think I went out to buy a newspaper and coffe for Joe and Frank and when I came back there was no one their. I looked for them all over till late. Then I dont remember so good but I think I got sleepy or sick. A nice cop brot me back home. Thats what my landlady Mrs Flynn says.

But I got a headache and a big lump on my head and black and blue all over. I think maybe I fell. Anyway I got a bad headache and Im sick and hurt all over. I dont think Ill drink anymore.

April 6 I beat Algernon! I dint even know I beat him until Burt the tester told me. Then the second time I lost because I got so exited I fell off the chair before I finished. But after that I beat him 8 more times. I must be getting smart to beat a smart mouse like Algernon. But I dont *feel* smarter.

I wanted to race Algernon some more but Burt said thats enough for one day. They let me hold him for a minit. Hes not so bad. Hes soft like a ball of cotton. He blinks and when he opens his eyes their black and pink on the eges.

I said can I feed him because I felt bad to beat him and I wanted to be nice and make frends. Burt said no Algernon is a very specshul mouse with an operashun like mine, and he was the first of all the animals to stay smart so long. He told me Algernon is so smart that every day he has to solve a test to get his food. Its a

Literary Analysis
First-Person Point of View
What do you learn about Charlie in this paragraph that you would not know if it were in third person?

thing like a lock on a door that changes every time Algernon goes in to eat so he has to lern something new to get his food. That made me sad because if he coudnt lern he woud be hungry.

I dont think its right to make you pass a test to eat. How woud Dr Nemur like it to have to pass a test every time he wants to eat. I think Ill be frends with Algernon.

April 9   Tonight after work Miss Kinnian was at the laboratory. She looked like she was glad to see me but scared. I told her dont worry Miss Kinnian Im not smart yet and she laffed. She said I have confidence in you Charlie the way you struggled so hard to read and right better than all the others. At werst you will have it for a littel wile and your doing something for sience.

We are reading a very hard book. I never read such a hard book before. Its called *Robinson Crusoe*[6] about a man who gets merooned on a dessert Iland. Hes smart and figers out all kinds of things so he can have a house and food and hes a good swimmer. Only I feel sorry because hes all alone and has no frends. But I think their must be somebody else on the iland because theres a picture with his funny umbrella looking at footprints. I hope he gets a frend and not be lonly.

April 10   Miss Kinnian teaches me to spell better. She says look at a word and close your eyes and say it over and over until you remember. I have lots of truble with *through* that you say *threw* and *enough* and *tough* that you dont say *enew* and *tew*. You got to say *enuff* and *tuff*. Thats how I use to write it before I started to get smart. Im confused but Miss Kinnian says theres no reason in spelling.

April 14   Finished Robinson Crusoe. I want to find out more about what happens to him but Miss Kinnian says thats all there is. *Why*

April 15   Miss Kinnian says Im lerning fast. She read some of the Progress Reports and she looked at me kind of funny. She says Im a fine person and Ill show them all. I asked her why. She said never mind but I shoudnt feel bad if I find out that everybody isnt nice like I think. She said for a person who god gave so little to you done more then a lot of people with brains they never even used. I said all my frends are smart people but there good. They like me and they never did anything that wasnt nice. Then she got something in her eye and she had to run out to the ladys room.

April 16   Today, I lerned, the comma, this is a comma (,) a period, with a tail, Miss Kinnian, says its importent, because, it makes writing, better, she said, somebody, coud lose, a lot of money, if a

✔ **Reading Check**

What is happening to Charlie?

---

6. **Robinson Crusoe** (kr$\overline{oo}$′ so) novel written in 1719 by Daniel Defoe, a British author.

comma, isnt, in the, right place, I dont have, any money, and I dont see, how a comma, keeps you, from losing it,

But she says, everybody, uses commas, so Ill use, them too,

April 17 I used the comma wrong. Its punctuation. Miss Kinnian told me to look up long words in the dictionary to lern to spell them. I said whats the difference if you can read it anyway. She said its part of your education so now on Ill look up all the words Im not sure how to spell. It takes a long time to write that way but I think Im remembering. I only have to look up once and after that I get it right. Anyway thats how come I got the word *punctuation* right. (Its that way in the dictionary). Miss Kinnian says a period is punctuation too, and there are lots of other marks to lern. I told her I thot all the periods had to have tails but she said no.

You got to mix them up, she showed? me" how. to mix! them(up,. and now; I can! mix up all kinds" of punctuation, in! my writing? There, are lots! of rules? to lern; but Im gettin'g them in my head.

One thing I? like about, Dear Miss Kinnian: (thats the way it goes in a business letter if I ever go into business) is she, always gives me' a reason" when—I ask. She's a gen'ius! I wish! I cou'd be smart" like, her;

(Punctuation, is; fun!)

April 18 What a dope I am! I didn't even understand what she was talking about. I read the grammar book last night and it explanes the whole thing. Then I saw it was the same way as Miss Kinnian was try-ing to tell me, but I didn't get it. I got up in the middle of the night, and the whole thing straightened out in my mind.

Miss Kinnian said that the TV working in my sleep helped out. She said I reached a plateau. Thats like the flat top of a hill.

After I figgered out how punctuation worked, I read over all my old Progress Reports from the beginning. Boy, did I have crazy spelling and punctuation! I told Miss Kinnian I ought to go over the pages and fix all the mistakes but she said, "No, Charlie, Dr. Nemur wants them just as they are. That's why he let you keep them after they were photostated, to see your own progress. You're coming along fast, Charlie."

That made me feel good. After the lesson I went down and played with Algernon. We don't race any more.

April 20 I feel sick inside. Not sick like for a doctor, but inside my chest it feels empty like getting punched and a heartburn at the same time.

I wasn't going to write about it, but I guess I got to, because its important. Today was the first time I ever stayed home from work.

Last night Joe Carp and Frank Reilly invited me to a party. There

Reading Strategy
Using Context to Verify Meaning What comparison does Charlie use to show the meaning of *plateau*? What plateau has Charlie reached?

were lots of girls and some men from the factory. I remembered how sick I got last time I drank too much, so I told Joe I didn't want anything to drink. He gave me a plain coke instead. It tasted funny, but I thought it was just a bad taste in my mouth.

We had a lot of fun for a while. Joe said I should dance with Ellen and she would teach me the steps. I fell a few times and I couldn't understand why because no one else was dancing besides Ellen and me. And all the time I was tripping because somebody's foot was always sticking out.

Then when I got up I saw the look on Joe's face and it gave me a funny feeling in my stomach. "He's a scream," one of the girls said. Everybody was laughing.

Frank said, "I ain't laughed so much since we sent him off for the newspaper that night at Muggsy's and ditched him."

"Look at him. His face is red."

"He's blushing. Charlie is blushing."

"Hey, Ellen, what'd you do to Charlie? I never saw him act like that before."

I didn't know what to do or where to turn. Everyone was looking at me and laughing and I felt naked. I wanted to hide myself. I ran out into the street and I threw up. Then I walked home. It's a funny thing I never knew that Joe and Frank and the others liked to have me around all the time to make fun of me.

Now I know what it means when they say "to pull a Charlie Gordon."

I'm ashamed.

PROGRESS REPORT 11

April 21   Still didn't go into the factory. I told Mrs. Flynn my landlady to call and tell Mr. Donnegan I was sick. Mrs. Flynn looks at me very funny lately like she's scared of me.

I think it's a good thing about finding out how everybody laughs at me. I thought about it a lot. It's because I'm so dumb and I don't even know when I'm doing something dumb. People think it's funny when a dumb person can't do things the same way they can.

Anyway, now I know I'm getting smarter every day. I know punctuation and I can spell good. I like to look up all the hard words in the dictionary and I remember them. I'm reading a lot now, and Miss Kinnian says I read very fast. Sometimes I even understand what I'm reading about, and it stays in my mind. There are times when I can close my eyes and think of a page and it all comes back like a picture.

Besides history, geography and arithmetic, Miss Kinnian said I should start to learn a few foreign languages. Dr. Strauss gave me some more tapes to play while I sleep. I still don't understand

Literary Analysis
First-Person Point of View How does the first-person point of view help you keep track of Charlie's development?

Reading Check

What does Charlie discover about why people laugh at him?

how that conscious and unconscious mind works, but Dr. Strauss says not to worry yet. He asked me to promise that when I start learning college subjects next week I wouldn't read any books on <u>psychology</u>—that is, until he gives me permission.

I feel a lot better today, but I guess I'm still a little angry that all the time people were laughing and making fun of me because I wasn't so smart. When I become intelligent like Dr. Strauss says, with three times my I.Q. of 68, then maybe I'll be like everyone else and people will like me and be friendly.

I'm not sure what an I.Q. is. Dr. Nemur said it was something that measured how intelligent you were—like a scale in the drugstore weighs pounds. But Dr. Strauss had a big arguement with him and said an I.Q. didn't weigh intelligence at all. He said an I.Q. showed how much intelligence you could get, like the numbers on the out-side of a measuring cup. You still had to fill the cup up with stuff.

Then when I asked Burt, who gives me my intelligence tests and works with Algernon, he said that both of them were wrong (only I had to promise not to tell them he said so). Burt says that the I.Q. measures a lot of different things including some of the things you learned already, and it really isn't any good at all.

So I still don't know what I.Q. is except that mine is going to be over 200 soon. I didn't want to say anything, but I don't see how if they don't know *what* it is, or *where* it is—I don't see how they know *how much* of it you've got.

Dr. Nemur says I have to take a *Rorshach Test* tomorrow. I wonder what *that* is.

April 22 I found out what a *Rorshach* is. It's the test I took before the operation—the one with the inkblots on the pieces of card-board. The man who gave me the test was the same one.

I was scared to death of those inkblots. I knew he was going to ask me to find the pictures and I knew I wouldn't be able to. I was thinking to myself, if only there was some way of knowing what kind of pictures were hidden there. Maybe there weren't any pic-tures at all. Maybe it was just a trick to see if I was dumb enough too look for something that wasn't there. Just thinking about that made me sore at him.

"All right, Charlie," he said, "you've seen these cards before, remember?"

"Of course I remember."

The way I said it, he knew I was angry, and he looked surprised. "Yes, of course. Now I want you to look at this one. What might this be? What do you see on this card? People see all sorts of things in these inkblots. Tell me what it might be for you—what it makes you think of."

I was shocked. That wasn't what I had expected him to say at all. "You mean there are no pictures hidden in those inkblots?"

psychology (sī kăl′ ə jē) *n.* science dealing with the mind and with mental and emotional processes

He frowned and took off his glasses. "What?"

"Pictures. Hidden in the inkblots. Last time you told me that everyone could see them and you wanted me to find them too."

He explained to me that the last time he had used almost the exact same words he was using now. I didn't believe it, and I still have the suspicion that he misled me at the time just for the fun of it. Unless—I don't know any more—could I have been *that* feeble-minded?

We went through the cards slowly. One of them looked like a pair of bats tugging at some thing. Another one looked like two men fencing with swords. I imagined all sorts of things. I guess I got carried away. But I didn't trust him any more, and I kept turning them around and even looking on the back to see if there was anything there I was supposed to catch. While he was making his notes, I peeked out of the corner of my eye to read it. But it was all in code that looked like this:

$$WF + A \; DdF\text{-}Ad \; orig. \; WF\text{-}A$$
$$SF + obj$$

The test still doesn't make sense to me. It seems to me that anyone could make up lies about things that they didn't really see. How could he know I wasn't making a fool of him by mentioning things that I didn't really imagine? Maybe I'll understand it when Dr. Strauss lets me read up on psychology.

April 25 I figured out a new way to line up the machines in the factory, and Mr. Donnegan says it will save him ten thousand dollars a year in labor and increased production. He gave me a $25 bonus.

I wanted to take Joe Carp and Frank Reilly out to lunch to celebrate, but Joe said he had to buy some things for his wife, and Frank said he was meeting his cousin for lunch. I guess it'll take a little time for them to get used to the changes in me. Everybody seems to be frightened of me. When I went over to Amos Borg and tapped him on the shoulder, he jumped up in the air.

People don't talk to me much any more or kid around the way they used to. It makes the job kind of lonely.

April 27 I got up the nerve today to ask Miss Kinnian to have dinner with me tomorrow night to celebrate my bonus.

At first she wasn't sure it was right, but I asked Dr. Strauss and he said it was okay. Dr. Strauss and Dr. Nemur don't seem to be getting along so well. They're arguing all the time. This evening when I came in to ask Dr. Strauss about having dinner with Miss Kinnian, I heard them shouting. Dr. Nemur was saying that it was *his* experiment and his research, and Dr. Strauss was shouting back that he contributed just as much, because he found me through Miss Kinnian and he performed the operation. Dr. Strauss

Literary Analysis
Point of View and Dynamic Character
Compare this entry with Charlie's first Rorschach test. What has changed?

Reading Check

What does Charlie learn about Dr. Nemur and Dr. Strauss?

▲ **Critical Viewing** Does Charlie seem to have made progress, judging from the details in this photograph? Explain. **[Interpret]**

said that someday thousands of neurosurgeons[7] might be using his technique all over the world.

Dr. Nemur wanted to publish the results of the experiment at the end of this month. Dr. Strauss wanted to wait a while longer to be sure. Dr. Strauss said that Dr. Nemur was more interested in the Chair[8] of Psychology at Princeton than he was in the experiment. Dr. Nemur said that Dr. Strauss was nothing but an opportunist who was trying to ride to glory on *his* coattails.

When I left afterwards, I found myself trembling. I don't know why for sure, but it was as if I'd seen both men clearly for the first time. I remember hearing Burt say that Dr. Nemur had a shrew of a wife who was pushing him all the time to get things published so that he could become famous. Burt said that the dream of her life was to have a big shot husband.

Was Dr. Strauss really trying to ride on his coattails?

April 28 I don't understand why I never noticed how beautiful Miss Kinnian really is. She has brown eyes and feathery brown hair that comes to the top of her neck. She's only thirty-four! I think from the beginning I had the feeling that she was an unreachable genius—and very, very old. Now, every time I see her she grows younger and more lovely.

We had dinner and a long talk. When she said that I was coming along so fast that soon I'd be leaving her behind, I laughed.

"It's true, Charlie. You're already a better reader than I am. You can read a whole page at a glance while I can take in only a few lines at a time. And you remember every single thing you read. I'm lucky if I can recall the main thoughts and the general meaning."

"I don't feel intelligent. There are so many things I don't understand."

She took out a cigarette and I lit it for her.

"You've got to be a *little* patient. You're accomplishing in days and weeks what it takes normal people to do in half a lifetime. That's what makes it so amazing. You're like a giant sponge now, soaking things in. Facts, figures, general knowledge. And soon you'll begin to connect them, too. You'll see how the different branches of learning are related. There are many levels, Charlie, like steps on a giant ladder that take you up higher and higher to see more and more of the world around you.

"I can see only a little bit of that, Charlie, and I won't go much higher than I am now, but you'll keep climbing up and up, and see more and more, and each step will open new worlds that you never even knew existed." She frowned. "I hope . . . I just hope to God—"

Reading Strategy
Using Context What restatement in this sentence helps you understand the meaning of the word *opportunist*?

Reading Check

What is Charlie's opinion of Dr. Nemur and Dr. Strauss?

---

7. neurosurgeons (nōō′ rō sʉr′ jənz) *n.* doctors who operate on the nervous system, including the brain and spine.
8. chair professorship.

"What?"

"Never mind, Charles. I just hope I wasn't wrong to advise you to go into this in the first place."

I laughed. "How could that be? It worked, didn't it? Even Algernon is still smart."

We sat there silently for a while and I knew what she was thinking about as she watched me toying with the chain of my rabbit's foot and my keys. I didn't want to think of that possibility any more than elderly people want to think of death. I *knew* that this was only the beginning. I knew what she meant about levels because I'd seen some of them already. The thought of leaving her behind made me sad.

I'm in love with Miss Kinnian.

PROGRESS REPORT 12

April 30 I've quit my job with Donnegan's Plastic Box Company. Mr. Donnegan insisted that it would be better for all concerned if I left. What did I do to make them hate me so?

The first I knew of it was when Mr. Donnegan showed me the petition. Eight hundred and forty names, everyone connected with the factory, except Fanny Girden. Scanning the list quickly, I saw at once that hers was the only missing name. All the rest demanded that I be fired.

Joe Carp and Frank Reilly wouldn't talk to me about it. No one else would either, except Fanny. She was one of the few people I'd known who set her mind to something and believed it no matter what the rest of the world proved, said or did—and Fanny did not believe that I should have been fired. She had been against the petition on principle and despite the pressure and threats she'd held out.

"Which don't mean to say," she remarked, "that I don't think there's something mighty strange about you, Charlie. Them changes. I don't know. You used to be a good, dependable, ordinary man—not too bright maybe, but honest. Who knows what you done to yourself to get so smart all of a sudden. Like everybody around here's been saying, Charlie, it's not right."

"But how can you say that, Fanny? What's wrong with a man becoming intelligent and wanting to acquire knowledge and understanding of the world around him?"

She stared down at her work, and I turned to leave. Without looking at me, she said: "It was evil when Eve listened to the snake and ate from the tree of knowledge. It was evil when she saw that she was naked. If not for that none of us would ever have to grow old and sick, and die."

Once again now I have the feeling of shame burning inside me. This intelligence has driven a wedge between me and all the people

Literary Analysis
Point of View and Dynamic Character
How does Fanny evaluate the changes that have occurred in Charlie?

I once knew and loved. Before, they laughed at me and despised me for my ignorance and dullness; now, they hate me for my knowledge and understanding. What do they want of me?

They've driven me out of the factory. Now I'm more alone than ever before . . .

May 15 Dr. Strauss is very angry at me for not having written any progress reports in two weeks. He's justified because the lab is now paying me a regular salary. I told him I was too busy thinking and reading. When I pointed out that writing was such a slow process that it made me impatient with my poor handwriting, he suggested that I learn to type. It's much easier to write now because I can type nearly seventy-five words a minute. Dr. Strauss continually reminds me of the need to speak and write simply so that people will be able to understand me.

I'll try to review all the things that happened to me during the last two weeks. Algernon and I were presented to the American Psychological Association sitting in convention with the World Psychological Association last Tuesday. We created quite a sensation. Dr. Nemur and Dr. Strauss were proud of us.

I suspect that Dr. Nemur, who is sixty—ten years older than Dr. Strauss—finds it necessary to see <u>tangible</u> results of his work. Undoubtedly the result of pressure by Mrs. Nemur.

Contrary to my earlier impressions of him, I realize that Dr. Nemur is not at all a genius. He has a very good mind, but it struggles under the <u>specter</u> of self-doubt. He wants people to take him for a genius. Therefore, it is important for him to feel that his work is accepted by the world. I believe that Dr. Nemur was afraid of further delay because he worried that someone else might make a discovery along these lines and take the credit from him.

Dr. Strauss on the other hand might be called a genius, although I feel that his areas of knowledge are too limited. He was educated in the tradition of narrow specialization; the broader aspects of background were neglected far more than necessary—even for a neurosurgeon.

I was shocked to learn that the only ancient languages he could read were Latin, Greek and Hebrew, and that he knows almost nothing of mathematics beyond the elementary levels of the calculus of variations. When he admitted this to me, I found myself almost annoyed. It was as if he'd hidden this part of himself in order to deceive me, pretending—as do many people I've discovered—to be what he is not. No one I've ever known is what he appears to be on the surface.

Dr. Nemur appears to be uncomfortable around me. Sometimes when I try to talk to him, he just looks at me strangely and turns away. I was angry at first when Dr. Strauss told me I was giving

Literary Analysis
Point of View and Dynamic Character
How does the first-person point of view allow the reader to measure the changes occurring in Charlie?

tangible (tan´ jə bəl) *adj.* that which can be understood; definite; objective

specter (spek´ tər) *n.* a ghost; frightening image

**Reading Check**

Why does Charlie lose his job?

Dr. Nemur an inferiority complex. I thought he was mocking me and I'm oversensitive at being made fun of.

How was I to know that a highly respected psychoexperimentalist like Nemur was unacquainted with Hindustani[9] and Chinese? It's absurd when you consider the work that is being done in India and China today in the very field of his study.

I asked Dr. Strauss how Nemur could refute Rahajamati's attack on his method and results if Nemur couldn't even read them in the first place. That strange look on Dr. Strauss' face can mean only one of two things. Either he doesn't want to tell Nemur what they're saying in India, or else—and this worries me—Dr. Strauss doesn't know either. I must be careful to speak and write clearly and simply so that people won't laugh.

May 18   I am very disturbed. I saw Miss Kinnian last night for the first time in over a week. I tried to avoid all discussions of intellectual concepts and to keep the conversation on a simple, everyday level, but she just stared at me blankly and asked me what I meant about the mathematical variance equivalent in Dorbermann's *Fifth Concerto.*

When I tried to explain she stopped me and laughed. I guess I got angry, but I suspect I'm approaching her on the wrong level. No matter what I try to discuss with her, I am unable to communicate. I must review Vrostadt's equations on *Levels of Semantic Progression.* I find that I don't communicate with people much any more. Thank God for books and music and things I can think about. I am alone in my apartment at Mrs. Flynn's boarding house most of the time and seldom speak to anyone.

May 20   I would not have noticed the new dishwasher, a boy of about sixteen, at the corner diner where I take my evening meals if not for the incident of the broken dishes.

They crashed to the floor, shattering and sending bits of white china under the tables. The boy stood there, dazed and frightened, holding the empty tray in his hand. The whistles and catcalls from the customers (the cries of "hey, there go the profits!" . . . "*Mazeltov!*" . . . and "well, he didn't work here very long . . ." which invariably seems to follow the breaking of glass or dishware in a public restaurant) all seemed to confuse him.

When the owner came to see what the excitement was about, the boy cowered as if he expected to be struck and threw up his arms as if to ward off the blow.

"All right! All right, you dope," shouted the owner, "don't just stand there! Get the broom and sweep that mess up. A broom . . . a broom, you idiot! It's in the kitchen. Sweep up all the pieces."

---

9. **Hindustani** (hin′ doo stä′ nē) *n.* a language of northern India.

Literary Analysis
Point of View
How does the first-person point of view make Charlie's attempts at communication sad?

refute (ri fyoot′) *v.* prove (an argument or statement) to be false by argument or evidence

▲ **Critical Viewing** Which details in the photograph reveal that Charlie has increased intelligence? **[Analyze]**

The boy saw that he was not going to be punished. His frightened expression disappeared and he smiled and hummed as he came back with the broom to sweep the floor. A few of the rowdier customers kept up the remarks, amusing themselves at his expense.

"Here, sonny, over here there's a nice piece behind you . . ."

"C'mon, do it again . . ."

"He's not so dumb. It's easier to break 'em than to wash 'em . . ."

As his vacant eyes moved across the crowd of amused onlookers, he slowly mirrored their smiles and finally broke into an uncertain grin at the joke which he obviously did not understand.

✔**Reading Check**

Is Charlie able to communicate well with Miss Kinnian? Explain.

I felt sick inside as I looked at his dull, vacuous smile, the wide, bright eyes of a child, uncertain but eager to please. They were laughing at him because he was mentally retarded.

And I had been laughing at him too.

Suddenly, I was furious at myself and all those who were smirking at him. I jumped up and shouted, "Shut up! Leave him alone! It's not his fault he can't understand! He can't help what he is! But . . . he's still a human being!"

The room grew silent. I cursed myself for losing control and creating a scene. I tried not to look at the boy as I paid my check and walked out without touching my food. I felt ashamed for both of us.

How strange it is that people of honest feelings and sensibility, who would not take advantage of a man born without arms or legs or eyes—how such people think nothing of abusing a man born with low intelligence. It infuriated me to think that not too long ago I, like this boy, had foolishly played the clown.

And I had almost forgotten.

I'd hidden the picture of the old Charlie Gordon from myself because now that I was intelligent it was something that had to be pushed out of my mind. But today in looking at that boy, for the first time I saw what I had been. *I was just like him!*

Only a short time ago, I learned that people laughed at me. Now I can see that unknowingly I joined with them in laughing at myself. That hurts most of all.

I have often reread my progress reports and seen the illiteracy, the childish naïvete,[10] the mind of low intelligence peering from a dark room, through the keyhole, at the dazzling light outside. I see that even in my dullness I knew that I was inferior, and that other people had something I lacked—something denied me. In my mental blindness, I thought that it was somehow connected with the ability to read and write, and I was sure that if I could get those skills I would automatically have intelligence too.

Even a feeble-minded man wants to be like other men.

A child may not know how to feed itself, or what to eat, yet it knows of hunger.

This then is what I was like. I never knew. Even with my gift of intellectual awareness, I never really knew.

This day was good for me. Seeing the past more clearly, I have decided to use my knowledge and skills to work in the field of increasing human intelligence levels. Who is better equipped for this work? Who else has lived in both worlds? These are my people. Let me use my gift to do something for them.

Tomorrow, I will discuss with Dr. Strauss the manner in which I can work in this area. I may be able to help him work out the

Literary Analysis
First-Person Point of View and Dynamic Character
How does Charlie now see himself?

illiteracy (il lit′ ər ə sē) *n.* inability to read or write

---

10. naïvete (nä ēv tā′) *n.* simplicity.

problems of widespread use of the technique which was used on me. I have several good ideas of my own.

There is so much that might be done with this technique. If I could be made into a genius, what about thousands of others like myself? What fantastic levels might be achieved by using this technique on normal people? On *geniuses*?

There are so many doors to open. I am impatient to begin.

PROGRESS REPORT 13

May 23 It happened today. Algernon bit me. I visited the lab to see him as I do occasionally, and when I took him out of his cage, he snapped at my hand. I put him back and watched him for a while. He was unusually disturbed and vicious.

May 24 Burt, who is in charge of the experimental animals, tells me that Algernon is changing. He is less cooperative; he refuses to run the maze any more; general motivation has decreased. And he hasn't been eating. Everyone is upset about what this may mean.

May 25 They've been feeding Algernon, who now refuses to work the shifting-lock problem. Everyone identifies me with Algernon. In a way we're both the first of our kind. They're all pretending that Algernon's behavior is not necessarily significant for me. But it's hard to hide the fact that some of the other animals who were used in this experiment are showing strange behavior.

Dr. Strauss and Dr. Nemur have asked me not to come to the lab any more. I know what they're thinking but I can't accept it. I am going ahead with my plans to carry their research forward. With all due respect to both of these fine scientists, I am well aware of their limitations. If there is an answer, I'll have to find it out for myself. Suddenly, time has become very important to me.

May 29 I have been given a lab of my own and permission to go ahead with the research. I'm on to something. Working day and night. I've had a cot moved into the lab. Most of my writing time is spent on the notes which I keep in a separate folder, but from time to time I feel it necessary to put down my moods and my thoughts out of sheer habit.

I find the *calculus of intelligence* to be a fascinating study. Here is the place for the application of all the knowledge I have acquired. In a sense it's the problem I've been concerned with all my life.

May 31 Dr. Strauss thinks I'm working too hard. Dr. Nemur says I'm trying to cram a lifetime of research and thought into a few weeks. I know I should rest, but I'm driven on by something inside

Literary Analysis
First-Person Point of View and Dynamic Character
How has Charlie changed up to this point in the story?

Reading Check

How has Algernon changed?

that won't let me stop. I've got to find the reason for the sharp regression in Algernon. I've got to know *if* and *when* it will happen to me.

June 4
Letter to Dr. Strauss (*copy*)
Dear Dr. Strauss:
Under separate cover I am sending you a copy of my report entitled, "The Algernon-Gordon Effect: A Study of Structure and Function of Increased Intelligence," which I would like to have you read and have published.

As you see, my experiments are completed. I have included in my report all of my formulae, as well as mathematical analysis in the appendix. Of course, these should be verified.

Because of its importance to both you and Dr. Nemur (and need I say to myself, too?) I have checked and rechecked my results a dozen times in the hope of finding an error. I am sorry to say the results must stand. Yet for the sake of science, I am grateful for the little bit that I here add to the knowledge of the function of the human mind and of the laws governing the artificial increase of human intelligence.

I recall your once saying to me that an experimental *failure* or the *disproving* of a theory was as important to the advancement of learning as a success would be. I know now that this is true. I am sorry, however, that my own contribution to the field must rest upon the ashes of the work of two men I regard so highly.
Yours truly,
Charles Gordon
encl.: rept.

June 5 I must not become emotional. The facts and the results of my experiments are clear, and the more sensational aspects of my own rapid climb cannot <u>obscure</u> the fact that the tripling of intelligence by the surgical technique developed by Drs. Strauss and Nemur must be viewed as having little or no practical applicability (at the present time) to the increase of human intelligence.

As I review the records and data on Algernon, I see that although he is still in his physical infancy, he has regressed mentally. Motor activity[11] is impaired; there is a general reduction of glandular activity; there is an accelerated loss of coordination.

There are also strong indications of progressive amnesia.

As will be seen by my report, these and other physical and mental deterioration <u>syndromes</u> can be predicted with statistically significant results by the application of my formula.

The surgical stimulus to which we were both subjected has resulted in an intensification and acceleration of all mental processes. The

---

11. **motor activity** movement; physical coordination.

obscure (əb skyoor´) *v.* conceal or hide

syndromes (sin´ drōmz´) *n.* a number of symptoms occurring together and characterizing a specific disease or condition

unforeseen development, which I have taken the liberty of calling the "Algernon-Gordon Effect," is the logical extension of the entire intelligence speedup. The hypothesis here proven may be described simply in the following terms: Artificially increased intelligence deteriorates at a rate of time directly proportional to the quantity of the increase.

I feel that this, in itself, is an important discovery.

As long as I am able to write, I will continue to record my thoughts in these progress reports. It is one of my few pleasures. However, by all indications, my own mental deterioration will be very rapid.

I have already begun to notice signs of emotional instability and forgetfulness, the first symptoms of the burnout.

June 10 Deterioration progressing. I have become absent-minded. Algernon died two days ago. Dissection shows my predictions were right. His brain had decreased in weight and there was a general smoothing out of cerebral convolutions as well as a deepening and broadening of brain fissures.

I guess the same thing is or will soon be happening to me. Now that it's definite, I don't want it to happen.

I put Algernon's body in a cheese box and buried him in the back yard. I cried.

June 15 Dr. Strauss came to see me again. I wouldn't open the door and I told him to go away. I want to be left to myself. I have become touchy and irritable. I feel the darkness closing in. I keep telling myself how important this <u>introspective</u> journal will be.

It's a strange sensation to pick up a book that you've read and enjoyed just a few months ago and discover that you don't remember it. I remembered how great I thought John Milton[12] was, but when I picked up *Paradise Lost* I couldn't understand it at all. I got so angry I threw the book across the room.

I've got to try to hold on to some of it. Some of the things I've learned. Oh, God, please don't take it all away.

June 19 Sometimes, at night, I go out for a walk. Last night I couldn't remember where I lived. A policeman took me home. I have the strange feeling that this has all happened to me before— a long time ago. I keep telling myself I'm the only person in the world who can describe what's happening to me.

June 21 Why can't I remember? I've got to fight. I lie in bed for days and I don't know who or where I am. Then it all comes back to me in a flash. Fugues of amnesia.[13] Symptoms of senility—

---

12. **John Milton** British poet (1608–1674) who wrote *Paradise Lost.*
13. **fugues** (fyo͞ogz) **of amnesia** (am ne′ zhə) periods of loss of memory.

second childhood. I can watch them coming on. It's so cruelly logical. I learned so much and so fast. Now my mind is deteriorating rapidly. I won't let it happen. I'll fight it. I can't help thinking of the boy in the restaurant, the blank expression, the silly smile, the people laughing at him. No—please—not that again . . .

June 22 I'm forgetting things that I learned recently. It seems to be following the classic pattern—the last things learned are the first things forgotten. Or is that the pattern? I'd better look it up again . . .

I reread my paper on the "Algernon-Gordon Effect" and I get the strange feeling that it was written by someone else. There are parts I don't even understand.

Motor activity impaired. I keep tripping over things, and it becomes increasingly difficult to type.

June 23 I've given up using the typewriter completely. My coordination is bad. I feel that I'm moving slower and slower. Had a terrible shock today.

Reading Strategy
Using Context What context clues help you verify the meaning of the word *coordination*?

◄ **Critical Viewing**
Charlie's boss says "Charlie Gordon, you got guts." How does this scene illustrate his boss's comment? **[Support]**

I picked up a copy of an article I used in my research, Krueger's "Uber psychische Ganzheit," to see if it would help me understand what I had done. First I thought there was something wrong with my eyes. Then I realized I could no longer read German. I tested myself in other languages. All gone.

June 30 A week since I dared to write again. It's slipping away like sand through my fingers. Most of the books I have are too hard for me now. I get angry with them because I know that I read and understood them just a few weeks ago.

I keep telling myself I must keep writing these reports so that somebody will know what is happening to me. But it gets harder to form the words and remember spellings. I have to look up even simple words in the dictionary now and it makes me impatient with myself.

Dr. Strauss comes around almost every day, but I told him I wouldn't see or speak to anybody. He feels guilty. They all do. But I don't blame anyone. I knew what might happen. But how it hurts.

July 7 I don't know where the week went. Todays Sunday I know because I can see through my window people going to church. I think I stayed in bed all week but I remember Mrs. Flynn bringing food to me a few times. I keep saying over and over Ive got to do something but then I forget or maybe its just easier not to do what I say Im going to do.

I think of my mother and father a lot these days. I found a picture of them with me taken at a beach. My father has a big ball under his arm and my mother is holding me by the hand. I dont remember them the way they are in the picture. All I remember is my father arguing with mom about money.

He never shaved much and he used to scratch my face when he hugged me. He said he was going to take me to see cows on a farm once but he never did. He never kept his promises . . .

July 10 My landlady Mrs Flynn is very worried about me. She said she doesnt like loafers. If Im sick its one thing, but if Im a loafer thats another thing and she wont have it. I told her I think Im sick.

I try to read a little bit every day, mostly stories, but sometimes I have to read the same thing over and over again because I dont know what it means. And its hard to write. I know I should look up all the words in the dictionary but its so hard and Im so tired all the time.

Then I got the idea that I would only use the easy words instead of the long hard ones. That saves time. I put flowers on Algernons grave about once a week. Mrs. Flynn thinks Im crazy to put flowers on a mouses grave but I told her that Algernon was special.

Literary Analysis
First-Person Point of View In this entry, how does the first-person point of view allow the reader to understand what Charlie is going through?

July 14 Its sunday again. I dont have anything to do to keep me busy now because my television set is broke and I dont have any money to get it fixed. (I think I lost this months check from the lab. I dont remember)

I get awful headaches and asperin doesnt help me much. Mrs. Flynn knows Im really sick and she feels very sorry for me. Shes a wonderful woman whenever someone is sick.

Literary Analysis
First-Person Point of View and Dynamic Character What changes do you see happening in Charlie's writing?

July 22 Mrs. Flynn called a strange doctor to see me. She was afraid I was going to die. I told the doctor I wasnt too sick and that I only forget sometimes. He asked me did I have any friends or relatives and I said no I dont have any. I told him I had a friend called Algernon once but he was a mouse and we used to run races together. He looked at me kind of funny like he thought I was crazy.

He smiled when I told him I used to be a genius. He talked to me like I was a baby and he winked at Mrs Flynn. I got mad and chased him out because he was making fun of me the way they all used to.

July 24 I have no more money and Mrs Flynn says I got to go to work somewhere and pay the rent because I havent paid for over two months. I dont know any work but the job I used to have at Donnegans Plastic Box Company. I dont want to go back there because they all knew me when I was smart and maybe they'll laugh at me. But I dont know what else to do to get money.

July 25 I was looking at some of my old progress reports and its very funny but I cant read what I wrote. I can make out some of the words but they dont make sense.

Miss Kinnian came to the door but I said go away I dont want to see you. She cried and I cried too but I wouldnt let her in because I didnt want her to laugh at me. I told her I didn't like her any more. I told her I didn't want to be smart any more. Thats not true. I still love her and I still want to be smart but I had to say that so shed go away. She gave Mrs. Flynn money to pay the rent. I dont want that. I got to get a job.

Please . . . please let me not forget how to read and write . . .

Literary Analysis
First-Person Point of View How do you know if Charlie is being honest with himself about Miss Kinnian in this paragraph?

July 27 Mr. Donnegan was very nice when I came back and asked him for my old job of janitor. First he was very suspicious but I told him what happened to me then he looked very sad and put his hand on my shoulder and said Charlie Gordon you got guts.

Everybody looked at me when I came downstairs and started working in the toilet sweeping it out like I used to. I told myself

Charlie if they make fun of you dont get sore because you remember their not so smart as you once thot they were. And besides they were once your friends and if they laughed at you that doesnt mean anything because they liked you too.

One of the new men who came to work there after I went away made a nasty crack he said hey Charlie I hear your a very smart fella a real quiz kid. Say something intelligent. I felt bad but Joe Carp came over and grabbed him by the shirt and said leave him alone or Ill break your neck. I didnt expect Joe to take my part so I guess hes really my friend.

Later Frank Reilly came over and said Charlie if anybody bothers you or trys to take advantage you call me or Joe and we will set em straight. I said thanks Frank and I got choked up so I had to turn around and go into the supply room so he wouldnt see me cry. Its good to have friends.

July 28 I did a dumb thing today I forgot I wasnt in Miss Kinnians class at the adult center any more like I use to be. I went in and sat down in my old seat in the back of the room and she looked at me funny and she said Charles. I dint remember she ever called me that before only Charlie so I said hello Miss Kinnian Im ready for my lesin today only I lost my reader that we was using. She startid to cry and run out of the room and everybody looked at me and I saw they wasnt the same pepul who use to be in my class.

Then all of a suddin I rememberd some things about the operashun and me getting smart and I said holy smoke I reely pulled a Charlie Gordon that time. I went away before she come back to the room.

Thats why Im going away from New York for good. I dont want to do nothing like that agen. I dont want Miss Kinnian to feel sorry for me. Evry body feels sorry at the factery and I dont want that eather so Im going someplace where nobody knows that Charlie Gordon was once a genus and now he cant even reed a book or rite good.

Im taking a cuple of books along and even if I cant reed them Ill practise hard and maybe I wont forget every thing I lerned. If I try reel hard maybe Ill be a littel bit smarter then I was before the operashun. I got my rabits foot and my luky penny and maybe they will help me.

If you ever reed this Miss Kinnian dont be sorry for me Im glad I got a second chanse to be smart becaus I lerned a lot of things that I never even new were in this world and Im grateful that I saw it all for a littel bit. I dont know why Im dumb agen or what I did wrong maybe its becaus I dint try hard enuff. But if I try and practis very hard maybe Ill get a littl smarter and know what all the words are. I remember a littel bit how nice I had a feeling with the blue book that has the torn cover when I red it. Thats why Im gonna keep trying to

Literary Analysis
First-Person Point of View and Dynamic Character How have Charlie's co-workers changed?

Reading Check

Why does Charlie decide to leave New York?

get smart so I can have that feeling agen. Its a good feeling to know things and be smart. I wish I had it rite now if I did I woud sit down and reed all the time. Anyway I bet Im the first dumb person in the world who ever found out somthing importent for sience. I remember I did somthing but I dont remember what. So I gess its like I did it for all the dumb pepul like me.

Goodbye Miss Kinnian and Dr Strauss and evreybody. And P.S. please tell Dr Nemur not to be such a grouch when pepul laff at him and he woud have more frends. Its easy to make frends if you let pepul laff at you. Im going to have lots of frends where I go.

P.P.S. Please if you get a chanse put some flowrs on Algernons grave in the bak yard . . .

Review and Assess

Thinking About the Selection

1. **Respond:** Was being part of the experiment good for Charlie? Why or why not?

2. **(a) Recall:** Who is Algernon? **(b) Compare:** Explain how Charlie's development parallels Algernon's. **(c) Interpret:** What is the meaning of the title of the story?

3. **(a) Recall:** Why does Charlie keep a journal? **(b) Evaluate:** How does Charlie's use of a journal contribute to the story's effectiveness?

4. **(a) Recall:** What does Charlie do when diners make fun of the dishwasher? **(b) Infer:** Why does he have such a strong reaction?

5. **(a) Compare and Contrast:** Name positive and negative results of Charlie's increased intelligence. **(b) Analyze:** How does Charlie feel about becoming more intelligent?

6. **(a) Recall:** How do Charlie's coworkers react to his increased intelligence? **(b) Draw Conclusions:** What are the reasons for their reactions? **(c) Make a Judgment:** Explain why you do or do not sympathize with their reactions.

7. **(a) Analyze:** When do you realize that Charlie's intelligence is not permanent? **(b) Apply:** What two details from the story reveal the progress of the reversal?

8. **(a) Contrast:** What is the difference between Charlie at the beginning of the story and Charlie at the end of the story? **(b) Apply:** Why does Charlie decide to leave New York? **(c) Predict:** What will happen to Charlie?

9. **Take a Position:** Do you think Charlie should have had the operation? Why or why not?

Daniel Keyes

(b. 1927)

Raised in Brooklyn, New York, writer and teacher Daniel Keyes has also been a photographer, a merchant seaman, and an editor. Keyes has written both fiction and nonfiction, including *The Minds of Billy Milligan* and *The Milligan Wars*, which are about a man with multiple-personality disorder. A meeting with a mentally-challenged young man gave Keyes the idea for "Flowers for Algernon." He began to wonder what would happen "if it were possible to increase human intelligence artificially." The central character, Charlie Gordon, is imaginary.

Review and Assess

Literary Analysis

First-Person Point of View

1. In a chart like the one shown, fill in the blanks to show the difference between Charlie's and another character's point of view.

Event, character, or situation	Charlie	Other character
Rorschach test	He thinks pictures are hidden in the inkblots.	You use your imagination to "find" the pictures.
Algernon's death		
Joe trips Charlie		

Connecting Literary Elements

2. On a timeline like the one shown, briefly describe Charlie before the operation, six weeks after the operation, and then three months after the operation.

Before Operation ·····▶ Six Weeks Later ·····▶ Three Months Later

3. How do Charlie's relationships with other people change before and after the operation?
4. How does Charlie's view of himself change?

Reading Strategy

Using Context

Copy each sentence. Underline the word or words that give context clues to the meaning of the italicized word. Then, write a new sentence using the italicized word.

5. He'd hidden this part of himself in order to *deceive* me, pretending—as do many people I've discovered—to be what he is not.
6. She said I reached a *plateau*. That's like the flat top of a hill.

Extend Understanding

7. **Science Connection:** What can scientists learn from failed experiments?

Quick Review

A story with a **first-person point of view** is told from the perspective of a character who participates in the action of the story. To review first-person point of view, see page 181.

A **dynamic character** grows and changes during the course of a literary work. A **static character** stays the same. To review character, see page 181.

The **context** of a word is the situation in which it is used—the surrounding words, sentences, and paragraphs. To review context, see page 181.

 Take It to the Net
www.phschool.com
Take the interactive self-test online to check your understanding of the selection.

Integrate Language Skills

Vocabulary Development Lesson

Word Analysis: Greek Root -psych-

The word root -psych- (pronounced *sike*) comes from the Greek word for "soul," but English words with this root usually refer to the mind. Combine this root with the suffix -*logy* and the suffix -*osis* to create two new words that are defined as follows:

1. "the study of the mind" _____
2. "an illness of the mind" _____

Spelling Strategy

The *s* sound in *psych* is spelled *ps,* and the *k* sound is spelled *ch.* Write the words in these sentences that follow one of these rules.

1. She used a pseudonym for her essay about chaos.
2. The chorus sang at the psychology convention.

Grammar Lesson

Verb Tenses

The **tense** of a verb shows the time of an action, state of being, or condition. There are six tenses. Each tense has a basic form.

Present:	I *own,* he/she/it *owns*
Past:	I *owned*
Future:	I *will own*
Present Perfect:	past action that continues: I *have owned*
Past Perfect	past action before another past event: I *had owned*
Future Perfect:	future action before another future event: I *will have owned*

Fluency: Sentence Completion

Use a word from the vocabulary list on page 181 to complete each sentence.

1. The professor taught a ____?____ course about common mental disorders.
2. In one case study, a man was haunted by the ____?____ of growing older.
3. The doctor achieved concrete, ____?____ results using psychotherapy.
4. No one could ____?____ the results.
5. No longer would rivals describe her studies and experiments as ____?____.
6. She was shy and ____?____.
7. She was troubled by her ____?____ and wanted to learn to read and write.
8. The source of her ____?____ was physical, not mental.

▶ *For more practice, see page R32, Exercise A.*
Practice Use the chart to help you label the tense of the italicized verbs in each sentence.

1. He *had turned* 37 before he *started.*
2. Charlie *knows* that soon he *will have forgotten* many things.
3. Charlie *will be* a different person.
4. Charlie *is* sad.
5. Frank *has helped* him.

Writing Application Change the incorrect verb tenses to the ones indicated in parentheses.

Charlie was racing (past) Algernon in mazes. Tomorrow, Charlie wins (future). He practices (future) tonight, and by tomorrow's race he is (future perfect) the fastest.

WG Prentice Hall Writing and Grammar Connection: Chapter 22, Section 2

Writing Lesson

Observation Journal

Write three journal entries in which Miss Kinnian tells events from her point of view.

Prewriting   Develop a list of events from the story.

Drafting   Write an account of each event, adding details that reflect how Miss Kinnian—not Charlie—would have thought, felt, or reacted.

Model: Support Ideas

Progress Report March 8. Now that I *recognize* the *potential danger* of the *experiment* , I wish Dr. Nemur and Dr. Strauss would not use Charlie. They do not even treat him like a human being. They talk about his low *IQ* right in front of him. He tried to write their *conversation* down. I wonder if he will read what he wrote someday and be angry with them.

> The words in italics show the difference between Charlie's entry and Miss Kinnian's. The writer shows the event through Miss Kinnian's eyes by including her thoughts and reactions.

Revising   Check to make sure you have used the correct verb tense. Review verb tenses on p. 212.

W͚G Prentice Hall Writing and Grammar Connection: Chapter 5, Section 3

Extension Activities

Listening and Speaking Hold a **group discussion** about whether or not Charlie should have been used in the experiment.

1. Prepare by finding examples from the story to support your argument.
2. Ask questions to make sure you understand what other group members are saying.
3. Before speaking to disagree with another group member, paraphrase or restate in your own words what the other person said. Ask if your paraphrase expresses what the speaker meant. Then, respond with your own point.

Research and Technology Write a brief **evaluation** of how nutrition, rest, and study contribute to academic performance.

1. Find facts or expert opinions on the influence of these factors on school success.
2. Write the evaluation, balancing researched opinions and statistics with opinions and examples from your own experience.
3. Conclude by summarizing your ideas and how they are or are not consistent with the researched facts.

 **Take It to the Net**   www.phschool.com

Go online for an additional research activity using the Internet.

READING INFORMATIONAL MATERIALS

Research Reports

About Research Reports

A research report presents information gathered from reference books, observations, interviews, or other sources. Examples of research reports include biographical sketches, which report high points in the life of a notable person, and documented essays, which use research to support a point or examine a trend.

By citing sources, a research writer lets others check the facts for themselves. A good research report also helps readers form an overall picture of the subject. The elements of an effective research report include

- an overall focus or main idea expressed in a thesis statement.
- information gathered from a variety of sources.
- clear organization and smooth transitions.
- facts and details to support each main point.
- accurate, complete citations identifying sources.

Reading Strategy

Question

To get the most out of reading research reports, ask questions. For instance, in the research report on the next page, the author explains that the Underground Railroad was an organization that helped slaves escape to freedom. You might ask, "Where did escaped slaves go?" If you read on, you will learn the answer.

As you read "The Underground Railroad," keep a list of questions on a chart like the one here. When you find the answers, record them in the chart as well. Asking questions and looking for answers will help you read in an active and focused way.

Questions	Answers
What was the Underground Railroad?	It was a secret network of people who helped slaves escape to freedom before the Civil War.
Why was it called the Underground Railroad if it was neither underground nor a railroad?	

A Ride for Liberty—The Fugitive Slaves, Eastman Johnson, The Brooklyn Museum of Art

THE UNDERGROUND RAILROAD

ROBERT W. PETERSON

Peterson's introduction includes a thesis statement giving his topic.

Before the Civil War, thousands of slaves escaped on this invisible train to freedom. The Underground Railroad wasn't under ground and it wasn't a railroad. But it was real just the same. And it was one of the brightest chapters in American history.

The Underground Railroad was a secret network of people who helped slaves flee to freedom before the Civil War (1861–1865). The slaves were black people from families who had been brought from Africa in chains. They were owned by their white masters and forced to work without pay.

Peterson organizes his points logically: First, he gives background on slavery. Next, he describes the operations of the Railroad. Then, he gives its history.

The first slaves arrived in Jamestown, Virginia, in 1619—the year before the Pilgrims landed at Plymouth, Massachusetts (Buckmater 11). Two hundred years later, there were nearly four million slaves in the United States (Siebert 378). Most worked on large plantations in the South. By then, slavery had been outlawed in most northern states.

Thousands of slaves ran away each year. Some fled to get away from harsh masters. Others wanted to enjoy liberty. The Underground Railroad was started to help them.

Its "stations" were homes, shops, and churches where runaway slaves were hidden and fed. The "agents" or "station-masters" were people—both black and white—who hated slavery. They wanted to help slaves get free.

Its "conductors" led or transported fugitives from station to station on their way to free states. They had to watch for slave catchers, who were paid to capture runaways and return them. Some conductors guided slaves all the way to Canada (Siebert 187) . . .

The Underground Railroad network covered all of the Northeast and went as far west as Kansas and Nebraska. Ohio had more stations than any other state. Thousands of runaway slaves crossed over the Ohio River into Ohio from Kentucky and what is now West Virginia (Siebert 134–135).

Not all fugitive slaves headed north to find freedom. A few went to Mexico. Some fled to Florida and were given refuge by Seminole Indians. Indians in other parts of the continent also sheltered runaway slaves. In Ohio, the Ottawa tribe took them in (Buckmaster 12, 35, 186, 187). In Ontario, Canada, Mohawk Chief Joseph Brant welcomed escaped slaves (Siebert 203) . . . .

We can only guess how many slaves used the Underground Railroad. Historians estimate the total at between 40,000 and 100,000 by the time the Civil War began in 1861 ("Underground Rails" 126). The war was fought in large part over the slavery issue.

In 1863, President Abraham Lincoln declared slaves free. That was the end of the Underground Railroad. There were no ceremonies and no celebrations. The invisible railroad ended as it had began—quietly and without fanfare.

Works Cited
Buckmaster, Henrietta. *Let My People Go.* Boston: Beacon Press, 1941.
Siebert, Wilbur H. *The Underground Railroad From Slavery to Freedom.* New York: Macmillan, 1898, reprinted 1992.
"Underground Railroad." *Encyclopedia Britannica,* vol. 12 15th ed., 1998.

Throughout the report, Peterson provides specific facts to create a picture of the scope of the Railroad. He documents specific facts with internal citations.

Peterson provides a "Works Cited" list that gives his sources in a standard format. Some reports include a **bibliography**—a list of all sources used, not just the ones cited.

Check Your Comprehension

1. Explain the following terms as they apply to the Underground Railroad: *stations*, *agents*, and *conductors*.
2. **(a)** Name three places that slaves went after escaping. **(b)** What attracted them to these places?
3. Describe how the Underground Railroad came to an end.

Applying the Reading Strategy

Question

4. If you had a question about the history of slavery, which paragraphs might you consult?
5. Name two questions that the fifth paragraph answers.
6. What questions did you have while reading? Where in the report did you find the answers?

Activity

Create a Bibliography

Choose a historical figure whom you find interesting and would like to learn more about, such as Harriet Tubman or Abraham Lincoln. Find five sources of information. Make a formatted bibliography. The chart here shows a standard format for citing books, encyclopedia entries, newspaper and magazine articles, and Internet sites.

Contrasting Informational Materials

Research Reports and Historical Fiction

MLA Style for Listing	
Book with one author	Pyles, Thomas. *The Orgins and Development of the English Language.* 2nd ed. New York: Harcourt Brace Jovanovich, Inc., 1971.
Article from an encyclopedia	Askeland, Donald R. (1991). "Welding." *World Book Encyclopedia.* 1991 ed.
Article from a weekly magazine	Wallace, Charles. "A Vodacious Deal." *Time* 14 Feb. 2000: 63.
Article from a newspaper	Thurow, Roger. "South Africans Who Fought for Sanctions Now Scrap for Investors." *Wall Street Journal* 11 Feb. 2000: A1.
Internet site	*National Association of Chewing Gum Manufacturers.* 19 Dec. 1999 <http://www.nacgm.org/consumer/funfacts.html>

In your library, find an example of historical fiction about the Underground Railroad. Read it, and answer the following questions:

1. Name two elements of the story that are historically accurate.
2. Name two elements of the story that are invented.
3. How is the historical fiction about the Underground Railroad different from the research report about the Underground Railroad?

Writing WORKSHOP

Description: Descriptive Essay

A **descriptive essay** presents a vivid picture of a place, event, object, or person. In this work- shop, you will write a descriptive essay focused on a topic that interests you.

Assignment Criteria Your descriptive essay should have the following characteristics:

- a clear, consistent organization
- a main impression reinforced by details
- strong sensory details—details of sight, sound, touch, smell, and taste

See the Rubric on page 221 for the criteria on which your descriptive essay may be assessed.

Prewriting

Choose a topic and focus your perspective. Choose as the topic of your description something, someone, or someplace you see frequently or have a clear memory of. Then, choose a perspective—a particular way of looking at the topic. Choosing one perspective will give a focus to your description. The diagram shows how one topic can be viewed from several perspectives.

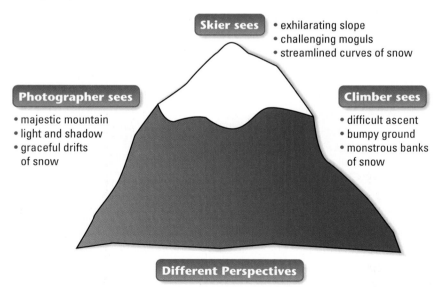

Skier sees
- exhilarating slope
- challenging moguls
- streamlined curves of snow

Photographer sees
- majestic mountain
- light and shadow
- graceful drifts of snow

Climber sees
- difficult ascent
- bumpy ground
- monstrous banks of snow

Different Perspectives

Gather sensory details. Sensory details about your topic—what you see, feel, taste, hear, or smell—will enrich your essay. For all or most of the senses, jot down a few words that apply to your topic.

Student Model

Before you begin drafting your descriptive essay, read this student model and review the characteristics of successful description.

Katie Hill
Baldwin Hills, California

The View From the Lift

At last I was back on my skis. After a soggy, hot summer that stayed hot through fall, I was finally feeling crisp cold air stinging my cheeks. The fresh tangy scent of the pine trees added a snap to the breeze.

As I waited by the lift, I listened to the swish and crunch of passing skiers moving along the line to board. When it was time for my dad and me to board, I leaned forward, waiting to feel the bump of the lift chair lifting me from my feet. I was lifted all right—but way off balance. I swung my legs and grasped at the chair, but the slick metal was too slippery for my gloves. Soon, I was half on the chair, held there by one hand on the arm rest, but the rest of me hung four feet above the ground, rocking and swaying as the chair moved forward lifting me five feet, then seven feet—and kept on creaking forward.

Even in my panic, I could hear the skiers below gasping as they realized what had happened. The lift lurched to a stop, but I was now eleven feet off the ground. When I looked down, the ground seemed as far away as if I were standing on top of my house. I could see the faces of the people waiting in line. Their mouths were open. Some faces looked stiff and frozen; other faces looked blank and dazed. I felt my Dad's hand grasping my loose hand but I didn't think he'd be able to pull me up. My boots felt like they were pulling my down. They had never felt so heavy.

My arms burned as I tried to help. I pulled on the arm of the lift while my dad pulled on the arm of me! I could see our frosty breath and hear our desperate gasps as we strained to get me back on the chair. Finally, I was. Although it seemed like the incident took hours, it only took a few seconds. When he saw I was safe, the lift attendant handed my dad and me our poles and we rode the lift the rest of the way up in silence. As I sat quietly, my breathing returned to normal and my heart stopped pounding like a balloon about to burst. The bitter metallic taste I noticed alerted me that I had bitten hard enough on my lip to make it bleed a little! I decided that if that was the worst injury I had from this experience, then I was pretty lucky.

The writer organizes her description in chronological or time order. She provides details in the order in which she experienced them.

The writer creates a main impression of danger and suspense. Details contribute to and strengthen that impression throughout the description.

The writer uses parallel structure to balance two actions and two descriptions.

Sensory details throughout the description help readers imagine the scene. Here, the writer provides details of physical sensation, sound, and taste.

Drafting

Organize the details to create a main impression. Shape your details into a coherent composition—an arrangement in which the pieces fit together logically. Several common methods of organization are shown on the chart.

Elaborate to build a main impression. Keeping your perspective in mind, choose one word that captures your subject. For example, a mountain described from the perspective of a skier could be captured in the word *exhilarating.* A painter might use the word *majestic.* Add details that connect, suggest, or build toward the word that captures your main impression.

Organizing a Descriptive Essay

Spatial Order - to describe places, scenes, or objects
— **Organize details by their physical arrangement**

Chronological Order - to describe events or processes
— **Organize details in the order in which events occur**

Order of Importance - to describe people, places, or objects
— **Begin with striking detail. Then organize from least important to most important.**

Revising

Revise for organization. Check to see if you have consistently followed your organizational plan. Make sure related details are grouped together rather than scattered throughout your essay. Use cutting and pasting to reorder details.

1. Make an extra printout or photocopy of your draft.

2. Look for related details that are far apart.

3. Cut each misplaced detail out of the copy of the draft.

4. Tape each detail in the correct position on your original draft.

5. Add a transition to show how the inserted detail connects to the one before or after it.

> My arms burned as I tried to help by pulling myself while my dad pulled too. I could see our frosty breath coming in short puffs as we both strained to get me back in the chair. Finally, I was. . . .
>
> *at the time*
> **Although it seemed like the incident took**
> *later*
> **hours, I realized it only took a few seconds.**

Revise for parallel structure. Sophisticated, effective writing uses parallelism, the joining of similar structures or sentence elements. Parallelism can be created by joining the same types of words and phrases: nouns with nouns, phrases with phrases, or clauses with clauses.

Not parallel: The colors included *brown, patches where it was green,* and *yellow.*

Parallel: The colors included *brown spots, green patches,* and *yellow streaks.*

Compare the model and the nonmodel. Why is the model more effective?

Nonmodel	Model
My arms burned as I tried to help. I pulled on the arm of the lift while on my arm, my dad pulled. I could see our frosty breath and hear how we gasped as we strained to get me back on the chair.	My arms burned as I tried to help. I pulled on the arm of the lift while my dad pulled on the arm of me! I could see our frosty breath and hear our desperate gasps as we strained to get me back on the chair.

Publishing and Presenting

Choose one of the following ways to share your writing with classmates or a wider audience.

Make a tape. If your subject is nearby, videotape the topic of your description and read your description aloud. Organize the video in the same order you organized your description so that your words match the images. Add music or sound effects that add to the main impression.

Build a booklet. Using artwork, cutouts, or photos, make a picture booklet based on your descriptive essay. Choose a particular audience, such as small children or older relatives.

Speaking Connection
To analyze the effect of descriptive details used in media, see the **Listening and Speaking Workshop: Critical Listening,** p. 222.

 Prentice Hall Writing and Grammar Connection: Chapter 5.

Rubric for Self-Assessment

Evaluate your descriptive essay using the following criteria and rating scale:

| Criteria | Rating Scale | | | | |
	Not very				Very
How clearly and consistently is the description organized?	1	2	3	4	5
How effectively are details used to create a main impression?	1	2	3	4	5
How vivid or strong are the sensory details?	1	2	3	4	5
How appropriately and effectively does the writer use parallelism?	1	2	3	4	5

Listening and Speaking WORKSHOP

Critical Listening

Television and radio offer drama, comedy, commercials, newscasts, and public-service announcements. Audiences: Beware. Do not listen passively. Practice questioning what pours into your brain. The form on this page can be used as a starting point for critical listening.

Consider the Speaker

In electronic journalism, the "speaker" is not always obvious. For example, in a newscast, the speaker may be the one doing the talking, but his or her material actually comes from a team of writers, a production staff, network executives, and news agencies like the Associated Press. Always consider the point of view of the people *behind* the words you hear. Evaluate the credibility of the speaker by considering these possibilities.

Hidden agendas. Sometimes the speaker may have a purpose that is not readily apparent. When you think this may be so, ask yourself, "Is the speaker trying to accomplish something that is not exactly what is being said?" In other words, is there a hidden agenda?

Speaker bias. Bias is the tendency to think in a certain way—no matter what. As you listen, consider whether information is presented in a slanted way or whether it takes several points of view into account.

Appealing techniques. Consider *how* the message appeals to its audience. For example, does a commercial suggest that *everyone* use its product? Does it cite experts or celebrities? Does it attempt to appeal to your age group, your desire to be popular, your well-being?

Ask Relevant Questions

Listening critically means, in part, questioning everything you hear. Here are a few tips for putting your questioning engine into gear.

- **Purpose** Is the purpose of what you are hearing to sell, inform, entertain, incite, or inspire—or a combination of these? Is the purpose clear?

- **Content** Do you understand what you see? Is it realistic or imaginative?

- **Delivery** Does the message move quickly or slowly? How loud is it? How much is verbal? How much is visual? What mood is created by the way the message is delivered?

Activity:
Critique a Commercial With a partner, view a television commercial with your most critical eye—and ear. After viewing, use the critique form to analyze what you have seen and heard. Then, discuss how the commercial affected you both.

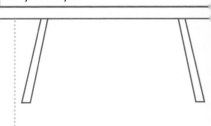

Commercial Critique
The Source
Hidden agendas?
Bias?
Techniques?
The Effects
Purpose:
Summary of content:
Delivery:
Answer the following questions:
What was the strength of this commercial?
What was its weakness?
Overall, was it effective?
Why or why not?

Assessment WORKSHOP

Analyzing Information

The reading sections of some tests require you to read a passage and answer multiple-choice questions by analyzing information. Use the following strategy to answer such questions.

- **Clarify the Question.** Some test questions require you not only to locate information in a passage but also to apply it. You may have to put information in categories, compare and contrast items, or determine causes and effects. Think about what the question is asking you to do, and then analyze the information you need in order to do it.

Sample Test Item

Directions: Read the passage, and then answer the question that follows.

Mr. and Mrs. Alvarez had left the babysitter this list of instructions:

1. Feed the children at 5:30. Warm up the soup that is in the refrigerator.
2. Let them watch half an hour of TV.
3. Be sure they brush their teeth and wash their faces and hands.
4. Read them a story of their choice.
5. Have them in bed by 8:00.

Martin fed the children on time. At 6:00, while cleaning up, he heard the TV. At 7:30, the children were still watching TV. Martin hurried them off to the bathroom and then tucked them into bed. Then he started his homework.

Which of the guidelines did Martin not follow?

A 1 and 2   **C** 2 and 3
B 2 and 4   **D** 3 and 5

Answer and Explanation

Comparing the list with the description of what Martin did, you see that he did 1, 3, and 5. He did not do 2 and 4, so **B** is correct.

Practice

Directions: Read the passage, and then answer the items that follow.

Erica made a list of the features she wanted in a new binder:

1. zipper closure
2. inside pockets for ruler and calculator
3. inside pouch for pens and pencils
4. subject dividers
5. inside pocket for loose papers

Then she saw this ad:

STUDY AID 3-RING BINDER
- Zips closed to keep paper from falling out
- Full-sized pockets inside back and front
- Inside pouch
- Available in a variety of colors
- Only $15.95!

1. Which of Erica's requirements is not mentioned in the ad?

   A 2   **B** 3   **C** 4   **D** 5

2. Erica's list would be more helpful to her process of choosing a new binder if it specified—

   A the brand she bought last year.
   B the price range she can afford.
   C the colors she likes.
   D the store where she usually shops.

Quest for Justice

Exploring the Theme

It is human nature to search for what we believe is right. The quest for justice occurs in many forms and in many places—from courtroom battles to international peacekeeping operations to efforts to settle disputes between friends. The selections in this unit explore ways in which people try to find or create what is just.

As you read, you can think about the struggles and determination of people and characters who have chosen to take an active role in bringing justice about.

◀ **Critical Viewing** What does this painting illustrate about the process of seeking justice? **[Analyze]**

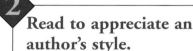
Why Read Literature?

The literature in this unit explores the theme of seeking justice—taking initiative for changing what seems unfair or destructive to people or things. Depending on the content, genre, and style of the works you plan to read, you will set various purposes for reading. Preview three of the purposes you might set before reading the works in this unit.

1 Read for the love of literature.

William Sidney Porter changed his name to O. Henry. Under this pen name, he became famous for his stories with surprise endings—many of them based on tales he heard in prison. Read one of these surprising stories, **"A Retrieved Reformation,"** page 242.

Toni Cade Bambara adopted the name "Bambara" after finding it written on a sketchbook in her great-grandmother's trunk. Growing up in Harlem, Bedford-Stuyvesant, and Queens, New York, and in Jersey City, New Jersey, she was encouraged to make the most of her imagination. Enjoy her story **"Raymond's Run,"** page 288.

2 Read to appreciate an author's style.

Henry Wadsworth Longfellow's poem about Paul Revere's ride is very famous, and very exciting, but it is not very accurate! Find out how Longfellow "jazzed up" history when you read **"Paul Revere's Ride,"** page 302.

What reason might Walt Whitman have had for shaping his stanzas like ships in a poem about Abraham Lincoln? Find out when you read **"O Captain! My Captain!,"** page 261.

3 Read for information.

You probably know some laws that protect people and their property, but did you know there are laws to protect trees? Read a legislative bill to protect oak woodlands when you read the **Analysis of a Legislative Bill,** page 283.

In Paul Revere's own account of his famous ride, he spends more time telling of his being captured than of his midnight adventure. Learn more about Revere's own impressions of his ride when you read his sworn account in **"Paul Revere's Deposition,"** page 311.

Take It to the Net
Visit the Web site for online instruction and activities related to each selection in this unit.
www.phschool.com

How to Read Literature

Strategies for Constructing Meaning

To fully understand a piece of writing, you must put words and ideas together in your mind so that they have meaning for you. Use these strategies to help yourself construct meaning:

1. Draw inferences.

Writers do not always tell you everything directly. Sometimes you need to draw inferences, or "read between the lines," to arrive at ideas the writer suggests but does not say. In this unit, you will practice thinking beyond the literal meaning of the words to get a fuller understanding of what the author means.

- Draw an inference by considering the implications of details that the writer includes or leaves out.

- Think about what this choice of details tells you about the author's opinions or purpose for writing.

2. Determine cause and effect.

To better understand the information presented to you, look for relationships among ideas. Cause and effect is one kind of relationship.

- A **cause** makes something happen.

- An **effect** is what happens—the result.

As you read the selections in this unit, you will learn to identify cause-and-effect relationships in fiction and nonfiction.

3. Ask questions.

Get at the meaning of text by asking yourself questions. Asking questions leads you to read more carefully and critically. Ask questions like the following:

- Why does it happen?
- Why does he do that?
- What does this mean?
- How does this fit in?

You can question the writer's motives and judgment. You can question why the writer gives you a particular bit of information. Then, read on to find out what happens. For example, you might question the sample passage at the right from O. Henry's "A Retrieved Reformation."

As you read the selections in this unit, review the reading strategies and look at the notes in the side columns. Use the suggestions to apply the strategies and construct meaning from the text.

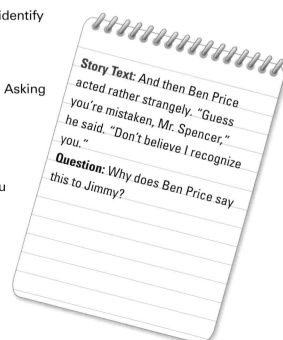

Story Text: And then Ben Price acted rather strangely. "Guess you're mistaken, Mr. Spencer," he said. "Don't believe I recognize you."

Question: Why does Ben Price say this to Jimmy?

Prepare to Read

Brown *vs.* Board of Education

 Take It to the Net

Visit www.phschool.com for interactive activities and instruction related to "Brown *vs.* Board of Education," including

- background
- graphic organizers
- literary elements
- reading strategies

Preview

Connecting to the Literature

The essay "Brown *vs.* Board of Education" tells of personal and public efforts to achieve equality and justice in education. Connect to the events in the essay by thinking about a time when you made an effort to change an unfair situation.

Background

In 1896, the court case *Plessy* vs. *Ferguson* upheld a law that allowed for "separate but equal" accommodations for whites and blacks on railroad cars. The results of this case were used to support segregation (the separation of races) in schools, hotels, transportation, and restaurants. It was not until the Supreme Court decision of *Brown* vs. *Board of Education* that segregation was declared unconstitutional.

Literary Analysis

Informative Essay

An **informative essay** is a short nonfiction piece that gives facts and details about a topic. "Brown *vs.* Board of Education" is an informative essay about the events surrounding a Supreme Court decision on segregation of schools. Use an outline like the one shown to take notes on the essay.

Connecting Literary Elements

Tone is the writer's attitude toward his or her readers and his or her subject. The tone of a work is shown in the writer's choice of language and details. In the following example, the author uses the words *important* and *oppressed*. These words reflect that the author has a serious attitude toward his topic and expects his readers to consider the information seriously.

> *Brown* vs. *Board of Education* signaled an *important* change in the struggle for civil rights. It signaled that the legal prohibitions that *oppressed* African Americans would have to fall.

Think about the following focus questions as you read:

1. What three words would you use to describe the tone of the essay?
2. What does the tone of the essay suggest about Myers's reasons for writing?

Reading Strategy

Analyzing Word Origins

Because modern legal practices have their roots in Roman law, many legal terms have Latin origins. For example, *legislature*, *legislate*, and *legal* have their roots in the Latin word *lex*, meaning "law." Learning the origins of these and other legal terms will help you remember their meanings. As you read, list the law-related words you encounter so that you can explore their origins once you have finished.

Vocabulary Development

elusive (i lo͞o′ siv) *adj.* hard to grasp or retain mentally (p. 231)

predominantly (prē däm′ ə nənt lē) *adj.* mainly; most noticeably (p. 231)

diligent (dil′ ə jənt) *adj.* careful and thorough (p. 233)

intangible (in tan′ jə bəl) *adj.* not able to be touched or grasped (p. 234)

unconstitutional (un′ kän stə to͞o′ shə nəl) *adj.* not in accordance with or permitted by the United States Constitution (p. 234)

deliberating (di lib′ ə rā tiŋ) *v.* thinking or considering very carefully (p. 235)

oppressed (ə prest′) *adj.* kept down by cruel or unjust use of power (p. 235)

Two Views

I. School Segregation in 1950s
  A. "Separate but Equal"
    1. *Plessy* v. *Ferguson* 1896
    2. de facto/de jure
  B. Unconstitutional
  C.
II. Thurgood Marshall
  A.
  B.
  C.
III. The Brown *vs.* Board of Education Decision
  A.
  B.

Brown vs. Board OF Education

Walter Dean Myers

▲ **Critical Viewing** In this photograph, a woman explains the significance of the ruling to her young daughter. What does the newspaper the woman is holding tell you about the impact of the ruling? **[Connect]**

There was a time when the meaning of freedom was easily understood. For an African crouched in the darkness of a tossing ship, wrists chained, men with guns standing on the decks above him, freedom was a physical thing, the ability to move away from his captors, to follow the dictates of his own heart, to listen to the voices within him that defined his values and showed him the truth of his own path. The plantation owners wanted to make the Africans feel helpless, inferior. They denied them images of themselves as Africans and told them that they were without beauty. They segregated them and told them they were without value.

Slowly, surely, the meaning of freedom changed to an <u>elusive</u> thing that even the strongest people could not hold in their hands. There were no chains on black wrists, but there were the shadows of chains, stretching for hundreds of years back through time, across black minds.

* * *

From the end of the Civil War in 1865 to the early 1950's, many public schools in both the North and South were segregated. Segregation was different in the different sections of the country. In the North most of the schools were segregated *de facto*;[1] that is, the law allowed blacks and whites to go to school together, but they did not actually always attend the same schools. Since a school is generally attended by children living in its neighborhood, wherever there were <u>predominantly</u> African-American neighborhoods there were, "in fact," segregated schools. In many parts of the country, however, and especially in the South, the segregation was *de jure*,[2] meaning that there were laws which forbade blacks to attend the same schools as whites.

The states with segregated schools relied upon the ruling of the Supreme Court in the 1896 *Plessy* vs. *Ferguson* case for legal justification: Facilities that were "separate but equal" were legal.

In the early 1950's the National Association for the Advancement of Colored People (N.A.A.C.P.) sponsored five cases that eventually reached the Supreme Court. One of the cases involved the school board of Topeka, Kansas.

Thirteen families sued the Topeka school board, claiming that to segregate the children was harmful to the children and, therefore, a violation of the equal protection clause of the Fourteenth Amendment. The names on the Topeka case were listed in alphabetical order, with the father of seven-year-old Linda Brown listed first.

"I didn't understand why I couldn't go to school with my playmates. I lived in an integrated neighborhood and played with

---

1. *de facto* (dē fak´ tō) Latin for "existing in actual fact."
2. *de jure* (dē jʉr´ ə) Latin for "by right or legal establishment."

elusive (i lōō´ siv) *adj.* hard to grasp or retain mentally

Reading Strategy
Analyzing Word Origins
Why do you think the writer uses two Latin terms in this paragraph that he then translates for the reader?

predominantly
(pri däm´ ə nənt lē) *adj.* mainly; most noticeably

✔**Reading Check**

What are segregated schools?

▲ **Critical Viewing** How is the classroom pictured above different from the classroom pictured at right? **[Contrast]**

children of all nationalities, but when school started they went to a school only four blocks from my home and I was sent to school across town," she says.

For young Linda the case was one of convenience and of being made to feel different, but for African-American parents it had been a long, hard struggle to get a good education for their children. It was also a struggle waged by lawyers who had worked for years to overcome segregation. The head of the legal team who presented the school cases was Thurgood Marshall.

* * *

The city was Baltimore, Maryland, and the year was 1921. Thirteen-year-old Thurgood Marshall struggled to balance the packages he was carrying with one hand while he tried to get his bus fare out of his pocket with the other. It was almost Easter, and the part-time job he had would provide money for flowers for his mother. Suddenly he felt a violent tug at his right arm that spun him around, sending his packages sprawling over the floor of the bus.

"Don't you never push in front of no white lady again!" an angry voice spat in his ear.

Thurgood turned and threw a punch . . . . The man charged into Thurgood, throwing punches that mostly missed, and tried to wrestle the slim boy to the ground. A policeman broke up the fight, grabbing Thurgood with one huge black hand and pushing him against the side of the bus. Within minutes they were in the local courthouse.

Thurgood was not the first of his family to get into a good fight. His father's father had joined the Union Army during the Civil War, taking the names Thorough Good to add to the one name he had in bondage. His grandfather on his mother's side was a man brought from Africa and, according to Marshall's biography, "so ornery that his owner wouldn't sell him out of pity for the people who might buy him, but gave him his freedom instead and told him to clear out of the county."

Thurgood's frequent scrapes earned him a reputation as a young boy who couldn't be trusted to get along with white folks.

His father, Will Marshall, was a steward at the Gibson Island Yacht Club near Baltimore, and his mother, Norma, taught in a segregated school. The elder Marshall felt he could have done more with his life if his education had been better, but there had been few opportunities available for African Americans when he had been a young man. When it was time for the Marshall boys to go to college, he was more than willing to make the sacrifices necessary to send them.

Young people of color from all over the world came to the United States to study at Lincoln University, a predominantly black institution in southeastern Pennsylvania. Here Marshall majored in predentistry, which he found boring, and joined the Debating Club, which he found interesting. By the time he was graduated at the age of twenty-one, he had decided to give up dentistry for the law. Three years later he was graduated, first in his class, from Howard University Law School.

At Howard there was a law professor, Charles Hamilton Houston, who would affect the lives of many African-American lawyers and who would influence the legal aspects of the civil rights movement. Houston was a great teacher, one who demanded that his students be not just good lawyers but great lawyers. If they were going to help their people—and for Houston the only reason for African Americans to become lawyers was to do just that—they would have to have absolute understanding of the law, and be <u>diligent</u> in the preparation of their cases. At the time, Houston was an attorney for the N.A.A.C.P. and fought against discrimination in housing and in jobs.

After graduation, Thurgood Marshall began to do some work for the N.A.A.C.P., trying the difficult civil rights cases. He not only knew about the effects of discrimination by reading about it, he

Literary Analysis
Informative Essay What facts about Thurgood's family do you learn here?

diligent (dil′ ə jənt) *adj.* careful and thorough

**Reading Check**

What is Marshall's profession, or job?

was still living it when he was graduated from law school in 1933. In 1936 Marshall began working full-time for the N.A.A.C.P., and in 1940 became its chief counsel.

It was Thurgood Marshall and a battery of N.A.A.C.P. attorneys who began to challenge segregation throughout the country. These men and women were warriors in the cause of freedom for African Americans, taking their battles into courtrooms across the country. They understood the process of American justice and the power of the Constitution.

In *Brown* vs. *Board of Education of Topeka,* Marshall argued that segregation was a violation of the Fourteenth Amendment—that even if the facilities and all other "tangibles" were equal, which was the heart of the case in *Plessy* vs. *Ferguson,* a violation still existed. There were <u>intangible</u> factors, he argued, that made the education unequal.

Everyone involved understood the significance of the case: that it was much more than whether black children could go to school with white children. If segregation in the schools was declared <u>unconstitutional</u>, then all segregation in public places could be declared unconstitutional.

Southerners who argued against ending school segregation were caught up, as then-Congressman Brooks Hays of Arkansas put it, in "a lifetime of adventures in that gap between law and custom." The law was one thing, but most Southern whites felt just as strongly about their customs as they did the law.

intangible (in tan´ jə bəl) *adj.* not able to be touched or grasped

unconstitutional (un´ kän stə tōō´ shə nəl) *adj.* not in accordance with or permitted by the U.S. Constitution

▲ **Critical Viewing** Thurgood Marshall is being sworn in as a Supreme Court justice as President Johnson looks on. What details show that this is a solemn, historic occasion? **[Interpret]**

Dr. Kenneth B. Clark, an African-American psychologist, testified for the N.A.A.C.P. He presented clear evidence that the effect of segregation was harmful to African-American children. Describing studies conducted by black and white psychologists over a twenty-year period, he showed that black children felt inferior to white children. In a particularly dramatic study that he had supervised, four dolls, two white and two black, were presented to African-American children. From the responses of the children to the dolls, identical in every way except color, it was clear that the children were rejecting the black dolls. African-American children did not just feel separated from white children, they felt that the separation was based on their inferiority.

Dr. Clark understood fully the principles and ideas of those people who had held Africans in bondage and had tried to make slaves of captives. By isolating people of African descent, by barring them from certain actions or places, they could make them feel inferior. The social scientists who testified at *Brown* vs. *Board of Education* showed that children who felt inferior also performed poorly.

The Justice Department argued that racial segregation was objectionable to the Eisenhower Administration and hurt our relationships with other nations.

* * *

On May 17, 1954, after <u>deliberating</u> for nearly a year and a half, the Supreme Court made its ruling. The Court stated that it could not use the intentions of 1868, when the Fourteenth Amendment was passed, as a guide to its ruling, or even those of 1896, when the decision in *Plessy* vs. *Ferguson* was handed down. Chief Justice Earl Warren wrote:

> We must consider public education in the light of its full development and its present place in American life throughout the nation. We must look instead to the effect of segregation itself on public education.

The Court went on to say that "modern authority" supported the idea that segregation deprived African Americans of equal opportunity. "Modern authority" referred to Dr. Kenneth B. Clark and the weight of evidence that he and the other social scientists had presented.

The high court's decision in Brown vs. Board of Education signaled an important change in the struggle for civil rights. It signaled clearly that the legal prohibitions that <u>oppressed</u> African Americans would have to fall. Equally important was the idea that the nature of the fight for equality would change. Ibrahima, Cinqué, Nat Turner, and George Latimer had struggled for freedom by fighting against their captors or fleeing from them. The 54th had fought for African freedom on the battlefields of the Civil

deliberating (di lib′ ə rā tiŋ) *v.* thinking or considering very carefully and fully

Reading Strategy
Analyzing Word Origins
To what language do you think you can trace the origin of *justice*? Why?

oppressed (ə prest′) *v.* kept down by cruel or unjust use of power

 **Reading Check**

What is the Supreme Court's ruling in *Brown* vs. *Board of Education?*

War. Ida B. Wells had fought for equality with her pen. Lewis H. Latimer and Meta Vaux Warrick had tried to earn equality with their work. In *Brown* vs. *Board of Education* Thurgood Marshall, Kenneth B. Clark, and the lawyers and social scientists, both black and white, who helped them had won for African Americans a victory that would bring them closer to full equality than they had ever been in North America. There would still be legal battles to be won, but the major struggle would be in the hearts and minds of people and "in that gap between law and custom."

In 1967 Thurgood Marshall was appointed by President Lyndon B. Johnson as an associate justice of the U.S. Supreme Court. He retired in 1991.

* * *

"I didn't think of my father or the other parents as being heroic at the time," Linda Brown says. "I was only seven. But as I grew older and realized how far-reaching the case was and how it changed the complexion of the history of this country, I was just thrilled that my father and the others here in Topeka were involved."

Review and Assess

Thinking About the Selection

1. **Respond:** How do you think the Supreme Court's decision in *Brown* vs. *Board of Education* has affected your life?

2. **(a) Recall:** Who was involved in the fight against segregation? **(b) Analyze:** Why were so many people willing to fight against school segregation? **(c) Apply:** Which of today's leaders lead the efforts for achieving justice for all people?

3. **(a) Recall:** What were the main claims made by parents in the lawsuit against the Topeka school board? **(b) Support:** What evidence did the lawyers present to support the case against segregation in schools? **(c) Evaluate:** Do you think that Thurgood Marshall was the best lawyer to present the case of *Brown* vs. *Board of Education*? Why or why not?

4. **(a) Recall:** What was the Supreme Court's decision in *Brown* vs. *Board of Education*? **(b) Apply:** Why is this Supreme Court case a significant event in American history?

5. **(a) Speculate:** What is the author's purpose in concluding his essay with Linda Brown's comments about the impact of this case? **(b) Make a Judgment:** Linda Brown says she did not think of her father as heroic at the time. Do you think any of the participants in this case are heroic? Explain.

Walter Dean Myers

(b. 1937)

A native of West Virginia, Walter Dean Myers was raised in New York City. His foster parents, the Deans, encouraged him to read, and from them he developed a lifelong love of books. Early in his life, Myers turned to writing poems and short stories as a way to overcome his painful shyness and a serious childhood speech problem.

Myers's career as an author began almost by chance in 1969 when he entered a writing contest. His story won a $500 prize. Since then, he has published more than sixty works for young people. He has won two Coretta Scott King Awards and two Newbery Honor Awards. Long interested in and concerned by the injustices suffered by African Americans, Myers has focused much of his writing on their experiences.

Review and Assess

Literary Analysis

Informative Essay

1. What are two facts that you learned about segregation in the United States from reading this **informative essay**?
2. What role does Marshall play in the fight against segregation?
3. Why is the title of the essay "*Brown* vs. *Board of Education*"?

Connecting Literary Elements

4. Use a cluster map like the one shown to record words, phrases, and details that reflect the author's attitude toward his subject and readers.

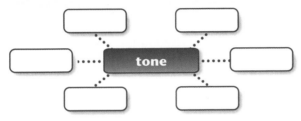

5. What three words would you use to describe the tone of the essay?
6. What does the tone of the essay suggest about Myers's reasons for writing the essay?

Reading Strategy

Analyze Word Origins

7. Enter the legal words you listed as you read on a chart like the one shown. Use the footnotes and a dictionary to complete the chart.

Word	Origin	Meaning
de jure		by right of law
de facto		
civil		
justice		

8. What origin do most or all of the words share?
9. Why do the law-related words share the same origin?

Extend Understanding

10. **Social Studies Connection:** What other events during the twentieth century had an impact on the civil rights movement in the United States? Explain.

Quick Review

An **informative essay** is a short nonfiction work that explains or gives information about a topic. To review informative essay, see page 229.

Tone is the writer's attitude toward the subject and the audience. To review tone, see page 229.

Word origins are the languages or cultures from which a word originally comes. To review word origins, see page 229.

 Take It to the Net
www.phschool.com
Take the interactive self-test online to check your understanding of the selection.

Integrate Language Skills

Vocabulary Development Lesson

Word Analysis: Latin Prefix in-

The word *intangible* is a combination of the Latin prefix *in-*, meaning "not," and *tangible*, meaning "able to be touched or felt." Therefore, *intangible* means "cannot be touched or defined."

Form words by adding *in-* to the following. Write a definition of each new word.

1. appropriate **2.** tolerant **3.** definite

Spelling Strategy

You may have to drop or change a letter before adding *-ed* to form the past tense of a verb. When a verb ends in silent *e*, drop the *e* before adding *-ed*:

escape + *-ed* = escaped

On your paper, add *-ed* to these verbs to form their past tense.

1. release **2.** exchange **3.** deliberate

Concept Development: Synonyms

Synonyms are words that have almost the same meaning. Write the word that is closest in meaning to the vocabulary word.

1. elusive: **(a)** hard to believe, **(b)** hard to hold, **(c)** frightening
2. predominantly: **(a)** mainly, **(b)** quickly, **(c)** unfairly
3. diligent: **(a)** respectful, **(b)** lazy, **(c)** hardworking
4. intangible: **(a)** weak, **(b)** concrete, **(c)** not solid
5. unconstitutional: **(a)** legal, **(b)** illegal, **(c)** illogical
6. deliberating: **(a)** considering, **(b)** noting, **(c)** waiting
7. oppressed: **(a)** cleansed, **(b)** beaten down, **(c)** hurried

Grammar Lesson

Adjectives

Adjectives are words that modify, or describe, nouns or pronouns. They tell about the nouns or pronouns they modify by answering the following questions:

- Which one?
- What kind?
- How many?
- How much?

In the following sentence, Myers uses adjectives to tell *what kind* of tug Thurgood Marshall felt and on *which* arm:

Suddenly he felt a *violent* tug at his *right* arm . . .

▶ *For more practice, see page R28, Exercise C.*
Practice Underline each adjective, and draw an arrow to the word it modifies.

1. His mother taught in a segregated school.
2. His short temper flared.
3. Marshall graduated first in his law class.
4. Thirteen families participated.
5. It was an important change.

Writing Application Copy the sentences. Add at least one adjective to each sentence.

1. Thurgood Marshall experienced discrimination as a boy.
2. He used his knowledge to pursue justice.
3. The case changed lives.

W͟G Prentice Hall Writing and Grammar Connection: Chapter 16, Section 1

Writing Lesson

Analysis of a Decision

Like most Supreme Court decisions, the decision in the case of *Brown* vs. *Board of Education* has had far-reaching effects. Do research to find out more about the decision and its impact. Then, in a brief essay, analyze the impact of the decision on life in the United States.

Prewriting   Review your research notes. Based on what you have found, write a single statement that expresses the overall impact of the decision. Then, organize specific examples in the order in which you will present and explain them.

Drafting   Begin with a quotation or a startling comparison to focus readers' attention on the significance of the decision. Then, present your examples and explanations of the impact of the decision.

Model: Strong Introduction
As President James Garfield once said, "Next in importance to freedom and justice is popular education, without which neither freedom nor justice can be permanently maintained."

> This writer begins with a powerful quotation to focus readers on the importance of any decision dealing with education.

Revising   Underline each specific example in one color. Underline explanations in another color. If you find you do not have enough examples, return to your notes or conduct more research to find more.

 Prentice Hall Writing and Grammar Connection: Chapter 11, Section 2

Extension Activities

Research and Technology Use a keyword search to find information on the Civil Rights movement, and develop a **timeline** of key events.

1. Begin by searching under some of the following key words:
   - Rosa Parks
   - integration
   - Civil Rights
2. Open the first four results for each search. Note dates, names, and other search topics.
3. Organize the information on a timeline.

Listening and Speaking Listen to a recording of a speech made by Thurgood Marshall during the *Brown* vs. *Board of Education* trial. (Ask a reference librarian to help you locate one.) After listening, **paraphrase** his speech.

 Take It to the Net   www.phschool.com

Go online for an additional research activity using the Internet.

Prepare to Read

A Retrieved Reformation

Young of the Town, 1933, Gerrit V. Sinclair, Williams American Art Galleries, Tennessee

Take It to the Net

Visit www.phschool.com for interactive activities and instruction related to "A Retrieved Reformation," including

- background
- graphic organizers
- literary elements
- reading strategies

Preview

Connecting to the Literature

A character in this short story meets a woman who inspires him to turn his life around. Before you read, think about reasons you've had for "turning over a new leaf."

Background

At the time of the story, the locks, dials, and levers of most safes were located on the outside. Safe crackers developed special tools and techniques to punch out these parts. Today, safes are built with their locks and bolts on the inside, making them much harder to break into.

Literary Analysis

Surprise Ending

O. Henry, the author of this story, is known for startling his readers with a **surprise ending**, an unexpected plot twist at the end of a story. Writers make surprise endings believable by including details that support the surprise ending without giving it away. As you read, use the following focus questions to help you examine O. Henry's use of this technique.

1. How do you think the story will end?
2. What clues lead you to expect this ending?

Connecting Literary Elements

Irony in literature involves surprising, interesting, or amusing contradictions. In "A Retrieved Reformation," O. Henry uses **irony of situation**—in which an event occurs that directly contradicts the expectations of the characters and the reader—to create a surprise ending. The reader believes that the conflict of the plot has already been resolved, but the main character's circumstances take an unexpected turn. The new circumstances change the outcome of the plot.

Reading Strategy

Asking Questions

You will have a better understanding of what you read if you **ask questions** about the characters and events. You might ask, for instance, why a character behaves in a certain way or what an action really means. Then, read on to find answers to your questions. Use a chart like the one shown to list your questions and the answers you find as you read "A Retrieved Reformation."

Vocabulary Development

assiduously (ə sij′ oo̅ wəs lē) *adv.* carefully and busily (p. 243)

virtuous (vur′ cho̅o̅ əs) *adj.* moral; upright (p. 243)

retribution (re′ trə byoo̅′ shən) *n.* punishment for wrongdoing (p. 245)

unobtrusively (un′ əb troo̅′ siv lē) *adv.* without calling attention to oneself (p. 247)

simultaneously (sī′ məl tā′ nē əs lē) *adv.* at the same time (p. 249)

anguish (aŋ′ gwish) *n.* great suffering from worry (p. 249)

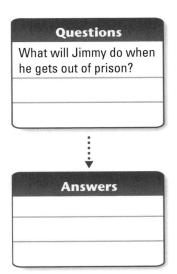

Questions

What will Jimmy do when he gets out of prison?

Answers

A RETRIEVED *Reformation*

O. Henry

▲ **Critical Viewing** What details in this photograph reveal that it was taken long ago? **[Connect]**

A guard came to the prison shoe-shop, where Jimmy Valentine was <u>assiduously</u> stitching uppers, and escorted him to the front office. There the warden handed Jimmy his pardon, which had been signed that morning by the governor. Jimmy took it in a tired kind of way. He had served nearly ten months of a four-year sentence. He had expected to stay only about three months, at the longest. When a man with as many friends on the outside as Jimmy Valentine had is received in the "stir" it is hardly worthwhile to cut his hair.

"Now, Valentine," said the warden, "you'll go out in the morning. Brace up, and make a man of yourself. You're not a bad fellow at heart. Stop cracking safes, and live straight."

"Me?" said Jimmy, in surprise. "Why, I never cracked a safe in my life."

"Oh, no," laughed the warden. "Of course not. Let's see, now. How was it you happened to get sent up on that Springfield job? Was it because you wouldn't prove an alibi for fear of compromising somebody in extremely high-toned society? Or was it simply a case of a mean old jury that had it in for you? It's always one or the other with you innocent victims."

"Me?" said Jimmy, still blankly <u>virtuous</u>. "Why, warden, I never was in Springfield in my life!"

"Take him back, Cronin," smiled the warden, "and fix him up with outgoing clothes. Unlock him at seven in the morning, and let him come to the bullpen.[1] Better think over my advice, Valentine."

At a quarter past seven on the next morning Jimmy stood in the warden's outer office. He had on a suit of the villainously fitting, ready-made clothes and a pair of the stiff, squeaky shoes that the state furnishes to its discharged compulsory guests.

The clerk handed him a railroad ticket and the five-dollar bill with which the law expected him to rehabilitate himself into good citizenship and prosperity. The warden gave him a cigar, and shook hands. Valentine, 9762, was chronicled on the books "Pardoned by Governor," and Mr. James Valentine walked out into the sunshine.

Disregarding the song of the birds, the waving green trees, and the smell of the flowers, Jimmy headed straight for a restaurant. There he tasted the first sweet joys of liberty in the shape of a chicken dinner. From there he proceeded leisurely to the depot and boarded his train. Three hours set him down in a little town

---

1. bullpen *n.* barred room in a jail, where prisoners are kept temporarily.

assiduously (ə sij′ oo wəs lē) *adv.* carefully and busily

virtuous (vur′ choo wəs) *adj.* moral; upright

Literary Analysis
Surprise Ending At this point in the story, what do you think the ending will be?

**Reading Check**

Where has Jimmy been for the past ten months?

near the state line. He went to the café of one Mike Dolan and shook hands with Mike, who was alone behind the bar.

"Sorry we couldn't make it sooner, Jimmy, me boy," said Mike. "But we had that protest from Springfield to buck against, and the governor nearly balked. Feeling all right?"

"Fine," said Jimmy. "Got my key?"

He got his key and went upstairs, unlocking the door of a room at the rear. Everything was just as he had left it. There on the floor was still Ben Price's collar-button that had been torn from that eminent detective's shirt-band when they had overpowered Jimmy to arrest him.

Pulling out from the wall a folding-bed, Jimmy slid back a panel in the wall and dragged out a dust-covered suitcase. He opened this and gazed fondly at the finest set of burglar's tools in the East. It was a complete set, made of specially tempered steel, the latest designs in drills, punches, braces and bits, jimmies, clamps, and augers,[2] with two or three novelties invented by Jimmy himself, in which he took pride. Over nine hundred dollars they had cost him to have made at —, a place where they make such things for the profession.

In half an hour Jimmy went downstairs and through the café. He was now dressed in tasteful and well-fitting clothes, and carried his dusted and cleaned suitcase in his hand.

"Got anything on?" asked Mike Dolan, genially.

"Me?" said Jimmy, in a puzzled tone. "I don't understand. I'm representing the New York Amalgamated Short Snap Biscuit Cracker and Frazzled Wheat Company."

This statement delighted Mike to such an extent that Jimmy had to take a seltzer-and-milk on the spot. He never touched "hard" drinks.

A week after the release of Valentine, 9762, there was a neat job of safe-burglary done in Richmond, Indiana, with no clue to the author. A scant eight hundred dollars was all that was secured. Two weeks after that a patented, improved, burglar-proof safe in Logansport was opened like a cheese to the tune of fifteen hundred dollars, currency; securities and silver untouched. That began to interest the rogue-catchers.[3] Then an old-fashioned bank-safe in Jefferson City became active and threw out of its crater an eruption of bank-notes amounting to five thousand dollars. The losses were now high enough to bring the matter up into Ben Price's class of work. By comparing notes, a remarkable similarity in the methods of the burglaries was noticed. Ben Price investigated the scenes of the robberies, and was heard to remark:

"That's Dandy Jim Valentine's autograph. He's resumed business. Look at that combination knob—jerked out as easy as pulling up a

Reading Strategy
Asking Questions What question could you ask yourself about Valentine's actions in this paragraph?

---

2. **drills . . . augers** (ô´ gərz) *n.* tools used in metalwork.
3. **rogue-catchers** *n.* police.

◀ **Critical Viewing**
What would appeal to Jimmy Valentine about this town? **[Deduce]**

radish in wet weather. He's got the only clamps that can do it. And look how clean those tumblers were punched out! Jimmy never has to drill but one hole. Yes, I guess I want Mr. Valentine. He'll do his bit next time without any short-time or clemency foolishness."

Ben Price knew Jimmy's habits. He had learned them while working up the Springfield case. Long jumps, quick getaways, no confederates,[4] and a taste for good society—these ways had helped Mr. Valentine to become noted as a successful dodger of <u>retribution</u>. It was given out that Ben Price had taken up the trail of the elusive cracksman, and other people with burglar-proof safes felt more at ease.

retribution
(reʹ trə byo͞oʹ shən) *n.* punishment for wrong-doing

One afternoon, Jimmy Valentine and his suitcase climbed out of the mail hack[5] in Elmore, a little town five miles off the railroad down in the blackjack country of Arkansas. Jimmy, looking like an athletic young senior just home from college, went down the board sidewalk toward the hotel.

A young lady crossed the street, passed him at the corner and entered a door over which was the sign "The Elmore Bank." Jimmy Valentine looked into her eyes, forgot what he was, and became another man. She lowered her eyes and colored slightly. Young men of Jimmy's style and looks were scarce in Elmore.

 **Reading Check**

What does Ben Price say when he visits the scene of the crime?

---

4. **confederates** (kən fedʹ ər its) *n.* accomplices.
5. **mail hack** *n.* horse and carriage used to deliver mail.

Jimmy collared a boy that was loafing on the steps of the bank as if he were one of the stockholders, and began to ask him questions about the town, feeding him dimes at intervals. By and by the young lady came out, looking royally unconscious of the young man with the suitcase, and went her way.

"Isn't that young lady Miss Polly Simpson?" asked Jimmy, with specious guile.[6]

"Naw," said the boy. "She's Annabel Adams. Her pa owns this bank. What'd you come to Elmore for? Is that a gold watch chain? I'm going to get a bulldog. Got any more dimes?"

Jimmy went to the Planters' Hotel, registered as Ralph D. Spencer, and engaged a room. He leaned on the desk and declared his platform[7] to the clerk. He said he had come to Elmore to look for a location to go into business. How was the shoe business, now, in the town? He had thought of the shoe business. Was there an opening?

The clerk was impressed by the clothes and manner of Jimmy. He, himself, was something of a pattern of fashion to the thinly gilded[8] youth of Elmore, but he now perceived his shortcomings. While trying to figure out Jimmy's manner of tying his four-in-hand,[9] he cordially gave information.

Yes, there ought to be a good opening in the shoe line. There wasn't an exclusive shoe store in the place. The dry-goods and general stores handled them. Business in all lines was fairly good. Hoped Mr. Spencer would decide to locate in Elmore. He would find it a pleasant town to live in, and the people very sociable.

Mr. Spencer thought he would stop over in the town a few days and look over the situation. No, the clerk needn't call the boy. He would carry up his suitcase, himself: it was rather heavy.

Mr. Ralph Spencer, the phoenix◆ that arose from Jimmy Valentine's ashes—ashes left by the flame of a sudden and alterative attack of love—remained in Elmore, and prospered. He opened a shoe store and secured a good run of trade.

Socially he was also a success, and made many friends. And he accomplished the wish of his heart. He met Miss Annabel Adams, and became more and more captivated by her charms.

At the end of a year the situation of Mr. Ralph Spencer was this: he had won the respect of the community, his shoe store was flourishing, and he and Annabel were engaged to be married in two weeks. Mr. Adams, the typical, plodding, country banker,

Literature in context Language Connection

◆ **Allusions: The Phoenix**

An allusion is a reference in a work of literature to a person, place, or thing in another artistic work (literature, art, music, history, painting, or mythology). For example, O. Henry writes, "Mr. Ralph Spencer, the phoenix that arose from Jimmy Valentine's ashes . . . ." The allusion here is to the phoenix, a mythical bird of the Arabian wilderness. It was believed to die in flames every 500 or 600 years. Then, the phoenix would be reborn, rising from its ashes. The allusion helps readers understand that Jimmy Valentine has completely reinvented himself as Ralph Spencer.

---

6. **specious guile** (spē´ shəs gīl´) *n.* crafty, indirect way of obtaining information.
7. **platform** *n.* here, a statement of intention.
8. **thinly gilded** *adj.* coated with a thin layer of gold; here, appearing well dressed.
9. **four-in-hand** *n.* necktie.

approved of Spencer. Annabel's pride in him almost equaled her affection. He was as much at home in the family of Mr. Adams and that of Annabel's married sister as if he were already a member.

One day Jimmy sat down in his room and wrote this letter, which he mailed to the safe address of one of his old friends in St. Louis:

Dear Old Pal:

I want you to be at Sullivan's place, in Little Rock, next Wednesday night, at nine o'clock. I want you to wind up some little matters for me. And, also, I want to make you a present of my kit of tools. I know you'll be glad to get them—you couldn't duplicate the lot for a thousand dollars. Say, Billy, I've quit the old business—a year ago. I've got a nice store. I'm making an honest living, and I'm going to marry the finest girl on earth two weeks from now. It's the only life, Billy—the straight one. I wouldn't touch a dollar of another man's money now for a million. After I get married I'm going to sell out and go West, where there won't be so much danger of having old scores brought up against me. I tell you, Billy, she's an angel. She believes in me; and I wouldn't do another crooked thing for the whole world. Be sure to be at Sully's, for I must see you. I'll bring along the tools with me.

Your old friend,
Jimmy.

Literary Analysis
Surprise Ending What conclusion do you expect will follow from these events?

On the Monday night after Jimmy wrote this letter, Ben Price jogged <u>unobtrusively</u> into Elmore in a livery buggy.[10] He lounged about town in his quiet way until he found out what he wanted to know. From the drugstore across the street from Spencer's shoe store he got a good look at Ralph D. Spencer.

"Going to marry the banker's daughter are you, Jimmy?" said Ben to himself, softly. "Well, I don't know!"

unobtrusively
(un′ əb tr$\overline{oo}$′ siv lē) *adv.*
without calling attention to oneself

The next morning Jimmy took breakfast at the Adamses. He was going to Little Rock that day to order his wedding suit and buy something nice for Annabel. That would be the first time he had left town since he came to Elmore. It had been more than a year now since those last professional "jobs," and he thought he could safely venture out.

Literary Analysis
Surprise Ending In what way can Ben Price change Jimmy's situation?

After breakfast quite a family party went downtown together—Mr. Adams, Annabel, Jimmy, and Annabel's married sister with her two little girls, aged five and nine. They came by the hotel where Jimmy still boarded, and he ran up to his room and brought along his suitcase. Then they went on to the bank. There stood Jimmy's horse and buggy and Dolph Gibson, who was going to drive him over to the railroad station.

All went inside the high, carved oak railings into the banking-

✔**Reading Check**
What does Jimmy decide to do with his life?

---

10. livery buggy *n.* horse and carriage for hire.

◀ **Critical Viewing**
Does the woman in this photograph share any qualities with Annabel, as described in the story? Explain. **[Connect]**

room—Jimmy included, for Mr. Adams's future son-in-law was welcome anywhere. The clerks were pleased to be greeted by the good-looking, agreeable young man who was going to marry Miss Annabel. Jimmy set his suitcase down. Annabel, whose heart was bubbling with happiness and lively youth, put on Jimmy's hat, and picked up the suitcase. "Wouldn't I make a nice drummer?"[11] said Annabel. "My! Ralph, how heavy it is! Feels like it was full of gold bricks."

"Lot of nickel-plated shoehorns in there," said Jimmy, coolly, "that I'm going to return. Thought I'd save express charges by taking them up. I'm getting awfully economical."

The Elmore Bank had just put in a new safe and vault. Mr. Adams was very proud of it, and insisted on an inspection by

---

11. drummer *n.* traveling salesman.

everyone. The vault was a small one, but it had a new, patented door. It fastened with three solid steel bolts thrown <u>simultaneously</u> with a single handle, and had a time lock. Mr. Adams beamingly explained its workings to Mr. Spencer, who showed a courteous but not too intelligent interest. The two children, May and Agatha, were delighted by the shining metal and funny clock and knobs.

While they were thus engaged Ben Price sauntered in and leaned on his elbow, looking casually inside between the railings. He told the teller that he didn't want anything; he was just waiting for a man he knew.

Suddenly there was a scream or two from the women, and a commotion. Unperceived by the elders, May, the nine-year-old girl, in a spirit of play, had shut Agatha in the vault. She had then shot the bolts and turned the knob of the combination as she had seen Mr. Adams do.

The old banker sprang to the handle and tugged at it for a moment. "The door can't be opened," he groaned. "The clock hasn't been wound nor the combination set."

Agatha's mother screamed again, hysterically.

"Hush!" said Mr. Adams, raising his trembling hand. "All be quiet for a moment. Agatha!" he called as loudly as he could. "Listen to me." During the following silence they could just hear the faint sound of the child wildly shrieking in the dark vault in a panic of terror.

"My precious darling!" wailed the mother. "She will die of fright! Open the door! Oh, break it open! Can't you men do something?"

"There isn't a man nearer than Little Rock who can open that door," said Mr. Adams, in a shaky voice. "My God! Spencer, what shall we do? That child—she can't stand it long in there. There isn't enough air, and, besides, she'll go into convulsions from fright."

Agatha's mother, frantic now, beat the door of the vault with her hands. Somebody wildly suggested dynamite. Annabel turned to Jimmy, her large eyes full of <u>anguish</u>, but not yet despairing. To a woman nothing seems quite impossible to the powers of the man she worships.

"Can't you do something, Ralph—*try*, won't you?"

He looked at her with a queer, soft smile on his lips and in his keen eyes.

"Annabel," he said, "give me that rose you are wearing, will you?"

Hardly believing that she heard him aright, she unpinned the bud from the bosom of her dress, and placed it in his hand. Jimmy stuffed it into his vest pocket, threw off his coat and pulled up his shirt sleeves. With that act Ralph D. Spencer passed away and Jimmy Valentine took his place.

"Get away from the door, all of you," he commanded, shortly.

He set his suitcase on the table, and opened it out flat. From that time on he seemed to be unconscious of the presence of

simultaneously
(sī′ məl tā′ nē əs lē) *adv.*
occurring at the same time

Reading Strategy
Asking Questions What question could you ask yourself about the situation in this paragraph?

anguish (aŋ′ gwish) *n.*
great suffering from worry

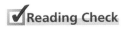**Reading Check**

What happens to Agatha?

anyone else. He laid out the shining, queer implements swiftly and orderly, whistling softly to himself as he always did when at work. In a deep silence and immovable, the others watched him as if under a spell.

In a minute Jimmy's pet drill was biting smoothly into the steel door. In ten minutes—breaking his own burglarious record—he threw back the bolts and opened the door.

Agatha, almost collapsed, but safe, was gathered into her mother's arms.

Jimmy Valentine put on his coat, and walked outside the railings toward the front door. As he went he thought he heard a far-away voice that he once knew call "Ralph!" But he never hesitated.

At the door a big man stood somewhat in his way.

"Hello, Ben!" said Jimmy, still with his strange smile. "Got around at last, have you? Well, let's go. I don't know that it makes much difference, now."

And then Ben Price acted rather strangely.

"Guess you're mistaken, Mr. Spencer," he said. "Don't believe I recognize you. Your buggy's waiting for you, ain't it?"

And Ben Price turned and strolled down the street.

Review and Assess

Thinking About the Selection

1. **Respond:** Would you have done what Ben Price did? Explain.

2. **(a) Recall:** Why is Jimmy Valentine in prison? **(b) Infer:** What is the prison warden's attitude toward Valentine's future? **(c) Contrast:** How is the warden's attitude different form Mike Dolan's attitude?

3. **(a) Recall:** What job does Valentine take after his release from prison? **(b) Infer:** What details suggest that he may be cracking safes as well? **(c) Draw Conclusions:** How do you know Valentine has given up safecracking for good?

4. **(a) Recall:** At what point in the story does Valentine have a change of heart? **(b) Deduce:** What causes this change? **(c) Support:** Find at least two details in the story that prove Valentine has really changed.

5. **(a) Recall:** Who is Ben Price? **(b) Infer:** Why does Price pretend not to know Valentine at the bank? **(c) Evaluate:** Does Price do the right thing? Explain.

6. **Make a Judgment:** Is Jimmy Valentine a good man? Explain.

O. Henry

(1862–1910)

O. Henry, who became one of America's best-known short-story writers, was born William Sydney Porter. His aunt Evelina nurtured his gift for storytelling by developing a game in which she would begin to tell a story and he would finish it. After growing up in Greensboro, North Carolina, Porter moved to Texas in 1882. There, he worked as a ranch hand, a bank teller, a writer and publisher of a humor magazine, and a reporter for the *Houston Post*. In 1898, he was sent to jail for embezzling bank funds. While in prison, he began to write short stories. It was there that he heard of a bank robber and safe-cracker who inspired the character of Jimmy Valentine, the hero of "A Retrieved Reformation."

Review and Assess

Literary Analysis

Surprise Ending

1. Complete a chart like the one shown to compare your expectations to the actual ending.

Ending I expect	O. Henry's Ending

2. What clues lead you to expect the ending you listed on your chart? Explain.
3. What details support the logic of the actual ending? Explain.
4. The surprise ending of this story arises from the decisions made by two characters—Jimmy and Ben. Use a graphic organizer like the one shown to examine those decisions and describe the character traits each one reveals.

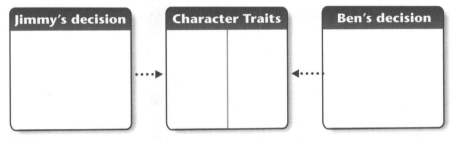

Connecting Literary Elements

5. Explain the **irony** of Jimmy having his tools with him when Agatha gets locked in the safe.
6. In what way does Ben Price almost ruin Jimmy?
7. In what way does Ben Price actually save Jimmy?

Reading Strategy

Asking Questions

8. You may have questioned whether Jimmy's "new life" in Elmore would last. What details in the story lead to your answer?
9. How does answering "Why does Ben Price let Jimmy go?" help you understand the story?

Extend Understanding

10. **Extend:** How could Jimmy use his skills to prevent robberies?

Quick Review

A **surprise ending** is an unexpected conclusion. To review surprise ending, see page 241.

Irony of situation occurs in a story when an event directly contradicts the expectations of the characters, the reader, or the audience. To review irony, see page 241.

Asking yourself **questions** about characters and events and then answering them can help you better understand a story.

 Take It to the Net
www.phschool.com
Take the interactive self-test online to check your understanding of the selection.

Integrate Language Skills

Vocabulary Development Lesson

Word Analysis: Latin Root -simul-

The word *simultaneously* contains the Latin word root -simul-, which means "same." *Simultaneously* means "at the same time." In a dictionary, find a word beginning with *simul* to fit each definition. Write each word.

1. to look or act the same
2. an image or experience that is almost the same as the real thing

Spelling Strategy

When you add -ion to verbs that end in *te*, you drop the *e* before adding -ion.

Add the -ion suffix to each word.

1. rehabilitate   2. promote   3. donate

Fluency: Sentence Completions

Complete each sentence with a vocabulary word from the list on page 241.

1. Detention is a type of ___?___.
2. Two things that occur at the same time happen ___?___.
3. If you are studying ___?___, you are studying carefully.
4. Tears can be a sign of ___?___.
5. Jimmy Valentine earned respect in Elmore by living a ___?___ life.
6. An elephant cannot move ___?___.

Grammar Lesson

Adjectives and Parallelism

Parallelism is the use of similar words, phrases, or structures for equal ideas. When juxtaposing two things—placing them in balance for emphasis—create parallel structure with the similar placement of adjectives.

> **Not parallel:** The heavy door was no match for the drill, which was light.
>
> **Parallel:** The heavy door was no match for the light drill.

When writing items in a series, use parallel placement of adjectives.

> **Not parallel:** His worn tools, complete concentration, and an attitude that was experienced silenced the group.
>
> **Parallel:** His worn tools, complete concentration, and experienced attitude silenced the group.

▶ *For more practice, see page R33, Exercise E.*

Practice Revise the sentences to create parallel structure through the placement of adjectives.

1. Jimmy's friendly manner, his smile that was charming, and his elegant clothes impressed the townspeople.
2. The sleepy town was about to become a place that was exciting.
3. Mr. Adams was a steady type but Jimmy was the type that was spontaneous.
4. Annabel was pretty, well-mannered, and she was charming.
5. Jimmy wore a gray vest, a wool coat, and a shirt that was pressed.

Writing Application Describe one of the characters. Use one sentence that includes nouns in a series. Include another in which you juxtapose a quality of the character with a quality of another character. Use parallel placement of adjectives.

W̶G̶ Prentice Hall Writing and Grammar Connection: Chapter 16, Section 1

Writing Lesson

Response to the Story

Write a response to the story in which you explain whether you agree or disagree with Ben Price's decision to let Jimmy go.

Prewriting   Jot down several reasons for your agreement or disagreement with Price's decision. Then, list details to support your reasons, using examples, analogies (comparisons that highlight the main quality of a situation by comparing it to something else that shares that quality), or other comparisons.

Model: Create an Analogy

What it is	What it is like
Price's decision to let Jimmy go	A fisherman putting the fish back into the water
Jimmy's second chance	Walking through a crowded intersection and just missing being hit by a truck

> This writer supports his or her conclusion by illustrating the positive aspects of Price's decision with analogies.

Drafting   Begin by stating your position either for or against Ben Price's action. Then, list your reasons, giving support for each one.

Revising   Look for places where changing the placement of adjectives will add variety to your sentences. Notice also places where you can create parallel structure for important ideas or descriptions.

WG Prentice Hall Writing and Grammar Connection: Chapter 12, Section 2

Extension Activities

Research and Technology Conduct research on the life and works of O. Henry. Explore questions about O. Henry, such as

- How did O. Henry choose his pen name?
- What other jobs besides writing did he pursue, and how did they contribute to his stories?

Share your group's findings with the rest of the class in an **oral report.**

Listening and Speaking Retell the story in the form of a television **news broadcast**. Include answers to the reporter's questions "who, what, when, where, why, and how." Organize the details of the report to meet the purpose of informing. Focus less on the love story and more on the facts of Jimmy's legal situation.

 **Take It to the Net**   www.phschool.com

Go online for an additional research activity using the Internet.

Prepare to Read

Emancipation ◆ O Captain! My Captain!

The First Reading of the Emancipation Proclamation before the Cabinet,
Courtesy of the Library of Congress

Take It to the Net

Visit www.phschool.com for interactive activities and instruction related to these selections, including
- background
- graphic organizers
- literary elements
- reading strategies

Preview

Connecting to the Literature

The subject of the biography and the poem you are about to read is Abraham Lincoln, considered by many people to be among the greatest leaders of all time. Think about what you already know about Lincoln. What are your impressions of him? Why?

Background

"Emancipation" is part of an award-winning full-length historical work, *Lincoln: A Photobiography*, written in 1987. "O Captain! My Captain!" is a poem written by the great American poet Walt Whitman—who served as a nurse during the Civil War—as a memorial to Lincoln after the president was assassinated.

Literary Analysis

Historical Context

The **historical context** of a literary work is the time period during which it is written or in which it takes place. Identify the events, attitudes, beliefs, and customs of the time period. Consider also the other literature of the time. These elements create the context, or situation in which a work is understood.

Create an organizer like the one shown here to analyze the cultural context of each work.

Comparing Literary Works

These two works are both about Lincoln. However, they differ in their scope—the range of details they present—and in their organization and purpose. To compare and contrast these works, ask yourself the following focus questions:

1. What details about Lincoln's life does each work include?
2. How are these details arranged to convey a message about Lincoln's historical importance?
3. What is the purpose, or goal, of each work?

Reading Strategy

Determining Cause and Effect

- A **cause** is an action, event, or situation that makes something happen.
- An **effect** is the result of a preceding event or situation.

As you read these selections, identify cause-and-effect relationships among events by asking yourself why events occur.

Vocabulary Development

alienate (āl′ yən āt′) *v.* make unfriendly; estrange (p. 257)

compensate (käm′ pən sāt′) *v.* repay (p. 257)

shackles (shak′ əls) *n.* a linked pair of metal fastenings, usually for the wrists or ankles of a prisoner (p. 258)

peril (per′ əl) *n.* exposure to harm or injury; danger (p. 258)

decisive (di sī′ siv) *adj.* having the power to settle a question or dispute (p. 258)

humiliating (hyo͞o mil′ ē āt′ iŋ) *adj.* embarrassing; undignified (p. 259)

exulting (eg zult′ iŋ) *v.* rejoicing (p. 261)

tread (tred) *n.* step (p. 262)

EMANCIPATION

from **Lincoln: A Photobiography**

Russell Freedman

President Abraham Lincoln was leading the country in 1862 during the Civil War. He was challenged to find the best means for preserving the Union. His troops had just been beaten in fierce battles in Virginia. He had tough military and political decisions to make.

The toughest decision facing Lincoln . . . was the one he had to make about slavery. Early in the war, he was still willing to leave slavery alone in the South, if only he could restore the Union. Once the rebellion was crushed, slavery would be confined to the Southern states, where it would gradually die out. "We didn't go into the war to put down slavery, but to put the flag back," Lincoln said. "To act differently at this moment would, I have no doubt, not only weaken our cause, but smack of bad faith."

Abolitionists were demanding that the president free the slaves at once, by means of a wartime proclamation. "Teach the rebels

Literary Analysis
Historical Context What different attitudes of people in this time period are discussed in this and the next paragraph?

and traitors that the price they are to pay for the attempt to abolish this Government must be the abolition of slavery," said Frederick Douglass, the famous black editor and reformer. "Let the war cry be down with treason, and down with slavery, the cause of treason!"

But Lincoln hesitated. He was afraid to <u>alienate</u> the large numbers of Northerners who supported the Union but opposed emancipation. And he worried about the loyal, slaveholding border states—Kentucky, Missouri, Maryland, and Delaware—that had refused to join the Confederacy. Lincoln feared that emancipation might drive those states into the arms of the South.

Yet slavery was the issue that had divided the country, and the president was under mounting pressure to do something about it. At first he supported a voluntary plan that would free the slaves gradually and <u>compensate</u> their owners with money from the federal treasury. Emancipation would begin in the loyal border states and be extended into the South as the rebel states were conquered. Perhaps then the liberated slaves could be resettled in Africa or Central America.

Lincoln pleaded with the border-state congressmen to accept his plan, but they turned him down. They would not part with their slave property or willingly change their way of life. "Emancipation in the cotton states is simply an absurdity," said a Kentucky congressman. "There is not enough power in the world to compel it to be done."

Lincoln came to realize that if he wanted to attack slavery, he would have to act more boldly. A group of powerful Republican

alienate (āl′ yən āt′) *v.* to make unfriendly; estrange

compensate (käm′ pən sāt′) *v.* to repay

Reading Check

Why did Lincoln enter the war?

senators had been urging him to act. It was absurd, they argued, to fight the war without destroying the institution that had caused it. Slaves provided a vast pool of labor that was crucial to the South's war effort. If Lincoln freed the slaves, he could cripple the Confederacy and hasten the end of the war. If he did not free them, then the war would settle nothing. Even if the South agreed to return to the Union, it would start another war as soon as slavery was threatened again.

Besides, enslaved blacks were eager to throw off their <u>shackles</u> and fight for their own freedom. Thousands of slaves had already escaped from behind Southern lines. Thousands more were ready to enlist in the Union armies. "You need more men," Senator Charles Sumner told Lincoln, "not only at the North, but at the South, in the rear of the rebels. You need the slaves."

All along, Lincoln had questioned his authority as president to abolish slavery in those states where it was protected by law. His Republican advisors argued that in time of war, with the nation in <u>peril</u>, the president did have the power to outlaw slavery. He could do it in his capacity as commander in chief of the armed forces. Such an act would be justified as a necessary war measure, because it would weaken the enemy. If Lincoln really wanted to save the Union, Senator Sumner told him, he must act now. He must wipe out slavery.

The war had become an endless nightmare of bloodshed and bungling generals. Lincoln doubted if the Union could survive without bold and drastic measures. By the summer of 1862, he had worked out a plan that would hold the loyal slave states in the Union, while striking at the enemies of the Union.

On July 22, 1862, he revealed his plan to his cabinet. He had decided, he told them, that emancipation was "a military necessity, absolutely essential to the preservation of the Union." For that reason, he intended to issue a proclamation freeing all the slaves in rebel states that had not returned to the Union by January 1, 1863. The proclamation would be aimed at the Confederate South only. In the loyal border states, he would continue to push for gradual, compensated emancipation.

Some cabinet members warned that the country wasn't ready to accept emancipation. But most of them nodded their approval, and in any case, Lincoln had made up his mind. He did listen to the objection of William H. Seward, his secretary of state. If Lincoln published his proclamation now, Seward argued, when Union armies had just been defeated in Virginia, it would seem like an act of desperation, "the last shriek on our retreat." The president must wait until the Union had won a <u>decisive</u> military victory in the East. Then he could issue his proclamation from a position of strength. Lincoln agreed. For the time being, he filed the document away in his desk.

Literary Analysis

Historical Context What does Freedman know as he writes the essay that people of Lincoln's time did not know?

shackles (shak′ əls) *n.* metal fastenings, usually a linked pair for the wrists or ankles of a prisoner

peril (per′ əl) *n.* exposure to harm or injury; danger

decisive (di sī′ siv) *adj.* having the power to settle a question or dispute

A month later, in the war's second battle at Bull Run, Union forces commanded by General John Pope suffered another humiliating defeat. "We are whipped again," Lincoln moaned. He feared now that the war was lost. Rebel troops under Robert E. Lee were driving north. Early in September, Lee invaded Maryland and advanced toward Pennsylvania.

Lincoln again turned to General George McClellan—Who else do I have? he asked—and ordered him to repel the invasion. The two armies met at Antietam Creek in Maryland on September 17 in the bloodiest single engagement of the war. Lee was forced to retreat back to Virginia. But McClellan, cautious as ever, held his position and failed to pursue the defeated rebel army. It wasn't the decisive victory Lincoln had hoped for, but it would have to do.

On September 22, Lincoln read the final wording of his Emancipation Proclamation to his cabinet. If the rebels did not return to the Union by January 1, the president would free "thenceforward and forever" all the slaves everywhere in the Confederacy. Emancipation would become a Union war objective. As Union armies smashed their way into rebel territory, they would annihilate slavery once and for all.

The next day, the proclamation was released to the press. Throughout the North, opponents of slavery hailed the measure, and black people rejoiced. Frederick Douglass, the black abolitionist, had criticized Lincoln severely in the past. But he said now: "We shout for joy that we live to record this righteous decree."

When Lincoln delivered his annual message to Congress on December 1, he asked support for his program of military emancipation:

"Fellow citizens, *we* cannot escape history. We of this Congress and this administration, will be remembered in spite of ourselves. . . . In *giving* freedom to the *slave,* we assure freedom to the *free*—honorable alike in what we give, and what we preserve."

On New Year's Day, after a fitful night's sleep, Lincoln sat at his White House desk and put the finishing touches on his historic decree. From this day forward, all slaves in the rebel states were "forever free." Blacks who wished to could now enlist in the Union army and sail on Union ships. Several all-black regiments were formed immediately. By the end of the war, more than 180,000 blacks—a majority of them emancipated slaves—had volunteered for the Union forces. They manned military garrisons and served as front-line combat troops in every theatre of the war.

The traditional New Year's reception was held in the White

humiliating
(hyōō mil′ ē āt′ iŋ) *adj.*
embarrassing; undignified

Reading Strategy
Determining Cause and Effect According to William H. Seward, how would the timing of the proclamation change its effect?

**Reading Check**

What does William H. Seward persuade Lincoln to do?

House that morning. Mary appeared at an official gathering for the first time since Willie's death[1], wearing garlands in her hair and a black shawl about her head.

During the reception, Lincoln slipped away and retired to his office with several cabinet members and other officials for the formal signing of the proclamation. He looked tired. He had been shaking hands all morning, and now his hand trembled as he picked up a gold pen to sign his name.

Ordinarily he signed "A. Lincoln." But today, as he put pen to paper, he carefully wrote out his full name. "If my name ever goes into history," he said then, "it will be for this act."

---

1. **Mary appeared . . . Willie's death** Mary Todd Lincoln was the President's wife. The couple's son William died in 1862 at the age of eleven.

Russell Freedman

(b. 1929)

If you like biographies, you may be familiar with the work of Russell Freedman. Freedman has written many critically acclaimed nonfiction books for young people that focus on great figures in American history, such as the Wright brothers, Crazy Horse, and Eleanor Roosevelt.

Freedman was born and grew up in San Francisco, California. After his discharge from the army, he worked as a reporter and editor for the Associated Press. He published his first book in 1961 and has been a full-time writer ever since. His *Lincoln: A Photobiography* won a Newbery Medal in 1988.

Review and Assess

Thinking About the Selection

1. **Respond:** Do you think President Lincoln ended slavery at the right time? Support your answer.
2. **(a) Recall:** What does Freedman say Lincoln's toughest decision as president was? **(b) Infer:** How is this decision related to Lincoln's ability to lead? **(c) Evaluate:** Does Freedman present Lincoln as a good leader? Explain.
3. **(a) Recall:** What consequences does Lincoln anticipate from certain northerners if he frees the slaves? **(b) Infer:** Why does Lincoln worry about Kentucky, Missouri, Maryland, and Delaware?
4. **(a) Recall:** Name two reasons that Lincoln decides to attack the issue of slavery. **(b) Synthesize:** Explain Lincoln's reasoning when he decides to issue the Emancipation Proclamation.
5. **(a) Recall:** What recommendation does Secretary of State William H. Seward make to Lincoln about when to publish his proclamation? **(b) Speculate:** Why does Lincoln choose to end slavery after the battle of Antietam Creek? **(c) Evaluate:** Does Lincoln achieve his goals by proclaiming emancipation at that time? Explain.
6. **Assess:** What, if any, act or achievement by an American president is as significant as Lincoln's Emancipation Proclamation?

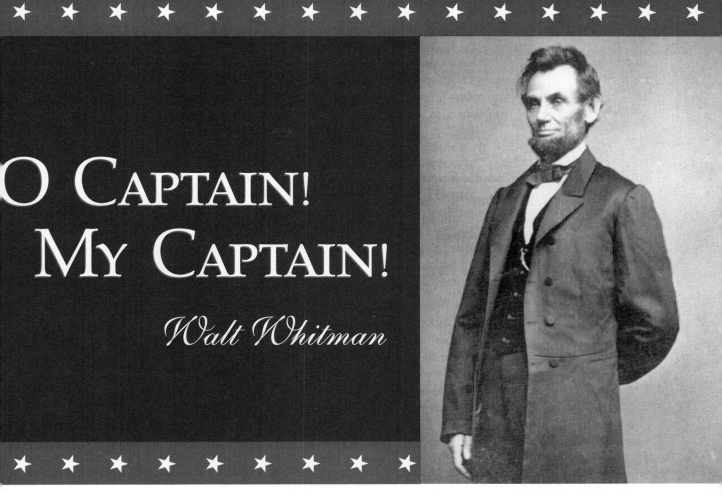

O CAPTAIN! MY CAPTAIN!

Walt Whitman

▲ **Critical Viewing** In what ways does Lincoln, as depicted in this photograph, exhibit leadership qualities? **[Interpret]**

O Captain! my Captain! our fearful trip is done,
The ship has weather'd every rack,[1] the prize we
    sought is won,
The port is near, the bells I hear, the people all
    <u>exulting</u>,
While follow eyes the steady keel,[2] the vessel grim
    and daring;
5   But O heart! heart! heart!
          O the bleeding drops of red,
             Where on the deck my Captain lies,
                Fallen cold and dead.

exulting (ig zult´ iŋ) *v.* rejoicing

☑ **Reading Check**

Why is the speaker upset?

---

1. rack *n.* great stress.
2. keel *n.* chief structural beam extending along the entire length of the bottom of a boat or ship and supporting the frame.

O Captain! my Captain! rise up and hear the bells;
10   Rise up—for you the flag is flung—for you the
      bugle trills,
For you bouquets and ribbon'd wreaths—for you
      the shores a-crowding,
For you they call, the swaying mass, their eager
      faces turning;
    Here Captain! dear father!
      This arm beneath your head!
15   It is some dream that on the deck,
          You've fallen cold and dead.

My Captain does not answer, his lips are pale
      and still,
My father does not feel my arm, he has no pulse
      nor will,
The ship is anchor'd safe and sound, its voyage
      closed and done,
20   From fearful trip the victor ship comes in with
      object won;
    Exult O shores, and ring O bells!
      But I with mournful <u>tread</u>,
        Walk the deck my Captain lies,
          Fallen cold and dead.

tread (tred) *n.* step

Review and Assess

Thinking About the Selection

1. **Respond:** How does this poem affect you?
2. **(a) Recall:** What has happened to the Captain?
   (b) Infer: Why does the timing of this event make it doubly unfortunate? **(c) Interpret:** How does the mood of the poem reflect what has happened?
3. **(a) Recall:** What words related to the sea and to sailing does the speaker of the poem use? **(b) Compare and Contrast:** In what ways does Lincoln's leadership of the country resemble a captain's role on a ship?
4. **(a) Recall:** What is the ship's destination? **(b) Interpret:** What is the "fearful trip" that the ship has "weathered"?
5. **(a) Recall:** How do the crowds of people respond to the Captain's arrival? **(b) Recall:** What feats has the Captain accomplished before the ship arrives? **(c) Draw Conclusions:** What kind of a leader does the speaker consider Lincoln?

Walt Whitman

(1819–1892)

Walt Whitman, one of America's greatest poets, began his career as a printer and journalist. In 1848, he began working on *Leaves of Grass*, a collection of poems about America. Because of its unusual style, commercial publishers refused to publish the book. However, Whitman printed a first edition with his own money in 1855. Since then, the style of Whitman's poetry has greatly influenced poets around the world.

During the Civil War, Whitman worked in military hospitals in Washington, D.C. Although he never formally met President Lincoln, he often saw the President at a distance in Washington. Lincoln's death moved Whitman to compose two famous poems, "O Captain! My Captain!" and "When Lilacs Last in the Dooryard Bloom'd."

Review and Assess

Literary Analysis

Historical Context

1. Explain why the knowledge that the nation was in a Civil War caused largely by the issue of slavery is critical to your understanding of "Emancipation."
2. Why was emancipation important not just morally, but politically as well? How does knowing this help you understand Lincoln's actions?
3. How does knowing that "O Captain! My Captain" was written just after Lincoln's death affect your response to it?

Comparing Literary Works

4. On a Venn diagram like this one, compare and contrast the portrayal of President Lincoln in these two selections. Consider similarities and differences in the way each work presents Lincoln as a president, as a man, and as a public figure.

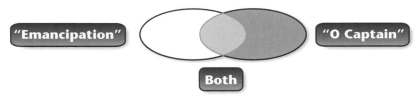

5. For what purposes do the authors write about Lincoln?
6. How do Freedman and Whitman feel about Lincoln as a leader?

Reading Strategy

Determining Cause and Effect

7. Use a diagram like the one below to identify three causes that had the effect of delaying the proclamation and two causes that eventually led to the proclamation.

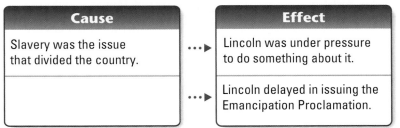

Cause		Effect
Slavery was the issue that divided the country.	...▶	Lincoln was under pressure to do something about it.
	...▶	Lincoln delayed in issuing the Emancipation Proclamation.

Extend Understanding

8. **Social Studies Connection:** If Lincoln were President today, what issues would he bring to national attention? Explain.

Quick Review

Historical context is the time period during which a literary work is written or set. To review historical context, see page 255.

A **cause** is an action, event, or situation that produces a result.

An **effect** is the result of a preceding event, or situation. To review causes and effects, see page 255.

 Take It to the Net
www.phschool.com
Take the interactive self-test online to check your understanding of these selections.

Integrate Language Skills

Vocabulary Development Lesson

Word Analysis: Latin Suffix -ate

The Latin suffix -ate means "to make or apply." Complete these sentences by adding the Latin suffix -ate to the noun or adjective in parentheses.

1. The smell of food can make a hungry person ___?___. (saliva)
2. Lincoln did not want to ___?___ people. (alien)

Spelling Strategy

When adding -ed or -ing to words that end with -ate, drop the e before adding any letters. Write new words indicated below.

1. create + -ing   2. devastate + -ed

Fluency: Definitions

On your paper, match each vocabulary word to its closest definition.

1. compensate
2. peril
3. decisive
4. humiliating
5. shackles
6. tread
7. exulting
8. alienate

a. great rejoicing
b. make unfriendly
c. step
d. restraints
e. danger
f. repay
g. crucial
h. hurtful to one's pride

Grammar Lesson

Adverbs and Sentence Variety

An **adverb** is a word that modifies, or describes, a verb, an adjective, or another adverb. Adverbs answer the questions *when*, *where*, *in what manner*, and *to what extent*.

"If Lincoln *really* wanted to save the Union . . . he must act *now*."
(*Really* tells to what extent he wanted; *now* tells when he must act.)

An adverb usually comes before the word it modifies, but it can also appear at the end or beginning of a sentence.

I have been feeling more energetic *lately*.
Lately, I have been feeling more energetic.

Vary the placement of adverbs to create sentence variety. However, check to make sure that it remains clear which word is being modified.

▶ *For more practice, see page R28, Exercise C.*
Practice Identify the adverb and the word modified in each of the following sentences. Then, revise each sentence to place the adverb at the beginning of the sentence.

1. Thousands of slaves had already escaped from behind Southern lines.
2. Lincoln carefully wrote out his full name.
3. I read a poem yesterday by Walt Whitman.
4. Lincoln finally issued the Emancipation Proclamation.
5. Lincoln spoke his mind decisively.

Writing Application Add at least one adverb to each sentence. Then, rewrite each sentence to vary the placement of the adverb.

1. Lincoln was cautious about freeing the slaves.
2. Many believed slavery caused the division between the North and the South.

W̶G Prentice Hall Writing and Grammar Connection: Chapter 16, Section 2

Writing Lesson

Description

"Emancipation" and "O Captain! My Captain!" both give unique insights into Lincoln's personality and character. Use details from the selections to write a brief description of Lincoln.

Prewriting   Use an organizer like the one shown to jot down qualities and traits of Lincoln that are mentioned in the selections. Group examples around main traits.

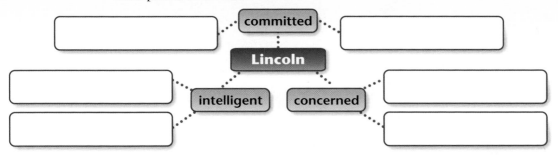

Drafting   Begin with a general statement about Lincoln's character. In the body of your description, use the main traits or ideas that you write in the larger spaces as the main ideas in paragraphs. Use details in the smaller spaces as the supporting details.

Revising   Delete or move details that do not support the main idea of a paragraph.

*W*G *Prentice Hall Writing and Grammar Connection: Chapter 6, Section 2*

Extension Activities

Listening and Speaking With a group, take turns delivering an **oral interpretation** of the Emancipation Proclamation (1863), the Declaration of Independence, or "O Captain! My Captain!"

1. Locate the work you will present through library resources or the Internet.
2. Listen to professional recordings, paying attention to the way the speaker uses his or her voice to create different effects.
3. Take turns delivering the work. Evaluate one another's delivery and the effect of volume, speed, and tone of voice.

Research and Technology Use the Internet to research Lincoln's presidency. Conduct a key word search to find sites. When using Internet search engines, type in specific words about your topic. Connectors such as AND, OR, and NOT help to narrow a search. For example, "Lincoln AND presidency" or "Lincoln NOT childhood" may provide sites about the topic, Lincoln's presidency. Write a **brief review** of the three best sites.

 **Take It to the Net**   www.phschool.com

Go online for an additional research activity using the Internet.

Prepare to Read

Gentleman of Río en Medio ◆ Saving the Wetlands

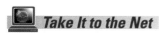
Take It to the Net

Visit www.phschool.com
for interactive activities
and instruction related to
these selections, including

- background
- graphic organizers
- literary elements
- reading strategies

Preview

Connecting to the Literature

Something that you find valuable may not be valuable to someone else. Each of these selections focuses on a person who finds value in nature—a value not shared by everyone.

Background

"Saving the Wetlands," by Barbara A. Lewis, focuses on the need to preserve wetlands—areas where the water level remains near or above the surface of the ground for most of the year. Types of wetlands include bogs, fens, marshes, and swamps. These areas are home to many kinds of plants and animals, including endangered species.

Literary Analysis
Resolution of a Conflict

In a narrative, a **conflict** is a struggle between two opposing forces. Often, a conflict takes the form of a problem that must be solved. The events in the narrative move toward the **resolution** of the conflict—the final outcome.

As you read, look for answers to the following focus questions:

1. What is the conflict or problem?
2. What do the characters do to resolve the conflict?

Comparing Literary Works

The way characters try to resolve a conflict will be influenced by a number of factors:

- the time period in which the character lives
- the character's motives—the reason he or she acts in a certain way
- the character's personality and past experiences

"Gentleman of Río en Medio" and "Saving the Wetlands" both present conflicts related to land ownership and the law. Use a graphic organizer like the one here to compare and contrast the way the characters deal with the conflict.

Gentleman		Wetlands
_____	time period	_____
_____	experiences	_____
_____	personality	_____
_____	motives	_____
	reactions to owning or sharing land	

Reading Strategy
Drawing Inferences

An **inference** is a reasonable conclusion that you can draw from given facts or clues. Look at the following example.

> It took months of negotiation to come to an understanding with the old man. He was in no hurry.

From these first two sentences in "Gentleman of Río en Medio," you can infer, or read between the lines, that the old man does not make quick decisions.

Vocabulary Development

negotiation (ni gō′ shē ā′ shən) *n.* discussion to reach an agreement (p. 269)

gnarled (närld) *adj.* knotty and twisted (p. 269)

innumerable (in n o͞o′ mər ə bəl) *adj.* too many to be counted (p. 269)

broached (brōcht) *v.* started a discussion about a topic (p. 270)

petition (pə tish′ ən) *n.* a formal document often signed by a number of people that makes a request of a person or group. (p. 275)

wizened (wiz′ ənd) *adj.* shriveled or withered (p. 276)

brandishing (bran′ dish iŋ) *v.* waving in a challenging way (p. 277)

GENTLEMAN OF RÍO EN MEDIO

Juan A. A. Sedillo

► **Critical Viewing**
Does the man in this painting look like someone who would "bow to all of us in the room"? Why or why not? **[Infer]**

The Sacristan of Trampas (detail), ca. 1915, Paul Burlin, Museum of Fine Arts, New Mexico

It took months of <u>negotiation</u> to come to an understanding with the old man. He was in no hurry. What he had the most of was time. He lived up in Río en Medio, (rē´ en mā dē ō) where his people had been for hundreds of years. He tilled the same land they had tilled. His house was small and wretched, but quaint. The little creek ran through his land. His orchard was <u>gnarled</u> and beautiful.

The day of the sale he came into the office. His coat was old, green and faded. I thought of Senator Catron,[1] who had been such a power with these people up there in the mountains. Perhaps it was one of his old Prince Alberts.[2] He also wore gloves. They were old and torn and his fingertips showed through them. He carried a cane, but it was only the skeleton of a worn-out umbrella. Behind him walked one of his <u>innumerable</u> kin—a dark young man with eyes like a gazelle.

The old man bowed to all of us in the room. Then he removed his hat and gloves, slowly and carefully. Chaplin[3] once did that in a picture, in a bank—he was the janitor. Then he handed his things to the boy, who stood obediently behind the old man's chair.

There was a great deal of conversation, about rain and about his family. He was very proud of his large family. Finally we got down to business. Yes, he would sell, as he had agreed, for twelve hundred dollars, in cash. We would buy, and the money was ready. "Don[4] Anselmo," I said to him in Spanish, "we have made a discovery. You remember that we sent that surveyor, that engineer, up there to survey your land so as to make the deed. Well, he finds that you own more than eight acres. He tells us that your land extends across the river and that you own almost twice as much as you thought." He didn't know that. "And now, Don Anselmo," I added, "these Americans are *buena gente*,[5] they are good people, and they are willing to pay you for the additional land as well, at the same rate per acre, so that instead of twelve hundred dollars you will get almost twice as much, and the money is here for you."

The old man hung his head for a moment in thought. Then he stood up and stared at me. "Friend," he said, "I do not like to have you speak to me in that manner." I kept still and let him have his say. "I know these Americans are good people, and that is why I have agreed to sell to them. But I do not care to be insulted. I have agreed to sell my house and land for twelve hundred dollars and that is the price."

I argued with him but it was useless. Finally he signed the deed and took the money but refused to take more than the amount agreed upon. Then he shook hands all around, put on his ragged gloves, took his stick and walked out with the boy behind him.

----

1. **Senator Catron** Thomas Benton Catron, senator from New Mexico, 1912–1917.
2. **Prince Alberts** long, double-breasted coats.
3. **Chaplin** Charlie Chaplin (1889–1977), actor and producer of silent films in the United States.
4. **Don** Spanish title of respect, similar to *sir* in English.
5. *buena gente* (bwā´ nä hen´ tā) Spanish for "good people."

negotiation
(ni gō´ shē ā´ shən) *n.* discussion to reach an agreement

gnarled (närld) *adj.* knotty and twisted

innumerable
(i nōō´ mər ə bəl) *adj.* too many to be counted

Reading Strategy
Drawing Inferences
In this paragraph, what inference can you draw about Don Anselmo?

**Reading Check**

What business are the people meeting about?

Springtime. c. 1928-29, Victor Higgins. Private collection, photo courtesy of the Gerald Peters Gallery, Santa Fe, NM.

◀ **Critical Viewing**
Does this orchard seem "gnarled and beautiful" to you? **[Evaluate]**

A month later my friends had moved into Río en Medio. They had replastered the old adobe house, pruned the trees, patched the fence, and moved in for the summer. One day they came back to the office to complain. The children of the village were overrunning their property. They came every day and played under the trees, built little play fences around them, and took blossoms. When they were spoken to they only laughed and talked back good-naturedly in Spanish.

I sent a messenger up to the mountains for Don Anselmo. It took a week to arrange another meeting. When he arrived he repeated his previous preliminary performance. He wore the same faded cutaway,[6] carried the same stick and was accompanied by the boy again. He shook hands all around, sat down with the boy behind his chair, and talked about the weather. Finally I <u>broached</u> the subject. "Don Anselmo, about the ranch you sold to these people. They are good people and want to be your friends and neighbors always. When you sold to them you signed a document, a deed, and in that deed you agreed to several things. One thing was that they were to have the complete possession of the property. Now, Don Anselmo, it seems that every day the children of the village overrun the orchard and spend most of their time there. We would like to know if you, as the most respected man in the village, could not stop them from doing so in order that these people may enjoy their new home more in peace."

Don Anselmo stood up. "We have all learned to love these Americans," he said, "because they are good people and good neighbors. I sold them my property because I knew they were good people, but I did not sell them the trees in the orchard."

broached (brōcht) *v.* started a discussion about a topic

Literary Analysis
Resolution of a Conflict
What is the conflict of the story?

---

6. cutaway (kut´ ə wā´) *n.* coat worn by men for formal daytime occasions.

This was bad. "Don Anselmo," I pleaded, "when one signs a deed and sells real property one sells also everything that grows on the land, and those trees, every one of them, are on the land and inside the boundaries of what you sold."

"Yes, I admit that," he said. "You know," he added, "I am the oldest man in the village. Almost everyone there is my relative and all the children of Río en Medio are my *sobrinos* and *nietos*,[7] my descendants. Every time a child has been born in Río en Medio since I took possession of that house from my mother I have planted a tree for that child. The trees in that orchard are not mine, *Señor*, they belong to the children of the village. Every person in Río en Medio born since the railroad came to Santa Fe owns a tree in that orchard. I did not sell the trees because I could not. They are not mine."

There was nothing we could do. Legally we owned the trees but the old man had been so generous, refusing what amounted to a fortune for him. It took most of the following winter to buy the trees, individually, from the descendants of Don Anselmo in the valley of Río en Medio.

---

7. **sobrinos** (sō brē′ nōs) **and nietos** (nyā′ tōs) Spanish for "nieces and nephews" and "grandchildren."

Juan A. A. Sedillo

(1902–1982)

A native of New Mexico, Juan A. A. Sedillo was a descendant of early Spanish colonists of the Southwest. In addition to being a writer, Sedillo served as a lawyer and judge and held a number of public offices.

Sedillo's story, "The Gentleman of Río en Medio," is based on an actual legal case that arose from a conflict over the value of a piece of property. Sedillo turned this case into a gentle tale that reveals the attitudes and culture of the people he knew so well.

Review and Assess

Thinking About the Selection

1. **Respond:** If you had bought Don Anselmo's land, would you be satisfied with the way things turned out? Why or why not?

2. **(a) Recall:** Who is the narrator of this story? **(b) Analyze:** What is the role of the narrator? **(c) Analyze:** How does the narrator's behavior affect the outcome?

3. **(a) Recall:** What does Don Anselmo discuss with the narrator before getting down to business? **(b) Infer:** What does this tell you about his personality? **(c) Connect:** What other details in the opening of the story indicate Don Anselmo's personality?

4. **(a) Recall:** Why does the narrator offer Don Anselmo more money? What is Don Anselmo's reaction? **(b) Compare and Contrast:** Compare and contrast the attitudes of Don Anselmo and the Americans toward money and what it can buy.

5. **(a) Recall** According to Don Anselmo, who owns the trees? **(b) Interpret:** Explain Don Anselmo's reasoning in your own words. **(c) Deduce:** How does Don Anselmo feel about the children and their parents?

Saving the **Wetlands**

Barbara A. Lewis

One day in 1987, Andy Holleman's family received a letter from a land developer. The letter announced the developer's plans to build 180 condominium[1] units near the Hollemans' home in Chelmsford, Massachusetts.

Twelve-year-old Andy snatched the letter and shouted, "He can't do that! He's talking about building right on top of the wetlands!"

Andy knew that several species living on that land were either endangered or on the Special Concern list of animals whose numbers are shrinking. He had spent much of his free time roaming the area, watching great blue herons bend their long, delicate legs in marshy waters, seeing blue-spotted salamanders slither past shy wood turtles, and hearing the red-tailed hawk's lonely call—*cree, cree.* He often ripped off his baseball cap and waved to salute their graceful flight.

"Mom, you've got to take me to the library," Andy insisted. "I need to find out everything I can about the land. We've got to fight this."

Cheryl Holleman, a school nurse, dropped her son off at the library. There Andy examined the master plan for their town. He dug into the Annotated Laws[2] for the state. And he discovered that the condos would take up 16.3 acres of land, one-half of which would cover and destroy the wetlands. A new sewage treatment plant, oil from driveways, and fertilizer runoff could all pollute the water system or penetrate the soil, contaminating both water and land.

Andy also learned that the proposed development sat on a stream which led into Russell Mill Pond. The pond fed into town wells. So it was possible that Chelmsford's drinking water could be contaminated, too. "Our drinking water was already terrible enough," Andy says, grinning.

He had his ammunition, and he had to do *something.* He thought of all the living things whose habitats would be destroyed by the condos: the ladyslippers, mountain laurels, fringed gentians, foxes, and snakes. And he knew he could count on his parents' support. They had always encouraged him to respect the environment.

Even now, when Cheryl needs Andy to do a chore, she doesn't bother looking for him in front of the TV. She knows she'll find him sprawled half off his bed or stretched across the floor, reading. Andy devours Audubon books about wildlife. He loves author Gerald Durrell's *The Drunken Forest* and *Birds, Beasts, and Other Relatives.* Sometimes, of course, he sneaks in a Stephen King thriller.

Literary Analysis
Resolution of a Conflict
What problem will Andy try to solve?

Reading Check

Why is Andy concerned about building on the wetlands?

---

1. **condominium** (kän´ də min´ ē əm) *n.* group of living units joined together; each unit is separately owned.
2. **Annotated** (an ō tāt´ əd) **Laws** laws with explanatory notes.

◀ **Critical Viewing** What animals do you think make their homes in this habitat? **[Speculate]**

Andy and his family have taken many nature walks in the wooded area by Russell Mill Pond. It's something they enjoy doing together—Andy, Cheryl, his dad, David, and his younger brother and sister, Nicholas and Elizabeth.

Andy remembers sitting on the glacial rocks by the stream in the middle of winter, eating baloney sandwiches. In the warmer months, he and Nicholas and Elizabeth played tag in the stream, jumping on the slippery rocks, soaking their shoes, socks, and jeans. When fall came, they gathered brilliant red leaves from swamp maples and golden oak, while their mother picked dried grape vines for wreaths. The children took their leaves home, pressed them between waxed paper, ironed them flat, then hung them on doorknobs and from picture frames.

The wetlands area where the developer wanted to build held other memories for Andy. Sometimes he ice-skated on the pond. Sometimes he made important discoveries.

"Once I brought home a huge baby crow," he says. "A baby crow is called a 'fledgling,' and this one was just learning to fly. It had fallen out of the nest. So I fed him popcorn and water that night, and built him a perch.

"Mom wouldn't let me keep him in the house while I was at school. But that was okay. He was able to fly away the next day to return to his home in the swamp."

When Andy was eleven, he found a skunk caught in a steel-jaw trap, the kind that rips animals' legs apart. Since he had been swimming with a

▼ **Critical Viewing**
In what way are the skunk pictured here and the hawk on page 276 alike? How are they different? **[Compare and Contrast]**

friend, Andy was wearing only his swim trunks and tattered sneakers—luckily, as it turned out.

He put on a diving mask, sneaked up behind the skunk, pressed the release button on the trap, and grabbed the startled skunk by the tail. Then he carried him upside-down for a quarter of a mile—all the way to his house. He knew that skunks can't spray when held by the tail.

Small children trailed behind him, holding their noses and giggling. A neighbor telephoned Andy's mother and said, "Go outside and watch. And shut your windows and doors behind you. Don't ask me to explain. Just do it."

By the time Andy arrived home, he was leading twenty dancing, squealing children, like the Pied Piper. The skunk dangled from his hand at arm's length.

"This is one animal you're not going to keep, Andrew," his mom called in a shrill voice.

His father, who was home from his job as a medical technologist, phoned the local animal shelter for advice.

"They said we could either let the skunk go in the woods, or bring it in to the shelter," David Holleman told his son. "You'd better let him go and let nature take its course. There is no way you're putting that animal in my car, and you certainly can't hold him out the window by his tail the whole way to the shelter."

"I let him go," Andy recalls. "His leg wasn't too bad, so it would probably heal by itself. Everyone thought I smelled pretty skunky, though. I bathed in vinegar, which smelled just as awful as the skunk to me. I finally came clean, but we had to throw my sneakers away."

Crows and skunks aren't the only creatures Andy has brought home from the wetlands. "My mother remembers an eighteen-inch snapping turtle which went to the bathroom all over the kitchen linoleum." He laughs. "I fed him raw hamburger."

Often Andy just wandered through the woods to think or to write a poem. Sometimes he sat quietly for hours, studying animal behavior. He spotted deer and red foxes. He captured salamanders, snakes, mice, and moles; after learning all he could from observing each animal, Andy carefully carried it back to its home in the woods.

The wetlands were too important to cover with concrete and steel. Andy couldn't allow Pontiacs and Toyotas to replace blue herons and shy wood turtles. He couldn't permit blaring car horns to muffle the *cree* of the red-tailed hawk.

"So I drafted a <u>petition</u> for the residents to sign to try to stop the developer from building," Andy says. "I walked around the neighborhood and collected 180 signatures. I told everyone to come to the public town meeting scheduled with the developer. I also collected about fifty signatures from students in the neighborhood and at McCarthy Middle School."

petition (pə tish´ ən) *n.* a formal document often signed by a number of people that makes a request of a person or group.

**Reading Check**

What kinds of things does Andy do as he wanders through the woods?

Only one or two people refused to sign the petition. "They acted like they thought I was too young, like I didn't know what I was doing. But almost everybody was really supportive."

Often Andy carried his petition around for an hour and collected only a few signatures—not because people didn't want to sign, but because they wanted to talk. They'd offer Andy a Coke and invite him in to discuss the problem. Andy spent a lot of time conversing with his neighbors.

An elderly lady named Agatha answered her door with long, bony fingers. Although she was <u>wizened</u> and thin with wild, white hair, Andy's enthusiasm breathed new life into her. She attended over forty meetings and became a real activist.

wizened (wiz´ ənd) *adj.* shriveled or withered

Once, on the way back from carrying his petition, Andy decided to detour through the swamp. He kicked up his heels with too much energy and tripped over a rotted log. He snatched helplessly at the pages of his petition as they tumbled into a muddy stream, but he managed to salvage them.

"It took a while for the pages to dry out," he recalls with a grin, "and then my mom had to iron them out flat. That's the last time I ever went through the swamp with something that wasn't waterproofed."

Andy sent copies of his petition to the Board of Selectmen,[3] the Conservation Commission, the Zoning Board of Appeals,[4] the Board of Health, and the land developer. He wrote letters to senators, representatives, and a TV anchorwoman. Although he received letters of support in return, no one did anything to help.

"When I called the Massachusetts Audubon Society and told them my problem with the wetlands and that no one was really helping me, the woman gave me no sympathy," Andy says. "She just told me, 'That's no excuse for *you*,' and went right on giving information. I learned that when you really believe in something, you have to stand up for it no matter how old you are."

Slowly, Andy's neighbors joined in, neighbors he had contacted with his petition. They organized into the Concord Neighborhood Association and raised $16,000 to hire a lawyer and an environmental consultant to fight the development of the wetlands.

On the night of the town meeting with the developer, over 250 people showed up. The meeting had to be moved to the basement of the Town Hall to make room for the crowd. And when the developer stood up and announced that *he* was the one who had invited everyone, the residents disagreed, saying, "No, it was Andy Holleman who invited us here."

---

3. **Board of Selectmen** group of persons elected to manage town affairs.
4. **Zoning Board of Appeals** group of persons who review problems dealing with construction in business and residential areas.

Andy had prepared a speech to give at the meeting. When it was time for him to speak, his stomach flipped, but he walked to the front of the room anyway, <u>brandishing</u> the brown shell of a wood turtle.

"You call yourself the Russell Mill Pond Realty Trust, Inc.," Andy began. "I don't understand how you can call yourself this when you're essentially polluting your own name." The residents responded with thunderous applause. White-haired Agatha winked at him and motioned a thumbs-up.

Andy continued. "We need the wetlands to prevent flooding and to purify the water through the mud," he said. "We need the plants and the creatures living there."

Nobody won that night's debate. In fact, the meetings continued for ten months. There were at least two meetings every week and sometimes more. Andy and either his mom or his dad attended every meeting—and Andy still got high grades in school. He spoke at most of the meetings.

In one meeting with the Board of Health, the developer arose and announced, "I'm not going to argue hydrogeological[5] facts with a thirteen-year-old!" Andy's parents were angry, but Andy just shrugged his shoulders.

Nine months after the first meeting, an important test called a "deep-hole test" was conducted in the swamp. The purpose of the test was to find out how quickly a hole dug in the swamp would fill up with water. If it filled up very fast, that would be a sign that the land was not suitable for building.

The developer, members of the Concord Neighborhood Association, and state environmental officials gathered to observe the test. The hole was dug—and it filled with water almost immediately. Andy grinned clear around his head.

The developer tried to withdraw his application to build on the wetlands, but the Zoning Board of Appeals wouldn't let him. Legally, that wouldn't have solved the problem. Someone else could have applied for the same kind of project, and Andy and his neighbors would have had to start fighting all over again. Instead, the Board totally denied the application. Their refusal prevented anyone from trying to build a big development on the wetlands.

When they got the news, Andy and the Concord Neighborhood Association cheered. Their battle was

---

5. hydrogeological (hī′ drō jē ə läj′ i kəl) *adj.* related to water and to the science of the nature and history of Earth.

◀ **Critical Viewing** In what way is a red-tailed hawk like this strong? In what ways is it fragile? **[Classify]**

brandishing (bran′ dish in) *v.* waving or exhibiting in a challenging way

Literary Analysis
Resolution of a Conflict
Is this a good way to resolve the conflict? Why or why not?

✓**Reading Check**

What happens when they conduct the "deep-hole test"?

over! And the wetlands were safe from large developers.

Soon after, the developer started building condos on an old drive-in movie lot—an acceptable site Andy had suggested in the beginning.

What did all of this mean to Andy? He became a celebrity. Even though he is modest and shy, he accepted invitations to speak at schools, community groups, and organizations. He received many awards, including the Young Giraffe Award for young people who "stick their necks out" for the good of others. His award was a free trip to the Soviet Union in July, 1990.

And what is Andy doing now? He's planning to go to college in a few years, where he'd like to study environmental law. Meanwhile, he's setting up a non-profit, tax-exempt fund to purchase the wetlands and any surrounding threatened land to preserve it forever. Then he can always wander by Russell Mill Pond, gathering autumn leaves from crimson swamp maples and golden oaks. He can watch the blue herons bend their long, delicate legs in marshy waters, and see blue-spotted salamanders slither safely past shy wood turtles. And he can hear the lonely cree of the red-tailed hawk as it soars freely, high above the pond, dipping its wings as if in salute to him. To Andy.

Review and Assess

Thinking About the Selection

1. **Respond:** What part of the environment do you care about most? Would you mount a campaign to save it? Explain.
2. **(a) Recall:** Why does Andy Holleman want to save the wetlands? **(b) Analyze:** Why does the narrator tell so much about Andy's experiences with the animals? **(c) Connect:** How do these accounts help us know Andy better?
3. **(a) Recall:** What is the first thing Andy does in his struggle against the developer? **(b) Contrast:** Contrast the two different types of reactions he gets. **(c) Assess:** Do you think Andy's age worked for or against him in his campaign to stop the developer? Explain.
4. **(a) Recall:** What test led to the rejection of the developer's application? **(b) Evaluate:** Explain why Andy was or was not successful.
5. **Hypothesize:** Suppose Andy had lost his fight. What would have happened to the wildlife and the wetlands?
6. **Take a Position:** What are your opinions about the balance between progress and development and preserving natural areas?

Barbara A. Lewis

(b. 1943)
Barbara Lewis never expected to be a writer. While teaching sixth grade in her home state of Utah, her class began a campaign to get rid of a hazardous waste site. Lewis was so impressed by her students' efforts that she decided to write about them.

Lewis believes that when it comes to taking social action, age does not matter. She wants young people to know that they can make a difference. To demonstrate this belief, she wrote *The Kid's Guide to Service Projects*, *The Kid's Guide to Social Action*, and *Kids With Courage*, a book that tells the stories of eighteen young people who spoke up for what they believed in.

Review and Assess

Literary Analysis

Resolution of a Conflict

1. What is the conflict or problem in each work?
2. What does each character do to resolve the conflict?
3. Identify "winners" and "losers" of the conflict in each selection on a chart like the one shown. Then, tell what each has gained or lost.

	Winners	Losers	What's Lost or Gained
"Gentleman of Río en Medio"			
"Saving the Wetlands"			

Comparing Literary Works

4. What are each character's motives, or reasons for acting as he or she does?
5. In what way do the customs, beliefs, and laws of the time period help or interfere with Andy's and Don Anselmo's struggles?
6. How do Andy's motives compare and contrast with Don Anselmo's?

Reading Strategy

Drawing Inferences

7. What can you infer about the Americans in "Gentleman of Río en Medio" based on the fact that they offer more money for Don Anselmo's land?
8. What inference can you make about Don Anselmo's character based on the fact that he will not accept the money?
9. Complete the chart to identify details that support the inferences shown.

Support	Inferences
	Andy enjoys spending time in the wetlands.
	The developer doesn't take Andy seriously.
	Andy will continue to work for the protection of natural lands.

Extend Understanding

10. **Career Connection:** Andy learned a great deal in his campaign to save the wetlands. Identify several careers he might pursue using the skills and knowledge he gained.

Quick Review

A **conflict** is a struggle between two opposing forces. The **resolution** is the outcome of the conflict. To review conflict and resolution, see page 267.

A character's or person's **motives** are the reasons he or she acts in a certain way.

When you **draw inferences,** you make an educated guess based on details in a story, essay, or article.

 Take It to the Net
www.phschool.com
Take the interactive self-test online to check your understanding of these selections.

Integrate Language Skills

Vocabulary Development Lesson

Word Analysis: Latin Root *-num-*

Words that contain the Latin word root *-num-*, as in *innumerable*, are related in meaning to the word *number*. *Innumerable* means "too many to be counted." Write the word from the list below that best completes each sentence.

enumerate   numerator   innumerable

1. The sky was dotted with ___?___ stars.
2. The ___?___ is the top number in a fraction.
3. The teacher will ___?___ the rules.

Spelling Strategy

The *n* sound you hear in the vocabulary word *gnarled* is spelled with a silent *g* preceding the *n*. Unscramble these *gn* words, and write them on your paper. Then, refer to a dictionary to write a definition for each one.

1. wagn   3. hnags
2. tnag   4. mogen

Grammar Lesson

Adjective or Adverb?

Good is an adjective. Use it after linking verbs including *looks*, *feels*, *seems*, *sounds*, and forms of *be*. *Well* is usually an adverb; occasionally it is used as an adjective.

Incorrect: The class behaved *good* all day.
Correct: The class behaved *well* all day.

Incorrect: That dress looks *well* on you.
Correct: That dress looks *good* on you.
Correct: She is not *well*.

Bad is an adjective. *Badly* is an adverb.

That loud music sounds *bad*.
I did *badly* on the test.

Concept Development: Synonyms

Synonyms are words that have almost the same meaning. For each numbered word, write the synonym from the three lettered choices.

1. negotiation: **a.** discussion, **b.** argument, **c.** opinion
2. gnarled: **a.** angry, **b.** intelligent, **c.** twisted
3. innumerable: **a.** countless, **b.** difficult, **c.** impossible
4. broached: **a.** mentioned, **b.** bejeweled, **c.** followed
5. petition: **a.** request, **b.** reply, **c.** complaint
6. wizened: **a.** wise, **b.** shriveled, **c.** empty
7. brandishing: **a.** waving, **b.** bragging, **c.** swaying

▶ *For more practice, see page R28, Exercise C.*

Practice Copy the following paragraph, proofreading and correcting errors in the use of *good*, *well*, *bad*, and *badly*.

There are only a few students in the orchestra this year. I think this is good because we have more time. I feel badly for the orchestra leader, though. I don't think the orchestra plays as good this year as last. It's not that they play bad, but they need practice. They sounded well last week. I hope they sound as good this week.

Writing Application Write a brief paragraph about a subject involving school or the environment. Use the following words at least once: *bad*, *badly*, *good*, and *well*.

*W**G* *Prentice Hall Writing and Grammar Connection: Chapter 25, Section 1*

Writing Lesson

Persuasive Speech

At a town meeting, Andy Holleman spoke persuasively against building on the wetlands. Write your own speech either for or against building on the wetlands.

Prewriting   Use periodical indexes to gather details about the effects of development on wetlands. A periodical index lists (alphabetically by subject) articles in magazines, newspapers, and journals. Look for articles that contain details, statistics, and quotations that support your position.

Drafting   Begin by stating your position. Then, support your position by organizing your reasons and details in order of importance. Conclude with your most powerful reason.

> *Reasons are numbered in order of importance. Each reason will be developed and supported in the body of the essay.*

Model: Organization

We need to clean up the abandoned fields and stream near the industrial park because 1) the area is unsightly, 2) the fields could be used as a sports field or playground, and 3) dangerous chemicals and other materials are polluting the stream and water table.

> By saving the most important issue until last, the speech will have more punch and is more likely to be remembered.

Revising   Add transitions to indicate the relative importance of each point. Common transitions for order of importance include *significantly, first, primarily, also, in addition, finally,* and *most importantly.*

W/G Prentice Hall Writing and Grammar Connection: Chapter 7, Section 2

Extension Activities

Listening and Speaking With another classmate, hold a **debate**—an organized discussion of two opposing viewpoints—about the issue of developing the wetlands in Andy's town.

- Match your vocabulary to your purpose. Accurately use words and technical terms that are specific to the topic.
- Use facial expressions to indicate distress, confidence, amazement, and other reactions.
- In your message, use reasons that will show your audience the benefits of supporting your position.

Research and Technology Identify a community problem, and work out a **community action** plan. To find problems, look at online or print newspapers, study bulletin board announcements, or call or write local environmental groups. Then, with several classmates, work out a plan for solving one of these problems. Consult with your teacher or other adults about putting the plan into action.

 Take It to the Net   www.phschool.com

Go online for an additional research activity using the Internet.

Public Documents

About Public Documents

Public documents include laws, government publications, legal notices, minutes, or notes, from public meetings, and other records of information that the public has a legal right to access.

An analysis of a **legislative bill** (a proposal for a law) is a public document. It summarizes the bill, tells what the current law is, explains what the bill would do if passed, and gives background on the issue that the bill addresses. It may also list organizations that support or oppose the bill. In California, a legislative bill analysis is prepared by legislative staff and submitted to the committee that is considering the bill. The committee uses the analysis to quickly gain an understanding of the bill and to begin discussing it.

Reading Strategy

Analyze Proposition and Support

An effective legislative bill presents a clear proposition—the proposed legislation—and supports the need for the legislation by providing background information. If the proposition or proposal is well-supported in the bill, then the support will show in the analysis.

As you read the following bill analysis, pay attention to the way the text is organized. The table shown here briefly explains the features and function of each part of the bill analysis.

Legislative Bill Analysis Structure	
Introductory Information	Information at the top of the bill analysis includes the bill number, the author of the bill, the committee considering the bill, and the chairperson of the committee.
Subject	This is the topic of the bill.
Issue	This section states the proposition of the document—that is, what the bill proposes.
Summary	This section lists details concerning what the bill will do if it is passed into law.
Background and Existing Law	This section explains the current law or practice and tells why changes are being proposed in the bill.
Proposed Law	This section tells how the current written laws will change if the bill passes.

Read the sample legislative bill analysis on the next two pages. Use the annotations to help you understand the meaning and purpose of the analysis.

Analysis of a Legislative Bill
California State Assembly
Senate Natural Resources and Wildlife

The author of a bill is the legislator, or lawmaker, who is proposing the bill.

BILL NO:	AB242
AUTHOR:	Thomson
VERSION:	Original: 2/19/99
	Amended: 5/28/99
FISCAL:	Yes
URGENCY:	No
CONSULTANT:	Neal Fishman
HEARING DATE:	6/22/99

SUBJECT:
Conservation of oak woodlands

ISSUE:
Should there be a new program within the Wildlife Conservation Board to grant funds to local agencies and nonprofit organizations to acquire conservation easements preserving oak woodlands? Should a fund be established in the State Treasury for receipt of funds for the conservation of oak woodlands?

Notice that here, the proposition is phrased as a series of questions. The writers of the bill would answer "yes" to every question.

An **easement** is the section of land on someone's property that is actually controlled by the government.

SUMMARY:
This bill would do all of the following:

1. Establish a program within the Wildlife Conservation Board to make grants to local government agencies, nonprofit organizations, park and open space districts, and resource conservation easements on oak woodlands and to develop local plans and public information activities which would encourage oak woodland conservation;

2. Create a fund in the State Treasury to receive money from public and private sources to carry out the program;

3. Require that the program be developed in consultation with the Board of Forestry, Department of Food and Agriculture, the University of California Integrated Hardwood Range Management Program, conservation groups and farming and ranching associations;

The "Summary" section includes numbered items so that the exact actions of the bill are clear to the reader.

4. Require that the board adopt criteria for making grants which would address long-term easement monitoring and a priority system for selecting projects "which achieve the greatest lasting conservation of oak woodlands";

5. Require that the program include cost share incentive payments to private property owners who agree to long-term easements and management practices that protect oaks;

6. Require that the program include public education and outreach that educates the public about the values of oak woodlands; and

7. Limit to 10% the amount of money that the Board could expend pursuant to this program on public education and local planning.

BACKGROUND & EXISTING LAW:

Oak woodlands, lands dominated by oak trees (*Quercus spp.*) make up about 10 percent of California. In all their varieties they make up California's most diverse ecosystem, providing habitat for approximately 2000 plant, 160 bird, 80 mammal, 80 amphibian and reptile and 5,000 insect species. These natural communities also help to stabilize and develop soil and maintain air and water quality.

Oak woodlands are not protected by the Forest Practices Act. They can be cut down for firewood or subdivisions without benefit of a timber harvest plan. They have marginal protection under the California Environmental Quality Act and the California Endangered Species Act. Some oak woodlands are protected by local planning and zoning ordinances.

Oak woodlands are under increasing threat due to development and cutting, mainly for firewood. An early 1980s study placed the conversion of oak woodlands at about 14,000 acres per year. This has accelerated over the past fifteen years. Current estimates are that about 60,000 acres per year have been cut averaged over the past five years. Additional lands have been converted to urban uses or fragmented in a way that reduces their habitat value.

PROPOSED LAW:

This bill would enact various uncodified legislative findings concerning the value of oak woodlands and the present condition of and threats to this habitat type. The bill would create the new program by adding Chapter 11 to Division 4 of the Public Resources Code, a division generally dealing with forest resources and the department of forestry.

An **incentive** is a reward offered ahead of time; something that stimulates one to take action or work harder; encouragement

The background of a bill often contains statistics that support the author's position.

Zoning ordinances are regulations dividing a community into areas determined by restrictions on types of construction, such as into residential and business zones.

This paragraph refers to an existing law code, explaining specifically how it would be altered if the bill is passed into law.

Check Your Comprehension

1. If this bill were to pass, what would the new program within the Wildlife Conservation Board do?
2. According to the bill analysis, why are oak woodlands important to California?
3. How are the oak woodlands endangered?

Applying the Reading Strategy

Analyze Proposition and Support

4. What is the proposition of Bill No. AB 242?
5. What information is given to support the proposition?
6. Are enough facts offered to convince you of the need for this law? Explain.

Activity

Deliver a Speech

Deliver a persuasive speech in which you support or oppose Bill No. AB 242. Make sure you include a clear thesis—a statement that conveys your position. Develop two or three arguments connected to your thesis, and provide detailed facts, reasons, and examples to support each argument. Use a chart like the one shown to anticipate the arguments of people who disagree with your position (called "counterarguments"), and address them using additional facts, reasoning, or examples.

Counterargument

My Arguments

At the current rate of woodlands conversion, thousands of animal and plant species will disappear in just a few years.

Counterarguments

There are thousands of species of animals and plants left in the country.

My Responses

If everyone had that attitude, we would destroy natural habitats all over the country without even trying to protect them.

Comparing Informational Materials

Bill Analyses and Newspaper

Find a newspaper article that reports on a woodland or other natural area. Compare the kinds of information provided in the article, pointing out similarities between that information and the details about California oak woodlands given in the bill analysis. Then, contrast the audiences and purposes of the two documents. Does the article present a proposition or try to persuade the reader to see things in a particular way? If not, what is its purpose?

Prepare to Read

Raymond's Run

Take It to the Net

Visit www.phschool.com for interactive activities and instruction related to "Raymond's Run," including
- background
- graphic organizers
- literary elements
- reading strategies

Preview

Connecting to the Literature

In "Raymond's Run," a young runner is determined to win a race—and learns an unexpected lesson about winning and respect. Connect with the character by recalling a time you learned an unexpected lesson.

Background

It is implied that the narrator's brother has Down's Syndrome—a condition that has both physical and mental symptoms. People with Down's Syndrome develop and progress more slowly than people without Down's. Nonetheless, people with Down's, like other people, continue to gain physical and mental skills throughout their lives. Focusing on a special interest or ability often helps a person with Down's Syndrome achieve his or her fullest potential.

Literary Analysis

Major and Minor Characters

Characters are the people (or animals) in a literary work.

- A **major character** is an important character in the story.
- **Minor characters** play smaller roles in the story's events but are necessary for the story to develop.

In this story, Squeaky, the narrator, is a major character. As you read, jot down notes on organizers like the one shown to indicate Squeaky's relationships with Raymond and Gretchen, two minor characters. At the top of each connecting line, write words and phrases that describe Squeaky's actions and attitudes from the beginning of the story. Write feelings from the end of the story near the bottom.

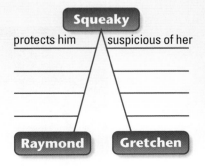

Connecting Literary Elements

Characterization is the process of creating and developing characters. Characters are developed through the characters' own actions, thoughts, and words; through the way other characters react to them; and through direct descriptions by the narrator or by other characters.

Use these focus questions to guide you as you read:

1. What does Squeaky say about herself?
2. What qualities are revealed through Squeaky's actions or through other characters' actions toward Squeaky?

Reading Strategy

Analyzing Idioms

Idioms are words and expressions that have a meaning in a particular language or region.

> **Example:** [It] drives my brother George *up the wall*.

You know George is not literally in a car going up a wall. Most speakers of English in the United States will recognize that phrase as meaning "It annoyed George a lot."

Find clues in the story that help you determine the meaning of idioms.

Vocabulary Development

prodigy (präd´ ə jē) *n.* a wonder; an unusually talented person (p. 290)

signify (sig´ nə fī) *v.* to show or make known, as by a sign or word (p. 291)

ventriloquist (ven tril´ ə kwist) *n.* someone who speaks through a puppet or dummy (p. 291)

periscope (per´ i skōp) *n.* instrument used in submarines to see objects on the surface (p. 293)

RAYMOND'S RUN

Toni Cade Bambara

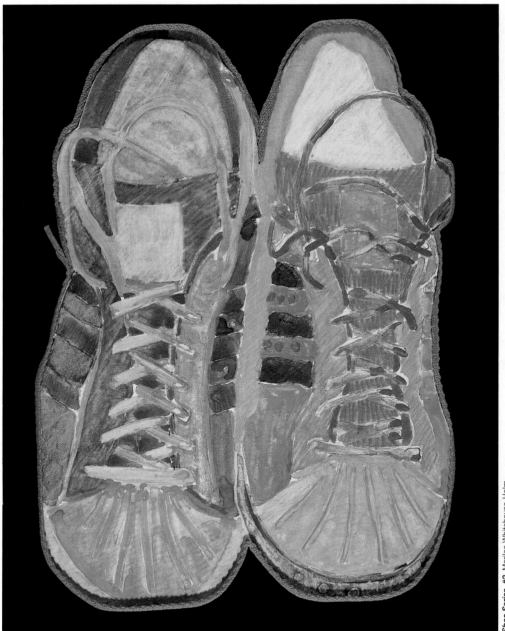

Shoe Series, #2, Marilee Whitehouse-Holm

I don't have much work to do around the house like some girls. My mother does that. And I don't have to earn my pocket money by hustling; George runs errands for the big boys and sells Christmas cards. And anything else that's got to get done, my father does. All I have to do in life is mind my brother Raymond, which is enough.

Sometimes I slip and say my little brother Raymond. But as any fool can see he's much bigger and he's older too. But a lot of people call him my little brother cause he needs looking after cause he's not quite right. And a lot of smart mouths got lots to say about that too, especially when George was minding him. But now, if anybody has anything to say to Raymond, anything to say about his big head, they have to come by me. And I don't play the dozens[1] or believe in standing around with somebody in my face doing a lot of talking. I much rather just knock you down and take my chances even if I am a little girl with skinny arms and a squeaky voice, which is how I got the name Squeaky. And if things get too rough, I run. And as anybody can tell you, I'm the fastest thing on two feet.

There is no track meet that I don't win the first place medal. I used to win the twenty-yard dash when I was a little kid in kindergarten. Nowadays, it's the fifty-yard dash. And tomorrow I'm subject to run the quarter-meter relay all by myself and come in first, second, and third. The big kids call me Mercury[2] cause I'm the swiftest thing in the neighborhood. Everybody knows that—except two people who know better, my father and me.

He can beat me to Amsterdam Avenue with me having a two fire-hydrant headstart and him running with his hands in his pockets and whistling. But that's private information. Cause can you imagine some thirty-five-year-old man stuffing himself into PAL[3] shorts to race little kids? So as far as everyone's concerned, I'm the fastest and that goes for Gretchen, too, who has put out the tale that she is going to win the first-place medal this year. Ridiculous. In the second place, she's got short legs. In the third place, she's got freckles. In the first place, no one can beat me and that's all there is to it.

I'm standing on the corner admiring the weather and about to take a stroll down Broadway so I can practice my breathing exercises, and I've got Raymond walking on the inside close to the buildings, cause he's subject to fits of fantasy and starts thinking he's a circus performer and that the curb is a tightrope strung high in the air.

---

1. **the dozens** game in which the players insult one another; the first to show anger loses.
2. **Mercury** in Roman mythology, the messenger of the gods, known for great speed.
3. **PAL** Police Athletic League.

◀ **Critical Viewing** Most young people, not just athletes, wear athletic shoes. What do athletic shoes symbolize to you? [**Generalize**]

Literary Analysis
Major and Minor Characters and Characterization What do you learn about Raymond from the narrator's words?

✔**Reading Check**
What is the speaker's most important responsibility?

And sometimes after a rain he likes to step down off his tightrope right into the gutter and slosh around getting his shoes and cuffs wet. Or sometimes if you don't watch him he'll dash across traffic to the island in the middle of Broadway and give the pigeons a fit. Then I have to go behind him apologizing to all the old people sitting around trying to get some sun and getting all upset with the pigeons fluttering around them, scattering their newspapers and upsetting the waxpaper lunches in their laps. So I keep Raymond on the inside of me, and he plays like he's driving a stage coach, which is O.K. by me so long as he doesn't run me over or interrupt my breathing exercises, which I have to do on account of I'm serious about my running, and I don't care who knows it.

Now some people like to act like things come easy to them, won't let on that they practice. Not me. I'll high prance down 34th Street like a rodeo pony to keep my knees strong even if it does get my mother uptight so that she walks ahead like she's not with me, don't know me, is all by herself on a shopping trip, and I am somebody else's crazy child.

Reading Strategy
Analyzing Idioms Why do you think the idiom *uptight* is used to describe a tense or nervous person?

Now you take Cynthia Procter for instance. She's just the opposite. If there's a test tomorrow, she'll say something like, "Oh, I guess I'll play handball this afternoon and watch television tonight," just to let you know she ain't thinking about the test. Or like last week when she won the spelling bee for the millionth time, "A good thing you got 'receive,' Squeaky, cause I would have got it wrong. I completely forgot about the spelling bee." And she'll clutch the lace on her blouse like it was a narrow escape. Oh, brother.

But of course when I pass her house on my early morning trots around the block, she is practicing the scales on the piano over and over and over and over. Then in music class she always lets herself get bumped around so she falls accidently on purpose onto the piano stool and is so surprised to find herself sitting there that she decides just for fun to try out the ole keys and what do you know—Chopin's[4] waltzes just spring out of her fingertips and she's the most surprised thing in the world. A regular <u>prodigy</u>. I could kill people like that.

prodigy (präd′ ə jē) *n.* a wonder; an unusually talented person

I stay up all night studying the words for the spelling bee. And you can see me any time of day practicing running. I never walk if I can trot, and shame on Raymond if he can't keep up. But of course he does, cause if he hangs back someone's liable to walk up to him and get smart, or take his allowance from him, or ask him where he got that great big pumpkin head. People are so stupid sometimes.

Literary Analysis
Characterization What do Squeaky's actions tell you about her character?

So I'm strolling down Broadway breathing out and breathing in on counts of seven, which is my lucky number, and here comes Gretchen and her sidekicks—Mary Louise who used to be a friend of mine when she first moved to Harlem from Baltimore and got

---

4. **Chopin** (shō pan′) Frédéric François Chopin (1810–1849), Polish composer and pianist.

beat up by everybody till I took up for her on account of her mother and my mother used to sing in the same choir when they were young girls, but people ain't grateful, so now she hangs out with the new girl Gretchen and talks about me like a dog; and Rosie who is as fat as I am skinny and has a big mouth where Raymond is concerned and is too stupid to know that there is not a big deal of difference between herself and Raymond and that she can't afford to throw stones. So they are steady coming up Broadway and I see right away that it's going to be one of those Dodge City[5] scenes cause the street ain't that big and they're close to the buildings just as we are. First I think I'll step into the candy store and look over the new comics and let them pass. But that's chicken and I've got a reputation to consider. So then I think I'll just walk straight on through them or even over them if necessary. But as they get to me, they slow down. I'm ready to fight, cause like I said I don't feature a whole lot of chit-chat, I much prefer to just knock you down right from the jump and save everybody a lotta precious time.

"You signing up for the May Day races?" smiles Mary Louise, only it's not a smile at all.

A dumb question like that doesn't deserve an answer. Besides, there's just me and Gretchen standing there really, so no use wasting my breath talking to shadows.

"I don't think you're going to win this time," says Rosie, trying to signify with her hands on her hips all salty, completely forgetting that I have whupped her many times for less salt than that.

"I always win cause I'm the best," I say straight at Gretchen who is, as far as I'm concerned, the only one talking in this ventriloquist-dummy routine.

Gretchen smiles, but it's not a smile, and I'm thinking that girls never really smile at each other because they don't know how and don't want to know how and there's probably no one to teach us how cause grown-up girls don't know either. Then they all look at Raymond who has just brought his mule team to a standstill. And they're about to see what trouble they can get into through him.

"What grade you in now, Raymond?"

"You got anything to say to my brother, you say it to me, Mary Louise Williams of Raggedy Town, Baltimore."

"What are you, his mother?" sasses Rosie.

"That's right, Fatso. And the next word out of anybody and I'll be *their* mother too." So they just stand there and Gretchen shifts from one leg to the other and so do they. Then Gretchen puts her hands on her hips and is about to say something with her freckle-face self but doesn't. Then she walks around me looking me up and down but keeps walking up Broadway, and her sidekicks follow her. So

---

5. Dodge City location of the television program *Gunsmoke*, which often presented a gunfight between the sheriff and an outlaw.

Literary Analysis

Characterization Will these girls be major or minor characters? Explain.

signify (sig′ nə fī) *v.* to show or make known, as by a sign or word

ventriloquist (ven tril′ ə kwist) *n.* someone who speaks through a puppet or dummy

**Reading Check**

What do Squeaky and the girls talk about?

me and Raymond smile at each other and he says, "Gidyap" to his team and I continue with my breathing exercises, strolling down Broadway toward the ice man on 145th with not a care in the world cause I am Miss Quicksilver herself.

I take my time getting to the park on May Day because the track meet is the last thing on the program. The biggest thing on the program is the May Pole dancing, which I can do without, thank you, even if my mother thinks it's a shame I don't take part and act like a girl for a change. You'd think my mother'd be grateful not to have to make me a white organdy dress with a big satin sash and buy me new white baby-doll shoes that can't be taken out of the box till the big day. You'd think she'd be glad her daughter ain't out there prancing around a May Pole getting the new clothes all dirty and sweaty and trying to act like a fairy or a flower or whatever you're supposed to be when you should be trying to be yourself, whatever that is, which is, as far as I am concerned, a poor black girl who really can't afford to buy shoes and a new dress you only wear once a lifetime cause it won't fit next year.

I was once a strawberry in a Hansel and Gretel pageant when I was in nursery school and didn't have no better sense than to dance on tiptoe with my arms in a circle over my head doing umbrella steps and being a perfect fool just so my mother and father could come dressed up and clap. You'd think they'd know better than to encourage that kind of nonsense. I am not a strawberry. I do not dance on my toes. I run. That is what I am all about. So I always come late to the May Day program, just in time to get my number pinned on and lay in the grass till they announce the fifty-yard dash.

I put Raymond in the little swings, which is a tight squeeze this year and will be impossible next year. Then I look around for Mr. Pearson, who pins the numbers on. I'm really looking for Gretchen if you want to know the truth, but she's not around. The park is jam-packed. Parents in hats and corsages and breast-pocket

Literary Analysis
Major and Minor Characters and Characterization What do Squeaky's reactions to the memory of her recital add to your understanding of her character?

handkerchiefs peeking up. Kids in white dresses and light-blue suits. The parkees unfolding chairs and chasing the rowdy kids from Lenox as if they had no right to be there. The big guys with their caps on backwards, leaning against the fence swirling the basketballs on the tips of their fingers, waiting for all these crazy people to clear out the park so they can play. Most of the kids in my class are carrying bass drums and glockenspiels[6] and flutes. You'd think they'd put in a few bongos or something for real like that.

Then here comes Mr. Pearson with his clipboard and his cards and pencils and whistles and safety pins and fifty million other things he's always dropping all over the place with his clumsy self. He sticks out in a crowd because he's on stilts. We used to call him Jack and the Beanstalk to get him mad. But I'm the only one that can outrun him and get away, and I'm too grown for that silliness now.

"Well, Squeaky," he says, checking my name off the list and handing me number seven and two pins. And I'm thinking he's got no right to call me Squeaky, if I can't call him Beanstalk.

"Hazel Elizabeth Deborah Parker," I correct him and tell him to write it down on his board.

"Well, Hazel Elizabeth Deborah Parker, going to give someone else a break this year?" I squint at him real hard to see if he is seriously thinking I should lose the race on purpose just to give someone else a break. "Only six girls running this time," he continues, shaking his head sadly like it's my fault all of New York didn't turn out in sneakers. "That new girl should give you a run for your money." He looks around the park for Gretchen like a periscope in a submarine movie. "Wouldn't it be a nice gesture if you were . . . to ahhh . . ."

I give him such a look he couldn't finish putting that idea into words. Grownups got a lot of nerve sometimes. I pin number seven to

---

6. glockenspiels (gläk´ ən spēlz) n. musical instruments with flat metal bars that make bell-like tones when struck with small hammers.

▲ **Critical Viewing**
What constitutes success in a race? Is the winner the only one who succeeds? Explain. **[Define]**

periscope (per´ ə skōp) n. an instrument used in submarines to see objects above the surface

✓ **Reading Check**
What is the only event of May Day that interests Squeaky?

myself and stomp away, I'm so burnt. And I go straight for the track and stretch out on the grass while the band winds up with "Oh, the Monkey Wrapped His Tail Around the Flag Pole," which my teacher calls by some other name. The man on the loudspeaker is calling everyone over to the track and I'm on my back looking at the sky, trying to pretend I'm in the country, but I can't, because even grass in the city feels hard as sidewalk, and there's just no pretending you are anywhere but in a "concrete jungle" as my grandfather says.

The twenty-yard dash takes all of two minutes cause most of the little kids don't know no better than to run off the track or run the wrong way or run smack into the fence and fall down and cry. One little kid, though, has got the good sense to run straight for the white ribbon up ahead, so he wins. Then the second-graders line up for the thirty-yard dash and I don't even bother to turn my head to watch cause Raphael Perez always wins. He wins before he even begins by psyching[7] the runners, telling them they're going to trip on their shoelaces and fall on their faces or lose their shorts or something, which he doesn't really have to do since he is very fast, almost as fast as I am. After that is the forty-yard dash which I use to run when I was in first grade. Raymond is hollering from the swings cause he knows I'm about to do my thing cause the man on the loudspeaker has just announced the fifty-yard dash, although he might just as well be giving a recipe for angel food cake cause you can hardly make out what he's saying for the static. I get up and slip off my sweat pants and then I see Gretchen standing at the starting line, kicking her legs out like a pro. Then as I get into place I see that ole Raymond is on line on the other side of the fence, bending down with his fingers on the ground just like he knew what he was doing. I was going to yell at him but then I didn't. It burns up your energy to holler.

Every time, just before I take off in a race, I always feel like I'm in a dream, the kind of dream you have when you're sick with fever and feel all hot and weightless. I dream I'm flying over a sandy beach in the early morning sun, kissing the leaves of the trees as I fly by. And there's always the smell of apples, just like in the country when I was little and used to think I was a choo-choo train, running through the fields of corn and chugging up the hill to the orchard. And all the time I'm dreaming this, I get lighter and lighter until I'm flying over the beach again, getting blown through the sky like a feather that weighs nothing at all. But once I spread my fingers in the dirt and crouch over the Get on Your Mark, the dream goes and I am solid again and am telling myself, Squeaky you must win, you must win, you are the fastest thing in the world, you can even beat your father up

▼ **Critical Viewing** Put yourself in the place of this race's winner. How must she feel? **[Speculate]**

---

7. psyching (sīk´ iŋ) *v.* slang for playing on a person's mental state.

Amsterdam if you really try. And then I feel my weight coming back just behind my knees then down to my feet then into the earth and the pistol shot explodes in my blood and I am off and weightless again, flying past the other runners, my arms pumping up and down and the whole world is quiet except for the crunch as I zoom over the gravel in the track. I glance to my left and there is no one. To the right a blurred Gretchen, who's got her chin jutting out as if it would win the race all by itself. And on the other side of the fence is Raymond with his arms down to his side and the palms tucked up behind him, running in his very own style, and it's the first time I ever saw that and I almost stop to watch my brother Raymond on his first run. But the white ribbon is bouncing toward me and I tear past it, racing into the distance till my feet with a mind of their own start digging up footfuls of dirt and brake me short. Then all the kids standing on the side pile on me, banging me on the back and slapping my head with their May Day programs, for I have won again and everybody on 151st Street can walk tall for another year.

"In first place . . ." the man on the loudspeaker is clear as a bell now. But then he pauses and the loudspeaker starts to whine. Then static. And I lean down to catch my breath and here comes Gretchen walking back, for she's overshot the finish line too, huffing and puffing with her hands on her hips taking it slow, breathing in steady time like a real pro and I sort of like her a little for the first time. "In first place . . ." and then three or four voices get all mixed up on the loudspeaker and I dig my sneaker into the grass and stare at Gretchen who's staring back, we both wondering just who did win. I can hear old Beanstalk arguing with the man on the loudspeaker and then a few others running their mouths about what the stopwatches say. Then I hear Raymond yanking at the fence to call me and I wave to shush him, but he keeps rattling the fence like a gorilla in a cage like in them gorilla movies, but then like a dancer or something he starts climbing up nice and easy but very fast. And it occurs to me, watching how smoothly he climbs hand over hand and remembering how he looked running with his arms down to his side and with the wind pulling his mouth back and his teeth showing and all, it occurred to me that Raymond would make a very fine runner. Doesn't he always keep up with me on my trots? And he surely knows how to breathe in counts of seven cause he's always doing it at the dinner table, which drives my brother George up the wall. And I'm smiling to beat the band cause if I've lost this race, or if me and Gretchen tied, or even if I've won, I can always retire as a runner and begin a whole new career as a coach with Raymond as my champion. After all, with a little more study I can beat Cynthia and her phony self at the spelling bee. And if I bugged my mother, I could get piano lessons and become a star. And I have a big rep as the baddest thing around. And I've got a roomful of ribbons and medals and awards. But what has Raymond got to call his own?

Reading Strategy
Analyzing Idioms What expression would you use to say you were proud? What idioms does Squeaky use?

Reading Check

What does Raymond do while Squeaky runs the race?

So I stand there with my new plans, laughing out loud by this time as Raymond jumps down from the fence and runs over with his teeth showing and his arms down to the side, which no one before him has quite mastered as a running style. And by the time he comes over I'm jumping up and down so glad to see him—my brother Raymond, a great runner in the family tradition. But of course everyone thinks I'm jumping up and down because the men on the loudspeaker have finally gotten themselves together and compared notes and are announcing "In first place—Miss Hazel Elizabeth Deborah Parker." (Dig that.) "In second place—Miss Gretchen P. Lewis." And I look over at Gretchen wondering what the "P" stands for. And I smile. Cause she's good, no doubt about it. Maybe she'd like to help me coach Raymond; she obviously is serious about running, as any fool can see. And she nods to congratulate me and then she smiles. And I smile. We stand there with this big smile of respect between us. It's about as real a smile as girls can do for each other, considering we don't practice real smiling every day, you know, cause maybe we too busy being flowers or fairies or strawberries instead of something honest and worthy of respect . . . you know . . . like being people.

Toni Cade Bambara

(1939–1995)
A native New Yorker, Toni Cade Bambara was educated in Europe and the United States. She taught at every level from preschool to college. As a writer, she often focused on her African American heritage, portraying her characters with affection. Her short stories have been collected in *Gorilla, My Love* (in which "Raymond's Run" appears), and *The Sea Birds Are Still Alive*. She also wrote a novel, *The Salt Eaters*. One critic wrote, "Bambara tells me more about being black through her quiet, proud, silly, tender, hip, acute, loving stories than any amount of literary [discussion] could hope to do. All of her stories share the affection that their narrator feels for the subject."

Review and Assess

Thinking About the Selection

1. **Respond:** If you were Squeaky, how would you feel after the race? Explain.
2. **(a) Recall:** What is the relationship between Raymond and Squeaky? **(b) Analyze:** How does Squeaky feel about taking care of Raymond?
3. **(a) Recall:** What does Mr. Pearson hint that Squeaky do in the race? **(b) Analyze:** Why does this suggestion make Squeaky angry? **(c) Speculate:** How would Gretchen feel if she knew what Mr. Pearson had hinted?
4. **(a) Recall:** What does Raymond do during the race? **(b) Connect:** How does this change Squeaky's view of Raymond? **(c) Deduce:** Why doesn't she care about the outcome of the race?
5. **(a) Draw Conclusions:** Why does Squeaky look down on most of the girls in her class? **(b) Evaluate:** Is her opinion justified? Why or why not? **(c) Apply:** What famous women do you think Squeaky would admire?
6. **(a) Interpret:** What is the meaning of the smile Squeaky and Gretchen exchange after the race? **(b) Speculate:** Will Squeaky and Gretchen become friends? Explain.

Review and Assess

Literary Analysis

Major and Minor Characters

1. What changes do you see in Squeaky as the story progresses?
2. Is Raymond a major or a minor character? Explain your answer.
3. How does Gretchen contribute to the story development?

Connecting Literary Elements

4. What details have other characters or Squeaky herself told you about Squeaky?
5. Which of Squeaky's qualities have you learned about through her actions or through other characters' actions toward her?
6. Use separate character wheels like the one shown to analyze Raymond and Gretchen.

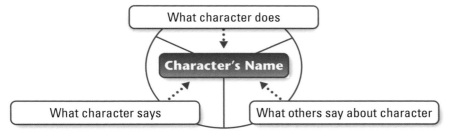

What character does

Character's Name

What character says

What others say about character

Reading Strategy

Analyzing Idioms

7. Use a chart like this one to analyze the idioms used in the story.

Idiom	Literal Meaning	Idiomatic Meaning
"I'm so burnt."		
"give someone else a break"		
"has a big mouth"		
"give you a run for your money"		

8. What idioms do you and your friends use to express approval of an idea or situation?

Extend Understanding

9. **Science Connection:** What properties of air do runners consider when they are dressing or preparing for a race?

Quick Review

A major character is one of the main or leading actors in a literary work. To review major character, see page 287.

A minor character plays a smaller role in a literary work but helps the story development. To review minor character, see page 287.

Characterization is the way a writer brings a character to life through actions, words, and descriptions. To review characterization, see page 287.

An **idiom** is a word or expression that has a meaning unique to a language or region.

 Take It to the Net
www.phschool.com
Take the interactive self-test online to check your understanding of the selection.

Integrate Language Skills

Vocabulary Development Lesson

Word Analysis: Greek Root -scope-

The Greek word root -scope-, meaning "to see," is used to form the names of several instruments used for seeing. Write a definition of each word.

1. periscope   **2.** telescope   **3.** microscope

Spelling Strategy

In almost all words that end in -gy, the vowel before the ending is o. Examples include *biology*, *ecology*, and *psychology*. There are some exceptions to the rule: *effigy*, *elegy*, and *strategy*.

Write the word that completes each sentence.

apology   biology   strategy

1. I made an ___?___ for my mistake.
2. Her winning ___?___ was to work hard.
3. Sports doctors study human ___?___.

Fluency: Definitions

On your paper, match each vocabulary word with its definition.

1. prodigy
2. signify
3. ventriloquist
4. periscope

a. person who speaks through a dummy or puppet
b. young person with unusual talent
c. to show or make known
d. instrument used in a submarine to see the ocean surface

Grammar Lesson

Prepositions

A **preposition** is a word that relates the noun or pronoun following it to another word in the sentence. Prepositions often show relationships in time (*before*, *after*) and in space (*above*, *beyond*). In "Raymond's Run," Squeaky says, "I'm the swiftest thing *in* the neighborhood. The preposition *in* relates *neighborhood* to *swiftest thing*.

Here are some other common prepositions:

about	across	against	around	as
behind	below	beside	between	down
for	from	into	near	of
over	toward	under	up	with

Some prepositions are made up of more than one word. Here are some examples:

according to	ahead of	as of	because of
in front of	instead of		

▶ *For more practice, see page R29, Exercise D.*

Practice Copy each sentence and underline the preposition. Draw an arrow between the two words that the preposition relates.

1. George runs errands for the big boys.
2. I'm standing on the corner.
3. He can beat me to Amsterdam Avenue.
4. Here comes Mr. Pearson with his clipboard.
5. We were too busy being strawberries instead of something honest.

Writing Application Copy this sentence three times, inserting a different preposition each time. Explain how the meaning changes.

The racers ran ___?___ the fence.

𝒲𝒢 *Prentice Hall Writing and Grammar Connection: Chapter 17*

Writing Lesson

Article About the Race

Write an article about the race. Include details that will help readers feel the excitement and suspense.

Prewriting   Write down details of what the crowd sees and details of what you imagine the racers are feeling. Think of one quotation each for Gretchen and Squeaky about their reactions to the race.

Model: Using Quotations

When you use a quotation, introduce it by identifying the speaker.
Gretchen gave us her reaction after the race, "I was worried.
This is the first time I've run against someone who is as serious
about racing as I am."

> The words of the speaker are set off in quotation marks. The comma separates the explanatory words from the character's exact words.

Drafting   Begin by describing the exciting finish. Then, go back and lead up to the moment Squeaky wins. Finally, use quotations about the event.

Revising   Add a quotation if you don't already have one. Use quotation marks and commas to punctuate the quotation.

W̶G *Prentice Hall Writing and Grammar Connection: Chapter 13, Section 2*

Extension Activities

Listening and Speaking Act out a **radio broadcast** of the race in the story.

1. Use precise language. For example, don't use *running* if you mean *jogging*.
2. Use action verbs like *flew, streaked,* and *plunged* to capture the movement.
3. Deliver your sportscast, using your voice and posture to convey some of the tense ending.

Writing Write a note from Squeaky to Gretchen in which Squeaky asks for Gretchen's help with Raymond's athletic training. Include details about why Squeaky wants to work with Raymond and why she thinks Gretchen would be a help.

Research and Technology Use the Internet to research the Special Olympics. Create an **informational brochure.**

1. Use a search engine to find appropriate sites. Get an exact match: Use quotation marks around the words: "Special Olympics."
2. Find topics that contain both words, not necessarily in that order by using a plus sign between the words: Special + Olympics.
3. When you find a site with good information, look for links to other sites.

 Take It to the Net   www.phschool.com

Go online for an additional research activity using the Internet.

Prepare to Read

Paul Revere's Ride

 Take It to the Net

Visit www.phschool.com
for interactive activities
and instruction related to
"Paul Revere's Ride,"
including

- background
- graphic organizers
- literary elements
- reading strategies

Preview

Connecting to the Literature

Henry Wadsworth Longfellow's poem, "Paul Revere's Ride," tells the story of an ordinary citizen who becomes a hero through an act of extraordinary courage. Prepare to read the poem by thinking of "everyday heroes" whom you know or have read about.

Background

What many people know—or think they know—about Paul Revere's famous ride on April 18, 1775, comes from Henry Wadsworth Longfellow's poem, "Paul Revere's Ride." The poem, however, is not a completely accurate account of events on that night.

Literary Analysis
Historical Characters

In literature, a **historical character** is usually a mix of fact and fiction based on a real person from history. An author may add or exaggerate details to make the historical character more dramatic or more human.

As you read "Paul Revere's Ride," notice the differences between the way the poem presents Paul Revere and the way a history book would present him. Use the following focus questions to guide you:

1. Which details in the poem illustrate Paul Revere's heroism?
2. Which of these details would probably not be found in a history textbook?

Connecting Literary Elements

Paul Revere has become more than a historical figure; he is a hero who represents courage. These lines from "Paul Revere's Ride" show that the poet is creating a heroic image.

> A voice in the darkness, a knock at the door,
> And a word that shall echo forevermore!

As you read, look for other details that add to the heroic image of Paul Revere. Jot them down on an organizer like this one.

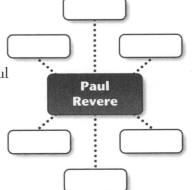

Reading Strategy
Recognizing the Author's Purpose

An **author's purpose** is his or her reason for writing. Common purposes include

- to entertain
- to instruct
- to persuade
- to inspire

The author's purpose influences the details that are included. If the author's purpose is to inspire, then details may exaggerate the character's brave and heroic deeds. If the author's purpose is to instruct, then details will be straightforward and factual.

As you read, notice the types of details Longfellow includes to achieve his purpose.

Vocabulary Development

stealthy (stel´ thē) *adj.* secretive; trying to avoid notice (p. 304)

somber (säm´ bər) *adj.* dark and gloomy (p. 304)

impetuous (im pech´ o͞o əs) *adj.* done suddenly with little thought (p. 304)

spectral (spek´ trəl) *adj.* phantomlike, ghostly (p. 304)

tranquil (tran´ kwil) *adj.* quiet or motionless; peaceful (p. 305)

aghast (ə gäst´) *adj.* feeling great horror or dismay (p. 305)

Paul Revere's Ride

Henry Wadsworth Longfellow

Listen, my children, and you shall hear
Of the midnight ride of Paul Revere,
On the eighteenth of April, in Seventy-five;
Hardly a man is now alive
5 Who remembers that famous day and year.

He said to his friend, "If the British march
By land or sea from the town to-night,
Hang a lantern aloft in the belfry arch[1]
Of the North Church tower as a signal light,—
10 One, if by land, and two, if by sea;
And I on the opposite shore will be,
Ready to ride and spread the alarm
Through every Middlesex village and farm,
For the country folk to be up and to arm."

15 Then he said, "Good night!" and with muffled oar
Silently rowed to the Charlestown shore,
Just as the moon rose over the bay,
Where swinging wide at her moorings[2] lay
The *Somerset,* British man-of-war;[3]
20 A phantom ship, with each mast and spar
Across the moon like a prison bar,
And a huge black hulk, that was magnified
By its own reflection in the tide.

Meanwhile, his friend, through alley and street,
25 Wanders and watches with eager ears,
Till in the silence around him he hears
The muster[4] of men at the barrack door,
The sound of arms, and the tramp of feet,
And the measured tread of the grenadiers,[5]
30 Marching down to their boats on the shore.

---

1. **belfry arch** (bel´ frē ärch) curved top of a tower or steeple that holds the bells.
2. **moorings** (mŏor´ iŋs) *n.* lines, cables, or chains that hold a ship to the shore.
3. **man-of-war** armed naval vessel; warship.
4. **muster** *n.* an assembly of troops summoned for inspection, roll call, or service.
5. **grenadiers** (gren´ ə dirz´) *n.* members of a special regiment or corps.

◀ **Critical Viewing** What details of this picture reflect the heroism and adventure communicated in the poem? **[Connect]**

Reading Strategy
Recognizing Author's Purpose In what way do these details create a heroic image?

Reading Check
What is Paul Revere going to do when the British arrive?

Then he climbed the tower of the Old North Church,
By the wooden stairs, with <u>stealthy</u> tread,
To the belfry-chamber overhead,
And startled the pigeons from their perch
35 On the <u>somber</u> rafters,[6] that round him made
Masses and moving shapes of shade,—
By the trembling ladder, steep and tall,
To the highest window in the wall,
Where he paused to listen and look down
40 A moment on the roofs of the town,
And the moonlight flowing over all.

Beneath, in the churchyard, lay the dead,
In their night-encampment on the hill,
Wrapped in silence so deep and still
45 That he could hear, like a sentinel's[7] tread,
The watchful night-wind, as it went
Creeping along from tent to tent,
And seeming to whisper, "All is well!"
A moment only he feels the spell
50 Of the place and the hour, and the secret dread
Of the lonely belfry and the dead;
For suddenly all his thoughts are bent
On a shadowy something far away,
Where the river widens to meet the bay,—
55 A line of black that bends and floats
On the rising tide, like a bridge of boats.

Meanwhile, impatient to mount and ride,
Booted and spurred, with a heavy stride
On the opposite shore walked Paul Revere.
60 Now he patted his horse's side,
Now gazed at the landscape far and near,
Then, <u>impetuous</u>, stamped the earth,
And turned and tightened his saddle-girth;[8]
But mostly he watched with eager search
65 The belfry-tower of the Old North Church,
As it rose above the graves on the hill,
Lonely and <u>spectral</u> and somber and still.
And lo! as he looks, on the belfry's height

stealthy (stel′ thē) *adj.*
artfully sly and secretive

somber (säm′ bər) *adj.*
dark and gloomy

impetuous (im pech′ ōō əs)
adj. done suddenly with
little thought

spectral (spek′ trəl) *adj.*
phantomlike; ghostly

---

6. rafters *n.* beams that slope from the ridge of a roof to the eaves and serve
to support the roof.
7. sentinel (sen′ ti nəl) *n.* guard.
8. girth (gurth) *n.* a band put around the belly of a horse for holding a saddle.

A glimmer, and then a gleam of light!
70 He springs to the saddle, the bridle he turns,
But lingers and gazes, till full on his sight
A second lamp in the belfry burns!

A hurry of hoofs in a village street,
A shape in the moonlight, a bulk in the dark,
75 And beneath, from the pebbles, in passing, a spark
Struck out by a steed flying fearless and fleet:
That was all! And yet, through the gloom and the light,
The fate of a nation was riding that night;
And the spark struck out by that steed in his flight,
80 Kindled the land into flame with its heat.
He has left the village and mounted the steep,[9]
And beneath him, <u>tranquil</u> and broad and deep,
Is the Mystic,[10] meeting the ocean tides;
And under the alders[11] that skirt its edge,
85 Now soft on the sand, now loud on the ledge,
Is heard the tramp of his steed as he rides.

It was twelve by the village clock,
When he crossed the bridge into Medford town.
He heard the crowing of the cock,
90 And the barking of the farmer's dog,
And felt the damp of the river fog,
That rises after the sun goes down.

It was one by the village clock,
When he galloped into Lexington.
95 He saw the gilded weathercock[12]
Swim in the moonlight as he passed,
And the meeting-house windows, blank and bare,
Gaze at him with a spectral glare,
As if they already stood <u>aghast</u>
100 At the bloody work they would look upon.

It was two by the village clock,
When he came to the bridge in Concord town.
He heard the bleating of the flock,
And the twitter of birds among the trees,
105 And felt the breath of the morning breeze

---

9. **steep** *n.* slope or incline having a sharp rise.
10. **Mystic** (mis´ tik) a river in Massachusetts.
11. **alders** (ôl´ dərz) *n.* trees and shrubs of the birch family.
12. **weathercock** (weth´ ər käk´) *n.* weathervane in the form of a rooster.

Reading Strategy
Recognizing Author's Purpose What details and comparisons does Longfellow use to heighten the significance of the ride?

tranquil (tran´ kwil) *adj.* quiet or motionless; peaceful

aghast (ə gäst´) *adj.* feeling great horror or dismay

✔**Reading Check**

What does Paul Revere see?

◀ **Critical Viewing**
Why would a church steeple like this one be ideal for a signal? **[Connect]**

Blowing over the meadows brown.
And one was safe and asleep in his bed
Who at the bridge would be first to fall,
Who that day would be lying dead,
110 Pierced by a British musket-ball.

You know the rest. In the books you have read,
How the British Regulars fired and fled,—
How the farmers gave them ball for ball,
From behind each fence and farm-yard wall,
115 Chasing the red-coats down the lane,
Then crossing the fields to emerge again
Under the trees at the turn of the road,
And only pausing to fire and load.

So through the night rode Paul Revere;
120 And so through the night went his cry of alarm
To every Middlesex village and farm,—
A cry of defiance and not of fear,
A voice in the darkness, a knock at the door,
And a word that shall echo forevermore!
125 For, borne on the night-wind of the Past,
Through all our history, to the last,
In the hour of darkness and peril and need,
The people will waken and listen to hear
The hurrying hoof-beats of that steed,
130 And the midnight message of Paul Revere.

Review and Assess

Thinking About the Selection

1. **Respond:** Does the poem capture the suspense and excitement of Paul Revere's ride? Explain.

2. **(a) Recall:** What is the reason for Paul Revere's ride?
   (b) Infer: Why is he willing to face danger to make this ride?

3. **(a) Recall:** Explain the signal plan. **(b) Apply:** Why is it important that Revere and his friend agree on the signals?
   (c) Evaluate: How effective is the signal plan? Explain.

4. **(a) Infer:** Why is Revere restless as he waits for the signal?
   (b) Draw Conclusions: How important is this ride to Paul Revere? To the country?

5. **(a) Interpret:** What does Longfellow mean when he writes, "The fate of a nation was riding that night"? **(b) Make a Judgment:** Does Paul Revere's ride accomplish its purpose? Explain.

Henry Wadsworth Longfellow

(1807–1882)

Henry Wadsworth Longfellow was one of the "fireside poets," writers whose popular poems were read aloud by nineteenth-century families gathered around the fireplace. He wrote several long poems on themes in American history in the style of old ballads. Many people can quote at least the first few lines of "Paul Revere's Ride," "The Wreck of the Hesperus," *The Song of Hiawatha*, or *Evangeline*. Born in what is now Maine, Longfellow showed his writing talent when he was a teenager, entering Bowdoin College at age fifteen. He traveled and studied in Europe, and he then taught modern languages at Bowdoin and Harvard. He also wrote a novel and essays.

Review and Assess

Literary Analysis

Historical Characters

1. In what historical situation does Paul Revere play a role?
2. Which details in the poem illustrate Paul Revere's heroism?
3. Which of these details would probably not be found in a textbook?
4. Use a Venn diagram like the one below to compare and contrast the poem with a factual account in a textbook or an encyclopedia. Write common elements in the shared section. Write details that are unique to each work in the outer parts of the circles.

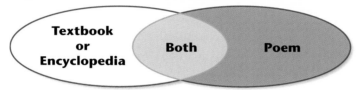

Textbook or Encyclopedia — Both — Poem

Connecting Literary Elements

5. What details in Longfellow's poem contribute to the sense of danger Paul Revere faces?
6. What is one drawback to reading only the poem?

Reading Strategy

Recognizing the Author's Purpose

7. What is Longfellow's purpose for writing "Paul Revere's Ride"?
8. Complete an organizer like the one shown to explore the relationship between the author's purpose and the details that are included in a work.

Author's Purpose

Detail — Detail — Detail

Final Result

Extend Understanding

9. **World Events Connection:** Are there opportunities today for the kind of heroism that Paul Revere displayed? Explain.

Quick Review

A **historical character** is a figure in literature who is based on a real person from the past and is portrayed with a mixture of fact and fiction. To review historical character, see page 301.

The **author's purpose** is his or her reason for writing. To review author's purpose, see page 301.

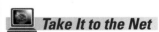 **Take It to the Net**
www.phschool.com
Take the interactive self-test online to check your understanding of the selection.

Integrate Language Skills

Vocabulary Development Lesson

Word Analysis: Latin Root -spec-

The Latin word root -spec- comes from the verb "to see." In the word *spectral*, for example, the root means "related to appearances or something seen." On your paper, match these words with their definitions

1. spectacles   a. band of colors found in light
2. spectrum   b. look at carefully
3. inspect   c. eyeglasses

Spelling Strategy

Sometimes the hard g sound is spelled *gh*, as in *ghastly*. On your paper, unscramble the letters to write words that contain the hard g sound spelled *gh*.

1. hogst   3. thasga   5. hettog
2. itteghaps   4. lough

Concept Development: Synonyms

Synonyms are words that express the same or very similar meanings. On your paper, match each vocabulary word in the left column with its synonym in the right.

1. stealthy   a. calm
2. somber   b. secret
3. impetuous   c. horrified
4. spectral   d. impulsive
5. tranquil   e. dark
6. aghast   f. ghostly

Replace each underlined word with a synonym from the left column above.

1. a <u>sneaky</u> burglar   3. a(n) <u>sudden</u> outburst
2. a <u>peaceful</u> scene   4. a <u>gloomy</u> mood

Grammar Lesson

Prepositional Phrases

A **prepositional phrase** is a group of words beginning with a preposition and ending with a noun or a pronoun. The noun or pronoun in the phrase is called the *object of the preposition*. A preposition is a word like *in, of, between,* or *from* that shows the relationship between the object of the preposition and another word in the sentence.

In the following lines from "Paul Revere's Ride," the prepositional phrase is underlined. The preposition is circled.

Listen, my children, and you shall hear
(of) the midnight ride (of) Paul Revere.

Practice Copy the following passages on your paper. Underline each prepositional phrase and circle the preposition that begins it.

1. . . . If the British march / by land or sea from the town tonight.
2. And I on the opposite shore will be
3. . . . in the silence around him he hears / The muster of men at the barrack door.
4. And startled the pigeons from their perch / On the somber rafters . . .
5. It was two by the village clock / When he came to the bridge in Concord town.

Writing Application Write a short summary of the events on the evening of April 18, 1775, using at least three of the following prepositions: on, across, until, during, of, like, at.

*W*_G *Prentice Hall Writing and Grammar Connection: Chapter 17/ Chapter 20, Section 1*

Writing Lesson

Comparison-and-Contrast Essay

Write a brief essay in which you compare and contrast Longfellow's poem with a historical account of the event. Explain why you think Longfellow presented details in a way that is not entirely factual.

Prewriting   Conduct research on the facts of the night Paul Revere took his ride. Take notes on details that differ from Longfellow's account.

Drafting   Begin with a general statement about the factual accuracy of Longfellow's account. In the body of your essay, give examples of the differences between the facts and the poem. Then, explain your own ideas about the reasons for the difference.

Model: Balance Details with Original Ideas

"Where he paused to listen and look down

A moment on the roofs of the town,

And the moonlight flowing over all."

> The writer balances the quotation with his or her own original thought on the significance of the details.

Even though they are not strictly factual, the pause and the moonlight give a spooky feeling that allows readers to experience the event, rather than just know about it.

Revising   Make sure that your quotations illustrate a point and that you have recorded them accurately.

W̶G Prentice Hall Writing and Grammar Connection: Chapter 8, Section 8.1

Extension Activities

Research and Technology   Research the events of April 18, 1775, when three people rode to warn the countryside. Draw or trace a **map of Boston** and the surrounding area, noting towns and landmarks mentioned in the poem. (Use a historical map if possible, because the Boston shoreline has changed.) On the map, trace the routes taken by Paul Revere, William Dawes, and Samuel Prescott. Compare your map to the route described in the poem.

Listening and Speaking   With a partner, perform a **recitation** of "Paul Revere's Ride."

1. Divide the stanzas to be memorized.
2. Practice delivering your stanzas expressively—using your voice to show the feeling of the words.
3. Perform your recitation.

 **Take It to the Net**   www.phschool.com

Go online for an additional research activity using the Internet.

Paul Revere: Fact and Fiction

Henry Wadsworth Longfellow wrote "Paul Revere's Ride" in 1861, long after Revere's historic ride. When the poem was published, it made Revere into a hero and his adventure into a legend. The story had not been well known, although Revere himself wrote several accounts of it. One is the "Deposition" you are about to read.

A Network of Spies During the autumn of 1774, Paul Revere and about thirty other patriots had formed a spy network to watch the movements of soldiers stationed in Boston to enforce British rule and make sure the colonists paid their taxes to the King. On Saturday, April 15, the day before Easter, Revere and others had noticed that British troops had been taken off the streets of Boston, and their small boats had been hauled in for repairs. They speculated that soon the grenadiers and infantry might be sent on an expedition to Lexington, about 15 miles away, and Concord, about 20 miles away. In Lexington, two prominent members of the patriots' Provincial Congress—Sam Adams and John Hancock—were visiting. In Concord, the defiant patriots had hidden arms and ammunition.

A Quiet Warning On Easter night, April 16, Revere rode quietly to Lexington to warn Adams and Hancock that they were in danger of being arrested. On his way back to Boston that night, Revere instructed patriots in Charlestown to watch for a lantern signal from the steeple of Old North Church. This would tell them what they would be responsible for telling Revere: which way the troops were traveling. On Tuesday afternoon, April 18, word leaked out that British officers had orders to patrol the roads that night between Cambridge and Concord. The patriots hastily put their plans in place. Robert Newman, the sexton of Old North Church, would give the lantern signal once he knew how the British would travel. Revere, the principal express rider, would take the fastest route to Lexington, first crossing the river by boat. As a backup plan, a second express rider, William Dawes, would take the longer route, by land.

The Ride Begins The moon was not yet high in the sky when Revere had two friends row him across the Charles River in a rowboat he had hidden. To avoid being seen by the British frigate Somerset, they crossed as far downriver as they could. In Charlestown, Revere was met by patriots who had spotted the flicker of Newman's two lanterns in the steeple—meaning that the British were also taking the faster route, crossing the river by boat. Revere was given a good horse, donated by one of Boston's wealthiest citizens. Then he began his ride.

Connecting the Poem and the Deposition

As you read Paul Revere's Deposition, notice how it differs, in facts, details, and mood, from Longfellow's poem. As one critic points out, Longfellow might have been Revere's best "publicity agent," but "[he] was a poet and not a historian." Paul Revere, on the other hand, was a patriot and not a writer. You will notice misspellings and errors in his draft, which has been left uncorrected for historical accuracy.

The Deposition: Draft

Paul Revere of Boston, in the Colony of the Massachusetts Bay in N. England of Lawfull age doth testifye and Say: that I was in Boston on the Evening of the 18th of April 1775, that I was sent for by Docr. Joseph Warren about 10 o'Clock that evening, and desired, "to go to Lexington and inform Mr. Samuel Adams, and Hon. John Hancock Esqr. That there was a number of Soldiers composed of the Light troops and Grenadiers marching to the bottom of the common,[1] where was a number Boats to receive them, and it was supposed, that they were going to Lexington, by the way of Watertown to take them, Mess. Adams and Hancock or to Concord." I proceeded imeaditly and was put across Charles River [by] Boat, and Landed at Charlestown Battery. Went into the Town and their got a Horse, while in Charlestown I was informed by Richd. Deavins Esqr. that he, that Evening after sun sett, mett 9 officers of Gages Army,[2] well mounted and Armed going to wards to Concord. I sett off (it was then about 11 o'Clock) the Moon Shone bright. I had got allmost over Charlestown Common towards Cambridge when I saw two officers on horse back standing under the shade of a Tree, In a narrow part of the Road. I got near enough to see their holsters and Cockades.[3] When one of them started his horse towards me and the other up the Road as I supposed to head me, I turned my horse short about and Rid upon full gallop for Mistick Road, he following me about 300 yards, and finding he could not catch me, stoped. I proceeded to Lexington throu Mistick, and awaked Messr. Adams and Hancock, and delivered my message. After I had been there about half an hour, Mr. Daws arrived, who came from Boston over the neck.[4] We sett of together for Concord, and were over-taken by a Young Gentleman named Prescot who belonged to Concord, and was going home. When we got about half way from Lexington to Concord, the Other two Stopped at a House to awake the Man. I kept along, when I had got about 200 Yards a head of them, I saw two officers under a Tree as before. I imeaditly called to my company to come up, saying here was two of them, (for I had told them, what Mr. Devens told me and of my being Stopped) in an Instant I saw four officers who rode up to me with their Pistols in their hands and said [...] Stop if you go an Inch farther you are a dead man, imeaditly Mr. Prescot came up, he turned the butt end of his whipp. We attempted to git thro' them but they kept before us and swore if we did not turn in to that pasture, they would Blow our brains out, (they had placed them selves opposite to a pair of Barrs and had taken the Barrs down) they forced us in, and when we had got in, Mr. Prescot said to me putt on, he turned to the left, I

---

1. **the common** Boston Common: a central "green," or park-like area, in Boston. In 1775, it was bordered on one side by the Charles River.
2. **Gages army** Gage was the British general in Boston.
3. **Cockades** *n.* rosettes or ribbons worn on hats as badges.
4. **the neck** in Revere's day, the town of Boston was situated at the end of a long, narrow spit of land, called Boston Neck.

turned to the Right, towards a wood in the bottom of the pasture, intending when I reached that, to jump my horse and Run afoot. Just as I reached it out started Six others on horseback, wrode up to me with their Pistols in their hands put them to my Breast siesed my bridle and ordered me to dismount, which I did. One of them who appeared to have the command there, and much of Gentleman, asked me where I came from, I told him, he asked me what time I left it, I told him, he said Sir may I crave[5] your Name, I answered my Name was Revere, he said what Paul Revere, I said yes, the others abused me much, but he told me not to be afraid, they should not hurt me. I told him they would miss their Aim. He said they should not, they were after som deserters that were on the Road. I told him I knew better, I knew what they were after, that I had alarmed the Country all the way up, and that their Boats had catched aground, and I should have 500 men their soon. He seemed supprised and rid imeaditly up to the Road to them that stopped me. They came down on full gallop, one of them (whom I have since learned was Major Mitcel of the 5th Regt.) clapd his pistol to My head, and said he was agoing to ask me some Questions, and if I did not tell the truth, he would blow my brains out. I replied that I calld my self a Man of Truth, and that he had stopped me on the high Way, and made me a prisoner I knew not by what right. I would tell the truth, for I was not afraid. He then asked me the same questions that the other did and many more but more particular, I gave him the same answers; after he and two more had spoke together in a low voice he orderd me to mount my horse, but they first searched me for Arms. When I had mounted, the Major rode up to me and took the reins out of my hand and said […] Sir you are not to ride with reins, and gave them to an officer upon my right to lead me. I asked him to let me have the reins, and I would not run from him, he said he would not trust me, he then orderd four men out of the Bushes, whom I found were Country men, which they had stopped and to mount their horses, and then Ordered us to march. He came up to me and said: "We are now going towards your friends and if you attempt to run, or we are insulted, we will blow your Brains out." I told him he might do as he pleased. When we had got into the road they formed a Circle and ordered the prisoners in the centre, and to lead me in front. We rode down to ward Lexington prittie smart.[6] I was often insulted by the officers calling me […] Rebel &c. &c. The Officer who ledd me said

The draft of Paul Revere's statement

▲ **Critical Viewing**
How can you tell that this is a picture of Paul Revere's draft of his account, rather than his final copy? **[Analyze]**

---

5. **crave** [krāv], *v.* ask.
6. **prittie smart** pretty smart: In other words, at a good pace; rapidly.

I was in a […] critical situation I told I was sensible of it. When We had got about a mile, I was delivered to a Serjant, who was Ordered to take out his Pistol (he rode with a hanger) and should I run to excecute the Major's Sentance. Whe[n] we got within about half a mile of Lexington meeting-house we heard a Gun fired, the Major asked what that was for, I told him to alarm the Country, he then Ordered the other 4 prisoners to dismount, which they did. They cut the Bridles and saddles off the Horses, drove them away, and told the men they might go about their Business. I asked the Major to dismiss he said he would not. He then ordered us to march. When we got within sight of the Meeting-house, we heard a Volley of Guns fired as I supposed at the Tavern, as an Alarm, the Major ordered a halt, he asked me ho[w] far it was to Cambridge. I told him, after Asking me a number of questions he Asked the Serjant if his horse was tired. He answered Yes, he ordered him to take My horse which he did. Then after cutting the Saddle and Bridle off the Serjants horse they told me they should make use of my horse for the Night and rode off, towards Cambridge. I then went to the house where I left Messr. Adams and Hancock and told them what had happined, thier Friends advised them to go out of the way, I went with them, went about two miles a cross road and their stopt, after resting my self I set off with another man, to go to the Tavern, to enquire wither the troops had come, or were coming. When we got there, a Man who has just come up the road, told us they were within two mile. We went into the Tavern to git a Trunk of Papers belonging to Col. Hancock, before we got out I saw the Ministearal Troops[7] from the chamber window, coming up the Road. We made haste, and had to pass thro our Militia, who were on a green behinde the Meeting house, to the Number as I suppose of 50 or 60. It was then Daylight. I passed thro' them, as I passed I heard the Command-ing officer, say words to this Effect "Lett the Troops pass by and donot molest them with out they bigin first." As I had to go a Cross road I had not got half gun shot distance, when the ministeral Troops appeard in Sight, behind the Meeting house. They made a short halt. When one Gun was fired, I saw the smoake in the front of them, they imeaditly gave a shout rann a few pace and then fired. I could distinguish first iregular firing and then platoons. At this time, I could not see our Militia, for they were covered by a house at the bottom of the Road.

---

7. Ministearal Troops the British troops.

Thematic Connection
What do we know now about the significance of that shot that Revere did not know when he wrote his account?

Connecting Literature and History

1. What events does Revere's deposition describe that Longfellow's poem does not?
2. Considering only the events that both the poem and the deposition describe, what differences of fact, detail, and mood do you notice between Revere's account and Longfellow's poem?
3. Why do you think Longfellow's poem made Revere a hero, while Revere's own account did not? Explain.

Prepare to Read

Always to Remember: The Vision of Maya Ying Lin

Take It to the Net

Visit www.phschool.com
for interactive activities
and instruction related to
"Always to Remember: The
Vision of Maya Ying Lin,"
including

- background
- graphic organizers
- literary elements
- reading strategies

Preview

Connecting to the Literature

"Always to Remember" introduces you to a young student of architecture who designed a powerful memorial to Americans killed or missing in the Vietnam War. Connect to the topic of the work by thinking about memorials and monuments you have seen and the impression they made on you.

Background

In 1961, President John F. Kennedy sent 3,000 military advisors to help the South Vietnamese government fight against communist rebels supported by North Vietnam. By 1968, the United States had more than 500,000 troops in Vietnam. In the United States, the war sparked massive protests. The nation became bitterly divided between those who supported the war and those who opposed it.

Literary Analysis

Biographical Profile

A biography tells the full story of a person's life. A **biographical profile** is a shorter piece of writing that often focuses on one important event or achievement in a person's life. As you read this profile, notice how Maya Lin's background has influenced her creative work.

> Her father, Henry Huan Lin, was a ceramicist of considerable reputation and dean of fine arts at Ohio University in Athens.

Look for other details that may have influenced Maya Lin's interests and abilities.

Connecting Literary Elements

The information about Maya Lin in this biographical profile is part of a longer article. The writer's purpose is to present a particular view of Maya Lin and of the memorial she designed. As you read, look for details that support a particular view, and identify what the view is.

Reading Strategy

Evaluating Internal Consistency of Text

You will better understand what you read if you are able to **evaluate the internal consistency,** or the logical relationships, in the text. To evaluate internal consistency, focus on questions like the following:

1. Are all the details connected to a few main ideas?
2. Is the text coherent—that is, does it hold together or does it seem like a collection of random ideas pulled together?

The chart at right shows consistent internal structure. You should be able to trace any detail in a selection along a path that leads up to the main topic. You should be able to find connections along the main ideas as well.

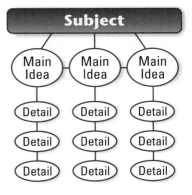

Vocabulary Development

criteria (krī tir′ ē ə) *n.* standards by which something is judged (p. 318)

registrants (rej′ is trənts) *n.* people who register to participate (p. 318)

harmonious (här mō′ nē əs) *adj.* combined in a pleasing, orderly way (p. 318)

anonymously (ə nän′ ə məs lē) *adv.* with the name withheld or secret (p. 319)

eloquent (el′ ə kwənt) *adj.* fluent, forceful, and persuasive (p. 319)

unanimous (yo͞o nan′ ə məs) *adj.* agreed to by all (p. 320)

conception (kən sep′ shən) *n.* an original idea, design, or plan (p. 322)

ALWAYS TO REMEMBER:

The Vision of Maya Ying Lin

Brent Ashabranner

In the 1960s and 1970s, the United States was involved in a war in Vietnam. Because many people opposed the war, Vietnam veterans were not honored as veterans of other wars had been. Jan Scruggs, a Vietnam veteran, thought that the 58,000 U.S. servicemen and women killed or reported missing in Vietnam should be honored with a memorial. With the help of lawyers Robert Doubek and John Wheeler, Scruggs worked to gain support for his idea. In 1980, Congress authorized the building of the Vietnam Veterans Memorial in Washington, D.C., between the Washington Monument and the Lincoln Memorial.

▶ **Critical Viewing**
Why do you think Lin designed the memorial with such a long walkway? **[Analyze]**

The memorial had been authorized by Congress "in honor and recognition of the men and women of the Armed Forces of the United States who served in the Vietnam War." The law, however, said not a word about what the memorial should be or what it should look like. That was left up to the Vietnam Veterans Memorial Fund, but the law did state that the memorial design and plans would have to be approved by the Secretary of the Interior, the Commission of Fine Arts, and the National Capital Planning Commission.

What would the memorial be? What should it look like? Who would design it? Scruggs, Doubek, and Wheeler didn't know, but they were determined that the memorial should help bring closer together a nation still bitterly divided by the Vietnam War. It couldn't be something like the Marine Corps Memorial showing

American troops planting a flag on enemy soil at Iwo Jima. It couldn't be a giant dove with an olive branch of peace in its beak. It had to soothe passions, not stir them up. But there was one thing Jan Scruggs insisted on: The memorial, whatever it turned out to be, would have to show the name of every man and woman killed or missing in the war.

The answer, they decided, was to hold a national design competition open to all Americans. The winning design would receive a prize of $20,000, but the real prize would be the winner's knowledge that the memorial would become a part of American history on the Mall in Washington, D.C. Although fund raising was only well started at this point, the choosing of a memorial design could not be delayed if the memorial was to be built by Veterans Day, 1982. H. Ross Perot contributed the $160,000 necessary to hold the competition, and a panel of distinguished architects, landscape architects, sculptors, and design specialists was chosen to decide the winner.

Announcement of the competition in October, 1980, brought an astonishing response. The Vietnam Veterans Memorial Fund received over five thousand inquiries. They came from every state in the nation and from every field of design; as expected, architects and sculptors were particularly interested.

Reading Strategy
Evaluating Internal Consistency of Text
How does this detail connect to the title?

✔ **Reading Check**

What is the purpose of the memorial?

Everyone who inquired received a booklet explaining the <u>criteria</u>. Among the most important: The memorial could not make a political statement about the war; it must contain the names of all persons killed or missing in action in the war; it must be in harmony with its location on the Mall.

A total of 2,573 individuals and teams registered for the competition. They were sent photographs of the memorial site, maps of the area around the site and of the entire Mall, and other technical design information. The competitors had three months to prepare their designs, which had to be received by March 31, 1981.

Of the 2,573 <u>registrants</u>, 1,421 submitted designs, a record number for such a design competition. When the designs were spread out for jury selection, they filled a large airplane hangar. The jury's task was to select the design which, in their judgment, was the best in meeting these criteria:

- a design that honored the memory of those Americans who served and died in the Vietnam War.
- a design of high artistic merit.
- a design which would be <u>harmonious</u> with its site, including visual harmony with the Lincoln Memorial and the Washington Monument.
- a design that could take its place in the "historic continuity" of America's national art.
- a design that would be buildable, durable, and not too hard to maintain.

criteria (krī tir´ ē ə) *n.* standards or tests by which something can be judged

registrants (rej´ is trənts) *n.* people who register to participate in something

harmonious (här mō´ nē əs) *adj.* combined in a pleasing, orderly arrangement

◀ **Critical Viewing**
What does the pictured veteran's reaction to the memorial tell you about its effectiveness? [**Draw Conclusions**]

The designs were displayed without any indication of the designer's name so that they could be judged <u>anonymously</u>, on their design merits alone. The jury spent one week reviewing all the designs in the airplane hangar. On May 1 it made its report to the Vietnam Veterans Memorial Fund; the experts declared Entry Number 1,026 the winner. The report called it "the finest and most appropriate" of all submitted and said it was "superbly harmonious" with the site on the Mall. Remarking upon the "simple and forthright" materials needed to build the winning entry, the report concludes:

> This memorial, with its wall of names, becomes a place of quiet reflection, and a tribute to those who served their nation in difficult times. All who come here can find it a place of healing. This will be a quiet memorial, one that achieves an excellent relationship with both the Lincoln Memorial and Washington Monument, and relates the visitor to them. It is uniquely horizontal, entering the earth rather than piercing the sky.
>
> This is very much a memorial of our own times, one that could not have been achieved in another time and place. The designer has created an <u>eloquent</u> place where the simple meeting of earth, sky and remembered names contain messages for all who will know this place.

anonymously
(ə nän′ ə məs lē) *adv.* with the name withheld or secret

eloquent (el′ ə kwənt) *adj.* fluent, forceful, and persuasive

☑ **Reading Check**

What criteria did the jury use to select the best design?

▲ **Critical Viewing**
What impact does the listing of names have on the viewer? [**Analyze**]

The eight jurors signed their names to the report, a <u>unanimous</u> decision. When the name of the winner was revealed, the art and architecture worlds were stunned. It was not the name of a national-ly famous architect or sculptor, as most people had been sure it would be. The creator of Entry Number 1,026 was a twenty-one-year-old student at Yale University. Her name—unknown as yet in any field of art or architecture—was Maya Ying Lin.

How could this be? How could an undergraduate student win one of the most important design competitions ever held? How could she beat out some of the top names in American art and architecture? Who was Maya Ying Lin?

unanimous
(yo͞o nan′ ə məs) *adj.*
agreeing completely;
united in opinion

Reading Strategy
Evaluating Internal
Consistency How does
the author make the
connection between
information about the wall
and information about
Maya Lin?

The answer to that question provided some of the other answers, at least in part. Maya Lin, reporters soon discovered, was a Chinese-American girl who had been born and raised in the small midwestern city of Athens, Ohio. Her father, Henry Huan Lin, was a ceramicist of considerable reputation and dean of fine arts at Ohio University in Athens. Her mother, Julia C. Lin, was a poet and professor of Oriental and English literature. Maya Lin's parents were born to culturally prominent families in China. When the Communists came to power in China in the 1940's, Henry and Julia Lin left the country and in time made their way to the United States. Maya Lin grew up in an environment of art and literature. She was interested in sculpture and made both small and large sculptural figures, one cast in bronze. She learned silversmithing and made jewelry. She was surrounded by books and read a great deal, especially fantasies such as *The Hobbit* and *Lord of the Rings*.[1]

But she also found time to work at McDonald's. "It was about the only way to make money in the summer," she said.

A covaledictorian at high school graduation, Maya Lin went to Yale without a clear notion of what she wanted to study and eventually decided to major in Yale's undergraduate program in architecture. During her junior year she studied in Europe and found herself increasingly interested in cemetery architecture. "In Europe there's very little space, so graveyards are used as parks," she said. "Cemeteries are cities of the dead in European countries, but they are also living gardens."

In France, Maya Lin was deeply moved by the war memorial to those who died in the Somme offensive in 1916 during World War I.[2] The great arch by architect Sir Edwin Lutyens is considered one of the world's most outstanding war memorials.

Back at Yale for her senior year, Maya Lin enrolled in Professor Andrus Burr's course in funerary (burial) architecture. The Vietnam Veterans Memorial competition had recently been announced, and although the memorial would be a cenotaph—a monument in honor of persons buried someplace else—Professor Burr thought that having his students prepare a design of the memorial would be a worthwhile course assignment.

Surely, no classroom exercise ever had such spectacular results.

After receiving the assignment, Maya Lin and two of her classmates decided to make the day's journey from New Haven, Connecticut, to Washington to look at the site where the memorial would be built. On

Literary Analysis
Biographical Profile
What details help you appreciate that Maya Lin is an ordinary young person?

✔**Reading Check**
Why is Maya Ying Lin famous?

---

1. *The Hobbit* and *Lord of the Rings* mythical novels by the English author and scholar J.R.R. Tolkien (1892–1973), chronicling the struggle between various good and evil kingdoms for possession of a magical ring that can shift the balance of power in the world.
2. **Somme offensive . . . World War I** a costly and largely unsuccessful Allied offensive that sustained roughly 615,000 casualties of British and French troops.

the day of their visit, Maya Lin remembers, Constitution Gardens was awash with a late November sun; the park was full of light, alive with joggers and people walking beside the lake.

"It was while I was at the site that I designed it," Maya Lin said later in an interview about the memorial with *Washington Post* writer Phil McCombs. "I just sort of visualized it. It just popped into my head. Some people were playing Frisbee. It was a beautiful park. I didn't want to destroy a living park. You use the landscape. You don't fight with it. You absorb the landscape. . . . When I looked at the site I just knew I wanted something horizontal that took you in, that made you feel safe within the park, yet at the same time reminding you of the dead. So I just imagined opening up the earth. . . ."

When Maya Lin returned to Yale, she made a clay model of the vision that had come to her in Constitution Gardens. She showed it to Professor Burr; he liked her conception and encouraged her to enter the memorial competition. She put her design on paper, a task that took six weeks, and mailed it to Washington barely in time to meet the March 31 deadline.

A month and a day later, Maya Lin was attending class. Her roommate slipped into the classroom and handed her a note. Washington was calling and would call back in fifteen minutes. Maya Lin hurried to her room. The call came. She had won the memorial competition.

conception (kən sep´ shən) *n.* an original idea, design, or plan

Review and Assess

Thinking About the Selection

1. **Respond:** What is your response to the design of the Vietnam Veterans Memorial?

2. **(a) Recall:** Why did people think that a Vietnam memorial was needed? **(b) Interpret:** What did the design of the memorial have to accomplish?

3. **(a) Recall:** How was the design for the memorial chosen? **(b) Infer:** How did this process increase Maya Lin's chances?

4. **(a) Recall:** Why did Maya Lin enter the competition? **(b) Draw Conclusions:** Why was her win so surprising?

5. **(a) Analyze:** How does Lin's design meet the criteria of the competition? **(b) Evaluate:** From the photographs, do you think the Vietnam Veterans Memorial succeeds as a memorial? Explain.

Brent Ashabranner

(b. 1921)
Brent Ashabranner, who lives in Williamsburg, Virginia, served in the military during World War II and knows what it's like to lose friends in battle. As a professional writer, he has drawn on his experiences as a Peace Corps advisor and from living overseas in Africa and Asia. He has written books on social issues for young adults, dealing with subjects such as migrant farm workers. The subject of the Vietnam Veterans Memorial appealed to Ashabranner because "It will make us remember that war . . . is about sacrifice and sorrow, not about glory and reward."

Review and Assess

Literary Analysis

Biographical Profile

1. List four of Maya Lin's personality traits. Then, use a chart like this one to show how those traits have influenced her work.

Personality Traits				
Character trait of Maya Ying Lin	Scholarly			
Event that shows trait				
Role that event played in her success				

2. How does the background information portion of this article contribute to the biographical profile?
3. How has family background influenced Maya Lin?

Connecting Literary Elements

4. What do you think the author's purpose was in writing "Always to Remember"—to inform, to persuade, or to entertain? On a chart like the one shown, identify details that support the purpose you have identified.

Detail	How it fits purpose

Reading Strategy

Evaluating Internal Consistency of Text

5. What main impression or idea do the details build toward?
6. Write one sentence to explain the link between one paragraph and the next for paragraphs 3–6 in the article.

   Example: The first paragraph, about the approval of the monument, leads to the second paragraph, about plans for its design.
7. How effectively does the writer support his view of Maya Lin and the memorial she designed?

Extend Understanding

8. **Apply:** Describe two other American monuments or memorials, and explain how their appearance is consistent with the image of the person or group honored.

Quick Review

A **biographical profile** is a piece of writing that often focuses on one event or achievement in a person's life. To review biographical profile, see page 315.

An **article** is a type of nonfiction writing that informs, entertains, or persuades.

The **internal consistency** of a work is its logic, organization, and coherence.

 Take It to the Net
www.phschool.com
Take the interactive self-test online to check your understanding of the selection.

Integrate Language Skills

Vocabulary Development Lesson

Word Analysis: Latin Plural Forms

Some English words derived from Latin keep their Latin plural forms. One is *criterion*, which means "a standard for judging." To form its plural, *criteria*, you change the *-on* to *-a*. For several Latin-based words ending in *-um*, form the plural by changing the *-um* to *-a*. Write the plural of each word. Check your answers with a dictionary.

   1. medium   **2.** datum   **3.** phenomenon

Spelling Strategy

Words ending in *-ant* and *-ent* sound alike but are spelled differently. Unscramble the letters to write words ending in *-ent* and *-ant*.

   1. quelonet   **2.** gristreant   **3.** trimnopen

Fluency: Definitions

Match each definition in the left column with the correct vocabulary word on the right.

1. without a known name **a.** unanimous
2. deeply expressive **b.** criteria
3. standards **c.** anonymously
4. those who register **d.** registrants
5. pleasingly arranged **e.** eloquent
6. in complete agreement **f.** harmonious
7. idea **g.** conception

Grammar Lesson

Prepositional Phrases as Adjectives and Adverbs

A **prepositional phrase** modifies another word in the sentence, functioning as either an adjective or an adverb.

- **Adjective:** They find it a <u>place</u> *of healing*. The phrase *of healing* modifies *place*.
- **Adverb:** The nation was bitterly <u>divided</u> *by the Vietnam War*. The phrase *by the Vietnam War* modifies *divided*.

You can add variety to your writing by beginning some sentences with prepositional phrases.

> *Of all the entries,* hers was best.

▶ *For more practice, see page R30, Exercise C.*
Practice Copy the following sentences. Underline each prepositional phrase. Then, identify the word it modifies, and tell whether the phrase is used as an adjective or adverb.

   1. American soldiers returned from the war.
   2. Between two famous monuments the Vietnam memorial stands.
   3. Announcement of the competition brought an astonishing response.
   4. Lin's design arrived near the deadline.
   5. During the year she studied in Europe.

Writing Application Add a prepositional phrase to the beginning of each sentence.

   1. Maya Lin received a call.
   2. The monument fits its environment.
   3. Many are affected by its quiet beauty.

 Prentice Hall Writing and Grammar Connection: Chapter 17/ Chapter 20, Section 1

Writing Lesson

Tourist Brochure for a Memorial

Create a brochure for the Vietnam Veterans Memorial or another memorial in Washington, D.C. Provide background, interesting facts, and a guide on features.

Prewriting   Prepare a layout for your brochure. Sketch in where photos would go. Jot notes for picture captions and text content in the appropriate places. Then, do research to fill out the spots in your brochure that are reserved for text.

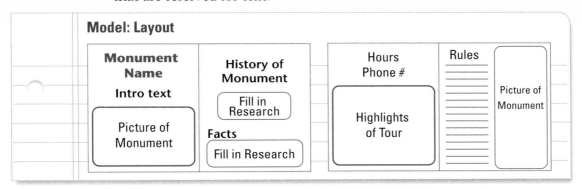

Model: Layout

Monument Name	History of Monument	Hours Phone #	Rules
Intro text	Fill in Research		
Picture of Monument	Facts	Highlights of Tour	Picture of Monument
	Fill in Research		

Drafting   Using a word-processing program, write the text of your brochure. Use formatting to create heads that stand out.

Revising   Ask a classmate to pretend he or she is a visitor to the monument and to evaluate the usefulness of your brochure. Consider your reviewer's suggestions and revise as needed.

WG Prentice Hall Writing and Grammar Connection: Chapter 11, Section 2

Extension Activities

Listening and Speaking Give a **tour guide's explanation** of the Vietnam Veteran's Memorial. Look carefully at the pictures in the book, or find some other pictures on the Internet, especially one that shows how the memorial fits into the ground. Review the selection to find information to use in your guided tour. Include details about:

- the goals and purposes of the monument.
- background on the designer.
- why it was constructed.

Research and Technology Conduct research on one of the other monuments in Washington. Compare and contrast the purpose and appearance of the two monuments. Include your own reactions to the memorials as well as information you have researched.

Writing Write a summary of the article. In addition to restating the main ideas, include your interpretation of the significance of the events described.

Take It to the Net   www.phschool.com

Go online for an additional research activity using the Internet.

READING INFORMATIONAL MATERIALS

Documentary Transcripts

About Transcripts

Transcripts are written records. Often, the word *transcript* refers to the written record of information originally communicated in a form other than writing—usually speech. Transcripts are a useful way to find information originally presented in one of the following ways:

- speeches
- interviews
- talk shows
- documentaries
- debates
- how-to programs

A transcript of a spoken presentation is an exact record of the words said. No comments on or interpretations of the words spoken are included. Formatting, such as color or a font change highlights who is speaking.

Transcripts are a source of information on a wide variety of topics. You can obtain transcripts in several ways.

- **Order from the source.** The network or station that originally broadcast the program may offer transcripts for a small fee to cover mailing.
- **Check with a librarian.** Many libraries keep transcripts of important public presentations, such as speeches or debates.
- **Search the Internet.** If you know the name of a program or event, search through the program title. If you are looking for information on a general topic, transcripts of related interviews or presentations will probably show up in a key word search.

Reading Strategy

Establish a Purpose for Reading

Reading without a purpose is like playing basketball without a basket—you have nothing to shoot for. **Establish a purpose for reading** and focus on appropriate details.

You might read "Accidental Entrepreneurs" for enjoyment. In that case, details about Castognaro's snoring will score high with you. You might read instead for help with problem-solving. In that case, Castognaro's transformation of a nuisance into a business idea will inspire you. You might also read to be informed, or to find models for your own writing.

As you read, use a graphic organizer like the one at right to list details that fit your purpose for reading.

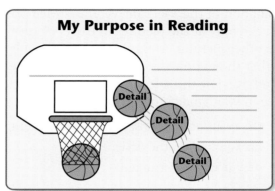

My Purpose in Reading

Detail
Detail
Detail

Accidental Entrepreneurs

Everything the host says, including his introduction of himself, is included in the transcript.

The documentary begins with an introduction describing the topic, and then introduces a specific example. Here, a particular entrepreneur is to be interviewed.

Bright red text sets off each speaker's name from the words he or she says. This formatting also makes it easy to see when speakers change.

DEREK MCGINTY, host: This is *All Things Considered*. I'm Derek McGinty.

The labor issues that concern most Americans are similar to those that prompted the UPS strike.[1] Pensions, job security, hourly pay. Though we may daydream about quitting our jobs altogether to strike out on our own, most of us never get an idea that we think would justify such a radical move.

But there are some people who stumble on inspiration in the midst of their everyday lives, and somehow, manage to turn that inspiration into their livelihoods.

NPR's Chris Arnold spoke with several of these accidental entrepreneurs[2] and has this report.

. . .

ARNOLD: . . . some people don't get hit with an innovative idea until much later in life. At 70 years old, Vincent Castognaro has just started a business to help people stop snoring. Vincent, whose friends call him Jimmy, says he's been snoring most of his life.

VINCENT CASTOGNARO, entrepreneur: So I was known as "Jimmy the Snorer." In my younger days, I was known as "Jimmy Dimples" because of my dimples, but later on, I was known as Jimmy the Snorer.

ARNOLD: Vincent grew up shining shoes and working in factories in Brooklyn, New York. He later moved out to Long Island, where he struggled to make a living as a cabinetmaker. For much of the last 25 years, Vincent and his wife Eleanor both have suffered with his snoring. He has a condition called sleep apnea, [ap nē ə] where the jaw slumps back during sleep, blocking a person's airway.

CASTOGNARO: Very, very uncomfortable for me. I would wake up with an extremely dry mouth in the morning. And all kinds of sore throats and problems of that type. And woozy during the day, sleepy. I could just simply close my eyes for two minutes

---

1. UPS strike On August 4, 1997, nearly 200,000 United Parcel Service workers went on strike.

2. entrepreneurs (än´ trə prə nʉrz´) *n.* people who start and manage their own businesses.

and I would end up falling asleep. It was drastic. It was really that bad. Naturally, it was uncomfortable for everybody else in the room, too.

ELEANOR CASTOGNARO, wife of Vincent: He used to snore terribly. I would have to get up and go in the living room and sleep on the couch.

ARNOLD: Vincent says surgery was too expensive and anti-snoring products on the market were too uncomfortable. One doctor recommended a machine with a mask that would strap around his head and pump air into his nose all night. Then, Vincent says he got an idea from a child dressed up as a vampire.

CASTOGNARO: One Halloween day, I saw some children with these imitation fang teeth in their mouth and that gave me, pretty much, the idea of what I thought would be necessary to keep my mouth closed.

ARNOLD: About this time, Vincent lost his cabinetry business. So with very little savings, he started to work full-time on inventing an anti-snoring mouthpiece to hold his jaw in place. He went to the library, found out what types of plastics were used for mouthguards, got some plaster for molds, and then started spending days on end in his basement wood shop working on his invention.

CASTOGNARO: Well, with trial and error, trial and error, I—by hand and with knives and files and sandpaper—I managed to make these two shapes. My wife and people that saw me thought I was a little bit cuckoo. But as the days and the months and the years went by, this thing started to really take shape.

> Because a transcript records exactly what is said, even repeated words and incomplete sentences are included.

ARNOLD: Along the way, Vincent became friends with an ex-aerospace engineer, who joined him as a partner. He went for tests at a sleep clinic and confirmed his mouthguard cured his snoring. They got a patent,[3] consulted the FDA,[4] and found several dentists through which to sell the devices. They've only been in business five months, so they're not yet turning a profit, but the mouthguards are selling and they think they could do well.

All of which makes Vincent very happy.

CASTOGNARO: It is the most incredible thing in my entire life. And again, like I say, I'm not a young kid anymore, and to have something like this happen, I can now, maybe, hopefully, say, well, now I can give something to my children.

ARNOLD: I'm Chris Arnold reporting.

---

3. patent a patent is a description of an invention filed with the government to protect the inventor from imitators.
4. FDA Food and Drug Administration, which regulates the sale of health items.

Check Your Comprehension

1. What is an "accidental entrepreneur"?
2. What is sleep apnea, and how did it cause a problem for the Castognaros?
3. How does Vincent Castognaro's invention solve the problem?

Applying the Reading Strategy

Establish a Purpose for Reading

4. Did you read the selection to be entertained, to solve a problem, to be informed, or as a model for your own writing?
5. What details in the transcript helped you accomplish your purpose?
6. What is one other purpose someone might have for reading this transcript?
7. What details would help the reader accomplish that purpose?

Activity

Locating Transcripts

Locate transcripts on a topic or person of interest to you, using the three different ways of locating transcripts identified on page 326. Try to find different types of transcripts. For example, find the transcript of a speech, an interview, and an informational program. Explain to a small group how you found the transcripts and the type of information contained in each.

Contrasting Informational Materials

Transcripts and Presentations

Compare and contrast a transcript to an oral presentation. Watch or listen to an informational program, a speech, or an interview. Based on what you observe and what you now know about transcripts, compare and contrast the characteristics of the two ways of communicating information. Explain the strengths and weaknesses of each form in each category shown on the graphic organizer.

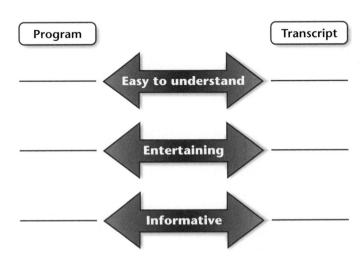

Writing WORKSHOP

Business Letter

A **business letter** is a document written for a formal purpose such as requesting information, stating a problem to do with a product or service, or placing an order. In this workshop, you will write a business letter.

Assignment Criteria. Your business letter should have the following characteristics:

- Correct business letter **format**
- A statement of **purpose**
- **Content** that is clear, concise, and focused
- **Support** for any points you make
- A **tone** that is appropriate for your audience

To preview the criteria on which your business letter may be assessed, see the Rubric on page 333.

Prewriting

Choose a topic. Make a list of problems you would like to solve or issues you would like to address by writing to a public official, business, or organization. Select the topic that interests you most.

Topic Ideas

- express a political opinion to my senator
- question my Internet service about the rate increase
- ask the mail-order company about a discounted price for the team's order of uniforms
- request a refund from the magazine publisher for my canceled subscription

---

Write a statement of purpose. Identify the main thing you want to accomplish in your letter. Write one statement to sum it up.

> **Example**
> **Statement of Purpose:** I want to voice my support for building an addition to the town library.

Plan your support. List the information you will use to explain and support your purpose. You may need to include concrete facts and examples. For example, if you are dissatisfied with a product, provide specific examples that will help your audience understand your problem.

Student Model

Before you begin drafting, read this student model and review the characteristics of an effective business letter.

1253 Campground Drive
Lawrence, IN 55555

November 10, 2002

Mark Gary
Unitron Corporation
Fourth Street
Lawrence, IN 55555

Dear Mr. Gary:

Community Students is a group of active, dedicated young people at Lawrence School who volunteer time to improve the quality of parks and other public spaces in our area. Last year Unitron generously supported our group and I hope we can count on your support again. Our next planned project is the improvement of Lees park. The plan includes the addition of two new benches and four picnic tables along the blacktopped walking path. In addition, we will plant four ornamental trees along the path.

Placing benches and tables near the blacktopped pathways will give greater accessibility for the physically challenged, the elderly, and parents pushing strollers. The trees will beautify the path.

Our group has scheduled bench and table building for January, February, and early March. Outdoor work is scheduled to begin in April. Planting is scheduled for late May and a final cleanup day is planned for June 1.

We have offers from Hahn Lumber and Fred's Nursery to give us materials and trees at a discount. We have raised $250.00 with our own fundraising activities. However, we need additional funding to meet the total budget for this project.

If you are willing to donate, please make out a check to Lawrence School Community Students. I have enclosed a flyer with more information about the group, including how you can contact us if you have questions.

Sincerely,

Jake Merkis

Jake Merkis
President, Community Students

In a block format business letter, the writer's address, the date, and the address of the person to whom the letter is written are aligned on the left side of the paper, with spaces between them.

The salutation addresses the person formally and is punctuated by a colon.

The body of the letter identifies the writer's purpose, to get a donation. The wording of the letter communicates a formal, professional tone, or attitude.

The writer offers support for his request by pointing out what the group has already accomplished toward the goal.

The closing *Sincerely* is common for business letters. *Respectfully yours* also communicates the appropriately formal tone. A business letter ends with both a handwritten signature and a typed name. Use your full name when signing a business letter.

Drafting

Keep to the format. A business letter must follow an appropriate format. This format will give your letter a professional look. Include each part of a business letter noted on the chart.

Draft the body. In the first paragraph, state your purpose for writing. Present your explanation or proposal, and supporting information, in the following paragraphs. To conclude, restate the purpose of your letter or indicate what will be done to follow up on it.

Present specific information. Whether you are explaining a problem or giving reasons for an opinion, specific information will make your letter easy to understand. Vague information might make the reader wonder exactly what you want or need.

Example

Vague: I have been having some problems with my VCR. Please tell me what I should do about it.

Specific: The rewind and fast-forward features of my VCR do not always function. Since it is still under warranty, I believe it should be fixed free of charge.

Revising

Revise for conciseness. Business letters should be brief and to the point. Review your letter for wordiness and unnecessary repetition. Cut and condense any passages that go on and on.

Heading: The writer's address and the date are placed in the upper left corner.
Inside address: The name and address of the recipient are placed below the heading, against the left margin.
Salutation: The salutation, or greeting to the recipient, is followed by a colon.
Examples: Dear Mr. Davies:
Dear Sir or Madam:
To Whom It May Concern:
Body: The main part of the letter presents the writer's purpose and the information that supports it.
Closing: The closing begins with a capital letter and ends with a comma.
Examples: Yours truly,
With best regards,
Sincerely,
Signature: The writer's name is typed below the closing. Between the closing and the typed name, the writer adds a handwritten signature.

Model: Revising to Be Concise

Community Students is a group of active, dedicated young people at Lawrence School who volunteer time to improve the quality of parks and other public spaces in our area. ~~You may think that people in middle school can't accomplish much but we can. We've done many excellent projects that have benefited the community.~~ Last year Unitron generously supported our group and I hope we can count on your support again.

> The writer realizes that Unitron is aware of the group's work. One sentence to jog Mr. Gary's memory is sufficient.

Revise for businesslike language. Business writing should not include slang, rude comments, or details from your personal life. Use serious, polite language that communicates respect.

Example

Non-professional tone: Your CD player is a rip-off. It broke and wrecked my party. I want my money back now.

Professional tone: This product does not work properly and would be too expensive to fix. Therefore I request that you refund my money promptly.

Compare the model and the nonmodel. Why is the model more effective than the nonmodel?

Nonmodel	Model
Hahn Lumber and Fred's Nursery will cut their prices for us. We've come up with $250.00 bucks with cake sales and stuff. We still need a lot of cash to get this project started, let alone finished.	We have offers from Hahn Lumber and Fred's Nursery to give us materials and trees at a discount. We have raised $250 with our own fundraising activities. However, we need additional funding to meet the total budget for this project.

Publishing and Presenting

Choose one of the following ways to share your writing with classmates or a wider audience.

Share your letter. Read your letter to a partner. Ask how he or she would respond to receiving it.

Send your letter. Print out an error-free copy on good-quality paper. Enclose it in a properly addressed envelope and mail it to the person or group to whom you wrote.

Prentice Hall Writing and Grammar Connection: Chapter 26, Section 3

Rubric for Self-Assessment

Evaluate your business letter using the following criteria and rating scale:

Criteria	Rating Scale Not very				Very
Is the letter's purpose clearly stated?	1	2	3	4	5
Is the content focused and concise?	1	2	3	4	5
How well does the letter follow correct format?	1	2	3	4	5
How professional and appropriate is the tone?	1	2	3	4	5

Listening and Speaking WORKSHOP

Delivering an Informational Presentation

In an **informational presentation,** you organize and deliver information orally—in spoken form. This workshop will help you prepare and deliver an effective informational presentation.

Be Organized

Like an essay, the content of an informational presentation should be logically organized. Organize your information in a way that most clearly shows your topic.

- **Chronological,** or time, order is good for explaining a process or for presenting a biography or a history.
- **Point by point.** Group related details such as "background" or "physical features."
- **Make an outline.** Prepare an outline of your presentation. Highlight words to be defined as explanations that are accompanied by visual aids so you do not forget to include these.

Be Precise

- **Use appropriate grammar.** Your audience will better understand your presentation if you stick to the rules. Save the slang and the fragments for casual conversation. Speak in complete sentences that are grammatically correct.
- **Use appropriate word choices.** Refer to the notes on your outline to accurately cite numbers, names, or quotations.

(Activity:)
Persuasive Speech
Following the suggestions above, deliver a two-to-three minute informational presentation on one of these topics:

- How to make a food you like
- An animal that makes a good pet
- How to get from your school to another location
- An exciting vacation destination

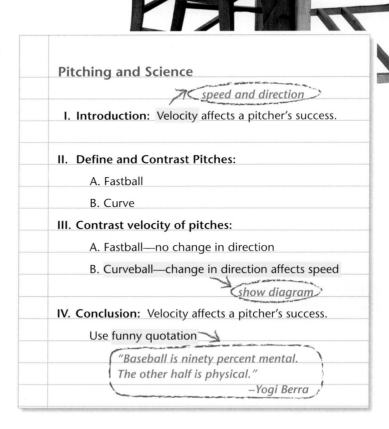

Pitching and Science

speed and direction

   I. Introduction: Velocity affects a pitcher's success.

   II. Define and Contrast Pitches:

      A. Fastball

      B. Curve

   III. Contrast velocity of pitches:

      A. Fastball—no change in direction

      B. Curveball—change in direction affects speed

show diagram

   IV. Conclusion: Velocity affects a pitcher's success.

   Use funny quotation

*"Baseball is ninety percent mental.
The other half is physical."*
—Yogi Berra

Assessment WORKSHOP

Identifying the Main Idea

The reading sections of some tests require you to read a passage and answer multiple-choice questions about main ideas.

Sometimes, the main idea of a passage is stated in a topic sentence, which may appear anywhere in the passage. Sometimes, the main idea is not stated directly but is implied, or suggested, by the details in the passage. Use what you have learned about making inferences to determine implied main ideas.

Test-Taking Strategy

After reading a passage, identify the main idea in your own mind before reading the choices. Select the choice that is closest to your idea.

Sample Test Item

Directions: Read the following passage, and then choose the answer that summarizes the author's message.

The platypus lives in the lakes and streams of eastern Australia. It looks like a duck-billed seal and acts like a lizard. Being a mammal, the platypus is warm-blooded and has fur. However, it also has some characteristics of a reptile. For example, instead of bearing live young, it lays eggs. Like a lizard, its legs are attached to the side of its body rather than underneath it.

1. What is the main idea of this passage?

    A The platypus lives in Australia.

    B Although it is a mammal, the platypus shares some characteristics with reptiles.

    C The platypus looks like a duck-billed seal.

    D The platypus is a graceful swimmer.

Answer and Explanation

A and C are details. D is not mentioned in the passage. **B** is the implied main idea of the passage.

Apply the Strategy

Directions: Answer the question based on this passage:

On Saturday, at 7:30 a.m., students began gathering in the school parking lot. Many carried home-baked goodies. Others brought pails, soap, sponges, and clothes. The students had formed a committee to raise money for the Tiny Tots Preschool, which had been severely damaged in a fire. With the car wash and bake sale, they hoped to raise funds to replace most of the school's books. By one o'clock, the students were counting their hard-earned money.

1. What is the main idea of the passage?

    A Students held a car wash and bake sale to benefit the Tiny Tots Preschool.

    B The Tiny Tots Preschool had fire damage.

    C Students like to help out in a crisis.

    D The students worked hard to earn money.

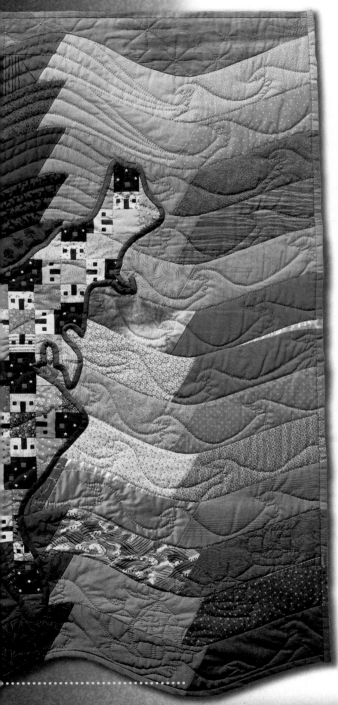

Exploring the Theme

Some people describe the United States as a melting pot, in which people from different cultures blend to become American. Others prefer the image of a mosaic, in which people retain their original heritage while joining American society. No matter whether you choose to celebrate Americans' similarities or differences, there's no disputing the fact that the United States is a rich nation—both in its people and in its geography and resources.

The selections in this unit explore what it means to live in this vast and diverse nation. In "Travels with Charley," John Steinbeck decides the best way to understand America is to travel its roads. Steinbeck encounters wildly different people and places that demonstrate why it is so difficult to come up with a single description of America or Americans.

◀ **Critical Viewing** How do the colors and patterns of this quilt serve as a metaphor, or symbol, for America? **[Infer]**

Why Read Literature?

Whenever you read, you have a purpose, or reason. Your purpose will vary, depending on the content, genre, and style of the work you plan to read. Preview three purposes you might set before reading works in this unit.

1 Read to be inspired.

When we are younger, it can be difficult for us to appreciate how much our parents do for us. Two poets, Robert Hayden and Evelyn Tooley Hunt, reflect back on how the thankless sacrifices of a parent allowed them to live a better life in **"Those Winter Sundays,"** page 400, and **"Taught Me Purple,"** page 398.

Martin Luther King, Jr.'s message of peace and justice brought out the best qualities in many people. Alice Walker discusses how King's eloquence and courage transformed her life in her inspirational essay, **"Choice: A Tribute to Dr. Martin Luther King, Jr.,"** page 364.

2 Read for information.

In 1920, more than eighty years ago, women won the right to vote. This right was achieved through a long and difficult struggle which is now largely forgotten. It is difficult to take this right for granted after reading the powerful words of early feminist Elizabeth Cady Stanton in **"Arguments in Favor of a Sixteenth Amendment,"** page 404.

3 Read for the love of literature.

The poet Emma Lazarus was from a wealthy family. Nevertheless, she still felt sympathy for the vast numbers of poor immigrants streaming into New York City in the late 19th century. Witness the words that have inspired countless numbers of new and established Americans when you read **"The New Colossus,"** page 372.

Memorable literature can sometimes capture a feeling with pinpoint accuracy. You may feel a flash of recognition as you experience the conflicted emotions of the young girl in Gish Jen's story, **"The White Umbrella,"** page 384.

 Take It to the Net

Visit the Web site for online instruction and activities related to each selection in this unit.

www.phschool.com

How to Read Literature

Interactive Reading Strategies

Interactive computer games can be more fun than simply watching television because you are more of an active participant. Interactive reading is similar. When you interact with the books you read, the experience becomes richer and more fun. Use these reading strategies to help you interact with the text.

1. Clarify details.

Most people encounter some moments of confusion when reading new material. When this happens, take time to clarify the details of the passage you have just read.

- Pause to think about what has happened in the story. Then reread the passage slowly and carefully to clear up any remaining confusion.
- If you still have questions, continue reading to see whether you can find answers in passages that lie farther ahead.

2. Recognize connotations of words.

A connotation is the implied, or suggested, meaning of a word or phrase. For example, if you call someone a "clown," you are probably relying on the connotation of the word—more than its literal meaning—to get your message across.

- To determine a connotation, notice how a word or phrase makes you feel.
- Classify the word or phrase as positive or negative, depending on its context and your past experience.

Phrase: "The wretched refuse of your teeming shore." — from "The New Colossus"

Feelings: Pity, disgust

Positive or negative? Negative (the noun *refuse* means "trash")

Connotation: These are the miserable people that nobody wants

3. Respond to a theme.

Poems and stories are most memorable when their themes generate an emotional reaction.

- Determine the main theme that the author is communicating.
- Note your reaction to the theme. You might respond with approval, anger, or any other type of emotion based on previous experience.

4. Predict

Predicting, or making guesses about what will happen later in a story, keeps you actively involved in a story. Use prediction to avoid missing details in a story that could be important and to check your understanding of what you have read.

As you read the selections in this unit, review the reading strategies and apply them to interact with the text.

Prepare to Read

from The People, Yes

Preview

Connecting to the Literature

Often, the stories told around a campfire blend reality and fantasy. In his poem, "The People, Yes," Carl Sandburg celebrates the stories cowboys and settlers used to tell around the campfire—tall tales and legends. Recall "camp" stories, tall tales, and other "tales" you have heard or told.

Background

This poem was published in 1936 during the Great Depression, a time of economic struggle that began in 1929 and lasted until World War II. In the poem, Sandburg recalls another critical era in American history: the age of Westward expansion, when tales of heroes with great strength inspired settlers who faced great hardships. Sandburg chose this subject matter to remind Americans of the courage and hope that are part of the American tradition.

Literary Analysis

Oral Tradition

The **oral tradition** is the passing on of stories from generation to generation by word of mouth. In his poem, Sandburg refers to many familiar American tales that were passed on in this way. Because this kind of storytelling is not as common as it once was, you may not recognize all the stories mentioned, but you can still see the humor in the exaggerations. Use these focus questions to guide you as you read:

1. How does Sandburg's use of language give his poem the quality of oral storytelling?
2. What is Sandburg's purpose in cataloging stories from the oral tradition?

Connecting Literary Elements

Sandburg's poem starts with the words, "They have yarns . . ." A **yarn** is another term for a "tall tale," a story that depends on claims that are so extreme and impossible that they are funny. Note the exaggeration in this example:

> . . . Of the man so tall *he must climb a ladder to shave himself,* . . .

A yarn may be based on actual people or events, but the storyteller wildly exaggerates some characteristics to create humor.

Reading Strategy

Recognizing Cultural References

Sandburg's references to American tall tales are examples of **cultural references**—details that reflect a writer's heritage, background, and traditions. Sandburg was a distinctly American voice—a poet who celebrated ordinary Americans and reveled in the American oral tradition. By referring to American folk heroes and tales, Sandburg captures many of the values and beliefs of American culture.

As you read, use a chart like this one to list references to folk heroes and tall tales and to record the qualities that you think Sandburg is trying to capture through these references.

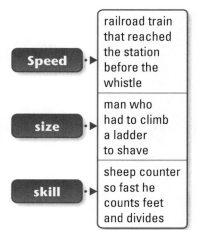

Vocabulary Development

mutineers (myo͞ot´ ən irz´) *n.* crew members on a ship who revolt against their officers (p. 343)

flue (flo͞o) *n.* pipe in a chimney that leads the smoke outside (p. 343)

Paul Bunyan, Rockwell Kent

▲ **Critical Viewing** Which aspects of this illustration of Paul Bunyan are realistic? Which aspects are exaggerated? **[Interpret]**

from THE PEOPLE, YES

Carl Sandburg

They have yarns
Of a skyscraper so tall they had to put hinges
On the two top stories so to let the moon go by,
Of one corn crop in Missouri when the roots
5 Went so deep and drew off so much water
The Mississippi riverbed that year was dry,
Of pancakes so thin they had only one side,
Of "a fog so thick we shingled the barn and six feet out on the
    fog,"
Of Pecos Pete straddling a cyclone in Texas and riding it to the
    west coast where "it rained out under him,"
10 Of the man who drove a swarm of bees across the Rocky
    Mountains and the Desert "and didn't lose a bee,"
Of a mountain railroad curve where the engineer
    in his cab can touch the caboose and spit in the
    conductor's eye,
Of the boy who climbed a cornstalk growing so fast he would
    have starved to death if they hadn't shot biscuits up to him,
Of the old man's whiskers: "When the wind was with him his
    whiskers arrived a day before he did,"
Of the hen laying a square egg and cackling, "Ouch!" and of
    hens laying eggs with the dates printed on them,
15 Of the ship captain's shadow: it froze to the deck one cold
    winter night,
Of <u>mutineers</u> on that same ship put to chipping rust with
    rubber hammers,
Of the sheep counter who was fast and accurate: "I just count
    their feet and divide by four,"
Of the man so tall he must climb a ladder to shave himself,
Of the runt so teeny-weeny it takes two men and a boy to see
    him,
Of mosquitoes: one can kill a dog, two of them a man,
Of a cyclone that sucked cookstoves out of the kitchen, up the
    chimney <u>flue</u>, and on to the next town,
Of the same cyclone picking up wagontracks in Nebraska and
    dropping them over in the Dakotas,
Of the hook-and-eye snake[1] unlocking itself into forty pieces,

---

1. **hook-and-eye snake** here, a snake that is fastened together with metal hooks.

Reading Strategy
Recognizing Cultural References What details in the poem reflect the poet's cultural heritage?

mutineers (myo͞ot′ ən irz′) *n.* people on a ship who revolt against their officers

flue (flo͞o) *n.* the pipe in a chimney that leads the smoke outside

**Reading Check**

What does the speaker list in the poem?

each piece two inches long, then in nine seconds flat
    snapping itself together again,
Of the watch swallowed by the cow—when they butchered her
    a year later the watch was running and had the correct
    time,

25 Of horned snakes, hoop snakes that roll themselves where
    they want to go, and rattlesnakes carrying bells instead of
    rattles on their tails,
Of the herd of cattle in California getting lost in a giant
    redwood tree that had hollowed out,
Of the man who killed a snake by putting its tail in its mouth
    so it swallowed itself,
Of railroad trains whizzing along so fast they reach the
    station before the whistle,
Of pigs so thin the farmer had to tie knots in their tails
    to keep them from crawling through the cracks in
    their pens,

30 Of Paul Bunyan's big blue ox, Babe, measuring between
    the eyes forty-two ax-handles and a plug of Star
    tobacco exactly,
Of John Henry's hammer and the curve of its swing and
    his singing of it as "a rainbow round my shoulder."

Review and Assess

Thinking About the Selection

1. **Respond:** Which tale sounds most interesting to you? Why?

2. **(a) Recall:** Identify three animals mentioned in these yarns.
(b) Infer: Why do tall tales often include unusual animals?
(c) Generalize: What characteristics do the people, animals, and things in these yarns share?

3. **(a) Recall:** Name three geographical locations mentioned in the yarns. **(b) Analyze:** What do these locations reveal about the origins of tall tales?

4. **(a) Recall:** Identify three people mentioned who have amazing abilities or skills. **(b) Compare:** In what way does each character's ability or skill contribute to survival?

5. **(a) Interpret:** Based on what you have read in this section, explain what you think the title of the poem means.
(b) Connect: What inspirational stories from recent times—true or fictional—could be used to give hope and courage?
(c) Evaluate: Are the heroes of the tall tales still inspirational or encouraging in today's world? Why or why not?

Carl Sandburg

(1878–1967)

Carl Sandburg was not only a folklorist and poet but also a journalist and historian. As a young man, he worked as a truck driver and farm worker. In the early 1900s, he became an active part of a Chicago writers' movement.

In his work, Sandburg focuses on the stories of ordinary Americans, using playful humor in his stories for children. He won a Pulitzer Prize in 1940 for a four-volume biography of Abraham Lincoln and again in 1951 for his *Complete Poems*. "The People, Yes" is an epic poem, published in 1936 when Americans were suffering the hardships of the Great Depression. The poem celebrates the American character and spirit.

Review and Assess

Literary Analysis

Oral Tradition

1. How does Sandburg's use of language give his poem the quality of oral storytelling?
2. What is Sandburg's purpose in cataloging stories from the oral tradition?
3. Complete a chart like the one shown. For each quality or concern that was important to the settlers of the West, identify two tales mentioned in Sandburg's poem that illustrate the quality or concern. Explain each answer.

Dangers of Nature	Hard Work	Cleverness

Connecting Literary Elements

4. On a chart like the one below, list three **yarns** referred to in the poem. Then explain how exaggeration may have been used to create each yarn based on an actual event.

Yarn	Actual Event	Exaggeration

Reading Strategy

Recognizing Cultural References

5. What American attitude or belief is reflected in the fact that tall tales make everything bigger than life?
6. What is Carl Sandburg's attitude toward the tall tales? How do you know?
7. Why would Sandburg include these tall tales in a poem he wrote to inspire courage and hope during the Great Depression?
8. What overall impression of the United States and its people does this poem convey? Support your answer with details from the poem.

Extend Understanding

9. **Evaluate:** How important is it for a country or a culture to have its own oral tradition? Explain.

Quick Review

The **oral tradition** includes all the songs, stories, and poems in a culture that are passed from generation to generation by word of mouth. To review oral tradition, see page 341.

A **yarn,** or tall tale, is a story or legend that creates humor through exaggerated actions and situations. To review yarns, see page 341.

Cultural references are details that connect a work to the writer's heritage, background, and traditions. To review a technique for recognizing cultural references, see page 341.

 Take It to the Net
www.phschool.com
Take the interactive self-test online to check your understanding of the selection.

Integrate Language Skills

Vocabulary Development Lesson

Word Analysis: Latin Suffix -eer

Add the suffix -eer to a word to form a noun that means "a person who does or works with [something]." For example, an *engineer* works with or operates an *engine*. Add the suffix -eer to each of these words. Then, use the word in a sentence.

1. auction   **2.** ballad   **3.** mutiny

Fluency: Sentence Completion

On your paper, write the vocabulary word from the list on page 341 that best completes each sentence.

1. Soot and ashes can clog the ___?___ of a chimney.

2. The ___?___ seized the ship and sailed to a deserted island.

Use each vocabulary word in a sentence about a tall tale or yarn mentioned in "The People, Yes."

Spelling Strategy

To make the plural of a word ending in -o, follow these rules:

- For most nouns ending in -o preceded by a vowel, add -s: radio + -s = radios
- For most nouns ending in -o preceded by a consonant, add -es: mosquito + -es = mosquitoes
- For most musical terms, add -s: piano + -s = pianos

Write the plurals of these words:

1. hero   **2.** potato   **3.** concerto   **4.** studio

Grammar Lesson

Subordinating Conjunctions

Conjunctions connect words or groups of words within a sentence. A **subordinating conjunction** connects two complete ideas and shows that one is dependent on the other.

> **Example:** *Although* redwood trees are huge, they are not large enough to hold a herd of cattle.

Common Subordinating Conjunctions			
after	although	as	as soon as
because	before	if	since
unless	until	when	when
while	whenever	whenever	while

▶ *For more practice, see page R29, Exercise E.*

Practice Revise the following passage by combining underlined words with another sentence. Use a subordinating conjunction to make the underlined clause dependent on the clause that comes before it. You may rearrange, remove, or add words or groups of words as needed.

Tall tales are part of American culture. <u>They are also known as yarns.</u> They are not the only examples of folk tales told in America. <u>They capture an important part of our American oral tradition.</u> Enslaved Africans brought with them many trickster stories. <u>The stories began to include "American" details.</u>

Writing Application Add a paragraph of your own that includes subordinating conjunctions.

W̸G̸ Prentice Hall Writing and Grammar Connection: Chapter 18, Section 18.1

Writing Lesson

Profile of a Legendary Figure

Write a profile—a short biographical article—of a legendary figure.

Prewriting   Research your subject's background, taking notes of interesting facts and stories. Prepare an "impression tree" to help you focus your main impression of the subject. First, list several adjectives to describe your subject. Combine specific words to form a more general description. Continue combining until you arrive at one overall word.

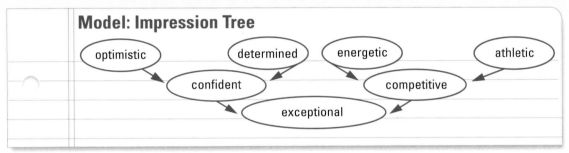

Model: Impression Tree

optimistic → confident
determined →
energetic → competitive
athletic →
confident → exceptional
competitive →

Drafting   Using your impression tree, write a thesis statement—a sentence that states the main idea of your profile. Then, use each adjective from your tree as the basis for a supporting paragraph. Give details and events from the subect's life that support the adjective you chose. Conclude with a restatement of your main impression.

Revising   Eliminate details that do not contribute to the main impression.

WG   *Prentice Hall Writing and Grammar Connection: Chapter 6, Section 4*

Extension Activities

Listening and Speaking Choose an American yarn and prepare and perform a **storytelling** for your class.

Use verbal feedback. Answer questions and respond to comments, but do not stray too far from the story or listeners will forget where the story left off.

Use nonverbal feedback. Watch faces and body language. People who are looking away or moving restlessly are not listening. Adjust your storytelling to make it more interactive if you see any of these signs.

Research and Technology In a small group, make a **collection of tall tales.** Each group should

- choose a legendary figure.
- use an Internet search engine or library resources to find different versions of tales, songs, and poems about the figure.

Collect the tales in a book and display it for the class to read. **[Group Activity]**

 **Take It to the Net**   www.phschool.com

Go online for an additional research activity using the Internet.

Prepare to Read

from Travels with Charley

 Take It to the Net

Visit www.phschool.com for interactive activities and instruction related to the excerpt from *Travels with Charley,* including

- background
- graphic organizers
- literary elements
- reading strategies

Preview

Connecting to the Literature

In *Travels with Charley,* John Steinbeck sets out with his dog, Charley, to meet people all across the United States and learn about their different views of life. Recall a person you have met who is very different from you or a place you have been that is very different from your home. Think about how these differences have shown you a new way of seeing things.

Background

As Steinbeck travels westward through the United States, he finds himself in the Badlands of North Dakota. The Badlands are a rugged region of fantastically shaped rock formations separated by valleys. In that barren landscape, few plants grow.

Literary Analysis

Travel Essay

A **travel essay** is a brief nonfiction work about a trip. Most travel essays include a combination of facts and personal impressions. Notice how John Steinbeck's personal impressions are reflected in this passage:

> On the Bismarck side it is an eastern landscape, eastern grass with the look and smell of eastern America. Across the Missouri it is pure west, with brown grass and water scorings and small outcrops.

Connecting Literary Elements

In his travel essay, Steinbeck uses the following types of **figurative language**—descriptive writing that is not meant to be taken literally. Examples are given in the chart on the right.

- **Metaphor:** Description of one item as if it were another, without using *like* or *as*.
- **Similes:** Comparison of two things using *like* or *as*.
- **Personification:** Nonhumans are given human characteristics.

As you read, keep these focus questions in mind:

1. In what way do comparisons make a description clearer?
2. What does figurative language add to Steinbeck's descriptions?

Metaphor
Steinbeck was a casual turtle, carrying his house on his back.
Simile
Charley has a roar *like* a lion
Personification
the grieving sky

Reading Strategy

Clarifying Details

When you do not completely understand a passage in a travel essay, use strategies to **clarify,** or make clear, the meaning. First, try to clarify without leaving the text.

- Look for footnotes or margin notes that give additional information.
- Recall similar words, place names, or expressions.
- Reread to discover details you may have missed.
- Read ahead to find additional details.

If the meaning remains unclear, use a resource such as a dictionary, a thesaurus, an atlas, or a reader's encyclopedia to clarify the meaning.

Vocabulary Development

diagnostic (dī′ əg näs′ tik) *adj.* providing evidence about the nature of something (p. 351)

peripatetic (per′ i pə tet′ ik) *adj.* moving from place to place (p. 351)

rigorous (rig′ ər əs) *adj.* very strict or harsh (p. 352)

inexplicable (in eks′ pli kə bəl) *adj.* not possible to explain (p. 354)

celestial (sə les′ chəl) *adj.* of the heavens; divine (p. 355)

from Travels with Charley

JOHN

▲ Critical Viewing
What impression of
traveling does this
picture give? [Analyze]

My plan was clear, concise, and reasonable, I think. For many
years I have traveled in many parts of the world. In America I live
in New York, or dip into Chicago or San Francisco. But New York
is no more America than Paris is France or London is England.
Thus I discovered that I did not know my own country. I, an
American writer, writing about America, was working from memory,
and the memory is at best a faulty, warpy reservoir. I had not
heard the speech of America, smelled the grass and trees and
sewage, seen its hills and water, its color and quality of light.
I knew the changes only from books and newspapers. But more
than this, I had not felt the country for twenty-five years. In
short, I was writing of something I did not know about, and it
seems to me that in a so-called writer this is criminal. My memories
were distorted by twenty-five intervening years.

Once I traveled about in an old bakery wagon, double-doored
rattler with a mattress on its floor. I stopped where people stopped
or gathered, I listened and looked and felt, and in the process had
a picture of my country the accuracy of which was impaired only
by my own shortcomings.

STEINBECK

So it was that I determined to look again, to try to rediscover this monster land. Otherwise, in writing, I could not tell the small <u>diagnostic</u> truths which are the foundations of the larger truth. One sharp difficulty presented itself. In the intervening twenty-five years my name had become reasonably well known. And it has been my experience that when people have heard of you, favorably or not, they change; they become, through shyness or the other qualities that publicity inspires, something they are not under ordinary circumstances. This being so, my trip demanded that I leave my name and my identity at home. I had to be <u>peripatetic</u> eyes and ears, a kind of moving gelatin plate.[1] I could not sign hotel registers, meet people I knew, interview others, or even ask searching questions. Furthermore, two or more people disturb the ecologic complex of an area. I had to go alone and I had to be self-contained, a kind of casual turtle carrying his house on his back.

With all this in mind I wrote to the head office of a great corporation which manufactures trucks. I specified my purpose and my

diagnostic (dī´ əg näs´ tik) *adj.* providing evidence about the nature of something

peripatetic (per´ i pə tet´ ik) *adj.* moving from place to place

 **Reading Check**

What is the narrator's plan?

---

1. gelatin plate sensitive glass plate used to reproduce pictures.

needs. I wanted a three-quarter-ton pick-up truck, capable of going anywhere under possibly <u>rigorous</u> conditions, and on this truck I wanted a little house built like the cabin of a small boat. A trailer is difficult to maneuver on mountain roads, is impossible and often illegal to park, and is subject to many restrictions. In due time, specifications came through, for a tough, fast, comfortable vehicle, mounting a camper top—a little house with double bed, a four-burner stove, a heater, refrigerator and lights operating on butane, a chemical toilet, closet space, storage space, windows screened against insects—exactly what I wanted. It was delivered in the summer to my little fishing place at Sag Harbor near the end of Long Island. Although I didn't want to start before Labor Day, when the nation settles back to normal living, I did want to get used to my turtle shell, to equip it and learn it. It arrived in August, a beautiful thing, powerful and yet lithe. It was almost as easy to handle as a passenger car. And because my planned trip had aroused some satiric remarks among my friends, I named it Rocinante, which you will remember was the name of Don Quixote's[2] horse.

Since I made no secret of my project, a number of controversies arose among my friends and advisers. (A projected journey spawns advisers in schools.) I was told that since my photograph was as widely distributed as my publisher could make it, I would find it impossible to move about without being recognized. Let me say in advance that in over ten thousand miles, in thirty-four states, I was not recognized even once. I believe that people identify things only in context. Even those people who might have known me against a background I am supposed to have, in no case identified me in Rocinante.

I was advised that the name Rocinante painted on the side of my truck in sixteenth-century Spanish script would cause curiosity and inquiry in some places. I do not know how many people recognized the name, but surely no one ever asked about it.

Next, I was told that a stranger's purpose in moving about the country might cause inquiry or even suspicion. For this reason I racked a shotgun, two rifles, and a couple of fishing rods in my truck, for it is my experience that if a man is going hunting or fishing his purpose is understood and even applauded. Actually, my hunting days are over. I no longer kill or catch anything I cannot

rigorous (rig´ ər əs) *adj.* very strict or harsh

Literary Analysis
Figurative Language What metaphor does Steinbeck use to emphasize qualities of the truck?

---

2. Don Quixote (dän´ kē hōt´ ē) hero of an early 17th-century satirical romance by Cervantes, who tries in a chivalrous but unrealistic way to rescue the oppressed and fight evil.

get into a frying pan; I am too old for sport killing. This stage setting turned out to be unnecessary.

It was said that my New York license plates would arouse interest and perhaps questions, since they were the only outward identifying marks I had. And so they did—perhaps twenty or thirty times in the whole trip. But such contacts followed an invariable pattern, somewhat as follows:

Local man: "New York, huh?"

Me: "Yep."

Local man: "I was there in nineteen thirty-eight—or was it thirty-nine? Alice, was it thirty-eight or thirty-nine we went to New York?"

Alice: "It was thirty-six. I remember because it was the year Alfred died."

Local man: "Anyway, I hated it. Wouldn't live there if you paid me."

There was some genuine worry about my traveling alone, open to attack, robbery, assault. It is well known that our roads are dangerous. And here I admit I had senseless qualms. It is some years since I have been alone, nameless, friendless, without any of the safety one gets from family, friends, and accomplices. There is no reality in the danger. It's just a very lonely, helpless feeling at first—a kind of desolate feeling. For this reason I took one companion on my journey—an old French gentleman poodle known as Charley. Actually his name is Charles le Chien.[3] He was born in Bercy on the outskirts of Paris and trained in France, and while he knows a little poodle-English, he responds quickly only to commands in French. Otherwise he has to translate, and that slows him down. He is a very big poodle, of a color called *bleu*, and he is blue when he is clean. Charley is a born diplomat. He prefers negotiation to fighting, and properly so, since he is very bad at fighting. Only once in his ten years has he been in trouble—when he met a dog who refused to negotiate. Charley lost a piece of his right ear that time. But he is a good watch dog—has a roar like a lion, designed to conceal from night-wandering strangers the fact that he couldn't bite his

Reading Check

Who accompanies the author?

---

3. **Charles le Chien** (shärl′ lə shē un′) French for "Charles the dog."

way out of a *cornet de papier*.[4] He is a good friend and traveling companion, and would rather travel about than anything he can imagine. If he occurs at length in this account, it is because he contributed much to the trip. A dog, particularly an exotic like Charley, is a bond between strangers. Many conversations en route began with "What degree of a dog is that?"

The techniques of opening conversation are universal. I knew long ago and rediscovered that the best way to attract attention, help, and conversation is to be lost.

* * *

The night was loaded with omens. The grieving sky turned the little water to a dangerous metal and then the wind got up—not the gusty, rabbity wind of the seacoasts I know but a great bursting sweep of wind with nothing to inhibit it for a thousand miles in any direction. Because it was a wind strange to me, and therefore mysterious, it set up mysterious responses in me. In terms of reason, it was strange only because I found it so. But a goodly part of our experience which we find <u>inexplicable</u> must be like that. To my certain knowledge, many people conceal experiences for fear of ridicule. How many people have seen or heard or felt something which so outraged their sense of what should be that the whole thing was brushed quickly away like dirt under a rug?

For myself, I try to keep the line open even for things I can't understand or explain, but it is difficult in this frightened time.

---

4. *cornet de papier* (kôr nā′ də pȧ pyā′) French for "paper bag."

354 ◆ *From Sea to Shining Sea*

▲ **Critical Viewing**
Why is the name "Badlands" appropriate for the region pictured here? **[Analyze]**

Literary Analysis
Figurative Language
How is the sky personified in the phrase "grieving sky"?

inexplicable
(in eks′ pli kə bəl) *adj.* not possible to explain

At this moment in North Dakota I had a reluctance to drive on that amounted to fear. At the same time, Charley wanted to go—in fact, made such a commotion about going that I tried to reason with him.

"Listen to me, dog. I have a strong impulse to stay amounting to <u>celestial</u> command. If I should overcome it and go and a great snow should close in on us, I would recognize it as a warning disregarded. If we stay and a big snow should come I would be certain I had a pipeline to prophecy."

Charley sneezed and paced restlessly. "All right, *mon cur*,[5] let's take your side of it. You want to go on. Suppose we do, and in the night a tree should crash down right where we are presently standing. It would be you who have the attention of the gods. And there is always that chance. I could tell you many stories about faithful animals who saved their masters, but I think you are just bored and I'm not going to flatter you." Charley leveled at me his most cynical eye. I think he is neither a romantic nor a mystic. "I know what you mean. If we go, and no tree crashes down, or stay and no snow falls—what then? I'll tell you what then. We forget the whole episode and the field of prophecy is in no way injured. I vote to stay. You vote to go. But being nearer the pinnacle of creation than you, and also president, I cast the deciding vote."

We stayed and it didn't snow and no tree fell, so naturally we forgot the whole thing and are wide open for more mystic feelings when they come. And in the early morning swept clean of clouds

celestial (sə les′ chəl) *adj.* of the heavens; divine

✓**Reading Check**

With whom does the narrator discuss his decision?

---

5. *mon cur* (mōn kʉr′) French slang for "my dear mutt."

and telescopically clear, we crunched around on the thick white ground cover of frost and got under way. The caravan of the arts was dark but the dog barked as we ground up to the highway.

Someone must have told me about the Missouri River at Bismarck, North Dakota, or I must have read about it. In either case, I hadn't paid attention. I came on it in amazement. Here is where the map should fold. Here is the boundary between east and west. On the Bismarck side it is eastern landscape, eastern grass, with the look and smell of eastern America. Across the Missouri on the Mandan side, it is pure west, with brown grass and water scorings and small outcrops. The two sides of the river might well be a thousand miles apart. As I was not prepared for the Missouri boundary, so I was not prepared for the Bad Lands. They deserve this name. They are like the work of an evil child. Such a place the Fallen Angels might have built as a spite to Heaven, dry and sharp, desolate and dangerous, and for me filled with foreboding. A sense comes from it that it does not like or welcome humans. But humans being what they are, and I being human, I turned off the highway on a shaley road and headed in among the buttes, but with a shyness as though I crashed a party. The road surface tore viciously at my tires and made Rocinante's overloaded springs cry with anguish. What a place for a colony of troglodytes, or better, of trolls. And here's an odd thing. Just as I felt unwanted in this land, so do I feel a reluctance in writing about it.

Presently I saw a man leaning on a two-strand barbed-wire fence, the wires fixed not to posts but to crooked tree limbs stuck in the ground. The man wore a dark hat, and jeans and long jacket washed palest blue with lighter places at knees and elbows. His pale eyes were frosted with sun glare and his lips scaly as snakeskin. A .22 rifle leaned against the fence beside him and on the ground lay a little heap of fur and feathers—rabbits and small birds. I pulled up to speak to him, saw his eyes wash over Rocinante, sweep up the details, and then retire into their sockets. And I found I had nothing to say to him. The "Looks like an early winter," or "Any good fishing hereabouts?" didn't seem to apply. And so we simply brooded at each other.

"Afternoon!"

"Yes, sir," he said.

"Any place nearby where I can buy some eggs?"

"Not real close by 'less you want to go as far as Galva or up to Beach."[6]

"I was set for some scratch-hen eggs."

"Powdered," he said. "My Mrs. gets powdered."

---

6. Galva . . . Beach cities in western North Dakota near the border of Montana.

"Lived here long?"

"Yep."

I waited for him to ask something or to say something so we could go on, but he didn't. And as the silence continued, it became more and more impossible to think of something to say. I made one more try. "Does it get very cold here winters?"

"Fairly."

"You talk too much."

He grinned. "That's what my Mrs. says."

"So long," I said, and put the car in gear and moved along. And in my rear-view mirror I couldn't see that he looked after me. He may not be a typical Badlander, but he's one of the few I caught.

A little farther along I stopped at a small house, a section of war-surplus barracks, it looked, but painted white with yellow trim, and with the dying vestiges of a garden, frosted-down geraniums and a few clusters of chrysanthemums, little button things yellow and red-brown. I walked up the path with the certainty that I was being regarded from behind the white window curtains. An old woman answered my knock and gave me the drink of water I asked for and nearly talked my arm off. She was hungry to talk, frantic to talk, about her relatives, her friends, and how she wasn't used to this. For she was not a native and she didn't rightly belong here. Her native clime was a land of milk and honey and had its share of apes and ivory and peacocks. Her voice rattled on as though she was terrified of the silence that would settle when I was gone. As she talked it came to me that she was afraid of this place and, further, that so was I. I felt I wouldn't like to have the night catch me here.

I went into a state of flight, running to get away from the unearthly landscape. And then the late afternoon changed everything. As the sun angled, the buttes and coulees, the cliffs and sculptured hills and ravines lost their burned and dreadful look and glowed with yellow and rich browns and a hundred variations of red and silver gray, all picked out by streaks of coal black. It was so beautiful that I stopped near a thicket of dwarfed and wind-warped cedars and junipers, and once stopped I was caught, trapped in color and dazzled by the clarity of the light. Against the descending sun the battlements were dark and clean-lined, while to the east, where the uninhibited light poured slantwise, the strange landscape shouted with color. And the night, far from being frightful, was lovely beyond thought, for the stars were close, and although there was no moon the starlight made a silver glow in the sky. The air cut the nostrils with dry frost. And for pure pleasure I collected a pile of dry dead cedar branches and built a small fire just to smell the perfume of the burning wood and to hear the excited crackle of the branches. My fire made a dome of

Literary Analysis
Figurative Language
What type of figurative language does Steinbeck use to describe the woman's native land?

✔**Reading Check**
What are the "Badlands"?

yellow light over me, and nearby I heard a screech owl hunting and a barking of coyotes, not howling but the short chuckling bark of the dark of the moon. This is one of the few places I have ever seen where the night was friendlier than the day. And I can easily see how people are driven back to the Bad Lands.

Before I slept I spread a map on my bed, a Charley-tromped map. Beach was not far away, and that would be the end of North Dakota. And coming up would be Montana, where I had never been. That night was so cold that I put on my insulated underwear for pajamas, and when Charley had done his duties and had his biscuits and consumed his usual gallon of water and finally curled up in his place under the bed, I dug out an extra blanket and covered him—all except the tip of his nose—and he sighed and wriggled and gave a great groan of pure ecstatic comfort. And I thought how every safe generality I gathered in my travels was canceled by another. In the night the Bad Lands had become Good Lands. I can't explain it. That's how it was.

Review and Assess

Thinking About the Selection

1. **Respond:** Would you have liked to join Steinbeck on his travels? Explain.
2. **(a) Recall:** Why does Steinbeck decide to make this trip? **(b) Interpret:** Explain what Steinbeck means when he says he "had not felt the country for twenty-five years." **(c) Synthesize:** What does Steinbeck hope to gain or learn from his trip?
3. **(a) Recall:** Who is Charley? **(b) Analyze:** What are Steinbeck's reasons for bringing Charley on the trip?
4. **(a) Recall:** What are Steinbeck's initial reactions to the Badlands? **(b) Contrast:** How do his feelings change as night falls?
5. **(a) Recall:** Identify two different people that Steinbeck meets on his journey. **(b) Compare and Contrast:** In what ways is each person similar to and different from Steinbeck? **(c) Generalize:** What generalization can you make about people in the United States based on Steinbeck's experience?
6. **(a) Compare and Contrast:** What can you learn from visiting a place that you cannot learn from reading about it? **(b) Make a Judgment:** Do you agree with Steinbeck that traveling around the country is the best way to learn about it? Explain. **(c) Assess:** In your opinion, does Steinbeck succeed in his aim to get reacquainted with America?

John Steinbeck

(1902–1968)

John Steinbeck's long and successful career made him one of America's best-loved authors. Drawing on his own upbringing in southern California, he often wrote with sympathy and humor about "ordinary" working Americans, such as fishermen and farm workers. *The Grapes of Wrath*, a dramatic story of people uprooted by the Great Depression, won the Pulitzer Prize in 1940. Several Steinbeck stories, including *East of Eden*, were made into films. He also wrote film scripts, including the one for his own book *The Red Pony*. Steinbeck won the Nobel Prize for Literature in 1962.

Review and Assess

Literary Analysis

Travel Essay

1. Explain how the excerpt from *Travels with Charley* fits the definition of a **travel essay**.
2. Prepare a chart like the one shown. Fill in details about the Badlands.

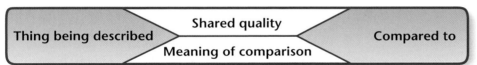

Subject	Facts	Descriptive details	Author's thoughts
By day			
By night			

Connecting Literary Elements

3. In the beginning of the essay, what kind of **figurative language** is Steinbeck using when he writes ". . . memory is at best a faulty, warpy reservoir."
4. Analyze the comparison by breaking it down on an organizer like the one shown here.

Thing being described | Shared quality / Meaning of comparison | Compared to

5. Identify and explain at least one example of metaphor, personification, and simile that Steinbeck uses.

Reading Strategy

Clarifying Details

6. Explain how you were able to **clarify** the meaning of the italicized words below. Go back to the page given, and tell what helped you discover the meaning.
   (a) On page 353: "Actually his name is *Charles le Chien*."
   (b) On page 352: "I named it Rocinante, which you will remember was the name of *Don Quixote's horse*."
   (c) On page 358: "*Beach* was not far away, and that would be the end of North Dakota."

Extend Understanding

7. **Take a Position:** Explain why it is or is not important for Americans to see and understand parts of the country where they do not live.

Quick Review

A **travel essay** is a brief nonfiction work about a trip. To review travel essays, see page 349.

Figurative language, such as metaphor, simile, and personification, is writing that is not meant to be taken literally. To review figurative language, see page 349.

Clarify details—make them clear—by using footnotes or margin notes, recalling similar details, rereading to discover missed information, or reading ahead to gather new details. To review this technique, see page 349.

 Take It to the Net
www.phschool.com
Take the interactive self-test online to check your understanding of the selection.

Integrate Language Skills

Vocabulary Development Lesson

Word Analysis: Greek Suffix -ic

The Greek suffix -ic means "like" or "related to" [something], as in diagnostic—"related to a diagnosis." Add -ic to noun bases to form adjectives:

patriot + -ic = patriotic

Write a definition for each of these words, including the definition of -ic in each answer.

1. photographic   2. fantastic   3. artistic

Spelling Strategy

The kw sound is spelled qu when it occurs at the beginning or in the middle of a word, as in quiet, inquire, and quest. Rewrite these phonetic spellings with the actual spelling of each word.

1. (kwiz)   2. (ri kwest)   3. (urth kwak)

Concept Development: Analogies

An analogy expresses a comparison between two ideas, situations, or words that are alike in one significant way, but different in most others. On your paper, write the vocabulary word that best completes each of these analogies.

1. Active is to athlete as ___?___ is to traveler.
2. Terrestrial is to Earth as ___?___ is to heavens.
3. Unsure is to uncertain as unexplainable is to ___?___.
4. X-ray is to ___?___ as computer is to electronic.
5. Harsh is to ___?___ as relaxed is to comfortable.

Grammar Lesson

Coordinating Conjunctions

A conjunction connects single words or groups of words. Coordinating conjunctions connect words of the same kind and equal rank, such as two nouns or two adjectives. They also can connect larger groups of words such as phrases or entire sentences. Common coordinating conjunctions are and, but, or, for, nor, so, and yet.

> **Connecting nouns:** If a man is going hunting or fishing, his purpose is understood.
>
> **Connecting verbs:** I listened and looked.
>
> **Connecting sentences:** The caravan of the arts was dark but the dog barked as we ground up to the highway.

▶ *For more practice, see page R29, Exercise E.*
Practice Copy these sentences and circle the coordinating conjunction in each.

1. I had to go alone and I had to be self-contained.
2. I specified my purpose and my needs.
3. I waited for him to ask, but he didn't.
4. I had to be peripatetic eyes and ears.
5. A stranger's purpose might cause inquiry or even suspicion.

Writing Application Using the coordinating conjunctions specified, write sentences according to the following instructions.

1. A sentence about Charley liking to travel/being good company using and
2. A sentence about Steinbeck/Charley using or
3. A sentence about the night/day in the Badlands using but

*W*G *Prentice Hall Writing and Grammar Connection: Chapter 18, Section 1*

Writing Lesson

Travel Essay

Recapture the look and feel of a trip you have taken by writing a travel essay, just as Steinbeck did.

Prewriting   Think of a specific place, incident, or event from your trip that you want to describe. Then, jot down sensory details that describe the sights, sounds, smells, tastes, and physical sensations of your experience.

Model: Using Sensory Details	
Sunrise Over the Lake	
Breeze from the lake	Birds singing
Waves lapping against boats	Intense colors: grayish blue lake
Fishy smell	Wet grass

> Details that appeal to the senses will bring the travel essay to life.

Drafting   Begin your essay with a description of the experience you have chosen, using the details you jotted down. Then, tell why you chose that particular experience. Why does it stick out in your mind? How do you feel about it?

Revising   Read your draft. Circle any details that do not contribute to the overall impression you are trying to convey. Then go back and eliminate or replace those details.

𝒲𝒢 *Prentice Hall Writing and Grammar Connection: Chapter 4, Section 3*

Extension Activities

Listening and Speaking With two or three classmates, prepare an **oral presentation** about the Badlands. Begin with details from Steinbeck's essay. Members of the group should

- each describe a different aspect of the Badlands.
- brainstorm precise nouns, colorful modifiers, and sensory details to describe it.
- use active verbs to enliven the presentation.

When you are ready give your presentation to the class.

Writing Steinbeck once said, "To my certain knowledge, many people conceal experiences for fear of ridicule." Write an **essay** in which you explain how this selection might have been different if Steinbeck had been one of those people.

Research and Technology Create a **map** of North Dakota's Badlands. Label the places that Steinbeck mentions in his essay. Post your complete map in the classroom.

 **Take It to the Net**   www.phschool.com

Go online for an additional research activity using the Internet.

Prepare to Read

Choice: A Tribute to Dr. Martin Luther King, Jr. ◆ Ellis Island ◆ Achieving the American Dream ◆ The New Colossus

Take It to the Net

Visit www.phschool.com for interactive activities and instruction related to these selections, including

- background
- graphic organizers
- literary elements
- reading strategies

Preview

Connecting to the Literature

Unless you are a Native American, you or your ancestors migrated to the United States from another country. The selections you are about to read give voice to the hopes and dreams that have prompted millions of people—possibly including your ancestors—to leave their native lands to start new lives in America.

Background

The literature in this group tells of the immigrants who came through Ellis Island, the chief immigration station of the eastern United States for seventy years. From 1892 to 1924, approximately sixteen million immigrants entered the United States through Ellis Island.

Literary Analysis

Epithet

An **epithet** is a phrase that points out a notable characteristic of a person or object. Like a nickname, it can substitute for the actual name—for example, *Honest Abe* and *Golden State*. In the following example, the epithet, shown in italics, immediately follows the thing it names.

> California, *the Golden State*, attracts many visitors.

Look for epithets as you read the works in this group. Notice how they shape your impressions of the people and things they describe.

Comparing Literary Works

One epithet for the United States is "the land of opportunity." Each of the writers in this group writes about the United States as a land of opportunity. Although the topic is similar, the treatment in each work is different. Use the following focus questions to help you identify similarities and differences in these works.

1. Which works seem to suggest that the United States is a land of opportunity, and which works seem to suggest that it is not?
2. Which work is most sentimental?

Reading Strategy

Recognizing Connotations of Words

The United States is called "a land of opportunity." The **connotations**, or ideas associated with these words, are positive.

As you read, look for words with strong connotations, either positive or negative, and write them in the chart. Then, describe the ideas associated with each word.

Words from Text	Connotations

Vocabulary Development

colossal (kə läs´ əl) *adj.* astonishingly large; extraordinary (p. 366)

conscience (kän´ shəns) *n.* recognition or inner sense of right and wrong (p. 366)

literally (lit´ ər əl ē) *adv.* actually; in fact (p. 366)

immigrate (im´ ə grāt) *v.* come into a foreign country to settle (p. 370)

apprehension (ap´ rə hen´ shən) *n.* fear that something bad will happen (p. 370)

immersed (i mʉrst´) *adj.* deeply involved in (p. 371)

ancestral (an ses´ trəl) *adj.* relating to one's ancestors (p. 371)

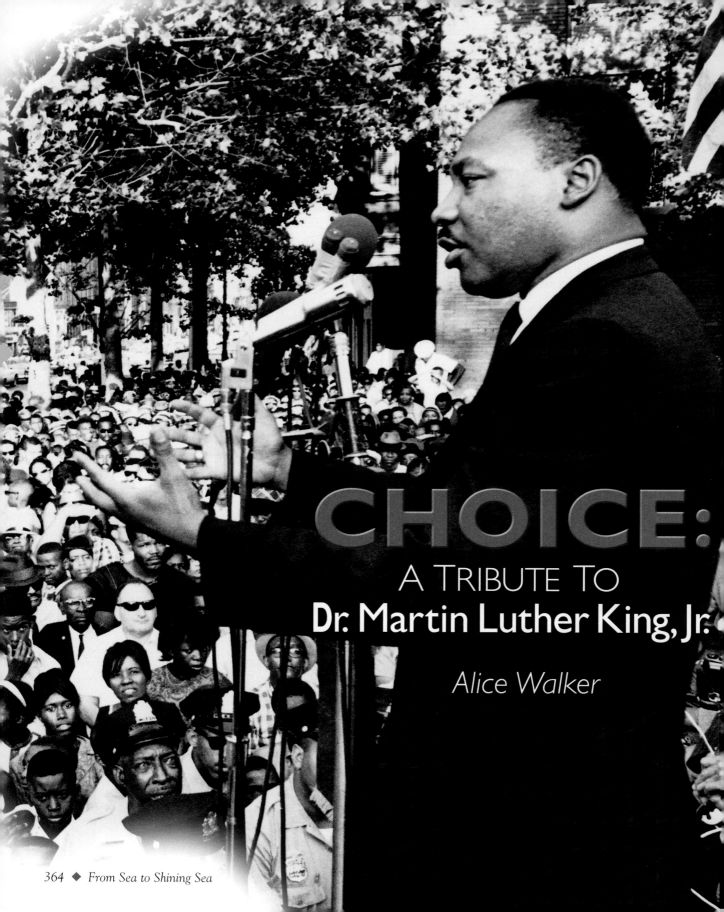

CHOICE:
A TRIBUTE TO
Dr. Martin Luther King, Jr.

Alice Walker

This address was made in 1973 at a Jackson, Mississippi, restaurant that had refused to serve people of color until forced to do so by the Civil Rights Movement a few years before.

❦

My great-great-great-grandmother walked as a slave from Virginia to Eatonton, Georgia—which passes for the Walker ancestral home—with two babies on her hips. She lived to be a hundred and twenty-five years old and my own father knew her as a boy. (It is in memory of this walk that I choose to keep and to embrace my "maiden" name, Walker.)

There is a cemetery near our family church where she is buried; but because her marker was made of wood and rotted years ago, it is impossible to tell exactly where her body lies. In the same cemetery are most of my mother's people, who have lived in Georgia for so long nobody even remembers when they came. And all of my great-aunts and -uncles are there, and my grandfather and grandmother, and, very recently, my own father.

If it is true that land does not belong to anyone until they have buried a body in it, then the land of my birthplace belongs to me, dozens of times over. Yet the history of my family, like that of all black Southerners, is a history of dispossession. We loved the land and worked the land, but we never owned it; and even if we bought land, as my great-grandfather did after the Civil War, it was always in danger of being taken away, as his was, during the period following Reconstruction.[1]

My father inherited nothing of material value from his father, and when I came of age in the early sixties I awoke to the bitter knowledge that in order just to continue to love the land of my birth, I was expected to leave it. For black people—including my parents—had learned a long time ago that to stay willingly in a beloved but brutal place is to risk losing the love and being forced to acknowledge only the brutality.

It is a part of the black Southern sensibility that we treasure memories; for such a long time, that is all of our homeland those of us who at one time or another were forced away from it have been allowed to have.

✔Reading Check

Why does the speaker believe that she needs to leave her birthplace?

---

1. Reconstruction period following the American Civil War (1867–1877) when the South was rebuilt and reestablished as part of the Union.

◀ **Critical Viewing** Judging from the size of the crowd, what can you infer about Dr. Martin Luther King, Jr.? **[Infer]**

I watched my brothers, one by one, leave our home and leave the South. I watched my sisters do the same. This was not un-usual; abandonment, except for memories, was the common thing, except for those who "could not do any better," or those whose strength or stubbornness was so <u>colossal</u> they took the risk that others could not bear.

In 1960, my mother bought a television set, and each day after school I watched Hamilton Holmes and Charlayne Hunter[2] as they struggled to integrate—fair-skinned as they were—the University of Georgia. And then, one day, there appeared the face of Dr. Martin Luther King, Jr. What a funny name, I thought. At the moment I first saw him, he was being handcuffed and shoved into a police truck. He had dared to claim his rights as a native son, and had been arrested. He displayed no fear, but seemed calm and serene, unaware of his own extraordinary courage. His whole body, like his <u>conscience</u>, was at peace.

At the moment I saw his resistance I knew I would never be able to live in this country without resisting everything that sought to disinherit me, and I would never be forced away from the land of my birth without a fight.

He was The One, The Hero, The One Fearless Person for whom we had waited. I hadn't even realized before that we *had* been waiting for Martin Luther King, Jr., but we had. And I knew it for sure when my mother added his name to the list of people she prayed for every night.

I sometimes think that it was <u>literally</u> the prayers of people like my mother and father, who had bowed down in the struggle for such a long time, that kept Dr. King alive until five years ago.[3] For years we went to bed praying for his life, and awoke with the question "Is the 'Lord' still here?"

The public acts of Dr. King you know. They are visible all around you. His voice you would recognize sooner than any other voice you have heard in this century—this in spite of the fact that certain municipal libraries, like the one in downtown Jackson, do not carry recordings of his speeches, and the librarians chuckle cruelly when asked why they do not.

You know, if you have read his books, that his is a complex and revolutionary philosophy that few people are capable of understanding fully or have the patience to embody in themselves.

---

2. **Hamilton Holmes and Charlayne Hunter** Hamilton Holmes and Charlayne Hunter made history in January 1961 by becoming the first two African Americans to attend the University of Georgia.
3. **until five years ago** Dr. Martin Luther King, Jr. (b. 1929); U.S. clergyman and leader in the civil rights movement from the mid-1950s until his death by assassination on April 4, 1968.

*L*iterature
in context   History Connectio

The March on Washington
One of the most dramatic days of the civil rights movement was August 28, 1963. Some 250,000 Americans gathered peacefully at the Lincoln Memorial in Washington, D.C., to show their solidarity with the hopes and goals of Dr. Martin Luther King, Jr., and other civil rights leaders. The highlight of the March on Washington was King's unforgettable "I Have a Dream" speech. He spoke eloquently about an America in which character would matter more than race. The march—the largest protest demonstration the country had ever seen—influenced the passage of civil rights legislation the following year.

colossal (kə läs′ əl) *adj.* astonishingly large; extraordinary

conscience (kän′ shəns) *n.* recognition or inner sense of right and wrong

literally (lit′ ər əl ē) *adv.* actually; in fact

Which is our weakness, which is our loss.

And if you know anything about good Baptist preaching, you can imagine what you missed if you never had a chance to hear Martin Luther King, Jr., preach at Ebeneezer Baptist Church.

You know of the prizes and awards that he tended to think very little of. And you know of his concern for the disinherited: the American Indian, the Mexican-American, and the poor American white—for whom he cared much.

You know that this very room, in this very restaurant, was closed to people of color not more than five years ago. And that we eat here together tonight largely through his efforts and his blood. We accept the common pleasures of life, assuredly, in his name.

But add to all of these things the one thing that seems to me second to none in importance: He gave us back our heritage. He gave us back our homeland; the bones and dust of our ancestors, who may now sleep within our caring *and* our hearing. He gave us the blueness of the Georgia sky in autumn as in summer; the colors of the Southern winter as well as glimpses of the green of vacation-time spring. Those of our relatives we used to invite for a visit we now can ask to stay. . . . He gave us full-time use of our woods, and restored our memories to those of us who were forced to run away, as realities we might each day enjoy and leave for our children.

He gave us continuity of place, without which community is ephemeral. He gave us home.   *1973*

Alice Walker

(b. 1944)
Alice Walker is a novelist, poet, and essayist whose writing often deals with social injustice, especially in the lives of several generations of African American women. Born in Georgia, Walker left the South to finish college in the Northeast. Perhaps her best-known novel is *The Color Purple* (1982), which won her a Pulitzer Prize and was made into a successful film in 1985. A number of her essays, including "Choice: A Tribute to Dr. Martin Luther King, Jr.," are collected in *In Search of Our Mothers' Gardens*.

Review and Assess

Thinking About the Selection

1. **Respond:** Would you have liked to hear this speech in person? Explain your response.

2. **(a) Recall:** Where is Walker making this speech?
   (b) Connect: What is significant about the location?

3. **(a) Recall:** Where did Walker first see Martin Luther King, Jr.?
   (b) Interpret: What did she realize about King?

4. **(a) Recall:** Before the civil rights movement, why did African Americans in the South feel disinherited? **(b) Evaluate:** According to Walker, what was King's most important gift to African Americans?

5. **(a) Interpret:** Why did many black Southerners move away from the South? **(b) Synthesize:** How does the black Southern experience compare with that of European immigrants?

Ellis Island

JOSEPH BRUCHAC

Beyond the red brick of Ellis Island
where the two Slovak children
who became my grandparents
waited the long days of quarantine,[1]
5   after leaving the sickness,
the old Empires of Europe,

---

1. quarantine (kwôr´ ən tēn) *n.* period, originally 40 days, during which an arriving vessel suspected of carrying contagious disease is detained in port in strict isolation to prevent any diseases from spreading.

Literary Analysis
Epithet What epithet does Bruchac use in this stanza of the poem?

a Circle Line ship slips easily
on its way to the island
of the tall woman, green
10 as dreams of forests and meadows
waiting for those who'd worked
a thousand years
yet never owned their own.

Like millions of others,
15 I too come to this island,
nine decades the answerer
of dreams.

Yet only one part of my blood
  loves that memory.
Another voice speaks
20 of native lands
within this nation.
Lands invaded
when the earth became owned.
Lands of those who followed
25 the changing Moon,
knowledge of the seasons
in their veins.

Joseph Bruchac

(b. 1942)

"Ellis Island" refers to Bruchac's own heritage as the son of an Abenaki Indian mother and a Slovak father. He grew up near the Adirondack Mountains and has juggled careers as a writer, story-teller, and editor. Bruchac has published more than fifty books, including collections of Native American stories.

Review and Assess

Thinking About the Selection

1. **Respond:** Which symbol of the United States is more meaningful to you—the Statue of Liberty or Ellis Island? Explain.

2. **(a) Recall:** Who are the ancestors of the speaker in "Ellis Island"? **(b) Interpret:** What does the speaker mean by the phrase "native lands within this nation"? **(c) Compare and Contrast:** How do his two sets of ancestors differ in their attitudes toward the land?

3. **(a) Analyze:** How does the speaker's dual ancestry influence his father's feelings toward Ellis Island? **(b) Apply:** Why does the speaker see the United States as a "land invaded"?

ACHIEVING THE AMERICAN DREAM

Mario Cuomo

In the Provincia di Salerno[1] just outside the Italian city of Naples, a laborer named Andrea Cuomo asked Immaculata Giordano to marry him. The young woman accepted under one condition: that the couple immigrate to the far-off land of her dreams—America. Andrea Cuomo agreed, and after marrying, the Cuomos made the long voyage to New York Harbor in the late 1920s. The young couple left the life, the language, the land, the family, and the friends they knew, arriving in Lady Liberty's shadow with no money, unable to speak English, and without any education. They were filled with both hope and apprehension.

All that my parents brought to their new home was their burning desire to climb out of poverty on the strength of their labor. They believed that hard work would bring them and their children better lives and help them achieve the American Dream.

At first, my father went to work in Jersey City, New Jersey, as a ditchdigger. After Momma and Poppa had three children, Poppa realized he needed to earn more to support his growing family. So he opened a small Italian American grocery store in South Jamaica, in the New York City borough of Queens.

By the time I was born in 1932, the store was open 24 hours a day, and it seemed as if Momma and Poppa were working there all the time. I can still see them waiting on customers and stocking shelves. And I can still smell and see and almost taste the food that brought in the customers: the provolone, the Genoa salami, the prosciutto,[2] the fresh bread, the fruits and vegetables. Our store gave our neighbors a delicious taste of Italy in New York.

My parents lacked the education to help us much with our schoolwork. But they taught us every single day, just by being who they were, about the values of family, hard work, honesty, and caring about others. These were not just Italian values, or American ones, but universal values that everyone can embrace.

◀ **Critical Viewing**
Do the facial expressions of the author and his mother reveal their determination to prosper? Explain.
[Deduce]

immigrate (im´ ə grāt) v. come into a foreign country to settle

apprehension (ap´ rə hen´ shən) n. fear; anxiety that something bad will happen

---

1. Provincia di Salerno (prō vin´ sē ə dē sə lär´ nō) region surrounding Salerno, a seaport in southern Italy.
2. prosciutto (prə shōōt´ ō) n. spicy Italian ham.

From my earliest days, I felt <u>immersed</u> in the culture and traditions of my parents' homeland. I grew up speaking Italian. I heard story after story from my parents and relatives about life in the Old Country.

Though not an immigrant myself, I saw the hardships Italian immigrants had to endure. I saw their struggle to make themselves understood in an alien language, their struggle to rise out of poverty, and their struggle to overcome the prejudices of people who felt superior because they or their ancestors had arrived earlier on this nation's shores.

As an Italian American, I grew up believing that America is the greatest country on earth, and thankful that I was born here. But at the same time, I have always been intensely proud that I am the son of Italian immigrants and that my Italian heritage helped make me the man I am.

The beauty of America is that I don't have to deny my past to affirm my present. No one does. We can love this nation like a parent and still embrace our <u>ancestral</u> home like cherished grandparents.

I like to tell the story of Andrea and Immaculata Cuomo because it tells us what America is about. Their story is the story not just of my parents, or of Italian immigrants at the beginning of this century, but of all immigrants. Our nation is renewed and strengthened by the infusion[3] of new Americans from around the world.

---

3. **infusion** (in fyōō′ zhən) *n.* addition.

immersed (i mʉrst′) *adj.* deeply involved in

ancestral (an ses′ trəl) *adj.* relating to one's ancestors

Mario Cuomo

(b. 1932)
Born in Queens, New York, Mario Cuomo has spent most of his career in public service. In "Achieving the American Dream," he describes how growing up in an Italian immigrant family influenced his views. Cuomo became New York Secretary of State in the late 1970s and was governor of the state from 1983 to 1995.

A leading thinker and speaker of the Democratic Party, Cuomo's keynote speech was a highlight of the 1984 Democratic National Convention. One of Cuomo's main concerns is that rich and poor work together to solve the country's problems.

Review and Assess

Thinking About the Selection

1. **Respond:** What is your reaction to Cuomo's story about his parents? Explain your response.

2. **(a) Recall:** Why do Cuomo's parents decide to emigrate?
   (b) Infer: What challenges do they face in the United States?

3. **(a) Recall:** How do the Cuomos make a living after they immigrate? **(b) Analyze Causes and Effects:** How does their lifestyle influence Mario Cuomo's attitudes and values?

4. **(a) Interpret:** What does Cuomo mean when he says " I don't have to deny my past to affirm my present." **(b) Deduce:** How has his background influenced his career?

5. **(a) Interpret:** What is "the American Dream"?
   (b) Make a Judgment: Have Mario Cuomo and his family achieved this dream? **(c) Evaluate:** Do you think it is possible for most people to achieve "The American Dream" today? Explain.

THE NEW COLOSSUS

Emma Lazarus

Not like the brazen giant of Greek fame,[1]
With conquering limbs astride from land to land;
Here at our sea-washed, sunset gates shall stand
A mighty woman with a torch, whose flame
5   Is the imprisoned lightning, and her name
Mother of Exiles. From her beacon-hand
Glows world-wide welcome; her mild eyes command
The air-bridged harbor that twin cities frame.
"Keep, ancient lands, your storied pomp!" cries she
10   With silent lips. "Give me your tired, your poor,
Your huddled masses yearning to breathe free,
The wretched refuse of your teeming shore.
Send these, the homeless, tempest-tost[2] to me,
I lift my lamp beside the golden door!"

---

1. brazen giant of Greek fame The Colossus of Rhodes, one of the Seven Wonders of the World, was a huge bronze statue built at the harbor of Rhodes in commemoration of the siege of Rhodes (305–304 B.C.).
2. tempest-tost (tem´ pist tôst) here, having suffered a turbulent ocean journey.

Review and Assess

Thinking About the Selection

1. **Respond:** Do you share the speaker's awe of the statue?
2. **(a) Recall:** What does the Statue of Liberty hold in her raised hand? **(b) Synthesize:** What does it represent to the world? **(c) Speculate:** What do you think the old Colossus looked like? **(d) Compare and Contrast:** How are the two statues alike and how are they different?
3. **(a) Recall:** In "The New Colossus," what does the Statue of Liberty say to newcomers? **(b) Apply:** What situations are the immigrants leaving?

Emma Lazarus

(1849–1887)

The famous last lines of Emma Lazarus's "The New Colossus" are written on the base of the Statue of Liberty.

Raised in New York City, Lazarus studied languages and the classics, publishing a book of poems and translations at age 17. She drew on her Jewish heritage for poems and plays, seeing America as a refuge for those persecuted in Europe.

Review and Assess

Literary Analysis

Epithet

1. Use an organizer like the one shown to explore the three different **epithets** used by Alice Walker to describe King.

Epithet	The One	The Hero	The One Fearless Person
Quality emphasized			
Overall impression			

2. What is the overall impression of Dr. King that Walker creates by using all three epithets?
3. In "The New Colossus," what qualities of the Statue of Liberty are emphasized by epithets?

Comparing Literary Works

4. Which works seem to suggest that the United States is a land of opportunity and which works seem to suggest that it is not? Support your answer.
5. How does the African American southern experience described by Alice Walker compare with the Italian immigrant experience described by Mario Cuomo?
6. Which work is most sentimental? Support your answer.

Reading Strategy

Recognizing Connotations of Words

7. In "Ellis Island," Bruchac speaks of "lands *invaded*." What are the **connotations** of *invaded*?
8. For the italicized word in each phrase, identify a word with more positive or more negative connotations.
   (a) "With *conquering* limbs astride from land to land . . ."
   (b) "The wretched refuse of your *teeming* shore . . ."

Extend Understanding

9. **Evaluate:** Do you agree with Cuomo's belief that a person need not deny his or her past to affirm his or her future? Explain.

Quick Review

An **epithet** is a word or phrase that points out an outstanding characteristic of a person or place. To review epithet, see page 363.

A **connotation** is the set of negative or positive ideas associated with a word. These associations go beyond its dictionary definition.

 Take It to the Net
www.phschool.com
Take the interactive self-test online to check your understanding of these selections.

Integrate Language Skills

Vocabulary Development Lesson

Word Analysis: Forms of *migrate*

The verb *migrate* means "to move from place to place." That meaning is included in other words related to it, such as *immigration, emigrate, migrant*, and *migratory*. On your own paper, complete these sentences using one of those related words.

1. The ___?___ workers picked cherries.
2. Cuomo's parents decided to ___?___ from Italy.
3. Most nations limit ___?___.
4. Canada geese are ___?___ birds.

Identify the part of speech for each form of *migrate*.

5. immigration
6. migratory
7. emigrate
8. migrant

Fluency: Definitions

Match each vocabulary word in Column 1 with the closest definition in Column 2.

1. ancestral   a. sense of right and wrong
2. apprehension   b. submerged
3. colossal   c. inherited from forebears
4. conscience   d. huge
5. immersed   e. anxiety about the future
6. immigrate   f. actually
7. literally   g. to move to a country

Spelling Strategy

One way to remember the spelling of a word is to find smaller words within it. For example, if you remember that *loss* appears in *colossal*, you will know which consonant is doubled. In each word below, identify a smaller word.

1. balloon   2. early   3. piece

Grammar Lesson

Correlative Conjunctions

Like coordinating conjunctions, **correlative conjunctions** are used to join words or groups of words of the same kind. These conjunctions, however, always appear in pairs and help indicate the relationship between ideas.

> **Examples:** They were filled with *both* hope *and* apprehension.
> This story is *not only* about my parents *but also* about the whole immigrant experience.

Common Correlative Conjunctions		
both . . . and	neither . . . nor	either . . . or
not only . . . but also		whether . . . or

▶ *For more practice, see page R29, Exercise E.*
Practice Copy the sentences. Underline the correlative conjunctions.

1. Bruchac's ancestors included both immigrants and Native Americans.
2. Neither Andrea nor Immaculata knew what to expect.
3. Cuomo learned values that were not only Italian and American but also universal.
4. Dr. King showed neither fear nor anger.
5. Dr. King gave back to African Americans both their heritage and their homeland.

Writing Application Write five sentences about the Statue of Liberty. Use different pairs of correlative conjunctions in each one.

 Prentice Hall Writing and Grammar Connection: Chapter 18, Section 1

Writing Lesson

Tribute

Alice Walker's essay about Dr. King is a tribute—a speech recognizing someone for outstanding accomplishments. Write a tribute about someone that shows your admiration for him or her.

Prewriting After you have chosen the subject of your tribute, brainstorm for a list of the qualities and deeds about him or her that you admire most.

Drafting Organize items in a logical order, such as least important to most important. Use transitions both within and at the beginning of paragraphs to show connections among ideas, such as time sequence.

Model: Transitions

At first, my father went to work in Jersey City, New Jersey, as a ditch digger. *After* Momma and Poppa had three children, Poppa realized he needed to earn more to support his growing family. *So* he opened a small Italian American grocery store . . . .

> *At first* and *after* are transition words that show time, and *so* indicates cause and effect.

Revising Underline the transition words you have used. Determine whether or not they make the connections between ideas clear. If not, change them or rephrase the sentence. Also look for places where you can add transitions.

WG *Prentice Hall Writing and Grammar Connection: Chapter 11, Section 2*

Extension Activities

Listening and Speaking Alice Walker originally delivered "Choice," her tribute to Dr. Martin Luther King, Jr., at a restaurant in Jackson, Mississippi. Follow these steps to present the **speech** to the class.

- Read the speech out loud at home or in another quiet place.
- Look for places where you should modulate your voice by varying its pitch or intensity. Speed up to build to an emotional high point. Slow down or pause for effect.
- Rehearse the speech several times.
- Read the speech aloud to your class.

Writing Write a brief **essay** in which you describe the qualities that you believe people must possess in order to leave their homeland to emigrate to the United States. If possible, quote lines from one or more selections.

Research and Technology Report on the life of Dr. King. Gather photos, news clippings, and, if possible, video- and audiotapes. Write text to explain and connect the pieces of your **multimedia report**. Present the report to the class.

 www.phschool.com

Go online for an additional research activity using the Internet.

Ellis Island and Angel Island

Three of the selections in this grouping deal with people immigrating to the United States. The ancestors of millions of present-day Americans immigrated to the United States in ships that sailed across the Atlantic and Pacific Oceans around the turn of the twentieth century. Before the ships' passengers could make this country their home, however, they had to pass through an immigration station. The best-known stations were at Ellis Island, in New York, and Angel Island, near San Francisco, California.

Life on the Passage

Embarking for the United States, whether from Europe or from Asia, was not a decision lightly made. In many families, a father or older brother or sister would come first, find work, and send money back home to other family members. Once on the ship, the trip could take from ten days to a few weeks. Many people could afford only a ticket in steerage, the lowest level of the ship. There, several hundred passengers shared cramped space with no fresh air, inadequate bathroom facilities, and terrible food. Diseases could spread quickly, and the immigrants were never sure whether they would reach their destination alive.

Ellis Island

Today, more than forty percent of living Americans (over 100 million people) have an ancestor who entered the United States through Ellis Island in New York Harbor. When a ship arrived, the passengers would enter a room called the Great Hall, where doctors and inspectors examined them. A myriad of voices speaking some thirty languages filled the air as immigrants answered questions about their health, their backgrounds, and their families. Immigrants who were healthy and passed inspection were ready to leave Ellis Island after a few hours. People who were sick with a curable disease were hospitalized until they were well, sometimes for weeks. Those with incurable diseases were deported back to their homeland.

Angel Island

In 1910, an immigration station that became known as the "Ellis Island of the West" opened on Angel Island in California. Officials anticipated that when the Panama Canal was completed in 1914, a flood of immigrants would arrive from Europe on ships traveling through the canal. World War I broke out in 1914, however, and such travel ceased. Immigrants from Asia, especially China, came instead. Like immigrants at Ellis Island, those at Angel Island could be detained, but there was an important difference. In order for people to be admitted to the United States through Angel Island, they had to prove that they had been born here or that their husband or father was a U.S. citizen. Most newcomers waited an average of two to three weeks. Some, however, stayed for several months, even up to two years. While they waited, some immigrants carved poetry on the walls of the detention center. That poetry can still be seen today. An example is shown behind the title on p. 376.

Thematic Connection
How do the two immigration stations discussed here connect to the theme "From Sea to Shining Sea"?

Living History

In 1940, the immigration station on Angel Island was closed. The station on Ellis Island closed in 1954. In both locations, the buildings through which thousands upon thousands of immigrants had passed would have been destroyed if it were not for a few individuals who thought they should be preserved as pieces of living history. Today, the buildings have been restored, and visitors can tour museums at both sites to learn what immigrants at the turn of the twentieth century withstood to start their lives anew in the land of promise.

Connecting Literature and Culture

1. Do you think the immigrants portrayed in the selections on pp. 368–372 came through Ellis Island or Angel Island? Explain.
2. How were the experiences of immigrants coming through the two stations similar and different?

Prepare to Read

A Ribbon for Baldy ◆ The White Umbrella

Girl in Car Window, Winson Trang, Courtesy of the artist

Take It to the Net

Visit www.phschool.com
for interactive activities
and instruction related to
these selections, including

- background
- graphic organizers
- literary elements
- reading strategies

Preview

Connecting to the Literature

In "A Ribbon for Baldy" and "The White Umbrella," you will read about two young people who work toward very different personal goals. Think about a time when you worked toward a goal and what the result was.

Background

In "A Ribbon for Baldy," the main character plants corn for his school science project. On a small farm, planting and harvesting may be done with hand tools rather than with machines. To prepare for planting, the land is cleared to a depth of about eight inches, plowed, and fertilized. Corn seeds are planted in early spring. The growing season is four to six months, so in Jesse Stuart's story, the narrator's corn, planted in April, would be ready to harvest in August.

Literary Analysis

Character Traits

Character traits are the qualities that make up a character's personality. A character's traits are revealed in the following ways:

- through the character's actions.
- through his or her thoughts and conversations with other characters.
- through descriptions by the narrator or by other characters.

As you read these selections, look for details that reveal character traits.

Comparing Literary Works

The main characters in these two stories come from very different backgrounds, but they share similar ideas and motivations. Use these focus questions to guide you in comparing and contrasting the two characters:

1. What similar challenges do the main characters in these stories face because of their families' situations?
2. How do each character's circumstances affect how he or she copes with the challenge?

Reading Strategy

Predicting

Understanding a character's traits can help you make **predictions,** or educated guesses. Your predictions may also be guided by your own experiences in similar situations or by hints that the author provides. Predicting gets you involved in a story.

As you read these two stories, compare your predictions with the actual outcomes. Use an organizer like the one shown to record your predictions and the actual outcomes.

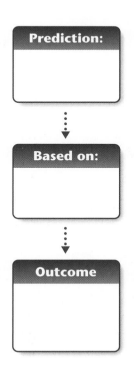

Vocabulary Development

surveyed (sʉr vād′) *v.* looked over in a careful way; examined; inspected (p. 381)

envelop (en vel′ əp) *v.* to wrap up; to cover completely (p. 381)

bargain (bär′ gən) *n.* something bought, offered, or sold at a price favorable to the buyer (p. 382)

discreet (di skrēt′) *adj.* careful about what one says or does; prudent (p. 385)

credibility (kred′ ə bil′ ə tē) *n.* believability (p. 386)

constellation (kän′ stə lā′ shən) *n.* group of stars named after, and thought to resemble, an object, an animal, or a mythological character (p. 387)

anxiously (aŋk′ shəs lē) *adv.* in a worried way (p. 388)

revelation (rev′ ə lā′ shən) *n.* something revealed; a disclosure of something not previously known or realized (p. 391)

A Ribbon for Baldy

JESSE STUART

The day Professor Herbert started talking about a project for each member of our General Science class, I was more excited than I had ever been. I wanted to have an outstanding project. I wanted it to be greater, to be more unusual than those of my classmates. I wanted to do something worthwhile, and something to make them respect me.

I'd made the best grade in my class in General Science. I'd made more yardage, more tackles and carried the football across the goal line more times than any player on my team. But making good grades and playing rugged football hadn't made them forget that I rode a mule to school, that I had worn my mother's shoes the first year and that I slipped away at the noon hour so no one would see me eat fat pork between slices of corn bread.

Every day I thought about my project for the General Science class. We had to have our project by the end of the school year and it was now January.

In the classroom, in study hall and when I did odd jobs on my father's 50 acres, I thought about my project. But it wouldn't come to me like an algebra problem or memorizing a poem. I couldn't think of a project that would help my father and mother to support us. One that would be good and useful.

"If you set your mind on something and keep on thinking about it, the idea will eventually come," Professor Herbert told us when Bascom Wythe complained about how hard it was to find a project.

One morning in February I left home in a white cloud that had settled over the deep valleys. I could not see an object ten feet in front of me in this mist. I crossed the pasture into the orchard and the mist began to thin. When I reached the ridge road, the light thin air was clear of mist. I looked over the sea of rolling white clouds. The tops of the dark winter hills jutted up like little islands.

I have to ride a mule, but not one of my classmates lives in a prettier place, I thought, as I <u>surveyed</u> my world. Look at Little Baldy! What a pretty island in the sea of clouds. A thin ribbon of cloud seemed to <u>envelop</u> cone-shaped Little Baldy from bottom to top like the new rope Pa had just bought for the windlass[1] over our well.

Then, like a flash—the idea for my project came to me. And what an idea it was! I'd not tell anybody about it! I wouldn't even tell my father, but I knew he'd be for it. Little Baldy wrapped in the white coils of mist had given me the idea for it.

I was so happy I didn't care who laughed at me, what anyone said or who watched me eat fat meat on corn bread for my lunch. I had an idea and I knew it was a wonderful one.

---

1. **windlass** (wind´ ləs) *n.* device for raising and lowering a bucket on a rope.

◀ **Critical Viewing** How much effort do you think it would take to plant and harvest a cornfield like this one? **[Draw Conclusions]**

Literary Analysis
Character Traits What traits are revealed in the narrator's thoughts about his project?

surveyed (sʉr vād´) *v.* looked over in a careful way; examined; inspected

envelop (en vel´ əp) *v.* to wrap up; to cover completely

Reading Check

Why does the speaker want to have the most outstanding project in the class?

"I've got something to talk over with you," I told Pa when I got home. "Look over there at that broom-sedge[2] and the scattered pines on Little Baldy. I'd like to burn the broom-sedge and briers and cut the pines and farm that this summer."

We stood in our barnlot and looked at Little Baldy.

"Yes, I've been thinkin' about clearin' that hill up someday," Pa said.

"Pa, I'll clear up all this south side and you clear up the other side," I said. "And I'll plow all of it and we'll get it in corn this year."

"Now this will be some undertakin'," he said. "I can't clear that land up and work six days a week on the railroad section. But if you will clear up the south side, I'll hire Bob Lavender to do the other side."

"That's a bargain," I said.

That night while the wind was still and the broom-sedge and leaves were dry, my father and I set fire all the way around the base. Next morning Little Baldy was a dark hill jutting high into February's cold, windy sky.

Pa hired Bob Lavender to clear one portion and I started working on the other. I worked early of mornings before I went to school. I hurried home and worked into the night.

Finn, my ten-year-old brother, was big enough to help me saw down the scattered pines with a crosscut.[3] With a handspike I started the logs rolling and they rolled to the base of Little Baldy.

By middle March, I had my side cleared. Bob Lavender had finished his too. We burned the brush and I was ready to start plowing.

By April 15th I had plowed all of Little Baldy. My grades in school had fallen off some. Bascom Wythe made the highest mark in General Science and he had always wanted to pass me in this subject. But I let him make the grades.

If my father had known what I was up to, he might not have let me do it. But he was going early to work on the railway section and he never got home until nearly dark. So when I laid Little Baldy off to plant him in corn, I started at the bottom and went around and around this high cone-shaped hill like a corkscrew. I was three days reaching the top. Then, with a hand planter, I planted the corn on moonlit nights.

---

2. **broom-sedge** (bro͞om′ sej) *n.* coarse grass used in making brooms.
3. **crosscut** (krôs′ kut) *n.* saw that cuts across the grain of the wood.

bargain (bär′ gən) *n.* something bought, offered, or sold at a price favorable to the buyer

▼ **Critical Viewing**
Which area of this terrain is cleared for planting? How can you tell? **[Deduce]**

When I showed my father what I'd done, he looked strangely at me. Then he said, "What made you do a thing like this? What's behind all of this?"

"I'm going to have the longest corn row in the world," I said. "How long do you think it is, Pa?"

"That row is over 20 miles," Pa said, laughing.

Finn and I measured the corn row with a rod pole and it was 23.5 miles long.

When it came time to report on our projects and I stood up in class and said I had a row of corn on our hill farm 23.5 miles long, everybody laughed. But when I told how I got the idea and how I had worked to accomplish my project, everybody was silent.

Professor Herbert and the General Science class hiked to my home on a Saturday in early May when the young corn was pretty and green in the long row. Two newspapermen from a neighboring town came too, and a photographer took pictures of Little Baldy and his ribbon of corn. He took pictures of me, of my home and parents and also of Professor Herbert and my classmates.

When the article and pictures were published, a few of my classmates got a little jealous of me but not one of them ever laughed at me again. And my father and mother were the proudest two parents any son could ever hope to have.

Jesse Stuart

(1906–1984)

Poet and novelist Jesse Stuart grew up in rural surroundings in eastern Kentucky. After high school, he worked for a circus and a steel mill before attending college. He then became a teacher and school superintendent. Stuart is known for his children's books, including *Red Mule*. Although he received many awards and honors in his lifetime, he was most proud of being a teacher. "First, last, always, I am a school teacher," he said. "I love the firing line of the classroom."

Review and Assess

Thinking About the Selection

1. **Respond:** What do you admire about the narrator, the main character of "A Ribbon for Baldy"?

2. **(a) Recall:** What three things does the boy do that make him different from his classmates? **(b) Analyze:** Why does he want to gain the respect of his classmates?

3. **(a) Recall:** Who or what is Little Baldy?
   (b) Connect: How does Little Baldy provide inspiration for a science project that the narrator considers worthwhile?
   (c) Deduce: Why does the narrator keep his project a secret from his father?

4. **(a) Recall:** What steps does the narrator take to complete his science project? **(b) Interpret:** When the narrator explains his project to the class, why are they silent?
   (c) Draw Conclusions: Does the narrator achieve his goals?

5. **(a) Speculate:** How do you think the narrator will feel about his classmates' opinion of him after the science project?
   (b) Support: Why do you think so?

The White Umbrella

Gish Jen

Girl in Car Window, Winson Trang, Courtesy of the artist

▲ **Critical Viewing** What inferences might you make about this story based on the painting above? **[Infer]**

When I was twelve, my mother went to work without telling me or my little sister.

"Not that we need the second income." The lilt of her accent drifted from the kitchen up to the top of the stairs, where Mona and I were listening.

"No," said my father, in a barely audible voice. "Not like the Lee family."

The Lees were the only other Chinese family in town. I remembered how sorry my parents had felt for Mrs. Lee when she started waitressing downtown the year before; and so when my mother began coming home late, I didn't say anything, and tried to keep Mona from saying anything either.

"But why shouldn't I?" she argued. "Lots of people's mothers work."

"Those are American people," I said.

"So what do you think we are? I can do the pledge of allegiance with my eyes closed."

Nevertheless, she tried to be <u>discreet</u>; and if my mother wasn't home by 5:30, we would start cooking by ourselves, to make sure dinner would be on time. Mona would wash the vegetables and put on the rice; I would chop.

For weeks we wondered what kind of work she was doing. I imagined that she was selling perfume, testing dessert recipes for the local newspaper. Or maybe she was working for the florist. Now that she had learned to drive, she might be delivering boxes of roses to people.

"I don't think so," said Mona as we walked to our piano lesson after school. "She would've hit something by now."

A gust of wind littered the street with leaves.

"Maybe we better hurry up," she went on, looking at the sky. "It's going to pour."

"But we're too early." Her lesson didn't begin until 4:00, mine until 4:30, so we usually tried to walk as slowly as we could. "And anyway, those aren't the kind of clouds that rain. Those are cumulus clouds."[1]

We arrived out of breath and wet.

"Oh, you poor, poor dears," said old Miss Crosman. "Why don't you call me the next time it's like this out? If your mother won't drive you, I can come pick you up."

"No, that's okay," I answered. Mona wrung her hair out on Miss Crosman's rug. "We just couldn't get the roof of our car to

---

1. **cumulus** (kyōōʹ myōō ləs) **clouds** *n.* fluffy, white clouds that usually indicate fair weather.

discreet (di skrētʹ) *adj.* careful about what one says or does; prudent

Reading Check

How does the narrator feel about the fact that her mother works?

close, is all. We took it to the beach last summer and got sand in the mechanism." I pronounced this last word carefully, as if the credibility of my lie depended on its middle syllable. "It's never been the same." I thought for a second. "It's a convertible."

"Well then make yourselves at home." She exchanged looks with Eugenie Roberts, whose lesson we were interrupting. Eugenie smiled good-naturedly. "The towels are in the closet across from the bathroom."

Huddling at the end of Miss Crosman's nine-foot leatherette couch, Mona and I watched Eugenie play. She was a grade ahead of me and, according to school rumor, had a boyfriend in high school. I believed it. . . . She had auburn hair, blue eyes, and, I noted with a particular pang, a pure white folding umbrella.

"I can't see," whispered Mona.

"So clean your glasses."

"My glasses *are* clean. You're in the way."

I looked at her. "They look dirty to me."

"That's because *your* glasses are dirty."

Eugenie came bouncing to the end of her piece.

"Oh! Just stupendous!" Miss Crosman hugged her, then looked up as Eugenie's mother walked in. "Stupendous!" she said again. "Oh! Mrs. Roberts! Your daughter has a gift, a real gift. It's an honor to teach her."

Mrs. Roberts, radiant with pride, swept her daughter out of the room as if she were royalty, born to the piano bench. Watching the way Eugenie carried herself, I sat up, and concentrated so hard on sucking in my stomach that I did not realize until the Robertses were gone that Eugenie had left her umbrella. As Mona began to play, I jumped up and ran to the window, meaning to call to them—only to see their brake lights flash then fade at the stop sign at the corner. As if to allow them passage, the rain had let up; a quivering sun lit their way.

The umbrella glowed like a scepter on the blue carpet while Mona, slumping over the keyboard, managed to eke out[2] a fair rendition of a catfight. At the end of the piece, Miss Crosman asked her to stand up.

"Stay right there," she said, then came back a minute later with a towel to cover the bench. "You must be cold," she continued. "Shall I call your mother and have her bring over some dry clothes?"

"No," answered Mona. "She won't come because she . . ."

"She's too busy," I broke in from the back of the room.

"I see." Miss Crosman sighed and shook her head a little. "Your glasses are filthy, honey," she said to Mona. "Shall I clean them for you?"

---

2. eke (ēk) **out** barely manage to play.

credibility (kred′ ə bil′ ə tē) *n.* believability

Reading Strategy
Predicting Predict what might happen with the white umbrella.

Sisterly embarrassment seized me. Why hadn't Mona wiped her lenses when I told her to? As she resumed abuse of the piano, I stared at the umbrella. I wanted to open it, twirl it around by its slender silver handle; I wanted to dangle it from my wrist on the way to school the way the other girls did. I wondered what Miss Crosman would say if I offered to bring it to Eugenie at school tomorrow. She would be impressed with my consideration for others; Eugenie would be pleased to have it back; and I would have possession of the umbrella for an entire night. I looked at it again, toying with the idea of asking for one for Christmas. I knew, however, how my mother would react.

"Things," she would say. "What's the matter with a raincoat? All you want is things, just like an American."

Sitting down for my lesson, I was careful to keep the towel under me and sit up straight.

"I'll bet you can't see a thing either," said Miss Crosman, reaching for my glasses. "And you can relax, you poor dear." She touched my chest, in an area where she never would have touched Eugenie Roberts. "This isn't a boot camp."[3]

When Miss Crosman finally allowed me to start playing I played extra well, as well as I possibly could. See, I told her with my fingers. You don't have to feel sorry for me.

"That was wonderful," said Miss Crosman. "Oh! Just wonderful."

An entire <u>constellation</u> rose in my heart.

"And guess what," I announced proudly. "I have a surprise for you."

Then I played a second piece for her, a much more difficult one that she had not assigned.

"Oh! That was stupendous," she said without hugging me. "Stupendous! You are a genius, young lady. If your mother had started you younger, you'd be playing like Eugenie Roberts by now!"

I looked at the keyboard, wishing that I had still a third, even more difficult piece to play for her. I wanted to tell her that I was the school spelling bee champion, that I wasn't ticklish, that I could do karate.

"My mother is a concert pianist," I said.

She looked at me for a long moment, then finally, without saying anything, hugged me. I didn't say anything about bringing the umbrella to Eugenie at school.

The steps were dry when Mona and I sat down to wait for my mother.

---

3. **boot camp** place where soldiers receive basic training and are disciplined severely.

constellation
(kän′ stə lā′ shən) *n.* group of stars named after, and thought to resemble, an object, an animal, or a mythological character

Reading Check

What thing of Eugenie's does the narrator wish were hers?

"Do you want to wait inside?" Miss Crosman looked <u>anxiously</u> at the sky.

"No," I said. "Our mother will be here any minute."

"In a while," said Mona.

"Any minute," I said again, even though my mother had been at least twenty minutes late every week since she started working.

According to the church clock across the street we had been waiting twenty-five minutes when Miss Crosman came out again.

"Shall I give you ladies a ride home?"

"No," I said. "Our mother is coming any minute."

"Shall I at least give her a call and remind her you're here? Maybe she forgot about you."

"I don't think she forgot," said Mona.

"Shall I give her a call anyway? Just to be safe?"

"I bet she already left," I said. "How could she forget about us?"

Miss Crosman went in to call.

"There's no answer," she said, coming back out.

"See, she's on her way," I said.

"Are you sure you wouldn't like to come in?"

"No," said Mona.

anxiously (aŋkʹ shəs lē) *adv.* In a worried way

▼ **Critical Viewing**
Are the girls in the photograph playing the piano in earnest or just having fun? Explain.
[Make a Judgment]

"Yes," I said. I pointed at my sister. "She meant yes too. She meant no, she wouldn't like to go in."

Miss Crosman looked at her watch. "It's 5:30 now, ladies. My pot roast will be coming out in fifteen minutes. Maybe you'd like to come in and have some then?"

"My mother's almost here," I said. "She's on her way."

We watched and watched the street. I tried to imagine what my mother was doing; I tried to imagine her writing messages in the sky, even though I knew she was afraid of planes. I watched as the branches of Miss Crosman's big willow tree started to sway; they had all been trimmed to exactly the same height off the ground, so that they looked beautiful, like hair in the wind.

It started to rain.

"Miss Crosman is coming out again," said Mona.

"Don't let her talk you into going inside," I whispered.

"Why not?"

"Because that would mean Mom isn't really coming any minute."

"But she isn't," said Mona. "She's working."

"Shhh! Miss Crosman is going to hear you."

"She's working! She's working! She's working!"

I put my hand over her mouth, but she licked it, and so I was wiping my hand on my wet dress when the front door opened.

"We're getting even *wetter*, " said Mona right away. "Wetter and wetter."

"Shall we all go in?" Miss Crosman pulled Mona to her feet. "Before you young ladies catch pneumonia? You've been out here an hour already."

"We're *freezing*." Mona looked up at Miss Crosman. "Do you have any hot chocolate? We're going to catch *pneumonia*."

"I'm not going in," I said. "My mother's coming any minute."

"Come on," said Mona. "Use your *noggin*."[4]

"Any minute."

"Come on, Mona," Miss Crosman opened the door. "Shall we get you inside first?"

"See you in the hospital," said Mona as she went in. "See you in the hospital with pneumonia."

I stared out into the empty street. The rain was pricking me all over; I was cold; I wanted to go inside. I wanted to be able to let myself go inside. If Miss Crosman came out again, I decided, I would go in.

She came out with a blanket and the white umbrella.

I could not believe that I was actually holding the umbrella, opening it. It sprang up by itself as if it were alive, as if that were what it wanted to do—as if it belonged in my hands, above my head. I stared up at the network of silver spokes, then spun the

Literary Analysis
Character Traits What different traits are shown by Mona's and the narrator's different reactions to the situation?

Reading Check

What are Mona and the narrator waiting for?

---

4. Use your *noggin* (näg´ in) informal expression for "use your head" or "think."

umbrella around and around and around. It was so clean and white that it seemed to glow, to illuminate everything around it.

"It's beautiful," I said.

Miss Crosman sat down next to me, on one end of the blanket. I moved the umbrella over so that it covered that too. I could feel the rain on my left shoulder and shivered. She put her arm around me.

"You poor, poor dear."

I knew that I was in store for another bolt of sympathy, and braced myself by staring up into the umbrella.

"You know, I very much wanted to have children when I was younger," she continued.

"You did?"

She stared at me a minute. Her face looked dry and crusty, like day-old frosting.

"I did. But then I never got married."

I twirled the umbrella around again.

"This is the most beautiful umbrella I have ever seen," I said. "Ever, in my whole life."

"Do you have an umbrella?"

"No. But my mother's going to get me one just like this for Christmas."

"Is she? I tell you what. You don't have to wait until Christmas. You can have this one."

"But this one belongs to Eugenie Roberts," I protested. "I have to give it back to her tomorrow in school."

"Who told you it belongs to Eugenie? It's not Eugenie's. It's mine. And now I'm giving it to you, so it's yours."

"It is?"

She hugged me tighter. "That's right. It's all yours."

"It's mine?" I didn't know what to say. "Mine?" Suddenly I was jumping up and down in the rain. "It's beautiful! Oh! It's beautiful!" I laughed.

Miss Crosman laughed too, even though she was getting all wet.

"Thank you, Miss Crosman. Thank you very much. Thanks a zillion. It's beautiful. It's *stupendous!*"

"You're quite welcome," she said.

"Thank you," I said again, but that didn't seem like enough. Suddenly I knew just what she wanted to hear. "I wish you were my mother."

Right away I felt bad.

"You shouldn't say that," she said, but her face was opening into a huge smile as the lights of my mother's car cautiously turned the corner. I quickly collapsed the umbrella and put it up my skirt, holding onto it from the outside, through the material.

"Mona!" I shouted into the house. "Mona! Hurry up! Mom's here!

Reading Strategy
Predicting Do you think the narrator will get to keep the umbrella? Why or why not?

I told you she was coming!"

Then I ran away from Miss Crosman, down to the curb. Mona came tearing up to my side as my mother neared the house. We both backed up a few feet, so that in case she went onto the curb, she wouldn't run us over.

"But why didn't you go inside with Mona?" my mother asked on the way home. She had taken off her own coat to put over me, and had the heat on high.

"She wasn't using her noggin," said Mona, next to me in the back seat.

"I should call next time," said my mother. "I just don't like to say where I am."

That was when she finally told us that she was working as a check-out clerk in the A&P. She was supposed to be on the day shift, but the other employees were unreliable, and her boss had promised her a promotion if she would stay until the evening shift filled in.

For a moment no one said anything. Even Mona seemed to find the <u>revelation</u> disappointing.

"A promotion already!" she said, finally.

I listened to the windshield wipers.

"You're so quiet." My mother looked at me in the rear view mirror. "What's the matter?"

"I wish you would quit," I said after a moment.

She sighed. "The Chinese have a saying: one beam cannot hold the roof up."

"But Eugenie Roberts's father supports their family."

She sighed once more. "Eugenie Roberts's father is Eugenie Roberts's father," she said.

As we entered the downtown area, Mona started leaning hard against me every time the car turned right, trying to push me over. Remembering what I had said to Miss Crosman, I tried to maneuver the umbrella under my leg so she wouldn't feel it.

"What's under your skirt?" Mona wanted to know as we came to a traffic light. My mother, watching us in the rear view mirror again, rolled slowly to a stop.

"What's the matter?" she asked.

"There's something under her skirt!" said Mona, pulling at me. "Under her skirt?"

Meanwhile, a man crossing the street started to yell at us. "Who do you think you are, lady?" he said. "You're blocking the whole crosswalk."

We all froze. Other people walking by stopped to watch.

"Didn't you hear me?" he went on, starting to thump on the hood with his fist. "Don't you speak English?"

My mother began to back up, but the car behind us honked.

revelation (rev´ ə lā´ shən) *n.* something revealed; a disclosure of something not previously known or realized

Literary Analysis
Character Traits What do the narrator's actions in this passage reveal about her?

Reading Check

What does Miss Crosman give the speaker and how does the speaker thank her?

Luckily, the light turned green right after that. She sighed in relief.

"What were you saying, Mona?" she asked.

We wouldn't have hit the car behind us that hard if he hadn't been moving too, but as it was our car bucked violently, throwing us all first back and then forward.

"Uh oh," said Mona when we stopped. "*Another* accident."

I was relieved to have attention diverted from the umbrella. Then I noticed my mother's head, tilted back onto the seat. Her eyes were closed.

"Mom!" I screamed. "Mom! Wake up!"

She opened her eyes. "Please don't yell," she said. "Enough people are going to yell already."

"I thought you were dead," I said, starting to cry. "I thought you were dead."

She turned around, looked at me intently, then put her hand to my forehead.

"Sick," she confirmed. "Some kind of sick is giving you crazy ideas."

As the man from the car behind us started tapping on the window, I moved the umbrella away from my leg. Then Mona and my mother were getting out of the car. I got out after them; and while everyone else was inspecting the damage we'd done, I threw the umbrella down a sewer.

Review and Assess

Thinking About the Selection

1. **Respond:** Were you surprised when the narrator threw away the umbrella at the end of the story? Why or why not?

2. **(a) Recall:** What excuse does the narrator give Miss Crosman for arriving at the piano lesson soaking wet? **(b) Infer:** Why does she hide the truth?

3. **(a) Recall:** Why is the narrator's mother late to pick up the sisters? **(b) Infer:** Why is the narrator bothered by her mother's lateness? **(c) Analyze:** Why does the narrator refuse to go back into Miss Crosman's house to get out of the rain?

4. **(a) Infer:** Why does Miss Crosman give the narrator the umbrella? **(b) Deduce:** How does Miss Crosman feel about children?

5. **(a) Recall:** How does the narrator feel about the white umbrella? **(b) Interpret:** What does the umbrella represent to the narrator? **(c) Draw Conclusions:** Why does the narrator throw away the umbrella at the end of the story?

Gish Jen

(b. 1956)

The daughter of Chinese immigrants, Gish Jen grew up in Yonkers and Scarsdale, New York, communities that had very few Asian Americans. Jen began writing fiction as an undergraduate at Harvard. After teaching English in China, she entered the University of Iowa writing program, where she wrote "The White Umbrella." Her first novel, *Typical American*, was published in 1991, and her second, *Mona in the Promised Land*, in 1996. Both of these novels deal with the clash of cultures that Asian Americans face in the United States.

Review and Assess

Literary Analysis
Character Traits
1. For each narrator, make a web like this one. Identify at least two character **traits** and two examples of details that reveal each trait.

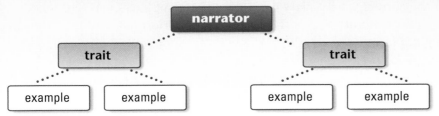

Comparing Literary Works
2. What similar challenges do the main characters in these stories face because of their families' situations?
3. How do each character's circumstances affect how he or she copes with the challenge?
4. What is similar about the two narrators' attempts to achieve respect? What is different? Use a Venn diagram like the one shown to compare and contrast their attempts.

"A Ribbon for Baldy"   Both   "The White Umbrella"

Reading Strategy
Predicting
5. What prediction did you make about the outcome of the narrator's project in "A Ribbon for Baldy"? Why?
6. (a) What predictions did you make about the narrator and the umbrella in "The White Umbrella"? Why? (b) Which predictions were accurate?

Extend Understanding
7. **Evaluate:** In your opinion, how important is the opinion of others? Do you think most students your age feel it is more important or less important than you do?
8. **Take a Position:** Do you agree or disagree that Americans place too much importance on things? Explain.

Quick Review

Character traits are the qualities of a character's personality. To review character traits, see page 379.

When you **predict,** you make educated guesses about what will happen in a story based on the information the author gives you. To review predicting, see page 379.

 Take It to the Net
www.phschool.com
Take the interactive self-test online to check your understanding of these selections.

Integrate Language Skills

Vocabulary Development Lesson

Word Analysis: Latin Root -cred-

Each of the words below contains the Latin root -cred-, meaning "believe." Rewrite the sentences, filling in the blank with the correct word.

a. incredibly   b. credit   c. credibility

1. She earned ___?___ for taking lessons.
2. The job was ___?___ difficult.
3. She told so many fibs that she didn't have much ___?___ with her friends.

Spelling Strategy

The *ksh* sound in *anxious* and in some other words is spelled *xi*. Write the following words, spelling the *sh* sound with the letters *xi*.

1. no___ous
2. comple___on
3. obno___ous
4. an___ously

Fluency: Sentence Completions

Review the words in the vocabulary list on page 379. Then, on your paper, write the vocabulary word that best completes each sentence.

1. The ___?___ Orion was visible in the sky.
2. He ___?___ the land before building a fence.
3. They waited ___?___ for their mom to arrive.
4. The story was so fantastic it had no ___?___.
5. At dusk, the fog would ___?___ the hilltop, making it invisible.
6. His solution to the problem came like a ___?___.
7. She was ___?___, telling no one about her job.
8. At the sale, she got a ___?___ on piano music.

Grammar Lesson

Subjects and Predicates

The **subject** of a sentence tells who or what the sentence is about. The **predicate** tells what the subject is or does.

Example: Our teacher, Professor Herbert, | talked about a project for each member of our General Science class.

The **simple subject** is the main noun or pronoun in the complete subject. The **simple predicate** is the verb or verb phrase in the predicate.

Example: The corn row | measured 23.5 miles long.

▶ *For more practice, see page R30, Exercise A.*
Practice Copy the sentences. Underline each subject once and each predicate twice. Circle each simple subject and simple predicate.

1. My mother went to work.
2. A gust of wind littered the street.
3. I could feel the rain on my left shoulder.
4. We burned the base of Little Baldy.
5. The boy worked into the night.

Writing Application Write five sentences, or tell a story, about one of these selections. Use simple subjects and simple predicates in your sentences.

W̸G Prentice Hall Writing and Grammar Connection: Chapter 19, Sections 1 and 2

Writing Lesson

Recommendation

A recommendation is a written statement about a person's abilities or accomplishments. Write a recommendation for the narrator of "A Ribbon for Baldy" or "The White Umbrella" for a job in a store.

Prewriting Make a list of the narrator's positive character traits. Jot down examples from the stories to support each trait.

Drafting Begin by stating the main quality that makes the narrator worth hiring. In your introductory paragraph, elaborate, or provide more details, about how that quality will help the narrator perform well on the job. Then, continue with other strong qualities in the paragraphs that follow, using examples to support your claims.

Revising Revise your word choice by adding specific information in place of vague references.

Model: Revising Word Choice

is a hard-working person
who would make   wonderful   , and he is always reliable.
Jesse ~~would be great as~~ a gardener. I've known him for a long time.
~~He's a great person!~~ He has had a lot of experience working on his
father's farm. For a school science project, he plowed the land and
planted a cornfield that consisted of one long, single row of corn.

W\G Prentice Hall Writing and Grammar Connection: Chapter 7, Section 2

Extension Activities

Listening and Speaking With a small group of classmates, prepare a **narrative presentation** about goals each of you is proud of achieving.

1. State the reasons you wanted to achieve your goal.
2. When you explain how you reached your goal, break the actions down into their smallest parts and choose precise verbs to name each action.
3. State the reasons you are proud you achieved your goal.

Research and Technology Use a search engine on the Internet to research how corn is normally planted. Look for agriculture sites or magazine articles or use an online encyclopedia.

Prepare a **list of sites** where others can find useful information.

 **Take It to the Net** www.phschool.com

Go online for an additional research activity using the Internet.

Prepare to Read

Taught Me Purple ◆ The City Is So Big ◆ Those Winter Sundays

Preview

Connecting to the Literature

The three poems in this grouping describe special people and places in the lives of the writers. Connect to these poems by thinking for a moment about people and places you see every day and how they influence you.

Background

Evelyn Tooley Hunt's poem, "Taught Me Purple," mentions a tenement, an apartment building that is low cost but run-down. Conditions in many tenements are crowded and dangerously substandard. They reflect one of the challenges of urban living—how to provide safe housing for millions of people living within a few square miles of one another.

Literary Analysis
Theme

In a work of literature, the **theme** is the central message or insight about life that the work conveys. To uncover the theme of a work, look carefully at specific details to see if they have some bigger meaning that can be applied to life in general. For instance, in the following lines from "Those Winter Sundays," the speaker realizes that as a boy, he did not appreciate all that his father had done for him.

> What did I know, what did I know
> of love's austere and lonely offices?

The specific experience of the speaker can be expanded into a general statement, such as "Appreciate the love shown in everyday actions." The organizer at right shows how to expand from specific to general ideas.

Personal Experience

speaker's feelings

speaker's reactions

lesson speaker learns

Theme

Comparing Literary Works

Certain themes recur throughout literary works from different ages and cultures. The three works you are about to read focus on two of the most common recurring themes: the importance of family and the role of individuality. As you read, compare and contrast the poems' explorations of these themes. Use the following focus questions to guide you:

1. What is conveyed about relationships and human interaction?
2. How are the messages about interaction different in each poem?

Reading Strategy
Responding to Theme

To get the most out of a work, you should **respond to the theme**—react to its message. The following are just a few of the ways you can respond to a theme:

- Decide if you agree or disagree with it.
- Look for ways to apply it to your own life.
- Identify other works or experiences that show if the theme is valid or not.

Vocabulary Development

tenement (ten´ ə mənt) *n.* here, a run-down apartment building (p. 398)

quake (kwāk) *v.* tremble or shake; shudder or shiver, as from fear or cold (p. 399)

banked (baŋt) *adj.* adjusted to burn slowly and long (p. 400)

chronic (krän´ ik) *adj.* continuing indefinitely; perpetual; constant (p. 400)

austere (ô stir´) *adj.* showing strict self-discipline; severe (p. 400)

Taught Me Purple

Evelyn Tooley Hunt

tenement (ten´ ə mənt) *n.*
here, a run-down apartment building

Evelyn Tooley Hunt

(b. 1904)

In 1961, Evelyn Tooley Hunt won the Sidney Lanier Memorial Award for her first collection of poems, *Look Again, Adam.* Her poems demonstrate a keen interest in other cultures. "I like to write from the inside of some culture other than my own," she says. She is best known for her variations of haiku, a type of Asian poetry, which she writes under the pen name of Tao-Li.

My mother taught me purple
    Although she never wore it.
Wash-gray was her circle,
    The <u>tenement</u> her orbit.

5 My mother taught me golden
    And held me up to see it,
Above the broken molding,
    Beyond the filthy street.

My mother reached for beauty
10   And for its lack she died,
Who knew so much of duty
    She could not teach me pride.

THE CITY IS SO BIG

Richard García

The city is so big
Its bridges quake with fear
I know, I have seen at night

The lights sliding from house to house
5   And trains pass with windows shining
Like a smile full of teeth

I have seen machines eating houses
And stairways walk all by themselves
And elevator doors opening and closing
10 And people disappear.

quake (kwāk) *v.* tremble or shake; shudder or shiver, as from fear or cold

Review and Assess

Thinking About the Selections

1. **Respond:** To which poem do you have a stronger reaction? Why?
2. **(a) Recall:** In "Taught Me Purple," what does the speaker say her mother taught her? **(b) Interpret:** What does each color represent to the speaker?
3. **(a) Recall:** What did the mother not teach the speaker? **(b) Infer:** Why not?
4. **(a) Recall:** In "The City Is So Big," what are two unusual events the speaker says he has seen? **(b) Interpret:** In your own words, explain what the speaker has actually seen.
5. **(a) Analyze:** What is the feeling behind most of the events or occurrences in the poem? **(b) Apply:** What is the mood or general feeling of the work? **(c) Draw Conclusions:** Explain how the speaker feels about the city.

Richard García

(b. 1941)
Richard García writes poetry for adults and children. His books include *The Flying Garcias* (1993) and a contemporary folk tale for children, *My Aunt Otilia's Spirits* (1978).

García is the Poet-in-Residence at the Children's Hospital in Los Angeles, California, where he leads poetry and art workshops for hospitalized children. He also teaches creative writing classes.

Those Winter Sundays

Robert Hayden

Sundays too my father got up early
and put his clothes on in the blueblack cold,
then with cracked hands that ached
from labor in the weekday weather made
5 banked fires blaze. No one ever thanked him.

I'd wake and hear the cold splintering, breaking.
When the rooms were warm, he'd call,
and slowly I would rise and dress,
fearing the chronic angers of that house,

10 Speaking indifferently to him,
who had driven out the cold
and polished my good shoes as well.
What did I know, what did I know
of love's austere and lonely offices?

banked (baŋt) *adj.* adjusted to burn slowly and long

chronic (krän´ ik) *adj.* continuing indefinitely; perpetual; constant

austere (ô stir´) *adj.* showing strict self-discipline; severe

Robert Hayden

(1913–1980)

Raised in a poor Detroit neighborhood, Robert Hayden became the first African American poet to be appointed as Consultant of Poetry to the Library of Congress. His poetry covers a wide range of subjects—from personal remembrances to celebrations of the history and achievements of African Americans.

Review and Assess

Thinking About the Selection

1. **Respond:** In what ways is the speaker's father in "Those Winter Sundays" admirable?

2. **(a) Recall:** What did the speaker's father do on winter Sunday mornings? **(b) Infer:** Why did the speaker's father get up early even on Sundays when he could have slept later?

3. **(a) Recall:** How did the speaker respond to his father when he was young? **(b) Infer:** How has his attitude toward his father's actions changed? **(c) Support:** Which lines emphasize the speaker's current attitude about his father's actions?

Review and Assess

Literary Analysis

Theme

1. In "Taught Me Purple," what is the relationship between the mother and the daughter?
2. What **theme** or message is expressed by this relationship?
3. Looking back on the situation in "Those Winter Sundays" as an adult, what does the speaker realize?
4. What general message about life can you make based on the speaker's realization?

Comparing Literary Works

5. What does each work convey about relationships and human interaction?
6. In each category, give each poem a rating from zero to five. (Zero means the idea does not apply at all. Five means it applies very strongly.) When you are finished, choose two poems and explain how the messages are the same or different.

	Love	Sacrifice	Identity	Work	Positive	Negative
"Taught Me Purple"		3				
"The City is So Big"		0				
"Those Winter Sundays"		5				

Reading Strategy

Responding to Theme

7. With which themes do you agree? With which do you disagree?
8. Which, if any, of the themes relates to your life? Explain.
9. For each work, identify another work of literature that has a similar theme. Explain the similarity.

Extend Understanding

10. **Cultural Connection:** Which of the three poems' themes seems most relevant for today's world? Explain.

Quick Review

The **theme** of a literary work is its central message, concern, or purpose. To review theme, see page 397.

 Take It to the Net
www.phschool.com
Take the interactive self-test online to check your understanding of these selections.

Integrate Language Skills

Vocabulary Development Lesson

Word Analysis: Greek Root *-chron-*

The word root *-chron-* comes from the Greek word for "time." *Chronic* means "continuing for a long period of time." Suggest a meaning for each of the words below. Then, use a dictionary to check your definitions.

1. chronicle **2.** chronological **3.** chronometer

Spelling Strategy

Some words, like *tenement* and *cemetery*, are spelled with three *e*'s. To remember how to spell these words, think of the three *e*'s in *remember!* Spell each of the following words correctly:

1. refirence **2.** elament **3.** independance

Grammar Lesson

Compound Subjects and Verbs

Sentences may have more than one subject or verb. A **compound subject** is two or more subjects that have the same verb and are linked by a coordinating conjunction such as *and* or *or*:

Compound Subject: That *mother and father* work hard for their children.

A **compound verb** is two or more verbs that have the same subject and are linked by a coordinating conjunction such as *and* or *or*:

Compound Verb: The city *lives* and *breathes* on its own.

Fluency: Sentence Completions

Review the vocabulary list on page 397. Then, write the vocabulary word that best completes each sentence.

1. The ___?___ was built to provide housing for the poor.
2. The room was so bare that it looked ___?___ and forbidding.
3. The ___?___ problem with the heat kept the rooms from ever getting warm enough.
4. A ___?___ fire will burn through the night.
5. When the radiator came on, the floors would ___?___ and the pipes would quiver.

▶ *For more practice, see page R30, Exercise B.*
Practice On your paper, combine the following sentence pairs by forming a compound subject or a compound verb. When you change the subject, make sure the verb agrees in number.

1. My father got up early. My father started the fire.
2. He did not speak much. I did not speak much.
3. Elevator doors open. Elevator doors close.
4. He drove out the cold. He polished my shoes.
5. The mother lives in a tenement. The daughter lives in a tenement, too.

Writing Application Write a paragraph containing one sentence about each of the poems in this section. Use at least one compound subject and one compound verb.

W̸G Prentice Hall Writing and Grammar Connection: Chapter 19, Section 3

Writing Lesson

Response to Poems

When you respond to literature, you react on a personal level to language and techniques as well as to ideas and themes. Choose two of the poems from this section, and write an essay in which you compare and contrast your response to each one.

Prewriting Reread the poems and jot down notes about your response to each. List how your responses to the two poems are similar and different.

Drafting Use comparison-and-contrast organization. You might write about one poem first and then the other. Alternatively, you might describe similarities between your responses to the two poems in one paragraph and differences in the next. Support your comparisons by citing passages from the poems.

Model: Comparison-and-Contrast Organization

I had different reactions to the last lines of the poems. The final lines of "Those Winter Sundays" made me feel sympathy for the speaker. By contrast, the final line of "The City Is So Big" made me feel tense.

> This writer states her similar reactions to the poems in one part of her response, and her different reactions to the poems in another.

Revising Check your notes to make sure you have included all of your points.

Prentice Hall Writing and Grammar Connection: Chapter 12, Section 3

Extension Activities

Listening and Speaking Prepare an **outline** for an informal speech about someone you admire. The following steps will help you:

- State your main point, the overall impression you want to give, in the introduction, or opening.
- In the body of your speech, give details and examples.
- Conclude with a summary of the reasons you admire your subject.

When you are ready, give your speech to the class.

Research and Technology With a group, develop a **magazine** that describes city life. Use magazines, newspapers, and online resources to gather information. Write articles using this information.

Writing Find a word in one of the poems that is critical to the poem's overall meaning. Then, write a brief essay in which you discuss why the writer chose this word and how the word relates to the poem's message.

 **Take It to the Net**   www.phschool.com

Go online for an additional research activity using the Internet.

Persuasive Speeches

About Persuasive Speeches

Like autobiographies and diaries, speeches can provide you with a first-hand view of historical events. In addition, they are a great source for learning about the various sides of political issues. When reading a speech:

- Remember that it was originally written to be presented orally to an audience.
- Try to understand the speaker's purpose, arguments, and evidence.
- Think about the other sides of the issue that the speaker may be ignoring.

Many speeches, such as political speeches, have a persuasive purpose. As a result, speakers often use carefully chosen words and details in order to convince the audience to agree with their position. Speakers also use a variety of techniques—including repetition and appeals to emotion—to influence listeners.

Reading Strategy

Analyzing Proposition and Support

Writers of speeches often make a *proposition*—a subject or statement to be discussed or debated—when they begin their speech. The proposition is the main point of the writer's speech. In order for a proposition to effectively persuade the reader or listener, it is necessary to present sufficient support:

- logical arguments
- facts
- expert opinions
- personal observations

Speaker's Proposition	What does the speaker want me to believe?
Supporting Details	How does the speaker support his or her argument?
Your Response	Did you "buy" the argument of the speaker? Why or why not?

When reading speeches critically, first identify the speaker's proposition or main point. Then, look for the details that support the proposition. Finally, you should evaluate the speech by looking at your own response. Were you influenced by the speaker to believe in his or her argument? Use a chart like the one shown to analyze Elizabeth Cady Stanton's proposition in "Arguments in Favor of a Sixteenth Amendment."

Arguments in Favor of a Sixteenth Amendment

Elizabeth Cady Stanton

Stanton introduces her topic with loaded language that makes her distaste for inequality evident.

The Republican party today congratulates itself on having carried the Fifteenth Amendment of the Constitution, thus securing "manhood suffrage" and estalishing an aristocracy of sex on this continent. As several bills secure Woman's Suffrage in the District and the Territories have been already presented in both houses of Congress, and as by Mr. Julian's bill, the question of so amending the Constitution as to extend suffrage to all the women of the country has been presented to the nation for consideration, it is not only the right but the duty of every thoughtful woman to express her opinion on a Sixteenth Amendment. While I hail the late discussions of Congress and the various bills presented as so many signs of progress, I am especially gratified with those of Messrs. Julian and Pomeroy, which forbid any State to deny the right of suffrage to any of its citizens on account of sex or color.

This fundamental principle of our government—the equality of all the citizens of the republic—should be incorporated in the Federal Constitution, there to remain forever. To leave this question to the States and partial acts of Congress, is to defer indefinitely its settlement, for what is done by this Congress may be repealed by the next; and politics in the several States differ so widely, that no harmonious action on any question can ever be secured, except as a strict party measure. Hence, we appeal to the party now in power, everywhere, to end this protracted debate on suffrage, and declare it the inalienable right of every citizen who is amenable to the laws of the land, who pays taxes and the penalty of crime. . . .

I urge a speedy adoption of a Sixteenth Amendment for the following reasons:

A government, based on the principle of caste and class, can not stand. The aristocratic idea, in any form, is opposed to the genius of our free institutions, to our own declaration of rights, and to the civilization of the age. All artificial distinctions, whether of family, blood, wealth, color, or sex, are equally oppressive to the subject classes, and equally destructive to national life and prosperity. Governments based on every form of aristocracy, on every degree and varety of inequality, have been tried in despotisms, monarchies, and republics, and all alike have perished. In the panorama of the past behold the mighty nations that have risen, one by one, but to fall. Behold their temples, thrones, and pyramids, their gorgeous palaces and stately monuments now crumbled all to dust. Behold every monarch in Europe at this very hour trembling on his throne. Behold the republics on this Western continent convulsed, distracted, divided, the hosts scattered, the leaders fallen, the scouts lost in the wilderness, the once inspired prophets blind and dumb, while on all sides the cry is echoed, "Republicanism is a failure," though that great principle of a government "by the people, of the people, for the people" has never been tried. Thus far, all nations have been built on caste and failed. Why, in this hour of reconstruction, with the experience of generations before us, make another experiment in the same direction? If serfdom, peasantry, and slavery have shattered kingdoms, deluged continents with blood, scattered republics like dust before the wind, and rent our own Union asunder, what kind of a government, think you, American statesmen, you can build, with the mothers of the race crouching at your feet, while iron-heeled peasants, serfs, and slaves, exalted by your hands, tread our inalienable rights into the dust? While all men, everywhere, are rejoicing in new-found liberties, shall woman alone be denied the rights, privileges, and immunities of citizenship?. . .

Of all kinds of aristocracy, that of sex is the most odious and unnatural; invading, as it does, our homes, desecrating our family altars, dividing those whom God has joined together, exalting the son above the mother who bore him, and subjugating, everywhere, moral power to brute force. Such a government would not be worth the blood and treasure so freely poured out in its long struggles for freedom. . . .

Stanton states her position by using concepts such as fairness and equality.

Stanton prepares her audience for the evidence she will use to support her proposition.

Stanton makes her case by portraying the opposite side as outdated and undemocratic in their thinking.

Stanton uses a rhetorical question here. A rhetorical question is one which the speaker has already answered or implied and with which the audience is expected to agree.

Checking Your Comprehension

1. What is the purpose of the Fifteenth Amendment? What would the Sixteenth Amendment add to it?
2. What bills did Messrs. Julian and Pomeroy present to Congress?
3. What does Stanton believe to be the fundamental principle of the government?
4. What does Stanton say about the aristocratic idea?
5. Why does Stanton believe that "no harmonious action on any question can ever be secured"?

Applying the Reading Strategy

Proposition and Support

6. What is Stanton's proposition?
7. What three details does she provide to support her proposition?
8. Why do you think Stanton provides examples of other governments?

Activity

Prepare a Speech

Use a chart like the one shown here to organize your thoughts for a speech in which you propose a plan, viewpoint, or suggested action. After outlining your plan, conduct research as needed to find statistics, expert opinions or other details that support your proposition.

Comparing Informational Materials

Speeches from the Past and Present

The speech given by Elizabeth Cady Stanton was given in the nineteenth century. Using the Internet, find a speech that was recently given about a proposed amendment or law. Evaluate the speech by identifying the proposition and the supporting details. Then, compare the two speeches by asking the following questions:

- Which speaker do you think is more effective in influencing readers?
- Which speaker backs up their argument more thoroughly?
- How is the language and style of the two time periods different?

When you are finished, present your comparison to the class.

Persuasive Essays

About Persuasive Essays

A **persuasive essay** is a written work in which a writer presents a case for or against a particular position. Some examples of persuasive essays are newspaper editorials and magazine commentary pages.

In a persuasive essay, each logical argument or striking phrase is like a step on a staircase leading to a window. As readers climb the staircase, they come closer to looking out this "window"—to seeing things from the writer's point of view. A persuasive essay has

- an issue with more than one side.
- a clear statement of the writer's position.
- a clear organization that builds toward a conclusion.
- evidence supporting the writer's position, including arguments, statistics, expert opinions, and personal observations.
- powerful verbal images and language.

Reading Strategy

Understand a Writer's Purpose

A writer's purpose—to inform, to entertain, to shape a viewpoint, to argue for or against a position—determines what facts, arguments, and images he or she selects. For instance, in the essay on the next page, "Darkness at Noon," the writer uses a series of anecdotes to support his argument that sighted people often make mistaken assumptions about the blind. As you read, keep track of these anecdotes in a chart like the one shown.

Writers often make their purpose clear by stating it in the introduction. Then, in the body of the essay, they explain the connection of each main point to their overall purpose. In "Darkness at Noon," the writer introduces a paragraph with the following sentence: "The toughest misconception of all is the view that because I can't see, I can't work." This connects the paragraph to his main purpose, which is to persuade people to treat the disabled fairly, especially in the workplace.

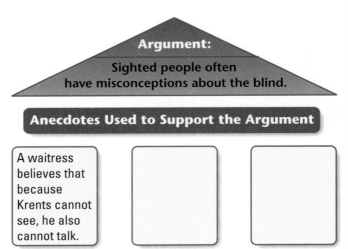

Argument:

Sighted people often have misconceptions about the blind.

Anecdotes Used to Support the Argument

A waitress believes that because Krents cannot see, he also cannot talk.

Darkness at Noon

Harold Krents

Blind from birth, I have never had the opportunity to see myself and have been completely dependent on the image I create in the eye of the observer. To date, it has not been narcissistic.

There are those who assume that since I can't see, I obviously also cannot hear. Very often people will converse with me at the top of their lungs, enunciating each word very carefully.

Conversely, people will also often whisper, assuming that since my eyes don't work, my ears don't either.

For example, when I go to the airport and ask the ticket agent for assistance to the plane, he or she will invariably pick up the phone, call a ground hostess, and whisper: "Hi, Jane, we've got a 76 here." I have concluded that the word *blind* is not used, for one of two reasons: Either they fear that if the dread word is spoken, the ticket agent's retina will immediately detach, or they are reluctant to inform me of my condition, of which I may not have been previously aware.

On the other hand, others know that of course I can hear, but believe that I can't talk. Often, therefore, when my wife and I go out to dinner, a waiter or waitress will ask Kit if "he would like a drink" to which I respond that "indeed he would."

This point was graphically driven home to me while we were in England. I had been given a year's leave of absence from my Washington law firm to study for a diploma in law at Oxford University. During the year I became ill and was hospitalized. Immediately after admission, I was wheeled down to the X-ray room. Just at the door sat an elderly woman— elderly I would judge from the sound of her voice. "What is his name?" the woman asked the orderly who had been wheeling me.

"What's your name?" the orderly repeated to me.

"Harold Krents," I replied.

"Harold Krents," he repeated.

"When was he born?"

"When were you born?"

"November 5, 1944," I responded.

"November 5, 1944," the orderly intoned.

The opening states the issue addressed by the essay: the perception of blind people by others. Since he does not state his position clearly in the opening, readers must infer it, or figure it out, from the examples he chooses and his attitude.

Examples from the author's own life serve as evidence for his argument. Such evidence, as well as powerful language, helps readers sympathize with the author's viewpoint.

This procedure continued for approximately five minutes, at which point even my saintlike disposition deserted me.

"Look," I finally blurted out, "this is absolutely ridiculous. Okay, granted I can't see, but it's got to have become pretty clear to both of you that I don't need an interpreter."

"He says he doesn't need an interpreter," the orderly reported to the woman.

The toughest misconception of all is the view that because I can't see, I can't work. I was turned down by over forty law firms because of my blindness, even though my qualifications included a cum laude degree from Harvard College and a good ranking in my Harvard Law School class.

The attempt to find employment, the continuous frustration of being told that it was impossible for a blind person to practice law, the rejection letters, based not on my lack of ability but rather on my disability, will always remain one of the most disillusioning experiences of my life.

Fortunately, this view of limitation and exclusion is beginning to change. On April 16, [1978,] the Department of Labor issued regulations that mandate equal-employment opportunities for the handicapped. By and large, the business community's response to offering employment to the disabled has been enthusiastic.

I therefore look forward to the day, with the expectation that it is certain to come, when employers will view their handicapped workers as a little child did me years ago when my family still lived in Scarsdale.

I was playing basketball with my father in our back yard according to procedures we had developed. My father would stand beneath the hoop, shout, and I would shoot over his head at the basket attached to our garage. Our next-door neighbor, aged five, wandered over into our yard with a playmate. "He's blind," our neighbor whispered to her friend in a voice that could be heard distinctly by dad and me. Dad shot and missed; I did the same. Dad hit the rim; I missed entirely; Dad shot and missed the garage entirely. "Which one is blind?" whispered back the little friend.

I would hope that in the near future, when a plant manager is touring the factory with the foreman and comes upon a handicapped and a non-handicapped person working together, his comment after watching them work will be, "Which one is disabled?"

Checking Your Comprehension

1. What disability does the writer have?
2. Name two misconceptions that sighted people have had about the writer.
3. **(a)** According to the writer, what is "the toughest misconception of all"? **(b)** Why does the writer find this misconception so difficult to handle?

Applying the Reading Strategy

Understand a Writer's Purpose

4. How does the introduction show that the writer's purpose is to persuade people to avoid inappropriate assumptions about people who cannot see?
5. The writer uses humor in the essay. Find one example of humor, and explain how this helps him accomplish his purpose.
6. What evidence does the writer use to support his argument that the disabled need fair treatment in the workplace?

Activity

Media Evaluation

Many perceptions are formed by the way people are portrayed in the media. Choose a movie or television program that has a person who is blind as a character. Watch the movie or program. Discuss with a partner how Harold Krents would react to the portrayal of the character.

Comparing Informational Materials

Persuasive Essays and Persuasive Speeches

Persuasive speeches use many of the same techniques as persuasive essays, such as logical arguments, charged language, and appeals to values and emotions. However, since they are meant to be heard as well as read, they often make greater use of speaking devices, such as repetition and emphasis. Compare persuasive speeches and persuasive essays using a chart like the one shown here.

	Persuasive Essay	Persuasive Speech
Purpose	To persuade readers	To persuade listeners
Format		
Techniques Used		

Writing WORKSHOP

Persuasion: Persuasive Composition

A **persuasive composition** is a written work in which a writer presents a case for or against a particular position in order to try to convince readers to agree with his or her ideas. In this workshop, you will write a persuasive composition on an issue of interest to you.

Assignment Criteria. Your persuasive composition should have the following characteristics:

- An issue that has more than one "side"
- A clear thesis statement that presents your position
- Detailed evidence, examples, and reasons in support of your position
- Arguments that anticipate reader's concerns and counterarguments
- Powerful words and vivid language

To preview the criteria on which your persuasive composition may be assessed, see the Rubric on page 415.

Prewriting

Choose a topic. For inspiration, check national and local news stories, or ask friends and family members to name topics that interest them. Here are a few broad categories to choose from:

- Laws that affect young people
- School rules
- Environmental issues
- Media influence

Know your audience. Choose details and a writing style that will appeal to your readers. To do this, create an audience profile to help you analyze your readers.

Conduct research. To support your proposal, present detailed evidence, examples, and reasons. Conduct interviews or surveys, or use the library or online research to gather quotations and facts from reliable sources.

Anticipate the counterarguments. Think about the arguments *against* your position. Plan ahead to answer concerns and meet opposing ideas head on with persuasive arguments of your own.

Audience Profile

Audience members: Classmates

Grade: 8th

Topic: Why rats make the best pets

Attitudes toward my topic: doubt, skepticism

Knowledge about my topic: limited

Interest in my topic: high

Student Model

Before you begin drafting your persuasive composition, read this student model and review the characteristics of a successful persuasive composition.

Joseph Bunke
Daytona Beach, Florida

Why Rats Make Better Pets Than Cats and Dogs

It has come to my attention as a pet owner and scholar that most pet owners own cats or dogs, and are repulsed by rodents—especially rats. A few years ago, we acquired a new family member after our pet snake refused to eat a rat. Since then, I have learned that rats are superior to cats and dogs in numerous ways, and I intend to show you how.

I believe that man's fear of rats stems mainly from an irrational fear of disease. This fear may have been legitimate back in the Middle Ages when fleas on street rats spread bubonic plague. Nowadays, rats have been domesticated, and pet rats are quite clean and free of disease. Their habitats are clean as well. Cats have litter boxes, true, but dogs have to be walked or let outside. A rat requires only a change of wood shavings in its cage once weekly. Also, since rats do not go outside of the house, their soft fur coats aren't exposed to much dirt, making them cleaner than cats and dogs.

Rats have nice personalities in addition to being so clean. They are affectionate and trusting towards humans, especially if they are exposed to humans before they are two months old. Rats, like dogs, can be trained to do tricks because they are very intelligent. I have yet to see a cat do tricks.

Then there's the issue of cost. Cats and dogs can cost several hundred dollars just to purchase. Then you have to pay monthly costs for basic needs like food, flea treatment (unless you want fleas), veterinary care, and repair expenses for the damage they inflict on your house. Rats cost much less. They cost only five dollars to purchase, require little or no veterinary attention, eat relatively anything, and are easy to entertain. You could realistically support three rats for the price of one cat or dog.

I personally think rats are great pets, but you can judge that for yourself. Think of it this way: Would you rather have a hulking mongrel who has to be watched all the time, a feline whose innocence conceals four sharp sets of claws, or a small, sweet, cheerful, clever rodent who loves people unconditionally? It's your choice, but if I were you I would choose a rodent.

Joseph has chosen the unpopular side of an issue that clearly has an opposing argument.

His thesis is clearly stated and sets up his persuasive arguments.

Given his controversial thesis, Joseph chooses to deal right away with readers' potential objections to rats.

He devotes each paragraph to examples of rats' superiority. Here he addresses cost.

Joseph's use of vivid language in this paragraph is intended to sway the reader.

Drafting

Begin with a strong introduction. Before you can persuade your reader, you must "hook" him or her. Try one of the lures, shown at right, as tempting bait.

Combine logic and emotion. Logic without emotion can be dry and bland. Emotion without logic is easily dismissed as empty and melodramatic. Successful persuasive writers use both.

- **Logic:** Take your readers step-by-step down a logical path. Let one point lead naturally to the next until together they reach the conclusion you have planned all along.

- **Emotion:** Brief stories or vivid descriptions can move readers to share your feelings. Words with strong connotations can pack a punch in just a few syllables. For example, calling an idea *irresponsible* or *childish* can be more effective than just calling it *mistaken*.

Save the best for last. Try a plan of attack called **Nestorian Order**. Begin with your second strongest point. Present other points and then—BOOM!—hit your reader with your strongest reason—a dramatic way to conclude.

Hooking Your Reader

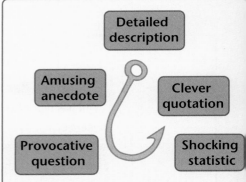

Revising

Revise for coherence. A good essay coheres, or holds together well. Read the last sentence of each paragraph followed by the first sentence of the next paragraph. If there is no obvious connection between the paragraphs, highlight the space between them. Add a word, phrase, or sentence that "glues" the paragraphs together. Use the following ideas to glue your paragraph together:

- Repeat a key word or phrase.
- Use a transitional word or phrase such as *similarly, however*, or *in addition.*
- Insert a sentence that takes your reader smoothly from one idea to the next.

Model: Making Paragraphs Stick Together

Rats have nice personalities in addition to being so clean.

Also, since rats do not go outside of the house, their soft fur coats aren't exposed to much dirt, making them cleaner than cats and dogs.

Rats are affectionate and trusting toward humans, especially if they are exposed to humans before they are two months old.

Joseph repeats a different form of the word "cleaner" in order to emphasize the connection between paragraphs.

Revise to repeat key words. Determine the most important words in your sentences. Try repeating them for emphasis. Use this strategy to create connections between sentences. Do not use it because you cannot think of another word.

Compare the model and the nonmodel. Why is the model more effective than the nonmodel?

Nonmodel	Model
Then there's the issue of cost. You can spend several hundred dollars just to purchase a cat or dog. Then you have to pay monthly fees for basic needs like . . .	Then there's the issue of cost. You might spend several hundred dollars just to purchase a cat or dog. Then you have to pay monthly costs like . . .

Publishing and Presenting

Choose one of these following ways to share your writing with classmates or a larger audience.

Record a speech. Use your persuasive composition as the basis for a speech that you tape-record and share with your classmates.

Publish a magazine. Combine your persuasive composition with other students' to create a class magazine that covers school, local, national, and worldwide issues. Give your magazine a title that will attract readers. Then, display it in your school library.

 Prentice Hall Writing and Grammar Connection: Chapter 7

Speaking Connection

To learn more about delivering a persuasive speech, see the **Listening and Speaking Workshop, page 416.**

Rubric for Self-Assessment

Evaluate your persuasive composition using the following criteria and rating scale:

Criteria	Rating Scale				
	Not very				Very
How clearly have you defined and stated your thesis?	1	2	3	4	5
How effective is the evidence you present?	1	2	3	4	5
How well do you address reader concerns and counterarguments?	1	2	3	4	5
How powerful and vivid is the language used in the essay?	1	2	3	4	5

Listening and Speaking WORKSHOP

Delivering a Persuasive Speech

A **persuasive speech** is a speech that attempts to persuade, or convince, the listener to adopt the speaker's opinion. A persuasive speech follows the same guidelines as persuasive compositions. (To review these, see the writing workshop, pp. 412–415.) It includes a well-defined thesis supported by detailed evidence, examples, and reasoning. Like a persuasive composition, it also anticipates listener concerns and counterarguments. However, a speech has additional dimensions and tools: careful preparation of speaking notes, as well as dramatic delivery.

Be Prepared

Prepare notes. When you prepare notes for your speech, do not write down everything you will say, word for word. Instead, prepare basic notes which will remind you of the main points you wish to cover, while still allowing you to speak spontaneously. The notes can be in outline form, with key points and details underlined or highlighted.

Rehearse. Rehearse the speech at least once, using your notes, so you will feel comfortable using them in front of an audience.

Use Your Voice and Body

Delivery can be a powerful persuasive element. Use these techniques to make a lasting impression on your audience.

Voice modulation. Adjust the sound of your voice to suit your audience and the place in which you are speaking. Use different intensities for drama and emphasis and to keep your audience engaged.

Tone. If possible, don't read your presentation. Use note cards to help you move from point to point, but speak as naturally and reasonably as you can.

Pace. In general, speak slowly. However, there may be times in which you speed your pace to create excitement or build suspense. Remember that your audience will only hear your speech once—and you want them to hear every word.

Use Your Body. Your audience is not just listening: they are also watching. While speaking make direct eye contact with your audience and gesture dramatically to emphasize key points.

> **Checklist for Persuasive Speeches**
> - ☐ Well-defined thesis
> - ☐ Detailed evidence
> - ☐ One opinion, many facts
> - ☐ Sound, logical reasoning
> - ☐ Listener concerns anticipated

Activity:
Persuasive Speech

Deliver a short persuasive speech to your classmates in which you take a stand on this question: "Should eighth graders be required to learn to swim before they can be promoted to ninth grade?" Prepare your speech by writing note cards with your main ideas.

Assessment WORKSHOP

Identifying the Best Summary

The reading sections of some tests require you to read a passage and answer multiple-choice questions in which you identify the best summary of that passage. Use the following strategies to answer such questions:

- Before choosing an answer, summarize the passage in your mind. Then, choose the summary that is closest to your own.
- Avoid choosing a summary that is true, but may include details that are unnecessary. The best summary is not necessarily the most detailed.

Sample Test Item

Directions: Read the passage, and then answer the question that follows.

The platypus lives in the lakes and streams of eastern Australia. It looks like a duck-billed seal and acts like a lizard. Being a mammal, the platypus is warm-blooded and has fur. However, it also has some characteristics of a reptile. For example, instead of bearing live young, it lays eggs. Like a lizard, its legs are attached to the side of its body rather than underneath it.

1. What is the best summary of the passage?

   A The platypus is a mammal that shares characteristics with reptiles.

   B The platypus is found in eastern Australia.

   C The platypus, found in Australia, is a mammal that lays eggs and has legs attached to its sides like a reptile.

   D Found in streams and lakes, the platypus is warm-blooded, fur-bearing, and egg-laying.

Answer and Explanation

A states the main idea but is not a summary. **B** and **D** don't include all the important information. *C* is correct.

▶ Practice

Directions: Read the passage, and then answer the question that follows.

On Saturday, at 7:30 A.M., students began gathering in the school parking lot. Many carried home-baked goodies. Others brought pails, soap, sponges, and clothes. The students had formed a committee to raise money for the Tiny Tots Preschool, which has been severely damaged in a fire. With the car wash and bake sale, they hoped to raise funds to replace most of the school's books. By one o'clock, the students were counting their hard-earned money.

1. What is the best summary of the passage?

   A Students brought food and cleaning supplies to the car wash and bake sale.

   B When a local preschool was damaged in a fire, students held a bake sale and car wash.

   C Students counted their money.

   D The Tiny Tots Preschool lost all of its books.

Reflections in the Store Window Glass, Yüan Lee

Exploring the Theme

Extraordinary occurrences happen in everyone's life. They serve as eye-opening jolts that shock us out of the ordinary and force us to look at the world differently. Sometimes we seek out these experiences, like when we leap off a high diving board or shiver our way through a chilling mystery novel or scary movie. But extraordinary occurrences are not only found in dramatic events. You can find the extraordinary in subtle changes as well. You might step outside one day and it seems—overnight— the tree that you barely noticed the day before has new leaves.

The selections in this unit revel in the feeling of awe that accompanies the extraordinary in the unusual and in the "everyday."

◄ **Critical Viewing** What aspects of this painting make it extraordinary? **[Connect]**

Why Read Literature?

Whenever you read, you have a purpose, or reason. You may start out reading with one purpose in mind and find it has changed halfway through. Or you may read a single work for multiple purposes. Preview three purposes you might set before reading works in this unit.

1 Read for the love of literature.

Did you know that the average person will spend two weeks over his or her lifetime waiting for the traffic light to change? Find out what interesting things happen during a traffic jam in May Swenson's poem **"Southbound on the Freeway,"** page 452.

Did you know that the first lamp was created in 70,000 B.C.? The original purpose of a lamp was to light up dark places and to end peoples' fears of the dark. Although its purpose hasn't changed, sometimes lights can actually cause someone to be afraid. See how lights affect Annie Dillard in the excerpt from her autobiography, *An American Childhood,* on page 424.

2 Read to be entertained.

Blue jays are a lot smarter than you would imagine. Did you know that blue jays' loud cries warn other birds and mammals of approaching predators? Read more about the incredible things blue jays can do in Mark Twain's **"What Stumped the Blue Jays,"** page 438.

If you heard the phrase "Elementary, my dear Watson," you would know immediately that Sherlock Holmes said it. But would you be surprised to know that, although his character says it in movies, he never really said it? Find out what else Holmes has to say in **"The Adventure of the Speckled Band,"** page 462.

3 Read for information.

Many people know that the microscope was invented by Leeuwenhoek, but did you know that he kept his method for making lenses a secret until his death at age ninety? Read about how to use a microscope on page 489.

Take It to the Net

Visit the Web site for online instruction and activities related to each selection in this unit.

www.phschool.com

How to Read Literature

Strategies for Reading Critically

Whenever you read a work that contains an author's ideas or opinions, it is wise to read the work critically. When you read critically, you examine and question the author's ideas, statements, and message to decide how you feel about their quality. Use the following strategies to help you read critically:

1. Recognize the author's purpose.

An author always writes with a particular purpose, or purposes, in mind. Recognizing these purposes will help you to evaluate if the work is successful or not.

- Start by asking why you think the author wrote the piece.

- Determine whether you think the author achieved the purpose or purposes. Support your opinion with evidence from the text.

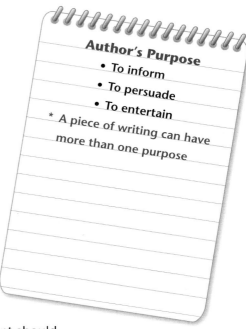

Author's Purpose
- To inform
- To persuade
- To entertain

* A piece of writing can have more than one purpose

2. Evaluate the text.

Once you fully understand a text, you are ready to evaluate it.

- **Check for logical organization.** A story should unfold in a way that is clearly understood. Arguments in persuasive pieces should build on each other and support the main point.

- **Check for consistency.** In fiction, the characters should not act in ways that seem out of keeping with their basic personalities. In a persuasive piece, one supporting argument should not contradict another.

3. Identify the evidence.

Evidence can take many forms, depending on what you are reading. If you are reading a mystery novel, evidence takes the form of clues. If you are reading a science report, evidence could be statistics or data that support the final conclusion.

- When reading fiction, use the evidence you collect to reach conclusions about what will happen next or to figure out the personality traits of a main character.

- In nonfiction, make sure that the author presents evidence that directly supports the conclusions. Make sure that the evidence cannot be interpreted in another way to support a different conclusion.

As you read the selections in this unit, review the reading strategies and look at the notes in the side column. Use the suggestions to interact with the text.

Prepare to Read

from An American Childhood

Take It to the Net

Visit www.phschool.com
for interactive activities
and instruction related to
An American Childhood,
including

- background
- graphic organizers
- literary elements
- reading strategies

Preview

Connecting to the Literature

In this excerpt from *An American Childhood*, Annie Dillard shares an eerie childhood experience that was at first frightening, then humorous. Get ready to share Dillard's experiences by recalling a time when an alarming noise or shadow turned out to be something no more threatening than the wind blowing a curtain.

Background

In this selection, Annie Dillard discovers that the strange motion of light she observes is caused by the reflection of light. When light is reflected, it bounces away from an object that it has run into. The direction of the bounce is determined by the direction of the "hit." The moving lights that Dillard sees are caused by the headlights of cars.

Literary Analysis

Vignette

This excerpt from *An American Childhood* is a **vignette**—a brief story that captures a memorable scene or experience described in precise detail. In the example below, precise details—words and phrases that give very specific information—are italicized.

> A car came *roaring down Edgerton Avenue in front of our house*, *stopped at the corner stop sign*, and passed on *shrieking* as its *engine shifted up the gears*.

As you read this excerpt from *An American Childhood*, use the details to get a clear image in your mind of what the author describes.

Connecting Literary Elements

To make a vignette interesting, some details are presented through metaphor. A **metaphor** is an implied comparison in which one thing is described as if it were another. Although metaphors are often brief, they may also be elaborate, lengthy comparisons. An **extended metaphor** is a comparison that is developed throughout the course of a work. This chart shows one comparison in an extended metaphor from the vignette.

Reading Strategy

Evaluating the Text

When you read, **evaluate** the text by judging how well the writer has communicated ideas. A paragraph or composition has **unity** when all of its parts relate to a single idea. Writing has **coherence** when ideas are organized in a logical order that shows readers the connections and the flow of ideas. Writing has **originality** when it presents ideas in a unique way. You can judge the **relevance** of a selection by determining whether the subject connects to your life or interest.

Use these focus questions to help you evaluate Dillard's vignette:

1. What is the main idea of Dillard's vignette?
2. What details of description add to the originality of Dillard's writing?

Detail from Text

It found the door, wall, and headboard; and it swiped them, charging them with its luminous glance.

What Is Compared

The lights moving through the room to a living thing searching for something

How It Connects

Earlier the light *flattened itself against the wall and slid into the room*. This new comparison adds to the impression of a hunter or predator.

Vocabulary Development

luminous (lo͞o′ mə nəs) *adj.* giving off light; shining; bright (p. 425)

ascent (ə sent′) *n.* the act of rising or climbing (p. 426)

contiguous (kən tig′ yo͞o əs) *adj.* in physical contact; next to (p. 427)

conceivably (kən sē′ və blē) *adv.* possibly (p. 427)

coincidental (kō in′ sə dent′ əl) *adj.* occurring without plan at the same time or place (p. 428)

elongate (i lôŋ′ gāt) *adj.* long and narrow (p. 428)

When I was five, growing up in Pittsburgh in 1950, I would not go to bed willingly because something came into my room. This was a private matter between me and it. If I spoke of it, it would kill me.

Who could breathe as this thing searched for me over the very corners of the room? Who could ever breathe freely again? I lay in the dark.

My sister Amy, two years old, was asleep in the other bed. What did she know? She was innocent of evil. Even at two she composed herself attractively for sleep. She folded the top sheet tidily under her prettily outstretched arm; she laid her perfect head lightly on an unwrinkled pillow, where her thick curls spread evenly in rays like petals. All night long she slept smoothly in a series of pleasant and serene, if artificial-looking, positions, a faint smile on her closed lips, as if she were posing

▲ Critical Viewing
What details of this photograph might be frightening to a young child, like the narrator?
[Analyze]

from

An American Childhood

Annie Dillard

for an ad for sheets. There was no messiness in her, no rough-ness for things to cling to, only a charming and charmed inno-cence that seemed then to protect her, an innocence I needed but couldn't muster. Since Amy was asleep, furthermore, and since when I needed someone most I was afraid to stir enough to wake her, she was useless.

I lay alone and was almost asleep when the thing entered the room by flattening itself against the open door and sliding in. It was a transparent, <u>luminous</u> oblong. I could see the door whiten at its touch; I could see the blue wall turn pale where it raced over it, and see the maple headboard of Amy's bed glow. It was a swift spirit; it was an awareness. It made noise. It had two joined parts, a head and a tail, like a Chinese dragon. It found the door, wall, and headboard; and it swiped them, charging them with its luminous glance. After its fleet, searching passage, things looked the same, but weren't.

luminous (loo' mə nəs) *adj.* giving off light; shining; bright

✓ **Reading Check**

What frightens the narrator?

I dared not blink or breathe; I tried to hush my whooping blood. If it found another awareness, it would destroy it.

Every night before it got to me it gave up. It hit my wall's corner and couldn't get past. It shrank completely into itself and vanished like a cobra down a hole. I heard the rising roar it made when it died or left. I still couldn't breathe. I knew—it was the worst fact I knew, a very hard fact—that it could return again alive that same night.

Sometimes it came back, sometimes it didn't. Most often, restless, it came back. The light stripe slipped in the door, ran searching over Amy's wall, stopped, stretched lunatic at the first corner, raced wailing toward my wall, and vanished into the second corner with a cry. So I wouldn't go to bed.

It was a passing car whose windshield reflected the corner streetlight outside. I figured it out one night.

Figuring it out was as memorable as the oblong itself. Figuring it out was a long and forced <u>ascent</u> to the very rim of being, to the membrane of skin that both separates and connects the inner life and the outer world. I climbed deliberately from the depths like a diver who releases the monster in his arms and hauls himself hand over hand up an anchor chain till he meets the ocean's sparkling membrane and bursts through it; he sights the sunlit, becalmed hull of his boat, which had bulked so ominously from below.

I recognized the noise it made when it left. That is, the noise it made called to mind, at last, my daytime sensations when a car passed—the sight and noise together. A car came roaring down hushed Edgerton Avenue in front of our house, stopped at the corner stop sign, and passed on shrieking as its engine shifted up the gears. What, precisely, came into the bedroom? A reflection from the car's oblong windshield. Why did it travel in two parts? The window sash split the light and cast a shadow.

Night after night I labored up the same long chain of reasoning, as

ascent (ə sent') *n.* the act of rising or climbing

Literary Analysis
Vignette and Extended Metaphor What comparison does Dillard draw in this passage?

night after night the thing burst into the room where I lay awake
and Amy slept prettily and my loud heart thrashed and I froze.

   There was a world outside my window and <u>contiguous</u> to it.
If I was so all-fired bright, as my parents, who had patently no
basis for comparison, seemed to think, why did I have to keep
learning this same thing over and over? For I had learned it a
summer ago, when men with jackhammers broke up Edgerton
Avenue. I had watched them from the yard; the street came up in
jagged slabs like floes. When I lay to nap, I listened. One restless
afternoon I connected the new noise in my bedroom with the
jackhammer men I had been seeing outside. I understood
abruptly that these worlds met, the outside and the inside. I
traveled the route in my mind: You walked downstairs from here,
and outside from downstairs. "Outside," then, was <u>conceivably</u>
just beyond my windows. It was the same world I reached by
going out the front or the back door. I forced my imagination
yet again over this route.

▲ **Critical Viewing**
Which word best
describes this
photograph of lights in
the night: threatening,
comforting, or useful?
Explain. **[Interpret]**

contiguous (kən tig´ yōō əs)
adj. in physical contact;
near or next to

conceivably (kən sē´ və blē)
adv. possibly

✔**Reading Check**

What is the cause of the
light?

from *An American Childhood* ◆ 427

The world did not have me in mind; it had no mind. It was a <u>coincidental</u> collection of things and people, of items, and I myself was one such item—a child walking up the sidewalk, whom anyone could see or ignore. The things in the world did not necessarily cause my overwhelming feelings; the feelings were inside me, beneath my skin, behind my ribs, within my skull. They were even, to some extent, under my control.

I could be connected to the outer world by reason, if I chose, or I could yield to what amounted to a narrative fiction, to a tale of terror whispered to me by the blood in my ears, a show in light projected on the room's blue walls. As time passed, I learned to amuse myself in bed in the darkened room by entering the fiction deliberately and replacing it by reason deliberately.

When the low roar drew nigh and the oblong slid in the door, I threw my own switches for pleasure. It's coming after me; it's a car outside. It's after me. It's a car. It raced over the wall, lighting it blue wherever it ran; it bumped over Amy's maple headboard in a rush, paused, slithered <u>elongate</u> over the corner, shrank, flew my way, and vanished into itself with a wail. It was a car.

coincidental
(kō in′ sə dent′ əl) *adj.*
occurring without plan at the same time or place

elongate (i lôŋ′ gāt) *adj.*
long and narrow

Annie Dillard

(b. 1945)
This excerpt is from *An American Childhood*, Annie Dillard's memoir about growing up. In it, she describes how her parents fostered her eagerness to explore the world. She also discusses the importance of books in her early life, emphasizing the relationship between reading and life.

An intense, creative writer, Dillard spends many hours carefully choosing and refining her words. Inspired partly by Henry David Thoreau's *Walden*, she spent four seasons living in a rural area of Virginia. There, she kept a journal in which she recorded her observations of nature and humanity. She edited the journal material to create *Pilgrim at Tinker Creek*, which won the 1975 Pulitzer Prize for general nonfiction.

Review and Assess

Thinking About the Selection

1. **Respond:** Do you find Dillard's childhood fears understandable? Explain.

2. **(a) Recall:** Who else is in Dillard's room when the mysterious event occurs? **(b) Compare and Contrast:** Why doesn't Amy react to the event in the same way?

3. **(a) Recall:** What happens to the thing before it reaches Dillard? **(b) Analyze:** Why does Dillard believe it can't find her? **(c) Contrast:** What is the real reason it doesn't reach her?

4. **(a) Recall:** What does Dillard finally figure out is the source of the event? **(b) Paraphrase:** What does this teach her about her place in the world? **(c) Infer:** After she figures out the mystery, Dillard sometimes pretends that she does not know the solution. Why?

5. **Speculate:** Why do you think Dillard chose to relate this particular childhood experience?

Review and Assess

Literary Analysis

Vignette

1. How does the opening line of Dillard's narrative grab a reader's interest?
2. Identify three details Dillard uses to describe the nightly event.
3. Why is this event so memorable to Dillard?

Connecting Literary Elements

4. In the **extended metaphor** she generates, to what does Dillard compare the unknown thing in her room?
5. What qualities of this thing are suggested by the words *swiped*, *charging*, and *glance*?
6. What effect does Dillard's use of this extended metaphor have on your response to the vignette? Explain.

Reading Strategy

Evaluating the Text

7. (a) What is the main idea of Dillard's vignette? (b) To **evaluate** the selection's **unity,** identify three details that contribute to the main idea.
8. Which paragraph maintains the selection's **coherence** during the shift between the description of the mystery and the explanation of it?
9. (a) What details of description add to the **originality** of Dillard's writing? (b) Given the subject, why is originality important to the success of the vignette?
10. What makes this selection relevant to young readers? Explain.
11. Using your answers to 7–10, rate Dillard's vignette in each category below. Use 1 as the lowest score and 5 as the highest. Explain your ratings.

 Unity and Coherence
 Logic
 Originality
 Relevance

Extend Understanding

12. **Science Connection:** Write two questions Dillard might have used to research the source of the light she saw.

Quick Review

A **vignette** is a sketch or brief narrative of a memorable scene. To review vignette, see page 423.

An **extended metaphor** is a metaphor that is developed through several comparisons. To review extended metaphor, see page 423.

When **evaluating the text,** you judge the unity, coherence, originality, and relevance. To review these qualities, see page 423.

 Take It to the Net
www.phschool.com
Take the interactive self-test online to check your understanding of the selection.

Integrate Language Skills

Vocabulary Development Lesson

Word Analysis: Latin Root -lum-

The word *luminous* contains the Latin word root *-lum-*, meaning "light." Something that is *luminous* reflects or produces a steady, glowing light. You will find *-lum-* in the words that follow. Predict the meaning of each word. Then, use a dictionary to check your definitions.

1. luminescence   2. illuminate   3. luminary

Spelling Strategy

Remember this helpful rule: Use *i* before *e* except after *c* or when sounded as *ay* as in *weigh*. Find the spelling error or errors in each sentence, and rewrite the sentences correctly.

1. The child was decieved by the sound of the shriek.
2. No one wants to recieve a visit from a fiend.
3. Her nieghbor's car made the light.

Concept Development: Synonyms or Antonyms

Review the vocabulary list on page 423. Then, decide how each word pair below is related.

On your paper, write **synonyms** for words similar in meaning and **antonyms** for words having opposite meanings.

1. luminous, dark
2. ascent, rise
3. contiguous, separated
4. conceivably, impossibly
5. coincidental, intentional
6. elongate, lengthen

Grammar Lesson

Inverted Sentences

In most English sentences, the subject comes before the verb. An **inverted sentence** is one in which the subject comes after the verb or some part of the predicate.

Writers sometimes invert, or reverse the order of, the subject and verb to draw attention to the subject or to create variety in their writing. Sentences beginning with *there* or *here* are in inverted order.

> **Examples:** There <u>was</u> a <u>world</u> outside my window and contiguous to it.
>
> Up the sidewalk <u>walked</u> a <u>child</u>.

▶ *For more practice, see page R30, Exercise A.*
Practice Identify the subject and verb in each sentence. Tell whether the sentence is inverted.

1. There was no messiness in her.
2. I heard the roar the thing made.
3. Through a window came the light.
4. Pounding against my chest was my heart.
5. A passing car stopped at the corner.

Writing Application Rewrite the following passage, inverting one of the sentences to create variety. Add two inverted sentences of your own.

One day, Paul and his friends discovered something unusual in the gully. A hornets' nest was hanging in a tree. They finally succeeded in knocking the nest down by throwing rocks at it.

W͗G Prentice Hall Writing and Grammar Connection: Chapter 19, Section 4

Writing Lesson

Vignette

Dillard recreates a childhood experience that entertains, gives an insight, and shares a significant moment from her life. Choose a childhood experience that you would like to share with others. Use it to write a vignette.

Prewriting   Choose an experience that is vivid in your memory. Your purpose will affect the way you present details. Look at the chart to see how an incident might be described to fulfill a variety of purposes. Then determine your purpose for your story.

Model: Learning to Ride a 2-wheeler

Purpose	Details to emphasize
To entertain with a humorous story	false starts; how I looked in all that safety equipment; how my sister looked running beside the bike
To show how my sister helped me	My sister yelling encouragement while running alongside; how tough she got when I wanted to quit; the ice pack
To warn about the importance of bike helmets	arguing with my sister over wearing the equipment; the crash that cracked the helmet—but not my head

Drafting   As you write your vignette, describe the experience you have chosen. Provide details that precisely tell your thoughts and feelings and what you saw and heard. Add metaphor to bring your description to life.

Revising   Look for places where you can strengthen details to unify support for your purpose. Eliminate details that distract from the main idea.

W/G Prentice Hall Writing and Grammar Connection: Chapter 4, Sections 1–7

Extension Activities

Listening and Speaking Present an **oral description** of ordinary sounds in ways that make them sound frightening. Follow these steps:

1. Think about the real sound. (*a motor*)
2. Use precise language and words that appeal to the senses. (*It's a loud, growly sound. Gets louder when car revs.*)
3. Use the details you identify in a description for the class. (*A threatening growl grows into an enraged roar!*)

Research and Technology With a group of classmates, prepare a **research report** on light and its various qualities and properties. Use print or online encyclopedias, science textbooks and science teachers. Share your findings with classmates. **[Group Activity]**

 **Take It to the Net**   www.phschool.com

Go online for an additional research activity using the Internet.

As a child, you may have been afraid of the dark. Perhaps you believed that there was a monster under your bed or in your closet. At one time or another, everyone suffers from this kind of irrational fear. We fear things we cannot explain or things we cannot see. Very often, we fear things that exist only in our imaginations.

In the excerpt from *An American Childhood*, Annie Dillard recalls a time when she was afraid to sleep in her bedroom because of a light that she couldn't explain. Until she figured out what caused the light, she was terrified every time she saw it.

Another writer who understands the feeling of being terrified is Stephen King. He makes a living by writing about the things that scare most people—and himself. In this interview with Lesley Stahl for the television news program *60 Minutes*, King talks about his work. As you read the transcript of the interview, notice the descriptions in parentheses. These details describe what you would see on the screen if you were watching the interview on television.

CBS News Archives
from

"Stephen King: His Books, His Life, His Wife"

LESLEY STAHL (CO-HOST): There's hardly anybody in America who hasn't read a Stephen King novel or seen a Stephen King movie. Let's face it, he's the world's best-selling novelist, the most successful horror writer in history. As we reported in February last year, even including entertainers, King is one of the highest paid in the country, earning more than $30 million in a single year. That's all because his mind works this way: A man screams . . .

STEPHEN KING (NOVELIST): . . . and this rat jumps into his mouth and gets halfway down his throat. And if you can imagine, OK, not just the taste of it and the rear legs sort of kicking in air, but the feel of the whiskers way back in your throat as it sort of gobbles away at your soft palate.

STAHL: You know what? I'm completely grossed out. You've accomplished . . .

KING: I'm sorry.

STAHL: No, you're not. That's what you wanted to do.

KING: No . . .

STAHL: Yes, this is . . .

KING: . . . I'm not sorry.

STAHL: Have you ever gone to a psychiatrist?

KING: No. No, I've never gone to a psychiatrist, because I feel like what you do at a psychiatrist is you pay $75, $90 an hour to get rid of your fears, whereas if I write them down, people pay me. It's good.

(footage of Stephen King thrillers; Stephen King working on a computer; Stephen King singing)

STAHL: (Voiceover) Since 1974, people have paid good money for 32 novels, five collections of short stories, nine screenplays and one non-fiction study of horror. Except for his birthday, the Fourth of July and Christmas, King writes at least four hours every day.

> voiceover *n.* voice commenting or narrating off camera, as for a television commercial

KING: The ideas come and they have to be let out. That's all. They just have to be let out.

(footage of King home)

STAHL: (Voiceover) All that stands between those ideas and the rest of the world are these wrought-iron[1] gates. King can afford to live anywhere, but the hometown of horror is Bangor, Maine.

No, this is not happening. This is not happening.

---

1. wrought-iron (rôt′ ī′ ərn) *n.* kind of iron that contains some slag and very little carbon; it is resistant to corrosion, tough, and ductile, and is used in fences, grating, rivets, etc.

KING: Bring me the ball.

(footage of King's Welsh Corgi[2])

STAHL: (Voiceover) A vicious canine beast also lives here.

KING: Oops! He stole the ball!

(footage of Stephen King with Corgi; excerpt from "Cujo")

STAHL: (Voiceover) In Stephen King's world, Welsh Corgis play basketball, and St. Bernards become demons, as in the movie "Cujo." He wants to scare us. But what scares him?

KING: Everything that scares you, everything that scares anybody. That's part of the reason for my success.

---

2. Welsh Corgi (kôr′ gē) *n.* any member of either of two breeds of short-legged dog with a foxlike head and erect ears, originally bred in Wales for herding cattle.

◄ **Critical Viewing**
Does Stephen King, seen here with his wife Tabitha, look like a writer of horror stories? Why or why not? **[Evaluate]**

STAHL: Well, for instance, is it true, or is this kind of part of your humor to tell us that you sleep with a night-light?

KING: So what if it is true? It's not hurting anybody. I tend to keep a night-light on, but, like anybody else—particularly if you're in a strange place—you don't want to stub your toe if you have to go to the bathroom in the night.

STAHL: It's not like anybody else. Trust me.

KING: No, no. It's like anybody else, or else I wouldn't be as successful as I am.

STAHL: Is his story that he sleeps with a night-light . . .

TABITHA KING (STEPHEN'S WIFE): Not true. Not true.

STAHL: Not true.

TABITHA KING: No.

(footage of Tabitha King)

STAHL: (Voiceover) Tabitha King is certain because she and her husband Stephen have been married for 26 years.

TABITHA KING: There's a lot of mythologizing.

STAHL: Yeah, but he . . . he created that.

TABITHA KING: And he encourages it. Yes, he does. He does. He encourages it.

KING: Tabby keeps the monsters away so . . . yeah, it's true. Over the years, you have kept a lot of monsters away.

Connecting Literature and Popular Culture

1. Describe Stephen King's accomplishments.
2. According to the interview, what scares Stephen King?
3. What do you think King would do with the oblong of light that moved around Dillard's room at night in the excerpt from *An American Childhood*?
4. How do you relate to Dillard's childhood fears?
5. Why do you think many people today enjoy stories of mystery, horror, and suspense?

Prepare to Read

What Stumped the Blue Jays ◆ Why Leaves Turn Color in the Fall

 Take It to the Net

Visit www.phschool.com for interactive activities and instruction related to these selections, including

- background
- graphic organizers
- literary elements
- reading strategies

Preview

Connecting to the Literature

In "What Stumped the Blue Jays," Mark Twain gives a humorous fictional account of blue jay behavior. In contrast, Diane Ackerman gives a serious—and factual—account of a natural event in "Why Leaves Turn Color in the Fall." Before reading, think of natural events that have entertained or impressed you.

Background

With blue-gray crests and a foot-long size, blue jays are easy to spot. Their loud, harsh voices also make them easy to hear. Blue jays eat nuts, seeds, and insects. These features of blue jays are reflected in the characters in Mark Twain's fictional account, "What Stumped the Blue Jays."

Literary Analysis

Author's Style

An **author's style** is the way he or she puts ideas into words. When you look at style, consider a writer's use of long or short sentences, level and type of vocabulary, and use of literary devices. Mark Twain's writing is known for these two elements of his style:

- Twain uses **colloquial language (**conversational and informal words) and dialect (the form of a language spoken in a particular region).
- Twain uses **humor,** words and ideas meant to be funny. He often exaggerates a character's traits or a situation to make readers laugh.

As you read, look for these and other qualities that define each author's unique style.

Comparing Literary Works

Even before you read the selections carefully, you will notice a difference between these writers' styles. In contrast to Twain's use of humorous language, Ackerman approaches her subject in a more serious manner. "Why Leaves Turn Color in the Fall" combines scientific and descriptive language to convey ideas. Use these focus questions to help you compare and contrast the writers' styles.

1. What ideas or topics do the two works have in common?
2. In what ways do the two authors use language differently?

Reading Strategy

Recognizing the Author's Purpose

Just as different authors have different styles, two authors may have different **purposes** or reasons for writing about a similar subject. For example, a writer may want to inform, explain, persuade, or entertain. As you read these works, use a chart like this one to determine each author's purpose in writing about nature.

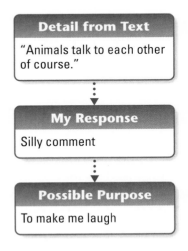

Detail from Text
"Animals talk to each other of course."

My Response
Silly comment

Possible Purpose
To make me laugh

Vocabulary Development

gratification (grat′ ə fi kā′ shən) n. satisfaction (p. 439)

countenance (koun′ tə nəns) n. the look on a person's face that shows his or her nature or feeling (p. 440)

singular (siŋ′ gyə lər) adj. unique; exceptional; extraordinary (p. 440)

guffawed (gə fôd′) v. laughed in a loud and coarse manner (p. 442)

macabre (mə käb′ rə) adj. gruesome; grim and horrible (p. 443)

camouflage (kam′ ə fläzh′) n. disguise or concealment (p. 444)

predisposed (prē′ dis pōzd′) adj. inclined; willing (p. 445)

capricious (kə prē′ shəs) adj. tending to change abruptly and without apparent reason (p. 445)

What Stumped the Blue Jays

MARK TWAIN

Animals talk to each other, of course. There can be no question about that; but I suppose there are very few people who can understand them. I never knew but one man who could. I knew he could, however, because he told me so himself. He was a middle-aged, simple-hearted miner who had lived in a lonely corner of California, among the woods and mountains, a good many years, and had studied the ways of his only neighbors, the beasts and the birds, until he believed he could accurately translate any remark which they made. This was Jim Baker. According to Jim Baker, some animals have only a limited education, and use only very simple words, and scarcely ever a comparison or a flowery figure; whereas, certain other animals have a large vocabulary, a fine command of language and a ready and fluent delivery; consequently these latter talk a great deal; they like it; they are conscious of their talent, and enjoy "showing off." Baker said, that after long and careful observation, he had come to the conclusion that the blue jays were the best talkers he had found among birds and beasts. Said he:—

"There's more *to* a blue jay than any other creature. He has got more moods, and more different kinds of feelings than any other creature; and mind you, whatever a blue jay feels, he can put into language. And no mere commonplace language, either, but rattling, out-and-out book-talk—and bristling with metaphor, too—just bristling! And as for command of language—why *you* never see a blue jay get stuck for a word. No man ever did. They just boil out of him! And another thing: I've noticed a good deal, and there's no bird, or cow, or anything that uses as good grammar as a blue jay. You may say a cat uses good grammar. Well, a cat does—but you let a cat get excited once; you let a cat get to pulling fur with another cat on a shed, nights, and you'll hear grammar that will give you the lockjaw. Ignorant people think it's the *noise* which fighting cats make that is so aggravating, but it ain't so; it's the sickening grammar they use.

Literary Analysis
Author's Style What details in this paragraph make Twain's writing humorous?

Now I've never heard a jay use bad grammar but very seldom; and when they do, they are as ashamed as a human; they shut right down and leave.

"When I first begun to understand jay language correctly, there was a little incident happened here. Seven years ago, the last man in this region but me, moved away. There stands his house,—been empty ever since; a log house, with a plank roof—just one big room, and no more; no ceiling—nothing between the rafters and the floor. Well, one Sunday morning I was sitting out here in front of my cabin, with my cat, taking the sun, and looking at the blue hills, and listening to the leaves rustling so lonely in the trees, and thinking of the home away yonder in the States, and I hadn't heard from in thirteen years, when a blue jay lit on that house, with an acorn in his mouth, and says, 'Hello, I reckon I've struck something.' When he spoke, the acorn dropped out of his mouth and rolled down the roof, of course, but he didn't care; his mind was all on the thing he had struck. It was a knothole in the roof. He cocked his head to one side, shut one eye and put the other one to the hole, like a 'possum looking down a jug; then he glanced up with his bright eyes, gave a wink or two with his wings—which sig-nifies <u>gratification</u>, you under-stand,—and says, 'It looks like a hole, it's located like a hole,—blamed if I don't believe it *is* a hole!'

"Then he cocked his head down and took another look; he glances up perfectly joyful, this time; winks his wings and his tail both, and says, 'O, no, this ain't no fat thing, I reckon! If I ain't in luck!—why it's a perfectly elegant hole!' So he flew down and got that acorn, and fetched it up and dropped it in, and was just tilting his head back, with the heavenliest smile on his face, when all of a sudden he was paralyzed into a listening attitude and that smile faded gradually

gratification
(grat′ ə fi kā′ shən)
n. satisfaction

✓**Reading Check**

What talent does the narrator say Jim Baker has?

▶ **Critical Viewing** Based on this photograph, what "personality" might a blue jay have? **[Draw Conclusions]**

out of his <u>countenance</u> like breath off'n a razor, and the queerest look of surprise took its place. Then he says, 'Why, I didn't hear it fall!' He cocked his eye at the hole again, and took a long look; raised up and shook his head; stepped around to the other side of the hole and took another look from that side; shook his head again. He studied a while, then he just went into the *details*—walked round and round the hole and spied into it from every point of the compass. No use. Now he took a thinking attitude on the comb of the roof and scratched the back of his head with his right foot a minute, and finally says, 'Well, it's too many for *me*, that's certain; must be a mighty long hole; however, I ain't got no time to fool around here, I got to 'tend to business; I reckon it's all right—chance it, anyway.'

"So he flew off and fetched another acorn and dropped it in, and tried to flirt his eye to the hole quick enough to see what become of it, but he was too late. He held his eye there as much as a minute; then he raised up and sighed, and says, 'Consound it, I don't seem to understand this thing, no way; however, I'll tackle her again.' He fetched another acorn, and done his level best to see what become of it, but he couldn't. He says, 'Well, I never struck no such a hole as this, before; I'm of the opinion it's a totally new kind of a hole.' Then he begun to get mad. He held in for a spell, walking up and down the comb of the roof and shaking his head and muttering to himself; but his feelings got the upper hand of him, presently, and he broke loose and cussed himself black in the face. I never see a bird take on so about a little thing. When he got through he walks to the hole and looks in again for half a minute; then he says, 'Well, you're a long hole, and a deep hole, and a mighty <u>singular</u> hole altogether—but I've started in to fill you, if it takes a hundred years!'

"And with that, away he went. You never see a bird work so since you was born. He laid into his work, and the way he hove acorns into that hole for about two hours and a half was one of the most exciting and astonishing spectacles I ever struck. He never stopped to take a look any more—he just hove 'em in and went for more. Well at last he could hardly flop his wings, he was so tuckered out. He comes a drooping down, once more, sweating like an ice-pitcher, drops his acorn in and says, 'Now I guess I've got the bulge on you by this time!' So he bent down for a look. If you'll believe me, when his head come up again he was just pale with rage. He says, 'I've shoveled acorns enough in there to keep the family thirty years, and if I can see a sign of one of 'em I wish I may land in a museum with a belly full of sawdust in two minutes!'

"He just had strength enough to crawl up on to the comb and lean his back agin the chimbly, and then he collected his impressions and begun to free his mind.

"Another jay was going by, and stops to inquire what was up. The sufferer told him the whole circumstance, and says, 'Now yonder's the hole, and if you don't believe me, go and

countenance
(koun′ tə nəns) *n.* the look on a person's face that shows his or her nature or feeling

▶ Critical Viewing
What features does this log house have in common with the log house described on page 439?
[Compare and Contrast]

singular (sin′ gyə lər) *adj.* unique; exceptional; extraordinary

look for yourself.' So this fellow went and looked, and comes back and says, 'How many did you say you put in there?' 'Not any less than two tons,' says the sufferer. The other jay went and looked again. He couldn't seem to make it out, so he raised a yell, and three more jays come. They all examined the hole, they all made the sufferer tell it over again, then they all discussed it, and got off as many leather-headed opinions about it as an average crowd of humans could have done.

"They called in more jays; then more and more, till pretty soon this whole region 'peared to have a blue flush about it. There must have been five thousand of them; and such another jawing and disputing and ripping and cussing, you never heard. Every jay in the whole lot put his eye to the hole and delivered a more chuckle-headed opinion about the mystery than the jay that went there before him. They examined the house all over, too. The door was standing half open, and at last one old jay happened to go and light on it and look in.

Literary Analysis
Author's Style Identify two characteristics of Twain's style in this passage.

**Reading Check**

What question are the blue jays trying to answer?

Of course that knocked the mystery galley-west in a second. There lay the acorns, scattered all over the floor. He flopped his wings and raised a whoop. 'Come here!' he says, 'Come here, everybody; hang'd if this fool hasn't been trying to fill up a house with acorns!' They all came a-swooping down like a blue cloud, and as each fellow lit on the door and took a glance, the whole absurdity of the contract that that first jay had tackled hit him home and he fell over backwards suffocating with laughter, and the next jay took his place and done the same.

"Well, sir, they roosted around here on the house-top and the trees for an hour, and <u>guffawed</u> over that thing like human beings. It ain't any use to tell me a blue jay hasn't got a sense of humor, because I know better. And memory, too. They brought jays here from all over the United States to look down that hole, every summer for three years. Other birds, too. And they could all see the point, except an owl that come from Nova Scotia to visit the Yosemite and he took this thing in on his way back. He said he couldn't see anything funny in it. But then he was a good deal disappointed about Yosemite too."

guffawed (gə fôd´) v. laughed in a loud and coarse manner

Review and Assess

Thinking About the Selection

1. **Respond:** Would you have liked to witness the scene described in the story? Why or why not?

2. **(a) Recall:** According to Jim Baker, what is so special about blue jays? **(b) Infer:** Why does he admire them? **(c) Support:** Give examples to support your opinion.

3. **(a) Recall:** Where does the blue jay drop the acorn? **(b) Analyze Causes and Effects:** Why can't he hear it drop? **(c) Interpret:** Based on this problem, explain the meaning of the title.

4. **(a) Distinguish:** What details in the story reflect facts about blue jays? **(b) Analyze:** What human characteristics does Twain give to blue jays? **(c) Evaluate:** How does using Jim Baker as the narrator make the story more or less entertaining?

5. **(a) Draw Conclusions:** Why do the blue jays keep coming back for years to look at the hole in the roof? **(b) Compare and Contrast:** How is the blue jays' reaction to the situation different from the owl's? **(c) Apply:** In what way do the birds show the different ways people might react to their mistakes?

6. **Evaluate:** Identify one situation from real life in which it is appropriate to laugh at a mistake and one situation in which it is not.

Mark Twain

(1835–1910)

Mark Twain wrote books that have become American classics, such as *The Adventures of Tom Sawyer* and *The Adventures of Huckleberry Finn*. Many of Twain's short stories and yarns are prized for his humorous, sometimes outrageous style.

Although Twain grew up near Hannibal, Missouri, and is most often associated with his books that center on the Mississippi River, his days as a reporter took him all across the country. "What Stumped the Blue Jays" combines Twain's humor with one of his favorite settings—the West.

Why Leaves Turn Color in the Fall

DIANE ACKERMAN

The stealth of autumn catches one unaware. Was that a goldfinch perching in the early September woods, or just the first turning leaf? A red-winged blackbird or a sugar maple closing up shop for the winter? Keen-eyed as leopards, we stand still and squint hard, looking for signs of movement. Early-morning frost sits heavily on the grass, and turns barbed wire into a string of stars. On a distant hill, a small square of yellow appears to be a lighted stage. At last the truth dawns on us: Fall is staggering in, right on schedule, with its baggage of chilly nights, <u>macabre</u> holidays, and spectacular, heart-stoppingly beautiful leaves. Soon the leaves will start cringing on the trees, and roll up in clenched fists before they actually fall off. Dry seedpods will rattle like tiny gourds. But first there will be weeks of gushing color so bright, so pastel, so confettilike, that people will travel up and down the East Coast just to stare at it —a whole season of leaves.

Where do the colors come from? Sunlight rules most living things with its golden edicts.[1] When the days begin to shorten, soon after the summer solstice on June 21, a tree reconsiders its leaves. All summer it feeds them so they can process sunlight, but in the dog days of summer the tree begins pulling nutrients back into its trunk

macabre (mə käb′ rə) *adj.* gruesome; grim and horrible

✔ Reading Check

What question will the writer answer?

---

1. edicts (ē′ dikts′) *n.* authority; order.

and roots, pares down, and gradually chokes off its leaves. A corky layer of cells forms at the leaves' slender petioles,[2] then scars over. Undernourished, the leaves stop producing the pigment chlorophyll,[3] and photosynthesis[4] ceases. Animals can migrate, hibernate, or store food to prepare for winter. But where can a tree go? It survives by dropping its leaves, and by the end of autumn only a few fragile threads of fluid-carrying xylem[5] hold leaves to their stems.

A turning leaf stays partly green at first, then reveals splotches of yellow and red as the chlorophyll gradually breaks down. Dark green seems to stay longest in the veins, outlining and defining them. During the summer, chlorophyll dissolves in the heat and light, but it is also being steadily replaced. In the fall, on the other hand, no new pigment is produced, and so we notice the other colors that were always there, right in the leaf, although chlorophyll's shocking green hid them from view. With their <u>camouflage</u> gone, we see these colors for the first time all year, and marvel, but they were always there, hidden like a vivid secret beneath the hot glowing greens of summer.

The most spectacular range of fall foliage occurs in the northeastern United States and in eastern China, where the leaves are robustly colored thanks in part to a rich climate. European maples don't achieve the same flaming reds as their American relatives, which thrive on cold nights and sunny days. In Europe, the warm, humid weather turns the leaves brown or mildly yellow. Anthocyanin, the pigment that gives apples their red and turns leaves red or red-violet, is produced by sugars that remain in the leaf after the supply of nutrients dwindles. Unlike the carotenoids, which color carrots, squash, and corn, and turn leaves orange and yellow, anthocyanin varies from year to year, depending on the temperature and amount of sunlight. The fiercest colors occur in years when the fall sunlight is strongest and the nights are cool and dry (a state of grace scientists find vexing to forecast). This is also why leaves appear dizzyingly bright and clear on a sunny fall day: The anthocyanin flashes like a marquee.

Not all leaves turn the same color. Elms, weeping willows, and the ancient ginkgo all grow radiant yellow, along with hickories, aspens, bottlebrush buckeyes, cottonweeds, and tall, keening poplars. Basswood turns bronze, birches bright gold. Water-loving maples put on a symphonic display of scarlets. Sumacs turn red, too, as do flowering dogwoods, black gums, and sweet gums. Though some oaks yellow, most turn a pinkish brown. The farmlands also change color, as tepees of cornstalks and bales of shredded-wheat-textured hay stand

camouflage (kam´ ə fläzh´) *n.* disguise or concealment

Literary Analysis
Author's Style In this passage about fall foliage ranges, would you call Ackerman's vocabulary mostly *scientific*, mostly *descriptive*, or mostly *bland*? Why?

---

2. **petioles** (pet´ ē ōls´) *n.* stalks of leaves.
3. **chlorophyll** (klôr´ ə fil´) *n.* green pigment found in plant cells. It is essential for the photosynthetic process.
4. **photosynthesis** (fōt´ ō sin´ thə sis) *n.* the production of organic substances; the transformation of radiant or light energy into chemical form.
5. **xylem** (zī´ ləm) *n.* woody tissue of a plant that carries water and minerals in the stems, roots, and leaves, giving support to softer tissues.

drying in the fields. In some spots, one slope of a hill may be green and the other already in bright color, because the hillside facing south gets more sun and heat than the northern one.

An odd feature of the colors is that they don't seem to have any special purpose. We are <u>predisposed</u> to respond to their beauty, of course. They shimmer with the colors of sunset, spring flowers, the tawny[6] buff of a colt's pretty rump, the shuddering pink of a blush. Animals and flowers color for a reason—adaptation to their environment—but there is no adaptive reason for leaves to color so beautifully in the fall any more than there is for the sky or ocean to be blue. It's just one of the haphazard marvels the planet bestows every year. We find the sizzling colors thrilling, and in a sense they dupe us. Colored like living things, they signal death and disintegration. In time, they will become fragile and, like the body, return to dust. They are as we hope our own fate will be when we die; not to vanish, just to sublime from one beautiful state into another. Though leaves lose their green life, they bloom with urgent colors, as the woods grow mummified day by day, and Nature becomes more carnal, mute, and radiant.

We call the season "fall," from the Old English *feallan*, to fall, which leads back through time to the Indo-European *phol*, which also means to fall. So the word and the idea are both extremely ancient, and haven't really changed since the first of our kind needed a name for fall's leafy abundance. As we say the word, we're reminded of that other Fall, in the Garden of Eden, when fig leaves never withered and scales fell from our eyes. Fall is the time when leaves fall from the trees, just as spring is when flowers spring up, summer is when we simmer, and winter is when we whine from the cold.

Children love to play in piles of leaves, hurling them into the air like confetti, leaping into soft unruly mattresses of them. For children, leaf fall is just one of the odder figments of Nature, like hailstones or snowflakes. Walk down a lane overhung with trees in the never-never land of autumn, and you will forget about time and death, lost in the sheer delicious spill of color. . . .

But how do the colored leaves fall? As a leaf ages, the growth hormone, auxin, fades, and cells at the base of the petiole divide. Two or three rows of small cells, lying at right angles to the axis of the petiole, react with water, then come apart, leaving the petioles hanging on by only a few threads of xylem. A light breeze, and the leaves are airborne. They glide and swoop, rocking in invisible cradles. They are all wing and may flutter from yard to yard on small whirlwinds or updrafts, swiveling as they go. Firmly tethered to earth, we love to see things rise up and fly—soap bubbles, balloons, birds, fall leaves. They remind us that the end of a season is <u>capricious</u>, as is the end of life. We especially like the way leaves rock, careen, and swoop as they fall.

---

6. tawny (tô′ nē) *adj.* brownish-yellow; tan.

predisposed
(prē′ dis pōzd′) *adj.*
inclined; willing

Reading Strategy
Recognizing the Author's Purpose What does this passage about children and leaves suggest that the author's purpose for writing might be?

capricious (kə prē′ shəs)
adj. tending to change abruptly and without apparent reason

✔**Reading Check**

What causes the reds and yellows in autumn leaves?

Why Leaves Turn Color in the Fall ◆ 445

Everyone knows the motion. Pilots sometimes do a maneuver called a "falling leaf," in which the plane loses altitude quickly and on purpose, by slipping first to the right, then to the left. The machine weighs a ton or more, but in one pilot's mind it is a weightless thing, a falling leaf. She has seen the motion before, in the Vermont woods where she played as a child. Below her the trees radiate gold, copper, and red. Leaves are falling, although she can't see them fall, as she falls, swooping down for a closer view.

At last the leaves leave. But first they turn color and thrill us for weeks on end. Then they crunch and crackle underfoot. They *shush*, as children drag their small feet through leaves heaped along the curb. Dark, slimy mats of leaves cling to one's heels after a rain. A damp, stuccolike mortar of semidecayed leaves protects the tender shoots with a roof until spring, and makes a rich humus. An occasional bulge or ripple in the leafy mounds signals a shrew or a field mouse tunneling out of sight. Sometimes one finds in fossil stones the imprint of a leaf, long since disintegrated, whose outlines remind us how detailed, vibrant, and alive are the things of this earth that perish.

Review and Assess

Thinking About the Selection

1. **Respond:** Which interested you more—the scientific details or the author's descriptions and language?

2. **(a) Recall:** Name two facts about leaves that Ackerman states in the selection. **(b) Speculate:** Do you think Ackerman's scientific knowledge about leaves comes from observation or research? Explain.

3. **(a) Recall:** Why do leaves fall off trees? **(b) Apply:** In what way does Ackerman apply this specific event to life in general?

4. **(a) Recall:** According to the author, in what two places are the changing colors of the leaves most spectacular? **(b) Compare and Contrast:** What weather conditions do these two places probably share? **(c) Question:** What questions might a reader who does not live in a place where leaves change color have?

5. **(a) Summarize:** In your own words, summarize Ackerman's explanation of why leaves change color. **(b) Evaluate:** Does a scientific explanation make the changing color of leaves more or less interesting or impressive? Explain.

6. **(a) Identify:** What are three things people do with fall leaves? **(b) Interpret:** What does Ackerman say is the reason people are attracted to falling leaves? **(c) Assess:** Do you agree with her or not? Explain.

Diane Ackerman

(b. 1948)

A native of Waukegan, Illinois, nature writer Diane Ackerman studied psychology, physiology, and English in college, eventually earning two master's degrees and a Ph.D. at Cornell University. She has published eight books of poems and more than ten books of nonfiction, including *A Natural History of the Senses*. Her literary skills and scientific training enable her to describe the natural world in a captivating way.

Review and Assess

Literary Analysis

Author's Style

1. Identify two examples of colloquial or conversational language in Mark Twain's story "What Stumped the Blue Jays."

2. What is one example of exaggeration for humor in "What Stumped the Blue Jays"?

3. Make an organizer like the one shown to analyze Diane Ackerman's writing style. In each box, write an example from her essay of the characteristic indicated by the label.

Comparing Literary Works

4. What ideas or topics do the two works have in common?

5. In what ways do the two authors use language differently?

6. Use a Venn diagram like this one to show how Twain's and Ackerman's styles are alike and how they are different. Consider subject, level of vocabulary, length of sentences, and use of description.

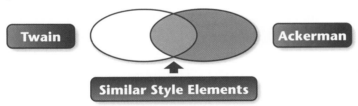

Reading Strategy

Recognizing the Author's Purpose

7. What is Twain's purpose for writing "What Stumped the Blue Jays"?

8. Describe two ways in which Ackerman informs the reader.

Extend Understanding

9. **Apply:** Identify one person to whom you would recommend each selection and explain your choices.

Quick Review

An **author's style** is a combination of the ideas the author expresses and the unique way the author expresses the ideas. To review style, see page 437.

An **author's purpose** is his or her reason for writing, such as to inform, to entertain, or to persuade. To review author's purpose, see page 437.

 Take It to the Net
www.phschool.com
Take the interactive self-test online to check your understanding of these selections.

Integrate Language Skills

Vocabulary Development Lesson

Word Analysis: Latin Root -grat-

The word *gratification* contains the Latin word root *-grat-*, which means "pleasing" or "satisfying." Write the following sentences, filling in the blanks with *gratitude*, *ungrateful*, or *gratified*.

1. Jim Baker was ___?___ that the blue jays used correct grammar.
2. The blue jay was filled with ___?___ for having discovered such a wonderful hole.
3. Only the owl was ___?___ for the privilege of viewing the site of the historic house.

Spelling Strategy

When you add a suffix beginning with a vowel to a word that ends in silent *e*, you drop the final *e*: dispose + -ed = disposed. Add the suffix to each word.

1. pace (-ed) 2. rake (-ing) 3. diverge (-ent)

Concept Development: Synonyms

On your paper, write the word whose meaning is closest to that of the vocabulary word.

1. camouflage: **a.** costume, **b.** forest, **c.** disguise
2. countenance: **a.** look, **b.** composure, **c.** stature
3. predisposed: **a.** wasted, **b.** receptive, **c.** changed
4. guffawed: **a.** groped, **b.** laughed, **c.** smiled
5. capricious: **a.** changeable, **b.** easy, **c.** flimsy
6. macabre: **a.** sad, **b.** grim, **c.** mediocre
7. gratification: **a.** honor, **b.** satisfaction, **c.** tip
8. singular: **a.** alone, **b.** chosen, **c.** unique

Grammar Lesson

Direct and Indirect Objects

A **direct object** is a noun or a pronoun that follows an action verb and answers *whom* or *what*.

> DO
> The leaves showed their <u>colors</u>.
> (Showed what? *colors*)

An **indirect object** is a noun or pronoun that answers *to whom*, *for whom*, *to what*, or *for what* after an action verb. All sentences with an indirect object also have a direct object:

> IO   DO
> Ackerman offers *readers* scientific <u>information</u>.
> (Offers what? *information* Offers information to whom? *readers*)

▶ *For more practice, see page R30, Exercise B.*
Practice On a sheet of paper, underline the indirect object once and the direct object twice in each sentence. Then, tell what question each noun or pronoun answers.

1. The colors give the trees a festive look.
2. Autumn's foliage sends us a message.
3. Ackerman gives readers facts about foliage.
4. She brings people fresh insights about the seasons.
5. Fall offers lovers of beauty a unique opportunity.

Writing Application Write three sentences about some aspect of nature using both direct and indirect objects in each sentence.

W︢G Prentice Hall Writing and Grammar Connection: Chapter 19, Section 5

Writing Lesson

Response to Author's Style and Purpose

Write a response to either Twain's story or to Ackerman's essay in which you describe and explain how you reacted to the author's style and purpose for writing.

Prewriting   Jot down your opinions of the author's style and purpose for writing, as well as details that support your opinions.

Drafting   Write a focus statement, a sentence that states your reaction to the author's style and purpose. Be specific in your reactions—connect your responses to specific references to the text.

Revising   In one color, underline each opinion or point you express. Use a second color to identify a text reference that illustrates your point. If you cannot find one, add some to show the connection between your opinions and the text.

Model: Citing Text References

Ackerman's writing is easy to enjoy and interesting to read because she mixes beautiful descriptions with factual information. In the following example, she follows facts with a poetic description. "Two or three rows of small cells . . . react with water, then come apart, leaving the petioles hanging on by only a few threads of xylem. *A light breeze, and the leaves are airborne. They glide and swoop, rocking in invisible cradles.*"

> The additional quotation from the text demonstrates the poetic descriptions in the work.

WG   *Prentice Hall Writing and Grammar Connection: Chapter 12, Sections 1–7*

Extension Activities

Listening and Speaking   In a group of three, stage an **author's chat show** for the class. One of you will be the host and the others will be the guests, Mark Twain and Diane Ackerman.

1. Jot down questions about the authors' purposes for writing, their views about nature, their unique styles, and so on.
2. Prepare to answer the host's questions.
3. Rehearse the chat show. Have the host pose his or her questions to the two authors, and give the guests an opportunity to answer them.

Research and Technology   Prepare a **nature guide** of birds and trees that are common in your area. Use various resources such as nature guides, print or online encyclopedias, interviews with local park rangers or naturalists, and the Internet. Include photographs or illustrations to help readers picture each bird you describe.

 **Take It to the Net**   www.phschool.com

Go online for an additional research activity using the Internet.

Prepare to Read

Southbound on the Freeway
Los New Yorks ◆ The Story-Teller

 Take It to the Net

Visit www.phschool.com
for interactive activities
and instruction related to
these selections, including

- background
- graphic organizers
- literary elements
- reading strategies

Preview

Connecting to the Literature

In the following poems, the perceptions of the speakers change ordinary people, places, and things into extraordinary ones. Connect to the story by thinking of a time your perceptions of a person or a situation changed, helping you to see something in a fresh new way.

Background

"Southbound on the Freeway" offers a unique viewpoint on cars. Little more than a hundred years ago, cars as we know them did not exist. Today much of our culture is based on cars. Highways crisscross the country, and the economy is based on oil. How would your daily life change without cars?

Literary Analysis

Free Verse

Free verse is poetry that is "free" of traditional structures. It usually does not have regular rhythms, rhyme patterns, or stanzas. Instead, it reflects the natural rhythms of speech. The following lines from "Los New Yorks" are written in free verse.

> I am going home now
> I am settled there with my fruits
> Everything tastes good today

Comparing Literary Works

"Southbound on the Freeway" and "Los New Yorks" are written in free verse. "The Story-Teller" is not free verse—it is structured in stanzas and uses a regular rhyme pattern. Compare and contrast the characteristics of the poems and your response to them. Use these focus questions to guide you:

1. Which poem sounds most like everyday speech? Which least?
2. How does each poem's structure support or help convey meaning?

Reading Strategy

Recognizing Word Origins

English **word origins** can be traced to a variety of sources and influences.

- **Latin and Greek:** Many English words—especially science and math words—come from Latin and Greek roots.
- **Conquest:** When the Normans (who spoke French) conquered England in 1066, they introduced many of their own words into the English language. Many English words in which *ou* is pronounced *oo* as in *school* have French origins.
- **Travel:** English explorers and travelers from countries where languages other than English are spoken have introduced a number of words borrowed from other languages.
- **Invented words:** New words are created to name new things.

As you read, look for words you think may come from other languages. Use a chart like the one shown to record your hunches. Then, use a good dictionary to follow up on your ideas.

Word	Latin/Greek	Conquest	Travel	Invented
freeway				
maracas				
galore				
diagram				
tour				

Vocabulary Development

transparent (trans par′ ənt) *adj.* capable of being seen through; clear (p. 452)

galore (gə lôr′) *adj.* in abundance; plentiful (p.455)

tropical (träp′ ə kəl) *adj.* very hot; sultry (p. 455)

romp (rämp) *n.* lively play or frolic (p. 455)

▲ **Critical Viewing** Judging from the painting, why might an alien mistake cars for Earth's inhabitants? **[Infer]**

SOUTHBOUND ON THE FREEWAY

May Swenson

A tourist came in from Orbitville,
parked in the air, and said:

The creatures of this star
are made of metal and glass.

5   Through the <u>transparent</u> parts
you can see their guts.

transparent (trans par´ ənt)
adj. capable of being
seen through; clear

Their feet are round and roll
on diagrams—or long

measuring tapes—dark
10 with white lines.

They have four eyes.
The two in the back are red.

Sometimes you can see a five-eyed
one, with a red eye turning
15 on the top of his head.
He must be special—

the others respect him,
and go slow,

when he passes, winding
20 among them from behind.

They all hiss as they glide,
like inches, down the marked

tapes. Those soft shapes,
shadowy inside

25 the hard bodies—are they
their guts or their brains?

Literary Analysis
Free Verse What
characteristics of free
verse do you find in
lines 15–18?

May Swenson

(1919–1989)

May Swenson
was born and
educated in
Utah. After
completing
college, she
moved to
New York City, where she
worked as an editor and as
a university lecturer.

Swenson believed that
poetry is based on the
desire to see things as
they are, rather than as
they appear. In "South-
bound on the Freeway,"
however, she portrays how
our culture might appear
to visiting aliens.

Review and Assess

Thinking About the Selection

1. **Respond:** Which images in "Southbound on the Freeway"
   appealed to you most? Why?
2. **(a) Recall:** Where does the "tourist" in "Southbound on the
   Freeway" live? **(b) Infer:** Why does Swenson use this term?
   (c) Deduce: What is the tourist describing?
3. **(a) Recall:** What kinds of creatures are mentioned in the
   poem? **(b) Compare and Contrast:** Compare and contrast the
   different kinds of creatures described.
4. **(a) Recall:** What question does the speaker ask in lines 25–26
   of "Southbound on the Freeway"? **(b) Relate:** What is the
   impact of this question on the reader? **(c) Interpret:** How
   would you answer the speaker's question?

Los New Yorks

Victor Hernández Cruz

New York City—Bird's Eye View, 1920, Joaquín Torres-García, Yale University Art Gallery

In the news that sails through the air
Like the shaking seeds of maracas[1]
I find you out

Suena[2]

5 You don't have to move here
Just stand on the corner
Everything will pass you by
Like a merry-go-round the red
bricks will swing past your eyes
10 They will melt
So   old
will move out by themselves

---

1. **maracas** (mə rä′ kəs) *n.* percussion instruments consisting of
a rattle with loose pebbles in it, which are shaken.
2. **Suena** (swā′ nə) Spanish for "It echoes."

▲ **Critical Viewing**
Do you have the feeling
that in the world of this
painting "Everything will
pass you by"? Explain.
[Assess]

Reading Strategy
Recognizing Word
Origins What language
does the word *maracas*
most likely come from?
What clues tell you what
maracas are?

Suena

I present you the tall skyscrapers
15 as merely huge palm trees with lights
Suena

The roaring of the trains is a fast guaguanco³
dance of the ages
20 Suena
Snow falls
Coconut chips <u>galore</u>
Take the train to Caguas⁴ and the bus is only ten cents
25 to Aguas Buenas⁵

Suena

A <u>tropical</u> wave settled here
And it is pulling the sun
with a <u>romp</u>
30 No one knows what to do

Suena

I am going home now
I am settled there with my fruits
Everything tastes good today
35 Even the ones that are grown here
Taste like they're from outer space
Walk y Suena⁶
Do it strange
Los New Yorks.

galore (gə lôr′) *adj.* in abundance; plentiful

tropical (träp′ ə kəl) *adj.* very hot; sultry

romp (rämp) *n.* lively play or frolic

---

3. **guaguanco** (gwə gwän′ kō) rumba, a dance with a complex rhythm.
4. **Caguas** (kä′ gwäs) city in the east-central region of Puerto Rico.
5. **Aguas Buenas** (ä′ gwäs bwā′ nəs) city in Puerto Rico, northwest of Caguas.
6. **y Suena** (ē swā′ nə) Spanish for "and make it echo."

Victor Hernández Cruz

(b. 1949)

Known as a "Nuyorican poet" (for his style of "New York Puerto Rican" verse), Victor Hernández Cruz was born in Puerto Rico but came to the United States when he was a young boy. Influenced by these two cultures, he examines both in his work. He says, "I compare smells and sounds, I explore the differences." Cruz began publishing his poetry in the San Francisco Bay area in the 1970s. His poetry often reads like music, in which the syllables act as chords and notes, producing catchy rhythms.

Review and Assess

Thinking About the Selection

1. **Respond:** Based on the details in this poem, would you like to visit "Los New Yorks"? Explain.

2. **(a) Recall:** Where is the speaker? **(b) Infer:** What two places is the speaker comparing? **(c) Support:** What evidence is there that the speaker has strong memories of another place?

3. **(a) Recall:** What Spanish word is repeated several times? **(b) Interpret:** What does its repetition indicate the speaker wants you to hear?

The Story - Teller

Mark Van Doren

He talked, and as he talked
Wallpaper came alive;
Suddenly ghosts walked,
And four doors were five;

5   Calendars ran backward,
And maps had mouths;
Ships went tackward[1]
In a great drowse;[2]

Trains climbed trees,
10 And soon dripped down
Like honey of bees
On the cold brick town.

He had wakened a worm
In the world's brain,
15 And nothing stood firm
Until day again.

Inspiration, Daniel Nevins

1. **tackward** (tak´ wərd) *adv.* against the wind.
2. **drowse** (drouz) *n.* sluggishness; doze.

◀ **Critical Viewing**
Does this painting capture the magical quality of the storyteller? Why or why not? **[Evaluate]**

Mark Van Doren

(1894–1972)

Mark Van Doren is best known as the winner of the 1940 Pulitzer Prize for Poetry for his *Collected Poems, 1922–38.* An English professor at Columbia University, he also wrote critical studies of major writers, including William Shakespeare, Henry David Thoreau, and Nathaniel Hawthorne. Among his more than 20 collections of poetry are *Spring Thunder and Other Poems, That Shining Place,* and *Winter Calligraphy.*

Review and Assess

Thinking About the Selection

1. **Respond:** Would you like to hear a story told by the storyteller? Why or why not?
2. **(a) Recall:** Name seven magical things that the storyteller in "The Story-Teller" can do. **(b) Infer:** Why is the storyteller able to do these magic things? **(c) Analyze Cause and Effect:** What happens as a result of what the storyteller does?
3. **(a) Recall:** When will things return to normal?
   (b) Interpret: What is the "worm" referred to in line 13?
   (c) Interpret: What is the "world's brain"? **(d) Analyze:** What is the message of "The Story-Teller"?

Review and Assess

Literary Analysis

Free Verse

1. How do the stanzas of "Los New Yorks" illustrate **free verse** form?
2. Identify two elements of "The Story-Teller" that show the poem is not written in free verse form.
3. On a T-chart like this one, list the characteristics of the two kinds of poetry with examples from the poems.

Free Verse	Traditional Poetry

Comparing Literary Works

4. Using a chart like this one, compare and contrast the poems.

Poem	Rhythm	Rhyme	Line and Stanza Length
"Southbound . . ."			2-line stanzas
"Los New Yorks"	has a musical beat		
"The Story-Teller"		regular *abab* rhyme scheme	

5. Which poem sounds most like everyday speech? Which least?
6. How does each poem's structure support or convey meaning?

Reading Strategy

Recognizing Word Origins

7. **(a)** What are three ways that words have entered the English language? **(b)** What are two ways that words may continue to enter the language? Why?
8. What are two words from the poems that were introduced into English by people traveling?
9. Why do you think it is important to understand the origins of words when you read?

Extend Understanding

10. **Make a Judgment:** Which of these poems has the most important message about contemporary American culture? Explain.

Quick Review

Free verse is poetry that usually does not have regular rhythms, rhyme patterns, or stanzas. It sounds more like conversational speech. To review free verse, see page 451.

Word origins are the sources or influences from which words come into a language. To review English word origins, see page 451.

 Take It to the Net
www.phschool.com
Take the interactive self-test online to check your understanding of these selections.

Integrate Language Skills

Vocabulary Development Lesson

Word Analysis: Latin Prefix *trans-*

The Latin prefix *trans-*, which means "through" or "across," is a key to the meaning of *transparent*, which means "clear enough to see through."

Determine the meaning of the following words with the prefix *trans-*: *transatlantic, transcontinental, transact, transform, transplant*. Then, on your paper, complete the sentences with one of these words.

1. Soon the ugly duckling will ____?____ into a graceful swan.
2. We took a ____?____ road trip.
3. Should we ____?____ this tree in the backyard?
4. Our ____?____ cruise took more than a week.
5. The two businessmen will ____?____ their agreement shortly.

Fluency: Definitions

Write the letter of the definition that matches the numbered vocabulary word.

1. galore
2. romp
3. transparent
4. tropical

a. hot and humid
b. may be seen through
c. noisy play
d. in great amounts

Spelling Strategy

When spelling words that end with *-cal* or *-cle*, remember that nouns usually end with *-cle*. Adjectives usually end with *-cal*. Write the correctly spelled word from each pair.

1. tropicle, tropical
2. icicle, icical
3. bicycle, bicycal
4. medical, medicle
5. historical, historicle
6. musical, musicle

Grammar Lesson

Predicate Adjectives

A **predicate adjective** is an adjective that comes after a linking verb (forms of *to be, taste, appear, smell, look, become, grow, sound, stay, remain*, or *seem*) and describes the subject.

> | | S | LV | PA |
> **Examples:** Their feet are round. . . .
> (The adjective *round* describes the subject *feet*.)
>
> | | S | | LV | PA |
> He must be *special*. . . .
> (The adjective *special* describes the subject *he*.)

▶ *For more practice, see page R31, Exercise A.*
Practice Write these sentences. Underline the predicate adjective. Circle the subject to which it refers.

1. The storyteller is almost magical.
2. The aliens looked strange.
3. The bricks in the city are red.
4. The skyscrapers seem tall.
5. The fresh, ripe fruit tastes good.

Writing Application Write a sentence that uses the idea in each phrase. Make the adjective a predicate adjective in the sentence.

1. talkative storyteller
2. red eyes
3. special creature
4. shadowy shapes
5. huge palm trees

W̶G̶ Prentice Hall Writing and Grammar Connection: Chapter 19, Section 5

Writing Lesson

Pros and Cons of Urban Living

Write a brief essay about the good and bad aspects of city life based on your reading of Cruz's poem and on your own experiences.

Prewriting   Make a T-chart of the pros and cons of urban living. Write positive points on one side of the chart and negative points on the other. Consider the social, economic, cultural, environmental, and geographic advantages and disadvantages.

Drafting   Using your T-chart, first address the disadvantages of city life. Then, address its advantages. Support your opinions with details and descriptions. Finally, identify and explain your preference. Choose words that convey an appropriate tone or attitude toward your subject.

Model: Using Appropriate Tone

One important advantage is access to culture, including *world-famous* museums, concerts by *renowned* musicians, and lectures by *influential* leaders in science, technology, and the arts.

> The words and phrases in italics help create an upbeat tone that reveals the writer's positive attitudes toward living in a city.

Revising   Circle any predicate adjectives. Check for correct grammar usage.

*W*G   *Prentice Hall Writing and Grammar Connection: Chapter 7, Sections 7.2–7.4*

Extension Activities

Listening and Speaking   With a small group, prepare two different **visual aids** for a presentation on New York City. Consider these possibilities:

- **Pie chart:** Show how things compare to each other in size and percentage.

- **Bar graph:** Compare numbers at different times or for different groups or places.

- **Maps:** Show physical relationships between streets or neighborhoods.

To learn more about visual aids, see the Assessment Workshop, p. 515.

Research and Technology   For one of the poets in this group, find and **summarize** two primary sources. Primary sources provide direct, first-hand knowledge of a subject. For example, you may find letters, interviews, or autobiographical writing. You can find these sources using periodical indexes, poetry journals, and Web sites. Summarize the information for the class.

 **Take It to the Net**   www.phschool.com

Go online for an additional research activity using the Internet.

Prepare to Read

The Adventure of the Speckled Band

Preview

Connecting to the Literature

One of the most beloved fictional detectives of all time is Sherlock Holmes. Think of a fictional detective from television or literature that you enjoy—such as Columbo, Harriet the Spy, or Inspector Gadget—and why you like that character. You may find as you read "The Adventure of the Speckled Band" that Holmes—imagined and created by Arthur Conan Doyle more than a century ago—embodies many of the same qualities you enjoy in your favorite characters.

Background

In "The Adventure of the Speckled Band," Sherlock Holmes uses deductive reasoning—analyzing evidence and drawing conclusions from it. This character is famous for making amazing deductions and then explaining them to his less-observant partner, Dr. Watson.

 Take It to the Net

Visit www.phschool.com for interactive activities and instruction related to "The Adventure of the Speckled Band," including
- background
- graphic organizers
- literary elements
- reading strategies

Literary Analysis

Mystery Story

A **mystery story** is a fictional tale about a crime or unexplained event. To solve a mystery, a character uses clues to arrive at a conclusion. In the following passage, clues to the mystery of the speckled band are italicized.

> The left arm of your *jacket is spattered with mud in* no less than *seven places. The marks are* perfectly *fresh.* There is *no vehicle save a dogcart which throws up mud in that way* . . .

From the clues, the conclusion can be drawn that the person wearing the jacket has been riding in a dogcart (a small cart drawn by a single horse). As you read this story, look for other clues that reveal unstated information.

Connecting Literary Elements

The **plot,** or arrangement of events, in a mystery centers around the detective's attempts to uncover clues that solve the mystery. This interaction between the character who has committed the crime and the character who is trying to solve the crime is the **conflict** (a struggle between two opposing forces). In this story, the conflict is resolved when the mystery is solved. As you read, use these focus questions to follow the plot toward its resolution.

1. What is the specific conflict in the mystery?
2. What event provides the resolution of the conflict?

Reading Strategy

Identifying the Evidence

Mystery writers know that readers enjoy trying to guess the solution to the mystery. To solve a mystery, **identify the evidence,** the details that can prove or disprove a conclusion. As you read this mystery, keep an evidence chart like this one to record details that may work together to provide a solution.

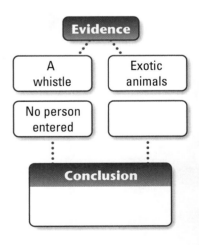

Vocabulary Development

defray (di frā´) *v.* to pay or furnish the money for (p. 465)

manifold (man´ ə fōld´) *adj.* many and varied (p. 465)

morose (mə rōs´) *adj.* gloomy; ill-tempered; sullen (p. 465)

convulsed (kən vulst´) *adj.* taken over by violent, involuntary spasms (p. 468)

imperturbably (im´ pər tur´ bə blē) *adv.* unexcitedly; impassively (p. 472)

reverie (rev´ ər ē) *n.* daydream (p. 477)

tangible (tan´ jə bəl) *adj.* having form and substance; can be touched or felt by touch (p. 478)

The Adventure of the Speckled Band

SIR ARTHUR CONAN DOYLE

On glancing over my notes of the seventy odd cases in which I have during the last eight years studied the methods of my friend Sherlock Holmes, I find many tragic, some comic, a large number merely strange, but none commonplace; for, working as he did rather for the love of his art than for the acquirement of wealth, he refused to associate himself with any investigation which did not tend towards the unusual, and even the fantastic. Of all these varied cases, however, I cannot recall any which presented more singular features than that which was associated with the well-known Surrey family of the Roylotts of Stoke Moran.

The events in question occurred in the early days of my association with Holmes when we were sharing rooms as bachelors in Baker Street. It is possible that I might have placed them upon record before but a promise of secrecy was made at the time, from which I have only been freed during the last month by the untimely death of the lady to whom the pledge was given. It is perhaps as well that the facts should now come to light, for I have reasons to know that there are widespread rumors as to the death of Dr. Grimesby Roylott which tend to make the matter even more terrible than the truth.

It was early in April in the year 1883 that I woke one morning to find Sherlock Holmes standing, fully dressed, by the side of my bed. He was a late riser, as a rule, and as the clock on the mantelpiece showed me that it was only a quarter past seven, I blinked up at him in some surprise, and perhaps just a little resentment, for I was myself regular in my habits.

"Very sorry to wake you up, Watson," said he, "but it's the common lot this morning. Mrs. Hudson has been awakened, she retorted upon me, and I on you."

"What is it, then—a fire?"

"No; a client. It seems that a young lady has arrived in a considerable state of excitement who insists upon seeing me. She is waiting now in the sitting room. Now, when young ladies wander about the metropolis at this hour of the morning, and get sleepy people up out of their beds, I presume that it is something very pressing which they have to communicate. Should it prove to be an interesting case, you would, I am sure, wish to follow it from the outset. I thought, at any rate, that I should call you and give you the chance."

"My dear fellow, I would not miss it for anything."

I had no keener pleasure than in following Holmes in his professional investigations, and in admiring the rapid deductions, as swift as intuitions, and yet always founded on a logical basis, with which he unraveled the problems which were submitted to him. I rapidly threw on my clothes and was ready in a few minutes to accompany my friend down to the sitting room. A lady dressed in black and heavily veiled, who had been sitting in the window, rose as we entered.

"Good morning, madam," said Holmes cheerily. "My name is Sherlock Holmes. This is my intimate friend and associate, Dr. Watson, before whom you can speak as freely as before myself. Ha! I am glad to see that Mrs. Hudson has had the good sense to light the fire. Pray draw up to it, and I shall order you a cup of hot coffee, for I observe that you are shivering."

◀ **Critical Viewing** What details indicate that the man is searching for clues? **[Analyze]**

Literary Analysis
Mystery Story Which character will be the one to analyze clues?

✔**Reading Check**

Why are Holmes and Watson awake at an early hour?

"It is not cold which makes me shiver," said the woman in a low voice, changing her seat as requested.

"What, then?"

"It is fear, Mr. Holmes. It is terror." She raised her veil as she spoke, and we could see that she was indeed in a pitiable state of agitation, her face all drawn and gray, with restless, frightened eyes, like those of some hunted animal. Her features and figure were those of a woman of thirty, but her hair was shot with premature gray, and her expression was weary and haggard. Sherlock Holmes ran her over with one of his quick, all-comprehensive glances.

"You must not fear," said he soothingly, bending forward and patting her forearm. "We shall soon set matters right, I have no doubt. You have come in by train this morning, I see."

"You know me, then?"

"No, but I observe the second half of a return ticket in the palm of your left glove. You must have started early, and yet you had a good drive in a dogcart[1] along heavy roads, before you reached the station."

The lady gave a violent start and stared in bewilderment at my companion.

"There is no mystery, my dear madam," said he, smiling. "The left arm of your jacket is spattered with mud in no less than seven places. The marks are perfectly fresh. There is no vehicle save a dogcart which throws up mud in that way, and then only when you sit on the left-hand side of the driver."

Reading Strategy
Identifying the Evidence
What evidence does Holmes use to draw conclusions about the means of transportation taken by the woman?

"Whatever your reasons may be, you are perfectly correct," said she. "I started from home before six, reached Leatherhead at twenty past, and came in by the first train to Waterloo. Sir, I can stand this strain no longer; I shall go mad if it continues. I have no one to turn to—none, save only one, who cares for me, and he, poor fellow, can be of little aid. I have heard of you, Mr. Holmes. I have heard of you from Mrs. Farintosh, whom you helped in the hour of her sore need. It was from her that I had your address. Oh, sir, do you not think that you could help me, too, and at least throw a little light through the dense darkness which surrounds me? At present it is out of my power to reward you for your service, but in a month or six weeks I shall be married, with the control of my own income, and then at least you shall not find me ungrateful."

Holmes turned to his desk and, unlocking it, drew out a small case book, which he consulted.

"Farintosh," said he. "Ah yes, I recall the case; it

---

1. **dogcart** small horse-drawn carriage with seats arranged back-to-back.

was concerned with an opal tiara. I think it was before your time, Watson. I can only say, madam, that I shall be happy to devote the same care to your case as I did to that of your friend. As to reward, my profession is its own reward; but you are at liberty to <u>defray</u> whatever expenses I may be put to, at the time which suits you best. And now I beg that you will lay before us everything that may help us in forming an opinion upon the matter."

"Alas!" replied our visitor, "the very horror of my situation lies in the fact that my fears are so vague, and my suspicions depend so entirely upon small points, which might seem trivial to another, that even he to whom of all others I have a right to look for help and advice looks upon all that I tell him about it as fancy. He does not say so, but I can read it from his soothing answers and averted eyes. But I have heard, Mr. Holmes, that you can see deeply into the <u>manifold</u> wickedness of the human heart. You may advise me how to walk amid the dangers which encompass me."

"I am all attention, madam."

"My name is Helen Stoner, and I am living with my stepfather, who is the last survivor of one of the oldest Saxon families in England: the Roylotts of Stoke Moran, on the western border of Surrey."

Holmes nodded his head. "The name is familiar to me," said he.

"The family was at one time among the richest in England, and the estates extended over the borders into Berkshire in the north, and Hampshire in the west. In the last century, however, four successive heirs were of a dissolute and wasteful disposition, and the family ruin was eventually completed by a gambler in the days of the Regency. Nothing was left save a few acres of ground, and the two-hundred-year-old house, which is itself crushed under a heavy mortgage. The last squire dragged out his existence there, living the horrible life of an aristocratic pauper; but his only son, my stepfather, seeing that he must adapt himself to the new conditions, obtained an advance from a relative, which enabled him to take a medical degree and went out to Calcutta, where, by his professional skill and his force of character, he established a large practice. In a fit of anger, however, caused by some robberies which had been perpetrated in the house, he beat his native butler to death and narrowly escaped a capital sentence. As it was, he suffered a long term of imprisonment and afterwards returned to England a <u>morose</u> and disappointed man.

◀ **Critical Viewing** What can you tell about the characters of Helen Stoner, Holmes, and Watson based on this illustration? **[Infer]**

defray (di frā´) *v.* to pay or furnish the money for

manifold (man´ ə fōld´) *adj.* many and varied

Reading Strategy
Identifying the Evidence
What clues do you find in this paragraph about the family?

morose (mə rōs´) *adj.* gloomy; ill-tempered; sullen

**Reading Check**

Why doesn't Helen Stoner ask anyone else but Holmes for help?

The Adventure of the Speckled Band ◆ 465

"When Dr. Roylott was in India he married my mother, Mrs. Stoner, the young widow of Major-General Stoner, of the Bengal Artillery. My sister Julia and I were twins, and we were only two years old at the time of my mother's remarriage. She had a considerable sum of money—not less than £1000² a year—and this she bequeathed to Dr. Roylott entirely while we resided with him, with a provision that a certain annual sum should be allowed to each of us in the event of our marriage. Shortly after our return to England my mother died—she was killed eight years ago in a railway accident near Crewe. Dr. Roylott then abandoned his attempts to establish himself in practice in London and took us to live with him in the old ancestral house at Stoke Moran. The money which my mother had left was enough for all our wants, and there seemed to be no obstacle to our happiness.

"But a terrible change came over our step-father about this time. Instead of making friends and exchanging visits with our neighbors, who had at first been overjoyed to see a Roylott of Stoke Moran back in the old family seat, he shut himself up in his house and seldom came out save to indulge in ferocious quarrels with who ever might cross his path. Violence of temper approaching to mania has been hereditary in the men of the family, and in my stepfather's case it had, I believe, been intensified by his long residence in the tropics. A series of disgraceful brawls took place, two of which ended in the police court, until at last he became the terror of the village, and the folks would fly at his approach, for he is a man of immense strength, and absolutely uncontrollable in his anger.

"Last week he hurled the local blacksmith over a parapet into a stream, and it was only by paying over all the money which I could gather together that I was able to avert another public exposure. He had no friends at all save the wandering gypsies, and he would give these vagabonds leave to encamp upon the few acres of bramble-covered land which represent the family estate, and would accept in return the hospitality of their tents, wandering away with them sometimes for weeks on end. He has a passion

▲ Critical Viewing
Which event in Roylott's life does this illustration depict? [Connect]

---

2. **£1000** one thousand pounds; £ is the symbol for pound or pounds, the British unit of money.

also for Indian animals, which are sent over to him by a corre-spondent, and he has at this moment a cheetah and a baboon, which wander freely over his grounds and are feared by the vil-lagers almost as much as is their master.

"You can imagine from what I say that my poor sister Julia and I had no great pleasure in our lives. No servant would stay with us, and for a long time we did all the work of the house. She was but thirty at the time of her death, and yet her hair had already begun to whiten, even as mine has."

"Your sister is dead, then?"

"She died just two years ago, and it is of her death that I wish to speak to you. You can understand that, living the life which I have described, we were little likely to see anyone of our own age and position. We had, however, an aunt, my mother's maiden sister, Miss Honoria Westphail, who lives near Harrow, and we were occasionally allowed to pay short visits at this lady's house. Julia went there at Christmas two years ago, and met there a major in the Marines, to whom she became engaged. My stepfather learned of the engagement when my sister returned and offered no objec-tion to the marriage; but within a fortnight of the day which had been fixed for the wedding, the terrible event occurred which has deprived me of my only companion."

Sherlock Holmes had been leaning back in his chair with his eyes closed and his head sunk in a cushion, but he half opened his lids now and glanced across at his visitor.

"Pray be precise as to details," said he.

"It is easy for me to be so, for every event of that dreadful time is seared into my memory. The manor house is, as I have already said, very old, and only one wing is now inhabited. The bedrooms in this wing are on the ground floor, the sitting rooms being in the central block of the buildings. Of these bedrooms the first is Dr. Roylott's, the second my sister's, and the third my own. There is no communication between them, but they all open out into the same corridor. Do I make myself plain?"

"Perfectly so."

"The windows of the three rooms open out upon the lawn. That fatal night Dr. Roylott had gone to his room early, though we knew that he had not retired to rest, for my sister was troubled by the smell of the strong Indian cigars which it was his custom to smoke. She left her room, therefore, and came into mine, where she sat for some time, chatting about her approaching wedding. At eleven o'clock she rose to leave me, but she paused at the door and looked back.

"'Tell me, Helen,' said she, 'have you ever heard anyone whistle in the dead of the night?'

"'Never,' said I.

Reading Strategy
Identifying the Evidence
What evidence points the finger of suspicion at Dr. Roylott?

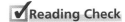Reading Check

Whose death does Helen Stoner want to investigate?

"'I suppose that you could not possibly whistle, yourself, in your sleep?'

"'Certainly not. But why?'

"'Because during the last few nights I have always, about three in the morning, heard a low, clear whistle. I am a light sleeper, and it has awakened me. I cannot tell where it came from—perhaps from the next room, perhaps from the lawn. I thought that I would just ask you whether you had heard it.'

"'No, I have not. It must be the gypsies in the plantation.'

"'Very likely. And yet if it were on the lawn, I wonder that you did not hear it also.'

"'Ah, but I sleep more heavily than you.'

"'Well, it is of no great consequence, at any rate.' She smiled back at me, closed my door, and a few moments later I heard her key turn in the lock."

"Indeed," said Holmes. "Was it your custom always to lock yourselves in at night?"

"Always."

"And why?"

"I think that I mentioned to you that the doctor kept a cheetah and a baboon. We had no feeling of security unless our doors were locked."

"Quite so. Pray proceed with your statement."

"I could not sleep that night. A vague feeling of impending misfortune impressed me. My sister and I, you will recollect, were twins, and you know how subtle are the links which bind two souls which are so closely allied. It was a wild night. The wind was howling outside, and the rain was beating and splashing against the windows. Suddenly, amid all the hubbub of the gale, there burst forth the wild scream of a terrified woman. I knew that it was my sister's voice. I sprang from my bed, wrapped a shawl round me, and rushed into the corridor. As I opened my door I seemed to hear a low whistle, such as my sister described, and a few moments later a clanging sound, as if a mass of metal had fallen. As I ran down the passage, my sister's door was unlocked, and revolved slowly upon its hinges. I stared at it horror-stricken, not knowing what was about to issue from it. By the light of the corridor lamp I saw my sister appear at the opening, her face blanched with terror, her hands groping for help, her whole figure swaying to and fro like that of a drunkard. I ran to her and threw my arms round her, but at that moment her knees seemed to give way and she fell to the ground. She writhed as one who is in terrible pain, and her limbs were dreadfully convulsed. At first I thought that she had not recognized me, but as I bent over her she suddenly shrieked out in a voice which I shall never forget, 'Oh, Helen! It was the band! The speckled band!' There was

---

Reading Strategy
Identifying the Evidence
How can you tell that Holmes considers the whistle a significant piece of evidence?

convulsed (kən vulst′) *adj.*
taken over by violent, involuntary spasms

something else which she would fain have said, and she stabbed with her finger into the air in the direction of the doctor's room, but a fresh convulsion seized her and choked her words. I rushed out, calling loudly for my stepfather, and I met him hastening from his room in his dressing gown. When he reached my sister's side she was unconscious, and though he poured brandy down her throat and sent for medical aid from the village, all efforts were in vain, for she slowly sank and died without having recovered her consciousness. Such was the dreadful end of my beloved sister."

"One moment," said Holmes; "are you sure about this whistle and metallic sound? Could you swear to it?"

"That was what the county coroner asked me at the inquiry. It is my strong impression that I heard it, and yet, among the crash of the gale and the creaking of an old house, I may possibly have been deceived."

"Was your sister dressed?"

"No, she was in her nightdress. In her right hand was found the charred stump of a match, and in her left a matchbox."

"Showing that she had struck a light and looked about her when the alarm took place. That is important. And what conclusions did the coroner come to?"

"He investigated the case with great care, for Dr. Roylott's conduct had long been notorious in the county, but he was unable to find any satisfactory cause of death. My evidence showed that the door had been fastened upon the inner side, and the windows were blocked by old-fashioned shutters with broad iron bars, which were secured every night. The walls were carefully sounded, and were shown to be quite solid all round, and the flooring was also thoroughly examined, with the same result. The chimney is wide, but is barred up by four large staples. It is certain, therefore, that my sister was quite alone when she met her end. Besides, there were no marks of any violence upon her."

"How about poison?"

"The doctors examined her for it, but without success."

"What do you think that this unfortunate lady died of, then?"

"It is my belief that she died of pure fear and nervous shock, though what it was that frightened her I cannot imagine."

"Were there gypsies in the plantation at the time?"

"Yes, there are nearly always some there."

▲ Critical Viewing
How well does this illustration convey Julia Stoner's face, "blanched with terror"? [Evaluate]

Literary Analysis
Mystery Story and Plot
What information do you know so far about the basic situation of this mystery story?

Reading Check
What does the coroner say about Julia's death?

"Ah, and what did you gather from this allusion to a band—a speckled band?"

"Sometimes I have thought that it was merely the wild talk of delirium, sometimes that it may have referred to some band of people, perhaps to these very gypsies in the plantation. I do not know whether the spotted handkerchiefs which so many of them wear over their heads might have suggested the strange adjective which she used."

Holmes shook his head like a man who is far from being satisfied.

"These are very deep waters," said he; "pray go on with your narrative."

"Two years have passed since then, and my life has been until lately lonelier than ever. A month ago, however, a dear friend, whom I have known for many years, has done me the honor to ask my hand in marriage. His name is Armitage—Percy Armitage—the second son of Mr. Armitage, of Crane Water, near Reading. My stepfather has offered no opposition to the match, and we are to be married in the course of the spring. Two days ago some repairs were started in the west wing of the building, and my bedroom wall has been pierced, so that I have had to move into the chamber in which my sister died, and to sleep in the very bed in which she slept. Imagine, then, my thrill of terror when last night, as I lay awake, thinking over her terrible fate, I suddenly heard in the silence of the night the low whistle which had been the herald of her own death. I sprang up and lit the lamp, but nothing was to be seen in the room. I was too shaken to go to bed again, however, so I dressed, and as soon as it was daylight I slipped down, got a dogcart at the Crown Inn, which is opposite, and drove to Leatherhead, from whence I have come on this morning with the one object of seeing you and asking your advice."

"You have done wisely," said my friend. "But have you told me all?"

"Yes, all."

"Miss Roylott, you have not. You are screening your stepfather."

"Why, what do you mean?"

For answer Holmes pushed back the frill of black lace which fringed the hand that lay upon our visitor's knee. Five little livid spots, the marks of four fingers and a thumb, were printed upon the white wrist.

"You have been cruelly used," said Holmes.

The lady colored deeply and covered over her injured wrist. "He is a hard man," she said, "and perhaps he hardly knows his own strength."

There was a long silence, during which Holmes leaned his chin upon his hands and stared into the crackling fire.

"This is a very deep business," he said at last. "There are a

Literary Analysis
Mystery Story Which of Holmes's ideas about the speckled band, if any, do you think might help solve the mystery? Why?

Literary Analysis
Mystery Story and Conflict In what way does Helen Stoner's situation intensify the conflict in the mystery?

thousand details which I should desire to know before I decide upon our course of action. Yet we have not a moment to lose. If we were to come to Stoke Moran today, would it be possible for us to look over these rooms without the knowledge of your stepfather?"

"As it happens, he spoke of coming into town today upon some most important business. It is probable that he will be away all day and that there would be nothing to disturb you. We have a house-keeper now, but I could easily get her out of the way."

"Excellent. You are not averse to this trip, Watson?"

"By no means."

"Then we shall both come. What are you going to do yourself?"

"I have one or two things which I would wish to do now that I am in town. But I shall return by the twelve o'clock train, so as to be there in time for your coming."

"And you may expect us early in the afternoon. I have myself some small business matters to attend to. Will you not wait and breakfast?"

"No, I must go. My heart is lightened already since I have confided my trouble to you. I shall look forward to seeing you again this afternoon." She dropped her thick black veil over her face and glided from the room.

"And what do you think of it all, Watson?" asked Sherlock Holmes, leaning back in his chair.

"It seems to me to be a most dark and sinister business."

"Dark enough and sinister enough."

"Yet if the lady is correct in saying that the flooring and walls are sound, and that the door, window, and chimney are impassable, then her sister must have been undoubtedly alone when she met her mysterious end."

"What becomes, then, of these nocturnal whistles, and what of the very peculiar words of the dying woman?"

"I cannot think."

"When you combine the ideas of whistles at night, the presence of a band of gypsies who are on intimate terms with this old doctor, the fact that we have every reason to believe that the doctor has an interest in preventing his stepdaughter's marriage, the dying allusion to a band, and, finally, the fact that Miss Helen Stoner heard a metallic clang, which might have been caused by one of those metal bars that secured the shutters, falling back into its place, I think that there is good ground to think that the mystery may be cleared along those lines."

"But what, then, did the gypsies do?"

"I cannot imagine."

"I see many objections to any such theory."

"And so do I. It is precisely for that reason that we are going to Stoke Moran this day. I want to see whether the objections are fatal, or if they may be explained away. But what in the name of the devil!"

Reading Strategy
Identifying the Evidence
What clues has Holmes already decided are important pieces of evidence?

✔**Reading Check**

Why does Helen Stoner feel she may be in danger?

The ejaculation had been drawn from my companion by the fact that our door had been suddenly dashed open, and that a huge man had framed himself in the aperture. His costume was a peculiar mixture of the professional and of the agricultural, having a black top hat, a long frock coat, and a pair of high gaiters,[3] with a hunting crop swinging in his hand. So tall was he that his hat actually brushed the crossbar of the doorway, and his breadth seemed to span it across from side to side. A large face, seared with a thousand wrinkles, burned yellow with the sun, and marked with every evil passion, was turned from one to the other of us, while his deep-set, bile-shot eyes, and his high, thin, fleshless nose, gave him somewhat the resemblance to a fierce old bird of prey.

"Which of you is Holmes?" asked this apparition.

"My name, sir; but you have the advantage of me," said my companion quietly.

"I am Dr. Grimesby Roylott, of Stoke Moran."

"Indeed, Doctor," said Holmes blandly. "Pray take a seat."

"I will do nothing of the kind. My stepdaughter has been here. I have traced her. What has she been saying to you?"

"It is a little cold for the time of the year," said Holmes.

"What has she been saying to you?" screamed the old man furiously.

"But I have heard that the crocuses promise well," continued my companion imperturbably.

"Ha! You put me off, do you?" said our new visitor, taking a step forward and shaking his hunting crop. "I know you, you scoundrel! I have heard of you before. You are Holmes, the meddler."

My friend smiled.

"Holmes, the busybody!"

His smile broadened.

"Holmes, the Scotland Yard Jack-in-office!"

Holmes chuckled heartily. "Your conversation is most entertaining," said he. "When you go out close the door, for there is a decided draft."

"I will go when I have said my say. Don't you dare to meddle with my affairs. I know that Miss Stoner has been here. I traced her! I am a dangerous man to fall foul of! See here." He stepped swiftly forward, seized the poker, and bent it into a curve with his huge brown hands.

"See that you keep yourself out of my grip," he snarled, and hurling the twisted poker into the fireplace he strode out of the room.

"He seems a very amiable person," said Holmes, laughing. "I am not quite so bulky, but if he had remained I might have shown him that my grip was not much more feeble than his own." As he spoke he picked up the steel poker and, with a sudden effort, straightened it out again.

imperturbably
(im′ pər tʉr′ bə blē) *adv.*
unexcitedly; impassively

---

3. gaiters (gāt′ ərz) *n.* cloth or leather coverings for the ankles and calves of legs

"Fancy his having the insolence to confound me with[4] the official detective force! This incident gives zest to our investigation, however, and I only trust that our little friend will not suffer from her imprudence in allowing this brute to trace her. And now, Watson, we shall order breakfast, and afterwards I shall walk down to Doctors' Commons, where I hope to get some data which may help us in this matter."

It was nearly one o'clock when Sherlock Holmes returned from his excursion. He held in his hand a sheet of blue paper, scrawled over with notes and figures.

"I have seen the will of the deceased wife," said he. "To determine its exact meaning I have been obliged to work out the present prices of the investments with which it is concerned. The total income, which at the time of the wife's death was little short of £1100, is now, through the fall in agricultural prices, not more than £750. Each daughter can claim an income of £250, in case of marriage. It is evident, therefore, that if both girls had married, this beauty would have had a mere pittance,[5] while even one of them would cripple him to a very serious extent. My morning's work has not been wasted, since it has proved that he has the very strongest motives for standing in the way of anything of the sort. And now, Watson, this is too serious for dawdling, especially as the old man is aware that we are interesting ourselves in his affairs; so if you are ready, we shall call a cab and drive to Waterloo. I should be very much obliged if you would slip your revolver into your pocket. An Eley's No. 2 is an excellent argument with gentlemen who can twist steel pokers into knots. That and a toothbrush are, I think, all that we need."

At Waterloo we were fortunate in catching a train for Leatherhead, where we hired a trap at the station inn and drove for four or five miles through the lovely Surrey lanes. It was a perfect day, with a bright sun and a few fleecy clouds in the heavens. The trees and wayside hedges were just throwing out their first green shoots, and the air was full of the pleasant smell of the moist earth. To me at least there was a strange contrast between the sweet promise of the spring and this sinister quest upon which we were engaged. My companion sat in the front of the trap, his arms folded, his hat pulled down over his eyes, and his chin sunk upon his breast, buried in the deepest thought. Suddenly, however, he started, tapped me on the shoulder, and pointed over the meadows.

"Look there!" said he.

A heavily timbered park stretched up in a gentle slope, thickening into a grove at the highest point. From amid the branches there jutted out the gray gables and high rooftop of a very old mansion.

---

4. **confound . . . with** mistake me for.
5. **pittance** (pit´ əns) n. small or barely sufficient allowance of money.

Literary Analysis
Mystery Story Do you think Dr. Roylott will be a formidable foe for Holmes to face? Why or why not?

Reading Strategy
Identifying the Evidence Is this motive by itself evidence of Dr. Roylott's guilt?

✓Reading Check
Which character does not want the girls to get married? Why?

The Adventure of the Speckled Band ◆ 473

"Stoke Moran?" said he.

"Yes, sir, that be the house of Dr. Grimesby Roylott," remarked the driver.

"There is some building going on there," said Holmes; "that is where we are going."

"There's the village," said the driver, pointing to a cluster of roofs some distance to the left; "but if you want to get to the house, you'll find it shorter to get over this stile, and so by the footpath over the fields. There it is, where the lady is walking."

"And the lady, I fancy, is Miss Stoner," observed Holmes, shading his eyes. "Yes, I think we had better do as you suggest."

We got off, paid our fare, and the trap rattled back on its way to Leatherhead.

"I thought it as well," said Holmes as we climbed the stile, "that this fellow should think we had come here as architects, or on some definite business. It may stop his gossip. Good afternoon, Miss Stoner. You see that we have been as good as our word."

Our client of the morning had hurried forward to meet us with a face which spoke her joy. "I have been waiting so eagerly for you," she cried, shaking hands with us warmly. "All has turned out splendidly. Dr. Roylott has gone to town, and it is unlikely that he will be back before evening."

"We have had the pleasure of making the doctor's acquaintance," said Holmes, and in a few words he sketched out what had occurred. Miss Stoner turned white to the lips as she listened.

"Good heavens!" she cried, "he has followed me, then."

"So it appears."

"He is so cunning that I never know when I am safe from him. What will he say when he returns?"

"He must guard himself, for he may find that there is someone more cunning than himself upon his track. You must lock yourself up from him tonight. If he is violent, we shall take you away to your aunt's at Harrow. Now, we must make the best use of our time, so kindly take us at once to the rooms which we are to examine."

The building was of gray, lichen-blotched[6] stone, with a high central portion and two curving wings, like the claws of a crab,

▼ **Critical Viewing**
Which figure in the illustration is Dr. Roylott? How do you know?
[Deduce]

---

6. **lichen-blotched** (lī´ kən blächt) *adj.* covered with patches of fungus.

thrown out on each side. In one of these wings the windows were broken and blocked with wooden boards, while the roof was partly caved in, a picture of ruin. The central portion was in little better repair, but the right-hand block was comparatively modern, and the blinds in the windows, with the blue smoke curling up from the chimneys, showed that this was where the family resided. Some scaffolding had been erected against the end wall, and the stonework had been broken into, but there were no signs of any workmen at the moment of our visit. Holmes walked slowly up and down the ill-trimmed lawn and examined with deep attention the outsides of the windows.

"This, I take it, belongs to the room in which you used to sleep, the center one to your sister's, and the one next to the main building to Dr. Roylott's chamber?"

"Exactly so. But I am now sleeping in the middle one."

"Pending the alterations, as I understand. By the way, there does not seem to be any very pressing need for repairs at that end wall."

"There were none. I believe that it was an excuse to move me from my room."

"Ah! that is suggestive. Now, on the other side of this narrow wing runs the corridor from which these three rooms open. There are windows in it, of course?"

"Yes, but very small ones. Too narrow for anyone to pass through."

"As you both locked your doors at night, your rooms were unapproachable from that side. Now, would you have the kindness to go into your room and bar your shutters?"

Miss Stoner did so, and Holmes, after a careful examination through the open window, endeavored in every way to force the shutter open, but without success. There was no slit through which a knife could be passed to raise the bar. Then with his lens he tested the hinges, but they were of solid iron, built firmly into the massive masonry. "Hum!" said he, scratching his chin in some perplexity. "My theory certainly presents some difficulties. No one could pass through these shutters if they were bolted. Well, we shall see if the inside throws any light upon the matter."

A small side door led into the whitewashed corridor from which the three bedrooms opened. Holmes refused to examine the third chamber, so we passed at once to the second, that in which Miss Stoner was now sleeping, and in which her sister had met with her fate. It was a homely little room, with a low ceiling and a gaping fireplace, after the fashion of old country houses. A brown chest of drawers stood in one corner, a narrow white-counterpaned bed in another, and a dressing table on the left-hand side of the window. These articles, with two small wickerwork chairs, made up all the furniture in the room save for a square of Wilton carpet in the center. The boards round and the paneling of the walls were of brown,

Reading Strategy
Identifying the Evidence
What evidence disproves Holmes's theory that someone might have entered through the window?

Reading Check

What room does Holmes examine first?

worm-eaten oak, so old and discolored that it may have dated from the original building of the house. Holmes drew one of the chairs into a corner and sat silent, while his eyes traveled round and round and up and down, taking in every detail of the apartment.

"Where does that bell communicate with?" he asked at last, pointing to a thick bell-rope which hung down beside the bed, the tassel actually lying upon the pillow.

"It goes to the housekeeper's room."

"It looks newer than the other things?"

"Yes, it was only put there a couple of years ago."

"Your sister asked for it, I suppose?"

"No, I never heard of her using it. We used always to get what we wanted for ourselves."

"Indeed, it seemed unnecessary to put so nice a bell-pull there. You will excuse me for a few minutes while I satisfy myself as to this floor." He threw himself down upon his face with his lens in his hand and crawled swiftly backward and forward, examining minutely the cracks between the boards. Then he did the same with the woodwork with which the chamber was paneled. Finally he walked over to the bed and spent some time in staring at it and in running his eye up and down the wall. Finally he took the bell-rope in his hand and gave it a brisk tug.

"Why, it's a dummy," said he.

"Won't it ring?"

"No, it is not even attached to a wire. This is very interesting. You can see now that it is fastened to a hook just above where the little opening for the ventilator is."

"How very absurd! I never noticed that before!"

"Very strange!" muttered Holmes, pulling at the rope. "There are one or two very singular points about this room. For example, what a fool a builder must be to open a ventilator into another room, when, with the same trouble, he might have communicated with the outside air!"

"That is also quite modern," said the lady.

"Done about the same time as the bell-rope?" remarked Holmes.

"Yes, there were several little changes carried out about that time."

"They seem to have been of a most interesting character—dummy bell-ropes, and ventilators which do not ventilate. With your permission, Miss Stoner, we shall now carry our researches into the inner apartment."

Dr. Grimesby Roylott's chamber was larger than that of his step-daughter, but was as plainly furnished. A camp bed, a small wooden shelf full of books, mostly of a technical character, an armchair beside the bed, a plain wooden chair against the wall, a round table, and a large iron safe were the principal things which met the eye.

Reading Strategy
Identifying the Evidence
What evidence does Holmes find that someone made special adjustments to the room?

Reading Strategy
Identifying the Evidence
What significance do you think the two clues in this passage about changes to the room might have?

Holmes walked slowly round and examined each and all of them with the keenest interest.

"What's in here?" he asked, tapping the safe.

"My stepfather's business papers."

"Oh! you have seen inside, then?"

"Only once, some years ago. I remember that it was full of papers."

"There isn't a cat in it, for example?"

"No. What a strange idea!"

"Well, look at this!" He took up a small saucer of milk which stood on the top of it.

"No; we don't keep a cat. But there is a cheetah and a baboon."

"Ah, yes, of course! Well, a cheetah is just a big cat, and yet a saucer of milk does not go very far in satisfying its wants, I daresay. There is one point which I should wish to determine." He squatted down in front of the wooden chair and examined the seat of it with the greatest attention.

"Thank you. That is quite settled," said he, rising and putting his lens in his pocket. "Hello! Here is something interesting!"

The object which had caught his eye was a small dog lash hung on one corner of the bed. The lash, however, was curled upon itself and tied so as to make a loop of whipcord.

"What do you make of that, Watson?"

"It's a common enough lash. But I don't know why it should be tied."

"That is not quite so common, is it? Ah, me! it's a wicked world, and when a clever man turns his brains to crime it is the worst of all. I think that I have seen enough now, Miss Stoner, and with your permission we shall walk out upon the lawn."

I had never seen my friend's face so grim or his brow so dark as it was when we turned from the scene of this investigation. We had walked several times up and down the lawn, neither Miss Stoner nor myself liking to break in upon his thoughts before he roused himself from his reverie.

"It is very essential, Miss Stoner," said he, "that you should absolutely follow my advice in every respect."

"I shall most certainly do so."

"The matter is too serious for any hesitation. Your life may depend upon your compliance."[7]

"I assure you that I am in your hands."

"In the first place, both my friend and I must spend the night in your room."

Both Miss Stoner and I gazed at him in astonishment.

"Yes, it must be so. Let me explain. I believe that that is the village inn over there?"

"Yes, that is the Crown."

Literary Analysis
Mystery Story and Conflict How does Holmes's statement about the world emphasize the nature of the conflict?

reverie (rev′ ər ē) *n.* daydream

Reading Check

Who will spend the night in Helen Stoner's room?

---

7. **compliance** (kəm plī′ əns) *n.* agreement to a request.

"Very good. Your windows would be visible from there?"

"Certainly."

"You must confine yourself to your room, on pretense of a headache, when your stepfather comes back. Then when you hear him retire for the night, you must open the shutters of your window, undo the hasp,[8] put your lamp there as a signal to us, and then withdraw quietly with everything which you are likely to want into the room which you used to occupy. I have no doubt that, in spite of the repairs, you could manage there for one night."

"Oh, yes, easily."

"The rest you will leave in our hands."

"But what will you do?"

"We shall spend the night in your room, and we shall investigate the cause of this noise which has disturbed you."

"I believe, Mr. Holmes, that you have already made up your mind," said Miss Stoner, laying her hand upon my companion's sleeve.

"Perhaps I have."

"Then, for pity's sake, tell me what was the cause of my sister's death."

"I should prefer to have clearer proofs before I speak."

"You can at least tell me whether my own thought is correct, and if she died from some sudden fright."

"No, I do not think so. I think that there was probably some more tangible cause. And now, Miss Stoner, we must leave you, for if Dr. Roylott returned and saw us our journey would be in vain. Goodbye, and be brave, for if you will do what I have told you, you may rest assured that we shall soon drive away the dangers that threaten you."

Sherlock Holmes and I had no difficulty in engaging a bedroom and sitting room at the Crown Inn. They were on the upper floor, and from our window we could command a view of the avenue gate, and of the inhabited wing of Stoke Moran Manor House. At dusk we saw Dr. Grimesby Roylott drive past, his huge form looming up beside the little figure of the lad who drove him. The boy had some slight difficulty in undoing the heavy iron gates, and we heard the hoarse roar of the doctor's voice and saw the fury with which he shook his clinched fists at him. The trap drove on, and a few minutes later we saw a sudden light spring up among the trees as the lamp was lit in one of the sitting rooms.

▲ **Critical Viewing**
What are the feelings of each character in this picture? **[Infer]**

tangible (tan´ jə bəl) *adj.* having form and substance; can be touched or felt by touch

---

8. **hasp** *n.* hinged metal fastening of a window.

"Do you know, Watson," said Holmes as we sat together in the gathering darkness, "I have really some scruples as to taking you tonight. There is a distinct element of danger."

"Can I be of assistance?"

"Your presence might be invaluable."

"Then I shall certainly come."

"It is very kind of you."

"You speak of danger. You have evidently seen more in these rooms than was visible to me."

"No, but I fancy that I may have deduced a little more. I imagine that you saw all that I did."

"I saw nothing remarkable save the bell-rope, and what purpose that could answer I confess is more than I can imagine."

"You saw the ventilator, too?"

"Yes, but I do not think that it is such a very unusual thing to have a small opening between two rooms. It was so small that a rat could hardly pass through."

"I knew that we should find a ventilator before ever we came to Stoke Moran."

"My dear Holmes!"

"Oh, yes, I did. You remember in her statement she said that her sister could smell Dr. Roylott's cigar. Now, of course that suggested at once that there must be a communication between the two rooms. It could only be a small one, or it would have been remarked upon at the coroner's inquiry. I deduced a ventilator."

"But what harm can there be in that?"

"Well, there is at least a curious coincidence of dates. A ventilator is made, a cord is hung, and a lady who sleeps in the bed dies. Does not that strike you?"

"I cannot as yet see any connection."

"Did you observe anything very peculiar about that bed?"

"No."

"It was clamped to the floor. Did you ever see a bed fastened like that before?"

"I cannot say that I have."

"The lady could not move her bed. It must always be in the same relative position to the ventilator and to the rope—or so we may call it, since it was clearly never meant for a bell-pull."

"Holmes," I cried, "I seem to see dimly what you are hinting at. We are only just in time to prevent some subtle and horrible crime."

"Subtle enough and horrible enough. When a doctor does go wrong he is the first of criminals. He has nerve and he has knowledge. Palmer and Pritchard were among the heads of their profession. This man strikes even deeper, but I think, Watson, that we shall be able to strike deeper still. But we shall have horrors enough before the night is over; for goodness' sake let us have a

Literary Analysis
Mystery Story What effect does potential danger have on the reader's interest in the story?

Reading Strategy
Identifying the Evidence What detail provides evidence that the bell pull is related to the crime?

Reading Check

What details about the room does Holmes point out to Watson?

quiet pipe and turn our minds for a few hours to something more cheerful."

About nine o'clock the light among the trees was extinguished, and all was dark in the direction of the Manor House. Two hours passed slowly away, and then, suddenly, just at the stroke of eleven, a single bright light shone out right in front of us.

"That is our signal," said Holmes, springing to his feet; "it comes from the middle window."

As we passed out he exchanged a few words with the landlord, explaining that we were going on a late visit to an acquaintance, and that it was possible that we might spend the night there. A moment later we were out on the dark road, a chill wind blowing in our faces, and one yellow light twinkling in front of us through the gloom to guide us on our somber errand.

There was little difficulty in entering the grounds; for unrepaired breaches gaped in the old park wall. Making our way among the trees, we reached the lawn, crossed it, and were about to enter through the window when out from a clump of laurel bushes there darted what seemed to be a hideous and distorted child, who threw itself upon the grass with writhing limbs and then ran swiftly across the lawn into the darkness.

"My God!" I whispered; "did you see it?"

Holmes was for the moment as startled as I. His hand closed like a vise upon my wrist in his agitation. Then he broke into a low laugh and put his lips to my ear.

"It is a nice household," he murmured. "That is the baboon."

I had forgotten the strange pets which the doctor affected. There was a cheetah, too; perhaps we might find it upon our shoulders at any moment. I confess that I felt easier in my mind when, after following Holmes's example and slipping off my shoes, I found myself inside the bedroom. My companion noiselessly closed the shutters, moved the lamp onto the table, and cast his eyes round the room. All was as we had seen it in the daytime. Then creeping up to me and making a trumpet of his hand, he whispered into my ear again so gently that it was all that I could do to distinguish the words:

"The least sound would be fatal to our plans."

I nodded to show that I had heard.

"We must sit without light. He would see it through the ventilator."

I nodded again.

"Do not go asleep; your very life may depend upon it. Have your pistol ready in case we should need it. I will sit on the side of the bed, and you in that chair."

I took out my revolver and laid it on the corner of the table.

Holmes had brought up a long thin cane, and this he placed upon the bed beside him. By it he laid the box of matches and the stump of a candle. Then he turned down the lamp, and we were left in darkness.

Literary Analysis
Mystery Story and Conflict
How can you tell that the plot is reaching the point at which the outcome of the story will be decided?

How shall I ever forget that dreadful vigil? I could not hear a sound, not even the drawing of a breath, and yet I knew that my companion sat open-eyed, within a few feet of me, in the same state of nervous tension in which I was myself. The shutters cut off the least ray of light, and we waited in absolute darkness. From outside came the occasional cry of a night bird, and once at our very window a long-drawn catlike whine, which told us that the cheetah was indeed at liberty. Far away we could hear the deep tones of the parish clock, which boomed out every quarter of an hour. How long they seemed, those quarters! Twelve struck, and one and two and three, and still we sat waiting silently for whatever might befall.

Suddenly there was the momentary gleam of a light up in the direction of the ventilator, which vanished immediately, but was suc-ceeded by a strong smell of burning oil and heated metal. Someone in the next room had lit a dark lantern.[9] I heard a gentle sound of movement, and then all was silent once more, though the smell grew stronger. For half an hour I sat with straining ears. Then suddenly another sound became audible—a very gentle, soothing sound, like that of a small jet of steam escaping continually from a kettle. The instant that we heard it, Holmes sprang from the bed, struck a match, and lashed furiously with his cane at the bell-pull.

"You see it, Watson?" he yelled. "You see it?"

But I saw nothing. At the moment when Holmes struck the light I heard a low, clear whistle, but the sudden glare flashing into my weary eyes made it impossible for me to tell what it was at which my friend lashed so savagely. I could, however, see that his face was deadly pale and filled with horror and loathing.

He had ceased to strike and was gazing up at the ventilator when suddenly there broke from the silence of the night the most horrible cry to which I have ever listened. It swelled up louder and louder, a hoarse yell of pain and fear and anger all mingled in the one dreadful shriek. They say that away down in the village, and even in the distant parsonage, that cry raised the sleepers from their beds. It struck cold to our hearts, and I stood gazing at Holmes, and he at me, until the last echoes of it had died away into the silence from which it rose.

"What can it mean?" I gasped.

"It means that it is all over," Holmes answered. "And perhaps, after all, it is for the best. Take your pistol, and we will enter Dr. Roylott's room."

With a grave face he lit the lamp and led the way down the corridor. Twice he struck at the chamber door without any reply from within. Then he turned the handle and entered, I at his heels, with the cocked pistol in my hand.

---

9. **dark lantern** lantern with a shutter that can hide the light.

**Literary Analysis
Mystery Story and Conflict**
Why does Holmes make this statement? How is the mystery over?

✔**Reading Check**

What do Holmes and Watson hear after Holmes strikes at the bell pull?

◄ **Critical Viewing**
Does this illustration
effectively bring to life
the story's climax?
Why or why not?
[Make a Judgment]

It was a singular sight which met our eyes. On the table stood a dark lantern with the shutter half open, throwing a brilliant beam of light upon the iron safe, the door of which was ajar. Beside this table, on the wooden chair, sat Dr. Grimesby Roylott, clad in a long gray dressing gown, his bare ankles protruding beneath, and his feet thrust into red heelless Turkish slippers. Across his lap lay the short stock with the long lash which we had noticed during the day. His chin was cocked upward and his eyes were fixed in a dreadful, rigid stare at the corner of the ceiling. Round his brow he had a peculiar yellow band, with brownish speckles, which seemed to be bound tightly round his head. As we entered he made neither sound nor motion.

"The band! the speckled band!" whispered Holmes.

I took a step forward. In an instant his strange headgear began to move, and there reared itself from among his hair the squat diamond-shaped head and puffed neck of a loathsome serpent.

"It is a swamp adder!" cried Holmes; "the deadliest snake in India. He has died within ten seconds of being bitten. Violence does, in truth, recoil upon the violent, and the schemer falls into the pit which he digs for another. Let us thrust this creature back into its den, and we can then remove Miss Stoner to some place of shelter and let the county police know what has happened."

As he spoke he drew the dog whip swiftly from the dead man's lap, and throwing the noose round the reptile's neck he drew it from its horrid perch and, carrying it at arm's length, threw it into the iron safe, which he closed upon it.

Such are the true facts of the death of Dr. Grimesby Roylott, of Stoke Moran. It is not necessary that I should prolong a narrative which has already run to too great a length by telling how we broke the sad news to the terrified girl, how we conveyed her by the morning train to the care of her good aunt at Harrow, of how the slow process of official inquiry came to the conclusion that the doctor met his fate while indiscreetly playing with a dangerous pet. The little which I had yet to learn of the case was told me by Sherlock Holmes as we traveled back next day.

Literary Analysis
Mystery Story and Conflict Who is the victor and who is the defeated in the conflict between the detective and the criminal in this mystery?

"I had," said he, "come to an entirely erroneous conclusion which shows, my dear Watson, how dangerous it always is to reason from insufficient data. The presence of the gypsies, and the use of the word band, which was used by the poor girl, no doubt to explain the appearance which she had caught a hurried glimpse of by the light of her match, were sufficient to put me upon an entirely wrong scent. I can only claim the merit that I instantly reconsidered my position when, however, it became clear to me that whatever danger threatened an occupant of the room could not come either from the window or the door. My attention was speedily drawn, as I have already remarked to you, to this ventilator, and to the bell-rope which hung down to the bed. The discovery that this was a dummy, and that the bed was clamped to the floor, instantly gave rise to the suspicion that the rope was there as a bridge for something passing through the hole and coming to the bed. The idea of a snake instantly occurred to me, and when I coupled it with my knowledge that the doctor was furnished with a supply of creatures from India, I felt that I was probably on the right track. The idea of using a form of poison which could not possibly be discovered by any chemical test was just such a one as would occur to a clever and ruthless man who had had an Eastern training. The rapidity with which such a poison would take effect would also, from his point of view, be an advantage. It would be a sharp-eyed coroner, indeed, who could distinguish the two little dark punctures which would show where the poison fangs had done their work. Then I thought of the whistle. Of course he must recall the snake before the morning light revealed it to the victim. He had trained it, probably by the use of the milk which we saw, to return to him when summoned. He would put it through this ventilator at the hour that he thought best, with the certainty that it would crawl down the rope and land on the bed. It might or might not bite the

Literary Analysis
Mystery Story What is the purpose of this "wrap up" of the mystery?

✔**Reading Check**

How does Dr. Roylott die?

The Adventure of the Speckled Band ◆ 483

occupant, perhaps she might escape every night for a week, but sooner or later she must fall a victim.

"I had come to these conclusions before ever I had entered his room. An inspection of his chair showed me that he had been in the habit of standing on it, which of course would be necessary in order that he should reach the ventilator. The sight of the safe, the saucer of milk, and the loop of whipcord were enough to finally dispel any doubts which may have remained. The metallic clang heard by Miss Stoner was obviously caused by her stepfather hastily closing the door of his safe upon its terrible occupant. Having once made up my mind, you know the steps which I took in order to put the matter to the proof. I heard the creature hiss as I have no doubt that you did also, and I instantly lit the light and attacked it."

"With the result of driving it through the ventilator."

"And also with the result of causing it to turn upon its master at the other side. Some of the blows of my cane came home and roused its snakish temper, so that it flew upon the first person it saw. In this way I am no doubt indirectly responsible for Dr. Grimesby Roylott's death, and I cannot say that it is likely to weigh very heavily upon my conscience."

Sir Arthur Conan Doyle

(1859–1930)

Born in Edinburgh, Scotland, Arthur Conan Doyle studied to be a medical doctor. However, one of his professors possessed an ability Doyle found amazing—he was able to guess with total accuracy details about his patients' lives. Doyle based his character Sherlock Holmes on this professor, and in 1887, he published his first Sherlock Holmes novel, *A Study in Scarlet*. He stopped practicing medicine in 1891, turning to a full-time literary career. He wrote four novels and fifty-six stories about Sherlock Holmes.

By 1894, Doyle was so fed up with this character that he wrote "The Final Problem," in which Holmes dies. However, public demand for more of Sherlock Holmes was so overwhelming that Doyle gave in and wrote *The Hound of the Baskervilles* in 1901, one of his most successful novels. This was followed, in 1905, by *Return of Sherlock Holmes*.

Review and Assess

Thinking About the Selection

1. **Respond:** Would you like to be Sherlock Holmes's partner? Why or why not?

2. **(a) Recall:** Why does Helen Stoner come to see Holmes? **(b) Compare and Contrast:** Name three ways in which Helen's situation when she comes to Holmes is similar to Julia's just before Julia's death.

3. **(a) Recall:** After Dr. Roylott's visit, what information does Holmes gather to start his investigation? **(b) Infer:** What motive does Holmes believe Dr. Roylott has for the crimes?

4. **(a) Recall:** How do Holmes and Watson spend the night at Stoke Moran? **(b) Analyze:** How does Dr. Roylott's plan backfire?

5. **(a) Recall:** What clues does Holmes use to solve the mystery? **(b) Speculate:** What do you think would have happened if Helen had not consulted Holmes?

6. **Make a Judgment:** Holmes says that he is indirectly responsible for Roylott's death. In your judgment, who is most responsible for Roylott's death? Explain.

Review and Assess

Literary Analysis

Mystery Story

1. To analyze elements in this **mystery story,** complete a diagram like this one with the appropriate details from the story.

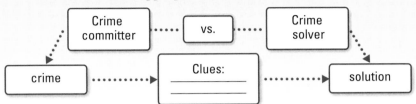

2. (a) How does Holmes outwit the criminal? (b) What role does Watson play?

Connecting Literary Elements

3. What is the specific **conflict** in the mystery?

4. Fill in a chart like the one below to indicate how the clues led Holmes to conclude that a snake was the murder weapon. Write the conclusion Holmes reaches as each new clue is added.

1. Danger can't come from a window	2. Bell pull is fake	3. Bed is bolted down	4. Doctor gets creatures from India
Conclusion from 1 + 2			
Conclusion from 1 + 2 + 3			
Conclusion from 1 + 2 + 3 + 4			

5. What is the high point at which the **plot** could turn out either way?
6. What event provides the **resolution** of the conflict?

Reading Strategy

Identifying the Evidence

7. Explain the significance of each of these clues: the dummy bellpull, the ventilator, and the bed anchored to the floor in Julia's room.
8. How does information about Roylott help solve the mystery?

Extend Understanding

9. **Career Connection**: How would you test an applicant who wants to enter a school for detectives?

Quick Review

A **mystery story** is a fictional tale about a crime or an unexplained event. To review the elements of a mystery story, see page 461.

The **plot** is a sequence of story events in which each event results from a previous one and causes the next. The plot centers around the **conflict**, or a struggle between opposing forces. To review plot and conflict, see page 461.

Evidence is a fact or detail that can prove or disprove a conclusion.

 Take It to the Net
www.phschool.com
Take the interactive self-test online to check your understanding of the selection.

Integrate Language Skills

Vocabulary Development Lesson

Word Analysis: Forms of *convulse*

The word *convulse* means "to shake violently." Write the form of *convulse, convulsions,* or *convulsive* to complete each sentence.

1. Her arm made one ___?___ twitch.
2. The frightening ___?___ will stop when the medicine takes effect.
3. Poisons can cause victims to ___?___.

Spelling Strategy

The *er* sound can be spelled *ur* and *er* —there are no sound clues to help you decide. Practice spelling words with *er* and *ur*. Rewrite the sentences, correcting any misspellings.

1. She reterned after curfew.
2. Do these clues purtain to this murdur case?
3. He spoke impurterbably.
4. The detective surprised his advursary.

Fluency: Sentence Completions

On your paper, write the vocabulary word from page 461 that best completes each sentence.

1. The basketball team felt ___?___ after its stunning defeat.
2. A loud crash in the office startled Chisho from a ___?___ about her upcoming vacation.
3. Caroline was suddenly ___?___ when she experienced an epileptic seizure.
4. Jamal will ___?___ the cost of a new CD player with his income from a part-time job.
5. Nick's minor skateboarding accident left him with ___?___ scratches.
6. I greatly admire my cousin's ___?___ talents in sports, music, and academics.
7. The grandmother reacted ___?___ when her grandson broke a plate.

Grammar Lesson

Predicate Nouns

A **predicate noun** appears after a linking verb and renames, identifies, or explains the subject of the sentence. The linking verb acts much like an equal sign between the subject and the noun that follows the verb.

> My *name* is *Sherlock Holmes.* (*name=Holmes*)
> *He* seems a very amiable *person.* (*he=person*)
> My sister *Julia* and *I* were *twins.* . . . (*Julia and I=twins*)

When creating parallel sentences to emphasize a situation or idea, use parallel predicate nouns.

Example: My name is Sherlock Holmes. His name is Dr. Watson.

▶ *For more practice, see page R30, Exercise A.*

Practice Write the subject and predicate noun in each of the following sentences. Then, tell whether the predicate noun renames, identifies, or explains the subject.

1. He was a late riser, as a rule. . . .
2. My name is Helen Stoner. . . .
3. I am a dangerous man to fall foul of!
4. . . . my profession is its own reward; . . .
5. He seems a very amiable person.

Writing Application Write a sentence with a predicate noun that renames each subject below.

1. Holmes	3. Roylott	5. Watson
2. Helen	4. snake	

𝒲G *Prentice Hall Writing and Grammar Connection: Chapter 19, Section 5*

Writing Lesson

Letter of Inquiry

Check the evidence in "The Adventure of the Speckled Band" by writing to an expert on reptiles and amphibians to ask questions about the details in the story.

Prewriting   Review the story to identify the specific questions you want to ask. For example, Holmes says that the swamp adder's victim is dead within moments of being bitten. You might want to ask the expert the range of time it takes for a swamp adder's venom to take effect.

Drafting   Use the standard business letter format for your letter, including the six elements identified below.

Model: Business Letter Format

Heading (letter writer's name, address, and date)

Inside address (letter receiver's name and address)

Salutation (Dear Ms. Redda)

Body (your explanation and questions)

Closing (Sincerely,)

Signature

> Business letters follow a set structure including these six elements.

Revising   Business letters should be error-free. Double-check that you have followed the correct format. For a sample business letter, see page R16.

Prentice Hall Writing and Grammar Connection: Chapter 11, Section 2

Extension Activities

Listening and Speaking With a group, prepare and perform a **radio play** based on "The Adventure of the Speckled Band."

1. Decide where sound effects will be used so that the speakers can adjust their volume or pause. Also practice enunciation—the clear pronunciation of words. When listeners cannot see you speak, they have a more difficult time understanding words.

2. Pace the narration, dialogue, and sound effects so that there are not long pauses.

Research and Technology Sir Arthur Conan Doyle has influenced many of today's mystery writers. Do a key word search using the Internet. Preview works by contemporary mystery writers in online bookstores. Read summaries and reviews, and prepare an **annotated list** of books. Share the titles you selected with your classmates.

 **Take It to the Net**   www.phschool.com

Go online for an additional research activity using the Internet.

Technical Directions

About Technical Directions

Every new piece of equipment or appliance comes with a set of directions. Directions tell you what the parts of the product are called, what those parts do, and how to use the product safely and effectively. The product may also come with other kinds of printed material, such as information about ordering extra parts, about the location of repair facilities in your region, and about related products that the manufacturer makes. It is extremely important to read through all of these materials, including the directions, before using a product for the first time. It is also important not to discard the written materials but to store them in a convenient place.

Reading Strategy

Following Directions

Before attempting to use a product you are not familiar with, it is important to read through all of the directions.

- If the directions do not already have numbered steps, then break them down into steps yourself and number them.

- Next, gather together any other equipment or tools you might need as you use the product.

- Finally, begin to follow the numbered steps, one at a time. Do not skip steps.

- If you have difficulty with a step, reread the instructions up to that point to see if you have misunderstood them or have followed a step incorrectly.

- Use any diagrams or illustrations to clarify difficult steps.

Using Diagrams and Illustrations

- Look over the picture
- Use the numbers, letters, and labels to identify each part of the picture
- Match the parts of the picture to the parts of the real thing

USING A MICROSCOPE

Most optical microscopes can magnify objects from about 50 up to 1,000 times their real size. The most powerful ones can magnify objects up to 200,000 times. You will find that optical microscopes are easy to use, especially once you know a little about them.

The heading and opening paragraph tell you what the product is and what it does.

Naming the parts

The picture shows the main parts of an optical microscope.

A typical optical microscope

1. Eyepiece. You look through this part. It contains a lens.

2. Body tube. On some microscopes this can be tilted.

3. Objective lenses. Most microscopes have three (see *Magnification*, next page).

4. Nosepiece. The objective lenses are attached to this.

5. Stage. Place the object you want to look at on here.

6. Focusing knob. Turn this to make the image sharp and clear.

7. Mirror. This reflects daylight or lamplight through a hole in the stage onto the object.

Before telling you how to use the product, the text tells you what its parts are called. Text like this is often accompanied by a diagram of the product.

WARNING:
Never point the microscope's mirror at the sun. Its strong rays can reflect off the mirror into your eye and make you blind.

Written materials that come with a product often give warnings about improper use of the product.

Setting up

Place the microscope on a table so that you can look down the eyepiece easily, without stretching or crouching over. You may be able to tilt your microscope's body tube to make it more comfortable for you to look through the eyepiece.

1. To light an object from above (called top lighting), place a lamp 8 inches away from the microscope.

2. Adjust the lamp so its light shines on the object. Alter the mirror so that no light shines through the stage.

3. To light an object from below (bottom lighting), adjust the lamp so the light shines under the stage.

4. Alter the mirror so that it reflects as much light as possible up through the stage and onto the object.

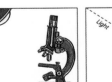 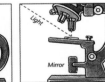

Directions are usually broken into numbered steps. Each step may be illustrated with a drawing or picture.

Feathers are easy to find and interesting to look at through a microscope (see right).

Magnification

Most optical microscopes have three objective lenses, which magnify the object by different amounts. They are called low, medium and high-power lenses.

A microscope's magnifying power is the power of the eyepiece and the objective lens multiplied together.

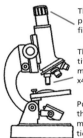

This eyepiece magnifies x10.

This objective lens magnifies x40.

Put together, the total magnification is x400.

Low to high power

The three pictures on the right show a wing feather viewed with low, medium and high-power lenses. In the first picture you can see the stem-like shaft that runs through the middle of the feather. The comb-like spikes growing out of the shaft are called barbs.

The next picture shows two rows of threads growing from each barb. These threads, or barbules, link together to make the feather strong and flexible, so that the bird can fly. You will see fewer barbs on body feathers, which are for warmth rather than flight.

The third picture shows how barbules attach to each other. The barbules shown in red have tiny hooks. These link into grooves on the barbules shown in yellow.

Shaft of feather

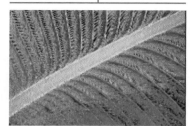

Optical microscope view of a wing feather, seen through a low-power lens.

A closer view of the feather, seen through a medium-power lens.

The feather, seen with a high-power lens.

Try viewing different types of feathers with your microscope.

Focusing

These four steps show you how to focus a microscope. Before you begin, turn the focusing knob to raise the lens as much as possible, then turn the nosepiece to select the lowest-power lens. Always start with this lens as it lets you see more of the object.

1. Place a specimen (such as the sugar grains shown here) in the middle of a microscope slide.

2. Put the slide on the stage, so the part you want to look at is over the hole. Light the specimen from below.

3. Turn the focusing knob to move the lens close to the slide. Make sure that it does not touch the slide.

4. Look through the eyepiece. Raise the lens until the specimen looks sharp and clear. It is now in focus.

Check Your Comprehension

1. What is the range of magnification of most optical microscopes?
2. What does the mirror on a microscope do?
3. What might happen if you did not read the Warning?
4. How do you determine a microscope's magnifying power?
5. When you begin to focus a microscope, which lens should you use? What position should the lens be in?

Applying the Reading Strategy

Following Directions

6. What should you do before you begin to follow the instructions for setting up a microscope?
7. Why is it important to have read the section on "Naming the parts" before reading the section on "Focusing"?
8. Why might the information in the section "Low to high power" be helpful to someone who has never used a microscope?
9. What other equipment might you need before you use the microscope?

Activity

Instruction Evaluation

With a partner, follow the instructions to use a microscope in your home or school. Evaluate how clearly these instructions explain the use of a microscope. Discuss your evaluation, then write a brief record of your conclusions.

Comparing Informational Materials

Directions for Multiple Products

Collect three or four sets of directions for operating a complex item. Examples might include the following:

- dishwasher
- portable CD player
- VCR
- television
- sports watch
- alarm clock
- washer or dryer

Read through each set of directions. Identify similarities in the organization and content of the directions. Explain any warnings given regarding the use of each product. Point out similarities in any drawings or diagrams that appear. Summarize your findings for the class.

Prepare to Read

A Glow in the Dark ◆
Mushrooms ◆ Southern Mansion ◆ The Bat

Preview

Connecting to the Literature

You have probably heard the expression "I couldn't believe my eyes." Think about a time when your eyes have played tricks on you. Then, read these selections to share unique, unexpected views of ordinary things that appear to be something they are not.

Background

Roethke's poem "The Bat" describes the behavior of a bat. In a process called echolocation, bats emit high-pitched cries, inaudible to the human ear. These cries are reflected back to the animal's sensitive ears by an obstacle. The bat changes its flight direction based on what it hears. For this reason, its flight path appears oddly random.

Literary Analysis

Tone

The **tone** of a literary work is the writer's attitude toward the subject and his or her audience. Tone can often be described in a single word, such as *formal, informal, serious, mysterious,* or *humorous.* Tone is revealed in the writer's choice of subject, choice of words, and even choice of sentence structure. In the following lines from "Mushrooms," the repetition and the contradictions create a mysterious tone:

> We are the shelves, we are/Tables, we are meek,/We are edible.

As you read, look for other indications of each author's attitude.

Comparing Literary Works

Even though each writer addresses the extraordinary, the tone of each of these selections is distinct. One writer uses words of mystery to generate a tone of eerie tension. Another makes gentle fun of a subject. Use the following focus questions to compare and contrast the tones of these works.

1. How does each author feel about the strangeness of the topic he or she describes?
2. In what ways is the tone of each work different from the tone of the other three works?

Reading Strategy

Using Restatement to Verify Meaning

You may sometimes encounter words whose meanings are hazy to you—you may have an idea of their meaning without being absolutely sure. Often, using the context or the words and phrases surrounding the unfamiliar word may help. You may find words or phrases that **restate**, or say in a different way, the meaning of the word in question. In the following example, the words in italics restate the meaning of the underlined word.

> . . . a cold-glowing green light with yellow edges that <u>diffused</u> the shape, *making it change and grow* as I watched.

Look for other restatements in these selections that help you verify the meanings of words. Analyze them using a chart like the one shown here.

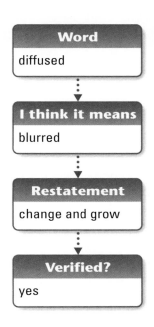

Word
diffused

I think it means
blurred

Restatement
change and grow

Verified?
yes

Vocabulary Development

diffused (di fyo͞ozd´) *v.* spread out widely into different directions (p. 496)

discreetly (dis krēt´ lē) *adv.* carefully; silently (p. 498)

acquire (ə kwīr´) *v.* to get; come to have as one's own (p. 498)

amiss (ə mis´) *adj.* wrongly placed; faulty or improper (p. 502)

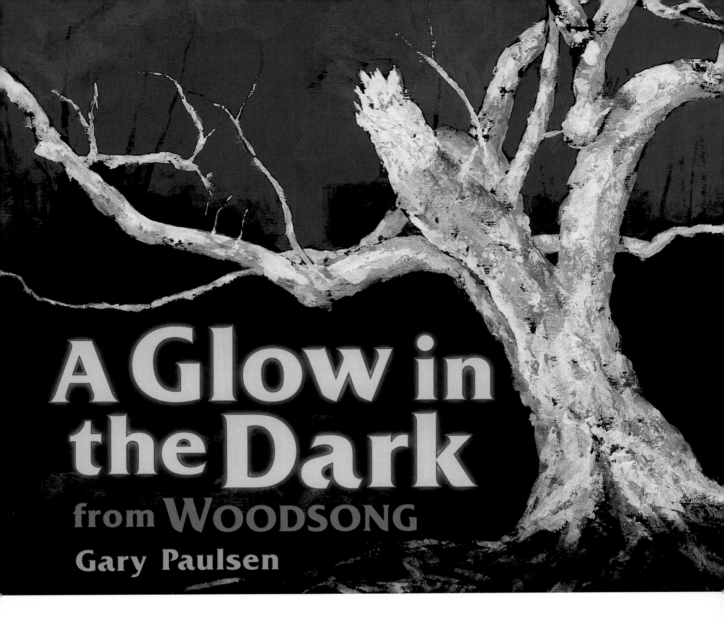

A Glow in the Dark

from WOODSONG

Gary Paulsen

There are night ghosts.

Some people say that we can understand all things if we can know them, but there came a dark night in the fall when I thought that was wrong, and so did the dogs.

We had been running all morning and were tired; some of the dogs were young and could not sustain a long run. So we stopped in the middle of the afternoon when they seemed to want to rest. I made a fire, set up a gentle, peaceful camp, and went to sleep for four hours.

It hadn't snowed yet so we had been running with a three-wheel cart, which meant we had to run on logging roads and open areas. I had been hard pressed to find new country to run in to keep the

▲ **Critical Viewing**
If you came upon this sight while alone in a dark forest, how might you react? [**Relate**]

young dogs from becoming bored and this logging trail was one we hadn't run. It had been rough going, with a lot of ruts and mud and the cart was a mess so I spent some time fixing it after I awakened, carving off the dried mud. The end result was we didn't get going again until close to one in the morning. This did not pose a problem except that as soon as I hooked the dogs up and got them lined out—I was running an eight-dog team—my head lamp went out. I replaced the bulb and tried a new battery, but that didn't help—the internal wiring was bad. I thought briefly of sleeping again until daylight but the dogs were slamming into the harnesses, screaming to run, so I shrugged and jumped on the rig and untied it. Certainly, I thought, running without a head lamp would not be the worst thing I had ever done.

Immediately we blew into the darkness and the ride was madness. Without a lamp I could not tell when the rig was going to hit a rut or a puddle. It was cloudy and fairly warm—close to fifty—and had rained the night before. Without the moon or even starlight I had no idea where the puddles were until they splashed me— largely in the face—so I was soon dripping wet. Coupled with that, tree limbs I couldn't see hit at me as we passed, almost tearing me off the back of the rig. Inside an hour I wasn't sure if I was up, down, or sideways.

And the dogs stopped.

They weren't tired, not even a little, judging by the way they had been ripping through the night, but they stopped dead.

I had just taken a limb in the face and was temporarily blinded. All I knew was that they had stopped suddenly and that I had to jam down on the brakes to keep from running over them. It took me a couple of seconds to clear my eyes and when I did, I saw the light.

In the first seconds I thought it was another person coming toward me. The light had an eerie green-yellow glow. It was quite bright and filled a whole part of the dark night ahead, down the trail. It seemed to be moving. I was in deep woods and couldn't think what a person would be doing there—there are no other teams where I train—but I was glad to see the light.

At first.

Then I realized the light was strange. It glowed and ebbed and seemed to fill too much space to be a regular light source. It was low to the ground, and wide.

I was still not frightened, and would probably not have become frightened except that the dogs suddenly started to sing.

Literary Analysis
Tone What details of this description of the darkness suggest an informal tone?

✓**Reading Check**
What happens to the narrator's headlamp?

I have already talked about some of their songs. Rain songs and first-snow songs and meat songs and come-back-and-stay-with-us songs and even puppy-training songs, but I had heard this song only once, when an old dog had died in the kennel. It was a death song.

And that frightened me.

They all sat. I could see them quite well in the glow from the light—the soft glow, the green glow, the ghost glow. It crept into my thinking without my knowing it: the ghost glow. Against my wishes I started thinking of all the things in my life that had scared me.

Ghosts and goblins and dark nights and snakes under the bed and sounds I didn't know and bodies I had found and graveyards under covered pale moons and death, death, death . . .

And they sang and sang. The cold song in the strange light. For a time I could do nothing but stand on the back of the wheeled rig and stare at the light with old, dusty terror.

But curiosity was stronger. My legs moved without my wanting them to move and my body followed them, along-side the team in the dark, holding to each dog like a security blanket until I reached the next one, moving closer to the light until I was at the front and there were no more dogs to hold.

The light had gotten brighter, seemed to pulse and flood back and forth, but I still could not see the source. I took another step, then another, trying to look around the corner, deeply feeling the distance from the dogs, the aloneness.

Two more steps, then one more, leaning to see around the corner and at last I saw it and when I did it was worse.

It was a form. Not human. A large, standing form glowing in the dark. The light came from within it, a cold-glowing green light with yellow edges that <u>diffused</u> the shape, making it change and grow as I watched.

I felt my heart slam up into my throat.

I couldn't move. I stared at the upright form and was sure it was a ghost, a being from the dead sent for me. I could not move and might not have ever moved except that the dogs had followed me,

$\mathcal{L}$iterature
in context Science Connection

♦**Phosphorescence**

Paulsen describes an eerie glow on the snowy landscape. He finally explains the glow as the result of phosphorus.

Phosphorus is a nonmetallic chemical element found in nature in compounds known as phosphates. During **phosphor-escence,** the process that makes phosphorus glow, phosphorus electrons absorb energy, causing them to become unstable. Light is produced as the electrons drop back to their original energy levels.

diffused (di fyo͞ozd´) v. spread out widely into different directions

► **Critical Viewing** Why might dog-sledding be popular with naturalists like Paulsen? **[Speculate]**

pulling the rig quietly until they were around my legs, peering ahead, and I looked down at them and had to laugh.

They were caught in the green light, curved around my legs staring at the standing form, ears cocked and heads turned sideways while they studied it. I took another short step forward and they all followed me, then another, and they stayed with me until we were right next to the form.

It was a stump.

A six-foot-tall, old rotten stump with the bark knocked off, glowing in the dark with a bright green glow. Impossible. I stood there with the dogs around my legs, smelling the stump and touching it with their noses. I found out later that it glowed because it had sucked phosphorus* from the ground up into the wood and held the light from day all night.

But that was later. There in the night I did not know this. Touching the stump, and feeling the cold light, I could not quite get rid of the fear until a black-and-white dog named Fonzie came up, smelled the stump, snorted, and relieved himself on it.

So much for ghosts.

Review and Assess

Thinking About the Selection

1. **Respond:** What might you have thought you were seeing if you saw the "green-yellow glow"?

2. **(a) Recall:** Where and when are Paulsen and his dogs running? **(b) Connect:** What is the significance of these details in connection with Paulsen's headlamp going out? **(c) Infer:** What does Paulsen's decision to continue reveal about his personality?

3. **(a) Recall:** Why do the dogs suddenly stop? **(b) Infer:** Why do they start to sing? **(c) Apply:** In what way does their singing increase Paulsen's fear?

4. **(a) Recall:** How does Paulsen use his dogs for support as he moves toward the glow? **(b) Support:** How do the dogs show that they trust Paulsen? **(c) Draw Conclusions:** Based on how he uses his dogs for support, how does Paulsen feel about his dogs?

5. **(a) Recall:** What does Paulsen later learn about why the stump glows? **(b) Speculate:** How would this information have helped Paulsen when he first saw the stump?

6. **Assess:** Do you think Paulsen shows good judgment and common sense? Explain why or why not.

Gary Paulsen

(b. 1939)
Gary Paulsen has won three Newbery Honor Awards—for his books *Hatchet, Dogsong,* and *The Winter Room*—as well as many other awards. He is the author of more than 175 books.

This selection comes from *Woodsong,* a true account of Paulsen's experiences as he trained for the Iditarod, a grueling dogsled race in the Alaskan wilderness. After running the race, Paulsen published *Winterdance: The Fine Madness of Running the Iditarod.*

MUSHROOMS

SYLVIA PLATH

Overnight, very
Whitely, <u>discreetly</u>,
Very quietly

Our toes, our noses
5 Take hold on the loam,[1]
<u>Acquire</u> the air.

Nobody sees us,
Stops us, betrays us;
The small grains make room.

10 Soft fists insist on
Heaving the needles,
The leafy bedding.

---

1. loam (lōm) *n.* any rich, dark soil.

discreetly (dis krēt′ lē) *adv.*
carefully; silently

acquire (ə kwīr′) *v.*
to get; come to have
as one's own

Even the paving.
Our hammers, our rams,
15 Earless and eyeless,
Perfectly voiceless,
Widen the crannies,
Shoulder through holes. We

Diet on water,
20 On crumbs of shadow,
Bland-mannered, asking
Little or nothing.
So many of us!
So many of us!

25 We are shelves, we are
Tables, we are meek,
We are edible,

Nudgers and shovers
In spite of ourselves.
30 Our kind multiplies:

We shall by morning
Inherit the earth.
Our foot's in the door.

◀ **Critical Viewing**
What stages of growth
can you observe in the
mushrooms on this page?
[Classify]

Review and Assess

Thinking About the Selection

1. **Respond:** Have your ideas about mushrooms changed since reading this poem? Why or why not?
2. **(a) Recall:** What human qualities do the mushrooms have? **(b) Infer:** What does this description suggest to you about how the mushrooms grow?
3. **(a) Recall:** What demands, if any, do the mushrooms make on their surroundings? **(b) Draw Conclusions:** What can you conclude about the mushrooms' ability to survive?
4. **(a) Recall:** How do the mushrooms overcome obstacles in their way? **(b) Deduce:** Why will this ability enable the mushrooms to "inherit the earth"?
5. **(a) Apply:** What message about strength do the mushrooms communicate by their example? **(b) Evaluate:** Do you think this message is true or not?

Sylvia Plath

(1932–1963)
Sylvia Plath was born in Boston. She developed an early interest in writing and published her first poem at the age of seventeen. Her *Collected Poems* won the Pulitzer Prize for Poetry in 1982.

Plath wrote about experiences that were deeply personal to her. Her poetry reveals a great capacity to experience emotion.

Southern Mansion

Arna Bontemps

▲ **Critical Viewing** Does this southern mansion appear to be deserted or inhabited? How can you tell? **[Deduce]**

Poplars[1] are standing there still as death
And ghosts of dead men
Meet their ladies walking
Two by two beneath the shade
5   And standing on the marble steps.

There is a sound of music echoing
Through the open door
And in the field there is
Another sound tinkling in the cotton:
10   Chains of bondmen[2] dragging on the ground.

The years go back with an iron clank,
A hand is on the gate,
A dry leaf trembles on the wall.
Ghosts are walking.
15   They have broken roses down
And poplars stand there still as death.

---

1. **Poplars** (päp´ lərz) *n.* trees of the willow family, with soft wood and flowers.
2. **bondmen** (bänd´ mən) *n.* slaves.

Literary Analysis
Tone What details indicate a condemning tone toward the time period described in the poem?

Review and Assess

Thinking About the Selection

1. **Respond:** Were you surprised by the descriptions in the poem? Why or why not?
2. **(a) Recall:** What is the scene described in Bontemps's poem? **(b) Infer:** What is strange and extraordinary about the scene?
3. **(a) Recall:** What words does Bontemps use to describe the poplars? **(b) Infer:** Why might he describe them in this way?
4. **(a) Recall:** How are the roses broken in the last stanza? **(b) Interpret:** What does this breaking of the roses represent?
5. **(a) Contrast:** What is the difference between the two sounds the speaker hears? **(b) Compare:** What do the sounds have in common? **(c) Interpret:** Explain how the lifestyle represented by one sound is maintained by the suffering represented by the other sound.

Arna Bontemps

(1902–1973)
Born in Louisiana and educated at the University of Chicago, Arna Bontemps was a university librarian for more than twenty years. Bontemps also had a career as an editor, a writer, teacher, and literary critic.

Bontemps wrote one of the most important records of African American life in the South during the Depression: *The Old South.* This collection of short stories combines fiction and personal memories.

Southern Mansion ◆ 501

THE BAT

Theodore Roethke

By day the bat is cousin to the mouse.
He likes the attic of an aging house.

His fingers make a hat about his head.
His pulse beat is so slow we think him dead.

5   He loops in crazy figures half the night
Among the trees that face the corner light.

But when he brushes up against a screen,
We are afraid of what our eyes have seen:

For something is <u>amiss</u> or out of place
10   When mice with wings can wear a human face.

amiss (ə mis′) *adj.* wrongly placed; faulty or improper

Review and Assess

Thinking About the Selection

1. **Respond:** What effect, if any, has this poem had on the way you feel about bats?

2. **(a) Recall:** To what animal does the speaker say the bat is related? **(b) Evaluate:** Is the statement accurate? Explain.

3. **(a) Recall:** Where does the bat spend its days? **(b) Interpret:** What is meant by the statement "His fingers make a hat about his head"?

4. **(a) Compare and Contrast:** How do the daytime and nighttime activities of the bat differ? **(b) Interpret:** Why is the description of the bat in the last stanza so strange?

Theodore Roethke

(1908–1963)

The son of a florist, young Theodore Roethke loved to play in the family greenhouse, where he developed a kinship with nature that he never lost. Roethke's poetry earned him the Bollingen Prize, the Pulitzer Prize, and the National Book Award.

Review and Assess

Literary Analysis

Tone

1. In "A Glow in the Dark," what are two details that reveal a humorous **tone** or attitude toward inexperience in the woods?
2. What details indicate that Paulsen expects his readers will understand his feelings about the episode?
3. Using a chart like the one shown, write a word or phrase that describes each writer's attitude toward his or her subject.

Poem	Mushrooms	Southern Mansions	The Bat
Lines	Nobody sees us,/stops us, betrays us;	A dry leaf trembles on the wall./Ghosts are walking./	By day the bat is cousin to the mouse,/He likes the attic of an aging house.
Tone			

Comparing Literary Works

4. How does each author feel about the strangeness of the topic he or she describes? Explain.
5. In what ways is the tone of each work different from the tone of the other three works?

Reading Strategy

Using Restatement to Verify Meaning

In items 6 and 7, identify the words that **restate** the meaning of the italicized word. (A restatement can appear before the italicized word.)

6. Something is *amiss* or out of place. . .
7. Our toes, our noses / Take hold on the loam. / *Acquire* the air.
8. Which sentence restates the meaning of *diffused*?
   (a) The light was diffused, but I could still see the shape clearly.
   (b) The light was diffused, it faded into shadow, then darkness.
9. Add words to reinforce the meaning of the italicized word.
   (a) The waitress *discreetly* checked the table.
   (b) The dogs cannot *sustain* a long run.

Extend Understanding

10. **Science Connection:** How does your understanding of phosphorescence help you understand Paulsen's writing?

Quick Review

Tone is the author's attitude toward his or her subject. To review tone, see page 493.

Restatement is saying the same thing again in different words. To review restatement, see page 493.

 Take It to the Net
www.phschool.com
Take the interactive self-test online to check your understanding of these selections.

Integrate Language Skills

Vocabulary Development Lesson

Word Analysis: Latin Prefix a-

The word *amiss*, which appears in "The Bat," means "wrongly placed." It begins with the Latin prefix *a-*, which can mean "on" or "in."

On your paper, complete these word equations that include the prefix *a-*. Then, define each word.

1. a- + board = ___?___
2. a- + side = ___?___
3. a- + ground = ___?___
4. a- + sleep = ___?___

Spelling Strategy

The sound *ak* can be spelled *acq*, as in *acquire*, or *aq*, as in *aqua*. Words having to do with water are usually spelled with *aq*. On your paper, complete the following words by adding *acq* or *aq*.

1. ___?___ uisition   3. ___?___uainted
2. ___?___uarium   4. ___?___uamarine

Fluency: Sentence Completions

Study the vocabulary list on page 493 and review the use of each word in the context of the selections. Then, on your paper, complete each sentence with a word from the vocabulary list.

1. We knew something was ___?___ when the cat raced across the room.
2. We disposed of the broken lamp ___?___ to avoid upsetting Mom.
3. We must ___?___ a new lamp immediately.
4. The filter ___?___ the ray of light, scattering it around the room.

Grammar Lesson

Appositive Phrases

An **appositive phrase** is made up of a noun or a pronoun plus modifiers and complements. It is placed near another noun or pronoun to explain or identify it. Appositive phrases are usually set off by commas or dashes. By providing explanatory information, appositives help clarify the relationship between ideas.

> I could see them quite well in the glow from the light—*the soft glow, the green glow, the ghost glow.* (modifies *glow*)

▶ *For more practice, see page R30, Exercise C.*

Practice Write the appositive phrases in each of the following.

1. The light came from within it, a cold-glowing green light with yellow edges. . . .
2. The dogs' song—a death song—echoed.
3. We are edible, / Nudgers and shovers / In spite of ourselves.
4. The mansion, a crumbling ruin, was outside Savannah.
5. A bat's screech, a noise undetectable by humans, helps it navigate in the darkness.

Writing Application Write a paragraph about one of the poems. Use an appositive phrase after the poet's name, the title of the poem, and one of the subjects of the poem.

WG Prentice Hall Writing and Grammar Connection: Chapter 20, Section 1

Writing Lesson

Comparison-and-Contrast Paper

Literature often presents ideas in vivid or new ways. Compare and contrast the way that one of the images—such as mushrooms or poplars—is presented with the way that you imagined or knew it to be before you read the selection.

Prewriting   Use a Venn diagram to gather information. In the left circle, list the way that the selections describe the image. In the right circle, list what you knew or imagined.

Drafting   First, state whether your impression is more similar to or different from the impression in the poem. Then, organize your paragraphs around the categories in your Venn diagram. When you provide details of your impressions, state your main points clearly.

Model: State Your Main Points Clearly

Vague: Bats have a special ability to navigate in darkness.

Clear: To navigate in darkness, *bats use echolocation, which operates like sonar in a submarine.*

> The words in italics state the main point in a more clear, detailed way.

Revising   Reread your draft to be sure you address each subject clearly. Add transitions such as *in contrast* or *similarly* to reinforce the comparisons and contrasts you make. Rephrase unclear or vague passages.

W͟G Prentice Hall Writing and Grammar Connection: Chapter 8, Sections 2 and 3

Extension Activities

Research and Technology Do a **multi-step Internet search** on one of the topics mentioned in the poems: phosphoresent glow, mushrooms, or bats.

1. Use your topic name in a keyword search.
2. Save links (by bookmarking or adding to favorites) to the sites that seem helpful.
3. Use hotlinks within useful sites to connect to other sources.

As you explain your search process to a partner, evaluate the sites and information you found. Then, identify one way you can make your next search more efficient.

Listening and Speaking Prepare an **oral presentation** in which you do a reading and interpretation of one of the poems.

- Use your voice to emphasize words that will make meaning clearer.
- Explain your interpretation of the poem's meaning.
- Ask listeners to share their reactions.

 **Take It to the Net**   www.phschool.com

Go online for an additional research activity using the Internet.

Instructions

About Instructions

Instructions explain how to do or make something. For example, instructions might explain how to make pancakes or repair a leaky faucet. The writer breaks down the process into a series of logical steps and explains them in the order in which the reader should do them. Most instructions include the following:

- a list of materials needed.
- clear explanations of any terms or materials that may be unfamiliar to readers.
- a series of logical steps explained in chronological, or time, order.
- charts, illustrations, and diagrams as necessary to make complicated procedures understandable.

Reading Strategy

Follow Steps in a Sequence

Instructions are arranged in chronological, or time, order. Many will give a list of materials before outlining the steps in the process. As you read instructions, pay close attention to transitional words, such as next and then, and numbers assigned to steps to indicate time sequence. For example, in "A Simple Shadow Puppet," the writer provides a list of materials before he explains the steps. Then, he outlines the four main steps involved in making a shadow puppet. Use the structure of a list of instructions to order your actions.

- First, gather materials.
- Skim the instructions and identify the main action in each step. Use an organizer like the one shown to identify the main action in each step of the instructions for making a shadow puppet.
- Read closely any step that seems difficult or confusing.
- When you are sure you understand what is required at each step, begin working, starting with step 1.

Making a Shadow Puppet

Preparation	Gather materials.
↓	
Step 1	Transfer design from paper to cardboard.
↓	
Step 2	
↓	
Step 3	
↓	
Step 4	

A Simple Shadow Puppet

David Currell

The introduction gives an overview of shadow puppets—what they are and how they are used.

Shadow puppets are normally flat, cutout figures held by a rod or wire and illuminated against a translucent screen, hence they're usually made from cardboard.

For a simple silhouette, black cardboard is ideal, but not essential. Any fairly strong board, such as that from a cereal box, will make a good puppet. Think about the size of your puppets in relation to the size of the screen, leaving space for all planned actions.

MATERIALS

A list of materials allows readers to make sure they have everything they need.

- Black cardboard
- Scissors
- Craft glue
- Glue brush
- 12-inch length of 3/8-inch diameter softwood dowel
- Thumbtack

1. Transfer the design from paper onto cardboard. For a screen that is 28 inches high, make puppets up to 12 inches high.

2. Cut out the shape with sharp scissors for a clean outline. If you wish, you can stiffen the cardboard by coating it with white glue.

Numbered steps, presented in chronological order, detail each step of the process of creating a shadow puppet.

3. Hold the puppet gently between your thumb and index finger, adjusting the position to find the point of balance. Attach the dowel control rod slightly above this point, so that there is just a little more weight below the control rod than above. This is to make sure that the puppet remains naturally upright, rather than tending to somersault as you operate it.

The author explains the control rod so readers understand the reason for this step.

4. Secure the rod to the puppet with the thumbtack, just above the point of balance. You will need to tap the thumbtack securely to make sure that the puppet turns with the rod and does not swing uncontrolled. With this type of control rod, the puppet cannot turn around, but it is very easy to make a duplicate facing in the opposite direction.

Photos help you see what actions and outcomes should look like.

DECORATION

You can add to the design of your shadow puppets by cutting out decorative or key shapes within the outline using a sharp craft knife or small, pointed scissors or by punching holes. You will find it helpful to study Japanese *wayang kulit* shadow puppets and Chinese figures, as they use cutout decoration to superb effect. Remember that these figures are made of leather that can hold its shape even when much of it has been removed, but do not cut away too much of your cardboard figures or they will be too weak to withstand a performance!

As an alternative to cutting out intricate decorations, you can cut away larger areas and cover the exposed sections with suitably textured materials that allow light to show through the design—for example, nets, lace, or paper doilies.

The writer places this section last because decorating is done after the puppet is made.

Check Your Comprehension

1. Explain why these cutout figures are called "shadow puppets."
2. What kind of board will make a sturdy shadow puppet?
3. What is the purpose of the control rod?
4. Why is it important to attach the control rod slightly above the puppet's point of balance?
5. What are two ways of adding to the design of a shadow puppet?

Applying the Reading Strategy

Follow Steps in a Sequence

6. Why do you think the writer begins the essay by explaining what shadow puppets are?
7. Step 1 says, "Transfer the design from paper onto cardboard." What must be done before this step can be completed?
8. What clue tells you that attaching the control rod comes after cutting out the shape of the puppet?
9. Why is it essential that step 3 comes before step 4?
10. Why does the writer end the essay with the "Decoration" section?

Activity

Rewrite a How-to Essay

Give a demonstration of how to make a shadow puppet. In an oral presentation, use transitional words, rather than numbers, to indicate sequence. Use words from the chart to indicate the order of steps as you give your demonstration.

Step	Words
Materials	Before you begin
1	First
2, 3, 4	Next, Then, After
Decoration	Finally, Lastly

Contrasting Informational Materials

Instructions and Manuals

A manual is a consumer document that often comes with a new product. For example, if you purchase a VCR or a computer game, you will probably find a manual in the box. The purpose of a manual is to explain how a product is used. Both instructions and manuals often contain the following features:

- illustrations or diagrams to clarify procedures
- explanations of unfamiliar terms
- a series of steps explained in chronological order

Instructions for activities can be found in books, magazines, and on the Internet.

Look at a manual for a product in your home. Notice the similarities to general instructions. Then, list four ways a manual is different from instructions for an activity.

Writing WORKSHOP

Exposition: Explanation of a Process

An **explanation of a process** is a work in which a writer divides an activity into a series of logical steps and explains them in the order in which a person should complete them. In this workshop, you will choose a process and write an explanation of how to accomplish it.

Assignment Criteria. Your explanation should have the following characteristics:

- A focused topic—a topic that can be fully explained in one essay
- Explanations of any terms or materials that may be unfamiliar to readers
- An explanation of activities necessary to complete the task, organized in chronological order
- Charts, illustrations, diagrams, or photographs that will enhance or clarify complicated procedures
- Formatting, such as headings and fonts that aid comprehension

See the Rubric on page 513 for the criteria on which your explanation may be assessed.

Prewriting

Choose a topic. To write an effective explanation of a process, choose a topic you know well. It must be narrow enough for readers to learn how to do it from an essay. "How to Build a Jet" is far too BIG! Here are some general ideas:

- How to prepare a food
- How to design a system
- How to operate a tool
- How to accomplish a personal goal

Make a timeline. First, divide the process you have chosen into distinct steps and consider how much time the entire process will take. Make a timeline to help yourself organize the sequence of steps your explanation will describe.

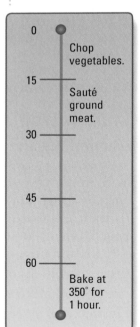

Gather visual aids. Remember that your readers may never have attempted the process you are explaining. Photographs or illustrations, with explanatory captions, will help them understand. Appropriate diagrams, charts, or maps can also help.

Define unusual terms. If your process is technical or unusual, define any terms with which your reader may be unfamiliar. If there are many, you can define the terms within the text or include a glossary at the end.

Student Model

Before you begin drafting your explanation of a process, read this student model and review the characteristics of successful explanation.

Joseph White
Tampa, Florida

Home Hydroponics

Hydroponics is the cultivation of plants in water containing dissolved inorganic nutrients rather than soil. If you are interested in how to take care of your plants in this type of system, continue reading.

Let's start with the basic terminology. First you need to know about pH. There is a way to measure the amount of **potential hydrogen (pH)** in the water. In chemistry, **pH is a measure of the acidity or alkalinity of a solution,** numerically equal to 7 for neutral solutions, increasing with increasing alkalinity and decreasing with increasing acidity. Plants need a pH balance. You can measure the pH in the water by using a tester to show the level of **alkalinity or acidity.** A good level of pH is 6.0 or a yellow to yellow-green color. If the pH is too high the test liquid will be blue, too low and the test liquid will be red. You can use pH down to decrease the level of pH. If the pH is too low, then use pH up. These are nutrient products you must purchase. You use a pH chart to match the color of the water's pH. Three drops of the tester liquid is put into a tube with the water. The tube is mixed and held up to the light to check the color. Once you know these basics, you're ready to move on to building a setup.

The first step in growing a healthy hydroponic plant is having the proper supplies:

- pH up and down
- rockwool
- small sprouts
- a small pump
- pH tester
- a tank
- test tubes

Rockwool is spun mineral wool fiber. First, the small sprouts are placed in the rockwool. It will hold water and retain sufficient air space to promote root growth. Add the water into the tank. Then, adjust the pump's nozzle into the water. The pump keeps adding thousands of tiny air bubbles to constantly circulate the nutrient solution across the plant's roots. The oxygen rich nutrient solution and the nutrient rich rockwool promote healthy and unrestricted root growth. Healthy root growth produces healthy, happy plants. The pH level in the water is tested so the water remains at the right level. Then you add the sprouts in the rockwool into the tank. Finally you turn the pump on so the plants will receive oxygen. Then every two days you check the pH level to make sure that it is at its correct level. These are the steps to creating your own hydroponics system and caring for the plants.

> Although the topic sounds complicated, it is simple enough to cover in one presentation.

> The writer begins by clearing up any unfamiliar terminology.

> In the body of the essay, the set up of a home hydroponics station is outlined.

> The writer carries his explanation through to the end of the project.

Drafting

Choose the best format. Experiment with formatting techniques that will help your reader understand. Here are a few suggestions:

- a brief overview or summary of the process at the beginning
- a list of necessary materials or ingredients
- headings to distinguish various steps or sections
- various fonts, in different sizes, to differentiate explanatory parts
- tips that are boxed or set off from the main text
- numbered points or bulleted lists
- a glossary of terms or a list of additional resources

Provide elaboration. A step that seems obvious to you may not be obvious to a reader who is new to the process. For example, the step *Chop vegetables* is not specific enough for someone who has never made lasagna. Include a glossary or list of terms that may be unfamiliar to readers.

List of Terms

- **Dice** green peppers into tiny chunks.
- **Slice** mushrooms thinly.
- **Chop** onions as small as possible.
- **Cut** black olives into quarters.

Define: *Dice, Slice, Chop, Cut*

Revising

Distinguish main steps and substeps. Highlight the main steps in one color. Highlight the substeps of each main step with another color. Review your highlighting to see if you need to provide elaboration or need to format information as a list or as sidebars.

Model: Highlighting to Clarify Steps

Rockwool is spun mineral wool fiber. First, place the small sprouts in the rockwool. Make sure they are securely tucked in so they don't float as soon as you put them in the water. The rockwool will hold water and retain sufficient air space to promote root growth. Add the water into the tank. Then, adjust the pump's nozzle in the water. The pump keeps adding thousands of tiny air bubbles to constantly circulate the nutrient solution across the plant's roots. The oxygen rich nutrient solution and the nutrient rich rockwool promotes healthy and unrestricted root growth. Healthy root growth produces healthy, happy plants. The pH level in the water is tested so the water remains at the right level. Then you add the sprouts in the rockwool into the tank. Finally you turn the pump on so the plants will receive oxygen. Check that the water is circulating but not gushing. Check the pH level every two days to make sure that it is at its correct level. These are the steps to creating your own hydroponics system and caring for the plants.

> The highlighting shows a balance between main steps, marked in yellow, and clarifying details, marked in green.

Vary sentence beginnings. After you have revised your paragraphs, look carefully at your sentences. Make sure you have not repeated the same sentence structure over and over. Combine some sentences, and change and add words to make your sentences more interesting and specific.

Compare the nonmodel and the model. Why is the model more effective than the nonmodel?

Nonmodel	Model
The pH is the first thing you need to know. The pH is the potential hydrogen (pH) in the water. The pH is a measure of the acidity or alkalinity of a solution, numerically equal to 7 for neutral solutions, increasing with increasing alkalinity and decreasing with increasing acidity. The plants need a pH balance.	First you need to know about pH. There is a way to measure the amount of potential hydrogen (pH) in the water. In chemistry, pH is a measure of the acidity or alkalinity of a solution, numerically equal to 7 for neutral solutions, increasing with increasing alkalinity and decreasing with increasing acidity. Plants need a pH balance.

Publishing and Presenting

Choose one of these ways to share your writing with classmates or a larger audience.

Make a brochure. Use the words and visual aids to create a brochure about your topic.

Do a demonstration. Turn your writing into an oral demonstration, complete with props and visual aids, that you present to your classmates.

*W*G *Prentice Hall Writing and Grammar Connection: Chapter 10*

Speaking Connection
To learn more about presenting an explanation of a process as a speech, see the **Listening and Speaking Workshop: Delivering an Informational Presentation,** page 334.

Rubric for Self-Assessment

Evaluate your explanation of a process, using the following criteria and rating scale:

Criteria	Rating Scale				
	Not very				Very
Is the essay focused on a topic that is appropriate to its length?	1	2	3	4	5
How clearly defined are terms that may be new to readers?	1	2	3	4	5
How clearly organized are the steps in the process?	1	2	3	4	5
How specifically is each step explained?	1	2	3	4	5
How well do visual aids clarify complicated procedures?	1	2	3	4	5
How well does formatting aid comprehension?	1	2	3	4	5

Listening and Speaking WORKSHOP

Evaluating an Informational Presentation

When you listen to an **informational presentation,** you may need to evaluate what you hear. Evaluating an informational presentation requires listening critically and carefully to determine the effectiveness of the presentation's content and the speaker's delivery. The following listening strategies, together with the form on this page, will help you get started.

Evaluate Credibility

A speaker's accuracy or authority should not be taken for granted. Do the following to evaluate his or her credibility.

Question the speaker's claims. Do not just accept what a speaker says as true. Question facts and details by asking questions at the end of the presentation. Be aware of the differences between facts and opinions. If a speaker does not support opinions with facts, consider the possible reasons.

Listen for loaded language. A speaker can "load" language in many ways. To influence an audience's reactions to information, he or she may include words with strongly positive or negative connotations or associations.

Recognize bias. A speaker may seem to be presenting factual information when he or she is also trying to sway your opinion. Listen carefully to identify evidence of an informational presenter's bias, or set opinions. By presenting only some facts, or partial facts, a speaker can give a biased view.

Evaluate Delivery

To evaluate a speaker's delivery, be aware of both verbal and nonverbal signals.

- **Voice modulation and inflection** An effective speaker uses variations in volume, tone, and pace to capture audience interest and emphasize particular points. Pay special attention when a speaker slows down, speeds up, or raises or lowers his or her voice.
- **Enunciation** You should be able to hear *every* word.
- **Nonverbal signals** At key points a good speaker looks up from his or her notes and makes eye contact with various audience members. The speaker uses body language, such as a shrug, a nod, pointing, or movement to communicate.

Activity:
Presentation and Feedback With a partner, watch an informational presentation either live or on television (infomercials are good examples). Use the feedback form to evaluate what you see and hear. Afterward, compare what each of you have observed.

Feedback Form for Persuasive Composition

Rating System
+ = Excellent   ✔ = Average   – = Weak

Content
Credibility of speaker's claims _____
Avoidance of loaded language _____
Absence of bias _____

Delivery
Voice modulation _____
Enunciation _____
Effectiveness of nonverbal signals_____

Answer the following questions:
Did you believe the speaker? Why or why not?
How well did the speaker inform you about the subject?
Did you learn more from verbal or nonverbal communication?

Assessment WORKSHOP

Interpreting Visual Aids

The reading sections of some tests require you to read a passage and answer multiple-choice questions about visual aids. Use the following strategies to help you answer such questions:

- **Study the key.** Visual aids present information with as few words as possible. Study the key to learn what each symbol stands for or what each axis or bar of a graph measures.
- **Clarify the question.** Questions about visual aids often require you to locate information, compare two items of information, or make calculations using the information. Read the question carefully so you are clear about what is being asked.

Sample Test Item

Directions: Answer the question based on the passage and the information in the graphic.

Tony prepared a bar graph to show how many boxes of greeting cards each class sold for the school fundraiser.

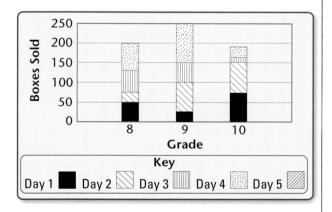

1. How many boxes did the eighth grade sell on Day 2?

   A 25   **C** 75

   B 50   **D** 100

Answer and Explanation

On Day 1, eighth-graders sold 50. On Day 2, the number went from 50 to 75, so 25 were sold. *A* is correct.

▶ Practice

Directions: Answer the question based on the passage and the information in the graphic.

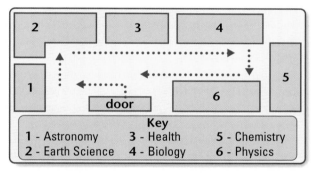

At the school science fair, Tanya, Alan, Dominic, and Gloria wanted to look at all four of their projects before looking at any other projects. Tanya's project was on the earth science table; Alan's was an astronomy project; Gloria did a physics experiment; and Dominic reported on a health issue.

1. If the four students follow the suggested flow of traffic, whose project will they see first?

   A Tanya's   **C** Alan's

   B Dominic's   **D** Gloria's

UNIT 6 Short Stories

Exploring the Genre

There is a feeling of anticipation when you open a short story. You know that, in the space of a few pages, you will meet new people and experience places and situations that may be quite different from your own. Reading the selections in this unit will give you a glimpse of what it might be like to live as another person in another place and time.

Despite their varied content, almost all short stories have the following element in common:

- **Plot:** the sequence of events that catches your interest and takes you through the story.

- **Characters:** the people, animals, or other beings that take part in the story's action.

- **Setting:** the time and place of a story's events.

- **Theme:** the message that the story conveys.

◀ **Critical Viewing** What do you imagine the people that live in this house are like? **[Infer]**

Why Read Literature?

You might read a short story for a variety of reasons. You may pick up a story because you already know and like the author. Or you might want to read about characters who resemble you—or are completely different. Preview three purposes you might choose before reading the selections in this unit.

1

Read for the love of literature.

Literature can open doors into cultures other than your own. To experience Sioux language and culture, read Virginia Driving Hawk Snede's **"The Medicine Bag,"** page 582.

Etiquette and custom play an important role in many cultures. In Japan, for example, eating in public, although commonplace now, was once considered a shocking breach of Japanese etiquette. It is also polite to initially refuse someone's offer of help. Traditionally, an offer is made three times. To read more about the importance of culture and etiquette in Japan, read Yoshiko Uchida's **"Tears of Autumn,"** page 564.

2

Read to appreciate an author's style.

If you have ever seen a James Bond movie, you are already familiar with the dryly ironic style of British author H. H. Munro (Saki). Like the famous secret agent, Munro also conceals his sense of humor with the cultivated attitude of the perfect gentleman. Discover the style of a true mischief-maker when you read Munro's **"The Story-Teller,"** page 576.

Did you know that the human heart beats 100,000 times every hour? The beating of the human heart is of special importance to Edgar Allan Poe's **"The Tell-Tale Heart,"** page 522. Poe's dark and disconcerting style makes a common occurence, a heart beating, into a frightening act.

3

Read for information.

Did you know that the longest speech ever given was 24 hours and 18 minutes long? Of course, most speeches are not that long. Speeches vary in many different ways, especially in length and purpose. To read a speech that is meant to inspire the American people, read **"Sharing in the American Dream"** by Colin Powell on page 598.

Take It to the Net

Visit the Web site for online instruction and activities related to each selection in this unit.

www.phschool.com

How to Read Literature

Strategies for Reading Fiction

Reading fiction is not hard work. All it takes is a willingness to plunge yourself into another world, to live through the same events as the characters, and to feel what they feel. The following are strategies to help you enjoy your reading:

1. Make predictions.

Predicting, or making guesses about what will happen later in a story, keeps you actively involved in a story. Use prediction to:

- Avoid missing details in a story that could prove important later.

- Sharpen your understanding of characters and their situations.

Keep a list of your predictions, like the one shown, to see how many are proved wrong or right.

2. Identify with a character.

Identifying with characters does not mean you have to agree with their choices or even like their personalities. It simply means that you should try to immerse yourself in their lives to feel what they feel. This will make the descriptions in the story more real. If you have trouble, relate the characters' experiences to events or situations you have experienced in the past and recall your reactions.

3. Ask questions.

Asking questions keeps you aware of what is going on in a story. While you are reading:

- Ask questions about the plot, theme, or characters.

- **Plot questions** center around what is happening in the story. **Theme questions** have to do with the underlying message the author is trying to communicate. **Character questions** revolve around why characters do what they do.

- Find answers to your questions by reading ahead or going back to reread passages more carefully for detail.

4. Draw inferences.

Make inferences to arrive at ideas that writers suggest, but do not say directly. To do this, consider what authors are saying and not saying by the details they select. Then use your inferences to predict how characters will react to certain situations.

As you read the selections in this unit, review the reading strategies and apply them to interact with the text.

Make Predictions

Story Detail: Man hides evidence

Prediction: He won't get caught

Wrong or Right?

Prepare to Read

The Tell-Tale Heart

M.C. Escher "Self-Portrait" © 1998 Cordon Art B.V. Baarn-Holland

Take It to the Net

Visit www.phschool.com for interactive activities and instruction related to "The Tell-Tale Heart," including

- background
- graphic organizers
- literary elements
- reading strategies

Preview

Connecting to the Literature.

You are lying in bed, trying to fall asleep, but a leaky faucet will not stop dripping. It seems to become louder and louder, filling the house. Anxiously, you wait for every drop. This common experience shows that, at times, your imagination can exaggerate what you hear or see. In this story, Edgar Allan Poe uses this type of experience to create terror.

Background

Edgar Allan Poe made the short story into an art form. He believed that the writer of a brief story could create a "unity of effect." Every element—from sentence rhythm to a character's personality—would help create a single impression on the reader. In this story, that impression is one of horror.

Literary Analysis
Plot

Edgar Allan Poe is known for the complex, often terrifying, plots of his short stories. **Plot** is the arrangement of events that tell a story. Most plots have the following parts:

1. **Exposition:** The situation is set up and background is provided.
2. **Conflict:** A struggle between two opposing forces.
3. **Rising action:** Events build toward the high point or climax.
4. **Climax:** The turning point at which it becomes clear how the conflict will turn out.
5. **Falling action:** The events that follow the climax.
6. **Resolution:** The conflict is resolved; the final outcome is achieved.

The diagram here shows traditional plot structure.

Climax

Rising Action

Falling Action

Exposition

Resolution

Connecting Literary Elements

A **symbol** is a person, place, or thing that, in addition to its literal meaning, has other layers of meaning. In "The Tell-Tale Heart," events are set in motion by the narrator's reaction to an old man's eye. The narrator's strong reaction is not only to the eye, but to the qualities and ideas the eye represents. As you read, think about the following focus questions:

1. What feelings does the narrator associate with the old man's eye?
2. What does the eye symbolize, or represent?

Reading Strategy
Making Predictions

Become actively involved in the story by **making predictions,** logical guesses about upcoming events. First, identify the meaningful details in what has already happened. Then, decide what is most likely to happen, based on what you know and on the pattern stories usually follow.

Vocabulary Development

acute (ə kyōōt′) *adj.* sensitive (p. 523)

dissimulation (di sim′ yə lā′ shən) *n.* hiding of one's feelings or purposes (p. 523)

profound (prō found′) *adj.* intellectually deep; getting to the bottom of the matter (p. 523)

sagacity (sə gas′ ə tē) *n.* high intelligence and sound judgment (p. 524)

crevice (krev′ is) *n.* a narrow opening (p. 525)

gesticulations (jes tik′ yōō lā′ shənz) *n.* energetic hand or arm movements (p. 527)

derision (di rizh′ ən) *n.* contempt; ridicule (p. 528)

The Tell-Tale HEART

EDGAR
ALLAN
POE

True!—nervous—very, very dreadfully nervous I had been and am; but why *will* you say that I am mad? The disease had sharpened my senses—not destroyed—not dulled them. Above all was the sense of hearing <u>acute</u>. I heard all things in the heaven and in the earth. I heard many things in hell. How, then, am I mad? Hearken![1] and observe how healthily—how calmly I can tell you the whole story.

It is impossible to say how first the idea entered my brain; but once conceived, it haunted me day and night. Object there was none. Passion there was none. I loved the old man. He had never wronged me. He had never given me insult. For his gold I had no desire. I think it was his eye! yes, it was this! One of his eyes resembled that of a vulture—a pale blue eye, with a film over it. Whenever it fell upon me, my blood ran cold; and so by degrees—very gradually—I made up my mind to take the life of the old man, and thus rid myself of the eye forever.

Now this is the point. You fancy me mad. Madmen know nothing. But you should have seen *me.* You should have seen how wisely I proceeded—with what caution— with what foresight—with what <u>dissimulation</u> I went to work! I was never kinder to the old man than during the whole week before I killed him. And every night, about midnight, I turned the latch of his door and opened it—oh, so gently! And then, when I had made an opening sufficient for my head, I put in a dark lantern, all closed, closed, so that no light shone out, and then I thrust in my head. Oh, you would have laughed to see how cunningly I thrust it in! I moved it slowly—very, very slowly, so that I might not disturb the old man's sleep. It took me an hour to place my whole head within the opening so far that I could see him as he lay upon his bed. Ha!—would a madman have been so wise as this? And then, when my head was well in the room, I undid the lantern cautiously—oh, so cautiously—cautiously (for the hinges creaked)—I undid it just so much that a single thin ray fell upon the vulture eye. And this I did for seven long nights—every night just at midnight—but I found the eye always closed; and so it was impossible to do the work; for it was not the old man who vexed me, but his evil eye. And every morning, when the day broke, I went boldly into the chamber, and spoke courageously to him, calling him by name in a hearty tone, and inquiring how he had passed the night. So you see he would have been a very <u>profound</u> old man, indeed, to suspect that every night, just at twelve, I looked in upon him while he slept.

Upon the eighth night I was more than usually cautious in opening the door. A watch's minute hand moves more quickly than did mine. Never, before that night, had I *felt* the extent of my own

---

1. Hearken (här´ kən) *v.* listen.

acute (ə kyo͞ot´) *adj.* sensitive

Literary Analysis
Plot What have you learned in the exposition?

dissimulation (di sim´ yə lā´ shən) *n.* hiding of one's feelings or purposes

profound (prō found´) *adj.* intellectually deep; getting to the bottom of the matter

Reading Check

How does the narrator describe himself?

The Tell-Tale Heart ◆ 523

A scene from "The Tell-Tale Heart," a U.P.A. short based on the Edgar Allan Poe story distributed by Columbia Pictures

▲ **Critical Viewing** What details of the scene in the picture might make you nervous, as the narrator is? **[Connect]**

powers—of my sagacity. I could scarcely contain my feelings of tri-umph. To think that there I was, opening the door, little by little, and he not even to dream of my secret deeds or thoughts. I fairly chuckled at the idea; and perhaps he heard me; for he moved on the bed suddenly, as if startled. Now you may think that I drew back—but no. His room was as black as pitch with the thick dark-ness (for the shutters were close fastened, through fear of rob-bers), and so I knew that he could not see the opening of the door, and I kept pushing it on steadily, steadily.

I had my head in, and was about to open the lantern, when my thumb slipped upon the tin fastening, and the old man sprang up in the bed, crying out—"Who's there?"

I kept quite still and said nothing. For a whole hour I did not move a muscle, and in the meantime I did not hear him lie down. He was still sitting up in the bed, listening;—just as I have done,

sagacity (sə gas′ ə tē) *n.* high intelligence and sound judgment

Literary Analysis
Plot In what way is the tension increasing?

night after night, hearkening to the deathwatches[2] in the wall.

Presently I heard a slight groan, and I knew it was the groan of mortal terror. It was not a groan of pain or of grief—oh, no!—it was the low stifled sound that arises from the bottom of the soul when overcharged with awe. I knew the sound well. Many a night, just at midnight, when all the world slept, it has welled up from my own bosom, deepening, with its dreadful echo, the terrors that distracted me. I say I knew it well. I knew what the old man felt, and pitied him, although I chuckled at heart.

I knew that he had been lying awake ever since the first slight noise, when he had turned in the bed. His fears had been ever since growing upon him. He had been trying to fancy them causeless, but could not. He had been saying to himself—"It is nothing but the wind in the chimney—it is only a mouse crossing the floor," or "it is merely a cricket which has made a single chirp." Yes, he has been trying to comfort himself with these suppositions: but he had found all in vain. *All in vain*; because Death, in approaching him, had stalked with his black shadow before him, and enveloped the victim. And it was the mournful influence of the unperceived shadow that caused him to feel—although he neither saw nor heard—to *feel* the presence of my head within the room.

When I had waited a long time, very patiently, without hearing him lie down, I resolved to open a little—a very, very little <u>crevice</u> in the lantern. So I opened it—you cannot imagine how stealthily, stealthily—until, at length, a single dim ray, like the thread of the spider, shot from out the crevice and fell upon the vulture eye.

It was open—wide, wide open—and I grew furious as I gazed upon it. I saw it with perfect distinctness—all a dull blue, with a hideous veil over it that chilled the very marrow in my bones; but I could see nothing else of the old man's face or person for I had directed the ray as if by instinct, precisely upon the spot.

And now—have I not told you that what you mistake for madness is but overacuteness of the senses?—now, I say, there came to my ears a low, dull, quick sound, such as a watch makes when enveloped in cotton. I knew *that* sound well, too. It was the beating of the old man's heart. It increased my fury, as the beating of a drum stimulates the soldier into courage.

But even yet I refrained and kept still. I scarcely breathed. I held the lantern motionless. I tried how steadily I could maintain the ray upon the eye. Meantime the hellish tattoo of the heart increased. It grew quicker and quicker, and louder and louder every instant. The old man's terror *must* have been extreme! It grew louder, I say, louder every moment!—do you mark me well? I have told you that I am nervous: so I am. And now at the dead

---

2. **deathwatches** (deth′ woch′ əz) *n.* wood-boring beetles whose heads make a tapping sound superstitiously regarded as an omen of death.

crevice (krev′ is) *n.* a narrow opening

Literary Analysis
Plot and Symbol Why is it important that the light shine directly on the eye and nowhere else?

**Reading Check**

What is the narrator's intention toward the old man? Why?

hour of the night, amid the dreadful silence of that old house, so strange a noise as this excited me to uncontrollable terror. Yet, for some minutes longer I refrained and stood still. But the beating grew louder, louder! I thought the heart must burst. And now a new anxiety seized me—the sound would be heard by a neighbor! The old man's hour had come! With a loud yell, I threw open the lantern and leaped into the room. He shrieked once—once only. In an instant I dragged him to the floor, and pulled the heavy bed over him. I then smiled gaily, to find the deed so far done. But, for many minutes, the heart beat on with a muffled sound. This, however, did not vex me; it would not be heard through the wall. At length it ceased. The old man was dead. I removed the bed and examined the corpse. Yes, he was stone, stone dead. I placed my hand upon the heart and held it there many minutes. There was no pulsation. He was stone dead. His eye would trouble me no more.

If still you think me mad, you will think so no longer when I describe the wise precautions I took for the concealment of the body. The night waned, and I worked hastily, but in silence. First of all I dismembered the corpse. I cut off the head and the arms and the legs.

Reading Strategy
Making Predictions Do you predict that the author will be this calm throughout the rest of the story? Why or why not?

▼ Critical Viewing
What part of the story does this drawing illustrate? **[Connect]**

A scene from "The Tell-Tale Heart," a U.P.A. short based on the Edgar Allan Poe story distributed by Columbia Pictures

I then took up three planks from the flooring of the chamber, and deposited all between the scantlings.[3] I then replaced the boards so cleverly, so cunningly, that no human eye—not even *his* —could have detected anything wrong. There was nothing to wash out—no stain of any kind—no blood-spot whatever. I had been too wary for that. A tub had caught all—ha! ha!

When I had made an end of these labors, it was four o'clock—still dark as midnight. As the bell sounded the hour, there came a knocking at the street door. I went down to open it with a light heart—for what had I *now* to fear? There entered three men, who introduced themselves, with perfect suavity, as officers of the police. A shriek had been heard by a neighbor during the night; suspicion of foul play had been aroused; information had been lodged at the police office, and they (the officers) had been deputed to search the premises.

I smiled—for *what* had I to fear? I bade the gentlemen welcome. The shriek, I said, was my own in a dream. The old man, I mentioned, was absent in the country. I took my visitors all over the house. I bade them search—search *well*. I led them, at length, to *his* chamber. I showed them his treasures, secure, undisturbed. In the enthusiasm of my confidence, I brought chairs into the room, and desired them *here* to rest from their fatigues, while I myself, in the wild audacity of my perfect triumph, placed my own seat upon the very spot beneath which reposed the corpse of the victim.

The officers were satisfied. My *manner* had convinced them. I was singularly at ease. They sat, and while I answered cheerily, they chatted of familiar things. But, ere long, I felt myself getting pale and wished them gone. My head ached, and I fancied a ringing in my ears: but still they sat and still chatted. The ringing became more distinct:—it continued and became more distinct: I talked more freely to get rid of the feeling: but it continued and gained definitiveness—until, at length, I found that the noise was *not* within my ears.

No doubt I now grew *very* pale—but I talked more fluently, and with a heightened voice. Yet the sound increased—and what could I do? It was a *low, dull, quick sound—much such a sound as a watch makes when enveloped in cotton.* I gasped for breath—and yet the officers heard it not. I talked more quickly—more vehemently; but the noise steadily increased. I arose and argued about trifles, in a high key and with violent gesticulations; but the noise steadily increased. Why *would* they not be gone? I paced the floor to and fro with heavy strides, as if excited to fury by the observations of the men—but the noise steadily increased. Oh! what *could* I do? I foamed—I raved—I swore! I swung the chair upon which I had

Reading Strategy
Making Predictions Will the police officers discover the crime? Explain.

Literary Analysis
Plot What new conflict is introduced here?

gesticulations
(jes tik´ yōō lā´ shənz) *n.* energetic hand or arm movements

✓**Reading Check**

What sound does the speaker hear?

---

3. **scantlings** (skant´ liŋz) *n.* small beams or timbers.

been sitting, and grated it upon the boards, but the noise arose over all, and continually increased. It grew louder—louder—*louder!* And still the men chatted pleasantly, and smiled. Was it possible they heard not?— no, no! They heard!—they suspected!— they *knew!* —they were making a mockery of my horror!—this I thought, and this I think. But anything was better than this agony! Anything was more tolerable than this <u>derision</u>! I could bear those hypocritical smiles no longer! I felt that I must scream or die!—and now again! hark! louder! louder! louder! *louder!*—

"Villains!" I shrieked, "dissemble⁴ no more! I admit the deed!—tear up the planks!—here, here!—it is the beating of his hideous heart!"

derision (di rizh´ ən) *n.* contempt; ridicule

---

4. **dissemble** (di sem´ bəl) *v.* conceal under a false appearance; to conceal the truth of one's true feelings or motives.

Review and Assess
Thinking About the Literature

1. **Respond:** At which point did you find the narrator most frightening?

2. **(a) Recall:** In order, retell the steps of the narrator's plan. **(b) Analyze:** Why does the narrator enjoy going through the steps of his plan each night? **(c) Contrast:** Contrast the narrator's opinion of himself with his opinion of the old man.

3. **(a) Recall:** Why does the narrator kill the old man? **(b) Draw Conclusions:** What does the narrator fear? **(c) Support:** What details in the story indicate his fears?

4. **(a) Recall:** How does the narrator behave in the presence of the police? **(b) Draw Conclusions:** What aspects of the narrator's behavior prove that he is insane? **(c) Analyze:** How would the story be different if the events in it were told by a police officer?

5. **(a) Recall:** What sound drives the narrator to confess to the crime? **(b) Apply:** Why do you think people sometimes confess or admit to having done something wrong, even if there is little chance that their wrongdoing will be discovered? **(c) Extend:** The "Tell-Tale Heart" in the title might be the old man's heart—or it might be the narrator's heart. Offer a brief explanation for both interpretations. Then, tell which interpretation you prefer and why.

6. **Take a Position:** Do you think the narrator should be put in prison or in a mental hospital for the criminally insane? Explain.

Edgar Allan Poe

(1809–1849)

If Poe's stories and poems deal with sorrow, crime, and horror, it may be because his own life was so troubled.

During his life, Poe endured personal tragedies, including the early death of his mother. Poe was raised, but never formally adopted, by Mr. and Mrs. John Allan of Richmond, Virginia. Poe quarreled often with John Allan, usually about Poe's spending and debt.

Poe is often called the inventor of the modern detective story. He was also one of the first writers or critics to suggest that short stories have a specific formula or pattern.

Though Poe's stories and poems attracted notice, they never gained him financial success. In 1849, two years after the death of his wife Virginia, Poe died penniless and alone.

Review and Assess

Literary Analysis

Plot

1. Explain the conflict between the young man and the old man.
2. What are two events that increase the tension of the conflict?
3. The **plot** of "The Tell-Tale Heart" has two related conflicts, each with its own climax. Make a chart like the one shown to identify relationships between these plot elements.

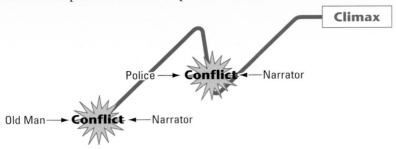

Connecting Literary Elements

4. Make a graphic organizer like the one shown to explore the symbolism of the eye. In the middle oval, write feelings and associations the narrator connects to the eye. Then, in the outer oval, write what you think the eye symbolizes.

5. What feelings and associations are connected to the old man's heart?
6. What does the heart symbolize or represent?

Reading Strategy

Making Predictions

7. What did you **predict** the young man would do about the eye?
8. Did you predict that the narrator would or would not get away with the murder? Why?

Extend Understanding

9. **Evaluate:** Explain why you think this story is more or less frightening than current horror movies or television programs.

Quick Review

Plot is the arrangement of events that tell a story. To review plot, see page 521.

A **symbol** is a person, place, or thing that in addition to its own meaning, has layers of meaning. To review symbol, see page 521.

 Take It to the Net

www.phschool.com

Take the interactive self-test online to check your understanding of the selection.

Integrate Language Skills

Vocabulary Development Lesson

Word Analysis: Latin Root *-found-*

Profound contains the Latin word root *-found-*, meaning "bottom." Show how each *-found-* word relates to starting from, or getting to, the "bottom."

1. Poe laid the *foundation* for the detective story.
2. He was *profound* in his knowledge of tales.
3. Critics regard him as one of the *founders* of American literature.

Spelling Strategy

The *zhun* sound at the end of a word is usually spelled *sion*. Unscramble the letters to write words with this ending.

1. snilliooc   2. soprivnio   3. driosine

Concept Development: Analogies

In word pairs, an **analogy** identifies a shared relationship between ideas that are otherwise unrelated. Complete each analogy with a vocabulary word from the list on page 521.

1. *Alert* is to *drowsy* as *praise* is to ___?___.
2. *Sweet* is to *sour* as *dull* is to ___?___.
3. *Marsh* is to *swamp* as *wisdom* is to ___?___.
4. *Contrary* is to *agreeable* as *frankness* is to ___?___.
5. *Paintbrush* is to *painting* as *hands* is to ___?___.
6. *Boring* is to *fascinating* as *shallow* is to ___?___.
7. *Summit* is to *peak* as *crack* is to ___?___.

Grammar Lesson

Adverb Clauses

An **adverb clause** is a subordinate clause that functions as an adverb. (An adverb modifies a verb, an adjective, or other adverb and answers the questions *when, where, how, why, to what extent,* or *under what conditions*.) A subordinate clause has a noun and a verb but cannot stand alone as a sentence.

Adverb clauses begin with subordinating conjunctions like *after, as, although, because, if, since, when, unless,* and *until*. In this example the adverb clause is italicized:

> *As the bell sounded the hour*, there came a knocking at the street door.

▶ *For more practice, see page R31, Exercise D.*
Practice On your paper, identify the adverb clause in each sentence. Then, tell which question it answers.

1. When the day broke, I went boldly into the chamber.
2. I could see him as he lay upon his bed.
3. He had been lying awake since the first slight noise.
4. When I had made an end of these labors, it was four o'clock.
5. The police suspected the narrator because he acted strangely.

Writing Application Write three sentences about the narrator's actions, using an adverb clause in each.

W̶G̶ Prentice Hall Writing and Grammar Connection: Chapter 20, Section 2

Writing Lesson

Response to Literature

Write a brief response to "The Tell-Tale Heart" in which you explain why you do or do not like Poe's short story, or why you like some parts and not others. Connect your responses to specific examples from the story.

Prewriting   Divide a piece of paper into three long sections, or columns. In the first column, make a list of features you do and don't like. In the second column, describe or explain the feature in literary terms. In the third column, explain why you feel the feature adds to or takes away from your enjoyment of the story.

Model: Gathering Details

Feature	Description	Explanation
Narrator	First-person frightening character	His telling makes the story more gripping.

Drafting   Begin with a statement of your overall response. Then, elaborate, or provide more details with the examples from your three-column list. Conclude with a statement that sums up your general feeling.

Revising   Underline each opinion you have expressed. If you did not provide at least one specific example from the story to support your opinion, add one now.

℘ *Prentice Hall Writing and Grammar Connection, Chapter 12 , Section 3*

Extension Activity

Research and Technology Write a brief **essay** in which you **analyze and evaluate** the illustrations on pages 524 and 526. Notice the following ways the artist creates an impression of sinister gloom. Look for the following details:

- sharp contrast between light and dark.
- large areas of complete darkness
- faces partially hidden in shadow

Evaluate how effectively these visual techniques achieve an impression appropriate to the story.

Listening and Speaking With a classmate, stage an **interview** between the narrator and a newspaper reporter.

- Develop a list of questions that you want to ask the narrator.
- Based on details from the story, prepare answers the narrator might give to these questions. (You may need to add invented details.)

 ***Take It to the Net***   www.phschool.com

Go online for an additional research activity using the Internet.

Prepare to Read

The Day I Got Lost ◆ Hamadi

 Take It to the Net

Visit www.phschool.com
for interactive activities
and instruction related to
these selections, including
- background
- graphic organizers
- literary elements
- reading strategies

Preview

Connecting to the Literature

People everywhere rush through their daily routines, racing from home to school or work, back home, and out again. However, these stories hint that sometimes it is those people who march to their own drummer—who are "outside" the norm—who find wisdom and peace. As you read these stories, notice which characters are able to remain calm in the everyday crisis of their worlds.

Background

Both these stories use a type of character from folk tales known as the wise fool. This character is a fool because he may forget his address, speak strangely, or wear unfashionable clothes. Yet this "fool" turns out to be wiser than the characters who seem to know where they are going.

Literary Analysis

Character

Characters are the people or animals who take part in the action of a literary work. They can be round, flat, dynamic, or static.

- **Round characters** have many character traits or qualities. A round character has an individual personality with a unique combination of likes and dislikes, opinions, beliefs, and attitudes.
- **Flat characters** have only one or two recognizable character traits or qualities. A flat character is a personality "type" that does not have unique opinions, beliefs, or attitudes.
- **Dynamic characters** change and grow as the story progresses.
- **Static characters** do not change or grow.

As you read, look for the different types of characters.

Comparing Literary Works

The characters, events, and ideas in a fictional work sometimes reflect the author's real life experiences, beliefs, or heritage. Read the author biographies on pages 538 and 546. Notice differences in the two stories that reflect the differences in the authors' backgrounds. The organizer shows a detail from each work that connects to each author's background. Look for other details as you read and add them to the organizers.

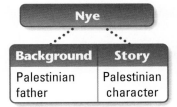

Nye	
Background	**Story**
Palestinian father	Palestinian character

Singer	
Background	**Story**
Writes in Yiddish	"Shlemiel" is a Yiddish word.

Reading Strategy

Identifying with a Character

When you **identify with a character,** you respond to story situations based on the character's background and experiences. Sometimes, you may have related or similar experience or background that can help you understand the character. As you read, ask yourself the following focus questions to help you identify with characters.

1. In what ways are this character's background and experiences similar to and different from mine?
2. What background or experiences influence the way this character behaves?

Vocabulary Development

forsaken (fər sā′ kən) *adj.* abandoned; desolate (p. 537)

brittle (brit′ əl) *adj.* stiff and unbending (p. 539)

lavish (lav′ ish) *adj.* showy; more than enough (p. 541)

refugees (ref′ yoo jēz′) *n.* people who flee from their homes in a time of trouble (p. 545)

melancholy (mel′ ən käl′ ē) *adj.* sad; depressed (p. 545)

The Day I Got Lost

Isaac Bashevis Singer

Windows, 1951, Charles Sheeler, Collection, Hirschl & Adler Galleries

It is easy to recognize me. See a man in the street wearing a too long coat, too large shoes, a crumpled hat with a wide brim, spectacles with one lens missing, and carrying an umbrella though the sun is shining, and that man will be me, Professor Shlemiel.[1] There are other unmistakable clues to my identity. My pockets are always bulging with newspapers, magazines, and just papers. I carry an overstuffed briefcase, and I'm forever making mistakes. I've been living in New York City for over forty years, yet whenever I want to go uptown, I find myself walking downtown, and when I want to go east, I go west. I'm always late and I never recognize anybody.

I'm always misplacing things. A hundred times a day I ask myself, Where is my pen? Where is my money? Where is my handkerchief? Where is my address book? I am what is known as an absent-minded professor.

For many years I have been teaching philosophy in the same university, and I still have difficulty in locating my classrooms. Elevators play strange tricks on me. I want to go to the top floor and I land in the basement. Hardly a day passes when an elevator door doesn't close on me. Elevator doors are my worst enemies.

In addition to my constant blundering and losing things, I'm forgetful. I enter a coffee shop, hang up my coat, and leave without it. By the time I remember to go back for it, I've forgotten where I've been. I lose hats, books, umbrellas, rubbers, and above all manuscripts. Sometimes I even forget my own address. One evening I took a taxi because I was in a hurry to get home. The taxi driver said, "Where to?" And I could not remember where I lived.

"Home!" I said.

"Where is home?" he asked in astonishment.

"I don't remember," I replied.

"What is your name?"

"Professor Shlemiel."

"Professor," the driver said, "I'll get you to a telephone booth. Look in the telephone book and you'll find your address."

He drove me to the nearest drugstore with a telephone booth in it, but he refused to wait. I was about to enter the store when I realized I had left my briefcase behind. I ran after the taxi, shouting, "My briefcase, my briefcase!" But the taxi was already out of earshot.

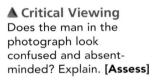

▲ **Critical Viewing**
Does the man in the photograph look confused and absent-minded? Explain. **[Assess]**

Reading Check

What is Professor Shlemiel's main weakness?

---

1. Shlemiel (shlə mēl′) version of the slang word *schlemiel*, an ineffectual, bungling person.

◀ **Critical Viewing** Explain the ways a person might get lost in a setting like the one shown in the painting. **[Summarize]**

In the drugstore, I found a telephone book, but when I looked under S, I saw to my horror that though there were a number of Shlemiels listed, I was not among them. At that moment I recalled that several months before, Mrs. Shlemiel had decided that we should have an unlisted telephone number. The reason was that my students thought nothing of calling me in the middle of the night and waking me up. It also happened quite frequently that someone wanted to call another Shlemiel and got me by mistake. That was all very well—but how was I going to get home?

I usually had some letters addressed to me in my breast pocket. But just that day I had decided to clean out my pockets. It was my birthday and my wife had invited friends in for the evening. She had baked a huge cake and decorated it with birthday candles. I could see my friends sitting in our living room, waiting to wish me a happy birthday. And here I stood in some drugstore, for the life of me not able to remember where I lived.

Then I recalled the telephone number of a friend of mine, Dr. Motherhead, and I decided to call him for help. I dialed and a young girl's voice answered.

"Is Dr. Motherhead at home?"

"No," she replied.

"Is his wife at home?"

"They're both out," the girl said.

"Perhaps you can tell me where they can be reached?" I said.

"I'm only the babysitter, but I think they went to a party at Professor Shlemiel's. Would you like to leave a message?" she said. "Who shall I say called, please?"

"Professor Shlemiel," I said.

"They left for your house about an hour ago," the girl said.

"Can you tell me where they went?" I asked.

"I've just told you," she said. "They went to your house."

"But where do I live?"

"You must be kidding!" the girl said, and hung up.

I tried to call a number of friends (those whose telephone numbers I happened to think of), but wherever I called, I got the same reply: "They've gone to a party at Professor Shlemiel's."

As I stood in the street wondering what to do, it began to rain. "Where's my umbrella?" I said to myself. And I knew the answer at once. I'd left it—somewhere. I got under a nearby canopy. It was now raining cats and dogs. It lightninged and thundered. All day it had been sunny and warm, but now that I was lost and my umbrella was lost, it had to storm. And it looked as if it would go on for the rest of the night.

To distract myself, I began to ponder the ancient philosophical

▲ **Critical Viewing**
Would Professor Shlemiel get lost in a place like this? Why or why not?
[Speculate]

problem. A mother chicken lays an egg, I thought to myself, and when it hatches, there is a chicken. That's how it has always been. Every chicken comes from an egg and every egg comes from a chicken. But was there a chicken first? Or an egg first? No philosopher has ever been able to solve this eternal question. Just the same, there must be an answer. Perhaps I, Shlemiel, am destined to stumble on it.

It continued to pour buckets. My feet were getting wet and I was chilled. I began to sneeze and I wanted to wipe my nose, but my handkerchief, too, was gone.

At that moment I saw a big black dog. He was standing in the rain getting soaked and looking at me with sad eyes. I knew immediately what the trouble was. The dog was lost. He, too, had forgotten his address. I felt a great love for that innocent animal. I called to him and he came running to me. I talked to him as if he were human. "Fellow, we're in the same boat," I said. "I'm a man shlemiel and you're a dog shlemiel. Perhaps it's also your birthday, and there's a party for you, too. And here you stand shivering and forsaken in the rain, while your loving master is searching for you everywhere. You're probably just as hungry as I am."

I patted the dog on his wet head and he wagged his tail. "Whatever happens to me will happen to you," I said. "I'll keep you with me until we both find our homes. If we don't find your master, you'll stay with me. Give me your paw," I said. The dog lifted his right paw. There was no question that he understood.

A taxi drove by and splattered us both. Suddenly it stopped and I heard someone shouting, "Shlemiel! Shlemiel!" I looked up and saw the taxi door open, and the head of a friend of mine appeared. "Shlemiel," he called. "What are you doing here? Who are you waiting for?"

"Where are you going?" I asked.

"To your house, of course. I'm sorry I'm late, but I was detained. Anyhow, better late than never. But why aren't you at home? And whose dog is that?"

"Only God could have sent you!" I exclaimed. "What a night! I've forgotten my address, I've left my briefcase in a taxi, I've lost my umbrella, and I don't know where my rubbers are."

"Shlemiel," my friend said, "if there was ever an absentminded professor, you're it!"

When I rang the bell of my apartment, my wife opened the door. "Shlemiel!" she shrieked. "Everybody is waiting for you. Where have you been? Where is your briefcase? Your umbrella? Your rubbers? And who is this dog?"

Our friends surrounded me. "Where have you been?" they cried. "We were so worried. We thought surely something had happened to you!"

"Who is this dog?" my wife kept repeating.

Literary Analysis
Character Why would the professor be considered a round character?

forsaken (fər sā′ kən) *adj.* abandoned; desolate

✔**Reading Check**
What is Professor Shlemiel looking for?

"I don't know," I said finally. "I found him in the street. Let's just call him Bow Wow for the time being."

"Bow Wow, indeed!" my wife scolded. "You know our cat hates dogs. And what about the parakeets? He'll scare them to death."

"He's a quiet dog," I said. "He'll make friends with the cat. I'm sure he loves parakeets. I could not leave him shivering in the rain. He's a good soul."

The moment I said this the dog let out a bloodcurdling howl. The cat ran into the room. When she saw the dog, she arched her back and spat at him, ready to scratch out his eyes. The parakeets in their cage began flapping their wings and screeching. Everybody started talking at once. There was pandemonium.

Would you like to know how it all ended?

Bow Wow still lives with us. He and the cat are great friends. The parakeets have learned to ride on his back as if he were a horse. As for my wife, she loves Bow Wow even more than I do. Whenever I take the dog out, she says, "Now, don't forget your address, both of you."

I never did find my briefcase, or my umbrella, or my rubbers. Like many philosophers before me, I've given up trying to solve the riddle of which came first, the chicken or the egg. Instead, I've started writing a book called *The Memoirs of Shlemiel*. If I don't forget the manuscript in a taxi, or a restaurant, or on a bench in the park, you may read them someday. In the meantime, here is a sample chapter.

Review and Assess

Thinking About the Literature

1. **Respond:** Have you ever known anyone who was a little like Professor Shlemiel? Explain.

2. **(a) Recall:** What does Professer Shlemiel do to try to find out his own address? **(b) Connect:** Why is this strategy unsuccessful? **(c) Interpet:** How does this behavior illustrate the Yiddish meaning of his name: "an ineffectual person"?

3. **(a) Recall:** Describe the dog that Professor Shlemiel finds. **(b) Compare:** How are the professor and the dog alike? **(c) Infer:** How does the professor seem to be rewarded for his kindness to the dog?

4. **(a) Recall:** How does the professor's wife react to the sight of the dog? **(b) Evaluate:** Does the professor give good persuasive reasons for keeping the dog? Explain.

5. **Analyze:** What is the wisest thing the professor says during the course of the story? Explain.

Isaac Bashevis Singer

(1904-1991)

Isaac Bashevis Singer came from a family of Jewish religious leaders in Poland. He grew up in Warsaw, Poland's capital, and received a Jewish education. However, Singer decided to become a writer instead of a religious leader.

In 1935, Singer left his home and moved to the United States. However, he described his lost home in the many Yiddish stories he wrote about Poland's Jews. Translated from English into Yiddish and other languages, these stories won him the Nobel Prize for Literature in 1978.

Hamadi
Naomi Shihab Nye

Susan didn't really feel interested in Saleh Hamadi until she was a freshman in high school carrying a thousand questions around. Why this way? Why not another way? Who said so and why can't I say something else? Those <u>brittle</u> women at school in the counselor's office treated the world as if it were a yardstick and they had tight hold of both ends.

Sometimes Susan felt polite with them, sorting attendance cards during her free period, listening to them gab about fingernail polish and television. And other times she felt she could run out of the building yelling. That's when she daydreamed about Saleh Hamadi, who had nothing to do with any of it. Maybe she thought of him as escape, the way she used to think about the Sphinx at Giza[1] when she was younger. She would picture the golden Sphinx sitting quietly in the desert with sand blowing around its face, never changing its expression. She would think of its wry, slightly crooked mouth and how her grandmother looked a little like that as she waited for her bread to bake in the old village north of Jerusalem. Susan's family had lived in Jerusalem for three years before she was ten and drove out to see her grandmother every weekend. They would find her patting fresh dough between her hands, or pressing cakes of dough onto the black rocks in the taboon, the rounded old oven outdoors. Sometimes she moved her lips as she worked. Was she praying? Singing a secret song? Susan had never seen her grandmother rushing.

Now that she was fourteen, she took long walks in America with her father down by the drainage ditch at the end of their street. Pecan trees shaded the path. She tried to get him to tell stories about his childhood in Palestine. She didn't want him to forget anything. She helped her American mother complete tedious kitchen tasks without complaining—rolling grape leaves around their lemony rice stuffing, scrubbing carrots for the roaring juicer. Some evenings when the soft Texas twilight pulled them all outside, she thought of her far-away grandmother and said, "Let's go see Saleh Hamadi.

---

1. Sphinx (sfiŋks) **at Giza** (gē´ zə) huge statue with the head of a man and the body of a lion, located near Cairo in northern Egypt.

Hamadi ◆ 539

Wouldn't he like some of that cheese pie Mom made?" And they would wrap a slice of pie and drive downtown. Somehow he felt like a good substitute for a grandmother, even though he was a man.

Usually Hamadi was wearing a white shirt, shiny black tie, and a jacket that reminded Susan of the earth's surface just above the treeline on a mountain—thin, somehow purified. He would raise his hands high before giving advice.

"It is good to drink a tall glass of water every morning upon arising!" If anyone doubted this, he would shake his head. "Oh Susan, Susan, Susan," he would say.

He did not like to sit down, but he wanted everyone else to sit down. He made Susan sit on the wobbly chair beside the desk and he made her father or mother sit in the saggy center of the bed. He told them people should eat six small meals a day.

They visited him on the sixth floor of the Traveler's Hotel, where he had lived so long nobody could remember him ever traveling. Susan's father used to remind him of the apartments available over the Victory Cleaners, next to the park with the fizzy pink fountain, but Hamadi would shake his head, pinching kisses at his spartan room. "A white handkerchief spread across a tabletop, my two extra shoes lined by the wall, this spells 'home' to me, this says 'mi casa.' What more do I need?"

Hamadi liked to use Spanish words. They made him feel expansive, worldly. He'd learned them when he worked at the fruits and vegetables warehouse on Zarzamora Street, marking off crates of apples and avocados on a long white pad. Occasionally he would speak Arabic, his own first language, with Susan's father and uncles, but he said it made him feel too sad, as if his mother might step into the room at any minute, her arms laden with fresh mint leaves. He had come to the United States on a boat when he was eighteen years old and he had never been married. "I married books," he said. "I married the wide horizon."

"What is he to us?" Susan used to ask her father. "He's not a relative, right? How did we meet him to begin with?"

Susan's father couldn't remember. "I think we just drifted together. Maybe we met at your uncle Hani's house. Maybe that old Maronite priest who used to cry after every service introduced us. The priest once shared an apartment with Kahlil Gibran[2] in New York—so he said. And Saleh always says he stayed with Gibran when he first got off the boat. I'll bet that popular guy Gibran has had a lot of roommates he doesn't even know about."

Susan said, "Dad, he's dead."

"I know, I know," her father said.

Literary Analysis
Character Is Hamadi a round character or a flat character? Explain.

---

2. Kahlil Gibran (kä lēl′ ji brän′) Lebanese novelist, poet, and artist who lived from 1883 to 1931; his most famous book is The Prophet.

Later Susan said, "Mr. Hamadi, did you really meet Kahlil Gibran? He's one of my favorite writers." Hamadi walked slowly to the window of his room and stared out. There wasn't much to look at down on the street—a bedraggled[3] flower shop, a boarded-up tavern with a hand-lettered sign tacked to the front, GONE TO FIND JESUS. Susan's father said the owners had really gone to Alabama.

Hamadi spoke patiently. "Yes, I met brother Gibran. And I meet him in my heart every day. When I was a young man—shocked by all the visions of the new world—the tall buildings—the wild traffic—the young people without shame—the proud mailboxes in their blue uniforms—I met him. And he has stayed with me every day of my life."

"But did you really meet him, like in person, or just in a book?"

He turned dramatically. "Make no such distinctions, my friend. Or your life will be a pod with only dried-up beans inside. Believe anything can happen."

Susan's father looked irritated, but Susan smiled. "I do," she said. "I believe that. I want fat beans. If I imagine something, it's true, too. Just a different kind of true."

Susan's father was twiddling with the knobs on the old-fashioned sink. "Don't they even give you hot water here? You don't mean to tell me you've been living without hot water?"

On Hamadi's rickety desk lay a row of different "Love" stamps issued by the post office.

"You must write a lot of letters," Susan said.

"No, no, I'm just focusing on that word," Hamadi said. "I particularly like the globe in the shape of a heart," he added.

"Why don't you take a trip back to his village in Lebanon?" Susan's father asked. "Maybe you still have relatives living there."

Hamadi looked pained. "'Remembrance is a form of meeting,' my brother Gibran says, and I do believe I meet with my cousins every day."

"But aren't you curious? You've been gone so long! Wouldn't you like to find out what has happened to everybody and everything you knew as a boy?" Susan's father traveled back to Jerusalem once every year to see his family.

"I would not. In fact, I already know. It is there and it is not there. Would you like to share an orange with me?"

His long fingers, tenderly peeling. Once when Susan was younger, he'd given her a lavish ribbon off a holiday fruit basket and expected her to wear it on her head. In the car, Susan's father said, "Riddles. He talks in riddles. I don't know why I have patience with him." Susan stared at the people talking and laughing in the next car. She did not even exist in their world.

---

3. **bedraggled** (bē drag′ əld) *adj.* limp and dirty, as if dragged through mud.

Reading Strategy

Identify with a Character
In what way might Susan's background influence her choice of favorite writer?

lavish (lav′ ish) *adj.* showy; more than enough

 **Reading Check**

Why does Susan like spending time with Hamadi?

Susan carried *The Prophet* around on top of her English textbook and her Texas history. She and her friend Tracy read it out loud to one another at lunch. Tracy was a junior—they'd met at the literary magazine meeting where Susan, the only freshman on the staff, got assigned to do proofreading. They never ate in the cafeteria; they sat outside at picnic tables with sack lunches, whole wheat crackers and fresh peaches. Both of them had given up meat.

Tracy's eyes looked steamy. "You know that place where Gibran says, 'Hate is a dead thing. Who of you would be a tomb?'

Susan nodded. Tracy continued. "Well, I hate someone. I'm trying not to, but I can't help it. I hate Debbie for liking Eddie and it's driving me nuts."

"Why shouldn't Debbie like Eddie?" Susan said. "*You* do."

Tracy put her head down on her arms. A gang of cheerleaders walked by giggling. One of them flicked her finger in greeting.

"In fact, we *all* like Eddie," Susan said. "Remember, here in this book—wait and I'll find it—where Gibran says that loving teaches us the secrets of our hearts and that's the way we connect to all of Life's heart? You're not talking about liking or loving, you're talking about owning."

Tracy looked glum. "Sometimes you remind me of a minister."

Susan said, "Well, just talk to me someday when *I'm* depressed."

Susan didn't want a boyfriend. Everyone who had boyfriends or girlfriends all seemed to have troubles. Susan told people she had a boyfriend far away, on a farm in Missouri, but the truth was, boys still seemed like cousins to her. Or brothers. Or even girls.

A squirrel sat in the crook of a tree, eyeing their sandwiches. When the end-of-lunch bell blared, Susan and Tracy jumped—it always seemed too soon. Squirrels were lucky; they didn't have to go to school.

Susan's father said her idea was ridiculous: to invite Saleh Hamadi to go Christmas caroling with the English Club. "His English is archaic,[4] for one thing, and he won't know any of the songs."

"How could you live in America for years and not know 'Joy to the World' or 'Away in a Manger'?"

"Listen, I grew up right down the road from 'Oh Little Town of Bethlehem' and I still don't know a single verse."

"I want him. We need him. It's boring being with the same bunch of people all the time."

So they called Saleh and he said he would come—"thrilled" was the word he used. He wanted to ride the bus to their house, he didn't want anyone to pick him up. Her father muttered, "He'll probably forget to get off." Saleh thought "caroling" meant they were going out

Reading Strategy
Identifying with a Character What experiences or reactions do you have in common with these characters?

---

4. archaic (är kā´ ik) *adj.* old-fashioned; out-of-date.

542 ◆ *Short Stories*

with a woman named Carol. He said, "Holiday spirit—I was just reading about it in the newspaper."

Susan said, "Dress warm."

Saleh replied, "Friend, my heart is warmed simply to hear your voice."

All that evening Susan felt light and bouncy. She decorated the coffee can they would use to collect donations to be sent to the children's hospital in Bethlehem. She had started doing this last year in middle school, when a singing group collected $100 and the hospital responded on exotic onion-skin stationery that they were "eternally grateful."

Her father shook his head. "You get something into your mind and it really takes over," he said. "Why do you like Hamadi so much all of a sudden? You could show half as much interest in your own uncles."

Susan laughed. Her uncles were dull. Her uncles shopped at the mall and watched TV. "Anyone who watches TV more than twelve minutes a week is uninteresting," she said.

Her father lifted an eyebrow.

"He's my surrogate grandmother," she said. "He says interesting things. He makes me think. Remember when I was little and he called me The Thinker? We have a connection." She added, "Listen, do you want to go too? It is not a big deal. And Mom has a *great* voice, why don't you both come?"

A minute later her mother was digging in the closet for neck scarves, and her father was digging in the drawer for flashlight batteries.

Saleh Hamadi arrived precisely on time, with flushed red cheeks and a sack of dates stuffed in his pocket. "We may need sustenance on our journey." Susan thought the older people seemed quite giddy as they drove down to the high school to meet the rest of the carolers. Strands of winking lights wrapped around their neighbors' drainpipes and trees. A giant Santa tipped his hat on Dr. Garcia's roof.

Her friends stood gathered in front of the school. Some were smoothing out song sheets that had been crammed in a drawer or cabinet for a whole year. Susan thought holidays were strange; they came, and you were supposed to feel ready for them. What if you could make up your own holidays as you went along? She had read about a woman who used to have parties to celebrate the arrival of fresh asparagus in the local market. Susan's friends might make holidays called Eddie Looked at Me Today and Smiled.

▲ **Critical Viewing**
Do the girls in the photograph seem to share qualities with Susan and Tracy? Explain.
[Compare and Contrast]

Reading Check

What activity does Susan invite the adults to join?

Two people were alleluia-ing in harmony. Saleh Hamadi went around the group formally introducing himself to each person and shaking hands. A few people laughed behind their hands when his back was turned. He had stepped out of a painting, or a newscast, with his outdated long overcoat, his clunky old men's shoes and elegant manners.

Susan spoke more loudly than usual. "I'm honored to introduce you to one of my best friends, Mr. Hamadi."

"Good evening to you," he pronounced musically, bowing a bit from the waist.

What could you say back but "Good evening, sir." His old–fashioned manners were contagious.

They sang at three houses which never opened their doors. They sang "We Wish You a Merry Christmas" each time they moved on. Lisa had a fine, clear soprano. Tracy could find the alto harmony to any line. Cameron and Elliot had more enthusiasm than accuracy. Lily, Rita, and Jeannette laughed every time they said a wrong word and fumbled to find their places again. Susan loved to see how her mother knew every word of every verse without looking at the paper, and her father kept his hands in his pockets and seemed more interested in examining people's mailboxes or yard displays than in trying to sing. And Saleh Hamadi—what language was he singing in? He didn't even seem to be pronouncing words, but humming deeply from his throat. Was he saying, "Om?" Speaking Arabic? Once he caught her looking and whispered, "That was an Aramaic word that just drifted into my mouth—the true language of the Bible, you know, the language Jesus Christ himself spoke."

By the fourth block their voices felt tuned up and friendly people came outside to listen. Trays of cookies were passed around and dollar bills stuffed into the little can. Thank you, thank you. Out of the dark from down the block, Susan noticed Eddie sprinting toward them with his coat flapping, unbuttoned. She shot a glance at Tracy, who pretended not to notice. "Hey, guys!" shouted Eddie. "The first time in my life I'm late and everyone else is on time! You could at least have left a note about which way you were going." Someone slapped him on the back. Saleh Hamadi, whom he had never seen before, was the only one who managed a reply. "Welcome, welcome to our cheery group!"

Eddie looked mystified. "Who is this guy?"

Susan whispered, "My friend."

Eddie approached Tracy, who read her song sheet intently just then, and stuck his face over her shoulder to whisper, "Hi." Tracy stared straight ahead into the air and whispered "Hi" vaguely, glumly. Susan shook her head. Couldn't Tracy act more cheerful at least? They were walking again. They passed a string of blinking reindeer and a wooden snowman holding a painted candle. Ridiculous!

Reading Strategy
Identifying with a Character How would you feel if you introduced Hamadi to your friends? Why?

Literary Analysis
Character How are Susan and Tracy affected by Eddie's presence?

Eddie fell into step beside Tracy, murmuring so Susan couldn't hear him anymore. Saleh Hamadi was flinging his arms up high as he strode. Was he power walking? Did he even know what power walking was? Between houses, Susan's mother hummed obscure songs people never remembered: "What Child Is This?" and "The Friendly Beasts."

Lisa moved over to Eddie's other side. "I'm so *excited* about you and Debbie!" she said loudly. "Why didn't she come tonight?"

Eddie said, "She has a sore throat."

Tracy shrank up inside her coat.

Lisa chattered on. "James said we should make our reservations *now* for dinner at the Tower after the Sweetheart Dance, can you believe it? In December, making a reservation for February? But otherwise it might get booked up!"

Saleh Hamadi tuned into this conversation with interest; the Tower was downtown, in his neighborhood. He said, "This sounds like significant preliminary planning! Maybe you can be an international advisor someday." Susan's mother bellowed, "Joy to the World!" and voices followed her, stretching for notes. Susan's father was gazing off into the sky. Maybe he thought about all the <u>refugees</u> in camps in Palestine far from doorbells and shutters. Maybe he thought about the horizon beyond Jerusalem when he was a boy, how it seemed to be inviting him, "Come over, come over." Well, he'd come all the way to the other side of the world, and now he was doomed to live in two places at once. To Susan, immigrants seemed bigger than other people, and always slightly <u>melancholy</u>. They also seemed doubly interesting. Maybe someday Susan would meet one her own age.

refugees (ref´ yōō jēz´) *n.* people who flee from their homes in a time of trouble

melancholy (mel´ ən käl´ ē) *adj.* sad; depressed

Reading Check
Who arrives late to the caroling?

◀ **Critical Viewing**
How would Saleh Hamadi fit in with this group of carolers? What might he say or do? **[Speculate]**

Two thin streams of tears rolled down Tracy's face. Eddie had drifted to the other side of the group and was clowning with Cameron, doing a tap dance shuffle. "While fields and floods, rocks hills and plains, repeat the sounding joy, repeat the sounding joy " Susan and Saleh Hamadi noticed her. Hamadi peered into Tracy's face, inquiring, "Why? Is it pain? Is it gratitude? We are such mysterious creatures, human beings!"

Tracy turned to him, pressing her face against the old wool of his coat, and wailed. The song ended. All eyes on Tracy, and this tall, courteous stranger who would never in a thousand years have felt comfortable stroking her hair. But he let her stand there, crying as Susan stepped up to stand firmly on the other side of Tracy, putting her arms around her friend. Hamadi said something Susan would remember years later, whenever she was sad herself, even after college, a creaky anthem sneaking back into her ear, "We go on. On and on. We don't stop where it hurts. We turn a corner. It is the reason why we are living. To turn a corner. Come, let's move."

Above them, in the heavens, stars lived out their lonely lives. People whispered, "What happened? What's wrong?" Half of them were already walking down the street.

Review and Assess
Thinking About the Literature

1. **Respond:** Would you like to know someone like Hamadi? Why or why not?

2. **(a) Recall:** What is Susan's memory of her grandmother? **(b) Infer:** Based on these memories, why do you think Susan feels Hamadi is a "surrogate grandmother"—a substitute for her grandmother who is so far away?

3. **(a) Recall:** What is Hamadi's explanation for having never married? **(b) Interpret:** What does Hamadi mean when he says, "I married the wide horizon"?

4. **(a) Paraphrase:** In your own words, explain Hamadi's position on whether or not he has met Kahlil Gibran. **(b) Evaluate:** Do you agree or disagree with Hamadi's position?

5. **(a) Infer:** Why does Susan invite Hamadi to go caroling with her and her friends? **(b) Draw Conclusions:** What are people's reactions to Hamadi's behavior as they carol?

6. **(a) Recall:** Why is Tracy upset during the caroling? **(b) Speculate:** Why does she turn to Hamadi for comfort? **(c) Evaluate:** How useful are Hamadi's words for Tracy's situation? **(d) Apply:** How useful are Hamadi's words in real life? Explain.

Naomi Shihab Nye

(b. 1952)

A poet and fiction writer, Naomi Shihab Nye is concerned with "paying attention to the world." Perhaps her travels and the richness of her heritage inspired her to "pay attention." She grew up in St. Louis as the daughter of a Palestinian father and an American mother. However, she has also lived in Jerusalem and Texas. The poems in *Words Under the Words* (1995) and the story "Hamadi" show that her imagination is well traveled, too.

Review and Assess

Literary Analysis

Character

1. What is Professor Shlemiel's most recognizable quality at the beginning of the story?

2. Has the **character** of Professor Shlemiel changed by the end of the story? Explain.

3. In "Hamadi," what are two pieces of evidence that show Susan has grown as a result of her interaction with Hamadi?

4. Create a chart like the one below to identify the types of characters in these stories. For each column, choose one of the words that best describes the character. In the box, write a reason for your choice. One example has been done for you.

Character	Static or Dynamic	Flat or Round
Shlemiel		
Susan	Dynamic—she is not as confused or unsure at the end of the story as she is at the beginning.	
Hamadi		
Tracy		

Comparing Literary Works

5. In what way do the characters and characters' names reflect each author's heritage?

6. How does each author feel about the importance of heritage? How is this attitude reflected in the author's story?

7. In what way does connecting the story to the author's background and heritage influence your understanding of each story?

Reading Strategy

Identifying With a Character

8. If you were Shlemiel in "The Day I Got Lost," would you have brought the dog home with you and kept it? Why or why not?

9. In "Hamadi," Susan invites Hamadi to go caroling with her. If you were Hamadi, why might you feel "thrilled" to go?

Extend Understanding

10. **Cultural Connection:** What do you think would be the most difficult adjustment for someone who had recently moved to the United States from another country? Explain.

Quick Review

Characters are the people or animals who take part in the action of a literary work. To review character, see page 533.

When you **identify with a character,** you respond to story situations based on the character's background and experiences.

 Take It to the Net

www.phschool.com
Take the interactive self-test online to check your understanding of these selections.

Integrate Language Skills

Vocabulary Development Lesson

Word Analysis: Greek Root -chol-

The word root -chol-, which means *bile* or *gall* (bitter fluids in the body), comes from the Greeks who believed that these bitter fluids caused negative feelings and bad health. On your paper, match each -chol- word in the first column with its meaning in the second column.

1. melancholy
2. cholesterol
3. choler

    a. anger or irritability
    b. a fatty substance that can clog arteries
    c. a deep sadness

Spelling Strategy

In final, unstressed syllables, the letters *f*, *g*, and *t* are usually followed by *le* rather than *el*. Write each misspelled word correctly on your paper.

1. rattel
2. tattle
3. satchel
4. haggel
5. marvle
6. gargel

Grammar Lesson

Adjective Clauses

An **adjective clause** is a subordinate clause that functions as an adjective; that is, it modifies a noun or a pronoun by telling *which one*, *what kind*, *how many*, or *how much*. Adjective clauses usually begin with a relative pronoun that relates the clause to the word it modifies. **Relative pronouns** are *who*, *whom*, *which*, *that*, and *whose*.

> Adjective Clauses
>
> Everyone <u>who had boyfriends or girlfriends</u> seemed to have troubles.

(The adjective clause modifies *everyone* by telling *which ones*—the ones with boyfriends or girlfriends.)

Concept Development: Context

Answer each question yes or no. Then, explain your answer.

1. Might you see a forsaken dog wandering in the streets?
2. Are brittle people usually open to new ideas?
3. Might you be noticed if you wore something lavish?
4. Do refugees usually live in fancy houses?
5. Does loss often create a feeling of melancholy?

▶ For more practice, see page R31, Exercise D.
Practice Identify the adjective clause in each sentence and the noun or pronoun it modifies.

1. Anyone who watches TV more than twelve minutes a week is uninteresting.
2. She had read about a woman who used to have parties to celebrate the arrival of fresh asparagus.
3. They sang at three houses which never opened their doors.
4. Hamadi had a jacket that reminded her of the earth's surface.
5. That was an Aramaic word that just drifted into my mouth.

Writing Application Retell the main events in one of the stories. Use at least three adjective clauses.

W̶G̶ Prentice Hall Writing and Grammar Connection: Chapter 20, Section 2

Writing Lesson

Dialogue

One way in which Singer and Nye reveal character is through **dialogue**, a conversation between two or more people. Write a dialogue between two characters in one of the stories. Incorporate action into your dialogue by describing gestures, actions, and expressions.

Prewriting Create a framework for your dialogue by deciding what the characters are discussing. Also, jot down a profile of each character. Then, think about how their personalities will influence their speech.

Model: Create Realistic Dialogue

Eddie looked mystified. "Who is this guy?"

Susan whispered, "My friend."

> To create realistic dialogue, imitate the informal way in which people usually speak. This informality includes the use of sentence fragments.

Drafting Begin by indicating the topic of the dialogue in the first speaker's words. Continue by writing words for each character to speak in turn. As you write your dialogue, say it aloud to make sure it sounds realistic and natural.

Revising Have two classmates act out your dialogue. Whenever it sounds unrealistic, have the speaker improvise a more natural way of saying the same thing. Then, include the improvisation in your dialogue.

W̲G Prentice Hall Writing and Grammar Connection: Chapter 5, Section 4

Extension Activities

Speaking and Listening Role-play a conversation between characters. Choose Susan and Tracy, Hamadi and Tracy, or Hamadi and Shlemiel. In the conversation, have each character respond to events in the story. Use language and word choice consistent with your character.

Writing Write a **character sketch** of one of the characters in these stories. Support your statements about the character with examples from the story.

Research and Technology In "The Day I Got Lost" and "Hamadi," characters in each story must navigate in their communities. Find a map of the area where you live. Use the map to provide **oral directions** on how to get from one place to another. Take turns with a partner giving the directions and providing feedback about how to improve the directions.

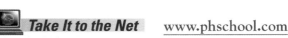 **Take It to the Net** www.phschool.com

Go online for an additional research activity using the Internet.

Internet Maps and Directions

About Internet Maps and Directions

You can find both maps and directions on Internet sites for hotels, museums, and other places of interest. Some Web sites even help you locate a specific street address. Internet maps have certain features that you do not find in printed maps. For example, you may be able to zoom in and out on an internet map:

- Zooming in brings you closer, showing more details.
- Zooming out gives you a bigger picture of the area around a site.

To make things easier for visitors, an organization's Web site may also give directions. These tell you how to get to the building you are seeking from major highways or by public transportation.

Reading Strategy

Analyzing Information

Written directions are packed with information and details. To follow directions to a place such as the Monterey Bay Aquarium, you must analyze the information carefully. Otherwise, you are likely to get lost. If you read directions carelessly, you may turn right instead of left, or go down the wrong street.

The Internet Web site on the next page gives directions to the Aquarium by five different routes: Highway 1 (from north or south), Route 101 (from north or south), or Route 68. Skim them to get the general idea. Then choose one route and analyze those directions. Consult the chart below for tips on reading a map with directions.

Tips for Reading a Map with Directions

To read directions effectively:			
	Find the location of your starting point on the map.		Notice major details in the directions, such as highway numbers or significant shifts in direction. Match them to the streets and highways on the map.
	Read each set of directions in order, while tracing your route along the map.		Keep in mind your basic direction so that if you get off track later, you will quickly realize your mistake.

Map and Directions
to the Monterey Bay Aquarium

Look at the map and read the directions carefully to find out where the aquarium is located and how to get to it from several different directions and highways. Both give additional information, such as where to park your car.

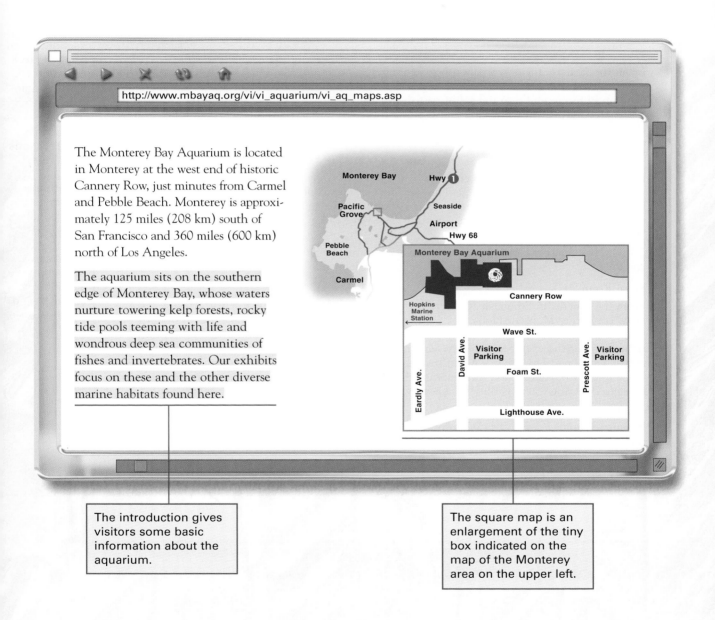

http://www.mbayaq.org/vi/vi_aquarium/vi_aq_maps.asp

The Monterey Bay Aquarium is located in Monterey at the west end of historic Cannery Row, just minutes from Carmel and Pebble Beach. Monterey is approximately 125 miles (208 km) south of San Francisco and 360 miles (600 km) north of Los Angeles.

The aquarium sits on the southern edge of Monterey Bay, whose waters nurture towering kelp forests, rocky tide pools teeming with life and wondrous deep sea communities of fishes and invertebrates. Our exhibits focus on these and the other diverse marine habitats found here.

Monterey Bay
Hwy 1
Pacific Grove
Seaside
Airport
Hwy 68
Pebble Beach
Carmel

Monterey Bay Aquarium
Hopkins Marine Station
Cannery Row
Wave St.
David Ave.
Visitor Parking
Prescott Ave.
Visitor Parking
Eardly Ave.
Foam St.
Lighthouse Ave.

The introduction gives visitors some basic information about the aquarium.

The square map is an enlargement of the tiny box indicated on the map of the Monterey area on the upper left.

http://www.mbayaq.org/vi/vi_aquarium/vi_aq_maps.asp

From Hwy. 1

From the North: Take Hwy. 1 South to Monterey; look for the Monterey Bay Aquarium sign and take the Monterey exit onto Fremont Street. Follow brown directional signs on Fremont to Camino El Estero and turn right. Just past the visitor information center, turn left on Del Monte Ave. and continue (in the right 2 lanes) past Fisherman's Wharf then through the tunnel. Follow the brown directional signs to Cannery Row parking and the aquarium. During summer months and major holiday periods, look for signs directing you to parking in downtown Monterey for The WAVE visitor shuttle.

From the South, you have two choices:

1. Look for the Monterey Bay Aquarium sign and exit Hwy. 1 at Munras Ave. in Monterey. Follow the brown directional signs to Cannery Row parking and the aquarium. During summer months and major holiday periods, look for signs directing you to free parking at Del Monte Center for The WAVE visitor shuttle.

2. Exit Hwy. 1 at Hwy. 68 West/Pacific Grove. Continue 4 miles to David Avenue, then turn right and follow David Ave. to the end. You'll see the aquarium and signs for parking on Cannery Row.

From Route 101

From the North: In Prunedale, take Hwy. 156 West/Monterey Peninsula to Hwy. 1 South. Take Hwy. 1 South to Monterey; look for the Monterey Bay Aquarium sign and take the Monterey exit onto Fremont Street. Follow brown directional signs on Fremont to Camino El Estero and turn right. Just past the visitor information center, turn left on Del Monte Ave. and continue (in the right 2 lanes) past Fisherman's Wharf then through the tunnel. Follow the brown directional signs to Cannery Row parking and the aquarium. During summer months and major holiday periods, look for signs directing you to parking in downtown Monterey for The WAVE visitor shuttle.

Catch the Wave!

In summer, you can catch the Waterfront Area Visitor Express (WAVE) and beat the parking problems around the aquarium!

Headings break up the directions into three sections, each applying to a different starting point.

Notice that the directions often refer to the aquarium's brown directional signs. That important detail can make the aquarium easier to find.

Check Your Comprehension

1. The Monterey Bay Aquarium is located near which two tourist sites?
2. What is the focus of the aquarium exhibits?
3. For which three highways does the Web site give directions?

Applying the Reading Strategy

Analyzing Information

Answer the following questions after analyzing the directions for how to get to the aquarium travelling on Route 101 from the North:

4. What exit should you take to get off Highway 1?
5. How will you know when to turn left onto Del Monte Avenue?
6. What will the brown directional signs tell you?

Activity

Planning a Field Trip

The Web site of the Monterey Bay Aquarium is a good example of a tourist attraction site. Use the Internet to plan a field trip to a similar tourist attraction, such as a museum or zoo.

- Use a search engine to find the home page of the attraction.
- Browse the site to find out what the attraction offers.
- Access the Web page with directions to the attraction.
- Use this page to design an information sheet for students and parents that describes the attraction and provides detailed travel directions.

Comparing Informational Materials

Printed Maps and Internet Maps

Compare the directions page for the Web site of the Monterey Bay Aquarium with a printed map. Use the questions in the chart shown to compare your findings with those of your classmates.

	Map on Web Page	Printed Map
What information is provided?		
Which map contains detailed directions?		
Which map would be easier to follow? Why?		

Prepare to Read

The Finish of Patsy Barnes ◆ Tears of Autumn

Take It to the Net

Visit www.phschool.com
for interactive activities
and instruction related to
these selections, including
- background
- graphic organizers
- literary elements
- reading strategies

Preview

Connecting to the Literature

These two stories will introduce you to new worlds. They will take you back in time one hundred years—to a thrilling horse race and to a ship sailing to California on a rough sea. As you read, take note of the details that the authors use to make these worlds come alive.

Background

"Tears of Autumn" takes place about a century ago, at a time when most Japanese families arranged marriages for their children. An older relative or family friend would help set up these unions. Before reaching an agreement, each family had to be satisfied that the other was worthy. When the bride and groom lived far apart, they often exchanged pictures before meeting.

Literary Analysis

Setting

The **setting** of a story is the time and place of the action. It may be indicated by details such as the customs and beliefs of the people, the clothes they wear and the language they use, and the weather, time of year, and physical features of the place. In the following example from the opening of "Tears of Autumn," details that indicate setting are shown in italics.

> *Hana Omiya* stood at the railing of the *small ship* that shuddered toward *America* in a *turbulent November sea*. She *shivered as* she pulled the folds of *her silk kimono* close to her throat . . .

As you read, look for other specific details that establish the setting of each story.

Comparing Literary Works

The **mood** of a work is the feeling it creates in the reader. The **tone** of a work is the author's attitude toward his or her subject.

Compare and contrast the effects of the different settings on the mood and tone of these works. Keep the following focus questions in mind as you read.

1. What details in the setting of each work contribute to the mood and the tone?
2. In which work are the mood and tone more influenced by the setting?

Reading Strategy

Asking Questions

Because a story introduces you to a new world, you will have questions as you read. As you ask yourself questions, be aware of the question-and-answer relationships. The chart shows the kinds of questions you might ask yourself—and the kinds of questions you might be asked to answer in class or on tests and where you will find the answers.

Question Answer Relationships (QAR)

In the Text
The answer is in the text.

In My Head
The answer comes from my own knowledge or experience.

In the Text and in My Head
The answer comes from a combination of information in the text and my own knowledge and experience.

Vocabulary Development

compulsory (kəm pul′ sə rē) *adj.* enforced; required (p. 557)

meager (mē′ gər) *adj.* lacking in some way; inadequate (p. 558)

obdurate (äb′ door it) *adj.* stubbornly persistent (p. 560)

diplomatic (dip′ lə mat′ ik) *adj.* tactful (p. 560)

turbulent (tʉr′ byoo lənt) *adj.* full of commotion; wild (p. 564)

affluence (af′ loo əns) *n.* wealth; abundance (p. 566)

degrading (dē grād′ iŋ) *adj.* insulting; dishonorable (p. 569)

The Finish
of
Patsy Barnes

Paul Laurence Dunbar

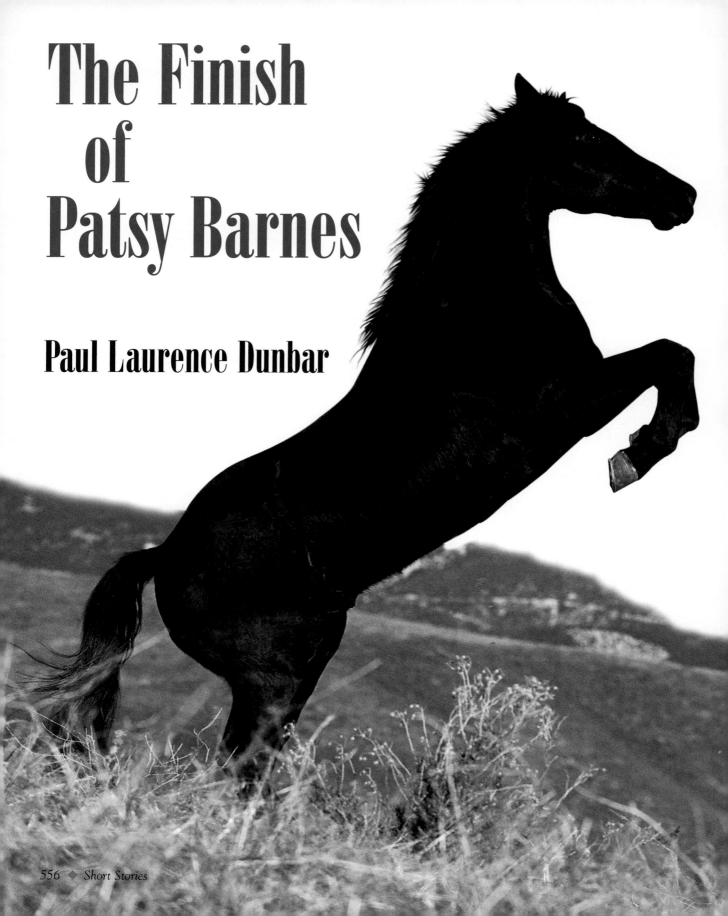

His name was Patsy Barnes, and he was a denizen of Little Africa.[1] In fact, he lived on Douglass Street. By all the laws governing the relations between people and their names, he should have been Irish—but he was not. He was colored, and very much so. That was the reason he lived on Douglass Street. The Negro has very strong within him the instinct of colonization and it was in accordance with this that Patsy's mother had found her way to Little Africa when she had come North from Kentucky.

Patsy was incorrigible. Even into the confines of Little Africa had penetrated the truant officer and the terrible penalty of the compulsory education law. Time and time again had poor Eliza Barnes been brought up on account of the shortcomings of that son of hers. She was a hard-working, honest woman, and day by day bent over her tub, scrubbing away to keep Patsy in shoes and jackets, that would wear out so much faster than they could be bought. But she never murmured, for she loved the boy with a deep affection, though his misdeeds were a sore thorn in her side.

She wanted him to go to school. She wanted him to learn. She had the notion that he might become something better, something higher than she had been. But for him school had no charms; his school was the cool stalls in the big livery stable[2] near at hand; the arena of his pursuits its sawdust floor; the height of his ambition, to be a horseman. Either here or in the racing stables at the Fair-grounds he spent his truant hours. It was a school that taught much, and Patsy was as apt a pupil as he was a constant attendant. He learned strange things about horses, and fine, sonorous oaths that sounded eerie on his young lips, for he had only turned into his fourteenth year.

A man goes where he is appreciated; then could this slim black boy be blamed for doing the same thing? He was a great favorite with the horsemen, and picked up many a dime or nickel for dancing or singing, or even a quarter for warming up a horse for its owner. He was not to be blamed for this, for, first of all, he was born in Kentucky, and had spent the very days of his infancy about the paddocks[3] near Lexington, where his father had sacrificed his life on account of his love for horses. The little fellow had shed no tears when he looked at his father's bleeding body, bruised and broken by the fiery young two-year-old he was

---

1. denizen of Little Africa someone who lives in an area heavily populated by African Americans.
2. livery (liv′ ər ē) **stable** *n.* place where horses are kept and fed.
3. paddocks (pad′ əks) *n.* enclosed areas near a stable in which horses are exercised.

◀ **Critical Viewing** Would you approach the pictured horse with eagerness or caution? Explain. **[Make a Decision]**

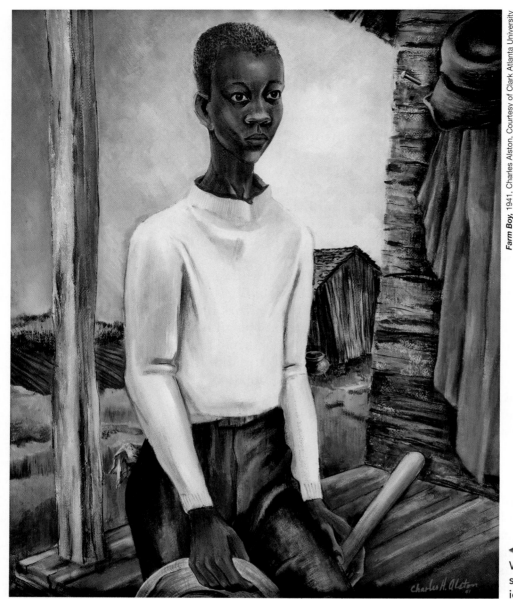

Farm Boy, 1941, Charles Alston, Courtesy of Clark Atlanta University

◀ **Critical Viewing**
What details of the story's setting can you identify in the picture?

trying to subdue. Patsy did not sob or whimper, though his heart ached, for over all the feeling of his grief was a mad, burning desire to ride that horse.

His tears were shed, however, when, actuated by the idea that times would be easier up North, they moved to Dalesford. Then, when he learned that he must leave his old friends, the horses and their masters, whom he had known, he wept. The comparatively <u>meager</u> appointments of the Fair-grounds at Dalesford proved a poor compensation for all these. For the first few weeks Patsy had dreams of running away—back to Kentucky and the horses and stables. Then after a while he settled himself with heroic resolution to make

meager (mē´ gər) *adj.* lacking in some way; inadequate

the best of what he had, and with a mighty effort took up the burden of life away from his beloved home.

Eliza Barnes, older and more experienced though she was, took up her burden with a less cheerful philosophy than her son. She worked hard, and made a scanty livelihood, it is true, but she did not make the best of what she had. Her complainings were loud in the land, and her wailings for her old home smote the ears of any who would listen to her.

They had been living in Dalesford for a year nearly, when hard work and exposure brought the woman down to bed with pneumonia.[4] They were very poor—too poor even to call in a doctor, so there was nothing to do but to call in the city physician. Now this medical man had too frequent calls into Little Africa, and he did not like to go there. So he was very gruff when any of its denizens called him, and it was even said that he was careless of his patients.

Patsy's heart bled as he heard the doctor talking to his mother:

"Now, there can't be any foolishness about this," he said. "You've got to stay in bed and not get yourself damp."

"How long you think I got to lay hyeah, doctah?" she asked.

"I'm a doctor, not a fortune-teller," was the reply. "You'll lie there as long as the disease holds you."

"But I can't lay hyeah long, doctah, case I ain't got nuffin' to go on."

"Well, take your choice: the bed or the boneyard."

Eliza began to cry.

"You needn't sniffle," said the doctor; "I don't see what you people want to come up here for anyhow. Why don't you stay down South where you belong? You come up here and you're just a burden and a trouble to the city. The South deals with all of you better, both in poverty and crime." He knew that these people did not understand him, but he wanted an outlet for the heat within him.

There was another angry being in the room, and that was Patsy. His eyes were full of tears that scorched him and would not fall. The memory of many beautiful and appropriate oaths came to him; but he dared not let his mother hear him swear. Oh! to have a stone—to be across the street from that man!

When the physician walked out, Patsy went to the bed, took his mother's hand, and bent over shamefacedly to kiss her. The little mark of affection comforted Eliza unspeakably. The mother-feeling overwhelmed her in one burst of tears. Then she dried her eyes and smiled at him.

"Honey," she said; "mammy ain' gwine lay hyeah long. She be all right putty soon."

Literary Analysis
Setting How do the doctor's words reveal some of the difficulties facing poor African Americans during the time when this story takes place?

✔**Reading Check**

Why doesn't Patsy like the doctor?

---

4. pneumonia (noo mōn´ yə) *n.* inflammation of the lungs.

"Nevah you min'," said Patsy with a choke in his voice. "I can do somep'n', an' we'll have an othah doctah."

"La, listen at de chile; what kin you do?"

"I'm goin' down to McCarthy's stable and see if I kin git some horses to exercise."

A sad look came into Eliza's eyes as she said: "You'd bettah not go, Patsy; dem hosses'll kill you yit, des lak dey did yo' pappy."

But the boy, used to doing pretty much as he pleased, was <u>obdurate</u>, and even while she was talking, put on his ragged jacket and left the room.

Patsy was not wise enough to be <u>diplomatic</u>. He went right to the point with McCarthy, the liveryman.

The big red-faced fellow slapped him until he spun round and round. Then he said, "Ye little devil, ye, I've a mind to knock the whole head off o' ye. Ye want harses to exercise, do ye? Well git on that un, 'an' see what ye kin do with him."

The boy's honest desire to be helpful had tickled the big, generous Irishman's peculiar sense of humor, and from now on, instead of giving Patsy a horse to ride now and then as he had formerly done, he put into his charge all the animals that needed exercise.

It was with a king's pride that Patsy marched home with his first considerable earnings.

They were small yet, and would go for food rather than a doctor, but Eliza was inordinately proud, and it was this pride that gave her strength and the desire of life to carry her through the days approaching the crisis of her disease.

As Patsy saw his mother growing worse, saw her gasping for breath, heard the rattling as she drew in the little air that kept going her clogged lungs, felt the heat of her burning hands, and saw the pitiful appeal in her poor eyes, he became convinced that the city doctor was not helping her. She must have another. But the money?

That afternoon, after his work with McCarthy, found him at the Fair-grounds. The spring races were on, and he thought he might get a job warming up the horse of some independent jockey. He hung around the stables, listening to the talk of men he knew and some he had never seen before. Among the latter was a tall, lanky man, holding forth to a group of men.

"No, suh," he was saying to them generally, "I'm goin' to withdraw my hoss, because thaih ain't nobody to ride him as he ought to be rode. I haven't brought a jockey along with me, so I've got to depend on pick-ups. Now, the talent's set again my hoss, Black Boy, because he's been losin' regular, but that hoss has lost for the want of ridin', that's all."

The crowd looked in at the slim-legged, raw-boned horse, and walked away laughing.

obdurate (äb´ door it) *adj.* stubbornly persistent

diplomatic (dip´ lə mat´ ik) *adj.* tactful; showing skill in dealing with people

Literary Analysis
Setting How is Eliza's medical treatment different than it would be in a modern setting?

"The fools!" muttered the stranger. "If I could ride myself I'd show 'em!"

Patsy was gazing into the stall at the horse.

"What are you doing thaih?" called the owner to him.

"Look hyeah, mistah," said Patsy, "ain't that a blue-grass hoss?"

"Of co'se it is, an' one o' the fastest that evah grazed."

"I'll ride that hoss, mistah."

"What do you know bout ridin'?"

"I used to gin'ally be' roun' Mistah Boone's paddock in Lexington, an'—"

"Aroun' Boone's paddock—what! Look here, if you can ride that hoss to a winnin' I'll give you more money than you ever seen before."

"I'll ride him."

Patsy's heart was beating very wildly beneath his jacket. That horse. He knew that glossy coat. He knew that raw-boned frame and those flashing nostrils. That black horse there owed something to the orphan he had made.

The horse was to ride in the race before the last. Somehow out of odds and ends, his owner scraped together a suit and colors* for Patsy. The colors were maroon and green, a curious combination. But then it was a curious horse, a curious rider, and a more curious combination that brought the two together.

Long before the time for the race Patsy went into the stall to become better acquainted with his horse. The animal turned its wild eyes upon him and neighed. He patted the long, slender head, and grinned as the horse stepped aside as gently as a lady.

"He sholy is full o' ginger," he said to the owner, whose name he had found to be Brackett.

"He'll show 'em a thing or two," laughed Brackett.

"His dam[5] was a fast one," said Patsy, unconsciously.

Brackett whirled on him in a flash. "What do you know about his dam?" he asked.

The boy would have retracted, but it was too late. Stammeringly he told the story of his father's death and the horse's connection therewith.

"Well," said Bracket, "if you don't turn out a hoodoo,[6] you're a winner, sure. But I'll be blessed if this don't sound like a story! But I've heard that story before. The man I got Black Boy from, no

Literature
in context Cultural Connection

♦ *Jockey's Colors*

Each jockey in a horse race wears a distinct combination of colors and patterns on the jacket and cap. These "colors" are provided by the owner of the horse. They are like a coat of arms—a registered emblem identified with the owner. A jockey who rides for several owners during a race-day will change colors each time he or she rides.

Reading Strategy
Asking Questions
Ask yourself, why does the black horse owe something to Patsy?

Reading Check

How does Patsy know the horse?

---

5. **dam** (dam) *n.* female parent of a four-legged animal.
6. **hoodoo** (hoo′ doo′) *n.* here, someone or something that causes bad luck.

matter how I got him, you're too young to understand the ins and outs of poker, told it to me."

When the bell sounded and Patsy went out to warm up, he felt as if he were riding on air. Some of the jockeys laughed at his getup, but there was something in him—or under him, maybe—that made him scorn their derision. He saw a sea of faces about him, then saw no more. Only a shining white track loomed ahead of him, and a restless steed[7] was cantering with him around the curve. Then the bell called him back to the stand.

They did not get away at first, and back they trooped. A second trial was a failure. But at the third they were off in a line as straight as a chalk-mark. There were Essex and Firefly, Queen Bess and Mosquito, galloping away side by side, and Black Boy a neck ahead. Patsy knew the family reputation of his horse for endurance as well as fire, and began riding the race from the first. Black Boy came of blood that would not be passed, and to this his rider trusted. At the eighth the line was hardly broken, but as the quarter was reached Black Boy had forged a length ahead, and Mosquito was at his flank. Then, like a flash, Essex shot out ahead under whip and spur, his jockey standing straight in the stirrups.

The crowd in the stand screamed; but Patsy smiled as he lay low over his horse's neck. He saw that Essex had made his best spurt. His only fear was for Mosquito, who hugged and hugged his flank. They were nearing the three-quarter post, and he was tightening his grip on the black. Essex fell back; his spurt was over. The whip fell unheeded on his sides. The spurs dug him in vain.

Black Boy's breath touches the leader's ear. They are neck and neck—nose to nose. The black stallion passes him.

Another cheer from the stand, and again Patsy smiles as they turn into the stretch. Mosquito has gained a head. The colored boy flashes one glance at the horse and rider who are so surely gaining upon him, and his lips close in a grim line. They are half-way down the stretch, and Mosquito's head is at the stallion's neck.

For a single moment Patsy thinks of the sick woman at home and what that race will mean to her, and then his knees close against the horse's sides with a firmer dig. The spurs shoot deeper into the steaming flanks. Black Boy shall win; he must win. The horse that has taken away his father shall give him back his

▲ **Critical Viewing**
Would Patsy have owned equipment like this? Why or why not? **[Infer]**

---

7. steed (stēd) *n.* high-spirited riding horse.

mother. The stallion leaps away like a flash, and goes under the wire—a length ahead.

Then the band thundered, and Patsy was off his horse, very warm and very happy, following his mount to the stable. There, a little later, Brackett found him. He rushed to him, and flung his arms around him.

"You little devil," he cried, "you rode like you were kin to that hoss! We've won! We've won!" And he began sticking banknotes at the boy. At first Patsy's eyes bulged, and then he seized the money and got into his clothes.

"Goin' out to spend it?" asked Brackett.

"I'm goin' for a doctah fu' my mother," said Patsy, "she's sick."

"Don't let me lose sight of you."

"Oh, I'll see you again. So long," said the boy.

An hour later he walked into his mother's room with a very big doctor, the greatest the druggist could direct him to. The doctor left his medicines and his orders, but, when Patsy told his story, it was Eliza's pride that started her on the road to recovery. Patsy did not tell his horse's name.

Review and Assess

Thinking About the Selection

1. **Respond:** What do you think will happen to Patsy and his mother?

2. **(a) Recall:** Instead of going to school, where does Patsy spend his time? **(b) Infer:** In what way do Patsy's reasons for spending time there change after his mother becomes ill? **(c) Draw Conclusions:** How does Patsy feel about his mother?

3. **(a) Recall:** What does the first doctor say to Eliza Barnes? **(b) Infer:** Why does he speak to Patsy's mother this way? **(c) Draw Conclusions:** What does this story suggest about the problems faced by Patsy and his mother?

4. **(a) Recall:** What happens to Patsy's father before the story begins? **(b) Infer:** Why does Patsy feel compelled to ride Black Boy? **(c) Evaluate:** Is Patsy's decision to ride the wild horse a good one? Why or why not?

5. **(a) Recall:** What does Patsy do with his earnings from the race? **(b) Interpret:** Why does Patsy decide not to tell his mother the name of the horse? **(c) Analyze:** In what way is Patsy's victory a triumph for both his mother and his father?

6. **Take a Position:** Who or what should provide assistance when very sick people cannot afford to pay medical bills?

Paul Laurence Dunbar

(1872–1906)

Paul Laurence Dunbar was born in Dayton, Ohio, the son of former slaves. The first African American to support himself as an author, Dunbar wrote poems, novels, and short stories.

At an early age, Dunbar won recognition for his poetry. His first book of poems, *Oak and Ivy*, was published in 1893. Written both in dialect and in standard English, his poems have continued to influence many writers. The title of Maya Angelou's autobiography, *I Know Why the Caged Bird Sings*, comes from Dunbar's poem "Sympathy."

Tears of Autumn

Yoshiko Uchida

Hana Omiya stood at the railing of the small ship that shuddered toward America in a turbulent November sea. She shivered as she pulled the folds of her silk kimono close to her throat and tightened the wool shawl about her shoulders.

She was thin and small, her dark eyes shadowed in her pale face, her black hair piled high in a pompadour that seemed too heavy for so slight a woman. She clung to the moist rail and breathed the damp salt air deep into her lungs. Her body seemed leaden and lifeless, as though it were simply the vehicle transporting her soul to a strange new life, and she longed with childlike intensity to be home again in Oka Village.

She longed to see the bright persimmon dotting the barren trees beside the thatched roofs, to see the fields of golden rice stretching to the mountains where only last fall she had gathered plum white mushrooms, and to see once more the maple trees lacing their flaming colors through the green pine. If only she could see a familiar face, eat a meal without retching, walk on solid ground, and stretch out at night on a *tatami* mat[1] instead of in a hard narrow bunk. She thought now of seeking the warm shelter of her bunk but could not bear to face the relentless smell of fish that penetrated the lower decks.

Why did I ever leave Japan? she wondered bitterly. Why did I ever listen to my uncle? And yet she knew it was she herself who had begun the chain of events that placed her on this heaving ship. It was she who had first planted in her uncle's mind the thought that she would make a good wife for Taro Takeda, the lonely man who had gone to America to make his fortune in Oakland, California.

It all began one day when her uncle had come to visit her mother.

"I must find a nice young bride," he had said, startling Hana with this blunt talk of marriage in her presence. She blushed and was ready to leave the room when her uncle quickly added, "My good friend Takeda has a son in America. I must find someone willing to travel to that far land."

This last remark was intended to indicate to Hana and her mother that he didn't consider this a suitable prospect for Hana,

turbulent (tur´ byoo lənt) *adj.* full of commotion; wild

Literary Analysis
Setting and Mood What mood or feeling is created by the contrast between Hana's home and the ship?

▶ **Critical Viewing** What kinds of emotions do you see on the faces of the newly arrived immigrants pictured here? **[Interpret]**

---

1. *tatami* (tə tä´ mē) **mat** *n.* floor mat woven of rice straw, traditionally used in Japanese homes.

who was the youngest daughter of what once had been a fine family. Her father, until his death fifteen years ago, had been the largest landholder of the village and one of its last samurai.[2] They had once had many servants and field hands, but now all that was changed. Their money was gone. Hana's three older sisters had made good marriages, and the eldest remained in their home with her husband to carry on the Omiya name and perpetuate the homestead. Her other sisters had married merchants in Osaka and Nagoya and were living comfortably.

Now that Hana was twenty-one, finding a proper husband for her had taken on an urgency that produced an embarrassing secretive air over the entire matter. Usually, her mother didn't speak of it until they were lying side by side on their quilts at night. Then, under the protective cover of darkness, she would suggest one name and then another, hoping that Hana would indicate an interest in one of them.

Her uncle spoke freely of Taro Takeda only because he was so sure Hana would never consider him. "He is a conscientious, hardworking man who has been in the United States for almost ten years. He is thirty-one, operates a small shop, and rents some rooms above the shop where he lives." Her uncle rubbed his chin thoughtfully. "He could provide well for a wife," he added.

"Ah," Hana's mother said softly.

"You say he is successful in this business?" Hana's sister inquired.

"His father tells me he sells many things in his shop—clothing, stockings, needles, thread, and buttons—such things as that. He also sells bean paste, pickled radish, bean cake, and soy sauce.

---

2. **samurai** (sam′ ə rī′) *n.* Japanese army officer or member of the military class.

Literary Analysis
Setting What attitudes toward marriage are part of the setting of this story?

✔**Reading Check**

Why is Hana traveling to America?

Tears of Autumn ◆ 565

A wife of his would not go cold or hungry."

They all nodded, each of them picturing this merchant in varying degrees of success and <u>affluence</u>. There were many Japanese emigrating to America these days, and Hana had heard of the picture brides who went with nothing more than an exchange of photographs to bind them to a strange man.

"Taro San[3] is lonely," her uncle continued. "I want to find for him a fine young woman who is strong and brave enough to cross the ocean alone."

"It would certainly be a different kind of life," Hana's sister ventured, and for a moment, Hana thought she glimpsed a longing ordinarily concealed behind her quiet, obedient face. In that same instant, Hana knew she wanted more for herself than her sisters had in their proper, arranged, and loveless marriages. She wanted to escape the smothering strictures of life in her village. She certainly was not going to marry a farmer and spend her life working beside him planting, weeding, and harvesting in the rice paddies until her back became bent from too many years of stooping and her skin was turned to brown leather by the sun and wind. Neither did she particularly relish the idea of marrying a merchant in a big city as her two sisters had done. Since her mother objected to her going to Tokyo to seek employment as a teacher, perhaps she would consent to a flight to America for what seemed a proper and respectable marriage.

Almost before she realized what she was doing, she spoke to her uncle. "Oji San, perhaps I should go to America to make this lonely man a good wife."

"You, Hana Chan?"[4] Her uncle observed her with startled curiosity. "You would go all alone to a foreign land so far away from your mother and family?"

"I would not allow it." Her mother spoke fiercely. Hana was her youngest and she had lavished upon her the attention and latitude that often befall the last child. How could she permit her to travel so far, even to marry the son of Takeda who was known to her brother?

But now, a notion that had seemed quite impossible a moment before was lodged in his receptive mind, and Hana's uncle grasped it with the pleasure that comes from an unexpected discovery.

"You know," he said looking at Hana, "it might be a very good life in America."

Hana felt a faint fluttering in her heart. Perhaps this lonely man in America was her means of escaping both the village and the encirclement of her family.

Her uncle spoke with increasing enthusiasm of sending Hana to become Taro's wife. And the husband of Hana's sister, who was

affluence (afʹ lo͞o əns) *n.* wealth; abundance

Reading Strategy
Asking Questions How would Hana's life in the United States be different from her life in Japan? How does your own experience help you answer the question?

---

3. **San** (sän) Japanese term added to names, indicating respect.
4. **Chan** (chän) Japanese term added to children's names.

head of their household, spoke with equal eagerness. Although he never said so, Hana guessed he would be pleased to be rid of her, the spirited younger sister who stirred up his placid life with what he considered radical ideas about life and the role of women. He often claimed that Hana had too much schooling for a girl. She had graduated from Women's High School in Kyoto, which gave her five more years of schooling than her older sister.

"It has addled her brain—all that learning from those books," he said when he tired of arguing with Hana.

A man's word carried much weight for Hana's mother. Pressed by the two men, she consulted her other daughters and their husbands. She discussed the matter carefully with her brother and asked the village priest. Finally, she agreed to an exchange of family histories and an investigation was begun into Taro Takeda's family, his education, and his health, so they would be assured there was no insanity or tuberculosis or police records concealed in his family's past. Soon Hana's uncle was devoting his energies entirely to serving as go-between for Hana's mother and Taro Takeda's father.

When at last an agreement to the marriage was almost reached, Taro wrote his first letter to Hana. It was brief and proper and gave no more clue to his character than the stiff formal portrait taken at his graduation from middle school. Hana's uncle had given her the picture with apologies from his parents, because it was the only photo they had of him and it was not a flattering likeness.

Hana hid the letter and photograph in the sleeve of her kimono and took them to the outhouse to study in private. Squinting in the dim light and trying to ignore the foul odor, she read and reread Taro's letter, trying to find the real man somewhere in the sparse unbending prose.

By the time he sent her money for her steamship tickets, she had received ten more letters, but none revealed much more of the man than the first. In none did he disclose his loneliness or his need, but Hana understood this. In fact, she would have recoiled from a man who bared his intimate thoughts to her so soon. After all, they would have a lifetime together to get to know one another.

So it was that Hana had left her family and sailed alone to America with a small hope trembling inside of her. Tomorrow, at last, the ship would dock in San Francisco and she would meet face to face the man she was soon to marry. Hana was overcome with excitement at the thought of being in America, and terrified of the meeting about to take place. What would she say to Taro Takeda when they first met, and for all the days and years after?

Hana wondered about the flat above the shop. Perhaps it would be luxuriously furnished with the finest of brocades and lacquers,[5] and

---

Literary Analysis
Setting and Tone How is the author's attitude toward the role of women different from the attitude of people during the time in which the story is set?

✓**Reading Check**

Why does Hana offer to marry Taro?

---

5. **brocades** (brō´ kādz´) **and lacquers** (lak´ ərz) *n.* brocades are rich cloths with raised designs; lacquers are highly polished, decorative pieces of wood.

▲ **Critical Viewing**
This painting depicts a Japanese village like the one Hana left. Why would her arrival at Angel Island cause her confusion and worry? **[Infer]**

perhaps there would be a servant, although he had not mentioned it. She worried whether she would be able to manage on the meager English she had learned at Women's High School. The overwhelming anxiety for the day to come and the violent rolling of the ship were more than Hana could bear. Shuddering in the face of the wind, she leaned over the railing and became violently and wretchedly ill.

By five the next morning, Hana was up and dressed in her finest purple silk kimono and coat. She could not eat the bean soup and rice that appeared for breakfast and took only a few bites of the yellow pickled radish. Her bags, which had scarcely been touched since she boarded the ship, were easily packed, for all they contained were her kimonos and some of her favorite books. The large willow basket, tightly secured by a rope, remained under the bunk, untouched since her uncle had placed it there.

She had not befriended the other women in her cabin, for they had lain in their bunks for most of the voyage, too sick to be company to anyone. Each morning Hana had fled the closeness of the sleeping quarters and spent most of the day huddled in a corner of the deck, listening to the lonely songs of some Russians also traveling to an alien land.

Literary Analysis
Setting and Mood What details contribute to the mood of uncertainty?

As the ship approached land, Hana hurried up to the deck to look out at the gray expanse of ocean and sky, eager for a first glimpse of her new homeland.

"We won't be docking until almost noon," one of the deckhands told her.

Hana nodded, "I can wait," she answered, but the last hours seemed the longest.

When she set foot on American soil at last, it was not in the city of San Francisco as she had expected, but on Angel Island, where all third-class passengers were taken. She spent two miserable days and nights waiting, as the immigrants were questioned by officials, examined for trachoma[6] and tuberculosis, and tested for hookworm.[7] It was a bewildering, <u>degrading</u> beginning, and Hana was sick with anxiety, wondering if she would ever be released.

On the third day, a Japanese messenger from San Francisco appeared with a letter for her from Taro. He had written it the day of her arrival, but it had not reached her for two days.

Taro welcomed her to America, and told her that the bearer of the letter would inform Taro when she was to be released so he could be at the pier to meet her.

The letter eased her anxiety for a while, but as soon as she was released and boarded the launch for San Francisco, new fears rose up to smother her with a feeling almost of dread.

The early morning mist had become a light chilling rain, and on the pier black umbrellas bobbed here and there, making the task of recognition even harder. Hana searched desperately for a face that resembled the photo she had studied so long and hard. Suppose he hadn't come. What would she do then?

Hana took a deep breath, lifted her head and walked slowly from the launch. The moment she was on the pier, a man in a black coat, wearing a derby and carrying an umbrella, came quickly to her side. He was of slight build, not much taller than she, and his face was sallow and pale. He bowed stiffly and murmured, "You have had a long trip, Miss Omiya. I hope you are well."

Hana caught her breath. "You are Takeda San?" she asked.

He removed his hat and Hana was further startled to see that he was already turning bald.

"You are Takeda San?" she asked again. He looked older than thirty-one.

"I am afraid I no longer resemble the early photo my parents gave you. I am sorry."

Hana had not meant to begin like this. It was not going well. "No, no," she said quickly. "It is just that I . . . that is, I am

---

6. **trachoma** (trə kō′ mə) *n.* contagious infection of the eyes.
7. **hookworm** (hʊʊk′ wʉrm′) *n.* disease caused by hookworms, small worms that attach themselves to the intestines.

degrading (dē grād′ iŋ) *adj.* insulting; dishonorable

Literary Analysis
Setting and Tone How does the description of Hana's behavior in a frightening setting reveal the author's admiration for her?

**Reading Check**

Why is Hana surprised at Takeda's appearance?

terribly nervous. . . ." Hana stopped abruptly, too flustered to go on.

"I understand," Taro said gently. "You will feel better when you meet my friends and have some tea. Mr. and Mrs. Toda are expecting you in Oakland. You will be staying with them until . . ." He couldn't bring himself to mention the marriage just yet and Hana was grateful he hadn't.

He quickly made arrangements to have her baggage sent to Oakland, then led her carefully along the rain-slick pier toward the streetcar that would take them to the ferry.

Hana shuddered at the sight of another boat, and as they climbed to its upper deck she felt a queasy tightening of her stomach.

"I hope it will not rock too much," she said anxiously. "Is it many hours to your city?"

Taro laughed for the first time since their meeting, revealing the gold fillings of his teeth. "Oakland is just across the bay," he explained. "We will be there in twenty minutes."

Raising a hand to cover her mouth, Hana laughed with him and suddenly felt better. I am in America now, she thought, and this is the man I came to marry. Then she sat down carefully beside Taro, so no part of their clothing touched.

Review and Assess

Thinking About the Selection

1. **Respond:** If you were Hana, would you feel you had made a mistake in coming to the United States?

2. **(a) Recall:** What career does Hana's mother prevent her from pursuing? **(b) Support:** In what other ways is Hana's life at home unappealing to her? **(c) Draw Conclusions:** Why does Hana agree to marry Taro?

3. **(a) Recall:** In what ways does Hana's family investigate Taro Takedo's family before arranging the marriage? **(b) Infer:** What is the purpose of these extensive investigations? **(c) Draw Conclusions:** Why is Hana's mother so hesitant to consent to the arrangement?

4. **(a) Recall:** Identify the key events in Hana's voyage to the United States. **(b) Infer:** In what ways is this journey courageous?

5. **(a) Recall:** What happens when Hana meets Taro? **(b) Interpret:** What does Taro's behavior toward Hana suggest about his personality? **(c) Draw Conclusions:** What does the end of the story suggest about Hana's future happiness?

6. **Evaluate:** What are the advantages and disadvantages of Hana's arranged marriage?

Yoshiko Uchida

(1921–1992)

Yoshiko Uchida experienced first-hand the discrimination that many Japanese Americans faced during World War II. She and her family spent a year in a Japanese American internment camp in Topaz, Utah. Allowed to leave to attend college, Uchida became a student of Japanese history and folklore.

Uchida became the first woman to write children's books about the internment experience. Her twenty-seven children's books include *Picture Bride, Journey to Topaz,* and *Desert Exile.* She said of her writing, "I hope to give young Asian Americans a sense of their past and to reinforce their self-esteem and self-knowledge."

Review and Assess

Literary Analysis

Setting

1. On a chart like the one shown here, fill in details of **setting** from each story for each category.

Story	Setting	Customs	Beliefs	Clothes
"Patsy Barnes"	1800s Northeast United States			
"Tears of Autumn"	1800s California			

2. Both Hana and Patsy originally come from a different "setting" than the ones they ultimately find themselves in. Describe the original setting for each character's story. Explain how each character feels about having left that time and place.

Comparing Literary Works

3. Both works take place in the United States in the nineteenth century, but the settings are different. Use a Venn diagram to compare and contrast the settings, the **moods** they create, and the **tone**—how the author seems to feel about each one.

"Tears" only   Common elements   "Finish" only

4. Explain how the similarities and differences in the settings contribute to the similarities and differences in the mood and tone of each work.

Reading Strategy

Asking Questions

5. Identify three **questions** you asked yourself as you were reading "Tears of Autumn." Explain whether the answer to each question is found in your head, in the text, or in your head and in the text.

6. How does asking and answering questions affect your understanding of the story?

Extend Understanding

7. **Evaluate:** Who took a bigger risk: Hana or Patsy? Explain.

8. **Social Studies Connection:** What were some financial and political reasons for arranged marriages during medieval and renaissance times in Europe?

Quick Review

Setting is the time and place in which the action of a story occurs. To review setting, see page 555.

The **mood** of a work is the feeling it creates in the reader.
The **tone** of the work is the author's attitude toward his or her subject.
To review mood and tone, see page 555.

Asking questions helps you to understand what you read.

 Take It to the Net
www.phschool.com
Take the interactive self-test online to check your understanding of these selections.

Integrate Language Skills

Vocabulary Development Lesson

Word Analysis: Latin Root *-flu-*

The word *affluence* contains the Latin root *-flu-*, means "flow." Explain how each of these *-flu-* words relates to the idea of flowing or movement.

1. influential
2. fluent
3. confluence
4. fluid

Spelling Strategy

The following words from the selection are also used in Social Studies. Read and spell each word aloud. Copy and answer each question.

emigrating   foreign   alien   immigrants

1. Which two words come from the Latin word *migrare*, meaning to move from one place to another?
2. Which three words are used to indicate or describe people from other countries?

Fluency: Definitions

On your paper, match each word in the first column with the word or phrase closest in meaning in the second column.

1. compulsory
2. meager
3. obdurate
4. diplomatic
5. turbulent
6. affluence
7. degrading

a. stubborn
b. disturbed and wild
c. wealth
d. required
e. making one feel worthless
f. scanty; skimpy
g. polite in dealing with people

Write a character description of Hana or Patsy. Use at least four of the vocabulary words in your description.

Grammar Lesson

Simple and Compound Sentences

A **simple sentence** consists of one independent clause. (An independent clause has a subject and a verb and can stand alone.)

   S   V
Patsy was incorrigible.

A **compound sentence** is two or more independent clauses joined by a comma and coordinating conjunction—*and, but, for, or, nor, so, yet*—or a semicolon.

      S   V   S V
His name was Patsy Barnes, and he was a denizen of Little Africa.

When you write, use a variety of sentence types, including simple and compound sentences.

▶ *For more practice, see page R30, Exercise C.*
Practice On your paper, copy each of these sentences. Indicate which sentences are simple and which are compound. Underline each independent clause.

1. She wanted him to go to school.
2. The little mark of affection comforted Eliza unspeakably.
3. The boy would have retracted, but it was too late.
4. He knew that raw-boned frame and those flashing nostrils.
5. They were nearing the three-quarter post, and he was tightening his grip on the black.

Writing Application Write a prediction about one of the main characters. Use two simple and two compound sentences.

W̶G̶ Prentice Hall Writing and Grammar Connection: Chapter 20, Section 2

Writing Lesson

Comparison and Contrast

In a brief essay, compare and contrast the ways each story shows the value of taking a chance.

Prewriting   Identify these details in each story: the qualities of the main character, the reasons he or she wants to achieve the goal, the goal, the risk, and the success of the outcome. In your introduction, identify each story's message about chance.

Drafting   Organize the body of your essay point by point. Make a point about a similarity or difference, then illustrate with examples from each selection. Then, move on to the next point.

Revising   In a formal comparison, avoid using the first-person pronoun *I*. Revise to make the viewpoint of your essay consistently third person (the viewpoint of an outside observer).

Model: Revising Point of View

However,

Both writers provide many details~~. I think~~ the setting in

"The Finish of Patsy Barnes" is much livelier~~. I liked~~ the
                      are especially appealing

descriptions of color and activity in the stables.

> The writer adjusts sentences to delete the use of the pronoun *I*.

𝑊𝐺 *Prentice Hall Writing and Grammar Connection: Chapter 8, Section 3*

Extension Activities

Listening and Speaking   Choose one of the characters, and write a **persuasive speech** either for or against the character's actions. Include facts that support your position. Facts are statements that can be proven true. Also include in your speech the opinions you form based on the facts. Opinions can be supported but not proved.

Fact: An unmarried Japanese woman in the 1800s would have continued to live in the home of one of her male family members.

Opinion: If Hana had stayed in Japan, she would have had a much duller and more difficult life.

Research and Technology   Research Hana's journey from Japan to Angel Island. Find answers to these and other questions:

1. What route did most ships take?
2. How many miles was the journey?
3. How many days did the journey take?

Present your findings in an **oral presentation** with charts or handouts.

 **Take It to the Net**   www.phschool.com

Go online for an additional research activity using the Internet.

Prepare to Read

The Story-Teller ◆ The Medicine Bag

Story Teller, Velino "Shije" Herrera, National Museum of American Art, Washington, D.C.

Take It to the Net

Visit www.phschool.com
for interactive activities
and instruction related to
these selections, including

- background
- graphic organizers
- literary elements
- reading strategies

Preview

Connecting to the Literature

Some gifts can be touched—like a ring passed down from a great-grandparent. Other gifts, just as valuable, cannot—a funny story or a family tradition. "The Story-Teller" involves a gift that cannot be touched, while "The Medicine Bag" involves both kinds of gifts. Think about gifts of both kinds that you have given or received.

Background

In "The Medicine Bag," a Native American boy receives his great-grandfather's medicine bag. For the Sioux Indians living on the Great Plains, medicine bags were sacred gifts. A personal medicine bag would contain symbolic items that were vitally important to the individual who chose them.

Literary Analysis

Theme

The **theme** of a story is its message, its insight into life. Some stories have a **stated theme**: the message of the story is directly stated by the author or a character. Other stories have an **implied theme**: the message of the story is suggested rather than directly stated. For instance, in this example, the grandfather's thoughts suggest that the story's theme deals with the importance of traditions.

> Grandpa thought he was going to die, and he had to follow the tradition of his family to pass the medicine bag, along with its history, to the oldest male child.

As you read each story, identify the message or insight the author wants you to get from the work.

Comparing Literary Works

"The Story-Teller" and "The Medicine Bag" both have implied themes. Determine each author's message by asking yourself how the details and events of the story work together to point toward one idea or message. Then, compare and contrast the themes by asking yourself the following focus questions:

1. What message does each work communicate about the passing along of values from adults to children?
2. What is the difference in the **tones** (the authors' attitudes) in which the messages are communicated?

Reading Strategy

Drawing Inferences

To figure out an implied theme, draw inferences. An **inference** is a logical conclusion reached by putting details together and determining what they mean or indicate. For example, if your teacher enters the room wearing a wet raincoat and carrying an umbrella, you can draw the inference that it is raining outside. The chart offers another example of putting details together to draw an inference.

Vocabulary Development

bachelor (bach′ ə lər) *n.* A man who has not married (p. 576)

resolute (rez′ ə lo͞ot′) *adj.* Fixed in purpose; resolved (p. 578)

listlessly (list′ lis lē) *adv.* Without interest; spiritlessly (p. 578)

authentic (ô then′ tik) *adj.* Genuine; real (p. 582)

procession (prō sesh′ ən) *n.* A group of people or things moving forward (p. 583)

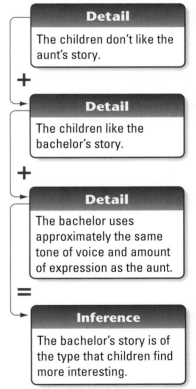

Detail

The children don't like the aunt's story.

+

Detail

The children like the bachelor's story.

+

Detail

The bachelor uses approximately the same tone of voice and amount of expression as the aunt.

=

Inference

The bachelor's story is of the type that children find more interesting.

The Story-Teller

SAKI

bachelor (bach´ ə lər)
n. a man who has
not married

It was a hot afternoon, and the railway carriage was correspondingly sultry, and the next stop was at Templecombe, nearly an hour ahead. The occupants of the carriage were a small girl, and a smaller girl, and a small boy. An aunt belonging to the children occupied one corner seat, and the further corner seat on the opposite side was occupied by a bachelor who was a stranger to their party, but the small girls and the small boy emphatically occupied the compartment. Both the aunt and the children were conversational in a limited, persistent way, reminding one of the attentions of a housefly that refused to be discouraged. Most of the aunt's remarks seemed to begin with "Don't," and nearly all of the children's remarks began with "Why?" The bachelor said nothing out loud.

"Don't, Cyril, don't," exclaimed the aunt, as the small boy began smacking the cushions of the seat, producing a cloud of dust at each blow.

"Come and look out of the window," she added.

The child moved reluctantly to the window. "Why are those sheep being driven out of that field?" he asked.

"I expect they are being driven to another field where there is more grass," said the aunt weakly.

"But there is lots of grass in that field," protested the boy; "there's nothing else but grass there. Aunt, there's lots of grass in that field."

Stirling Station, 1887, William Kennedy, Collection of Andrew McIntosh Patrick, UK

▲ **Critical Viewing** Basing your answer on the details in this painting, describe what rail travel was like in the early 1900s in England. **[Draw Conclusions]**

"Perhaps the grass in the other field is better," suggested the aunt fatuously.[1]

"Why is it better?" came the swift, inevitable question.

"Oh, look at those cows!" exclaimed the aunt. Nearly every field along the line had contained cows or bullocks, but she spoke as though she were drawing attention to a rarity.

"Why is the grass in the other field better?" persisted Cyril.

The frown on the bachelor's face was deepening to a scowl. He was a hard, unsympathetic man, the aunt decided in her mind. She was utterly unable to come to any satisfactory decision about the grass in the other field.

Reading Check

Who is traveling in the railway carriage?

---

1. fatuously (fach′ o̅o̅ wəs lē) *adv.* in a foolish way.

The smaller girl created a diversion by beginning to recite "On the Road to Mandalay."[2] She only knew the first line, but she put her limited knowledge to the fullest possible use. She repeated the line over and over again in a dreamy but <u>resolute</u> and very audible voice; it seemed to the bachelor as though someone had had a bet with her that she could not repeat the line aloud two thousand times without stopping. Whoever it was who had made the wager was likely to lose his bet.

"Come over here and listen to a story," said the aunt, when the bachelor had looked twice at her and once at the communication cord.

The children moved <u>listlessly</u> toward the aunt's end of the carriage. Evidently her reputation as a story-teller did not rank high in their estimation.

In a low, confidential voice, interrupted at frequent intervals by loud, petulant[3] questions from her listeners, she began an unenterprising and deplorably uninteresting story about a little girl who was good, and made friends with everyone on account of her goodness, and was finally saved from a mad bull by a number of rescuers who admired her moral character.

"Wouldn't they have saved her if she hadn't been good?" demanded the bigger of the small girls. It was exactly the question that the bachelor had wanted to ask.

"Well, yes," admitted the aunt lamely, "but I don't think they would have run quite so fast to her help if they had not liked her so much."

"It's the stupidest story I've ever heard," said the bigger of the small girls, with immense conviction.

"I didn't listen after the first bit, it was so stupid," said Cyril.

The smaller girl made no actual comment on the story, but she had long ago recommenced a murmured repetition of her favorite line.

"You don't seem to be a success as a story-teller," said the bachelor suddenly from his corner.

The aunt bristled in instant defense at this unexpected attack.

"It's a very difficult thing to tell stories that children can both understand and appreciate," she said stiffly.

"I don't agree with you," said the bachelor.

"Perhaps *you* would like to tell them a story," was the aunt's retort.

"Tell us a story," demanded the bigger of the small girls.

"Once upon a time," began the bachelor, "there was a little girl called Bertha, who was extraordinarily good."

The children's momentarily aroused interest began at once to flicker; all stories seemed dreadfully alike, no matter who told them.

"She did all that she was told, she was always truthful, she kept her clothes clean, ate milk puddings as though they were jam tarts, learned her lessons perfectly, and was polite in her manners."

resolute (rez´ ə loot´) *adj.* fixed in purpose; resolved

listlessly (list´ lis lē) *adv.* without interest; spiritlessly

Reading Strategy
Drawing Inferences
What inference can you draw about the aunt based on the children's misbehavior?

Literary Analysis
Theme What message is suggested by the children's disinterest in the beginning of the bachelor's story?

---

2. **"On the Road to Mandalay"** poem by Rudyard Kipling.
3. **petulant** (pech´ oo lənt) *adj.* impatient.

"Was she pretty?" asked the bigger of the small girls.

"Not as pretty as any of you." said the bachelor, "but she was horribly good."

There was a wave of reaction in favor of the story; the word horrible in connection with goodness was a novelty that commended itself. It seemed to introduce a ring of truth that was absent from the aunt's tales of infant life.

"She was so good," continued the bachelor, "that she won several medals for goodness, which she always wore, pinned on to her dress. There was a medal for obedience, another medal for punctuality, and a third for good behavior. They were large metal medals and they clinked against one another as she walked. No other child in town where she lived had as many as three medals, so everybody knew that she must be an extra good child."

"Horribly good," quoted Cyril.

"Everybody talked about her goodness, and the Prince of the country got to hear about it, and he said that as she was so very good she might be allowed once a week to walk in his park, which was just outside the town. It was a beautiful park, and no children were ever allowed in it, so it was a great honor for Bertha to be allowed to go there."

"Were there any sheep in the park?" demanded Cyril.

"No," said the bachelor, "there were no sheep."

"Why weren't there any sheep?" came the inevitable question arising out of that answer.

The aunt permitted herself a smile, which might almost have been described as a grin.

"There were no sheep in the park," said the bachelor, "because the Prince's mother had once had a dream that her son would either be killed by a sheep or else by a clock falling on him. For that reason the Prince never kept a sheep in his park or a clock in his palace."

The aunt suppressed a gasp of admiration.

"Was the Prince killed by a sheep or by a clock?" asked Cyril.

"He is still alive, so we can't tell whether the dream will come true," said the bachelor unconcernedly; "anyway, there were no sheep in the park, but there were lots of little pigs running all over the place."

"What color were they?"

"Black with white faces, white with black spots, black all over, gray with white patches, and some were white all over."

The story-teller paused to let a full idea of the park's treasures sink into the children's imaginations; then he resumed:

"Bertha was rather sorry to find that there were no flowers in the park. She had promised her aunts, with tears in her eyes, that she would not pick any of the kind Prince's flowers, and she had meant to keep her promise, so of course it made her feel silly to find that there were no flowers to pick."

Reading Strategy
Drawing Inferences
From what details can you draw the inference that the bachelor understands children?

Reading Check

What does the stranger think he can do better than the aunt?

"Why weren't there any flowers?"

"Because the pigs had eaten them all," said the bachelor promptly. "The gardeners had told the Prince that you couldn't have pigs and flowers, so he decided to have pigs and no flowers."

There was a murmur of approval at the excellence of the Prince's decision; so many people would have decided the other way.

"There were lots of other delightful things in the park. There were ponds with gold and blue and green fish in them, and trees with beautiful parrots that said clever things at a moment's notice, and hummingbirds that hummed all the popular tunes of the day. Bertha walked up and down and enjoyed herself immensely, and thought to herself: 'If I were not so extraordinarily good, I should not have been allowed to come into this beautiful park and enjoy all that there is to be seen in it,' and her three medals clinked against one another as she walked and helped to remind her how very good she really was. Just then an enormous wolf came prowling into the park to see if it could catch a fat little pig for its supper."

"What color was it?" asked the children, amid an immediate quickening of interest.

"Mud color all over, with a black tongue and pale gray eyes that gleamed with unspeakable ferocity. The first thing that it saw in the park was Bertha; her pinafore⁴ was so spotlessly white and clean that it could be seen from a great distance. Bertha saw the wolf and saw that it was stealing toward her, and she began to wish that she had never been allowed to come into the park. She ran as hard as she could, and the wolf came after her with huge leaps and bounds. She managed to reach a shrubbery of myrtle bushes, and she hid herself in one of the thickest of the bushes. The wolf came sniffing among the branches, its black tongue lolling out of its mouth and its pale gray eyes glaring with rage. Bertha was terribly frightened, and thought to herself: 'If I had not been so extraordinarily good, I should have been safe in the town at this moment.' However, the scent of the myrtle was so strong that the wolf could not sniff out where Bertha was hiding, and the bushes were so thick that he might have hunted about in them for a long time without catching sight of her, so he thought he might as well go off and catch a little pig instead. Bertha was trembling very much at having the wolf prowling and sniffing so near her, and as she trembled the medal for obedience clinked against the medals for good conduct and punctuality. The wolf was just moving away when he heard the sound of the medals clinking and stopped to listen; they clinked again in a bush quite near him. He dashed into the bush, his pale gray eyes gleaming with ferocity and triumph, and dragged Bertha out and devoured her to the last morsel. All that was left of her were her

---

4. **pinafore** (pin´ ə fôr´) *n.* an apronlike garment worn over a dress.

shoes, bits of clothing, and the three medals for goodness."

"Were any of the little pigs killed?"

"No, they all escaped."

"The story began badly," said the smaller of the small girls, "but it had a beautiful ending."

"It is the most beautiful story that I ever heard," said the bigger of the small girls, with immense decision.

"It is the *only* beautiful story I have ever heard," said Cyril.

A dissentient[5] opinion came from the aunt.

"A most improper story to tell to young children! You have undermined the effect of years of careful teaching."

"At any rate," said the bachelor, collecting his belongings preparatory to leaving the carriage, "I kept them quiet for ten minutes, which was more than you were able to do."

"Unhappy woman!" he observed to himself as he walked down the platform of Templecombe station; "for the next six months or so those children will assail her in public with demands for an improper story!"

---

5. **dissentient** (di sen´ shənt) *adj.* differing from the majority.

Literary Analysis
Theme What does the contrast between the two stories suggest about this story's theme?

Review and Assess
Thinking About the Selection

1. **Respond:** Did you like the bachelor's story? Why or why not?

2. **(a) Recall:** What are three things the children do before the story is told? **(b) Infer:** Why do the children do these things?

3. **(a) Recall:** What questions do the children ask the aunt? **(b) Analyze:** Why are the children unsatisfied with her answers? **(c) Evaluate:** How well or poorly thought out are the aunt's responses?

4. **(a) Recall:** What does the bachelor do when the aunt cannot control the children? **(b) Infer:** What does his reaction indicate? **(c) Extend:** To whom is his reaction more directed—the aunt or the children? Explain.

5. **(a) Recall:** What does the bachelor say he was able to accomplish that the aunt could not? **(b) Compare and Contrast:** How were the bachelor's and the aunt's motives in trying to entertain the children similar? How were they different? **(c) Evaluate:** The aunt says the bachelor's story was improper for children. Do you agree or disagree? Explain.

6. **Take a Position:** Do you think there should be government or industry regulations that judge the age appropriateness of entertainment such as movies or music? Why or why not?

Saki (H. H. Munro)

(1870–1916)

Long before today's celebrities started using single names, H. H. Munro became famous under the pen name of Saki. Born to British parents in Burma (now Myanmar), Saki was sent to England to be raised by two aunts and a grandmother after his mother died.

Saki made his name as a witty newspaper writer in London. He also became famous for his humorous short stories, which often had surprise endings. Saki's own life, too, ended with a surprise twist. After surviving many serious illnesses, he died as a soldier in World War I.

The Story-Teller ◆ 581

The Medicine Bag

Virginia Driving Hawk Sneve

My kid sister Cheryl and I always bragged about our Sioux[1] grandpa, Joe Iron Shell. Our friends, who had always lived in the city and only knew about Indians from movies and TV, were impressed by our stories. Maybe we exaggerated and made Grandpa and the reservation sound glamorous, but when we'd return home to Iowa after our yearly summer visit to Grandpa, we always had some exciting tale to tell.

We always had some <u>authentic</u> Sioux article to show our listeners. One year Cheryl had new moccasins[2] that Grandpa had made. On another visit he gave me a small, round, flat, rawhide drum that was decorated with a painting of a warrior riding a horse. He taught me a real Sioux chant to sing while I beat the drum with a leather-covered stick that had a feather on the end. Man that really made an impression.

We never showed our friends Grandpa's picture. Not that we were ashamed of him, but because we knew that the glamorous tales we told didn't go with the real thing. Our friends would have laughed at the picture because Grandpa wasn't tall and stately like TV Indians. His hair wasn't in braids but hung in stringy, gray strands on his neck, and he was old. He was our great-grandfather, and he didn't live in a tepee,[3] but all by himself in a part log, part tarpaper shack on the Rosebud Reservation[4] in South Dakota. So when Grandpa came to visit us, I was so ashamed and embarrassed I could've died.

There are a lot of yippy poodles and other fancy little dogs in our neighborhood, but they usually barked singly at the mailman from

▲ Critical Viewing
Do you think the medicine bag pictured was manufactured or handmade? How can you tell? [Infer]

authentic (ô then′ tik) *adj.* genuine; real

---

1. **Sioux** (sōō) *n.* Native American tribes of the northern plains of the United States and nearby southern Canada.
2. **moccasins** (mäk′ ə sənz) *n.* heelless slippers of soft, flexible leather.
3. **tepee** (tē′ pē) *n.* cone-shaped tent of animal skins; used by the Plains Indians.
4. **Rosebud Reservation** small Indian reservation in southcentral South Dakota.

the safety of their own yards. Now it sounded as if a whole pack of mutts were barking together in one place.

I got up and walked to the curb to see what the commotion was. About a block away I saw a crowd of little kids yelling, with the dogs yipping and growling around someone who was walking down the middle of the street.

I watched the group as it slowly came closer and saw that in the center of the strange <u>procession</u> was a man wearing a tall black hat. He'd pause now and then to peer at something in his hand and then at the houses on either side of the street. I felt cold and hot at the same time as I recognized the man. "Oh, no!" I whispered. "It's Grandpa!"

I stood on the curb, unable to move even though I wanted to run and hide. Then I got mad when I saw how the yippy dogs were growling and nipping at the old man's baggy pant legs and how wearily he poked them away with his cane. "Stupid mutts," I said as I ran to rescue Grandpa.

When I kicked and hollered at the dogs to get away, they put their tails between their legs and scattered. The kids ran to the curb where they watched me and the old man.

"Grandpa," I said and felt pretty dumb when my voice cracked. I reached for his beat-up old tin suitcase, which was tied shut with a rope. But he set it down right in the street and shook my hand.

"*Hau, Takoza,* Grandchild," he greeted me formally in Sioux.

All I could do was stand there with the whole neighborhood watching and shake the hand of the leather-brown old man. I saw how his gray hair straggled from under his big black hat, which had a drooping feather in its crown. His rumpled black suit hung like a sack over his stooped frame. As he shook my hand, his coat fell open to expose a bright red satin shirt with a beaded bolo tie[5] under the collar. His get-up wasn't out of place on the reservation, but it sure was here, and I wanted to sink right through the pavement.

"Hi," I muttered with my head down. I tried to pull my hand away when I felt his bony hand trembling, and looked up to see fatigue in his face. I felt like crying. I couldn't think of anything to say so I picked up Grandpa's suitcase, took his arm, and guided him up the driveway to our house.

Mom was standing on the steps. I don't know how long she'd been watching, but her hand was over her mouth and she looked as if she couldn't believe what she saw. Then she ran to us.

"Grandpa," she gasped. "How in the world did you get here?"

She checked her move to embrace Grandpa and I remembered that such a display of affection is unseemly to the Sioux and would embarrass him.

procession (prō sesh′ ən) *n.* a group of people or things moving forward

Reading Strategy
Drawing Inferences
What details allow you to make the inference that the narrator is embarrassed?

**Reading Check**

Who arrives on the narrator's street?

---

5. **bolo** (bō′ lō) **tie** *n.* string tie held together with a decorated sliding device.

"*Hau*, Marie," he said as he shook Mom's hand. She smiled and took his other arm.

As we supported him up the steps, the door banged open and Cheryl came bursting out of the house. She was all smiles and was so obviously glad to see Grandpa that I was ashamed of how I felt.

"Grandpa!" she yelled happily. "You came to see us!"

Grandpa smiled, and Mom and I let go of him as he stretched out his arms to my ten-year-old sister, who was still young enough to be hugged.

"*Wicincala*, little girl," he greeted her and then collapsed.

He had fainted. Mom and I carried him into her sewing room, where we had a spare bed.

After we had Grandpa on the bed, Mom stood there helplessly patting his shoulder.

"Shouldn't we call the doctor, Mom?" I suggested, since she didn't seem to know what to do.

"Yes," she agreed with a sigh. "You make Grandpa comfortable, Martin."

I reluctantly moved to the bed. I knew Grandpa wouldn't want to have Mom undress him, but I didn't want to, either. He was so skinny and frail that his coat slipped off easily. When I loosened his tie and opened his shirt collar, I felt a small leather pouch that hung from a thong[6] around his neck. I left it alone and moved to remove his boots. The scuffed old cowboy boots were tight, and he moaned as I put pressure on his legs to jerk them off.

I put the boots on the floor and saw why they fit so tight. Each one was stuffed with money. I looked at the bills that lined the boots and started to ask about them, but Grandpa's eyes were closed again.

Mom came back with a basin of water. "The doctor thinks Grandpa is suffering from heat exhaustion," she explained as she bathed Grandpa's face. Mom gave a big sigh, "Oh, *hinh*, Martin. How do you suppose he got here?"

We found out after the doctor's visit. Grandpa was angrily sitting up in bed while Mom tried to feed him some soup.

"Tonight you let Marie feed you, Grandpa," spoke my dad, who had gotten home from work just as the doctor was leaving. "You're not really sick," he said as he gently pushed Grandpa back against the pillows. "The doctor said you just got too tired and hot after your long trip."

---

6. **thong** *n.* narrow strip of leather.

Literature in context Social Studies Connection

The Sioux

The Sioux used to live throughout the northern plains of North America. However, tension developed and increased between the Sioux and the United States government in the mid-1800s. In 1868, a treaty established the boundaries of the Great Sioux Nation Reservation and guaranteed that white settlers would stay out of the territory. When the U. S. government violated the treaty, many Sioux decided to fight. Led by the famous chiefs Sitting Bull and Crazy Horse, they defeated General George Custer and his troops at Little Big Horn. Eventually, however, the Sioux were overpowered. Today, many Sioux live on reservations in North and South Dakota, Nebraska, Montana, Minnesota, and Wyoming.

Grandpa relaxed, and between sips of soup, he told us of his journey. Soon after our visit to him, Grandpa decided that he would like to see where his only living descendants lived and what our home was like. Besides, he admitted sheepishly, he was lonesome after we left.

I knew that everybody felt as guilty as I did—especially Mom. Mom was all Grandpa had left. So even after she married my dad, who's a white man and teaches in the college in our city, and after Cheryl and I were born, Mom made sure that every summer we spent a week with Grandpa.

I never thought that Grandpa would be lonely after our visits, and none of us noticed how old and weak he had become. But Grandpa knew, and so he came to us. He had ridden on buses for two and a half days. When he arrived in the city, tired and stiff from sitting for so long, he set out, walking, to find us.

He had stopped to rest on the steps of some building downtown, and a policeman found him. The cop, according to Grandpa, was a good man who took him to the bus stop and waited until the bus came and told the driver to let Grandpa out at Bell View Drive. After Grandpa got off the bus, he started walking again. But he couldn't see the house numbers on the other side when he walked on the sidewalk, so he walked in the middle of the street. That's when all the little kids and dogs followed him.

I knew everybody felt as bad as I did. Yet I was so proud of this eighty-six-year-old man, who had never been away from the reservation, having the courage to travel so far alone.

"You found the money in my boots?" he asked Mom.

"Martin did," she answered, and roused herself to scold. "Grandpa, you shouldn't have carried so much money. What if someone had stolen it from you?"

Grandpa laughed. "I would've known if anyone tried to take the boots off my feet. The money is what I've saved for a long time—a hundred dollars—for my funeral. But you take it now to buy groceries so that I won't be a burden to you while I am here."

"That won't be necessary, Grandpa," Dad said. "We are honored to have you with us, and you will never be a burden. I am only sorry that we never thought to bring you home with us this summer and spare you the discomfort of a long trip."

Grandpa was pleased. "Thank you," he answered. "But do not feel bad that you didn't bring me with you, for I would not have come then. It was not time." He said this in such a way that no one could argue with him. To Grandpa and the Sioux, he once told me, a thing would be done when it was the right time to do it, and that's the way it was.

"Also," Grandpa went on, looking at me, "I have come because it is soon time for Martin to have the medicine bag."

Reading Check

Why does Grandpa come to the city?

We all knew what that meant. Grandpa thought he was going to die, and he had to follow the tradition of his family to pass the medicine bag, along with its history, to the oldest male child.

"Even though the boy," he said still looking at me, "bears a white man's name, the medicine bag will be his."

I didn't know what to say. I had the same hot and cold feeling that I had when I first saw Grandpa in the street. The medicine bag was the dirty leather pouch I had found around his neck. "I could never wear such a thing," I almost said aloud. I thought of having my friends see it in gym class or at the swimming pool and could imagine the smart things they would say. But I just swallowed hard and took a step toward the bed. I knew I would have to take it.

But Grandpa was tired. "Not now, Martin," he said, waving his hand in dismissal. "It is not time. Now I will sleep."

So that's how Grandpa came to be with us for two months. My friends kept asking to come see the old man, but I put them off. I told myself that I didn't want them laughing at Grandpa. But even as I made excuses, I knew it wasn't Grandpa that I was afraid they'd laugh at.

Nothing bothered Cheryl about bringing her friends to see Grandpa. Every day after school started, there'd be a crew of giggling little girls or round-eyed little boys crowded around the old man on the patio, where he'd gotten in the habit of sitting every afternoon.

Grandpa would smile in his gentle way and patiently answer their questions, or he'd tell them stories of brave warriors, ghosts, animals; and the kids listened in awed silence. Those little guys thought Grandpa was great.

Finally, one day after school, my friends came home with me because nothing I said stopped them. "We're going to see the great Indian of Bell View Drive," said Hank, who was supposed to be my best friend. "My brother has seen him three times so he oughta be well enough to see us."

When we got to my house, Grandpa was sitting on the patio. He had on his red shirt, but today he also wore a fringed leather vest that was decorated with beads. Instead of his usual cowboy boots, he had solidly beaded moccasins on his feet that stuck out of his black trousers. Of course, he had his old black hat on—he was seldom without it. But it had been brushed, and the feather in the beaded headband was proudly erect, its tip a brighter white. His hair lay in silver strands over the red shirt collar.

I stared just as my friends did, and I heard one of them murmur, "Wow!"

Grandpa looked up, and, when his eyes met mine, they twinkled as if he were laughing inside. He nodded to me, and my face got all hot. I could tell that he had known all along I was afraid he'd embarrass me in front of my friends.

"*Hau, hoksilas,* boys," he greeted and held out his hand.

Literary Analysis
Theme What does Martin's reaction to the medicine bag reveal about his attitude toward his Sioux heritage?

My buddies passed in a single file and shook his hand as I introduced them. They were so polite I almost laughed. "How, there, Grandpa," and even a "How-do-you-do, sir."

"You look fine, Grandpa," I said as the guys sat on the lawn chairs or on the patio floor.

"*Hanh*, yes," he agreed. "When I woke up this morning, it seemed the right time to dress in the good clothes. I knew that my grandson would be bringing his friends."

"You guys want some lemonade or something?" I offered. No one answered. They were listening to Grandpa as he started telling how he'd killed the deer from which his vest was made.

Grandpa did most of the talking while my friends were there. I was so proud of him and amazed at how respectfully quiet my buddies were. Mom had to chase them home at supper time. As they left, they shook Grandpa's hand again and said to me,

"Martin, he's really great!"

"Yeah, man! Don't blame you for keeping him to yourself."

"Can we come back?"

But after they left, Mom said, "No more visitors for a while, Martin. Grandpa won't admit it, but his strength hasn't returned. He likes having company, but it tires him."

That evening Grandpa called me to his room before he went to sleep. "Tomorrow," he said, "when you come home, it will be time to give you the medicine bag."

I felt a hard squeeze from where my heart is supposed to be and was scared, but I answered, "OK, Grandpa."

All night I had weird dreams about thunder and lightning on a high hill. From a distance I heard the slow beat of a drum. When I woke up in the morning, I felt as if I hadn't slept at all. At school it seemed as if the day would never end and, when it finally did, I ran home.

Grandpa was in his room, sitting on the bed. The shades were down, and the place was dim and cool. I sat on the floor in front of Grandpa, but he didn't even look at me. After what seemed a long time he spoke.

"I sent your mother and sister away. What you will hear today is only for a man's ears. What you will receive is only for a man's hands." He fell silent, and I felt shivers down my back.

"My father in his early manhood," Grandpa began, "made a vision quest[7] to find a spirit guide for his life. You cannot understand how it was in that time, when the great Teton Sioux were first made to stay on the reservation. There was a strong need for guidance from *Wakantanka*,[8] the Great Spirit. But too many of the young men were filled with despair and hatred. They thought it was hopeless to

---

7. **vision quest** a search for a revelation that would aid understanding.
8. **Wakantanka** (wä´ kən tank´ ə) *n.* the Sioux religion's most important spirit—the creator of the world.

Literary Analysis
Theme Why does Martin have a change of heart about Grandpa when his friends come to visit?

☑ **Reading Check**
What does Grandpa want to give Martin? Why?

The Medicine Bag ◆ 587

search for a vision when the glorious life was gone and only the hated confines of a reservation lay ahead. But my father held to the old ways.

"He carefully prepared for his quest with a purifying sweat bath, and then he went alone to a high butte top[9] to fast and pray. After three days he received his sacred dream—in which he found, after long searching, the white man's iron. He did not understand his vision of finding something belonging to the white people, for in that time they were the enemy. When he came down from the butte to cleanse himself at the stream below, he found the remains of a campfire and the broken shell of an iron kettle. This was a sign that reinforced his dream. He took a piece of the iron for his medicine bag, which he had made of elk skin years before, to prepare for his quest.

"He returned to his village, where he told his dream to the wise old men of the tribe. They gave him the name *Iron Shell*, but neither did they understand the meaning of the dream. The first Iron Shell kept the piece of iron with him at all times and believed it gave him protection from the evils of those unhappy days.

"Then a terrible thing happened to Iron Shell. He and several other young men were taken from their homes by the soldiers and sent far away to a white man's boarding school. He was angry and lonesome for his parents and the young girl he had wed before he

Literary Analysis
Theme What message is implied in Grandpa's story about the first Iron Shell?

---

9. butte (byo͞ot) **top** *n.* top of a steep hill standing alone in a plain.

▲ **Critical Viewing** How does this scene fit the image of a vision quest as described on page 588? Explain. **[Connect]**

was taken away. At first Iron Shell resisted the teacher's attempts to change him, and he did not try to learn. One day it was his turn to work in the school's blacksmith shop. As he walked into the place, he knew that his medicine had brought him there to learn and work with the white man's iron.

"Iron Shell became a blacksmith and worked at the trade when he returned to the reservation. All of his life he treasured the medicine bag. When he was old, and I was a man, he gave it to me, for no one made the vision quest any more."

Grandpa quit talking, and I stared in disbelief as he covered his face with his hands. His shoulders were shaking with quiet sobs, and I looked away until he began to speak again.

"I kept the bag until my son, your mother's father, was a man and had to leave us to fight in the war across the ocean. I gave him the bag, for I believed it would protect him in battle, but he did not take it with him. He was afraid that he would lose it. He died in a faraway place."

Again Grandpa was still, and I felt his grief around me.

"My son," he went on after clearing his throat, "had only a daughter, and it is not proper for her to know of these things."

He unbuttoned his shirt, pulled out the leather pouch, and lifted it over his head. He held it in his hand, turning it over and over as if memorizing how it looked.

"In the bag," he said as he opened it and removed two objects, "is the broken shell of the iron kettle, a pebble from the butte, and a

**Reading Check**

What happened when Grandpa's son did not take the medicine bag?

piece of the sacred sage."[10] He held the pouch upside down and dust drifted down.

"After the bag is yours you must put a piece of prairie sage within and never open it again until you pass it on to your son." He replaced the pebble and the piece of iron, and tied the bag.

I stood up, somehow knowing I should. Grandpa slowly rose from the bed and stood upright in front of me holding the bag before my face. I closed my eyes and waited for him to slip it over my head. But he spoke.

"No, you need not wear it." He placed the soft leather bag in my right hand and closed my other hand over it. "It would not be right to wear it in this time and place where no one will understand. Put it safely away until you are again on the reservation. Wear it then, when you replace the sacred sage."

Grandpa turned and sat again on the bed. Wearily he leaned his head against the pillow. "Go," he said. "I will sleep now."

"Thank you, Grandpa," I said softly and left with the bag in my hands.

That night Mom and Dad took Grandpa to the hospital. Two weeks later I stood alone on the lonely prairie of the reservation and put the sacred sage in my medicine bag.

---

10. **sage:** (sāj) *n.* plant belonging to the mint family.

Review and Assess
Thinking About the Selection

1. **Respond:** What items do you own that have a special meaning for you? Explain.
2. **(a) Recall:** Describe how each family member welcomes Grandpa. **(b) Analyze:** What causes Martin's shame when Grandpa appears? **(c) Interpret:** How can Martin feel both ashamed and proud of Grandpa?
3. **(a) Recall:** What three reasons for coming does Grandpa give? **(b) Support:** How do the events of the story support Grandpa's idea that things will be done when it is "the right time"?
4. **(a) Recall:** How does Martin's attitude toward the medicine bag change after his friends visit Grandpa? **(b) Compare and Contrast:** In what way does the Sioux heritage Martin brags about differ at first from the Sioux heritage Grandpa describes to him?
5. **(a) Recall:** What does Martin do at the very end of the story? **(b) Draw Conclusions:** What does Martin's final action in the story reveal about his relationship to his heritage?
6. **(a) Evaluate:** Is Martin ready by the end of the story to receive his grandfather's gift? **(b) Apply:** Using examples from the story and from life, explain how some "gifts" are also responsibilities.

Virginia Driving Hawk Sneve

(b. 1933)
Virginia Driving Hawk Sneve grew up on the Rosebud Reservation in South Dakota where she listened to storytellers tell traditional legends and folktales. After having her own children, she became inspired to become a children's author because she realized that few children's books at the time accurately portrayed Native American culture.

A writer and teacher, Sneve has won many awards for her fiction. In novels like *Jimmy Yellow Hawk* and *High Elk's Treasure*, she draws on her intimate knowledge of Sioux life. Her Sioux heritage also plays an important role in "The Medicine Bag."

Review and Assess

Literary Analysis

Theme

1. What details in "The Story-Teller" suggest the **theme** that entertainment and instruction are two different things?
2. What insight about tradition and heritage does the "The Medicine Bag" reveal?
3. The organizer below shows how details work together to suggest the theme of "The Story-Teller." Create one like it to show how details work together to suggest the theme of "The Medicine Bag."

Theme	Instruction is not entertainment.			
Details	Aunt's story is boring	Aunt's story is instructive	Bachelor's story is not instructive	Bachelor's story is interesting

Comparing Literary Works

4. Use an organizer like the one shown to identify similarities and differences in the themes of the two works.

Medicine Bag   **Storyteller**

Differences   **Similarities**   **Differences**

5. In what ways does the **tone,** or author's attitude, in each work affect how seriously you take the message?

Reading Strategy

Drawing Inferences

6. From which details in "The Story-Teller" can you **infer** that the bachelor understands children?
7. From what details in "The Medicine Bag" can you infer that family is very important to Martin's grandfather?

Extend Understanding

8. **Social Studies Connection: (a)** Identify a time period in history that is characterized most by tradition and keeping things the same. **(b)** Identify another time period that is characterized most by change and the birth of new ideas.

Quick Review

The **theme** of a story is its message, its insight into life. To review theme, see page 575.

An **inference** is a logical conclusion reached by putting details together and determining what they mean or indicate.

 Take It to the Net
www.phschool.com
Take the interactive self-test online to check your understanding of these selections.

Integrate Language Skills

Vocabulary Development Lesson

Word Analysis: Suffix -less

The suffix *-less* means "without." Explain how adding the suffix *-less* to each of these positive qualities turns them into negative ones:

1. care   2. faith   3. rest

Spelling Strategy

When a noun refers to a person or thing that does something, you spell the final *ur* sound *or*:

direct + or   = director

On your paper, write the noun that corresponds to each verb:

1. collect   2. connect   3. process

Grammar Lesson

Complex Sentences

A **complex sentence** contains one independent clause and one or more subordinate clauses. A subordinate clause cannot stand alone. An independent clause can.

> INDEPENDENT CLAUSE
> One year Cheryl had *new* moccasins
>
> SUBORDINATE CLAUSE
> that Grandpa had made.

When you use complex sentences to express equal ideas, arrange the clauses to achieve parallel structure. When you are juxtaposing ideas—setting them side by side to call attention to a similarity or difference, you should use parallel structure. In the following example, Martin's two feelings are juxtaposed.

Not parallel: Although Martin was proud, shame was another feeling he had.

Parallel: Although Martin was proud, he was also ashamed.

Fluency: Sentence Completions

On your paper, fill in each blank with a suitable word from the list on page 575.

1. Despite problems, Grandpa is ___?___ in locating his family.
2. The children approached ___?___ to hear the boring story.
3. The ___?___ had never met a woman he wanted to marry.
4. The Sioux medicine bag that the museum displayed had been examined by experts and was ___?___.
5. The ___?___ consisted of three kids, a dog, and Grandpa.

▶ *For more practice, see page R31, Exercise E.*
Practice Identify the independent and subordinate clauses in the following complex sentences.

1. It's difficult to tell stories that children can both understand and appreciate.
2. "I kept them quiet for ten minutes, which was more than you were able to do."
3. When I kicked and hollered at the dogs to get away, they scattered.
4. Mom and I carried him into her sewing room, where we had a spare bed.

Writing Application Revise the following paragraph. Combine sentences to introduce complex sentences for variety. Establish or improve parallel structure where appropriate.

I oppose the proposal. It will increase traffic. Parking will be a problem. In addition, the residents will pay higher taxes. Unfortunately, the residents are not the ones who will benefit. The facility will be used mostly by non-residents.

W͜G Prentice Hall Writing and Grammar Connection: Chapter 20, Section 2

Writing Lesson

Book Jacket Text

Write the text that might appear on a book jacket for "The Story-Teller" or "The Medicine Bag." In your jacket text, include previews of characters, plot, and setting, and include a comparison to another writer or work of literature.

Prewriting Look over several book jackets to get an idea of the types of details they include. Then, use hexagonal writing to generate details you can include in your jacket copy.

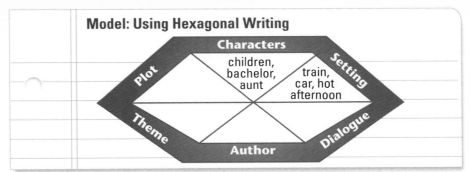

Model: Using Hexagonal Writing

Plot / Characters / Setting
children, bachelor, aunt / train, car, hot afternoon
Theme / Author / Dialogue

Drafting Begin with a positive statement that includes the book's title and use the author's full name. In separate paragraphs, develop details of character, setting, plot, and comparison to another work.

Revising Look for places where you have not supported your points. Add examples as needed.

𝒲𝒢 Prentice Hall Writing and Grammar Connection: Chapter 12, Section 2

Extension Activities

Listening and Speaking Use the bachelor's tale to **tell a story** for a small group of younger children. Pay attention to audience feedback.

1. Notice restlessness: It is a nonverbal cue that attention is wandering. Regain attention by introducing some audience participation, such as having the audience repeat lines of the story.

2. Answer questions: Questions are a verbal cue that a listener wants more information.

3. Watch facial expressions:. If you see confusion, restate events or ideas in a simpler way.

Research and Technology Research traditional and contemporary Sioux customs and beliefs. Share your findings in an **oral report.** Use resources such as the following:

- history books
- print or online encyclopedias
- the Internet
- magazines and newspapers

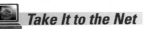 **Take It to the Net**   www.phschool.com

Go online for an additional research activity using the Internet.

The children in Saki's story are critical listeners who demand a tale with details, characters, and events that startle and spark their imaginations. They pronounce the bachelor's tale "beautiful" because it meets these criteria, and they call the aunt's tale "stupid" because it does not.

Pat Mora is a Mexican-American writer who has given a lot of thought to what makes a piece of writing good, and to what makes the creative process rewarding for both writer and audience. Her introduction to *My Own True Name* is a letter addressed to a "fellow writer"—you! In it, she explains how writers find interesting things to write about. She explains why she writes, what inspires her, and why she thinks you might be inspired to write, too.

As you read "Dear Fellow Writer," think about Mora's ideas about the sources and subject matter of good creative writing. Ask yourself how her ideas and assumptions compare and contrast with those of Saki's storytellers.

Dear Fellow Writer

from
My Own True Name

Pat Mora

Dear Fellow Writer,

A blank piece of paper can be exciting and intimidating. Probably every writer knows both reactions well. I know I do. I wanted to include a letter to you in this book because I wish I could talk to you individually. I'd say: Listen to your inside self, your private voice. Respect your thoughts and feelings and ideas. You—yes, you—play with sounds. With language(s), explore the wonder of being alive.

Living hurts, so sometimes we write about a miserable date, a friend who betrayed us, the death of a parent. Some days, though, we're so full of joy we feel like a kite. We can fly! Whether we write for ourselves or to share our words, we discover ourselves when we truly write: when we dive below the surface. It's never easy to really reveal ourselves in school, but remember that writing is practice. Without practice, you will never learn to hear and sing your own unique song.

I have always been a reader, which is the best preparation for becoming a writer. When I was in grade school in El Paso, Texas (where I was born), I read comic books and mysteries and magazines and library books. I was soaking up language.

I've always liked to write, too—but I was a mother before I began to create regular time for my writing. Was it that I didn't think that I had anything important to say? Was it that I didn't believe that I could say anything that well? Was it that when I was in school we never studied a writer who was like me—bilingual, a Mexican American—and so somehow I decided that "people like me" couldn't be writers?

I have a large poster of an American Indian storyteller right above my desk. Children are climbing all over her, just as my sisters and my brother and I climbed over *nuestra tía*, our aunt, Ignacia Delgado, the aunt we called Lobo. She was our storyteller. Who is yours? Would you like to

▼ **Critical Viewing** Why would a writer be inspired by a storyteller sculpture such as this one? **[Connect]**

be a storyteller? Would you like to write or paint or draw or sing your stories?

I became a writer because words give me so much pleasure that I have always wanted to sink my hands and heart into them, to see what I can create, what will rise up, what will appear on the page. I've learned that some writers are quiet and shy, others noisy, others just plain obnoxious. Some like enchiladas and others like sushi; some like rap and others like *rancheras*.[1] Some write quickly, and some are as slow as an elderly man struggling up a steep hill on a windy day.

I'll tell you a few of our secrets.

The first is that we all read. Some of us like mysteries and some of us like memoirs, but writers are readers. We're curious to see what others are doing with words, but—what is more important— we like what happens to us when we open a book, how we journey into the pages.

---

1. *rancheras* a type of popular Latino music.

◄ **Critical Viewing**
In what ways is this boy following Pat Mora's advice? **[Connect]**

Another secret is that we write often. We don't just talk about writing. We sit by ourselves inside or outside, writing at airports or on kitchen tables, even on napkins.

We're usually nosy and very good at <u>eavesdropping</u>. Just ask my three children! And writers are collectors. We collect facts and phrases and stories: the names of cacti, the word for cheese in many languages.

In the last twenty years, I've spent more and more time writing my own books for children and adults. I have received many rejections and will probably receive many more, darn it. I just keep writing—and revising. Revising is now one of my favorite parts of being a writer, though I didn't always feel that way. I enjoy taking what I've written—a picture or a book or a poem—and trying to make the writing better, by changing words or rhythm. Sometimes by starting over!

Writing is my way of knowing myself better, of hearing myself, of discovering what is important to me and what makes me sad, what makes me different, what makes me *me*—of discovering my own true name. And writing makes me less lonely. I have all these words in English and Spanish whispering or sometimes shouting at me, just waiting for me to put them to work, to combine them so that they leap over mountains on small hooves or slip down to the sandy bottom of the silent sea.

And you? Maybe these poems—taken from my collections *Chants, Borders,* and *Communion,* along with some new poems written for this book, for you—will tempt you to write your own poems about a special person or a special place, about a gray fear or a green hope. What are your blooms, your thorns, your roots?

Remember, my friend, never speak badly of your writing. Never make fun of it. Bring your inside voice out and let us hear you on the page. Come, join the serious and sassy family of writers.

eavesdropping
(ēvz´drãp´iṇ) *n.* secretly listening to the private conversation of others.

Pat Mora

(b. 1942)

In her work, Pat Mora explores the experience of cultural diversity, as well as her own experience as a Mexican American woman. Born in El Paso, Texas, she was raised partly by her grandmother and her Aunt "Lobo." Although she considers herself a Southwesterner, she travels widely, giving presentations and poetry readings. From 1983 to 1984, she hosted a National Public Radio show called "Voice: The Mexican-American in Perspective." Her award-winning writings include numerous volumes of poetry and essays, a memoir, and books for children.

Connecting Literature Past and Present

1. What kinds of things inspire Pat Mora to write? What factors seem to inspire Saki's bachelor to tell his story?

2. How does Pat Mora's purpose for writing compare with the storytelling purpose of the aunt and bachelor in Saki's story?

3. Do you think Saki and Pat Mora might have similar or different ideas about what makes a story interesting? Explain.

Inspirational Speeches

About Inspirational Speeches

A speaker gives an **inspirational speech** to elicit an emotional response from an audience. You might hear an inspirational speech at a graduation ceremony or in the locker room of a football team at halftime. When you *read* an inspirational speech it is often easier to judge the speaker's methods more objectively than when you *hear it*. Whether you read or hear a speech, analyze and evaluate the speaker's message, rather than reacting on a purely emotional level.

An inspirational speech contains the following characteristics:
- a dramatic opening that introduces the topic
- use of language and imagery that has emotional impact for the audience
- a clear notion of what the speaker wants the audience to do
- a concluding paragraph that ends on an emotional high note

Reading Strategy

Evaluating the Speaker's Message

Evaluating the message of a speech can help you form an opinion about the speaker's position. To find the speaker's message, summarize the main idea of the speech in a single sentence. The main idea can usually be found in the opening and closing paragraphs. Once you have done this, record your personal reaction to the speaker's message. Also, note any aspects of the speaker's position with which you agree or disagree. Finally, determine whether you ultimately agree or disagree with the speaker's message. Use the chart to guide you.

Speaker's Message
Summary: The speaker's message is _____.

Emotional Reaction
When I read the speech I felt _____ _____.

Analysis
I thought the speaker's message was flawed/made sense because _____.

Final Evaluation
I agree/disagree with the speaker because _____ _____.

From **Sharing in the American Dream**
Colin Powell

Powell introduces his topic with a dramatic comparison between the nation's founders and the volunteers whom he is addressing.

Over 200 years ago, a group of volunteers gathered on this sacred spot to found a new nation. In perfect words, they voiced their dreams and aspirations of an imperfect world. They pledged their lives, their fortune and their sacred honor to secure inalienable rights given by God for life, liberty and pursuit of happiness—pledged that they would provide them to all who would inhabit this new nation.

They look down on us today in spirit, with pride for all we have done to keep faith with their ideals and their sacrifices. Yet, despite all we have done, this is still an imperfect world. We still live in an imperfect society. Despite more than two centuries of moral and material progress, despite all our efforts to achieve a more perfect union, there are still Americans who are not sharing in the American Dream. There are still Americans who wonder: is the journey there for them, is the dream there for them, or, whether it is, at best, a dream deferred.

The great American poet, Langston Hughes, talked about a dream deferred, and he said, "What happens to a dream deferred? Does it dry up like a raisin in the sun, or fester like a sore and then run? Does it stink like rotten meat or crust and sugar over like a syrupy sweet? Maybe it just sags, like a heavy load. Or, does it explode?"…

So today, we gather here today to pledge that the dream must no longer be deferred and it will never, as long as we can do anything about it, become a dream denied. That is why we are here, my friends. We gather here to pledge that those of us who are more fortunate will not forsake those who are less fortunate. We are a compassionate and caring people. We are a generous people. We will reach down, we will reach back, we will reach across to help our brothers and sisters who are in need.

Above all, we pledge to reach out to the most vulnerable members of the American family, our children. As you've heard, up to 15 million young Americans today are at risk...

In terms of numbers the task may seem staggering. But if we look at the simple needs that these children have, then the task is manageable, the goal is achievable. We know what they need. They need an adult caring person in their life, a safe place to learn and grow, a healthy start, marketable skills and an opportunity to serve so that early in their lives they learn the virtue of service so that they can reach out then and touch another young American in need.

These are basic needs that we commit ourselves to today, we promise today. We are making America's promise today to provide to those children in need. This is a grand alliance. It is an alliance between government and corporate America and nonprofit America, between our institutions of faith, but especially between individual Americans.

You heard the governors and the mayors, and you'll hear more in a little minute that says the real answer is for each and every one of us, not just here in Philadelphia, but across this land—for each and every one of us to reach out and touch someone in need.

All of us can spare 30 minutes a week or an hour a week. All of us can give an extra dollar. All of us can touch someone who doesn't look like us, who doesn't speak like us, who may not dress like us, but needs us in their lives. And that's what we all have to do to keep this going.

And so there's a spirit of Philadelphia here today. There's a spirit of Philadelphia that we saw yesterday in Germantown. There is a spirit of Philadelphia that will leave Philadelphia tomorrow afternoon and spread across this whole nation—30 governors will go back and spread it; over 100 mayors will go back and spread it, and hundreds of others, leaders around this country who are watching will go back and spread it. Corporate America will spread it, nonprofits will spread it. And each and every one of us will spread it because it has to be done, we have no choice. We cannot leave these children behind if we are going to meet the dreams of our founding fathers.

And so let us all join in this great crusade. Let us make sure that no child in America is left behind, no child in America has their dream deferred or denied. We can do it. We can do it because we are Americans. . . .

> Powell first states the purpose of his speech here as an emotional appeal for greater volunteerism.

> Powell addresses concerns his listeners may have.

> The speaker uses practical arguments in this paragraph to support his main message.

> Powell ends his speech dramatically with a patriotic call to action.

Check Your Comprehension

1. Who does Powell say are looking down on the volunteers in the audience?
2. Why does Powell claim that America has not yet lived up to its ideals?
3. Why does the speaker use the cause of children to illustrate the potential of volunteerism?
4. What is Powell claiming we all can spare 30 minutes to do?

Applying the Reading Strategy

Evaluating the Speaker's Message

5. How would you summarize Powell's message?
6. Are there any problems with the arguments he uses?
7. To what types of emotions does this speech appeal?
8. How does Powell use patriotism to reinforce his message?
9. Do you agree or disagree with his basic message?

Activity

Evaluating a Political Speech

With your classmates, watch a political speech that is designed to inspire action on a specific social issue. Evaluate the speech. To do this:

- briefly summarize the speaker's purpose and point of view.
- note the speaker's arguments and how he or she uses dramatic language to sway emotions.
- decide whether you agree or disagree with the speaker.
- compare and discuss your evaluation with your classmates.

Contrasting Informational Texts

Inspirational Speeches and News Reports

Inspirational speeches and news reports differ in format and purpose. Consider the differences between these two informational texts. Then, use a chart like the one shown to list the major differences.

	Powell's Speech	**News Report**
Purpose		To offer facts about a current event
Content	• Outlines the need for volunteerism • Explains how volunteers will bring about change	• • •
Format		

Writing WORKSHOP

Narration: Short Story

A **short story** is a brief narrative that describes fictional characters and events. In this workshop, you will create a short story.

Assignment Criteria. Your short story should have the following characteristics:

- one or more **characters,** developed throughout the story
- a clear **setting,** a time and place in which action occurs, described with sensory details
- a **conflict** or problem faced by a main character
- a **plot** that develops the conflict and leads to a climax, or turning point, and a resolution of the conflict
- a **theme**—an idea or question about life or human nature—that is reflected in the story's plot

To preview the criteria on which your short story may be assessed, see the Rubric on page 605.

Prewriting

Choose a type of story. Decide what kind of story you would like to write. There are several kinds:

- **Realistic stories** reflect the everyday lives of ordinary people.
- **Character studies** emphasize character development instead of complicated plot developments.
- **Genre stories**—including science-fiction, detective, and horror stories—are designed to elicit a special reaction, like wonder, suspense, or horror.

Begin with a character. Get to know your main character by drawing a picture, listing details, or asking and answering questions such as "How do you spend your time?" or "Who are your friends?"

Picture the scene. Picture your character in a particular time and place. Make a chart of sensory images to weave through your story. Use all five senses to help readers experience the setting as real.

SIGHT	open window; curtains blowing
SOUND	music, laughter
SMELL	neighbors' barbecue
TOUCH	breeze from window

Invent a situation. Envision your character in a situation that will make your story compelling to readers. Imagine a scenario in which characters must confront a force of nature or resolve a sticky dilemma while enduring emotions such as fear, guilt, or grief. Build in tension that culminates in a crisis.

Student Model

Before you begin drafting your short story, read this portion of a student model and review the characteristics of successful fiction. The full text is available at www.phschool.com

Nick Meyer
Maplewood, New Jersey

A Constitution of My Own

I slowly opened the stained, thick envelope I had found in my grandparents' house in the lining of a painting of George Washington. I looked inside cautiously and all I saw was dust. I dropped the envelope on the floor and walked away. But something told me to take another look. I slowly opened the attic door for the second time. It creaked and sputtered dust like a car. I walked over to the folded envelope and dumped the contents on the floor. On the top of the gray pile of dust was a folded piece of yellow paper. I started to open it, and I gasped at what I saw. It was . . . a copy of the Constitution of the United States!

*　　*　　*

Slowly, I walked to the attic door and started to descend the stairs. But I stopped: "No point in getting excited if it's false." Slowly I started again, making sure not to go too fast so my grandma wouldn't get suspicious . . . . I didn't want to tell her about the document until I could confirm that it was authentic.

"Grandma?"

"Yes, honey, what can I do for you?" said my grandma, with a smile as big as the sun on her face.

"Where did you get the painting in the attic? I mean of George Washington?" My grandma stood for a few seconds with arms folded on her shovel. She had a puzzled look on her face, and I started to wonder if the painting had "just appeared" there.

"Well, your grandpa got that painting from his granddad, and his grandpa . . . The reason I hesitate, though, is because I don't know where it came from," said my grandma. She didn't have the young expression on her face anymore. And it added to the mystery even more.

*　　*　　*

I walked the stone path again, and listened to the high-pitched calls of the birds. I was lost in thought about my great-great—I don't know how many greats—but I was thinking about my grandpas. What if George Washington had given him that copy himself? . . .

The main character in this story is the first-person narrator.

Sensory details establish an effective setting.

The problem faced by the narrator is how to find out the origin of the document without letting anyone else know he has it.

Plot developments center around the discovery of the document and the narrator's efforts to find its origin.

The theme of this piece involves the excitement of connecting with the distant past.

Drafting

Show, do not tell. Do not tell your reader that the basketball game is exciting. Show it with details such as a ticking clock, a tied score, and the deafening roar of a crowd stomping on wooden bleachers. Let dynamic verbs and carefully chosen adjectives and adverbs do the work.

Use dialogue. Distinguish your individual characters by giving them individual voices and patterns of speech. Write dialogue that moves the action forward. Make sure your characters interact and display a wide range of emotions through their dialogue.

Build to a climax. In the beginning, give your readers information, called **exposition**, to help them understand the situation. Develop the conflict, event by event, until you reach the turning point or climax, the point of highest tension when your story turns toward its logical conclusion. Use a plot diagram like the one shown to help you construct your story.

One day George discovers Martha and Henry trapped by a bull.

Climax

Martha refuses to marry George because he is an uneducated farmer.

George distracts the bull, and Henry runs away.

Introduce George, Martha, and Henry the school teacher.

Rising Action

Falling Action

Struck by George's bravery, Martha agrees to marry him.

Resolution

Exposition   Conflict Introduced

Revising

Revise to develop characters. Look for places where you can add more details to flesh out your characters.

1. Review your draft, highlighting situations and events to which a character would have a strong reaction.

2. Ask yourself: What gestures, words, facial expressions, thoughts, memories, or actions will reflect this reaction?

3. In the margin, jot down answers to these questions.

4. When you have finished marking up your draft, review these marginal notes and decide which details to include.

Model: Developing your Character

crumbling, yellow

It was . . . a copy of the Constitution of the United States! I ran my hands over the dry, yellow paper looking to see if it was real. It was.

Nick adds a physical detail that allows us to picture the document in the previous sentence.

Revise to include action verbs. Linking verbs simply connect a subject with a word that describes it. Action verbs are often a more exciting alternative. To replace linking verbs, highlight all forms of *be* and other linking verbs (*feel, look, appear, become, grow, remain*) and try to rewrite your sentences using action verbs.

Example: Coretta looked white as a sheet.
The blood drained from Coretta's face.

Compare the model and the nonmodel. Why is the model more effective than the nonmodel?

Nonmodel	Model
I started to open it, and I was surprised by what I saw.	I started to open it, and I gasped at what I saw.

Publishing and Presenting

Choose one of these ways to share your writing with classmates or a larger audience.

Tell your story aloud. Hold a storytelling event in which several students tell their stories aloud. Make posters announcing the event and invite other classes.

Submit your story. Send your story to a national magazine, online journal, or contest that solicits student writing. Ask your teacher or librarian for suggestions.

W̶G Prentice Hall Writing and Grammar Connection: Chapter 5

Speaking Connection

To learn more about delivering a short story orally, see the **Listening and Speaking Workshop: Storytelling,** page 606.

Rubric for Self-Assessment

Evaluate your short story using the following criteria and rating scale:

Criteria	Rating Scale Not very ——— Very				
How clearly does the story show a conflict or problem faced by a main character?	1	2	3	4	5
How well does the story develop a particular theme?	1	2	3	4	5
How well is the character developed throughout the story?	1	2	3	4	5
How successfully does the plot build to a climax?	1	2	3	4	5
Is the conflict interesting enough to make readers care how it turns out?	1	2	3	4	5

Listening and Speaking WORKSHOP

Storytelling

Effective **storytelling** has much in common with effective story writing. (To review the characteristics of good short story writing, see the Writing Workshop, p. 602.) Along with narrative techniques—such as the use of descriptive details that appeal to all five senses—good storytellers use dramatic techniques to entertain their audience and bring their stories to life. The following strategies and the checklist on this page can help you polish your storytelling delivery.

Use Your Voice

There is no one way to tell a story. Your voice, with its wide range of sounds, is the tool that breathes life into the narrative and makes it your own.

Experiment with pacing and volume. Use your voice as if it were a musical instrument. Make it sound loud or soft, high or low, fast or slow, bold or timid, depending upon the effect you wish to create in the story. If you speak rapidly, remember to enunciate, pronouncing all the words clearly.

Make dialogue come to life. Have fun with your characters' conversation. Help your audience recognize each character by making each voice unique.

Dramatize sounds. If a character sneezes, sneeze. If another screams, do so with abandon. Do not be shy. Sound effects, like the slamming of a door or the hooting of an owl, will add to your story's mood.

Use Your Body

Good storytellers use their bodies to make characters unique and actions vivid.

Get physical. Practice in front of a mirror to get the best facial expressions and hand motions to punctuate your narrative. Use your arms, legs, feet, and back. Jump around, reach for the sky, or scratch your head if you are puzzled. Be an actor.

Add a prop. A carefully chosen prop, such as a medicine bag or an old briefcase, can give your story focus.

Move around. Vary your stance as you tell your story. Where your story calls for it, you can sit, kneel, crouch, walk around, spin, or jump up and click your heels.

Activity: Storytelling Choose a story from this unit and practice retelling it in your own words. Use the checklist here to help you experiment with different effects you can achieve. Tell your story to family members, classmates, or friends.

Checklist for Storytelling Delivery

Sound Effects
- ☐ Pacing
- ☐ Volume
- ☐ Characters' dialogue
- ☐ Other sound effects

Visual Effects
- ☐ Body language
- ☐ Props
- ☐ Varied stance

Identifying Cause and Effect

The reading sections of some tests require you to read a passage and answer multiple-choice questions about cause-and-effect relationships. Use the following strategies to answer such questions:

- You can distinguish between cause and effect when you determine what is making something happen (the cause) and what is happening (the effect).

- One cause may have several effects, and one effect may have multiple causes.

- Do not confuse time sequence with cause and effect. Even if one event follows another, the first event does not necessarily cause the second one.

Test-Taking Strategies

- Look for words such as *because, the reason for,* or *in order to* that signal cause-and-effect relationships.
- Verify cause and effect by determining whether the cause was necessary for the effect to happen.

Sample Test Item

Directions: Read the following passage, and then choose the letter of the best possible answer.

Tigers are an endangered species. In 1999 there were fewer than seven thousand of them living in the wild. These few are dying off fast as a result of illegal hunting and loss of habitat. When land is cleared to make room for a growing human population, tigers have less land on which to hunt and raise their young. To save wild tigers, governments need to protect tiger habitats and impose stricter hunting penalties.

1. In order to prevent tigers from dying out, governments need to—

   A clear land

   B encourage hunters

   C protect habitats

   D place tigers in zoos

Answer and Explanation

C is correct. **A** and **B** are not actions, or causes, that will have the effect of protecting tigers. **D** is not mentioned in the passage.

▶ Practice

Directions: Read the following passage, and then choose the letter of the best possible answer.

The extra half-hour of practice each day had paid off. Maya could hear the improvement in her violin playing. She was sure that her new-found confidence would result in her being more relaxed at the audition for Senior Orchestra. Just as she was about to raise her bow for the first note, she heard a ping. One of her strings had snapped. Maya's face fell. "Don't worry," smiled the director. "I always bring an extra set of strings to auditions. We'll have your violin restrung in a jiffy."

1. Maya's new confidence was a result of—

   A being more relaxed at the audition

   B getting a new string

   C extra practice each day

   D the director's friendly attitude

Nonfiction

Still Life #31, 1963, Tom Wesselmann, Frederick P. Weisman Art Foundation, ©Tom Wesselmann/Licensed by VAGA, New York, NY

Exploring the Genre

Whatever you want to know, there is a non-fiction book to provide the information. Nonfiction expands our minds with in-depth information, compelling us to ask more and more questions about how things work and why. The subject matter of nonfiction is reality—the reality of people, events, places, and scientific exploration. Whether you want to learn more about someone's life, a historical event, a travel destination, or the origin of our species, you can turn to nonfiction.

◀ **Critical Viewing** How might this painting be related to the theme of nonfiction? **[Connect]**

Why Read Literature?

Whenever you read nonfiction, you have a purpose, or reason. Your purpose will vary, depending on what type of information and enjoyment you expect to get out of the reading. Preview three purposes you might set before reading works in this unit.

 1

Read for the love of literature.

John Hersey's writing often looks at the impact of war from the perspective of human suffering. His most famous work, *Hiroshima*, tells the gripping story of the suffering caused by the dropping of the atomic bomb. Read Hershey's piece about a Polish prisoner's incredible escape from certain death in **"Not to Go With the Others,"** page 639.

Nonfiction writing often teaches us something new. Bruce Brooks takes on the role of teacher in a thought-provoking essay on wasps that is half memoir, half biology lesson. Find out how wasps build their intricate nests when you read **"Animal Craftsmen,"** page 614.

2

Read for information.

Imagine saying at the age of seventy-five that all of your work before you turned seventy was worthless! That is what the Japanese artist Katsushika Hokusai did. Learn more about this fascinating artist who created thirty thousand works in the span of ninety years in **"Hokusai: The Old Man Mad About Drawing,"** page 636.

Have you ever heard your parents say that watching too much television will "rot your brain"? If so, you may not agree with Robert MacNeil's similar view on the effects of watching television. But at least you will be well prepared to debate the issue with your parents after reading MacNeil's essay, **"The Trouble with Television,"** page 668.

3

Read to be entertained.

Sometimes the rules of traditional sports are just too uninspiring for the active minds of young children. When this happens, they add a creative twist or two of their own, bending the rules slightly to suit their own needs. You may not recognize the game, but you will doubtless be entertained, when you read Lionel García's childhood memoir, **"Baseball,"** page 624.

Take It to the Net

Visit the Web site for online instruction and activities related to each selection in this unit.
www.phschool.com

How to Read Literature

Strategies for Reading Nonfiction

Nonfiction is writing about real events, people, and places. That does not mean, however, that you should accept everything a writer tells you. When reading, it is important to judge the facts for yourself and form your own interpretations. In this unit, you will learn to use the following strategies to help you:

1. Identify the author's purpose.

Nonfiction authors have a reason, or purpose, for writing. The details and information they present support this purpose. In this unit, you will learn strategies for identifying the author's purpose and recognizing how that purpose influences the information the author chooses to include.

2. Identify the author's main points.

Ask yourself what the author wants you to learn or think as a result of reading the nonfiction piece. Look in the beginning and concluding sections of the piece for clues. Choose points that the author develops throughout the entire selection.

3. Evaluate logic.

In order for a nonfiction piece to be persuasive, its arguments have to be logical. If the arguments are not logical, they are said to contain *logical flaws*.

- Make sure that authors use arguments that support their main points and do not conflict with one another.

- Check if the author overstates his or her arguments by leaving out evidence that might contradict his or her main points.

Evaluate Logic

Main Argument: Television has a negative effect on the minds of viewers.

Support: Television encourages lazy thinking.

Logical Flaw: Overly broad statement that ignores educational programs and TV movies that are thought-provoking.

Support: Literacy rates are down, while television viewership is high.

Logical Flaw: Leaves out possibility that literacy rates may be low for other reasons.

4. Evaluate the author's presentation.

Evaluating an author's presentation involves analyzing the various choices the author made when writing the piece.

- **Organization:** The way in which the information is arranged.

- **Support:** An author should support his or her main points with facts. If an author makes broad statements but does not back them up, note this in your evaluation.

- **Interest level:** Just because a nonfiction piece presents facts does not mean it has to be flat or boring. An author should still use provocative language, anecdotes, and information to hold your interest.

As you read the selections in this unit, review the reading strategies and look at the notes in the side column. Use the suggestions to interact with the text.

Prepare to Read

Animal Craftsmen

Take It to the Net

Visit www.phschool.com for interactive activities and instruction related to "Animal Craftsmen," including

- background
- graphic organizers
- literary elements
- reading strategies

Preview

Connecting to the Literature

If you have ever marveled at a perfect spider web or been fascinated by a caterpillar's cocoon, then you have witnessed the amazing abilities that Bruce Brooks analyzes in "Animal Craftsmen."

Background

Author Bruce Brooks had finished writing a book about designs in nature when he realized it needed a beginning. That led him to write this essay. "So I went back to the incident that had started my interest," Brooks says, "and I simply told that story, hoping my readers would get a similar sense of starting up." The object that inspires the essay is an unlikely one—the intricate, sculptured nest of mud wasps.

Literary Analysis

Reflective Essay

An essay is a short nonfiction work about an idea or topic. There are many types of essays. One type is the **reflective essay**, an essay in which the writer expresses his or her thoughts about a subject of personal interest. The writer may retell personal experiences that relate to the subject, sharing his or her insights and interpretations, as in this example from Brooks's essay:

> There's nothing wrong with trying to empathize with an animal, but we shouldn't forget that ultimately animals live *animal* lives.

After describing his own experience as a child, Bruce Brooks broadens its meaning into a lesson for both himself and his readers.

Connecting Literary Elements

Because a reflective essay expresses the writer's personal responses, it shows the **author's perspective**, the viewpoint from which the work is written. That perspective—a result of attitudes, beliefs, and customs that the writer brings to an experience—affects the way he or she presents and interprets incidents.

Look at this chart that shows Brooks's perspective. As you read, consider how his perspective

- shapes how he describes things.
- affects his reactions to what he describes.

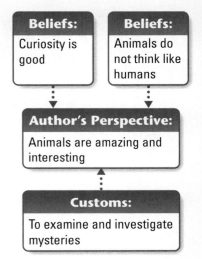

Beliefs: Curiosity is good

Beliefs: Animals do not think like humans

Author's Perspective: Animals are amazing and interesting

Customs: To examine and investigate mysteries

Reading Strategy

Evaluating the Author's Presentation

A writer's perspective on a subject affects the way he or she organizes and presents the material. Brooks writes from the perspective of someone who loves and has knowledge of nature. Because his perspective is both informational and emotional, he includes both. Evaluate how effectively he presents his material by considering these focus questions as you read:

1. How clearly are main ideas identified?
2. How effectively are examples used to illustrate main ideas?

Vocabulary Development

subtle (sut´ əl) *adj.* fine, hard to detect (p. 615)

infusion (in fyoo´ zhən) *n.* act of putting one substance into another (p. 615)

habitable (hab´ ə tə bəl) *adj.* fit to live in (p. 616)

empathy (em´ pə thē) *n.* ability to share another's thoughts or feelings (p. 617)

Animal Craftsmen

BRUCE BROOKS

One evening, when I was about five, I climbed up a ladder on the outside of a rickety old tobacco barn at sunset. The barn was part of a small farm near the home of a country relative my mother and I visited periodically; though we did not really know the farm's family, I was allowed to roam, poke around, and conduct sudden studies of anything small and harmless. On this evening, as on most of my jaunts, I was not looking for anything; I was simply climbing with an open mind. But as I balanced on the next-to-the-top rung and inhaled the spicy stink of the tobacco drying inside, I *did* find something under the eaves[1] —something very strange.

It appeared to be a kind of gray paper sphere, suspended from the dark planks by a thin stalk, like an apple made of ashes hanging on its stem. I studied it closely in the clear light. I saw that the bottom was a little ragged, and open. I could not tell if it had been torn, or if it had been made that way on purpose—for it was clear to me, as I studied it, that this thing had been *made*. This was no fruit or fungus.[2] Its shape, rough but trim; its intricately[3]

▲ **Critical Viewing** What about this spiderweb do you find "awesome"? Explain. **[Evaluate]**

---

1. **eaves** (ēvz) *n.* lower edges of a roof.
2. **fungus** (fuṇ´ gəs) *n.* vegetable-like organism such as a mushroom, which lives on other living beings.
3. **intricately** (in´ tri kit lē) *adv.* in a complex, highly detailed way.

colored surface with <u>subtle</u> swirls of gray and tan; and most of all the uncanny adhesiveness with which the perfectly tapered stem stuck against the rotten old pine boards—all of these features gave evidence of some intentional design. The troubling thing was figuring out who had designed it, and why.

I assumed the designer was a human being: someone from the farm, someone wise and skilled in a craft that had so far escaped my curiosity. Even when I saw wasps entering and leaving the thing (during a vigil I kept every evening for two weeks), it did not occur to me that the wasps might have fashioned it for themselves. I assumed it was a man-made "wasp house" placed there expressly for the purpose of attracting a family of wasps, much as the "martin hotel," a giant birdhouse on a pole near the farmhouse, was maintained to shelter migrant[4] purple martins who returned every spring. I didn't ask myself why anyone would want to give wasps a bivouac;[5] it seemed no more odd than attracting birds.

As I grew less wary of the wasps (and they grew less wary of me), and as my confidence on the ladder improved, I moved to the upper rung and peered through the sphere's bottom. I could see that the paper swirled in layers around some secret center the wasps inhabited, and I marveled at the delicate hands of the craftsman who had devised such tiny apertures[6] for their protection.

I left the area in the late summer, and in my imagination I took the strange structure with me. I envisioned unwrapping it, and in the middle finding—what? A tiny room full of bits of wool for sleeping, and countless manufactured pellets of scientifically determined wasp food? A glowing blue jewel that drew the wasps at twilight, and gave them a cool <u>infusion</u> of energy as they clung to it overnight? My most definite idea was that the wasps lived in a small block of fine cedar the craftsman had drilled full of holes, into which they slipped snugly, rather like the bunks aboard submarines in World War II movies.

As it turned out, I got the chance to discover that my idea of the cedar block had not been wrong by much. We visited our relative again in the winter. We arrived at night, but first thing in the morning I made straight for the farm and its barn. The shadows under the eaves were too dense to let me spot the sphere from far off. I stepped on the bottom rung of the ladder—slick with frost—and climbed carefully up. My hands and feet kept slipping, so my eyes stayed on the rung ahead, and it was not until I was secure at the top that I could look up. The sphere was gone.

I was crushed. That object had fascinated me like nothing I had come across in my life; I had even grown to love wasps because of it. I sagged on the ladder and watched my breath eddy[7] around

---

4. **migrant** (mī´ grənt) *adj.* moving from one region to another with the changing seasons.
5. **bivouac** (biv´ wak´) *n.* temporary shelter.
6. **apertures** (ap´ ər chərz) *n.* openings.
7. **eddy** (ed´ ē) *v.* move in a circular motion.

subtle (sut´ əl) *adj.* fine, hard to detect

Literary Analysis
Author's Perspective
What is Brooks's attitude toward the nest?

infusion (in fyoo´ zhən) *n.* the act of putting one substance into another

**Reading Check**
Who does Brooks assume had designed the nest?

the blank eaves. I'm afraid I pitied myself more than the apparently homeless wasps.

But then something snapped me out of my sense of loss: I recalled that I had watched the farmer taking in the purple martin hotel every November, after the birds left. From its spruce appearance when he brought it out in March, it was clear he had cleaned it and repainted it and kept it out of the weather. Of course he would do the same thing for *this* house, which was even more fragile. I had never mentioned the wasp dwelling to anyone, but now I decided I would go to the farm, introduce myself, and inquire about it. Perhaps I would even be permitted to handle it, or, best of all, learn how to make one myself.

I scrambled down the ladder, leaping from the third rung and landing in the frosty salad of tobacco leaves and windswept grass that collected at the foot of the barn wall. I looked down and saw that my left boot had, by no more than an inch, just missed crushing the very thing I was rushing off to seek. There, lying dry and separate on the leaves, was the wasp house.

I looked up. Yes. I was standing directly beneath the spot where the sphere had hung—it was a straight fall. I picked up the wasp house, gave it a shake to see if any insects were inside, and, discovering none, took it home.

My awe of the craftsman grew as I unwrapped the layers of the nest. Such beautiful paper! It was much tougher than any I had encountered, and it held a curve (something my experimental paper airplanes never did), but it was very light, too. The secret at the center of the swirl turned out to be a neatly made fan of tiny cells, all of the same size and shape, reminding me of the heart of a sunflower that had lost its seeds to birds. The fan hung from the sphere's ceiling by a stem the thickness of a pencil lead.

The rest of the story is a little embarrassing. More impressed than ever, I decided to pay homage to the creator of this <u>habitable</u> sculpture. I went boldly to the farmhouse. The farmer's wife answered my knock. I showed her the nest and asked to speak with the person in the house who had made it. She blinked and frowned. I had to repeat my question twice before she understood what I believed my mission to be; then, with a gentle laugh, she dispelled my illusion about an ingenious old papersmith fond of wasps. The nest, she explained, had been made entirely by the insects themselves, and wasn't that amazing?

Well, of course it was. It still is. I needn't have been so embarrassed—the structures that animals build, and the sense of design they display, *should* always astound us. On my way home from the farmhouse, in my own defense I kept thinking, "But *I* couldn't build anything like this! Nobody could!"

The most natural thing in the world for us to do, when we are confronted with a piece of animal architecture, is to figure out if we

habitable (hab´ ə tə bəl) *adj.* fit to live in

Literary Analysis
Reflective Essay What impact does Brooks's discovery have on him?

could possibly make it or live in it. Who hasn't peered into the dark end of a mysterious hole in the woods and thought, "It must be pretty weird to live in there!" or looked up at a hawk's nest atop a huge sycamore and shuddered at the thought of waking up every morning with nothing but a few twigs preventing a hundred-foot fall. How, we wonder, do those twigs stay together, and withstand the wind so high?

It is a human tendency always to regard animals first in terms of ourselves. Seeing the defensive courage of a mother bear whose cubs are threatened, or the cooperative determination of a string of ants dismantling a stray chunk of cake, we naturally use our own behavior as reference for our <u>empathy</u>. We put ourselves in the same situation and express the animal's action in feelings—and words—that apply to the way people do things.

Sometimes this is useful. But sometimes it is misleading. Attributing human-like intentions to an animal can keep us from looking at the *animal's* sense of itself in its surroundings—its immediate and future needs, its physical and mental capabilities, its genetic[8] instincts. Most animals, for example, use their five senses in ways that human beings cannot possibly understand or express. How can a forty-two-year-old nearsighted biologist have any real idea what a two-week-old barn owl sees in the dark? How can a sixteen-year-old who lives in the Arizona desert identify with the muscular jumps improvised by a waterfall-leaping salmon in Alaska? There's nothing wrong with trying to empathize with an animal, but we shouldn't forget that ultimately animals live *animal* lives.

Animal structures let us have it both ways—we can be struck with a strange wonder, and we can empathize right away, too. Seeing a vast spiderweb, taut and glistening between two bushes, it's easy to think, "I have no idea how that is done; the engineering is awesome." But it is just as easy to imagine climbing across the bright strands, springing from one to the next as if the web were a new Epcot attraction, the Invisible Flying Flexible Space Orb. That a clear artifact of an animal's wits and agility[9] stands right there in front of us—that we can touch it, look at it from different angles, sometimes take it home—inspires our imagination as only a strange reality can. We needn't move into a molehill to experience a life of darkness and digging; our creative wonder takes us down there in a second, without even getting our hands dirty.

---

8. **genetic** (jə net′ ik) *adj.* inherited biologically.
9. **agility** (ə jil′ ə tē) *n.* ability to move quickly and easily.

▲ **Critical Viewing**
In what way does this wasps' nest look like "an apple made of ashes hanging on its stem"? **[Connect]**

empathy (em′ pə thē) *n.* ability to share another's emotions, thoughts, or feelings

✓ **Reading Check**
How does Brooks discover how the nest was really made?

But what if we discover some of the mechanics of how the web is made? Once we see how the spider works (or the humming bird, or the bee), is the engineering no longer awesome? This would be too bad: we don't want to lose our sense of wonder just because we gain understanding.

And we certainly do *not* lose it. In fact, seeing how an animal makes its nest or egg case or food storage vaults has the effect of increasing our amazement. The builder's energy, concentration, and athletic adroitness are qualities we can readily admire and envy. Even more startling is the recognition that the animal is working from a precise design in its head, a design that is exactly replicated time after time. This knowledge of architecture—knowing where to build, what materials to use, how to put them together—remains one of the most intriguing mysteries of animal behavior. And the more *we* develop that same knowledge, the more we appreciate the instincts and intelligence of the animals.

Review and Assess

Thinking About the Literature

1. **Respond:** Do you share the author's feeling that animal behavior is fascinating? Consider why or why not.

2. **(a) Recall:** As a child, what does Brooks assume about the "wasp house"? **(b) Infer:** What do you learn about Brooks when he reports having thought, "Perhaps I would be permitted to handle (the nest), or, best of all, learn how to make one myself"? **(c) Speculate:** What might Brooks's youthful assumption show about human estimates of animal ability?

3. **(a) Recall:** How does Brooks discover the truth about the wasps' nest? **(b) Analyze Cause and Effect:** What is his reaction? **(c) Connect:** In terms of the rest of the essay, what are the results of the discovery?

4. **(a) Recall:** According to Brooks, how do people usually react to seeing animal structures like nests? **(b) Draw Conclusions:** What does this show about the human imagination? **(c) Apply:** Identify two examples of people attributing human reactions and feelings to animals

5. **(a) Interpret:** What understanding does Brooks want his readers to have? **(b) Speculate:** What does this essay tell you about Brooks as a person?

6. **Take a Position:** Brooks suggests that people should not attribute human emotions, abilities, or reactions to animals. Do you agree or disagree with Brooks? Explain.

Bruce Brooks

(b. 1950)
Bruce Brooks is a versatile writer who has written both fiction and nonfiction. Brooks has worked as a newspaper reporter and a magazine writer. In addition to writing, he has worked as a printer and a teacher. Born in Washington, D.C., he spent much of his childhood in North Carolina and graduated from college there.

Brooks's first novel, *The Moves Make the Man*, was a Newbery Honor book in 1985, as was *What Hearts* in 1993. Nonfiction books include the award-winning *On the Wing* and *Nature by Design*, in which "Animal Craftsmen" appears. Brooks has also been a teacher and a reporter. He says, "I have an affinity for independence, for loners, for smart people who are watchers."

Review and Assess

Literary Analysis

Reflective Essay

1. List two statements in which Brooks shares his thoughts, feelings, or opinions.
2. What words can you suggest to describe Brooks's feelings about the natural world? Complete a word web like this one to show his reactions to nature. The chart has been started for you.

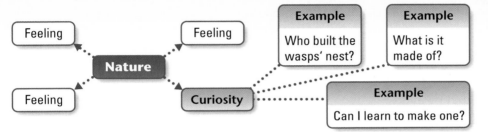

Feeling — Nature — Feeling

Feeling — Curiosity

Example Who built the wasps' nest?

Example What is it made of?

Example Can I learn to make one?

Connecting Literary Elements

3. Does the author think that understanding nature makes it less wonderful? Explain.
4. How does Brooks's perspective affect his reactions to the wasps' nest as a boy?
5. In what way is Brooks's childhood perspective on nature similar to and different from his adult perspective?

Reading Strategy

Evaluating the Author's Presentation

6. What are the main points Brooks makes in his essay?
7. How clearly are these main ideas expressed?
8. How effectively are examples used to illustrate main ideas? Use a chart like the one below to help you answer.

Animal Craftsmen	
Main Point: Animals use many skills to survive	Examples: spider's web
Main Point:	Examples:

Extend Understanding

9. **Science Connection:** In what way does the wasps' nest show the connection between structure and function?

Quick Review

A **reflective essay** is a short nonfiction work in which a writer expresses his or her thoughts on a subject. To review reflective essays, see page 613.

The **author's perspective** is the viewpoint from which he or she writes the work. To review author's perspective, see page 613.

 Take It to the Net
www.phschool.com
Take the interactive self-test online to check your understanding of the selection.

Integrate Language Skills

Vocabulary Development Lesson

Related Words: *Habitable*

The nest built by the mud wasps in "Animal Craftsmen" is *habitable*—"suitable to live in." The word *habitable* comes from the Latin word *habitare*, which means "to inhabit" or "to dwell." Complete the following sentences using one of these three words that share the same Latin origin:

inhabit   inhabitant   habitat

1. The Arctic is the natural ____?____ of polar bears.
2. The writer was fascinated by every ____?____ of the wasps' nest.
3. Purple martins ____?____ the bird house.

Fluency: Definitions

On your paper, match the vocabulary word in the first column with the word or phrase closest to its meaning in the second column.

1. subtle   a. livable
2. infusion   b. shared feeling
3. habitable   c. injection
4. empathy   d. slight

Spelling Strategy

The letter *b* is silent in the word *subtle* and in a number of other English words. Each clue below points to a word that contains a silent *b*. Write the words on your paper.

1. This person fixes water pipes and sinks.
2. You use this to untangle your hair.
3. This word can mean a tree branch or your arm.

Grammar Lesson

Nominative Case Pronouns

Pronouns in English have three forms, or cases—nominative, objective, and possessive. Which case to use depends on the pronoun's grammatical use in a sentence. If a pronoun is a subject or a predicate pronoun (renames subject after a linking verb), you use the **nominative case.**

Nominative Case Pronouns

I, we, you, he, she, it, they

As subject: *He* climbed up a ladder.

As predicate pronoun: The *finder* of the wasps' nest was *he.*

▶ *For more practice, see page R32, Exercise B.*
Practice Write the nominative pronoun or pronouns in each sentence. After each one write S (for subject) or PP (predicate pronoun).

1. I took the strange structure with me.
2. We visited our relative again in the winter.
3. They discovered that the owner of the birdhouse was he.
4. She blinked and frowned.
5. It was they who built the nests.

Writing Application Write a sentence using each of these pronouns in the way indicated.

1. she (predicate pronoun)
2. they (subject)
3. we (subject)

W͟G Prentice Hall Writing and Grammar Connection: Chapter 23

Writing Lesson

Summary

Find and read an article or explanation related to one of the topics discussed by Brooks. Write a summary—a brief restatement and interpretation of the main points.

Prewriting   Check a variety of sources for information on your topic. Choose one article or explanation to read. On a photocopy, highlight the main points.

Drafting   Write your summary. Include one or two of the most important highlighted details from the beginning, one or two from the middle, and one or two from the end.

Model: Combine Related Details

The spider makes its web of silk, which it produces from a sac in its body. ~~The web silk is very strong.~~ ⟨ ⟩ *strong* First, the spider makes a simple framework from the ∧ web silk. Then. . .

> The fact that the web silk is strong can be incorporated as an adjective into another sentence.

Revising   A summary should be brief and to the point. Evaluate the importance of each detail. Eliminate any that are not related to many ideas in the article.

WG *Prentice Hall Writing and Grammar Connection: Chapter 21, Section 21.3*

Extension Activities

Listening and Speaking Give an **oral response** to Bruce Brooks's essay.

1. Identify your overall response to the essay. For example, you might say that you could relate to the ideas he expressed.
2. Give reasons for your response.
3. Use examples from the text to support each reason you point out.
4. Write your points and examples on note cards and refer to them as you speak.

Writing Write a **letter to the author** sharing your reactions to the essay and telling him about any childhood experiences that relate to the points he makes.

Research and Technology Research another animal, either an animal mentioned in the essay or another, that builds carefully engineered nests or other structures.

- Use the Internet, periodicals, and other science resources to find out about the animal's habitat, its lifestyle, and how it builds.
- Combine your research with drawings or photographs to make a **poster** for display.

 **Take It to the Net**   www.phschool.com

Go online for an additional research activity using the Internet.

Prepare to Read

Baseball ◆ *from* One Writer's Beginnings

 Take It to the Net

Visit www.phschool.com
for interactive activities
and instruction related to
these selections, including
• background
• graphic organizers
• literary elements
• reading strategies

Preview

Connecting to the Literature

In these two selections, Eudora Welty and Lionel García share memories of very different childhood experiences. Think about the many ways childhood experiences can influence people's lives—what they learn to like or dislike, abilities they discover, beliefs and attitudes they develop.

Background

In "One Writer's Beginnings," Eudora Welty discusses an error in her thinking and writing over the movement of the moon in the sky. Although the moon is associated with nighttime, in its "new moon" phase it rises with the sun! The only time that the moon rises in the east as the sun sets in the west is the time closest to the full moon phase.

Literary Analysis
Autobiographical Writing

Autobiographical writing is writing in which the writer tells the story of his or her own life. The writer uses the first person, referring to himself or herself with the pronoun "I." The reader sees people and events in the author's life through the author's eyes. Look at this example.

> The night sky over my childhood Jackson was velvety black. I could see the full constellations in it and call their names; . . .

In *One Writer's Beginnings* and "Baseball," Eudora Welty and Lionel García tell stories about memorable events in their childhoods.

Comparing Literary Works

Although both these selections are about their authors' childhoods, the ideas are treated differently. Welty focuses on a lesson she learned and how her imagination developed. García's story focuses on action, characters, and factual description, more like a short story. Both writers use humor, but in different ways.

Use the following focus questions to guide you in completing a Venn diagram like this one.

1. What are the key events or points in each narrative?
2. How do the childhood priorities of the two writers compare?

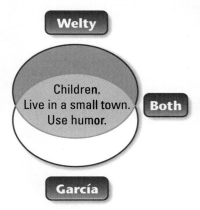

Reading Strategy
Understand the Author's Purpose

Authors write for many reasons:

- To stir your thoughts and emotions
- To explain or persuade
- To share experiences in a way that speaks to the reader

In order to **understand the author's purpose,** ask yourself "Why is the writer telling me this?"

Vocabulary Development

devices (di vīs´ ez) *n.* techniques or means for working things out (p. 625)

evaded (ē vād´ əd) *v.* avoided (p. 625)

visible (viz´ ə bəl) *adj.* able to be seen (p. 629)

reigning (rān´ iŋ) *adj.* ruling (p. 630)

respectively (ri spek´ tiv lē) *adv.* in the order named (p. 630)

constellations (kän´ stə lā´ shəns) *n.* groups of stars that have traditionally been thought to form the outline of a picture (p. 630)

eclipses (i klips´ əz) *n.* events in which the shadow of the moon or Earth obscures the view of the moon or sun (p. 630)

BASEBALL

Lionel G. García

We loved to play baseball. We would take the old mesquite[1] stick and the old ball across the street to the parochial[2] school grounds to play a game. Father Zavala enjoyed watching us. We could hear him laugh mightily from the screened porch at the rear of the rectory[3] where he sat.

The way we played baseball was to rotate positions after every out. First base, the only base we used, was located where one would normally find second base. This made the batter have to run past the pitcher and a long way to first baseman, increasing the odds of getting thrown out. The pitcher stood in line with the batter, and with

▲ **Critical Viewing**
How can you tell that these children are enjoying the game of baseball? **[Support]**

---

1. **mesquite** (mes´ kēt´) thorny shrub of North America.
2. **parochial** (pə rō´ kē əl) *adj.* supported by a church.
3. **rectory** (rek´ tər ē) *n.* residence for priests.

first base, and could stand as close or as far from the batter as he or she wanted. Aside from the pitcher, the batter and the first baseman, we had a catcher. All the rest of us would stand in the outfield. After an out, the catcher would come up to bat. The pitcher took the position of catcher, and the first baseman moved up to be the pitcher. Those in the outfield were left to their own <u>devices</u>. I don't remember ever getting to bat.

There was one exception to the rotation scheme. I don't know who thought of this, but whoever caught the ball on the fly would go directly to be the batter. This was not a popular thing to do. You could expect to have the ball thrown at you on the next pitch.

There was no set distance for first base. First base was wherever Matías or Juan or Cota tossed a stone. They were the law. The distance could be long or short depending on how soon we thought we were going to be called in to eat. The size of the stone marking the base mattered more than the distance from home plate to first base. If we hadn't been called in to eat by dusk, first base was hard to find. Sometimes someone would kick the stone farther away and arguments erupted.

When the batter hit the ball in the air and it was caught that was an out. So far so good. But if the ball hit the ground, the fielder had two choices. One, in keeping with the standard rules of the game, the ball could be thrown to the first baseman and, if caught before the batter arrived at the base, that was an out. But the second, more interesting option allowed the fielder, ball in hand, to take off running after the batter. When close enough, the fielder would throw the ball at the batter. If the batter was hit before reaching first base, the batter was out. But if the batter <u>evaded</u>

◀ **Critical Viewing** What does it feel like to learn a new skill or game? **[Relate]**

Literary Analysis
Autobiography What do the opening paragraphs tell you about the writer's background?

devices (di vīs´ ez) *n.* technique or means for working things out

evaded (ē vād´ əd) *v.* avoided

✔**Reading Check**

What is unusual about how García played baseball?

being hit with the ball, he or she could either run to first base or run back to home plate. All the while, everyone was chasing the batter, picking up the ball and throwing it at him or her. To complicate matters, on the way to home plate the batter had the choice of running anywhere possible to avoid getting hit. For example, the batter could run to hide behind the hackberry trees[4] at the parochial school grounds, going from tree to tree until he or she could make it safely back to home plate. Many a time we would wind up playing the game past Father Zavala and in front of the rectory half a block away. Or we could be seen running after the batter several blocks down the street toward town, trying to hit the batter with the ball. One time we wound up all the way across town before we cornered Juan against a fence, held him down, and hit him with the ball. Afterwards, we all fell laughing in a pile on top of each other, exhausted from the run through town.

The old codgers, the old shiftless men who spent their day talking at the street corners, never caught on to what we were doing. They would halt their idle conversation just long enough

▼ **Critical Viewing**
How do young players adapt the game of baseball to their own neighborhood or circumstances? **[Generalize]**

---

4. hackberry trees fruit-bearing trees of the elm family.

to watch us run by them, hollering and throwing the old ball at the batter.

It was the only kind of baseball game Father Zavala had ever seen. What a wonderful game it must have been for him to see us hit the ball, run to a rock, then run for our lives down the street. He loved the game, shouting from the screened porch at us, pushing us on. And then all of a sudden we were gone, running after the batter. What a game! In what enormous stadium would it be played to allow such freedom over such an expanse of ground?

My uncle Adolfo, who had pitched for the Yankees and the Cardinals in the majors, had given us the ball several years before. Once when he returned for a visit, he saw us playing from across the street and walked over to ask us what we were doing.

"Playing baseball," we answered as though we thought he should know better. After all, he was the professional baseball player.

He walked away shaking his head. "What a waste of a good ball," we heard him say, marveling at our ignorance.

Review and Assess

Thinking About the Literature

1. **Respond:** Would you have liked to play baseball with García and his friends, even though they did not follow the rules? Why or why not?

2. **(a) Recall:** What equipment do García and his friends have for their game? **(b) Infer:** What can you tell about García's background and neighborhood?

3. **(a) Recall:** Where was first base in the game? **(b) Analyze Cause and Effect:** What were some results of this decision?

4. **(a) Recall:** Did anyone actually win or lose Garcia's game? **(b) Connect:** How do you think García and his friends came to develop the rules of this game?

5. **(a) Recall:** How do Father Zavala and uncle Adolfo each respond to the game? **(b) Distinguish:** Why do they react so differently toward this version of baseball? **(c) Make a Judgment:** Would anyone else in this story have agreed with Adolfo's statement, "What a waste of a good ball"? **(d) Take a Position:** What is your reaction to Adolfo's remark? Do you agree with him? Why or why not?

6. **Speculate:** García and his friends thought they were playing baseball. If they had found out how real baseball is played, do you think they would have changed their game? Explain your answer.

Lionel G. García

(b. 1935)
Lionel García's novels and short stories focus on the lives of Mexican Americans, showing both their problems and their joys. García was born in San Diego, Texas, and as a child lived with his grandfather, a goatherd. He then became a veterinarian, teaching himself to write after working hours. "A writer's job is to present people as they are," he says, "usually to the surprise of the reader." His books include *I Can Hear the Cowbells Ring* (1994), in which "Baseball" appears.

from
One Writer's Beginnings

Eudora Welty

Learning stamps you with its moments. Childhood's learning is made up of moments. It isn't steady. It's a pulse.

In a children's art class, we sat in a ring on kindergarten chairs and drew three daffodils that had just been picked out of the yard; and while I was drawing, my sharpened yellow pencil and the cup of the yellow daffodil gave off whiffs just alike. That the pencil doing the drawing should give off the same smell as the flower it drew seemed part of the art lesson—as shouldn't it be? Children, like animals, use all their senses to discover the world. Then artists come along and discover it the same way, all over again. Here and there, it's the same world. Or now and then we'll hear from an artist who's never lost it.

In my sensory[1] education I include my physical awareness of the *word*. Of a certain word, that is; the connection it has with what it stands for. At around age six, perhaps, I was standing by myself in our front yard waiting for supper, just at that hour in a late summer day when the sun is already below the horizon and the risen full moon in the <u>visible</u> sky stops being chalky and begins to take on light. There comes the moment, and I saw it then, when the moon goes from flat to round. For the first time it met my eyes as a globe. The word "moon" came into my mouth as though fed to me out of a silver spoon. Held in my mouth the moon became a word. It had the roundness of a Concord grape Grandpa took off his vine and gave me to suck out of its skin and swallow whole, in Ohio.

This love did not prevent me from living for years in foolish error about the moon. The new moon just appearing in the west was the rising moon to me. The new should be rising. And in

Literary Analysis
Autobiography How do you know that the writer is telling her own story?

visible (viz´ ə bəl) *adj.* able to be seen

✔**Reading Check**

What does the writer observe as a child late on a summer day?

---

1. sensory (sen´ sər ē) *adj.* appealing to the senses of sight, hearing, smell, taste, and touch.

◀ **Critical Viewing** Why has the moon, especially as seen here, been an object of fascination throughout the centuries? **[Infer]**

early childhood the sun and moon, those opposite <u>reigning</u> powers, I just as easily assumed rose in east and west <u>respectively</u> in
their opposite sides of the sky, and like partners in a reel[2] they
advanced, sun from the east, moon from the west, crossed over
(when I wasn't looking) and went down on the other side. My
father couldn't have known I believed that when bending behind
me and guiding my shoulder, he positioned me at our telescope in
the front yard and, with careful adjustment of the focus, brought
the moon close to me.

The night sky over my childhood Jackson was velvety black. I
could see the full <u>constellations</u> in it and call their names; when I
could read, I knew their myths. Though I was always waked for
<u>eclipses</u> and indeed carried to the window as an infant in arms
and shown Halley's Comet[3] in my sleep, and though I'd been
taught at our diningroom table about the solar system and knew
the earth revolved around the sun, and our moon around us, I
never found out the moon didn't come up in the west until I was a
writer and Herschel Brickell, the literary critic, told me after I misplaced it in a story. He said valuable words to me about my new
profession: "Always be sure you get your moon in the right part
of the sky."

---

2. **reel** (rēl) *n.* lively Scottish dance.
3. **Halley's Comet** famous comet that reappears every 76 years.

reigning (rān´ in) *adj.*
ruling

respectively (ri spek´ tiv lē)
adv. in the order named

constellations
(kän´ stə lā´ shəns) *n.*
collections of stars

eclipses (i klips´ əz) *n.*
here, lunar eclipses: when
the moon is obscured by
the Earth's shadow

Review and Assess

Thinking About the Literature

1. **Respond:** Would you like to have known Eudora Welty as
   a child?

2. **(a) Recall:** How, according to Welty, do children learn about
   the world? **(b) Infer:** How do these insights apply to her life
   as a writer?

3. **(a) Recall:** How does Welty learn about the moon, stars, and
   planets? **(b) Speculate:** Why does Welty describe the word
   "moon" as having the quality of roundness?

4. **(a) Recall:** What mistake does Welty make about the
   movements of the moon? **(b) Interpret:** How does her
   imagination make this mistake seem logical?

5. **(a) Evaluate:** What does Welty learn in art class about the
   senses? **(b) Draw Conclusions:** How do the experiences in
   this essay relate to the title *One Writer's Beginnings*?
   (c) Evaluate: What kinds of experiences do you think a
   good writer needs to have in his or her past?

Eudora Welty

(1909–2001)

Eudora Welty
was born in
Jackson,
Mississippi,
and spent most
of her long life
there. Her novels
and short stories
focus mainly on people and
places in the southern
United States, and are written with careful observation
and gentle humor. In her
own words, she admired stories "about the interior of
our lives" told "with love."
Welty's 1972 novel, *The
Optimist's Daughter*, won a
Pulitzer Prize. She was
awarded a Presidential
Medal of Freedom in 1980.
The book *One Writer's
Beginnings*, which became a
bestseller, grew out of lectures she gave at Harvard
University in 1983.

Review and Assess

Literary Analysis

Autobiographical Writing

1. What do you think motivated each author to write about his or her childhood?
2. Identify two memories that Welty describes. Use a chart like this one to show why each memory is important to her.

Author's Memory	Importance to Author

3. What do you learn about García's boyhood from his account?

Comparing Literary Works

4. What are the two most important events or points in each narrative?
5. In what ways are the childhood priorities of the two writers similar and different?

Reading Strategy

Identify Author's Purpose

6. What kinds of details does Welty include about writing?
7. What feelings do these details reveal?
8. What is Welty's purpose in writing about her misunderstanding related to the moon?
9. Complete an organizer like the one shown to analyze the author's purpose for writing "Baseball."

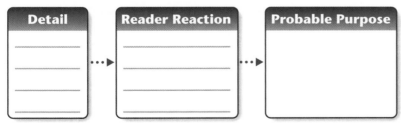

Extend Understanding

10. **Take a Position:** What do you think is the best balance of organized, supervised group activities and free time for a person your age? For a child of seven? Explain the difference, using details from the works to support your answer.

Quick Review

Autobiographical writing is narrative writing from the writer's own life, told by the writer. To review autobiographical writing, see page 623.

The **author's purpose** is his or her reason for writing. To review author's pupose, see page 623.

 Take It to the Net
www.phschool.com
Take the interactive self-test online to check your understanding of these selections.

Integrate Language Skills

Vocabulary Development Lesson

Word Analysis: Latin Root -vis-

The Latin root -vis- refers to "seeing," as in *visible*. On your paper, replace each word or phrase in parentheses with a word containing -vis-.

1. During the day the moon is usually almost (not able to be seen).
2. A pitcher needs good (eyesight).

Spelling Strategy

Practice spelling words that follow this rule:

Put *i* before *e* except after *c*, or when sounded as *a* as in *neighbor* and *weigh*.

Supply the missing letters in these sentences.

1. Welty rec____?____ved advice from a critic.
2. Garcia and his fr____?____nds were the r____?____gning neighborhood champions.

Fluency: True or False?

Write whether each statement is true or false. Explain your answers.

1. The moon becomes most *visible* at dawn and in the morning light.
2. Welty's *reigning* passion is for words.
3. She assumed the sun and moon rose in the east and the west, *respectively*.
4. A dark night sky makes it more difficult to see the *constellations*.
5. *Eclipses* of the moon occur when the moon passes through the Earth's shadow.
6. For her education, Welty's parents left her to her own *devices*.
7. As a girl, Welty successfully *evaded* learning anything about the stars and planets.

Grammar Lesson

Objective Case Pronouns

Personal pronouns have three cases: nominative, objective, or possessive—depending on their use in a sentence. If the pronoun is a direct object, an indirect object, or the object of a preposition, use the **objective case.** Objective pronouns are *me, you, him, her, it, us, them.*

Direct object: We could hear *him* laugh mightily.

Indirect object: He gave *me* a baseball bat.

Object of a preposition: He shouted at *us* from the screened porch.

▶ *For more practice, see page R33, Exercise E.*

Practice Copy the sentences and correct errors in pronoun usage. Explain each change by telling whether the pronoun functions as a direct object, indirect object, or object of a preposition.

1. Grandpa gave I a grape from his vine.
2. Everyone was chasing the batter, picking up the ball and throwing it at he or her.
3. My uncle Adolfo had given we the ball.
4. She told we a story.
5. He gave the baseball to Tom and I. He wanted to help he and me to improve.

Writing Application Write a paragraph about a baseball game. Include at least five errors in pronoun usage. Exchange paragraphs with a classmate, and correct the errors that each of you has introduced.

W̸G Prentice Hall Writing and Grammar Connection: Chapter 23

Writing Lesson

Annotated Rule Book

Write the rule book for the game of baseball that García and his friends play.

Prewriting   Review the story to find the rules García outlines. Organize them in a logical order. Then, identify gaps and make up rules to fill the gaps.

Drafting   Organize the rules in a logical way. For instance, group together rules that apply to hitting the ball or to getting a runner out.

Revising   Check the organization of your rules. If necessary, rearrange a rule to group it with other, similar rules.

Model: Revise for Organization

A batter can be called out in the following ways:

1. Missing the ball three times
2. Hitting the ball into the intersection
3. When running from second to third, the runner has to be tagged out
4. Hitting the ball into the air and having it be caught.

> Rule three in the list of ways a batter can be called out should be moved because it is not a rule about how a batter can be called out.

Prentice Hall Writing and Grammar Connection: Chapter 10, Section 10.3

Extension Activities

Listening and Speaking With two classmates, form a panel to **evaluate the objectivity** of a local sportscaster or news reporter. Watch out for bias and slanted reporting—reporting that presents only one side or favors one side. Begin by making a list of 5 or 6 criteria for making your judgment. For example:

- Does an announcer praise only players from one team?
- Does he or she seem to favor the home team?
- Does a reporter give both sides of an issue?

Keep your own scores as you watch or listen to a broadcast. Compare your ratings with the others on your panel and share them with the class. **[Group Activity]**

Research and Technology Find an article online or in the library about one of these writers, or about his or her work.

- Write a **summary** of the article.
- Explain how the comments in the article do or do not apply to the work you have read here.

Writing Using García's piece as a model, write an **autobiographical account** of one of your favorite childhood games.

 **Take It to the Net**   www.phschool.com

Go online for an additional research activity using the Internet.

Prepare to Read

Hokusai: The Old Man Mad About Drawing ◆ Not to Go With the Others

VII, Fuji in clear weather. One of the "Thirty-six Views of Fuji," Hokusai, British Museum

Preview

Connecting to the Literature

People we admire may have exceptional talents. Some have great courage and some inspire strong emotional connections. You will meet two people in these biographies—Katsushika Hokusai and Frantizek Zaremski—who are likely to fit your definition of admirable.

Background

In "Not to Go With the Others," Frantizek Zaremski is put in a Gestapo prison during World War II. The Gestapo was a German military police force. Its main role was to persecute those whom the ruling Nazi party considered enemies—Jews, Catholics, political opponents, Gypsies, the mentally ill, and others. The Gestapo operated outside the law. Its officers had the power to imprison people without trials. Many Gestapo prisoners were tortured, sent to concentration camps, or executed.

Literary Analysis

Biographical Narrative

These selections are **biographical narratives**—works of nonfiction in which a writer tells about another person's life. The writer takes facts and details about a subject's life and weaves them into an intriguing story. Like fiction writers, writers of biographies try to catch your interest. The passage below contains facts, but it also presents a compelling situation that makes you want to find out more.

> In the third year of the war, Frantizek Zaremski was arrested by the invaders on a charge of spreading underground literature—. . . .

Comparing Literary Works

Biographical narratives range in length from a brief article to several volumes. They differ in treatment and style, too. Even short selections can vary in scope—how much of a person's life they actually describe.

- "Hokusai: The Old Man Mad About Drawing" summarizes highlights and incidents of the subject's entire life.
- "Not to Go With the Others" describes one central event or turning point in its subject's life.

Use these questions to compare and contrast the two works.

1. What qualities of his subject does each writer emphasize?
2. Which writer presents the more detailed picture of his subject?

Reading Strategy

Identify the Author's Main Points

One important strategy in reading nonfiction is to track the **author's main points.** Ask yourself what the writer wants you to know or think as a result of reading this piece of nonfiction. Identify the main points of individual paragraphs, and you can more easily see the intent of the entire work. Fill in a chart like this one to track main points as you read.

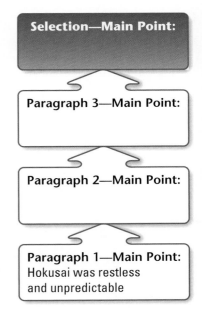

Selection—Main Point:

Paragraph 3—Main Point:

Paragraph 2—Main Point:

Paragraph 1—Main Point: Hokusai was restless and unpredictable

Vocabulary Development

apprenticed (ə prenʹ tist) *v.* contracted to learn a trade from a skilled worker (p. 637)

engulfing (en gulfʹ iŋ) *adj.* flowing over and swallowing (p. 638)

mania (māʹ nē ə) *n.* uncontrollable enthusiasm (p. 638)

feigned (fānd) *v.* pretended (p. 640)

ensued (en sood̄ʹ) *v.* came afterward; followed immediately (p. 640)

dispatched (di spachtʹ) *v.* disposed of; put to death (p. 640)

pretense (prē tensʹ) *n.* false appearance; act of pretending (p. 640)

immersed (im murstʹ) *adj.* submerged, under water (p. 641)

Hokusai:
The Old Man Mad About Drawing

Stephen Longstreet

▲ **Critical Viewing** What do you appreciate most about this work by Hokusai? **[Assess]**

Of all the great artists of Japan, the one Westerners probably like and understand best is Katsushika Hokusai. He was a restless, unpredictable man who lived in as many as a hundred different houses and changed his name at least thirty times. For a very great artist, he acted at times like P. T. Barnum[1] or a Hollywood producer with his curiosity and drive for novelty.

Hokusai was born in 1760 outside the city of Edo[2] in the province of Shimofusa. He was <u>apprenticed</u> early in life to a mirror maker and then worked in a lending library, where he was fascinated by the woodcut illustrations of the piled-up books. At eighteen he became a pupil of Shunsho, a great artist known mainly for his prints of actors. Hokusai was soon signing his name as Shunro, and for the next fifteen years he, too, made actor prints, as well as illustrations for popular novels. By 1795 he was calling himself Sori and had begun working with the European copper etchings which had become popular in Japan. Every time Hokusai changed his name, he changed his style. He drew, he designed fine surimino (greeting prints), he experimented with pure landscape.

Hokusai never stayed long with a period or style, but was always off and running to something new. A great show-off, he painted with his fingers, toothpicks, a bottle, an eggshell; he worked left-handed, from the bottom up, and from left to right. Once he painted two sparrows on a grain of rice. Commissioned by a shogun (a military ruler in 18th century Japan) to decorate a door of the Temple of Dempo-ji, he tore it off its hinges, laid it in the courtyard, and painted wavy blue lines on it to represent running water, then dipped the feet of a live rooster in red seal ink and chased the bird over the painted door. When the shogun came to see the finished job, he at once saw the river Tatsuta and the falling red maple leaves of autumn. Another time Hokusai used a large broom dipped into a vat of ink to draw the full-length figure of a god, over a hundred feet long, on the floor of a courtyard.

When he was fifty-four, Hokusai began to issue books of his sketches, which he called *The Manga*.

---

1. **P. T. Barnum** Phineas Taylor Barnum (1810–1891); U.S. showman and circus operator.
2. **Edo** (ē′ dō) former name of Tokyo.

The Great Wave off Kangawa, Katsushika Hokusai, The Metropolitan Museum of Art, New York, NY

apprenticed (ə pren′ tist) *v.* contracted to learn a trade under a skilled worker

Reading Strategy
Identify Author's Main Points What point do all these actions make about Hokusai's creative mind?

Reading Check

In what time period did Hokusai paint?

He found everything worth sketching: radish grinders, pancake women, street processions, jugglers, and wrestlers. And he was already over sixty when he began his great series, *Thirty-six Views of Fuji*, a remarkable set of woodcut prints that tell the story of the countryside around Edo: people at play or work, great waves <u>engulfing</u> fishermen, silks drying in the sun, lightning playing on great mountains, and always, somewhere, the ash-tipped top of Fuji.

Hokusai did thirty thousand pictures during a full and long life. When he was seventy-five he wrote:

From the age of six I had a <u>mania</u> for drawing the shapes of things. When I was fifty I had published a universe of designs. But all I have done before the age of seventy is not worth bothering with. At seventy-five I have learned something of the pattern of nature, of animals, of plants, of trees, birds, fish, and insects. When I am eighty you will see real progress. At ninety I shall have cut my way deeply into the mystery of life itself. At a hundred I shall be a marvelous artist. At a hundred and ten everything I create, a dot, a line, will jump to life as never before. To all of you who are going to live as long as I do, I promise to keep my word. I am writing this in my old age. I used to call myself Hokusai, but today I sign myself "The Old Man Mad About Drawing."

He didn't reach a hundred and ten, but he nearly reached ninety. On the day of his death, in 1849, he was cheerfully at work on a new drawing.

engulfing (en gulf´ in) *adj.* flowing over and swallowing

mania (mā´ nē ə) *n.* uncontrollable enthusiasm

Review and Assess

Thinking About the Literature

1. **Respond:** What do you admire most about Hokusai? Explain.

2. **(a) Recall:** How many jobs and names had the artist had by the year 1795? **(b) Connect:** How does this pattern fit with his later approach to life?

3. **(a) Recall:** Identify five different styles of art that Hokusai used. **(b) Interpret:** How do these relate to his stated ambitions for his old age?

4. **(a) Recall:** What were some of the subjects of *The Manga* and *Thirty-six Views of Fuji*? **(b) Infer:** What do these subjects say about life in Japan at the time?

5. **(a) Evaluate:** What kind of person was Hokusai? **(b) Speculate:** What do you think Hokusai would paint or draw if he were living today?

Stephen Longstreet

(1907–2002)

Stephen Longstreet wrote in many different genres and under several different names. His fiction and nonfiction works include social histories, historical novels, screenplays, television scripts, art criticism, and detective stories. This biography of Hokusai reflects Longstreet's own interest in art, as he studied painting in several European cities. Living in Europe in the 1920s, he met such well-known artists as Marc Chagall, Henri Matisse, and Pablo Picasso.

NOT to Go With the Others

John Hersey

In the third year of the war, Frantizek Zaremski was arrested by the invaders on a charge of spreading underground literature— specifically, for carrying about his person a poem a friend from Gdynia[1] had given him, which began: *Sleep, beloved Hitler, planes will come by night . . .*

After he had spent six weeks of a three-year sentence for this crime in the Gestapo[2] prison at Inowroczon, Zaremski was sent to Kalice[3] to do carpentry. By bad luck, at the time when his term expired, the Russians had broken through at the Vistula, and his captors, instead of releasing him, took him, in their general panic, to the transfer camp for Polish political prisoners at Rodogoszcz,[4] where he was placed in Hall Number Four with nine hundred men. Altogether there were between two and three thousand men and women—no Jews, only "Aryan"[5] Poles suspected or convicted of political activity—in the prison.

Late in the evening of Wednesday, January 17, 1945, three days before Lódź was to fall to the Russians, all the prisoners were gathered on the third and fourth floors of the main building, even those who were sick, and there they all lay down on wooden bunks and floors to try to sleep. At about two in the morning guards came and ordered the inmates to get up for roll call.

They divided the prisoners into groups of about twenty each and lined up the groups in pairs. Zaremski was in the second group.

Literary Analysis
Biographical Narrative
What circumstances send Zaremski to the camp?

Reading Check

Why was Zaremski arrested?

---

1. **Gdynia** (gə din´ ē ə) a city in the northern region of Poland.
2. **Gestapo** (gə stä´ pō) the secret police force of the German Nazi state, notorious for its terrorism and brutality.
3. **Inowroczon** (ē nəv rô´ zôn´) . . . **Kalice** (kä´ lish) cities in the central region of Poland.
4. **Rodogoszcz** (rô dô gôzh´) a suburb of the city of Lódź.
5. **"Aryan"** (âr´ ē ən) in Naziism, people of northern European descent who were said to possess racially superior traits and capacities for government, social organization, and civilization, while the non-Aryan peoples, such as the Jews, were seen as being inferior.

SS[6] men led it down concrete stairs in a brickwalled stairwell at one end of the building and halted it on a landing of the stairway, near a door opening into a large loft on the second floor. The first group had apparently been led down to the ground floor.

Someone gave an order that the prisoners should run in pairs into the loft as fast as they could. When the first pairs of Zaremski's group ran in, SS men with their backs to the wall inside the room began to shoot at them from behind. Zaremski's turn came. He ran in terror. A bullet burned through his trouser leg. Another grazed his thigh. He fell down and <u>feigned</u> death.

Others, from Zaremski's and later groups, ran into the hall and were shot and fell dead or wounded on top of Zaremski and those who had gone first. At one time Zaremski heard the Polish national anthem being sung somewhere.

Finally the running and shooting ended, and there <u>ensued</u> some shooting on the upper floors, perhaps of people who had refused to run downstairs.

SS men with flashlights waded among the bodies, shining lights in the faces of the prostrate victims. Any wounded who moaned or moved, or any whose eyes reacted when the shafts of light hit their faces, were <u>dispatched</u> with pistol shots. Somehow Zaremski passed the test of <u>pretense</u>.

As dawn began to break, Zaremski heard the iron doors of the main building being locked, and he heard some sort of grenades or bombs being thrown into the lowest hall and exploding there; they seemed to him to make only smoke, but they may have been incendiaries.[7] Later, in any case, the ground floor began to burn.

feigned (fānd) *v.* pretended

ensued (en sōōd´) *v.* came afterward; followed immediately

dispatched (di spacht´) *v.* put an end to; killed

pretense (prē tens´) *n.* false showing; pretending

---

6. **SS** abbreviation of the German *Schutzstaffel*, meaning "protective rank." They were a quasi-military unit of the Nazi party used as a special police force
7. **incendiaries** (in sen´ dē er´ ēz) bombs made with a chemical substance that cause a large fire when exploded.

Perhaps benzine or petrol[8] had been poured around. Zaremski was still lying among the bodies of others.

There were several who were still alive, and they began jumping out of the burning building, some from windows on the upper stories. A few broke through a skylight to the roof, tied blankets from the prisoners' bunks into long ropes and let themselves down outside. Zaremski, now scurrying about the building, held back to see what would happen. Those who jumped or climbed down were shot at leisure in the camp enclosure by SS men in the turrets on the walls, and Zaremski decided to try to stay inside.

On the fourth floor, at the top of the reinforced concrete staircase, in the bricked stairwell at the end of the building, Zaremski found the plant's water tank, and for a time he and others poured water over the wounded lying on the wooden floors in the main rooms. Later Zaremski took all his clothes off, soaked them in the tank, and put them back on. He lay down and kept pouring water over himself. He put a soaked blanket around his head.

The tank was a tall one, separated from the main room by the stairwell's brick wall, and when the fire began to eat through the wooden floor of the fourth story and the heat in the stairwell grew unbearable, Zaremski climbed up and got right into the water in the tank. He stayed <u>immersed</u> there all day long. Every few minutes he could hear shots from the wall turrets. He heard floors of the main halls fall and heard the side walls collapse. The staircase shell and the concrete stairs remained standing.

It was evening before the shooting and the fire died down. When he felt sure both had ended, Zaremski pulled himself out of the tank and lay awhile on the cement floor beside it. Then, his strength somewhat restored, he made his way down the stairs, and on the way he found six others who were wounded but could walk.

The seven went outside. Dusk. All quiet. They thought the Germans had left, and they wanted to climb the wall and escape. The first three climbed up and dropped away in apparent safety, but then the lights flashed on in the turrets and bursts of firing broke out. Three of the remaining four decided to take their chances at climbing out after total darkness; they did not know whether the first three had been killed or had escaped. Only Zaremski decided to stay.

The three climbed, but this time the lights came sooner, and the guards killed all three while they were still scaling the wall.

Zaremski crept into the camp's storehouse in a separate building. Finding some damp blankets, he wrapped them around himself and climbed into a big box, where he stayed all night. Once during the night he heard steps outside the building, and in the early morning

---

8. **benzine** (ben´ zēn´) . . . **petrol** (pet´ rəl) clear, poisonous, highly flammable liquid fuels.

◀ **Critical Viewing** What does this photograph reveal about conditions in Gestapo prisons? **[Infer]**

Literary Analysis
Biographical Narrative
What does his decision to stay inside show about Zaremski?

immersed (im mʉrst´) v. plunged into; submerged

**Reading Check**
What happens after the doors of the main building are locked?

Not to Go With the Others ◆ 641

he heard walking again. This time the footsteps approached the storeroom door. The door opened. The steps entered. Through the cracks of the box Zaremski sensed that the beam of a flashlight was probing the room. Zaremski could hear box tops opening and slamming and a foot kicking barrels. He held the lid of his box from the inside. Steps came near, a hand tried the lid, but Zaremski held tight, and the searcher must have decided the box was locked or nailed down. The footsteps went away.

Later two others came at different times and inspected the room, but neither tried Zaremski's box; the third hunter locked the door from the outside.

Much later Zaremski heard a car start and drive away.

Much later still—some time on the nineteenth of January in the year of victory—Zaremski heard the Polish language being spoken, even by the voices of women and children. He jumped out of the box and broke the window of the storehouse and climbed out to his countrymen.

▲ Critical Viewing
What does this photograph suggest about the prisoners' states of mind? [Infer]

John Hersey

(1914–1993)

Born in China to parents who were missionaries, John Hersey worked as a correspondent and editor for several news magazines. His articles and books often document the human side of world events, particularly in World War II. *Hiroshima* (1946) is a dramatic account of the dropping of the atomic bomb and its aftermath. Other works include *The Wall* (1950), a novel about the Jewish resistance in the Warsaw ghetto, and *A Bell for Adano* (1944), which won a Pulitzer Prize.

Review and Assess

Thinking About the Literature

1. **Respond:** What would you have done in Zaremski's situation?

2. **(a) Recall:** For what crime did the Gestapo arrest Zaremski? **(b) Deduce:** What does this show about the Nazi regime?

3. **(a) Recall:** Why is Zaremski later sent to a camp for political prisoners? **(b) Connect:** What happens at this camp?

4. **(a) Recall:** What are Zaremski's hiding places during his escape? **(b) Infer:** Why does he hide instead of going over the prison wall? **(c) Analyze Cause and Effect:** What is the effect of this decision?

5. **(a) Evaluate:** What characteristics helped Zaremski survive this ordeal? **(b) Make a Judgment:** Was Zaremski's escape lucky? Explain.

Review and Assess

Literary Analysis

Biographical Narrative

1. Why are Hokusai and Zaremski good subjects for a biographical narrative?
2. What character traits of his subject does each writer emphasize? Fill in a chart like this one for each subject.

3. Find two details in "Hokusai: The Old Man Mad about Drawing" that help create a strong impression of his character.

Comparing Literary Works

4. How do Longstreet and Hersey differ in the way they show the personalities of their subjects? Fill in a chart like this one.

Subject	Quality	Example
Hokusai		
Zaremski		

5. What qualities of his subject does each writer emphasize?
6. Which writer covers more time in his subject's life? Explain.
7. Which writer provides more detail about a significant time in the writer's life? Explain.
8. Which writer presents the more detailed picture of his subject? Why?

Reading Strategy

Identify Author's Main Points

9. What is Stephen Longstreet's main point, that is, what does he most want you to remember about Hokusai?
10. What are the most important ideas in the selection by Hersey?
11. How does the title, "Not to Go with the Others," relate to the main point of the selection?

Extend Understanding

12. **Evaluate:** Do either of these two men qualify as heroes? As role-models? Explain.

Quick Review

A **biographical narrative** is an account of a person's life written by someone other than the subject. Coverage of the subject's life may vary, from a single event to an entire lifetime. To review biographical narrative, see page 635.

An author's **main points** are his or her most important ideas.

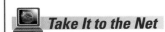 **Take It to the Net**

www.phschool.com

Take the interactive self-test online to check your understanding of these selections.

Integrate Language Skills

Vocabulary Development Lesson

Word Analysis: Latin Prefix *en-*

The Latin prefix *en-* can mean "in/into," "cover with," or "cause to be." Use one of these *en-* words to complete each of the sentences below.

enrich   enjoy   enclosed

1. The prisoners were in an _____?_____ room.
2. Later, Zaremski could _____?_____ his freedom.
3. Stories like this _____?_____ our lives.

Spelling Strategy

The letter *g* is often silent when it comes before the letter *n*, as in *feigned.* Unscramble the words in parentheses.

1. Small insect (tagn)   3. A pattern (singed)
2. Rule (ernig)   4. Chew (gawn)

Fluency: Definitions

Match the vocabulary word in Column A with the best definition in Column B.

Column A	Column B
1. apprenticed	a. simulated; shammed
2. engulfing	b. deception
3. mania	c. put to death
4. feigned	d. learned a trade
5. ensued	e. extreme enthusiasm
6. dispatched	f. swallowing up
7. pretense	g. followed
8. immersed	h. submerged

Grammar Lesson

Using *Who* and *Whom*

Many people have trouble choosing between the pronouns *who* and *whom.*

- *Who* is the nominative case. Use it for the subject in a sentence or a clause.
- *Whom* is the objective case. Use it as a direct object, an indirect object, or the object of a preposition.

Subject: *Who* knew that Hokusai would live to be nearly ninety?
Subject in a Clause: To all of you *who* are going to live as long as I do. . .
Direct Object: Hokusai was an artist *whom* others imitated. (Others imitated *whom*.)
Object of a Preposition: For *whom* did he paint the temple door?

▶ *For more practice, see page R33, Exercise E.*
Practice Identify any errors in the use of *who* or *whom* in these sentences.

1. The prisoners whom were still alive jumped out of the burning building.
2. To who did Zaremski tell his plan?
3. Who betrayed Zaremski?
4. Zaremski found others whom were wounded but could still walk.
5. He was a man who people admired.

Writing Application Revise the following passage to eliminate errors with *who* or *whom.*

Rita admired artists whom were willing to try new techniques. She never knew with who she might be discussing a new technique. Therefore, she made sure she knew who was showing new work.

𝒲𝒢 *Prentice Hall Writing and Grammar Connection: Chapter 23*

Writing Lesson

Response to Art

Now that you are acquainted with Hokusai, respond to his work. Look back at the pictures of Mount Fuji and the Great Wave on pages 634 and 637. Then write a brief essay in response to these works. Your response can be positive, negative, or mixed.

Prewriting   Choose one or two paintings as a focus. Make notes of what you like (or dislike) about them. Then make a generalization about Hokusai and your responses to him. Use that as your central theme.

Drafting   Start your essay by stating your central point. Give evidence and examples to support your ideas. In this model, examples support the underlined statement:

> ### Model: Support with Examples
>
> Hokusai liked to show ordinary people at work. He sketched carpenters and barrelmakers. He painted fishermen in their boats and women diving for shellfish.

Revising   Reread your response to Hokusai's art. If necessary, add more examples to strengthen the points you have made.

WG Prentice Hall Writing and Grammar Connection: Chapter 7, Section 7.2

Extension Activities

Listening and Speaking Learn more about Hokusai's paintings and drawings by looking in books about Japanese prints. With a group, **evaluate techniques** he uses to affect viewer's impressions.

1. Review the biographical account to identify any techniques mentioned.
2. Find one or two articles on the Internet or in art books that discuss his techniques and the impressions he was attempting to create.
3. As a group, evaluate whether he achieved a particular impression.

Research and Technology Use the Internet and museum resources to find primary sources (firsthand accounts and documents, such as newspapers of the times, interviews, and letters) to prepare an **exhibit** about Poland's role in the Second World War. Make copies of the primary sources for your exhibit. Add captions or labels.

 **Take It to the Net** www.phschool.com

Go online for an additional research activity using the Internet.

Prepare to Read

Forest Fire ◆ Debbie

 Take It to the Net

Visit www.phschool.com
for interactive activities
and instruction related to
these selections, including
  • background
  • graphic organizers
  • literary elements
  • reading strategies

Preview

Connecting to the Literature

We have all observed funny, interesting, or frightening things that we relate to family and friends. In "Debbie" by James Herriot and "Forest Fire" by Anaïs Nin, the writers relate some surprises of everyday life to their readers.

Background

Though Nin describes time-tested strategies used in fighting forest fires, today's firefighters use the latest technology to combat wildfires. Airplanes and helicopters are often used to gather data and spray fire retardant. NASA's Firefly system uses airplanes to fly an infrared scanner over a fire. The information is relayed to a satellite and then to firefighters on the ground who use it to fight fires more efficiently.

Literary Analysis

Essays

An **essay** is a short nonfiction work about a particular subject. Here are two kinds of essays you will read:

- "Forest Fire" is a **descriptive essay** in which the author describes events and feelings by including images and details that show how things look, sound, smell, taste, or feel.
- A **narrative essay** such as "Debbie" tells a true story about real people. You learn about them through their actions, words, and thoughts, as you do with fictional characters.

As you read these selections, look for characteristics of each type of essay.

Comparing Literary Works

As you read these essays, compare and contrast the writers' views of humanity's relationships with nature. Also, compare Herriot's and Nin's views with those held by Bruce Brooks in "Animal Craftsmen" on page 614. Use these questions to guide you as you read:

1. In what ways are Herriot's and Nin's views of animals and the natural world similar?
2. In what ways are their views different?

Reading Strategy

Setting a Purpose for Reading

Nonfiction can sometimes overwhelm you with its wealth of factual information. A good way to focus your reading is by **setting a purpose** before you read. Read the first paragraph of an essay, and then stop to set a purpose for reading the rest.

To help you keep your purpose in mind, work on a KWL chart like this one as you read each essay. Write what you know about the topic in the top row. List your purpose—what you want to get out of the essay—in the second row. Write what you learned in the third.

K	**What I Know**
	Why a forest fire is so dangerous
W	**What I Want to know**
	How a forest fire is stopped
L	**What I Learned**
	?

Vocabulary Development

evacuees (ē vak′ yōō ēz′) *n.* people who leave a place, especially because of danger (p. 648)

tenacious (tə nā′ shəs) *adj.* holding on firmly (p. 650)

dissolution (dis′ ə lōō′ shən) *n.* the act of breaking down and crumbling (p. 650)

privations (prī vā′ shənz) *n.* deprivation or lack of common comforts (p. 656)

Forest Fire

Anaïs Nin

A man rushed in to announce he had seen smoke on Monrovia Peak.[1] As I looked out of the window I saw the two mountains facing the house on fire. The entire rim burning wildly in the night. The flames, driven by hot Santa Ana winds[2] from the desert, were as tall as the tallest trees, the sky already tinted coral, and the crackling noise of burning trees, the ashes and the smoke were already increasing. The fire raced along, sometimes descending behind the mountain where I could only see the glow, sometimes descending toward us. I thought of the foresters in danger. I made coffee for the weary men who came down occasionally with horses they had led out, or with old people from the isolated cabins. They were covered with soot from their battle with the flames.

At six o'clock the fire was on our left side and rushing toward Mount Wilson. Evacuees from the cabins began to arrive and had

---

1. **Monrovia** (mən rō´ vē ə) **Peak** mountain in southwest California.
2. **Santa** (san´ tə) **Ana** (an´ ə) **winds** hot desert winds from the east or northeast in southern California.

Reading Strategy
Setting a Purpose for Reading After reading the first paragraph of this essay, what purpose for reading the rest did you set?

evacuees (ē vak´ yoo ēz´) *n.* people who leave a place, especially because of danger

▲ **Critical Viewing**
Why are forest fires such dangerous occurrences? Refer to details in the photograph in your response. **[Deduce]**

to be given blankets and hot coffee. The streets were blocked with fire engines readying to fight the fire if it touched the houses. Policemen and firemen and guards turned away the sightseers. Some were relatives concerned over the fate of the foresters, or the pack station family. The policemen lighted flares, which gave the scene a theatrical, tragic air. The red lights on the police cars twinkled alarmingly. More fire engines arrived. Ashes fell, and the roar of the fire was now like thunder.

We were told to ready ourselves for evacuation. I packed the diaries. The saddest spectacle, beside that of the men fighting the fire as they would a war, were the animals, rabbits, coyotes, mountain lions, deer, driven by the fire to the edge of the mountain, taking a look at the crowd of people and panicking, choosing rather to rush back into the fire.

The fire now was like a ring around Sierra Madre,[3] every mountain was burning. People living at the foot of the mountain were packing their cars. I rushed next door to the Campion children, who had been left with a baby-sitter, and got them into the car. It was impossible to save all the horses. We parked the car on the field below us. I called up the Campions, who were out for the evening, and reassured them. The baby-sitter dressed the children warmly. I made more coffee. I answered frantic telephone calls.

All night the fire engines sprayed water over the houses. But the fire grew immense, angry, and rushing at a speed I could not believe. It would rush along and suddenly leap over a road, a trail, like a monster, devouring all in its path. The firefighters cut breaks in the heavy brush, but when the wind was strong enough, the fire leaped across them. At dawn one arm of the fire reached the back of our houses but was finally contained.

☑ **Reading Check**

How is the author affected by the forest fire?

---

3. **Sierra** (sē er′ ə) **Madre** (mä′ drā) mountain range.

But high above and all around, the fire was burning, more vivid than the sun, throwing spirals of smoke in the air like the smoke from a volcano. Thirty-three cabins burned, and twelve thousand acres of forest still burning endangered countless homes below the fire. The fire was burning to the back of us now, and a rain of ashes began to fall and continued for days. The smell of the burn in the air, acrid and pungent and <u>tenacious</u>. The dragon tongues of flames devouring, the flames leaping, the roar of destruction and <u>dissolution</u>, the eyes of the panicked animals, caught between fire and human beings, between two forms of death. They chose the fire. It was as if the fire had come from the bowels of the earth, like that of a fiery volcano, it was so powerful, so swift, and so ravaging. I saw trees become skeletons in one minute, I saw trees fall, I saw bushes turned to ashes in a second, I saw weary, ash-covered men, looking like men returned from war, some with burns, others overcome by smoke.

The men were rushing from one spot to another watching for recrudescence.[4] Some started backfiring up the mountain so that the ascending flames could counteract the descending ones.

As the flames reached the cities below, hundreds of roofs burst into flame at once. There was no water pressure because all the fire hydrants were turned on at the same time, and the fire departments were helpless to save more than a few of the burning homes.

The blaring loudspeakers of passing police cars warned us to prepare to evacuate in case the wind changed and drove the fire in our direction. What did I wish to save? I thought only of the diaries. I appeared on the porch carrying a huge stack of diary volumes, preparing to pack them in the car. A reporter for the Pasadena *Star News* was taking pictures of the evacuation. He came up, very annoyed with me. "Hey, lady, next time could you bring out something more important than all those old papers? Carry some clothes on the next trip. We gotta have human interest in these pictures!"

Literary Analysis
Essays What effect does this vivid description have on you?

tenacious (tə nā´ shəs) *adj.* holding on firmly

dissolution (dis´ ə loo͞´ shən) *n.* the act of breaking down and crumbling

---

4. **recrudescence** (rē´ kro͞o des´ əns) *n.* fresh outbreak of something that has been inactive.

A week later, the danger was over.

Gray ashy days.

In Sierra Madre, following the fire, the January rains brought floods. People are sandbagging their homes. At four A.M. the streets are covered with mud. The bare, burnt, naked mountains cannot hold the rains and slide down bringing rocks and mud. One of the rangers must now take photographs and movies of the disaster. He asks if I will help by holding an umbrella over the cameras. I put on my raincoat and he lends me hip boots which look to me like seven-league boots.

We drive a little way up the road. At the third curve it is impassable. A river is rushing across the road. The ranger takes pictures while I hold the umbrella over the camera. It is terrifying to see the muddied waters and rocks, the mountain disintegrating. When we are ready to return, the road before us is covered by large rocks but the ranger pushes on as if the truck were a jeep and forces it through. The edge of the road is being carried away.

I am laughing and scared too. The ranger is at ease in nature, and without fear. It is a wild moment of danger. It is easy to love nature in its peaceful and consoling moments, but one must love it in its furies too, in its despairs and wildness, especially when the damage is caused by us.

Review and Assess

Thinking About the Literature

1. **Respond:** What would you bring with you if firefighters asked you to evacuate your home?

2. **(a) Recall:** Describe the setting—the time and place—of the fire. **(b) Infer:** Why is a fire in this setting particularly dangerous? **(c) Analyze Causes and Effects:** What are the effects of the fire?

3. **(a) Recall:** What does Nin rescue from the fire? **(b) Recall:** How does Nin help others during this ordeal? **(c) Draw Conclusions:** What do Nin's actions during the evacuation reveal about her as a person?

4. **(a) Recall:** List three details or images Nin uses to describe the fire. **(b) Interpret:** What is the effect on you of Nin's use of figurative language to describe the fire?

5. **(a) Recall:** What other natural disaster do the people in this essay have to face? **(b) Connect:** How is the new disaster related to the effects of the fire? **(c) Draw Conclusions:** What conclusion does Nin draw from observing these disasters?

Anaïs Nin

(1903–1977)

A native of France, Anaïs Nin moved to the United States when she was eleven. During the voyage to her new home in New York City, she began writing in a diary, a practice that she continued throughout her life. Although she wrote novels and short stories, Nin was best known for *The Diary of Anaïs Nin,* her series of published diaries spanning sixty years. "Forest Fire," from the fifth diary, illustrates how Nin looked at life, as she said, "as an adventure and a tale." The incident she wrote about in this essay happened while she was living in Sierra Madre, California.

Debbie

James Herriot

I first saw her one autumn day when I was called to see one of Mrs. Ainsworth's dogs, and I looked in some surprise at the furry black creature sitting before the fire.

"I didn't know you had a cat," I said.

The lady smiled. "We haven't, this is Debbie."

"Debbie?"

"Yes, at least that's what we call her. She's a stray. Comes here two or three times a week and we give her some food. I don't know where she lives but I believe she spends a lot of her time around one of the farms along the road."

"Do you ever get the feeling that she wants to stay with you?"

Literary Analysis
Essays How can you tell that this is a narrative essay?

"No." Mrs. Ainsworth shook her head. "She's a timid little thing. Just creeps in, has some food then flits away. There's something so appealing about her but she doesn't seem to want to let me or anybody into her life."

I looked again at the little cat. "But she isn't just having food today."

"That's right. It's a funny thing but every now and again she slips through here into the lounge and sits by the fire for a few minutes. It's as though she was giving herself a treat."

"Yes . . . I see what you mean." There was no doubt there was something unusual in the attitude of the little animal. She was sitting bolt upright on the thick rug which lay before the fireplace in which the coals glowed and flamed. She made no effort to curl up or wash herself or do anything other than gaze quietly ahead. And there was something in the dusty black of her coat, the half-wild scrawny look of her, that gave me a clue. This was a special event in her life, a rare and wonderful thing; she was lapping up a comfort undreamed of in her daily existence.

As I watched she turned, crept soundlessly from the room and was gone.

"That's always the way with Debbie," Mrs. Ainsworth laughed. "She never stays more than ten minutes or so, then she's off."

Mrs. Ainsworth was a plumpish, pleasant-faced woman in her forties and the kind of client veterinary surgeons dream of; well off, generous, and the owner of three cosseted[1] Basset hounds. And it only needed the habitually mournful expression of one of the dogs to deepen a little and I was round there posthaste.[2] Today one of the Bassets had raised its paw and scratched its ear a couple of times and that was enough to send its mistress scurrying to the phone in great alarm.

So my visits to the Ainsworth home were frequent but undemanding, and I had ample opportunity to look out for the little cat that had intrigued me. On one occasion I spotted her nibbling

▲ **Critical Viewing** Would you think the cat in this photograph was "a timid little thing"? Why or why not? **[Assess]**

✓ **Reading Check**
Who is Debbie?

---

1. **cosseted** (käs´ it əd) *adj.* pampered; indulged.
2. **posthaste** (pōst´ hāst´) *adv.* with great speed.

daintily from a saucer at the kitchen door. As I watched she turned and almost floated on light footsteps into the hall then through the lounge door.

The three Bassets were already in residence, draped snoring on the fireside rug, but they seemed to be used to Debbie because two of them sniffed her in a bored manner and the third merely cocked a sleepy eye at her before flopping back on the rich pile.

Debbie sat among them in her usual posture; upright, intent, gazing absorbedly into the glowing coals. This time I tried to make friends with her. I approached her carefully but she leaned away as I stretched out my hand. However, by patient wheedling[3] and soft talk I managed to touch her and gently stroked her cheek with one finger. There was a moment when she responded by putting her head on one side and rubbing back against my hand but soon she was ready to leave. Once outside the house she darted quickly along the road then through a gap in a hedge and the last I saw was the little black figure flitting over the rain-swept grass of a field.

"I wonder where she goes," I murmured half to myself.

Mrs. Ainsworth appeared at my elbow. "That's something we've never been able to find out."

It must have been nearly three months before I heard from Mrs. Ainsworth, and in fact I had begun to wonder at the Bassets' long symptomless run when she came on the phone.

It was Christmas morning and she was apologetic. "Mr. Herriot, I'm so sorry to bother you today of all days. I should think you want a rest at Christmas like anybody else." But her natural politeness could not hide the distress in her voice.

"Please don't worry about that," I said. "Which one is it this time?"

"It's not one of the dogs. It's . . . Debbie."

"Debbie? She's at your house now?"

"Yes. . . but there's something wrong. Please come quickly."

Driving through the marketplace I thought again that Darrowby on Christmas Day was like Dickens come to life; the empty square with the snow thick on the cobbles and hanging from the eaves of the fretted[4] lines of roofs; the shops closed and the colored lights of the Christmas trees winking at the windows of the clustering

---

3. **wheedling** (hwēd´ liŋ) *v.* gentle, constant persuading.
4. **fretted** (fret´ əd) *adj.* decoratively arranged.

Reading Strategy
Setting a Purpose for Reading Based on the opening paragraphs, what is the most appropriate purpose for reading this essay?

▼ **Critical Viewing**
In what ways might an energetic kitten stir up the life of Basset hounds like these? **[Speculate]**

houses, warmly inviting against the cold white bulk of the fells[5] behind.

Mrs. Ainsworth's home was lavishly decorated with tinsel and holly, rows of drinks stood on the sideboard and the rich aroma of turkey and sage and onion stuffing wafted[6] from the kitchen. But her eyes were full of pain as she led me through to the lounge.

Debbie was there all right, but this time everything was different. She wasn't sitting upright in her usual position; she was stretched quite motionless on her side, and huddled close to her lay a tiny black kitten.

I looked down in bewilderment. "What's happened here?"

"It's the strangest thing," Mrs. Ainsworth replied. "I haven't seen her for several weeks then she came in about two hours ago—sort of staggered into the kitchen, and she was carrying the kitten in her mouth. She took it through to the lounge and laid it on the rug and at first I was amused. But I could see all was not well because she sat as she usually does, but for a long time— over an hour—then she lay down like this and she hasn't moved."

I knelt on the rug and passed my hand over Debbie's neck and ribs. She was thinner than ever, her fur dirty and mudcaked. She did not resist as I gently opened her mouth. The tongue and mucous membranes were abnormally pale and the lips ice-cold against my fingers. When I pulled down her eyelid and saw the dead white conjunctiva[7] a knell[8] sounded in my mind.

I palpated[9] the abdomen with a grim certainty as to what I would find and there was no surprise, only a dull sadness as my fingers closed around a hard lobulated[10] mass deep among the viscera.[11] Massive lymphosarcoma.[12] Terminal and hopeless. I put my stethoscope on her heart and listened to the increasingly faint, rapid beat then I straightened up and sat on the rug looking sightlessly into the fireplace, feeling the warmth of the flames on my face.

Mrs. Ainsworth's voice seemed to come from afar. "Is she ill, Mr. Herriot?"

I hesitated. "Yes . . . yes, I'm afraid so. She has a malignant growth." I stood up. "There's

Literary Analysis
Essays What does Mrs. Ainsworth's **story** reveal about Debbie's personality?

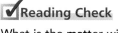
Reading Check

What is the **matter** with Debbie?

---

5. **fells** *n.* rocky or barren hills.
6. **wafted** (waf´ təd) *v.* moved lightly through the air.
7. **conjunctiva** (kän´ jəŋk tī´ və) *n.* lining of the inner surface of the eyelids.
8. **knell** (nel) *n.* sound of a bell slowly ringing, as for a funeral.
9. **palpated** (pal´ pāt ed) *v.* examined by touching.
10. **lobulated** (läb´ yoo lā´ təd) *adj.* subdivided.
11. **viscera** (vis´ ər ə) *n.* internal organs.
12. **lymphosarcoma** (lim´ fō sär kō´ mə) *n.* malignant tumor in the tissue.

absolutely nothing I can do. I'm sorry."

"Oh!" Her hand went to her mouth and she looked at me wide-eyed. When at last she spoke her voice trembled. "Well, you must put her to sleep immediately. It's the only thing to do. We can't let her suffer."

"Mrs. Ainsworth," I said. "There's no need. She's dying now—in a coma—far beyond suffering."

She turned quickly away from me and was very still as she fought with her emotions. Then she gave up the struggle and dropped on her knees beside Debbie.

"Oh, poor little thing!" she sobbed and stroked the cat's head again and again as the tears fell unchecked on the matted fur. "What she must have come through. I feel I ought to have done more for her."

For a few moments I was silent, feeling her sorrow, so discordant among the bright seasonal colors of this festive room. Then I spoke gently.

"Nobody could have done more than you," I said. "Nobody could have been kinder."

"But I'd have kept her here—in comfort. It must have been terrible out there in the cold when she was so desperately ill—I daren't think about it. And having kittens, too—I . . . I wonder how many she did have?"

I shrugged. "I don't suppose we'll ever know. Maybe just this one. It happens sometimes. And she brought it to you, didn't she?"

"Yes . . . that's right . . . she did . . . she did." Mrs. Ainsworth reached out and lifted the bedraggled black morsel. She smoothed her finger along the muddy fur and the tiny mouth opened in a soundless miaow. "Isn't it strange? She was dying and she brought her kitten here. And on Christmas Day."

I bent and put my hand on Debbie's heart. There was no beat.

I looked up. "I'm afraid she's gone." I lifted the small body, almost feather light, wrapped it in the sheet which had been spread on the rug and took it out to the car.

When I came back Mrs. Ainsworth was still stroking the kitten. The tears had dried on her cheeks and she was brighteyed as she looked at me.

"I've never had a cat before," she said.

I smiled. "Well, it looks as though you've got one now."

And she certainly had. That kitten grew rapidly into a sleek handsome cat with a boisterous nature which earned him the name of Buster. In every way he was the opposite to his timid little mother. Not for him the privations of the secret outdoor life; he stalked the rich carpets of the Ainsworth home like a king and the ornate collar he always wore added something more to his presence.

Literary Analysis
Essay How does Herriot's use of dialogue help you picture the action?

privations (prī vā′ shənz) *n.* deprivation or lack of common comforts

On my visits I watched his development with delight but the occasion which stays in my mind was the following Christmas Day, a year from his arrival.

I was out on my rounds as usual. I can't remember when I haven't had to work on Christmas Day because the animals have never got round to recognizing it as a holiday; but with the passage of the years the vague resentment I used to feel has been replaced by philosophical acceptance. After all, as I tramped around the hillside barns in the frosty air I was working up a better appetite for my turkey than all the millions lying in bed or slumped by the fire.

I was on my way home, bathed in a rosy glow. I heard the cry as I was passing Mrs. Ainsworth's house.

"Merry Christmas, Mr. Herriot!" She was letting a visitor out of the front door and she waved at me gaily. "Come in and have a drink to warm you up."

I didn't need warming up but I pulled in to the curb without hesitation. In the house there was all the festive cheer of last year and the same glorious whiff of sage and onion which set my gastric[13] juices surging. But there was not the sorrow; there was Buster.

He was darting up to each of the dogs in turn, ears pricked, eyes blazing with devilment, dabbing a paw at them then streaking away.

Mrs. Ainsworth laughed. "You know, he plagues the life out of them. Gives them no peace."

She was right. To the Bassets, Buster's arrival was rather like the intrusion of an irreverent outsider into an exclusive London club. For a long time they had led a life of measured grace; regular sedate walks with their mistress, superb food in ample quantities and long snoring sessions on the rugs and armchairs. Their days followed one upon another in unruffled calm. And then came Buster.

He was dancing up to the youngest dog again, sideways this time, head on one side, goading him. When he started boxing with both paws it was too much even for the Basset. He dropped his dignity and rolled over with the cat in a brief wrestling match.

"I want to show you something." Mrs. Ainsworth lifted a hard rubber ball from the sideboard and went out to the garden, followed by Buster. She threw the ball across the lawn and the cat bounded after it over the frosted grass, the muscles rippling under the black sheen of his coat. He seized the ball in his teeth, brought it back to his mistress, dropped it at her feet and waited expectantly. She threw it and he brought it back again.

---

13. **gastric** (gas´ trik) *adj.* of the stomach.

✓ Reading Check

How does Buster come into Mrs. Ainsworth's life?

I gasped incredulously. A feline retriever!

The Bassets looked on disdainfully. Nothing would ever have induced them to chase a ball, but Buster did it again and again as though he would never tire of it.

Mrs. Ainsworth turned to me. "Have you ever seen anything like that?"

"No," I replied. "I never have. He is a most remarkable cat."

She snatched Buster from his play and we went back into the house where she held him close to her face, laughing as the big cat purred and arched himself ecstatically against her cheek.

Looking at him, a picture of health and contentment, my mind went back to his mother. Was it too much to think that that dying little creature with the last of her strength had carried her kitten to the only haven of comfort and warmth she had ever known in the hope that it would be cared for there? Maybe it was.

But it seemed I wasn't the only one with such fancies. Mrs. Ainsworth turned to me and though she was smiling her eyes were wistful.

"Debbie would be pleased," she said.

I nodded. "Yes, she would . . . It was just a year ago today she brought him, wasn't it?"

"That's right." She hugged Buster to her again. "The best Christmas present I ever had."

James Herriot

(1916–1995)

Born in England and raised in Scotland, James Herriot (the pen name of James Alfred Wight) wrote many memorable true stories about his fifty years as a veterinarian. The incidents Herriot describes, such as the one in "Debbie," have filled more than ten books, including *All Creatures Great and Small* and *All Things Wise and Wonderful*, and inspired a popular television series. Although he did not start writing until he was fifty, he found a natural talent for describing the people and animals that enriched his career. As Herriot told one interviewer: "I think it was the fact that I liked it so much that made the writing just come out of me automatically."

Review and Assess

Thinking About the Literature

1. **Respond:** How would you have reacted if Debbie had left you her newborn kitten?

2. **(a) Recall:** Describe Debbie and her life. **(b) Infer:** Why does Debbie never stay with Mrs. Ainsworth for long?

3. **(a) Recall:** How does Buster come to live with Mrs. Ainsworth? **(b) Speculate:** Why might Debbie have chosen to bring her kitten to Mrs. Ainsworth's home?

4. **(a) Recall:** How does the Ainsworth household change after Buster's arrival? **(b) Compare and Contrast:** How is Buster different from his mother?

5. **(a) Recall:** What thoughts do Herriot and Mrs. Ainsworth share at the end of the essay? **(b) Interpret:** Why do you think Mrs. Ainsworth calls Buster "the best Christmas present" she ever had?

Review and Assess

Literary Analysis

Essay

1. **(a)** Which character do you think is most fully drawn in Herriot's essay? **(b)** Tell how Herriot brings this character to life.
2. On a chart like the one below, analyze the different impression Nin creates with different images and comparisons. Consider whether each impression is positive or negative, frightening or beautiful.

Image	Impression
Monster, devouring all in its path	
More vivid than the sun	
Dragon tongue of flames	

Comparing Literary Works

3. In what ways are Herriot's and Nin's views of animals and the natural world similar?
4. In what ways are their views different?
5. Compare and contrast the messages in "Debbie," "Forest Fire," and "Animal Craftsmen," on page 614. Use a chart like this one to help you get started.

Essays	Messages
"Debbie"	
"Forest Fire"	
"Animal Craftsmen"	

Reading Strategy

Setting a Purpose for Reading

6. What was your purpose for reading each essay? Why?
7. Did you shift or extend your purpose while reading either of the essays? If so, explain how and why.
8. When do you think it is helpful to change your purpose for reading?

Extend Understanding

9. **Career Connection:** What qualities and training do you think it takes to be a successful veterinarian like James Herriot?

Quick Review

An **essay** is a short nonfiction work about a particular subject.
A **narrative essay** tells the story of a true event.
A **descriptive essay** presents a detailed view of an incident or experience.

Setting a purpose helps you focus your reading and makes it easier to identify and remember information.

 Take It to the Net
www.phschool.com
Take the interactive self-test online to check your understanding of these selections.

Integrate Language Skills

Vocabulary Development Lesson

Word Analysis: Latin Root -vac-

The Latin root -vac-, which appears in the word *evacuees* in "Forest Fire," means "empty." An *evacuee* is someone who is removed from a place, leaving that place empty.

Complete each sentence with the most appropriate word containing the root -vac-.

vacuum	evacuate	vacant
vacuous	vacated	

1. After the forest fire, the town was ___?___ .
2. The suction of the backdraft left a ___?___ inside the room.
3. We were forced to ___?___ when the fire reached our property line.
4. The police ___?___ the area quickly as the fire spread.
5. Phil had a ___?___ expression when he visited the ruins.

Concept Development: Antonyms

An **antonym** is an opposite. Identify the word most opposite in meaning to the first word.

1. privations: **a.** riches, **b.** limits, **c.** public
2. evacuees: **a.** helpers, **b.** fears, **c.** inhabitants
3. tenacious: **a.** wild, **b.** brilliant, **c.** weak
4. dissolution: **a.** height, **b.** growth, **c.** visible

Spelling Strategy

The *j* sound can be spelled with a *g*, as in the word *ravaging*. Rewrite these sentences, correcting misspelled words.

1. The averaje pet owner should not keep an endanjered species as a pet.
2. An experienced veterinarian can diagnose a problem with an animal's dijestive system and tell whether or not surjery is needed.

Grammar Lesson

Pronoun and Antecedent Agreement

A personal pronoun such as *I*, *you*, or *it* must **agree** with its antecedent—the word or group of words for which a pronoun stands—in gender (masculine, feminine, or neither) and number (singular or plural).

> *Buster* did it again and again as though *he* would never tire of it.

(The personal pronoun *he* agrees with the singular masculine antecedent *Buster*.)

▶ *For more practice, see page R32, Exercise B.*
Practice Rewrite each sentence, correcting errors in pronoun and antecedent agreement.

1. The people were slow to abandon his homes.
2. The fire spread quickly, destroying all of the people's homes in their path.
3. Mrs. Ainsworth threw the ball, and the cat bounded after them.
4. He rushed next door to the Campion children and got her into the car.
5. The firefighters were weary after its long day fighting the fire.

Writing Application Write sentences with pronouns that agree with the antecedents below.

1. Mrs. Ainsworth   2. Buster   3. firefighters

W̶G Prentice Hall Writing and Grammar Connection: Chapter 24, Section 2

Writing Lesson

Persuasive Letter

Often, devastating forest fires are ignited by human carelessness—perhaps a match thrown into the woods or a still-smoldering campfire. Write a letter to the editor of your local newspaper about the importance of fire prevention.

Prewriting   Do research to gather facts, details, statistics, and quotations to support your position. If possible, call your local fire department for information. Take notes on what you learn.

Drafting   Use your notes to draft the letter. Begin with a clear statement of your position, and follow with logical arguments and supporting evidence such as statistics and expert opinions. Use powerful language and images to make a strong impression.

	Model: Connotative Language	Powerful words such as *senseless, waste,* and *precious,* are meant to provoke an emotional response in a reader.
	To prevent the senseless waste of precious park land, I urge our town board to ban campfires and the use of outdoor barbecue grills during drought season.	

Revising   Check your letter to see whether you can make any of your language stronger to appeal to the emotions of your readers.

WG Prentice Hall Writing and Grammar Connection: Chapter 7, Sections 1–7

Extension Activities

Listening and Speaking Research, plan, and deliver a **persuasive speech** in support of a local animal shelter. In your speech, give the following information:

- how many animals the shelter rescues yearly
- why the shelter's efforts are important
- how members of your community can help by donating money, volunteering services, or adopting a pet

Use anecdotal evidence—evidence in the form of true stories—gathered from the shelter's staff to strengthen your argument. Deliver the speech to your classmates.

Research and Technology James Herriot's stories have been used as the basis for movies and a television series. Write an **analysis** of "Debbie" explaining why you think it would or would not be a good story for a visual medium like television.

Writing Using "Forest Fire" as a model, write a descriptive essay about something memorable that you witnessed.

 **Take It to the Net**   www.phschool.com

Go online for an additional research activity using the Internet.

Warranties and Product Directions

About Warranties and Product Directions

When you buy a new product—from a video game to a vacuum cleaner—you also receive several important documents. You might just leave them in the box, but that would be a mistake. Those documents help you use a product safely and correctly. They also protect your rights as a buyer.

- The first document to read is the product directions. Many products can be dangerous if you install or use them incorrectly. The directions on page 664, for example, contain several warnings about using a fire extinguisher.

- The product warranty is another important document. It explains what the manufacturer promises you, the buyer. A warranty lasts for a certain amount of time, usually one to five years. It says what parts or services the maker will provide and under what conditions. Because a warranty is a kind of legal contract, it is written in formal, legal language. Before reading a warranty, get acquainted with these terms.

Warranty Terms	
express/implied	express means stated outright implied means unstated but assumed (terms are opposite in meaning)
breach	failure to live up to an agreement
liable	responsible
consequential	resulting from an action

Reading Strategy

Following Technical Directions

To get information from technical directions, you must read them carefully. This is one situation in which skimming does not work. If you do not understand and follow directions exactly, your new product may not work correctly. Even worse, it may hurt you or someone around you. Here are tips for following directions:

- Read all the directions through carefully before starting. Then go back and read each one as you are performing the action.
- Pay careful attention to details.
- Notice verbs in particular because they tell you what actions to take.
- Do each step in the exact order given in the directions.
- Do not skip any steps.
- Pay attention to warnings or "danger" signs in the directions.

Fire Extinguisher Warranty

The following warranty for a fire extinguisher would be included with the directions and other materials packaged with a new fire extinguisher. Whenever you purchase a new product, you should read the warranty. Some warranties must be signed and returned in order to be activated.

The title tells what kind of warranty the manufacturer offers.

This paragraph gives the general terms of the warranty and of the product to which it applies. It puts limits on what the manufacturer will do.

This section tells you reasons for which the company would not be responsible for repairs.

LIMITED WARRANTY

BRK Brands, Inc. ("BRK") the maker of First Alert® brand product, warrants that for a period of five years from the date of purchase, this product will be free from defects in material and workmanship. BRK, its option, will repair or replace this product or any component of the product found to be defective during the warranty period. Replacement will be made with a new or remanufactured product or component. If the product is no longer available, replacement may be made with a similar product of equal or greater value. This is your exclusive warranty.

This warranty is valid for the original retail purchaser from the date of initial retail purchase and is not transferable. Keep the original sales receipt. Proof of purchase is required to obtain warranty performance. BRK dealers, service centers, or retail stores selling BRK products do not have the right to alter, modify or any way change the terms and conditions of this warranty.

This warranty does not cover normal wear of parts or damage resulting from any of the following: negligent use or misuse of the product, use on improper voltage or current, use contrary to the operating instructions, disassembly, repair or alteration by anyone other than BRK or an authorized service center. Further, the warranty does not cover acts of God, such as fire, flood, hurricanes and tornadoes.

BRK shall not be liable for any incidental or consequential damages caused by the breach of any express or implied warranty. Except to the extent prohibited by applicable law, any implied warranty of merchantability or fitness for a particular purpose is limited in duration to the duration of the above warranty. Some states, provinces, or jurisdictions do not allow the exclusion or limitation of incidental or consequential damages or limitations on how long an implied warranty lasts, so the above limitations or exclusion may not apply to you. This warranty gives you specific legal rights, and you may also have other rights that vary from state to state, or province to province.

How to operate your extinguisher in a fire emergency

DANGER!

Make sure your extinguisher may be safely and effectively used on the small fire you want to fight. Always use extreme caution when fighting any fire. Fight a fire only where there is a clear escape path to allow you to get out safely if the fire gets worse.

TO FIGHT THE FIRE

WARNING!

This unit will not operate with mounting bracket attached. The extinguisher must be removed from the mounting bracket or it cannot discharge its contents to fight a fire.

1. Remove the extinguisher from the mounting bracket.
2. Hold the unit firmly with the nozzle facing away from you. Pull out the pin to break the "Safety Seal." You won't be able to squeeze the trigger until the safety seal is removed.
3. Stand back 6 feet (2 meters) from the fire and make sure the fire is not between you and your exit.
4. Hold the extinguisher upright and aim the nozzle at the base of the fire.
5. Press and hold the trigger to discharge the powder.
6. Sweep the spray at the base of the burning material, using quick side-to-side motions. (If the spray scatters the fire, move back.)
7. Move slowly towards the fire as the extinguisher spray pushes the fire back. Maintain a 6-foot (2-meter) distance between you and the front of the fire at all times.
8. Completely discharge the contents of the extinguisher and make sure the fire is completely out. Flashbacks are common with fires.
9. For kitchen fires on a kitchen stove, turn off the stove immediately if possible, otherwise as soon as it is safe.
10. If you suspect a fire had an electrical origin, shut off the electrical power, if possible, without eliminating your escape route. Do not touch electrical wires or appliances.
11. After you have completely discharged your extinguisher, leave the building and close all the doors behind you.

This section gives you information about how to deal safely with a fire.

Color and boldface are used to emphasize important information such as warnings.

Pictures or diagrams are used to show details.

Check Your Comprehension

1. What kind of fires is this extinguisher designed to fight? When should you NOT use this extinguisher?
2. Where should you stand when using this fire extinguisher?
3. How do you activate the fire extinguisher?
4. For how long is the warranty on the extinguisher valid?
5. How do state laws affect the terms of the warranty?

Applying the Reading Strategy

Following Technical Directions

Paraphrasing, or putting technical directions in your own words, can often make them easier to understand. Write a paraphrase of the main action of each step from 1–11.

Activity

Fire Extinguisher Demonstration

In class, demonstrate how to use a fire extinguisher safely. (Use a water bottle or similar container to represent the extinguisher.) Restate the technical directions in your own words. Begin by reviewing the safety warnings. Then demonstrate each step, using both words and gestures. When you have finished, ask classmates to evaluate how clearly you have interpreted these technical directions. Have you explained the directions well enough for someone else to use the fire extinguisher safely? When other students have made the same demonstration, compare the effectiveness of each one.

Comparing Informational Materials

Comparing Manuals

Get copies of the directions or instruction manuals for products such as a computer, a portable CD player, a camp stove, or a bookshelf you assemble yourself. Compare these different documents by completing a chart like the one shown.

	Product 1	Product 2
Technical terms		
Number of steps		
Safety warnings		
Use of diagrams		
Ease of use		

Prepare to Read

The Trouble with Television ◆ The American Dream

 Take It to the Net

Visit www.phschool.com
for interactive activities
and instruction related to
these selections, including
- background
- graphic organizers
- literary elements
- reading strategies

Preview

Connecting to the Literature

Think about how many hours a day the television set is turned on in your home. In "The Trouble with Television," you will learn what one well-respected journalist thinks about the effects of too much time spent watching television.

Background

According to Robert MacNeil, Americans watch too much television. The A. C. Nielson Co. has stated that in 1998, the average American watched nearly four hours of television every day. At that rate, a seventy-year old person who began watching television at the age of five has spent ten years sitting in front of the set!

Literary Analysis

Persuasive Techniques

Persuasive techniques are strategies used to affect an audience's reaction to the persuasive message. Writers use persuasive techniques to convince readers or listeners to think or act in a certain way. These techniques include the following:

- supporting points with facts, statistics, and quotations
- using words that have strong emotional impact
- repeating key ideas or beliefs
- using slogans or chants that can stir an audience to action

In this passage from "The Trouble with Television," for example, MacNeil uses statistics to support his point: "If you fit the statistical averages, by the age of 20 you will have been exposed to at least 20,000 hours of television."

Comparing Literary Works

Writers use a range of persuasive techniques, depending on the audience they are trying to influence. Compare and contrast the persuasive techniques used in these two works. Use a chart like this one to record the persuasive techniques each writer uses. Then, compare the results.

Persuasive Techniques
Supporting Evidence:
Persuasive Language:
Repetition:
Slogans:

Reading Strategy

Evaluating Logic

Evaluating a writer's logic, or reasoning, helps you test the soundness of the argument and make a judgment about the ideas that have been presented. To judge MacNeil's and King's essays, for example, think about whether they support their opinions with clear examples and reliable facts and draw logical conclusions based on evidence. Use these questions to guide you as you read:

1. What facts or examples do MacNeil and King present to support their arguments?
2. Do the writers draw logical conclusions based on solid evidence?

Vocabulary Development

diverts (dī vʉrts´) *v.* amuse, entertain (p. 669)

usurps (yo͞o sʉrps´) *v.* takes over (p. 669)

august (ô gust´) *adj.* honored (p. 670)

pervading (pər vād´ iŋ) *v.* spreading throughout (p. 670)

antithesis (an tith´ ə sis) *n.* contrast or opposition of thought (p. 673)

paradoxes (par´ ə däks´ es) *n.* things that seem to be contradictory (p. 673)

devoid (di void´) *adj.* completely without; lacking (p. 674)

The Trouble with Television

Robert MacNeil

It is difficult to escape the influence of television. If you fit the statistical averages, by the age of 20 you will have been exposed to at least 20,000 hours of television. You can add 10,000 hours for each decade you have lived after the age of 20. The only things Americans do more than watch television are work and sleep.

Calculate for a moment what could be done with even a part of those hours. Five thousand hours, I am told, are what a typical college undergraduate spends working on a bachelor's degree. In 10,000 hours you could have learned enough to become an astronomer or engineer. You could have learned several languages fluently. If it appealed to you, you could be reading Homer[1] in the original Greek or Dostoevski[2] in Russian. If it didn't, you could have walked around the world and written a book about it.

The trouble with television is that it discourages concentration. Almost anything interesting and rewarding in life requires some constructive, consistently applied effort. The dullest, the least gifted of us can achieve things that seem miraculous to those who never concentrate on anything. But television encourages us to apply no effort. It sells us instant gratification. It <u>diverts</u> us only to divert, to make the time pass without pain.

Television's variety becomes a narcotic,[3] not a stimulus.[4] Its serial, kaleidoscopic[5] exposures force us to follow its lead. The viewer is on a perpetual guided tour: thirty minutes at the museum, thirty at the cathedral, then back on the bus to the next attraction—except on television, typically, the spans allotted are on the order of minutes or seconds, and the chosen delights are more often car crashes and people killing one another. In short, a lot of television <u>usurps</u> one of the most precious of all human gifts, the ability to focus your attention yourself, rather than just passively surrender it.

Capturing your attention—and holding it—is the prime motive of most television programming and enhances its role as a profitable advertising vehicle. Programmers live in constant fear of losing anyone's attention—anyone's. The surest way to avoid doing so is to keep everything brief, not to strain the attention of anyone but instead to provide constant stimulation through variety, novelty, action and movement. Quite simply, television operates on the appeal to the short attention span.

It is simply the easiest way out. But it has come to be regarded as a given, as inherent[6] in the medium[7] itself: as an imperative, as

---

1. **Homer** (hō′ mər) Greek epic poet of the eighth century B.C.
2. **Dostoevski** (dôs′ tô yef′ skē) Fyodor (fyô′ dôr) Dostoevski (1821–1881) Russian novelist.
3. **narcotic** (när kät′ ik) *n.* something that has a soothing effect.
4. **stimulus** (stim′ yə ləs) *n.* something that rouses to action.
5. **kaleidoscopic** (kə lī′ də skäp′ ik) *adj.* constantly changing.
6. **inherent** (in hir′ ənt) *adj.* natural.
7. **medium** (mē′ dē əm) *n.* means of communication.

◀ **Critical Viewing** What effect does watching television seem to be having on this girl? [**Make a Judgment**]

Literary Analysis
Persuasive Techniques
What support does MacNeil cite before he ever states the point of his argument?

diverts (dī vʉrts′) *v.* distracts

usurps (yoo sʉrps′) *v.* takes over

✔**Reading Check**
What is MacNeil's attitude toward television?

though General Sarnoff, or one of the other <u>august</u> pioneers of video, had bequeathed to us tablets of stone commanding that nothing in television shall ever require more than a few moments' concentration.

In its place that is fine. Who can quarrel with a medium that so brilliantly packages escapist entertainment as a mass-marketing tool? But I see its values now <u>pervading</u> this nation and its life. It has become fashionable to think that, like fast food, fast ideas are the way to get to a fast-moving, impatient public.

In the case of news, this practice, in my view, results in inefficient communication. I question how much of television's nightly news effort is really absorbable and understandable. Much of it is what has been aptly described as "machine gunning with scraps." I think its technique fights coherence.[8] I think it tends to make things ultimately boring and dismissable (unless they are accompanied by horrifying pictures) because almost anything is boring and dismissable if you know almost nothing about it.

I believe that TV's appeal to the short attention span is not only inefficient communication but decivilizing as well. Consider the casual assumptions that television tends to cultivate: that complexity must be avoided, that visual stimulation is a substitute for thought, that verbal precision is an anachronism.[9] It may be old-fashioned, but I was taught that thought is words, arranged in grammatically precise ways.

There is a crisis of literacy in this country. One study estimates that some 30 million adult Americans are "functionally illiterate" and cannot read or write well enough to answer a want ad or understand the instructions on a medicine bottle.

Literacy may not be an inalienable human right, but it is one that the highly literate Founding Fathers might not have found unreasonable or even unattainable. We are not only not attaining it as a nation, statistically speaking, but we are falling further and further short of attaining it. And, while I would not be so simplistic as to suggest that television is the cause, I believe it contributes and is an influence.

---

8. coherence (kō hir´ əns) *n.* the quality of being connected in an intelligible way.
9. anachronism (ə nak´ rə niz´ əm) *n.* anything that seems to be out of its proper place in history.

▲ **Critical Viewing**
What does this photograph suggest about the process of watching television?

august (ô gust´) *adj.*
honored

pervading (pər vād´ iŋ) *v.*
spreading throughout

Literary Analysis
Persuasive Techniques
What persuasive techniques does MacNeil use in this paragraph?

Everything about this nation—the structure of the society, its forms of family organization, its economy, its place in the world—has become more complex, not less. Yet its dominating communications instrument, its principal form of national linkage, is one that sells neat resolutions to human problems that usually have no neat resolutions. It is all symbolized in my mind by the hugely successful art form that television has made central to the culture, the thirty-second commercial: the tiny drama of the earnest housewife who finds happiness in choosing the right toothpaste.

When before in human history has so much humanity collectively surrendered so much of its leisure to one toy, one mass diversion? When before has virtually an entire nation surrendered itself wholesale to a medium for selling?

Some years ago Yale University law professor Charles L. Black, Jr. wrote: ". . . forced feeding on trivial fare is not itself a trivial matter." I think this society is being force fed with trivial fare, and I fear that the effects on our habits of mind, our language, our tolerance for effort, and our appetite for complexity are only dimly perceived. If I am wrong, we will have done no harm to look at the issue skeptically and critically, to consider how we should be resisting it. I hope you will join with me in doing so.

Reading Strategy
Evaluating Logic Does this paragraph seem logical to you? Why or why not?

Robert MacNeil

(b. 1931)
Born in Montreal, Canada, Robert MacNeil worked on a children's show for the Canadian Broadcasting Corporation early in his career. After becoming a broadcast journalist, MacNeil went to public television to host his own news analysis program, which grew into the highly regarded *MacNeil/Lehrer NewsHour*. The show differed from other news programs by offering more in-depth reports.

MacNeil retired as co-anchor of the PBS *MacNeil/Lehrer NewsHour* in 1995. An acclaimed author, he has published two memoirs, *The Right Place at the Right Time* and *Wordstruck,* and has drawn on his years of experience in the field of broadcast journalism to write the novel *Breaking News.*

Review and Assess

Thinking About the Literature

1. **Respond:** Is television a waste of time or a valuable source of information? Explain.

2. **(a) Recall:** According to MacNeil, what is the biggest trouble with television? **(b) Draw Conclusions:** How might everyday life be different if people watched less television? Explain.

3. **(a) Recall:** To what growing crisis in the United States does MacNeil believe television contributes? **(b) Evaluate:** Are MacNeil's arguments justified? Explain.

4. **(a) Recall:** What positive aspects of the medium of television does MacNeil mention? **(b) Speculate:** If MacNeil were the president of a television network, what changes in the programming might he make?

5. **(a) Recall:** What three "decivilizing" assumptions does MacNeil say that television programs encourage in the viewer? **(b) Apply:** Do you think television could be improved? How? **(c) Make a Judgment:** To what degree is television a valuable or a destructive element in society? Explain.

The American Dream

~ MARTIN LUTHER KING, Jr. ~

A merica is essentially a dream, a dream as yet unfulfilled. It is a dream of a land where men of all races, of all nationalities and of all creeds can live together as brothers. The substance of the dream is expressed in these sublime words, words lifted to cosmic proportions: "We hold these truths to be self-evident, that all men are created equal, that they are endowed by their Creator with certain unalienable rights, that among these are life, liberty, and pursuit of happiness."[1] This is the dream.

One of the first things we notice in this dream is an amazing universalism. It does not say some men, but it says all men. It does not say all white men, but it says all men, which includes black men. It does not say all Gentiles, but it says all men, which includes Jews. It does not say all Protestants, but it says all men, which includes Catholics.

And there is another thing we see in this dream that ultimately distinguishes democracy and our form of government from all of the totalitarian regimes[2] that emerge in history. It says that each individual has certain basic rights that are neither conferred by nor derived from the state. To discover where they came from it is necessary to move back behind the dim mist of eternity, for they are God-given. Very seldom if ever in the history of the world has a sociopolitical document expressed in such profoundly eloquent and unequivocal language the dignity and the worth of human personality. The American dream reminds us that every man is heir to the legacy of worthiness.

Ever since the Founding Fathers of our nation dreamed this noble dream, America has been something of a schizophrenic[3] personality, tragically divided against herself. On the one hand we have proudly professed the principles of democracy, and on the other hand we have sadly practiced the very <u>antithesis</u> of those principles. Indeed slavery and segregation have been strange <u>paradoxes</u> in a nation founded on the principle that all men are created equal. This is what the Swedish sociologist, Gunnar Myrdal, referred to as the American dilemma.

But the shape of the world today does not permit us the luxury of an anemic democracy. The price America must pay for the continued exploitation of the Negro and other minority groups is the price of its own destruction. The hour is late; the clock of destiny is ticking out. It is trite, but urgently true, that if America is to remain a first-class nation she can no longer have second-class citizens. Now, more than ever before, America is challenged to bring her noble dream into reality, and those who are working to implement the American dream are the true saviors of democracy.

---

1. **"We hold these . . . pursuit of happiness"** from the Declaration of Independence, which declares the American colonies free and independent of Great Britain.
2. **totalitarian** (tō tal´ ə ter´ ē ən) **regimes** governments or states in which one political party or group maintains complete control under a dictatorship.
3. **schizophrenic** (skit´ se fren´ ik) *adj.* characterized by a separation between the thought processes and emotions.

Literary Analysis
Persuasive Techniques
Why does King cite the Declaration of Independence?

antithesis (an tith´ ə sis) *n.* contrast or opposition of thought

paradoxes (par´ ə däks´ es) *n.* things that seem to be contradictory

Reading Check

What is the dream that King is expressing?

Now may I suggest some of the things we must do if we are to make the American dream a reality. First I think all of us must develop a world perspective if we are to survive. The American dream will not become a reality <u>devoid</u> of the larger dream of a world of brotherhood and peace and good will. The world in which we live is a world of geographical oneness and we are challenged now to make it spiritually one.

Man's specific genius and technological ingenuity has dwarfed distance and placed time in chains. Jet planes have compressed into minutes distances that once took days and months to cover. It is not common for a preacher to be quoting Bob Hope, but I think he has aptly described this jet age in which we live. If, on taking off on a non-stop flight from Los Angeles to New York City, you develop hiccups, he said, you will hic in Los Angeles and cup in New York City. That is really *moving*. If you take a flight from Tokyo, Japan, on Sunday morning, you will arrive in Seattle, Washington, on the preceding Saturday night. When your friends meet you at the airport and ask you when you left Tokyo, you will have to say, "I left tomorrow." This is the kind of world in which we live. Now this is a bit humorous but I am trying to laugh a basic fact into all of us: the world in which we live has become a single neighborhood.

Through our scientific genius we have made of this world a neighborhood; now through our moral and spiritual development we must make of it a brotherhood. In a real sense, we must all learn to live together as brothers, or we will all perish together as fools. We must come to see that no individual can live alone; no nation can live alone. We must all live together; we must all be concerned about each other.

devoid (di void') *adj.* completely without; lacking

Martin Luther King, Jr.

(1929–1968)
The son and grandson of Baptist ministers, Reverend Dr. Martin Luther King, Jr., followed the family tradition and became a clergyman. An impassioned activist for justice, King's first well-publicized venture into civil rights occurred in 1955. After Rosa Parks refused to give up her bus seat to a white person as required by the law, King led a successful boycott of buses in Montgomery, Alabama. Eight years later, King led a civil rights march in Washington, D.C. There, he delivered his famous "I Have a Dream" speech.

In 1964, King was awarded the Nobel Peace Prize. He continued to fight for racial equality until his tragic death at the age of 39. In the spring of 1968, King was shot and killed in Memphis, Tennessee, where he had gone to support striking city workers.

Review and Assess

Thinking About the Literature

1. **Respond:** What is your "American dream"?

2. **(a) Recall:** According to King, what historic document reveals "the American dream"? **(b) Interpret:** What is the significance of the lines King recites from this document?

3. **(a) Recall:** What does King think will happen if the United States continues to exploit minority groups? **(b) Infer:** Explain what King means when he speaks of the "American dilemma."

4. **(a) Recall:** King talks about the impact of rapid travel on the world. What does he say has been a result of this ability to travel? **(b) Analyze:** According to King, what is the difference between a neighborhood and a brotherhood?

5. **(a) Recall:** What does King think must be done if the American dream is to become a reality? **(b) Assess:** Do you agree? Explain.

Review and Assess

Literary Analysis

Persuasive Techniques

1. What persuasive technique does MacNeil use to support the claim he makes in the title of his essay?
2. What technique is King employing when he quotes Bob Hope?
3. Find two examples of repetition in King's speech.
4. For each work, complete a chart like the one shown to identify examples of each author's use of persuasive techniques.

Main Points	Persuasive Technique	Example
Americans watch too much television.	Statistics	Average American watches 10,000 hours per decade.

Comparing Literary Works

5. Which author uses a greater variety of persuasive techniques to make his case? Explain and give examples.
6. Which selection do you think employs these persuasive techniques more effectively? Why?
7. On the whole, which selection is more persuasive? Why?

Reading Strategy

Evaluating Logic

8. What are two facts or examples MacNeil presents to support his argument in "The Trouble with Television"?
9. What are two facts or examples King uses to support his point?
10. Do you think that each of these authors has used sound logic in developing his argument? Why or why not? To help you evaluate, record facts and examples on a scale like this one.

> "The Trouble with Television"   "The American Dream"

Extend Understanding

11. **Math Connection:** Calculate the number of hours of television you watch per day, per week, and per year. Do your television-watching habits support the points MacNeil makes? Explain.

Quick Review

Persuasive techniques are strategies used to affect an audience's reaction to the persuasive message. To review persuasive techniques, see page 667.

Evaluating logic involves analyzing and questioning what an author says to make a judgment about whether the ideas expressed are valid. To review evaluating logic, see page 667.

 Take It to the Net
www.phschool.com
Take the interactive self-test online to check your understanding of these selections.

Integrate Language Skills

Vocabulary Development Lesson

Word Analysis: Greek Prefix *anti-*

The Greek prefix *anti-* means "opposed to," "against," or "opposite." Combined with *thesis*, "a statement supported by argument," *antithesis* refers to a statement or concept that is the opposite of another.

On a sheet of paper, combine the following words with the prefix *anti-*, and define the new word:

    1. climax   **2.** septic   **3.** social

Spelling Strategy

If the *oy* sound is in the middle of a word, it is spelled *oi*, as in the word *devoid*. At the end of a word, it is spelled *oy*, as in the word *toy*.

Choose the correct spelling of each word.

    1. annoi annoy   **3.** coil   coyl

    2. avoid avoyd   **4.** turmoyl turmoil

Grammar Lesson

Pronoun Agreement With Indefinite Subjects

Pronouns must agree with their antecedents in both number and gender, even when the antecedent is indefinite—not referring to a specific person.

If the antecedent is *anybody, anyone, each, either, everybody, everyone, neither, nobody, no one, one, someone,* or *somebody,* use a singular pronoun:

> *Each person* must do what *he* or *she* (not *they*) thinks is right.

> *Everyone* can help in *his* or *her* own way.

If the antecedent is *both, few, many, others,* or *several,* use a plural pronoun to refer to it:

> *Both* citizens pursued *their* American dreams.

Fluency: Definitions

Copy the two rows of words onto a separate sheet of paper. Then match each numbered word with the lettered word or phrase closest in meaning.

Column A	Column B
1. diverts	a. spreading throughout
2. usurps	b. opposing idea
3. august	c. empty
4. pervading	d. distracts, amuses
5. antithesis	e. seizes power
6. paradoxes	f. seemingly contradictory statements
7. devoid	g. honored

▶ For more practice, see page R28, Exercise A.
Practice Identify which of the sentences below contain errors in pronoun usage.

    1. Each of the programs reached their audience.

    2. Nobody volunteered to give up their favorite television show.

    3. Many spend his or her time watching television.

    4. Give each person their civil rights.

    5. Few of the adults turned off their television sets.

Writing Application Revise each of the incorrect sentences you identified in the above exercise to eliminate the errors.

WG *Prentice Hall Writing and Grammar Connection: Chapter 24, Section 2*

Writing Lesson

Written Directions

A VCR allows people to choose what they watch based on their interests, rather than on what happens to be on when they have time to watch. Write a set of directions in which you explain to other students how to program a VCR.

Prewriting   Locate a VCR manual that includes how-to instructions. Carefully read the directions. Then, list important details you will include in your own directions for other students.

Drafting   Present your directions as a series of numbered steps in chronological order. Include drawings or diagrams.

Model: Chronological Order

1. Press "menu."
2. Select "clock."
3. Look for the blinking light.

Revising   Have a classmate read your directions to check whether you have left out any steps. If possible, have him or her "test" your instructions by following them to program a clock on a VCR.

 Prentice Hall Writing and Grammar Connection: Chapter 10, Sections 1–7

Extension Activities

Listening and Speaking Deliver King's **speech** to your class.

1. Memorize all or part of "The American Dream."
2. Rehearse your recitation.
   - Use volume for emphasis. Begin softly and increase the loudness of your voice as you build to an important point.
   - Vary your pitch—how high or low you make your voice.
   - Adjust your pace—the rate of speed you use when you speak—to show a sense of urgency.
3. Present the speech to your classmates.

Research and Technology With a partner, interview ten adults and ten students about the number of hours they spend each week viewing televised sporting events, dramas, comedies, news, movies, and educational programs. Then, chart your results on a **television-watching graph** and present your findings to your classmates. **[Group Activity]**

Writing Write an **evaluation** of the effectiveness of King's speech. Base your evaluation on how effectively he supports his points and on his use of persuasive techniques.

 **Take It to the Net**   www.phschool.com

Go online for an additional research activity using the Internet.

from A Painted House

Robert MacNeil clearly remembers the days before television was invented. But for anyone too young to remember, it may be hard to imagine how suddenly—and significantly—this invention forever changed things for the average American. Think of it: many people, especially those who lived in rural areas, had never seen all sorts of entertainments we now take for granted—including the World Series!

In his novel, *A Painted House*, John Grisham tells a story he says was "inspired by my childhood in rural Arkansas." The year is 1952; the place is Arkansas. The narrator is a seven-year-old boy named Luke who helps his family farm eighty acres of cotton fields that they rent. When the cotton is ripe, they hire migrant farm workers from the Ozarks and Mexico, to help them harvest it. During the six weeks of picking cotton, Luke grows up in important ways. In the excerpt you are about to read, his world suddenly grows larger, in a way he can never reverse and could never have predicted.

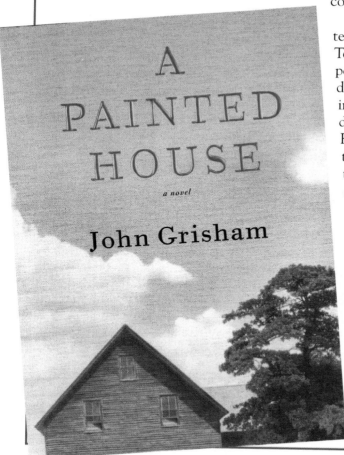

Robert NacNeil's perspective on television in "The Trouble With Television" is mostly negative. His position is that it "diverts us only to divert." In other words, he is claiming that most television programs do not offer much to think about. Further, he asserts, or puts forward, the idea that the wide variety of television programs fosters a short attention span.

As you read the excerpt from *A Painted House*, think about how Grisham's portrayal of television differs from MacNeil's. Although he gives only a brief glimpse at the narrator's experience with television, the perspective is mostly positive.

Compare and contrast these two perspectives on television. Think about what your own opinions are in relationship to those of the writers.

from A Painted House

John Grisham

After lunch Pappy said abruptly, "Luke, we're goin' to town. The trailer's full."

The trailer wasn't completely full, and we never took it to the gin[1] in the middle of the day. But I wasn't about to object. Something was up.

There were only four trailers ahead of us when we arrived at the gin. Usually, at this time of the harvest, there would be at least ten, but then we always came after supper, when the place was crawling with farmhands. "Noon's a good time to gin,"[2] Pappy said.

He left the keys in the truck, and as we were walking away he said, "I need to go to the Co-op. Let's head to Main Street." Sounded good to me.

The town of Black Oak had three hundred people, and virtually all of them lived within five minutes of Main Street. I often thought how wonderful it would be to have a neat little house on a shady street, just a stone's throw from Pop and Pearl's and the Dixie theater, with no cotton anywhere in sight.

Halfway to Main, we took an abrupt turn. "Pearl wants to see you," he said, pointing at the Watsons' house just to our right. I'd never been in Pop and Pearl's house, never had any reason to enter, but I'd seen it from the outside. It was one of the few houses in town with some bricks on it.

"What?" I asked, completely bewildered.

He said nothing, and I just followed.

Pearl was waiting at the door. When we entered I could smell the rich, sweet aroma of something baking, though I was too confused to realize she was preparing a treat for me. She gave me a pat on the head and winked at Pappy. In one corner of the room, Pop was bent at the waist, his back to us, fiddling with something. "Come here, Luke," he said, without turning around.

I'd heard that they owned a television. The first one in our county had been purchased a year earlier by Mr. Harvey Gleeson, the

---

1. gin (jin) *n.* cotton gin: a machine that separates the seeds and seed hulls from the fibers of cotton.

2. gin (jin) *v.* to remove the seeds from cotton with a gin.

◀ **Critical Viewing**
Why do you think sports
events were some of
the earliest television
broadcasts? **[Deduce]**

owner of the bank, but he was a <u>recluse</u>, and no one had yet seen
his television, as far as we knew. Several church members had
kinfolks in Jonesboro who owned televisions, and whenever they
went there to visit they came back and talked nonstop about this
wonderful new invention. Dewayne had seen one inside a store
window in Blytheville, and he'd strutted around school for an
<u>insufferable</u> period of time.

"Sit here," Pop said, pointing to a spot on the floor, right in front
of the set. He was still adjusting knobs. "It's the World Series," he
said. "Game three, Dodgers at Yankee Stadium."

My heart froze; my mouth dropped open. I was too stunned to
move. Three feet away was a small screen with lines dancing
across it. It was in the center of a dark, wooden cabinet with the
word Motorola scripted in chrome just under a row of knobs. Pop
turned one of the knobs, and suddenly we heard the scratchy
voice of an announcer describing a ground ball to the shortstop.

recluse (rek´ loōs) *n.* A
hermit; someone who
withdraws from the world
to live in solitude and
seclusion.

insufferable (in suf´ ər ə bəl)
adj. unbearable;
intolerable.

Then Pop turned two knobs at once, and the picture became clear.

It was a baseball game. Live from Yankee Stadium, and we were watching it in Black Oak, Arkansas!

Chairs moved behind me, and I could feel Pappy inching closer. Pearl wasn't much of a fan. She busied herself in the kitchen for a few minutes, then emerged with a plate of chocolate cookies and a glass of milk. I took them and thanked her. They were fresh from the oven and smelled delicious. But I couldn't eat, not right then.

Ed Lopat was pitching for the Yankees, Preacher Roe for the Dodgers. Mickey Mantle, Yogi Berra, Phil Rizzuto, Hank Bauer, Billy Martin with the Yankees, and Pee Wee Reese, Duke Snider, Roy Campanella, Jackie Robinson, and Gil Hodges with the Dodgers. They were all there in Pop and Pearl's living room, playing before sixty thousand fans in Yankee Stadium. I was <u>mesmerized</u> to the point of being mute. I simply stared at the television, watching but not believing.

"Eat the cookies, Luke," Pearl said as she passed through the room. It was more of a command than an invitation, and I took a bite of one.

"Who are you pullin' for?" asked Pop.

"I don't know," I mumbled, and I really didn't. I had been taught to hate both teams. And it had been easy hating them when they were away in New York, in another world. But now they were in Black Oak, playing the game I loved, live from Yankee Stadium. My hatred vanished. "Dodgers, I guess," I said.

"Always pull for the National League," Pappy said behind me.

We pulled our empty trailer back to the farm, and I picked cotton until quitting time. During supper the adults gave me the floor. I talked nonstop about the game and the commercials and everything I'd seen on Pop and Pearl's television.

Modern America was slowly invading rural Arkansas.

mesmerized (mes′mə rīzd) *adj.* hypnotized; enthralled.

John Grisham

(b. 1955)

When John Grisham was growing up in Arkansas, his family moved often. Every time they settled in a new town, Grisham would immediately go to the public library and get a library card. He loved to read, although he never imagined he would one day write novels that sold millions of copies. In fact, he got a D in English composition! After college, he pursued a career as a lawyer. He was elected to the Mississippi House of Representatives, where he served for six years. Today he is known as a best-selling author of mystery, crime, and suspense fiction. Many of his novels, including *The Firm* and *The Pelican Brief*, have been made into films.

Connecting Literature and Culture

1. In the excerpt from *A Painted House*, in what ways does television seem to be a positive thing, from Luke's point of view?

2. How do you think John Grisham might respond to Robert MacNeil's comments about television? Explain your reasoning.

3. How does television change the way Luke thinks about the Dodgers?

4. How might television change the way that Luke thinks about the world?

5. In what ways does television influence culture?

6. In what ways does literature influence culture?

Cause-and-Effect Essays

About Cause-and-Effect Essays

Expository writing is writing that informs or explains. A cause-and-effect essay is a specific type of expository writing that explains the reasons something happened or its results. For example, historical essays explain the impact of key developments in the past, and news reports explain the causes and effects of current events or developments. Effective cause-and-effect essays include

- a clear explanation of how one or more events or situations resulted in another event or situation.
- a thorough presentation of facts, statistics, and other details that support the explanation presented.
- a clear and consistent organization that makes it easy to follow the connections among events and details.

Reading Strategy

Identify Connections Among Causes and Effects

The key to understanding a cause-and-effect essay is paying close attention to the relationships among the details. Writers include many words that indicate causes and effects. These may include verbs—for example, *causes*, *produces*, and *affects*—and transitions—*because of*, *as a result*, or *for this reason*. For example, in "Why Is the Sea Blue?" the author writes, "The time of year also affects the ocean's color." The verb *affects* indicates a connection between season and water color. As you read, record connections among causes and effects in a chart like the one shown here.

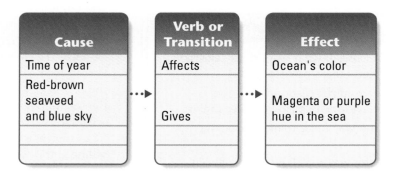

Cause	Verb or Transition	Effect
Time of year	Affects	Ocean's color
Red-brown seaweed and blue sky	Gives	Magenta or purple hue in the sea

Why Is the Sea Blue?

Denis Wallis

All color in the world comes from light. Without light, we would see no color in the greenest grass, a peacock's feather, a bunch of flowers, or a brilliant rainbow. Three factors determine the colors we see: the light itself, the material it falls on, and the ability of the human eye to distinguish colors.

A beam of light appears to us to have no color. Shine it through a prism, and it breaks down into a spread of colors resembling those in a rainbow. Indeed, that is why rainbows appear in the sky: a shower of raindrops acts to open up the full spectrum of light into all its different and wonderful wavelengths.

We see a ripe tomato as being bright red because its skin reflects the red light in the spectrum, and absorbs all other colors. Grass isn't in itself colored green, nor are other objects in our world in a myriad variety of colors. Their surface texture reflects light of a particular wavelength. That is why some objects appear to change color if they are tilted towards or away from the light. A shiny fabric, for example, may look green from one angle and blue from another.

If the light source is changed, an object's color may alter. A woman buying some curtains is wise to take them into daylight: fluorescent store lights have more blue light; sunshine increases the amount of red in a fabric.

Travelers know that the seas appear to be a dark green in some places and turquoise blue in others. The Mediterranean is renowned for its dark-blue color. The sky and its reflection in water account partly for the sea's color. On gray and stormy days of heavy cloud, the water looks leaden.

When light strikes water, much is reflected, possibly causing glare. Of the light that penetrates the surface, some is absorbed; the rest is broken up and scattered back towards the surface that gives the sea its color.

> The writer explains the effects of light striking water.

Different wavelengths of light penetrate to different depths. If the water is clear, the red and yellow wavelengths of light are soon absorbed, leaving only blue-green light to be scattered back. That is why clear seas appear bluer.

The time of year also affects the ocean's color. If the water is rich in nutrients, as it may become through chemicals carried down by rivers, it may encourage spring and summer weed growths. Fine particles suspended in the water will alter its color. Blooms of algae, for example, can suddenly turn seas red.

A combination of red-brown seaweed and blue sky sometimes gives seas such as the Mediterranean a magenta or purple hue. Runoff from coastal rivers, bringing a range of different vegetable and mineral particles, may cause the sea to look red-brown on one day and almost yellow on another. And close to shore any light-colored sand will make the water look blue-green rather than blue.

> Here, the writer explains why the sea sometimes appears purple, red-brown, yellow, or blue-green.

If you don't agree with a companion that the sea is a brilliant blue, the cause undoubtedly lies in your eyes. Our perception of color varies according to how light-sensitive cells are distributed in the retina. What looks like dark blue to one person may be gray-blue to another.

Check Your Comprehension

1. What three factors determine the colors we see?
2. Why do rainbows appear in the sky?
3. Why do some objects appear to change color if they are tilted toward or away from the light?
4. What happens when light strikes water?
5. Why might two people describe the same sea as different colors?

Applying the Reading Strategy

Identify Connections Among Causes and Effects

6. What factors cause us to see tomatoes as red and grass as green?
7. How does light give the sea its color?
8. How can the time of year affect the ocean's color?
9. (a) Name one color other than blue that the sea might appear to be. (b) Explain what causes the sea to appear this way.
10. How does the human eye affect our perception of color?

Activity

Charting Causes and Effects

Choose a current event that you find interesting, such as a local election or a major sports upset. In the newspaper or on the Internet, find an article about the event. Read the article, and identify the event's causes and some of its likely effects. Make a chart or diagram to show the causes and effects.

Contrasting Informational Materials

Cause-and-Effect Essays and Scientific Reports

Scientific reports are another type of cause-and-effect writing. They explain the results of an experiment or analyze the causes and effects of a natural event. For example, you might read a scientific report on the study of a new pain medication or the causes of an earthquake. You can find scientific reports in science journals or in the science section of a newspaper.

Find a scientific report in your library or on the Internet. Read the report, and then compare and contrast it with the cause-and-effect essay you read here. Answer the following questions:

1. Who is the intended audience of each selection?
2. How does the audience affect the language the writer uses?
3. How does the audience affect the level of complexity in the selection?
4. After reading the selections, name at least one question that you still have about each topic.

Writing WORKSHOP

Research: Research Report

A research report presents information gathered from a variety of primary and secondary resources. By citing these sources, a research writer lets others check the facts for themselves. In this workshop, you will write a research report based on information from a variety of sources.

Assignment Criteria. Your research report should have the following characteristics:

- An overall focus or main idea expressed in a thesis
- Important ideas, concepts, and direct quotations from a variety of sources
- Information from both primary and secondary sources
- Charts, maps, graphs, or other visual displays
- A clear organization and smooth transitions
- Accurate, complete citations identifying sources

See the Rubric on page 691 for the criteria on which your research report may be assessed.

Prewriting

Choose a topic. Brainstorm for ideas by asking yourself questions such as these:

- What interesting people do I want to know more about?
- What places would I like to visit?
- What intriguing things or events do I want to explore?

Example:
Interesting People: Benjamin Franklin
Jackie Robinson
Grandma Rose
Virginia Woolf

Narrow your topic. Answer questions like the ones shown in the chart. The example shows how the topic "Benjamin Franklin" can be focused.

Use a variety of primary and secondary sources. Use both primary sources (firsthand or original accounts, such as interview transcripts and newspaper articles) and secondary sources (accounts that are not original, such as encyclopedia entries) in your research.

General Topic: Benjamin Franklin

- In what general category does your topic belong?

  Inventor, Founding Father

- How is your topic similar to or different from other topics in this category?

  People still know Franklin's sayings, unlike words of other Founding Fathers; Jefferson was also an inventor.

- Narrowed Topic

  The variety of Franklin's accomplishments.

Student Model

Before you begin drafting your research report, read this portion of the student model report and review the characteristics of a successful research report. To read the full report, visit **www.phschool.com.**

Tyler Quinn
Fair Oaks, CA

Civil Rights: The March Continues

There are many significant events in the history of the United States. One event in particular stands out because it broke the racial barriers forever. This monumental event is called the Civil Rights Act of 1964, aka CRA.

The purpose of this act was to tell all the people henceforth that no person in the United States shall: on the grounds of race, color, or national origin be excluded from participation in, be denied the benefits of, or be otherwise subjected to discrimination.

History of the Civil Rights Act The origins of this movement go back more than a century to the Dred Scott decision. Dred Scott was a black slave in the slave state of Missouri. The circumstances of his court decision concerned his travels with a man who held him in servitude. Scott traveled to the free state of Illinois, as well as to the free state of Wisconsin. Upon his arrival back in Missouri, he claimed to be a free man, based upon his temporary status as a free man in Illinois and Wisconsin. He claimed he had achieved freedom and sued for his freedom from his former slave owner in the Missouri State Supreme Court. There the court ruled against him on the grounds that he was still in this man's servitude. He then took his case to the Missouri circuit court, where they also ruled against him on the same basis as the Missouri Supreme Court.

A Growing Concern Approximately forty years later, another case like the Dred Scott case came along. In 1896, *Plessy* v. *Ferguson* became a lightning rod for the public's attention to equal rights. Louisiana had passed a law requiring railroad companies to provide separate but equal cars for black passengers and white passengers. African American leaders protested, claiming this solution violated the equal protection clause of the new 14th amendment. They decided to challenge the constitutionality of the law in court and chose a man by the name of Homer Plessy to be the test case. Plessy bought a train ticket and insisted on riding in the whites-only car. He was arrested and then convicted. He then appealed his case to the Supreme Court. The question in front of the Supreme Court was whether Louisiana law

> The overall focus—the impact of the Civil Rights Act—is identified in the first paragraph.

> The report is organized chronologically: The writer begins with the origins of the civil rights movement and then reports its progress.

violated the equal protection clause. Since the law required that blacks and whites have equal facilities, the court concluded that no unfair discrimination had taken place. Louisiana law was declared Constitutional.

*   *   *

[During the desegregation of schools] A group by the name of the White Citizen's Council promised massive resistance. A noteworthy example would be that of the Little Rock Crisis in Arkansas on December 4, 1957. The Arkansas Governor dispatched the National Guard to prevent nine black students from enrolling in Central High School. This incident attracted so much attention that eventually Dwight D. Eisenhower ordered the army to escort the students through school. But the army could not be there all the time. As one student wrote: "They couldn't be everywhere. They couldn't be with us for example in the ladies bathroom. They couldn't be with us in gym. . . ." (Hampton 35)

One of the most publicized events of the Civil Rights movement was the Montgomery boycott in December of 1955. Rosa Parks, an African American woman, refused to give up her seat to a white man, in spite of an Alabama law requiring that she do so. Although Rosa Parks has said that she was simply tired, to many African Americans, she became a symbol of strength and dignity. Some who were not active in the movement before were inspired by her example. (Brown interview)

> Primary sources provide a first-hand look at a historic situation. Credit information from primary sources as well as from secondary sources.

*   *   *

Bibliography

1. Brown, John. Personal interview. 7 Nov. 1999.

2. Hampton, Henry, and Steve Fayer. *Voices of Freedom*. London: Bantam Books, 1990.

3. King, Mary. *Freedom Song*. New York: William Morrow and Company, 1987.

4. Bender, David L. *The Civil Rights Movement*. San Diego: Greenhaven Press, 1996.

5. Canton, Andrew, et al. *America Pathways to the Present*. New Jersey: Prentice Hall, 1999.

6. *Civil Rights*. <http://members.aol.com/Pflaumen3/civilright.html>

All sources used are listed at the end of the paper in a Bibliography. To see how different sources should be listed, see Citing Sources and Preparing Manuscript, pages R12–R13.

You may some-times use a Works Cited list instead of a Bibliography. (See pages R12–R13.) Find out which one your teacher prefers.

Take detailed notes. Paraphrase important information by writing it in your own words. Remember that you must give credit for both direct quotes and paraphrased ideas, so record the publication information of each source you use.

Drafting

Define your thesis. Sum up the point of your paper in a sentence, called a **thesis statement**. For example, in a report on Franklin D. Roosevelt, your thesis statement might read, "In his presidency, Roosevelt showed the same characteristic he showed in fighting his disability—determination." Include your thesis statement in the introduction to your report.

Make an outline. Write a formal outline for your report before you begin to draft. Use Roman numerals for your most important points and capital letters for the details that support them. Make sure every point on your outline supports your thesis statement.

Display information on charts, maps, and graphs. Enhance your report by adding a visual display such as a chart, map, or graph. For example, if a section of your report contains a large amount of statistics, display this information in an organized and easy-to-read chart.

Outline

I. Introductions

II. First main point
   A. Supporting detail #1
      1. Example
      2. Example
      3. Example
   B. Supporting detail #2
   C. Supporting detail #3

III. Second main point

Revising

Revise for unity. **Unity** is the quality of written work in which all the parts fit together in a complete, self-contained whole. Review your report to check unity.

1. Make sure that every paragraph develops your thesis statement. Eliminate paragraphs that seem related, but that do not build toward the point expressed in your thesis statement.

2. Identify the main idea of each paragraph. Often, a **topic sentence** will directly state that main idea. If a paragraph does not contain a topic sentence, consider adding one—a single sentence that expresses the main idea.

3. Eliminate any sentences that do not support or explain the topic sentence or main idea.

Check your citations. An internal citation appears in parentheses. It includes the author's last name and the page number on which the information appears. The citation directly follows the information from the source cited.

> **Example:** "The Duke of Lancaster in 1888 controlled more than 163,000 acres of British countryside" (Pool 163).

Remember that you must credit the source of other people's ideas or research, even if you restate the information in your own words.

> **Example:** Historians estimate that the Underground Railroad was traveled by between 40,000 and 100,000 slaves by the time the Civil War began ("Underground Railroad" 126).

Publishing and Presenting

Choose one of these ways to share your writing with classmates or a larger audience.

Share your report with a large audience. Do some research to determine which organizations (historical societies, fan clubs, and so on) might be interested in the topic of your report. Submit a copy of your report to one of these groups for publication in its newsletter or on its Web site.

Participate in a panel discussion. Join with classmates who have written on a similar subject, and organize a panel discussion. Each student should present his or her report and respond to questions and comments from other panel members.

Prentice Hall Writing and Grammar Connection: Chapter 11

Speaking Connection

To learn about delivering a research report as a speech, see the **Listening and Speaking Workshop: Delivering a Research Presentation**, page 692.

Rubric for Self-Assessment

Evaluate your research report, using the following criteria and rating scale:

Criteria	Rating Scale Not very				Very
How well is the main idea expressed in a thesis?	1	2	3	4	5
How well does the report include information from a variety of sources?	1	2	3	4	5
How well does the report combine information from both primary and secondary sources?	1	2	3	4	5
How well does the report include charts, maps, graphs, or other visual displays?	1	2	3	4	5
How clear is the organization, including transitions?	1	2	3	4	5
How accurate and complete are the citations?	1	2	3	4	5

Writing Workshop ◆ 691

Listening and Speaking WORKSHOP

Delivering a Research Presentation

A research report presents information gathered from a variety of primary and secondary resources. An effective **research presentation** has most of the same characteristics as a successful research report. (To review the characteristics of a successful research report, see the writing workshop, pp. 686–691.) The following strategies will help you to deliver an effective research presentation.

Consider Content

Make your thesis clear. Present your thesis early in your presentation. For emphasis and clarity, you may want to write it on the chalkboard or on a poster. Make sure that every part of your presentation supports it.

Include a variety of perspectives. Your presentation should include ideas, concepts, and direct quotations from multiple sources. Try to paraphrase and summarize all relevant perspectives on the topic, especially when they differ dramatically, to give your audience a thorough picture of your topic.

Use both primary and secondary sources. Use both primary sources (firsthand or original accounts, such as interview transcripts) and secondary sources (accounts that are not original, such as encyclopedia entries) in your presentation. Consider the nature and value of each source before you use it.

Make use of visual aids. Charts, maps, graphs, and other visual aids allow you to present lots of information quickly and concisely. Visual aids can also make your presentation more attractive and engaging.

Consider Delivery

Make eye contact. Speak from notes rather than reading directly from your essay. Look up from your notes and make eye contact with the audience to emphasize key points.

Enunciate clearly. Your audience should be able to hear every word you say. Speak loudly enough to be heard in the back of the room.

Use an appropriate pace. Speak more slowly than you do in everyday conversation. Your sentences will be longer and more complex than usual, so give your audience the chance to digest them.

Activity:
Radio News Segment
With a partner, prepare a brief research presentation on a local event that you find interesting, such as the winning streak of the high school softball team or the opening of a new play at the community theater. Include at least one interview as part of your research. When you finish, tape record your presentation in the form of a story on a radio news broadcast.

Checklist for Delivering a Research Presentation

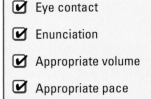

Content
☑ Clear thesis
☑ Variety of perspectives
☑ Primary sources
☑ Secondary sources
☑ Visual aids

Delivery
☑ Use of notes
☑ Eye contact
☑ Enunciation
☑ Appropriate volume
☑ Appropriate pace

Distinguish Fact From Opinion

The reading sections of some tests require you to read a passage and answer multiple-choice questions about fact and opinion. Use the following strategies to help you answer such questions:

- A fact can be proved true by a reliable source, such as an unbiased book or an expert.
- An opinion is a statement of belief.

Sample Test Item

Directions: Read the poster, and then answer the question that follows.

Bob Giles *for*
Student Council President
Why vote for Bob?

✔ Bob was SC treasurer last year.

✔ Bob is captain of the football team.

✔ Bob is well liked by everyone.

● Bob's opponent has no school spirit.

● Bob's opponent is a one-issue candidate.

● Bob's opponent is new to the school.

Bob Giles will put this school on the map!

---

1. Which of the following is an OPINION?
  A Bob is captain of the football team.
  B His opponent has no school spirit.
  C His opponent is new to the school.
  D Bob was SC treasurer last year.

Answer and Explanation

Research can prove that *A, C,* and *D* are true. *B* is an opinion.

▶ Practice

Directions: Read the passage, and then answer the questions that follow.

Dear Editor:

I am writing to protest the new city law that dogs must be on leashes at all times. Everyone knows dogs deserve to run free. They can't enjoy running at a human's pace. I know the law is designed to keep dogs from annoying people and fighting with other dogs. However, my dog is obedient and has never been in a fight. The leash law is unfair to well-behaved dogs. It was passed by dog-haters!

A Dog Lover

1. Which of these statements is a FACT?
  A The leash law is unfair to well-behaved dogs.
  B My dog has never been in a fight.
  C Everyone knows dogs deserve to run free.
  D Dogs can't enjoy running at a human's pace.

2. Which statement is an example of propaganda?
  A The law is designed to keep dogs from annoying people.
  B I'm writing to protest the new city law.
  C My dog has never been in a fight.
  D It was passed by dog-haters!

Ballet Rehearsal, 1944, oil on canvas, Steven Spurrier, Phillips, The International Fine Art Auctioneers

Exploring the Genre

Watching a play gives you one perspective on plot, setting, and character. Reading a play gives you an entirely different perspective. Gone are the elaborate stage sets, period costumes, and talented actors. All that is left are words of dialogue on a page and a few stage directions. When you read a play, you fill in what is missing with your imagination. As you read the play in this unit, *The Diary of Anne Frank*, use the following drama elements to help you imagine the action:

- **Stage Directions:** These notes convey information about sound effects, actions, sets, and characters' personalities and ways of speaking.

- **Dialogue:** Conversations between characters, through which most of a play's action takes place.

- **Plot:** Most dramas contain a plot in which events unfold, rise to a climax, and end in a resolution.

- **Theme**: A theme is the central message the playwright conveys to the audience.

◀ **Critical Viewing** Which details in this painting give you an indication of the type of performance being rehearsed? **[Analyze]**

Why Read Literature?

People do not always read a dramatic work for just a single purpose. You might read a play for multiple reasons. You might wish to know more about the historical setting of a play, you might read to be moved by its subject, or you might pick up the play because you have enjoyed other works by the same playwright. Preview a list of purposes you might choose for reading *The Diary of Anne Frank*, page 700.

1 Read for the love of literature.

Anne Frank had no idea when she was writing her diary that her words would reach millions of people. Left behind when the police arrested her family, the diary was found after the war and published. Since then, this compelling story of a young girl in hiding has been adapted as a play and made into a documentary. See why Anne's story inspires in all its forms when you read the play *The Diary of Anne Frank.*

2 Read for information.

The abrupt changes in mood in Anne Frank's story make no sense without the historical backdrop of World War II and the Holocaust. The Allies' military successes against Hitler in 1943 and 1944 gave Anne's family some cause for hope in the midst of a desperate situation. Understand how historical events can have a crucial impact on lives when you read *The Diary of Anne Frank.*

3 Read to be inspired.

Since it was first published in 1947, *The Diary of Anne Frank* has sold over twenty-five million copies in fifty-five languages. One factor in its success is that Anne gives a human face to the millions who died from Nazi brutality. As you read, think of the turbulent events swirling around Anne Frank—and how she retained her faith and courage even in the face of fear and prejudice.

Take It to the Net

Visit the Web site for online instruction and activities related to each selection in this unit.
www.phschool.com

How to Read Literature

Strategies for Reading Drama

The one thing that distinguishes dramas from other types of literature is that they are meant to be performed. The written script is merely a blueprint, or guide, that allows the actors and you, the reader, to understand the playwright's vision. When you read a drama, use the following strategies to interact with the text:

1. Analyze the historical context.

When playwrights write dramas, they frequently assume that you have basic knowledge of the historical events behind the play's action. To increase your awareness of context:

- Identify the time and place in which a play takes place.

- Research the period. Some sources for historical information are encyclopedias, Web sites, and historical documentaries.

- Determine how the politics and culture of the time may have influenced the attitudes of characters in the play. Establish relationships between historical events (causes) and characters' actions (effects).

2. Picture the action.

Part of the challenge and fun of reading a play—instead of seeing it on stage—is visualizing the action.

- Read stage directions closely for clues about setting, how characters are moving, and, occasionally, the way that characters will say a particular line.

- Use details in the stage directions and dialogue to help you form a mental picture of the way the characters look, move, talk, and interact with one another. Use the chart shown to help you picture the character.

Character: Peter Van Daan

Details Provided: Spends a lot of time in his room with his cat, only kissed a girl once.

Character Profile:
- Awkward and shy
- Has bad posture
- Blushes easily when talking to girls

- Imagine you are the director of the play. Think about stage sets, characters' clothing, and how you would tell the actors to play their parts and relate to each other.

As you read the play in this unit, review the reading strategies in order to interact with the text.

Prepare to Read

The Diary of Anne Frank, Act I

 Take It to the Net

Visit www.phschool.com for interactive activities and instruction related to *The Diary of Anne Frank,* Act I, including

- background
- graphic organizers
- literary elements
- reading strategies

Preview

Connecting to the Literature

You probably don't think twice about turning on a radio or CD player when you want to hear music, stepping out your front door to go to school, or walking down the street with your friends. In this drama, you will find out what life is like for a girl who can't do any of these things. Her life depends on avoiding all the things she is used to doing.

Background

In the early 1940s, the armies of Nazi Germany swept across Europe, conquering and occupying many countries. The Nazi occupation of the Netherlands, and the persecution of the Jews there, is the background for *The Diary of Anne Frank,* a play by Frances Goodrich and Albert Hackett based on the actual diary of a young German-Jewish girl living in Holland.

Literary Analysis

Staging

The **staging** of a play includes its physical features—scenery, costumes, lighting, and sound, as well as the actors' movements and the way they speak. These details are indicated in the **stage directions**. Stage directions are usually printed in italics and set in brackets. The stage directions here describe the setting of the play.

> *A narrow steep flight of stairs at the back leads up to the attic. The rooms are sparsely furnished with a few chairs, cots, a table or two.*

Directors and actors use stage directions to help them produce the drama. Readers use the stage directions to help them visualize the characters, the scenes, and the action that would occur on stage.

Connecting Literary Elements

The stage directions in *The Diary of Anne Frank* describe the on-stage setting. In this, and other literary works, however, the events take place in a larger setting as well—a time and place in the world—a **historical context**. The historical context of a work includes the time, place, customs, political forces, cultural attitudes, and major events of the period. As you read, use the timeline shown here to help you track the events that form the backdrop for the play.

Reading Strategy

Analyzing the Effect of Historical Context

The historical context of the play creates a mood, or feeling, of danger and tension. Some characters react by helping others avoid danger. Other characters react selfishly in the face of danger.

As you read, use these focus questions to help you analyze other effects of the historical context on the mood and meaning of *The Diary of Anne Frank*.

1. What are the political forces and cultural attitudes of the setting?
2. What is Anne's reaction to these forces and attitudes?

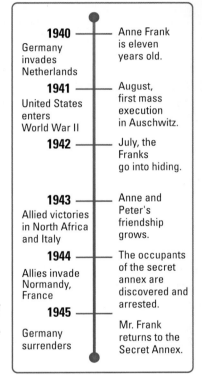

1940
Germany invades Netherlands

1941
United States enters World War II

1942

1943
Allied victories in North Africa and Italy

1944
Allies invade Normandy, France

1945
Germany surrenders

Anne Frank is eleven years old.

August, first mass execution in Auschwitz.

July, the Franks go into hiding.

Anne and Peter's friendship grows.

The occupants of the secret annex are discovered and arrested.

Mr. Frank returns to the Secret Annex.

Vocabulary Development

conspicuous (kən spik′ yōō əs) *adj.* noticeable (p. 704)

mercurial (mər kyōōr′ ē əl) *adj.* quick or changeable in behavior (p. 705)

unabashed (un ə basht′) *adj.* unashamed (p. 708)

insufferable (in suf′ ər ə bəl) *adj.* unbearable (p. 715)

meticulous (mə tik′ yōō ləs) *adj.* extremely careful about details (p. 725)

fatalist (fā′ tə list) *n.* one who believes events are determined by fate (p. 735)

ostentatiously (äs′ tən tā′ shəs lē) *adv.* in a showy way (p. 740)

The Diary of Anne Frank

**Frances Goodrich
and Albert Hackett**

CHARACTERS

MR. FRANK	MRS. FRANK
MIEP	MARGOT FRANK
MRS. VAN DAAN	ANNE FRANK
MR. VAN DAAN	MR. KRALER
PETER VAN DAAN	MR. DUSSEL

Act I

Scene 1

[*The scene remains the same throughout the play. It is the top floor of a warehouse and office building in Amsterdam, Holland. The sharply peaked roof of the building is outlined against a sea of other rooftops, stretching away into the distance. Nearby is the belfry[1] of a church tower, the Westertoren, whose carillon[2] rings out the hours. Occasionally faint sounds float up from below: the voices of children playing in the street, the tramp of marching feet, a boat whistle from the canal.*

The three rooms of the top floor and a small attic space above are exposed to our view. The largest of the rooms is in the center, with two small rooms, slightly raised, on either side. On the right is a bathroom, out of sight. A narrow steep flight of stairs at the back leads up to the attic. The rooms are sparsely furnished with a few chairs, cots, a table or two. The windows are painted over, or covered with makeshift blackout curtains.[3] In the main room there is a sink, a gas ring for cooking and a woodburning stove for warmth.

The room on the left is hardly more than a closet. There is a skylight in the sloping ceiling. Directly under this room is a small steep stairwell, with steps leading down to a door. This is the only entrance from the building below. When the door is opened we see that it has been concealed on the outer side by a bookcase attached to it.

The curtain rises on an empty stage. It is late afternoon, November 1945.

The rooms are dusty, the curtains in rags. Chairs and tables are overturned.

The door at the foot of the small stairwell swings open. MR. FRANK *comes up the steps into view. He is a gentle, cultured European in his middle years. There is still a trace of a German accent in his speech.*

He stands looking slowly around, making a supreme effort at self-control. He is weak, ill. His clothes are threadbare.

After a second he drops his rucksack[4] on the couch and moves slowly about. He opens the door to one of the smaller rooms, and then abruptly closes it again, turning away. He goes to the window at the back, looking off at the Westertoren as its carillon strikes the hour of six, then he moves restlessly on.

From the street below we hear the sound of a barrel organ[5] and children's voices at play. There is a many-colored scarf hanging from a nail. MR. FRANK *takes it, putting it around his neck. As he starts back*

Literary Analysis

Staging What impression of this character do you get from the description?

**Reading Check**

When and where does the opening of this play take place?

---

1. belfry (bel´ frē) *n.* the part of a tower that holds the bells.
2. carillon (kar´ ə län´) *n.* a set of stationary bells, each producing one note of the scale.
3. blackout curtains draperies that conceal all lights that might otherwise be visible to enemy air raiders at night.
4. rucksack (ruk´ sak´) *n.* knapsack or backpack.
5. barrel organ *n.* mechanical musical instrument played by turning a crank.

for his rucksack, his eye is caught by something lying on the floor. It is a woman's white glove. He holds it in his hand and suddenly all of his self-control is gone. He breaks down, crying.

We hear footsteps on the stairs. MIEP GIES *comes up, looking for* MR. FRANK. MIEP *is a Dutch girl of about twenty-two. She wears a coat and hat, ready to go home. She is pregnant. Her attitude toward* MR. FRANK *is protective, compassionate.*]

MIEP. Are you all right, Mr. Frank?

MR. FRANK. [*Quickly controlling himself*] Yes, Miep, yes.

MIEP. Everyone in the office has gone home . . . It's after six. [*Then pleading*] Don't stay up here, Mr. Frank. What's the use of torturing yourself like this?

MR. FRANK. I've come to say good-bye . . . I'm leaving here, Miep.

MIEP. What do you mean? Where are you going? Where?

MR. FRANK. I don't know yet. I haven't decided.

MIEP. Mr. Frank, you can't leave here! This is your home! Amsterdam is your home. Your business is here, waiting for you . . . You're needed here . . . Now that the war is over, there are things that . . .

MR. FRANK. I can't stay in Amsterdam, Miep. It has too many memories for me. Everywhere there's something . . . the house we lived in . . . the school . . . that street organ playing out there . . . I'm not the person you used to know, Miep. I'm a bitter old man. [*Breaking off*] Forgive me. I shouldn't speak to you like this . . . after all that you did for us . . . the suffering . . .

MIEP. No. No. It wasn't suffering. You can't say we suffered. [*As she speaks, she straightens a chair which is overturned.*]

MR. FRANK. I know what you went through, you and Mr. Kraler. I'll remember it as long as I live. [*He gives one last look around.*] Come, Miep. [*He starts for the steps, then remembers his rucksack, going back to get it.*]

MIEP. [*Hurrying up to a cupboard*] Mr. Frank, did you see? There are some of your papers here. [*She brings a bundle of papers to him.*] We found them in a heap of rubbish on the floor after . . . after you left.

MR. FRANK. Burn them. [*He opens his rucksack to put the glove in it.*]

MIEP. But, Mr. Frank, there are letters, notes . . .

MR. FRANK. Burn them. All of them.

MIEP. Burn this? [*She hands him a paper-bound notebook.*]

MR. FRANK. [*quietly*] Anne's diary. [*He opens the diary and begins to read.*] "Monday, the sixth of July, nineteen forty-two." [*To* MIEP] Nineteen forty-two. Is it possible, Miep? . . . Only three years ago. [*As he continues his reading, he sits down on the couch.*] "Dear Diary, since you and I are going to be great friends, I will start by telling you about myself. My name is Anne Frank. I am thirteen years old. I was born in Germany the twelfth of June, nineteen twenty-nine. As my family is Jewish, we emigrated to Holland when Hitler came to power."

[*As* MR. FRANK *reads on, another voice joins his, as if coming from the air. It is* ANNE'S VOICE.]

MR. FRANK and **ANNE**. "My father started a business, importing spice and herbs. Things went well for us until nineteen forty. Then the war came, and the Dutch capitulation,[6] followed by the arrival of the Germans. Then things got very bad for the Jews."

[MR. FRANK'S VOICE *dies out.* ANNE'S VOICE *continues alone. The lights dim slowly to darkness. The curtain falls on the scene.*]

ANNE'S VOICE. You could not do this and you could not do that. They forced Father out of his business. We had to wear yellow stars.[7] I had to turn in my bike. I couldn't go to a Dutch school any more. I couldn't go to the movies, or ride in an automobile, or even on a street-car, and a million other things. But somehow we children still managed to have fun. Yesterday Father told me we were going into hiding. Where, he wouldn't say. At five o'clock this morning Mother woke me

---

6. **capitulation** (kə pich′ ə lā′ shən) *n.* surrender
7. **yellow stars** Stars of David, which are six-pointed stars that are symbols of Judaism. The Nazis ordered all Jews to wear them sewn to their clothing so that Jews could be easily identified.

Reading Strategy
Analyzing the Effect of Historical Context Anne is referring to Adolf Hitler, the German dictator who persecuted Jews and spread war through Europe. What other key details of the historical context do you learn here?

☑**Reading Check**

Who is Anne Frank and what have you learned about her?

▲ **Critical Viewing** This photograph captures the Frank family out for a walk with friends. How would you describe their mood, judging from their expressions? **[Connect]**

and told me to hurry and get dressed. I was to put on as many clothes as I could. It would look too suspicious if we walked along carrying suitcases. It wasn't until we were on our way that I learned where we were going. Our hiding place was to be upstairs in the building where Father used to have his business. Three other people were coming in with us . . . the Van Daans and their son Peter . . . Father knew the Van Daans but we had never met them . . .

[*During the last lines the curtain rises on the scene. The lights dim on.* ANNE'S VOICE *fades out.*]

Scene 2

[*It is early morning, July 1942. The rooms are bare, as before, but they are now clean and orderly.*

MR. VAN DAAN, *a tall, portly[8] man in his late forties, is in the main room, pacing up and down, nervously smoking a cigarette. His clothes and overcoat are expensive and well cut.*

MRS. VAN DAAN *sits on the couch, clutching her possessions, a hatbox, bags, etc. She is a pretty woman in her early forties. She wears a fur coat over her other clothes.*

PETER VAN DAAN *is standing at the window of the room on the right, looking down at the street below. He is a shy, awkward boy of sixteen. He wears a cap, a raincoat, and long Dutch trousers, like "plus fours."[9] At his feet is a black case, a carrier for his cat.*

The yellow Star of David is <u>conspicuous</u> on all of their clothes.]

MRS. VAN DAAN. [*Rising, nervous, excited*] Something's happened to them! I know it!

MR. VAN DAAN. Now, Kerli!

MRS. VAN DAAN. Mr. Frank said they'd be here at seven o'clock. He said . . .

MR. VAN DAAN. They have two miles to walk. You can't expect . . .

MRS. VAN DAAN. They've been picked up. That's what's happened. They've been taken . . .

[MR. VAN DAAN *indicates that he hears someone coming.*]

MR. VAN DAAN. You see?

[PETER *takes up his carrier and his schoolbag, etc., and goes into the main room as* MR. FRANK *comes up the stairwell from below.* MR. FRANK *looks much younger now. His movements are brisk, his manner confident. He wears an overcoat and carries his hat and a small cardboard box. He crosses to the* VAN DAANS, *shaking hands with each of them.*]

MR. FRANK. Mrs. Van Daan, Mr. Van Daan, Peter. [*Then, in explanation of their lateness*] There were too many of the Green Police[10] on the streets . . . we had to take the long way around.

---

8. **portly** (pôrt′ lē) *adj.* large, heavy, and dignified.
9. **plus fours** *n.* loose knickers worn for active sports.
10. **Green Police** Nazi police, who wore green uniforms.

Literary Analysis
Staging What do these details tell you about the members of the Van Daan family?

Reading Strategy
Analyzing the Effect of Historical Context What is the meaning of the yellow Star of David on the characters' clothes?

conspicuous
(kən spik′ yo͞o əs) *adj.* noticeable

[*Up the steps come* MARGOT FRANK, MRS. FRANK, MIEP *(not pregnant now) and* MR. KRALER. *All of them carry bags, packages, and so forth. The Star of David is conspicuous on all of the* FRANKS' *clothing.* MARGOT *is eighteen, beautiful, quiet, shy.* MRS. FRANK *is a young mother, gently bred, reserved. She, like* MR. FRANK, *has a slight German accent.* MR. KRALER *is a Dutchman, dependable, kindly.*

As MR. KRALER *and* MIEP *go upstage to put down their parcels,* MRS. FRANK *turns back to call* ANNE.]

MRS. FRANK. Anne?

[ANNE *comes running up the stairs. She is thirteen, quick in her movements, interested in everything,* <u>mercurial</u> *in her emotions. She wears a cape, long wool socks and carries a schoolbag.*]

MR. FRANK. [*Introducing them*] My wife, Edith. Mr. and Mrs. Van Daan . . . their son, Peter . . . my daughters, Margot and Anne.

[MRS. FRANK *hurries over, shaking hands with them.*]

[ANNE *gives a polite little curtsy as she shakes* MR. VAN DAAN'S *hand. Then she immediately starts off on a tour of investigation of her new home, going upstairs to the attic room.*

MIEP *and* MR. KRALER *are putting the various things they have brought on the shelves.*]

MR. KRALER. I'm sorry there is still so much confusion.

MR. FRANK. Please. Don't think of it. After all, we'll have plenty of leisure to arrange everything ourselves.

MIEP. [*To* MRS. FRANK] We put the stores of food you sent in here. Your drugs are here . . . soap, linen here.

MRS. FRANK. Thank you, Miep.

MIEP. I made up the beds . . . the way Mr. Frank and Mr. Kraler said. [*She starts out.*] Forgive me. I have to hurry. I've got to go to the other side of town to get some ration books[11] for you.

MRS. VAN DAAN. Ration books? If they see our names on ration books, they'll know we're here.

MR. KRALER. There isn't anything . . .

MIEP. Don't worry. Your names won't be on them. [*As she hurries out*] I'll be up later.

MR. FRANK. Thank you, Miep.

MRS. FRANK. [*To* MR. KRALER] It's illegal, then, the ration books? We've never done anything illegal.

MR. FRANK. We won't be living here exactly according to regulations.

---

11. ration books (rash′ ən books) *n.* books of stamps given to ensure the even distribution of scarce items, especially in wartime. Stamps as well as money must be given to obtain an item that is scarce.

mercurial (mər kyōōr′ ē əl) *adj.* quick or changeable in behavior

Reading Strategy
Analyzing the Effect of Historical Context What is the importance of having ration books?

✔**Reading Check**
Why are the Franks late?

The Diary of Anne Frank, Act I ◆ 705

[*As* MR. KRALER *reassures* MRS. FRANK, *he takes various small things, such as matches, soap, etc., from his pockets, handing them to her.*]

MR. KRALER. This isn't the black market,[12] Mrs. Frank. This is what we call the white market . . . helping all of the hundreds and hundreds who are hiding out in Amsterdam.

[*The carillon is heard playing the quarter-hour before eight.* MR. KRALER *looks at his watch.* ANNE *stops at the window as she comes down the stairs.*]

ANNE. It's the Westertoren!

MR. KRALER. I must go. I must be out of here and downstairs in the office before the workmen get here. [*He starts for the stairs leading out.*] Miep or I, or both of us, will be up each day to bring you food and news and find out what your needs are. Tomorrow I'll get you a better bolt for the door at the foot of the stairs. It needs a bolt that you can throw yourself and open only at our signal. [*To* MR. FRANK] Oh . . . You'll tell them about the noise?

MR. FRANK. I'll tell them.

MR. KRALER. Good-bye then for the moment. I'll come up again, after the workmen leave.

MR. FRANK. Good-bye, Mr. Kraler.

MRS. FRANK. [*Shaking his hand*] How can we thank you?

[*The others murmur their good-byes.*]

MR. KRALER. I never thought I'd live to see the day when a man like Mr. Frank would have to go into hiding. When you think—

[*He breaks off, going out.* MR. FRANK *follows him down the steps, bolting the door after him. In the interval before he returns,* PETER *goes over to* MARGOT, *shaking hands with her. As* MR. FRANK *comes back up the steps,* MRS. FRANK *questions him anxiously.*]

MRS. FRANK. What did he mean, about the noise?

MR. FRANK. First let us take off some of these clothes.

[*They all start to take off garment after garment. On each of their coats, sweaters, blouses, suits, dresses, is another yellow Star of David.* MR. *and* MRS. FRANK *are underdressed quite simply. The others wear several things, sweaters, extra dresses, bathrobes, aprons, nightgowns, etc.*]

MR. VAN DAAN. It's a wonder we weren't arrested, walking along the streets . . . Petronella with a fur coat in July . . . and that cat of Peter's crying all the way.

ANNE. A cat?

[*Finally, as they have all removed their surplus clothes, they look to* MR. FRANK, *waiting for him to speak.*]

---

12. black market illegal way of buying scarce items without ration stamps.

Literary Analysis
Staging What is the effect of hearing the church bells ringing outside the attic?

Literary Analysis
Staging Why are the Stars of David key details in the description of the characters' costumes?

MR. FRANK. Now. About the noise. While the men are in the building below, we must have complete quiet. Every sound can be heard down there, not only in the workrooms, but in the offices too. The men come at about eight-thirty, and leave at about five-thirty. So, to be perfectly safe, from eight in the morning until six in the evening we must move only when it is necessary, and then in stockinged feet. We must not speak above a whisper. We must not run any water. We cannot use the sink, or even, forgive me, the w.c.[13] The pipes go down through the workrooms. It would be heard. No trash . . .

[MR. FRANK *stops abruptly as he hears the sound of marching feet from the street below. Everyone is motionless, paralyzed with fear.* MR. FRANK *goes quietly into the room on the right to look down out of the window.* ANNE *runs after him, peering out with him. The tramping feet pass without stopping. The tension is relieved.* MR. FRANK, *followed by* ANNE, *returns to the main room and resumes his instructions to the group.*] . . . No trash must ever be thrown out which might reveal that someone is living up here . . . not even a potato paring. We must burn everything in the stove at night. This is the way we must live until it is over, if we are to survive.

[*There is silence for a second.*]

MRS. FRANK. Until it is over.

MR. FRANK. [*Reassuringly*] After six we can move about . . . we can talk and laugh and have our supper and read and play games . . . just as we would at home. [*He looks at his watch.*] And now I think it would be wise if we all went to our rooms, and were settled before eight o'clock. Mrs. Van Daan, you and your husband will be upstairs. I regret that there's no place up there for Peter. But he will be here, near us. This will be our common room, where we'll meet to talk and eat and read, like one family.

MR. VAN DAAN. And where do you and Mrs. Frank sleep?

MR. FRANK. This room is also our bedroom.

[*Together*] { **MRS. VAN DAAN.** That isn't right. We'll sleep here and you take the room upstairs.

MR. VAN DAAN. It's your place.

MR. FRANK. Please. I've thought this out for weeks. It's the best arrangement. The only arrangement.

MRS. VAN DAAN. [*To* MR. FRANK] Never, never can we thank you. [*Then to* MRS. FRANK] I don't know what would have happened to us, if it hadn't been for Mr. Frank.

MR. FRANK. You don't know how your husband helped me when I came to this country . . . knowing no one . . . not able to speak the language. I can never repay him for that. [*Going to* VAN DAAN] May I help you with your things?

---

13. w.c. water closet; bathroom.

Reading Strategy
Analyzing the Effect of Historical Context Why is the sound of marching feet so alarming to the families?

☑ **Reading Check**

When and why must the Franks and the others be quiet?

MR. VAN DAAN. No. No. [*To* MRS. VAN DAAN] Come along, *liefje*.[14]

MRS. VAN DAAN. You'll be all right, Peter? You're not afraid?

PETER. [*Embarrassed*] Please, Mother.

[*They start up the stairs to the attic room above.* MR. FRANK *turns to* MRS. FRANK.]

MR. FRANK. You too must have some rest, Edith. You didn't close your eyes last night. Nor you, Margot.

ANNE. I slept, Father. Wasn't that funny? I knew it was the last night in my own bed, and yet I slept soundly.

MR. FRANK. I'm glad, Anne. Now you'll be able to help me straighten things in here. [*To* MRS. FRANK *and* MARGOT] Come with me . . . You and Margot rest in this room for the time being.

[*He picks up their clothes, starting for the room on the right.*]

MRS. FRANK. You're sure . . . ? I could help . . . And Anne hasn't had her milk . . .

MR. FRANK. I'll give it to her. [*To* ANNE *and* PETER] Anne, Peter . . . it's best that you take off your shoes now, before you forget.

[*He leads the way to the room, followed by* MARGOT.]

MRS. FRANK. You're sure you're not tired, Anne?

ANNE. I feel fine. I'm going to help Father.

MRS. FRANK. Peter, I'm glad you are to be with us.

PETER. Yes, Mrs. Frank.

[MRS. FRANK *goes to join* MR. FRANK *and* MARGOT.]

[*During the following scene* MR. FRANK *helps* MARGOT *and* MRS. FRANK *to hang up their clothes. Then he persuades them both to lie down and rest. The* VAN DAANS *in their room above settle themselves. In the main room* ANNE *and* PETER *remove their shoes.* PETER *takes his cat out of the carrier.*]

ANNE. What's your cat's name?

PETER. Mouschi.

ANNE. Mouschi! Mouschi! Mouschi! [*She picks up the cat, walking away with it. To* PETER] I love cats. I have one . . . a darling little cat. But they made me leave her behind. I left some food and a note for the neighbors to take care of her . . . I'm going to miss her terribly. What is yours? A him or a her?

PETER. He's a tom. He doesn't like strangers. [*He takes the cat from her, putting it back in its carrier.*]

ANNE. [<u>*Unabashed*</u>] Then I'll have to stop being a stranger, won't I? Where did you go to school?

Literary Analysis
Staging How do the characters' actions in this scene move the action along?

unabashed (un ə basht´) *adj.* unashamed

---

14. liefje (lēf´ hyə) Dutch for "little love."

PETER. Jewish Secondary.

ANNE. But that's where Margot and I go! I never saw you around.

PETER. I used to see you . . . sometimes . . .

ANNE. You did?

PETER. . . . In the school yard. You were always in the middle of a bunch of kids. [*He takes a penknife from his pocket.*]

ANNE. Why didn't you ever come over?

PETER. I'm sort of a lone wolf. [*He starts to rip off his Star of David.*]

ANNE. What are you doing?

PETER. Taking it off.

ANNE. But you can't do that. They'll arrest you if you go out without your star.

[*He tosses his knife on the table.*]

PETER. Who's going out?

ANNE. Why, of course! You're right! Of course we don't need them any more. [*She picks up his knife and starts to take her star off.*] I wonder what our friends will think when we don't show up today?

PETER. I didn't have any dates with anyone.

ANNE. Oh, I did. I had a date with Jopie to go and play ping-pong at her house. Do you know Jopie de Waal?

PETER. No.

ANNE. Jopie's my best friend. I wonder what she'll think when she telephones and there's no answer? . . . Probably she'll go over to the house . . . I wonder what she'll think . . . we left everything as if we'd suddenly been called away . . . breakfast dishes in the sink . . . beds not made . . . [*As she pulls off her star, the cloth underneath shows clearly the color and form of the star.*] Look! It's still there!

[PETER *goes over to the stove with his star.*]

What're you going to do with yours?

PETER. Burn it.

ANNE. [*She starts to throw hers in, and cannot.*] It's funny, I can't throw mine away. I don't know why.

PETER. You can't throw . . . ? Something they branded you with . . . ? That they made you wear so they could spit on you?

ANNE. I know. I know. But after all, it is the Star of David, isn't it?

[*In the bedroom, right,* MARGOT *and* MRS. FRANK *are lying down.* MR. FRANK *starts quietly out.*]

PETER. Maybe it's different for a girl.

[MR. FRANK *comes into the main room.*]

Literary Analysis
Staging What is the significance of the characters ripping off their Stars of David?

Reading Check

What are Anne and Peter doing as they are talking?

MR. FRANK. Forgive me, Peter. Now let me see. We must find a bed for your cat. [*He goes to a cupboard.*] I'm glad you brought your cat. Anne was feeling so badly about hers. [*Getting a used small washtub*] Here we are. Will it be comfortable in that?

PETER. [*Gathering up his things*] Thanks.

MR. FRANK. [*Opening the door of the room on the left*] And here is your room. But I warn you, Peter, you can't grow any more. Not an inch, or you'll have to sleep with your feet out of the skylight. Are you hungry?

PETER. No.

MR. FRANK. We have some bread and butter.

PETER. No, thank you.

MR. FRANK. You can have it for luncheon then. And tonight we will have a real supper . . . our first supper together.

PETER. Thanks. Thanks. [*He goes into his room. During the following scene he arranges his possessions in his new room.*]

MR. FRANK. That's a nice boy, Peter.

ANNE. He's awfully shy, isn't he?

MR. FRANK. You'll like him, I know.

ANNE. I certainly hope so, since he's the only boy I'm likely to see for months and months.

[MR. FRANK *sits down, taking off his shoes.*]

MR. FRANK. Annele,[15] there's a box there. Will you open it?

[*He indicates a carton on the couch.* ANNE *brings it to the center table. In the street below there is the sound of children playing.*]

ANNE. [*As she opens the carton*] You know the way I'm going to think of it here? I'm going to think of it as a boarding house. A very peculiar summer boarding house, like the one that we—[*She breaks off as she pulls out some photographs.*] Father! My movie stars! I was wondering where they were! I was looking for them this morning . . . and Queen Wilhelmina![16] How wonderful!

MR. FRANK. There's something more. Go on. Look further. [*He goes over to the sink, pouring a glass of milk from a thermos bottle.*]

ANNE. [*Pulling out a pasteboard-bound book*] A diary! [*She throws her arms around her father.*] I've never had a diary. And I've always longed for one. [*She looks around the room.*] Pencil, pencil, pencil, pencil. [*She starts down the stairs.*] I'm going down to the office to get a pencil.

Literary Analysis
Staging What does this speech tell you about Mr. Frank as a person?

▼ Critical Viewing
Why do you think Jews were forced to wear yellow stars like this one? **[Infer]**

---

15. **Annele** (än′ ə lə) nickname for Anne.
16. **Queen Wilhelmina** (wil′ hel mē′ nə) Queen of the Netherlands from 1890 to 1948.

MR. FRANK. Anne! No! [*He goes after her, catching her by the arm and pulling her back.*]

ANNE. [*Startled*] But there's no one in the building now.

MR. FRANK. It doesn't matter. I don't want you ever to go beyond that door.

ANNE. [*Sobered*] Never . . . ? Not even at nighttime, when everyone is gone? Or on Sundays? Can't I go down to listen to the radio?

MR. FRANK. Never. I am sorry, Anneke.[17] It isn't safe. No, you must never go beyond that door.

[*For the first time* ANNE *realizes what "going into hiding" means.*]

ANNE. I see.

MR. FRANK. It'll be hard, I know. But always remember this, Anneke. There are no walls, there are no bolts, no locks that anyone can put on your mind. Miep will bring us books. We will read history, poetry, mythology. [*He gives her the glass of milk.*] Here's your milk. [*With his arm about her, they go over to the couch, sitting down side by side.*] As a matter of fact, between us, Anne, being here has certain advantages for you. For instance, you remember the battle you had with your mother the other day on the subject of overshoes? You said you'd rather die than wear overshoes? But in the end you had to wear them? Well now, you see, for as long as we are here you will never have to wear over-shoes! Isn't that good? And the coat that you inherited from Margot, you won't have to wear that any more. And the piano! You won't have to practice on the piano. I tell you, this is going to be a fine life for you!

[ANNE'S *panic is gone.* PETER *appears in the doorway of his room, with a saucer in his hand. He is carrying his cat.*]

PETER. I . . . I . . . I thought I'd better get some water for Mouschi before . . .

MR. FRANK. Of course.

[*As he starts toward the sink the carillon begins to chime the hour of eight. He tiptoes to the window at the back and looks down at the street below. He turns to* PETER, *indicating in pantomime that it is too late.* PETER *starts back for his room. He steps on a creaking board. The three of them are frozen for a minute in fear. As* PETER *starts away again,* ANNE *tiptoes over to him and pours some of the milk from her glass into the saucer for the cat.* PETER *squats on the floor, putting the milk before the cat.* MR. FRANK *gives* ANNE *his fountain pen, and then goes into the room at the right. For a second* ANNE *watches the cat, then she goes over to the center table, and opens her diary.*

In the room at the right, MRS. FRANK *has sat up quickly at the sound of the carillon.* MR. FRANK *comes in and sits down beside her on the settee, his arm comfortingly around her.*

---

17. **Anneke** (än´ ə kə) nickname for "Anne."

Reading Strategy
Analyzing the Effect of Historical Context Why is Anne forbidden to go downstairs?

Reading Strategy
Analyzing the Effect of Historical Context Why is eight o'clock too late for Peter to run water?

**Reading Check**

What does Anne's father give to her?

Upstairs, in the attic room, MR. *and* MRS. VAN DAAN *have hung their clothes in the closet and are now seated on the iron bed.* MRS. VAN DAAN *leans back exhausted.* MR. VAN DAAN *fans her with a newspaper.*

ANNE *starts to write in her diary. The lights dim out, the curtain falls.*

In the darkness ANNE'S VOICE *comes to us again, faintly at first, and then with growing strength.*]

ANNE'S VOICE. I expect I should be describing what it feels like to go into hiding. But I really don't know yet myself. I only know it's funny never to be able to go outdoors . . . never to breathe fresh air . . . never to run and shout and jump. It's the silence in the nights that frightens me most. Every time I hear a creak in the house, or a step on the street outside, I'm sure they're coming for us. The days aren't so bad. At least we know that Miep and Mr. Kraler are down there below us in the office. Our protectors, we call them. I asked Father what would happen to them if the Nazis found out they were hiding us. Pim said that they would suffer the same fate that we would . . . Imagine! They know this, and yet when they come up here, they're always cheerful and gay as if there were nothing in the world to bother them . . . Friday, the twenty-first of August, nineteen forty-two. Today I'm going to tell you our general news. Mother is unbearable. She insists on treating me like a baby, which I loathe. Otherwise things are going better. The weather is . . .

[*As* ANNE'S VOICE *is fading out, the curtain rises on the scene.*]

Scene 3

[*It is a little after six o'clock in the evening, two months later.*

MARGOT *is in the bedroom at the right, studying.* MR. VAN DAAN *is lying down in the attic room above.*

The rest of the "family" is in the main room. ANNE *and* PETER *sit opposite each other at the center table, where they have been doing their lessons.* MRS. FRANK *is on the couch.* MRS. VAN DAAN *is seated with her fur coat, on which she has been sewing, in her lap. None of them are wearing their shoes.*

Their eyes are on MR. FRANK, *waiting for him to give them the signal which will release them from their day-long quiet.* MR. FRANK, *his shoes in his hand, stands looking down out of the window at the back, watching to be sure that all of the workmen have left the building below.*

After a few seconds of motionless silence, MR. FRANK *turns from the window.*]

MR. FRANK. [*Quietly, to the group*] It's safe now. The last workman has left.

[*There is an immediate stir of relief.*]

ANNE. [*Her pent-up energy explodes.*] WHEE!

MR. FRANK. [*Startled, amused*] Anne!

MRS. VAN DAAN. I'm first for the w.c.

Literary Analysis
Staging How does the use of Anne's voice as she writes in the diary provide key details for readers and viewers?

Literary Analysis
Staging How do the changes in the characters' positions and activities indicate that this scene does not begin where the last one left off?

712 ◆ *Drama*

[*She hurries off to the bathroom.* MRS. FRANK *puts on her shoes and starts up to the sink to prepare supper.* ANNE *sneaks* PETER'S *shoes from under the table and hides them behind her back.* MR. FRANK *goes in to* MARGOT'S *room.*]

MR. FRANK. [*To* MARGOT] Six o'clock. School's over.

[MARGOT *gets up, stretching.* MR. FRANK *sits down to put on his shoes. In the main room* PETER *tries to find his.*]

PETER. [*To* ANNE] Have you seen my shoes?

ANNE. [*Innocently*] Your shoes?

PETER. You've taken them, haven't you?

ANNE. I don't know what you're talking about.

PETER. You're going to be sorry!

ANNE. Am I?

[PETER *goes after her.* ANNE, *with his shoes in her hand, runs from him, dodging behind her mother.*]

MRS. FRANK. [*Protesting*] Anne, dear!

PETER. Wait till I get you!

ANNE. I'm waiting!

[PETER *makes a lunge for her. They both fall to the floor.* PETER *pins her down, wrestling with her to get the shoes.*]

Don't! Don't! Peter, stop it. Ouch!

MRS. FRANK. Anne! . . . Peter!

[*Suddenly* PETER *becomes self-conscious. He grabs his shoes roughly and starts for his room.*]

ANNE. [*Following him*] Peter, where are you going? Come dance with me.

PETER. I tell you I don't know how.

ANNE. I'll teach you.

PETER. I'm going to give Mouschi his dinner.

ANNE. Can I watch?

PETER. He doesn't like people around while he eats.

ANNE. Peter, please.

PETER. No! [*He goes into his room.* ANNE *slams his door after him.*]

MRS. FRANK. Anne, dear, I think you shouldn't play like that with Peter. It's not dignified.

ANNE. Who cares if it's dignified? I don't want to be dignified.

[MR. FRANK *and* MARGOT *come from the room on the right.* MARGOT *goes to help her mother.* MR. FRANK *starts for the center table to correct* MARGOT'S *school papers.*]

Literary Analysis
Staging What does the action of this scene show about the changing relationship between Anne and Peter?

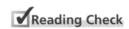**Reading Check**

What does Anne take from Peter?

MRS. FRANK. [*To* ANNE] You complain that I don't treat you like a grownup. But when I do, you resent it.

ANNE. I only want some fun . . . someone to laugh and clown with . . . After you've sat still all day and hardly moved, you've got to have some fun. I don't know what's the matter with that boy.

MR. FRANK. He isn't used to girls. Give him a little time.

ANNE. Time? Isn't two months time? I could cry. [*Catching hold of* MARGOT] Come on, Margot . . . dance with me. Come on, please.

MARGOT. I have to help with supper.

ANNE. You know we're going to forget how to dance . . . When we get out we won't remember a thing.

[*She starts to sing and dance by herself.* MR. FRANK *takes her in his arms, waltzing with her.* MRS. VAN DAAN *comes in from the bathroom.*]

MRS. VAN DAAN. Next? [*She looks around as she starts putting on her shoes.*] Where's Peter?

ANNE. [*As they are dancing*] Where would he be!

MRS. VAN DAAN. He hasn't finished his lessons, has he? His father'll kill him if he catches him in there with that cat and his work not done.

[MR. FRANK *and* ANNE *finish their dance. They bow to each other with extravagant formality.*]

Anne, get him out of there, will you?

ANNE. [*At* PETER'S *door*] Peter? Peter?

PETER. [*Opening the door a crack*] What is it?

ANNE. Your mother says to come out.

PETER. I'm giving Mouschi his dinner.

MRS. VAN DAAN. You know what your father says. [*She sits on the couch, sewing on the lining of her fur coat.*]

PETER. For heaven's sake, I haven't even looked at him since lunch.

MRS. VAN DAAN. I'm just telling you, that's all.

ANNE. I'll feed him.

PETER. I don't want you in there.

MRS. VAN DAAN. Peter!

PETER. [*To* ANNE] Then give him his dinner and come right out, you hear?

[*He comes back to the table.* ANNE *shuts the door of* PETER'S *room after her and disappears behind the curtain covering his closet.*]

MRS. VAN DAAN. [*To* PETER] Now is that any way to talk to your little girl friend?

PETER. Mother . . . for heaven's sake . . . will you please stop saying that?

MRS. VAN DAAN. Look at him blush! Look at him!

Literary Analysis
Staging How do the stage directions let you envision the action?

PETER. Please! I'm not . . . anyway . . . let me alone, will you?

MRS. VAN DAAN. He acts like it was something to be ashamed of. It's nothing to be ashamed of, to have a little girl friend.

PETER. You're crazy. She's only thirteen.

MRS. VAN DAAN. So what? And you're sixteen. Just perfect. Your father's ten years older than I am. [*To* MR. FRANK] I warn you, Mr. Frank, if this war lasts much longer, we're going to be related and then . . .

MR. FRANK. *Mazeltov!*[18]

MRS. FRANK. [*Deliberately changing the conversation*] I wonder where Miep is. She's usually so prompt.

[*Suddenly everything else is forgotten as they hear the sound of an automobile coming to a screeching stop in the street below. They are tense, motionless in their terror. The car starts away. A wave of relief sweeps over them. They pick up their occupations again.* ANNE *flings open the door of* PETER'S *room, making a dramatic entrance. She is dressed in* PETER'S *clothes.* PETER *looks at her in fury. The others are amused.*]

ANNE. Good evening, everyone. Forgive me if I don't stay. [*She jumps up on a chair.*] I have a friend waiting for me in there. My friend Tom. Tom Cat. Some people say that we look alike. But Tom has the most beautiful whiskers, and I have only a little fuzz. I am hoping . . . in time . . .

PETER. All right, Mrs. Quack Quack!

ANNE. [*Outraged—jumping down*] Peter!

PETER. I heard about you . . . How you talked so much in class they called you Mrs. Quack Quack. How Mr. Smitter made you write a composition . . . "'Quack, Quack,' said Mrs. Quack Quack."

ANNE. Well, go on. Tell them the rest. How it was so good he read it out loud to the class and then read it to all his other classes!

PETER. Quack! Quack! Quack . . . Quack . . . Quack . . .

[ANNE *pulls off the coat and trousers.*]

ANNE. You are the most intolerable, <u>insufferable</u> boy I've ever met!

[*She throws the clothes down the stairwell.* PETER *goes down after them.*]

PETER. Quack, Quack, Quack!

MRS. VAN DAAN. [*To* ANNE] That's right, Anneke! Give it to him!

ANNE. With all the boys in the world . . . Why I had to get locked up with one like you! . . .

PETER. Quack, Quack, Quack, and from now on stay out of my room!

[*As* PETER *passes her,* ANNE *puts out her foot, tripping him. He picks himself up, and goes on into his room.*]

---

18. **Mazeltov** (mä′ zəl tōv′) "good luck" in Hebrew and Yiddish.

Reading Strategy
Evaluating the Effect of Historical Context Why does the sound of the car stopping frighten everyone?

insufferable
(in suf′ ər ə bəl) *adj.*
unbearable

Reading Check

How does Peter react when his mother calls Anne his girlfriend?

MRS. FRANK. [*Quietly*] Anne, dear . . . your hair. [*She feels* ANNE'S *forehead.*] You're warm. Are you feeling all right?

ANNE. Please, Mother. [*She goes over to the center table, slipping into her shoes.*]

MRS. FRANK. [*Following her*] You haven't a fever, have you?

ANNE. [*Pulling away*] No. No.

MRS. FRANK. You know we can't call a doctor here, ever. There's only one thing to do . . . watch carefully. Prevent an illness before it comes. Let me see your tongue.

ANNE. Mother, this is perfectly absurd.

MRS. FRANK. Anne, dear, don't be such a baby. Let me see your tongue. [*As* ANNE *refuses,* MRS. FRANK *appeals to* MR. FRANK] Otto . . . ?

MR. FRANK. You hear your mother, Anne.

[ANNE *flicks out her tongue for a second, then turns away.*]

MRS. FRANK. Come on—open up! [*As* ANNE *opens her mouth very wide*] You seem all right . . . but perhaps an aspirin . . .

MRS. VAN DAAN. For heaven's sake, don't give that child any pills. I waited for fifteen minutes this morning for her to come out of the w.c.

ANNE. I was washing my hair!

MR. FRANK. I think there's nothing the matter with our Anne that a ride on her bike, or a visit with her friend Jopie de Waal wouldn't cure. Isn't that so, Anne?

[MR. VAN DAAN *comes down into the room. From outside we hear faint sounds of bombers* going over and a burst of ack-ack.*][19]

MR. VAN DAAN. Miep not come yet?

MRS. VAN DAAN. The workmen just left, a little while ago.

MR. VAN DAAN. What's for dinner tonight?

MRS. VAN DAAN. Beans.

MR. VAN DAAN. Not again!

MRS. VAN DAAN. Poor Putti! I know. But what can we do? That's all that Miep brought us.

[MR. VAN DAAN *starts to pace, his hands behind his back.* ANNE *follows behind him, imitating him.*]

ANNE. We are now in what is known as the "bean cycle." Beans boiled, beans en casserole, beans with strings, beans without strings . . .

---

19. **ack-ack** (ak´ ak´) *n.* slang for an anti-aircraft gun's fire.

Literature in context World Events Connection

◆ Air Raids

When Anne's family hears the sound of bombers and anti-aircraft guns overhead, they are hearing a familiar sound of the time. World War II was the first major war to involved the massive aerial bombardment of cities. Often, the first sound to alert city residents to an air attack was the wailing of an air raid siren. This meant, "Take cover!" Then the drone of bomber engines and the dull booming of anti-aircraft fire would take over— the sounds that Anne hears. Finally, there might be the sound of bombs exploding or a plane going down in flames. These were sounds heard by many families, including Anne's throughout Europe. This was the soundtrack of war.

Bombers like this B-17 Flying Fortress filled the skies over Germany during World War II.

Reading Strategy
Analyzing the Effect of Historical Context What is the effect of the distant sounds of a bombing raid?

[PETER *has come out of his room. He slides into his place at the table, becoming immediately absorbed in his studies.*]

MR. VAN DAAN. [*To* PETER] I saw you . . . in there, playing with your cat.

MRS. VAN DAAN. He just went in for a second, putting his coat away. He's been out here all the time, doing his lessons.

MR. FRANK. [*Looking up from the papers*] Anne, you got an excellent in your history paper today . . . and very good in Latin.

ANNE. [*Sitting beside him*] How about algebra?

MR. FRANK. I'll have to make a confession. Up until now I've managed to stay ahead of you in algebra. Today you caught up with me. We'll leave it to Margot to correct.

ANNE. Isn't algebra *vile*, Pim!

MR. FRANK. Vile!

MARGOT. [*To* MR. FRANK] How did I do?

ANNE. [*Getting up*] Excellent, excellent, excellent, excellent!

MR. FRANK. [*To* MARGOT] You should have used the subjunctive[20] here . . .

MARGOT. Should I? . . . I thought . . . look here . . . I didn't use it here . . .

[*The two become absorbed in the papers.*]

ANNE. Mrs. Van Daan, may I try on your coat?

MRS. FRANK. No, Anne.

MRS. VAN DAAN. [*Giving it to* ANNE] It's all right . . . but careful with it. [ANNE *puts it on and struts with it.*] My father gave me that the year before he died. He always bought the best that money could buy.

ANNE. Mrs. Van Daan, did you have a lot of boy friends before you were married?

MRS. FRANK. Anne, that's a personal question. It's not courteous to ask personal questions.

MRS. VAN DAAN. Oh I don't mind. [*To* ANNE] Our house was always swarming with boys. When I was a girl we had . . .

MR. VAN DAAN. Oh, no. Not again!

MRS. VAN DAAN. [*Good-humored*] Shut up!

[*Without a pause, to* ANNE, MR. VAN DAAN *mimics* MRS. VAN DAAN, *speaking the first few words in unison with her.*]

One summer we had a big house in Hilversum. The boys came buzzing round like bees around a jam pot. And when I was sixteen! . . . We were wearing our skirts very short those days and I had good-looking legs. [*She pulls up her skirt, going to* MR. FRANK.] I still have 'em.

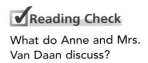

Reading Check

What do Anne and Mrs. Van Daan discuss?

---

20. subjunctive (səb juŋk′ tiv) *n.* a particular form of a verb.

I may not be as pretty as I used to be, but I still have my legs. How about it, Mr. Frank?

MR. VAN DAAN. All right. All right. We see them.

MRS. VAN DAAN. I'm not asking you. I'm asking Mr. Frank.

PETER. Mother, for heaven's sake.

MRS. VAN DAAN. Oh, I embarrass you, do I? Well, I just hope the girl you marry has as good. [*Then to* ANNE] My father used to worry about me, with so many boys hanging round. He told me, if any of them gets fresh, you say to him . . . "Remember, Mr. So-and-So, remember I'm a lady."

ANNE. "Remember, Mr. So-and-So, remember I'm a lady." [*She gives* MRS. VAN DAAN *her coat.*]

MR. VAN DAAN. Look at you, talking that way in front of her! Don't you know she puts it all down in that diary?

MRS. VAN DAAN. So, if she does? I'm only telling the truth!

[ANNE *stretches out, putting her ear to the floor, listening to what is going on below. The sound of the bombers fades away.*]

MRS. FRANK. [*Setting the table*] Would you mind, Peter, if I moved you over to the couch?

ANNE. [*Listening*] Miep must have the radio on.

[PETER *picks up his papers, going over to the couch beside* MRS. VAN DAAN.]

MR. VAN DAAN. [*Accusingly, to* PETER] Haven't you finished yet?

PETER. No.

MR. VAN DAAN. You ought to be ashamed of yourself.

PETER. All right. All right. I'm a dunce. I'm a hopeless case. Why do I go on?

MRS. VAN DAAN. You're not hopeless. Don't talk that way. It's just that you haven't anyone to help you, like the girls have. [*To* MR. FRANK] Maybe you could help him, Mr. Frank?

MR. FRANK. I'm sure that his father . . . ?

MR. VAN DAAN. Not me. I can't do anything with him. He won't listen to me. You go ahead . . . if you want.

MR. FRANK. [*Going to* PETER] What about it, Peter? Shall we make our school coeducational?

MRS. VAN DAAN. [*Kissing* MR. FRANK] You're an angel, Mr. Frank. An angel. I don't know why I didn't meet you before I met that one there. Here, sit down, Mr. Frank . . . [*She forces him down on the couch beside* PETER.] Now, Peter, you listen to Mr. Frank.

MR. FRANK. It might be better for us to go into Peter's room.

[PETER *jumps up eagerly, leading the way.*]

Literary Analysis

Staging What do the stage directions reveal about the Van Daans' relationship?

Literary Analysis

Staging What more do her actions show about Mrs. Van Daan?

MRS. VAN DAAN. That's right. You go in there, Peter. You listen to Mr. Frank. Mr. Frank is a highly educated man.

[*As* MR. FRANK *is about to follow* PETER *into his room,* MRS. FRANK *stops him and wipes the lipstick from his lips. Then she closes the door after them.*]

ANNE. [*On the floor, listening*] Shh! I can hear a man's voice talking.

MR. VAN DAAN. [*To* ANNE] Isn't it bad enough here without your sprawling all over the place?

[ANNE *sits up.*]

MRS. VAN DAAN. [*To* MR. VAN DAAN] If you didn't smoke so much, you wouldn't be so bad-tempered.

MR. VAN DAAN. Am I smoking? Do you see me smoking?

MRS. VAN DAAN. Don't tell me you've used up all those cigarettes.

MR. VAN DAAN. One package. Miep only brought me one package.

MRS. VAN DAAN. It's a filthy habit anyway. It's a good time to break yourself.

MR. VAN DAAN. Oh, stop it, please.

MRS. VAN DAAN. You're smoking up all our money. You know that, don't you?

MR. VAN DAAN. Will you shut up?

[*During this,* MRS. FRANK *and* MARGOT *have studiously kept their eyes down. But* ANNE, *seated on the floor, has been following the discussion interestedly.* MR. VAN DAAN *turns to see her staring up at him.*]

And what are you staring at?

ANNE. I never heard grownups quarrel before. I thought only children quarreled.

MR. VAN DAAN. This isn't a quarrel! It's a discussion. And I never heard children so rude before.

ANNE. [*Rising, indignantly*] I, rude!

MR. VAN DAAN. Yes!

MRS. FRANK. [*Quickly*] Anne, will you get me my knitting?

[ANNE *goes to get it.*]

I must remember, when Miep comes, to ask her to bring me some more wool.

MARGOT. [*Going to her room*] I need some hairpins and some soap. I made a list. [*She goes into her bedroom to get the list.*]

MRS. FRANK. [*To* ANNE] Have you some library books for Miep when she comes?

▼ Critical Viewing
The photograph shows the front view of the building in which the Franks hid. Why was this location a good one for hiding? **[Assess]**

✓ Reading Check
What happens between Mr. and Mrs. Van Daan in this scene?

ANNE. It's a wonder that Miep has a life of her own, the way we make her run errands for us. Please, Miep, get me some starch. Please take my hair out and have it cut. Tell me all the latest news, Miep. [*She goes over, kneeling on the couch beside* MRS. VAN DAAN] Did you know she was engaged? His name is Dirk, and Miep's afraid the Nazis will ship him off to Germany to work in one of their war plants. That's what they're doing with some of the young Dutchmen . . . they pick them up off the streets—

MR. VAN DAAN. [*Interrupting*] Don't you ever get tired of talking? Suppose you try keeping still for five minutes. Just five minutes.

[*He starts to pace again. Again* ANNE *follows him, mimicking him.* MRS. FRANK *jumps up and takes her by the arm up to the sink, and gives her a glass of milk.*]

MRS. FRANK. Come here, Anne. It's time for your glass of milk.

MR. VAN DAAN. Talk, talk, talk. I never heard such a child. Where is my . . . ? Every evening it's the same talk, talk, talk. [*He looks around.*] Where is my . . . ?

MRS. VAN DAAN. What're you looking for?

MR. VAN DAAN. My pipe. Have you seen my pipe?

MRS. VAN DAAN. What good's a pipe? You haven't got any tobacco.

MR. VAN DAAN. At least I'll have something to hold in my mouth! [*Opening* MARGOT's *bedroom door*] Margot, have you seen my pipe?

MARGOT. It was on the table last night.

[ANNE *puts her glass of milk on the table and picks up his pipe, hiding it behind her back.*]

MR. VAN DAAN. I know. I know. Anne, did you see my pipe? . . . Anne!

MRS. FRANK. Anne, Mr. Van Daan is speaking to you.

ANNE. Am I allowed to talk now?

MR. VAN DAAN. You're the most aggravating . . . The trouble with you is, you've been spoiled. What you need is a good old-fashioned spanking.

ANNE. [*Mimicking* MRS. VAN DAAN] "Remember, Mr. So-and-So, remember I'm a lady." [*She thrusts the pipe into his mouth, then picks up her glass of milk.*]

MR. VAN DAAN. [*Restraining himself with difficulty*] Why aren't you nice and quiet like your sister Margot? Why do you have to show off all the time? Let me give you a little advice, young lady. Men don't like that kind of thing in a girl. You know that? A man likes a girl who'll listen to him once in a while . . . a domestic girl, who'll keep her house shining for her husband . . . who loves to cook and sew and . . .

ANNE. I'd cut my throat first! I'd open my veins! I'm going to be remarkable! I'm going to Paris . . .

Literary Analysis
Staging What do the stage directions reveal about the characters here?

Reading Strategy
Analyzing the Effect of Historical Context What cultural attitudes does Mr. Van Daan show in this speech?

MR. VAN DAAN. [*Scoffingly*] Paris!

ANNE. . . . to study music and art.

MR. VAN DAAN. Yeah! Yeah!

ANNE. I'm going to be a famous dancer or singer . . . or something wonderful.

[*She makes a wide gesture, spilling the glass of milk on the fur coat in* MRS. VAN DAAN'S *lap.* MARGOT *rushes quickly over with a towel.* ANNE *tries to brush the milk off with her skirt.*]

MRS. VAN DAAN. Now look what you've done . . . you clumsy little fool! My beautiful fur coat my father gave me . . .

ANNE. I'm so sorry.

MRS. VAN DAAN. What do you care? It isn't yours . . . So go on, ruin it! Do you know what that coat cost? Do you? And now look at it! Look at it!

ANNE. I'm very, very sorry.

MRS. VAN DAAN. I could kill you for this. I could just kill you!

[MRS. VAN DAAN *goes up the stairs, clutching the coat.* MR. VAN DAAN *starts after her.*]

MR. VAN DAAN. Petronella . . . *Liefje! Liefje!* . . . Come back . . . the supper . . . come back!

MRS. FRANK. Anne, you must not behave in that way.

ANNE. It was an accident. Anyone can have an accident.

MRS. FRANK. I don't mean that. I mean the answering back. You must not answer back. They are our guests. We must always show the greatest courtesy to them. We're all living under terrible tension.

[*She stops as* MARGOT *indicates that* VAN DAAN *can hear. When he is gone, she continues.*]

That's why we must control ourselves . . . You don't hear Margot getting into arguments with them, do you? Watch Margot. She's always courteous with them. Never familiar. She keeps her distance. And they respect her for it. Try to be like Margot.

ANNE. And have them walk all over me, the way they do her? No, thanks!

MRS. FRANK. I'm not afraid that anyone is going to walk all over you, Anne. I'm afraid for other people, that you'll walk on them. I don't know what happens to you, Anne. You are wild, self-willed. If I had ever talked to my mother as you talk to me . . .

ANNE. Things have changed. People aren't like that any more. "Yes, Mother." "No, Mother." "Anything you say, Mother." I've got to fight things out for myself! Make something of myself!

MRS. FRANK. It isn't necessary to fight to do it. Margot doesn't fight, and isn't she . . . ?

Reading Strategy
Analyzing the Effect of Historical Context How is the characters' situation affecting them?

Reading Check

What happens to Mrs. Van Daan's fur coat and how does she react?

ANNE. [*Violently rebellious*] Margot! Margot! Margot! That's all I hear from everyone . . . how wonderful Margot is . . . "Why aren't you like Margot?"

MARGOT. [*Protesting*] Oh, come on, Anne, don't be so . . .

ANNE. [*Paying no attention*] Everything she does is right, and everything I do is wrong! I'm the goat around here! . . . You're all against me! . . . And you worst of all!

[*She rushes off into her room and throws herself down on the settee, stifling her sobs.* MRS. FRANK *sighs and starts toward the stove.*]

MRS. FRANK. [*To* MARGOT] Let's put the soup on the stove . . . if there's anyone who cares to eat. Margot, will you take the bread out?

[MARGOT *gets the bread from the cupboard.*]

I don't know how we can go on living this way . . . I can't say a word to Anne . . . she flies at me . . .

MARGOT. You know Anne. In half an hour she'll be out here, laughing and joking.

MRS. FRANK. And . . . [*She makes a motion upwards, indicating the* VAN DAANS.] . . . I told your father it wouldn't work . . . but no . . . no . . . he had to ask them, he said . . . he owed it to him, he said. Well, he knows now that I was right! These quarrels! . . . This bickering!

MARGOT. [*With a warning look*] Shush. Shush.

[*The buzzer for the door sounds.* MRS. FRANK *gasps, startled.*]

MRS. FRANK. Every time I hear that sound, my heart stops!

MARGOT. [*Starting for* PETER'S *door*] It's Miep. [*She knocks at the door.*] Father?

[MR. FRANK *comes quickly from* PETER'S *room.*]

MR. FRANK. Thank you, Margot. [*As he goes down the steps to open the outer door*] Has everyone his list?

MARGOT. I'll get my books. [*Giving her mother a list*] Here's your list.

[MARGOT *goes into her and* ANNE'S *bedroom on the right.* ANNE *sits up, hiding her tears, as* MARGOT *comes in.*]

Miep's here.

[MARGOT *picks up her books and goes back.* ANNE *hurries over to the mirror, smoothing her hair.*]

MR. VAN DAAN. [*Coming down the stairs*] Is it Miep?

MARGOT. Yes. Father's gone down to let her in.

MR. VAN DAAN. At last I'll have some cigarettes!

MRS. FRANK. [*To* MR. VAN DAAN] I can't tell you how unhappy I am about Mrs. Van Daan's coat. Anne should never have touched it.

MR. VAN DAAN. She'll be all right.

MRS. FRANK. Is there anything I can do?

MR. VAN DAAN. Don't worry.

[*He turns to meet* MIEP. *But it is not* MIEP *who comes up the steps. It is* MR. KRALER, *followed by* MR. FRANK. *Their faces are grave.* ANNE *comes from the bedroom.* PETER *comes from his room.*]

MRS. FRANK. Mr. Kraler!

MR. VAN DAAN. How are you, Mr. Kraler?

MARGOT. This is a surprise.

MRS. FRANK. When Mr. Kraler comes, the sun begins to shine.

MR. VAN DAAN. Miep is coming?

MR. KRALER. Not tonight.

[KRALER *goes to* MARGOT *and* MRS. FRANK *and* ANNE, *shaking hands with them.*]

MRS. FRANK. Wouldn't you like a cup of coffee? . . . Or, better still, will you have supper with us?

MR. FRANK. Mr. Kraler has something to talk over with us. Something has happened, he says, which demands an immediate decision.

MRS. FRANK. [*Fearful*] What is it?

[MR. KRALER *sits down on the couch. As he talks he takes bread, cabbages, milk, etc., from his briefcase, giving them to* MARGOT *and* ANNE *to put away.*]

MR. KRALER. Usually, when I come up here, I try to bring you some bit of good news. What's the use of telling you the bad news when there's nothing that you can do about it? But today something has happened . . . Dirk . . . Miep's Dirk, you know, came to me just now. He tells me that he has a Jewish friend living near him. A dentist. He says he's in trouble. He begged me, could I do anything for this man? Could I find him a hiding place? . . . So I've come to you . . . I know it's a terrible thing to ask of you, living as you are, but would you take him in with you?

MR. FRANK. Of course we will.

MR. KRALER. [*Rising*] It'll be just for a night or two . . . until I find some other place. This happened so suddenly that I didn't know where to turn.

MR. FRANK. Where is he?

MR. KRALER. Downstairs in the office.

MR. FRANK. Good. Bring him up.

MR. KRALER. His name is Dussel . . . Jan Dussel.

▲ **Critical Viewing**
What kind of personality would you say Mrs. Frank had, based on details in this photograph? [**Infer**]

✔**Reading Check**
What does Mr. Kraler ask of Mr. Frank?

The Diary of Anne Frank, Act I ◆ 723

MR. FRANK. Dussel . . . I think I know him.

MR. KRALER. I'll get him.

[*He goes quickly down the steps and out.* MR. FRANK *suddenly becomes conscious of the others.*]

MR. FRANK. Forgive me. I spoke without consulting you. But I knew you'd feel as I do.

MR. VAN DAAN. There's no reason for you to consult anyone. This is your place. You have a right to do exactly as you please. The only thing I feel . . . there's so little food as it is . . . and to take in another person . . .

[PETER *turns away, ashamed of his father.*]

MR. FRANK. We can stretch the food a little. It's only for a few days.

MR. VAN DAAN. You want to make a bet?

MRS. FRANK. I think it's fine to have him. But, Otto, where are you going to put him? Where?

PETER. He can have my bed. I can sleep on the floor. I wouldn't mind.

MR. FRANK. That's good of you, Peter. But your room's too small . . . even for *you.*

ANNE. I have a much better idea. I'll come in here with you and Mother, and Margot can take Peter's room and Peter can go in our room with Mr. Dussel.

MARGOT. That's right. We could do that.

MR. FRANK. No, Margot. You mustn't sleep in that room . . . neither you nor Anne. Mouschi has caught some rats in there. Peter's brave. He doesn't mind.

ANNE. Then how about *this?* I'll come in here with you and Mother, and Mr. Dussel can have my bed.

MRS. FRANK. *No. No. No!* Margot will come in here with us and he can have her bed. It's the only way. Margot, bring your things in here. Help her, Anne.

[MARGOT *hurries into her room to get her things.*]

ANNE. [*To her mother*] Why Margot? Why can't I come in here?

MRS. FRANK. Because it wouldn't be proper for Margot to sleep with a . . . Please, Anne. Don't argue. Please.

[ANNE *starts slowly away.*]

MR. FRANK. [*To* ANNE] You don't mind sharing your room with Mr. Dussel, do you, Anne?

ANNE. No. No, of course not.

MR. FRANK. Good.

Reading Strategy

Analyzing the Effect of Historical Context Why does Mrs. Frank agree to allow another person to come to the hiding place when she has just finished complaining that it is too crowded?

[ANNE *goes off into her bedroom, helping* MARGOT. MR. FRANK *starts to search in the cupboards.*]

Where's the cognac?

MRS. FRANK. It's there. But, Otto, I was saving it in case of illness.

MR. FRANK. I think we couldn't find a better time to use it. Peter, will you get five glasses for me?

[PETER *goes for the glasses.* MARGOT *comes out of her bedroom, carrying her possessions, which she hangs behind a curtain in the main room.* MR. FRANK *finds the cognac and pours it into the five glasses that* PETER *brings him.* MR. VAN DAAN *stands looking on sourly.* MRS. VAN DAAN *comes downstairs and looks around at all the bustle.*]

MRS. VAN DAAN. What's happening? What's going on?

MR. VAN DAAN. Someone's moving in with us.

MRS. VAN DAAN. In here? You're joking.

MARGOT. It's only for a night or two . . . until Mr. Kraler finds him another place.

MR. VAN DAAN. Yeah! Yeah!

[MR. FRANK *hurries over as* MR. KRALER *and* DUSSEL *come up.* DUSSEL *is a man in his late fifties,* meticulous, *finicky . . . bewildered now. He wears a raincoat. He carries a briefcase, stuffed full, and a small medicine case.*]

MR. FRANK. Come in, Mr. Dussel.

MR. KRALER. This is Mr. Frank.

DUSSEL. Mr. Otto Frank?

MR. FRANK. Yes. Let me take your things. [*He takes the hat and briefcase, but* DUSSEL *clings to his medicine case.*] This is my wife Edith . . . Mr. and Mrs. Van Daan . . . their son, Peter . . . and my daughters, Margot and Anne.

[DUSSEL *shakes hands with everyone.*]

MR. KRALER. Thank you, Mr. Frank. Thank you all. Mr. Dussel, I leave you in good hands. Oh . . . Dirk's coat.

[DUSSEL *hurriedly takes off the raincoat, giving it to* MR. KRALER. *Underneath is his white dentist's jacket, with a yellow Star of David on it.*]

DUSSEL. [*To* MR. KRALER] What can I say to thank you . . . ?

MRS. FRANK. [*To* DUSSEL] Mr. Kraler and Miep . . . They're our life line. Without them we couldn't live.

MR. KRALER. Please. Please. You make us seem very heroic. It isn't that at all. We simply don't like the Nazis. [*To* MR. FRANK, *who offers him a drink*] No, thanks. [*Then going on*] We don't like their methods. We don't like . . .

Literary Analysis

Stage Directions What does this description show about Mr. Dussel?

meticulous (mə tik´ yoo ləs) *adj.* extremely careful about details

✔**Reading Check**

Who is Mr. Dussel and why does he come to live with the Franks?

The Diary of Anne Frank, Act I ◆ 725

MR. FRANK. [*Smiling*] I know. I know. "No one's going to tell us Dutchmen what to do with our Jews!"

MR. KRALER. [*To* DUSSEL] Pay no attention to Mr. Frank. I'll be up tomorrow to see that they're treating you right. [*To* MR. FRANK] Don't trouble to come down again. Peter will bolt the door after me, won't you, Peter?

PETER. Yes, sir.

MR. FRANK. Thank you, Peter. I'll do it.

MR. KRALER. Good night. Good night.

GROUP. Good night, Mr. Kraler. We'll see you tomorrow, etc., etc.

[MR. KRALER *goes out with* MR. FRANK, MRS. FRANK *gives each one of the "grownups" a glass of cognac.*]

MRS. FRANK. Please, Mr. Dussel, sit down.

[MR. DUSSEL *sinks into a chair.* MRS. FRANK *gives him a glass of cognac.*]

DUSSEL. I'm dreaming. I know it. I can't believe my eyes. **Mr.** Otto Frank here! [*To* MRS. FRANK] You're not in Switzerland* then? A woman told me . . . She said she'd gone to your house . . . the door was open, everything was in disorder, dishes in the sink. She said she found a piece of paper in the wastebasket with an address scribbled on it . . . an address in Zurich. She said you must have escaped to Zurich.

ANNE. Father put that there purposely . . . just so people would think that very thing!

DUSSEL. And you've been *here* all the time?

MRS. FRANK. All the time . . . ever since July.

[ANNE *speaks to her father as he comes back.*]

ANNE. It worked, Pim . . . the address you left! Mr. Dussel says that people believe we escaped to Switzerland.

MR. FRANK. I'm glad. . . . And now let's have a little drink to welcome Mr. Dussel.

[*Before they can drink,* MR. DUSSEL *bolts his drink.* MR. FRANK *smiles and raises his glass.*]

To Mr. Dussel. Welcome. We're very honored to have you with us.

MRS. FRANK. To Mr. Dussel, welcome.

[*The* VAN DAANS *murmur a welcome. The "grownups" drink.*]

MRS. VAN DAAN. Um. That was good.

MR. VAN DAAN. Did Mr. Kraler warn you that you won't get much to eat

here? You can imagine . . . three ration books among the seven of us . . . and now you make eight.

[PETER *walks away, humiliated. Outside a street organ is heard dimly.*]

DUSSEL. [*Rising*] Mr. Van Daan, you don't realize what is happening outside that you should warn me of a thing like that. You don't realize what's going on . . .

[*As* MR. VAN DAAN *starts his characteristic pacing,* DUSSEL *turns to speak to the others.*]

Right here in Amsterdam every day hundreds of Jews disappear . . . They surround a block and search house by house. Children come home from school to find their parents gone. Hundreds are being deported . . . people that you and I know . . . the Hallensteins . . . the Wessels . . .

MRS. FRANK. [*In tears*] Oh, no. No!

DUSSEL. They get their call-up notice . . . come to the Jewish theater on such and such a day and hour . . . bring only what you can carry in a rucksack. And if you refuse the call-up notice, then they come and drag you from your home and ship you off to Mauthausen.[21] The death camp!

MRS. FRANK. We didn't know that things had got so much worse.

DUSSEL. Forgive me for speaking so.

ANNE. [*Coming to* DUSSEL] Do you know the de Waals? . . . What's become of them? Their daughter Jopie and I are in the same class. Jopie's my best friend.

DUSSEL. They are gone.

ANNE. Gone?

DUSSEL. With all the others.

ANNE. Oh, no. Not Jopie!

[*She turns away, in tears.* MRS. FRANK *motions to* MARGOT *to comfort her.* MARGOT *goes to* ANNE, *putting her arms comfortingly around her.*]

MRS. VAN DAAN. There were some people called Wagner. They lived near us . . . ?

MR. FRANK. [*Interrupting, with a glance at* ANNE] I think we should put this off until later. We all have many questions we want to ask . . . But I'm sure that Mr. Dussel would like to get settled before supper.

DUSSEL. Thank you. I would. I brought very little with me.

MR. FRANK. [*Giving him his hat and briefcase*] I'm sorry we can't give you a room alone. But I hope you won't be too uncomfortable. We've had to make strict rules here . . . a schedule of hours . . . We'll tell you after supper. Anne, would you like to take Mr. Dussel to his room?

---

21. Mauthausen (maùt´ haù´ zən) village in Austria that was the site of a Nazi concentration camp.

Reading Strategy
Analyzing the Effect of Historical Context How does Dussel's news affect the people who have been in hiding?

Reading Check

What kind of news does Dussel bring and how does it affect Anne?

ANNE. [*Controlling her tears*] If you'll come with me, Mr. Dussel? [*She starts for her room.*]

DUSSEL. [*Shaking hands with each in turn*] Forgive me if I haven't really expressed my gratitude to all of you. This has been such a shock to me. I'd always thought of myself as Dutch. I was born in Holland. My father was born in Holland, and my grandfather. And now . . . after all these years . . . [*He breaks off.*] If you'll excuse me.

[DUSSEL *gives a little bow and hurries off after* ANNE. MR. FRANK *and the others are subdued.*]

ANNE. [*Turning on the light*] Well, here we are.

[DUSSEL *looks around the room. In the main room* MARGOT *speaks to her mother.*]

MARGOT. The news sounds pretty bad, doesn't it? It's so different from what Mr. Kraler tells us. Mr. Kraler says things are improving.

MR. VAN DAAN. I like it better the way Kraler tells it.

[*They resume their occupations, quietly.* PETER *goes off into his room. In* ANNE'S *room,* ANNE *turns to* DUSSEL.]

ANNE. You're going to share the room with me.

DUSSEL. I'm a man who's always lived alone. I haven't had to adjust myself to others. I hope you'll bear with me until I learn.

ANNE. Let me help you. [*She takes his briefcase.*] Do you always live all alone? Have you no family at all?

DUSSEL. No one. [*He opens his medicine case and spreads his bottles on the dressing table.*]

ANNE. How dreadful. You must be terribly lonely.

DUSSEL. I'm used to it.

ANNE. I don't think I could ever get used to it. Didn't you even have a pet? A cat, or a dog?

DUSSEL. I have an allergy for fur-bearing animals. They give me asthma.

ANNE. Oh, dear. Peter has a cat.

DUSSEL. Here? He has it here?

ANNE. Yes. But we hardly ever see it. He keeps it in his room all the time. I'm sure it will be all right.

DUSSEL. Let us hope so. [*He takes some pills to fortify himself.*]

ANNE. That's Margot's bed, where you're going to sleep. I sleep on the sofa there. [*Indicating the clothes hooks on the wall*] We cleared these off for your things. [*She goes over to the window.*] The best part about this room . . . you can look down and see a bit of the street and the canal. There's a houseboat . . . you can see the end of it . . . a bargeman lives there with his family . . . They have a baby and he's just beginning to walk and I'm so afraid he's going to fall into the canal some day. I watch him. . . .

▲ **Critical Viewing**
What details of Dussel's appearance suggest that he is meticulous, as described in the stage directions on page 725? **[Analyze]**

728 ◆ *Drama*

DUSSEL. [*Interrupting*] Your father spoke of a schedule.

ANNE. [*Coming away from the window*] Oh, yes. It's mostly about the times we have to be quiet. And times for the w.c. You can use it now if you like.

DUSSEL. [*Stiffly*] No, thank you.

ANNE. I suppose you think it's awful, my talking about a thing like that. But you don't know how important it can get to be, especially when you're frightened . . . About this room, the way Margot and I did . . . she had it to herself in the afternoons for studying, reading . . . lessons, you know . . . and I took the mornings. Would that be all right with you?

DUSSEL. I'm not at my best in the morning.

ANNE. You stay here in the mornings then. I'll take the room in the afternoons.

DUSSEL. Tell me, when you're in here, what happens to me? Where am I spending my time? In there, with all the people?

ANNE. Yes.

DUSSEL. I see. I see.

ANNE. We have supper at half past six.

DUSSEL. [*Going over to the sofa*] Then, if you don't mind . . . I like to lie down quietly for ten minutes before eating. I find it helps the digestion.

ANNE. Of course. I hope I'm not going to be too much of a bother to you. I seem to be able to get everyone's back up.

[DUSSEL *lies down on the sofa, curled up, his back to her.*]

DUSSEL. I always get along very well with children. My patients all bring their children to me, because they know I get on well with them. So don't you worry about that.

[ANNE *leans over him, taking his hand and shaking it gratefully.*]

ANNE. Thank you. Thank you, Mr. Dussel.

[*The lights dim to darkness. The curtain falls on the scene.* ANNE'S *voice comes to us faintly at first, and then with increasing power.*]

ANNE'S VOICE. . . . And yesterday I finished Cissy Van Marxvelt's latest book. I think she is a first-class writer. I shall definitely let my children read her. Monday the twenty-first of September, nineteen forty-two. Mr. Dussel and I had another battle yesterday. Yes, Mr. Dussel! According to him, nothing, I repeat . . . nothing, is right about me . . . my appearance, my character, my manners. While he was going on at me I thought . . . sometime I'll give you such a smack that you'll fly right up to the ceiling! Why is it that every grownup thinks he knows the way to bring up children? Particularly the grownups that never had any. I keep wishing that Peter was a girl instead of a boy. Then I would have someone to talk to. Margot's a darling, but she takes everything too seriously. To pause for a moment on the subject of Mrs. Van Daan. I must tell you that

Reading Strategy
Analyzing the Effect of Historical Context How long have the families been in hiding?

**Reading Check**

Which aspects of her daily routine does Anne discuss with Dussel?

her attempts to flirt with father are getting her nowhere. Pim, thank goodness, won't play.

[*As she is saying the last lines, the curtain rises on the darkened scene.* ANNE'S VOICE *fades out.*]

Scene 4

[*It is the middle of the night, several months later. The stage is dark except for a little light which comes through the skylight in* PETER'S *room.*

Everyone is in bed. MR. *and* MRS. FRANK *lie on the couch in the main room, which has been pulled out to serve as a makeshift double bed.*

MARGOT *is sleeping on a mattress on the floor in the main room, behind a curtain stretched across for privacy. The others are all in their accustomed rooms.*

From outside we hear two drunken soldiers singing "Lili Marlene." A girl's high giggle is heard. The sound of running feet is heard coming closer and then fading in the distance. Throughout the scene there is the distant sound of airplanes passing overhead.

A match suddenly flares up in the attic. We dimly see MR. VAN DAAN. *He is getting his bearings. He comes quickly down the stairs, and goes to the cupboard where the food is stored. Again the match flares up, and is as quickly blown out. The dim figure is seen to steal back up the stairs.*

There is quiet for a second or two, broken only by the sound of airplanes, and running feet on the street below.

Suddenly, out of the silence and the dark, we hear ANNE *scream.*]

ANNE. [*Screaming*] No! No! Don't . . . don't take me!

[*She moans, tossing and crying in her sleep. The other people wake, terrified.* DUSSEL *sits up in bed, furious.*]

DUSSEL. Shush! Anne! Shush!

ANNE. [*Still in her nightmare*] Save me! Save me!

[*She screams and screams.* DUSSEL *gets out of bed, going over to her, trying to wake her.*]

DUSSEL. Quiet! Quiet! You want someone to hear?

[*In the main room* MRS. FRANK *grabs a shawl and pulls it around her. She rushes in to* ANNE, *taking her in her arms.* MR. FRANK *hurriedly gets up, putting on his overcoat.* MARGOT *sits up, terrified.* PETER'S *light goes on in his room.*]

MRS. FRANK. [*To* ANNE, *in her room*] Hush, darling, hush. It's all right. It's all right. [*Over her shoulder to* DUSSEL] Will you be kind enough to turn on the light, Mr. Dussel? [*Back to* ANNE] It's nothing, my darling. It was just a dream.

[DUSSEL *turns on the light in the bedroom.* MRS. FRANK *holds* ANNE *in her arms. Gradually* ANNE *comes out of her nightmare still trembling with horror.* MR. FRANK *comes into the room, and goes quickly to the window, looking out to be sure that no one outside has heard* ANNE'S *screams.* MRS.

◄ **Critical Viewing**
Why might the designers of this stamp have chosen such a happy photograph of Anne? **[Speculate]**

FRANK *holds* ANNE, *talking softly to her. In the main room* MARGOT *stands on a chair, turning on the center hanging lamp. A light goes on in the* VAN DAANS' *room overhead.* PETER *puts his robe on, coming out of his room.*]

DUSSEL. [*To* MRS. FRANK, *blowing his nose*] Something must be done about that child, Mrs. Frank. Yelling like that! Who knows but there's somebody on the streets? She's endangering all our lives.

MRS. FRANK. Anne, darling.

DUSSEL. Every night she twists and turns. I don't sleep. I spend half my night shushing her. And now it's nightmares!

[MARGOT *comes to the door of* ANNE'S *room, followed by* PETER. MR. FRANK *goes to them, indicating that everything is all right.* PETER *takes* MARGOT *back.*]

MRS. FRANK. [*To* ANNE] You're here, safe, you see? Nothing has happened. [*To* DUSSEL] Please, Mr. Dussel, go back to bed. She'll be herself in a minute or two. Won't you, Anne?

DUSSEL. [*Picking up a book and a pillow*] Thank you, but I'm going to the w.c. The one place where there's peace!

[*He stalks out.* MR. VAN DAAN, *in underwear and trousers, comes down the stairs.*]

MR. VAN DAAN. [*To* DUSSEL] What is it? What happened?

DUSSEL. A nightmare. She was having a nightmare!

MR. VAN DAAN. I thought someone was murdering her.

DUSSEL. Unfortunately, no.

[*He goes into the bathroom.* MR. VAN DAAN *goes back up the stairs.* MR. FRANK, *in the main room, sends* PETER *back to his own bedroom.*]

 **Reading Check**

What reaction does Anne's screaming elicit from Dussel?

MR. FRANK. Thank you, Peter. Go back to bed.

[PETER *goes back to his room.* MR. FRANK *follows him, turning out the light and looking out the window. Then he goes back to the main room, and gets up on a chair, turning out the center hanging lamp.*]

MRS. FRANK. [*To* ANNE] Would you like some water? [ANNE *shakes her head.*] Was it a very bad dream? Perhaps if you told me . . . ?

ANNE. I'd rather not talk about it.

MRS. FRANK. Poor darling. Try to sleep then. I'll sit right here beside you until you fall asleep. [*She brings a stool over, sitting there.*]

ANNE. You don't have to.

MRS. FRANK. But I'd like to stay with you . . . very much. Really.

ANNE. I'd rather you didn't.

MRS. FRANK. Good night, then.

[*She leans down to kiss* ANNE. ANNE *throws her arm up over her face, turning away.* MRS. FRANK, *hiding her hurt, kisses* ANNE'S *arm.*]

You'll be all right? There's nothing that you want?

ANNE. Will you please ask Father to come.

MRS. FRANK. [*After a second*] Of course, Anne dear.

[*She hurries out into the other room.* MR. FRANK *comes to her as she comes in.*]

Sie verlangt nach Dir! [22]

MR. FRANK. [*Sensing her hurt*] Edith, *Liebe, schau . . .*[23]

MRS. FRANK. *Es macht nichts! Ich danke dem lieben Herrgott, dass sie sich wenigstens an Dich wendet, wenn sie Trost braucht! Geh hinein, Otto, sie ist ganz hysterisch vor Angst.*[24] [*As* MR. FRANK *hesitates*] *Geh zu ihr.*[25]

[*He looks at her for a second and then goes to get a cup of water for* ANNE. MRS. FRANK *sinks down on the bed, her face in her hands, trying to keep from sobbing aloud.* MARGOT *comes over to her, putting her arms around her.*]

She wants nothing of me. She pulled away when I leaned down to kiss her.

---

22. **Sie verlangt nach Dir** (sē fer´ laŋt´ näk dir) German for "She is asking for you."
23. **Liebe, schau** (lē´ bə shou) German for "Dear, look."
24. **Es macht . . . vor Angst** German for "It's all right. I thank dear God that at least she turns to you when she needs comfort. Go in, Otto, she is hysterical because of fear."
25. **Geh zu ihr** (gē tsoo ēr) German for "Go to her."

▲ **Critical Viewing** This photograph shows the block of Amsterdam in which the Franks hid. The inset shows the building they lived in close up. Why do you think the Franks chose to remain in Amsterdam, in hiding, rather than flee to Switzerland? [**Draw Conclusions**]

MARGOT. It's a phase . . . You heard Father . . . Most girls go through it . . . they turn to their fathers at this age . . . they give all their love to their fathers.

MRS. FRANK. You weren't like this. You didn't shut me out.

MARGOT. She'll get over it . . .

[*She smooths the bed for* MRS. FRANK *and sits beside her a moment as* MRS. FRANK *lies down. In* ANNE'S *room* MR. FRANK *comes in, sitting down by* ANNE. ANNE *flings her arms around him, clinging to him. In the distance we hear the sound of ack-ack.*]

ANNE. Oh, Pim. I dreamed that they came to get us! The Green Police! They broke down the door and grabbed me and started to drag me out the way they did Jopie.

MR. FRANK. I want you to take this pill.

**Reading Check**

What was in Anne's dream that scared her so much?

The Diary of Anne Frank, Act I ◆ 733

ANNE. What is it?

MR. FRANK. Something to quiet you.

[*She takes it and drinks the water. In the main room* MARGOT *turns out the light and goes back to her bed.*]

MR. FRANK. [*To* ANNE] Do you want me to read to you for a while?

ANNE. No. Just sit with me for a minute. Was I awful? Did I yell terribly loud? Do you think anyone outside could have heard?

MR. FRANK. No. No. Lie quietly now. Try to sleep.

ANNE. I'm a terrible coward. I'm so disappointed in myself. I think I've conquered my fear . . . I think I'm really grown-up . . . and then something happens . . . and I run to you like a baby . . . I love you, Father. I don't love anyone but you.

MR. FRANK. [*Reproachfully*] Annele!

ANNE. It's true. I've been thinking about it for a long time. You're the only one I love.

MR. FRANK. It's fine to hear you tell me that you love me. But I'd be happier if you said you loved your mother as well . . . She needs your help so much . . . your love . . .

ANNE. We have nothing in common. She doesn't understand me. Whenever I try to explain my views on life to her she asks me if I'm constipated.

MR. FRANK. You hurt her very much just now. She's crying. She's in there crying.

ANNE. I can't help it. I only told the truth. I didn't want her here . . . [*Then, with sudden change*] Oh, Pim, I was horrible, wasn't I? And the worst of it is, I can stand off and look at myself doing it and know it's cruel and yet I can't stop doing it. What's the matter with me? Tell me. Don't say it's just a phase! Help me.

MR. FRANK. There is so little that we parents can do to help our children. We can only try to set a good example . . . point the way. The rest you must do yourself. You must build your own character.

ANNE. I'm trying. Really I am. Every night I think back over all of the things I did that day that were wrong . . . like putting the wet mop in Mr. Dussel's bed . . . and this thing now with Mother. I say to myself, that was wrong. I make up my mind, I'm never going to do that again. Never! Of course I may do something worse . . . but at least I'll never do that again! . . . I have a nicer side, Father . . . a sweeter, nicer side. But I'm scared to show it. I'm afraid that people are going to laugh at me if I'm serious. So the mean Anne comes to the outside and the good Anne stays on the inside, and I keep on trying to switch them around and have the good Anne outside and the bad Anne inside and be what I'd like to be . . . and might be . . . if only . . . only . . .

[*She is asleep.* MR. FRANK *watches her for a moment and then turns off the light, and starts out. The lights dim out. The curtain falls on the scene.* ANNE'S VOICE *is heard dimly at first, and then with growing strength.*]

ANNE'S VOICE. . . . The air raids are getting worse. They come over day and night. The noise is terrifying. Pim says it should be music to our ears. The more planes, the sooner will come the end of the war. Mrs. Van Daan pretends to be a <u>fatalist</u>. What will be, will be. But when the planes come over, who is the most frightened? No one else but Petronella! . . . Monday, the ninth of November, nineteen forty-two. Wonderful news! The Allies have landed in Africa. Pim says that we can look for an early finish to the war. Just for fun he asked each of us what was the first thing we wanted to do when we got out of here. Mrs. Van Daan longs to be home with her own things, her needle-point chairs, the Beckstein piano her father gave her . . . the best that money could buy. Peter would like to go to a movie. Mr. Dussel wants to get back to his dentist's drill. He's afraid he is losing his touch. For myself, there are so many things . . . to ride a bike again . . . to laugh till my belly aches . . . to have new clothes from the skin out . . . to have a hot tub filled to overflowing and wallow in it for hours . . . to be back in school with my friends . . .

[*As the last lines are being said, the curtain rises on the scene. The lights dim on as* ANNE'S VOICE *fades away.*]

Scene 5

[*It is the first night of the Hanukkah*[26] *celebration.* MR. FRANK *is standing at the head of the table on which is the Menorah.*[27] *He lights the Shamos,*[28] *or servant candle, and holds it as he says the blessing. Seated listening is all of the "family," dressed in their best. The men wear hats,* PETER *wears his cap.*]

MR. FRANK. [*Reading from a prayer book*] "Praised be Thou, oh Lord our God, Ruler of the universe, who has sanctified us with Thy commandments and bidden us kindle the Hanukkah lights. Praised be Thou, oh Lord our God, Ruler of the universe, who has wrought wondrous deliverances for our fathers in days of old. Praised be Thou, oh Lord our God, Ruler of the universe, that Thou has given us life and sustenance and brought us to this happy season." [MR. FRANK *lights the one candle of the Menorah as he continues.*] "We kindle this Hanukkah light to celebrate the great and wonderful deeds wrought through the zeal with which God filled the hearts of the heroic Maccabees, two thousand years ago. They fought against indifference, against tyranny and oppression, and they restored our Temple to us. May these lights remind us that we should ever look to God, whence cometh our help." Amen.

---

fatalist (fā´ tə list) *n.* one who believes that all events are determined by fate and cannot be changed

Reading Strategy
Analyzing the Effect of Historical Context What does Anne's narration tell the audience about the progress of the war?

Literary Analysis
Staging What is the importance to the families of this Hanukkah ritual?

✔**Reading Check**
Why are the families celebrating?

---

26. **Hanukkah** (khä´ noo kä´) *n.* Jewish celebration that lasts eight days.
27. **Menorah** (mə nō´ rə) *n.* a candle holder with nine candles, used during Hanukkah.
28. **Shamos** (shä´ məs) *n.* the candle used to light the others in a menorah.

ALL. Amen.

[MR. FRANK *hands* MRS. FRANK *the prayer book.*]

MRS. FRANK. [*Reading*] "I lift up mine eyes unto the mountains, from whence cometh my help. My help cometh from the Lord who made heaven and earth. He will not suffer thy foot to be moved. He that keepeth thee will not slumber. He that keepeth Israel doth neither slumber nor sleep. The Lord is thy keeper. The Lord is thy shade upon thy right hand. The sun shall not smite thee by day, nor the moon by night. The Lord shall keep thee from all evil. He shall keep thy soul. The Lord shall guard thy going out and thy coming in, from this time forth and forevermore." Amen.

ALL. Amen.

[MRS. FRANK *puts down the prayer book and goes to get the food and wine.* MARGOT *helps her.* MR. FRANK *takes the men's hats and puts them aside.*]

DUSSEL. [*Rising*] That was very moving.

ANNE. [*Pulling him back*] It isn't over yet!

MRS. VAN DAAN. Sit down! Sit down!

ANNE. There's a lot more, songs and presents.

DUSSEL. Presents?

MRS. FRANK. Not this year, unfortunately.

MRS. VAN DAAN. But always on Hanukkah everyone gives presents . . . everyone!

DUSSEL. Like our St. Nicholas' Day.[29]

[*There is a chorus of "no's" from the group.*]

MRS. VAN DAAN. No! Not like St. Nicholas! What kind of a Jew are you that you don't know Hanukkah?

MRS. FRANK. [*As she brings the food*] I remember particularly the candles . . . First one, as we have tonight. Then the second night you light two candles, the next night three . . . and so on until you have eight candles burning. When there are eight candles it is truly beautiful.

MRS. VAN DAAN. And the potato pancakes.

MR. VAN DAAN. Don't talk about them!

MRS. VAN DAAN. I make the best *latkes* you ever tasted!

MRS. FRANK. Invite us all next year . . . in your own home.

MR. FRANK. God willing!

MRS. VAN DAAN. God willing.

Reading Strategy
Analyzing the Effect of Historical Context How do world events make this Hanukkah different from others that the characters have celebrated?

---

29. **St. Nicholas' Day** December 6, the day Christian children in Holland receive gifts.

MARGOT. What I remember best is the presents we used to get when we were little . . . eight days of presents . . . and each day they got better and better.

MRS. FRANK. [*Sitting down*] We are all here, alive. That is present enough.

ANNE. No, it isn't. I've got something . . . [*She rushes into her room, hurriedly puts on a little hat improvised from the lamp shade, grabs a satchel bulging with parcels and comes running back.*]

MRS. FRANK. What is it?

ANNE. Presents!

MRS. VAN DAAN. Presents!

DUSSEL. Look!

MR. VAN DAAN. What's she got on her head?

PETER. A lamp shade!

ANNE. [*She picks out one at random.*] This is for Margot. [*She hands it to* MARGOT, *pulling her to her feet.*] Read it out loud.

MARGOT. [*Reading*]
  "You have never lost your temper.
  You never will, I fear,
  You are so good.
  But if you should,
  Put all your cross words here."

[*She tears open the package.*] A new crossword puzzle book! Where did you get it?

ANNE. It isn't new. It's one that you've done. But I rubbed it all out, and if you wait a little and forget, you can do it all over again.

MARGOT. [*Sitting*] It's wonderful, Anne. Thank you. You'd never know it wasn't new.

[*From outside we hear the sound of a streetcar passing.*]

ANNE. [*With another gift*] Mrs. Van Daan.

MRS. VAN DAAN. [*Taking it*] This is awful . . . I haven't anything for anyone . . . I never thought . . .

MR. FRANK. This is all Anne's idea.

MRS. VAN DAAN. [*Holding up a bottle*] What is it?

ANNE. It's hair shampoo. I took all the odds and ends of soap and mixed them with the last of my toilet water.

MRS. VAN DAAN. Oh, Anneke!

ANNE. I wanted to write a poem for all of them, but I didn't have time. [*Offering a large box to* MR. VAN DAAN] Yours, Mr. Van Daan, is really something . . . something you want more than anything. [*As she waits for him to open it*] Look! Cigarettes!

Literary Analysis
Staging What effect does the sound of a streetcar have in this scene?

**Reading Check**

Why do the gifts Anne gives mean so much to the people receiving them?

MR. VAN DAAN. Cigarettes!

ANNE. Two of them! Pim found some old pipe tobacco in the pocket lining of his coat . . . and we made them . . . or rather, Pim did.

MRS. VAN DAAN. Let me see . . . Well, look at that! Light it, Putti! Light it.

[MR. VAN DAAN *hesitates.*]

ANNE. It's tobacco, really it is! There's a little fluff in it, but not much.

[*Everyone watches intently as* MR. VAN DAAN *cautiously lights it. The cigarette flares up. Everyone laughs.*]

PETER. It works!

MRS. VAN DAAN. Look at him.

MR. VAN DAAN. [*Spluttering*] Thank you, Anne. Thank you.

[ANNE *rushes back to her satchel for another present.*]

ANNE. [*Handing her mother a piece of paper*] For Mother, Hanukkah greeting.

[*She pulls her mother to her feet.*]

MRS. FRANK. [*She reads*] "Here's an I.O.U. that I promise to pay. Ten hours of doing whatever you say. Signed, Anne Frank." [MRS. FRANK, *touched, takes* ANNE *in her arms, holding her close.*]

DUSSEL. [*To* ANNE] Ten hours of doing what you're told? Anything you're told?

ANNE. That's right.

DUSSEL. You wouldn't want to sell that, Mrs. Frank?

MRS. FRANK. Never! This is the most precious gift I've ever had!

[*She sits, showing her present to the others.* ANNE *hurries back to the satchel and pulls out a scarf, the scarf that* MR. FRANK *found in the first scene.*]

ANNE. [*Offering it to her father*] For Pim.

MR. FRANK. Anneke . . . I wasn't supposed to have a present! [*He takes it, unfolding it and showing it to the others.*]

ANNE. It's a muffler . . . to put round your neck . . . like an ascot, you know. I made it myself out of odds and ends . . . I knitted it in the dark each night, after I'd gone to bed. I'm afraid it looks better in the dark!

MR. FRANK. [*Putting it on*] It's fine. It fits me perfectly. Thank you, Annele.

[ANNE *hands* PETER *a ball of paper with a string attached to it.*]

ANNE. That's for Mouschi.

PETER. [*Rising to bow*] On behalf of Mouschi, I thank you.

ANNE. [*Hesitant, handing him a gift*] And . . . this is yours . . . from Mrs. Quack Quack. [*As he holds it gingerly in his hands*] Well . . . open it . . . Aren't you going to open it?

PETER. I'm scared to. I know something's going to jump out and hit me.

ANNE. No. It's nothing like that, really.

MRS. VAN DAAN. [*As he is opening it*] What is it, Peter? Go on. Show it.

ANNE. [*Excitedly*] It's a safety razor!

DUSSEL. A what?

ANNE. A razor!

MRS. VAN DAAN. [*Looking at it*] You didn't make that out of odds and ends.

ANNE. [*To* PETER] Miep got it for me. It's not new. It's second-hand. But you really do need a razor now.

DUSSEL. For what?

ANNE. Look on his upper lip . . . you can see the beginning of a mustache.

DUSSEL. He wants to get rid of that? Put a little milk on it and let the cat lick it off.

PETER. [*Starting for his room*] Think you're funny, don't you.

DUSSEL. Look! He can't wait! He's going in to try it!

PETER. I'm going to give Mouschi his present!

[*He goes into his room, slamming the door behind him.*]

MR. VAN DAAN. [*Disgustedly*] Mouschi, Mouschi, Mouschi.

[*In the distance we hear a dog persistently barking.* ANNE *brings a gift to* DUSSEL.]

ANNE. And last but never least, my roommate, Mr. Dussel.

DUSSEL. For me? You have something for me?

[*He opens the small box she gives him.*]

ANNE. I made them myself.

DUSSEL. [*Puzzled*] Capsules! Two capsules!

ANNE. They're ear-plugs!

DUSSEL. Ear-plugs?

ANNE. To put in your ears so you won't hear me when I thrash around at night. I saw them advertised in a magazine. They're not real ones . . . I made them out of cotton and candle wax. Try them . . . See if they don't work . . . see if you can hear me talk . . .

DUSSEL. [*Putting them in his ears*] Wait now until I get them in . . . so.

ANNE. Are you ready?

DUSSEL. Huh?

ANNE. Are you ready?

DUSSEL. Oh! They've gone inside! I can't get them out! [*They laugh as*

Reading Check

What does Anne give Mr. Dussel?

MR. DUSSEL *jumps about, trying to shake the plugs out of his ears. Finally he gets them out. Putting them away*] Thank you, Anne! Thank you!

[*Together*] {
  MR. VAN DAAN. A real Hanukkah!

  MRS. VAN DAAN. Wasn't it cute of her?

  MRS. FRANK. I don't know when she did it.

  MARGOT. I love my present.

ANNE. [*Sitting at the table*] And now let's have the song, Father . . . please . . . [*To* DUSSEL] Have you heard the Hanukkah song, Mr. Dussel? The song is the whole thing! [*She sings.*] "Oh, Hanukkah! Oh, Hanukkah! The sweet celebration . . ."

MR. FRANK. [*Quieting her*] I'm afraid, Anne, we shouldn't sing that song tonight. [*To* DUSSEL] It's a song of jubilation, of rejoicing. One is apt to become too enthusiastic.

ANNE. Oh, please, please. Let's sing the song. I promise not to shout!

MR. FRANK. Very well. But quietly now . . . I'll keep an eye on you and when . . .

[*As* ANNE *starts to sing, she is interrupted by* DUSSEL, *who is snorting and wheezing.*]

DUSSEL. [*Pointing to* PETER] You . . . You!

[PETER *is coming from his bedroom,* <u>ostentatiously</u> *holding a bulge in his coat as if he were holding his cat, and dangling* ANNE's *present before it.*]

How many times . . . I told you . . . Out! Out!

MR. VAN DAAN. [*Going to* PETER] What's the matter with you? Haven't you any sense? Get that cat out of here.

PETER. [*Innocently*] Cat?

MR. VAN DAAN. You heard me. Get it out of here!

PETER. I have no cat. [*Delighted with his joke, he opens his coat and pulls out a bath towel. The group at the table laugh, enjoying the joke.*]

DUSSEL. [*Still wheezing*] It doesn't need to be the cat . . . his clothes are enough . . . when he comes out of that room . . .

MR. VAN DAAN. Don't worry. You won't be bothered any more. We're getting rid of it.

DUSSEL. At last you listen to me. [*He goes off into his bedroom.*]

MR. VAN DAAN. [*Calling after him*] I'm not doing it for you. That's all in your mind . . . all of it! [*He starts back to his place at the table.*] I'm doing it because I'm sick of seeing that cat eat all our food.

PETER. That's not true! I only give him bones . . . scraps . . .

MR. VAN DAAN. Don't tell me! He gets fatter every day! Damn cat looks better than any of us. Out he goes tonight!

ostentatiously
(äs′ tən tā′ shəs lē) *adv.*
in a showy way

Literary Analysis
Staging What does Peter's joke about the cat show about Mr. Dussel?

PETER. No! No!

ANNE. Mr. Van Daan, you can't do that! That's Peter's cat. Peter loves that cat.

MRS. FRANK. [*Quietly*] Anne.

PETER. [To MR. VAN DAAN] If he goes, I go.

MR. VAN DAAN. Go! Go!

MRS. VAN DAAN. You're not going and the cat's not going! Now please . . . this is Hanukkah . . . Hanukkah . . . this is the time to celebrate . . . What's the matter with all of you? Come on, Anne. Let's have the song.

ANNE. [*Singing*]
   "Oh, Hanukkah! Oh, Hanukkah! The sweet celebration."

MR. FRANK. [*Rising*] I think we should first blow out the candle . . . then we'll have something for tomorrow night.

MARGOT. But, Father, you're supposed to let it burn itself out.

MR. FRANK. I'm sure that God understands shortages. [*Before blowing it out*] "Praised be Thou, oh Lord our God, who hast sustained us and permitted us to celebrate this joyous festival."

[*He is about to blow out the candle when suddenly there is a crash of something falling below. They all freeze in horror, motionless. For a few seconds there is complete silence.* MR. FRANK *slips off his shoes. The others noiselessly follow his example.* MR. FRANK *turns out a light near him. He motions to* PETER *to turn off the center lamp.* PETER *tries to reach it, realizes he cannot and gets up on a chair. Just as he is touching the lamp he loses his balance. The chair goes out from under him. He falls. The iron lamp shade crashes to the floor. There is a sound of feet below, running down the stairs.*]

MR. VAN DAAN. [*Under his breath*] Oh, oh!

[*The only light left comes from the Hanukkah candle.* DUSSEL *comes from his room.* MR. FRANK *creeps over to the stairwell and stands listening. The dog is heard barking excitedly.*]

Do you hear anything?

MR. FRANK. [*In a whisper*] No. I think they've gone.

MRS. VAN DAAN. It's the Green Police. They've found us.

MR. FRANK. If they had, they wouldn't have left. They'd be up here by now.

MRS. VAN DAAN. I know it's the Green Police. They've gone to get help. That's all. They'll be back!

MRS. VAN DAAN. Or it may have been the Gestapo,[30] looking for papers . . .

---

30. **Gestapo** (gə stä′ pō) *n.* the secret police force of the German Nazi state, known for its terrorism and atrocities.

Reading Strategy
Analyzing the Effect of Historical Context What might be happening downstairs? Why is Peter's fall so dangerous?

**Reading Check**

What happens to interrupt the Hanukkah celebration?

MR. FRANK. [*Interrupting*] Or a thief, looking for money.

MRS. VAN DAAN. We've got to do something . . . Quick! Quick! Before they come back.

MR. VAN DAAN. There isn't anything to do. Just wait.

[MR. FRANK *holds up his hand for them to be quiet. He is listening intently. There is complete silence as they all strain to hear any sound from below. Suddenly* ANNE *begins to sway. With a low cry she falls to the floor in a faint.* MRS. FRANK *goes to her quickly, sitting beside her on the floor and taking her in her arms.*]

MRS. FRANK. Get some water, please! Get some water!

[MARGOT *starts for the sink.*]

MR. VAN DAAN. [*Grabbing* MARGOT] No! No! No one's going to run water!

MR. FRANK. If they've found us, they've found us. Get the water.

[MARGOT *starts again for the sink.* MR. FRANK, *getting a flashlight*] I'm going down.

[MARGOT *rushes to him, clinging to him.* ANNE *struggles to consciousness.*]

MARGOT. No, Father, no! There may be someone there, waiting . . . It may be a trap!

MR. FRANK. This is Saturday. There is no way for us to know what has happened until Miep or Mr. Kraler comes on Monday morning. We cannot live with this uncertainty.

MARGOT. Don't go, Father!

MRS. FRANK. Hush, darling, hush.

[MR. FRANK *slips quietly out, down the steps and out through the door below.*]

Margot! Stay close to me.

[MARGOT *goes to her mother.*]

MR. VAN DAAN. Shush! Shush!

[MRS. FRANK *whispers to* MARGOT *to get the water.* MARGOT *goes for it.*]

MRS. VAN DAAN. Putti, where's our money? Get our money. I hear you can buy the Green Police off, so much a head. Go upstairs quick! Get the money!

MR. VAN DAAN. Keep still!

MRS. VAN DAAN. [*Kneeling before him, pleading*] Do you want to be dragged off to a concentration camp? Are you going to stand there and wait for them to come up and get you? Do something, I tell you!

MR. VAN DAAN. [*Pushing her aside*] Will you keep still!

[*He goes over to the stairwell to listen.* PETER *goes to his mother, helping*

Reading Strategy
Analyzing the Effect of Historical Context Why does Mr. Frank go downstairs?

her up onto the sofa. There is a second of silence, then ANNE *can stand it no longer.*]

ANNE. Someone go after Father! Make Father come back!

PETER. [*Starting for the door*] I'll go.

MR. VAN DAAN. Haven't you done enough?

[*He pushes* PETER *roughly away. In his anger against his father* PETER *grabs a chair as if to hit him with it, then puts it down, burying his face in his hands.* MRS. FRANK *begins to pray softly.*]

ANNE. Please, please, Mr. Van Daan. Get Father.

MR. VAN DAAN. Quiet! Quiet!

[ANNE *is shocked into silence.* MRS. FRANK *pulls her closer, holding her protectively in her arms.*]

MRS. FRANK. [*Softly, praying*] "I lift up mine eyes unto the mountains, from whence cometh my help. My help cometh from the Lord who made heaven and earth. He will not suffer thy foot to be moved . . . He that keepeth thee will not slumber . . ."

[*She stops as she hears someone coming. They all watch the door tensely.* MR. FRANK *comes quietly in.* ANNE *rushes to him, holding him tight.*]

MR. FRANK. It was a thief. That noise must have scared him away.

MRS. VAN DAAN. Thank goodness!

MR. FRANK. He took the cash box. And the radio. He ran away in such a hurry that he didn't stop to shut the street door. It was swinging wide open. [*A breath of relief sweeps over them.*] I think it would be good to have some light.

MARGOT. Are you sure it's all right?

MR. FRANK. The danger has passed.

[MARGOT *goes to light the small lamp.*]

▲ **Critical Viewing** What evidence in this photograph of Anne Frank can you find that reveals Anne's exuberant personality? **[Connect]**

Reading Check

Who had made the noise that interrupted the celebration?

Don't be so terrified, Anne. We're safe.

DUSSEL. Who says the danger has passed? Don't you realize we are in greater danger than ever?

MR. FRANK. Mr. Dussel, will you be still!

[MR. FRANK *takes* ANNE *back to the table, making her sit down with him, trying to calm her.*]

DUSSEL. [*Pointing to* PETER] Thanks to this clumsy fool, there's someone now who knows we're up here! Someone now knows we're up here, hiding!

MRS. VAN DAAN. [*Going to* DUSSEL] Someone knows we're here, yes. But who is the someone? A thief! A thief! You think a thief is going to go to the Green Police and say . . . I was robbing a place the other night and I heard a noise up over my head? You think a thief is going to do that?

DUSSEL. Yes. I think he will.

MRS. VAN DAAN. [*Hysterically*] You're crazy!

[*She stumbles back to her seat at the table.* PETER *follows protectively, pushing* DUSSEL *aside.*]

DUSSEL. I think some day he'll be caught and then he'll make a bargain with the Green Police . . . if they'll let him off, he'll tell them where some Jews are hiding!

[*He goes off into the bedroom. There is a second of appalled silence.*]

MR. VAN DAAN. He's right.

ANNE. Father, let's get out of here! We can't stay here now . . . Let's go . . .

MR. VAN DAAN. Go! Where?

MRS. FRANK. [*Sinking into her chair at the table*] Yes. Where?

MR. FRANK. [*Rising, to them all*] Have we lost all faith? All courage? A moment ago we thought that they'd come for us. We were sure it was the end. But it wasn't the end. We're alive, safe.

[MR. VAN DAAN *goes to the table and sits.* MR. FRANK *prays.*]

"We thank Thee, oh Lord our God, that in Thy infinite mercy Thou hast again seen fit to spare us." [*He blows out the candle, then turns to* ANNE.] Come on, Anne. The song! Let's have the song!

[*He starts to sing.* ANNE *finally starts falteringly to sing, as* MR. FRANK *urges her on. Her voice is hardly audible at first.*]

ANNE. [*Singing*]
"Oh, Hanukkah! Oh, Hanukkah! The sweet . . . celebration . . ."

[*As she goes on singing, the others gradually join in, their voices still shaking with fear.* MRS. VAN DAAN *sobs as she sings.*]

GROUP. "Around the feast . . . we . . . gather
In complete . . . jubilation . . .
Happiest of sea . . . sons
Now is here.
Many are the reasons for good cheer."

[DUSSEL *comes from the bedroom. He comes over to the table, standing beside* MARGOT, *listening to them as they sing.*]

"Together/We'll weather/Whatever tomorrow may bring."

[*As they sing on with growing courage, the lights start to dim.*]

"So hear us rejoicing/And merrily voicing/The Hanukkah song that we sing./Hoy!"

[*The lights are out. The curtain starts slowly to fall.*]

"Hear us rejoicing/And merrily voicing/The Hanukkah song that we sing."

[*They are still singing, as the curtain falls.*]

Literary Analysis
Staging What is the effect of this song as a finale to the act?

Review and Assess

Thinking About the Selection

1. **Respond:** The families must follow strict rules to keep from being discovered. Which would be the hardest rules for you to follow? Why?

2. **(a) Recall:** In Scene 1, what objects does Mr. Frank find in the secret rooms? **(b) Connect:** How do these objects connect with the rest of the act?

3. **(a) Recall:** Who are the people in hiding? **(b) Analyze Cause and Effect:** How might their relationship affect the way they get along?

4. **(a) Recall:** How are Margot and Anne different? **(b) Compare and Contrast:** How does the difference between them affect their relationship with their parents?

5. **(a) Recall:** What happens to Anne in the middle of the night? **(b) Analyze Cause and Effect:** What does this event reveal about Anne?

6. **(a) Recall:** What special meaning does Hanukkah have for the families? **(b) Deduce:** What do Anne's Hanukkah presents show about her? **(c) Interpret:** How do the others react to getting presents?

7. **Evaluate:** Anne's father tells her, "There are...no locks anyone can put on your mind." How does Anne prove that this is true?

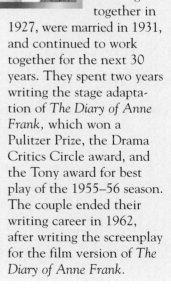

**Frances Goodrich
Albert Hackett**

**(1890–1984)
(1900–1995)**
Frances Goodrich and Albert Hackett began their careers acting in vaudeville and silent films, then turned to playwriting. They began working together in 1927, were married in 1931, and continued to work together for the next 30 years. They spent two years writing the stage adaptation of *The Diary of Anne Frank,* which won a Pulitzer Prize, the Drama Critics Circle award, and the Tony award for best play of the 1955–56 season. The couple ended their writing career in 1962, after writing the screenplay for the film version of *The Diary of Anne Frank.*

The Diary of Anne Frank, Act I ◆ 745

Review and Assess

Literary Analysis

Staging

1. Why is setting important in making the Franks' situation clear?
2. Analyze the **staging** for each scene in the act by completing a chart like the one below.

Act 1	Scenery	Lighting	Sound	Costumes	Characters
Scene 1	3 top-floor rooms, stairs up to attic Dust, torn curtains	Dim light, late afternoon	Church bells	Frank: worn suit, knapsack	Mr. Frank Miep

3. Name three offstage sound effects used in Act I. What does each contribute to the drama?

Connecting Literary Elements

4. What three details from Act I are clues to the **historical context** of *The Diary of Anne Frank?* Use a chart like the one shown here to record your answers.

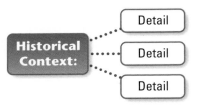

5. How is staging used to show the historical context of the play?

Reading Strategy

Analyzing the Effect of Historical Context

6. What are the political forces and cultural attitudes of this time and place?
7. What is Anne's reaction to these forces and attitudes?
8. In what way do the details of the historical setting taking place outside the attic enhance the meaning of the events occurring within the play?

Extend Understanding

9. **Evaluate:** Could the events in this play have taken place at a different time in history? Why or why not?

Quick Review

The **staging** of a play includes all the physical effects—scenery, costumes, lighting, sound effects, and actors' movements —that bring the drama to life. To review staging, see page 699.

The **historical context** of a work includes the culture, politics, and events of the time in which it is set. To review historical context, see page 699.

 Take It to the Net
www.phschool.com
Take the interactive self-test online to check your understanding of the play.

Integrate Language Skills

Vocabulary Development Lesson

Word Analysis: Prefixes *in-* and *un-*

When you add the prefix *in-* or *un-* to a word, the result is a word with the opposite meaning.

Write the opposite of each word by adding the prefix indicated. Write a sentence for each word you make.

    1. secure (in)   **2.** bearable (un)

Spelling Strategy

Learn the exceptions to the *i* before *e* rule. They include *either/neither, seize, weird, foreign,* and *their.* Unscramble the letters to spell two additional exceptions.

    1. sliruee   **2.** thighe

Grammar Lesson

Subject and Verb Agreement

A verb must agree with its subject in number, either singular or plural. Verbs change in form to agree with their subjects. The singular form of a verb ends in *s*, but the plural form does not.

> **Singular:** The scene *remains* the same. . .
>
> **Plural:** All the characters *remain* in the room.

Fluency: Definitions

Write the vocabulary word from the list on page 699 that is closest in meaning to the definition provided.

    1. changeable
    2. very visible
    3. person who believed that she could not change her destiny
    4. in a showy manner
    5. not shy
    6. very careful
    7. impossible to tolerate
    8. free time

▶ *For more practice, see page R32, Exercise C.*

Practice Rewrite these sentences using the form of the verb that agrees with the subject.

    1. The curtain (fall, falls) on the scene.
    2. They (strain, strains) to hear any sound.
    3. Mrs. Frank (begin, begins) to pray softly.
    4. They (remove, removes) their shoes.
    5. A flight of stairs (lead, leads) to the attic.

Writing Application Write three sentences of your own about the action in the play, making sure that each subject and verb agree in number.

𝒲𝒢 *Prentice Hall Writing and Grammar Connection: Chapter 24, Section 24.1*

Extension Activities

Biographical Writing Use information from the play, plus your imagination, to write a **biographical sketch** of a character from the play. Describe the character's personality, way of moving, habits, and attitudes.

Listening and Speaking Choose a **dramatic speech** from the play and deliver it as the character whose part it is.

 Take It to the Net   www.phschool.com

Go online for an additional research activity using the Internet.

Prepare to Read

The Diary of Anne Frank, Act II

Literary Analysis

Plot and Subplot

The **plot** of a play is the arrangement of related events that lead to a climax or highpoint. In addition to the main plot, a play may also have one or more **subplots**, or secondary stories. These develop within the framework of the main plot and may contribute to its resolution. In *The Diary of Anne Frank*, for example, the growing relationship between Anne and Peter is a subplot. To trace elements of the plot, use these focus questions as you read:

1. Where does the climax of the plot occur?
2. What are two subplots in the play?

Connecting Literary Elements

In a drama, the **dialogue**—the conversation among the characters—carries the action of the plot. It moves events along to the climax and the resolution. Dialogue also reveals the personalities and motives of the characters, as in the following example:

> **Peter:** I thought you were fine just now. You know just how to talk to them. I'm no good . . . I never can think . . . especially when I'm mad . . .

Reading Strategy

Picturing the Action

When you see a live performance of a play, the actors, setting, and dialogue all help to bring the drama to life. When you read a play, however, you picture the scene and hear the characters in your mind. Watch for details that describe how the characters look and move and speak. As you read each scene, use a chart like the one shown to keep track of "sights" and "sounds" that are important in the play.

Act II, Scene 1	
Visual Images	**Sounds**
1. People reading quietly	1. Ann's voice
2. Late afternoon light	2. Church bells
3. Warm clothing	3. Door buzzer

Vocabulary Development

inarticulate (in ̍ är tik ́ yə lit) *adj.* unable to express oneself (p. 753)

apprehension (ap ́ rə hen ́ shən) *n.* a fearful feeling about the future (p. 754)

intuition (in ́ tōō wish ́ ən) *n.* ability to sense or know immediately, without reasoning (p. 760)

indignant (in dig ́ nənt) *adj.* filled with anger at meanness or injustice (p. 762)

stealthily (stel ́ thi lē) *adv.* in a secretive way, avoiding being noticed (p. 766)

ineffectually (in ́ e fek ́ chōō ə lē) *adv.* without producing the desired result (p. 774)

Act II

Scene 1

[*In the darkness we hear* ANNE'S VOICE, *again reading from the diary.*]

ANNE'S VOICE. Saturday, the first of January, nineteen forty-four. Another new year has begun and we find ourselves still in our hiding place. We have been here now for one year, five months and twenty-five days. It seems that our life is at a standstill.

[*The curtain rises on the scene. It is late afternoon. Everyone is bundled up against the cold. In the main room* MRS. FRANK *is taking down the laundry which is hung across the back.* MR. FRANK *sits in the chair down left, reading.* MARGOT *is lying on the couch with a blanket over her and the many-colored knitted scarf around her throat.* ANNE *is seated at the center table, writing in her diary.* PETER, MR. *and* MRS. VAN DAAN *and* DUSSEL *are all in their own rooms, reading or lying down.*

As the lights dim on, ANNE'S VOICE *continues, without a break.*]

ANNE'S VOICE. We are all a little thinner. The Van Daans' "discussions" are as violent as ever. Mother still does not understand me. But then I don't understand her either. There is one great change, however. A change in myself. I read somewhere that girls of my age don't feel quite certain of themselves. . . .

[*We hear the chimes and then a hymn being played on the carillon outside. The buzzer of the door below suddenly sounds. Everyone is startled.* MR. FRANK *tiptoes cautiously to the top of the steps and listens. Again the buzzer sounds, in* MIEP'*s V-for-Victory signal.*][1]

MR. FRANK. It's Miep!

[*He goes quickly down the steps to unbolt the door.* MRS. FRANK *calls upstairs to the* VAN DAANS *and then to* PETER.]

MRS. FRANK. Wake up, everyone! Miep is here!

[ANNE *quickly puts her diary away.* MARGOT *sits up, pulling the blanket around her shoulders.* MR. DUSSEL *sits on the edge of his bed, listening, disgruntled.* MIEP *comes up the steps, followed by* MR. KRALER. *They bring flowers, books, newspapers, etc.* ANNE *rushes to* MIEP, *throwing her arms affectionately around her.*]

Miep . . . and Mr. Kraler . . . What a delightful surprise!

MR. KRALER. We came to bring you New Year's greetings.

MRS. FRANK. You shouldn't . . . you should have at least one day to

---

1. **V-for-Victory signal** three short rings and one long one (the letter V in Morse code).

Literary Analysis
Plot and Subplot What subplot is indicated in this diary entry?

**Reading Check**
What has changed in the year and a half that Anne has been in hiding?

The Diary of Anne Frank, Act II ◆ 749

yourselves. [*She goes quickly to the stove and brings down teacups and tea for all of them.*]

ANNE. Don't say that, it's so wonderful to see them! [*Sniffing at* MIEP's *coat*] I can smell the wind and the cold on your clothes.

MIEP. [*Giving her the flowers*] There you are. [*Then to* MARGOT, *feeling her forehead*] How are you, Margot? . . . Feeling any better?

MARGOT. I'm all right.

ANNE. We filled her full of every kind of pill so she won't cough and make a noise. [*She runs into her room to put the flowers in water.* MR. *and* MRS. VAN DAAN *come from upstairs. Outside there is the sound of a band playing.*]

MRS. VAN DAAN. Well, hello, Miep. Mr. Kraler.

MR. KRALER. [*Giving a bouquet of flowers to* MRS. VAN DAAN] With my hope for peace in the New Year.

PETER. [*Anxiously*] Miep, have you seen Mouschi? Have you seen him anywhere around?

MIEP. I'm sorry, Peter. I asked everyone in the neighborhood had they seen a gray cat. But they said no.

[MRS. FRANK *gives* MIEP *a cup of tea.* MR. FRANK *comes up the steps, carrying a small cake on a plate.*]

MR. FRANK. Look what Miep's brought for us!

MRS. FRANK. [*Taking it*] A cake!

MR. VAN DAAN. A cake! [*He pinches* MIEP's *cheeks gaily and hurries up to the cupboard.*] I'll get some plates.

[DUSSEL, *in his room, hastily puts a coat on and starts out to join the others.*]

MRS. FRANK. Thank you, Miepia. You shouldn't have done it. You must have used all of your sugar ration for weeks. [*Giving it to* MRS. VAN DAAN] It's beautiful, isn't it?

MRS. VAN DAAN. It's been ages since I even saw a cake. Not since you brought us one last year. [*Without looking at the cake, to* MIEP] Remember? Don't you remember, you gave us one on New Year's Day? Just this time last year? I'll never forget it because you had "Peace in nineteen forty-three" on it. [*She looks at the cake and reads*] "Peace in nineteen forty-four!"

MIEP. Well, it has to come sometime, you know. [*As* DUSSEL *comes from his room*] Hello, Mr. Dussel.

MR. KRALER. How are you?

◀ **Critical Viewing** Behind the bookcase is the staircase leading to the attic in which the Franks hid. How does this photograph of the setting contribute to your understanding of the suspense and tension in the play? **[Relate]**

Literary Analysis
Plot and Subplot How does **Mrs.** Van Daan's speech **show** that time has passed **while** they were in hiding?

☑**Reading Check**
What **does** Miep bring for everyone?

MR. VAN DAAN. [*Bringing plates and a knife*] Here's the knife, *liefje.* Now, how many of us are there?

MIEP. None for me, thank you.

MR. FRANK. Oh, please. You must.

MIEP. I couldn't.

MR. VAN DAAN. Good! That leaves one . . . two . . . three . . . seven of us.

DUSSEL. Eight! Eight! It's the same number as it always is!

MR. VAN DAAN. I left Margot out. I take it for granted Margot won't eat any.

ANNE. Why wouldn't she!

MRS. FRANK. I think it won't harm her.

MR. VAN DAAN. All right! All right! I just didn't want her to start coughing again, that's all.

DUSSEL. And please, Mrs. Frank should cut the cake.

[*Together*] { **MR. VAN DAAN.** What's the difference?

MRS. VAN DAAN. It's not Mrs. Frank's cake, is it, Miep? It's for all of us.

DUSSEL. Mrs. Frank divides things better.

[*Together*] { **MRS. VAN DAAN.** [*Going to* DUSSEL] What are you trying to say?

MR. VAN DAAN. Oh, come on! Stop wasting time!

MRS. VAN DAAN. [*To* DUSSEL] Don't I always give everybody exactly the same? Don't I?

MR. VAN DAAN. Forget it, Kerli.

MRS. VAN DAAN. No. I want an answer! Don't I?

DUSSEL. Yes. Yes. Everybody gets exactly the same . . . except Mr. Van Daan always gets a little bit more.

[VAN DAAN *advances on* DUSSEL, *the knife still in his hand.*]

MR. VAN DAAN. That's a lie!

[DUSSEL *retreats before the onslaught of the* VAN DAANS.]

MR. FRANK. Please, please! [*Then to* MIEP] You see what a little sugar cake does to us? It goes right to our heads!

MR. VAN DAAN. [*Handing* MRS. FRANK *the knife*] Here you are, Mrs. Frank.

MRS. FRANK. Thank you. [*Then to* MIEP *as she goes to the table to cut the cake*] Are you sure you won't have some?

MIEP. [*Drinking her tea*] No, really, I have to go in a minute.

[*The sound of the band fades out in the distance.*]

PETER. [*To* MIEP] Maybe Mouschi went back to our house . . . they say

Reading Strategy
Picturing the Action
What expressions do you picture on the faces of Van Daan, Dussel, and Mr. Frank during this disagreement?

that cats . . . Do you ever get over there . . . ? I mean . . . do you suppose you could . . . ?

MIEP. I'll try, Peter. The first minute I get I'll try. But I'm afraid, with him gone a week . . .

DUSSEL. Make up your mind, already someone has had a nice big dinner from that cat!

[PETER *is furious,* <u>inarticulate</u>. *He starts toward* DUSSEL *as if to hit him.* MR. FRANK *stops him.* MRS. FRANK *speaks quickly to ease the situation.*]

MRS. FRANK. [*To* MIEP] This is delicious, Miep!

MRS. VAN DAAN. [*Eating hers*] Delicious!

MR. VAN DAAN. [*Finishing it in one gulp*] Dirk's in luck to get a girl who can bake like this!

MIEP. [*Putting down her empty teacup*] I have to run. Dirk's taking me to a party tonight.

ANNE. How heavenly! Remember now what everyone is wearing, and what you have to eat and everything, so you can tell us tomorrow.

MIEP. I'll give you a full report! Good-bye, everyone!

MR. VAN DAAN. [*To* MIEP] Just a minute. There's something I'd like you to do for me.

[*He hurries off up the stairs to his room.*]

MRS. VAN DAAN. [*Sharply*] Putti, where are you going? [*She rushes up the stairs after him, calling hysterically.*] What do you want? Putti, what are you going to do?

MIEP. [*To* PETER] What's wrong?

PETER. [*His sympathy is with his mother.*] Father says he's going to sell her fur coat. She's crazy about that old fur coat.

DUSSEL. Is it possible? Is it possible that anyone is so silly as to worry about a fur coat in times like this?

PETER. It's none of your darn business . . . and if you say one more thing . . . I'll, I'll take you and I'll . . . I mean it . . . I'll . . .

[*There is a piercing scream from* MRS. VAN DAAN *above. She grabs at the fur coat as* MR. VAN DAAN *is starting downstairs with it.*]

MRS. VAN DAAN. No! No! No! Don't you dare take that! You hear? It's mine!

[*Downstairs* PETER *turns away, embarrassed, miserable.*]

My father gave me that! You didn't give it to me. You have no right. Let go of it . . . you hear?

[MR. VAN DAAN *pulls the coat from her hands and hurries downstairs.* MRS. VAN DAAN *sinks to the floor, sobbing. As* MR. VAN DAAN *comes into the main room the others look away, embarrassed for him.*]

inarticulate (in´ är tik´ yə lit) *adj.* speechless or unable to express oneself

Literary Analysis
Plot and Subplot What is the subplot concerning Mr. and Mrs. Van Daan?

**Reading Check**

Why does Peter get angry with Dussel?

The Diary of Anne Frank, Act II ◆ 753

MR. VAN DAAN. [*To* MR. KRALER] Just a little—discussion over the advisability of selling this coat. As I have often reminded Mrs. Van Daan, it's very selfish of her to keep it when people outside are in such desperate need of clothing . . . [*He gives the coat to* MIEP.] So if you will please to sell it for us? It should fetch a good price. And by the way, will you get me cigarettes. I don't care what kind they are . . . get all you can.

MIEP. It's terribly difficult to get them, Mr. Van Daan. But I'll try. Good-bye.

[*She goes.* MR. FRANK *follows her down the steps to bolt the door after her.* MRS. FRANK *gives* MR. KRALER *a cup of tea.*]

MRS. FRANK. Are you sure you won't have some cake, Mr. Kraler?

MR. KRALER. I'd better not.

MR. VAN DAAN. You're still feeling badly? What does your doctor say?

MR. KRALER. I haven't been to him.

MRS. FRANK. Now, Mr. Kraler! . . .

MR. KRALER. [*Sitting at the table*] Oh, I tried. But you can't get near a doctor these days . . . they're so busy. After weeks I finally managed to get one on the telephone. I told him I'd like an appointment . . . I wasn't feeling very well. You know what he answers . . . over the telephone . . . Stick out your tongue! [*They laugh. He turns to* MR. FRANK *as* MR. FRANK *comes back.*] I have some contracts here . . . I wonder if you'd look over them with me . . .

MR. FRANK. [*Putting out his hand*] Of course.

MR. KRALER. [*He rises*] If we could go downstairs . . . [MR. FRANK *starts ahead;* MR. KRALER *speaks to the others.*] Will you forgive us? I won't keep him but a minute. [*He starts to follow* MR. FRANK *down the steps.*]

MARGOT. [*With sudden foreboding*] What's happened? Something's happened! Hasn't it, Mr. Kraler?

[MR. KRALER *stops and comes back, trying to reassure* MARGOT *with a pretense of casualness.*]

MR. KRALER. No, really. I want your father's advice . . .

MARGOT. Something's gone wrong! I know it!

MR. FRANK. [*Coming back, to* MR. KRALER] If it's something that concerns us here, it's better that we all hear it.

MR. KRALER. [*Turning to him, quietly*] But . . . the children . . . ?

MR. FRANK. What they'd imagine would be worse than any reality.

[*As* MR. KRALER *speaks, they all listen with intense* <u>apprehension</u>. MRS. VAN DAAN *comes down the stairs and sits on the bottom step.*]

MR. KRALER. It's a man in the storeroom . . . I don't know whether or not you remember him . . . Carl, about fifty, heavy-set, nearsighted . . . He came with us just before you left.

Literary Analysis
Plot and Subplot What do you learn about the plot from this dialogue between Mr. Kraler and Mr. Frank?

apprehension
(ap′ rə hen′ shən) *n.* a fearful feeling about the future; dread

MR. FRANK. He was from Utrecht?

MR. KRALER. That's the man. A couple of weeks ago, when I was in the storeroom, he closed the door and asked me . . . how's Mr. Frank? What do you hear from Mr. Frank? I told him I only knew there was a rumor that you were in Switzerland. He said he'd heard that rumor too, but he thought I might know something more. I didn't pay any attention to it . . . but then a thing happened yesterday . . . He'd brought some invoices to the office for me to sign. As I was going through them, I looked up. He was standing staring at the bookcase . . . your bookcase. He said he thought he remembered a door there . . . Wasn't there a door there that used to go up to the loft? Then he told me he wanted more money. Twenty guilders[2] more a week.

MR. VAN DAAN. Blackmail!

MR. FRANK. Twenty guilders? Very modest blackmail.

MR. VAN DAAN. That's just the beginning.

DUSSEL. [*Coming to* MR. FRANK] You know what I think? He was the thief who was down there that night. That's how he knows we're here.

MR. FRANK. [*To* MR. KRALER] How was it left? What did you tell him?

MR. KRALER. I said I had to think about it. What shall I do? Pay him the money? . . . Take a chance on firing him . . . or what? I don't know.

DUSSEL. [*Frantic*] Don't fire him! Pay him what he asks . . . keep him here where you can have your eye on him.

MR. FRANK. Is it so much that he's asking? What are they paying nowadays?

MR. KRALER. He could get it in a war plant. But this isn't a war plant. Mind you, I don't know if he really knows . . . or if he doesn't know.

MR. FRANK. Offer him half. Then we'll soon find out if it's blackmail or not.

DUSSEL. And if it is? We've got to pay it, haven't we? Anything he asks we've got to pay!

MR. FRANK. Let's decide that when the time comes.

MR. KRALER. This may be all my imagination. You get to a point, these days, where you suspect everyone and everything. Again and again . . . on some simple look or word, I've found myself . . .

[*The telephone rings in the office below.*]

MRS. VAN DAAN. [*Hurrying to* MR. KRALER] There's the telephone! What does that mean, the telephone ringing on a holiday?

MR. KRALER. That's my wife. I told her I had to go over some papers in my office . . . to call me there when she got out of church. [*He starts out.*] I'll offer him half then. Good-bye . . . we'll hope for the best!

---

2. **guilders** (gil′ dərz) *n.* monetary units of the Netherlands.

Reading Strategy
Picturing the Action
What details in Mr. Kraler's story help you picture the incident with the man in the storeroom?

Reading Check

Why is Dussel so concerned about paying the man in the storeroom?

The Diary of Anne Frank, Act II ◆ 755

[*The group calls their good-byes halfheartedly.* MR. FRANK *follows* MR. KRALER *to bolt the door below. During the following scene,* MR. FRANK *comes back up and stands listening, disturbed.*]

DUSSEL. [*To* MR. VAN DAAN] You can thank your son for this . . . smashing the light! I tell you, it's just a question of time now.

[*He goes to the window at the back and stands looking out.*]

MARGOT. Sometimes I wish the end would come . . . whatever it is.

MRS. FRANK. [*Shocked*] Margot!

[ANNE *goes to* MARGOT, *sitting beside her on the couch with her arms around her.*]

MARGOT. Then at least we'd know where we were.

MRS. FRANK. You should be ashamed of yourself! Talking that way! Think how lucky we are! Think of the thousands dying in the war, every day. Think of the people in concentration camps.

ANNE. [*Interrupting*] What's the good of that? What's the good of thinking of misery when you're already miserable? That's stupid!

MRS. FRANK. Anne!

[*As* ANNE *goes on raging at her mother,* MRS. FRANK *tries to break in, in an effort to quiet her.*]

ANNE. We're young, Margot and Peter and I! You grownups have had your chance! But look at us . . . If we begin thinking of all the horror in the world, we're lost! We're trying to hold onto some kind of ideals . . . when everything . . . ideals, hopes . . . everything, are being destroyed! It isn't our fault that the world is in such a mess! We weren't around when all this started! So don't try to take it out on us! [*She rushes off to her room, slamming the door after her. She picks up a brush from the chest and hurls it to the floor. Then she sits on the settee, trying to control her anger.*]

MR. VAN DAAN. She talks as if we started the war! Did we start the war?

[*He spots* ANNE'S *cake. As he starts to take it,* PETER *anticipates him.*]

PETER. She left her cake.

[*He starts for* ANNE'S *room with the cake. There is silence in the main room.* MRS. VAN DAAN *goes up to her room, followed by* VAN DAAN. DUSSEL *stays looking out the window.* MR. FRANK *brings* MRS. FRANK *her cake. She eats it slowly, without relish.* MR. FRANK *takes his cake to* MARGOT *and sits quietly on the sofa beside her.* PETER *stands in the doorway of* ANNE'S *darkened room, looking at her, then makes a little movement to let her know he is there.* ANNE *sits up, quickly, trying to hide the signs of her tears.* PETER *holds out the cake to her.*]

You left this.

ANNE. [*Dully*] Thanks.

[PETER *starts to go out, then comes back.*]

Reading Strategy
Picturing the Action
What do the actions in this stage direction show about the characters' relationships?

▲ **Critical Viewing**
This photograph shows a wall in Anne Frank's room. In what ways does Anne's room resemble a typical teenager's room today? **[Relate]**

PETER. I thought you were fine just now. You know just how to talk to them. You know just how to say it. I'm no good . . . I never can think . . . especially when I'm mad . . . That Dussel . . . when he said that about Mouschi . . . someone eating him . . . all I could think is . . . I wanted to hit him. I wanted to give him such a . . . a . . . that he'd . . . That's what I used to do when there was an argument at school . . . That's the way I . . . but here . . . And an old man like that . . . it wouldn't be so good.

ANNE. You're making a big mistake about me. I do it all wrong. I say too much. I go too far. I hurt people's feelings . . .

[DUSSEL *leaves the window, going to his room.*]

PETER. I think you're just fine . . . What I want to say . . . if it wasn't for you around here, I don't know. What I mean . . .

[PETER *is interrupted by* DUSSEL'S *turning on the light.* DUSSEL *stands in the doorway, startled to see* PETER. PETER *advances toward him forbiddingly.* DUSSEL *backs out of the room.* PETER *closes the door on him.*]

ANNE. Do you mean it, Peter? Do you really mean it?

PETER. I said it, didn't I?

ANNE. Thank you, Peter!

Reading Check

Why does Peter admire Anne?

[*In the main room* MR. *and* MRS. FRANK *collect the dishes and take them to the sink, washing them.* MARGOT *lies down again on the couch.* DUSSEL, *lost, wanders into* PETER'S *room and takes up a book, starting to read.*]

PETER. [*Looking at the photographs on the wall*] You've got quite a collection.

ANNE. Wouldn't you like some in your room? I could give you some. Heaven knows you spend enough time in there . . . doing heaven knows what . . .

PETER. It's easier. A fight starts, or an argument . . . I duck in there.

ANNE. You're lucky, having a room to go to. His lordship is always here . . . I hardly ever get a minute alone. When they start in on me, I can't duck away. I have to stand there and take it.

PETER. You gave some of it back just now.

ANNE. I get so mad. They've formed their opinions . . . about everything . . . but we . . . we're still trying to find out . . . We have problems here that no other people our age have ever had. And just as you think you've solved them, something comes along and bang! You have to start all over again.

PETER. At least you've got someone you can talk to.

ANNE. Not really. Mother . . . I never discuss anything serious with her. She doesn't understand. Father's all right. We can talk about everything . . . everything but one thing. Mother. He simply won't talk about her. I don't think you can be really intimate with anyone if he holds something back, do you?

PETER. I think your father's fine.

ANNE. Oh, he is, Peter! He is! He's the only one who's ever given me the feeling that I have any sense. But anyway, nothing can take the place of school and play and friends of your own age . . . or near your age . . . can it?

PETER. I suppose you miss your friends and all.

ANNE. It isn't just . . . [*She breaks off, staring up at him for a second.*] Isn't it funny, you and I? Here we've been seeing each other every minute for almost a year and a half, and this is the first time we've ever really talked. It helps a lot to have someone to talk to, don't you think? It helps you to let off steam.

PETER. [*Going to the door*] Well, any time you want to let off steam, you can come into my room.

ANNE. [*Following him*] I can get up an awful lot of steam. You'll have to be careful how you say that.

PETER. It's all right with me.

ANNE. Do you mean it?

Literary Analysis
Plot and Subplot What subplot is being developed here?

Reading Strategy
Picturing the Action How do you picture this scene between Anne, Peter, and Dussel?

PETER. I said it, didn't I?

[*He goes out.* ANNE *stands in her doorway looking after him. As* PETER *gets to his door he stands for a minute looking back at her. Then he goes into his room.* DUSSEL *rises as he comes in, and quickly passes him, going out. He starts across for his room.* ANNE *sees him coming, and pulls her door shut.* DUSSEL *turns back toward* PETER'S *room.* PETER *pulls his door shut.* DUSSEL *stands there, bewildered, forlorn.*

The scene slowly dims out. The curtain falls on the scene. ANNE'S VOICE *comes over in the darkness . . . faintly at first, and then with growing strength.*]

ANNE'S VOICE. We've had bad news. The people from whom Miep got our ration books have been arrested. So we have had to cut down on our food. Our stomachs are so empty that they rumble and make strange noises, all in different keys. Mr. Van Daan's is deep and low, like a bass fiddle. Mine is high, whistling like a flute. As we all sit around waiting for supper, it's like an orchestra tuning up. It only needs Toscanini[3] to raise his baton and we'd be off in the Ride of the Valkyries.[4] Monday, the sixth of March, nineteen forty-four. Mr. Kraler is in the hospital. It seems he has ulcers. Pim says we are his ulcers. Miep has to run the business and us too. The Americans have landed on the southern tip of Italy. Father looks for a quick finish to the war. Mr. Dussel is waiting every day for the warehouse man to demand more money. Have I been skipping too much from one subject to another? I can't help it. I feel that spring is coming. I feel it in my whole body and soul. I feel utterly confused. I am longing . . . so longing . . . for everything . . . for friends . . . for someone to talk to . . . someone who understands . . . someone young, who feels as I do . . .

[*As these last lines are being said, the curtain rises on the scene. The lights dim on.* ANNE'S VOICE *fades out.*]

Scene 2

[*It is evening, after supper. From outside we hear the sound of children playing. The "grownups," with the exception of* MR. VAN DAAN, *are all in the main room.* MRS. FRANK *is doing some mending,* MRS. VAN DAAN *is reading a fashion magazine.* MR. FRANK *is going over business accounts.* DUSSEL, *in his dentist's jacket, is pacing up and down, impatient to get into his bedroom.* MR. VAN DAAN *is upstairs working on a piece of embroidery in an embroidery frame.*

In his room PETER *is sitting before the mirror, smoothing his hair. As the scene goes on, he puts on his tie, brushes his coat and puts it on, preparing himself meticulously for a visit from* ANNE. *On his wall are now hung some of* ANNE'S *motion picture stars.*

---

3. Toscanini (täs´ kə nē´ nē) Arturo Toscanini, a famous Italian American orchestra conductor.
4. Ride of the Valkyries (val´ kir´ ēz) a stirring selection from an opera by Richard Wagner, a German composer.

Literary Analysis
Plot and Subplot How do details from Anne's diary increase the tension of the plot?

Reading Check

What is the bad news that causes a change in Anne's living situation?

In her room ANNE *too is getting dressed. She stands before the mirror in her slip, trying various ways of dressing her hair.* MARGOT *is seated on the sofa, hemming a skirt for* ANNE *to wear.*

In the main room DUSSEL *can stand it no longer. He comes over, rapping sharply on the door of his and* ANNE'S *bedroom.*]

ANNE. [*Calling to him*] No, no, Mr. Dussel! I am not dressed yet.

[DUSSEL *walks away, furious, sitting down and burying his head in his hands.* ANNE *turns to* MARGOT.]

How is that? How does that look?

MARGOT. [*Glancing at her briefly*] Fine.

ANNE. You didn't even look.

MARGOT. Of course I did. It's fine.

ANNE. Margot, tell me, am I terribly ugly?

MARGOT. Oh, stop fishing.

ANNE. No. No. Tell me.

MARGOT. Of course you're not. You've got nice eyes . . . and a lot of animation, and . . .

ANNE. A little vague, aren't you?

[*Outside,* MRS. FRANK, *feeling sorry for* DUSSEL, *comes over, knocking at the girls' door.*]

MRS. FRANK. [*Outside*] May I come in?

MARGOT. Come in, Mother.

MRS. FRANK. [*Shutting the door behind her*] Mr. Dussel's impatient to get in here.

ANNE. Heavens, he takes the room for himself the entire day.

MRS. FRANK. [*Gently*] Anne, dear, you're not going in again tonight to see Peter?

ANNE. [*Dignified*] That is my intention.

MRS. FRANK. But you've already spent a great deal of time in there today.

ANNE. I was in there exactly twice. Once to get the dictionary, and then three-quarters of an hour before supper.

MRS. FRANK. Aren't you afraid you're disturbing him?

ANNE. Mother, I have some <u>intuition</u>.

MRS. FRANK. Then may I ask you this much, Anne. Please don't shut the door when you go in.

ANNE. You sound like Mrs. Van Daan! [*She picks up her blouse, putting it on.*]

MRS. FRANK. No. No. I don't mean to suggest anything wrong. I only

Literary Analysis
Plot and Subplot What does this exchange show about the relationship between Anne and her mother?

intuition (in´ tōō wish´ ən) *n.* ability to know immediately, without reasoning

wish that you wouldn't expose yourself to criticism . . . that you wouldn't give Mrs. Van Daan the opportunity to be unpleasant.

ANNE. Mrs. Van Daan doesn't need an opportunity to be unpleasant!

MRS. FRANK. Everyone's on edge, worried about Mr. Kraler. This is one more thing . . .

ANNE. I'm sorry, Mother. I'm going to Peter's room. I'm not going to let Petronella Van Daan spoil our friendship.

[MRS. FRANK *hesitates for a second, then goes out, closing the door after her. She gets a pack of playing cards and sits at the center table, playing solitaire. In* ANNE'S *room* MARGOT *hands the finished skirt to* ANNE. *As* ANNE *is putting it on,* MARGOT *takes off her high-heeled shoes and stuffs paper in the toes so that* ANNE *can wear them.*]

MARGOT. [*To* ANNE] Why don't you two talk in the main room? It'd save a lot of trouble. It's hard on Mother, having to listen to those remarks from Mrs. Van Daan and not say a word.

ANNE. Why doesn't she say a word? I think it's ridiculous to take it and take it.

MARGOT. You don't understand Mother at all, do you? She can't talk back. She's not like you. It's just not in her nature to fight back.

ANNE. Anyway . . . the only one I worry about is you. I feel awfully guilty about you. [*She sits on the stool near* MARGOT, *putting on* MARGOT'S *high-heeled shoes.*]

MARGOT. What about?

ANNE. I mean, every time I go into Peter's room, I have a feeling I may be hurting you. [MARGOT *shakes her head.*] I know if it were me, I'd be wild. I'd be desperately jealous, if it were me.

MARGOT. Well, I'm not.

ANNE. You don't feel badly? Really? Truly? You're not jealous?

MARGOT. Of course I'm jealous . . . jealous that you've got something to get up in the morning for . . . But jealous of you and Peter? No.

[ANNE *goes back to the mirror.*]

ANNE. Maybe there's nothing to be jealous of. Maybe he doesn't really like me. Maybe I'm just taking the place of his cat . . . [*She picks up a pair of short white gloves, putting them on.*] Wouldn't you like to come in with us?

MARGOT. I have a book.

[*The sound of the children playing outside fades out. In the main room* DUSSEL *can stand it no longer. He jumps up, going to the bedroom door and knocking sharply.*]

DUSSEL. Will you please let me in my room!

Reading Strategy
Picturing the Action
What is the effect of picturing the actions of Mrs. Frank and Anne and Margot at the same time?

Reading Check

Why does Anne suspect that Margot is jealous of her?

ANNE. Just a minute, dear, dear Mr. Dussel. [*She picks up her mother's pink stole and adjusts it elegantly over her shoulders, then gives a last look in the mirror.*] Well, here I go . . . to run the gauntlet.[5]

[*She starts out, followed by* MARGOT.]

DUSSEL. [*As she appears—sarcastic*] Thank you so much.

[DUSSEL *goes into his room.* ANNE *goes toward* PETER'S *room, passing* MRS. VAN DAAN *and her parents at the center table.*]

MRS. VAN DAAN. My God, look at her!

[ANNE *pays no attention. She knocks at* PETER'S *door.*]

I don't know what good it is to have a son. I never see him. He wouldn't care if I killed myself.

[PETER *opens the door and stands aside for* ANNE *to come in.*]

Just a minute, Anne. [*She goes to them at the door.*] I'd like to say a few words to my son. Do you mind?

[PETER *and* ANNE *stand waiting.*]

Peter, I don't want you staying up till all hours tonight. You've got to have your sleep. You're a growing boy. You hear?

MRS. FRANK. Anne won't stay late. She's going to bed promptly at nine. Aren't you, Anne?

ANNE. Yes, Mother . . . [*To* MRS. VAN DAAN] May we go now?

MRS. VAN DAAN. Are you asking me? I didn't know I had anything to say about it.

MRS. FRANK. Listen for the chimes, Anne dear.

[*The two young people go off into* PETER'S *room, shutting the door after them.*]

MRS. VAN DAAN. [*To* MRS. FRANK] In my day it was the boys who called on the girls. Not the girls on the boys.

MRS. FRANK. You know how young people like to feel that they have secrets. Peter's room is the only place where they can talk.

MRS. VAN DAAN. Talk! That's not what they called it when I was young.

[MRS. VAN DAAN *goes off to the bathroom.* MARGOT *settles down to read her book.* MR. FRANK *puts his papers away and brings a chess game to the center table. He and* MRS. FRANK *start to play. In* PETER'S *room,* ANNE *speaks to* PETER, *indignant, humiliated.*]

ANNE. Aren't they awful? Aren't they impossible? Treating us as if we were still in the nursery.

[*She sits on the cot.* PETER *gets a bottle of pop and two glasses.*]

Reading Strategy
Picturing the Action How do these stage directions help you picture what the characters are doing?

indignant (in dig´ nənt) *adj.* filled with anger over some meanness or injustice

---

5. to run the gauntlet (gônt´ lit) formerly, to pass between two rows of men who struck at the offender with clubs as he passed; here, a series of troubles or difficulties.

PETER. Don't let it bother you. It doesn't bother me.

ANNE. I suppose you can't really blame them . . . they think back to what *they* were like at our age. They don't realize how much more advanced we are . . . When you think what wonderful discussions we've had! . . . Oh, I forgot. I was going to bring you some more pictures.

PETER. Oh, these are fine, thanks.

ANNE. Don't you want some more? Miep just brought me some new ones.

PETER. Maybe later. [*He gives her a glass of pop and, taking some for himself, sits down facing her.*]

ANNE. [*Looking up at one of the photographs*] I remember when I got that . . . I won it. I bet Jopie that I could eat five ice-cream cones. We'd all been playing ping-pong . . . We used to have heavenly times . . . we'd finish up with ice cream at the Delphi, or the Oasis, where Jews were allowed . . . there'd always be a lot of boys . . . we'd laugh and joke . . . I'd like to go back to it for a few days or a week. But after that I know I'd be bored to death. I think more seriously about life now. I want to be a journalist . . . or something. I love to write. What do you want to do?

PETER. I thought I might go off some place . . . work on a farm or something . . . some job that doesn't take much brains.

ANNE. You shouldn't talk that way. You've got the most awful inferiority complex.

PETER. I know I'm not smart.

ANNE. That isn't true. You're much better than I am in dozens of things . . . arithmetic and algebra and . . . well, you're a million times better than I am in algebra. [*With sudden directness*] You like Margot, don't you? Right from the start you liked her, liked her much better than me.

PETER. [*Uncomfortably*] Oh, I don't know.

[*In the main room* MRS. VAN DAAN *comes from the bathroom and goes over to the sink, polishing a coffee pot.*]

ANNE. It's all right. Everyone feels that way. Margot's so good. She's sweet and bright and beautiful and I'm not.

PETER. I wouldn't say that.

ANNE. Oh, no, I'm not. I know that. I know quite well that I'm not a beauty. I never have been and never shall be.

PETER. I don't agree at all. I think you're pretty.

ANNE. That's not true!

PETER. And another thing. You've changed . . . from at first, I mean.

ANNE. I have?

PETER. I used to think you were awful noisy.

Literary Analysis
Plot and Subplot In what way is the subplot involving Anne and Peter related to Anne's question about Margot?

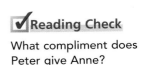
Reading Check

What compliment does Peter give Anne?

ANNE. And what do you think now, Peter? How have I changed?

PETER. Well . . . er . . . you're . . . quieter.

[*In his room* DUSSEL *takes his pajamas and toilet articles and goes into the bathroom to change.*]

ANNE. I'm glad you don't just hate me.

PETER. I never said that.

ANNE. I bet when you get out of here you'll never think of me again.

PETER. That's crazy.

ANNE. When you get back with all of your friends, you're going to say . . . now what did I ever see in that Mrs. Quack Quack.

PETER. I haven't got any friends.

ANNE. Oh, Peter, of course you have. Everyone has friends.

PETER. Not me. I don't want any. I get along all right without them.

ANNE. Does that mean you can get along with-out me? I think of myself as your friend.

PETER. No. If they were all like you, it'd be different.

[*He takes the glasses and the bottle and puts them away. There is a second's silence and then* ANNE *speaks, hesitantly, shyly.*]

ANNE. Peter, did you ever kiss a girl?

PETER. Yes. Once.

ANNE. [*To cover her feelings*] That picture's crooked.

[PETER *goes over, straightening the photograph.*]

Was she pretty?

PETER. Huh?

ANNE. The girl that you kissed.

PETER. I don't know. I was blind-folded. [*He comes back and sits down again.*] It was at a party. One of those kissing games.

ANNE. [*Relieved*] Oh. I don't suppose that really counts, does it?

▼ **Critical Viewing**
Does this photograph of Peter Van Daan seem to capture his personality? Explain. **[Assess]**

PETER. It didn't with me.

ANNE. I've been kissed twice. Once a man I'd never seen before kissed me on the cheek when he picked me up off the ice and I was crying. And the other was Mr. Koophuis, a friend of Father's who kissed my hand. You wouldn't say those counted, would you?

PETER. I wouldn't say so.

ANNE. I know almost for certain that Margot would never kiss anyone unless she was engaged to them. And I'm sure too that Mother never touched a man before Pim. But I don't know . . . things are so different now . . . What do you think? Do you think a girl shouldn't kiss anyone except if she's engaged or something? It's so hard to try to think what to do, when here we are with the whole world falling around our ears and you think. . . well . . . you don't know what's going to happen tomorrow and . . . What do you think?

PETER. I suppose it'd depend on the girl. Some girls, anything they do's wrong. But others . . . well . . . it wouldn't necessarily be wrong with them.

[*The carillon starts to strike nine o'clock.*]

I've always thought that when two people . . .

ANNE. Nine o'clock. I have to go.

PETER. That's right.

ANNE. [*Without moving*] Good night.

[*There is a second's pause, then* PETER *gets up and moves toward the door.*]

PETER. You won't let them stop you coming?

ANNE. No. [*She rises and starts for the door.*] Sometimes I might bring my diary. There are so many things in it that I want to talk over with you. There's a lot about you.

PETER. What kind of thing?

ANNE. I wouldn't want you to see some of it. I thought you were a nothing, just the way you thought about me.

PETER. Did you change your mind, the way I changed my mind about you?

ANNE. Well . . . You'll see . . .

[*For a second* ANNE *stands looking up at* PETER, *longing for him to kiss her. As he makes no move she turns away. Then suddenly* PETER *grabs her awkwardly in his arms, kissing her on the cheek.* ANNE *walks out dazed. She stands for a minute, her back to the people in the main room. As she regains her poise she goes to her mother and father and* MARGOT, *silently kissing them. They murmur their good nights to her. As she is about to open her bedroom door, she catches sight of* MRS. VAN DAAN. *She goes quickly to her, taking her face in her hands and kissing her first on one cheek and then on the other. Then she hurries off into*

Literary Analysis

Plot and Subplot What is happening in the subplot about Peter and Anne?

Literary Analysis

Plot and Subplot and Dialogue How does this dialogue between Anne and Peter advance the subplot?

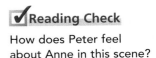

Reading Check

How does Peter feel about Anne in this scene?

The Diary of Anne Frank, Act II ◆ 765

her room. MRS. VAN DAAN *looks after her, and then looks over at* PETER'S *room. Her suspicions are confirmed.*]

MRS. VAN DAAN. [*She knows.*] Ah hah!

[*The lights dim out. The curtain falls on the scene. In the darkness* ANNE'S VOICE *comes faintly at first and then with growing strength.*]

ANNE'S VOICE. By this time we all know each other so well that if anyone starts to tell a story, the rest can finish it for him. We're having to cut down still further on our meals. What makes it worse, the rats have been at work again. They've carried off some of our precious food. Even Mr. Dussel wishes now that Mouschi was here. Thursday, the twentieth of April, nineteen forty-four. Invasion fever is mounting every day. Miep tells us that people outside talk of nothing else. For myself, life has become much more pleasant. I often go to Peter's room after supper. Oh, don't think I'm in love, because I'm not. But it does make life more bearable to have someone with whom you can exchange views. No more tonight. P.S. . . . I must be honest. I must confess that I actually live for the next meeting. Is there anything lovelier than to sit under the skylight and feel the sun on your cheeks and have a darling boy in your arms? I admit now that I'm glad the Van Daans had a son and not a daughter. I've outgrown another dress. That's the third. I'm having to wear Margot's clothes after all. I'm working hard on my French and am now reading *La Belle Nivernaise.*[6]

[*As she is saying the last lines—the curtain rises on the scene. The lights dim on, as* ANNE'S VOICE *fades out.*]

Scene 3

[*It is night, a few weeks later. Everyone is in bed. There is complete quiet. In the* VAN DAANS' *room a match flares up for a moment and then is quickly put out.* MR. VAN DAAN, *in bare feet, dressed in underwear and trousers, is dimly seen coming* <u>stealthily</u> *down the stairs and into the main room, where* MR. *and* MRS. FRANK *and* MARGOT *are sleeping. He goes to the food safe and again lights a match. Then he cautiously opens the safe, taking out a half-loaf of bread. As he closes the safe, it creaks. He stands rigid.* MRS. FRANK *sits up in bed. She sees him.*]

MRS. FRANK. [*Screaming*] Otto! Otto! *Komme schnell!*[7]

[*The rest of the people wake, hurriedly getting up.*]

MR. FRANK. *Was ist los? Was ist passiert?*[8]

[DUSSEL, *followed by* ANNE, *comes from his room.*]

MRS. FRANK. [*As she rushes over to* MR. VAN DAAN] *Er stiehlt das Essen!*[9]

Reading Strategy
Picture the Action What do you picture while Anne is speaking at the end of the scene?

stealthily (stel′ thi lē′) *adv.* in a secretive or sneaky way

---

6. *La Belle Nivernaise* a story by Alphonse Daudet, a French author.
7. *Komme schnell!* (käm′ ə shnel) German for "Come quick!"
8. *Was ist los? Was ist passiert?* (väs ist los väs ist päs′ ērt) German for "What's the matter? What happened?"
9. *Er stiehlt das Essen!* (er stēlt däs es′ ən) German for "He steals food!"

DUSSEL. [*Grabbing* MR. VAN DAAN] You! You! Give me that.

MRS. VAN DAAN. [*Coming down the stairs*] Putti . . . Putti . . . what is it?

DUSSEL. [*His hands on* VAN DAAN'S *neck*] You dirty thief . . . stealing food . . . you good-for-nothing . . .

MR. FRANK. Mr. Dussel! Oh! Help me, Peter!

[PETER *comes over, trying, with* MR. FRANK, *to separate the two struggling men.*]

PETER. Let him go! Let go!

[DUSSEL *drops* MR. VAN DAAN, *pushing him away. He shows them the end of a loaf of bread that he has taken from* VAN DAAN.]

DUSSEL. You greedy, selfish . . . !

[MARGOT *turns on the lights.*]

MRS. VAN DAAN. Putti . . . what is it?

[*All of* MRS. FRANK'S *gentleness, her self-control, is gone. She is outraged, in a frenzy of indignation.*]

MRS. FRANK. The bread! He was stealing the bread!

DUSSEL. It was you, and all the time we thought it was the rats!

MR. FRANK. Mr. Van Daan, how could you!

MR. VAN DAAN. I'm hungry.

MRS. FRANK. We're all of us hungry! I see the children getting thinner and thinner. Your own son Peter . . . I've heard him moan in his sleep, he's so hungry. And you come in the night and steal food that should go to them . . . to the children!

MRS. VAN DAAN. [*Going to* MR. VAN DAAN *protectively*] He needs more food than the rest of us. He's used to more. He's a big man.

[MR. VAN DAAN *breaks away, going over and sitting on the couch.*]

MRS. FRANK. [*Turning on* MRS. VAN DAAN] And you . . . you're worse than he is! You're a mother, and yet you sacrifice your child to this man . . . this . . . this . . .

MR. FRANK. Edith! Edith!

[MARGOT *picks up the pink woolen stole, putting it over her mother's shoulders.*]

MRS. FRANK. [*Paying no attention, going on to* MRS. VAN DAAN] Don't think I haven't seen you! Always saving the choicest bits for him! I've watched you day after day and I've held my tongue. But not any longer! Not after this! Now I want him to go! I want him to get out of here!

[*Together*] {
    MR. FRANK. Edith!

    MR. VAN DAAN. Get out of here?

    MRS. VAN DAAN. What do you mean?

Reading Check

Why does Mrs. Van Daan defend her husband when he is caught stealing bread?

MRS. FRANK. Just that! Take your things and get out!

MR. FRANK. [*To* MRS. FRANK] You're speaking in anger. You cannot mean what you are saying.

MRS. FRANK. I mean exactly that!

[MRS. VAN DAAN *takes a cover from the* FRANKS' *bed, pulling it about her.*]

MR. FRANK. For two long years we have lived here, side by side. We have respected each other's rights . . . we have managed to live in peace. Are we now going to throw it all away? I know this will never happen again, will it, Mr. Van Daan?

MR. VAN DAAN. No. No.

MRS. FRANK. He steals once! He'll steal again!

[MR. VAN DAAN, *holding his stomach, starts for the bathroom.* ANNE *puts her arms around him, helping him up the step.*]

MR. FRANK. Edith, please. Let us be calm. We'll all go to our rooms . . . and afterwards we'll sit down quietly and talk this out . . . we'll find some way . . .

MRS. FRANK. No! No! No more talk! I want them to leave!

MRS. VAN DAAN. You'd put us out, on the streets?

MRS. FRANK. There are other hiding places.

MRS. VAN DAAN. A cellar . . . a closet. I know. And we have no money left even to pay for that.

MRS. FRANK. I'll give you money. Out of my own pocket I'll give it gladly. [*She gets her purse from a shelf and comes back with it.*]

MRS. VAN DAAN. Mr. Frank, you told Putti you'd never forget what he'd done for you when you came to Amsterdam. You said you could never repay him, that you . . .

MRS. FRANK. [*Counting out money*] If my husband had any obligation to you, he's paid it, over and over.

MR. FRANK. Edith, I've never seen you like this before. I don't know you.

MRS. FRANK. I should have spoken out long ago.

DUSSEL. You can't be nice to some people.

MRS. VAN DAAN. [*Turning on* DUSSEL] There would have been plenty for all of us, if *you* hadn't come in here!

MR. FRANK. We don't need the Nazis to destroy us. We're destroying ourselves.

[*He sits down, with his head in his hands.* MRS. FRANK *goes to* MRS. VAN DAAN.]

MRS. FRANK. [*Giving* MRS. VAN DAAN *some money*] Give this to Miep. She'll find you a place.

Literary Analysis
Plot and Subplot What does Mr. Frank's speech show about his character?

Literary Analysis
Plot and Subplot How does Mr. Van Daan's action increase the tension of the plot?

ANNE. Mother, you're not putting Peter out. Peter hasn't done anything.

MRS. FRANK. He'll stay, of course. When I say I must protect the children, I mean Peter too.

[PETER *rises from the steps where he has been sitting.*]

PETER. I'd have to go if Father goes.

[MR. VAN DAAN *comes from the bathroom.* MRS. VAN DAAN *hurries to him and takes him to the couch. Then she gets water from the sink to bathe his face.*]

MRS. FRANK. [*While this is going on*] He's no father to you . . . that man! He doesn't know what it is to be a father!

PETER. [*Starting for his room*] I wouldn't feel right. I couldn't stay.

MRS. FRANK. Very well, then. I'm sorry.

ANNE. [*Rushing over to* PETER] No, Peter! No!

[PETER *goes into his room, closing the door after him.* ANNE *turns back to her mother, crying.*]

I don't care about the food. They can have mine! I don't want it! Only don't send them away. It'll be daylight soon. They'll be caught . . .

MARGOT. [*Putting her arms comfortingly around* ANNE] Please, Mother!

MRS. FRANK. They're not going now. They'll stay here until Miep finds them a place. [*To* MRS. VAN DAAN] But one thing I insist on! He must never come down here again! He must never come to this room where the food is stored! We'll divide what we have . . . an equal share for each!

[DUSSEL *hurries over to get a sack of potatoes from the food safe.* MRS. FRANK *goes on, to* MRS. VAN DAAN]

You can cook it here and take it up to him.

[[DUSSEL *brings the sack of potatoes back to the center table.*]

MARGOT. Oh, no. No. We haven't sunk so far that we're going to fight over a handful of rotten potatoes.

DUSSEL. [*Dividing the potatoes into piles*] Mrs. Frank, Mr. Frank, Margot, Anne, Peter, Mrs. Van Daan, Mr. Van Daan, myself . . . Mrs. Frank . . .

[*The buzzer sounds in* MIEP's *signal.*]

MR. FRANK. It's Miep! [*He hurries over, getting his overcoat and putting it on.*]

MARGOT. At this hour?

MRS. FRANK. It is trouble.

MR. FRANK. [*As he starts down to unbolt the door*] I beg you, don't let her see a thing like this!

Reading Strategy
Picture the Action How do you picture the scene as Dussel starts to divide the food?

**Reading Check**

Why does Mrs. Frank insist the Van Daans must leave?

MR. DUSSEL. [*Counting without stopping*] . . . Anne, Peter, Mrs. Van Daan, Mr. Van Daan, myself . . .

MARGOT. [*To* DUSSEL] Stop it! Stop it!

DUSSEL. . . . Mr. Frank, Margot, Anne, Peter, Mrs. Van Daan, Mr. Van Daan, myself, Mrs. Frank . . .

MRS. VAN DAAN. You're keeping the big ones for yourself! All the big ones . . . Look at the size of that! . . . And that! . . .

[DUSSEL *continues on with his dividing.* PETER, *with his shirt and trousers on, comes from his room.*]

MARGOT. Stop it! Stop it!

[*We hear* MIEP'S *excited voice speaking to* MR. FRANK *below.*]

MIEP. Mr. Frank . . . the most wonderful news! . . . The invasion has begun!

MR. FRANK. Go on, tell them! Tell them!

[MIEP *comes running up the steps ahead of* MR. FRANK. *She has a man's raincoat on over her nightclothes and a bunch of orange-colored flowers in her hand.*]

MIEP. Did you hear that, everybody? Did you hear what I said? The invasion has begun! The invasion!

[*They all stare at* MIEP, *unable to grasp what she is telling them.* PETER *is the first to recover his wits.*]

PETER. Where?

MRS. VAN DAAN. When? When, Miep?

MIEP. It began early this morning . . .

[*As she talks on, the realization of what she has said begins to dawn on them. Everyone goes crazy. A wild demonstration takes place.* MRS. FRANK *hugs* MR. VAN DAAN.]

MRS. FRANK. Oh, Mr. Van Daan, did you hear that?

[DUSSEL *embraces* MRS. VAN DAAN. PETER *grabs a frying pan and parades around the room, beating on it, singing the Dutch National Anthem.* ANNE *and* MARGOT *follow him, singing, weaving in and out among the excited grown-ups.* MARGOT *breaks away to take the flowers from* MIEP *and distribute them to everyone. While this pandemonium is going on* MRS. FRANK *tries to make herself heard above the excitement.*]

MRS. FRANK. [*To* MIEP] How do you know?

MIEP. The radio . . . The B.B.C.![10] They said they landed on the coast of Normandy![11]

---

10. B.B.C. British Broadcasting Corporation.
11. Normandy (nôr'mən dē) a region in northwest France, on the English Channel.

Literature in context   World Events Connection

Normandy Invasion

The invasion that took place on June 6, 1944 in Normandy gave many families, like the Franks, a sense of renewed hope. The assault across the English Channel into France took many months of careful planning because most of the coastline was bristling with German guns and troops. But the Allies were successful in fooling the Germans about where and when the attack would occur. Once the intense fighting was over and the Allied foothold in France was secured, Germany's total defeat was only a matter of time. The liberation of Amsterdam from Nazi rule was less than a year away. If Anne's family could continue to escape detection for a little longer, they would be saved.

The landing at Normandy

PETER. The British?

MIEP. British, Americans, French, Dutch, Poles, Norwegians . . . all of them! More than four thousand ships! Churchill spoke, and General Eisenhower! D-Day they call it!

MR. FRANK. Thank God, it's come!

MRS. VAN DAAN. At last!

MIEP. [*Starting out*] I'm going to tell Mr. Kraler. This'll be better than any blood transfusion.

MR. FRANK. [*Stopping her*] What part of Normandy did they land, did they say?

MIEP. Normandy . . . that's all I know now . . . I'll be up the minute I hear some more! [*She goes hurriedly out.*]

MR. FRANK. [*To* MRS. FRANK] What did I tell you? What did I tell you?

[MRS. FRANK *indicates that he has forgotten to bolt the door after* MIEP. *He hurries down the steps.* MR. VAN DAAN, *sitting on the couch, suddenly breaks into a convulsive*[12] *sob. Everybody looks at him, bewildered.*]

MRS. VAN DAAN. [*Hurrying to him*] Putti! Putti! What is it? What happened?

MR. VAN DAAN. Please, I'm so ashamed.

[MR. FRANK *comes back up the steps.*]

DUSSEL. Oh!

MRS. VAN DAAN. Don't, Putti.

MARGOT. It doesn't matter now!

MR. FRANK. [*Going to* MR. VAN DAAN] Didn't you hear what Miep said? The invasion has come! We're going to be liberated! This is a time to celebrate! [*He embraces* MRS. FRANK *and then hurries to the cupboard and gets the cognac and a glass.*]

MR. VAN DAAN. To steal bread from children!

MRS. FRANK. We've all done things that we're ashamed of.

ANNE. Look at me, the way I've treated Mother . . . so mean and horrid to her.

MRS. FRANK. No, Anneke, no.

[ANNE *runs to her mother, putting her arms around her.*]

ANNE. Oh, Mother, I was. I was awful.

MR. VAN DAAN. Not like me. No one is as bad as me!

DUSSEL. [*To* MR. VAN DAAN] Stop it now! Let's be happy!

Reading Check

What is the good news that the families in hiding receive?

---

12. **convulsive** (kən vul′ siv) *adj.* having an involuntary contraction or spasm of the muscles; shuddering.

MR. FRANK. [*Giving* MR. VAN DAAN *a glass of cognac*] Here! Here! Schnapps! L'chaim![13]

[VAN DAAN *takes the cognac. They all watch him. He gives them a feeble smile.* ANNE *puts up her fingers in a V-for-Victory sign. As* VAN DAAN *gives an answering V-sign, they are startled to hear a loud sob from behind them. It is* MRS. FRANK, *stricken with remorse. She is sitting on the other side of the room.*]

MRS. FRANK. [*Through her sobs*] When I think of the terrible things I said . . .

[MR. FRANK, ANNE *and* MARGOT *hurry to her, trying to comfort her.* MR. VAN DAAN *brings her his glass of cognac.*]

MR. VAN DAAN. No! No! You were right!

MRS. FRANK. That I should speak that way to you! . . . Our friends! . . . Our guests! [*She starts to cry again.*]

DUSSEL. Stop it, you're spoiling the whole invasion!

[*As they are comforting her, the lights dim out. The curtain falls.*]

ANNE'S VOICE. [*Faintly at first and then with growing strength*] We're all in much better spirits these days. There's still excellent news of the invasion. The best part about it is that I have a feeling that friends are coming. Who knows? Maybe I'll be back in school by fall. Ha, ha! The joke is on us! The warehouse man doesn't know a thing and we are paying him all that money! . . . Wednesday, the second of July, nineteen forty-four. The invasion seems temporarily to be bogged down. Mr. Kraler has to have an operation, which looks bad. The Gestapo have found the radio that was stolen. Mr. Dussel says they'll trace it back and back to the thief, and then, it's just a matter of time till they get to us. Everyone is low. Even poor Pim can't raise their spirits. I have often been downcast myself . . . but never in despair. I can shake off everything if I write. But . . . and that is the great question . . . will I ever be able to write well? I want to so much. I want to go on living even after my death. Another birthday has gone by, so now I am fifteen. Already I know what I want. I have a goal, an opinion.

---

13. **Schnapps! L'chaim!** (shnäps lə khä´ yim) German for "a drink," and a Hebrew toast meaning "To life."

▲ Critical Viewing
This is a page of Anne Frank's diary. Judging from its appearance, was Anne a careful writer or a careless one? Explain. **[Deduce]**

[*As this is being said—the curtain rises on the scene, the lights dim on, and* ANNE'S VOICE *fades out.*]

Scene 4

[*It is an afternoon a few weeks later . . . Everyone but* MARGOT *is in the main room. There is a sense of great tension.*

Both MRS. FRANK *and* MR. VAN DAAN *are nervously pacing back and forth,* DUSSEL *is standing at the window, looking down fixedly at the street below.* PETER *is at the center table, trying to do his lessons.* ANNE *sits opposite him, writing in her diary.* MRS. VAN DAAN *is seated on the couch, her eyes on* MR. FRANK *as he sits reading.*

The sound of a telephone ringing comes from the office below. They all are rigid, listening tensely. DUSSEL *rushes down to* MR. FRANK.]

DUSSEL. There it goes again, the telephone! Mr. Frank, do you hear?

MR. FRANK. [*Quietly*] Yes. I hear.

DUSSEL. [*Pleading, insistent*] But this is the third time, Mr. Frank! The third time in quick succession! It's a signal! I tell you it's Miep, trying to get us! For some reason she can't come to us and she's trying to warn us of something!

MR. FRANK. Please. Please.

MR. VAN DAAN. [*To* DUSSEL] You're wasting your breath.

DUSSEL. Something has happened, Mr. Frank. For three days now Miep hasn't been to see us! And today not a man has come to work. There hasn't been a sound in the building!

MRS. FRANK. Perhaps it's Sunday. We may have lost track of the days.

MR. VAN DAAN. [*To* ANNE] You with the diary there. What day is it?

DUSSEL. [*Going to* MRS. FRANK] I don't lose track of the days! I know exactly what day it is! It's Friday, the fourth of August. Friday, and not a man at work. [*He rushes back to* MR. FRANK, *pleading with him, almost in tears.*] I tell you Mr. Kraler's dead. That's the only explanation. He's dead and they've closed down the building, and Miep's trying to tell us!

MR. FRANK. She'd never telephone us.

DUSSEL. [*Frantic*] Mr. Frank, answer that! I beg you, answer it!

MR. FRANK. No.

MR. VAN DAAN. Just pick it up and listen. You don't have to speak. Just listen and see if it's Miep.

Literary Analysis
Plot and Subplot In what way does the ringing telephone serve as a turning point in the plot?

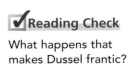

Reading Check

What happens that makes Dussel frantic?

The Diary of Anne Frank, Act II ◆ 773

DUSSEL. [*Speaking at the same time*] Please . . . I ask you.

MR. FRANK. No. I've told you, no. I'll do nothing that might let anyone know we're in the building.

PETER. Mr. Frank's right.

MR. VAN DAAN. There's no need to tell us what side you're on.

MR. FRANK. If we wait patiently, quietly, I believe that help will come.

[*There is silence for a minute as they all listen to the telephone ringing.*]

DUSSEL. I'm going down.

[*He rushes down the steps.* MR. FRANK *tries* <u>ineffectually</u> *to hold him.* DUSSEL *runs to the lower door, unbolting it. The telephone stops ringing.* DUSSEL *bolts the door and comes slowly back up the steps.*]

    Too late.

[MR. FRANK *goes to* MARGOT *in* ANNE'S *bedroom.*]

MR. VAN DAAN. So we just wait here until we die.

MRS. VAN DAAN. [*Hysterically*] I can't stand it! I'll kill myself! I'll kill myself!

MR. VAN DAAN. Stop it!

[*In the distance, a German military band is heard playing a Viennese waltz.*]

MRS. VAN DAAN. I think you'd be glad if I did! I think you want me to die!

MR. VAN DAAN. Whose fault is it we're here?

[MRS. VAN DAAN *starts for her room. He follows, talking at her.*]

    We could've been safe somewhere . . . in America or Switzerland. But no! No! You wouldn't leave when I wanted to. You couldn't leave your things. You couldn't leave your precious furniture.

MRS. VAN DAAN. Don't touch me!

[*She hurries up the stairs, followed by* MR. VAN DAAN. PETER, *unable to bear it, goes to his room.* ANNE *looks after him, deeply concerned.* DUSSEL *returns to his post at the window.* MR. FRANK *comes back into the main room and takes a book, trying to read.* MRS. FRANK *sits near the sink, starting to peel some potatoes.* ANNE *quietly goes to* PETER'S *room, closing the door after her.* PETER *is lying face down on the cot.* ANNE *leans over him, holding him in her arms, trying to bring him out of his despair.*]

ANNE. Look, Peter, the sky. [*She looks up through the skylight.*] What a lovely, lovely day! Aren't the clouds beautiful? You know what I do when it seems as if I couldn't stand being cooped up for one more minute? I think myself out. I think myself on a walk in the park where I used to go with Pim. Where the jonquils and the crocus and the violets grow down the slopes. You know the most

ineffectually
(in´ e fek´ cho͞o ə lē) *adv.* without producing the desired effect

Literary Analysis
Plot and Subplot What does the Van Daans' continuing bickering show about their characters?

wonderful part about *thinking* yourself out? You can have it any way you
like. You can have roses and violets
and chrysanthemums all blooming at
the same time . . . It's funny . . . I
used to take it all for granted . . . and
now I've gone crazy about everything
to do with nature. Haven't you?

PETER. I've just gone crazy. I think if
something doesn't happen soon . . . if
we don't get out of here . . . I can't
stand much more of it!

ANNE. [*Softly*] I wish you had a religion,
Peter.

PETER. No, thanks! Not me!

ANNE. Oh, I don't mean you have to be
Orthodox[14] . . . or believe in heaven and
hell and purgatory[15] and things . . . I
just mean some religion . . . it doesn't
matter what. Just to believe in
something! When I think of all that's
out there . . . the trees . . . and flowers
. . . and seagulls . . . when I think of
the dearness of you, Peter . . . and the

goodness of the people we know . . . Mr. Kraler, Miep, Dirk, the vegetable man, all risking their lives for us every day . . . When I think of
these good things, I'm not afraid any more . . . I find myself, and God,
and I . . .

[PETER *interrupts, getting up and walking away.*]

PETER. That's fine! But when I begin to think, I get mad! Look at us,
hiding out for two years. Not able to move! Caught here like . . . waiting for them to come and get us . . . and all for what?

ANNE. We're not the only people that've had to suffer. There've always
been people that've had to . . . sometimes one race . . . sometimes
another . . . and yet . . .

PETER. That doesn't make me feel any better!

ANNE. [*Going to him*] I know it's terrible, trying to have any faith . . .
when people are doing such horrible . . . But you know what I sometimes think? I think the world may be going through a phase, the way
I was with Mother. It'll pass, maybe not for hundreds of years, but

▲ **Critical Viewing**
In what ways is Anne
Frank deserving of being
honored on a postage
stamp? [**Connect**]

Reading Strategy
Picture the Action What
do you picture in this
scene as Peter and Anne
try to deal with their
fright?

☑**Reading Check**

What kinds of things does
Anne think about to lose
her fear?

---

14. **Orthodox** (ôr´ thə däks´) *adj.* strictly observing the rites and traditions of Judaism.
15. **purgatory** (pʉr´gə tôr´ ē) *n.* a state or place of temporary punishment.

some day . . . I still believe, in spite of everything, that people are really good at heart.

PETER. I want to see something now . . . Not a thousand years from now! [*He goes over, sitting down again on the cot.*]

ANNE. But, Peter, if you'd only look at it as part of a great pattern . . . that we're just a little minute in the life . . . [*She breaks off.*] Listen to us, going at each other like a couple of stupid grownups! Look at the sky now. Isn't it lovely?

[*She holds out her hand to him.* PETER *takes it and rises, standing with her at the window looking out, his arms around her.*]

Some day, when we're outside again, I'm going to . . .

[*She breaks off as she hears the sound of a car, its brakes squealing as it comes to a sudden stop. The people in the other rooms also become aware of the sound. They listen tensely. Another car roars up to a screeching stop.* ANNE *and* PETER *come from* PETER'S *room.* MR. *and* MRS. VAN DAAN *creep down the stairs.* DUSSEL *comes out from his room. Everyone is listening, hardly breathing. A doorbell clangs again and again in the building below.* MR. FRANK *starts quietly down the steps to the door.* DUSSEL *and* PETER *follow him. The others stand rigid, waiting, terrified.*

In a few seconds DUSSEL *comes stumbling back up the steps. He shakes off* PETER's *help and goes to his room.* MR. FRANK *bolts the door below, and comes slowly back up the steps. Their eyes are all on him as he stands there for a minute. They realize that what they feared has happened.* MRS. VAN DAAN *starts to whimper.* MR. VAN DAAN *puts her gently in a chair, and then hurries off up the stairs to their room to collect their things.* PETER *goes to comfort his mother. There is a sound of violent pounding on a door below.*]

MR. FRANK. [*Quietly*] For the past two years we have lived in fear. Now we can live in hope.

[*The pounding below becomes more insistent. There are muffled sounds of voices, shouting commands.*]

MEN'S VOICES. *Auf machen! Da drinnen! Auf machen! Schnell! Schnell! Schnell!*[16] etc., etc.

[*The street door below is forced open. We hear the heavy tread of footsteps coming up.* MR. FRANK *gets two school bags from the shelves, and gives one to* ANNE *and the other to* MARGOT. *He goes to get a bag for* MRS. FRANK. *The sound of feet coming up grows louder.* PETER *comes to* ANNE, *kissing her good-bye, then he goes to his room to collect his things. The buzzer of their door starts to ring.* MR. FRANK *brings* MRS. FRANK *a bag. They stand together, waiting. We hear the thud of gun butts on the door, trying to break it down.*

Reading Strategy
Picture the Action As you read the stage directions, how do you picture each person as they listen to the Nazi police at the door?

Literary Analysis
Plot and Subplot and Dialogue How does Mr. Frank's speech contribute to the resolution of the plot?

---

16. *Auf machen! . . . Schnell!* (ouf mäk´ ən dä dri´ nən ouf mak´ ən shnəl shnəl shnəl) German for "Open up, you in there, open up, quick, quick, quick."

ANNE *stands, holding her school satchel, looking over at her father and mother with a soft, reassuring smile. She is no longer a child, but a woman with courage to meet whatever lies ahead.*

The lights dim out. The curtain falls on the scene. We hear a mighty crash as the door is shattered. After a second ANNE'S VOICE *is heard.*]

ANNE'S VOICE. And so it seems our stay here is over. They are waiting for us now. They've allowed us five minutes to get our things. We can each take a bag and whatever it will hold of clothing. Nothing else. So, dear Diary, that means I must leave you behind. Good-bye for a while. P.S. Please, please, Miep, or Mr. Kraler, or anyone else. If you should find this diary, will you please keep it safe for me, because some day I hope . . .

[*Her voice stops abruptly. There is silence. After a second the curtain rises.*]

Scene 5

[*It is again the afternoon in November, 1945. The rooms are as we saw them in the first scene.* MR. KRALER *has joined* MIEP *and* MR. FRANK. *There are coffee cups on the table. We see a great change in* MR. FRANK. *He is calm now. His bitterness is gone. He slowly turns a few pages of the diary. They are blank.*]

MR. FRANK. No more. [*He closes the diary and puts it down on the couch beside him.*]

MIEP. I'd gone to the country to find food. When I got back the block was surrounded by police . . .

MR. KRALER. We made it our business to learn how they knew. It was the thief . . . the thief who told them.

[MIEP *goes up to the gas burner, bringing back a pot of coffee.*]

MR. FRANK. [*After a pause*] It seems strange to say this, that anyone could be happy in a concentration camp. But Anne was happy in the camp in Holland where they first took us. After two years of being shut up in these rooms, she could be out . . . out in the sunshine and the fresh air that she loved.

MIEP. [*Offering the coffee to* MR. FRANK] A little more?

MR. FRANK. [*Holding out his cup to her*] The news of the war was good. The British and Americans were sweeping through France. We felt sure that they would get to us in time. In September we were told that we were to be shipped to Poland . . . The men to one camp. The women to another. I was sent to Auschwitz.[17] They went to Belsen.[18] In January we were freed, the few of us who were left.

---

17. Auschwitz (oush′ vits) Nazi concentration camp in Poland that was notorious as an extermination center.
18. Belsen (bel′ zən) village in Germany that, with the village of Bergen, was the site of Bergen-Belsen, a Nazi concentration camp and extermination center.

Literary Analysis
Plot and Subplot What is the outcome of the plot?

The war wasn't yet over, so it took us a long time to get home. We'd be sent here and there behind the lines where we'd be safe. Each time our train would stop . . . at a siding, or a crossing . . . we'd all get out and go from group to group . . . Where were you? Were you at Belsen? At Buchenwald?[19] At Mauthausen? Is it possible that you knew my wife? Did you ever see my husband? My son? My daughter? That's how I found out about my wife's death . . . of Margot, the Van Daans . . . Dussel. But Anne . . . I still hoped . . . Yesterday I went to Rotterdam. I'd heard of a woman there . . . She'd been in Belsen with Anne . . . I know now.

[*He picks up the diary again, and turns the pages back to find a certain passage. As he finds it we hear* ANNE'S VOICE.]

ANNE'S VOICE. In spite of everything, I still believe that people are really good at heart. [MR. FRANK *slowly closes the diary.*]

MR. FRANK. She puts me to shame.

[*They are silent.*]

---

19. **Buchenwald** (boo′ ken wôld′) notorious Nazi concentration camp and extermination center in central Germany.

Anne Frank

(1929–1945)

Born in Germany, Anne Frank moved with her parents and older sister to Amsterdam to escape the Nazi regime. After Hitler's troops occupied the Netherlands, Jews there were also persecuted. In July 1942, when the family went into hiding, Anne took the diary she had received for her thirteenth birthday, just a month earlier. After an informer betrayed the families in August 1944, all were sent to concentration camps. Anne and Margot both died of typhus at the Bergen-Belsen camp early in 1945. Her father, the only survivor, had parts of the diary published in 1947. Today, the "Secret Annex" is a museum, drawing thousands of visitors each year.

Review and Assess

Thinking About the Selection

1. **Respond:** What do you like best about Anne Frank? How would you like having her as a friend?

2. **(a) Recall:** What is the time span of Act II? **(b) Interpret:** How have the characters changed since the end of Act I? **(c) Support:** How do you know that Anne has changed?

3. **(a) Recall:** How does the relationship between Anne and Peter change during Act II? **(b) Infer:** In what way does their friendship help Anne live through a difficult time? **(c) Analyze Cause and Effect:** How does Anne and Peter's relationship affect the others?

4. **(a) Recall:** What disturbing news does Mr. Kraler bring on New Year's Day? **(b) Connect:** What hint does this give about the ending of the play?

5. **(a) Recall:** What happens to the families at the end of Scene 4? **(b) Recall:** When does Scene 5 occur? **(c) Draw Conclusions:** How can Anne believe that "in spite of everything . . . people are really good at heart"? **(d) Interpret:** What does Mr. Frank mean by his last line: "She puts me to shame."

Review and Assess

Literary Analysis

Plot and Subplot
1. What is the conflict of the main **plot**?
2. On a graphic organizer like the one shown, plot the major events of *The Diary of Anne Frank* scene by scene, starting with Act I, Scene 2.

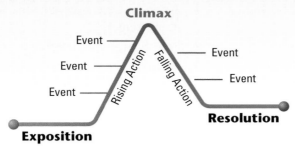

3. What are two subplots in *The Diary of Anne Frank?*
4. Create a plot diagram for one of those two subplots.

Connecting Literary Elements
5. Make an organizer like the one shown here. For each purpose shown, provide one example of **dialogue** that achieves the purpose.

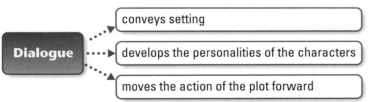

6. After Mr. Van Daan is caught stealing food, what does the dialogue among the eight people reveal about their personalities?

Reading Strategy

Picture the Action
7. Which details from the stage directions at the beginning of Act II, Scene 2, call to mind visual images?
8. Which details of Act II, Scene 4, heighten the suspense by appealing to your sense of hearing?

Extend Understanding
9. **World Events Connection:** Are there places in the world today where people in certain groups have to go into hiding?

Quick Review

The **plot** of a drama is the connected sequence of events in which each event results from a previous one and causes the next, leading to a climax and a resolution. A play may also have **subplots,** stories that are secondary to the main plot. To review **plot** and **subplot** see page 748.

Dialogue—the conversations between characters—moves the plot along and reveals character. To review dialogue, see page 748.

Picture the action of the play as you read—view the play in your mind by using your imagination and gathering clues from the stage directions and dialogue.

 Take It to the Net
www.phschool.com
Take the interactive self-test online to check your understanding of the play.

Integrate Language Skills

Vocabulary Development Lesson

Concept Development: Forms of *effect*

As a noun, the word *effect* means "result." Complete each sentence by writing the correct form of *effect: effective, ineffective, effect.*

1. The audience's tears and applause showed that the play was very ___?___.
2. The staging had a powerful ___?___ .
3. One critic, however, complained that the actor playing Mr. Frank was ___?___.

Spelling Strategy

When the "choo" sound appears in the middle of a word, it is sometimes spelled *tu*, as in *situation* and *ineffectual*. To practice spelling the "choo" sound with *tu*, unscramble the words in parentheses. Write the words on your paper.

1. a great amount of money (routfen)
2. real, true (latcua)

Fluency: Word Choice

Write the best vocabulary word from the list on page 748 to replace the underlined word or phrase in each sentence.

1. Anne became <u>angry</u> at Mrs. Van Daan's unfair remarks.
2. Peter's cat moved <u>secretively</u> up the stairs.
3. At first, Peter's shyness with Anne made him <u>unable to express himself.</u>
4. Sounds in the office below filled everyone with <u>dread.</u>
5. Anne's <u>quick insight</u> helped her win Peter's friendship.
6. Mr. Van Daan tried <u>without result</u> to persuade his wife to flee to Switzerland.

Grammar Lesson

Verb Agreement With Indefinite Pronouns

A verb must agree with its subject in number. Sometimes, though, you may have trouble deciding whether a subject is singular or plural. One confusing kind of subject is the **indefinite pronoun,** a pronoun that does not refer to a particular person, place, or thing. Some of these indefinite pronouns are always singular and take a singular verb. Others are always plural.

Singular Pronouns anybody, anyone, everybody, everyone, nobody, somebody, someone

Plural Pronouns both, few, many, others, several

> **Example:** *Someone* is here. (singular)
> *Others* are waiting. (plural)

▶ For more practice, see page R32, Exercise C.
Practice Revise these sentences to eliminate errors in subject-verb agreement. Not all sentences have errors.

1. Everyone are on edge, worried about Mr. Kraler.
2. Few knows where the Franks are hiding.
3. If anyone start to tell a story, the others can finish it.
4. Everyone is listening.
5. Many is touched by Anne's story.

Writing Application Write a two-paragraph review of the play. Use the indefinite pronouns *everyone, someone, anyone,* and *others,* making sure the subjects and verbs agree.

𝒲𝒢 *Prentice Hall Writing and Grammar Connection: Chapter 24, Sections 1 and 2*

Writing Lesson

Story Scene with Dialogue

Rewrite a scene from the play as a narrative that includes dialogue.

Prewriting   Decide on your scene. Make notes about the characters and the feelings and qualities you want to show.

Drafting   Begin your narrative with a brief exposition—a section in which you set up and explain the situation. Then, tell story events in order. Develop parts of the story scene through dialogue.

Model: Incorporating Dialogue

Once again, Anne and Peter were bickering. Mrs. Frank tried to ignore the noise, but when the argument turned into a wrestling match she had to speak up. "Anne! . . . Peter!" she exclaimed. Embarrassed, Peter headed for his room.

"Peter, where are you going?" cried Anne. "Come dance with me."

"I tell you, I don't know how, " growled Peter.

> After setting up the situation, the writer uses dialogue from the play to show interaction between characters. In between characters' words, the writer tells what characters do and what they think and feel.

Revising   Revise your narrative to improve word choice. In sections of dialogue where you want to indicate the way characters speak, replace *said* with a more precise verb, such as *shouted*, *whispered*, or *cried*.

*W*G *Prentice Hall Writing and Grammar Connection: Chapter 5*

Extension Activities

Research and Technology   Work with a group to create a **bulletin board display** about the experiences of specific Jewish individuals or communities in Europe during World War II. Use primary sources to give a human perspective to your display. Primary sources include

- records of journals
- newspaper articles
- government documents

Write captions that identify the sources you used. **[Group Activity]**

Listening and Speaking   Think about the theme or message of *The Diary of Anne Frank* and about the way in which you respond to the play. Develop a statement that explains your reactions. Then prepare and deliver your **oral response** to the play. Support your response by connecting to the playwrights' writing techniques and to specific references from the text.

 **Take It to the Net**   www.phschool.com

Go online for an additional research activity using the Internet.

READING INFORMATIONAL MATERIALS

Summaries

About Summaries

A **summary** is a statement of the main ideas and major details in a written or dramatic work. You will find summaries in many sources.

- Newspapers and magazines carry short "capsule" summaries of current movies.
- An encyclopedia of English literature includes detailed summaries of important books and other literary works, such as Shakespeare's plays and Jane Austen's novels.
- Scientific research reports usually begin with a summary, or "abstract," of the researchers' findings.

Summaries are very useful for quickly previewing or reviewing a work. Writing your own summaries helps you remember what you have read. Since summaries remove most of the detail, reading a summary can never replace the experience of reading the complete book, play, or article.

Reading Strategy

Comparing an Original Text and a Summary

A summary should give the reader a good idea of what the original work was about. A good summary should meet several tests:

- It must capture the main ideas of the work and present them accurately.
- It should include those details that are crucial to the plot or important in understanding the characters.

The Diary of Anne Frank		
	Act I	Act II
Major Events		
Summary		

- It should convey the underlying meaning of the work.

If you looked up *The Diary of Anne Frank* in an encyclopedia of drama or American literature, you would find a plot summary similar to the one included on the following pages. As you read the summary, use a chart like the one shown here to keep track of the major points and details it includes.

The Diary of Anne Frank

Authors: Frances Goodrich
         Albert Hackett
  Genre: Drama
    Date: 1954
Characters: Mr. Frank, Mrs. Frank,
Margot Frank, Anne Frank,
Mr. Van Daan, Mrs. Van Daan,
Peter Van Daan, Mr. Dussel,
Miep, Mr. Kraler

Anne Frank Fonds, Basel/Archive Photos

Overview: The main action of the play occurs between July 1942 and August 1944 during the Nazi occupation of the Netherlands. Two short opening and closing scenes, featuring Anne Frank's father, are set in November 1945 and frame the action. The play has one set—several small attic rooms above an office building in Amsterdam. The Franks, the Van Daans, and Dussel go into hiding in this "Secret Annex," waiting until the war is over in hopes of avoiding arrest by the Nazis. Two courageous non-Jewish Dutch friends, Miep (Gies) and Mr. Kraler, bring the families food and other supplies. Most of the action revolves around the daily realities of living in hiding and the tensions created by so many people living in such a confined space. Excerpts from Anne's diary frame the scenes, giving insight into her thoughts as a young woman coming of age in these unusual circumstances. Eventually, they are discovered and German soldiers arrive at the door.

In a short final scene in November 1945. Mr. Kraler has joined Miep and Mr. Frank. Frank briefly tells about life in the camps, and how he learned that all the others have died.

He then reads from Anne's diary: "In spite of everything, I still believe that people are really good at heart."

This summary of the play begins with an overview, which introduces the characters and supplies background information.

◆ ◆ ◆

The Diary of a Young Girl by Anne Frank

Author: Anne(lies) (Marie) Frank (1929–1945) *also known as:* Anne (lies) (Marie) Frank and Annalies Marie Frank
 Genre: war memoir
  Date: 1947
[English translation, 1952; originally published in the Netherlands as *Het achterhuis*]

Notice that the summary includes a quotation that captures a theme of the play.

Information not vital to the story is set separately.

Plot

"It's a wonder I haven't abandoned all my ideals, they seem so absurd and impractical. Yet I cling to them because I still believe, in spite of everything, that people are truly good at heart." This is just one of the extraordinarily mature statements recorded by a German-Jewish girl living in Holland while hiding from Nazi persecution during World War II. Anne Frank was thirteen years old when she made her first diary entry and fifteen when she wrote the final one. The entries in between are neither the work of a professional writer nor the scribblings of a teenage girl. They are, instead, a document of World War II and a testimony to the strength and nobility of the human spirit—even when confronted with the most evil of evils.

Anne, her sister, Margot, and their parents, Mr. and Mrs. Otto Frank, moved from Germany to Holland when Anne was four years old. Her father was a successful businessman, and the Frank family made many friends in their new home. After the outbreak of war in Europe, it soon became apparent that the Jews were to be treated differently from other citizens. In 1940, Anne was transferred from the school she attended in Amsterdam to a Jewish lyceum. That May, Germany invaded the Netherlands and crushed all outward Dutch resistance.

Day by day, life became more dangerous for the Jews in Holland. A special law required them to wear a yellow, six-pointed Star of David on their clothing, labeling them as a persecuted group. Mr. Frank began to formulate plans for the family to leave the country, but by the summer of 1942, the Gestapo—Hitler's police force—began raiding apartments looking for Jews to send to concentration camps. In July of that year, the Franks went into hiding with another family—Mr. and Mrs. Van Daan (their real family name was Van Pels, but Anne changed it in the diary) and their son, Peter—on the third floor of a secret apartment, where they spent the next two years in self-imposed exile.

These two years are detailed in Anne's diary, in which she recorded not only the daily happenings in her life but also her own philosophy as it evolved against a background of unspeakable horror. Anne reveals an astonishing awareness of human nature and of her own abilities in her entries. Despite the horror and fear that each day brought her, she was able to keep alive her spirit and determination. In her diary, she reveals her thoughts to an imaginary friend she called Kitty, a name she got from a Dutch novel for girls that was popular at the time.

The apartment hideout was discovered by the Germans on August 4, 1944. Both families were arrested and deported to concentration camps. Of them all, only Otto Frank survived. The Franks' two friends who served as links to the outside world during their two years of exile were also sent to concentration camps, but they survived. Anne and her sister died in March, 1945, at Bergen-Belsen camp, two months before the Allies liberated Holland and two months before her sixteenth birthday.

Although her papers spilled out onto the floor when the Nazis raided the apartment, Anne's writing survived because the soldiers considered it to be of no importance. Friends of the Franks found the diary papers and gave them to Otto Frank after he returned from the camps. The first edition of the diary was published in 1947, and there have been a number of editions afterward, including the most authoritative to date: *The Diary of a Young Girl: The Definitive Edition*, published in 1995.

A good summary will also give you an idea of the historical context of plot events.

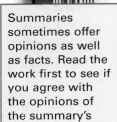

Summaries sometimes offer opinions as well as facts. Read the work first to see if you agree with the opinions of the summary's author.

Summaries describe the events of a story, including the ending. That is why summaries should be read *after* the work, whenever possible.

Check Your Comprehension

1. What information about setting and staging does the summary include?
2. Which does the summary emphasize more—plot action or characterization?

Applying the Reading Strategy

Comparing an Original Text and a Summary

After reading the summary of the play, glance through *The Diary of Anne Frank* again.

3. Did the summary's author leave anything important out of the summary?
4. What did the summary leave out that was in the original text?
5. How does the experience of reading a summary differ from reading the full text?

Activity

Writing a Summary

Think back on a movie you have seen recently. Then, write a one- or two-paragraph summary of it. If you need help in remembering details, consult newspaper movie reviews or go online to read other people's summaries and reviews of the same movie. Remember, you are not writing a critique of the movie, just a summary of the main ideas and action.

Comparing Informational Materials

Comparing the Summaries of a Play and a Book

As you know, the stage version of *The Diary of Anne Frank* was based on Anne's actual diary. Compare the summary of the orginal book version of *The Diary of a Young Girl* with the summary of the play. Complete a chart like the one shown.

1. What information does the summary of the book include that is not in the summary of the play?
2. Which summary tells you more about the events in the hiding place?
3. Which summary tells you more about Anne herself? Why do you think this is true?

Summarize	Book	Play
Information Included		
Similarities		
Key Differences		

CONNECTIONS
Literature and Film

Picturing the Holocaust

Hundreds of books, plays, and films have pictured the horrors of the Holocaust and its victims. Otto Frank miraculously survived the Nazi death camp, Auschwitz, and returned to Amsterdam. Through the urging of friends, Mr. Frank decided to publish his daughter Anne's diary of life in hiding. Many other survivors kept diaries or wrote memoirs of their experiences. Other writers have used their imaginations to create novels and plays about suffering, survival, and heroism in the Nazi concentration camps.

Italian actor-director Roberto Benigni decided to approach the Holocaust from a different perspective—humor. Benigni was already a popular comic actor, director, and screenwriter. In *Life Is Beautiful*—in Italian, *La vita è bella*—he plays Guido, an Italian Jew who protects his young son from the brutality of a concentration camp by pretending it is all a game. His desperate efforts turn Guido into a hero. Benigni intended the film as a fable, not a realistic story. Still, he knew that people might think that his approach was disrespectful to those who had suffered or lost their lives in the Holocaust. Audiences around the world, however, loved the mixture of laughter and tragedy. *Life Is Beautiful* won dozens of awards, including the 1998 Academy Awards for best actor and best foreign-language film.

Now a Major Motion Picture from Miramax Films

LIFE IS BEAUTIFUL
(LA VITA È BELLA)

A Screenplay

ROBERTO BENIGNI AND VINCENZO CERAMI

from Life Is Beautiful

GUIDO, *a bookshop owner who loves to clown around, has been sent to a concentration camp along with his wife,* DORA; *their young son,* JOSHUA; *his* UNCLE; *and other Jews from the town. In this scene, the train carrying the prisoners has just arrived at the camp.* GUIDO *and* JOSHUA *are lined up with the other men outside the camp barracks.*

Scene 49

The Camp, Guido's Barracks—Ext.-Int., Day

In a ragged line, the men walk slowly alongside a gray wall in front of the prisoners' dormitories. Nearly all carry a suitcase, a bundle, or a bag which they must leave at the door of their assigned dormitory before entering. German soldiers check that order is maintained. The dormitories are squalid buildings with small, barred windows from behind which disheveled, white faces with large, spooky eyes watch the proceedings. GUIDO, *almost at a run, catches up to* UNCLE *and* JOSHUA, *who are walking unsteadily. He takes the child by the hand; on* GUIDO'S *face is an expression of the utmost calm.*

GUIDO.	So, Joshua, how goes it? You're happy, right? Get a load of this place. How are you doing? A little tired?
JOSHUA.	Yes. I didn't like the train.
GUIDO.	No? Then we'll take the bus home. . . . [*yells loudly to the others on line*] Listen, guys, we're taking the bus back! The bus with seats! [*to* JOSHUA] I told them!
JOSHUA.	[*to himself*] Yes, it's better.
GUIDO.	I think so too.

[*At the first door, the Germans choose some prisoners, take their baggage, and order them to enter. When those barracks are full, the line moves on.*]

GUIDO.	Look at that organization! Did you see those soldiers? You

Thematic Connection
How do the stage directions show a reality that contrasts with what Guido says?

Connections: from Life Is Beautiful ◆ 787

have to stand in line to get in. People try to sneak in every which way, but they have to stand in line outside, and the guards check everyone. Look, they didn't let those two in!

[*In fact, two prisoners are taken away mysteriously.*]

Thematic Connection
How do Guido and Mr. Frank each try to ease the impact of difficult circumstances?

GUIDO. Don't worry, though, they'll let us in, I reserved! See, Joshua? We're going to have a great time!

JOSHUA. Daddy, what's the name of this game?

GUIDO. Right! The name of the game? It's the thing game, the one I told you about! We're all playing, got it? The men here, the women over there. Then there are the soldiers. Then they'll give us the schedule. Not so easy, is it? No, not easy. If you make a mistake, they send you right home. But if you win, you get first prize.

JOSHUA. What do you win, Daddy?

GUIDO. [*hesitates*] You win—first prize! I told you!

JOSHUA. Yes, but what's the prize?

[*GUIDO is having a hard time.*]

GUIDO. It's . . . it's . . .

[*UNCLE comes to his rescue.*]

UNCLE. A tank!

JOSHUA. I already have a tank!

GUIDO. No, a real one. Brand new!

[*JOSHUA stops, open-mouthed.*]

JOSHUA. A real one?

[*He is ecstatic.*]

No!

GUIDO. Yes! I didn't want to tell you.

JOSHUA. How do you get to come in first?

GUIDO. I'll tell you later.

JOSHUA. A real tank!

GUIDO. A real one!

[*At the next door, the soldiers make some prisoners enter,* GUIDO *and* JOSHUA *among these. But* UNCLE *is forced to continue walking with the other men.*]

JOSHUA. Where is Uncle going?

GUIDO. To another team, it's all been planned. [*He waves.*] 'Bye, Uncle!

[*As they enter the barracks, they stop, frightened. It is a filthy, nauseating room with dank stone walls and dull light coming through the small windows. Bunk beds, piled three high, line the walls around a small space in the center of the room where the new arrivals are crowded together. About half the beds in the room are taken by emaciated, silent young men aged by fatigue. Here and there, faces peek out from the covers, smiling in friendship and solidarity.* GUIDO *has to recharge, because* JOSHUA *is about to burst into tears. He rubs his hands together exaggeratedly.*]

GUIDO. [*pleased*] Ah, didn't I tell you? Is this amazing, or what? [*loudly*] We reserved two singles!

[*He and* JOSHUA *go to the first free bed they find on the bottom row.*]

GUIDO. Quickly, or they'll take our space.

[*Father and son will share a bed, the first available bunk they find in the bottom row. The two bunks above are already taken. The little boy is sad—he doesn't like this place. He sits down on the bed, with tears in his eyes. His father sees.*]

GUIDO. Okay, we sleep here, we'll snuggle up. Joshua!
JOSHUA. It's ugly here, it stinks. I want to go to Mommy!
GUIDO. We will.
JOSHUA. I'm hungry.
GUIDO. We're going to eat, Joshua.
JOSHUA. And they're really mean, they yell.
GUIDO. They have to, there's a big prize, so they have to be really tough because everybody wants that tank, Joshua!
JOSHUA. So what do you have to do? Can I see Mommy?
GUIDO. When the game's over.

[BARTHOLOMEW, *a longtime prisoner, thin as a rail inside his striped uniform, looks down from the highest bunk bed and listens sorrowfully.*]

JOSHUA. And when is the game over?
GUIDO. You have to get a—a thousand points. Whoever gets them first wins the tank.
JOSHUA. The tank? I don't believe it. [*He whimpers.*] Do we get a snack?
GUIDO. [*surprised*] A snack? We'll see. Let me ask, we're all friends here.

Thematic Connection
How does Joshua's reaction to circumstances differ from Anne's? How does the difference in their ages affect their reactions?

[*He looks up and sees* BARTHOLOMEW, *who has been listening to the conversation.*]

> GUIDO. Well, look who's here! See who's here! It's what's-his-name. . . .
>
> BARTHOLOMEW. Bartholomew.
>
> GUIDO. Uh, Bartholomew, has the bread and jelly man come by yet?

[BARTHOLOMEW, *his expression unchanged, nods his head.*]

> GUIDO. I knew it, we missed him! He'll come by again, won't he?

[BARTHOLOMEW *shrugs his shoulders.*]

[*Just then an* SS CORPORAL *comes in with two armed soldiers. The* CORPORAL *is a pudgy man with a stern air about him. He looks over his shoulder as though waiting for someone. But he's in a hurry.*]

> CORPORAL. [*in German*] Any of you Italians speak German?

[*No one says a word, they are too frightened.* GUIDO *says in a whisper to* BARTHOLOMEW,]

> GUIDO. [*whispering*] What did he say?
>
> BARTHOLOMEW. [*very softly*] He's looking for someone who speaks German. He's going to explain the camp rules.

[GUIDO *promptly raises his hand.*]

> BARTHOLOMEW. [*very softly*] You speak German?

[*The* CORPORAL *motions* GUIDO *to come stand next to him.*]

> GUIDO. [*very softly as he moves*] No.

[GUIDO *takes his place next to the* CORPORAL, *who immediately starts yelling loudly at the prisoners.*]

> CORPORAL. [*in German*] Attention! I'm only going to say this once!

[*He looks at* GUIDO, *waiting for a translation.*]

Thematic Connection
Why do you think Bartholomew goes along with Guido's make-believe?

GUIDO.	Okay, the game begins! If you're here, you're here, if you're not, you're not!
CORPORAL.	[*in German*] You are here for one reason, and one reason only!
GUIDO.	[*in Italian*] The first one to get a thousand points wins a real tank!
CORPORAL.	[*in German*] To work!
GUIDO.	Lucky man!

[*The prisoners are trying to understand what the* CORPORAL *and* GUIDO *are talking about, but only* JOSHUA *gets it. He is standing very still, eyes popping. The* CORPORAL *points to the yard outside.*]

CORPORAL.	[*in German*] Any sabotage is punishable by death, sentence carried out right here in the yard, by machine gun in the back!

[*He points to his own back.*]

GUIDO.	Scores will be announced every morning on the loudspeakers outside! Whoever is last has to wear a sign—here on his back!

[*Imitating the* CORPORAL's *gesture, he points to his own back.*]

CORPORAL.	[*in German*] You are privileged to work for our great Germany, building our great empire!
GUIDO.	We play the mean guys, the ones who yell! Whoever's scared loses points!

[*The* CORPORAL *gets tougher. He holds up three fingers.*]

CORPORAL.	[*in German*] There are three very important rules. One: Never attempt escape. Two: Obey all orders without asking questions. Three: Any attempt at organized riot will be punished by hanging. [*loudly*] Is that clear?
GUIDO.	You can lose all your points for any one of three things. One: If you cry. Two: If you ask to see your mother. Three: If you're hungry and ask for a snack! [*loudly*] Forget it!

Thematic Connection
Why is Guido saying something other than what the corporal says?

Thematic Connection
Why do you think Guido makes up these rules?

Connections: from Life Is Beautiful ◆ 791

CORPORAL. [*in German*] You should be happy to work here. Follow the rules and nothing bad will happen to you.

GUIDO. It's easy to be disqualified for hunger. Just yesterday, I lost forty points because I absolutely had to have a jelly sandwich.

CORPORAL. [*in German*] Obey orders!

GUIDO. Apricot jelly!

[*A German soldier whispers something in the* CORPORAL'S *ear. He nods.*]

CORPORAL. [*in German*] One more thing:

GUIDO. He wanted strawberry!

CORPORAL. [*in German*] When you hear this whistle . . .

[*He sticks his fingers in his mouth to imitate the whistle.*]

CORPORAL. [*in German*] . . . everyone out of the dormitory immediately!

[GUIDO *sticks his fingers in his mouth.*]

GUIDO. Never ask for lollipops! You can't have any, they're for us only!

CORPORAL. [*in German*] And form two lines!

GUIDO. I ate twenty yesterday!

CORPORAL. [*in German*] In absolute silence!

GUIDO. What a bellyache!

CORPORAL. [*in German*] Every morning . . .

GUIDO. But they were so good!

CORPORAL. [*in German*] . . . roll call!

GUIDO. Just forget it!

CORPORAL. [*in German*] Every two weeks you get a day of rest, no work.

GUIDO. Okay, it's tough, but it's fun, too.

[*The prisoners look lost—they don't get it. But* JOSHUA *is paying attention, not missing a single word.*]

CORPORAL. [*in German*] That's it. Anything else you want to know, ask the veteran prisoners.

GUIDO. Yesterday, for example, I played ring-around-the-rosy all day. Today, I'm playing hide-and-seek. A million laughs.

[*As he is about to leave, the* CORPORAL *turns and adds.*]

CORPORAL. [*in German*] And that's all I have to say.

GUIDO. Sorry, gotta run.

[*The CORPORAL points into the distance.*]

CORPORAL. [*in German*] The work areas are there. But you'll figure out the layout here soon enough.

[*The CORPORAL goes toward the exit.*]

GUIDO. I'm playing hide-and-seek, gotta go before they find me.

[*The CORPORAL leaves, followed by the soldiers, who close the door. After a moment or two, the new prisoners rally around GUIDO.*]

A YOUNG MAN. I'm sorry, but…

[*GUIDO goes to JOSHUA.*]

GUIDO. [*to the young man*]. Don't ask me, ask Bartholomew, he knows everything! Don't forget to tell me what he said too.

[*Everyone goes toward BARTHOLOMEW, who climbs down from his bunk.*]

GUIDO. [*to BARTHOLOMEW*] Later, tell me what the guard said.

[*JOSHUA's face has a completely new expression on it. He is absolutely convinced that all this is one big game.*]

JOSHUA. A thousand points?
GUIDO. I told you! We're going to have fun.

Roberto Benigni

Roberto Benigni, who co-authored the script for *Life Is Beautiful* with Vincenzo Cerami, was born in Tuscany, Italy, in 1952. He did not experience World War II, but his father had been a prisoner in a Nazi labor camp. His father's stories helped inspire *Life Is Beautiful*. Even as a young boy, Benigni loved the movies. His hero, Charlie Chaplin, inspired Benigni's own style of slapstick comedy. He made his first film in 1976 and a few years later began to direct. His popular Italian films include *Johnny Stecchino* and *The Monster*. "Doing this was a risk," he says about *Life Is Beautiful*. "But my duty is to make something I love. And I love this." He often works with real-life wife, Nicoletta Braschi (Dora in the film).

Connecting Literature and Film

1. How does the humor in this film scene compare or contrast with the way in which humor is used in *The Diary of Anne Frank*?

2. Recall the scene in which Anne gives everyone Hanukkah presents. Do you think she would have understood Guido's impulse to use humor to resist brutality?

3. While Anne and Peter are teenagers, Joshua is only a little boy. How does this difference in age affect their responses to events?

READING INFORMATIONAL MATERIALS

About Responses to Literature

A written **response to literature** is an essay that discusses a particular aspect of a book, short story, essay, article, or poem. An author might respond to the beauty of a poem, the plot of an exciting story, or the lack of character development in a play. When reading a response to literature, it is necessary to look for the following details:

- A strong, interesting focus
- A clear organization that groups related details
- Supporting details for each main idea
- A summary of important features of the work
- A judgment about the value of the work

Reading Strategy

Identifying Evidence

The writer of a response to literature or another piece of nonfiction should provide evidence to support each main point. A writer does not always supply proven facts as evidence. Instead, a writer might offer details and expectations that support the writer's opinion.

As you read nonfiction critically, you should identify the evidence for better understanding. For instance, May Lamberton Becker, the author of "Introducing Natty Bumppo," says that Natty Bumppo takes you "completely into his time and place." The evidence she gives for this claim are her summaries of his adventures: he lives with Indians, works as an army scout, and travels west. This evidence shows that Bumppo was involved in many aspects of the pioneer life of his time.

Before you read "Introducing Natty Bumppo," make a chart like the one below. Fill in the chart, as you read, to make sure you understand the author's main points and support.

Author's Main Point	Evidence	Explanation

Daniel Day-Lewis as Natty Bumppo.

Introducing Natty Bumppo

May Lamberton Becker

The author indicates what her focus will be and offers a strong, clear thesis.

There is no hero in American fiction who takes you with him into his time and place more completely than Natty Bumppo on his life journey through the five Leatherstocking Tales.

He strides into *The Deerslayer* a young hunter brought up among the Delaware Indians, getting experience in Indian warfare in the wilderness of northern New York State in the seventeen-forties. The perfect woodsman, he needs plenty of room; loving the forest, he has the keen senses and cool nerve needed to keep alive there.

In *The Last of the Mohicans: A Narrative of 1757* he is in the prime of life and at the top of his powers as a scout in the campaign of Fort William Henry. In *The Pathfinder* he falls in love, but you remember that less than you do the defense of the blockhouse.

In *The Pioneers* civilization is beginning to catch up with the old scout. Leatherstocking, free hunter of the forest, is arrested for shooting deer out of season. In *The Prairie* he has retired still further to the western plains; frontiersman still, nearly ninety and still able to deal with forest fires and the buffalo stampedes, the last tremendous effort of his life is to rise from his sickbed as the sun goes down, answer "Here," and fall back, dead. Generous, resourceful, not so fond of traders as of Indians, his way through these five romances has been that of the pioneer through a period when America was taking shape. . . .

Few of us now take the adventures in order. We meet Natty Bumppo head-on in *The Last of the Mohicans* with Chingachgook and Uncas, holding our breaths from one escape to the other, hating to let the older men go on the last page, even if Uncas has gone beyond our reach. So when we find that Chingachgook is in another story, we read *The Deerslayer*. After that we take them any way they come, but *Mohicans* stays the longest. All over the world this story has leaped out of the book and become part of the lives of boys. Reading it for the first time is an experience no one should miss. I never knew anyone who could quite forget it.

> The author's organization in this section is **chronological.** It follows the order of the life story of the main character.

> The author offers evidence for this statement by explaining the order in which the books are usually read. She does not tell the reader how she aquired this knowledge.

> Here the author offers a judgment of the value of the work.

A scene from the movie *The Last of the Mohicans*

Check Your Comprehension

1. Who is Natty Bumppo?
2. What is Natty Bumppo's role in *The Deerslayer*?
3. In how many books does Natty Bumppo appear?
4. What happens to Natty Bumppo in *The Pioneers*?

Applying the Reading Strategy

Identifying the Evidence

5. What evidence does Becker provide to support her point that "civilization is beginning to catch up with" Natty Bumppo?
6. How does Becker describe Bumppo's role throughout the novels in which he appears?
7. What evidence does Becker provide to support her statement that "Few of us now take the adventures in order"? Is it convincing?

Activity

Identifying Evidence in Fiction

Use a chart like the one provided to help you analyze a fictional story you have just read. Find at least five instances when the author supplies the reader with information and then gives the evidence to support it.

Information from Text	Evidence

Comparing Informational Materials

Different Types of Responses to Literature

In addition to a standard literary essay, there are other types of responses to literature. There are *book reviews* and *letters to an author*.

- A book review gives readers the critic's impression of a book, encouraging them to either read it or avoid reading it. The review can be presented orally or in written form.

- Letters to an author explain what a reader found enjoyable or disappointing in an author's work.

Find an example of each type of response and compare its characteristics with another response.

Writing WORKSHOP

Response to Literature: Critical Review

A **critical review** is a piece of writing that analyzes and evaluates the value of a book, story, article, play or poem. The review might show why a story is powerful, point out the complexities of a poem, or analyze the shortcomings of a play. In this workshop, you will write a critical review that evaluates a work of literature.

Assignment Criteria. Your critical review should have the following characteristics:

- A strong, interesting focus on an aspect of the work
- An interpretation based on careful reading and your own responses to the writer's techniques
- Supporting details based on specific textual references, references to other works and authors, or personal knowledge
- A discussion of the effects of a literary work on an audience

To preview the criteria on which your critical review may be assessed, see the Rubric on page 801.

Prewriting

Choose a topic. Look in the literature section of a library or consult your reading journal and **browse** through the titles there. Flip through works you have already read or new works by familiar authors. Choose the work you find most interesting as your topic.

Start brainstorming. To gather details about your topic, use a graphic organizer like the one shown. Look through the work—and consult your own experience—to find details for each part of the hexagon.

Look for literary elements. As you plan your review, include references to the various literary elements and terms you have learned to apply to different kinds of literature. Here are a few suggestions:

Novels and Short Stories: plot, character, theme, setting, point of view, suspense, foreshadowing, climax, narrator

Poetry: rhyme, rhythm, alliteration, metaphor, simile, onomatopoeia, personification, speaker

Drama: act, scene, stage directions, dialogue, plot, character, theme, setting, suspense, climax

Nonfiction: point of view, exposition, analogy, anecdote, description, main ideas

Using a Hexagon

Personal Knowledge
- "Nobody"—Movie stars don't always like being famous.
- "Flowers"—People who have Alzheimer's disease may not recognize their own family.

Summary
- "Nobody"—The narrator is excited to be a "nobody."
- "Flowers"—Flowers don't even know that others appreciate them.

Themes
- "Nobody"—being humble and quiet is a good thing. A lot of people want to be famous but end up happy.
- "Flowers"—Being too quiet makes you miss out on life

What I liked or didn't like
- I like these poems because they make me think about their hidden meanings.

Similarities to Other Works
- "Nobody" reminds me of a movie about a princess who wants to be a regular person.
- "Flowers" reminds me of an article about a blind man who does not even know what he looks like.

Author's Technique
- In both poems, the author uses examples taken from nature to prove her point.

Student Model

Before you begin drafting your critical review, read this student model and review the characteristics of a successful critical review.

Katie O'Connell
Indianapolis, Indiana

The Ransom of Red Chief

"The Ransom of Red Chief" is a short story written by William Sidney Porter, also known as O. Henry. This story is about two criminals who kidnap a ten-year-old terror and try to ransom him back to his father. I found the story entertaining because of its surprising twists and turns.

> The opening paragraph provides background on the work and the author, and provides the reader with an assessment of the work.

At the beginning of the story the author creates a mood of criminal mischief and intrigue. Two men plotting to kidnap a ten-year-old little boy ask the boy if he wants some candy and a ride. They assume any kid could be lured with candy. This little boy cannot. Instead, he catches one of the men neatly in the eye with a piece of brick. This makes both men angry and they struggle with the boy, who puts up quite a fight.

Later in the story when the two men have the little boy in custody at a cave, they start a little game. The boy becomes Red Chief and the two men, Snake Eye and Old Hank. The boy tells Old Hank that he is to be scalped at daybreak and Snake Eye is to be broiled at the stake. The mood turns lighter and more humorous at this point in the story, when both men realize that they may have taken on more than they could chew by kidnapping this terror. Neither man knows what to expect next with such a wild boy.

> The reviewer supplies carefully chosen supporting details from the text to support her assessment.

As the days go by, the men grow tired of the boy and decide they must go to town and write the ransom letter. The mood quickly changes to desperation. The two men have had enough of the little boy's fun and games. They write and send the letter to his father, Ebenezer Dorset, and wait for the reply. The next night they get the surprising reply that he won't pay the ransom for his own son. They are just so tired of the boy that they offer the father $250.00 to take him back.

"The Ransom of Red Chief" ends on a surprising note, which is typical of the story in general. I think we all know someone who is similar to the little boy in "The Ransom of Red Chief." The figure of the little boy who looks innocent, but is a mischievous troublemaker, can be found on television shows and in popular cartoons. O. Henry's humorous description of the situation of the little boy is what sets this story apart and makes it enjoyable for me.

> The reviewer includes personal observations and responses that clearly relate to the literature.

Drafting

Find and define your focus. Using your notes, pinpoint the effect that the work had on you. Choose an evaluation that you can support with specific examples in the text. Use your own insights to define a focus that relates to the meaning of the work and its effect on the reader. Express this focus in one topic sentence that appears in your first paragraph.

Provide supporting details. As you draft, refer to your notes to find support for your focus and main ideas. Include details such as:

- **Quotations:** These provide supporting examples of your main ideas.
- **Description:** A powerful description can help readers picture settings, characters, or events.
- **Personal observations:** Telling about your own experience as a reader strengthens your argument.

Summarize your assessment. Finish your draft with an evaluation of the work as a whole, and restate your main idea about the work's impact on the reader.

Revising

Circle your strongest point. Look over your draft and locate your strongest idea.

1. Read your draft aloud to a classmate. Ask your classmate to help you identify main ideas.

2. Circle these main ideas, and choose the strongest.

3. Consider moving this point to the end of your review. The review will then build to the high point in your writing, and you can end your review with a powerful closing.

Model: Circling Your Strongest Point

O. Henry's mischievous little boy is actually a common character in popular media. It is O. Henry's description of the boy, his witty dialogue, and clever plot that set this story apart for me.

> Katie selects an insight about the character of the little boy as her strongest point to place at the end.

Revise to emphasize a point. To provide additional emphasis for main points, repeat a key word or phrase. Repetition also helps to link together ideas and provides smooth transitions.

Compare the nonmodel and the model. Why is one more effective than the other?

Nonmodel	Model
I found the story entertaining because of its many changes in mood and surprising twists and turns.	I found the story entertaining because of its many changes in mood and surprising twists and turns.
At the beginning of the story, the author wants you to be intrigued by the characters.	At the beginning of the story, the author creates a mood of criminal mischief and intrigue.

Publishing and Presenting

Choose one of these ways to share your writing with classmates or a larger audience.

Post a review board. Arrange the critical reviews of the class on a bulletin board in your school or local library. If possible, include an eye-catching picture with each review.

"Teens Review" column. Contact a local newspaper and arrange for a series of critical reviews by teenagers to be published.

 Prentice Hall Writing and Grammar Connection: Chapter 4.

 Speaking Connection

To learn more about delivering a critical review as a speech, see the **Listening and Speaking Workshop: Delivering an Oral Response to Literature,** page 802.

Rubric for Self-Assessment

Evaluate your critical review using the following criteria and rating scale:

Criteria	Rating Scale				
	Not very				Very
How well does the review focus on an interesting aspect of the work?	1	2	3	4	5
How clearly is the interpretation based on careful reading and insight?	1	2	3	4	5
How well does the review rely on specific textual references, references to other works and authors, or personal knowledge for support?	1	2	3	4	5
How well does the review describe the effects of a literary work on its audience?	1	2	3	4	5

Listening and Speaking WORKSHOP

Delivering an Oral Response to Literature

Like a good written critical review (see Writing Workshop, pages 798-801), an **oral response to literature** is an opportunity to express your ideas about a book, short story, play, poem, or article. It is not simply a summary of the literature. Use your oral response to discuss the *meaning* of the work and present interesting personal insights you gathered from your reading.

Develop Your Response

Interpret a reading by providing insight. A good oral response begins with a careful and thorough reading—and *rereading*—of the text:

- Note which passages of the text seem most important, or affect you most strongly.
- Focus on how the author produced this reaction in you.
- Begin with a brief summary of the work, but do not stop there. Base your response on insight, not just literal understanding.

Make comparisons. It is appropriate to make comparisons to other literary works or authors to make your points, but keep your focus on the work you are reviewing.

Outline main points and supporting details. Organize your information into an outline like the one here. Group your details under main points and subtopics. Arrange the topics in logical order.

Speak Effectively

Practice your delivery. Before you deliver your response, rehearse it on your own or with a friend or family member. Do not try to memorize what you will say. Instead, use notes that show your key points and use them to guide your presentation.

Use nonverbal techniques. Gesture, move your body, and use facial expressions to animate your presentation and add emphasis. Relax and have fun with your presentation so your audience can do the same.

Activity:
Videotape a review

Choose a piece of literature you have enjoyed. Imagine that you are a reviewer for a major television network. Videotape your response using the tips above. Share your review with your classmates.

"Hamadi"—Several Stories in One

A. *Susan's story*
   1. Relationship to family
   2. Relationship to Hamadi
   3. View of caroling night

B. *Tracy's story*
   1. Relationship to Susan
   2. Relationship to Eddie
   3. View of caroling night

C. *Hamadi's story*
   1. Relationship to Susan
   2. Relationship to Susan's father
   3. View of caroling night

The writing sections of some tests require you to read a passage and answer multiple-choice questions about sentence construction. Use the following strategies to help you answer such questions:

● **Recognize Incomplete Sentences and Run-on Sentences** An incomplete sentence does not express a complete thought. Correct an incomplete sentence by making sure it has a subject and a verb. A run-on sentence is made up of two or more sentences without the proper punctuation between them. Correct a run-on sentence by adding the correct punctuation and, if necessary, a conjunction.

● **Combine Sentences** Sometimes two short sentences sound better if they are combined. When you join two short sentences on a test, make sure that they are closely related in subject matter.

Test-Taking Strategies

● If you are confused about what the subject or action is in a sentence, it may be incomplete.

● Recognize a run-on sentence by the breathless sensation you get from reading a sentence without enough pauses.

Sample Test Item

Directions: Read the following sentences and then choose the letter of the sentence that is correctly written.

1. **A** Abraham Lincoln rescued a turkey. That was supposed to be killed for Thanksgiving.

   B Abraham Lincoln rescued a turkey that was supposed to be killed for Thanksgiving.

   C Abraham Lincoln rescued a turkey it was supposed to be killed for Thanksgiving.

   D Abraham Lincoln rescued a turkey killed for Thanksgiving.

Answer and Explanation

B is the correct answer because it combines two short related sentences. The second part of **A** is an incomplete sentence. **C** is a run-on sentence. **D** is an incomplete sentence.

Practice

Directions: Choose the best way to rewrite the underlined sentence. If it needs no change, choose "Correct as is."

An animal's tongue can be very useful. (1) A gecko wipes its eyelids with its tongue a giraffe's tongue strips leaves from a tree.

1. **A** A gecko wipes its eyelids with its tongue, a giraffe's tongue strips leaves from trees.

   B A gecko wipes its eyelids with its tongue but a giraffe's tongue strips leaves from trees.

   C A gecko wipes its eyelids with its tongue. A giraffe's tongue strips leaves from trees.

   D Correct as is

©Reginald Wickham

Exploring the Genre

In poetry, language is used in special ways to create vivid, memorable, and sometimes musical impressions. Poems may capture a single moment in time, take you into a world of make-believe, or tell the story of a person's life. As you explore the poems in this unit, you will become familiar with the following terms:

- **Narrative poetry** tells a story. A *ballad* is one type of narrative poem.

- **Lyric poetry** expresses personal thoughts and feelings.

- **Poetic form** is the structure of a poem—its pattern of lines, stanzas, and rhyme. A *haiku,* a *sonnet,* and a *concrete poem* have different poetic forms.

- **Poetic purpose** is the intention of a poem. An *ode,* an *elegy,* and an *epic* are written to achieve different poetic purposes.

- **Sound devices** are elements such as *rhyme, rhythm, alliteration,* and *onomatopoeia* that give poetry a musical quality.

- **Imagery** is descriptive detail that appeals to the senses.

- **Figurative language** uses *simile, metaphor,* or *personification* to say things in ways that are not meant to be taken literally.

◀ **Critical Viewing** What details in this picture might appeal to a poet? **[Analyze]**

Why Read Literature?

Your purpose for reading naturally varies, depending on the content, genre, and style of the work you plan to read. You might read a sonnet for the love of literature. You might read a haiku to appreciate the author's style. You might read a ballad to be entertained. Review three of the purposes you might set before reading the works in this unit.

1

Read for the love of literature.

Pablo Neruda once wrote a poem about his socks! In his collection *Odes to Opposites,* he explores other unusual poetic subjects. Read **"Ode to Enchanted Light,"** page 848.

There is a tree in Africa that is populated by bats and blossoms only in moonlight. Read about Walter de la Mare's fascination with moonlight in his poem **"Silver,"** page 868.

2

Read to appreciate an author's style.

There is a village in Turkey where the people communicate through whistling. This unique language allows the villagers to communicate over distances of up to one mile! Read **"Forgotten Language,"** page 869, by Shel Silverstein to see how his unique style is used to describe unknown languages.

Did you know that January is the top-selling month of the year for buying chicken soup? Read how John Updike presents images of January in his poem **"January,"** page 839.

3

Read for information.

Since 1896, the beginning of the modern Olympics, only Greece and Australia have participated in every game! The Olympics is an event that reaches all areas of the world. Read about an unusual competition at the Japan Olympics 1988 in **"Haiku for the Olympics,"** page 864.

Take It to the Net

Visit the Web site for online instruction and activities related to each selection in this unit.
www.phschool.com

How to Read Literature

Use Strategies for Reading Poetry

Poetry is unlike other types of literature. Poets use language imaginatively to create images, tell stories, explore feelings and experiences, and suggest meanings. They choose and combine words carefully to enable you to see your world in a fresh or unusual way. They may also use rhythm and rhyme to create musical effects in a poem. In this unit you will learn strategies to help you to appreciate and enjoy the poetry you read.

1. Read the lines according to punctuation.

Punctuation marks are like traffic signals to the reader of poetry. They tell you when to pause, for how long, and when to stop. Look for sentences or complete thoughts in a poem. If there is no punctuation mark at the end of a line, read on without pausing or stopping.

For example, the first line of "The Secret Heart" contains no end punctuation. Therefore, you would read on without pausing until you get to the period at the end of the second line:

"Across the years he could recall
His father one way best of all."

2. Paraphrase.

Restate the lines of poetry in your own words. Capture the meaning behind the lines by identifying the main images and ideas.

3. Identify the speaker.

The speaker in poetry is the voice that the poet creates to communicate his or her message. Sometimes the speaker is identified; sometimes the speaker is a nameless voice; and sometimes the speaker is the poet. In this unit you will read a variety of poems with different speakers.

4. Draw inferences.

Poetry often expresses things in indirect ways. To get at the sense of the poem, you may need to draw inferences, or reach conclusions based on evidence in the poem's details, sound devices, or images.

5. Use your senses.

Poetry is full of images that appeal to your senses of sight, hearing, taste, smell, and touch. Identify those images as you read, and pause to experience and appreciate their appeal.

As you read the selections in this unit, review the reading strategies and look at the notes in the side column. Use the suggestions to apply the strategies and interact with the text.

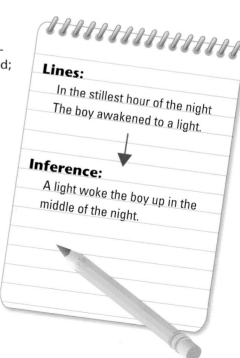

Lines:

In the stillest hour of the night
The boy awakened to a light.

Inference:

A light woke the boy up in the middle of the night.

Prepare to Read

The Secret Heart

Preview

Connecting to the Literature

Our minds hold thousands of memories, but some stand out as if the events happened yesterday. In "The Secret Heart," Robert P. Tristram Coffin describes one man's memory of a single vivid moment from his childhood.

Background

Robert Coffin's poem, "The Secret Heart," describes a person's heart. Traditionally, the heart is associated with love. Valentines are often decorated with hearts, and Cupid, the Roman god of love, is represented as shooting his arrow through a heart. The heart is also associated with love in expressions like "dear to my heart," "sweetheart," and "heartache."

Literary Analysis

Symbols

A **symbol** is an object, person, or idea that stands for something beyond itself. A symbol usually has several layers of meaning. For example, the heart at right shows several ideas represented by the heart in "The Secret Heart." Writers use symbols as a kind of poetic shorthand to make a point or reinforce the theme or message. As you read "The Secret Heart," look for the meanings indicated on the organizer to appreciate several layers of meaning for the heart and flame.

Connecting Literary Elements

Any form of poetry can use a symbol to express an idea, but some poems organize ideas with specific structures. Two structures you will frequently encounter in reading poetry are couplets and stanzas.

- A **couplet** is a pair of rhyming lines.
- A **stanza** is a group of lines that are meant to be read as a unit.

In "The Secret Heart," each couplet forms a two-line stanza.

His two hands were curved apart
In the semblance of a heart.

He wore, it seemed to his small son
A bare heart on his hidden one.

These two stanzas, each made of one couplet, describe the main symbol in the poem. Notice how other stanzas in the poem express a single main idea. While reading, think about the following focus questions:

1. In this poem, how do couplets and stanzas achieve the same purpose?
2. What important idea is expressed in the first stanza?

Reading Strategy

Reading Poetry

When you read poetry, pay attention to the punctuation in each stanza. If there is no punctuation mark at the end of the first line of a couplet, read on without pausing or stopping. If there is a comma, pause briefly. If there is a period, come to a stop. In "The Secret Heart," each couplet is punctuated as a sentence. The thought is not complete until you read to the end of the second line in each couplet.

Vocabulary Development

kindled (kin′ dəld) *v.* stirred up; awakened (p. 811)

semblance (sem′ bləns) *n.* look or appearance (p. 812)

THE SECRET HEART

Robert P. Tristram Coffin

Across the years he could recall
His father one way best of all.

In the stillest hour of night
The boy awakened to a light.

5   Half in dreams, he saw his sire[1]
With his great hands full of fire.

The man had struck a match to see
If his son slept peacefully.

He held his palms each side the spark
10 His love had <u>kindled</u> in the dark.

---

1. **sire** (sīr) *n.* father.

◀ **Critical Viewing** What sort of mood do the
colors in this photograph evoke? Explain. **[Interpret]**

kindled (kin′ dəld) *v.*
stirred up; awakened

His two hands were curved apart
In the <u>semblance</u> of a heart.

He wore, it seemed to his small son,
A bare heart on his hidden one.

15 A heart that gave out such a glow
No son awake could bear to know.

It showed a look upon a face
Too tender for the day to trace.

One instant, it lit all about,
20 And then the secret heart went out.

But it shone long enough for one
To know that hands held up the sun.

semblance (sem′ bləns) *n.*
look or appearance

Review and Assess

Thinking About the Selection

1. **Respond:** Should the father have been less secretive about his love? Why or why not?

2. **(a) Recall:** Whose memory is described in the poem?
   (b) Contrast: What is the difference between the boy's interpretation of the events and the speaker's interpretation?
   (c) Compare: What quality do both the boy and the speaker recognize in the father?

3. **(a) Recall:** What event is recalled in the poem? **(b) Infer:** The boy is "half in dreams" during the incident. How might being half asleep affect his impressions?

4. **(a) Recall:** What does the boy discover about his father?
   (b) Interpret: What is the look in lines 17 and 18 that is too tender for the day to trace? **(c) Apply:** The poet suggests that the father does not show his love for his son as openly during the day. Why do you think this is?

5. **Extend:** In what ways does society encourage or discourage people to show their love for family and friends?

Robert P. Tristram Coffin

(1892–1955)

Robert P. Tristram Coffin grew up on a farm in Brunswick, Maine. He attended Bowdoin College and Oxford University, where he was a Rhodes scholar. After serving in World War I, he became a professor at Wells College. Later, he returned to his alma mater, Bowdoin, where he was a professor of English from 1934 until his death. Besides publishing more than 40 books of poetry, prose, essays, and biographies during his lifetime, Coffin was an artist who created etchings and sketches. He won the Pulitzer Prize for Poetry in 1936.

Review and Assess

Literary Analysis

Symbols

1. What does the "glowing heart" represent to the boy?
2. What does it represent for the speaker?
3. Copy the graphic organizer. Add details associated with "glowing" and with "heart." Use details from your organizer to explain how the glowing heart has several layers of meaning.

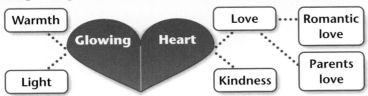

Connecting Literary Elements

4. What is the difference between a couplet and a stanza?
5. What important idea is expressed in the first stanza?
6. Explain how in this poem couplets and stanzas achieve the same purpose.
7. Copy the chart. Under each stanza number, identify the rhyming words that are used in the couplet.

1	2	3	4	5	6	7	8	9	10	11

8. Which stanzas contain rhymes that sound like the same words but are not?
9. Why are these two stanzas especially important to the meaning of the poem?

Reading Strategy

Reading Poetry

10. Why would you read on, without stopping, at the end of line 7?
11. Where would you pause when reading lines 19 and 20? Where would you stop? Why?

Extend Understanding

12. **Extend:** How do you think the poet feels about his own father? Explain.

Quick Review

A **symbol** is an object, person, or idea that stands for something beyond itself. To review symbols, see page 809.

A **stanza** is a formal division of lines in a poem. Each stanza is thought of as one unit. A **couplet** is two lines of poetry that rhyme with each other. To review stanza and couplet, see page 809.

 Take It to the Net
www.phschool.com
Take the interactive self-test online to check your understanding of the selection.

Integrate Language Skills

Vocabulary Development Lesson

Word Analysis: Latin Root -semble-

The Latin word root *-semble-* means "to seem" or "to appear." Complete each sentence with one of these words containing *-semble-*:

resemblance   resembling   resemble

1. When he cupped his hands around the burning match, he made a shape ___?___ a fiery heart.
2. The ___?___ between the twin boys was almost startling.
3. The child hoped that he would ___?___ his father when he grew up.

Fluency: Sentence Completions

Complete each sentence with the correct word from the vocabulary list.

1. The boy's drawing had the ___?___ of a boat, but he had added artistic details.
2. The description of the villain ___?___ the young boy's interest in the story.

Spelling Strategy

The roots *-semble-*, *-icle-*, and the suffix *-able* all spell the *uhl* sound with *le* in the last, unaccented syllable. Practice spelling words with these endings. Unscramble the letters to spell words ending in *le*.

1. clearpit   2. breemsel   3. alavalieb

Grammar Lesson

Comparative and Superlative Forms of Modifiers

Adjectives modify or describe nouns or pronouns. **Adverbs** modify verbs, adjectives, or other adverbs. Both adjectives and adverbs have different forms, which can be used to compare people, places, and things.

The **comparative** form of adjectives and adverbs compares two items. The **superlative** form compares more than two items.

Positive	Comparative	Superlative
fast	faster	fastest
speedy	speedier	speediest
sadly	more sadly	most sadly

Avoid double comparisons such as *more sadder* or *most cleanest*.

▶ *For more practice, see page R31, Exercise D.*

Practice Copy the sentences. Underline each modifier. Label it comparative or superlative. Then, circle the word that it modifies.

1. In the stillest hour of the night . . .
2. His father loved him more dearly than anything else.
3. He was happier than anyone.
4. It was his most cherished memory.
5. Of the two, it is the harder poem.

Writing Application Proofread and edit the following passage, correcting errors with modifiers.

The poem describes the boy's more vivid memory of his father. There is no memory more better than this one. The father too, probably has happiest memories of his son's boyhood. For instance, each night his son seemed to sleep most peacefully than the night before.

 Prentice Hall Writing and Grammar Connection: Chapter 25, Section 1

Writing Lesson

Evaluation of a Symbol

"The Secret Heart" uses the symbol of a glowing heart. A rich, effective symbol can be interpreted on more than one level. In a brief essay, evaluate whether the symbol of the glowing heart is effective in offering several related layers of meaning.

Prewriting First, identify the layers of meaning you want to discuss. Then, answer the questions below to gather details to help you decide whether the glowing heart is a rich and effective symbol.

Model: Gathering Details to Support Judgments:

- In what other works is a heart used as a symbol?
  Does this seem stronger, weaker, or equal to those uses?

- What symbols are used in other works to represent love?
  Are they more, less, or as effective as the heart?

> The questions in blue italics will lead you to evaluate the symbol within the context of other works.

Drafting Begin by stating whether or not you think the glowing heart is an effective symbol. Give your explanation, and organize your support. Follow each opinion or judgment with an example, a detail, or a comparison.

Revising Check that you have given enough reasons to support your ideas. Look for comparisons you have used, and make sure you have chosen the correct form of the modifying words.

WG Prentice Hall Writing and Grammar Connection: Chapter 12, Section 4

Extension Activities

Listening and Speaking Present an **oral response** to the poem. Begin by stating whether you think the poem does or does not have a powerful emotional effect. Read aloud lines from the poem to illustrate your points.

Writing As the man who remembers his father, write a letter to the father. Tell him your memory and what it means to you. In the letter, include details provided in the poem.

Research and Technology "The Secret Heart" expresses the value of love and family. Create a **quotation booklet** with the same theme or display several quotations on a classroom bulletin board. To find appropriate material, look online at parenting pages or at quotations Web sites. In addition, use print products like parenting magazines or dictionaries of quotations.

 **Take It to the Net** www.phschool.com

Go online for an additional research activity using the Internet.

Prepare to Read

The Wreck of the Hesperus ◆ The Centaur

Benares, Marshall Johnson, Courtesy, Peabody Essex Museum, Salem, Mass. Photo by Mark Sexton.

 Take It to the Net

Visit www.phschool.com for interactive activities and instruction related to these selections, including
- background
- graphic organizers
- literary elements
- reading strategies

Preview

Connecting to the Literature

Shipwrecks and adventures at sea have been popular topics for stories and songs since ancient times. Before reading, think about contemporary examples from literature, music, and movies that show the interest in the dangers of the ocean.

Background

Henry Wadsworth Longfellow's journal entry of December 17, 1839, tells of his horror on reading about a schooner called the *Hesperus*, which had been wrecked off Norman's Woe, a reef near Gloucester, Massachusetts. Twenty bodies were washed ashore, one of them tied to a piece of the wreckage. A few weeks later, Longfellow wrote "The Wreck of the Hesperus."

Literary Analysis

Narrative Poems and Ballads

A **narrative poem** tells a story. Like a short story, a narrative poem has a plot, setting, and characters. Unlike a story, however, a narrative poem is written in verse. Ideas are organized in stanzas rather than paragraphs. Both poems in this group are narrative.

A **ballad** is a specific type of narrative poem based on the ancient custom of telling stories in songs. A ballad usually has as its subject an adventure, a romance, or a dramatic event told in a serious, formal way. Repetition and elaborate language give most ballads a songlike quality. "The Wreck of the Hesperus" is a ballad.

Comparing Literary Works

All narrative poems tell a story. The tone and mood with which the stories are told can vary greatly. **Mood** is the feeling a reader gets from the work. **Tone** is the feeling the writer brings to the work—his or her attitude toward the topic and the reader. Most ballads have a serious tone, like the formal songs they are modeled after. Compare and contrast the mood and tone of "The Wreck of the Hesperus" and "The Centaur."

1. What is the subject or topic of each poem?
2. How do the differences in topic contribute to the differences in mood and tone?

Reading Strategy

Reading Lines According to Punctuation

The sophisticated sentence structure of "The Wreck of the Hesperus" and the wandering thoughts of the speaker in "The Centaur" are marked with a variety of **punctuation** beyond the period and the question mark. Knowing how and why these marks are used will help you read the poems accurately and fluently. As you read, look for and read according to the marks shown on the chart.

Vocabulary Development

scornful (skôrn´ fəl) *adj.* full of contempt or disdain (p. 820)

gale (gāl) *n.* strong wind (p. 820)

breakers (brāk´ ərz) *n.* waves that break into foam (p. 822)

cinched (sincht) *v.* bound firmly; tightly fastened (p. 825)

canter (kan´ ter) *v.* ride at a smooth, gentle pace (p. 825)

negligent (neg´ le jent) *adj.* without care or attention; indifferent (p. 826)

, Comma

Indicates a small break in thought or delivery

Pause briefly

; Semicolon

Connects complete thoughts of equal weight

Pause and use tone of voice to give equal emphasis to both thoughts

! Exclamation point

Indicates intensity of emotion

Read with great emotion, often as if calling out

— Dash

Shows a thought is not finished

Read with voice trailing off as if not finished speaking

THE WRECK OF THE HESPERUS

HENRY WADSWORTH LONGFELLOW

It was the schooner[1] Hesperus,
    That sailed the wintry sea;
And the skipper had taken his little daughter,
    To bear him company.

5   Blue were her eyes as the fairy-flax,[2]
    Her cheeks like the dawn of day,
And her bosom white as the hawthorn buds
    That ope in the month of May.

---

1. schooner (sko͞on′ ər) *n.* ship with two or more masts.
2. fairy-flax slender plant with delicate blue flowers.

Benares, Marshall Johnson, Courtesey, Peabody Essex Museum, Salem, Mass. Photo by Mark Sexton

▲ **Critical Viewing** What details in this painting convey the roughness of the sea? **[Connect]**

The skipper he stood beside the helm,
10   His pipe was in his mouth,
And he watched how the veering flaw[3] did blow
        The smoke now West, now South.

Then up and spake an old sailor,
        Had sailed to the Spanish Main,[4]
15 "I pray thee, put into yonder port,
        For I fear a hurricane.

✔**Reading Check**

Who does the skipper bring on the ship?

"Last night the moon had a golden ring,
    And tonight no moon we see!"
The skipper he blew a whiff from his pipe,
20   And a <u>scornful</u> laugh laughed he.

Colder and colder blew the wind,
    A <u>gale</u> from the Northeast,
The snow fell hissing in the brine,
    And the billows frothed like yeast.

25 Down came the storm, and smote amain,[5]
    The vessel in its strength;
She shuddered and paused, like a frighted steed,
    Then leaped her cable's length.

"Come hither! come hither! my little daughter,
30   And do not tremble so;
For I can weather the roughest gale,
    That ever wind did blow."

He wrapped her warm in his seaman's coat
    Against the stinging blast;
35 He cut a rope from a broken spar,[6]
    And bound her to the mast.

"O father! I hear the church-bells ring,
    O say, what may it be?"
"'Tis a fog-bell on a rock-bound coast!—"
40   And he steered for the open sea.

"O father! I hear the sound of guns,
    O say, what may it be?"
"Some ship in distress, that cannot live
    In such an angry sea!"

45 "O father! I see a gleaming light,
    O say, what may it be?"
But the father answered never a word,
    A frozen corpse was he.

scornful (skôrn′ fəl) *adj.* full of contempt or disdain

gale (gāl) *n.* strong wind

Literary Analysis
Ballads and Narratives
What details give the poem a song-like quality?

Reading Check

Why doesn't the skipper answer the last question?

The Lookout — "All's Well," Winslow Homer, Courtesy, Museum of Fine Arts, Boston, MA

▲ **Critical Viewing** What details in this painting suggest a sense of peril or fear? **[Connect]**

Lashed to the helm, all stiff and stark,
50   With his face turned to the skies,
The lantern gleamed through the gleaming snow
      On his fixed and glassy eyes.

Then the maiden clasped her hands and prayed
      That savèd she might be;
55 And she thought of Christ, who stilled the wave,
      On the Lake of Galilee.[7]

And fast through the midnight dark and drear
      Through the whistling sleet and snow,
Like a sheeted ghost, the vessel swept
60   Towards the reef of Norman's Woe.

And ever the fitful gusts between
      A sound came from the land;
It was the sound of the trampling surf,
      On the rocks and the hard sea-sand.

65 The <u>breakers</u> were right beneath her bows,
      She drifted a dreary wreck,
And a whooping billow swept the crew
      Like icicles from her deck.

She struck where the white and fleecy waves
70   Looked soft as carded[8] wool,
But the cruel rocks, they gored[9] her side
      Like the horns of an angry bull.

Her rattling shrouds,[10] all sheathed in ice,
      With the masts went by the board;
75 Like a vessel of glass, she stove[11] and sank,
      Ho! ho! the breakers roared!

Literary Analysis
Ballads and Narratives
What is the problem at
the center of the plot?

breakers (brāk´ ərz) *n.*
waves that break into
foam

---

7. Lake of Galilee (gal´ ə lē´) lake in northeastern Israel.
8. carded combed.
9. gored pierced.
10. shrouds ropes or wires stretched from the ship's side to the mast.
11. stove broke.

At daybreak, on the bleak sea-beach,
     A fisherman stood aghast,
To see the form of a maiden fair,
80   Lashed close to a drifting mast.

The salt sea was frozen on her breast,
     The salt tears in her eyes;
And he saw her hair, like the brown sea-weed,
     On the billows fall and rise.

85 Such was the wreck of the Hesperus,
     In the midnight and the snow!
Christ save us all from a death like this,
     On the reef of Norman's Woe!

Review and Assess

Thinking About the Selection

1. **Respond:** What would you say to the skipper about his decision not to listen to the old sailor's advice?

2. **(a) Recall:** What warning does the old sailor give the skipper? **(b) Compare and Contrast:** Compare and contrast the attitudes of the skipper and the old sailor about the sea and its dangers. **(c) Deduce:** Why do you think the old sailor is afraid of what might happen?

3. **(a) Recall:** What event happens just before the skipper steers for the open sea? **(b) Infer:** Why does he head for the open sea rather than toward land? **(c) Make a Judgment:** Does the skipper act responsibly?

4. **(a) Recall:** What finally happens to the Hesperus? **(b) Draw Conclusions:** What character trait in the skipper leads to the shipwreck? **(c) Assess:** Would you trust someone like the skipper? Why or why not?

5. **(a) Recall:** What happens to everyone on board, including the skipper's daughter and the old sailor? **(b) Interpret:** What is the message or theme of this poem? **(c) Support:** Which of the speaker's lines or words are the strongest indication of the theme?

6. **Take a Stand:** Is the skipper responsible for his daughter's death? Why or why not?

Henry Wadsworth Longfellow

(1807–1882)

Longfellow was the most popular poet of his time. When he entered a room, people stood up and gentlemen took off their hats. He published his first poem when he was thirteen. At fifteen, he entered Bowdoin College, where he excelled as a student. His ballad "The Song of Hiawatha" sold over a million copies in his lifetime.

Longfellow became known as one of the "fireside poets," whose works were frequently read by families who gathered around the fireplace for an evening of reading and discussion.

The Centaur [1]

May Swenson

The summer that I was ten—
Can it be there was only one
summer that I was ten? It must

have been a long one then—
5   each day I'd go out to choose
a fresh horse from my stable

which was a willow grove
down by the old canal.
I'd go on my two bare feet.

---

1. **Centaur** (sen´ tôr´) mythological creature with a man's head, trunk, and arms, and a horse's body and legs.

► **Critical Viewing**
How do the actions of the girl in the photograph compare with the actions of the poem's speaker? **[Compare and Contrast]**

10 But when, with my brother's jack-knife,
    I had cut me a long limber horse
    with a good thick knob for a head,

    and peeled him slick and clean
    except a few leaves for the tail,
15 and <u>cinched</u> my brother's belt

    around his head for a rein,
    I'd straddle and <u>canter</u> him fast
    up the grass bank to the path,

    trot along in the lovely dust
20 that talcumed[2] over his hoofs,
    hiding my toes, and turning

    his feet to swift half–moons.
    The willow knob with the strap
    jouncing between my thighs

---

2. **talcumed** (tal´ kəmd´) *v.* blew like fine powder.

cinched (sincht) *v.* bound firmly; tightly fastened

canter (kan´ tər) *v.* ride at a smooth, gentle pace

✔ **Reading Check**

What does the speaker recall herself pretending?

25 was the pommel[3] and yet the poll[4]
    of my nickering pony's head.
    My head and my neck were mine,

    yet they were shaped like a horse.
    My hair flopped to the side
30 like the mane of a horse in the wind.

    My forelock swung in my eyes,
    my neck arched and I snorted.
    I shied and skittered and reared,

    stopped and raised my knees,
35 pawed at the ground and quivered.
    My teeth bared as we wheeled

    and swished through the dust again.
    I was the horse and the rider,
    and the leather I slapped to his rump

40 spanked my own behind.
    Doubled, my two hoofs beat—
    a gallop along the bank,

    the wind twanged in my mane,
    my mouth squared to the bit.
45 And yet I sat on my steed

    quiet, <u>negligent</u> riding,
    my toes standing the stirrups,
    my thighs hugging his ribs.

    At a walk we drew up to the porch.
50 I tethered him to a paling.[5]
    Dismounting, I smoothed my skirt

negligent (neg´ lə jənt) *adj.*
without care or attention;
indifferent

---

3. **pommel** (päm´ əl) *n.* the rounded knob on the front part of a
saddle.
4. **poll** head or mane (the long hair growing from the top of a
horse).
5. **paling** (pāl´ iŋ) *n.* fence.

Horse in the Countryside, 1910, Franz Marc, Museum Folkwang Essen, Essen, Germany

▲ **Critical Viewing** How does this painting reflect the magic of the speaker's imaginary world? **[Interpret]**

and entered the dusky hall.
My feet on the clean linoleum
left ghostly toes in the hall.

55   *Where have you been?* said my mother.
Been riding, I said from the sink,
and filled me a glass of water.

What's that in your pocket? she said.
Just my knife. It weighted my pocket
60   and stretched my dress awry.

Go tie back your hair, said my mother,
and *Why is your mouth all green?*
*Rob Roy, he pulled some clover
as we crossed the field,* I told her.

Review and Assess

Thinking About the Selection

1. **Respond:** If you could have a conversation with the narrator of "The Centaur," what would you want to talk about? Why?

2. **(a) Recall:** The speaker says she got a fresh horse from her stable. What is the "stable"? **(b) Infer:** How does the speaker's imagination influence her actions?

3. **(a) Recall:** What clues does the poet give that the narrator has mentally become one with her "horse"? **(b) Infer:** How does the narrator's comment that Rob Roy "pulled some clover" explain her green mouth?

4. **(a) Recall:** What is the narrator doing as she talks to her mother in the kitchen? **(b) Compare and Contrast:** Compare and contrast the narrator's actions as a daughter to her actions as "the horse and the rider." **(c) Speculate:** Why do you think Swenson chose to present such a comparison and contrast in the poem?

5. **(a) Infer:** How does the natural world enhance the speaker's life? **(b) Interpret:** How does the poem's title reflect this transformation? **(c) Draw Conclusions:** Why do you think the poet only uses the word centaur in the title—not the text—of the poem? **(d) Evaluate:** Do you think "The Centaur" is an appropriate title for this poem? Why?

May Swenson

(1919–1989)

May Swenson was born in Logan, Utah, and later attended Utah State University. After working for a while as a newspaper reporter, she moved to New York City, where she worked as an editor and as a college lecturer. Her poems were published in such magazines as *The New Yorker, Harper's,* and *The Nation.*

Review and Assess

Literary Analysis

Narrative Poems and Ballads

1. Give examples of two characteristics that make these narrative poems different from prose narratives.
2. On a chart like the one shown, record the specific narrative characteristics of each poem.

	Characters	**Setting**	**Story**
Hesperus			
Centaur			

Comparing Literary Works

3. On a chart like the one below, circle the best description of the language level and language conventions used in each poem. Language level for "The Wreck of the Hesperus" is done for you.

	"The Wreck of the Hesperus"	**"The Centaur"**
Language level	(formal)	formal
	informal	informal
Language Conventions	follows all rules	follows all rules
	not tied to rules	not tied to rules

4. In what ways do language level and language conventions show the differences in the writers' attitudes toward their subjects?
5. Which poem has a more formal and serious topic, tone, and mood?

Reading Strategy

Reading Lines According to Punctuation

6. Identify the punctuation marks used in the first and last stanza of each poem and explain how each mark affects the way you read the stanza.

Extend Understanding

7. **Social Studies Connection:** In medieval times, ballads were sung at banquets and feasts. What were the main topics of ballads during the middle ages? Why do you think the story songs of these times focused on these topics?

Quick Review

Narrative poetry tells a story. **Ballads** are a specific type of narrative poetry based on the ancient custom of telling stories in song. To review narrative poems and ballads, see page 817.

Mood is the feeling a reader gets from a work. **Tone** is the author's attitude toward the topic and the reader. To review mood and tone, see page 817.

 Take It to the Net

www.phschool.com
Take the interactive self-test online to check your understanding of these selections.

Integrate Language Skills

Vocabulary Development Lesson

Word Analysis: Suffix -ful-

The suffix -ful-, as in *scornful*, can mean "full of" or "having the qualities of." Complete each sentence with the most appropriate word from this list: *beautiful, cheerful, fearful, successful, peaceful*.

1. Work hard, and you'll be ___?___.
2. Don't be ___?___; the dog won't bite.
3. The painting of the sunset was ___?___.
4. The tune she whistled was ___?___.
5. The sleeping baby had a ___?___ look.

Spelling Strategy

When you write words with the suffix -ful, do not double the final *l*. Complete the following words by adding -ful.

1. master___?___   2. play___?___
3. event___?___   4. use___?___

Concept Development: Synonyms

Write the letter of the word that is closest in meaning to the numbered word.

1. breakers
   a. lights
   b. repairs
   c. waves
2. canter
   a. scold
   b. run
   c. crawl
3. cinched
   a. tied
   b. cut
   c. cheated
4. gale
   a. valley
   b. wind
   c. innocence
5. negligent
   a. careless
   b. fast
   c. slow
6. scornful
   a. respectful
   b. sneering
   c. lucky

Grammar Lesson

Comparisons with *more* and *most*

With longer adjectives and adverbs, make comparisons by adding *more* or *most*.

Comparative: Compares two.
Of the two poems, which is *more* interesting?
Superlative: Compares more than two.
It was the *most* dangerous storm in years.

When you juxtapose qualities, or balance them against each other, use parallel structure. Make the parts of your comparison parallel by using the same level of comparison.

Not Parallel: This poem is more formal but that poem is the most interesting.

Parallel: This poem is more formal but that poem is more interesting.

▶ *For more practice, see page R34, Exercise D.*
Practice Write *more* or *most* to complete each sentence.

1. This tale is ___?___ serious than that one.
2. He is the ___?___ fearful sailor ever.
3. This is the ___?___ useful type of wood.
4. Beth is ___?___ adventurous than Mary.
5. She thinks that the centaur is the ___?___ fascinating mythological figure.

Writing Application Write a paragraph about a fierce storm like the one in "The Wreck of the Hesperus." Use parallel structure in sentences that juxtapose elements.

W̶G *Prentice Hall Writing and Grammar Connection: Chapter 25, Section 1*

Writing Lesson

Comparison and Contrast of Two Poems

In an essay, compare and contrast "The Wreck of the Hesperus" and "The Centaur."

Prewriting List similarities and differences in subject, mood, language level and types of details. Jot notes about how readers will react to these features.

Drafting Begin by writing an introduction in which you present the two works and state whether, overall, they are more similar or different. In the body of your essay, explain the points that are similar and different. Describe how the similarities and differences will affect readers' reactions. Develop and support your main points by following these steps:

- State your points.
- Extend the ideas.
- Elaborate with examples, explanations, supporting facts, or other details.

Model: Support Points

S Both poems help readers picture characters' actions.

E Each gives specific details about what characters do.

E For example, Longfellow says the skipper wrapped his daughter "warm in his seaman's coat." Swenson's speaker tells how she rode her horse: "I'd straddle and canter him fast."

Revising Underline each main point. Evaluate whether you have extended and elaborated each statement of a main point.

Prentice Hall Writing and Grammar Connection: Chapter 8

Extension Activities

Research and Technology Make a mythological creature **poster.** To find resources on the Internet, search on the key word *mythical* or *mythological* added to the word *character*, *beast*, or *creature*.

Writing Write a brief response explaining which of these poems you preferred. In your response, give specific examples from the poem.

Listening and Speaking With a partner, perform a **dramatic reading** of "The Wreck of the Hesperus" for the class. Read different passages with different pacing and emphasis. Discuss the effects on your audience of each way of reading.

 **Take It to the Net**   www.phschool.com

Go online for an additional research activity using the Internet.

Prepare to Read

Harlem Night Song ◆ Blow, Blow, Thou Winter Wind ◆ love is a place ◆ January

 **Take It to the Net**

Visit www.phschool.com
for interactive activities
and instruction related to
these selections, including

- background
- graphic organizers
- literary elements
- reading strategies

Preview

Connecting to the Literature

You can be walking along, having an ordinary day, when suddenly a gust of wind or the sight of a flock of birds makes you notice the beauty of the world around you. The poets in this group capture such moments in verse. Read the poems to share the beauties they notice.

Background

Poets sometimes refer to the light of the moon. The moon, however, does not shine with its own light; it reflects the light of the sun. So, in "Harlem Night Song," when Langston Hughes writes, "Moon is shining," he is actually describing the moon's bright reflection of the sun's light. From Earth, we always see the same side of the moon, but the amount of illumination on that side varies, depending on the moon's position in relation to Earth and the sun.

Literary Analysis

Lyric Poetry

Lyric poetry expresses the thoughts and feelings of a single speaker—the person "saying" the poem. A lyric poem is very musical: The sounds of the words create a pleasant harmonious effect. The poem focuses on a single image or idea. On a chart like the one shown, record the main image or idea in each poem.

Lyric Poetry	Image or Idea
"Harlem Night Song"	
"Blow, Blow, Thou Winter Wind"	
"love is a place"	
"January"	

Comparing Literary Works

All of the poems you are about to read are lyric poems. However, the poems address different topics and are written in different structures.

Notice how these characteristics differ among the selections. Use these focus questions to guide you as you read:

1. What attitudes toward love and friendship are expressed in "Harlem Night Song" and "Blow, Blow, Thou Winter Wind"?
2. How are the subjects of "Blow, Blow, Thou Winter Wind" and "January" similar and different?

Reading Strategy

Identifying the Speaker

A lyric poem focuses on the thoughts and feelings of a single **speaker**—the person saying the poem.

- Sometimes the speaker is the poet.
- Sometimes the speaker is an imaginary character created by the poet.

Clues that will help you recognize the speaker include the word choice used in the poem and the attitudes expressed. This way of speaking and these attitudes may or may not be those of the poet. As you read, look for details that help you identify the speaker of the poem.

Vocabulary Development

roam (rōm) v. go aimlessly; wander (p. 835)

keen (kēn) adj. having a sharp cutting edge (p. 836)

feigning (fān′ iŋ) v. pretending (p. 836)

HARLEM NIGHT SONG

LANGSTON HUGHES

Relics, Martin Lewis, Philadelphia Museum of Art, Philadelphia, PA

Come,
Let us <u>roam</u> the night together
Singing.

I love you.

5 Across
The Harlem[1] roof-tops
Moon is shining.
Night sky is blue.
Stars are great drops
10 Of golden dew.

Down the street
A band is playing.

I love you.

Come,
15 Let us roam the night together
Singing.

_____

1. **Harlem** (här´ ləm) *n.* section of New York City in
the northern part of Manhattan.

◀**Critical Viewing** In what ways has the artist captured the spirit of the night in
this drawing? **[Interpret]**

roam (rōm) *v.* go aim-
lessly; wander

Review and Assess

Thinking About the Selection

1. **Respond:** What emotions do the sights and sounds of your
   neighborhood arouse in you?
2. **(a) Recall:** What does the speaker urge the listener to do
   as they "roam the night together"? **(b) Interpret:** Why
   would the speaker suggest this activity?
3. **(a) Infer:** Why does the speaker feel so full of life?
   (b) Analyze: Which word best describes the speaker's
   view of his surroundings: distracting, inspiring, or beautiful?
4. **(a) Connect:** How are the stanzas that say "I love you"
   related to what happens in the other stanzas?
   (b) Speculate: Do you think the speaker of the poem lives in
   Harlem? Explain your answer.

Langston Hughes

(1902–1967)

Langston
Hughes wrote
poems, stories,
plays, essays,
histories, and
songs. As a song-
writer, he wrote
the lyrics for Kurt
Weill's music for *Street
Scene,* a successful 1947
Broadway musical.

BLOW, BLOW, THOU WINTER WIND

William Shakespeare

Blow, blow, thou winter wind.
Thou art not so unkind
    As man's ingratitude.
Thy tooth is not so keen,
5   Because thou art not seen,
    Although thy breath be rude.[1]
Heigh-ho! Sing, heigh-ho! unto the green holly.
Most friendship is feigning, most loving mere folly.
    Then, heigh-ho, the holly!
10   This life is most jolly.

Freeze, freeze, thou bitter sky,
That dost not bite so nigh
    As benefits forgot.

keen (kēn) *adj.* having a sharp cutting edge

feigning (fān´ iŋ) *v.* pretending

---

1. rude *adj.* rough; harsh.

Though thou the waters warp,[2]
15 Thy sting is not so sharp
As friend remembered not.
Heigh-ho! Sing, heigh-ho! unto the green holly.
Most friendship is feigning, most loving mere folly.
Then, heigh-ho, the holly!
20 This life is most jolly.

---

2. **warp** v. freeze.

Review and Assess

Thinking About the Selection

1. **Respond:** Do you share the view of friendship expressed by the speaker in this poem? Explain.

2. **(a) Recall:** To whom is the speaker speaking in each of these stanzas? **(b) Interpret:** What does the speaker mean when he repeats "This life is most jolly"?

3. **(a) Recall:** What does the speaker say is more unkind than the winter wind and sharper than the sting of the bitter sky? **(b) Infer:** How does the speaker feel about friendship and love?

4. **(a) Compare and Contrast:** Explain what the poem suggests about the harshness of nature compared to the pain of human relationships. **(b) Speculate:** Based on the poem, what do you think happened to the speaker to make him feel this way?

5. **Take a Stand:** Do you think the speaker should allow the pain of a past experience to grow into bitterness?

William Shakespeare

(1564–1616)

Probably the most famous author in English literature, William Shakespeare was born in Stratford-on-Avon, a small town in England. The son of a glovemaker, Shakespeare made his living as an actor and writer. Although born in Stratford, he moved to London as a young man, and spent most of his adult life there. His plays were performed in special presentations for Queen Elizabeth I, as well as his theater—*The Globe*. Although written centuries ago, plays such as *Romeo and Juliet* continue to capture audiences today. In addition to writing thirty-seven plays, he also wrote poems and songs.

JANUARY

John Updike

The Magpie, 1869, Claude Monet, Musée d'Orsay, Paris, France

▲ **Critical Viewing** Compare and contrast the artist's concept of winter with Updike's. **[Compare and Contrast]**

The days are short,
    The sun a spark
Hung thin between
    The dark and dark.

5   Fat snowy footsteps
    Track the floor,
And parkas pile up
    Near the door.

The river is
10   A frozen place
Held still beneath
    The trees' black lace.

The sky is low.
    The wind is gray.
15 The radiator
    Purrs all day.

Literary Analysis
Lyric Poetry In what ways is this poem musical?

Review and Assess

Thinking About the Selection

1. **Respond:** Which image in "January" best conveys to you the essence of that month? Why?

2. **(a) Recall:** What is the sun compared to in the first stanza of the poem? **(b) Interpret:** Explain the image "dark and dark" in line 4.

3. **(a) Interpret:** Why do the trees appear to be made of black lace? **(b) Compare and Contrast:** How does this image contrast visually with other parts of the poem?

4. **(a) Infer:** What sense besides sight does the poem appeal to? **(b) Draw Conclusions:** Would you describe the speaker's attitude toward winter as positive or negative? Explain.

John Updike

(b.1932)
Best known as a Pulitzer Prize-winning novelist, John Updike is also an essayist, poet, and editor. Updike's quartet of novels, including *Rabbit, Run; Rabbit Redux; Rabbit Is Rich;* and *Rabbit at Rest,* is considered to be one of the great chronicles of modern life.

The Nest, 1893, Constant Montald, Musées Royaux des Beaux-Arts de Belgique, Bruxelles-Koninklijke Musea voor Schone Kunsten van Belgie, Brussels, Belgium

▲ **Critical Viewing** In what ways does this painting bring to life the phrase "brightness of peace"? **[Interpret]**

love is a place

E.E. Cummings

love is a place
& through this place of
love move
(with brightness of peace)
5   all places

yes is a world
& in this world of
yes live
(skillfully curled)
10   all worlds

E. E. Cummings

(1894–1962)

The E. E. in Cummings's name stands for Edward Estlin. During World War I, before the United States had entered the war, he joined a volunteer ambulance corps in France. There, his unusual style of writing got him in trouble. His letters home looked suspicious to French censors and he was arrested and imprisoned for three months as a spy.

Today, Cummings is known for the playful, experimental nature of his poetry. He uses mostly lower case letters, unusual punctuation, and unique arrangements of words. Cummings once said that poetry is "the only thing that matters." In his poems, he celebrates families, parents, children, and fun.

Review and Assess

Thinking About the Selection

1. **Respond:** What do you think of Cummings's statements that "love is a place" and "yes is a world"?

2. **(a) Recall:** What does the speaker say moves through the "place of / love" and lives in "this world of / yes"?
   (b) Interpret: What does he mean by saying these things?

3. **(a) Interpret:** What do you think the speaker means when he describes "all worlds" in "this world of / yes" as being "skillfully curled"? **(b) Draw Conclusions:** Would you say that the speaker is satisfied with the world as it is? Explain.

4. **(a) Analyze:** In what ways does Cummings celebrate nature in this poem? **(b) Speculate:** If Cummings had added a third stanza to the poem, what do you think its first word might have been? Why?

Review and Assess

Literary Analysis

Lyric Poetry

1. What is the main image or idea of each poem?
2. For both "Blow, Blow, Thou Winter Wind" and "January," give one example of a line with musical quality.

Comparing Literary Works

3. Compare and contrast the attitudes toward love and friendship of the speakers in "Harlem Night Song" and in "Blow, Blow, Thou Winter Wind."
4. Complete a chart like the one shown to explore the other similarities and differences in the structures of the poems.

Poem	Stanzas—Regular or Irregular?	Line Length
"Harlem Night Song"		
"Blow, Blow, Thou Winter Wind"		
"love is a place"		
"January"		

5. Is the structure of lyric poetry as important as the feelings and qualities associated with it? Explain your answer.

Reading Strategy

Identifying the Speaker

6. Using a chart like the one shown, jot down what you know about each poem's speaker and how you know it.

Poem	Speaker	Evidence
"Harlem Night Song"	is a person who loves the sights and sounds of Harlem.	
"Blow, Blow, Thou Winter Wind"		
"love is a place"		
"January"		

Extend Understanding

7. **Cultural Connection:** Based on "Harlem Night Song," what features of an urban setting do you think city residents might find beautiful that rural residents might not?

Quick Review

Lyric poetry is highly musical poetry that focuses on a single image or idea. To review lyric poetry, see page 833.

The **speaker** of a poem is the character or voice assumed by the poet, which may or may not be the voice of the poet himself or herself. To review the speaker, see page 833.

 Take It to the Net
www.phschool.com
Take the interactive self-test online to check your understanding of these selections.

Integrate Language Skills

Vocabulary Development Lesson

Word Analysis: Multiple-Meaning Word *keen*

In "Blow, Blow, Thou Winter Wind," the adjective *keen* means "having a sharp cutting edge." However, this adjective can have any of the following meanings:

 a. having a sharp cutting edge
 b. mentally sharp and quick
 c. eager; enthusiastic

On your paper, match each use of *keen* with the letter of the correct meaning from the list above.

1. Because a hawk has *keen* eyesight, it can spot the movement of a mouse from a great height.
2. After an afternoon of building snow figures, I am *keen* to drink a mug of warm cocoa.
3. A *keen* knife can slice through a tomato easily.

Fluency: Sentence Completions

On your paper, write the vocabulary word that best completes each sentence.

1. ____?____ sleep, the child kept her eyes closed.
2. David has a ____?____ interest in music.
3. Be careful when you ____?____ the streets at night.

Spelling Strategy

When choosing between *ei* and *ie*, follow this rule: Put *i* before *e* except after *c* or when sounded like *ay* as in *neighbor* and *weigh*. On your paper, complete the following words by adding *ei* or *ie*.

1. sl__?__gh
2. c__?__ling
3. fr__?__nd
4. n__?__ce
5. rec__?__ve
6. b__?__ge

Grammar Lesson

Comparisons of Modifiers

Some modifiers have **irregular forms for comparisons:** they change form to show degrees of comparison, rather than just adding the ending *–ed*.

Positive	Comparative	Superlative
bad	worse	worst
good	better	best
well	better	best
little	less	least
many, much	more	most

► *For more practice, see page R31, Exercise D.*

Practice Copy the sentences. Underline the modifiers and label them comparative or superlative.

1. Most friendship is feigning.
2. Winter is the least friendly season.
3. More stars are visible with a telescope than without.
4. Give me less war and more peace.
5. The moon looked better over the water than over the land.

Writing Application To each sentence, add a second part, in which you use a different form of comparison of the italicized modifier.

1. I saw *many* colors reflected in the water.
2. She felt *good* today.
3. It is a *bad* season for skiing.

W̶G̶ Prentice Hall Writing and Grammar Connection: Chapter 25, Section 1

Writing Lesson

Profile of a Poet

Choose one poet from this group. Write a brief profile in which you discuss his work.

Prewriting Research the poet's poetry. On the basis of several of his poems, take notes about the qualities of the poet's work that make his style unique and influential.

Drafting Develop a thesis statement—the main point you want to make. Include it in your first paragraph. Support your thesis statement with specific examples from the poems. Use language and sentence structure that reflect an appropriate tone—an attitude toward your subject.

Model: Use an Appropriate Tone

E. E. Cummings often wrote whimsical poems with surprising comparisons. One example is "who knows if the moon's," in which the poet describes the moon as a hot-air balloon.

> Sophisticated vocabulary such as *whimsical* and *surprising comparisons* and a complex sentence contribute to a formal, academic tone appropriate for a profile of a poet.

Revising Review your thesis statement, and check to make sure each main point supports it in some way. Be sure your tone is appropriate and consistent.

𝒲ᴳ *Prentice Hall Writing and Grammar Connection: Chapter 3, Section 3*

Extension Activities

Research and Technology With a small group, create a **poets' timeline** on which you mark the lifespans of the four poets in this section.

1. Measure a timeline in half centuries.
2. Use different colors to make bars or lines marking the lifetime of each poet. (The lifetimes of some poets will overlap. Use a separate line for each poet's color.)
3. Do research and record world events that happened during each poet's lifetime.

With the group, discuss how the events and other poets on the timeline may have influenced each poets writing. **[Group Activity]**

Listening and Speaking Perform a **reading** of two or more of the poems in this grouping to the class. Prepare a "reading copy" of the poems on which you mark words to be emphasized and places to pause. Rehearse, then perform your reading for the class.

Writing Write a **literary analysis** of one of the poems. Identify and explain literary techniques used in the poem. Define any literary terms you use.

 **Take It to the Net**   www.phschool.com

Go online for an additional research activity using the Internet.

Prepare to Read

Ode to Enchanted Light ◆ Two Haiku ◆
She Dwelt Among the Untrodden Ways ◆ Harriet Beecher Stowe ◆
from John Brown's Body ◆ 400-Meter Free Style

 Take It to the Net

Visit www.phschool.com
for interactive activities
and instruction related to
these selections, including
- background
- graphic organizers
- literary elements
- reading strategies

Preview

Connecting to the Literature

Some days start out great—you arrive early at the bus stop, the weather
is great, and you are prepared for every class. Then something happens—
the bus does not show up, you are late for a test, or it starts to rain and
you do not have an umbrella. Life is full of ups and downs, and poets capture the full range of emotions that result. The poems in this group show
a variety of feelings. As you read, notice the words and images the speakers in the poems use to show their feelings.

Background

The poems "Harriet Beecher Stowe" and "John Brown's Body" have as
their subjects two famous people associated with the Civil War. Both
opposed slavery—Stowe through her writing and Brown through his
attacks on slave-holders and military posts.

Literary Analysis

Form and Purpose

The poems in this group represent several **forms**, or types, of poetry that are identified by their unique characteristics.

Some forms are set apart by their unique structure. Others are defined by their **purpose**, the goal of the poem, the reason the poet writes it. On the next two pages, you can find more detail about the forms of the poems in this group. As you read, notice the characteristics of each form as shown in the representative poem in this group.

Comparing Literary Works

Compare and contrast the poems in this group, based on their purposes and structures.

1. Which two poems have the most similar topics?
2. What are the differences in the ways these poems present their topics?

Reading Strategy

Drawing Inferences

No matter what form a poem takes, much of what the poet is communicating will be suggested rather than stated. To interpret the author's message, **draw inferences**—make logical guesses—based on details in the works. In the following example, italicized details allow you to draw an inference about the speaker's feelings. The chart shows how the details lead to the inference. Use a chart like it to draw inferences while reading other poems.

> American muse, whose *strong and diverse* heart
> So many men have tried to understand
> But *only made it smaller* with their art,
> Because *you are as various as your land.*

Details

– strong and diverse
– only made it smaller
– you are as various as your land

⬇

What does the combination of details suggest?

⬇

Inference

The speaker admires the size and diversity of the American muse, or spirit

Vocabulary Development

untrodden (un träd′'n) *adj.* not walked upon (p. 850)

muse (myōōz) *n.* spirit of inspiration (p. 851)

essence (es′əns) *n.* fundamental nature; most important quality (p. 852)

semblences (sem′ bləns əz) *n.* appearances (p. 852)

complacent (kəm plā′sənt) *adj.* self-satisfied (p. 853)

cunningly (kun′ iŋ lē) *adv.* skillfully (p. 854)

extravagance (ik strav′ ə gəns) *n.* wastefulness (p. 855)

nurtures (nʉr′ chərz) *v.* nourishes (p. 855)

Forms of Poetry

Each form of poetry has specific purposes and characteristics. A form is usually defined in terms of purpose and characteristics.

Purpose: The goal of the poem; the reason it is written

Subject and Theme: The topic and the message the poem communicates

Tone: The poet's attitude toward the subject and/or the reader

Rhyme: The use of words that have the same ending vowel and consonant sounds—for example, poem/home

Rhythm: The arrangement of stressed and unstressed syllables in a line

Lines and Stanzas: The number and arrangement of lines and groups of lines to create an appearance on the page or to group thoughts

Ode

An ode is a single, unified strain of exalted verse with a single purpose and dealing with a single theme. Read "Ode to Enchanted Light," page 848.

Purpose: To celebrate a single object or idea

Subject and Theme: An ode can be about any subject. Pablo Neruda has written odes to socks and salt.

Tone: Elaborate and dignified, the ode glorifies and celebrates its subject with a formal tone.

Rhyme and Rhythm: May or may not have end rhyme or regular rhythm

Lines and Stanzas: Number and length can vary. Odes are usually long with varying line lengths.

Haiku

A haiku is a short poem. Haiku originated in Japan, but people around the world enjoy writing and reading these very short poems. Read two haiku by Bashō and Moritake, page 849.

Subject and Theme: Anything, but usually nature

Tone: Serious

Rhyme and Rhythm: Does not rhyme. Does not have regular rhythm

Lines and Stanzas: Each haiku has three lines. The first line is five syllables, the second line is seven syllables, and the third line goes back to five syllables.

Elegy

An elegy is a formal poem that reflects on death or another solemn theme. Read "She Dwelt Among the Untrodden Ways," page 850.

Purpose: To memorialize a person or reflect on a subject

Subject and Theme: The death of a particular person or another serious subject such as war

Tone: Formal and serious

Rhyme and Rhythm: May or may not have end rhyme. May or may not have a regular rhythm

Lines and Stanzas: Vary

Herons and Reeds, Japanese, Asian Art Museum of San Francisco, CA

Sonnet A sonnet is a fourteen-line poem that follows a specified rhyme scheme. Read "Harriet Beecher Stowe," page 853.

Purpose: Varies, but often the purpose of a sonnet is to praise

Subject and Theme: Can vary; many sonnets are written about love

Tone: Usually formal and serious

Rhyme: Has a definite rhyme scheme. The type of rhyme scheme a sonnet has places it into an even smaller category of Petrarchan (Italian) sonnets or Shakespearean (English) sonnets [abbaabbacdecde or abbaabbacdcdcd].

Rhythm: Iambic pentameter (an unstressed beat followed by a stressed beat)

Lines and Stanzas: All sonnets have fourteen lines. Petrarchan sonnets have two stanzas: an **octet** (eight-line stanza) followed by a **sextet** (six-line stanza). Shakespearean sonnets have four stanzas: three **quatrains** (four-line stanzas) followed by a **couplet** (a pair of lines that can function as a stanza).

Epic An epic is a long narrative poem. It often begins with an appeal to a muse—the beings that the ancient Greeks believed governed inspiration in the arts. After the appeal to the muse, an epic usually begins *in medias res*—in the middle of the action. Read "John Brown's Body," page 851.

Purpose: To tell an exciting or inspiring story

Subject and Theme: Hero of imposing stature and national or international importance

Tone: Serious and elevated

Rhyme and Rhythm: Usually doesn't have end rhyme. May or may not have a regular rhythm

Lines and Stanzas: Usually has many lines and stanzas

Concrete Poem In a concrete poem, the words are arranged on the page to make a shape that suggests the topic of the poem. Read "400-Meter Freestyle," page 854.

Purpose: To connect ideas and appearance

Subject and Theme: Anything

Tone: Often playful or lighthearted

Rhyme and Rhythm: Does not necessarily rhyme. Usually does not have regular rhythm

Lines and Stanzas: The arrangement of lines and groups of lines depends entirely on the shape the poet wishes to make.

Ode to Enchanted Light

Pablo Neruda

Under the trees light
has dropped from the top of the sky,
light
like a green
5 latticework of branches,
shining
on every leaf,
drifting down like clean
white sand.

10 A cicada sends
its sawing song
high into the empty air.

The world is
a glass overflowing
15 with water.

Pablo Neruda

(1904–1973)

This Chilean poet may be the only poet ever to write a poem to his socks! Throughout his life, he kept his ear tuned to the songs of common objects and, through poetry, showed their beauty and uniqueness. His ability to create interest in everyday experiences is shown in "Ode to Enchanted Light." Neruda's passion for life fueled a large body of work. In 1971, he was awarded the Nobel Prize for Literature.

Two Haiku

The lightning flashes!
And slashing through the darkness,
A night-heron's[1] screech.

Bashō

The falling flower
I saw drift back to the branch
Was a butterfly.

Moritake

---

1. **night-heron** (nit′ her′ ən) *n.*: A large
wading bird with a long neck and long legs
that is active at night

Matsuo Bashō

(1644–1694)

Japanese poet
Matsuo Bashō
is widely
regarded as
the greatest of
haiku poets. He
began writing
poetry at age nine,
and at the age of thirty, he
founded a school for the
study of haiku.

Moritake

(1452–1540)

A priest as well as a
poet, Moritake is
considered one of the
leading Japanese poets of
the sixteenth century.

Review and Assess

Thinking About the Selections

1. **Respond:** Which haiku were you better able to envision?
Why?

2. **(a) Recall:** What is the subject of the haiku by Bashō?
(b) Connect: In what way do the sight and sound work
together?

3. **(a) Recall:** What does Moritake describe in his haiku?
(b) Compare: What are the similarities between the two
things he mentions? **(c) Evaluate:** How effective is his
comparison in helping you envision his subject?

4. **Make a Judgment:** Do you think a good haiku would be easy
or difficult to write? Why?

She Dwelt Among the Untrodden Ways

William Wordsworth

She dwelt among the <u>untrodden</u> ways
  Beside the springs of Dove,
A maid whom there were none to praise,
  And very few to love.

5 A violet by a mossy stone
  Half-hidden from the eye!
—Fair as a star, when only one
  Is shining in the sky.

  She lived unknown, and few could know
10 When Lucy ceased to be;
But she is in her grave, and, oh,
  The difference to me!

untrodden (un träd′ n) *adj.*
not walked on

Review and Assess

Thinking About the Selection

1. **Respond:** Would you like to be described by the words in this poem? Why or why not?

2. **(a) Recall:** Who is the subject of the poem? **(b) Deduce:** What has happened to her? **(c) Draw Conclusions:** How does the speaker feel about the subject and what has happened to her?

3. **(a) Connect:** To what does the poet compare the subject of the poem? **(b) Analzye:** What personality qualities are suggested by these comparisons? **(c) Extend:** What comparisons could you add that would suggest these same qualities?

4. **(a) Speculate:** Why does the poet write this poem about the subject? **(b) Evaluate:** Is the subject important enough to write a poem about? Explain.

William Wordsworth

(1770–1850)

William Wordsworth began his literary career as a "revolutionary" poet. What seemed outrageous at the time was Wordsworth's use of simple language to memorialize remarkable moments in everyday life. He proposed that poets should use "a selection of language really used by men." He is also known for defining poetry in a way that influenced generations of writers that followed. According to Wordsworth, poetry is "emotion recollected in tranquillity."

INVOCATION

from John Brown's Body

Stephen Vincent Benét

American <u>muse</u>, whose strong and diverse heart
So many men have tried to understand
But only made it smaller with their art,
Because you are as various as your land,

5 As mountainous-deep, as flowered with blue rivers,
Thirsty with deserts, buried under snows,
As native as the shape of Navajo quivers,
And native, too, as the sea–voyaged rose.

Swift runner, never captured or subdued,
10 Seven–branched elk beside the mountain stream,
That half a hundred hunters have pursued
But never matched their bullets with the dream,

Where the great huntsmen failed, I set my sorry
And mortal snare for your immortal quarry.

15 You are the buffalo-ghost, the broncho-ghost
With dollar-silver in your saddle-horn,
The cowboys riding in from Painted Post,
The Indian arrow in the Indian corn,

And you are the clipped velvet of the lawns
20 Where Shropshire grows from Massachusetts sods,
The grey Maine rocks—and the war-painted dawns
That break above the Garden of the Gods.

The prairie-schooners crawling toward the ore
And the cheap car, parked by the station-door.

25 Where the skyscrapers lift their foggy plumes

muse (myo͞oz) *n.* spirit thought to inspire a poet or other artist

Reading Check

What is the speaker describing?

Of stranded smoke out of a stony mouth
You are that high stone and its arrogant fumes,
And you are ruined gardens in the South

And bleak New England farms, so winter-white
30　Even their roofs look lonely, and the deep
The middle grainland where the wind of night
Is like all blind earth sighing in her sleep.

A friend, an enemy, a sacred hag
With two tied oceans in her medicine-bag.

35　They tried to fit you with an English song
And clip your speech into the English tale.
But, even from the first, the words went wrong,
The catbird pecked away the nightingale.

The homesick men begot high-cheekboned things
40　Whose wit was whittled with a different sound
And Thames and all the rivers of the kings
Ran into Mississippi and were drowned.

All these you are, and each is partly you,
And none is false, and none is wholly true.

45　So how to see you as you really are,
So how to suck the pure, distillate, stored
Essence of essence from the hidden star
And make it pierce like a riposting sword.

For, as we hunt you down, you must escape
50　And we pursue a shadow of our own
That can be caught in a magician's cape
But has the flatness of a painted stone.

Never the running stag, the gull at wing,
The pure elixir, the American thing.

55　And yet, at moments when the mind was hot
With something fierier than joy or grief,
When each known spot was an eternal spot
And every leaf was an immortal leaf,

I think that I have seen you, not as one,
60　But clad in diverse semblances and powers,
Always the same, as light falls from the sun,
And always different, as the differing hours.

essence (es´ əns) *n.*
most important quality

semblances (sem´ bləns əs)
n. outward form or
appearance

Stephen Vincent Benét

(1898–1943)

Born in
Bethelehem,
Pennsylvania,
Benét grew up
listening to his
father's evening
poetry readings.
His interest in
American history and folklore provided subjects and
themes for much of his
work, including *John
Brown's Body*. He was
awarded the Pulitzer Prize
for this American epic.
(He was awarded another
Pulitzer after his death for
the unfinished American
epic *Western Star*.) In addition to poetry, Benét wrote
plays, operas, and even a
motion picture!

Harriet Beecher Stowe

PAUL LAURENCE DUNBAR

She told the story, and the whole world wept
  At wrongs and cruelties it had not known
  But for this fearless woman's voice alone.
  She spoke to the consciences that long had slept:
5 Her message, Freedom's clear reveille, swept
  From heedless hovel to <u>complacent</u> throne.
  Command and prophecy were in the tone
  And from its sheath the sword of justice leapt.
Around two peoples swelled the fiery wave,
10 But both came forth transfigured from the flame
Blest be the hand that dared be strong to save,
  And blest be she who in our weakness came—
  Prophet and priestess! At one stroke she gave
  A race to freedom and herself to fame.

complacent (kəm plā´ sənt)
adj. self-satisfied, smug

Review and Assess

Thinking About the Selections

1. **Respond:** Would you want to meet the subject or writer of either poem? Why or why not?

2. **(a) Recall:** What is Stowe's achievement? **(b) Interpret:** What "two peoples" are transfigured by her work? **(c) Draw Conclusions:** Why does her work require strength?

3. **(a) Evaluate:** Do you feel Harriet Beecher Stowe's writing can be judged according to contemporary standards? Why or why not? **(b) Make a Judgment:** Is Dunbar's poem about Harriet Beecher Stowe meaningful to people today? Why or why not?

4. **(a) Recall:** To whom is Benét's invocation addressed? **(b) Analzye:** Why does the speaker have difficulty describing the subject?

5. **(a) Interpret:** To what period in American history is the speaker referring with these words: "They tried to fit you with an English song/And clip your speech into an English tale"? **(b) Contrast:** Based on details in the poem, how is "American" different from "English"?

Paul Laurence Dunbar

(1872–1906)

Dunbar was the son of former slaves. Encouraged by his mother, he began writing at an early age. Some of his poems are written in formal language; others are written in dialect. Dunbar found value in both forms of expression, but was discouraged when readers or critics focused on only one or the other of his styles.

He was inspired by Harriet Beecher Stowe's epic work *Uncle Tom's Cabin* and in his own work honored people who contributed to the struggle for African American rights.

400-Meter

Maxine Kumin

The **gun** full swing the swimmer catapults and cracks
      s
      i
      x
feet **away** onto that perfect glass he catches at
a
n
d
throws behind him scoop[1] after scoop <u>cunningly</u> moving
      t
      h
      e
water **back** to move him forward. Thrift is his wonderful
  s
  e
  c
5 ret; **he** has schooled out all <u>extravagance</u>. No muscle

cunningly (kun´ iŋ lē) *adv.*
skillfully

extravagance
(ik strav´ ə gəns)
n. wastefulness

---

1. scoop (sko͞op) *n.* the amount taken up; in this case, with a cupped hand.

▼ **Critical Viewing**
What words would you
choose to describe the
swimmer pictured here?
[Interpret]

Free Style

        r
         i
          p
ples without compensation wrist cock³ to heel snap to
h
i
s
mobile mouth that siphons³ in the air that <u>nurtures</u>
                h
                 i
                  m
at half an inch above sea level so to speak. The
h
e
astonishing whites of the soles of his feet rise
              a
               n
                d

10 salute us on the turns. He flips, converts, and is gone
a
l
l

---

nurtures (nʉr′ chərz) v. nourishes

☑ **Reading Check**

What is the subject of the poem doing?

2. **wrist cock** the tilted position of the wrist.
3. **siphons** (sī′ fənz) v. draws; pulls.

in one. We watch him for signs. His arms are steady at

$$t$$
$$h$$
$$e$$

catch, his cadent[4] feet tick in the stretch, they know

$$t$$
$$h$$
$$e$$

lesson well. Lungs know, too; he does not list[5] for

$$a$$
$$i$$
$$r$$

he drives along on little sips carefully expended

$$b$$
$$u$$
$$t$$

15   that plum[6] red heart pumps hard cries hurt how soon

$$i$$
$$t$$
$$s$$

near one more and makes its final surge   Time 4:25:9

---

4. **cadent** (kā´ dənt) *adj.* rhythmic beating.
5. **list** (list) *v.* tilt to one side.
6. **plum** (plum) *adj.* here, first class.

Review and Assess

Thinking About the Selection

1. **Respond:** How does the shape of "400-Meter Freestyle" affect your reading?

2. **(a) Recall:** With what action does the poem begin?
   (b) Analyze: What is the impact of beginning with this event?

3. **(a) Distinguish:** Would you classify this poem as more narrative or more descriptive? **(b) Support:** What details from the poem support your opinion?

4. **(a) Interpret:** Why does Kumin end the poem with the swimmer's racing time? **(b) Assess:** Is the swimmer's racing time an appropriate ending? Why or why not?
   (c) Connect: What other sport do you think would make a good subject for a poem? Why?

5. **Take a Position:** Do you think the amount of training time involved for swimmers and other athletes to be competitive is worth the things they give up? Why or why not?

Maxine Kumin

(b. 1925)
In addition to poetry, Maxine Kumin has written novels, essays, and children's books. Much of her work includes images and ideas from her life on her New Hampshire farm. In 1973, she won the Pulitzer Prize for *Up Country: Poems of New England*. She is admired for her poetic craftsmanship—many of her poems are carefully structured in traditional poetic patterns. In "400-Meter Freestyle" Kumin takes a more playful approach, while still demonstrating her ability to fit words into a form.

Review and Assess

Literary Analysis

Form and Purpose

1. How does "Harriet Beecher Stowe" follow the rules of its form?
2. What feature of an epic is shown in the section of *John Brown's Body?*
3. What is the specific purpose of "Ode to Enchanted Light"?

Comparing Literary Works

4. Copy the following chart. In the blank spaces, write a statement that makes a connection between the topics or purposes of the two poems pointing to the space.

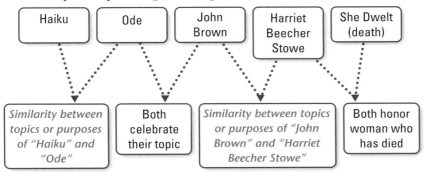

5. Which two poems have the most similar topic or purpose?
6. What are the differences in the way the two poems present their topics or achieve their purposes ?

Reading Strategy

Draw Inferences

7. In "She Dwelt Among the Untrodden Ways," what inference can you draw about the relationship between Lucy and the speaker?
8. Do you think Paul Laurence Dunbar and Stephen Vincent Benét would like each other? Explain why or why not based on inferences you draw from the subjects of their poems.

Extend Understanding

9. **Social Studies Connection:** What people or events from American history support the descriptions of the American muse in Benét's poem as large and diverse?
10. **Make a Judgment:** Which of these poems would you recommend to another reader? Why?

Quick Review

Form is a type of poetry that is identified by unique characteristics. To review form and purpose, see page 845.

The **purpose** of a poem is the reason the poet writes it.

An **inference** is a logical conclusion based on clues.

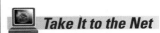
Take It to the Net
www.phschool.com
Take the interactive self-test online to check your understanding of these selections.

Integrate Language Skills

Vocabulary Development Lesson

Concept Development: Use Words in Context

The **context** of a word is the situation in which it is used. For words that have more than one meaning, the surrounding words and phrases help you understand the meaning in a particular sentence. Read the following sets of sentences. Copy the two sentences that use the word in the same way.

1. **a.** Benét calls upon the American *muse*. **b.** A writer may *muse* for a while before beginning to write. **c.** Most epics begin with an appeal to a *muse*.

2. **a.** The United States has a *diverse* population. **b.** Maxine Kumin writes on *diverse* subjects. **c.** The two writers followed *diverse* courses.

Word Analysis: Word Relationships

Explain how the meanings of the words in each pair are related.

1. untrodden; tread
2. complacent; placate
3. muse; musing
4. essence; essential
5. semblances; resemble
6. cunningly; canny
7. extravagance; extra
8. nurtures; nutrition

Spelling Strategy

The *z* sound in the sound *ooz* is sometimes spelled with an *se* at the end of a word. Proofread the passage. Correct any misspellings of words that contain the *z* sound. Consult a dictionary if you are not sure.

Figuring out the meaning of the poem is not difficult if you use the cluse. Of course, you can refuze to see the hints. Some hints may seem like a rues. You could accuse the poets of trying to confues you.

Grammar Lesson

Punctuating Coordinate Adjectives

Adjectives that modify the same noun separately and equally are **coordinate adjectives.**

> **Example:** American muse, whose strong and diverse heart…

Use a comma to separate coordinate adjectives. To test whether two adjectives are coordinate, switch the order of the adjectives. If the new order still makes sense, the adjectives are coordinate. Do not use a comma between adjectives whose order cannot be reversed.

▶ *For more practice, see page R32, Exercise B.*

Practice Write the sentences. Punctuate the coordinate adjectives correctly.

1. You are the clipped velvet lawn.
2. Benét's long historical poem won the Pulitzer.
3. The thorough accurate work also contains fictional characters
4. The traditional epic beginning is an invocation to the muse.
5. In it, the speaker describes the colorful varied images that suggest America.

Writing Application Write a sentence to describe each poem. In at least three of your sentences, use coordinate adjectives.

W͞G Prentice Hall Writing and Grammar Connection: Chapter 28

Writing Lesson

Poem

Write a poem in one of the forms you have learned about in this group.

Prewriting Make lists of family, friends, pets, special places, and special things. Choose one of the items on your lists as a topic. Then, identify details that could be used in the different forms of poetry. Choose the form for which you have the most details. (See pages 846–847.)

Model Topic: my dog

Ode	Sonnet	Epic	Concrete
Elevated qualities that create a single effect	rhymes	adventures	Visual effects
Loyal, faithful, trusting	Play/day Trust/must/just	Swimming in the river Chasing the woodchuck	Wagging tail Big paws

The chart shows the different details that could be used to make the same topic work in different forms. You only need to generate details for the form you choose.

Drafting Use your details to write in your chosen form. To review the characteristics of the different forms, see pages 846 and 847.

Revising Add or delete words or details to make your poem more closely fit the form you choose.

WG Prentice Hall Writing and Grammar Connection: Chapter 8, Section 3

Extension Activities

Research and Technology Prepare a collection of poems that illustrate the different forms.

1. Use a search engine with the form as a keyword.
2. Go to a poetry site and use the site map to find the forms.
3. Look for the name of each form in the index of a print poetry anthology.

Choose one example of each form in each of the resources. Print the examples you find online. Make a photocopy of the examples you find in print resources. Share your collection with the class.

Listening and Speaking Plan two **poetry presentations:** One for an audience of students your own age and one for an audience of younger children.

1. Choose one of the poems in this group for each audience.
2. Identify the main points you want your audience to remember about the poem.
3. Identify terms or vocabulary that may need to be defined or explained.

 **Take It to the Net**   www.phschool.com

Go online for an additional research activity using the Internet.

Directions and Warranties

About Directions and Warranties

When you buy a new product, two important documents usually come with it. To be a smart consumer, you need to understand both of those documents. Sometimes, however, they are written in difficult or complicated language. You need to make sure you know the words and terms they use.

- The first document is an instruction manual or sheet of directions. These tell you how to use a tool or product correctly and safely. Without them, you might break the product, hurt yourself, or never figure out how to use it.
- The second document is the product warranty. It tells you your rights as a buyer of this product. It sets out the conditions under which the maker will replace or repair the product. Some warranties are printed along with the directions. Some appear on a card that you sign and mail back to the company.

Reading Strategy

Following Operating Instructions

Product operating instructions are a specialized form of writing that require careful reading. They explain the step-by-step technique for using a new product. You cannot read directions in the same way that you read a story or even a nonfiction article. You need to notice each detail and the order in which the steps are given.

- Read all the directions completely before starting to follow them.
- Look for clues such as bold type or capital letters. These are signposts that point out specific sections or important information.
- If the directions include diagrams, use them to locate and name the parts of the product. Knowing the name of each part makes it easier to follow directions.
- Notice the details carefully.
- Follow each step in the exact order given in the directions. You can use a chart like this one to keep track of the steps as you read.
- Don't skip any steps.
- When reading warranties, be sure you understand the legal language.

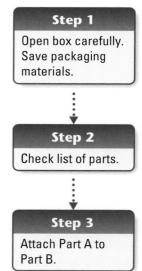

Step 1
Open box carefully. Save packaging materials.

Step 2
Check list of parts.

Step 3
Attach Part A to Part B.

Diagrams play an important part in understanding directions. Compare the product with the diagram before starting to operate it. If other diagrams are given as you work through the directions, examine them carefully.

These items describe the basic settings for the stopwatch. They tell you what the three knobs—S1, S2, S3—control.

Bold type is often used for the headings of major sections in directions. The bold type helps you find the section you need quickly.

In addition to giving steps for operating the product, directions often include additional information to help you use it. Here, the directions tell you when and how to replace the stopwatch battery.

HOW TO OPERATE

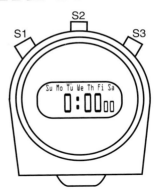

1. Time display in hours, minutes, seconds, and day of week—normal time display state
2. Calendar display in month, date, day of week, and snooze—hold down S3
3. Alarm time display and disarm —hold down S1
4. Alarm on (on) off (off)—hold down S1 and S3
5. Chime on (all day-flags on) off (all day-flags off)—hold down S1 and S2

TO SET TIME AND CALENDAR—press S2 three times
—select flashing digit(s) to be set by depressing S1 and then advance figure by depressing S3 (fast advance by holding down S3 for more than 2 seconds)
—select 12/24-hour cycle option when setting normal time hour by advancing figure to "A" for 12-hour mode or "H" for 24-hour mode
—press S2 once again to return to time display state

TO SET ALARM TIME—press S2 twice
—set alarm hour and minutes in the same way as above
—press S2 once again to return to time display state

This mode counts in 1/100th of a second intervals for the first 30 minutes of timing (29min 59sec) and then in one-second increments up to a max of 24 hours (23hr:50min 59sec).

TO ENTER STOPWATCH MODE—press S2 in time display state
1. Start/Stop—press S3 once
2. Split (Lap) time—press S1 to "freeze" elapsed time display while counting, and press S1 again to resume timing
3. **RESET**—press S1 when the stopwatch stops counting; to return to time display state, press S2 once again

When readout becomes dim or no longer displays, it is time to replace the battery. Unscrew the small screws on the back of the case; the battery is held down by a metal strip. Loosen strip with a small screwdriver, remove battery, and replace with a new one (UCC No. 392 or SR41W). Tighten battery strip and close case.

A warranty always states how long it lasts. Here, both the heading and the first sentence set the time at 24 months.

Warranties usually set strict conditions on what the warranty covers and what the manufacturer will or will not repair or replace. This sentence specifically excludes certain parts of the watch.

A warranty usually includes instructions for sending the product back for repair or replacement. This warranty gives the buyer extremely specific directions.

24 MONTH LIMITED WARRANTY

The Advance Watch Co. Ltd. warranties that it will repair any failure due to defects to materials and/or workmanship free of charge for a period of twenty-four (24) months from when it was purchased. This limited warranty does not cover replacement of crystal, battery components in lieu of repair. This warranty does not cover any failure to function properly due to misuse such as water immersion or severe shock. If your watch ever needs service, wrap it carefully in tissue paper or a similar soft material and pack it in a mailing carton. Send it via insured Parcel Post to:

LCD SERVICE
25800, Sherwood
Warren, MI 48091-4160

Include a brief note explaining what is wrong. Be sure to print your name and address clearly. Enclose a check or money order for $5.95 to cover the cost of return postage and handling. If the warranty period has expired we will examine your watch and notify you of the repair charges before proceeding.

Check Your Comprehension

1. Which knob do you press to set the alarm time? How many times?
2. When you are in stopwatch mode, how do you set the stopwatch to "Start/Stop"?
3. What signal shows that it is time to replace the battery?
4. How long does the warranty on the stopwatch last?
5. What watch parts will not be replaced under this warranty?

Applying the Reading Strategy

Following Operating Instructions

The time display on the stopwatch diagram in the directions reads "0:00 00." Your first step in using the stopwatch is to set it to the right time: hour, minute, and seconds. Study the directions and explain how you would set an imaginary watch at 8:45 and 30 seconds, as in this diagram. Assume that you are using a 12-hour clock.

6. Find the section of the directions that tells you how "To Set Time and Calendar." What is the first thing to do?
7. When the numbers in the display are flashing, what is the next step to take?
8. What letter do you choose to put the stopwatch in 12-hour mode, not a 24-hour clock?
9. What do you do to return to the time display state?

Activity

Demonstrating How to Operate a Product

Bring to class a tool, a game, or another product that you already know how to use so you can demonstrate how to use it to the class. First, write down directions or make notes about each step as if you were going to teach someone who had never seen such an object before. Then, explain the product to the class, using both words and gestures to show each step in the directions. At the end of your presentation, have your classmates evaluate your directions. Were they clear and easy to follow?

Comparing Informational Materials

Instructions and Warranties

Although instructions and warranties both come with new products, they are written and read for different purposes. Explain the differences in the reasons they are written and the reasons they are read. Show how this affects the type of information included with examples from the documents here.

Haiku such as those by Bashō and Moritake have been written for four centuries. Especially in Japan, the writing of haiku is commonly practiced as a challenging and popular art. Many Japanese occasionally compose haiku as greetings or to celebrate special occasions.

Haiku
for the Olympics
Translated by Laurent Mabesoone

Jumping in the air,
The skier looks like a bridge
Between sky and earth!
    by *Yukiko Kuzama*
    Obuse Town

Crossing the ski course
In the twinkling of an eye:
The morning squirrel!
    by *Kazuko Ohyama*
    Shinano Town

Dazzled by the snow
We are competing together
On the slope of peace!
    by *Yoko Kiyota*
    Iida

Little by little
A girl becomes a flower
Spinning on the ice!
    by *Nobuko Agata*
    Nagano City

Even the plains and mountains
Are competing for the Games:
Each has a white dress!
    by *Mue Ohta*
    Toyoshina Town

"One Haiku for the Olympics"

In February and March, 1998, the Winter Olympic and Paralympic Games were held in Nagano, Japan. Nagano Prefecture is proud to be the birthplace of a world-famous master haiku poet, Kobayashi Issa, who lived from 1763 to 1828.

To welcome visitors to the Olympics, the people of Nagano were invited to create "one haiku for the Olympics" and enter it in a poetry competition. People sent over 1,600 poems to the Haiku Poets' Association of Nagano Prefecture, who selected the one hundred best haiku.

Composed originally in Japanese, the one hundred haiku were translated into English and French, then printed on 7,500 small flags. As a welcome to visitors throughout the Winter Olympics, the flags decorated local businesses and information centers. People around the world who could not visit Nagano in person could read the haiku on the official website of the XVIII Winter Olympic Games.

A Shared Philosophy

Traditional haiku, like those by Bashō and Moritake, make use of an image or comparison that suggests harmony in nature and expresses the poet's mood or insight at a particular moment in time. The haiku composed for the Olympics follow this formula while celebrating a related theme of the Olympic Games: harmony among diverse people, gathered in one season and one place to play.

Connecting Literature and Culture

1. Give examples of images in the haiku on page 864 that suggest a theme of harmony. What type of harmony does each haiku writer celebrate?

2. Which of the haiku on page 864 are most similar in mood or technique to the haiku by Bashō? Which ones have more in common with the haiku by Moritake? Explain.

3. In what ways did haiku promote harmony during the 1998 Winter Olympics?

Prepare to Read

Silver ◆ Forgotten Language ◆ Drum Song ◆
If I can stop one Heart from breaking

Egrets in Summer, 1940–45, N.C. Wyeth, Courtesy of Metropolitan Life Insurance Company, New York, NY

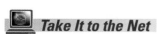

Take It to the Net

Visit www.phschool.com for interactive activities and instruction related to these selections, including
- background
- graphic organizers
- literary elements
- reading strategies

Preview

Connecting to the Literature

Sometimes with a friend, you just need to share a glance—then you both nod or burst out laughing. You share a secret language. Connect to the poems in this grouping by thinking about how each speaks to you as a friend, telling you something secret or surprising.

Background

In "Drum Song," Wendy Rose writes of women taking part in ceremonial dances still performed on First and Second Mesas of the Hopi reservation in Arizona, and at pueblos in New Mexico. During dances like the corn dance—to celebrate the planting of crops—dancers move in a line to the beat of drums. The drums, made of animal hide stretched over a wooden frame, are struck with a padded stick and make a deep, low sound. Gourd rattles may be filled with dried corn kernels, beans, and squash seeds.

Literary Analysis

Sound Devices

Poets use **sound devices** such as the following to create musical effects in poems.

- **Rhyme:** Using the same vowel and consonant sound at the end of two words.
- **Repetition:** Using the same word or phrase more than once.
- **Alliteration:** Using the same consonant at the beginning of words.

Listen for these sound devices as you read.

Comparing Literary Works

As you read the poems in this grouping, think about how each poet has used rhyme, repetition, and alliteration. Notice also how line length and word choice affect the sound of a poem. Read the poems aloud and use the following focus question to guide you as you read:

1. What types of musical effects do the sound devices in each poem create?

Reading Strategy

Interpret Meaning

You can interpret the meaning of a poem by looking for words and ideas the poet emphasizes. Common literary devices used to emphasize particular words or phrases include

- **alliteration:** using several words with the same initial consonant sound
- **repetition:** using a word or phrase more than once

Some poets use unconventional spelling, word choice, capitalization, or punctuation to call attention to certain words or lines. Emily Dickinson, for example is known for capitalizing words and using dashes, often in unexpected ways. As you read, use a chart like the one shown to take notes about the devices that contribute to the poem's meaning by emphasizing particular words, phrases, or images.

	Device	**Emphasis or Effect**
Silver	alliteration	
Forgotten Language	repetition	
Drum Song	repetition	
If I can stop	unconventional capitalization	

Vocabulary Development

vertical (vur´ ti kel) *adj.* straight up and down; upright (p. 870)

burrow (bur´ o) *n.* passage or hole for shelter (p. 871)

gourd (gôrd) *n.* dried, hollowed-out shell of fruits such as melons and pumpkins (p. 871)

Silver

Walter de la Mare

Slowly, silently, now the moon
Walks the night in her silver shoon;[1]
This way, and that, she peers, and sees
Silver fruit upon silver trees;
5 One by one the casements catch
Her beams beneath the silvery thatch;
Couched in his kennel, like a log,
With paws of silver sleeps the dog;
From their shadowy coat the white breasts peep
10 Of doves in a silver-feathered sleep;
A harvest mouse goes scampering by,
With silver claws, and silver eye;
And moveless fish in the water gleam,
By silver reeds in a silver stream.

---

1. **shoon** (sho͞on) *n.* old-fashioned word for "shoes."

Review and Assess

Thinking About the Selection

1. **Respond:** Describe a moment when a natural phenomenon—like a sunset, a snowfall, or light in a forest—seemed to change the setting around you.

2. **(a) Recall:** Describe the "silver scene" in "Silver."
(b) Analyze Causes and Effects: Describe the effects of the moon's walk through the night. **(c) Generalize:** How has the moon transformed this scene?

3. **(a) Recall:** Find four details in "Silver" that contribute to an image of stillness. **(b) Draw Conclusions:** Which of these details contribute to the poem's magical atmosphere, or mood? Explain.

Walter de la Mare

(1873–1956)

Walter de la Mare was a British poet and novelist. After graduating from St. Paul's Cathedral Choir School in London, he worked for eighteen years as a clerk in the statistics department of a big oil company. Later, a government grant allowed him to write full time. De la Mare believed that the world beyond human experience could best be understood through the imagination. His poems, found in books like *The Listeners and Other Poems*, often stress the magical and mysterious. They delight children and adults alike.

Forgotten Language

Shel Silverstein

Once I spoke the language of the flowers,
Once I understood each word the caterpillar said,
Once I smiled in secret at the gossip of the starlings,[1]
And shared a conversation with the housefly
        in my bed.
5   Once I heard and answered all the questions
        of the crickets,
And joined the crying of each falling dying
        flake of snow,
Once I spoke the language of the flowers . . .
        How did it go?
        How did it go?

---

1. **starlings** (stär´ liŋz) *n.* dark-colored birds with a short tail, long wings, and a sharp, pointed bill.

Review and Assess

Thinking About the Selection

1. **Respond:** Describe a time when something in nature "spoke" to you.

2. **(a) Recall:** Name six things from nature that spoke to the speaker in Silverstein's poem. **(b) Infer:** What language did they speak? **(c) Draw Conclusions:** How does this language differ from a language like English or Spanish? Explain.

3. **(a) Recall:** What does Silverstein ask at the end of "Forgotten Language"? **(b) Deduce:** Why does he repeat the question? **(c) Connect:** What evidence of Silverstein's forgotten language do you find in "Silver"?

Shel Silverstein

(1932–1999)

Silverstein was a poet, a writer of children's books, a cartoonist, a folk singer, and a composer. Children and adults around the world have enjoyed his poetry collection *Where the Sidewalk Ends* and his fable *The Giving Tree.* The critic William Cole has written that Silverstein's poems are "tender, funny, sentimental, philosophical, and ridiculous in turn, and they're for all ages."

Drum Song

Wendy Rose

Crawling Turtle II, Barry Wilson

▲ **Critical Viewing** What physical characteristics of the turtle allow it to go from "land to rock to water"? **[Connect]**

Listen. Turtle
     your flat round feet
     of four claws each
     go slow, go steady,
5   from rock to water
     to land to rock to
water.

Listen. Woodpecker
     you lift your red head
10   on wind, perch
     on <u>vertical</u> earth
     of tree bark and
branch.

vertical (vʉr´ ti kəl) *adj.* straight up and down; upright

Listen. Snowhare[1]
15   your belly drags,
    your whiskers dance
    bush to <u>burrow</u>
    your eyes turn up
    to where owls
20 hunt.

Listen. Women
    your tongues melt,
    your seeds are planted
    mesa[2] to mesa a shake
25   of <u>gourds</u>,
    a line of mountains
    with blankets
    on their
hips.

burrow (bʉr´ ō) *n.* passage or hole for shelter

gourds (gôrdz) *n.* dried, hollowed-out shell of fruits such as melons and pumpkins

---

1. Snowhare (snō´ her) *n.* snowshoe hare, a large rabbitlike animal whose color changes from brown in summer to white in winter and whose broad feet resemble snowshoes.
2. mesa (mā´ sə) *n.* small, high plateau with steep sides.

Review and Assess

Thinking About the Selection

1. **Respond:** How might performing or hearing "Drum Song" help you better understand the natural world?

2. **(a) Recall:** What is each of the animals in "Drum Song" doing? **(b) Infer:** How is each animal's physical description related to the way it moves?

3. **(a) Recall:** What three animals are mentioned before the women? **(b) Connect:** What is the point of mentioning each animal in its habitat?

4. **(a) Recall:** What word does the speaker repeat at the beginning of each stanza? **(b) Infer:** To whom does the speaker address this word?

5. **Support:** Find details that support this description of "Drum Song": It tells how creatures go about living in the natural world, and its rhythm is like the pulse of daily life.

Wendy Rose

(b. 1948)

Wendy Rose believes that "For everything in this universe there is a song to accompany its existence; writing is another way of singing these songs." Rose sings songs in both words and gestures. A well-published poet, she also managed a museum bookstore and lectured at the University of California. As a visual artist, she designs postcards, posters, T-shirts, and bookbags.

If I can stop one Heart from breaking

Emily Dickinson

If I can stop one Heart from breaking
I shall not live in vain
If I can ease one Life the Aching
Or cool one Pain

5 Or help one fainting Robin
Unto his Nest again
I shall not live in Vain.

Review and Assess

Thinking About the Selection

1. **Respond:** What makes you feel that you have not lived "in vain"?

2. **(a) Recall:** In "If I can stop one Heart . . . ," what four things will keep the speaker from living in vain? **(b) Interpret:** What do these four things tell you about what Dickinson thinks is important in life?

3. **(a) Recall:** What does the speaker hope to accomplish? **(b) Draw Conclusions:** Judging by this poem, what do you think Dickinson wanted poetry to do? **(c) Support:** Explain.

4. **(a) Apply:** What types of things can people in today's world do to live the words of Dickinson's poem? **(b) Assess:** Do many people share the feelings Dickinson expresses? Explain.

Emily Dickinson

(1830–1886)

Dickinson led a quiet life in Amherst, Massachusetts. She published only a few poems in her lifetime. However, she secretly wrote 1,775 lyric poems that made her one of the founders of American poetry. Sparkling with thought and feeling, these poems show how active her inner life really was.

Review and Assess

Literary Analysis

Sound Devices

1. What sound devices does each poem include? Use a chart like the one shown to record examples.

Poem	Rhyme	Repetition	Alliteration
"Silver"	moon/shoon		casements/catch
"Forgotten Language"		"Once I" x 5	
"Drum Song"			
"If I can..."			

2. What are two examples of rhyme used in "Silver"? Why do you think the poet wanted to call attention to the rhyming words?

3. Give two examples from "Drum Song" in which the poem's sounds remind you of a drum beat.

4. What device does Emily Dickinson use to emphasize the importance of helping others?

Comparing Literary Works

5. What types of musical effects do the sound devices in each poem create?

6. Which poem do you find most musical? Why?

Reading Strategy

Interpreting Meaning

7. What literary device is used to emphasize the question at the end of "Forgotten Language"? Explain.

8. What words does Emily Dickinson capitalize in the third and fourth line of "If I can stop . . ."? Why are these words important to the meaning?

Extend Understanding

9. **Take a Position:** Argue for or against the idea expressed in Emily Dickinson's poem. To what extent do you think people are responsible for helping one another?

Quick Review

Poets use **sound devices**, such as **rhyme, repetition,** and **alliteration**, to create musical effects in poems. To review sound devices, see page 867.

 Take It to the Net
www.phschool.com
Take the interactive self-test online to check your understanding of these selections.

Integrate Language Skills

Vocabulary Development Lesson

Concept Development: Word Pairs

Some words with opposite meanings are thought of in pairs, like *vertical* and *horizontal*. Each sentence below includes a pair of opposites that are usually thought of in pairs. Use what the sentence tells you about the first word to determine the meaning of the second word.

1. If *convex* means "curving outward," *concave* means ____?____.
2. If *longitude* is "a measure of east-west distance using lines drawn through the Earth's poles and at right angles to the equator," *latitude* is ____?____.
3. If *introverted* means mostly "keeping to one's self," *extroverted* means ____?____.
4. If *nocturnal* refers to animals that are active during the night, then *diurnal* probably refers to ____?____.

Fluency: True or False?

On your paper, answer each question true or false. Then, explain your answer.

1. To cross a street, you would go in a *vertical* direction.
2. Animals that like to *burrow* can be found in the ground.
3. A *gourd* is grown from seeds.

Spelling Strategy

The long *o* sound may be spelled *ow*, as in *low* and *burrow*. On your paper, write these sentences, filling in the blanks with the correct spelling for the long *o* sound.

1. Look at the furr____?____s on the poet's forehead.
2. He feels sorr____?____ because he has forgotten a language.
3. I borr____?____ed several books from my brother.
4. The fruit in the trees gl____?____ed in the moonlight.

Grammar Lesson

End Marks

- **Periods** are used at the end of sentences that make statements or give commands.
  Statement: Wendy Rose is a poet.
  Command: Read the poem.
- **Question marks** are used at the end of questions.
  Question: Which poem did you read?
- **Exclamation points** are used at the end of exclamatory sentences or after some interjections.
  Exclamatory sentence: I love that movie!
  Interjection: Aha!

▶ *For more practice, see page R34, Exercise A.*

Practice Copy the following sentences. Add end-marks. Use exclamation marks where appropriate.

1. The snowhare moves awkwardly
2. Who speaks the language
3. No Don't touch that
4. When was this written
5. Finish your paper by Monday

Writing Application Write two questions and two statements about the poems.

𝒲𝒢 *Prentice Hall Writing and Grammar Connection: Chapter 16, Section 2*

Writing Lesson

Biographical Sketch of Emily Dickinson

Emily Dickinson was famous not only for her poems, but for the type of life she lived. Write a biographical sketch of her based on details found through research. Include quotations from her poems that reflect qualities of her life and personality.

Prewriting   Begin with a keyword search of Dickinson's first and last name on the Web. Look especially for primary source documents: writings of people who took part in or observed events firsthand. Use secondary sources (writings that interpret and comment on events not observed firsthand) to learn the full story you need to pull the pieces together.

Model: Framing Quotation

Thomas Johnson felt that Dickinson's letters were a form of poetry. He wrote that they ". . . leave the reader in doubt where the letter leaves off and the poem begins." (*Letters* 1: xv) These words show that all Dickinson's writing contains some poetry.

> The writer tells what the quotation is about, gives the quotation, and follows up by commenting on the quotation.

Drafting   Within your draft, use a quotation from a literary critic or another poet that offers a viewpoint on Emily Dickinson, the person or the poet. To get the most power from the words, frame a quotation: Introduce the quotation, give the quotation, follow up on the quotation.

Revising   Revise to eliminate unneccessary clutter around quotations. Although you do want to introduce it and follow up on it, you don't want to overwhelm it.

Prentice Hall Writing and Grammar Connection: Chapter 11, Section 2

Extension Activities

Research and Technology   Prepare a **poetry interpretation**. Use the Internet to find background that helps you interpret one of the poems in this group.

To begin your search, type in the poet's name or the poem title as a key word. Look or the following types of information:

- biological information on the poet
- literary criticism on the poet's work

Choose relevant information and use it to support your interpretation of the poem.

Listening and Speaking   A poem deserves to be heard. Choose one poem from this grouping to use in a **poetry recitation.** Practice by reading the poem aloud, over and over. Note on a copy of the poem where you will pause, stop, or stress particular words or sounds.

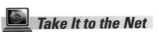 **Take It to the Net**   www.phschool.com

Go online for an additional research activity using the Internet.

Prepare to Read

New World ◆ Lyric 17 ◆
For My Sister Molly Who in the Fifties

 Take It to the Net

Visit www.phschool.com
for interactive activities
and instruction related to
these selections, including

- background
- graphic organizers
- literary elements
- reading strategies

Preview

Connecting to the Literature

In your purse or wallet, you may carry around photos with a special meaning for you. They may show people who have touched your life or places where you feel at home. The images are out of sight but always near. These poems might be compared to wallets or purses: They hold images of people, places, or ideas that the poets want to keep close.

Background

N. Scott Momaday's poem, "New World," describes the passage of a day. Day and night are caused by the rotation of Earth on its axis. This rotation exposes a region to the sun, creating daylight. Meanwhile, the opposite side of Earth is shaded from the sun, creating night. A single day results from a complete spin of the Earth—which takes not twenty-four hours, but twenty-three hours, fifty-six minutes, and four seconds!

Literary Analysis

Imagery

Poets help you understand a scene by using **imagery,** words and phrases that appeal to your senses. Often, an image appeals to your sense of sight. Many images will also appeal to your other senses of hearing, touch, taste, or smell. In the following example, the imagery of the warm loam appeals to the sense of touch. The swarm of bees suggests a buzzing that appeals to the sense of hearing.

> . . . turtles/enter/slowly/into/the warm/dark loam./Bees hold/
> the swarm.

Comparing Literary Works

The imagery a poet uses often reflects his or her culture, heritage, and traditions. Native American poet N. Scott Momaday uses images of trees, animals, and landscapes that are familiar to him as a Kiowa Indian from the southwestern United States. The respect and admiration with which he describes these images reflect the reverence for nature that is part of his Native American heritage.

Review the details of each poet's background shown at right. As you read, connect details from the poems to details from the poets' background. Use the following focus questions to guide you.

1. What does each poet seem to believe about his or her topic?
2. How do the images and ideas connect to the poets' backgrounds?

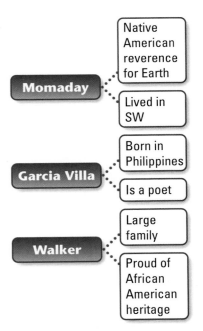

Reading Strategy

Using Your Senses

Use your senses to fully experience imagery. Call on your own sense memories to see, hear, taste, smell, and touch what the words are describing.

As you read the images the poets present, pay special attention to the specific sensory details they point out. Use the details and your imagination to enter into the experience of the poem.

Vocabulary Development

hover (huv´ ər) v. hang as if suspended in the air (p. 878)

glistens (glis´ ənz) v. shines; sparkles (p. 878)

borne (bôrn) v. carried (p. 878)

low (lō) v. make the typical sound that a cow makes; moo (p. 878)

recede (ri sēd´) v. move away (p. 879)

luminance (lōō´ mə nəns) n. brightness; brilliance (p. 881)

New World

N. Scott Momaday

1.

First Man,
behold:
the earth
glitters
5 with leaves;
the sky
glistens
with rain.
Pollen[1]
10 is borne
on winds
that low
and lean
upon
15 mountains.
Cedars
blacken
the slopes—
and pines.

2.

20 At dawn
eagles
hie[2] and
hover
above
25 the plain
where light
gathers
in pools.
Grasses
30 shimmer
and shine.
Shadows
withdraw
and lie
35 away
like smoke.

hover (huv´ ər) v. hang as
if suspended in the air

glistens (glis´ ənz) v.
shines; sparkles

borne (bôrn) v. carried

low (lō) v. make the typical sound that a cow
makes; moo

---

1. pollen (päl´ ən) *n.* yellow, powderlike male cells formed in the stamen of a flower.
2. hie (hī) *v.* hurry or hasten.

3.

At noon
turtles
enter
40 slowly
into
the warm
dark loam.[3]
Bees hold
45 the swarm.
Meadows
<u>recede</u>
through planes
of heat
50 and pure
distance.

4.

At dusk
the gray
foxes
55 stiffen
in cold;
blackbirds
are fixed
in the
60 branches.
Rivers
follow
the moon,
the long
65 white track
of the
full moon.

recede (ri sēd′) **v. move away**

---

3. loam (lōm) *n.* rich, dark soil.

Review and Assess

Thinking About the Selection

1. **Respond:** How is the world you live in different from and similar to the one described in the poem?

2. **(a) Recall:** What are three things described in the opening of the poem? **(b) Infer:** Why does the speaker want "First Man" to see these things? **(c) Deduce:** Whom does the character "First Man" represent?

3. **(a) Recall:** What are the three times of day identified in the poem? **(b) Analyze:** Why does the poet describe these three times of day? **(c) Interpret:** What might the three times of day represent?

4. **(a) Analyze:** What is the main point of the poem?
   (b) Interpret: Explain how the title relates to the meaning of the poem. **(c) Apply:** In what way is the world "new" every day?

5. **Make a Judgment:** Land is used in the United States for many purposes and needs. As related to land use in what order of importance would you place protected habitats, energy, and housing?

N. Scott Momaday

(b. 1934)

A Kiowa Indian, N. Scott Momaday is known for his poetry, his essays, and his Pulitzer Prize-winning novel, *House Made of Dawn* (1968).

Momaday says that "New World" was inspired by ". . . the realization of himself in the New World, [where] the Indian has assumed a deep ethical regard for the earth and sky, a reverence for the natural world . . . ."

Lyric 17

José Garcia Villa

First, a poem must be magical,
Then musical as a sea-gull.
It must be a brightness moving
And hold secret a bird's flowering.
5   It must be slender as a bell,
And it must hold fire as well.
It must have the wisdom of bows
And it must kneel like a rose.
It must be able to hear
10 The <u>luminance</u> of dove and deer.
It must be able to hide
What it seeks, like a bride.
And over all I would like to hover
God, smiling from the poem's cover.

luminance (lōō´ mə nəns) *n.*
brightness; brilliance

Review and Assess

Thinking About the Selection

1. **Respond:** In answer to "Lyric 17," tell what you think "a poem must be."

2. **(a) Recall:** According to "Lyric 17," what are three qualities a poem must have and some things a poem must be able to do?
   (b) Distinguish: Locate two lines that seem to express opposite ideas of what a poem should do or be.

3. **(a) Recall:** Identify three similes in the poem. **(b) Infer:** What do these comparisons help you understand about Garcia Villa's definition of poetry?

4. **(a) Connect:** In what ways does Garcia Villa's definition make poetry seem mysterious? **(b) Draw Conclusions:** Is "Lyric 17" effective as a definition of poetry?
   (c) Support: Why or why not?

José Garcia Villa

(1904–1997)
Garcia Villa was born in Manila, in the Philippines, and emigrated to the United States in 1930. He published several volumes of poetry and was honored by the Poetry Society of America in 1959. "Lyric 17" reflects the judgment of one critic, who said that Villa's poems come "straight from the poet's being, from his blood, from his spirit, as a fire breaks from wood, or as a flower grows from its soil."

For My Sister Molly Who in the Fifties

Alice Walker

For my Sister Molly Who in the Fifties
Once made a fairy rooster from
Mashed potatoes
Whose eyes I forget
5   But green onions were his tail
And his two legs were carrot sticks
A tomato slice his crown.
Who came home on vacation
When the sun was hot
10 and cooked
and cleaned
And minded least of all
The children's questions
A million or more
15 Pouring in on her
Who had been to school
And knew (and told us too) that certain
Words were no longer good
And taught me not to say us for we
20 No matter what "Sonny said" up the
road.

FOR MY SISTER MOLLY WHO IN THE FIFTIES
Knew Hamlet well and read into the night
And coached me in my songs of Africa
25 A continent I never knew
But learned to love
Because "they" she said could carry
A tune
And spoke in accents never heard
30 In Eatonton.[1]

---

1. **Eatonton** (ēt′ ən tən) town in Georgia.

◀ **Critical Viewing** How would you describe the relationship between the girls in the photograph? **[Infer]**

Reading Check

What are two things the speaker appreciates about her sister?

Who read from *Prose and Poetry*
And loved to read "Sam McGee from Tennessee"
On nights the fire was burning low
And Christmas wrapped in angel hair[2]
35 And I for one prayed for snow.

WHO IN THE FIFTIES
Knew all the written things that made
Us laugh and stories by
The hour Waking up the story buds
40 Like fruit. Who walked among the flowers
And brought them inside the house
And smelled as good as they
And looked as bright.
Who made dresses, braided
45 Hair. Moved chairs about
Hung things from walls
Ordered baths
Frowned on wasp bites
And seemed to know the endings
50 Of all the tales
I had forgot.

---

2. **angel hair** fine, white, filmy Christmas tree decoration.

Review and Assess

Thinking About the Selection

1. **Respond:** Have you looked up to someone the way the speaker looked up to her sister? Explain.

2. **(a) Recall:** How does Molly help take care of the house? **(b) Infer:** Why does the speaker admire the way that Molly takes care of the house?

3. **(a) Recall:** Name three ways in which Molly takes physical care of the younger children. **(b) Analyze:** How do Molly's actions reveal her creative spirit? **(c) Analyze:** How does Molly awaken the creative spirit of the children?

4. **(a) Recall:** List three things the speaker learns from Molly. **(b) Infer:** How does Molly awaken the speaker's creative spirit?

5. **(a) Recall:** Describe the relationship between the speaker and Molly. **(b) Make a Judgment:** Is the speaker successful in expressing her relationship with her sister? **(c) Support:** Why or why not?

Alice Walker

(b. 1944)
Alice Walker, the youngest of eight children, grew up in Georgia, where her parents were farmers. Her novel *The Color Purple* is based on true stories about her great-grandmother and on research Walker did at Spelman College. Many of Walker's poems deal with her African American heritage. This interest can be seen in "For My Sister Molly Who in the Fifties," which is from *Revolutionary Petunias and Other Poems*.

Review and Assess

Literary Analysis

Imagery

1. Choose two examples of imagery in "New World" that appeal to a total of three or more senses.
2. What imagery does the poet use to describe poetry in "Lyric 17"?
3. From the imagery used in "For My Sister Molly . . . ," what can you conclude about what the speaker thinks was most important about her relationship with Molly?

Comparing Literary Works

4. What does each poet seem to believe about his or her topic?
5. How do the images and ideas connect to the poets' background?
6. Which of these poems uses images most successfully?

Reading Strategy

7. To what senses does the imagery in "Lyric 17" most appeal?
8. Explain how the poem "For My Sister Molly Who in the Fifties" recalls the sounds, smells, and sensations of the speaker's youth.
9. Use a Venn diagram to compare the senses appealed to in two of the poems.

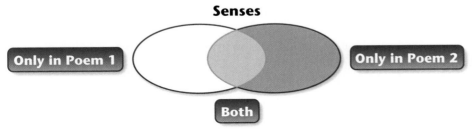

Senses

Only in Poem 1   Only in Poem 2

Both

Extend Understanding

10. **Cultural Connection:** N. Scott Momaday has stated that "New World" was inspired by ". . . the realization of himself in the New World, [where] the Indian has assumed a deep ethical regard for the earth and sky, a reverence for the natural world." Identify the parts of the natural world that Momaday describes. Explain why you think he chooses to describe these areas.

Quick Review

Imagery is a word or phrase that appeals to one or more of the five senses. To review imagery, see page 877.

When you use your **senses** to experience imagery, you call on your own sense memories to see, hear, taste, smell, and touch what the words are describing.

 Take It to the Net
www.phschool.com
Take the interactive self-test online to check your understanding of these selections.

Integrate Language Skills

Vocabulary Development Lesson

Word Analysis: Latin Root -cede-

Sometimes the Latin root -cede- is spelled -ceed. Match the -cede or -ceed ("to go") words in the first column with their meanings in the second column:

1. recede	a. to go apart
2. secede	b. to go forward
3. proceed	c. to go back

Spelling Strategy

Three words ending in the *seed* sound are spelled *ceed*: *exceed*, *succeed*, and *proceed*. In all other words, this ending sound is spelled *cede*. Identify and correct the misspelled words:

1. secede	3. recede	5. succede
2. preceed	4. exceed	

Fluency: Context

Write a sentence that is a response to each direction:

1. Use the word *glistens* to describe a lake.
2. Describe a flying kite using the word *borne*.
3. Use the word *low* in a description of barnyard sounds.
4. Paint a word picture of a hawk using the word *hover*.
5. Using the word *recede*, describe a glacier's movement.
6. Use the word *luminance* to compare a flashlight and a firefly.

Grammar Lesson

Punctuation and Capitalization of Dialogue and Quotations

- A speaker's words are enclosed in quotation marks.
    She said, "I like the poem."
- The speaker's first word is usually capitalized.
- The punctuation for a speaker's words falls inside the quotation marks.
- If the speaker's words are a statement that is not the end of the larger sentence, a comma separates the speaker's words from the rest of the sentence. Other types of sentences are punctuated as usual. The comma separating the speaker's words from the "tag" always comes before the nearest quotation mark.
    She said, "We read that poem."
    "We read that poem," she said.
    "Who read the poem?" she asked.

▶ *For more practice, see page R35, Exercise D.*
Practice Copy each sentence, correcting capitalization and punctuation as needed.

1. Walker's sister read *Hamlet* to her I told my sister.
2. What do you want to do she asked.
3. Molly said dinner is almost ready
4. She asked what are you doing
5. Wait Alice called. I'll come, too

Writing Application Write an imaginary dialogue between Walker and her sister. Punctuate dialogue correctly.

ʍͭ *Prentice Hall Writing and Grammar Connection: Chapter 23*

Writing Lesson

Free-Verse Poem

Two poems in this group are free verse. They are unrhymed and do not make use of regular rhythms. Write your own free-verse poem using imagery from your own background and experience. Develop one dominant or overriding image to tie the poem together.

Prewriting   Choose a scene, experience, or memory. Freewrite about your choice—set down all the ideas and details that come to mind. Then, circle details that are related and can work toward a dominant image.

Model: Selecting Details for a Dominant Image

We ride our bikes in the schoolyard after school. The blacktop is cracked and uneven, so sometimes the bikes skid. The bells from the school ring every hour, even when we're not there. We can hear them as we ride around the yard. We circle on our bikes and watch each other try new tricks.

> The circled details can work together to create the image of a group of bikeriders circling and racing on uneven pavement.

Drafting   Arrange the details you have selected into lines of your poem. Group related details near each other.

Revising   Look for places where you can add details to strengthen your dominant image. Delete details that distract from that image.

WG *Prentice Hall Writing and Grammar Connection: Chapter 5, Section 2*

Extension Activities

Research and Technology To find out more about how heritage and background contribute to a writer's work, do an **on-line search.**

1. Use the Internet, a library database, or CD-ROM to locate the author's published works. Key the author's name to begin your search.
2. When you locate a primary source, try to find out what type of literature it contains. For example, perhaps you have found a novel or a work of nonfiction. Jot down notes about your author.
3. Share your findings with your classmates.

Listening and Speaking Prepare a **research presentation** on one of the five senses. In your presentation, answer the following questions:

1. How does this sense work?
2. Why is this sense important?
3. How do you keep this sense healthy?

Deliver your presentation to your classmates, using charts or diagrams to illustrate your information.

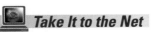 **Take It to the Net**   www.phschool.com

Go online for an additional research activity using the Internet.

Prepare to Read

The Dark Hills ◆ Incident in a Rose Garden

 Take It to the Net

Visit www.phschool.com for interactive activities and instruction related to these selections, including

- background
- graphic organizers
- literary elements
- reading strategies

Preview

Connecting to the Literature

A movie *star*, a *shutterbug*, a *bookworm*: These phrases are so common that you automatically adjust your interpretation when you read or hear them—you understand that they do not mean a ball of burning gas, an insect, or a worm. In these poems, the poets use similar imaginative expressions. These expressions may not be as familiar as the others, but they are powerfully descriptive.

Background

Donald Justice's poem, "Incident in a Rose Garden," was inspired by this traditional story set in Southwest Asia: A servant meets Death in the marketplace of Baghdad. Believing Death is after him, the servant flees to Samarra. The servant's employer asks Death why she threatened him. Death says she did not threaten the servant: She was surprised to see him in Baghdad because she had an appointment with him that night in Samarra!

Literary Analysis

Figurative Language

Figurative language is writing or speech that is not meant to be taken literally. A **simile** is a comparison of two apparently unlike items that uses the word *like* or *as*. A **metaphor** is a description of one item as if it were another, without using *like* or *as*. **Personification** is a description of something nonhuman as if it were human.

Use a chart like the one shown to identify figures of speech as you read.

Comparing Literary Works

Several of the figures of speech you encounter in these poems will be ways of referring to mortality—the inability to live forever. The theme, or central idea of each work, relates to mortality. Compare and contrast the different approaches the writers take, figures of speech they use, and themes of the works. Use the following focus questions to guide your comparison.

1. What expressions, phrases, or words do the different works use to refer to mortality and death?

2. What are the differences in what each poet says about death?

Reading Strategy

Comparing and Contrasting

Figurative language communicates unexpected comparisons between unlike things. Depending on a poem's theme, tone, and purpose, it may use figurative language in ways calculated to surprise or otherwise impress the reader.

When reading these poems, compare and contrast the two poems' use of personification. In each poem, picture the things being compared. No matter how different they are, search for the hidden similarities the poet has identified.

Passage

"Where sunset hovers like a sound
Of golden horns . . ."

Figure of Speech

Simile: uses the word *like*

Compares what?

Sunset is compared to horn music.

Vocabulary Development

hovers (huv´ ərz) *v.* suspends; lingers (p. 891)

legions (lē´ jənz) *n.* large number; multitude (p. 891)

scythe (sīth) *n.* long tool with a single-edged blade used in cutting tall grass (p. 892)

beckoned (bek´ ənd) *v.* summoned by a silent motion; called (p. 892)

gestures (jes´ chərz) *n.* movements used to convey an idea, emotion, or intention (p. 894)

The Dark Hills

EDWIN ARLINGTON ROBINSON

Dark hills at evening in the west,
Where sunset <u>hovers</u> like a sound
Of golden horns that sang to rest
Old bones of warriors under ground,
5　Far now from all the bannered ways
Where flash the <u>legions</u> of the sun,
You fade—as if the last of days
Were fading, and all wars were done.

◀ **Critical Viewing**
Are the hills in this photograph inviting or forbidding? Explain. **[Assess]**

hovers (huv′ erz) v. suspends; lingers

legions (lē′ jənz) n. larger number; multitude

Review and Assess

Thinking About the Selection

1. **Respond:** Briefly describe a time when you saw the sun in a fresh way—whether at dawn, midday, or sunset.

2. **(a) Recall:** To what does Robinson compare the sunset in "The Dark Hills"? **(b) Relate:** How does this comparison help you experience the sunset?

3. **(a) Recall:** Find three descriptive details in "The Dark Hills." **(b) Interpret:** What overall feeling do the details in "The Dark Hills" create?

4. **(a) Recall:** What did the "golden horns" sing "to rest" in the poem? **(b) Speculate:** Why do you think the poet includes this image in the poem?

5. **(a) Infer:** Whom does the speaker address at the end of the poem? **(b) Support:** How do you know? **(c) Draw Conclusions:** What does the comparison in lines 7-8 reveal about the speaker's mood or experience? Explain.

Edwin Arlington Robinson

(1869–1935)

Robinson was raised in Gardiner, Maine. This small town served as the model for Tilbury Town, the fictional setting of his finest poems. Many of his poems grew out of his childhood observations of Gardiner and focus on people's inner struggles.

Incident in a ROSE GARDEN

DONALD JUSTICE

Gardener: Sir, I encountered Death
Just now among our roses.
Thin as a <u>scythe</u> he stood there.

                I knew him by his pictures.
5   He had his black coat on,
                Black gloves, a broad black hat.

                I think he would have spoken.
                Seeing his mouth stood open.
                Big it was, with white teeth.

10   As soon as he <u>beckoned</u>, I ran.
                I ran until I found you.
                Sir, I am quitting my job.

                I want to see my sons
                Once more before I die.
15   I want to see California.

scythe (sīth) *n.* long tool with a single-edged blade used in cutting tall grass

beckoned (bek´ ənd) *v.* summoned by a silent motion; called

China Roses, Broadway, Alfred William Parsons, Christopher Wood Gallery, London, UK

▲ **Critical Viewing** Why would a figure like Death be so startling to encounter in a setting such as this? **[Connect]**

Master:	Sir, you must be that stranger
	Who threatened my gardener.
	This is my property, sir.

	I welcome only friends here.
20 *Death:*	Sir, I knew your father.
	And we were friends at the end.

	As for your gardener,
	I did not threaten him.
	Old men mistake my <u>gestures</u>.

25	I only meant to ask him
	To show me to his master.
	I take it you are he?

gestures (jes´ chərz) *n.* movements used to convey an idea, emotion, or intention

Review and Assess

Thinking About the Selection

1. **Respond:** Do you find this poem amusing or alarming? Explain.

2. **(a) Recall:** What did Death want to ask the Gardener?
   (b) Infer: In what way do lines 25–27 give you a surprising view of the Gardener's flight?

3. **(a) Recall:** Paraphrase what Death says to the master.
   (b) Infer: What does Death mean when he says to the Master, "I knew your father./ And we were friends at the end."?

4. **(a) Recall:** What does Death do to make the Gardener run away? **(b) Speculate:** Why do you think old men "mistake" Death's gestures?

5. **(a) Recall:** Whom does Death really want? **(b) Draw Conclusions:** The Master is full of pride. What lesson does he learn from his encounter with Death?

Donald Justice

(b. 1925)

Donald Justice was awarded the Pulitzer Prize for his *Selected Poems* and the Bollingen Prize for his lifetime achievement in poetry.

Review and Assess

Literary Analysis

Figurative Language

1. What simile does Justice use to describe Death? How does this simile help you picture Death and his role in the poem?
2. Do both poems include **personification**, or only one? Explain.

Comparing Literary Works

3. What expressions, phrases, or words do the different works use to refer to mortality and death?
4. What are the differences in what each poet says about death?
5. How similar or different are the ideas or attitudes about mortality that each poem presents? Use a Venn diagram like the one shown to plan your response.

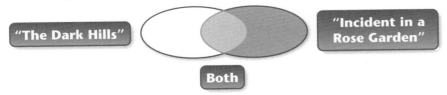

"The Dark Hills"   Both   "Incident in a Rose Garden"

Reading Strategy

Comparing and Contrasting

6. In "The Dark Hills," to what humans are the colors of the sunset compared?
7. Describe your response to the imagery that Robinson uses. Use a web like the one shown to note your reactions.

My Response

Image — dark hills at evening

Image — Sunset hovers

The Dark Hills

Image — old bones of warriors under ground

Image — last of days...fading

8. Would your response to Justice's poem have been different if Death had appeared in a more sinister setting? Why or why not?

Extend Understanding

9. **Science Connection:** Find out how dust particles in the atmosphere contribute to the vivid colors of the sunset.

Quick Review

Figurative language is language that is not meant to be taken literally. Examples include **simile, metaphor,** and **personification.** To review figurative language, see page 889.

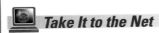

Take It to the Net
www.phschool.com
Take the interactive self-test online to check your understanding of these selections.

Integrate Language Skills

Vocabulary Development Lesson

Word Analysis: Commonly Confused Words

Note these commonly confused words: *continuously* ("without interruption") and *continually* ("frequently repeated"); *beside* ("next to") and *besides* ("in addition to"); and *imply* ("suggest") and *infer* ("deduce"). Copy the following passage, correcting any misused italicized words.

> The Gardener *implies* from the stranger's behavior that danger threatens. Death then stands *besides* the Master, saying that old men *continually* mistake his gestures.

Spelling Strategy

Pronounce each syllable before writing or spelling multisyllable words. Write the following words in syllables. If necessary, use a dictionary.

1. unrecompensed   2. continuously

Fluency: Definitions

On your paper, answer each question below.

1. What is the difference between *hovers* and *soars*?
2. What is the difference between *legions* and *several*?
3. What is the difference between *unrecompensed* and *paid*?
4. What is the difference between *continuously* and *continually*?
5. What is the difference between *scythe* and *ax*?
6. What is the difference between *beckoned* and *dismissed*?

Grammar Lesson

Capitalization of Titles

Capitalize the first word and all other other important words in a title. Words not capitalized in titles include articles (*a, an, the*), conjunctions (*and, or, but*), and prepositions (such as *to, with, for,* or *in*). Verbs are always capitalized.

Use quotation marks for the titles of shorter works, such as poems and short story titles. Underline or set in italics the titles of longer works, such as books, plays, and movies, and the titles of artworks.

> **Book**: The Pearl
> **Short Story**: "Tears of Autumn"
> **Poem**: "The Dark Hills"
> **Magazine**: Time
> **Painting**: Girl with a Watering Can

▶ *For more practice, see page R35, Exercise D.*

Practice On your paper, rewrite the following titles, adding any missing capitalization.

1. landscape with two oaks (painting)
2. death of a salesman (play)
3. "the charge of the light brigade" (poem)
4. a hero is nothing but a sandwich (book)
5. "the finish of patsy barnes" (short story)

WG *Prentice Hall Writing and Grammar Connection: Chapter 27, Exercise 10*

Writing Lesson

Comparison and Contrast

Write an essay in which you compare and contrast the mood, or feeling, of "The Dark Hills" and the mood of "Incident in a Rose Garden."

Prewriting Review the poems, noting devices each poet has used to convey a particular mood or atmosphere. Use a chart like the one shown to organize your ideas.

Model: Organize Ideas

TONE

Imagery		Rhyme		Figurative Language	
"Dark"	"Incident"	"Dark"	"Incident"	"Dark"	"Incident"

Drafting Organize your essay using the "block" method: First, present all the facts and supporting details about one poem's mood. Then, present all the facts and details about the second poem's mood.

Revising Review your essay to check the organization of the paragraphs.

WG Prentice Hall Writing and Grammar Connection: Chapter 8, Section 3

Extension Activities

Research and Technology Use the Internet to **research** the folk tale on which Justice's poem is based. Use key words to narrow your search on the Internet. For example, try typing *folk tales + Asia*. Keep notes on the research methods you use to locate the folk tale—including the key words.

After you complete your research, write a brief explanation and evaluation of your search process. Identify the steps you performed and indicate what you will do differently to make your next search more effective.

Listening and Speaking Develop a **presentation** of your reaction to "The Dark Hills."

1. Read the poem again.
2. Jot down notes about specific lines or phrases you react to.
3. Present your response to your classmates. Explain your overall reaction to the poem, supporting it with the particular examples you have noted.

 **Take It to the Net** www.phschool.com

Go online for an additional research activity using the Internet.

READING INFORMATIONAL MATERIALS

Comparison-and-Contrast Essays

About Comparison-and-Contrast Essays

A comparison-and-contrast essay uses factual details to analyze the similarities and differences between two or more persons, places, or things. For example, a magazine might feature a comparison-and-contrast essay about two books on the same topic or two candidates for mayor. Comparison-and-contrast essays can help readers look at the things being compared in a new way. Comparison-and-contrast essays include

- a topic involving two or more things that are in some ways similar and in other ways different.
- an introduction that presents the main point of the essay and body paragraphs that include details showing similarities and differences.
- an organization that highlights the points of comparison.

Reading Strategy

Identifying Main Points

In a comparison-and-contrast essay, the main points are the main similarities and differences that the writer examines. By identifying the writer's main points, you can more easily grasp the information he or she provides. For instance, in "Are Animals Smart?" you might identify one main idea as follows: Animals' feeling are not simply human traits mimicked by lesser creatures.

Often, writers introduce their main points in the first paragraph. In the introduction of "Are Animals Smart?" Brooks identifies the two items he is comparing: animals and humans. Many writers state their main points clearly in the topic sentence of the paragraph in which they introduce them. As you read the comparison-and-contrast essay on the next page, identify the main points and record them in a chart like the one shown here.

Humans	Main Points	Animals
Have emotions	1. emotions 2. structures 3. intelligence 4.	genuine emotions (as real as human emotions)

Are Animals Smart?
Bruce Brooks

Even when we are careful to see an animal's actions in terms of its own life, we still notice that many animal qualities are obvious as correlates to our own experiences. We are not mistaken in giving these qualities the same names. We can tell when a cat is suspicious, a bird afraid, a dog lonesome. Why not say so? The mistake may be that we presume in the first place that these are human traits crudely mimicked by lesser creatures, and that by sharing our words we are elevating animal behavior above its lowly place. Who is to say humans invented suspiciousness or fear, and that we therefore own its copyright?

Animal structures allow us the same kind of correlation. We can see that a snail shell is like armor, a spiderweb like a fishnet, an ovenbird's nest like a house. But the comparison of things that are designed and made strikes deeper than does a comparison of feelings. These artifacts lead us to consider whether animals possess the most controversial quality of all, the one we imagine sets us furthest apart from the less-refined, more elemental life of creatures: intelligence.

> In the introduction, Brooks identifies the two items he is comparing: animals and humans.

Most of us would say: People are smart. Animals are . . . well, something else. When a two-year-old human child uses a yard stick to scoop a cookie off a high kitchen counter, we praise the child's native brightness but accept it as a mere step in the development of intellect. But when a bolas spider swings a strand of silk with a sticky globule on the end at a passing insect and hauls the bug in to eat, we treat it more as a bit of luck, an accidental discovery the spider managed, improbably, to repeat and pass on by instinct—a naïve sort of act, far from intellectual. . . .

It is true that human intelligence goes far beyond that of insects and birds and amphibians and reptiles and fishes and crustaceans and mollusks and our fellow mammals. We have the freedom of improvisation where the animal has the boundary of instinct. We can improvise structures when we need them; with a few exceptions, animals cannot. The ability to improvise to create new solutions to immediate problems and to plan innovative strategies without reference to others is a profoundly individual talent: each one of us can do it because we can think alone. The restrictiveness of instinct is the opposite: it shows that each wasp or panda or octopus is essentially a member of a species that behaves as a group in a certain way.

> Here, Brooks compares instances in which humans and animals solve a problem (getting food) in inventive ways.

> In this paragraph, Brooks compares human intelligence with animal intelligence.

Check Your Comprehension

1. Why does Brooks believe it is wrong to call animals' emotions "human traits crudely mimicked by lesser creatures"?
2. According to Brooks, what is the difference between things that are "designed" and things that are "made"?
3. When a spider spins a web, why don't we think of it as "smart"?
4. According to the writer, in what way does human intelligence go beyond that of animals?
5. What does Brooks mean when he says that only humans have "the ability to improvise"?

Applying the Reading Strategy

Identifying Main Points

6. In the first paragraph, what human and animal trait does Brooks examine?
7. (a) What main point is addressed in the third paragraph? (b) What transition sentence introduces this point?
8. In the final paragraph, what two types of intelligence does Brooks compare and contrast?

Activity

Compare and Contrast Encyclopedia Entries

Choose two animals that you might consider adopting as pets and find an encyclopedia entry on each one. Read the entries and compare the animals from the angle of a prospective pet owner. Focus on main points that a pet owner would consider, such as the animals' needs for food, shelter, and exercise. Record your findings on a chart like the one here.

Comparing and Contrasting

Animal A
Food
Shelter
Exercise

Animal B
Food
Shelter
Exercise

Contrasting Informational Materials

Comparison-and-Contrast Essays and Comparative Reviews

Comparative reviews compare two or more books or movies and then make a recommendation. People often consult such reviews before choosing which one to read or attend. Examine a comparative review and contrast it with the essay you read here. Answer the following questions:

1. What is the purpose of each document?
2. How does its purpose affect what information is included?
3. How does its purpose affect the way the information is organized?

Writing WORKSHOP

Exposition: Comparison-and-Contrast Essay

A **comparison-and-contrast essay** uses factual details to analyze the similarities and differences between two or more persons, places, or things. These essays help readers—and writers—look at the subjects in new ways.

Assignment Criteria. Your comparison-and-contrast essay should have the following characteristics:

- A topic involving two or more subjects that are different in some ways and similar in other ways
- An introduction that presents the main point of the essay and body paragraphs that include details showing similarities and differences
- An organization that highlights the points of comparison and contrast

See the Rubric on page 905 for the criteria on which your comparison-and-contrast essay may be assessed.

Prewriting

Choose a topic. The two subjects you choose should be related in some way. It may be helpful to choose two or more subjects from one category, such as these:

- competitive products
- popular music
- films on the same topic
- vacation spots
- people you know
- countries or towns

Gather details. Make notes on as many descriptive details, facts, statistics, and other examples as you can. If necessary, use reference books, newspapers, magazines, Internet sites, or documentaries. Talk to experts or visit museums. Take careful notes about everything you hear, read, or see.

Make a Venn diagram. Draw two overlapping circles as shown here. Jot similarities in the center section. Note differences in the outer sections of each circle. Use this diagram as a working document to record ideas and observations throughout your writing process.

Draft a thesis statement. When you are satisfied that you have gathered enough details, review your notes. Write one good sentence that expresses what you want to show in your composition. Using strong, vivid language, write clearly and precisely. This thesis statement should appear in the introduction of your composition.

Example:
Thesis Statement: Buses and trains are both good ways to get around a city, but each has advantages and disadvantages.

Buses   **Subways**

above ground
comfortable
see where
you're going
get caught in
traffic

faster than
walking
cheap
don't have
to park

underground
claustrophobic
can't see where
you're going
avoid traffic

Both

Student Model

Before you begin drafting, read this student model and review the characteristics of a successful comparison-and-contrast essay.

Carolyn Sienko
Williamston, Michigan

Comparing Struggles for Equality

The civil rights movement of the 1950s and 1960s had a lot in common with the women's suffrage movement that began with the Seneca Falls Convention in 1848. Both movements involved a group of people who were denied rights and who fought to obtain those rights.

Although in most ways the two struggles were similar, the specific rights each group fought for were different. Women wanted the right to vote in elections, the right to own property in their own names, and the right to keep their own wages. African Americans fought for the end to segregation. They wanted to be treated with equal rights in schools, jobs, and public places like buses and restaurants.

Both movements protested in nonviolent ways. They held marches, boycotts, and demonstrations to raise the public's consciousness and get the laws changed. In 1917, Alice Paul and other women picketed at the White House. In 1963, more than 200,000 Americans, led by Dr. Martin Luther King, Jr., marched on Washington, D.C. They wanted Congress to pass laws to end discrimination.

Both movements were about equality. In the Declaration of Independence it states: "We hold these truths to be self-evident, that all men are created equal; that they are endowed by the Creator with certain unalienable rights; that among these are life, liberty, and the pursuit of happiness." Both groups felt that they were being denied rights that were given to them by this statement from the Declaration of Independence.

Both groups were able to change the laws so that they could have their rights. Women were given the right to vote in 1920 by Amendment 19 to the Constitution. The Civil Rights Act of 1964 outlawed discrimination in hiring and ended segregation in public places.

In conclusion, the civil rights movement of the 1950s and 1960s and the women's suffrage movement were both about equality under the law. They are both good examples of how much it takes to change the laws. It is good to know, however, that the laws can be changed.

Carolyn begins her essay with a thesis statement that introduces the two groups she is comparing and indicates that she will focus more on similarities.

The writer identifies the differences in the specific rights being sought before calling out similarities.

Carolyn uses point-by-point organization to compare the movements.

The conclusion restates the introduction.

Drafting

Select an effective organization. There are two good ways to organize a comparison-and-contrast composition. Your audience, purpose, and topic will influence the method that you choose.

- **Block method** In this method, a writer presents all the details about one subject first, followed by all the details about the next subject, and so on.

- **Point-by-point method** In this method, a writer covers one aspect of both subjects, then moves on to another aspect of both subjects, and so on.

Layer ideas using SEE. To develop the main point of a supporting paragraph in your composition, follow these steps:

- *State* the topic of the paragraph.

- *Extend* the idea by restating it a new way, applying it to a particular case, or contrasting it with another point.

- *Elaborate* with specific examples, facts, statistics, explanations, or quotations.

Block

I. Buses
    a. cheaper
    b. more routes
    c. better views
II. Trains
    a. better seats
    b. faster
    c. quieter

Point-by-Point

I.   Introduction
II. Costs of each
III. Accessibility of each
IV. View from each
V.   Disadvantages of each

Revising

Color-code to check organization and balance. Reread your draft. Use one color to highlight details about one of your subjects. Use another color to highlight details about the other. If you have more of one color, add details on the subject about which you have written less. Consider whether your highlights show a consistent organization, using either the block method or the point-by-point method.

Model: Check Balance

Both groups were able to change the laws so that they could have their rights. Women were given the right to vote in 1920 by Amendment 19 to the Constitution. ∧ *The Civil Rights Act of 1964 outlawed discrimination in hiring and ended segregation in public places. This law helped both groups.*

> Carolyn added a fact that supported both subjects.

Add supporting details. Copy your thesis onto an index card. Run the card down your draft as you read it, one line at a time. Find any details that do not directly support your thesis. Delete the details or rewrite them to develop your main idea. Note how this writer caught a detail that did not add to a comparison of buses and trains.

> **Example:** Buses cost 85¢ a ride. ~~Of course, you can walk for free or take a cab that costs $1.00 for each quarter mile.~~ Trains cost $1.25.

Compare the model and nonmodel. Why is the model more effective than the nonmodel?

Nonmodel	Model
Both movements protested in nonviolent ways. Sometimes the response to these marches was violent. Many people were injured.	*Both movements protested in nonviolent ways. They held marches, boycotts, and demonstrations to raise the public's consciousness and get the laws changed.*

Publishing and Presenting

Choose one of these ways to share your writing with classmates or a larger audience.

Publish a column. If you have compared and contrasted subjects of local interest, such as two restaurants or several stores, submit your essay to your local newspaper.

Start a family tradition. If you have compared and contrasted two subjects of interest to your family—two uncles, two birthdays, two vacations—read your essay aloud at a family gathering.

 Prentice Hall Writing and Grammar Connection: Chapter 8

 Speaking Connection

To learn more about comparing and contrasting media messages, see the **Listening and Speaking Workshop: Evaluating Media Messages,** page 906.

Rubric for Self-Assessment

Evaluate your comparison-and-contrast essays, using the following criteria and rating scale:

Criteria	Rating Scale				
	Not very				Very
How clearly does the essay cover two or more appropriate subjects?	1	2	3	4	5
How well does the introduction present a judgment or thesis?	1	2	3	4	5
How well do the body paragraphs include factual details that support the thesis?	1	2	3	4	5
How clear, consistent, and appropriate is the organization?	1	2	3	4	5
How well are the interpretations and inferences based on careful observations and insights?	1	2	3	4	5

Every day, you face hundreds of media messages: from television, radio, billboards, print ads, videotapes, even on the Internet. It is important to question the ideas in these messages. Practice being an active and critical audience by following these suggestions.

Evaluate Technique

Look critically at images. The media flash images at us at amazing speeds and levels of complexity. Some are graphic; others are realistic; still others are digitally created or enhanced. All are intended to catch your attention and keep you watching. Be aware of how certain images are designed to appeal to a particular audience.

Listen critically to words and sounds. What are the key words in the message? Be aware, too, of music and sound effects that add emotion. What overall mood does the creator of the message intend to instill in the audience?

Observe "tricks of the trade." Some messages suggest that you jump on a bandwagon. Others use celebrity spokespeople. Still others use statistics and fact to impress an audience. Recognizing media techniques will make you a smarter viewer.

Evaluate Credibility

As you receive a media message, analyze the believability of what you observe. Think about not only what *is* expressed, but also what is *not* expressed.

Hidden agendas Sometimes, messages are hidden underneath comedy, drama, or flashy visual effects. Look beyond the surface of a media message. Which values and ideas are being presented?

Slant or bias Often, complex subjects are presented from only one point of view. For example, political ads or public service announcements may address only one side of a controversial issue. As a viewer, be aware that you may not have been fully informed about an issue.

> **Feedback Form for Media Messages**
>
> **Techniques**
> • What are the key images? _____
> • What are the key words? _____
> • What media presentation techniques do you observe? _____
>
> **Credibility**
> • Is there a hidden agenda? _____
> • Is there bias or slant? _____
> • How would you rate the credibility of this message?
>   ____ Excellent ____ Good ____ Fair ____ Poor
> • Give a reason for your rating: _____
> _____

(Activity:)
Presentation and Feedback With a partner, choose an example of a short media message such as a commercial. Use the Feedback Form above to evaluate what you see and hear. Share your evaluation with your classmates.

Assessment WORKSHOP

Appropriate Usage

The writing sections of some tests require you to read a passage and answer multiple-choice questions about appropriate usage. Use the following strategies to help you answer such questions:

- Use the correct form of a word. Do not confuse adjectives and adverbs. Pay attention to the case of the pronouns.
- Use correct agreement. Verbs should agree with subjects. Pronouns should agree with antecedents.
- Use correct verb tense and form.

Test-Taking Strategies

- Read each question carefully to determine what is being asked.
- Try each answer choice and eliminate those that are wrong.

Sample Test Item

Directions: Read each question and choose the word or words that belong in the space.

1. The directions were very _____ .

   A confusion   **C** confused

   B confusing   **D** confuse

2. This book encourages readers to think _____.

   A creative   **C** creatively

   B more creative   **D** most creatively

3. The Wilsons and _____ took a vacation.

   A us   **C** ourselves

   B we   **D** ourself

Answers and Explanations

1. An adjective is needed. **B** and **C** are both adjectives, but *confused* would mean the directions experienced confusion. **B** is correct.

2. An adverb is needed to modify the verb *think*. **C** and **D** are both adverbs, but **D** is the superlative form, used only in comparisons. **C** is correct.

3. The type of pronoun required in this sentence is part of a compound subject, so the answer is **B**.

Practice

Directions: Read the passage and choose the word or words that belong in each space.

Everyone I know __(1)__ Helen Keller was an __(2)__ person. Although she __(3)__ her sight and hearing at the age of nineteen months, __(4)__ learned to communicate with the whole world. With the help of __(5)__ teacher, Anne Sullivan, Keller went to college.

1. **A** think   **C** thinking

   B thinks   **D** have thought

2. **A** amaze   **C** amazed

   B amazement   **D** amazing

3. **A** has losed   **C** will lost

   B losed   **D** lost

4. **A** her   **C** hers

   B she   **D** herself

5. **A** its   **C** his

   B their   **D** her

Exploring the Genre

T he American folk tradition is a rich collection of literature that grew out of the oral tradition. These stories amaze, teach, and amuse the reader of today just as they did the listener of generations ago. As you read this unit, you will encounter the following types of folk literature:

- **Myths** are ancient tales about beings, ancestors, fictional heroes, and themes that reveal the beliefs and attitudes of a culture.

- **Folk tales** are stories from a particular region that are told in the language of the common people and are passed down through the generations to teach a lesson or to entertain.

- **Tall tales** often tell of life on the American frontier and contain larger-than-life characters who take part in, or witness, fantastic events.

◀ **Critical Viewing** What details in this painting suggest that it portrays an ordinary individual in an American setting? **[Interpret]**

Why Read Literature?

Your purpose, or reason, for reading folk literature will vary, depending on the content and style of the work you plan to read. For example, you might read a myth to find out what a particular culture believed about the origins of the universe. You might read a tall tale to get a good laugh. Preview three purposes you might set before reading the works in this unit.

1

Read for the love of literature.

In some Native American cultures, the mythical character Coyote is a sly trickster who is always up to something. But did you know that coyotes have two known weaknesses? They sleep heavily and they look back while running away. See what the coyote is up to in the Zuni tale, **"Coyote Steals the Sun and Moon,"** page 920.

Did you know that when a possum is attacked, it rolls over and plays dead? To see how Brer Possum reacts to a threatening situation, read **"Brer Possum's Dilemma,"** page 917.

2

Read to be entertained.

To hear the "king of the wild frontier" tell it, getting a good night's sleep could be an awful challenge. Discover why when you read **"Davy Crockett's Dream,"** page 948.

When John Henry vowed to work faster than a machine, his will was as strong as steel. Learn what happened as a result when you read the ballad **"John Henry,"** page 934.

Did you know that cyclones spin counterclockwise north of the equator and clockwise south of the equator? This is called the Coriolis Effect. Read about a disruptive cyclone in **"Pecos Bill: The Cyclone,"** page 938.

3

Read for information.

The footprints left by the Apollo astronauts will not erode since there is no wind or water on the moon. The footprints should last up to two million years! To read more about astronauts' firsts, read **"The Right Stuff,"** page 954.

Take It to the Net

Visit the Web site for online instruction and activities related to each selection in this unit.

www.phschool.com

How to Read Literature

Use Strategies for Reading Folk Literature

Folk literature is older than recorded history. Its tales, stories, legends, and myths have been passed down for many generations. Because these tales were told orally, they often contain repetition (making them easier to remember) and dialect (specialized vocabulary and grammar of a region). As you explore the folk literature in this unit, use the following strategies to guide your reading:

1. Understand the cultural context.

You will better understand the action and characters of a story if you know the culture from which it comes. For example, a Mexican American tale—a *cuento*—reveals different beliefs and customs than a Native American tale. Look at the following example based on "Chicoria":

> **Folk Tale Passage:** Instead, [the rancher] asked that a chair be brought and placed by the wall where Chicoria was to sit. The rich ranchers began to eat without inviting Chicoria.

> **Cultural Context:** In the culture of the big ranches, when California belonged to Mexico, there was a large gulf between rich and poor in social status.

2. Recognize the storyteller's purpose.

Storytellers often use folk tales to transmit beliefs or values. Some tales serve to explain scientific mysteries or natural occurrences. As you read, consider what message the story might be conveying to listeners.

- Examine the details of the tale for clues to the storyteller's purpose.
- Look for a message or moral near the story's end.

3. Predict.

Folk literature is predictable. Good characters and deeds are rewarded; bad characters are either banished or reformed. This pattern makes it easy for you to predict the story's outcome or message.

As you read the selections in this unit, review the reading strategies and apply them to interact with the text.

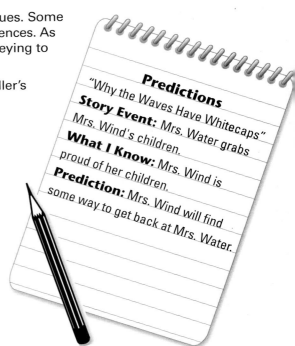

Predictions

"Why the Waves Have Whitecaps"

Story Event: Mrs. Water grabs Mrs. Wind's children.

What I Know: Mrs. Wind is proud of her children.

Prediction: Mrs. Wind will find some way to get back at Mrs. Water.

Prepare to Read

Chicoria ◆ Brer Possum's Dilemma ◆ Coyote Steals the Sun and Moon ◆ Why the Waves Have Whitecaps

Cosmic Canine, John Nieto, Courtesy of the artist

Take It to the Net

Visit www.phschool.com
for interactive activities
and instruction related to
these selections, including
- background
- graphic organizers
- literary elements
- reading strategies

Preview

Connecting to the Literature

When you watch a television program in which one of the characters gets into trouble because of something he or she did, the message is usually pretty clear—others should not do what the character does. Long before television, people had a similar way of passing along lessons and messages: through stories, such as the ones you are about to read.

Background

"Why the Waves Have Whitecaps," recounted by Zora Neale Hurston, gives a folk explanation for whitecaps—waves with white-foam tops. Scientifically, wind causes waves on the water's surface. As an ocean wave nears the shore—where the water is shallower—the height of the wave increases. When the wind has driven the wave to its highest point, the wave breaks up into water droplets. The droplets reflect light and appear to be white—thus, whitecaps.

Literary Analysis

Folk Tale

A **folk tale** is a story that has been passed by word of mouth from generation to generation within a cultural group. Many folk tales have been written down for all to enjoy. Folk tales usually have several of the following characteristics:

- They are entertaining.
- They explain something in nature.
- They teach a lesson.
- They express a belief or a custom of the culture that created it.
- They use dialect, or the specialized vocabulary and grammar of a region.

Comparing Literary Works

The following stories are folk tales from a variety of cultures. As you read, compare and contrast the elements they contain and the messages they convey. Use the following focus questions to guide you:

1. What is the purpose of each tale—to entertain, to explain something in nature, or to teach a lesson?
2. What similarities can you find among the characters?
3. What common threads can you find among the messages the tales convey?

Reading Strategy

Understanding the Cultural Context

Folk tales reflect the values and beliefs of the cultures from which they come. As you read, look for details within the myth to help you **understand the cultural context** of the story. For example, in these works, details about animal behavior, the weather, and the change of seasons may lead you to understand that the culture originating these tales was agricultural, depending on nature for survival. Use a chart like the one here to record details.

Detail	What it Shows
Coyote steals the sun and moon.	Importance of light to culture.

Vocabulary Development

cordially (kôr′ jə lē) *adv.* in a warm and friendly way (p. 915)

haughty (hôt′ ē) *adj.* proud of oneself and scornful of others (p. 915)

commenced (kə menst′) *v.* started; began (p. 917)

pitiful (pət′ i fəl) *adj.* deserving compassion or sympathy (p. 919)

shriveled (shriv′ əld) *v.* dried up; withered (p. 922)

pursuit (pər so͞ot′) *n.* following in order to overtake and capture (p. 922)

CHICORIA

Adapted in Spanish by José Griego y Maestas
Retold in English by Rudolfo A. Anaya

Invitation to the Dance (el convite), Theodore Gentilz, The Daughters of the Republic of Texas Library, San Antonio, Texas

There were once many big ranches in California, and many New Mexicans went to work there. One day one of the big ranch owners asked his workers if there were any poets in New Mexico.

"Of course, we have many fine poets," they replied. "We have old Vilmas,[1] Chicoria,[2] Cinfuegos,[3] to say nothing of the poets of Cebolleta[4] and the Black Poet."

"Well, when you return next season, why don't you bring one of your poets to compete with Gracia[5]—here none can compare with him!"

When the harvest was done the New Mexicans returned home. The following season when they returned to California they took with them the poet Chicoria, knowing well that in spinning a rhyme or in weaving wit there was no *Californio*[6] who could beat him.

As soon as the rancher found out that the workers had brought Chicoria with them, he sent his servants to invite his good neighbor and friend to come and hear the new poet. Meanwhile, the cooks set about preparing a big meal. When the maids began to dish up the plates of food, Chicoria turned to one of the servers and said, "Ah, my friends, it looks like they are going to feed us well tonight!"

The servant was surprised. "No, my friend," he explained, "the food is for *them*. We don't eat at the master's table. It is not permitted. We eat in the kitchen."

"Well, I'll bet I can sit down and eat with them," Chicoria boasted.

"If you beg or if you ask, perhaps, but if you don't ask they won't invite you," replied the servant.

"I never beg," the New Mexican answered. "The master will invite me of his own accord, and I'll bet you twenty dollars he will!"

So they made a twenty-dollar bet and they instructed the serving maid to watch if this self-confident New Mexican had to ask the master for a place at the table. Then the maid took Chicoria into the dining room. Chicoria greeted the rancher <u>cordially</u>, but the rancher appeared <u>haughty</u> and did not invite Chicoria to sit with him and his guest at the table. Instead, he asked that a chair be brought and placed by the wall where Chicoria was to sit. The rich ranchers began to eat without inviting Chicoria.

1. **Vilmas** (vēl´ mäs)
2. **Chicoria** (chē kō´ rē ä)
3. **Cinfuegos** (sin fwä´ gōs)
4. **Cebolleta** (sā bō´ yä tä)
5. **Gracia** (grä´ sē ä)
6. **Californio** (kä lē fôr´ nyō) *n.* Spanish for "person from California."

◀ **Critical Viewing** Are the men on horseback welcomed or feared? Explain. **[Draw Conclusions]**

Reading Strategy
Understanding the Cultural Context What do the details in this section tell you about the relationship between New Mexicans and *Californios*?

cordially (kôr´ jə lē) *adv.* in a warm and friendly way

haughty (hôt´ ē) *adj.* proud of oneself and scornful of others

✓**Reading Check**
What does Chicoria say he will do?

So it is just as the servant predicted, Chicoria thought. The poor are not invited to share the rich man's food!

Then the master spoke: "Tell us about the country where you live. What are some of the customs of New Mexico?"

"Well, in New Mexico when a family sits down to eat each member uses one spoon for each biteful of food," Chicoria said with a twinkle in his eyes.

The ranchers were amazed that the New Mexicans ate in that manner, but what Chicoria hadn't told them was that each spoon was a piece of tortilla[7]: one fold and it became a spoon with which to scoop up the meal.

"Furthermore," he continued, "our goats are not like yours."

"How are they different?" the rancher asked.

"Here your nannies[8] give birth to two kids, in New Mexico they give birth to three!"

"What a strange thing!" the master said. "But tell us, how can the female nurse three kids?"

"Well, they do it exactly as you're doing it now: While two of them are eating the third one looks on."

The rancher then realized his lack of manners and took Chicoria's hint. He apologized and invited his New Mexico guest to dine at the table. After dinner, Chicoria sang and recited his poetry, putting Gracia to shame. And he won his bet as well.

---

7. **tortilla** (tôr tē´ yə) *n.* thin, round pancake of cornmeal or flour.
8. **nannies** (nan´ ēz) *n.* female goats.

Review and Assess

Thinking About the Selection

1. **Respond:** Who did you think would win the bet—the servant or Chicoria? Why?

2. **(a) Recall:** How does the server respond when Chicoria says he expects to be fed well at the rancher's table? **(b) Connect:** What determines who sits with the rancher at dinner and who does not? **(c) Analyze:** Why does Chicoria assume that he will eat at the rancher's table?

3. **(a) Recall:** What bet does Chicoria make with the servants? **(b) Interpret:** What does his statement "I never beg" show about his character? **(c) Speculate:** What do you think the servants expect will happen to him?

4. **(a) Recall:** What does Chicoria say about New Mexican goats? **(b) Analyze:** Why does he tell this story?

5. **Make a Judgment:** Do you think the rancher's thoughtlessness should be excused? Why or why not?

José Griego y Maestas

(b. 1949)

José Griego y Maestas is an expert in bilingual education and Hispanic folklore. The dean of instruction at Northern New Mexico Community College, he is also a story-teller, and he sometimes performs with his daughters, who are actors in New Mexico community theater.

Rudolfo A. Anaya

(b. 1937)

New Mexico resident Rudolfo Anaya, an acclaimed writer of short stories and novels that evoke the culture of the Hispanic people, translated the folk tales collected by José Griego y Maestas into English. One of Anaya's most celebrated books is *Bless Me, Ultima*, a novel set in New Mexico.

Brer Possum's Dilemma

Jackie Torrence

Back in the days when the animals could talk, there lived ol' Brer[1] Possum. He was a fine feller. Why, he never liked to see no critters[2] in trouble. He was always helpin' out, a-doin' somethin' for others.

Ever' night, ol' Brer Possum climbed into a persimmon tree, hung by his tail, and slept all night long. And each mornin', he climbed outa the tree and walked down the road to sun 'imself.

One mornin', as he walked, he come to a big hole in the middle of the road. Now, ol' Brer Possum was kind and gentle, but he was also nosy, so he went over to the hole and looked in. All at once, he stepped back, 'cause layin' in the bottom of that hole was ol' Brer Snake with a brick on his back.

Brer Possum said to 'imself, "I best git on outa here, 'cause ol' Brer Snake is mean and evil and lowdown, and if I git to stayin' around 'im, he jist might git to bitin' me."

So Brer Possum went on down the road.

But Brer Snake had seen Brer Possum, and he <u>commenced</u> to callin' for 'im.

"Help me, Brer Possum."

Brer Possum stopped and turned around. He said to 'imself, "That's ol' Brer Snake a-callin' me. What do you reckon he wants?"

Well, ol' Brer Possum was kindhearted, so he went back down the road to the hole, stood at the edge, and looked down at Brer Snake.

"Was that you a-callin' me? What do you want?"

Brer Snake looked up and said, "I've been down here in this hole for a mighty long time with this brick on my back. Won't you help git it offa me?"

Brer Possum thought.

"Now listen here, Brer Snake. I knows you. You's mean and evil and lowdown, and if'n I was to git down in that hole and git to liftin' that brick offa your back, you wouldn't do nothin' but bite me."

Ol' Brer Snake just hissed.

commenced (kə menst') *v.* started; began

---

1. **Brer** (brʉr) dialect for "brother," used before a name.
2. **critters** dialect for "creatures"; animals.

✔Reading Check

What does Brer Snake want Brer Possum to do?

"Maybe not. Maybe not. Maaaaaaaybe not."

Brer Possum said, "I ain't sure 'bout you at all. I jist don't know. You're a-goin' to have to let me think about it."

So ol' Brer Possum thought—he thought high, and he thought low—and jist as he was thinkin', he looked up into a tree and saw a dead limb a-hangin' down. He climbed into the tree, broke off the limb, and with that ol' stick, pushed that brick offa Brer Snake's back. Then he took off down the road.

Brer Possum thought he was away from ol' Brer Snake when all at once he heard somethin'.

"Help me, Brer Possum."

Brer Possum said, "Oh, no, that's him agin."

But bein' so kindhearted, Brer Possum turned around, went back to the hole, and stood at the edge.

"Brer Snake, was that you a-callin' me? What do you want now?"

Ol' Brer Snake looked up outa the hole and hissed.

"I've been down here for a mighty long time, and I've gotten a little weak, and the sides of this ol' hole are too slick for me to climb. Do you think you can lift me outa here?"

Brer Possum thought.

"Now, you jist wait a minute. If'n I was to git down into that hole and lift you outa there, you wouldn't do nothin' but bite me."

Brer Snake hissed.

"Maybe not. Maybe not. Maaaaaaaybe not."

Brer Possum said, "I jist don't know. You're a-goin' to have to give me time to think about this."

So ol' Brer Possum thought.

And as he thought, he jist happened to look down there in that hole and see that ol' dead limb. So he pushed the limb underneath ol' Brer Snake and he lifted 'im outa the hole, way up into the air, and throwed 'im into the high grass.

Brer Possum took off a-runnin' down the road.

Well, he thought he was away from ol' Brer Snake when all at once he heard somethin'.

"Help me, Brer Possum."

Brer Possum thought, "That's him agin."

But bein' so kindhearted, he turned around, went back to the hole, and stood there a-lookin' for Brer Snake. Brer Snake crawled outa the high grass just as slow as he could, stretched 'imself out across the road, rared up,[3] and looked at ol' Brer Possum.

Then he hissed. "I've been down there in that ol' hole for a mighty

▲ **Critical Viewing**
What human characteristics does the snake in this illustration exhibit?
[Interpret]

---

3. rared up dialect for "reared up."

918 ◆ *The American Folk Tradition*

long time, and I've gotten a little cold 'cause the sun didn't shine. Do you think you could put me in your pocket and git me warm?"

Brer Possum said, "Now you listen here, Brer Snake. I knows you. You's mean and evil and lowdown, and if'n I put you in my pocket you wouldn't do nothin' but bite me."

Brer Snake hissed.

"Maybe not. Maybe not. Maaaaaaaybe not."

"No sireee. Brer Snake. I knows you. I jist ain't a-goin' to do it."

But jist as Brer Possum was talkin' to Brer Snake, he happened to git a real good look at 'im. He was a-layin' there lookin' so <u>pitiful</u>, and Brer Possum's great big heart began to feel sorry for ol' Brer Snake.

"All right," said Brer Possum. "You must be cold. So jist this once I'm a-goin' to put you in my pocket."

So ol' Brer Snake coiled up jist as little as he could, and Brer Possum picked 'im up and put 'im in his pocket.

Brer Snake laid quiet and still—so quiet and still that Brer Possum even forgot that he was a-carryin' 'im around. But all of a sudden, Brer Snake commenced to crawlin' out, and he turned and faced Brer Possum and hissed.

"I'm a-goin' to bite you."

But Brer Possum said, "Now wait a minute. Why are you a-goin' to bite me? I done took that brick offa your back, I got you outa that hole, and I put you in my pocket to git you warm. Why are you a-goin' to bite me?"

Brer Snake hissed.

"You knowed I was a snake before you put me in you pocket."

And when you're mindin' your own business and you spot trouble, don't never trouble trouble 'til trouble troubles you.

pitiful (pit′ i fəl) *adj.* deserving compassion or sympathy

Jackie Torrence

(b. 1944)
Widely known to audiences as "the Story Lady," Jackie Torrence has written several collections of folk tales and stories for children, including *The Accidental Angel*, *My Grandmother's Treasure*, and *Classic Children's Tales*. A popular and entertaining reader, Torrence has recorded many of her stories on compact discs and videotapes.

Review and Assess

Thinking About the Selection

1. **Respond:** Is Brer Snake to be blamed for his behavior? Why or why not?

2. **(a) Recall:** What words does Torrence use to describe Brer Possum? **(b) Infer:** Is Brer Possum meant to look foolish or simply big-hearted? Explain. **(c) Compare and Contrast:** In what ways are Brer Possum and Brer Snake different?

3. **(a) Recall:** What is the last request Brer Snake makes of Brer Possum? **(b) Deduce:** Why might Brer Possum think it is safe to honor Brer Snake's request?

4. **(a) Recall:** What does Brer Snake say he will do? **(b) Make a Judgment:** Who is to blame for Brer Possum's problem? Explain. **(c) Apply:** How does the message of this story apply to people?

COYOTE STEALS THE SUN AND MOON

—Zuñi Myth—

Retold by Richard Erdoes and Alfonso Ortiz

Cosmic Canine, John Nieto, Courtesy of the artist

Coyote is a bad hunter who never kills anything. Once he watched Eagle hunting rabbits, catching one after another—more rabbits than he could eat. Coyote thought, "I'll team up with Eagle so I can have enough meat." Coyote is always up to something.

"Friend," Coyote said to Eagle, "we should hunt together. Two can catch more than one."

"Why not?" Eagle said, and so they began to hunt in partnership. Eagle caught many rabbits, but all Coyote caught was some little bugs.

At this time the world was still dark; the sun and moon had not yet been put in the sky. "Friend," Coyote said to Eagle, "no wonder I can't catch anything; I can't see. Do you know where we can get some light?"

"You're right, friend, there should be some light," Eagle said. "I think there's a little toward the west. Let's try and find it."

And so they went looking for the sun and moon. They came to a big river, which Eagle flew over. Coyote swam, and swallowed so much water that he almost drowned. He crawled out with his fur full

▲ Critical Viewing
Why might the artist have chosen to depict Coyote as multicolored? [Infer]

of mud, and Eagle asked, "Why don't you fly like me?"

"You have wings; I just have hair," Coyote said. "I can't fly without feathers."

At last they came to a pueblo,[1] where the Kachinas◆ happened to be dancing. The people invited Eagle and Coyote to sit down and have something to eat while they watched the sacred dances. Seeing the power of the Kachinas, Eagle said, "I believe these are the people who have light."

Coyote, who had been looking all around, pointed out two boxes, one large and one small, that the people opened whenever they wanted light. To produce a lot of light, they opened the lid of the big box, which contained the sun. For less light they opened the small box, which held the moon.

Coyote nudged Eagle. "Friend, did you see that? They have all the light we need in the big box. Let's steal it."

"You always want to steal and rob. I say we should just borrow it."

"They won't lend it to us."

"You may be right," said Eagle. "Let's wait till they finish dancing and then steal it."

After a while the Kachinas went home to sleep, and Eagle scooped up the large box and flew off. Coyote ran along trying to keep up, panting, his tongue hanging out. Soon he yelled up to Eagle, "Ho, friend, let me carry the box a little way."

"No, no," said Eagle, "you never do anything right."

He flew on, and Coyote ran after him. After a while Coyote shouted again: "Friend, you're my chief, and it's not right for you to carry the box; people will call me lazy. Let me have it."

"No, no, you always mess everything up." And Eagle flew on and Coyote ran along.

So it went for a stretch, and then Coyote started again. "Ho, friend, it isn't right for you to do this. What will people think of you and me?"

"I don't care what people think. I'm going to carry this box."

Again Eagle flew on and again Coyote ran after him. Finally Coyote begged for the fourth time: "Let me carry it. You're the chief, and I'm just Coyote. Let me carry it."

Eagle couldn't stand any more pestering. Also, Coyote had asked him four times, and if someone asks four times, you'd better give

Kachinas

◆ The Kachina dancers mentioned in the story serve as links between the earthly world and the spirit world in Hopi Indian culture. Every year, between late December and July, Hopi men and women spend days apart in preparation for the ceremony. During the ceremony, dancers perform, wearing masks representing various supernatural beings, or Kachinas.

The dancers play a central role in Hopi religion, where the blessings of the powerful spirits are sought every year for a good harvest and good fortune. Children are given miniature versions of the Kachinas made of cottonwood and fabric, and special food is eaten. This old tradition is still observed by Hopi people today.

A Hopi Kachina dancer

✔**Reading Check**

What do Coyote and Eagle take?

---

1. **pueblo** (pweb´ lō) Native American village in the southwestern United States.

him what he wants. Eagle said, "Since you won't let up on me, go ahead and carry the box for a while. But promise not to open it."

"Oh, sure, oh yes, I promise." They went on as before, but now Coyote had the box. Soon Eagle was far ahead, and Coyote lagged behind a hill where Eagle couldn't see him. "I wonder what the light looks like, inside there," he said to himself. "Why shouldn't I take a peek? Probably there's something extra in the box, something good that Eagle wants to keep to himself."

And Coyote opened the lid. Now, not only was the sun inside, but the moon also. Eagle had put them both together, thinking that it would be easier to carry one box than two.

As soon as Coyote opened the lid, the moon escaped, flying high into the sky. At once all the plants <u>shriveled</u> up and turned brown. Just as quickly, all the leaves fell off the trees, and it was winter. Trying to catch the moon and put it back in the box, Coyote ran in <u>pursuit</u> as it skipped away from him. Meanwhile the sun flew out and rose into the sky. It drifted far away, and the peaches, squashes, and melons shriveled up with cold.

Eagle turned and flew back to see what had delayed Coyote. "You fool! Look what you've done!" he said. "You let the sun and moon escape, and now it's cold." Indeed, it began to snow, and Coyote shivered. "Now your teeth are chattering," Eagle said, "and it's your fault that cold has come into the world."

It's true. If it weren't for Coyote's curiosity and mischief making, we wouldn't have winter; we could enjoy summer all the time.

shriveled (shriv´ əld) *v.* dried up; withered

pursuit (pər sōōt´) *n.* following in order to overtake and capture

Review and Assess

Thinking About the Selection

1. **Respond:** What advice would you like to give to Eagle?

2. **(a) Recall:** Why does Coyote want to team up with Eagle? **(b) Compare and Contrast:** Contrast the attitudes of Eagle and Coyote. **(c) Connect:** How does each character's attitude relate to his actions?

3. **(a) Recall:** How does Coyote finally get the box? **(b) Infer:** What does Coyote's behavior tell you about his character?

4. **(a) Distinguish:** Which details in this story have a factual basis? Which ones do you think are invented? **(b) Support:** How do you know which is which?

5. **(a) Recall:** What element of nature does this story explain? **(b) Analyze:** In what way does the story caution the reader to respect nature?

Richard Erdoes
Alfonso Ortiz

(b. 1912)
(1939–1997)
For their book *American Indian Myths and Legends,* Richard Erdoes and Alfonso Ortiz collected many stories over a period of twenty-five years. Some of the stories in the book "were jotted down at pow-wows, around campfires, even inside a moving car." Richard Erdoes was born in Vienna, Austria. Alfonso Ortiz was born in San Juan, a Tewa pueblo in New Mexico.

Why the Waves Have WHITECAPS

ZORA NEALE HURSTON

Wind and Geometry, 1978, David True, Courtesy of the artist

▲ **Critical Viewing** In this painting, which force would you say is stronger—the wind or the water? Explain. **[Make a Judgment]**

De wind is a woman, and de water is a woman too. They useter[1] talk together a whole heap. Mrs. Wind useter go set down by de ocean and talk and patch and crochet.

They was jus' like all lady people. They loved to talk about their chillun, and brag on 'em.

✔**Reading Check**

What two characters enjoy talking to each other?

---

1. useter (yoo′ stə) *v.* dialect for "used to."

Why the Waves Have Whitecaps ◆ 923

Mrs. Water useter say, "Look at *my* chillun! Ah got de biggest and de littlest in de world. All kinds of chillun. Every color in de world, and every shape!"

De wind lady bragged louder than de water woman:

"Oh, but Ah got mo' different chilluns than anybody in de world. They flies, they walks, they swims, they sings, they talks, they cries. They got all de colors from de sun. Lawd, my chillun sho is a pleasure. 'Tain't nobody got no babies like mine."

Mrs. Water got tired of hearin' 'bout Mrs. Wind's chillun so she got so she hated 'em.

One day a whole passle of her chillun come to Mrs. Wind and says: "Mama, wese thirsty. Kin we go git us a cool drink of water?"

She says, "Yeah chillun. Run on over to Mrs. Water and hurry right back soon."

When them chillun went to squinch they thirst Mrs. Water grabbed 'em all and drowned 'em.

When her chillun didn't come home, de wind woman got worried. So she went on down to de water and ast for her babies.

"Good evenin' Mis' Water, you see my chillun today?"

De water woman tole her, "No-oo-oo."

Mrs. Wind knew her chillun had come down to Mrs. Water's house, so she passed over de ocean callin' her chillun, and every time she call de white feathers would come up on top of de water. And dat's how come we got white caps on waves. It's de feathers comin' up when de wind woman calls her lost babies.

When you see a storm on de water, it's de wind and de water fightin' over dem chillun.

Zora Neale Hurston

(1891–1960)

Zora Neale Hurston was among the first Americans to collect and publish African American folklore. She re-created and interpreted the folk tales that she had heard while growing up in Eatonville, Florida, and used the local dialect in her tales. She also wrote novels, short stories, and magazine articles.

Review and Assess

Thinking About the Selection

1. **Respond:** What did you enjoy most about "Why the Waves Have Whitecaps"?

2. **(a) Recall:** What are Mrs. Wind and Mrs. Water doing at the beginning of the story? **(b) Analyze:** In what ways are their activities like those of many ordinary people?

3. **(a) Recall:** How would you describe the relationship between Mrs. Wind and Mrs. Water at the beginning of the story? **(b) Infer:** What made their relationship change?

4. **(a) Recall:** According to the story, what are the whitecaps on the waves? **(b) Deduce:** Do you think the outcome of the story was inevitable? Explain.

Review and Assess

Literary Analysis

Folk Tale

1. Identify the characteristics of a folk tale that you find in "Why the Waves Have Whitecaps."
2. What can you learn about life in the Southwest from the details and events in "Chicoria"?
3. In "Brer Possum's Dilemma," how do words like *a-callin'* and *a-lookin'* indicate that this tale came from the oral tradition?

Comparing Literary Works

4. What is the main purpose in each folk tale?
5. **(a)** In which selection is cleverness or trickery a good thing? **(b)** In which selection is trickery bad? Explain.
6. What similarities can you find among the characters?
7. Using a graphic organizer like the one shown, identify the common threads you find in the messages each tale conveys.

	Problem	Resolution	Message
Folk Tale			

Reading Strategy

Understanding the Cultural Context

8. Whom do you think readers of "Chicoria" are meant to admire more—Chicoria or the New Mexican servants? Explain.
9. In "Coyote Steals the Sun and Moon," the snows of winter come when coyote loses the sun, and this causes great suffering. What does this tell you about the people's way of life?
10. Which two selections communicate the belief that curiosity can get a person in trouble? Explain.

Extend Understanding

11. **Science Connection:** What behaviors of Brer Possum, Brer Snake, Coyote, and Eagle do you think might mirror the behaviors of the real-life animals that these characters are based on?

Integrate Language Skills

Vocabulary Development Lesson

Concept Development: Using Synonyms

Synonyms are words with the same basic meaning. Rewrite each sentence, replacing each italicized word with a synonym from the vocabulary words listed on page 913.

1. The lady of the manor was *snobbish*.
2. The ceremony *began* at noon.
3. They welcomed us *hospitably*.
4. The snake looked *pathetic*.

Spelling Strategy

Some words have more letters than you expect. Pay attention to silent letters and vowel combinations. Practice spelling the following words.

haughty   pursuit

1. Which word has a silent *gh*?
2. Which spells the long *u* sound with *ui*?

Fluency: Sentence Completions

On your paper, write the word from the vocabulary list that best completes each sentence.

The town festival ____?____ with a large and tasty barbecue, followed by a series of races. With great pride, the mayor ____?____ welcomed all townsfolk and promised each competitor a prize. Runners in each age group raced as fast as they could in ____?____ of a first-place medal. Some of the winners were ____?____ toward those who won the prize for last place, a rather ____?____ potted plant with somewhat ____?____ leaves.

Grammar Lesson

Commas in a Series and in Compound Sentences

Use **commas** to separate three or more words, phrases, or elements in a **series.** Include a comma before the final conjunction in the series.

Commas in Series: Ol' Brer Possum *climbed into a persimmon tree, hung by his tail,* and *slept all night long.*

In compound sentences, use commas to separate two independent clauses that are joined by a coordinating conjunction (*and, but, or, for,* or *nor*). Insert the comma before the coordinating conjunction.

Commas in a Compound Sentence: *He flew on,* and *Coyote ran after him.*

▶ For more practice, see page R34, Exercise A.
Practice Copy these sentences and add commas where necessary.

1. There were big ranches in California and New Mexicans went to work there.
2. Possum could help Brer Snake get out of the hole or he could walk away.
3. Brer Snake crawled out of Brer Possum's pocket turned to face him and hissed.
4. Mrs. Water grabbed the children drowned them and lied to Mrs. Wind.
5. They went on but now he had the box.

Writing Application   In a paragraph, summarize the actions Chicoria took to get invited to eat. Include at least one series and one compound sentence, using commas correctly.

W̶G̶ Prentice Hall Writing and Grammar Connection: Chapter 26, Section 2

Writing Lesson

Letter of Inquiry

Write a letter of inquiry, a letter requesting information, to the chairperson of the anthropology department of the nearest university, asking where to find information about Native American, African American, or Mexican American culture to gain background for one of these folk tales.

Prewriting   Use the standard business letter format including a heading with your name, address, and the date; an inside address indicating the name and address of the recipient; a salutation or greeting; the body of your letter; a closing; and your signature. For more information on writing, see pages 330–333. For another model, see page R16.

Model: Using an Effective Format

Dear Dr. Belascoe:

My class is currently studying American folk literature.

> In a business letter using block format, each element starts at the left margin.

Drafting   Write concisely. Let the reader know immediately what information you want.

Revising   Check the spellings of names and places, especially the name of the person receiving your letter. Correct any errors before you send your letter.

Prentice Hall Writing and Grammar Connection: Chapter 3, Section 2

Extension Activities

Listening and Speaking Make up a **new folk tale.** In addition to a plot, or sequence of events, include the following:

- description of the background and characters
- a comparison of your various characters
- dialogue that your characters might speak (including dialect, if appropriate)

Practice telling the tale aloud. Then, tell it to a classmate. Have your classmate share your tale with the class. Finally, discuss the subtle changes that occurred from one telling to the next.

Writing: Prepare a **newspaper story** based on one of the tales presented here.

Research and Technology Compile a **collection of folk tales** from a single culture. Use CD-ROMs and the Internet to find folk tales from the culture you have chosen. When searching on the Internet, narrow your search with AND. For example, use: "folk tales AND Finland" to find a more specific list of sites.

 **Take It to the Net**   www.phschool.com

Go online for an additional research activity using the Internet.

READING INFORMATIONAL MATERIALS

Bylaws

About Bylaws

If you have ever belonged to a club or other kind of organization, you might have read their bylaws. **Bylaws** are the rules adopted by members of a club, society, or corporation. Bylaws generally apply to (1) the time and place of meetings and (2) the methods of voting.

When reading bylaws critically, it is important to know for what kind of organization they are written. This will help you determine their purpose. Also, you should remember that bylaws are a legal, technical document with a formal structure and vocabulary. The bylaws are usually broken down into articles, sections, and clauses.

- An article is the main point of each bylaw.
- Sections are the details that support the articles.
- Clauses provide additional support for the sections.

Frequently, there is also a glossary, so that readers know the precise definition of each term as it is used in the document.

Apply the Reading Strategy

Reading Technical Documents

Reading technical documents can be an intimidating experience. The language used may be complex and highly specialized. The reader may need to have prior knowledge of the subject in order to understand the information given. Here are some strategies to help you read and understand technical documents.

- Use the glossary; make a photocopy and keep it next to you while you read.
- If there isn't a glossary, make sure you have a dictionary to look up unfamiliar words.
- Take notes and summarize main ideas in your own words.
- Before reading, it may be useful to skim the document in order to familiarize yourself with the format and headings.

Copy the chart provided into your notebook. Use it to help you read the bylaws of the Student Senate.

Bylaws of Student Senate

Who is the audience? _____

What is their purpose? _____

Unfamiliar words and definitions _____

_____

Section Heads

Article 1 - _____

Section A _____

_____

Section B _____

_____

Student Government Bylaws

Article I–Student Senate

Section A: The purposes of the Student Senate shall be to function as a channel for student views on campus affairs and other areas of student concerns, to represent the student body and serve as a unified voice in speaking for the students, to serve as a front where the student body may be addressed, and to establish continuity of student government.

Section B: To fulfill these goals, the Senate shall have power to appoint delegates to serve as representatives of the Senate and the Student Body, to grant or revoke charters, to apportion funds granted to the student body by the Board of Trustees of Hartwick College and any other funds which the Senate may from time to time acquire, to make rules concerning the liquidation of defunct campus-student organizations, and to exercise all other powers granted to the Senate by this constitution or which are appropriate or usual to a student governing body.

The first section of bylaws will often offer a definition. In this case, the role of the Senate is defined.

Article II–Student Senate Elections

These headings divide the major topics from one another.

Section A: The election of the officers of the Student Senate shall be conducted in the spring term on at least two (2) days in the second week of April. Election for officers must be by majority vote. If majority is not obtained, a run-off election between the top two (2) candidates shall be held.

Section B: The qualifications for the candidates for the Presidency and other elected offices shall be a valid petition, residency in the Oneonta area for the full term of office, and be a registered student at Hartwick College.

Section C: Clause One—The Senate Executive Board shall determine the number of Senators needed to comply with the representational policies of the Senate outlined in the bylaws.

Clause Two–Any residence may petition the Senate for increased Senator representation. The validity of the request will be determined by Senate acceptance. Any student residing in a residence which is not otherwise entitled to Senator representation shall, at their request, be assigned by the Senate to residences where they will vote and be represented.

Clause Three–Senator elections may be reviewed by the Senate to ensure that established election procedures have been followed. The term of office for Senators shall end at the last regular Senate meeting of the current school year.

Section D: All officers, senators-elect, and justices of the several campus-wide courts shall be installed at the first Senate meeting they attend following their election. The following oath shall be administered while the right hand is raised:

"Do you solemnly swear to faithfully execute the office to which you are elected or appointed and that you will uphold the Constitution of the Student Body of Hartwick College?"

If the appointee or officer agrees to this oath, he or she shall respond "I will."

Section E: Clause One—In case of a tie in any election conducted by the Senate, the election shall be reheld within one week. All campus-wide elections shall be by secret ballot and by plurality vote. Names of the candidates shall be listed alphabetically. Write-in votes shall be allowed for all offices. Ballots shall be kept for a period of thirty (30) days following the election.

Clause Two—In the event that vacancies in these offices occur, the Senate shall appoint, within one week, an acting officer to fill the vacant position and make known the appointment to the student body. If, within two (2) school weeks of the appointment, at least one candidate shall come forth with a valid petition for the vacant office, then the Senate shall within five (5) school weeks from the date of appointment conduct a special election for that office. Otherwise, the appointed officer shall serve as if duly elected in an open election.

Article III—Student Rights

Section A: No student shall be expelled or suffer disciplinary action unless proceedings and hearings of the College Judicial System and subsidiary judicial boards are consistent with minimal standards of due process as here defined.

1. All charges must be in writing and presented to the student at the notification of the hearing.
2. Charges shall be specific as to nature, time, and place of alleged infraction.
3. The student shall be informed of his/her rights (including the right to appeal) at the time he/she is charged.
4. The defendant shall be afforded at least three days' notice of a hearing.
5. The defendant shall have the right to a speedy trial.
6. Hearings on constitutionality shall be open to the student body.
7. The defendant shall have the right to be accompanied by an advisor, who may confer with and assist the defendant.
8. The defendant shall be presumed innocent until proven guilty.
9. The defendant shall have the opportunity to answer accusations and to submit the testimony of witnesses on his/her own behalf.
10. All evidence and testimony shall be introduced in the presence of the accused.
11. No person shall be twice put in jeopardy of punishment for the same offense.
12. Decisions of the Court shall be rendered to the defendant, and to the appropriate officers of the student senate, within forty-eight (48) hours of the end of deliberations.
13. Deliberations of the Court shall be done in private. No verdict may be reached by the Court unless the same majority present during the hearings shall be present during the deliberations among the justices. In such a case where all justices necessary are not present, the lack of a valid reason shall be cause for dismissal.

Check Your Comprehension

1. What are two purposes of the Student Senate?
2. When does the term of office for Senators end?
3. How many days' notice must a defendant be given before a hearing?

Applying the Reading Strategy

Reading Technical Documents

4. Summarize the main point of Article II, Section E, Clause 1.
5. Which article and section supply information about the qualifications needed for candidates to be elected? What are the qualifications?
6. Summarize Article III, number 12.

Activity

Mock Trial

After reading the bylaws of the Student Senate, conduct a mock trial using the Student Rights section. Determine the charge against the student, then assign one team to the prosecution and one to the defense. The rest of the students can serve as the Student Senate members in charge of the hearing. All parties can ask questions and should refer to the bylaws, whenever possible, to make their case.

Comparing and Contrasting Informational Materials

Bylaws and Constitutions

Bylaws sometimes look like another type of technical document: constitutions. The similarity between these two documents is in the formatting and formal language. They are both technical documents and are therefore laid out in a structured format with headings and numbering.

Otherwise, bylaws and constitutions are actually quite different. Constitutions differ from bylaws in their purpose and use. A constitution is a statement that outlines the agreed basic principles of a formal organization. Bylaws address the specific legal aspects of running an organization. They also differ from one another in that a constitution can only be changed when almost all of the members agree. In order to change bylaws, there only needs to be a majority vote.

Find an example of a constitution and compare it to the Student Senate Bylaws using the chart shown.

	Constitutions	Bylaws
Example		
Purpose		
Intended Audience		

Prepare to Read

John Henry ◆ Pecos Bill: The Cyclone ◆
Paul Bunyan of the North Woods ◆ Davy Crockett's Dream

Hammer in His Hand, Palmer C. Hayden, Museum of African American Art, Los Angeles, CA

Take It to the Net

Visit www.phschool.com for interactive activities and instruction related to these selections, including
- background
- graphic organizers
- literary elements
- reading strategies

Preview

Connecting to the Literature

Think about people from real life who perform heroic deeds that amaze and surprise you. The tales in this group—the traditional tale "John Henry," "Paul Bunyan of the North Woods" by Carl Sandburg, "Pecos Bill: The Cyclone" by Harold W. Felton, and "Davy Crockett's Dream" by Davy Crockett—are about several such larger-than-life heroes.

Background

John Henry is believed to have been an actual person who was employed by the Chesapeake and Ohio Railway. Railroad companies boomed during the late 1800s. The Union Pacific Railroad began building tracks west from Omaha, Nebraska, and the Central Pacific Railroad began building tracks east from Sacramento, California. In 1869, the tracks met and were joined with a golden spike, creating the first transcontinental railroad.

Literary Analysis

Cultural Context

The **cultural context** of a literary work includes the traditions, attitudes, and beliefs of the time and place from which the work comes. (Although the works in this group were written down by specific authors, they are retellings of stories from the oral tradition.) The following example reveals some of the cultural context of "Pecos Bill: The Cyclone."

> On this particular Fourth of July, the celebration had gone off fine. The speeches were loud and long. The contests and games were hard fought.

Look for other details that reveal the cultural context of each selection.

Comparing Literary Works

These selections are **tall tales**—humorous stories that exaggerate details to bigger-than-life proportions. Most tall tales have their origins in the American West, during the time that it was still a new frontier. Because survival in such a harsh setting depended on skill and strength, many tall tales exaggerate these qualities.

Compare and contrast these tall tales, noting the values each expresses through its use of exaggeration. Begin by looking for answers to the following focus questions:

1. Which tales exaggerate a character's skill or cleverness?
2. Which tales exaggerate a character's strength?

Reading Strategy

Predicting

Tall tales, like other folk tales, develop in predictable patterns. You can **predict** that the characters will perform exaggerated or even impossible feats. After reading a few paragraphs of each selection, use a chart like the one shown to predict the kinds of events about which the stories will tell.

Selection	
Character traits and other details	Predictions

Vocabulary Development

usurped (yōō surpt´) v. took power or authority away from (p. 941)

invincible (in vin´ sə bəl) adj. unbeatable (p. 942)

futile (fyōōt´ əl) adj. useless; hopeless (p. 942)

inexplicable (in eks´ pli kə bəl) adj. unexplainable (p. 943)

skeptics (skep´ tiks) n. people who frequently doubt and question matters generally accepted. (p. 943)

granite (gran´ it) adj. made of granite, a very hard rock (p. 946)

commotion (kə mō´ shən) n. noisy movement (p. 946)

JOHN HENRY
TRADITIONAL

John Henry was a lil baby,
Sittin' on his mama's knee,
Said: 'The Big Bend Tunnel on the C. & O. road
Gonna cause the death of me,
5   Lawd, Lawd, gonna cause the death of me.'

Cap'n says to John Henry,
'Gonna bring me a steam drill 'round,
Gonna take that steam drill out on the job,
Gonna whop that steel on down,
10   Lawd, Lawd, gonna whop that steel on down.'

John Henry tol' his cap'n,
Lightnin' was in his eye:
'Cap'n, bet yo' las, red cent on me,
Fo' I'll beat it to the bottom or I'll die,
15   Lawd, Lawd, I'll beat it to the bottom or I'll die.'

Sun shine hot an' burnin',
Wer'n't no breeze a-tall,
Sweat ran down like water down a hill,
That day John Henry let his hammer fall,
20   Lawd, Lawd, that day John Henry let his hammer fall.

John Henry went to the tunnel,
An' they put him in the lead to drive,
The rock so tall an' John Henry so small,
That he lied down his hammer an' he cried,
25   Lawd, Lawd, that he lied down his hammer an' he cried.

Literary Analysis
Cultural Context and Tall Tales In what way does John Henry's boast fit the exaggerated portrayals of a tall tale?

▼ **Critical Viewing**
What elements of this photo show the speed and power of a locomotive? **[Interpret]**

John Henry started on the right hand,
The steam drill started on the lef'—
'Before I'd let this steam drill beat me down,
I'd hammer my fool self to death,
30   Lawd, Lawd, I'd hammer my fool self to death.'

John Henry had a lil woman,
Her name were Polly Ann,
John Henry took sick an' had to go to bed,
Polly Ann drove steel like a man,
35   Lawd, Lawd, Polly Ann drove steel like a man.

John Henry said to his shaker,[1]
'Shaker, why don' you sing?
I'm throwin' twelve poun's from my hips on down,
Jes' listen to the col' steel ring,
40   Lawd, Lawd, jes' listen to the col' steel ring.'

Oh, the captain said to John Henry,
'I b'lieve this mountain's sinkin' in.'
John Henry said to his captain, oh my!
'Ain' nothin' but my hammer suckin' win',
45   Lawd, Lawd, ain' nothin' but my hammer suckin' win'.'

---

1. shaker (shā´ kər) *n.* person who sets the spikes and places the drills for a steel-driver to hammer.

Reading Strategy
Predicting Which do you think will win the contest—John Henry or the steam drill? Explain.

✔**Reading Check**

What is John Henry competing against?

He Layed Down His Hammer and Cried, 1944–47, Palmer C. Hayden, Museum of African American Art, Los Angeles, CA

◀ **Critical Viewing**
Does this painting depict John Henry as a superhero or as a man? Explain. **[Evaluate]**

Reading Strategy
Predicting What do you think will be the outcome of the competition? Why?

John Henry tol' his shaker,
'Shaker, you better pray,
For, if I miss this six-foot steel,
Tomorrow'll be yo' buryin' day,
50 Lawd, Lawd, tomorrow'll be yo' buryin' day.'

John Henry tol' his captain,
'Look yonder what I see—
Yo' drill's done broke an' yo' hole's done choke,
An' you cain' drive steel like me,
55 Lawd, Lawd, an' you cain' drive steel like me.'

The man that invented the steam drill,
Thought he was mighty fine.
John Henry drove his fifteen feet,
An' the steam drill only made nine,
60 Lawd, Lawd, an' the steam drill only made nine.

The hammer that John Henry swung,
It weighed over nine pound;
He broke a rib in his lef'-han' side,
An' his intrels[2] fell on the groun',
65 Lawd, Lawd, an' his intrels fell on the groun'.

All the womens in the Wes',
When they heared of John Henry's death,
Stood in the rain, flagged the eas'-boun' train,
Goin' where John Henry fell dead,
70 Lawd, Lawd, goin' where John Henry fell dead.

John Henry's lil mother,
She was all dressed in red,
She jumped in bed, covered up her head,
Said she didn' know her son was dead,
75 Lawd, Lawd, didn' know her son was dead.

Dey took John Henry to the graveyard,
An' they buried him in the san',
An' every locomotive come roarin' by,
Says, 'There lays a steel-drivin' man,
80 Lawd, Lawd, there lays a steel-drivin' man.'

---

2. intrels (en´ trālz) *n.* entrails; internal organs.

Review and Assess

Thinking About the Selection

1. **Respond:** Do you admire John Henry's decision to challenge the steam engine in a steel driving match? Why or why not?

2. **(a) Recall:** What does John Henry promise his captain?
   (b) Analyze: How do the first few stanzas build the drama of the contest?

3. **(a) Infer:** How important is it to John Henry to beat the steam engine? **(b) Support:** What details lead you to make this inference?

4. **(a) Speculate:** Why do you think people pay tribute to John Henry? **(b) Deduce:** What do their tributes tell you about his character?

5. **(a) Interpret:** What qualities of John Henry make him a folk hero? **(b) Draw Conclusions:** Do folk heroes need to be "larger than life"? Explain.

Pecos Bill: The Cyclone

Harold W. Felton

One of Bill's greatest feats, if not the greatest feat of all time, occurred unexpectedly one Fourth of July. He had invented the Fourth of July some years before. It was a great day for the cowpunchers.[1] They had taken to it right off like the real Americans they were. But the celebration had always ended on a dismal note. Somehow it seemed to be spoiled by a cyclone.

Bill had never minded the cyclone much. The truth is he rather liked it. But the other celebrants ran into caves for safety. He invented cyclone cellars for them. He even named the cellars. He called them "'fraid holes." Pecos wouldn't even say the word "afraid." The cyclone was something like he was. It was big and strong too. He always stood by musing[2] pleasantly as he watched it.

The cyclone caused Bill some trouble, though. Usually it would destroy a few hundred miles of fence by blowing the postholes away. But it wasn't much trouble for him to fix it. All he had to do was to go and get the postholes and then take them back and put the fence posts in them. The holes were rarely ever blown more than twenty or thirty miles.

In one respect Bill even welcomed the cyclone, for it blew so hard it blew the earth away from his wells. The first time this happened, he thought the wells would be a total loss. There they were, sticking up several hundred feet out of the ground. As wells they

1. **cowpunchers** (kou´ pun chərz) n. cowboys.
2. **musing** (myo͞oz´ ing) adj. thinking deeply.

▲ **Critical Viewing**
Does this cyclone seem capable of destroying "a few hundred miles of fence"? Explain. **[Assess]**

Literary Analysis
Cultural Context Identify three characteristics of the culture that produced this tale.

were useless. But he found he could cut them up into lengths and sell them for postholes to farmers in Iowa and Nebraska. It was very profitable, especially after he invented a special posthole saw to cut them with. He didn't use that type of posthole himself. He got the prairie dogs to dig his for him. He simply caught a few gross[3] of prairie dogs and set them down at proper intervals. The prairie dog would dig a hole. Then Bill would put a post in it. The prairie dog would get disgusted and go down the row ahead of the others and dig another hole. Bill fenced all of Texas and parts of New Mexico and Arizona in this manner. He took a few contracts and fenced most of the Southern Pacific right of way too. That's the reason it is so crooked. He had trouble getting the prairie dogs to run a straight fence.

As for his wells, the badgers dug them. The system was the same as with the prairie dogs. The labor was cheap so it didn't make much difference if the cyclone did spoil some of the wells. The badgers were digging all of the time anyway. They didn't seem to care whether they dug wells or just badger holes.

One year he tried shipping the prairie dog holes up north, too, for postholes. It was not successful. They didn't keep in storage and they couldn't stand the handling in shipping. After they were installed they seemed to wear out quickly. Bill always thought the difference in climate had something to do with it.

✔**Reading Check**

Where does Pecos Bill get the postholes he sells to farmers in Iowa and Nebraska?

---

3. gross (grōs) *n.* twelve dozen.

It should be said that in those days there was only one cyclone. It was the first and original cyclone, bigger and more terrible by far than the small cyclones of today. It usually stayed by itself up north around Kansas and Oklahoma and didn't bother anyone much. But it was attracted by the noise of the Fourth of July celebration and without fail managed to put in an appearance before the close of the day.

On this particular Fourth of July, the celebration had gone off fine. The speeches were loud and long. The contests and games were hard fought. The high point of the day was Bill's exhibition with Widow Maker, which came right after he showed off Scat and Rat. People seemed never to tire of seeing them in action. The mountain lion was almost useless as a work animal after his accident, and the snake had grown old and somewhat infirm, and was troubled with rheumatism in his rattles. But they too enjoyed the Fourth of July and liked to make a public appearance. They relived the old days.

Widow Maker had put on a good show, bucking as no ordinary horse could ever buck. Then Bill undertook to show the gaits[4] he had taught the palomino.[5] Other mustangs[6] at that time had only two gaits. Walking and running. Only Widow Maker could pace. But now Bill had developed and taught him other gaits. Twenty-seven in all. Twenty-three forward and three reverse. He was very proud of the achievement. He showed off the slow gaits and the crowd was eager for more.

He showed the walk, trot, canter, lope, jog, slow rack, fast rack, single foot, pace, stepping pace, fox trot, running walk and the others now known. Both men and horses confuse the various gaits nowadays. Some of the gaits are now thought to be the same, such as the rack and the single foot. But with Widow Maker and Pecos Bill, each one was different. Each was precise and to be distinguished from the others. No one had ever imagined such a thing.

Then the cyclone came! All of the people except Bill ran into the 'fraid holes. Bill was annoyed. He stopped the performance. The remaining gaits were not shown. From that day to this horses have used no more than the gaits Widow Maker exhibited that day. It is unfortunate that the really fast gaits were not shown. If they were, horses might be much faster today than they are.

Bill glanced up at the cyclone and the quiet smile on his face faded into a frown. He saw the cyclone was angry. Very, very angry indeed.

The cyclone had always been the center of attention. Everywhere it

---

4. gaits (gāts) *n.* foot movements of a horse.
5. palomino (pal′ ə mē′ nō) *n.* a light-tan or golden-brown horse with a cream-colored mane and tail.
6. mustangs (mus′ taŋz) *n.* wild horses.

went people would look up in wonder, fear and amazement. It had been the undisputed master of the country. It had observed Bill's rapid climb to fame and had seen the Fourth of July celebration grow. It had been keeping an eye on things all right.

In the beginning, the Fourth of July crowd had aroused its curiosity. It liked nothing more than to show its superiority and power by breaking the crowd up sometime during the day. But every year the crowd was larger. This preyed on the cyclone's mind. This year it did not come to watch. It deliberately came to spoil the celebration. Jealous of Bill and of his success, it resolved to do away with the whole institution of the Fourth of July once and for all. So much havoc and destruction would be wrought that there would never be another Independence Day Celebration. On that day, in future years, it would circle around the horizon leering[7] and gloating. At least, so it thought.

The cyclone was resolved, also, to do away with this bold fellow who did not hold it in awe and run for the 'fraid hole at its approach. For untold years it had been the most powerful thing in the land. And now, here was a mere man who threatened its position. More! Who had <u>usurped</u> its position!

When Bill looked at the horizon and saw the cyclone coming, he recognized the anger and rage. While a cyclone does not often smile, Bill had felt from the beginning that it was just a grouchy fellow who never had a pleasant word for anyone. But now, instead of merely an unpleasant character, Bill saw all the viciousness of which an angry cyclone is capable. He had no way of knowing that the cyclone saw its kingship tottering and was determined to stop this man who threatened its supremacy.

But Bill understood the violence of the onslaught even as the monster came into view. He knew he must meet it. The center of the cyclone was larger than ever before. The fact is, the cyclone had been training for this fight all winter and spring. It was in best form and at top weight. It headed straight for Bill intent on his destruction. In an instant it was upon him. Bill had sat quietly and silently on the great pacing mustang. But his mind was working rapidly. In the split second between his first sight of the monster and the time for action he had made his plans. Pecos Bill was ready! Ready and waiting!

Green clouds were dripping from the cyclone's jaws. Lightning flashed from its eyes as it swept down upon him. Its plan was to envelop Bill in one mighty grasp. Just as it was upon him, Bill turned Widow Maker to its left. This was a clever move for the cyclone was right-handed, and while it had been training hard to get its left in shape, that was not its best side. Bill gave rein to his mount. Widow Maker wheeled and turned on a dime which

usurped (yōō surpt′) v. took power or authority away from

Reading Check

Why is the cyclone angry with Bill?

---

7. leering (lir′ ing) *adj.* looking with malicious triumph.

Pecos had, with great foresight[8] and accuracy, thrown to the ground to mark the exact spot for this maneuver. It was the first time that anyone had thought of turning on a dime. Then he urged the great horse forward. The cyclone, filled with surprise, lost its balance and rushed forward at an increased speed. It went so fast that it met itself coming back. This confused the cyclone, but it did not confuse Pecos Bill. He had expected that to happen. Widow Maker went into his twenty-first gait and edged up close to the whirlwind. Soon they were running neck and neck.

At the proper instant Bill grabbed the cyclone's ears, kicked himself free of the stirrups and pulled himself lightly on its back. Bill never used spurs on Widow Maker. Sometimes he wore them for show and because he liked the jingling sound they made. They made a nice accompaniment for his cowboy songs. But he had not been singing, so he had no spurs. He did not have his rattlesnake for a quirt.[9] Of course there was no bridle. It was man against monster! There he was! Pecos Bill astride a raging cyclone, slick heeled and without a saddle!

The cyclone was taken by surprise at this sudden turn of events. But it was undaunted. It was sure of itself. Months of training had given it a conviction that it was <u>invincible</u>. With a mighty heave, it twisted to its full height. Then it fell back suddenly, twisting and turning violently, so that before it came back to earth, it had turned around a thousand times. Surely no rider could ever withstand such an attack. No rider ever had. Little wonder. No one had ever ridden a cyclone before. But Pecos Bill did! He fanned the tornado's ears with his hat and dug his heels into the demon's flanks and yelled, "Yipee-ee!"

The people who had run for shelter began to come out. The audience further enraged the cyclone. It was bad enough to be disgraced by having a man astride it. It was unbearable not to have thrown him. To have all the people see the failure was too much! It got down flat on the ground and rolled over and over. Bill retained his seat throughout this ruse.[10] Evidence of this desperate but <u>futile</u> stratagem[11] remains today. The great Staked Plains, or as the Mexicans call it, *Llano Estacado* is the result. Its small, rugged mountains were covered with trees at the time. The rolling of the cyclone destroyed the mountains, the trees, and almost everything else in the area. The destruction was so

---

8. **foresight** (fôr′ sīt) *n.* the act of seeing beforehand.
9. **quirt** (kwurt) *n.* short-handled riding whip with a braided rawhide lash.
10. **ruse** (ro͞oz) *n.* trick.
11. **stratagem** (strat′ ə jəm) *n.* plan for defeating an opponent.

Literature in context Science Connection

Cyclones

If Pecos Bill were wrestling a *real* cyclone, or tornado, his arms might need to be hundreds of yards long (and very strong) just to get a hold of one! Cyclones have been spotted that were over a mile wide and spread damage along a fifty mile path. A cyclone is an area of rapidly spinning winds that is associated with severe thunderstorms. The rotating winds can reach speeds of 250 mph and are capable of lifting even very heavy objects into the column of circulating air. The scientific cause of cyclones involves warm and cold masses of air colliding with abrupt changes in wind speed and direction. Unlike Pecos Bill, most people are smart enough to take shelter underground when they see a cyclone coming.

invincible (in vin′ sə bəl) *adj.* unbeatable

futile (fyo͞ot′ əl) *adj.* useless; hopeless

complete, that part of the country is flat and treeless to this day. When the settlers came, there were no landmarks to guide them across the vast unmarked space, so they drove stakes in the ground to mark the trails. That is the reason it is called "Staked Plains." Here is an example of the proof of the events of history by careful and painstaking research. It is also an example of how seemingly <u>inexplicable</u> geographical facts can be explained.

It was far more dangerous for the rider when the cyclone shot straight up to the sky. Once there, the twister tried the same thing it had tried on the ground. It rolled on the sky. It was no use. Bill could not be unseated. He kept his place, and he didn't have a sky hook with him either.

As for Bill, he was having the time of his life, shouting at the top of his voice, kicking his opponent in the ribs and jabbing his thumb in its flanks. It responded and went on a wild bucking rampage over the entire West. It used all the bucking tricks known to the wildest broncos as well as those known only to cyclones. The wind howled furiously and beat against the fearless rider. The rain poured. The lightning flashed around his ears. The fight went on and on. Bill enjoyed himself immensely. In spite of the elements he easily kept his place. . . .

The raging cyclone saw this out of the corner of its eye. It knew then who the victor was. It was twisting far above the Rocky Mountains when the awful truth came to it. In a horrible heave it disintegrated! Small pieces of cyclone flew in all directions. Bill still kept his seat on the main central portion until that rained out from under him. Then he jumped to a nearby streak of lightning and slid down it toward earth. But it was raining so hard that the rain put out the lightning. When it fizzled out from under him, Bill dropped the rest of the way. He lit in what is now called Death Valley. He hit quite hard, as is apparent from the fact that he so compressed the place that it is still two hundred and seventy-six feet below sea level. The Grand Canyon was washed out by the rain, though it must be understood that this happened after Paul Bunyan had given it a good start by carelessly dragging his ax behind him when he went west a short time before.

The cyclones and the hurricanes and the tornadoes nowadays are the small pieces that broke off of the big cyclone Pecos Bill rode. In fact, the rainstorms of the present day came into being in the same way. There are always <u>skeptics</u>, but even they will recognize the logic of the proof of this event. They will recall that even now it almost always rains on the Fourth of July. That is because the rainstorms of today still retain some of the characteristics of the giant cyclone that met its comeuppance at the hands of Pecos Bill.

inexplicable
(in eks´ pli kə bəl) *adj.*
unexplainable

Literary Analysis
Cultural Context Do you think the original storytellers believed these explanations? Explain.

skeptics (skep´ tiks) *n.* people who frequently doubt and question matters generally accepted

✔**Reading Check**

What did Bill do with the cyclone?

Bill lay where he landed and looked up at the sky, but he could see no sign of the cyclone. Then he laughed softly as he felt the warm sand of Death Valley on his back. . . .

It was a rough ride though, and Bill had resisted unusual tensions and pressures. When he got on the cyclone he had a twenty-dollar gold piece and a bowie knife[12] in his pocket. The tremendous force of the cyclone was such that when he finished the ride he found that his pocket contained a plugged nickel[13] and a little pearl-handled penknife. His two giant six-shooters were compressed and transformed into a small water pistol and a popgun.

It is a strange circumstance that lesser men have monuments raised in their honor. Death Valley is Bill's monument. Sort of a monument in reverse. Sunk in his honor, you might say. Perhaps that is as it should be. After all, Bill was different. He made his own monument. He made it with his hips, as is evident from the great depth of the valley. That is the hard way.

---

12. **bowie** (bō´ ē) **knife** a strong, single-edged hunting knife named after James Bowie (1799–1836), a soldier.
13. **plugged nickel** fake nickel.

Review and Assess

Thinking About the Selection

1. **Respond:** Which parts of the story did you find humorous? Explain.

2. **(a) Recall:** Describe three human characteristics of the cyclone. **(b) Infer:** Name one way in which the cyclone resembles Pecos Bill himself.

3. **(a) Recall:** Why does Bill call the cyclone cellars "'fraid holes"? **(b) Interpret:** What do you learn about the character of Pecos Bill from his reaction to the cellars?

4. **(a) Analyze:** Explain the meaning of these sentences: "Death Valley is Bill's monument. Sort of a monument in reverse." **(b) Speculate:** How large do you think Pecos Bill is? How can you tell?

5. **(a) Recall:** What word is Bill unwilling to say aloud? **(b) Draw Conclusions:** How does his resolve never to say this word explain why he is a folk hero?

Harold W. Felton

(1902–1991)

Harold William Felton practiced law and worked for the Internal Revenue Service, yet he became increasingly interested in the legends and folklore of the United States. He published collections of stories about folk heroes and the cowboys of the West, including *Legends of Paul Bunyan*, which contains more than one hundred stories about the great logging hero.

Paul Bunyan
of the North Woods

Carl Sandburg

Who made Paul Bunyan, who gave him birth as a myth, who joked him into life as the Master Lumberjack, who fashioned him forth as an apparition[1] easing the hours of men amid axes and trees, saws and lumber? The people, the bookless people, they made Paul and had him alive long before he got into the books for those who read. He grew up in shanties, around the hot stoves of winter, among socks and mittens drying, in the smell of tobacco smoke and the roar of laughter mocking the outside weather. And some of Paul came overseas in wooden bunks below decks in sailing vessels. And some of Paul is old as the hills, young as the alphabet.

---

1. **apparition** (ap´ ə rish´ ən) *n.* a strange figure appearing suddenly or in an extraordinary way.

The Pacific Ocean froze over in the winter of the Blue Snow and Paul Bunyan had long teams of oxen hauling regular white snow over from China. This was the winter Paul gave a party to the Seven Axmen. Paul fixed a <u>granite</u> floor sunk two hundred feet deep for them to dance on. Still, it tipped and tilted as the dance went on. And because the Seven Axmen refused to take off their hob-nailed boots, the sparks from the nails of their dancing feet lit up the place so that Paul didn't light the kerosene lamps. No women being on the Big Onion river at that time the Seven Axmen had to dance with each other, the one left over in each set taking Paul as a partner. The <u>commotion</u> of the dancing that night brought on an earthquake and the Big Onion river moved over three counties to the east.

One year when it rained from St. Patrick's Day till the Fourth of July, Paul Bunyan got disgusted because his celebration on the Fourth was spoiled. He dived into Lake Superior and swam to where a solid pillar of water was coming down. He dived under this pillar, swam up into it and climbed with powerful swimming strokes, was gone about an hour, came splashing down, and as the rain stopped, he explained, "I turned the darn thing off." This is told in the Big North Woods and on the Great Lakes, with many particulars.

Two mosquitoes lighted on one of Paul Bunyan's oxen, killed it, ate it, cleaned the bones, and sat on a grub shanty picking their teeth as Paul came along. Paul sent to Australia for two special bumblebees to kill these mosquitoes. But the bees and the mosquitoes intermarried; their children had stingers on both ends. And things kept getting worse till Paul brought a big boatload of sorghum² up from Louisiana and while all the

Paul Bunyan Carrying a Tree on His Shoulder and an Ax in His Hand

▲ **Critical Viewing**
What impression of Paul Bunyan does this illustration convey?
[Summarize]

granite (gran′ it) *adj.* made of granite, a very hard rock

commotion (kə mō′ shən) *n.* noisy movement

---

2. sorghum (sôr′ gəm) *n.* tropical grasses bearing flowers and seeds, grown for use as grain or syrup.

bee-mosquitoes were eating at the sweet sorghum he floated them down to the Gulf of Mexico. They got so fat that it was easy to drown them all between New Orleans and Galveston.

Paul logged on the Little Gimlet in Oregon one winter. The cookstove at that camp covered an acre of ground. They fastened the side of a hog on each snowshoe and four men used to skate on the griddle while the cook flipped the pancakes. The eating table was three miles long; elevators carried the cakes to the ends of the table where boys on bicycles rode back and forth on a path down the center of the table dropping the cakes where called for.

Benny, the Little Blue Ox of Paul Bunyan, grew two feet every time Paul looked at him, when a youngster. The barn was gone one morning and they found it on Benny's back; he grew out of it in a night. One night he kept pawing and bellowing for more pancakes, till there were two hundred men at the cookshanty stove trying to keep him fed. About breakfast time Benny broke loose, tore down the cookshanty, ate all the pancakes piled up for the loggers' breakfast. And after that Benny made his mistake; he ate the red hot stove; and that finished him. This is only one of the hot-stove stories told in the North Woods.

Review and Assess

Thinking About the Selection

1. **Respond:** Which tall tale about Paul Bunyan is your favorite? Why?
2. **(a) Recall:** What are two of the feats Paul Bunyan performs? **(b) Infer:** What qualities and abilities are valued in this tale?
3. **(a) Recall:** Where does Sandburg say Paul Bunyan came from? **(b) Interpret:** Interpret the following statement: "And some of Paul is old as the hills, young as the alphabet."
4. **(a) Classify:** Identify actions that show Bunyan's cleverness and actions that show his strength. **(b) Support:** Explain how he combines cleverness and strength to achieve his purpose.
5. **(a) Compare and Contrast:** How is "Paul Bunyan of the North Woods" both similar to and different from the folk tales in the preceding group of selections? **(b) Generalize:** What generalization can you make about tall tales based on your reading of this tale?

Carl Sandburg

(1878–1967)

The work of Carl Sandburg—especially the poetry for which he is best known—seemed to speak directly to many of the people of his time. It celebrated the lives and spirit of ordinary Americans of that era. In addition to his work as a poet, Sandburg was also a journalist, an author of children's books, and a historian. Sandburg received two Pulitzer Prizes—one in 1939 for his biography of Abraham Lincoln and one in 1951 for his *Complete Poems*.

Davy Crockett's Dream

Davy Crockett

One day when it was so cold that I was afeard to open my mouth, lest I should freeze my tongue, I took my little dog named Grizzle and cut out for Salt River Bay to kill something for dinner. I got a good ways from home afore I knowed where I was, and as I had swetted some before I left the house my hat froze fast to my head, and I like to have put my neck out of joint in trying to pull it off. When I sneezed the icicles crackled all up and down the inside of my nose, like when you walk over a bog in winter time. The varmints was so scarce that I couldn't find one, and so when I come to an old log hut that had belonged to some squatter that had ben reformed out by the nabors, I stood my rifle up agin one of the door posts and went in. I kindled up a little fire and told Grizzle I was going to take a nap. I piled up a heap of chestnut burs for a pillow and straitened myself out on the ground, for I can curl closer than a rattlesnake and lay straiter than a log. I laid with the back of my head agin the hearth, and my eyes looking up chimney so that I could see when it was noon by the sun, for Mrs. Crockett was always rantankerous[1] when I staid out over the time. I got to sleep before Grizzle had done warming the eend of his nose, and I had swallowed so much cold wind that it laid hard on my stomach, and as I laid gulping and belching the wind went out of me and roared up chimney like a young whirlwind. So I had a pesky dream, and kinder thought, till I waked up, that I was floating down the Massassippy in a holler tree, and I hadn't room to stir my legs and arms no more than they were withed together with young saplings. While I was there and want able to help myself a

---

1. **rantankerous** (ran taŋ´ kər əs) *adj.* dialect for *cantankerous*, meaning "wildly and noisily upset."

◀ **Critical Viewing** Does Davy Crockett, pictured here, look as if he might use "a heap of chestnut burs" for a pillow? Explain. **[Assess]**

Literary Analysis
Cultural Context What does the first paragraph reveal about the author's traditions and attitudes?

✔**Reading Check**

What does Crockett do in the old log hut?

feller called Oak Wing that lived about twenty miles off, and that I had give a most almighty licking once, cum and looked in with his blind eye that I had gouged out five years before, and I saw him looking in one end of the hollow log, and he axed me if I wanted to get out. I told him to tie a rope to one of my legs and draw me out as soon as God would let him and as much sooner as he was a mind to. But he said he wouldn't do it that way, he would ram me out with a pole. So he took a long pole and rammed it down agin my head as if he was ramming home the cattridge in a cannon. This didn't make me budge an inch, but it pounded my head down in between my shoulders till I look'd like a turcle with his head drawn in. This started my temper a trifle, and I ript and swore till the breath boiled out of the end of the log like the steam out of the funnel pipe of a steemboat. Jest then I woke up, and seed my wife pulling my leg, for it was enermost sundown and she had cum arter me. There was a long icicle hanging to her nose, and when she tried to kiss me, she run it right into my eye. I told her my dreem, and sed I would have revenge on Oak Wing for pounding my head. She said it was all a dreem and that Oak was not to blame; but I had a very diffrent idee of the matter. So I went and talked to him, and told him what he had done to me in a dreem, and it was settled that he should make me an apology in his next dreem, and that wood make us square,[2] for I don't like to be run upon when I'm asleep, any more than I do when I'm awake.

2. **square** even.

Review and Assess

Thinking About the Selection

1. **Respond:** Do you think you would like Davy Crockett if you met him? Why or why not?

2. **(a) Recall:** Identify at least two examples of exaggeration in this tale. **(b) Connect:** Describe how these exaggerations add humor to the tale.

3. **(a) Recall:** How do Crockett and Oak Wing settle the matter of the dream? **(b) Draw Conclusions:** How does this settlement indicate that this is a tall tale?

4. **(a) Analyze:** Do you think that Crockett's descriptions are meant to be taken literally? **(b) Interpret:** How does your answer explain Crockett's anger toward Oak Wing?

5. **(a) Analyze:** How does Crockett's dialect—his regional pronunciation of words and differences in grammar—affect the narration of the tale? **(b) Modify:** How would the story be different if it had been written in Standard English?

Davy Crockett

(1786–1836)

Davy Crockett was a celebrated frontiersman, a soldier in the Texas Army, and a Tennessee congressman. His tall tales strongly influenced the comic tradition and legendary history of the western frontier. He fought at the Alamo for Texan independence and was killed there by Mexican troops.

Davy Crockett was also known as a family man and a politician with integrity. His autobiography has been called "clever fiction."

Review and Assess

Literary Analysis

Cultural Context

1. **(a)** Use a chart like the one shown to note at least four examples of **cultural context** that you find in these works. **(b)** Then, select an adjective to describe the image of the American West of the 1800s each example conveys.

Identify Cultural Context

Selection	Element of Cultural Context	Image Conveyed
"John Henry"		
"Pecos Bill"		
"Paul Bunyan"		
"Davy Crockett"		

2. Based on these selections, what personal qualities did people in the American West of the 1800s value?

Comparing Literary Works

3. Review these **tall tales**, noting **(a)** two examples of exaggerated characters, **(b)** two examples of exaggerated events, and **(c)** two examples of exaggerated descriptions of the landscape or the weather.

4. For each story, how do these uses of exaggeration help to emphasize a cultural belief or value?

5. If you were to tell one of these tall tales as an ordinary story, which descriptions of characters or events would you change or omit? Why?

Reading Strategy

Predicting

6. What details early in "John Henry" might lead you to **predict** that Henry's contest with the steam drill will cause his death?

7. What prediction can you make about "Pecos Bill: The Cyclone" based on the first two paragraphs?

8. Did you predict that Davy Crockett might interpret his dream literally? Why or why not?

Extend Understanding

9. **Math Connection:** If the rock through which the railroad tunnel was being built were two miles thick, how many days would it take John Henry and the steam drill to drill through it? (Assume the contest in "John Henry" took place in one day.)

Quick Review

The **cultural context** of a literary work is the traditions, attitudes, and beliefs of the time and place in which the work originated. To review cultural context, see page 933.

Tall tales are humorous stories that use exaggeration. To review tall tales, see page 933.

When you **predict**, you use details from the text to guess about future story events. To review predicting, see page 933.

 Take It to the Net
www.phschool.com
Take the interactive self-test online to check your understanding of these selections.

Integrate Language Skills

Vocabulary Development Lesson

Word Analysis: Forms of *skeptic*

Knowing that *skeptic* means "a person who doubts what others accept as true," you can figure out the meaning of related words. Complete the following sentences with words related to *skeptic*:

skeptically   skeptical   skepticism

1. She remained ___?___ about bungee jumping, even though several people assured her that it was safe.
2. Before signing the standard lease, the renter ___?___ reviewed the contract again.
3. Even though we assure him, my grandfather expresses ___?___ that the latest technological devices will work.

Grammar Lesson

Commas in Complex Sentences

A **complex sentence** consists of one independent clause and one or more subordinate clauses. Subordinate clauses are separated from the independent clause with commas when they are introductory clauses or when they are not essential to the meaning of the sentence.

As John Henry grew a bit older, he practiced swinging the hammer.

The crowd cheered loudly for John Henry, *who was well ahead of the steam drill*.

Commas are not used when a subordinate clause is essential to the meaning of a sentence.

The person *who grieved the longest for John Henry* was his mother.

Fluency: Sentence Definitions

On your paper, match each vocabulary word with its definition.

1. granite   a. doubters
2. commotion   b. useless
3. usurped   c. took power
4. invincible   d. unexplainable
5. futile   e. hard stone
6. inexplicable   f. unbeatable
7. skeptics   g. disturbance

Spelling Strategy

Most multisyllable words with the *m* sound in the middle, like *commotion*, are spelled with two *m*s, not one. Practice this rule by correcting the spelling of the following words:

1. comitment 2. comander 3. accomodate

▶ *For more practice, see page R34, Exercise A.*

Practice On your paper, rewrite the following sentences, adding commas where necessary.

1. When he saw the pillar of water Paul Bunyan swam up into it.
2. Benny who was Bunyan's ox grew rapidly.
3. If the cyclone reappeared Pecos Bill was determined to meet it head-on.
4. The small cyclones that we see today are pieces of the original cyclone.
5. When he awoke from his dream Davy Crockett wanted revenge against the man who had rammed the pole against his head.

Writing Application Add a subordinate clause to each sentence above. Use commas as needed.

W̶G *Prentice Hall Writing and Grammar Connection: Chapter 20, Section 2, and Chapter 26, Section 2*

Writing Lesson

Résumé for John Henry

When John Henry was a "lil baby," he already knew he was destined to be a steel-driver, helping to build the railroad. Write a résumé that he might use to search for a job. Use your sense of humor to compose an exaggerated version of a standard résumé, but choose formal language as you draft.

Prewriting   Make notes about the kinds of experience and training John Henry might include in his résumé. List jobs he might have had before becoming a steel-driver.

Drafting   Include John Henry's name, address, and phone number at the top of the page. Then, use the headings *Qualifications*, *Work Experience*, *Education*, and *Awards* to organize his experience and training.

Model: Drafting

Qualifications

Possess amazing physical strength and strong sense of competition.

Enjoy besting machines at their games.

Work Experience

1851-52   Well-digger, Tom's Well Service

Served as one-man team digging wells for homesteaders.

1850-51   Performer, Bob's Circus

Challenged machines to duels. Always won.

Revising   Ask a classmate to read the résumé and identify sections lacking information. Add details to complete John Henry's profile.

WG Prentice Hall Writing and Grammar Connection: Chapter 3, Section 3

Extension Activities

Research and Technology In "Pecos Bill: The Cyclone," the hero is said to have created many natural wonders. With a small group of classmates, research scientific explanations for the origins for the Great Plains, Death Valley, and the Grand Canyon. Then, write a brief **report** that compares and contrasts the tall-tale and scientific versions of these origins. Share your report with the class. **[Group Activity]**

Listening and Speaking Continue the oral tradition by presenting a **tall tale** of your own. Be sure your story has a beginning, middle, and end, and include the following elements: dialogue, action, and description.

 **Take It to the Net**   www.phschool.com

Go online for an additional research activity using the Internet.

CONNECTIONS
Literature and History

Heroes: Fiction and Fact

Some folk heroes, like John Henry, seemed larger than life even when they were alive, and grow larger as the stories of their feats are told. Legendary heroes like Paul Bunyan and Pecos Bill are "joked . . . into life," as Carl Sandburg says, by people telling tall tales to pass the time. Davy Crockett was a real man who became a legendary hero by telling tall tales about himself and his adventures in the unsettled American lands known as "the wild frontier."

The New Frontier

By the middle of the twentieth century, virtually all large tracts of land in the United States had been developed and populated. When John F. Kennedy was elected President in 1960, he began using the term "The New Frontier." He said Americans needed to think of ways to replace the frontier that no longer existed. As one replacement, Kennedy suggested Americans begin thinking about exploring the last frontier—the moon.

"The Right Stuff"

One of the biggest news topics of the 1960s was the preparation for the first flight to the moon. Tom Wolfe later wrote a book about the former test pilots who were selected and the rigorous training they underwent for the trip into space. It was a difficult and very dangerous job, requiring levels of ability and courage that few people had. The outstanding qualities needed to be an astronaut were known as "the right stuff." This phrase became the title of Wolfe's book.

The following excerpt from *The Right Stuff* tells how Alan Shepard was elevated to the status of a hero following a ground-breaking rocket flight—going 5,134 miles per hour for 15 minutes, 28 seconds, at an altitude of 116.5 statute miles. As you read, think about the qualities that make Alan Shepard a modern American hero.

▶ **Critical Viewing** This photograph captures Alan Shepard being honored in a parade. What evidence shows that he had become a hero of the people? **[Connect]**

from THE RIGHT STUFF

Tom Wolfe

Glenn[1] and the others now watched from the sidelines as Al Shepard[2] was hoisted out of their midst and installed as a national hero on the order of a Lindbergh.[3] That was the way it looked. As soon as his technical debriefings[4] had been completed, Shepard was flown straight from Grand Bahama Island to Washington. The next day the six also-rans[5] joined him there. They stood by as President Kennedy gave Al the Distinguished Service Medal in a ceremony in the Rose Garden of the White House. Then they followed in his wake as Al sat up on the back of an open limousine waving to the crowds along Constitution Avenue. Tens of thousands of people had turned out to watch the motorcade, even though it had been arranged with barely twenty-four hours' notice. They were screaming to Al, reaching out, crying, awash with awe and gratitude. It took the motorcade half an hour to travel the one mile from the White House to the Capitol. Al sometimes seemed to have transistors in his solar plexus.[6] But not now; now he seemed truly moved. They adored him. He was on . . . the Pope's balcony . . . Thirty minutes of it . . . The next day New York City gave Al a ticker-tape parade up Broadway. There was Al on the back ledge of the limousine, with all that paper snow and confetti coming down, just the way you used to see it in the Movietone News in the theaters. Al's hometown, Derry, New

Shepard's Flight
Altitude: 116.5 statute miles
Duration: 15 min., 28 sec.
Distance: 303 statue miles
Velocity: 5,134 m.p.h.

---

1. **Glenn** John Herschel Glenn, Jr. (b. 1921); first American to orbit the Earth (1962).
2. **Shepard** Alan B. Shepard, Jr. (1923–1998); on May 5, 1961, he became the first U.S. astronaut to travel in space.
3. **Lindbergh** (lind´ bərg): Charles Augustus Lindbergh (1902–1974); U.S. navigator who made the first nonstop flight from New York to Paris in 1927.
4. **debriefings** information given concerning a flight or mission just completed.
5. **also-rans** nonwinners in a race, competition, or election.
6. **seemed to have transistors in his solar plexus** showed little or no emotion.

Hampshire, which was not much more than a village, gave Al a parade, and it drew the biggest crowd the state had ever seen. Army, Navy, Marine, Air Force, and National Guard troops from all over New England marched down Main Street, and aerobatic teams of jet fighters flew overhead. The politicians thought New Hampshire was entering Metro Heaven and came close to renaming Derry "Spacetown U.S.A." before they got hold of themselves. In the town of Deerfield, Illinois, a new school was named for Al, overnight, just like that. Then Al started getting tons of greeting cards in the mail, cards saying "Congratulations to Alan Shepard, Our First Man in Space!" That was already printed on the cards, along with NASA's address. All the buyers had to do was sign them and mail them. The card companies were cranking these things out. Al was that much of a hero.

Next to Gagarin's[7] orbital flight, Shepard's little mortar lob to Bermuda, with its five minutes of weightlessness, was no great accomplishment. But that didn't matter. The flight had unfolded like a drama, the first drama of *single combat* in American history. Shepard had been the tiny underdog, sitting on top of an American rocket—*and our rockets always blew up*—challenging the omnipotent Soviet Integral.[8] The fact that the entire thing had been televised, starting a good two hours before the liftoff, had generated the most feverish suspense. And then he had gone through with it. He let them light the fuse. *He hadn't resigned.* He hadn't even panicked. He handled himself perfectly. He was as great a daredevil as Lindbergh, and he was purer; he did it all for his country. Here was a man . . . with the right stuff.

---

7. **Gagarin** Yuri Gagarin (1934–1968), a Soviet astronaut, became the first human being to orbit the Earth on April 12, 1961.
8. **omnipotent Soviet Integral** Soviet propaganda claimed that American rockets always blew up.

Connecting Literature and History

1. What details in the selection make Alan Shepard seem like a heroic figure?
2. What does Alan Shepard have in common with John Henry, Paul Bunyan, Pecos Bill, and Davy Crockett? How is his type of heroism different from theirs?
3. What does this selection suggest about heroism and how heroes are made?

Tom Wolfe

(b. 1931)
Tom Wolfe began his career as a reporter in Springfield, Massachusetts, in 1956. He later worked for the *Washington Post* and the *New York Herald Tribune*. His first collection of articles, published in 1965, was entitled *The Kandy-Kolored Tangerine-Flake Streamline Baby*. He has since published eleven books of nonfiction and three novels. He is best known for his style of humorously criticizing some of the more foolish things that Americans do.

READING INFORMATIONAL MATERIALS

Training Manuals

About Training Manuals

Training manuals are written instructions that are designed to help new employees learn job skills. Employers do not expect their employees to come into the workplace knowing everything about their new jobs. That is why they set up training programs, which gradually ease new employees into their new work environment. The training manuals are an important part of this process, since they allow employees to learn on their own—at their own pace.

Training manuals vary in content and form, depending on the type of job that they are designed to teach. Manuals are only a part of most training programs. Many training programs now involve some combination of computer-based and on-the-job training, along with reading training manuals.

Training manuals share the following characteristics:

- A clear indication of what skill or skills are being taught
- Guidelines on how to prepare for your task
- Logical instructions on how to perform the task
- Details that demonstrate what to expect when carrying out the task
- Troubleshooting instructions that explain how to solve common problems

Reading Strategy

Making Inferences

Understanding what you read sometimes requires some thoughtful detective work. Attentive readers use the information the author provides to make inferences. Making inferences requires you to "read between the lines" to arrive at ideas the author suggests, but does not say directly. Make an inference by:

1. Considering the details that the author includes or does not include.
2. Drawing conclusions, based on what this choice of details tells you about the author's purpose in writing.

Use the chart shown to record details and the kinds of conclusions you can draw from them.

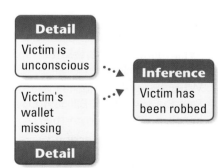

Crime Solving Problems for the Modern Detective

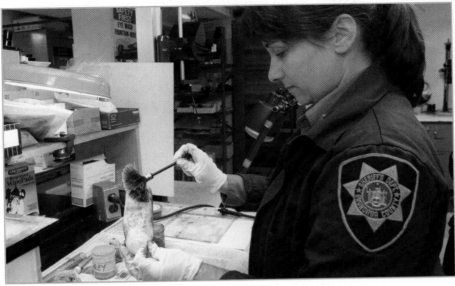

This information was adapted from the workbook of the California Commission on Peace Officer Standards and Training for the "Forensic Technology for Law Enforcement" Telecourse.

The purpose of crime scene investigation is to help establish what happened (crime scene reconstruction) and to identify the responsible person. This is done by carefully documenting the conditions at a crime scene and recognizing all relevant physical evidence. The ability to recognize and properly collect physical evidence is oftentimes critical to both solving and prosecuting violent crimes. It is no exaggeration to say that in the majority of cases, the law enforcement officer who protects and searches a crime scene plays a critical role in determining whether physical evidence will be used in solving or prosecuting violent crimes.

Despite Hollywood's portrayal, crime scene investigation is a difficult and time-consuming job. There is no substitute for a careful and thoughtful approach. An investigator must not leap to an immediate conclusion as to what happened based upon limited information but must generate several different theories of the crime, keeping the ones that are not eliminated by incoming

The opening paragraph describes the set of job skills that the article will teach. It also explains how the task of crime scene investigation is accomplished and the role that trained officers play.

In this sentence, the reader is meant to make the inference that Hollywood's portrayal of crime scene investigations is unrealistic.

information at the scene. Reasonable inferences[1] about what happened are produced from the scene appearance and information from witnesses. These theories will help guide the investigator to document specific conditions and recognize valuable evidence. Documenting crime scene conditions can include immediately recording transient[2] details such as lighting (on/off), drapes (open/closed), weather, or furniture moved by medical teams. Certain evidence such as shoeprints or gunshot residue is fragile and if not collected immediately can easily be destroyed or lost. The scope of the investigation also extends to considerations of arguments which might be generated in this case and documenting conditions which would support or refute these arguments.

In addition, it is important to be able to recognize what should be present at a scene but is not (victim's vehicle/wallet) and objects which appear to be out of place (ski mask) and might have been left by the assailant. It is also important to determine the full extent of a crime scene. A crime scene is not merely the immediate area where a body is located or where an assailant concentrated his activities but can also encompass a vehicle and access/escape routes.

Although there are common items which are frequently collected as evidence (fingerprints, shoeprints, or bloodstains), literally any object can be physical evidence. Anything which can be used to connect a victim to a suspect or a suspect to a victim or crime scene is relevant physical evidence. Using the "shopping list" approach (collecting bloodstains, hairs, or shoeprints) will probably not result in recognizing the best evidence. For example, collecting bloodstains under a victim's body or shoeprints from emergency personnel will rarely answer important questions. Conversely, a single matchstick (usually not mentioned as physical evidence) recovered on the floor near a victim's body can be excellent physical evidence since it can be directly tied to a matchbook found in a suspect's pocket.

Since a weapon or burglar tool is easily recognized as significant physical evidence, it is frequently destroyed by the perpetrator.[3] Sometimes the only remaining evidence is microscopic evidence consisting of hairs, fibers, or other small traces the assailant unknowingly leaves behind or takes with him. Although this evidence is effectively collected when the clothing of the victim or suspect is taken, protocols (involving tape lifts) should be in place so as not to lose this fragile evidence.

> The article describes a common mistake that forensic investigators make and suggests how to avoid this pitfall.

---

1. **inferences** conclusions arrived at through reason
2. **transient** (tran´ sē ənt) *adj.* temporary
3. **perpetrator** (pur pə trāt ər) *n.* one who commits a crime

Check Your Comprehension

1. What is the basic purpose of a crime scene investigation?
2. Why is it vital to document crime scene conditions immediately?
3. Why are certain objects frequently destroyed by the perpetrator?

Applying the Reading Strategy

Making Inferences

4. What can you infer might happen if a law enforcement officer were to jump to conclusions based on limited evidence?
5. Why would it be important to note if a crime victim's wallet were missing?
6. What is the author assuming about the reader when he uses the term "reasonable inferences"?

Activity

Casebook

One way of sharpening your powers of observation and inference can be achieved by picking up a clever detective story or mystery. As you read:

- Keep track of your suspicions about who will eventually get charged with the crime in a casebook or journal.
- Support each theory you develop by interpreting evidence from the book.
- Confirm or refute your final theories at the conclusion of the book.
- Then, go back and read your casebook to see which inferences were correct or where you were led astray.

Comparing Informational Texts

Training Manuals and Textbooks

A training manual and a textbook are both designed to educate. They differ, though, in what they teach and how that information is used. The training manual is focused on a specific set of job-related skills, while textbooks have a more general purpose. Complete a chart like the one shown to explore their differences more fully.

	Training Manual	Literature Textbook
Purpose		
Content		
Format and Organization		

Writing WORKSHOP

Exposition: Guidelines and Rules

Guidelines and rules give the boundaries within which a person or group operates. Like rules, guidelines lead someone through a process or activity. Guidelines list the main ideas or steps in a task, point by point, so that the reader can easily refer to the guidelines while performing the task. In this workshop, you will write clear and complete guidelines.

Assignment Criteria. Your guidelines should have the following characteristics:

● A focused topic that can be fully explained in the length of an essay

● The steps or key ideas needed to complete the activity, presented in a logical order and clearly described

● Tips and strategies that consider all factors and variables of the task

● Text features (headings, fonts, bullets) to aid comprehension

To preview the criteria on which your guidelines may be assessed, see the Rubric on page 965.

Prewriting

Choose a topic. To write effective guidelines, you should know your topic well. Make sure it is simple enough to be covered in a few pages, yet complex enough to require detailed explanations. To begin, **list** activities you know a lot about and might enjoy explaining to someone else.

Examples:

● skateboarding ● creating a personal Web site
● making lasagna ● taking photographs
● washing a dog

Subdivide your topic. Divide your topic into pieces and then choose a method of organization. For example, if your guidelines are how-to directions, use chronological order. An example of how-to guidelines for writing haiku, a Japanese poetic form, is shown at right. Safety tips or suggestions should be in order of importance. A flowchart might be best for guidelines for designing a system or process.

Consider your audience. Determine how much your audience knows about your subject, especially when it comes to specialized terms. For example, guidelines for making lasagna will differ depending on whether they are written for children or adults. Tailor your guidelines to the needs and knowledge level of your audience.

	Guidelines for Writing Haiku
	Audience: Third Graders
🌳	Concentrate on a single image or idea.
	Draft a sentence or two.
123	Count syllables.
📖	Experiment with word choices.
	Move words around.
☀	Look for the surprise.

Student Model

Before you begin drafting your guidelines, read this student model and review the characteristics of successful guidelines.

Sean G. Denard
Naperville, Illinois

Band Rules

For a band to be successful, it must have rules. Following the rules is essential for projecting a professional image and sound for the band.

ATTENDANCE

- Band members must attend all practices.
- Missing more than two practices might mean that the band member might not be allowed to perform. Band members missing a practice must bring a signed note with a legitimate excuse for the absence.
- Band members must always be on time for practice.
- Attending concerts in time to warm up is a necessary requirement.

PRACTICE

- Band members must practice at least 30 minutes daily.
- Members must be familiar with their parts when attending rehearsals.
- Band members who don't know their parts will be assigned additional practice.

INSTRUMENTS

- Band members must keep their instruments tuned and in good condition. They must repair instruments that are defective.
- Members are responsible for bringing their instruments to practices and performances.

COURTESY

- It's vital for band members not to be rude or disrespectful to other members or to the conductor.
- Band members must pay attention to the conductor and not talk during practices or performances.
- The first time members violate a rule, they will not be allowed to perform in a concert. If they continue to violate rules, they will be asked to leave the band.

The topic is manageable and can be addressed in a single page.

Categories of information are called out with capital letters

To help readers, the author uses bullets for quick reference to essential information.

The author uses clear language to emphasize important rules.

The last bullet tells readers the consequences of not following these rules.

Drafting

Elaborate by "exploding the moment." As you draft, you may find that your explanations need more details before your readers will understand exactly what is required. Circle important details that need elaboration. Add details that answer questions such as *What kind? How much? How long?* and *To what degree?*

Formatting

The following formatting can be used to differentiate sections of your document.

Boldface	**Color**
<u>Underscore</u>	**Size**
ALL CAPITALS	• Bullets

Choose the best format. Use headings to emphasize the key points in your guidelines. Using two different fonts may aid comprehension. Italics, underlining, or boldface can give your guidelines a clean, crisp look and highlight key words and phrases. Consider adding pictures, diagrams, or other visual aids if it will help the reader's understanding.

Revising

Revise to include supporting details. If a set of guidelines is too general, it might be of little use to the reader. Make sure that you support each guideline with enough detail to allow the reader to accomplish the task. To do this, use one color highlighter to mark each guideline. Then, use another method to mark the supporting details within each guideline. Review your highlighting.

- Does every guideline have enough supporting details?
- Does every detail clearly support a guideline?
- Are your guidelines arranged in logical order?

Model: Supporting With Details

Band members missing a practice must bring a signed note with a legitimate excuse for the absence.

Missing more than two practices might mean that the band member might not be allowed to perform.

Sean clarifies the rule about missing practices by offering a supporting detail.

Evaluate repeated words. Read your draft aloud, listening and looking for repeated words. Circle them. Evaluate each use to determine whether you might replace an overused word with a synonym or even rewrite the sentence to avoid the repetition.

Example: Fill the *water* tub with tepid water. Make sure the *water* is not too hot.
Fill the tub with tepid water. Make sure it isn't too hot.

Compare the nonmodel and the model. Why is the model more effective than the nonmodel?

Nonmodel	Model
• Band members must always be on time for practice.	• Band members must always be on time for practice.
• Band members must attend concerts and arrive in time to warm up.	• Attending concerts in time to warm up is a requirement.

Publishing and Presenting

Choose one of these ways to share your writing with classmates or a larger audience.

Give a demonstration. Share your guidelines with a listening audience by presenting them as an oral presentation. Use visual aids to support what you say and engage your audience.

Submit your guidelines to a publication. Search either in print or online for a publication that is appropriate to your topic. Submit your guidelines to an editor and cross your fingers that you will see your name on a byline!

 Speaking Connection

To learn more about delivering guidelines in a speech, see the **Listening and Speaking Workshop: Multimedia Presentation,** page 966.

 Prentice Hall Writing and Grammar Connection: Chapter 28, Section 2

Rubric for Self-Assessment

Evaluate your expository set of guidelines using the following criteria and rating scale:

Criteria	Rating Scale				
	Not very				Very
How well are the guidelines focused on one appropriate topic?	1	2	3	4	5
How appropriate is the system of organization you chose?	1	2	3	4	5
How complete and clear are the supporting details?	1	2	3	4	5
How well does the format aid comprehension?	1	2	3	4	5
How clear, precise, and concise is the language?	1	2	3	4	5

Listening and Speaking WORKSHOP

Multimedia Presentation

In a **multimedia presentation**, the speaker enhances an oral presentation by using various forms of media to illustrate main points. With careful planning and creativity, a multimedia presentation can be informative and memorable.

Prepare

Define your ideas. As with a research report, your presentation should flow from a sound and well-written thesis, a clear statement of your main idea. Every detail in your presentation must relate to this thesis. Write a single statement to express your main idea.

Use primary and secondary sources to support your ideas. As you research, record important ideas, concepts, and direct quotations from primary and secondary sources.

- Primary sources give direct contemporary evidence.
- Secondary sources are observations or summaries made later.

Examples of each type of source are listed in the chart shown.

Primary Media Sources	Secondary Media Sources
• taped broadcasts • photographs/slides • first-person accounts • recorded interviews • documentaries	• video documentaries • audio tapes • CD-ROMs • Internet sites

Get equipment ready. As you plan your presentation, list the equipment you will need. For example, you might list tape recorders, slide projectors, and software. Then, familiarize yourself with the equipment.

Present

Decide which media to use. Base your decision on what you think would make the greatest impact on your audience. Incorporate photographs, charts, maps, multimedia software, and graphs. A variety of visual aids will keep your audience interested and will let you express a lot of information quickly.

Be dramatic. Using multimedia in your presentaion will allow you to be even more dramatic. Set up a photograph with a dramatic description of the setting or events behind it. Remember, if you are excited about your presentation, you can interest your audience as well.

Activity:
Make an Infomercial Using the tips above, prepare a multimedia presentation about some aspect of your school. Consider topics such as these:

- a club
- a sports team
- an upcoming event
- school lunches
- a new teacher
- an exciting new class

Assessment WORKSHOP

Spelling, Capitalization, and Punctuation

The writing sections of some tests require you to read a passage and answer multiple-choice questions about spelling, capitalization, and punctuation. Use the following strategies to help you answer such questions:

Recognize Spelling Errors Check the spelling of each word in the passage. Pay special attention to double consonants (*worry*, not *wory*), irregular verbs (*dealt*, not *dealed*), and words with -ie- or -ei-.

Recognize Capitalization Errors Make sure that the first word in a sentence or a quotation is capitalized, that proper nouns are capitalized, and that no words are capitalized unnecessarily.

Recognize Punctuation Errors Check end punctuation and determine whether quotation marks and parentheses are closed.

Sample Test Item

Directions: Read the passage and decide which type of error, if any, appears in each sentence.

(1) Windmills are old and new. (2) The first ones were used more then a thousand years ago in Persia. (3) Modern windmills called wind turbines convert wind energy into electricity. (4) some are powered by the wind produced by speeding cars.

1. **A** Spelling error   **C** Punctuation error
   B Capitalization error **D** No error

2. **A** Spelling error   **C** Punctuation error
   B Capitalization error **D** No error

3. **A** Spelling error   **C** Punctuation error
   B Capitalization error **D** No error

4. **A** Spelling error   **C** Punctuation error
   B Capitalization error **D** No error

Answers and Explanations

For sentence 1, there are no errors, so **D** is correct. For sentence 2, *then* should be *than*, so **A** is correct. For sentence 3, "called wind turbines" should be set off with commas, so **C** is correct. For sentence 4, *some* should be capitalized, so **B** is correct.

▶ Practice

Directions: Read the passage and decide which type of error, if any, appears in each sentence.

(1) Yellowstone national Park has something for everyone. (2) Hikers, boaters, skiers campers and photographers can all find lots of ways to have fun. (3) In 1872, Yellowstone became the country's first national park. (4) More than one hundred years later, it is still impresing visitors.

1. **A** Spelling error   **C** Punctuation error
   B Capitalization error **D** No error

2. **A** Spelling error   **C** Punctuation error
   B Capitalization error **D** No error

3. **A** Spelling error   **C** Punctuation error
   B Capitalization error **D** No error

4. **A** Spelling error   **C** Punctuation error
   B Capitalization error **D** No error

RESOURCES

Handbooks

Indexes

Following are some suggestions for longer works that will give you the opportunity to experience the fun of sustained reading. Each of the suggestions further explores one of the themes in this book. All of the titles are included in the **Prentice Hall Literature Library**, featuring the **Penguin Literature Library.**

You may want to consult your teacher before choosing one of these longer works.

Unit 1: Coming of Age

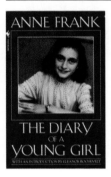

The Diary of a Young Girl
Anne Frank, translated by B. M. Mooyaart-Doubleday
Bantam Books 1952, 1967

In 1942, with Nazis occupying Holland, a thirteen-year-old Jewish girl and her family flee their home in Amsterdam and go into hiding. For the next two years, until their whereabouts are betrayed to the Gestapo, they and another family live in the "Secret Annex" of an old office building. Cut off from the outside world, they face hunger and boredom in addition to the constant tension of living in confined quarters and the ever-present threat of discovery and death. In her diary, Anne Frank recorded vivid impressions of her experiences during this period.

Someone is Hiding on Alcatraz Island
Eve Bunting
Berkley Books, 1984

When Danny saves an old woman from a mugger's attack, he does not expect to tangle with the toughest guys in school, the Outlaws. It turns out that the mugger he fought off is the Outlaw leader's brother. Desperation overcomes Danny's paralyzing fear and he tries to escape by heading to Alcatraz Island, the site of a notorious federal prison that once housed some of the country's most dangerous criminals. Once on the island, terror must give way to action when Danny realizes the Outlaws have followed him.

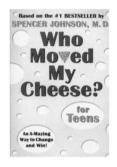

Who Moved My Cheese? for Teens
Spencer Johnson, M.D.
G. P. Putnam's Sons, 2002

This simple story is meant to help people deal with the changes in their lives. In it, four characters live in a "Maze" and look for "Cheese" to nourish them and make them happy. "Cheese" is a symbol that stands for what you want to achieve in life—whether it is doing well at school, making a team, or just feeling good about yourself. The "Maze" is where you look for what you want. In the story, the characters are faced with unexpected change, and they deal with it in different ways. The original version of *Who Moved My Cheese?* has sold over one million copies worldwide.

Boy: Tales of Childhood
Roald Dahl
Puffin Books, 1984

This nonfiction book covers selected events from Roald Dahl's childhood. Dahl's upbringing was, by any standard, eccentric. In *Boy,* he describes some of his adventures at boarding school, the car accident in which he almost lost his nose, and the "Great Mouse Plot" of 1924. Aside from being entertaining, *Boy* helps readers understand Dahl's reasons for choosing some of the subjects of his novels. The book also reveals that several characters in Dahl's novels are based on real people who had a powerful impact on the author's early life.

Famous All Over Town
Danny Santiago
Plume, 1983

Rudy "Chato" Medina lives in East Los Angeles, California, in a Mexican American neighborhood. Chato's street is threatened by the expansion of the "S.P.," the Southern Pacific Railroad, once a giant among American railroad companies. During its history, the S.P. battled with residents over access to land for rail routes. As Chato's family does in the story, residents often lost their battles to this corporate giant.

Unit 2: Meeting Challenges

I, Juan de Pareja with Connected Readings
Elizabeth Borton de Treviño
Pearson Prentice Hall, 2000

Diego Velázquez (1599–1660) was an important Spanish painter who lived and worked for much of his life at the court of King Philip IV of Spain. Juan de Pareja is the slave of Diego Velázquez. Juan helps his master in his studio by preparing paints and stretching canvases. However, Juan is an artist, too. He has taught himself by watching his master's technique. Although such work is forbidden to slaves, Juan cannot keep his secret any longer.

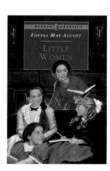

Little Women
Louisa May Alcott
Puffin Books, 1997

This is a story of family, hope, dreams, and growing up, as four devoted sisters search for romance and find maturity in Civil War era New England. Meg, Jo, Beth, and Amy March manage to lead interesting lives despite the fact that their father has gone off to war and their family lacks money. Whether they are putting on a play or forming a secret society, their cheerfulness is infectious. The March family in *Little Women* is based on the author's own family; the character of Jo is based on Louisa herself. Louisa's sisters, Anna, Elizabeth, and May, were the models for Jo's sisters in the book.

Hatchet
Gary Paulsen
Simon & Schuster, 1987

Thirteen-year-old Brian Robeson is on his way to visit his father when the single-engine plane in which he is flying crashes. Suddenly, Brian finds himself alone in the Canadian wilderness with nothing but the clothes he is wearing, a tattered windbreaker, and the hatchet his mother has given him as a gift. Along with these items, he carries the terrible secret that has been tearing him apart ever since his parents' divorce. But now Brian has no time for anger, self-pity, or despair. It will take all his know-how and determination—and all the courage he can muster—to survive.

The Golden Goblet
Eloise Jarvis McGraw
Puffin Books, 1961

This novel is set in ancient Egypt during the reign of Amenhotep III (ca. 1391–ca. 1353 B.C.). Ranofer, an orphan boy, lives with his evil half brother Gebu following the death of their father. Gebu is a stonecutter, and he forces Ranofer to leave his work as a goldsmith's apprentice to work with him at the stonecutting shop. There, Ranofer discovers a dangerous secret about Gebu and puts himself in danger in order to stop his brother's criminal behavior.

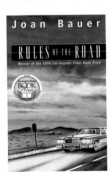

Rules of the Road
Joan Bauer
Puffin Books, 1998

Jenna Boller is the best employee at her branch of Gladstone's Shoes—she can sell anybody *anything*. Her family problems, however, are harder to handle, and there are times when Jenna wishes she could just get out of town and take a break. When Madeline Gladstone, the elderly president of Gladstone Shoe Stores, offers Jenna a job as her driver for the summer, Jenna leaps at the chance—right into the driver's seat. This begins a cross-country adventure from Chicago to Dallas, during which Jenna and Mrs. Gladstone learn about the rules of the road *and* the rules of life.

Unit 3:
Quest for Justice

The Pearl
John Steinbeck
Penguin Books, 1973

Like his father and grandfather before him, Kino is a diver, gathering pearls from the Gulf beds that once brought great wealth to the kings of Spain. On a day like any other, Kino emerges from the sea with a pearl as large as a sea gull's egg, as "perfect as the moon." The poverty-stricken Kino believes that he has found good fortune that will enable him to provide for his family. His wife, Juana, however, fears that the pearl might bring trouble and begs Kino to throw it back into the ocean for her sake and for the welfare of their son. Kino refuses, and the tragic events that follow change their lives forever.

The House of Dies Drear with Connected Readings
Virginia Hamilton
Pearson Prentice Hall, 2000

The house of Dies Drear is not just a new home for the Small family, but an important part of the nation's history. The house, a stop on the Underground Railroad, was built by the abolitionist Dies Drear. Thirteen-year-old Thomas Small finds the house and its surroundings full of mystery. He encounters secret passageways, finds bizarre symbols left by an intruder, and flees in fear from an old man living in the forest. The novel traces the steps Thomas and his family take to solve the mystery surrounding their new home.

They Had a Dream
Jules Archer
Puffin Books, 1993

The people profiled in this book lived in different cities and eras, but they all shared the goal of ending racial discrimination. Frederick Douglass was born a slave and became a leading abolitionist of his time. Marcus Garvey left his home in Jamaica to bring his vision of racial equality to the United States. Martin Luther King, Jr., best known for his efforts in the civil rights movement of the 1950s and 1960s, spread his message of nonviolent protest to thousands of Americans. Malcolm X was drawn to the religion of Islam and believed radicalism was the only way to shake African Americans out of accepting their status as second-class citizens. All four men were instrumental in achieving racial tolerance and social equality for African Americans.

Why We Can't Wait
Martin Luther King, Jr.
Signet Classic, 1964

In 1963, in Birmingham, Alabama, Dr. Martin Luther King, Jr., launched a civil rights campaign that demonstrated to the world the power of nonviolent direct action. *Why We Can't Wait* recounts not only the Birmingham campaign, but also examines the history of the civil rights struggle and the tasks that future generations must accomplish to bring about full equality for African Americans. Dr. King's eloquent analysis of these events propelled the civil rights movement from lunch-counter sit-ins and prayer marches to the forefront of the American consciousness.

The Sherlock Holmes Mysteries
Sir Arthur Conan Doyle
Signet Classic, 1984

In each of these twenty-two stories, fictional detective Sherlock Holmes uses his amazing powers of deduction to solve crimes. Conan Doyle's clever Sherlock Holmes tales not only helped establish the mystery and the short story as popular modern literary forms, but also offered ideas that furthered the study of criminology. The stories take place in England in the late 1800s, when Victoria was queen and the British empire was at its height. In those days, the streets of London were still lit by gas lamps, homes were heated mainly by fireplaces, and communication was by letter or telegram.

Unit 4: From Sea to Shining Sea

The Call of the Wild
Jack London
Tor Books, 1986

In 1897, Jack London joined the Gold Rush in Canada's Yukon Territory. After returning to his native California in 1898, London decided to earn his living as a writer. He wrote *The Call of the Wild* in 1903, setting the novel in the Yukon. In the story, a dog named Buck, half St. Bernard and half German shepherd, is kidnapped from his safe California home and thrown into a life-and-death struggle in the frozen Arctic wilderness. Buck learns many hard lessons when he is forced to become a sled dog—the lesson of the lash, of the cold, of near-starvation, and of cruelty. However, his last owner, John Thornton, teaches Buck the greatest lesson of all—the power of love and loyalty.

Behind the Blue and Gray: The Soldier's Life in the Civil War
Delia Ray
Puffin Books, 1991

Whether they wore Union blue or Confederate gray, the inexperienced recruits of the Civil War quickly learned to endure the hardships of army life. They experienced the horrors of battle, rampant disease, makeshift hospitals and prison camps, and even boredom. Drawing on letters, diaries, eyewitness accounts, and many vintage photographs, this book explores the lives of soldiers from all walks of life—from members of the African American Northern regiments to young boys who lied about their age to enlist.

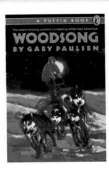

Woodsong
Gary Paulsen
Puffin Books, 1990

When Gary Paulsen travels with his sled dogs, he is up against the most unforgiving side of nature. Facing the brutally cold Minnesota wilderness is a challenge he is determined to survive. After that, the ultimate test is Alaska's Iditarod. Alone, with only his dogs for company, Paulsen begins a thousand-mile trek through frozen Arctic wasteland—a journey that may cost him his life. Because he has been a hunter and a trapper, Paulsen thinks he knows about the outdoors. Instead, he discovers he knows very little until he opens himself to the realities of predators and prey, and to the lessons taught to him by the animals he encounters and the sled dogs he trains and races.

Life on the Mississippi
Mark Twain
Penguin Books, 1984

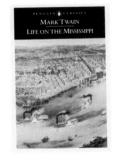

In the 1850s, Mark Twain worked as an apprentice boat pilot on the Mississippi River, accumulating experiences and taking notes that would become the foundation for the book he would write thirty years later. This book is no ordinary guided tour, for every page expresses the structure, style, and high humor that is the very essence of Twain the writer. Filled with Twain's observations and commentaries on the culture and society of the great river valley, the book is a wonderful collection of lively anecdotes, tall tales, and character sketches; historical facts and information; and reminiscences of the author's boyhood and experiences as a steamboat pilot.

Native American Literature
Prentice Hall Literature Library
Pearson Prentice Hall, 2000

This anthology explores the experiences of Native Americans throughout North America—from the Penobscot people of New England to the pueblos, or villages, of the American Southwest and from the Eskimos in Alaska to the Mayan and Aztec civilizations of Central America. The authors include great leaders of the past as well as present-day writers. Joseph Bruchac (b. 1942), for example, is a noted reteller of Native American myths and legends, some of which he learned from his Abenaki mother. Red Cloud (1822–1909) was an important leader of the Oglala branch of the Lakota people. Kiowa author N. Scott Momaday (b. 1934) won the 1969 Pulitzer Prize for his masterful novel of Native American experience, *House Made of Dawn.*

Unit 5:
Extraordinary Occurrences

20,000 Leagues Under the Sea
Jules Verne, translated by Mendor T. Brunetti
Signet Classic, 1969

When a ship hunting a deadly sea monster is destroyed in an explosion, a French scientist, his sidekick, and a Canadian harpoonist are the only survivors. They are then swallowed up by a technological monster—a submarine. The men take part in an underwater odyssey commanded by the madman Captain Nemo. This novel, written in 1870, laid the foundation for much of today's science fiction in its accurate prediction of future technological advances.

The Story of My Life
Helen Keller
Signet Classic, 1988

Helen Keller's triumph over blindness, deafness, and muteness has become one of the most inspiring and well-known stories of our time. Here, in a book first published when she was a young woman, is Helen Keller's own story. Her words offer a unique look directly into the heart of an exceptional woman and reveal her struggles and joys, including the memorable moment when she finally understands that her teacher's finger-spelled letters *w-a-t-e-r* mean the cold fluid rushing over her hand. Keller was always a compassionate advocate for the handicapped, and her sincere and eloquent memoir is deeply moving for the sighted and the blind, the hearing and the deaf, and the young and the old.

Ordeal by Sea:
The Tragedy of the
U.S.S. *Indianapolis*
Thomas Helm
Signet, 2001

At midnight on July 30, 1945, the heavy cruiser U.S.S. *Indianapolis,* having just delivered the Hiroshima atom bomb to the island of Tinian, hurried to rendezvous with the Pacific fleet. One minute later, a Japanese torpedo slammed into her starboard bow. The ship began sinking rapidly, the order to abandon ship was given, and 1,196 men went into the water. By the time help arrived, 317 remained. What happened during those five awful days would become the stuff of legend—*and* nightmare.

Around the World
in Eighty Days
**Jules Verne, translated by
Jacqueline Rogers**
Signet Classic, 1991

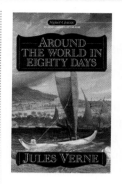

An English gentleman makes an amazing bet—he will travel around the world in eighty days or forfeit his life's savings. Phileas Fogg and his faithful manservant, Jean Passepartout, embark on a fantastic journey into a world filled with danger and beauty. On the exotic shores of India, the heroic travelers rescue a beautiful Raja's wife from ritual sacrifice. Later, on the rugged American frontier, their train is ambushed by an angry Sioux tribe. Fogg's mission is further complicated by an incredible case of mistaken identity that sends a Scotland Yard detective in hot pursuit. These are just a few of the many exciting adventures readers encounter in this classic novel.

The War of the Worlds
H. G. Wells
Signet Classic, 1986

"No one would have believed in the last years of the nineteenth century that this world was being watched keenly and closely by intelligences greater than man's and yet as mortal as his own. . . ." So begins *The War of the Worlds,* the science-fiction classic that first proposed the possibility of intelligent life on other planets. This compelling tale describes the Martian invasion of Earth. Ten huge and tireless creatures land in England, and complete chaos erupts. Using their fiery heat rays and crushing strength, the heartless aliens just may succeed in silencing all opposition.

abyss (ə bis´) *n.* great depth

acquire (ə kwīr´) *v.* to get, come to have as one's own

acute (ə kyōōt´) *adj.* sensitive

aerobatic (er´ ə bat´ ik) *adj.* performing loops, rolls, etc., with an airplane; stunt-like

affluence (af´ lōō əns) *n.* wealth; abundance

aggregation (ag´ grə gā´ shən) *n.* group or mass of distinct objects or individuals

aghast (ə gäst´) *adj.* feeling great horror

alienate (āl yən āt´) *v.* to make unfriendly

amiss (ə mis´) *adj.* wrongly placed; faulty

ancestral (an ses´ trəl) *adj.* of or inherited from one's forefathers or ancestors

anguish (aŋ´ gwish) *n.* great worry

anonymously (ə nän´ ə məs lē) *adv.* with the name withheld or secret

antithesis (an tith´ ə sis) *n.* contrast or opposition of thought

anxiously (aŋk´ shəs lē) *adv.* in a worried way

apprehension (ap´ rə hen´ shən) *n.* 1 anxiety that something bad will happen; 2 perception

apprenticed (ə pren´ tist) *v.* contracted to learn a trade under a skilled worker

arduous (är´ jōō əs) *adj.* difficult to do; laborious

ascent (ə sent´) *n.* the act of climbing or rising

assiduously (ə sij´ ōō wəs lē) *adv.* carefully and busily

august (ô gust´) *adj.* honored

austere (ô stir´) *adj.* showing strict self-discipline

authentic (ô then´ tik) *adj.* genuine; real

bachelor (bach´ ə lər) *n.* a man who has not married

banked (baŋkt) *adj.* adjusted to burn slowly and long

bargain (bär´ gən) *n.* agreement, contract

barren (bar´ ən) *adj.* sterile; empty

beckoned (bek´ ənd) *v.* summoned by a silent motion; called

benediction (ben´ ə dik´ shən) *n.* blessing

benign (bi nīn´) *adj.* kindly

blunders (blun´ dərz) *n.* careless mistakes

borne (bôrn) *v.* carried

brandishing (bran´ dish iŋ) *v.* waving or exhibiting in a challenging way

breakers (brāk´ ərs) *n.* waves that break into foam

brittle (brit´ əl) *adj.* stiff and unbending in manner; lacking warmth

broached (brōcht) *v.* started a discussion about a topic

burrow (bur´ ō) *n.* passage or hole for shelter

cajoling (kə jōl´ iŋ) *v.* coaxing gently

camouflage (kam´ ə fläzh´) *n.* disguise or concealment

canter (kan´ tər) *v.* ride at a gentle pace

capricious (kə prē´ shəs) *adj.* tending to change abruptly and without apparent reason

catapults (kat´ ə pults´) *v.* launches; leaps

celestial (sə les´ chəl) *adj.* of heaven; divine

chronic (krän´ ik) *adj.* continuing indefinitely; perpetual; constant

cinched (sincht) *v.* bound firmly; tightly fastened

coincidental (kō in´ sə dent´ əl) *adj.* occurring at the same time or place

colossal (kə läs´ əl) *adj.* astonishingly great

commenced (kə menst´) *v.* started; began

commotion (kə mō´ shən) *n.* noisy movement

compensate (käm´ pən sāt´) *v.* to repay

competent (käm´ pə tənt) *adj.* well qualified and capable

complacent (kəm plā´ sənt) *adj.* self-satisfied

compounded (käm pound´ əd) *adj.* mixed or combined

compulsory (kəm pul´ sə rē) *adj.* enforced; required

conceivably (kən sē´ və blē) *adv.* possibly

conception (kən sep´ shən) *n.* an original idea, design, plan, etc.

configuration (kən fig´ yōō rā´ shən) *n.* structure; arrangement

conscience (kän´ shəns) *n.* knowledge or sense of right and wrong

conspicuous (kən spik´ yōō əs) *adj.* noticeable

constellation (kän´ stə lā´ shən) *n.* group of stars named after an object, an animal, or character

contiguous (kən tig´ yōō əs) *adj.* in physical contact; near or next to

convulsed (kən vulst´) *adj.* taken over by violent, involuntary spasms

cordially (kôr´ jəl lē) *adv.* warm and friendly

couched (koucht) *v.* put into words; expressed

countenance (koun´ tə nəns) *n.* the look on a person's face that shows his or her nature

credibility (kred´ ə bil´ ə tē) *n.* believability

crevice (krev´ is) *n.* a narrow opening

criteria (krī tir´ ē ə) *n.* standards or tests by which something can be judged

cunningly (kun´ iŋ lē) *adv.* skillfully

decisive (de sī´ siv) *adj.* having the power to settle a question

defray (di frā´) *v.* to pay or furnish the money for

degrading (dē grād´ iŋ) *adj.* insulting; dishonorable

deliberating (di lib´ ə rā tiŋ) *v.* thinking or considering very carefully and fully

derision (di rizh´ ən) *n.* contempt; ridicule

descent (dē sent´) *n.* the act of climbing down

devices (di vīs´ ez) *n.* ways of amusing yourself

devoid (di void´) *adj.* completely without

devoured (di vourd´) *v.* ate greedily

diagnostic (dī´ əg näs´ tik) *adj.* providing a distinguishing sign

diffused (di fyōōsd´) *v.* spread out widely into different directions

diligent (dil´ ə jənt) *adj.* done with careful, steady effort; hardworking

diplomatic (dip´ lə mat´ ik) *adj.* tactful; showing skill in dealing with people

discreet (di skrēt´) *adj.* careful about what one says or does; prudent

discreetly (di skrēt´ lē) *adv.* carefully; silently

disheveled (di shev´ əld) *adj.* untidy; messy

dispatched (di spacht´) *v.* put an end to; killed

dissimulation (di sim´ yə lā´ shən) *n.* hiding of one's feelings or purposes

dissolution (dis´ ə lōō´ shən) *n.* the act of breaking down and crumbling

diverged (dī vurjd´) *v.* branched off

diverse (dī vurs´) *adj.* varied

diverts (dī vurts´) *v.* distracts

eavesdropping (ēvz´ dräpin) *n.* secretly listening to the private conversation of others.

eclipses (i klips´ əz) *n.* here, lunar eclipses; when the moon is obscured by the Earth's shadow

elongate (i lôŋ´ gāt) *adj.* long and narrow

eloquent (el´ ə kwənt) *adj.* fluent, forceful, and persuasive

elusive (i lōō´ siv) *adj.* hard to grasp or retain mentally

emancipated (i man´ sə pā´ təd) *v.* freed from the control or power of another

empathy (em´ pə thē) *n.* ability to share another's emotions, thoughts, or feelings

encompasses (en kum´ pəs´ sez) *v.* contains; includes

engulfing (en gulf´ iŋ) *v.* flowing over and swallowing

ensued (en sōōd´) *v.* came afterward

envelop (en vel´ əp) v. to wrap up; cover completely

essence (es´ əns) n. fundamental nature

etiquette (et´ i kit) n. rules for behavior

evacuees (ē vak´ yoo ēz´) n. people who leave a place, especially because of danger

evaded (i vād´ əd) v. avoided

exertion (eg zur´ shən) n. energetic activity

exhausted (eg zôst´ əd) v. used up; expended completely

extravagance (ek strav´ ə gəns) n. a spending of more than is necessary; wastefulness

exulting (eg zult´ iŋ) v. rejoicing

fastidious (fas tid´ ē əs) adj. refined in an oversensitive way, so as to be easily disgusted or displeased

fatalist (fā´ tə list) n. one who believes that all events are determined by fate

feigning (fān´ iŋ) v. pretending

fertile (fur´ təl) adj. rich; fruitful

fiscal (fis´ kəl) adj. having to do with finances

flue (floo) n. the pipe in a chimney that leads the smoke outside

forsaken (fər sā´ kən) adj. abandoned

fugitives (fyoo´ ji tivs) n. people fleeing

furrows (fur´ ōz) n. deep wrinkles

furtive (fur´ tiv) adj. sly or done in secret

futile (fyoot´ əl) adj. ineffective; useless

gale (gāl) n. strong wind

galore (gə lôr´) adj. in abundance; plentiful

gesticulations (jes tik´ yoo lā´ shənz) n. energetic hand or arm movements

gestures (jes´ chərs) n. movements used to convey an idea, emotion, or intention

gin (jin) n. cotton gin; a machine that separates the seeds from cotton

glistens (glis´ ənz) v. shines; sparkles

gnarled (närld) adj. knotty and twisted, as the trunk of an old tree

gourds (gôrdz) n. dried, hollowed-out shell of fruit

granite (gran´ it) adj. made of granite, a very hard rock

gratification (grat´ ə fi kā´ shən) n. satisfaction

guffawed (gə fôd´) v. laughed in a loud and coarse manner

guttural (gut´ ər əl) adj. made in the back of the throat

habitable (hab´ ə tə bəl) adj. fit to live in

harmonious (här mō´ nē əs) adj. combined in a pleasing, orderly arrangement

harnessed (här´ nist) v. tied; bound

haughty (hôt´ ē) adj. proud of oneself and scornful of others

heedless (hēd´ lis) adj. unmindfully careless

hefted (hef´ tid) v. lifted; tested the weight of

hemisphere (hem´ i sfir´) n. half of a sphere; dome

hover (huv´ ər) v. flutter in the air; linger

humiliating (hyoo mil´ ē āt iŋ) adj. embarrassing, undignified

illiteracy (il lit´ ər ə sē) n. inability to read or write

immersed (im murst´) adj. deeply involved in

immersed (im murst´) v. plunged into; submerged

immigrate (im´ ə grät) v. come into a foreign country to make a new home

imperturbably (im´ pər tur´ bə blē) adv. unexcitedly; impassively

impetuous (im pech´ oo əs) adj. moving with great force or violence; done suddenly with little thought

implemented (im´ plə mənt´ əd) v. put into effect

implications (im´ pli kā´ shəns) n. possible conclusions

inarticulate (in´ är tik´ yə lit) adj. speechless or unable to express oneself

incentive (in sent´ iv) n. something that stimulates one to action; encouragement

incredulously (in krej´ oo ləs lē) adv. with doubt or disbelief

indicative (in dik´ ə tiv) adj. giving a suggestion; showing

indignant (in dig´ nənt) adj. filled with anger over some meanness or injustice

indomitable (in däm´ it ə bəl) adj. not easily discouraged

indulgent (in dul´ jənt) adj. very mild and tolerant; not strict or critical

ineffectually (in´ e fek´ choo ə lē) adv. without producing the desired effect

inexplicable (in eks´ pli kə bəl) adj. unexplainable

infuse (in fyooz´) v. put into

infusion (in fyoo´ zhən) n. the act of putting one thing into another

innumerable (i noo´ mər ə bəl) adj. too many to be counted

inquiry (in´ kwə rē) n. an investigation or examination

inscrutable (in skroot´ ə bəl) adj. impossible to see or understand

insolently (in´ sə lənt lē) adv. boldly disrespectful in speech or behavior

insufferable (in suf´ ər ə bəl) adj. unbearable

intangible (in tan´ jə bəl) adj. not able to be touched or grasped

interaction (in´ tər ak´ shən) n. actions that affect each other

intimate (in´ tə mət) adj. private or personal

intimation (in´ tə mā´ shən) n. hint or suggestion

intolerant (in täl´ ər ənt) adj. not able or willing to accept

introspective (in´ trō spekt´ iv) adj. inward looking; thoughtful

intuition (in´ too wish´ ən) n. ability to know immediately, without reasoning

invincible (in vin´ sə bəl) adj. unbeatable

judicious (joo dish´ əs) adj. showing sound judgment; wise and careful

kindled (kin´ dəld) v. stirred up; awakened

keen (kēn) adj. having a sharp cutting edge

latching (lach´ iŋ) v. attaching oneself to

lavish (lav´ ish) adj. showy; more than enough

legions (lē´ jəns) n. large number; multitude

leisure (lezh´ ər) n. free and unoccupied time

lilting (lilt´ iŋ) adj. singing or speaking with a light, graceful rhythm

listlessly (list´ lis lē) adv. without interest

literally (lit´ ər əl ē) adv. actually; in fact

looming (loom´ iŋ) adj. ominous and awe-inspiring

low (lō) v. make the typical sound that a cow makes; moo

luminance (loo´ mə nəns) n. brightness, brilliance

luminous (loo´ mə nəs) adj. giving off light; shining; bright

macabre (mə käb´ rə) adj. gruesome; grim

maneuver (mə noo´ vər) n. series of planned steps

mania (mā´ nē ə) n. uncontrollable enthusiasm

manifestly (man´ ə fest´ lē) adv. clearly

manifold (man´ ə fōld´) adj. many and varied

marginal (mär´ jə nəl) adj. limited; minimal

meager (mē´ gər) adj. lacking in some way; inadequate

melancholy (mel´ ən käl ē) adj. sad

membrane (mem´ brān) n. a thin, soft sheet or layer serving as a covering

mercurial (mər kyoor´ ē əl) adj. quick or changeable in behavior

mesmerized (mez´ mər izd) adj. hypnotized; enthralled

meticulous (mə tik´ yoo ləs) adj. extremely careful about details

microbes (mī´ krōbes´) n. extremely small organisms

misinterpret (mis´ in tur´ prit) v. to understand or explain incorrectly

mistrusted (mis´ trust´ əd) v. doubted

molding (mōl´ diŋ) n. ornamental woodwork that projects from the walls of a room

morose (mə rōs´) adj. gloomy; ill-tempered

mosquitoes (mə skēt´ ōz) n. insects

muse (myo͞oz) *n.* spirit of inspiration

mutineers (myo͞ot´ ən irz´) *n.* people on a ship who revolt against their officers

mutinous (myo͞ot´ ən əs) *adj.* rebellious

negligent (neg´ lə jənt) *adj.* without care or attention; indifferent

negotiation (ni gō´ shē ā´ shən) *n.* discussion to reach an agreement

nurtures (nʉr´ chərz) *v.* nourishes

obdurate (äb´ do͞or it) *adj.* stubbornly persistent

obscure (əb skyoor´) *v.* conceal or hide

oppressed (ə prest´) *adj.* kept down by cruel or unjust use of power

orators (ôr´ ət ərz) *n.* public speakers

ostentatiously (äs´ tən tā´ shəs lē) *adv.* in a showy way

pandemonium (pan də mō´ nē əm) *n.* a scene of wild disorder

paradoxes (par´ ə däks´ es) *n.* things that seem to be contradictory

peril (per´ əl) *n.* exposure to harm or injury

peripatetic (per´ i pə tet´ ik) *adj.* moving from place to place; walking about

periscope (per´ ə skōp´) *n.* an instrument used to see objects not in a direct line from the viewer

pervading (pər vād´ iŋ) *v.* spreading throughout

petition (pə tish´ ən) *n.* a formal document that makes a request

pitiful (pit´ i fəl) *adj.* deserving compassion

precipitate (prē sip´ ə tāt´) *v.* cause to happen before expected or desired

predisposed (prē´ dis pōzd´) *adj.* inclined

predominantly (pri däm´ ə nənt lē) *adj.* mainly; most noticeably

presentable (prē zent´ ə bəl) *adj.* in proper order for being seen

pretense (prē tens´) *n.* false showing; pretending

pretext (prē´ tekst) *n.* false reason or motive used to hide a real intention

privations (prī vā´ shənz) *n.* deprivation or lack of common comforts

procession (prō sesh´ ən) *n.* a group of people or things moving forward

prodigy (präd´ ə jē) *n.* a wonder; an unusually talented person

profound (prō found´) *adj.* intellectually deep; getting to the bottom of the matter

prominent (präm´ ə nənt) *adj.* widely and favorably known

psychology (sī käl´ ə jē) *n.* science dealing with mental and emotional processes

pursuit (pər so͞ot´) *n.* following in order to overtake and capture

quake (kwāk) *v.* to tremble or shake; to shudder or shiver, as from fear or cold

radial (rā´ dē əl) *adj.* branching out in all directions from a common center

ravaging (rav´ ij iŋ) *adj.* severely damaging

recede (ri sēd´) *v.* move away; fade

receding (ri sēd´ iŋ) *v.* moving back

recluse (rek´ lo͞os) *n.* a hermit

refugees (ref´ yo͞o jēz) *n.* people who flee from their homes in a time of trouble

refute (ri fyo͞ot´) *v.* prove to be false by argument or evidence

registrants (rej´ is trənts) *n.* people who register to participate in something

reigning (rān´ iŋ) *adj.* ruling

renounced (re nounst´) *v.* gave up

resolute (rez´ ə lo͞ot´) *adj.* fixed in purpose; resolved

respectively (ri spek´ tiv lē) *adv.* in the order named

retribution (re´ trə byo͞o´ shən) *n.* punishment for wrongdoing

revelation (rev´ ə lā´ shən) *n.* something revealed

reverie (rev´ ər ē) *n.* daydream

rigorous (rig´ ər əs) *adj.* very strict or harsh

riveted (riv´ it əd) *adj.* fastened or made firm

rivulets (riv´ yo͞o lits) *n.* little streams

roam (rōm) *v.* go aimlessly; wander

romp (rämp) *n.* lively play or frolic

runt (runt) *n.* the smallest animal in a litter

sagacity (sə gas´ ə tē) *n.* high intelligence and sound judgment

sarcastic (sär kas´ tik) *adj.* speaking with sharp mockery intended to hurt another

sauntering (sân´ tər iŋ) *v.* walking slowly and confidently

scolded (skōld´ əd) *v.* criticized harshly

scornful (skôrn´ fəl) *adj.* full of contempt

scythe (sīth) *n.* long tool with a single-edged blade

seductive (si duk´ tiv) *adj.* tempting; enticing

semblance (sem´ bləns) *n.* look or appearance

semblences (sem bləns iz) *n.* appearances

shackles (shak´ əls) *n.* metal fastenings for the wrists or ankles of a prisoner

shriveled (shriv´ əld) *v.* dried up; withered

shunned (shund) *v.* avoided

signify (sig´ nə fī) *v.* to show or make known, as by a sign, words, etc.

simultaneously (sī məl tā´ nē əs lē) *adv.* at the same time

singular (siŋ´ gyə lər) *adj.* unique; exceptional; extraordinary

skeptics (skep´ tiks) *n.* people who frequently doubt and question

smoldering (smōl´ dər iŋ) *adj.* burning or smoking without flame

somber (säm´ bər) *adj.* dark and gloomy

specter (spek´ tər) *n.* disturbing thoughts

spectral (spek´ trəl) *adj.* phantomlike; ghostly

spontaneously (spän tā´ nē əs lē) *adv.* resulting from a natural feeling

stalwart (stôl´ wərt) *adj.* resolute; firm

stealthy (ste´ thē) *adj.* artfully sly and secretive

stoic (stō´ ik) *adj.* calm and unbothered in spite of suffering

strife (strīf) *n.* conflict

sturdy (stʉr´ dē) *adj.* firm; strong

subtle (sut´ əl) *adj.* delicate; fine

supple (sup´ əl) *adj.* flexible and pliant

surveyed (sʉr vād´) *v.* looked over in a careful way; examined

swarthy (swôr´ *th*ē) *adj.* having a dark complexion

syndromes (sin´ drōmz) *n.* a number of symptoms occurring

tangible (tan´ jə bəl) *adj.* having form and substance; that can be touched or felt by touch; that can be understood; definite

taut (tôt) *adj.* tightly stretched

telecommunicator (tel´ i kə myo͞o´ ni kā tər) *n.* one who practices communication by electronic means

tenacious (tə nā´ shəs) *adj.* holding on firmly

tenement (ten´ ə mənt) *n.* here, a rundown apartment building

thoroughly (thʉr´ ō lē) *adv.* accurately and with regard to detail

transparent (trans par´ ənt) *adj.* capable of being seen through; clear

tread (tred) *n.* step

tranquil (tran´ kwil) *adj.* quiet or motionless

tropical (träp´ ə kəl) *adj.* very hot; sultry

turbulent (tʉr´ byo͞o lənt) *adj.* full of commotion; wild

unabashed (un ə basht´) *adj.* unashamed

unanimous (yo͞o nan´ ə məs) *adj.* agreeing completely; united in opinion

unconstitutional (un´ kän stə to͞o´ shə nəl) *adj.* not in accordance with or permitted by U.S. law

unfurled (un fʉrld´) *adj.* unfolded

unobtrusively (un´ əb tro͞o´ siv lē) *adv.* without calling attention to oneself

unremitting (un ri mit´ iŋ) *adj.* not stopping

untrodden (un träd´ ´n) *adj.* not walked upon

usurped (yo͞o sʉrpt´) *v.* took power or authority away from

usurps (yo͞o sʉrps´) *v.* takes over

ventriloquist (ven tril´ ə kwist) *n.* someone who speaks through a puppet or dummy

vertical (vʉr´ ti kəl) *adj.* straight up and down; upright

virtuous (vʉr´ cho͞o wəs) *adj.* moral; upright

visible (viz´ ə bəl) *adj.* able to be seen

wan (wän) *adj.* pale

wizened (wiz´ ənd) *v.* shriveled or withered

TIPS FOR IMPROVING READING FLUENCY

When you were younger, you learned to read. Then, you read to expand your experiences or for pure enjoyment. Now, you are expected to read to learn. As you progress in school, you are given more and more material to read. The tips on these pages will help you improve your reading fluency, or your ability to read easily, smoothly, and expressively.

Keeping Your Concentration

One common problem that readers face is the loss of concentration. When you are reading an assignment, you might find yourself rereading the same sentence several times without really understanding it. The first step in changing this behavior is to notice that you do it. Becoming an active, aware reader will help you get the most from your assignments. Practice using these strategies:

- Cover what you have already read with a note card as you go along. Then, you will not be able to reread without noticing that you are doing it.
- Set a purpose for reading beyond just completing the assignment. Then, read actively by pausing to ask yourself questions about the material as you read.
- Use the Reading Strategy instruction and notes that appear with each selection in this textbook.
- Stop reading after a specified period of time (for example, 5 minutes) and summarize what you have read. To help you with this strategy, use the Reading Check questions that appear with each selection in this textbook. Reread to find any answers you do not know.

Reading Phrases

Fluent readers read phrases rather than individual words. Reading this way will speed up your reading and improve your comprehension. Here are some useful ideas:

- Experts recommend rereading as a strategy to increase fluency. Choose a passage of text that is neither too hard nor too easy. Read the same passage aloud several times until you can read it smoothly. When you can read the passage fluently, pick another passage and keep practicing.
- Read aloud into a tape recorder. Then, listen to the recording, noting your accuracy, pacing, and expression. You can also read aloud and share feedback with a partner.
- Use the *Prentice Hall Listening to Literature* audiotapes or CDs to hear the selections read aloud. Read along silently in your textbook, noticing how the reader uses his or her voice and emphasizes certain words and phrases.

**Reading Check**
What common problem do many readers face?

**Reading Check**
In what ways will reading phrases rather than individual words affect your reading?

Understanding Key Vocabulary

If you do not understand some of the words in an assignment, you may miss out on important concepts. Therefore, it is helpful to keep a dictionary nearby when you are reading. Follow these steps:

- Before you begin reading, scan the text for unfamiliar words or terms. Find out what those words mean before you begin reading.
- Use context—the surrounding words, phrases, and sentences—to help you determine the meanings of unfamiliar words.
- If you are unable to understand the meaning through context, refer to the dictionary.

Paying Attention to Punctuation

When you read, pay attention to punctuation. Commas, periods, exclamation points, semicolons, and colons tell you when to pause or stop. They also indicate relationships between groups of words. When you recognize these relationships you will read with greater understanding and expression. Look at the chart below.

Punctuation Mark	Meaning
comma	brief pause
period	pause at the end of a thought
exclamation point	pause that indicates emphasis
semicolon	pause between related but distinct thoughts
colon	pause before giving explanation or examples

Using the Reading Fluency Checklist

Use the checklist below each time you read a selection in this textbook. In your Language Arts journal or notebook, note which skills you need to work on and chart your progress each week.

Reading Fluency Checklist

❏ Preview the text to check for difficult or unfamiliar words.
❏ Practice reading aloud.
❏ Read according to punctuation.
❏ Break down long sentences into the subject and its meaning.
❏ Read groups of words for meaning rather than reading single words.
❏ Read with expression (change your tone of voice to add meaning to the word).

Reading is a skill that can be improved with practice. The key to improving your fluency is to read. The more you read, the better your reading will become.

✔ **Reading Check**

Why should you look up words you do not know when reading an assignment?

HIGH-FREQUENCY WORDS

Approximately fifty percent of the words you read will be the same one hundred words. Learning to instantly recognize **high-frequency words**—words that are used often in print—will greatly improve your reading fluency. Learn to instantly recognize the words on this page. Practice any that give you trouble.

the	said	could	things	large	still	seemed	second
of	there	people	our	must	learn	next	later
and	use	my	just	big	should	hard	miss
a	an	than	name	even	American	open	idea
to	each	first	good	such	world	example	enough
in	which	water	sentence	because	high	beginning	eat
is	she	been	man	turned	ever	life	face
you	do	called	think	here	near	always	watch
that	how	who	say	why	add	those	far
it	their	oil	great	asked	food	both	Indians
he	if	sit	where	went	between	paper	rally
was	will	now	help	men	own	together	almost
for	up	find	through	read	below	got	let
on	other	long	much	need	country	group	above
are	about	down	before	land	plants	often	girl
as	out	day	line	different	last	run	sometimes
with	many	did	right	home	school	important	mountains
his	then	get	too	us	father	until	cut
they	them	come	means	move	keep	children	young
I	these	made	old	try	trees	side	talk
at	so	may	any	kind	never	feet	soon
be	some	part	same	hand	started	car	list
this	her	over	tell	picture	city	miles	song
have	would	new	boy	again	earth	night	being
from	make	sound	following	change	eyes	walked	leave
or	like	take	came	off	light	white	family
one	him	only	want	play	thought	sea	it's
had	into	little	show	spell	head	began	
by	time	work	also	air	under	grow	
words	has	know	around	away	story	took	
but	look	place	form	animals	saw	river	
not	two	years	three	house	left	four	
what	more	live	small	point	don't	carry	
all	write	me	set	page	few	state	
were	go	back	put	letters	while	once	
we	see	give	end	mother	along	book	
when	number	most	does	answer	might	hear	
your	no	very	another	found	close	stop	
can	way	after	well	study	something	without	

LITERARY TERMS HANDBOOK

ALLITERATION *Alliteration* is the repetition of initial consonant sounds. Writers use alliteration to draw attention to certain words or ideas, to imitate sounds, and to create musical effects.

ALLUSION An *allusion* is a reference to a well-known person, place, event, literary work, or work of art. Understanding what a writer is saying often depends on recognizing allusions.

ANALOGY An *analogy* makes a comparison between two or more things that are similar in some ways but otherwise unalike.

ANECDOTE An *anecdote* is a brief story about an interesting, amusing, or strange event. Writers tell anecdotes to entertain or to make a point.

ANTAGONIST An *antagonist* is a character or a force in conflict with a main character, or protagonist.

See *Conflict* and *Protagonist.*

ATMOSPHERE *Atmosphere,* or *mood,* is the feeling created in the reader by a literary work or passage.

AUTHOR'S ARGUMENT An *author's argument* is the position he or she puts forward, supported by reasons.

AUTOBIOGRAPHY An *autobiography* is the story of the writer's own life, told by the writer. Autobiographical writing may tell about the person's whole life or only a part of it.

Because autobiographies are about real people and events, they are a form of nonfiction. Most autobiographies are written in the first person.

See *Biography, Nonfiction,* and *Point of View.*

BALLAD A *ballad* is a songlike poem that tells a story, often one dealing with adventure and romance. Most ballads are written in four- to six-line stanzas and have regular rhythms and rhyme schemes. A ballad often features a refrain—a regularly repeated line or group of lines.

See *Oral Tradition* and *Refrain.*

BIOGRAPHY A *biography* is a form of nonfiction in which a writer tells the life story of another person. Most biographies are written about famous or admirable people. Although biographies are nonfiction, the most effective ones share the qualities of good narrative writing.

See *Autobiography* and *Nonfiction.*

CHARACTER A *character* is a person or an animal that takes part in the action of a literary work. The main, or *major,* character is the most important character in a story, poem, or play. A *minor* character is one who takes part in the action but is not the focus of attention.

Characters are sometimes classified as flat or round. A *flat character* is one-sided and often stereotypical. A *round character,* on the other hand, is fully developed and exhibits many traits—often both faults and virtues. Characters can also be classified as dynamic or static. A *dynamic character* is one who changes or grows during the course of the work. A *static character* is one who does not change.

See *Characterization, Hero/Heroine,* and *Motive.*

CHARACTERIZATION *Characterization* is the act of creating and developing a character. Authors use two major methods of characterization—*direct* and *indirect.* When using *direct* characterization, a writer states the *characters' traits,* or characteristics.

When describing a character indirectly, a writer depends on the reader to draw conclusions about the character's traits. Sometimes the writer tells what other participants in the story say and think about the character.

See *Character* and *Motive.*

CLIMAX The climax, also called the turning point, is the high point in the action of the plot. It is the moment of greatest tension, when the outcome of the plot hangs in the balance.

See *Plot.*

COMEDY A *comedy* is a literary work, especially a play, which is light, often humorous or satirical, and ends happily. Comedies frequently depict ordinary characters faced with temporary difficulties and conflicts. Types of comedy include *romantic comedy,* which involves problems among lovers, and the *comedy of manners,* which satirically challenges social customs of a society.

CONCRETE POEM A *concrete poem* is one with a shape that suggests its subject. The poet arranges the letters, punctuation, and lines to create an image, or picture, on the page.

CONFLICT A *conflict* is a struggle between opposing forces. Conflict is one of the most important elements of stories, novels, and plays because it causes the action. There are two kinds of conflict: external and internal. An *external conflict* is one in which a character struggles against some outside force, such as another person. Another kind of external conflict may occur between a character and some force in nature.

An *internal conflict* takes place within the mind of a character. The character struggles to make a decision, take an action, or overcome a feeling.

See *Plot.*

CONNOTATIONS The *connotation* of a word is the set of ideas associated with it in addition to its explicit meaning. The connotation of a word can be personal, based on individual experiences. More often, cultural connotations—those recognizable by most people in a group—determine a writer's word choices.

See also *Denotation.*

COUPLET A *couplet* is two consecutive lines of verse with end rhymes. Often, a couplet functions as a stanza.

DENOTATION The *denotation* of a word is its dictionary meaning, independent of other associations that the word may have. The denotation of the word *lake*, for example, is "an inland body of water." "Vacation spot" and "place where the fishing is good" are connotations of the word *lake.*

See also *Connotation.*

DESCRIPTION A *description* is a portrait, in words, of a person, place, or object. Descriptive writing uses images that appeal to the five senses—sight, hearing, touch, taste, and smell.

See *Image.*

DEVELOPMENT See *Plot.*

DIALECT *Dialect* is the form of a language spoken by people in a particular region or group. Dialects differ in pronunciation, grammar, and word choice. The English language is divided into many dialects. British English differs from American English.

DIALOGUE A *dialogue* is a conversation between characters. In poems, novels, and short stories, dialogue is usually set off by quotation marks to indicate a speaker's exact words.

In a play, dialogue follows the names of the characters, and no quotation marks are used.

DRAMA A *drama* is a story written to be performed by actors. Although a drama is meant to be performed, one can also read the script, or written version, and imagine the action. The *script* of a drama is made up of dialogue and stage directions. The *dialogue* is the words spoken by the actors. The *stage directions,* usually printed in italics, tell how the actors should look, move, and speak. They also describe the setting, sound effects, and lighting.

Dramas are often divided into parts called *acts.* The acts are often divided into smaller parts called *scenes.*

DYNAMIC CHARACTER See *Character.*

ELEGY An *elegy* is a solemn and formal lyric poem about death. It may mourn a particular person or reflect on a serious or tragic theme, such as the passing of youth, beauty, or a way of life.

See *Lyric Poem.*

EPIC POEM An *epic* is a long narrative poem about the adventures of gods or a hero. An epic is serious in tone and broad in theme. It offers a portrait of the culture in which it was produced. The earliest known epics were created in ancient Greece and Rome and are part of the oral tradition.

Epic conventions are traditional characteristics of epic poems, including an opening statement of the theme; an appeal for supernatural help in telling the story (an invocation); a beginning "in the middle of things"; long lists of people and things; accounts of past events; and repeated epithets.

See *Oral Tradition* and *Epithets.*

EPITHET An *epithet* is a word or phrase that states a characteristic quality of a person or thing.

ESSAY An *essay* is a short nonfiction work about a particular subject. Most essays have a single major focus and a clear introduction, body, and conclusion.

There are many types of essays. An *informal essay* uses casual, conversational language. A *historical essay* gives facts, explanations, and insights about historical events. An *expository essay* explains an idea by breaking it down. A *narrative essay* tells a story about a real-life experience. An *informational essay* explains a process. A *persuasive essay* offers an opinion and supports it.

See *Exposition, Narration,* and *Persuasion.*

EXPOSITION In the plot of a story or a drama, the *exposition,* or introduction, is the part of the work that introduces the characters, setting, and basic situation.

See *Plot.*

EXPOSITORY WRITING *Expository writing* is writing that explains or informs.

EXTERNAL CONFLICT See *Conflict.*

EXTENDED METAPHOR In an *extended metaphor,* as in a regular metaphor, a subject is spoken or written of as though it were something else. However, extended metaphor differs from regular metaphor in that several connected comparisons are made.

See *Metaphor.*

FABLE A *fable* is a brief story or poem, usually with animal characters, that teaches a lesson, or moral. The moral is usually stated at the end of the fable.

See *Irony* and *Moral.*

FANTASY A *fantasy* is highly imaginative writing that contains elements not found in real life. Examples of fantasy include stories that involve supernatural elements, stories that resemble fairy tales, stories that deal with imaginary places and creatures, and science-fiction stories.

See *Science Fiction.*

FICTION *Fiction* is prose writing that tells about imaginary characters and events. Short stories and novels are works of fiction. Some writers base their fiction on actual events and people, adding invented characters, dialogue, settings, and plots. Other writers rely on imagination alone.

See *Narration, Nonfiction,* and *Prose.*

FIGURATIVE LANGUAGE *Figurative language* is writing or speech that is not meant to be taken literally. The many types of figurative language are known as *figures of speech.* Common figures of speech include metaphor, personification, and simile. Writers use figurative language to state ideas in vivid and imaginative ways.

See *Metaphor, Personification, Simile,* and *Symbol.*

FIGURE OF SPEECH See *Figurative Language.*

FLASHBACK A *flashback* is a scene within a story that interrupts the sequence of events to relate events that occurred in the past.

FLAT CHARACTER See *Character.*

FOLK TALE A *folk tale* is a story composed orally and then passed from person to person by word of mouth. Folk tales originated among people who could neither read nor write. These people entertained one another by telling stories aloud—often dealing with heroes, adventure, magic, or romance. Eventually, modern scholars collected these stories and wrote them down. Folk tales reflect the cultural beliefs and environments from which they come.
See *Fable, Legend, Myth,* and *Oral Tradition.*

FOOT See *Meter.*

FORESHADOWING *Foreshadowing* is the author's use of clues to hint at what might happen later in the story. Writers use foreshadowing to build their readers' expectations and to create suspense.

FREE VERSE *Free verse* is poetry not written in a regular, rhythmical pattern, or meter. The poet is free to write lines of any length or with any number of stresses, or beats. Free verse is therefore less constraining than *metrical verse,* in which every line must have a certain length and a certain number of stresses.
See *Meter.*

GENRE A *genre* is a division or type of literature. Literature is commonly divided into three major genres: poetry, prose, and drama. Each major genre is, in turn, divided into lesser genres, as follows:
1. *Poetry:* lyric poetry, concrete poetry, dramatic poetry, narrative poetry, epic poetry

2. *Prose:* fiction (novels and short stories) and nonfiction (biography, autobiography, letters, essays, and reports)
3. *Drama:* serious drama and tragedy, comic drama, melodrama, and farce

See *Drama, Poetry,* and *Prose.*

HAIKU The *haiku* is a three-line Japanese verse form. The first and third lines of a haiku each have five syllables. The second line has seven syllables. A writer of haiku uses images to create a single, vivid picture, generally of a scene from nature.

HERO/HEROINE A *hero* or *heroine* is a character whose actions are inspiring, or noble. Often heroes and heroines struggle to overcome the obstacles and problems that stand in their way. Note that the term *hero* was originally used only for male characters, while heroic female characters were always called *heroines.* However, it is now acceptable to use *hero* to refer to females as well as to males.

HISTORICAL FICTION In *historical fiction* real events, places, or people are incorporated into a fictional or made up story.

IDIOM An *idiom* is an expression that has a meaning particular to a language or region. For example, in "Seventh Grade" Gary Soto uses the idiom "making a face," which means to contort one's face in an unusual, usually unattractive, way.

IMAGES *Images* are words or phrases that appeal to one or more of the five senses. Writers use images to describe how their subjects look, sound, feel, taste, and smell. Poets often paint images, or word pictures, that appeal to your senses. These pictures help you to experience the poem fully.

IMAGERY See *Image.*

INTERNAL CONFLICT See *Conflict.*

IRONY *Irony* is the general name given to literary techniques that involve surprising, interesting, or amusing contradictions.

JOURNAL A *journal* is a daily, or periodic, account of events and the writer's thoughts and feelings about those events. Personal journals are not normally written for publication, but sometimes they do get published later with permission from the author or the author's family.

LEGEND A *legend* is a widely told story about the past—one that may or may not have a foundation in fact. Every culture has its own legends—its familiar, traditional stories.

See *Folk Tale, Myth,* and *Oral Tradition.*

LETTERS A *letter* is a written communication from one person to another. In personal letters, the writer shares information and his or her thoughts and feelings with one other person or group. Although letters are not normally written for publication, they sometimes do get published later with the permission of the author or the author's family.

LIMERICK A *limerick* is a humorous, rhyming, five-line poem with a specific meter and rhyme scheme. Most limericks have three strong stresses in lines 1, 2, and 5 and two strong stresses in lines 3 and 4. Most follow the rhyme scheme *aabba.*

LYRIC POEM A *lyric poem* is a highly musical verse that expresses the observations and feelings of a single speaker. It creates a single, unified impression.

MAIN CHARACTER See *Character.*

MEDIA ACCOUNTS *Media Accounts* are reports, explanations, opinions, or descriptions written for television, radio, newspapers, and magazines. While some media accounts report only facts, others include the writer's thoughts and reflections.

METAPHOR A *metaphor* is a figure of speech in which something is described as though it were something else. A metaphor, like a simile, works by pointing out a similarity between two unlike things.

See *Extended Metaphor* and *Simile.*

METER The *meter* of a poem is its rhythmical pattern. This pattern is determined by the number of *stresses,* or beats, in each line. To describe the meter of a poem, read it emphasizing the beats in each line. Then, mark the stressed and unstressed syllables, as follows:

My fath | er was | the first | to hear |

As you can see, each strong stress is marked with a slanted line (´) and each unstressed syllable with a horseshoe symbol (ˇ). The weak and strong stresses are then divided by vertical lines (|) into groups called *feet.*

MINOR CHARACTER See *Character.*

MOOD *Mood,* or *atmosphere,* is the feeling created by a literary work or passage. Writers use many devices to create mood, including images, dialogue, setting, and plot. Often, a writer creates a mood at the beginning of a work that he or she sustains throughout. Sometimes, however, the mood of the work changes dramatically.

MORAL A *moral* is a lesson taught by a literary work. A fable usually ends with a moral that is directly stated. A poem, novel, short story, or essay often suggests a moral that is not directly

stated. The moral must be drawn by the reader, based on other elements in the work.

See *Fable.*

MOTIVATION See *Motive.*

MOTIVE A *motive* is a reason that explains or partially explains a character's thoughts, feelings, actions, or speech. Writers try to make their characters' motives, or motivations, as clear as possible. If the motives of a main character are not clear, then the character will not be believable.

Characters are often motivated by needs, such as food and shelter. They are also motivated by feelings, such as fear, love, and pride. Motives may be obvious or hidden.

MYTH A *myth* is a fictional tale that explains the actions of gods or heroes or the origins of elements of nature. Myths are part of the oral tradition. They are composed orally and then passed from generation to generation by word of mouth. Every ancient culture has its own mythology, or collection of myths. Greek and Roman myths are known collectively as *classical mythology.*

See *Oral Tradition.*

NARRATION *Narration* is writing that tells a story. The act of telling a story is also called narration. Each piece is a *narrative.* A story told in fiction, nonfiction, poetry, or even in drama is called a narrative.

See *Narrative, Narrative Poem,* and *Narrator.*

NARRATIVE A *narrative* is a story. A narrative can be either fiction or nonfiction. Novels and short stories are types of fictional narratives. Biographies and autobiographies are nonfiction narratives. Poems that tell stories are also narratives.

See *Narration* and *Narrative Poem.*

NARRATIVE POEM A *narrative poem* is a story told in verse. Narrative poems often have all the elements of short stories, including characters, conflict, and plot.

NARRATOR A *narrator* is a speaker or a character who tells a story. The narrator's perspective is the way he or she sees things. A *third-person narrator* is one who stands outside the action and speaks about it. A *first-person narrator* is one who tells a story and participates in its action.

See *Point of View.*

NONFICTION *Nonfiction* is prose writing that presents and explains ideas or that tells about real people, places, objects, or events. Autobiographies, biographies, essays, reports, letters, memos, and newspaper articles are all types of nonfiction.

See *Fiction.*

NOVEL A *novel* is a long work of fiction. Novels contain such elements as characters, plot, conflict, and setting. The writer of novels, or novelist, develops these elements. In addition to its main plot, a novel may contain one or more subplots, or independent, related stories. A novel may also have several themes. See *Fiction* and *Short Story.*

NOVELLA A fiction work that is longer than a short story but shorter than a novel.

ODE An *ode* is a formal lyric poem with a serious theme. It is usually long and may be written for a private occasion or a public ceremony. Odes often honor people, commemorate events, or respond to natural scenes.

See *Lyric Poem.*

ONOMATOPOEIA *Onomatopoeia* is the use of words that imitate sounds. *Crash, buzz, screech, hiss, neigh, jingle,* and *cluck* are examples of onomatopoeia. *Chickadee, towhee,* and *whippoorwill* are onomatopoeic names of birds.

Onomatopoeia can help put the reader in the activity of a poem.

ORAL TRADITION *Oral tradition* is the passing of songs, stories, and poems from generation to generation by word of mouth. Folk songs, folk tales, legends, and myths all come from the oral tradition. No one knows who first created these stories and poems.

See *Folk Tale, Legend,* and *Myth.*

PERSONIFICATION *Personification* is a type of figurative language in which a nonhuman subject is given human characteristics.

PERSPECTIVE See *Narrator* and *Point of View.*

PERSUASION *Persuasion* is used in writing or speech that attempts to convince the reader or listener to adopt a particular opinion or course of action. Newspaper editorials and letters to the editor use persuasion. So do advertisements and campaign speeches given by political candidates.

See *Essay.*

PLAYWRIGHT A *playwright* is a person who writes plays. William Shakespeare is regarded as the greatest playwright in English literature.

PLOT *Plot* is the sequence of events in which each event results from a previous one and causes the next. In most novels, dramas, short stories, and narrative poems, the plot involves both characters and a central conflict. The plot usually begins with an *exposition* that introduces the setting, the characters, and the basic situation. This is followed by the *inciting incident,* which

introduces the central conflict. The conflict then increases during the *development* until it reaches a high point of interest or suspense, the *climax.* The climax is followed by the *falling action,* or end, of the central conflict. Any events that occur during the falling action make up the *resolution* or *denouement.*

Some plots do not have all of these parts. Some stories begin with the inciting incident and end with the resolution.

See *Conflict.*

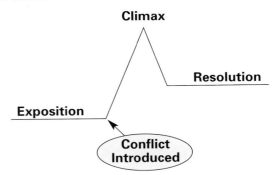

POETRY *Poetry* is one of the three major types of literature, the others being prose and drama. Most poems make use of highly concise, musical, and emotionally charged language. Many also make use of imagery, figurative language, and special devices of sound such as rhyme. Major types of poetry include *lyric poetry, narrative poetry,* and *concrete poetry.*

See *Concrete Poem, Genre, Lyric Poem,* and *Narrative Poem.*

POINT OF VIEW Point of view is the perspective, or vantage point, from which a story is told. It is either a narrator outside the story or a character in the story. *First-person point of view* is told by a character who uses the first person pronoun "I."

The two kinds of *third-person point of view,* limited and omniscient, are called "third person" because the narrator uses third-person pronouns such as *he* and *she* to refer to the characters. There is no "I" telling the story.

In stories told from the *omniscient third-person point of view,* the narrator knows and tells about what each character feels and thinks.

In stories told from the *limited third-person point of view,* the narrator relates the inner thoughts and feelings of only one character, and everything is viewed from this character's perspective.

In works written from a *subjective* point of view, the writer includes opinions and feelings. A work written from an *objective* point of view includes only facts, or an account of events.

See *Narrator.*

PROBLEM See *Conflict.*

PROSE *Prose* is the ordinary form of written language. Most writing that is not poetry, drama, or song is considered prose.

Prose is one of the major genres of literature and occurs in two forms—fiction and nonfiction.

See *Fiction, Genre,* and *Nonfiction.*

PROTAGONIST The *protagonist* is the main character in a literary work. Often, the protagonist is a person, but sometimes it can be an animal.

See *Antagonist* and *Character.*

REFRAIN A *refrain* is a regularly repeated line or group of lines in a poem or a song.

REPETITION *Repetition* is the use, more than once, of any element of language—a sound, word, phrase, clause, or sentence. Repetition is used in both prose and poetry.

See *Alliteration, Meter, Plot, Rhyme,* and *Rhyme Scheme.*

RESOLUTION The *resolution* is the outcome of the conflict in a plot.

See *Plot.*

RHYME *Rhyme* is the repetition of sounds at the ends of words. Poets use rhyme to lend a songlike quality to their verses and to emphasize certain words and ideas. Many traditional poems contain *end rhymes,* or rhyming words at the ends of lines.

Another common device is the use of *internal rhymes,* or rhyming words within lines. Internal rhyme also emphasizes the flowing nature of a poem.

See *Rhyme Scheme.*

RHYME SCHEME A *rhyme scheme* is a regular pattern of rhyming words in a poem. To indicate the rhyme scheme of a poem, one uses lowercase letters. Each rhyme is assigned a different letter, as follows in the first stanza of "Dust of Snow," by Robert Frost:

The way a crow	*a*
Shook down on me	*b*
The dust of snow	*a*
From a hemlock tree	*b*

Thus, the stanza has the rhyme scheme *abab.*

RHYTHM *Rhythm* is the pattern of stressed and unstressed syllables in spoken or written language.

See *Meter.*

ROUND CHARACTER See *Character.*

SCENE A *scene* is a section of uninterrupted action in the act of a drama.

See *Drama.*

SCIENCE FICTION *Science fiction* combines elements of fiction and fantasy with scientific fact. Many science-fiction stories are set in the future.

SENSORY LANGUAGE *Sensory language* is writing or speech that appeals to one or more of the five senses.

See *Image.*

SETTING The *setting* of a literary work is the time and place of the action. The setting includes all the details of a place and time—the year, the time of day, even the weather. The place may be a specific country, state, region, community, neighborhood, building, institution, or home. Details such as dialects, clothing, customs, and modes of transportation are often used to establish setting. In most stories, the setting serves as a backdrop—a context in which the characters interact. Setting can also help to create a feeling, or atmosphere.

See *Atmosphere.*

SHORT STORY A *short story* is a brief work of fiction. Like a novel, a short story presents a sequence of events, or plot. The plot usually deals with a central conflict faced by a main character, or protagonist. The events in a short story usually communicate a message about life or human nature. This message, or central idea, is the story's theme.

See *Conflict, Plot,* and *Theme.*

SIMILE A *simile* is a figure of speech that uses like or as to make a direct comparison between two unlike ideas. Everyday speech often contains similes, such as "pale as a ghost," "good as gold," "spread like wildfire," and "clever as a fox."

SONNET A *sonnet* is a fourteen-line lyric poem with a single theme. Sonnets vary, but they are usually written in iambic pentameter, following one of two traditional patterns.

The *Petrarchan,* or *Italian, sonnet* is divided into two parts: an eight-line octave and six-line sestet. The octave rhymes *abba abba,* while the sestet usually rhymes *cde cde.* The two parts of this sonnet work together. The octave raises a question, states a problem, or presents a brief narrative, and the sestet answers the question, solves the problem, or comments on the narrative.

The *Shakespearean,* or *English, sonnet* has three four-line quatrains plus a concluding two-line couplet. The rhyme scheme is usually *abab cdcd efef gg.* Usually, each of the three quatrains explores a different variation of the main theme. Then the couplet presents a summarizing or concluding statement.

See *Lyric Poem* and *Stanza.*

SOLILOQUY A *soliloquy* is a long speech, in a play or in a prose work, made by a character who is alone. The character reveals his or her private thoughts and feelings to the audience or reader.

SPEAKER The *speaker* is the imaginary voice a poet uses when writing a poem. The speaker is the character who tells the poem. This character, or voice, often is not identified by name. There can be important differences between the poet and the poem's speaker.

See *Narrator.*

STAGE DIRECTIONS *Stage directions* are notes included in a drama to describe how the work is to be performed or staged. Stage directions are usually printed in italics and enclosed within parentheses or brackets. Some stage directions describe the movements, costumes, emotional states, and ways of speaking of the characters.

STAGING *Staging* includes the setting, the lighting, the costumes, special effects, music, dance, and so on that go into putting on a stage performance of a drama.

See *Drama.*

STANZA A *stanza* is a formal division of lines in a poem and is considered as a unit. Many poems are divided into stanzas that are separated by spaces. Stanzas often function just as paragraphs do in prose. Each stanza states and develops a single main idea.

Stanzas are commonly named according to the number of lines found in them, as follows:

- *Couplet:* two-line stanza
- *Tercet:* three-line stanza
- *Quatrain:* four-line stanza
- *Cinquain:* five-line stanza
- *Sestet:* six-line stanza
- *Heptastich:* seven-line stanza
- *Octave:* eight-line stanza

STATIC CHARACTER See *Character.*

SURPRISE ENDING A *surprise ending* is a conclusion that is unexpected. The reader has certain expectations about the ending based on details in the story. Often, a surprise ending is *forshadowed,* or subtly hinted at, in the course of the work.

See *Foreshadowing* and *Plot.*

SUBPLOT A *subplot* is a secondary story line that complicates or adds depth to the main plot.

SUSPENSE *Suspense* is a feeling of anxious uncertainty about the outcome of events in a literary work. Writers create suspense by raising questions in the minds of their readers.

SYMBOL A *symbol* is anything that stands for or represents something else. Symbols are common in everyday life. A dove with an olive branch in its beak is a symbol of peace. A blindfolded woman holding a balanced scale is a symbol of justice. A crown is a symbol of a king's status and authority.

TALL TALE Most *tall tales* come out of the oral tradition of the American frontier. They typically involve characters with highly exaggerated abilities and qualities.

See *Legend, Myth, Oral Tradition,* and *Yarn.*

THEME The *theme* is a central message, concern, or purpose in a literary work. A theme can usually be expressed as a generalization, or a general statement, about human beings or about life. The theme of a work is not a summary of its plot. The theme is the writer's central idea.

Although a theme may be stated directly in the text, it is more often presented indirectly. When the theme is stated indirectly, or implied, the reader must figure out what the theme is by looking carefully at what the work reveals about people or about life.

TONE The *tone* of a literary work is the writer's attitude toward his or her audience and subject. The tone can often be described by a single adjective, such as *formal* or *informal, serious* or *playful, bitter,* or *ironic.* Factors that contribute to the tone are word choice, sentence structure, line length, rhyme, rhythm and repetition.

TRAGEDY A *tragedy* is a work of literature, especially a play, that results in a catastrophe for the main character. In ancient Greek drama, the main character was always a significant person—a king or a hero—and the cause of the tragedy was a tragic flaw, or weakness, in his or her character. In modern drama, the main character can be an ordinary person, and the cause of the tragedy can be some evil in society itself. The purpose of tragedy is not only to arouse fear and pity in the audience, but also, in some cases, to convey a sense of the grandeur and nobility of the human spirit.

TURNING POINT See *Climax.*

VIGNETTE A *vignette* is a vivid literary sketch or brief narrative of a scene or event that was memorable to the writer. It may be part of a longer work.

YARN A *yarn* is a folk tale—usually, a tall tale—about far-fetched characters and events.

See *Tall Tale.*

RUBRICS

What is a rubric?

A rubric is a tool, often in the form of a chart or a grid, that helps you assess your work. Rubrics are particularly helpful for writing and speaking assignments.

To help you or others assess, or evaluate, your work, a rubric offers several specific criteria to be applied to your work. Then the rubric helps you or an evaluator indicate your range of success or failure according to those specific criteria. Rubrics are often used to evaluate writing for standardized tests.

Using a rubric will save you time, focus your learning, and improve the work you do. When you know what the rubric will be before you begin writing a persuasive essay, for example, as you write you will be aware of specific criteria that are important in that kind of an essay. As you evaluate the essay before giving it to your teacher, you will focus on the specific areas that your teacher wants you to master— or on areas that you know present challenges for you. Instead of searching through your work randomly for any way to improve it or correct its errors, you will have a clear and helpful focus on specific criteria.

How are rubrics constructed?

Rubrics can be constructed in several different ways.

- Your teacher may assign a rubric for a specific assignment.
- Your teacher may direct you to a rubric in your textbook.
- Your teacher and your class may construct a rubric for a particular assignment together.
- You and your classmates may construct a rubric together.
- You may create your own rubric with criteria you want to evaluate in your work.

How will a rubric help me?

A rubric will help you assess your work on a scale. Scales vary from rubric to rubric but usually range from 6 to 1, 5 to 1, or 4 to 1, with 6, 5, or 4 being the highest score and 1 being the lowest. If someone else is using the rubric to assess your work, the rubric will give your evaluator a clear range within which to place your work. If you are using the rubric yourself, it will help you make improvements to your work.

What are the types of rubrics?

- A **holistic rubric** has general criteria that can apply to a variety of assignments. See p. R22 for an example of a holistic rubric.
- An **analytic rubric** is specific to a particular assignment. The criteria for evaluation address the specific issues important in that assignment. See p. R21 for examples of analytic rubrics.

SAMPLE ANALYTIC RUBRICS

Rubric With a 4-point Scale

The following analytic rubric is an example of a rubric to assess a persuasive essay.
It will help you evaluate audience and purpose, organization, elaboration, and use of language.

	Audience/Purpose	Organization	Elaboration	Use of Language
4	Demonstrates highly effective word choice; clearly focused on task.	Uses clear, consistent organizational strategy.	Provides convincing, well-elaborated reasons to support the position.	Incorporates transitions; includes very few mechanical errors.
3	Demonstrates good word choice; states focus on persuasive task.	Uses clear organizational strategy with occasional inconsistencies.	Provides two or more moderately elaborated reasons to support the position.	Incorporates some transitions; includes few mechanical errors.
2	Shows some good word choices; minimally states focus on persuasive task.	Uses inconsistent organizational strategy; presentation is not logical.	Provides several reasons but few are elaborated; only one elaborated reason.	Incorporates few transitions; includes many mechanical errors.
1	Shows lack of attention to persuasive task.	Demonstrates lack of organizational strategy.	Provides no specific reasons or does not elaborate.	Does not connect ideas; includes many mechanical errors.

Rubric With a 6-point Scale

The following analytic rubric is an example of a rubric to assess a persuasive essay.
It will help you evaluate presentation, position, evidence, and arguments.

	Presentation	Position	Evidence	Arguments
6	Essay clearly and effectively addresses an issue with more than one side.	Essay clearly states a supportable position on the issue.	All evidence is logically organized, well presented, and supports the position.	All reader concerns and counterarguments are presented effectively.
5	Most of essay addresses an issue that has more than one side.	Essay clearly states a position on the issue.	Most evidence is logically organized, well presented, and supports the position.	Most reader concerns and counterarguments are presented effectively.
4	Essay adequately addresses issue that has more than one side.	Essay adequately states a position on the issue.	Many parts of evidence support the position; some evidence is out of order.	Many reader concerns and counterarguments are presented adequately.
3	Essay addresses issue with two sides but does not present second side clearly.	Essay states a position on the issue, but the position is difficult to support.	Some evidence supports the position, but some evidence is out of order.	Some reader concerns and counterarguments are presented.
2	Essay addresses issue with two sides but does not present second side.	Essay states a position on the issue, but the position is not supportable.	Not much evidence supports the position, and what is included is out of order.	A few reader concerns and counterarguments are presented.
1	Essay does not address issue with more than one side.	Essay does not state a position on the issue.	No evidence supports the position.	No reader concerns or counterarguments are presented.

SAMPLE HOLISTIC RUBRIC

Holistic rubrics such as this one are sometimes used to assess writing assignments on standardized tests. Notice that the criteria for evaluation are focus, organization, support, and use of conventions.

Points	Criteria
6 Points	• The writing is strongly focused and shows fresh insight into the writing task. • The writing is marked by a sense of completeness and coherence and is organized with a logical progression of ideas. • A main idea is fully developed, and support is specific and substantial. • A mature command of the language is in evidence, and the writing may employ characteristic creative writing strategies. • Sentence structure is varied, and writing is free of all but purposefully used fragments. • Virtually no errors in writing conventions appear.
5 Points	• The writing is clearly focused on the task. • The writing is well organized and has a logical progression of ideas, though there may be occasional lapses. • A main idea is well developed and supported with relevant details. • Command of the language is mature. • Sentence structure is varied, and the writing is free of fragments, except when used purposefully. • Writing conventions are followed correctly.
4 Points	• The writing is clearly focused on the task, but extraneous material may intrude at times. • A clear organizational pattern is present, though lapses may occur. • A main idea is adequately supported, but development may be uneven. • Sentence structure is generally free of fragments but shows little variation. • Writing conventions are generally followed correctly.
3 Points	• Writing is generally focused on the task, but extraneous material may intrude at times. • An organizational pattern is evident, but writing may lack a logical progression of ideas. • Support for the main idea is generally present but is sometimes illogical. • Sentence structure is generally free of fragments, but there is almost no variation. • The work generally demonstrates a knowledge of writing conventions, with occasional misspellings.
2 Points	• The writing is related to the task but generally lacks focus. • There is little evidence of organizational pattern, and there is little sense of cohesion. • Support for the main idea is generally inadequate, illogical, or absent. • Sentence structure is unvaried, and serious errors may occur. • Errors in writing conventions and spelling are frequent.
1 Point	• The writing may have little connection to the task and is generally unfocused. • There has been little attempt at organization or development. • The paper seems fragmented, with no clear main idea. • Sentence structure is unvaried, and serious errors appear. • Poor word choice and poor command of the language obscure meaning. • Errors in writing conventions and spelling are frequent.
Unscorable	The paper is considered unscorable if • The response is unrelated to the task or is simply a rewording of the prompt. • The response has been copied from a published work. • The student did not write a response. • The response is illegible. • The words in the response are arranged with no meaning. • There is an insufficient amount of writing to score.

STUDENT MODEL

Persuasive Writing

This persuasive essay, which would receive a top score according to a persuasive rubric, is a response to the following writing prompt, or assignment:

Most young people today spend more than 5 hours a day watching television. Many adults worry about the effects on youth of seeing too much television violence. Write a persuasive piece in which you argue against or defend the effects of television watching on young people. Be sure to include examples to support your views.

Until the television was invented, families spent their time doing different activities. Now most families stay home and watch TV. Watching TV risks the family's health, reduces the children's study time, and is a bad influence on young minds. Watching television can be harmful.

> The writer clearly states a position in the first paragraph.

The most important reason why watching TV is bad is that the viewers get less exercise. For example, instead of watching their favorite show, people could exercise for 30 minutes. If people spent less time watching TV and more time exercising, then they could have healthier bodies. My mother told me a story about a man who died of a heart attack because he was out of shape from watching television all the time. Obviously, watching TV can put a person's health in danger.

> Each paragraph provides details that support the writer's main points.

Furthermore, watching television reduces children's study time. For example, children would spend more time studying if they didn't watch television. If students spent more time studying at home, then they would make better grades at school. Last week I had a major test in science, but I didn't study because I started watching a movie. I was not prepared for the test and my grade reflected my lack of studying. Indeed, watching television is bad because it can hurt a student's grades.

Finally, watching TV can be a bad influence on children. For example, some TV shows have inappropriate language and too much violence. If children watch programs that use bad language and show violence, then they may start repeating these actions because they think the behavior is "cool." In fact, it has been proven that children copy what they see on TV. Clearly, watching TV is bad for children and it affects children's behavior.

In conclusion, watching television is a bad influence for these reasons: It reduces people's exercise time and students' study time and it shows children inappropriate behavior. Therefore, people should take control of their lives and stop allowing television to harm them.

> The conclusion restates the writer's position.

TYPES OF WRITING

NARRATION

Whenever writers tell any type of story, they are using **narration.** While there are many kinds of narration, most narratives share certain elements, such as characters, a setting, a sequence of events, and, often, a theme.

Autobiographical writing tells the story of an event or person in the writer's life.

Biographical writing is a writer's account of another person's life.

Short story A short story is a brief, creative narrative—a retelling of events arranged to hold a reader's attention.

A few types of short stories are: realistic stories, fantasy, science-fiction stories, and adventure stories.

DESCRIPTION

Descriptive writing is writing that creates a vivid picture of a person, place, thing, or event. Descriptive writing can stand on its own or be part of a longer work, such as a short story.

Descriptive writing includes descriptions of people or places, remembrances, observations, vignettes, and character profiles.

PERSUASION

Persuasion is writing or speaking that attempts to convince people to accept a position or take a desired action. When used effectively, persuasive writing has the power to change people's lives. As a reader and a writer, you will find yourself engaged in many forms of persuasion.

Forms of persuasive writing include persuasive essays, advertisements, persuasive letters, editorials, persuasive speeches, and public-service announcements.

EXPOSITORY WRITING

Expository writing is writing that informs or explains. The information you include in expository writing is factual or based on fact. Effective expository writing reflects a well-thought-out organization—one that includes a clear introduction, body, and conclusion. The organization should be appropriate for the type of exposition you are writing. Here are some types of exposition.

Comparison-and-Contrast essay A comparison-and-contrast essay analyzes the similarities and differences between two or more things.

Cause-and-Effect essay A cause-and-effect essay is expository writing that explains the reasons why something happened or the results an event or situation will probably produce. You may examine several causes of a single effect or several effects of a single cause.

Problem-and-Solution essay The purpose of a problem-and-solution essay is to describe a problem and offer one or more solutions to it. It describes a clear set of steps to achieve a result.

How-to essay A how-to essay explains how to do or make something. You break the process down into a series of logical steps and explain the steps in order.

Summary A summary is a brief statement of the main ideas and significant supporting details presented in a piece of writing. A summary should include

- main events, ideas, or images.
- connections among significant details.
- your own words.
- underlying meaning rather than superficial details.
- background information, such as setting or characters.

RESEARCH WRITING

Writers often use outside research to gather information and explore subjects of interest. The product of that research is called **research writing.** Good research writing does not simply repeat information. It guides readers through a topic, showing them why each fact matters and creating an overall picture of the subject. Here are some types of research writing.

Research report A research report presents information gathered from reference books, observations, interviews, or other sources.

Biographical report A biographical report examines the high points and achievements in the life of a notable person. It includes dates, details, and main events in the person's life as well as background on the period in which the person lived. The writer may also make educated guesses about the reasons behind events in the person's life.

Multimedia report A multimedia report presents information gathered from a variety of reliable sources, both print and nonprint. A wide range of materials are available, such as tape recorders, videocameras, slides, photographs, overhead projectors, prerecorded music and sound effects, digital imaging, graphics software, computers, spreadsheets, data bases, electronic resources, and web sites.

I-Search report An I-Search report begins with a topic of immediate concern to you and provides well-researched information on that topic. Unlike a research report, it tells the story of your exploration of the topic, using the pronoun *I*. It explains

- your purpose in learning about the topic.
- the story of how you researched it.
- an account of what you learned.

RESPONSE TO LITERATURE

A **response to literature** is an essay or other type of writing that discusses and interprets what is of value in a book, short story, essay, article, or poem. You take a careful, critical look at various important elements in the work.

In addition to the standard literary essay, here are some other types of responses to literature.

Literary Criticism Literary criticism is the result of literary analysis—the examination of a literary work or a body of literature. In literary criticism, you make a judgment or evaluation by looking carefully and critically at various important elements in the work. You then attempt to explain how the author has used those elements and how effectively they work together to convey the author's message.

Book or movie reviews A book review gives readers an impression of a book, encouraging them either to read it or to avoid reading it. A movie review begins with a basic response to whether or not you enjoyed the movie, and then explains the reasons why or why not.

Letter to an author People sometimes respond to a work of literature by writing a letter to the writer. It lets the writer know what a reader found enjoyable or disappointing in a work. You can praise the work, ask questions, or offer constructive criticism.

Comparisons of works A comparison of works highlights specific features of two or more works by comparing them.

CREATIVE WRITING

Creative writing blends imagination, ideas, and emotions, and allows you to present your own unique view of the world. Poems, plays, short stories, dramas,

and even some cartoons are examples of creative writing. Here are some types of creative writing.

Lyric Poem A lyric poem uses sensory images, figurative language, and sound devices to express deep thoughts and feelings about a subject. Writers give lyric poems a musical quality by employing sound devices, such as rhyme, rhythm, alliteration, and onomatopoeia.

Narrative poem A narrative poem is similar to a short story in that it has a plot, characters, and a theme. However, a writer divides a narrative poem into stanzas, usually composed of rhyming lines that have a definite rhythm, or beat.

Song lyrics Song lyrics, or words to accompany a song contain many elements of poetry—rhyme, rhythm, repetition, and imagery. In addition, song lyrics convey emotions, as well as interesting ideas.

Drama A drama or a dramatic scene is a story that is intended to be performed. The story is told mostly through what the actors say (dialogue) and what they do (action).

PRACTICAL AND TECHNICAL DOCUMENTS

Practical writing is fact-based writing that people do in the workplace or in their day-to-day lives. A business letter, memorandum, school form, job application, and a letter of inquiry are a few examples of practical writing.

Technical documents are fact-based documents that identify the sequence of activities needed to design a system, operate a tool, follow a procedure, or explain the bylaws of an organization. You encounter technical writing every time you read a manual or a set of instructions.

In the following descriptions, you'll find tips for tackling several types of practical and technical writing.

Business letter A formal letter that follows one of several specific formats. (See page R28).

News release A news release, also called a press release, announces factual information about upcoming events. A writer might send a news release to a local newspaper, local radio station, TV station, or other media that will publicize the information.

Guidelines Guidelines give information about how people should act or provide tips on how to do something.

Process explanation A process explanation is a step-by-step explanation of how to do something. Your explanation should be clear and specific and might include diagrams or other illustrations to further clarify the process.

Proofreading and Preparing Manuscript

Before preparing a final copy, proofread your manuscript. The chart shows the standard symbols for marking corrections to be made.

Proofreading Symbols	
insert	∧
delete	⌿
close space	⌒
new paragraph	¶
add comma	⌃
add period	⊙
transpose (switch)	∿
change to cap	a̲
change to lower case	A̸

- Choose a standard, easy-to-read font.
- Type or print on one side of unlined 8 1/2" x 11" paper.
- Set the margins for the side, top, and bottom of your paper at approximately one inch. Most word-processing programs have a default setting that is appropriate.
- Double-space the document.
- Indent the first line of each paragraph.
- Number the pages in the upper right corner.

Follow your teacher's directions for formatting formal research papers. Most papers will have the following features:

- Title page
- Table of Contents or Outline
- Works-Cited List

Avoiding Plagiarism

Whether you are presenting a formal research paper or an opinion paper on a current event, you must be careful to give credit for any ideas or opinions that are not your own. Presenting someone else's ideas, research, or opinion as your own—even if you have rephrased it in different words—is *plagiarism*, the equivalent of academic stealing, or fraud.

Do not use the ideas or research of others in place of your own. Read from several sources to draw your own conclusions and form your own opinions. Incorporate the ideas and research of others to support your points. Credit the source of the following types of support:

- Statistics
- Direct quotations
- Indirectly quoted statements of opinions
- Conclusions presented by an expert
- Facts available in only one or two sources

Crediting Sources

When you credit a source, you acknowledge where you found your information and you give your readers the details necessary for locating the source themselves. Within the body of the paper, you provide a short citation, a footnote number linked to a footnote, or an endnote number linked to an endnote reference. These brief references show the page numbers on which you found the information. Prepare a reference list at the end of the paper to provide full bibliographic information on your sources. These are two common types of reference lists:

- A **bibliography** provides a listing of all the resources you consulted during your research.
- A **works-cited list** indicates the works you have referenced in your paper.

The chart on the next page shows the Modern Language Association format for crediting sources. This is the most common format for papers written in the content areas in middle school and high school. Unless instructed otherwise by your teacher, use this format for crediting sources.

MLA Style for Listing Sources

Book with one author	Pyles, Thomas. *The Origins and Development of the English Language.* 2nd ed. New York: Harcourt Brace Jovanovich, Inc., 1971.
Book with two or three authors	McCrum, Robert, William Cran, and Robert MacNeil. *The Story of English.* New York: Penguin Books, 1987.
Book with an editor	Truth, Sojourner. *Narrative of Sojourner Truth.* Ed. Margaret Washington. New York: Vintage Books, 1993.
Book with more than three authors or editors	Donald, Robert B., et al. *Writing Clear Essays.* Upper Saddle River, NJ: Prentice-Hall, Inc., 1996.
A single work from an anthology	Hawthorne, Nathaniel. "Young Goodman Brown." *Literature: An Introduction to Reading and Writing.* Ed. Edgar V. Roberts and Henry E. Jacobs. Upper Saddle River, NJ: Prentice-Hall, Inc., 1998. 376–385. [Indicate pages for the entire selection.]
Introduction in a published edition	Washington, Margaret. Introduction. *Narrative of Sojourner Truth.* By Sojourner Truth. New York: Vintage Books, 1993. v–xi.
Signed article in a weekly magazine	Wallace, Charles. "A Vodacious Deal." *Time* 14 Feb. 2000: 63.
Signed article in a monthly magazine	Gustaitis, Joseph. "The Sticky History of Chewing Gum." *American History* Oct. 1998: 30–38.
Unsigned editorial or story	"Selective Silence." Editorial. *Wall Street Journal* 11 Feb. 2000: A14. [If the editorial or story is signed, begin with the author's name.]
Signed pamphlet	[Treat the pamphlet as though it were a book.]
Pamphlet with no author, publisher, or date	*Are You at Risk of Heart Attack?* n.p. n.d. [n.p. n.d. indicates that there is no known publisher or date]
Filmstrip, slide program, or videotape	*The Diary of Anne Frank.* Dir. George Stevens. Perf. Millie Perkins, Shelley Winters, Joseph Schildkraut, Lou Jacobi, and Richard Beymer. Twentieth Century Fox, 1959.
Radio or television program transcript	"Nobel for Literature." Narr. Rick Karr. *All Things Considered.* National Public Radio. WNYC, New York. 10 Oct. 2002. Transcript.
Internet	*National Association of Chewing Gum Manufacturers.* 19 Dec. 1999 <http://www.nacgm.org/consumer/funfacts.html> [Indicate the date you accessed the information. Content and addresses at Web sites change frequently.]
Newspaper article	Thurow, Roger. "South Africans Who Fought for Sanctions Now Scrap for Investors." *Wall Street Journal* 11 Feb. 2000: A1+ [For a multipage article, write only the first page number on which it appears, followed by a plus sign.]
Personal interview	Smith, Jane. Personal interview. 10 Feb. 2000.
CD (with multiple publishers)	Simms, James, ed. *Romeo and Juliet.* By William Shakespeare. CD-ROM. Oxford: Attica Cybernetics Ltd.; London: BBC Education; London: HarperCollins Publishers, 1995.
Article from an encyclopedia	Askeland, Donald R. "Welding." *World Book Encyclopedia.* 1991 ed.

Formatting Business Letters

Business letters follow one of several acceptable formats. In **block format** each part of the letter begins at the left margin. A double space is used between paragraphs. In **modified block format**, some parts of the letter are indented to the center of the page. No matter which format is used, all letters in business format have a heading, an inside address, a salutation, or greeting, a body, a closing, and a signature. These parts are shown and annotated on the model business letter below, formatted in modified block style.

Model Business Letter

In this letter, Yolanda Dodson uses modified block format to request information.

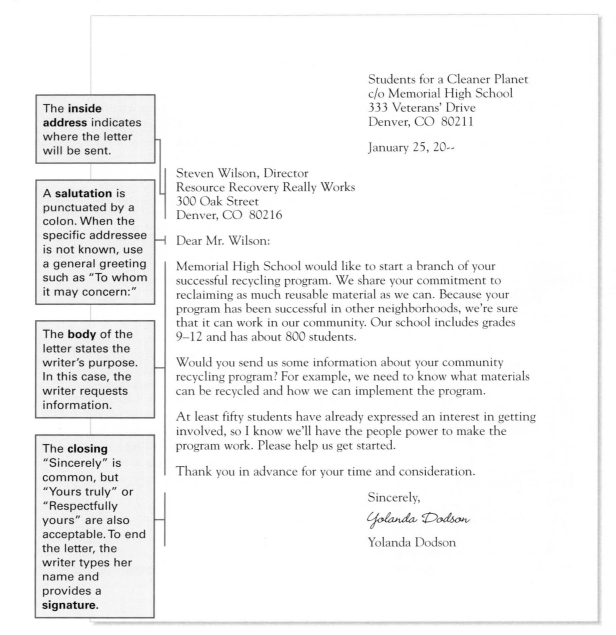

The **inside address** indicates where the letter will be sent.

A **salutation** is punctuated by a colon. When the specific addressee is not known, use a general greeting such as "To whom it may concern:"

The **body** of the letter states the writer's purpose. In this case, the writer requests information.

The **closing** "Sincerely" is common, but "Yours truly" or "Respectfully yours" are also acceptable. To end the letter, the writer types her name and provides a **signature**.

Students for a Cleaner Planet
c/o Memorial High School
333 Veterans' Drive
Denver, CO 80211

January 25, 20--

Steven Wilson, Director
Resource Recovery Really Works
300 Oak Street
Denver, CO 80216

Dear Mr. Wilson:

Memorial High School would like to start a branch of your successful recycling program. We share your commitment to reclaiming as much reusable material as we can. Because your program has been successful in other neighborhoods, we're sure that it can work in our community. Our school includes grades 9–12 and has about 800 students.

Would you send us some information about your community recycling program? For example, we need to know what materials can be recycled and how we can implement the program.

At least fifty students have already expressed an interest in getting involved, so I know we'll have the people power to make the program work. Please help us get started.

Thank you in advance for your time and consideration.

Sincerely,

Yolanda Dodson

Yolanda Dodson

Writing Friendly Letters

A friendly letter is much less formal than a business letter. It is a letter to a friend, a family member, or anyone with whom the writer wants to communicate in a personal, friendly way. Most friendly letters are made up of five parts:

- the heading
- the salutation, or greeting
- the body
- the closing
- the signature

The purpose of a friendly letter is often one of the following:

- to share personal news and feelings
- to send or to answer an invitation
- to express thanks

Model Friendly Letter

In this friendly letter, Betsy thanks her grandparents for a birthday present and gives them some news about her life.

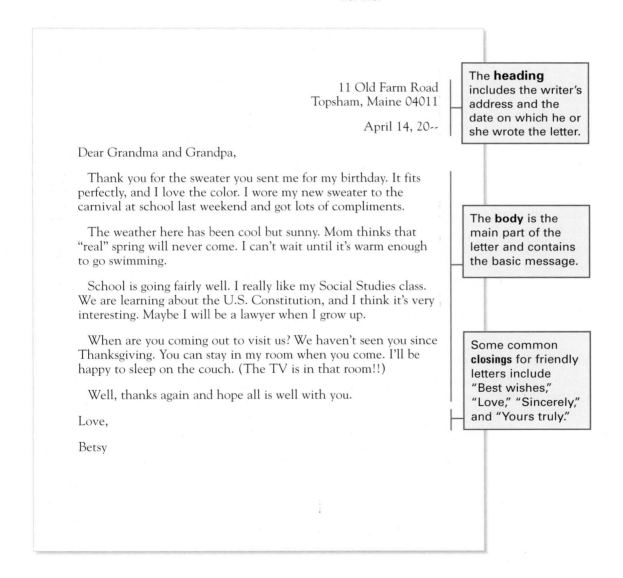

11 Old Farm Road
Topsham, Maine 04011

April 14, 20--

The **heading** includes the writer's address and the date on which he or she wrote the letter.

Dear Grandma and Grandpa,

Thank you for the sweater you sent me for my birthday. It fits perfectly, and I love the color. I wore my new sweater to the carnival at school last weekend and got lots of compliments.

The weather here has been cool but sunny. Mom thinks that "real" spring will never come. I can't wait until it's warm enough to go swimming.

School is going fairly well. I really like my Social Studies class. We are learning about the U.S. Constitution, and I think it's very interesting. Maybe I will be a lawyer when I grow up.

When are you coming out to visit us? We haven't seen you since Thanksgiving. You can stay in my room when you come. I'll be happy to sleep on the couch. (The TV is in that room!!)

Well, thanks again and hope all is well with you.

Love,

Betsy

The **body** is the main part of the letter and contains the basic message.

Some common **closings** for friendly letters include "Best wishes," "Love," "Sincerely," and "Yours truly."

Key Word Search

Before you begin a search, you should identify your specific topic. To make searching easier, narrow your subject to a key word or a group of **key words.** These are your search terms, and they should be as specific as possible. For example, if you are looking for information about your favorite musical group, you might use the band's name as a key word. You might locate such information as band member biographies, the group's history, fan reviews of concerts, and hundreds of sites with related names containing information that is irrelevant to your search. Depending on your research needs you might need to narrow your search.

How to Narrow Your Search

If you have a large group of key words and still don't know which ones to use, write out a list of all the words you are considering. Once you have completed the list, scrutinize it. Then, delete the words that are least important to your search, and highlight those that are most important.

These **key search connectors** can help you fine-tune your search:

AND: narrows a search by retrieving documents that include both terms. For example: *baseball AND playoffs*

OR: broadens a search by retrieving documents including any of the terms. For example: *playoffs OR championships*

NOT: narrows a search by excluding documents containing certain words. For example: *baseball NOT history*

Tips for an Effective Search

1. Keep in mind that search engines can be case-sensitive. If your first attempt at searching fails, check your search terms for misspellings and try again.

2. If you are entering a group of key words, present them in order, from the most important to the least important key word.

3. Avoid opening the link to every single page in your results list. Search engines present pages in descending order of relevancy. The most useful pages will be located at the top of the list. However, read the description of each link before you open the page.

4. When you use some search engines, you can find helpful tips for specializing your search. Take the opportunity to learn more about effective searching.

Tips for Evaluating Internet Sources

Consider who constructed and who now maintains the Web page. Determine whether this author is a reputable source. Often, the URL endings indicate a source.

- Sites ending in *.edu* are maintained by educational institutions.
- Sites ending in *.gov* are maintained by government agencies (federal, state, or local).
- Sites ending in *.org* are normally maintained by nonprofit organizations and agencies.
- Sites with a *.com* ending are commercially or personally maintained.

Other Ways to Search

How you search should be tailored to what you are hoping to find. If you are looking for data and facts, use reference sites before you jump onto a simple search engine. For example, you can find reference sites to provide definitions of words, statistics about almost any subject, biographies, maps, and concise information on many topics. Some useful online reference sites:

Online libraries

Online periodicals

Almanacs

Encyclopedias

You can also use other electronic sources such as CD-ROMs. Ask a reference librarian to help you locate and use the full range of electronic resources.

Respecting Copyrighted Material

Because the Internet is a relatively new and quickly growing medium, issues of copyright and ownership arise almost daily. As laws begin to govern the use and reuse of material posted online, they may change the way that people can access or reprint material.

Text, photographs, music, and fine art printed online may not be reproduced without acknowledged permission of the copyright owner.

Applying Spelling Rules

Choosing Between *ie* and *ei*

When a word has a long *e* sound, use *ie*. When a word has a long *a* sound, use *ei*. When a word has a long *e* sound preceded by the letter *c*, use *ei*.

Long *e* Sound	Long *a* Sound	Long *e* Sound Preceded by *c*
believe	freight	deceive
grief	reign	receive

Exceptions: either, neither, seize, weird

Choosing the Ending *-cede, -ceed,* or *-sede*

There are ten words that end with this sound. You will need to memorize their spellings.

-cede Words	*-ceed* Words	*-sede* Words
accede	exceed	supersede
concede	proceed	
intercede	succeed	
precede		
recede		
secede		

Adding Prefixes

A *prefix* is one or more syllables added at the beginning of a word to form a new word. Adding a prefix to a word does not usually change the spelling of the original word.

re- + place = replace

un- + fair = unfair

mis- + spell = misspell

dis- + appear = disappear

il- + legal = illegal

Adding Suffixes

A *suffix* is one or more syllables added at the end of a word to form a new word. Adding a suffix often involves a spelling change in the original word.

Adding Suffixes That Begin With a Consonant

When adding a suffix that begins with a consonant—such as *-ly, -ness, -less, -ment,* and *-ful*—you usually do not change the spelling of the original word.

calm + *-ly* = calmly

open + *-ness* = openness

time + *-less* = timeless

employ + *-ment* = employment

help + *-ful* = helpful

Except for *truly, argument, judgment, daily*

Exceptions: If a word ends in *y* preceded by a consonant, change the *y* to *i* before adding these suffixes:

ready + *-ly* = readily

busy + *-ness* = business

Except for *shyness, slyly, spryness*

Adding Suffixes to Words That End in Silent *e*

If a word ends in a silent *e*, drop the *e* before adding a suffix that begins with a vowel.

love + *-able* = lovable

Except for *changeable, agreeable, useable*

Adding Suffixes That Begin With a Vowel to Words That End in *y*

When adding a suffix that begins with a vowel to a word that ends in *y* preceded by a consonant, change the *y* to *i* before adding the suffix.

greedy + *-er* = greedier

worry + *-ed* = worried

Exceptions: Do not change the *y* to *i* if the suffix begins with *i*—*carrying, babyish*

When adding a suffix that begins with a vowel to a word that ends in *y* preceded by a vowel, keep the *y* before adding the suffix.

portray + *-al* = portrayal

obey + *-ed* = obeyed

Exceptions: paid (not *payed*), said (not *sayed*), laid (not *layed*), gaiety (not *gayety*)

Doubling the Final Consonant Before Adding a Suffix

If a one-syllable word ends in a single consonant preceded by a single vowel, double the final consonant before adding a suffix that begins with a vowel.

stop + -ed = stopped

dim + -ing = dimming

Exceptions: Words that end in *x, y,* or *w* (*mixer, prayed, flowing*)

If a word of more than one syllable ends in a single consonant preceded by a single vowel and the accent is on the final syllable, double the final consonant before adding a suffix that begins with a vowel.

omit + -ed = omitted

occur + -ence = occurrence

Exceptions: Words in which the accent shifts when the suffix is added (*prefer—preference*)

Do not double the final consonant if the accent is not on the last syllable.

travel + -ing = traveling

endanger + -ed = endangered

Forming the Plurals of Nouns

Forming Regular Plurals The rules below apply to most nouns whose plurals are formed in regular ways.

Noun Ending	Rule	Examples
s, ss, x, z, *zz, sh, ch*	Add *-es*	circus, circuses lass, lasses fox, foxes waltz, waltzes buzz, buzzes bush, bushes church, churches
o preceded by a consonant	Add *-es*	potato, potatoes hero, heroes *Exceptions:* Musical terms— solo, solos piano, pianos
o preceded by a vowel	Add *-s*	radio, radios patio, patios
y preceded by a consonant	Change *y* to *i* and add *-es*	party, parties enemy, enemies
y preceded by a vowel	Add *-s*	key, keys convoy, convoys
ff	Add *-s*	staff, staffs sheriff, sheriffs
fe	Change *f* to *v* and add *-es*	life, lives knife, knives
f	Add *-s*	chief, chiefs roof, roofs
	OR	
	Change *f* to *v* and add *-es*	leaf, leaves shelf, shelves

Forming Irregular Plurals The plurals of some nouns are formed in irregular ways. You will need to memorize these:

goose, geese	foot, feet
man, men	woman, women
ox, oxen	child, children
tooth, teeth	mouse, mice
deer, deer	sheep, sheep

Forming Plurals of Compound Nouns Most one-word compound nouns have regular plural forms. If one part of a compound word is irregular, the plural form will also be irregular.

flashlight, flashlights (regular)

handful, handfuls (regular)

stepchild, stepchildren (irregular)

The plurals of most compound nouns written with hyphens or as separate words are formed by making the modified word—the word being described—plural.

mother-in-law, mothers-in-law

Web site, Web sites

Forming Plurals of Proper Nouns To form the plurals of proper nouns, follow the same rules as with common nouns. In most cases, simply add -s to the proper noun. Add -es if the name ends in *s, ss, x, z, sh,* or *ch.*

> There are two Anns in our class.
>
> All of the Coxes arrived in one car.

For proper nouns ending in *y*, just add -s. Do not change the *y* to *i* and add -es.

> The Kennedys live in the house on the corner.
>
> There are two Kansas Citys; one in Missouri and one in Kansas.

Forming Plurals of Signs and Symbols Use an apostrophe and an -s to write the plurals of numbers, symbols, letters, and words used to name themselves.

> Business names often include &'s.
>
> All of the 6's were written as 9's.
>
> She received only *A*'s and *B*'s.
>
> You used too many *and*'s in this sentence.

Writing Numbers

Spelling Out Numbers If a number begins a sentence, spell it out.

> *Twenty-two* players are on the field during a football game.

Within a sentence, spell out numbers that can be written in one or two words.

> There are *fifty-two* weeks in a year.

Spell out numbers used to indicate place or order.

> Shelley came in *second* in the race.
>
> This is the *fifth* day in a row that it has rained.

Using Numerals Use numerals for longer numbers that come within a sentence.

> Approximately *875* people attended the game.

If you include both small and large numbers in the same sentence, write them in the same way. It is best to use numerals.

> During a *12*-hour period, we counted *680* cars crossing the intersection.

Suggestions for Improving Your Spelling

Start a Personal Spelling List

Select the words that you have difficulty spelling, enter them in a special area in your notebook, and study them regularly. Add new words to your list, and cross out words you have mastered. You may find many of the words on your list among the Commonly Misspelled Words on the next page of this textbook.

Sound Out Difficult Words

Say the words aloud. Then, sound them out syllable by syllable as you study how to spell them.

Devise Memory Aids

Underline the part of a word that gives you the most trouble. Then, develop a memory device to help you remember the correct spelling.

Word	Memory Aid
de<u>ss</u>ert	My de<u>ss</u>ert is me<u>ss</u>y.
lib<u>r</u>ary	lib<u>r</u>ary b<u>r</u>anch
ne<u>c</u>essary	Only one <u>c</u> is ne<u>c</u>essary.

Look for Roots and Derivatives

Many words have common *roots*. Look for the root inside a word to help you focus on its spelling. Then, use the root to help you spell related words.

> <u>bene</u>fit, <u>bene</u>ficial, <u>bene</u>factor
>
> pre<u>ferr</u>ed, re<u>ferr</u>ed, in<u>ferr</u>ed
>
> de<u>cide</u>, in<u>cide</u>nt, ac<u>cide</u>nt
>
> trans<u>mit</u>, trans<u>miss</u>ion, ad<u>mit</u>, ad<u>miss</u>ion

A *derivative* is a word that is formed from another word. Once you know how to spell a base word—the word from which the others are formed—you can more easily learn to spell its derivatives.

> de<u>ci</u>de, de<u>ci</u>sion, de<u>ci</u>sive
>
> <u>cau</u>tion, <u>cau</u>tious, pre<u>cau</u>tion
>
> regu<u>l</u>ar, regu<u>l</u>ation, regu<u>l</u>ate
>
> stron<u>g</u>, stren<u>g</u>th, stren<u>g</u>then

Commonly Misspelled Words

The words listed on this page are ones that cause spelling problems for many people. As you review the list, check to see how many of the words give you trouble in your own writing. Then, try some of the suggestions for improving your spelling discussed on the previous page.

abbreviate	bicycle	criticize	grammar	naturally	realize
absence	bookkeeper	cylinder	grievance	necessary	really
absolutely	boulevard	deceive	guarantee	negotiate	receipt
accelerate	brief	decision	guard	neighbor	recipe
accidentally	brilliant	defendant	guidance	neutral	recognize
accurate	bruise	definitely	handkerchief	nickel	recommend
ache	bulletin	delinquent	harass	niece	rehearse
achievement	buoy	dependent	height	ninety	relevant
acquaintance	bureau	descendant	humorous	noticeable	reminiscence
adequate	bury	description	hygiene	nuclear	renowned
advertisement	buses	desirable	immediately	nuisance	repetition
aerial	business	dessert	immigrant	obstacle	restaurant
aggravate	cafeteria	dining	independent	occasion	rhythm
agreeable	calendar	disappoint	individual	occurrence	ridiculous
aisle	campaign	disastrous	inflammable	omitted	sandwich
all right	canceled	discipline	interfere	opinion	satellite
aluminum	candidate	eighth	irritable	opportunity	schedule
amateur	captain	eligible	jewelry	optimistic	scissors
analysis	career	embarrass	judgment	outrageous	secretary
analyze	carriage	enthusiastic	knowledge	pamphlet	siege
ancient	cashier	entrepreneur	laboratory	parallel	sincerely
anecdote	category	envelope	lawyer	paralyze	solely
anniversary	ceiling	environment	legible	parentheses	sponsor
anonymous	cemetery	equipped	legislature	particularly	subtle
answer	census	equivalent	leisure	patience	superintendent
anxiety	certain	especially	liable	permanent	surveillance
apologize	characteristic	exaggerate	library	permissible	susceptible
appall	chauffeur	excel	license	perseverance	tariff
appearance	clothes	excellent	lieutenant	persistent	temperamental
appreciate	colonel	exercise	lightning	perspiration	theater
appropriate	column	existence	likable	persuade	threshold
architecture	commercial	extraordinary	liquefy	phenomenon	truly
argument	commitment	familiar	literature	physician	unmanageable
associate	committee	fascinating	maintenance	pneumonia	unwieldy
athletic	competitor	February	marriage	possession	usage
attendance	condemn	fiery	mathematics	prairie	usually
awkward	congratulate	financial	maximum	preferable	valuable
banquet	conscience	fluorescent	meanness	prejudice	various
bargain	conscious	foreign	mediocre	prerogative	vegetable
barrel	convenience	forfeit	mileage	privilege	voluntary
battery	cooperate	fourth	millionaire	probably	volunteer
beautiful	correspondence	fragile	minuscule	procedure	weight
beggar	counterfeit	gauge	miscellaneous	pronunciation	weird
beginning	courageous	genius	mischievous	psychology	whale
behavior	courteous	genuine	misspell	pursue	wield
benefit	criticism	government	mortgage	questionnaire	yield

Parts of Speech

Nouns A **noun** is the name of a person, place, or thing. A **common noun** names any one of a class of people, places, or things. A **proper noun** names a specific person, place, or thing.

Common Nouns	Proper Nouns
writer	Francisco Jiménez
city	Los Angeles

Pronouns A **pronoun** is a word that stands for a noun or for a word that takes the place of a noun.

A **personal pronoun** refers to (1) the person speaking, (2) the person spoken to, or (3) the person, place, or thing spoken about.

	Singular	Plural
First Person	I, me, my, mine	we, us, our, ours
Second Person	you, your, yours	you, your, yours
Third Person	he, him, his, she, her, hers, it, its	they, them, their, theirs

A **demonstrative pronoun** directs attention to a specific person, place, or thing.

These are the juiciest pears I have ever tasted.

An **interrogative pronoun** is used to begin a question.

Who is the author of "Jeremiah's Song"?

An **indefinite pronoun** refers to a person, place, or thing, often without specifying which one.

Many of the players were tired.

Everyone bought something.

Verbs A **verb** is a word that expresses time while showing an action, a condition, or the fact that something exists.

An **action verb** indicates the action of someone or something.

A **linking verb** connects the subject of a sentence with a noun or a pronoun that renames or describes the subject.

A **helping verb** can be added to another verb to make a single verb phrase.

Adjectives An **adjective** describes a noun or a pronoun or gives a noun or a pronoun a more specific meaning. Adjectives answer the questions *what kind, which one, how many, how much.*

The articles *the, a,* and *an* are adjectives. *An* is used before a word beginning with a vowel sound.

A noun may sometimes be used as an adjective.

family home   *science* fiction

Adverbs An **adverb** modifies a verb, an adjective, or another adverb. Adverbs answer the questions *where, when, in what way,* or *to what extent.*

Prepositions A **preposition** relates a noun or a pronoun following it to another word in the sentence.

Conjunctions A **conjunction** connects other words or groups of words.

A **coordinating conjunction** connects similar kinds or groups of words.

Correlative conjunctions are used in pairs to connect similar words or groups of words.

both Grandpa *and* Dad   *neither* they *nor* I

Interjections An **interjection** is a word that expresses feeling or emotion and functions independently of a sentence.

"Ah!" says he—

Phrases, Clauses, and Sentences

Sentences A **sentence** is a group of words with two main parts: a complete subject and a complete predicate. Together, these parts express a complete thought.

We read that story last year.

A **fragment** is a group of words that does not express a complete thought.

"Not right away."

Subject The **subject** of a sentence is the word or group of words that tells whom or what the sentence is about. The **simple subject** is the essential noun, pronoun, or group of words acting as a noun that cannot be left out of the complete subject. A **complete subject** is the simple subject plus any modifiers. In the following example, the complete subject is underlined. The simple subject is italicized.

Pony express *riders* carried packages more than 2,000 miles.

A **compound subject** is two or more subjects that have the same verb and are joined by a conjunction.

> Neither the *horse nor the driver* looked tired.

Predicate The **predicate** of a sentence is the verb or verb phrase that tells what the complete subject of the sentence does or is. The **simple predicate** is the essential verb or verb phrase that cannot be left out of the complete predicate. A **complete predicate** is the simple predicate plus any modifiers or complements. In the following example, the complete predicate is underlined. The simple predicate is italicized.

> Pony express riders *carried* packages more than 2,000 miles.

A **compound predicate** is two or more verbs that have the same subject and are joined by a conjunction.

> She *sneezed and coughed* throughout the trip.

Complement A **complement** is a word or group of words that completes the meaning of the predicate of a sentence. Five different kinds of complements can be found in English sentences: *direct objects, indirect objects, objective complements, predicate nominatives* and *predicate adjectives.*

A **direct object** is a noun, pronoun, or group of words acting as a noun that receives the action of a transitive verb.

> We watched the *liftoff.*

An **indirect object** is a noun, pronoun, or group of words that appears with a direct object and names the person or thing that something is given to or done for.

> He sold the *family* a mirror.

An **objective complement** is an adjective or noun that appears with a direct object and describes or renames it.

> I called Meg my *friend.*

A **subject complement** is a noun, pronoun, or adjective that appears with a linking verb and tells something about the subject. A subject complement may be a *predicate nominative* or a *predicate adjective.*

A **predicate nominative** is a noun or pronoun that appears with a linking verb and renames, identifies, or explains the subject.

> Kiglo was the *leader.*

A **predicate adjective** is an adjective that appears with a linking verb and describes the subject of a sentence.

> Roko became *tired.*

Simple Sentence A **simple sentence** consists of a single independent clause.

Compound Sentence A **compound sentence** consists of two or more independent clauses joined by a comma and a coordinating conjunction or by a semicolon.

Complex Sentence A **complex sentence** consists of one independent clause and one or more subordinate clauses.

Compound-Complex Sentence A **compound-complex sentence** consists of two or more independent clauses and one or more subordinate clauses.

Declarative Sentence A **declarative sentence** states an idea and ends with a period.

Interrogative Sentence An **interrogative sentence** asks a question and ends with a question mark.

Imperative Sentence An **imperative sentence** gives an order or a direction and ends with either a period or an exclamation mark.

Exclamatory Sentence An **exclamatory sentence** conveys a strong emotion and ends with an exclamation mark.

Phrases A **phrase** is a group of words, without a subject and a verb, that functions in a sentence as one part of speech.

A **prepositional phrase** is a group of words that includes a preposition and a noun or a pronoun that is the object of the preposition.

> near the town   with them

An **adjective phrase** is a prepositional phrase that modifies a noun or a pronoun by telling *what kind* or *which one.*

> Mr. Sanderson brushed his hands over the shoes in the window . . . .

An **adverb phrase** is a prepositional phrase that modifies a verb, an adjective, or an adverb by pointing out *where, when, in what manner,* or *to what extent.*

> The trees were black where the bark was wet.

An **appositive phrase** is a noun or a pronoun with modifiers, placed next to a noun or a pronoun to add information and details.

> The story, *a tale of adventure,* takes place in the Yukon.

A **participial phrase** is a participle modified by an adjective or an adverb phrase or accompanied by a complement. The entire phrase acts as an adjective.

> *Running at top speed,* he soon caught up with them.

An **infinitive phrase** is an infinitive with modifiers, complements, or a subject, all acting together as a single part of speech.

> At first I was too busy enjoying my food *to notice how the guests were doing.*

Clauses A **clause** is a group of words with its own subject and verb.

An **independent clause** can stand by itself as a complete sentence.

> "I think it belongs to Rachel."

A **subordinate clause** has a subject and a verb but cannot stand by itself as a complete sentence; it can only be part of a sentence.

> "Although it was late"

Using Verbs and Pronouns

Principal Parts A verb has four **principal parts**: the *present,* the *present participle,* the *past,* and the *past participle.*

Regular verbs form the past and past participle by adding -*ed* to the present form.

> **Present**: walk
> **Present Participle**: (am) walking
> **Past**: walked
> **Past Participle**: (have) walked

Irregular verbs form the past and past participle by changing form rather than by adding -*ed.*

> **Present**: go
> **Present Participle**: (am) going
> **Past**: gone
> **Past Participle**: (have) gone

Verb Tense A **verb tense** tells whether the time of an action or condition is in the past, the present, or the future. Every verb has six tenses: *present, past, future, present perfect, past perfect,* and *future perfect.*

The **present tense** shows actions that happen in the present.

The **past tense** shows actions that have already happened.

The **future tense** shows actions that will happen.

The **present perfect tense** shows actions that begin in the past and continue to the present.

The **past perfect tense** shows a past action or condition that ended before another past action.

The **future perfect tense** shows a future action or condition that will have ended before another begins.

Pronoun Case The **case** of a pronoun is the form it takes to show its use in a sentence. There are three pronoun cases: *nominative, objective,* and *possessive.*

The **nominative case** is used to name or rename the subject of the sentence. The nominative case pronouns are *I, you, he, she, it, we, you, they.*

> **As the subject:** *She* is brave.
> **Renaming the subject:** The leader is *she.*

The **objective case** is used as the direct object, indirect object, or object of a preposition. The objective case pronouns are *me, you, him, her, it, us, you, them.*

> **As a direct object:** Tom called *me.*
> **As an indirect object:** My friend gave *me* advice.
> **As an object of preposition:** The coach gave pointers to *me.*

The **possessive case** is used to show ownership. The possessive pronouns are *my, your, his, her, its, our, their, mine, yours, his, hers, its, ours, theirs.*

Subject-Verb Agreement To make a subject and a verb agree, make sure that both are singular or both are plural. Two or more singular subjects joined by *or* or *nor* must have a singular verb. When singular and plural subjects are joined by *or* or *nor,* the verb must agree with the closest subject.

> *He is* at the door.
> *They drive* home every day.
> Both *pets are* hungry.
> Either the *chairs* or the *table is* on sale.

Pronoun-Antecedent Agreement Pronouns must agree with their antecedents in number and gender. Use singular pronouns with singular antecedents and plural pronouns with plural antecedents. Many errors in pronoun-antecedent agreement occur when a plural pronoun is used to refer to a singular antecedent for which the gender is not specified.

Incorrect: Everyone did their best.
Correct: Everyone did his or her best.

The following indefinite pronouns are singular: *anybody, anyone, each, either, everybody, everyone, neither, nobody, no one, one, somebody, someone.*

The following indefinite pronouns are plural: *both, few, many, several.*

The following indefinite pronouns may be either singular or plural: *all, any, most, none, some.*

Glossary of Common Usage

accept, except *Accept* is a verb that means "to receive" or "to agree to." *Except* is a preposition that means "other than" or "leaving out." Do not confuse these two words.

Aaron sadly *accepted* his father's decision to sell Zlateh.

Everyone *except* the fisherman and his wife had children.

affect, effect *Affect* is normally a verb meaning "to influence" or "to bring about a change in." *Effect* is usually a noun, meaning "result."

among, between *Among* is usually used with three or more items. *Between* is generally used with only two items.

bad, badly Use the predicate adjective *bad* after linking verbs such as *feel, look,* and *seem.* Use *badly* whenever an adverb is required.

Mouse does not feel *bad* about tricking Coyote.

In the myth, Athene treats Arachne *badly.*

beside, besides *Beside* means "at the side of" or "close to." *Besides* means "in addition to."

can, may The verb *can* generally refers to the ability to do something. The verb *may* generally refers to permission to do something.

different from, different than *Different from* is generally preferred over *different than.*

farther, further Use *farther* when you refer to distance. Use *further* when you mean "to a greater degree or extent" or "additional."

fewer, less Use *fewer* for things that can be counted. Use *less* for amounts or quantities that cannot be counted.

good, well Use the predicate adjective *good* after linking verbs such as *feel, look, smell, taste,* and *seem.* Use *well* whenever you need an adverb.

hopefully You should not loosely attach this adverb to a sentence, as in "*Hopefully,* the rain will stop by noon." Rewrite the sentence so *hopefully* modifies a specific verb. Other possible ways of revising such sentences include using the adjective *hopeful* or a phrase like "everyone *hopes* that."

its, it's The word *its* with no apostrophe is a possessive pronoun. The word *it's* is a contraction for *it is.* Do not confuse the possessive pronoun *its* with the contraction *it's,* standing for "it is" or "it has."

lay, lie Do not confuse these verbs. *Lay* is a transitive verb meaning "to set or put something down." Its principal parts are *lay, laying, laid, laid. Lie* is an intransitive verb meaning "to recline." Its principal parts are *lie, lying, lay, lain.*

leave, let Be careful not to confuse these verbs. *Leave* means "to go away" or "to allow to remain." *Let* means "to permit."

like, as *Like* is a preposition that usually means "similar to" or "in the same way as." *Like* should always be followed by an object. Do not use *like* before a subject and a verb. Use *as* or *that* instead.

loose, lose *Loose* can be either an adjective (meaning "unattached") or a verb (meaning "to untie"). *Lose* is always a verb (meaning "to fail to keep, have, or win").

many, much Use *many* to refer to a specific quantity. Use *much* for an indefinite amount or for an abstract concept.

of, have Do not use *of* in place of *have* after auxiliary verbs like *would, could, should, may, might,* or *must.*

raise, rise *Raise* is a transitive verb that usually takes a direct object. *Rise* is intransitive and never takes a direct object.

set, sit *Set* is a transitive verb meaning "to put (something) in a certain place." Its principal parts are *set, setting, set, set*. *Sit* is an intransitive verb meaning "to be seated." Its principal parts are *sit, sitting, sat, sat*.

than, then The conjunction *than* is used to connect the two parts of a comparison. Do not confuse *than* with the adverb *then,* which usually refers to time.

that, which, who Use the relative pronoun *that* to refer to things or people. Use *which* only for things and *who* only for people.

their, there, they're *Their* is a possessive adjective and always modifies a noun. *There* is usually used either at the beginning of a sentence or as an adverb. *They're* is a contraction for "they are."

to, too, two *To* is a preposition that begins a prepositional phrase or an infinitive. *Too*, with two *o*'s, is an adverb and modifies adjectives and other adverbs. *Two* is a number.

when, where, why Do not use *when, where,* or *why* directly after a linking verb such as *is.* Reword the sentence.

Faulty:	Suspense is *when* an author increases the reader's tension.
Revised:	An author uses suspense to increase the reader's tension.
Faulty:	A biography is *where* a writer tells the life story of another person.
Revised:	In a biography, a writer tells the life story of another person.

who, whom In formal writing, remember to use *who* only as a subject in clauses and sentences and *whom* only as an object.

Capitalization and Punctuation Rules

Capitalization

1. Capitalize the first word of a sentence.
   Young Roko glances down the valley.
2. Capitalize all proper nouns and adjectives.
   Mark Twain   Amazon River   Thanksgiving Day
   Montana   October   Italian

3. Capitalize a person's title when it is followed by the person's name or when it is used in direct address.
   Doctor   General Khokhotov   Mrs. Price
4. Capitalize titles showing family relationships when they refer to a specific person, unless they are preceded by a possessive noun or pronoun.
   Granny-Liz   Margie's mother
5. Capitalize the first word and all other key words in the titles of books, periodicals, poems, stories, plays, paintings, and other works of art.
   from *Tom Sawyer*   "Grandpa and the Statue"
   "Breaker's Bridge"   "The Spring and the Fall"
6. Capitalize the first word and all nouns in letter salutations and the first word in letter closings.
   Dear Willis,   Yours truly,

Punctuation

End Marks

1. Use a **period** to end a declarative sentence, an imperative sentence, and most abbreviations.
2. Use a **question mark** to end a direct question or an incomplete question in which the rest of the question is understood.
3. Use an **exclamation mark** after a statement showing strong emotion, an urgent imperative sentence, or an interjection expressing strong emotion.

Commas

1. Use a comma before the conjunction to separate two independent clauses in a compound sentence.
2. Use commas to separate three or more words, phrases, or clauses in a series.
3. Use commas to separate adjectives of equal rank. Do not use commas to separate adjectives that must stay in a specific order.
4. Use a comma after an introductory word, phrase, or clause.
5. Use commas to set off parenthetical and nonessential expressions.
6. Use commas with places and dates made up of two or more parts.
7. Use commas after items in addresses, after the salutation in a personal letter, after the closing in all letters, and in numbers of more than three digits.

Semicolons

1. Use a semicolon to join independent clauses that are not already joined by a conjunction.

2. Use a semicolon to join independent clauses or items in a series that already contain commas.

> The Pengelly family had no say in the choosing of Lob; he came to them in the second way. . . .

Colons

1. Use a colon before a list of items following an independent clause.

2. Use a colon in numbers giving the time, in salutations in business letters, and in labels used to signal important ideas.

Quotation Marks

1. A direct quotation represents a person's exact speech or thoughts and is enclosed in quotation marks.

2. An **indirect quotation** reports only the general meaning of what a person said or thought and does not require quotation marks.

3. Always place a comma or a period inside the final quotation mark of a direct quotation.

4. Place a question mark or an exclamation mark inside the final quotation mark if the end mark is part of the quotation; if it is not part of the quotation, place it outside the final quotation mark.

Titles

1. Underline or italicize the titles of long written works, movies, television and radio shows, lengthy works of music, paintings, and sculptures.

2. Use quotation marks around the titles of short written works, episodes in a series, songs, and titles of works mentioned as parts of collections.

Hyphens

1. Use a **hyphen** with certain numbers, after certain prefixes, with two or more words used as one word, and with a compound modifier that comes before a noun.

Apostrophes

1. Add an **apostrophe** and *s* to show the possessive case of most singular nouns.

2. Add an apostrophe to show the possessive case of plural nouns ending in *s* and *es*.

3. Add an apostrophe and *s* to show the possessive case of plural nouns that do not end in *s* or *es*.

4. Use an apostrophe in a contraction to indicate the position of the missing letter or letters.

GRAMMAR, USAGE, AND MECHANICS EXERCISES

Parts of Speech

Exercise A Identifying Nouns and Pronouns Identify the nouns and pronouns in the following sentences. Label each noun *collective, compound, common,* or *proper,* as well as *singular* or *plural.* Label each pronoun *personal, demonstrative, relative, interrogative,* or *indefinite.*

1. The Great Lakes form a group of five freshwater lakes in North America.
2. They form part of the border between the United States and Canada, while one lies fully within the United States.
3. This means that the Canadian province of Ontario borders four lakes.
4. Their primary outlet is the St. Lawrence River, which flows to the Atlantic Ocean.
5. The lake system holds twenty percent of the world's fresh water.
6. The resources help cities, such as Chicago and Toronto, in North America's heartland.
7. The shoreline of the Great Lakes provides many recreational areas for people of the United States and Canada.
8. Which is the largest Great Lake?
9. Lake Superior, which is the largest freshwater lake in the world, is the largest in surface area.
10. It is also the highest above sea level.

Exercise B Recognizing Verbs Write the verbs in the following sentences, and label each one *action* or *linking* and *transitive* or *intransitive.* Include and underline all helping verbs.

1. Lake Superior has an irregular coastline with several large bays.
2. Rocky cliffs, some rising one thousand feet high, line the northern shore.
3. The Pictured Rocks, near Munising, Michigan, are colorful sandstone cliffs.
4. Large forests containing streams and rivers border the lake in some places.
5. The Nipigon River flows into Lake Superior from the north.

6. The lake also receives the St. Louis River from the west.
7. The St. Marys River connects Lake Superior to Lake Huron.
8. This river is navigable through the Sault Sainte Marie Canals.
9. Lake Superior rarely freezes over, but ice closes many ports during the winter.
10. Étienne Brulé, a French explorer, probably had discovered the lake in 1610.

Exercise C Recognizing Adjectives and Adverbs Label the underlined words in the following sentences *adjective* or *adverb.* Then, write the word each one modifies.

1. Lake Huron is the <u>second</u> largest of the five Great Lakes.
2. The <u>maximum</u> length of Lake Huron is <u>nearly</u> 200 miles.
3. It receives water from Lake Michigan <u>only</u> through the Straits of Mackinac.
4. The population of <u>several</u> fish species was <u>seriously</u> reduced in the mid-twentieth century.
5. <u>Government</u> programs have since helped the <u>fishing</u> industry recover.
6. Lake Huron is <u>heavily</u> used by shipping vessels, especially those carrying <u>iron</u> ore.
7. In <u>early</u> April the ice melts, reopening the <u>main</u> ports to navigation.
8. The Huron confederacy of the <u>Iroquois</u> family <u>historically</u> inhabited the area east of Lake Huron.
9. Their population declined <u>quickly</u> after <u>European</u> explorers arrived.
10. <u>Jesuit</u> missionaries <u>initially</u> settled the shoreline in 1638.

Exercise D Recognizing Prepositions

Identify the prepositions in the following sentences. Then, write the object of each preposition.

1. Lake Erie, with an area of 9,910 square miles, is the fourth largest of the Great Lakes.
2. It has an average depth of only 62 feet.
3. Because it is so shallow, the lake is quickly stirred by storms.
4. Lake Erie was polluted by the dumping of industrial wastes by industries, cities, and farms.
5. Since the United States and Canada agreed to clean up the lake in 1972, the quality of the water has improved greatly and the supply of fish has increased.

Exercise E Recognizing Conjunctions and Interjections

Identify the conjunctions and interjections in the following sentences. Label the conjunctions *coordinating, correlative,* or *subordinating.*

1. Hey, who discovered Lake Erie before the French built fur-trading posts?
2. During the French and Indian War, Great Britain won control of the lake.
3. Not only did Jay's Treaty divide control of the lake, but also Lake Erie was the scene of a battle in the War of 1812.
4. Wow! The Americans triumphed over the British.
5. Now, Lake Erie serves as a channel for a great deal of freight shipping even though navigation can be hazardous.
6. Yes, both the St. Lawrence Seaway and the Erie Canal service the lake.
7. Products—including iron ore, steel, and coal—travel from various ports.
8. Several states are involved in this trade, but ice closes the lake for the winter.
9. The Niagara River and the Welland Canal feed into Lake Ontario.
10. Neither Cattaraugus Creek nor the Raisin River feeds large amounts of water into Lake Erie.

Exercise F Identifying All the Parts of Speech

Write the part of speech of each underlined word in the following paragraph. Be specific.

Lake Michigan is the only Great Lake that lies <u>entirely</u> within the United States. <u>Oh</u>, it <u>touches</u> Michigan, Wisconsin, and Illinois. The Chicago Sanitary and Ship Canal connects the lake to the Mississippi River. <u>Green Bay</u> is <u>located</u> on the <u>western</u> shore, and Grand Traverse Bay is on the eastern shore. <u>These</u> form the main <u>indentations</u> <u>in</u> the lake.

Exercise G Revising Sentences

Rewrite the following sentences, adding the part of speech indicated.

1. Buffalo, New York, (verb) on Lake Erie.
2. (pronoun) was founded (preposition) the Dutch in 1803.
3. The site was chosen (conjunction) it lay at the western end of an important Indian trail.
4. Buffalo is the (noun) of two United States presidents—Millard Fillmore and Grover Cleveland.
5. The Erie Canal (verb) from Lake Erie at Buffalo (preposition) the Hudson River at Troy, New York.

Exercise H Writing Application

Write a short narrative about a body of water with which you are familiar. Include nouns, pronouns, verbs, adjectives, adverbs, prepositions, conjunctions, and interjections, and underline at least one example of each. Then, label each word's part of speech as specifically as possible.

Phrases, Clauses, and Sentences

▶ **Exercise A** Recognizing Basic Sentence Parts Copy the following sentences, underlining each simple subject once and each simple predicate twice. Circle the complements, and label each *direct object, indirect object, predicate noun,* or *predicate adjective.* Then, identify the function of each sentence as *declarative, imperative, interrogative,* or *exclamatory.*

1. I really enjoy sports like water polo!
2. It is a fast-paced game in a swimming pool.
3. The two versions of water polo have slightly different rules and regulations.
4. The international rules and the collegiate rules are used at different levels of competition.
5. Does the water polo ball resemble a soccer ball?
6. Toss me the ball!
7. Will you and Sam play all four periods of the game?
8. The two-minute break gives us time to rest.
9. The way you score goals is awesome!
10. That was an amazing shot from the middle of the pool!

▶ **Exercise B** Revising Basic Sentences Revise the sentences below according to the directions in parentheses. In your new sentences, underline each simple subject once and each simple predicate twice. Circle each complement.

1. Water polo involves skills similar to swimming. (Rewrite, creating a compound subject.)
2. Swimming uses body parts to move. Those body parts are the hands and feet. (Combine, creating a compound direct object.)
3. Humans take strokes in the water. They do not use a walking motion, as animals do. (Combine, creating a compound verb.)

4. Strokes are usually quick. They are also powerful. (Combine by creating a compound predicate adjective.)
5. David gave me a swimming lesson, and he gave one to Mary. (Rewrite, creating a compound indirect object.)

▶ **Exercise C** Identifying Phrases and Clauses Label the phrases in the following sentences *adjective prepositional, adverb prepositional, appositive, participial, gerund,* or *infinitive.* Label each clause *adjective* or *adverb.* Then, identify the structure of the sentence as *simple, complex, compound,* or *compound-complex.*

1. The crawl stroke, which is also called the freestyle, was developed by an English swimmer; it was first used in the 1870s.
2. Moving the arm through the air and water pulls the swimmer through the water.
3. The swimmer tries to kick continuously while he or she makes the arm movements.
4. Turning the head to one side, the swimmer takes a breath of air and exhales underwater.
5. Harry Hebner, an American swimmer, competed with an alternating arm backstroke in 1912.
6. The backstroke, which involves turning the back to the water, resembles the crawl.
7. Known since the seventeenth century, the breaststroke is the oldest style of swimming.
8. The swimmer, who lies face down in the water, moves forward after making a series of horizontal movements.
9. The butterfly stroke brings both arms over the head; then, they are pulled backward through the water.
10. For the dolphin leg kick, which is more difficult, the swimmer needs to keep the feet together.

Exercise D Revising to Combine Sentences With Phrases and Clauses Rewrite the sentences below according to the instructions given in parentheses. Underline the newly created sentence part.

1. Waterskiing can be a recreational sport. It can be competitive. (Combine by creating an adjective clause.)
2. The sport was invented in 1939. That was the year the first tournament was held. (Combine by creating an adverb clause.)
3. Skiers are towed across the water, and they are towed by motorboats. (Rewrite, creating an adverb prepositional phrase.)
4. Fins are located on the underside of skis. They add stability. (Combine by creating a participial phrase.)
5. The skier crouches, and the boat begins acceleration. (Rewrite, creating an infinitive phrase.)
6. A skier needs strong arms. A skier also needs strong legs. (Create a compound sentence.)
7. The skier streaks across the water. He or she causes waves to form. (Begin with a participial phrase.)
8. Waterskiing is an activity I have always loved. It is a true summertime sport. (Combine using an appositive phrase.)
9. I think about our week at the lake. In May, I begin thinking about it. (Combine by replacing the object of a preposition.)
10. Get the boat powered up. I am on my way! (Rewrite, creating an adverb clause.)

Exercise E Revising a Passage Revise the following sentences, combining or shortening sentences to add variety, and correcting usage problems.

In synchronized swimming, a set of choreographed maneuvers. The reason this sport is appealing is because the music is used to showcase the athlete's skills. Synchronized swimming is not a sport only about grace and beauty, but it is also about great athletic skill, which is something that is needed by those who participate in the sport. Having impressive strength, agility, and timing, most spectators enjoy watching the sport. The figures competition is when swimmers perform several combinations of movements. Judges award points. They base their judgments on the athlete's timing, height, stability, and control. The free routines last from two to five minutes, the swimmers perform their own choreography of figures and strokes. By using original movements, routines are enhanced by the swimmers. Musical interpretation and the presentation of the performance effect the judges' artistic-impression marks. Water ballet was a sport in the early twentieth century. Synchronized swimming developed from that.

Exercise F Writing Application Write a short description of a water sport or activity that you have enjoyed doing or watching. Be sure to vary the lengths and structures of your sentences. Underline each simple subject once and each simple predicate twice. Then, circle at least three phrases and three clauses. Try to avoid fragments, run-ons, double negatives, misplaced modifiers, and the common usage problems you have studied.

Usage

▶ **Exercise A** Using Verbs Choose the verb or verb phrase that makes each sentence correct. Identify its principal part and tense.

1. The digging of the Mississippi River was (did, done) by glaciers during the last Ice Age.
2. Several Native American groups had (set, sat) their communities on the banks of the Mississippi.
3. If we had lived in earlier times, we would have (saw, seen) a different landscape from the one we see today.
4. The Mississippi River has (play, played) a central role in the development of North America.
5. A major portion of freight shipments have (gone, went) down this river.
6. More freight has (traveling, traveled) on the Mississippi than on any other inland waterway in North America.
7. The river will (continue, continues) to be of great economic importance to cities from Saint Paul to New Orleans.
8. The teacher (says, said) that if measured from Lake Itasca, the Mississippi River is 2,540 miles long.
9. However, if one was (measured, measuring) the river from the headwaters of the Missouri River, a major tributary, its length totals 3,710 miles.
10. After it (passes, passed) New Orleans, the river branches into smaller channels in the delta.

▶ **Exercise B** Identifying the Case of Pronouns Identify the case of each pronoun in the following sentences as *subject, objective,* or *possessive.*

1. The Ojibwa, Natchez, and Choctaw made (them, their) homes along the Mississippi River.
2. As settlers moved in, the Native Americans and (they, them) briefly shared this territory.

3. The Algonquin word *missisipioui*, meaning "big water," gave the river (their, its) name.
4. Exploring the landscape in 1541, Hernando de Soto was the first European to see (its, it).
5. French explorers Louis Jolliet and Jacques Marquette followed (he, him) in 1673.
6. (They, Their) were succeeded by La Salle, (who, whom) claimed the entire Mississippi Valley for France.
7. The French gave the Mississippi (their, its) first European settlements when (it, they) founded New Orleans, St. Louis, and other cities in the early eighteenth century.
8. By the 1830s, farmers and settlers encouraged the steamboat trade because it made (they, them) more prosperous.
9. The golden age of steamboats attracted those (who, whom) wanted to serve as a boat captain or pilot.
10. Mark Twain wrote about (him, his) own experiences on and around the Mississippi River.

▶ **Exercise C** Making Verbs Agree With Subjects Choose the correct word or words from the choices in parentheses, and write them on your paper.

1. Several species of fish, especially catfish, (thrive, thrives) in the Mississippi River.
2. Commercial fishermen harvest (it, them) very successfully.
3. The flood plain in the delta area (form, forms) an extensive wetlands area.
4. (They are, It is) an important habitat for migratory birds.
5. Grains, soybeans, cotton, and rice (grow, grows) in the flood plains.
6. The rich soil from periods of erosion and deposition supports (it, them).
7. Coal, sand, gravel, and other bulk products (constitutes, constitute) the important cargoes that travel the river.
8. The region north of Saint Paul, due to (its, their) Falls of Saint Anthony, is not navigable.
9. Dams or locks have been built, so (they, it) provide a navigation channel from Saint Paul to St. Louis.

10. St. Louis, near the junction of the Missouri River, (link, links) the Mississippi with the Great Plains.

Exercise D Using Modifiers Write the form of the adjective or adverb indicated in parentheses.

1. The Missouri River is the Mississippi's (long—superlative) tributary.
2. (Initially—positive), the Mississippi River begins at Lake Itasca in Minnesota.
3. There, it is (only—positive) twelve feet wide and (barely—positive) two feet deep.
4. Much of the river is now (navigable—comparative) than before due to dredging and engineering efforts.
5. There are now (few—comparative) hazards for large vessels.
6. Barge traffic increased (steadily—positive) during the twentieth century.
7. At the delta area, the river splits into (small—comparative) channels called distributaries before entering the gulf.
8. The Mississippi River system is the (large—superlative) drainage system in North America.
9. There is a (vast—positive) network of levees built to limit the river's flooding.
10. However, there is concern that the levees may have caused (great—comparative) damage in 1993.

Exercise E Revising Sentences to Eliminate Usage Errors Rewrite the following sentences, correcting any usage errors.

1. The Monongahela River and the Allegheny River joins together at Pittsburgh, forming the Ohio River.
2. It provides slightly fewer than half of the Mississippi River's water.
3. The Ohio River winds southeast where they borders on five different states.
4. Cities like Pittsburgh, Cincinnati, and Louisville lay alongside the river.
5. They owed much of their growth to it proximity.
6. Now, there was little shipping conducted out of these cities.
7. Currently, bulk products like coal are just shipped on the Ohio River.
8. A series of thirteen dams and locks ensure the passage of commercial vessels.
9. The products are loaded onto barges, which carry it to nearby electric plants along the river.
10. The river is frequented by local residents whom use it for recreational activities.

Exercise F Writing Application Write a short description of a trip you have taken on or near a body of water. Be sure that the words in your sentences follow the rules of agreement and that your modifiers are used correctly. Then, list your verbs and verb phrases, identifying their tense. Make a list of the personal pronouns, and label the case of each one.

Mechanics

Exercise A Using End Marks, Commas, Semicolons, and Colons Copy the following sentences, inserting the appropriate end marks, commas, semicolons, and colons.

1. Cocoa beans grow in a specific location hot humid climates
2. After harvesting and roasting the cocoa beans what is the next step for making chocolate
3. The beans are crushed into an unsweetened substance consequently sugar may be added to the mixture
4. Emulsifiers are included for smoothness and cocoa butter is added or removed
5. Most American companies make one kind of chocolate milk chocolate
6. Other types of chocolate include baking chocolate cocoa powder and eating chocolate
7. Hey White chocolate is not really chocolate
8. Did you know that no part of the cocoa bean is used in making white chocolate
9. It still tastes really good
10. The original cocoa bean mash in its ingredients is called unsweetened chocolate it is also called baking chocolate

Exercise B Using All the Rules of Punctuation Copy the following sentences, inserting the appropriate end marks, commas, semicolons, colons, quotation marks, underlining, hyphens, and apostrophes. All quoted material is underlined.

1. Did you know that butter is made out of cream
2. It is skimmed off the top of whole milk with a cream ladle a large spoon with holes in it
3. The milk runs through the holes but the cream does not
4. The cream is chilled and soured next the mixture needs to reach room temperature
5. Then it is poured into the most well known piece of equipment the churn
6. Wow My hands got tired separating the butter from the buttermilk
7. Grandmother said It can take from one-half hour to forever to separate
8. We work the butter with a butter paddle, and we use clean water to wash it
9. Before putting it in the molds we sprinkle in some salt
10. In the book Little House in the Big Woods Laura Ingalls Wilder writes about making butter

Exercise C Using Capitalization Copy the following sentences, capitalizing letters where appropriate.

1. christopher columbus, who sailed for queen isabella in 1492, discovered chili peppers.
2. Columbus saw that they were popular in south america and mexico, and so he brought them to spain.
3. columbus's discovery influenced cooking worldwide.
4. indian, thai, and japanese cooking quickly embraced these peppers.
5. also, szechwan-style chinese cooking is spicy and uses peppers.
6. even colonists in the americas began using chili peppers.
7. however, it was not until the twentieth century that people in the united states began exploring chilies.
8. in 1975, the hellfire cookbook was published, which contained only hot and spicy recipes.
9. the chili pepper encyclopedia explains that there are many different levels of spiciness.
10. people are not aware of the variety of peppers and their flavors.
11. the habanero chile is native to the yucatan peninsula and the caribbean islands.
12. it is fifty times hotter than the jalapeno, which is used throughout the united states in nachos.
13. the serrano is a pepper cultivated in mexico that turns from green to red to yellow as it grows.

14. in the american southwest, it is used in several popular snacks.
15. the poblana chile is a dark-green, triangular–shaped chile used in *mole* sauces.

▶ **Exercise D** Using Capitalization and Punctuation Copy the following dialogue, inserting the appropriate capitalization, punctuation, and indentation.

1. rob what kind of salad dressing do you want on your salad asked karin
2. rob answered i usually choose italian or creamy italian
3. have you ever tried plain oil and vinegar it is a distinct taste, but very good
4. well, what kind of oil do they mean asked rob
5. olive oil is the best choice for salads it has a distinct flavor and is very smooth karin answered
6. wait just a second is it really made out of olives
7. karin responded yes countries like italy greece and spain have been making and using olive oil for thousands of years.
8. i have seen olive oil in the stores said rob sometimes it is very dark, and sometimes it looks much lighter
9. the book the joy of cooking explained that it can depend on the type of olive that was used and also on how pure the oil really is karin explained
10. then rob asked does that affect the taste of the oil
11. many factors affect the taste replied karin from the number of times it was pressed to the length of time it has mellowed
12. well karin how does one choose an oil to use on salad
13. it is important to look for oil that has been cold pressed and contains little acid
14. i think i would be interested in trying some it is such a historical product said rob
15. you have made a good choice here drizzle this on your salad and then i will use it

▶ **Exercise E** Proofreading for Errors in Punctuation and Capitalization Read the following passage. Then, rewrite it, correcting all errors in punctuation and capitalization.

Cooking is a fun, and useful hobby. Whether you cook fancy meals or simple ones, you can enjoy the results of your work. If you are interested in getting started i have several helpful books "the joy of cooking" "meals on a budget" and "market fresh meals". Are you interested in borrowing any of them. Start with simple meals then move on to the more complicated ones.

▶ **Exercise F** Writing Application Write a short dialogue between you and a friend about your favorite foods. Be sure to use correct capitalization and punctuation.

You use communication every day in writing, speaking, listening, and viewing. Having strong communication skills will benefit you both in and out of school. Many of the assignments accompanying the literature in this textbook involve speaking, listening, and viewing. This handbook identifies some of the terminology related to the oral and visual communication you experience every day and the assignments you may do in conjunction with the literature in this book.

Communication

You use speaking and listening skills every day. When you talk with your friends, teachers, or parents, or when you interact with store clerks, you are communicating orally. In addition to everyday conversation, oral communication includes class discussions, speeches, interviews, presentations, debates, and performances. When you communicate, you usually use more than your voice to get your message across. For example, you use one set of skills in face-to-face communication and another set of skills in a telephone conversation.

The following terms will give you a better understanding of the many elements that are part of communication:

BODY LANGUAGE refers to the use of facial expressions, eye contact, gestures, posture, and movement to communicate a feeling or an idea.

CONNOTATION is the set of associations a word calls to mind. The connotations of the words you choose influence the message you send. For example, most people respond more favorably to being described as "slim" rather than as "skinny." The connotation of *slim* is more appealing than that of *skinny*.

EYE CONTACT is direct visual contact with another person's eyes.

FEEDBACK is the set of verbal and nonverbal reactions that indicate to a speaker that a message has been received and understood.

GESTURES are the movements made with arms, hands, face, and fingers to communicate.

LISTENING is understanding and interpreting sound in a meaningful way. You listen differently for different purposes.

Listening for key information: For example, when a teacher gives an assignment, or when someone gives you directions to a place, you listen for key information.

Listening for main points: In a classroom exchange of ideas or information, or while watching a television documentary, you listen for main points.

Listening critically: When you evaluate a performance, song, or a persuasive or political speech, you listen critically, questioning and judging the speaker's message.

MEDIUM is the material or technique used to present a visual image. Common media include paint, clay, and film.

NONVERBAL COMMUNICATION is communication without the use of words. People communicate nonverbally through gestures, facial expressions, posture, and body movements. Sign language is an entire language based on nonverbal communication.

PROJECTION is speaking in such a way that the voice carries clearly to an audience. It's important to project your voice when speaking in a large space like a classroom or an auditorium.

VIEWING is observing, understanding, analyzing, and evaluating information presented through visual means. You might use the following questions to help you interpret what you view:

- What subject is presented?
- What is communicated about the subject?
- Which parts are factual? Which are opinion?
- What mood, attitude, or opinion is conveyed?
- What is your emotional response?

VOCAL DELIVERY is the way in which you present a message. Your vocal delivery involves all of the following elements:

Volume: the loudness or quietness of your voice

Pitch: the high or low quality of your voice

Rate: the speed at which you speak; also called pace

Stress: the amount of emphasis placed on different syllables in a word or on different words in a sentence

All of these elements individually, and the way in which they are combined, contribute to the meaning of a spoken message.

Speaking, Listening, and Viewing Situations

Here are some of the many types of situations in which you apply speaking, listening, and viewing skills:

AUDIENCE Your audience in any situation refers to the person or people to whom you direct your message. An audience can be a group of people observing a performance or just one person. When preparing for any speaking situation, it's useful to analyze your audience, so that you can tailor your message to them.

CHARTS AND GRAPHS are visual representations of statistical information. For example, a pie chart might indicate how the average dollar is spent by government, and a bar graph might compare populations in cities over time.

DEBATE A debate is a formal public-speaking situation in which participants prepare and present arguments on opposing sides of a question, stated as a **proposition.**

The two sides in a debate are the *affirmative* (pro) and the *negative* (con). The affirmative side argues in favor of the proposition, while the negative side argues against it. Each side has an opportunity for *rebuttal,* in which they may challenge or question the other side's argument.

DOCUMENTARIES are nonfiction films that analyze news events or other focused subjects. You can watch a documentary for the information on its subject.

GRAPHIC ORGANIZERS summarize and present information in ways that can help you understand the information. Graphic organizers include charts, outlines, webs, maps, lists, and diagrams. For example, a graphic organizer for a history chapter might be an outline. A Venn diagram is intersecting circles that display information showing how concepts are alike and different.

GROUP DISCUSSION results when three or more people meet to solve a common problem, arrive at a decision, or answer a question of mutual interest. Group discussion is one of the most widely used forms of interpersonal communication in modern society.

INTERVIEW An interview is a form of interaction in which one person, the interviewer, asks questions of another person, the interviewee. Interviews may take place for many purposes: to obtain information, to discover a person's suitability for a job or a college, or to inform the public of a notable person's opinions.

MAPS are visual representations of Earth's surface. Maps may show political boundaries and physical features and provide information on a variety of other topics. A map's title and its key identify the content of the map.

ORAL INTERPRETATION is the reading or speaking of a work of literature aloud for an audience. Oral interpretation involves giving expression to the ideas, meaning, or even the structure of a work of literature. The speaker interprets the work through his or her vocal delivery. **Storytelling**, in which a speaker reads or tells a story expressively, is a form of oral interpretation.

PANEL DISCUSSION is a group discussion on a topic of interest common to all members of a panel and to a listening audience. A panel is usually composed of four to six experts on a particular topic who are brought together to share information and opinions.

PANTOMIME is a form of nonverbal communication in which an idea or a story is communicated completely through the use of gesture, body language, and facial expressions, without any words at all.

POLITICAL CARTOONS are drawings that comment on important political or social issues. Often, these cartoons use humor to convey a message about their subject. Viewers use their own knowledge of events to evaluate the cartoonist's opinion.

READERS THEATRE is a dramatic reading of a work of literature in which participants take parts from a story or play and read them aloud in expressive voices. Unlike a play, however, sets and costumes are not part of the performance, and the participants remain seated as they deliver their lines.

ROLE PLAY To role-play is to take the role of a person or character and act out a given situation, speaking, acting, and responding in the manner of the character.

SPEECH A speech is a talk or address given to an audience. A speech may be **impromptu**—delivered on the spur of the moment with no preparation—or formally prepared and delivered for a specific purpose or occasion.

- *Purposes:* The most common purposes of speeches are to persuade, to entertain, to explain, and to inform.

- *Occasions:* Different occasions call for different types of speeches. Speeches given on these occasions could be persuasive, entertaining, or informative, as appropriate.

VISUAL REPRESENTATION refers to informative texts, such as newspapers and advertisements, and entertaining texts, such as magazines. Visual representations use elements of design—such as texture and color, shapes, drawings, and photographs—to convey the meaning, message, or theme.

Indexes

Index of Authors and Titles

Page numbers in *italics* refer to biographical information.

Index of Skills

GRAMMAR, USAGE, AND MECHANICS

VOCABULARY

Index of Features

Massachusetts Historical Society From *Paul Revere's Three Accounts of His Famous Ride* by Paul Revere. Copyright © 1968 by The Massachusetts Historical Society. Used by permission.

N. Scott Momaday "New World" from *The Gourd Dancers* by N. Scott Momaday, copyright © 1976 by N. Scott Momaday. Used by permission of the author.

Monterey Bay Aquarium Foundation "Locating the Monterey Bay Aquarium" from Monterey Bay Aquarium Web site (www.mbayaq.org). Copyright © 2000 The Monterey Bay Aquarium. Reproduced by permission of the Monterey Bay Aquarium Foundation.

National Public Radio "Accidental Entrepreneurs" by Chris Arnold. © Copyright NPR 1997. The audio and text of a news report by NPR's Chris Arnold was originally broadcast on National Public Radio's "All Things Considered" on August 19, 1997, and is used with the permission of National Public Radio, Inc. Any unauthorized duplication is strictly prohibited.

The New York Times "Darkness at Noon" by Harold Krents, originally published in The New York Times, May 26, 1978. Used by permission.

W. W. Norton & Company, Inc., "400-Meter Free Style" from *Selected Poems 1960-1990* by Maxine Kumin. Copyright © 1959 and renewed 1987 by Maxine Kumin. Reprinted by permission of W.W. Norton & Company, Inc.

Naomi Shihab Nye "Hamadi" by Naomi Shihab Nye, copyright © 1993 by Naomi Shihab Nye. First published in *American Street.*

Julio Noboa "Identity" by Julio Noboa Polanco from *The Rican, Journal of Contemporary Puerto Rican Thought,* copyright 1973. Used by permission.

Harold Ober Associates, Inc. "Southern Mansion" by Arna Bontemps, published in *Personals.* Copyright 1949 by Arna Bontemps and Langston Hughes. Copyright renewed 1976 by Alberta Bontemps and George Houston Bass. Used by permission.

Pantheon Books, a division of Random House, Inc. "Coyote Steals the Sun and Moon" from *American Indian Myths and Legends* edited by Richard Erdoes and Alfonso Ortiz, copyright © 1984 by Richard Erdoes and Alfonso Ortiz. Used by permission of Pantheon Books, a division of Random House, Inc.

Robert W. Peterson "Riding the Underground Railroad" by Robert W. Peterson, from *Boys' Life,* February 1993. By permission of the author.

Random House, Inc. "Why Leaves Turn Color in the Fall" from *A Natural History of the Senses* by Diane Ackerman. Copyright © 1990 by Diane Ackerman. From *The Diary of Anne Frank* by Frances Goodrich and Albert Hackett, copyright © 1956 by Albert Hackett, Frances Goodrich Hackett and Otto Frank. From *I Know Why the Caged Bird Sings* by Maya Angelou, copyright © 1969 and renewed 1997 by Maya Angelou. "Raymond's Run" from *Gorilla, My Love* by Toni Cade Bambara, copyright © 1971 by Toni Cade Bambara. Used by permission of Random House, Inc.

The Reader's Digest Association, Inc. "Why is the sea blue?" by Denis Wallis et al. from *Why in the World?,* copyright © 1994 The Reader's Digest Association Limited. Used by permission of the Reader's Digest Association, Inc., Pleasantville, NY, www.rd.com.

Marian Reiner for the Jesse Stuart Foundation "A Ribbon for Baldy" by Jesse Stuart from *A Jesse Stuart Reader,* selected and introduced by Jesse Stuart. Copyright 1956 Esquire, Inc., © 1963 McGraw-Hill Book Company. © Renewed 1984, 1991 Jesse Stuart and the Jesse Stuart Foundation. Reprinted by permission of Marian Reiner for the Jesse Stuart Foundation.

Wendy Rose "Drum Song" by Wendy Rose, from *The Halfbreed Chronicles and Other Poems.* Copyright © 1985 by Wendy Rose. Used by permission of the author.

Russell & Volkening, Inc. "Harriet Tubman: Guide to Freedom" from *Harriet Tubman: Conductor on the Underground Railroad* by Ann Petry. Copyright © 1955 by Ann Petry, renewed 1983 by Ann Petry.

Russell & Volkening, Inc., for Pat Mora "Dear Fellow Writer" by Pat Mora from *My Own True Name.* Text © 2000 by Pat Mora.

St. Martin's Press, Inc., and Harold Ober Associates, Inc. "Debbie" from *All Things Wise and Wonderful* by James Herriot. Copyright © 1976, 1977 by James Herriot.

Scovil Chichak Galen Literary Agency, Inc., and the author "The Secret" by Arthur C. Clarke from *The Wind from the Sun: Stories of the Space Age,* published by Victor Gollancz Ltd. Copyright © 1962, 1963, 1964,1965, 1967, 1970, 1971, 1972 by Arthur C. Clarke. Reprinted by permission of the author and the author's agent, Scovil Chichak Galen Literary Agency, Inc.

Scribner, a division of Simon & Schuster, Inc., and The Estate of Robert P. Tristram Coffin c/o June Coffin "The Secret Heart" from *The Collected Poems of Robert P. Tristram Coffin* by Robert P. Tristram Coffin. Copyright © 1939 by Macmillan Publishing Company, copyright renewed © 1967 by Margaret Coffin Halvosa. Reprinted with the permission of Scribner, a Division of Simon & Schuster, Inc. and The Estate of Robert P. Tristram Coffin c/o June Coffin.

John Seabrook From "E-Mail from Bill Gates" from *Deeper: Adventures on the Net* by John Seabrook, first published in *The New Yorker,* January 1994. Copyright John Seabrook. Used by permission of the author.

Simon & Schuster Books for Young Readers, an imprint of Simon & Schuster Children's Publishing Division From *Hatchet* by Gary Paulsen. Copyright © 1987 by Gary Paulsen. Reprinted with the permission of Simon & Schuster Books for Young Readers, an imprint of Simon & Schuster Children's Publishing Division. "The Old Grandfather and His Little Grandson" from *Twenty-Two Russian Tales for Young Children* by Leo Tolstoy, selected, translated, and with an afterword by Miriam Morton. Translation copyright © 1969 Miriam Morton. "A Glow in the Dark" from *Woodsong* by Gary Paulsen. Text copyright © 1990 Gary Paulsen. "Southbound on the Freeway" by May Swenson from *The Complete Poems to Solve* by May Swenson. Text copyright © 1993 by The Literary Estate of May Swenson. (Originally appeared in *The New Yorker,* 1963). "The Centaur" by May Swenson from *The Complete Poems to Solve* by May Swenson. Copyright © 1956 by May Swenson; copyright renewed 1984 by May Swenson. Reprinted with the permission of Simon & Schuster Books for Young Readers, an imprint of Simon & Schuster Children's Publishing Division.

The Society of Authors for the Literary Trustees of Walter de la Mare "Silver" and "All but Blind" by Walter de la Mare from *The Complete Poems of Walter de la Mare,* 1969. Used by permission of The Literary Trustees of Walter de la Mare and the Society of Authors as their representative.

Helen Thomson *California State Assembly Senate Natural Resources and Wildlife* by Assemblywoman Helen Thomson, from *California State Senate Natural Resources and Wildlife,* Bill No.: AB242. Used by permission.

Jackie Torrence "Brer Possum's Dilemma" by Jackie Torrence, copyright © 1988 by Jackie Torrence, published in *Homespun: Tales from America's Favorite Storytellers* by Jimmy Neil Smith. Reprinted by permission of the author.

The Estate of Yoshiko Uchida c/o The Bancroft Library, Admin Offices "Tears of Autumn" from *The Forbidden Stitch* by Yoshiko Uchida. Copyright © 1989 by Yoshiko Uchida. Coutesy of the Bancroft Library, University of California, Berkeley.

University Press of Virginia "Harriet Beecher Stowe" by Paul Laurence Dunbar from *The Collected Poetry of Paul Laurence Dunbar,* Joanne M. Braxton, ed. (Charlottesville: University Press of Virginia, 1993). Used by permission.

University of Tennessee Press "Davy Crockett's Dream" by Davy Crockett, from *The Tall Tales of Davy Crockett: The Second Nashville Series of Crockett Almanacs, 1839-1841.* Copyright © 1987 by the University of Tennessee Press. Used by permission of the University of Tennessee Press.

Usborne Publishing Ltd. "Using a Microscope" by Kirsteen Rogers from *The Complete Book of the Microscope.* Copyright © Usborne Publishing Ltd., 1998. Used by permission of Usborne Publishing Ltd., 83–85 Saffron Hill, London EC1N8RT.

Viking Penguin, Inc., A Division of Penguin Putnam, Inc. From *Travels With Charley* by John Steinbeck. Copyright © 1961, 1962 by The Curtis Publishing Co., © 1962 by John Steinbeck, renewed © 1990 by Elaine Steinbeck, Thom Steinbeck, and John Steinbeck IV. "The Choice" by Dorothy Parker, copyright 1926, copyright renewed 1954 by Dorothy Parker, from *The Portable Dorothy Parker* by Dorothy Parker, edited by Brendan Gill. Used by permission of Viking Penguin, a division of Penguin Putnam, Inc.

Estate of Jose Garcia Villa, c/o John Edwin Cowen, Literary Trustee "Lyric 17" by Jose Garcia Villa from *Have Come, Am Here.* Copyright 1942 by Jose Garcia Villa, copyright renewed © 1969 by Jose Garcia Villa. Used by permission.

Virginia Driving Hawk Sneve "The Medicine Bag" by Virginia Driving Hawk Sneve, published in *Boy's Life,* March 1975. Reprinted by permission of the author.

William Morris Agency "Flowers for Algernon" copyright © 1957 by Daniel Keys. All rights reserved. CAUTION: Professionals and amateurs are hereby warned that "Flowers for Algernon" is subject to a royalty. It is fully protected under the copyright laws of the United States of America and of all countries covered by the International Copyright Union (including the Dominion of Canada and the rest of the British Commonwealth), the Berne Convention, the Pan-American Copyright Convention, and the Universal Copyright Convention as well as all countries with which the United States has reciprocal copyright relations. All rights, radio broadcasting, television, video or sound recording, all other forms of mechanical or electronic reproduction, such as CD-ROM, CD-I, information storage and retrieval systems and photocopying, and the rights of translation into foreign languages, are strictly reserved. Particular emphasis is laid upon the matter of readings, permission for which must be secured from the Author's agent in writing. Inquiries concerning rights should be addressed to: William Morris Agency, Inc., 1325 Avenue of the Americas, New York, NY 10019, ATTN: Mel Berger. "Achieving the American Dream" by Mario M. Cuomo, Introduction from *The Italian Family Album.* Copyright © 1994 by Mario M. Cuomo.

Note: Every effort has been made to locate the copyright owner of material reprinted in this book. Omissions brought to our attention will be corrected in subsequent printings.

CREDITS

Cover and Title Page *The Abundance of Summer*, oil on canvas, Tim Solliday, Courtesy of the artist **vi** Corel Professional Photos CD-ROM™ **vii** SuperStock **viii–ix** Fotopic/Omni-Photo Communications, Inc. **x** AP/Wide World Photos **xi (t.)** Phil Dotson/Photo Researchers, Inc. **xi (b.)** Steve Kraseman/DRK Photo **xii (t.)** Jerry Jacka Photography **xii (b.)** ©The Stock Market/Tom Bean **xiii** Mike Mazzaschi/Stock, Boston **xiv** UPI/CORBIS-BETTMANN **xiv–xv** Shelley Rotner/Omni-Photo Communications, Inc. **xvii** Bob Rowan, Progressive Image/CORBIS **1** *The Cat*, Robert Vickrey, egg tempera, 36" x 48 1/8", ©Robert Vickrey/Licensed by VAGA, New York, **2 (t.l.)** *Remembrance (Erinnerung)*, ca. 1918, Marc Chagall, Solomon R. Guggenheim Museum, New York, Gift, Solomon R. Guggenheim Museum, 1941, Photograph by David Heald © Solomon R. Guggenheim Foundation, New York (FN 41.440). ©2000 Artists Rights Society (ARS), New York/ADAGP, Paris. **2 (t.r.)** Michael Agliolo/International Stock Photography, Ltd. **2 (b.)** Corel Professional Photos CD-ROM™ **4** Courtesy National Archives **6** *Drummer Boy*, Julian Scott, N.S. Mayer **9** Courtesy National Archives **12** Thomas Victor **16** Courtesy National Archives **19** CORBIS-BETTMANN **20, 22** SuperStock **24** Courtesy of the Library of Congress **26** AP/Wide World Photos **30** *Parkville, Main Street (Missouri)*, 1933, Gale Stockwell, National Museum of American Art, Washington, DC/Art Resource, NY **32** ©FPG International LLC **35** *Woman in Calico*, 1944, William Johnson, National Museum of American Art, Washington DC/Art Resource, NY **38** Henry McGee/Globe Photos **42** ©The Stock Market/Alan Goldsmith **44–45** Corel Professional Photos CD-ROM™ **45 (b.)** Dimitri Kessel/Life Magazine **46** Robert Maier/Animals Animals **47** ©Faber & Faber Ltd **48 (t.)** Corel Professional Photos CD-ROM™ **48 (b.)** The Granger Collection, New York **52, 55** Michael Agliolo/International Stock Photography, Ltd. **58 (b.)** Microsoft Corporation **58 (t.)** The New Yorker **66** *Second Circle Dance*, Phoebe Beasley, 36" x 36" collage **68** *Woman with White Kerchief (Uygur)*, Painting by Lunda Hoyle Gill **69** Photo by Catherine Ling Hinds **70** *El Pan Nuestro (Our Daily Bread)*, Ramon Frade, oil on canvas, 60 1/4" x 38 3/4", Instituto de Cultura Puertorriquena, San Juan, Photo courtesy Squibb Galleries, New Jersey **71** Arte Público Press / University of Houston **72** *L. N. Tolstoi*, I. E. Repin, Sovfoto/Eastfoto **76** Digital Imagery ©Copyright 2001 PhotoDisc, Inc. **78** *Alfred, Lord Tennyson*, c.1840, S. Laurence, By courtesy of the National Portrait Gallery, London **79** New York Public Library **80** Courtesy of the Library of Congress **85** ©Jack Jr Hoehn/Index Stock Photography, Ltd. **94–95** *The Idleness of Sisyphus*, 1981, Sandro Chia, oil on canvas, in two parts, overall, 10' 2" x 12' 8 1/4" (307 x 386.7 cm); top panel: 6'9" x 12' 1 1/4" (104.5 x 386.7 cm). The Museum of Modern Art, New York. Acquired through the Carter Burden, Barbara Jakobson, and Saidie A. May funds and purchase. Photograph ©1998 The Museum of Modern Art, New York. **96 (l.)** NASA **96 (r.)** Harriet Tubman Quilt made by the Negro History Club of Marin City and Sausalito, CA, 1951, 120 x 96 inches, cotton appliqued. Designed by Ben Irvin. Gift of the Howard Thurman Educational Trust to the permanent collection of the Robert W. Woodruff Library, Atlanta University Center, Atlanta, GA **98** *The Great Mississippi Steamboat Race*, 1870, Currier & Ives, The Granger Collection, New York **100** *Looking down the Mississippi River at Hannibal*, MO, George L. Crosby, Mark Twain Home and Museum **103** Courtesy US Army Corp of Engineers **105** *The Champions of the Mississippi*, Currier & Ives, Scala/Art Resource, New York **106** From *The Book of the Great South* by Edward King, 1875. Photo by Silver Burdett Ginn **108** *Samuel Langhorne Clemens (Mark Twain)* (detail), 1935, Frank Edwin Larson, The National Portrait Gallery, Smithsonian Institution, Washington, D.C./Art Resource, New York **116** Digital Imagery ©Copyright 2001 PhotoDisc, Inc. **118, 120** NASA **122–123** Digital Imagery ©Copyright 2001 PhotoDisc, Inc. **124** CORBIS-BETTMANN **128** *Forward*, 1967, Jacob Lawrence, North Carolina Museum of Art, Raleigh, Purchased with funds from the State of North Carolina. **130** Harriet Tubman Quilt made by the Negro History Club of Marin City and Sausalito, CA, 1951, 120 x 96 inches, cotton appliqued. Designed by Ben Irvin. Gift of the Howard Thurman Educational Trust to the permanent collection of the Robert W. Woodruff Library, Atlanta University Center, Atlanta, GA **134** *Harriet Tubman Series*, # 16, Jacob Lawrence, Hampton University Museum, Hampton, Virginia **138** AP/Wide World Photos **144** *The Landing of Columbus*, 1876, Currier & Ives, The Harry T. Peters Collection, Museum of the City of New York **145** The Granger Collection, New York **146** *A New Beginning*, oil, 24 x 36, Duane Bryers, Courtesy of the artist **147** AP/Wide World Photos **148–149** United Nations **150 (t.)** *East Side Main Plaza, San Antonio, Texas*, 1844, William G.M. Samuel, Courtesy of Bexar County and the Witte Museum, San Antonio, Texas **150 (b.)** Juan Guzman/LIFE Magazine©TIME Inc. **154** Corel Professional Photos CD-ROM™ **156** ©Anchorage Museum/Alaska Stock Images **159** Shelley Rotner/Omni-Photo Communications, Inc. **160** ©Anchorage Museum/Alaska Stock Images **162** CORBIS-Bettmann **166, 167** © Ric Ergenbright/CORBIS **168** Corel Professional Photos CD-ROM™ **169** Flannery Literary, photo © Ruth Wright Paulsen 1993 **170, 172** *Empire State*, Tom Christopher, Vicki Morgan Associates **175** *Minnie*, 1930, William Johnson, National Museum of American Art, Washington, DC/Art Resource, NY **176** New York Public Library **180** Photofest **182** ©Cinerama/Archive Photos **184** Archiv Medizinischer Verlag Hams Huber, Bern und Stuttgart **187, 188** Photofest **196** ©Cinerama/Archive Photos **201, 206** Photofest **210** Harry Snaveley **215** *A Ride for Liberty—The Fugitive Slaves*, Eastman Johnson, The Brooklyn Museum of Art, Gift of Miss Gwendolyn O.L. Conkling **218** Ken Karp/PH Photo **218** Comstock, Inc. **224–225** *Trial by Jury*, 1964, Thomas Hart Benton, oil on canvas; 30" x 40" (76.0 x 1010.7cm), The Nelson-Atkins Museum of Art, Kansas City, Missouri, bequest of the artist. ©T.H. Benton and R.P. Benton Testamentary Trusts/Licensed by VAGA, New York, NY **226 (t.)** James Lemass/Gamma Liaison **226 (b.)** Paul Fusco/Magnum Photos, Inc. **228** AP/Wide World Photos **230** UPI/CORBIS-Bettmann **232 (t.)** Lass/Archive Photos **232 (b.)** Will Hart **234** Courtesy of the Library of Congress **235** Digital Imagery ©Copyright 2001 PhotoDisc, Inc. **236** John Craig Photo **240** *Young of the Town*, 1933, oil on board, Gerrit V. Sinclair, Williams American Art Galleries, Tennessee **242** New York State Historical Association, Cooperstown, New York **245** Culver Pictures, Inc. **248 (t.)** New York State Historical Association, Cooperstown, New York **248 (b.)** ©Michelle Garrett/CORBIS **250** CORBIS-Bettmann **254** *The First reading of the Emancipation Proclamation before the Cabinet*, Courtesy of the Library of Congress **256 (l.)** CORBIS **256 (r.)** Louis A. Warren Lincoln Library and Museum, Fort Wayne, Indiana **257 (l.)** ©CORBIS **257 (r.)** Louis A. Warren Lincoln Library and Museum, Fort Wayne, Indiana **260** Photograph by Charles Osgood, Copyrighted 5/23/88, Chicago Tribune Company, All rights reserved. Used with permission. **261** Courtesy National Archives **262** Courtesy of the Library of Congress **266** Paul Fusco/Magnum Photos, Inc. **268 (b.)** *The Sacristan of Trampas* (detail), ca. 1915, Paul Burlin, Collection of the Museum of Fine Arts, Museum of New Mexico, 1922 **268 (t.)** Fotopic/Omni-Photo Communications, Inc. **270** *Springtime*, c. 1928–29, Victor Higgins, oil on canvas, 24 x 20 inches. Private collection, photo courtesy of the Gerald Peters Gallery, Santa Fe, NM **271** Courtesy Raul Sedillo **272** ©The Stock Market/Randy Ury **274, 275, 276** Dr. E.R. Degginger **278** Free Spirit Publishing **283** Corel Professional Photos CD-ROM™ **286** ©Otto Greule/Allsport **288** *Shoe Series, #2*, Private collection/Marilee Whitehouse-Holm/ SuperStock **292–293** Audrey Gottlieb/Monkmeyer **294** Steven E. Sutton/Duomo Photography, Inc. **296** Nikky Finney **300** James Lemass/ Gamma Liaison **302–303** Bettmann/CORBIS **304** David Binder/Stock, Boston **306** *Henry Wadsworth Longfellow* (detail), Thomas B. Read, The National Portrait Gallery, Smithsonian Institution, Washington, D.C./Art Resource, New York **310** *Paul Revere*, John Singleton Copley, Courtesy, Museum of Fine

Credits ◆ R61

Staff Credits

The people who made up the *Prentice Hall Literature: Timeless Voices, Timeless Themes* team—representing design services, editorial, editorial services, market research, marketing services, media resources, online services & multimedia development, production services, project office, and publishing processes—are listed below. Bold type denotes the core team members.

Susan Andariese, Rosalyn Arcilla, Laura Jane Bird, Betsy Bostwick, **Anne M. Bray,** Evonne Burgess, **Louise B. Capuano, Pam Cardiff,** Megan Chill, Ed Cordero, Laura Dershewitz, Philip Fried, **Elaine Goldman,** Barbara Goodchild, Barbara Grant, **Rebecca Z. Graziano, Doreen Graizzaro,** Dennis Higbee, **Leanne Korszoloski,** Ellen Lees, David Liston, Mary Luthi, **George Lychock,** Gregory Lynch, Sue Lyons, **William McAllister,** Frances Medico, Gail Meyer, Jessica S. Paladini, Wendy Perri, Carolyn Carty Sapontzis, **Melissa Shustyk,** Annette Simmons, Alicia Solis, Robin Sullivan, Cynthia Sosland Summers, Lois Teesdale, Elizabeth Torjussen, Doug Utigard, Bernadette Walsh, Helen Young

The following persons provided invaluable assistance and support during the production of this program.

Gregory Abrom, Robert Aleman, Diane Alimena, Michele Angelucci, Gabriella Apolito, Penny Baker, Sharyn Banks, Anthony Barone, Barbara Blecher, Helen Byers, Rui Camarinha, Lorelee J. Campbell, John Carle, Cynthia Clampitt, Jaime L. Cohen, Martha Conway, Dina Curro, Nancy Dredge, Johanna Ehrmann, Josie K. Fixler, Steve Frankel, Kathy Gavilanes, Allen Gold, Michael E. Goodman, Diana Hahn, Kerry L. Harrigan, Jacki Hasko, Evan Holstrom, Beth Hyslip, Helen Issackedes, Cathy Johnson, Susan Karpin, Raegan Keida, Stephanie Kota, Mary Sue Langan, Elizabeth Letizia, Christine Mann, Vickie Menanteaux, Kathleen Mercandetti, Art Mkrtchyan, Karyl Murray, Kenneth Myett, Stefano Nese, Kim Ortell, Lissette Quinones, Erin Rehill-Seker, Patricia Rodriguez, Mildred Schulte, Adam Sherman, Mary Siener, Jan K. Singh, Diane Smith, Barbara Stufflebeem, Louis Suffredini, Lois Tatarian, Tom Thompkins, Lisa Valente, Ryan Vaarsi, Linda Westerhoff, Jeff Zoda

Prentice Hall gratefully acknowledges the following teachers who provided student models for consideration in the program.

Barbara Abel, Dawn Akuna, Kathy Allen, Joan Anderson, Amy Bales, Lisa Cobb, Ann Collier-Buchanan, Janice Crews, Denise Donahue, Becky Dressler, Nicci Durban, Nancy Fahner, Margo Graf, Jan Graham, Carleen Hemric, Karen Hurley, Max Hutto, Lenore Hynes, Kim Johnson, Gail Kidd, Ashley MacDonald, Maureen MacDonald, Akiko Morimoto, Judy Plouff, Charlene Revels, Lynn Richter, Kathleen Riley, Sandy Shannon, Marilyn Shaw, Cheryl Spivak, Lynn Striepe, John Tierney, Vanna Turner, Pam Walden, Holly Ward, Jennifer Watson, Joan West, Virginia Wong